Apply Here — Bureau of Alcohol, Tobacco, and Firearms

Typical Positions:
Special agent, explosives expert, firearms specialist, bomb-scene investigator, liquor law violations investigator, fingerprint identification specialist, intelligence specialist, and forensic chemist.

Employment Requirements:
GS-5 special agent applicants must meet the same employment requirements as most other federal agents, including (1) Pass the Treasury Enforcement Agent Examination, (2) a field interview, (3) a full field background investigation leading to successful certification for a top-secret clearance, and (4) a bachelor's degree from an accredited college or university.

Other Requirements:
Other general requirements for employment as a federal officer apply. Applicants must (1) be a U.S. citizen, (2) be between 21 and 37 years old, (3) have good physical health, (4) hold a current, valid U.S. driver's license, (5) pass a polygraph examination, and (6) have eyesight of no less than 20/100 uncorrected, and correctabe to at least 20/30 in one eye and 20/20 in the other. New agents undergo eight weeks of specialized training at the Federal Law Enforcement Training Center in Glynco, Georgia.

Salary:
A bachelor's degree qualifies applicants for appointment at GS-5, although some appointments are made at GS-7. GS-9 appointments require a master's degree, two full academic years of progressively higher-level graduate education, or one year of specialized experience equivalent to the next lower grade in the federal service. Depending on geographic area of assignment, this salary can be raised from 16% to 30% above the established base level.

Benefits:
Benefits include (1) 13 days of sick leave annually, (2) two and a half to five weeks of paid vacation and ten paid federal holidays each year, (3) federal health and life insurance, and (4) a comprehensive retirement program.

Direct Inquiries To:
Bureau of Alcohol, Tobacco, and Firearms
Personnel Division, Room 4100
650 Massachusetts Ave., N.W.
Washington, DC 20226
Phone: (202) 927-5690
Website: http://atf.treas.gov

Source:
Bureau of Alcohol, Tobacco and Firearms

Career Opportunities — U.S. Secret Service

Typical Positions:
Special agent, Uniformed Division police officer, and special officer. Clerical and administrative positions are also available.

Employment Requirements:
Applicants for appointment at the GS-5 level must (1) pass the Treasury Enforcement Agent Examination, (2) have a bachelor's degree from an accredited college or university, (3) be in excellent physical condition, including at least 20/40 vision in each eye, correctable to 20/20, and (4) pass a thorough background investigation. Appointment at the GS-7 level also requires (1) one additional year of specialized experience, (2) a bachelor's degree with superior academic achievement, or (3) one year of graduate study in a related field, such as police science, police administration, criminology, law, law enforcement, business administration, accounting, economics or finance.

"Specialized experience" is defined as responsible criminal investigative or comparable experience that required (1) the exercise of tact, resourcefulness, and judgment in collecting, assembling, and developing facts, evidence, and other pertinent data through investigative techniques that include personal interviews, (2) the ability to make oral and written reports and presentations of personally conducted or personally directed investigations, and (3) the ability to analyze and evaluate evidence and arrive at sound conclusions.

"Superior academic achievement" is defined as meeting one or more of the following criteria: (1) a B average (3.0 on a 4.0 scale) for all courses completed at the time of application or for all courses during the last two years of the undergraduate curriculum, (2) a B+ average (3.5 on a 4.0 scale) for all courses in the major field of study or for all courses in the major during the last two years of the undergraduate curriculum, (3) a rank in the upper third of the applicant's undergraduate class or major subdivision (for example, school of liberal arts), and (4) membership in an honorary scholastic society that meets the requirements of the Association of College Honor Societies.

Other Requirements:
Applicants must also have a valid driver's license, submit to urinalysis testing for the presence of illegal drugs, and be able to qualify for top-secret security clearance. Applications are not accepted earlier than nine months prior to graduation.

Salary:
Special agents are appointed at GS-5 or GS-7, depending on qualifications. A high-cost-area supplement ranging from 4% to 16% is paid in some geographic areas.

Benefits:
Benefits include (1) 13 days of sick leave annually, (2) two and a half to five weeks of paid vacation and ten paid federal holidays each year, (3) federal health and life insurance, and (4) a comprehensive retirement program.

Direct Inquiries To:
U.S. Secret Service
Personnel Division
1800 G St., N.W.
Washington, DC 20223
Phone: (888) 813-8777
Website: http://www.treas.gov/usss

Source:
U.S. Secret Service

criminal justice today

7th edition

**An Introductory Text
for the Twenty-first Century**

Frank Schmalleger, Ph.D.
Professor Emeritus
The University of North Carolina at Pembroke

Foreword by
James P. Levine
John Jay College of Criminal Justice
The City University of New York

Prentice Hall

Upper Saddle River, New Jersey 07458

Library of Congress Cataloging-in-Publication Data
Schmalleger, Frank.
    Criminal Justice Today: an introductory text for the twenty-first century/Frank
Schmalleger; foreword by James P. Levine.—7th ed.
        p. cm.
    Includes indexes.
    ISBN 0-13-045064-2
    1. Criminal justice, Administration of—United States. I. Title.
HV9950.S35 2003
364.973—dc21

                                2001059252

Photo Credits
Part Openers: Jean Marc Giboux, Liaison, Getty Images, Inc.; Charles Rotkin, CORBIS; Sal Maiome, SuperStock, Inc.; AP/Wide World Photos; Donna Binder, Impact Visuals Photo & Graphics, Inc.
Chapter Openers: © Jeffry Scott, Impact Visuals, PNI: Gary Walts, Syracuse Newspapers, The Image Works; Edouard Beme, Stone, Getty Images, Inc.; David Young-Wolff, PhotoEdit; Michael Newman, PhotoEdit; AP/Wide World Photos; David McNew, Getty Images, Inc.; Shaun Egan, Stone, Getty Images, Inc.; John Neubauer, PhotoEdit; Michael Newman, PhotoEdit; Alan Levenson, PictureQuest, eMotion, Inc.; Kwame Zikomo, SuperStock, Inc.; Bob Daemmrich, The Image Works; Jim Corwin, Stone, Getty Images, Inc.; © Owen Franken, CORBIS; Ian Waldie, Reuters NewMedia, Inc., CORBIS; Tim Lynch, Index Stock Imagery, Inc.

Publisher: Jeff Johnston
Executive Assistant and Supervisor: Glenda Rock
Executive Editor: Kim Davies
Editorial Assistant: Korrine Dorsey
Managing Editor: Mary Carnis
Production Management: Janet Bolton
Interior Design: Amanda Kavanagh/ARK Design
Production Liaison: Barbara Marttine Cappuccio
Director of Manufacturing and Production: Bruce Johnson
Manufacturing Buyer: Cathleen Petersen
Creative Director: Cheryl Asherman
Cover Design Coordinator: Miguel Ortiz
Formatting: Carlisle Communications
Electronic Art Creation: Carlisle Communications
Printer/Binder: Von Hoffman
Copy Editor: Judith Mara Riotto
Proofreader: Maine Proofreading Services
Cover Design: Blair Brown
Cover Image: Carl Glover/Tony Stone
Cover Printer: Phoenix

Pearson Education LTD.
Pearson Education Australia PTY, Limited
Pearson Education Singapore, Pte. Ltd
Pearson Education North Asia Ltd
Pearson Education Canada, Ltd.
Pearson Educación de Mexico, S.A. de C.V.
Pearson Education—Japan
Pearson Education Malaysia, Pte. Ltd

Prentice Hall

10 9 8 7 6 5 4 3 2 1
ISBN 0-13-045064-2
ISBN 0-13-048295-1

For Harmonie Star-Schmalleger
—my beautiful wife and other self

The publisher and the author of this textbook jointly donate a portion of sales proceeds to research and education in the field of crime and justice.

Thematic Approach

Three themes underlie this book and provide a conceptual framework to help students understand the American criminal justice system of today and of tomorrow. These themes (1) contrast the constitutional and procedural rights of individuals with the need for public order and personal safety; (2) explore the role of technology as it helps in the fight against crime while simultaneously providing new criminal opportunities for high-technology offenders; and (3) examine the challenge of multiculturalism and diversity as they contribute to the complex social and cultural framework within which the criminal justice system must operate.

CJ Today Exhibit 13–3

Federal Oversight of the Texas Prison System: A Timeline

1972: Inmate David Ruiz and several other prisoners file a civil rights suit against the Texas Department of Corrections (now called the Texas Department of Criminal Justice), alleging constitutional violations.

October 2, 1978–September 20, 1979: The *Ruiz* case is tried in Houston.

December 10, 1980: U.S. District Court Judge William Wayne Justice finds that confinement in the Texas prison system constitutes cruel and unusual punishment. He cites overcrowding, understaffing, brutality by guards and inmate-guards known as building tenders, substandard medical care, and uncontrolled physical abuse among inmates.

January 12, 1981: The judge orders improvements to be made to the system and sets deadlines.

April 19, 1981: Judge Justice appoints a special master to supervise compliance.

April 1982: The state agrees to halt the building tender system and to hire additional correctional officers.

January–June 1983: The Texas legislature passes laws intended to reduce the prison population.

November 1987: Texas voters authorize $500 million in bonds for prison construction.

March 31, 1990: The special master's office is closed.

November 1990: Texas voters approve $672 million in bonds to build 25,300 prison beds and 12,000 drug- and alcohol-treatment beds.

February 1992: Inmates' attorneys and the Texas Board of Criminal Justice reach an agreement. Texas Attorney General Dan Morales rejects it.

May 1, 1992: Morales offers a settlement proposal.

July 14, 1992: Inmates' attorneys accept the proposal.

December 11, 1992: Judge Justice signs the settlement.

January 21, 1999: Judge Justice begins a hearing to determine whether Texas prisons should be freed of federal court oversight.

March 1, 1999: Judge Justice decides to maintain oversight of the prison system.

March 20, 2001: The 5th U.S. Circuit Court of Appeals reverses Judge Justice's ruling, ending oversight but giving him 90 days to review the matter.

June 18, 2001: Judge Justice says that the Texas prison system has improved but that oversight is still needed in the areas of "conditions of confinement in administrative segregation, the failure to provide reasonable safety to inmates against assault and abuse, and the excessive use of force by correctional officers." Judge Justice discontinues federal oversight of other aspects of the prison system, including health services and staffing.

Source: Adapted from Ed Timms, "Judge to Lessen Oversight of Texas Prisons," *Dallas Morning News,* June 19, 2001. Reprinted with permission. Web posted at http://www.dallasnews.com/archive. Accessed March 12, 2002.

CJ Today Exhibits

The day-to-day practices of personnel within the criminal justice system and the expectations that professional associations, judicial bodies, and government decision-makers hold for professional justice system participants are the focus of CJ Today Exhibits. Codes of professional ethics, laws and statutes, precedent-setting court decisions, and government-issued enforcement guidelines can all be found in this book's many CJ Today Exhibits.

CJ Today News

"Big Brother" Cameras on Watch for Criminals

TAMPA—In spirited family groupings and knots of raucous collegians, as many as 35,000 visitors stroll the blocked-off avenues of Tampa's historic Ybor City entertainment district on a busy Saturday night.

As the revelers canvass the neon-lit storefronts for an appealing disco, bar or restaurant, they walk past curbside warning signs reading "Area Under Video Monitoring." And if their glances wander to tall poles placed every block or so, the visitors can see 36 surveillance cameras swiveling silently.

At a nearby command post, police officers viewing 10 video screens are doing more than watching for street fracases. They are using sophisticated face-recognition technology to scan the crowds for wanted criminals. The practice is fueling a nationwide debate over whether Big Brother is behind the camera.

Since June 29, 2001, surveillance cameras have been linked to a computer that randomly compares pedestrians' faces with 1,000 database images of known felons and teenage runaways.

Critics say the identification technique erodes privacy rights and raises the specter of government tracking individuals' movements. The American Civil Liberties Union is in rare alliance with conservative House Republican leader Dick Armey in saying that the software should be banned.

But surveillance advocates say the face-recognition software enhances public safety. "If it is Big Brother, it's Big Brother watching out for you," says Virginia Beach, Va., Police Chief Jay Jacocks, who is lobbying city officials to install a Tampa-style system in his city.

Like fingerprinting and DNA analysis, face-recognition technology is a form of biometrics, the science of identifying people by unique physical characteristics. The automated software measures 80 facial features, converts them to a mathematical formula and searches the database for a match.

To privacy watchdogs, the digitized facial inspections being done by police lengthen a list of high-technology threats to anonymity:

■ Employers and the FBI are monitoring e-mail and Web browsing.

■ Car-rental companies are using global positioning satellites to detect and fine speeders.

■ In 40 cities, automatic cameras trigger citations for running red lights.

In Tampa, "merely by walking down the street, a person is in essence put into an electronic police lineup without even knowing it," ACLU Associate Director Gregory Nojeim says. "If this isn't Big Brother, I don't know what is."

Four towns so far in Ybor (pronounced EE-bore) City, the computer has sounded an alarm signaling an apparent match, but police viewing a monitor have decided the faces were different. Police have not detained anyone.

Tampa is getting a free, 1-year trial of the FaceIt software made by Visionics Corp. of New Jersey. The City Council, which approved the deal in May, 2001, without a hearing, has been having second thoughts amid a public uproar. Two weeks ago, the council deadlocked 3-3 over asking Mayor Dick Greco to scrap the contract. Another vote is scheduled for today. However the advisory vote goes, Greco says he'll continue the experiment.

In a second weekend of protests, 25 activists from the Green Party and other groups marched Saturday night on Ybor City's Seventh Avenue and chanted, "Big Bro, hell, no." One demonstrator was costumed as a computer monitor with Greco's face onscreen. Public opinion in Ybor City is deeply split over the technology, which as configured here prevents wholesale tracking by deleting images that don't match mug shots.

"Safety was the intent, and safety is exactly what it did: keep the troublemakers off the streets," says Jason Fernandez, managing partner of a restaurant in Ybor City.

"If it can help parents find out that their missing child is alive, then it's fine," says Mary Thurston, 34, a computer technician. "If you have something to hide, you shouldn't be out in public, right?"

But Jonathan Kish, 22, a stage technician visiting from Atlanta, says, "I don't want these people spying on me."

Nora Lee Smith, 41, a Tampa sales rep, says, "The cameras are not effective. They should use the money for more police patrol."

In 1998, British officials combined FaceIt with 300 surveillance cameras in London's gritty borough of Newham. Friday, London police chasing down a computer match arrested a man on a warrant for street crime, one of "less than 10" such arrests locally, says Bob Lack, Newham security director. Similar surveillance is under way in Birmingham, England, along Israel's Gaza boundary and at 80 U.S. casinos. The airport near Reykjavik, Iceland, is installing it.

Using another company's software, Tampa first tried face-scanning in January, 2001, at Super Bowl XXXV and in Ybor City before the game. The ACLU dubbed the event the Snooper Bowl. Checking 100,000 faces at stadium turnstiles against 1,700 criminals in the database, the system registered 19 hits. Supervisors considered only one resemblance worth dispatching an officer to find the suspect, an alleged ticket scalper, who vanished.

Untested legally, face-recognition surveillance probably would withstand Supreme Court scrutiny, says Erwin Chemerinsky, a law professor at the University of Southern California. "We have no reasonable expectation of privacy in a public place—that we're not going to be seen, or that our picture won't be taken," he says.

On June 11, 2001, the Supreme Court weighed high-tech searches in *Kyllo vs. United States,* a 5-4 opinion written by Justice Antonin Scalia. The ruling: Police must obtain a search warrant before employing imaging techniques not readily available to the public to snoop inside a home.

Left open was the question of using advanced technology on public streets. "Whether or not it's illegal, it's deeply troubling," says Jeffrey Rosen, a George Washington University law professor and author of *The Unwanted Gaze: The Destruction of Privacy in America.*

Federal agents in the *Kyllo* arrest in 1992 used an infrared imager to detect heat from lamps used to grow marijuana indoors. As Scalia noted, the government now is financing development of far more advanced snooping methods.

The Pentagon's Defense Advanced Research Projects Agency is administering a $50 million program, HumanID, to improve face-recognition capability. The goal is to guard U.S. embassies and military

Audio Extras!

Hear it straight from Frank Schmalleger! Using the latest Web technology, readers can listen to the author introduce each chapter and hear him identify important criminal justice issues addressed in the text.

CJ Today News Boxes

We keep you informed with featured stories from the Associated Press, the *New York Times,* and *USA Today!* This book contains up-to-date and current articles on today's hottest topics, such as genetic crimes, cybercrime, juvenile justice, cross-national crime, and terrorism. But this new edition doesn't stop there. Each CJ Today News box provides a link to the Talk Justice online news feed, allowing you to read the latest in breaking crime and justice news.

Crime and Justice News Feed

Read the latest in crime and justice news, constantly updated, at the Talk Justice online news feed. Maintained by Frank Schmalleger and powered by Moreover.com, stories from the feed relate directly to subjects discussed in this textbook. Visit the Crime and Justice online news feed at http://crimenews.info, or access it through the Companion Website that accompanies this book. Remember to refresh your browser regularly to see breaking headlines as events happen.

Individual Rights versus Public Order Boxes

Designed to illustrate the central theme of this text, these boxes, found in most chapters, highlight the challenges faced by the American criminal justice system as it attempts to control crime while simultaneously respecting the constitutional and other legal rights of individuals. Individual Rights versus Public Order boxes portray the American justice system as one of *crime control through due process.* In so doing, they provide a conceptual framework for understanding the justice system—both now and in the future.

INDIVIDUAL RIGHTS VERSUS PUBLIC ORDER

Fairness in Policing

[This chapter builds upon the following theme: For police action to be "just," it must recognize the rights of individuals while holding them accountable to the social obligations defined by law. It is important to realize that many democratically inspired legal restraints upon the police stem from the Bill of Rights, which comprises the first ten amendments to the U.S. Constitution. Such restraints help ensure individual freedoms in our society and prevent the development of a "police state" in America.

In police work and elsewhere, the principles of individual liberty and social justice are cornerstones upon which the American way of life rests. Ideally, the work of police agencies, as well as the American system of criminal justice, is to ensure justice while guarding liberty. The liberty-justice issue is the dual thread which holds the tapestry of the justice system together—from the simplest daily activities of police on the beat to the often complex and lengthy renderings of the U.S. Supreme Court.

For the criminal justice system as a whole, the question becomes, How can individual liberties be maintained in the face of the need for official action, including arrest, interrogation, incarceration, and the like? The answer is far from simple, but it begins with the recognition that liberty is a double-edged sword, entailing obligations as well as rights.

? DISCUSSION QUESTIONS

1. What does it mean to say that "for police action to be 'just,' it must recognize the rights of individuals while holding them accountable to the social obligations defined by law"? How can police agencies accomplish this? What can individual officers do to help their agencies in this regard?
2. This box asks, "How can individual liberties be maintained in the face of the need for official action, including arrest, interrogation, incarceration, and the like?" What's your answer?
3. What does it mean to say, as this box does, that "liberty is a double-edged sword, entailing obligations as well as rights"?

CJ Futures

[Technocorrections]

In the twenty-first century, the technological forces that have made cell phones ubiquitous will converge with the forces of law and order to create what some have called *technocorrections.* The correctional establishment—the managers of the jail, prison, probation, and parole systems and their sponsors in elected office—is seeking more cost-effective ways to increase public safety as the number of people under correctional supervision continues to grow. Technocorrections will be defined by a correctional establishment that takes advantage of all the potential offered by the new technologies to reduce the costs of supervising criminal offenders and to minimize the risk they pose to society.

Emerging technologies in three areas will soon be central elements of technocorrections: electronic tracking and location systems, pharmacological treatments, and genetic and neurobiologic risk assessments. While these technologies may significantly increase public safety, we must also be mindful of the threats they pose to democratic principles. The critical challenge will be to learn how to take advantage of new technological opportunities applicable to the corrections field while minimizing their threats.

Tracking and Location Systems

Electronic tracking and location systems are the technology perhaps most familiar to correctional practitioners today. Most states use electronic monitoring—either with the older bracelets that communicate through a device connected to telephone lines or with more modern versions based on cellular or satellite tracking. With such technology, correctional officials can continuously track offenders' locations and use that information to supervise their movements. As this technology expands, it will enable correctional officials to define geographic areas from which offenders are prohibited and to furnish tracking devices to potential victims (such as battered wives). The devices will set "safe zones" that trigger alarms or warning notices upon approach of the offender.

Tiny cameras might also be integrated into tracking devices to provide live video of offenders' locations and activities. Miniature electronic devices implanted in the body to signal the location of offenders at all times, to create unique identifiers that trigger alarms, and to monitor key bodily functions that affect unwanted behaviors are under development and are close to becoming reality.[1]

Pharmacological Treatments

Pharmacological breakthroughs—new "wonder drugs" being developed to control behavior in correctional and noncorrectional settings—will also be a part of technocorrections. Correctional officials are already familiar with some of these drugs, as many are currently used to treat mentally ill offenders. Yet these drugs could also be used to control mental conditions affecting undesirable behaviors even for offenders who are not mentally ill. Research into the relationship between levels of the neurotransmitter serotonin and violent behavior continues to be refined. Findings to date seem to indicate that people who have low levels of serotonin are more prone than others to impulsive, violent acts, especially when they abuse alcohol.[2] (See Chapter 3 for more information.) Not long ago, the National Academy of Sciences (NAS) recommended a new emphasis in biomedical research on violence as a means to understand the biological roots of violent behavior.[3] The NAS reports that research findings from animal and human studies "point to several features of the nervous system as promising sites" for discovering reliable biological "markers" for violent behavior and designing preventive therapies.[4]

It is only a matter of time before research findings in this area lead to the development of drugs to control neurobiological processes. These drugs could become correctional tools to manage violent offenders and perhaps even to prevent violence. Such advances are related to the third area of technology that will affect corrections: genetic and neurobiological risk-assessment technologies.

Risk-Assessment Technologies

Correctional officials today are familiar with DNA profiling of offenders, particularly sex offenders. This, however, is just the beginning of the correctional application of gene-related technologies. The Human Genome Project, supported by the National Institutes of Health and the Department of Energy, is about to be completed. A map of the 3 billion chemical bases that make up human DNA will be created, and high-powered "sequencer" machines will be able to analyze the map faster than any human researcher.[5] Emerging as a powerhouse of the high-tech economy, the biotechnology industry will drive developments in this area.

Gene "management" technologies are already widely used in agriculture and are increasingly used in medicine. The progression is likely to continue, with applications in psychiatric and behavioral management. Researchers are investigating the genetic—or inherited—basis of behavior, including antisocial and criminal behavior. Studies of twins, for example, have revealed similarities in behavior attributable to a genetic effect.[6] Eventually, the genetic roots of human behavior could be profiled.

Neurobiological research is taking the same path, although thus far no neurobiological patterns specific enough to be reliable biological markers for violent behavior have been uncovered. Is it possible that breakthroughs in these areas will lead to the development of risk-assessment tools that use genetic or neurobiological profiles to identify children who have a propensity toward addiction or violence? Might they also be capable of identifying males with a propensity for sex offending? We may soon be able to link genetic and neurobiological traits with social and environmental factors to reliably predict who is at risk for addiction, sex offending, violent behavior, or crime in general.

Attempts will surely be made to develop genetic or neurobiological tests for assessing risks posed by individuals. This is already done for the risk of contracting certain diseases. Demand for risk assessments of individuals will come from correctional officials under pressure to prevent violent recidivism. Once under correctional control, specific offenders could be identified, on the basis of such testing and risk assessment, as likely violent recidivists. The group so classified could be placed under closer surveillance or declared a danger to themselves and society and be civilly committed to special facilities for indeterminate periods. In other words, incarceration could assume a more preventive role.

CJ Futures Boxes

These informative boxes, illustrating a secondary theme of this book, lead readers into the future of the criminal justice enterprise and help prepare them for work in the twenty-first century.

Multiculturalism and Diversity in America Boxes

Illustrating a second subtheme of this book, these boxes explain how multiculturalism and social diversity present special challenges to, as well as opportunities for, the American system of criminal justice.

Multiculturalism and Diversity in America

[Policing a Multicultural Society]

Members of some culturally diverse groups have backgrounds, values, and perspectives that, while not directly supportive of law-breaking, contrast sharply with those of many police officials. Robert M. Shustra, a well-known writer on multicultural law enforcement, says that police officers "need to recognize the fact of poor police-minority relations historically, including *unequal* treatment under the law."[1] Moreover, says Shustra, "many officers and citizens are defensive with each other because their contact is tinged with negative historical 'baggage.'"

In other words, even though discrimination in the enforcement of the criminal law may not be commonplace today, it *was* in the past—and perceptions built upon past experience are often difficult to change. Moreover, if the function of law enforcement is to "protect and serve" law-abiding citizens from all backgrounds, then it becomes vital for officers to understand and respect differences in habits, customs, beliefs, patterns of thought, and traditions.[2] Hence, as Shustra says, "The acts of approaching, communicating, questioning, assisting, and establishing trust with members of different groups require special knowledge and skills that have nothing to do with the fact that 'the law is the law' and must be enforced equally. Acquiring sensitivity, knowledge, and skills leads to [an increased appreciation for the position of others] that will contribute to improved communications with members of all groups."[3]

How can police officers acquire greater sensitivity to the issues involved in policing a diverse multicultural society? Some researchers suggest that law enforcement officers of *all* backgrounds begin by exploring their own prejudices. Prejudices, which are judgments or opinions formed before facts are known and which usually involve negative or unfavorable thoughts about groups of people, can lead to discrimination. Hence, most citizens, including police officers, should be able to reduce their tendency to discriminate against those who are different by exploring and uprooting their own personal prejudices.

One technique for identifying prejudices is cultural awareness training. As practiced in some police departments today, cultural awareness training explores the impact of culture on human behavior—and especially law-breaking behavior. Cultural awareness training generally involves four stages:[4]

- *Clarifying the relationship between cultural awareness and police professionalism.* As Shustra explains it, "The more professional a peace officer is, the more sophisticated he or she is in responding to people of all backgrounds and the more successful he or she is in cross-cultural contact."[5]
- *Recognizing personal prejudices.* In the second stage of cultural awareness training, participating officers are asked to recognize and identify their own personal prejudices and biases. Once prejudices have been identified, trainers strive to show how they can affect daily behavior.
- *Acquiring sensitivity to police-community relations.* In this stage of training, participating officers learn about historical and existing community perceptions of the police. Training can often be enhanced through the use of carefully chosen and well-qualified guest speakers or participants from minority communities.
- *Developing interpersonal relations skills.* The goal of this last stage of training is to assist with the development of positive verbal and nonverbal communications skills necessary for successful interaction with community members. Many trainers believe that basic skills training will result in the continuing development of such skills because officers will quickly begin to see the benefits (in terms of lessened interpersonal conflict) of effective interpersonal skills.

[1] Robert M. Shusta et al., *Multicultural Law Enforcement: Strategies for Peacekeeping in a Diverse Society,* 2d ed. (Upper Saddle River, N.J.: Prentice Hall, 2002), p. 4.
[2] Ibid., p. 16.
[3] Ibid., p. 4.
[4] Ibid., pp. 104–106.
[5] Ibid., p. 4.

WHAT WOULD YOU DO?

The CD-ROM scenario for Chapter 6 builds on concepts of sovereign immunity and police civil liability. It is derived from a real-life incident involving a police officer's high speed chase of a bank robbery suspect. The actual case eventually found its way to the U.S. Supreme Court, with unfavorable consequences for the on-the-scene officer and his department. Use the CD-ROM found in the back of your textbook to work through this scenario, and see if you can make better decisions than the responding officer did.

What Would You Do? Boxes

These chapter-specific boxes, new to this edition, ask students to work through the interactive scenarios found on the CD-ROM included with the book. Each scenario is based on a real-life U.S. Supreme Court case and asks students what they would do at critical points in the decision-making process.

CJ Cybrary

Known as "the world's crime and justice directory" on the Web, the CJ Cybrary (or cyberlibrary) contains approximately 12,000 fully searchable and annotated links leading to crime- and justice-related sites on the Web and across the world. Thousands of other Cybrary links provide instant access to crime and justice documents from places like the National Criminal Justice Reference Service, the Bureau of Justice Statistics, the U.S. Department of Justice, the National Institute of Justice, and the Office of Juvenile Justice and Delinquency Prevention.

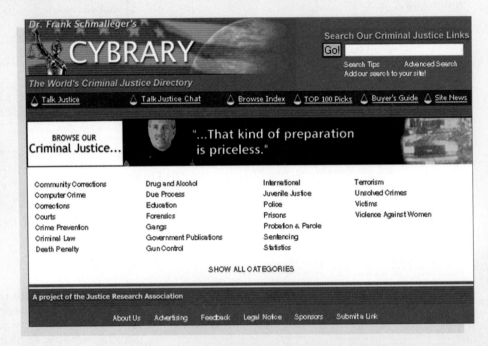

have been added since opening day.[100] At the memorial, an interactive video system provides visitors with brief biographies and photographs of officers who have died. Tour the memorial by visiting **WebExtra! 6-3** at cjtoday.com.

As the memorial shows, police work is, by its very nature, dangerous. Although many officers never once fire their weapons in the line of duty, it is also plain that some officers

Web Extras!

End aimless Net surfing and the frustration that accompanies dead and moved links! Integrated throughout the text, Web Extras! take readers to important crime and justice websites, which are continuously maintained and updated at cjtoday.com. *Criminal Justice Today* contains over 300 Web Extras!, including

- Academy of Criminal Justice Sciences
- Access to Justice Network
- American Bar Association
- American Judicature Society
- American Probation and Parole Association
- American Society for Industrial Security
- Bureau of Justice Assistance
- Bureau of Justice Statistics
- Computer Security Institute
- Cornell University's Legal Information Institute
- Corrections Connection
- Court TV
- Death Penalty Information Center
- Drug Enforcement Administration
- Federal Bureau of Investigation
- Federal Bureau of Prisons
- International Association of Chiefs of Police
- National Center for State Courts
- National Center for Victims of Crime
- National Council on Crime and Delinquency
- National Criminal Justice Reference Service
- National Institute of Justice
- National Youth Gang Center
- Office for Victims of Crime
- Office of Juvenile Justice and Delinquency Prevention
- Office of National Drug Control Policy
- Terrorism Research Center
- U.S. Supreme Court
- U.S. Department of Justice

Library Extras!

Library Extras! make suggested readings fun! Located at the end of every chapter and available in full on cjtoday.com, the more than 100 Library Extras! in *Criminal Justice Today* are electronic documents that expand upon the material presented in the book. Library Extras! are authored and produced by agencies as diverse as the Federal Bureau of Investigation, the Police Executive Research Forum, the National Institute of Justice, the Bureau of Justice Statistics, the Office of Justice Programs, the Office of National Drug Control Policy, the Office of Juvenile Justice and Delinquency Prevention, the National Institute of Corrections, the National Center for the Analysis of Violent Crimes, the National Center for Women and Policing, the United Nations, and the U.S. Department of State. Library Extras! include

- *Annual Report on Drug Use Among Adult and Juvenile Arrestees*
- *"Broken Windows" and Police Discretion*
- *Capital Punishment*
- *The Challenge of Crime in a Free Society: Looking Back Looking Forward*
- *Community Policing in Action*
- *Convicted by Juries, Exonerated by Science: Case Studies in the Use of DNA Evidence to Establish Innocence after Trial*
- *Correctional Populations in the United States*
- *Creating a New Criminal Justice System in the 21st Century*
- *Criminal Justice 2000*
- *Critical Criminal Justice Issues: Task Force Reports from the American Society of Criminology*
- *Full Report of the Prevalence, Incidence, and Consequences of Violence Against Women*
- *Global Report on Crime and Justice*
- *Indicators of School Crime and Safety*

- *Law Enforcement Management and Administrative Statistics*
- *Minorities in the Criminal Justice System*
- *National Assessment of Structured Sentencing*
- *National Crime Victimization Survey: Criminal Victimization*
- *National Drug Control Strategy*
- *National Household Survey on Drug Abuse*
- *On the Job Stress in Policing*
- *Patterns of Global Terrorism*
- *Perspectives on Crime and Justice*
- *Prevalence, Incidence, and Consequences of Violence Against Women: Findings From the National Violence Against Women Survey*
- *Preventing Crime: What Works, What Doesn't and What's Promising*
- *Racially Biased Policing: A Principled Response*
- *Recruiting and Retaining Women: A Self-Assessment Guide for Law Enforcement*
- *The School Shooter: A Threat Assessment Perspective*
- *Uniform Crime Reports*
- *Violent Victimization and Race*
- *Women in Criminal Justice: A Twenty Year Update*
- *Women in Prison*
- *World Factbook of Criminal Justice Systems*

Library Extras!

Library Extra! 9–1   *Improving Criminal Justice Systems through Expanded Strategies and Innovative Collaborations: Report of the National Symposium on Indigent Defense* (OJP, 1999).
Library Extra! 9–2   *National Survey of Indigent Defense Systems* (BJS, 2001).
Library Extra! 9–3   *State-Funded Indigent Defense Services, 1999* (NIJ, 2001).
Library Extra! 9–4   *The Convergence of Race, Ethnicity, Gender, and Class on Court Decisionmaking* (NIJ, 2000).
Library Extra! 9–5   *Standards and Measures in Court Performance* (NIJ, 2000).

To explore these resources online, go to the Library Extras! area of the *Criminal Justice Today* Companion Website at cjtoday.com. You should also check the author's "Late Picks" online for newly released documents and updated Library Extras! You can find Late Picks at http://cjtoday.com/latepicks.htm.

It is also important to recognize that the decision of the Supreme Court in the *Weeks* case was binding, at the time, only upon federal officers, because it was federal agents who were involved in the illegal seizure. Read the *Weeks* decision in its entirety at **Library Extra! 7–1** at cjtoday.com.

Web Quests!

Web Quests!, found at the end of each chapter, are Web-based assignments that show how to use the Web to research topics in the criminal justice area. Web Quests! include virtual visits to

- The American Probation and Parole Association
- Cornell University's Legal Information Institute
- The Corrections Connection

- The Federal Bureau of Investigation
- The Federal Judiciary
- The National Criminal Justice Reference Service
- The National Center for State Courts
- The Office of National Drug Control Policy
- The U.S. Sentencing Commission
- The U.S. Supreme Court

Web Quest!

Visit the National Criminal Justice Reference Service (NCJRS) at http://www.ncjrs.org. Click on the "Keyword Search" option, then on "Help Text" to view tips on performing effective searches, modifying search queries, and interpreting search results. Write a description of the search techniques available under "Keyword Search," including wild-card, proximity, concept, Boolean, and pattern searching. What does the help text suggest you do if you find too much in your search? If you find too little?

Frank Schmalleger, Ph.D., is Professor Emeritus at the University of North Carolina at Pembroke, where he chaired the Department of Sociology, Social Work, and Criminal Justice for nearly 20 years. He currently serves as director of the Justice Research Association, a private consulting firm and think tank focusing on issues of crime and justice. Dr. Schmalleger is also founder and codirector of the Criminal Justice Distance Learning Consortium (http://cjcentral.com/cjdlc).

Dr. Schmalleger holds degrees from the University of Notre Dame and Ohio State University, having earned both a master's degree (1970) and a doctorate in sociology (1974) from Ohio State University with a special emphasis in criminology. He served as an adjunct professor at Webster University in St. Louis, Missouri, where he helped develop the university's graduate program in Security Administration and Loss Prevention. He taught courses in that curriculum for more than a decade. Schmalleger also taught in the New School for Social Research's online graduate program, helping build the world's first electronic classrooms in support of distance learning through computer telecommunications. An avid Web developer, Schmalleger is the creator of a number of award-winning websites, including some that support this textbook (http://www.prenhall.com/schmalleger; http://cjtoday.com; and http://cybrary.info).

Frank Schmalleger is the author of numerous articles and many books, including the widely used *Criminology Today* (Prentice Hall, 2002); *Criminal Justice: A Brief Introduction* (Prentice Hall, 2002); *Criminal Law Today* (Prentice Hall, 2002); *The Definitive Guide to Criminal Justice and Criminology on the World Wide Web* (Prentice Hall, 2002); *Corrections in the Twenty-first Century* (Glencoe, 2001), coauthored with John Smykla; *Crime and the Justice System in America: An Encyclopedia* (Greenwood, 1997); and *Trial of the Century: People of the State of California vs. Orenthal James Simpson* (Prentice Hall, 1996).

Schmalleger is the founding editor of the journal *The Justice Professional.* He has served as editor for the Prentice Hall series *Criminal Justice in the Twenty-First Century* and as imprint adviser for Greenwood Publishing Group's criminal justice reference series.

Schmalleger's philosophy of both teaching and writing can be summed up in these words: "To communicate knowledge we must first catch, then hold, a person's interest—be it student, colleague, or policymaker. Our writing, our speaking, and our teaching must be relevant to the problems facing people today, and they must—in some way—help solve those problems."

The first edition of this textbook appeared in print more than ten years ago. At that time, I chose what seemed to be a rather unique subtitle: *An Introductory Text for the Twenty-first Century*. The subtitle was unusual not only because the new century was still more than a decade away, but because other introductory criminal justice authors seemed to be writing about the past and not the future. I wanted my subtitle to speak to students and professors. I wanted it to say, "This is a book that, while it owes a legacy to the past, is not bound by it. This is a book that will prepare students of justice for the world of the future—a soon-to-be vital and real world with almost limitless possibilities in which they will live and work."

Since then, of course, much has changed. *Criminal Justice Today* is now in its seventh edition. The twenty-first century is here, and thinking about the future has become routine.

As I write this preface to the seventh edition, I think of how the first edition of this text was a standard ink-on-paper hardcover book with sparsely placed black-and-white photographs. I reflect on how it has since evolved into a multimedia-rich, information-filled, experiential package that brings up-to-the-minute learning opportunities to today's students in printed form, on the Web, via CD-ROM, and through other digital formats. I think of how it makes extensive use of technologically enhanced learning environments, and I hope that it has contributed, at least in some small way, to the growth and continuing maturation of those environments.

The seventh edition of this learning package (for it is no longer merely a book) is intimately integrated with today's "wired" world. *Criminal Justice Today* has evolved into a multifaceted learning experience that, I believe, sets the standard for a new generation of educational tools that integrate text-based information and electronic media in ways not possible only a short while ago.

Although you can still hold this book in your hands, the printed pages are but a representation of the multitude of learning possibilities that accompany it. The *Criminal Justice Today* Companion Website (http://www.cjtoday.com), for example, adds a wealth of constantly updated news, statistics, legal information, and diverse opinions to the core text. The *Criminal Justice Today* e-mail discussion groups, message boards, and Talk Justice facility make it possible for students and professors to interact with one another and with others across the nation and around the world who share an interest in criminal justice and in crime prevention. Our criminal justice Cybrary (http://cybrary.info) provides a fully searchable gold mine of thousands of up-to-the-minute justice-specific websites and publications to facilitate research, writing, and learning. WebCT® and Blackboard® templates and fully developed content for this textbook, as well as the online teaching possibilities provided by the *Criminal Justice Today* Companion Website, allow classes to be taught entirely online, so students can study criminal justice subject matter from virtually anywhere.

While much has changed over seven editions, this text remains true to its original purpose. In the preface to the first edition, I wrote that the purpose of this book is "to teach criminal justice students the fundamental tried-and-true concepts of an evolving discipline, to give them the critical-thinking skills necessary to effectively apply those concepts to the real world, and to apply those concepts and skills to today's problems and to the emerging issues of tomorrow." In Chapter 1 of that edition, I promised that this book would "describe in detail the criminal justice system, while helping students develop an appreciation for the delicacy of the balancing act now facing it." I pointed out that the fundamental question for the future would be "how to ensure the existence of, and effectively manage, a justice system which is as fair to the individual as it is supportive of the needs of society." Finally, I asked, "Is justice for all a reasonable expectation of today's system of criminal justice?" The seventh edition remains true to these roots, yet has blossomed in ways unanticipated a decade ago.

As it was from the start, *Criminal Justice Today* is intended for use by students everywhere who are beginning the study of criminal justice. The seventh edition incorporates and supports the best contemporary principles guiding the study of our discipline. The educational principles underlying the Academy of Criminal Justice Sciences' recent explorations into the accreditation arena (via the ACJS Ad Hoc Committee on Minimum Standards for Criminal Justice Education), for example, are incorporated into this text, as are some of the state-specific guidelines for criminal justice education.

In summary, *Criminal Justice Today* is intended not as a simple description of what has already taken place in the field (although it contains plenty of descriptions and lots of historical information), but as a visual and thoughtful guide to the study and practice of criminal justice today, a road map through the criminal justice system of the twenty-first century, and a bridge between past and future.

Frank Schmalleger, Ph.D.
Professor Emeritus
The University of North Carolina at Pembroke

Using the *Exploring Criminal Justice Today* CD-ROM

The *Exploring Criminal Justice Today* CD-ROM contained in your textbook is as entertaining as it is useful. Designed to help you learn about daily practices in the criminal justice system, the CD facilitates a number of independent learning activities that you can use to enhance study sessions, to build knowledge of key concepts, to quiz yourself on course material, and to learn about important U.S. Supreme Court cases of relevance to each chapter. Your instructor may require you to complete assignments from material found on the disc and may ask you to submit those assignments via e-mail or on paper. Specific features of the CD-ROM include

- **Interactive scenarios.** These multimedia interactive scenarios are designed to improve your justice-related decision-making skills. Each simulation is based on a real-life court case, and each contains links to abbreviated on-disc court opinions.
- **Study review games.** These chapter-specific vocabulary-building games focus on the key terms listed at the start of each chapter and help you remember crucial concepts and associated definitions.
- **Electronic exercises.** Each practice quiz contains multiple-choice and true-false questions intended to help you assess your understanding of course material.
- **Glossary.** The terms in the disc-based glossary parallel the definitions of important terminology used in the book. If you have any questions about the definition of a key term, just check this glossary.
- **Web links.** If you are connected to the Internet while using the *Exploring Criminal Justice Today* CD-ROM, you will be able to browse the Web and link to important criminal justice sites from within other areas of the disc.

Exploring Criminal Justice Today CD-ROM System Requirements

PC

- **Color monitor (adjust settings inside Control Panel/Display/Settings):**
  Color palette: 256 colors (True Color 32-bit recommended)
  Desktop area: at least 800 x 600
  Font size: small fonts
- **Minimum system requirements: Pentium/266 MHz, with 24 MB of RAM**
  Multimedia-equipped PC, with 4x (or faster) CD-ROM drive
- **Operating Systems:** Windows98, Windows 2000, Windows XP, or higher

Macintosh

- **Color monitor (adjust settings inside Control Panel/Display/Settings):**
  Color palette: 256 colors (True Color 32-bit recommended)
  Desktop area: 800 x 600
  Enable sounds
- **Minimum system requirements:** PowerPC or above, with 24 MB of RAM
  Multimedia-equipped Macintosh, with 4x (or faster) CD-ROM drive
- **Operating System:** System OS 8.0 or above

Using *Criminal Justice Today* World Wide Web Features

Criminal Justice Today is supported by a widely acclaimed award-winning website accessible at http://cjtoday.com. Once you arrive at the site, click on the cover of your book to enter. The feature-rich seventh edition website builds upon a strong tradition of standard-setting excellence in Web-based media. It offers the following special features:

- **Electronic syllabus.** Check here to see if your instructor has created an online syllabus. If so, refer to it to keep track of reading assignments, test dates, term papers, and other coursework. The electronic syllabus posted by your instructor may also contain links to Web-based media, such as online lectures, and to sites chosen by your instructor for you to view.

- **Audio Extras!** Hear the author introduce each chapter. Audio chapter introductions require Real Player™ (also referred to as Real One™) or Windows Media Player™ software.

- **Chapter learning objectives.** Set your study goals for each chapter with chapter-specific learning objectives. Use these objectives to maintain your focus on important materials as you read the text.

- **Practice review questions.** Prepare for tests and assess your knowledge of critical content with online review questions. Use these true-false and multiple-choice questions to test yourself as often as you want, and watch your scores improve.

- **Electronic homework.** Respond to online essay questions, and e-mail your answers to your instructor for grading. Electronic homework makes it possible for you to demonstrate your knowledge of core concepts while it helps save trees!

- **Chapter summaries.** Review chapter materials with online summaries of key points. Bulleted summaries allow for quick and easy access to critical content and can help you remember important chapter information.

- **Web Quests!** Work your way through comprehensive Web-based chapter projects, and learn how to do criminal justice research on the Internet. Web Quests! make studying enjoyable and open the door to a wealth of electronic information.

- **Web Extras!** Visit sites that are closely related to the topics you are studying. Web Extras! provide a virtual criminal justice tour of the Internet, with visits to police, courts, and corrections sites on the Web.

- **Library Extras!** Read carefully selected documents from the Bureau of Justice Statistics, the National Institute of Justice, the Bureau of Justice Assistance, the Federal Bureau of Investigation, and other agencies at the *Criminal Justice Today* electronic library. Library Extras! are continually updated to bring you the latest in criminal justice research and data.

- **Crime and justice news.** Stay up-to-the-minute with late-breaking crime and justice news from the Talk Justice online news feed available at http://crimenews.info. Continually updated stories provide complete coverage of current events in the crime and justice field.

- **Careers center.** Use the careers feature to find the best-paying jobs in the justice profession. If you aren't sure that you want to work in the justice system, the careers center can help you decide your future.

- **Message boards.** Discuss criminal justice issues with students and professors from across the country and around the world. Our boards allow you to read and post messages whenever you are connected to the Internet.

■ **E-mail discussion list.** Join our e-mail discussion list at http://groups.yahoo.com/group/CJToday, and stay abreast of what other students are talking about. E-mail discussions are a handy way to stay current on issues in the field and to share your thoughts with others. You can also begin an e-mail study group to review text materials with students in other colleges.

■ **Dr. Frank Schmalleger's Cybrary.** Find what you're looking for on the Web with Dr. Frank Schmalleger's cyberlibrary of criminal justice links (http://cybrary.info). Containing over 12,000 crime and justice sites in its fully searchable database, the Cybrary is well known on the Internet as "the world's crime and justice directory."

■ **Electronic glossary.** Use this Web-based glossary as a study aid to help you understand key concepts and other text materials. Our glossary includes standardized terminology from the criminal justice, criminology, law, and corrections fields.

■ **Twenty-first-century criminal justice.** Learn what the criminal justice system of tomorrow will be like, and see how the principles that undergird today's system will influence the justice system of the future.

■ **The U.S. Constitution.** Review the full text of the U.S. Constitution, including all amendments. Use this feature to research the constitutionally protected rights of those facing processing by the justice system.

CONTENTS

CONTENTS

CONTENTS

CONTENTS

ADJUDICATION   323   part three

CONTENTS

CORRECTIONS   449

part four

CONTENTS

CONTENTS

CONTENTS

My thanks to all who assisted in so many different ways in the development of this textbook. The sacrifice of time made by my wife, Harmonie, as I worked endlessly in my study is very much appreciated. Thanks also to Cheryl Asherman, Robin Baliszewski, Janet Bolton, Barbara Cappuccio, Carey Davies, Mary Carnis, Kim Davies, Sarah Holle, Jeff Johnston, Craig Marcus, Frank Mortimer (aka "Krazy Elvis"), Miguel Ortiz, Amy Peltier, Cathleen Petersen, Jessica Pfaff, Ilene Sanford, Carol Sykes, and all the Prentice Hall staff—true professionals who make the task of manuscript development enjoyable. My supplements author, Steve Chermak, is extremely talented, and I am grateful to him for using his skills in support of this new edition. Thanks also to personal assistant Laura Joyce for her capable handling of numerous details. The keen eye of copy editor Judith Mara Riotto is beyond compare, and this book is much richer for her efforts. Thanks, too, to Sarah Nordin for her excellent work on this book's PowerPoint presentation package.

From its inception, this edition has benefited considerably from the suggestions of Clem Bartollas, Terry Hutchins, Jess Maghan, Bill Ruefle, and Richard Zevitz and from suggestions made by Herman Woltring of the U.N. Crime Prevention and Criminal Justice Branch. I am grateful, as well, to the manuscript reviewers involved in this and previous editions for holding me to the fire when I might have opted for a less rigorous coverage of some topics—and to Bryan J. Vila, whose definitive works on criminal justice policy are as useful to me as they are to the discipline! A special thanks goes to Darl Champion of Methodist College, Jim Smith at West Valley College, and Derald D. Hunt, Associate Dean Emeritus of Coast Community College District, for their insightful suggestions as this new edition got under way. Manuscript reviewers who have contributed to the development of *Criminal Justice Today* include

Howard Abadinsky
Saint Xavier University
Chicago, IL

Reed Adams
Mt. Olive College
Mt. Olive, NC

Gordon Armstrong
Oakland Community College
Auburn Hills, MI

Kevin Barrett
Palomar College
San Marcos, CA

Clemens Bartollas
University of Northern Iowa
Cedar Falls, IA

Larry Bassi
State University of New York (SUNY)
  Brockport
Brockport, NY

Richard Becker
North Harris College
Houston, TX

Michael Blankenship
East Tennessee State University
Johnson City, TN

W. Garret Capune
California State University—Fullerton
Fullerton, CA

Darl Champion
Methodist College
Fayettville, NC

Art Chete
Central Florida Community College
Ocala, FL

Geary Chlebus
James Sprunt Community College
Kenansville, NC

Lora C. Clark, J.D.
Pitt Community College
Greenville, NC

Jon E. Clark
Temple University
Philadelphia, PA

Warren Clark
California State University
Anaheim, CA

Ellen G. Cohn
Florida International University
Miami, FL

Gary Colboth
California State University—Long
  Beach
Long Beach, CA

Mark L. Dantzker
University of Texas—Pan American
Edinburgh, TX

Jannette O. Domingo
John Jay College of Criminal Justice
New York, NY

Vicky Doworth
Montgomery College
Rockville, MD

Steven Egger
University of Springfield
Springfield, IL

Ron Fagan
Pepperdine University
Malibu, CA

Michael Gray
Wor-Wic Community College
Salisbury, MD

Alex Greenberg
Niagra County Community College
Sanborn, NY

Richard Guymon
Maplewoods Community College
Kansas City, MO

Julia Hall
Drexel University
Philadelphia, PA

Ed Heischmidt
Rend Lake College
Ina, IL

Dennis Hoffman
University of Nebraska at Omaha
Omaha, NE

Michael Hooper
California Department of Justice
Sacramento, CA

Derald D. Hunt
Coast Community College District
Costa Mesa, CA

Terry Hutchins
Former Special Assistant to the
    Chancellor
The University of North Carolina at
    Pembroke
Pembroke, NC

William D. Hyatt
Western Carolina University
Cullowhee, NC

Nicholas H. Iron
County College of Morris
Randolph, NJ

Galen M. Janeksela
University of Tennessee at
    Chattanooga
Chattanooga, TN

Terry L. Johnson
Owens Community College
Toledo, OH

David M. Jones
University of Wisconsin—Oshkosh
Oshkosh, WI

Victor Kappeler
Eastern Kentucky State University
Richmond, KY

P. Ray Kedia
Grambling State University
Grambling, LA

Debra Kelly
Longwood College
Farmville, VA

Lloyd Klein
Louisiana State University—
    Shreveport
Shreveport, LA

Sylvia Kuennen
Briar Cliff College
Sioux City, IA

Karel Kurst-Swanger
Oswego State University of New York
Oswego, NY

Hamid R. Kusha
Texas A&M International University
Laredo, TX

Joan Luxenburg
University of Central Oklahoma
Edmond, OK

Michael Lyman
Columbia College
Columbia, MO

Thomas P. McAninch
Scott Community College
Bettendorf, IA

Jess Maghan
University of Illinois at Chicago
Chicago, IL

Richard H. Martin
Elgin Community College
Elgin, IL

David C. May
Eastern Kentucky University
Richmond, KY

G. Larry Mays
New Mexico State University
Las Cruces, NM

Susan S. McGuire
San Jacinto College North
Houston, TX

Robert J. Meadows
California Lutheran University
Thousand Oaks, CA

Jim Mezhir
Niagara County Community College
Sanborn, NY

Rick Michelson
Grossmont College
El Cajon, CA

Harv Morley
California State University
Long Beach, CA

Roslyn Muraskin
C. W. Post Campus of Long Island
Brookville, NY

Charles Myles
California State University at Los
    Angeles
Los Angeles, CA

Bonnie Neher
Harrisburg Area Community College
Harrisburg, PA

David Neubauer
University of New Orleans—Lakefront
New Orleans, LA

P. J. Ortmier
Grossmont College
El Cajon, CA

David F. Owens
Onondaga Community College
Syracuse, NY

Michael J. Palmiotto
Wichita State University
Wichita, KS

Lance Parr
Grossmont College
El Cajon, CA

William H. Parsonage
Penn State University
University Park, PA

Ken Peak
University of Nevada—Reno
Reno, NV

Joseph M. Pellicciotti
Indiana University Northwest
Gary, IN

Roger L. Pennel
Central Missouri State University
Warrensburg, MO

Joseph L. Peterson
University of Illinois at Chicago
Chicago, IL

Morgan Peterson
Palomar College
San Marcos, CA

Gary Prawel
Keuka College
Keuka Park, NY

Philip J. Reichel
University of Northern Colorado
Greely, CO

Albert Roberts
Rutgers University
New Brunswick, NJ

Carl E. Russell
Scottsdale Community College
Scottsdale, AZ

Benson Schaffer
IVAMS Arbitration and Mediation
    Services
Pomona, CA

Stephen J. Schoenthaler
California State University, Stanislaus
Turlock, CA

Jeff Schrink
Indiana State University
Terre Haute, IN

Judith M. Sgarzi
Mount Ida College
Newton, MA

Ira Silverman
University of South Florida
Tampa, FL

Jim Smith
West Valley Community College
Saratoga, CA

Loretta J. Stalans
Loyola University Chicago
Chicago, IL

Z. G. Standing Bear
Colorado State University
Fort Collins, CO

Mark A. Stetler
Montgomery College
Conroe, TX

B. Grant Stitt
University of Nevada—Reno
Reno, NV

Robert W. Taylor
University of North Texas
Denton, TX

Lawrence F. Travis III
University of Cincinnati
Cincinnati, OH

Bryan Vila
University of Wyoming
Laramie, WY

Ron Vogel
California State University Long Beach
Long Beach, CA

John Vollmann, Jr.
Miami-Dade Community College
Miami, FL

David Whelan
Western Carolina University
Cullowhee, NC

Lois Wims
Salve Regina University
Newport, RI

L. Thomas Winfree, Jr.
New Mexico State University
Las Cruces, NM

Herman Woltring
UN Crime Prevention and Criminal
    Justice Branch
Vienna, Austria

John M. Wyant
Illinois Central College
East Peoria, IL

Richard Zevitz
Marquette University
Milwaukee, WI

My thanks to each and every one! I would also like to extend a special thanks to the following individuals for their invaluable comments and suggestions along the way: Avon Burns, Kathy Cameron-Hahn, Gene Evans at New Jersey's Camden County College, Joe Graziano, Donald J. Melisi, Phil Purpura, John Robich, Ted Skotnicki, Tom Thackery, Joe Trevalino, Howard Tritt, Bill Tyrrell, Tim Veiders, and Bob Winslow.

Jean E. Sexton and Lucy H. Hartley, both very fine librarians, helped uncover information otherwise irretrievable. Thanks are also due everyone who assisted in artistic arrangements, including Michael L. Hammond of the Everett (Washington) Police Department, Sergeant Michael Flores of the New York City Police Department's Photo Unit, Assistant Chief James M. Lewis of the Bakersfield (California) Police Department, Monique Smith of the National Institute of Justice, and Tonya Matz of the University of Illinois at Chicago—all of whom were especially helpful in providing a wealth of photo resources. I am especially indebted to University of Illinois Professor Joseph L. Peterson for assistance with sections on scientific evidence, and to George W. Knox of the National Gang Crime Research Center for providing valuable information on gangs and gang activity.

I'd also like to acknowledge J. Harper Wilson, Chief of the FBI's Uniform Crime Reporting Program; Nancy Carnes of the same program; Mark Reading of the Drug Enforcement Administration's Office of Intelligence; Kristina Rose at the National Criminal Justice Reference Service; Marilyn Marbrook and Michael Rand at the Office of Justice Programs; Wilma M. Grant of the U.S. Supreme Court's Project Hermes; Ken Kerle at the American Jail Association; Lisa Bastian, survey statistician with the National Crime Victimization Survey Program; Steve Shackelton with the U.S. Parks Service; Ronald T. Allen, Steve Chaney, Bernie Homme, and Kenneth L. Whitman, all with the California Peace Officer Standards and Training Commission; Dianne Martin at the Drug Enforcement Administration; and George J. Davino of the New York City Police Department for their help in making this book both timely and accurate.

Last, but by no means least, Taylor Davis, H. R. Delaney, Jannette O. Domingo, Al Garcia, Rodney Hennigsen, Norman G. Kittel, Robert O. Lampert, and Joseph M. Pellicciotti, should know that their writings, contributions, and valuable suggestions at the earliest stages of manuscript development continue to be very much appreciated. Thank you, each and everyone!

Frank Schmalleger, Ph.D.

Criminal justice is a ubiquitous phenomenon in the lives of Americans. Newspapers and television are saturated with crime stories that rivet the attention of average citizens. The country spends about $150 billion annually on police, prisons, and courts, and well over 2 million people work in the criminal justice system. Concerns about security in the aftermath of the horrific terrorist attacks of September 11, 2001, have magnified even further the impact of law enforcement on American society. Because the nation is steeped in criminal justice matters, it is incumbent on educators to give students an accurate portrayal of how our massive, far-reaching justice system really works.

Frank Schmalleger does just that. *Criminal Justice Today* presents a wealth of materials on the functioning of the criminal justice system and the crime problems the system is intended to address. The prose is engaging, the graphics are stunning, the case studies are vivid, and the ample linkages to relevant websites are quite informative. Complex legal concepts, difficult theoretical ideas, and complicated statistical findings are presented in a very accessible manner.

Another virtue of the book is its scholarly foundation. The technological wonders of the Internet and the appeal of multicolored visual aids are never substituted for solid, well-documented analysis. Classic studies like Jerome Skolnick's study of policing and Gresham Sykes's analysis of prisons are discussed; articles in criminal justice periodicals are referenced; legal citations are plentiful. Virtually every chapter has more than 150 endnotes.

Criminal Justice Today is aptly titled: It is thoroughly up-to-date. The latest statistics, recent court decisions, and current research findings are included. Successive revisions of the text have kept even minor details accurate; for example, Schmalleger notes that the federal government's Drug Use Forecasting system (DUF), which uses urine tests to measure drug consumption, is now called the Arrestee Drug Abuse Monitoring system (ADAM). Schmalleger has painstakingly rewritten *Criminal Justice Today* to incorporate changes in law, policy, and knowledge. The seventh edition is in all respects, as the subtitle indicates, a text for the twenty-first century.

As contemporary as this text is, it is also rooted in the past. Schmalleger does a nice job of providing students with historical background which explains the evolution of modern institutions. Preventive police patrol is thus traced back to its nineteenth-century British progenitor Robert Peel, from whom the term *bobbies* is derived as a nickname for British police officers. The chapter on prisons shows how virtually every generation's wave of penal reform in the United States has become the next generation's scourge. Allusions to the past help students grasp the persistence of traditional practices as well as the impetus for change.

Criminal Justice Today is not only about today and yesterday; it is most assuredly a book about tomorrow. Every chapter is replete with discussion of the critical policy debates confronting the American criminal justice system. Among the many issues covered are whether hate crimes should carry extra punishment, whether sobriety checkpoints to identify drunk drivers should be permitted, whether peremptory challenges of prospective jurors should be eliminated, and whether "three strikes and you're out" sentencing laws are sound. Wherever possible, empirical data are introduced to shed light on the matters in dispute, but there is also clear recognition of the ethical dilemmas raised by such questions. The enduring conflict between the competing ideals of crime control and due process emerges again and again in the discussion, as well it should.

Students introduced to these profoundly important questions will surely come away from reading the text with more informed positions. Schmalleger avoids polemics in candidly presenting controversial issues like racial profiling and capital punishment; he lets readers think through their own points of view. Whether they wind up pursuing criminal justice careers or simply responding to criminal justice matters as citizens, having grappled with competing ideas will enable them to develop more sophisticated opinions. *Criminal Justice Today* equips students to respond more intelligently to election campaigns, which are often engulfed by crime and justice issues.

Criminal justice has come of age as a respected academic discipline with an established body of knowledge and rigorous methodological standards. The National Institute of Justice, which provides federal funding for research, is now about three decades old; peer-refereed criminal justice journals reporting empirical studies have proliferated; the number of doctoral programs in the field of criminal justice has grown; membership in the two major professional associations in the field, the Academy of Criminal Justice Sciences and the American Society of Criminology, has dramatically increased; and the number of students majoring in criminal justice at the undergraduate and graduate levels has soared. Introductory criminal justice textbooks need to reflect this enhanced professionalism—which is exactly what *Criminal Justice Today* does.

I have taught basic courses in criminal justice many times. While I am now primarily involved in graduate education, were I to return to the undergraduate classroom I would be happy to use Frank Schmalleger's book. It would make teaching an inherently fascinating subject even more exciting, without sacrificing the careful exposition of ideas which is the heart and soul of higher education. In terms of both academic quality and student-friendliness, *Criminal Justice Today* hits the mark.

James P. Levine
Dean of Graduate Studies and Research
John Jay College of Criminal Justice
The City University of New York

[*Justice is truth in action!*]

—Benjamin Disraeli (1804–1881)

[*Injustice anywhere is a threat to justice everywhere.*]

—Martin Luther King, Jr. (1929–1968)

part one

■ Goals of the Criminal Justice System

Common law, constitutional, statutory, and humanitarian rights of the accused:

- Justice for the individual
- Personal liberty
- Dignity as a human being
- The right to due process

These individual rights must be effectively balanced against these community concerns:

- Social justice
- Equality before the law
- The protection of society
- Freedom from fear

How does our system of justice work toward balance?

Crime in America

The Will of the People Is the Best Law

The great American statesman and orator Daniel Webster (1782–1852) once wrote, "Justice is the great interest of man on earth. It is the ligament which holds civilized beings and civilized nations together." Although Webster lived in a relatively simple time with few problems and many shared rules, justice has never been easily won. Unlike Webster's era, society today is highly complex and populated by groups with a wide diversity of interests. It is within this challenging context that the daily practice of American criminal justice occurs.

The criminal justice system has three central components: police, courts, and corrections. The history, the activities, and the legal environment surrounding the police are discussed in Part 2 of this book. Part 3 describes the courts, and Part 4 deals with prisons, probation, and parole. Part 5 provides a guide to the future of the justice system and of enforcement agencies. We begin here in Part 1, however, with an overview of that grand ideal that we call *justice*, and we consider how the justice ideal relates to the everyday practice of criminal justice in the United States today. To that end, in the four chapters that make up this section, we will examine how and why laws are made. We will look at the wide array of interests that impinge upon the justice system, and we will examine closely the dichotomy that distinguishes citizens who are primarily concerned with individual rights from those who emphasize the need for individual responsibility and social accountability. In the pages that follow, we will see how justice can mean protection from the power of the state to some people, and vengeance to others. In this section, we will also lay the groundwork for the rest of the text by painting a picture of crime in America today, suggesting possible causes for it, and showing how policies for dealing with crime have evolved.

As you read about the complex tapestry that is the practice of criminal justice in America today, you will see a system in flux, perhaps less sure of its values and purpose than at any time in its history. You may also catch the sense, however, that very soon a new and reborn institution of justice may emerge from the ferment that now exists. Whatever the final outcome, it can only be hoped that *justice*, as proffered by the American system of criminal justice, will be sufficient to hold our civilization together—and to allow it to prosper well into the twenty-first century and beyond.

What Is
Criminal Justice?

LEARNING OBJECTIVES

After reading this chapter, you should be able to

■ Explain how media reports of crime have led to increased public concern about criminal activity

■ Identify the central theme and the two sub-themes around which this textbook is built

■ Highlight the differences between the individual-rights and public-order perspectives

■ Discuss the nature of justice, and list various types of justice

■ Explain the structure of the criminal justice system and the differences between the consensus and conflict models

■ Describe the process of American criminal justice, including the stages of criminal case processing

■ Describe the meaning of due process of law, and identify where guarantees of due process can be found in the American legal system

■ Explain the difference between the academic disciplines of criminal justice and criminology

■ Explain how multiculturalism and diversity present special challenges to, and opportunities for, the American system of criminal justice

chapter 1

The rights guaranteed to criminal suspects, defendants, offenders, and prisoners were not included in the Bill of Rights for the benefit of criminals. They are fundamental political rights that protect all Americans from governmental abuse of power. These rights are found in the Fourth, Fifth, Sixth, Eighth, and Fourteenth Amendments. They include the guarantee against unreasonable search and seizure, the right to reasonable bail, the right to due process of law, and the right to be free from cruel and unusual treatment. This "bundle of rights" is indispensable to a free society.

—American Civil Liberties Union[1]

The Constitution is not a suicide pact.

—Former Secretary of State Warren Christopher, after terrorists destroyed the World Trade Center in New York City in 2001[2]

Key Concepts

[Terms]

arraignment	criminal justice	multiculturalism
bail	criminal justice system	preliminary hearing
booking	criminology	probable cause
civil justice	due process	public-order advocate
concurrent sentence	due process model	social control
conflict model	grand jury	social justice
consecutive sentence	indictment	trial
consensus model	individual rights	USA PATRIOT Act of 2001
crime	individual-rights advocate	warrant
crime-control model	justice	

Hear the author discuss this chapter at **cjtoday.com**

Introduction

On September 11, 2001, kamikaze-like zealots hijacked four commercial airliners laden with fuel and crashed two of them into New York City's 110-story twin World Trade Center (WTC) towers. The towers collapsed shortly afterward, their steel girders softened from the intense fires that the crashes produced. The third commandeered airliner crashed into the Pentagon, and the fourth crashed into the Pennsylvania countryside after passengers wrestled with the hijackers. The attacks were carried out by nineteen militant Islamic fanatics thought to be under the control of terrorist leader Osama bin Laden and his Al Qaeda organization. Bin Laden apparently hoped to damage America's long-held sense of security and to pull the world into a final conflict that he and his followers believed would lead to an Armageddon. The attacks left nearly 3,000 people dead or missing and caused billions of dollars in property damage.

The fuel-fed infernos that consumed the World Trade Center and part of the Pentagon left behind what was arguably the nation's largest-ever crime scene. The attacks were the most destructive criminal activity ever to have been perpetrated on U.S. soil. Within days of the attacks, President George W. Bush declared a worldwide war on terrorism and created a new Cabinet-level position of Director of the Office of Homeland Security—a position that was quickly filled by then-Governor Tom Ridge of Pennsylvania.

Beginning soon after the attacks, hundreds of thousands of calls poured into the offices of federal, state, and local law enforcement agencies from people who had information to share. That information, along with evidence collected at the scenes, interviews with airline employees, and efforts to track the activities of the terrorists before the attack, soon produced the largest and most intense criminal investigation ever undertaken in this country.[3] The Federal Bureau of Investigation (FBI), the U.S. Secret Service, the Immigration and Naturalization Service, the U.S. Border Patrol, U.S. Customs, and the Bureau of Alcohol, Tobacco, and Firearms were the most visible of the enforcement agencies involved in the investigation. Many county, state, and city law enforcement agencies also fielded thousands of calls and followed numerous leads in an attempt to track down suspected remaining terrorist cells. Telephone records; bank accounts; e-mail messages; websites; credit card and rental car receipts; aircraft, railway, and bus manifests; Arabic-language newspapers and publications; computer disks; and the records of flight-training schools that had instructed the terrorists were all scoured by investigators looking for information.

To effectively scrutinize the immense amount of information that was uncovered, and to avoid information overload, law enforcement personnel investigating the terrorist attacks employed a tool known as *intelligence link analysis*. Intelligence link analysis uses centralized computers to create complex flowcharts highlighting information that appears to link perpetrators to criminal incidents and to possible accomplices. Data collected from financial records, intercepted electronic communications, and interviews with potential associates of

> The criminal justice system is composed of a sprawling bureaucracy with many separate agencies that are largely autonomous and independent.
>
> —Gary LaFree, Ph.D., University of New Mexico

The 110-story twin towers of the World Trade Center burning after Islamic terrorists commandeered two commercial jetliners and crashed them into the buildings on September 11, 2001. Both buildings collapsed within hours, killing nearly 3,000 people. Another 262 people aboard the airplanes died. Terrorism is a criminal act that may involve mass murder, arson, destruction of property, kidnapping, hijacking, conspiracy, and other offenses.

AP/Wide World Photos

the hijackers, combined with other interviews and evidence searches, were fed into the software model, allowing agents to produce evidence linking the hijackers to a criminal network with outposts in Britain, Germany, Spain, the United Arab Emirates, and the United States.[4] A massive dragnet, based partly on the results of the analysis, was created by police agencies across the United States and in Europe, resulting in the arrest of more than 400 people within two weeks of the attacks.

The terrorist attacks hold many lessons as well as challenges for students of criminal justice. The most critical issue could be found in the ensuing debate between advocates of individual rights and freedom and others wanting to ensure collective security and crime prevention. This issue, which fed TV talk shows and newspaper editorials nationwide following the attacks, asks Americans to determine what rights, freedoms, and conveniences (if any) they are willing to sacrifice to increase personal and public safety. It also anticipates the theme upon which this book is based (discussed at length later in this chapter).

Another lesson has come in the form of heightened recognition of terrorism as a potentially horrendous **crime**. Many states and the federal government have laws outlawing terrorism, although terrorism itself can involve many other kinds of crimes. In the case of the World Trade Center and Pentagon attacks, for example, the crimes committed include murder, kidnapping, hijacking, grand theft, felonious assault, battery, conspiracy, and arson.

A third lesson, the need for relevant multicultural skills among justice agency personnel, emerged from the inability of investigators to effectively interpret important

> People expect both safety and justice and do not want to sacrifice one for the other.
>
> —Christopher Stone, President and Director, the Vera Institute of Justice

crime

Conduct in violation of the criminal laws of a state, the federal government, or a local jurisdiction, for which there is no legally acceptable justification or excuse.

President George W. Bush viewing an "intelligence link analysis" printout a month after the September 11, 2001, terrorist attacks on the World Trade Center and the Pentagon. Intelligence link analysis allows investigators to create large flowcharts with lines connecting suspected criminals and possible accomplices. The flowchart is expanded as new information arrives.

AP/Wide World Photos

phone conversations, e-mail communications, and written documents—all of which were in Arabic. "You are getting these huge amounts of material and have no way to translate it," said one New York City official.[5] Peter S. Probst, a former terrorism expert for the Department of Defense and the Central Intelligence Agency, noted that "wiretaps do you no good if you have no one who can translate, or can be able to understand what they are hearing."[6] In response, FBI Director Robert S. Mueller III immediately created special positions within the FBI for people proficient in English and Arabic, Farsi, or Pashto.[7]

Because the values, interests, language, and motivation of foreign conspirators often differ substantially from those of most Americans, defending against transnational crime and heading off terrorist attacks can be especially difficult. Law enforcement agencies whose members possess a wide range of multicultural skills, including the ability to speak or read languages other than English, are probably best equipped to detect and thwart such crimes.

Although law enforcement and security agencies were unable to prevent the September 11 attacks, many have since moved from a reactive to a proactive posture in the fight against terrorism. As a result, law enforcement agencies throughout the country are now using information gathered from a wide variety of intelligence activities to anticipate and plan for growing threats to public safety. An especially important new tool in the law enforcement arsenal is the federal **USA PATRIOT Act of 2001**,[8] largely enacted as a legislative response to terrorism. The law is officially known as the Uniting and Strengthening America by Providing Appropriate Tools Required to Intercept and Obstruct Terrorism Act of 2001 (from which the acronym *USA PATRIOT* is derived). The law dramatically increases the investigatory authority of federal, state, and local police agencies, although sometimes only temporarily. The expanded police powers created under the legislation are not limited to investigations of terrorist activity, but apply to many different criminal offenses. See Chapter 7 for a detailed description of the legislation.

The section of text that follows traces the history of crime and criminality in this country during the past fifty years. As you read about these crimes, you might ask yourself, "What do crimes like these do to America's sense of well-being, and what might such crimes mean for the future of the American way of life and for our criminal justice system?" Learn more about crime fears via **Library Extra! 1–1** at cjtoday.com.

USA PATRIOT Act of 2001

A federal law (Public Law 107–56), enacted in response to terrorist attacks on the World Trade Center and the Pentagon occurring on September 11, 2001. The law, officially titled the Uniting and Strengthening America by Providing Appropriate Tools Required to Intercept and Obstruct Terrorism Act, substantially broadens the investigative authority of law enforcement agencies throughout America and is applicable to many crimes other than terrorism.

Library EXTRA!

Crime in the Last Half Century

The last half century has been especially influential in shaping the nature of crime and the American criminal justice system of today. What we call *criminal activity* has undoubtedly been with us since the dawn of history, and crime control has long been a primary concern of politicians and government leaders worldwide.

In America, crime waves have come and gone, including an 1850–1880 crime wave that was apparently related to social upheaval caused by large-scale immigration, and the wave of widespread organized criminal activity associated with the Prohibition years of the early twentieth century.[9] Following World War II, however, American crime rates remained relatively stable until the 1960s.

The 1960s and 1970s saw a burgeoning concern with the rights of ethnic and racial minorities, women, the physically and mentally challenged, and many other groups. The civil rights movement of the period emphasized equality of opportunity and respect for individuals, regardless of race, color, creed, or personal attributes. As new laws were passed and suits filed, court involvement in the movement grew. Soon a plethora of hard-won individual rights and prerogatives, based upon the U.S. Constitution, the Bill of Rights, and new federal and state legislation, were recognized and guaranteed. By the 1980s, the civil rights movement had profoundly affected all areas of social life—from education through employment to the activities of the criminal justice system.

This emphasis on **individual rights** was accompanied by a dramatic increase in reported criminal activity. "Traditional" crimes, such as murder, rape, and assault, as reported by the FBI, increased astronomically during the 1970s and into the 1980s. Many theories were advanced to explain this virtual explosion of observed criminality. A few doubted the accuracy of "official" accounts, claiming that any actual rise in crime was much less than that portrayed in the reports. Some analysts of American culture, however, suggested that newfound freedoms combined with the long-pent-up hostilities of the socially and economically deprived to produce social disorganization and increased criminality.

By the mid-1980s, popular perceptions identified one particularly insidious form of criminal activity—the dramatic increase in the sale and use of illicit drugs—as a threat to the very fabric of American society. Cocaine, and later laboratory-processed "crack," had spread to every corner of America. The country's borders were inundated with smugglers intent on reaping quick fortunes. Large cities became havens for drug gangs, and many inner-city areas were all but abandoned to highly armed and well-financed racketeers. Some famous personalities succumbed to the allure of drugs, and athletic teams and sporting events became focal points for drug busts. Drugs quickly spread to younger users. Even small-town elementary schools found themselves facing the specter of campus drug dealing and associated violence.

Worse still were the seemingly ineffective governmental measures intended to stem the drug tide. Drug peddlers, with their huge reserves of money, were often able to escape prosecution or to wrangle plea bargains to avoid imprisonment. Public anger grew, fueled by constant media coverage of such "miscarriages of justice."

By the close of the 1980s, neighborhoods and towns were fighting for their communal lives. Cities experienced dramatic declines in property values, and residents wrestled with the eroding quality of life. Huge rents had been torn in the national social fabric. The American way of life, long taken for granted, was under the gun. Traditional values appeared in danger of going up in smoke along with the "crack" now being smoked openly in some parks and resorts. Looking for a way to stem the tide of increased criminality, many took up the call for "law and order." In response, President Ronald Reagan created a "drug czar" Cabinet-level position to coordinate the "war on drugs." Careful thought was given at the highest levels to using the military to patrol the sea-lanes and air corridors through which many of the illegal drugs entered the country. President George Bush, who followed Reagan into office, quickly embraced and expanded the government's antidrug efforts.

The 1990s began with the arrest of serial murderer Jeffrey Dahmer, and the shocking details of his crimes later became public. Dahmer, who killed as many as 15 young men in sexually motivated attacks, cannibalized some of his victims and kept the body parts of others in his refrigerator. Dahmer's crimes, along with those of other serial killers, are discussed in more detail in Chapter 2.

In 1992, the videotaped beating of Rodney King, an African-American motorist, at the hands of Los Angeles–area police officers, splashed across TV screens throughout the country and shifted the public's focus onto issues of police brutality and the effective

---

individual rights

The rights guaranteed to all members of American society by the U.S. Constitution (especially those found in the first ten amendments to the Constitution, known as the *Bill of Rights*). These rights are especially important to criminal defendants facing formal processing by the criminal justice system.

When you know both the accuser and the accused, as we so often do, the conflict between civil rights and victims' rights is seldom completely black or white. And it is the gray areas in between that make the debate so difficult.

—Columnist Vicki Williams, writing on crime in a small American town

management of law enforcement personnel. As the King incident seemed to show, when racial minorities come face-to-face with agents of the American criminal justice system, something less than justice may be the result. Although initially acquitted by a California jury—which contained no black members—two of the officers who beat King were convicted in a 1993 federal courtroom of violating his civil rights.[10] The incident and trials are described in more detail in Chapter 7.

The year 1993 saw an especially violent encounter in Waco, Texas, among agents of the Bureau of Alcohol, Tobacco, and Firearms (ATF), the Federal Bureau of Investigation, and members of cult leader David Koresh's Branch Davidian. The fray, which began when ATF agents assaulted Koresh's fortresslike compound, leaving four agents and six cultists dead, ended 51 days later with the fiery deaths of Koresh and 71 of his followers, many of whom were children. The assault on Koresh's compound led to a congressional investigation and charges that the ATF and the FBI had been ill-prepared to deal successfully with large-scale domestic resistance and had reacted more out of alarm and frustration than wisdom. Attorney General Janet Reno refused to blame agents for misjudging Koresh's intentions, although 11 Davidians were later acquitted of charges that they had murdered the federal agents.

By the mid-1990s, however, a strong shift away from the claimed misdeeds of the criminal justice system began, and a newfound emphasis on individual accountability began to blossom among an American public fed up with crime and fearful of their own victimization. Growing calls for enhanced responsibility quickly began to replace the previous emphasis on individual rights. As a juggernaut of conservative opinion made itself felt on the political scene, Senator Phil Gramm of Texas observed that the public wants to "grab violent criminals by the throat, put them in prison [and] stop building prisons like Holiday Inns."[11]

It was probably the public's perception of growing crime rates, coupled with a belief that offenders frequently went unpunished or that many received only a judicial slap on the wrist, that led to the burgeoning emphasis on responsibility and punishment. However, a few spectacular crimes which received widespread coverage in the news media heightened the public's sense that crime in the United States was out of hand and that new measures were needed to combat it. In 1993, for example, James Jordan, father of Chicago Bulls' basketball superstar Michael Jordan, was killed in a cold-blooded robbery by two young men with long criminal records. Jordan's death, which seemed to be the result of a chance encounter, helped rivet the nation's attention on what appeared to be the increasing frequency of random and senseless violence.

In that same year, a powerful bomb ripped apart the basement of one of the twin World Trade Center buildings in New York City. The explosion, which killed five and opened a 100-foot crater through four sublevels of concrete, displaced 50,000 workers, including employees at the commodities exchanges that handle billions of dollars' worth of trade in oil, gold, coffee, and sugar.[12]

> Everywhere across the nation, we are more concerned with ensuring that criminal activity does not repeat itself, rather than keeping criminal activity from occurring in the first place.
>
> —Tony Fabelo, Executive Director, Texas Criminal Justice Policy Council

Also in 1993, the heart-wrenching story of Polly Klaas splashed across the national media. Twelve-year-old Polly was kidnapped from a slumber party at her home while her mother and little sister slept in the next room. Two other girls were left bound and gagged after a bearded stranger broke into the Klaas home in Petaluma, California. Despite efforts by hundreds of uniformed officers and 4,000 volunteers, attempts to find the girl proved fruitless. Nine weeks later, just before Christmas, an ex-con named Richard Allen Davis was arrested and charged with Polly's murder. Investigators found that Davis's life read like a litany of criminal activity and that Polly's death was due at least partially to the failure of the criminal justice system to keep a dangerous man behind bars. Three years later, in 1996, Davis was convicted of Polly's murder and was sentenced to death.

In 1994, the attention of the nation was riveted on proceedings in the Susan Smith case. Smith, a South Carolina mother, confessed to drowning her two young boys (ages one and three years) by strapping them into child-safety seats and rolling the family station wagon off a pier and into a lake. Smith, who appears to have been motivated by the demands of an extramarital love affair, had originally claimed that a black man had carjacked her vehicle with the boys still inside. This was also the year in which seven-year-old Megan Kanka was brutally murdered by convicted sex offender Jesse K. Timmendequas.

Senseless violence linked to racial hatred stunned the nation during the 1995 trial of Colin Ferguson. Ferguson, who was eventually convicted of killing six passengers and wounding 19 others during what prosecutors claimed was a racially motivated shooting rampage on a Long Island Railroad commuter train in 1993, maintained his innocence throughout the trial, even though he was identified by more than a dozen eyewitnesses, including some whom he had shot.

In 1995, the double-murder trial of former football superstar and media personality O. J. Simpson received much national exposure, with daily reports on the trial appearing on television and in newspapers throughout the country. Simpson was acquitted of the brutal murders of his ex-wife Nicole and her friend Ronald Goldman. Simpson had hired a team of lawyers whom some referred to as "the million-dollar defense"—an action many people saw as akin to buying justice. In a 1997 civil trial, however, a California jury found Simpson liable for the death of Goldman and the "battery" of his former wife, and he was ordered to pay $33.5 million in damages.

Perhaps no one criminal incident gripped the psyche of the American people and later galvanized the policy-making efforts of legislators during the 1990s more than the 1995 bombing of the Alfred P. Murrah Federal Building in Oklahoma City by antigovernment extremist Timothy McVeigh. One hundred sixty-eight people died in the bombing, 19 of them children. Hundreds more were wounded, and millions of dollars' worth of property was destroyed. McVeigh was executed in the U.S. penitentiary in Terre Haute, Indiana, on June 11, 2001.

The attack on the Oklahoma City federal building was followed by a bombing at the 1996 Olympics in Atlanta that killed one person and injured 111. Both events caused Americans to realize that the very freedoms that allow the United States to serve as a model of democracy for the rest of the world make it possible for terrorist or terrorist-affiliated groups to operate within the country relatively unencumbered.

The strangulation murder of six-year-old JonBenet Ramsey, the young "beauty queen" killed at Christmastime 1996 in her family's Boulder, Colorado, home added to the national sense that no one is safe. (See **Web Extra! 1–1** at cjtoday.com for more information.) In 1997, the roadside murder of 27-year-old Ennis Cosby, son of well-known entertainer Bill Cosby, heightened the public's fear of random violence. A 1997 killing spree attributed to Andrew Cunanan, which ended in his suicide (and which claimed the life of world-renowned fashion designer Gianni Versace and five other men), galvanized the nation as the public participated in a media-led hunt for the alleged killer.

In 1998, 21-year-old Matthew Shepard, a shy and slightly built University of Wyoming college student, was savagely beaten to death by two men, Aaron James McKinney and Russell Arthur Henderson, both of whom were also 21.[13] Shepard, who was gay, had been lured from a bar to a remote location outside of town. He suffered 18 blows to the head and had been pistol-whipped with a .357-caliber Magnum revolver. Shepard's body had been tied so tightly to a barbed-wire fence that sheriff's deputies had trouble cutting it free. The blood on Shepard's face had been partially washed away by tears—a sign that he had lived for some time after the beating. The killing outraged many Americans and helped focus the nation's attention on hate crimes.

The Columbine High School massacre in Colorado and the Wedgwood Baptist Church shootings in Fort Worth, Texas, provided a stunningly violent backdrop to 1999. The Columbine shooting left 14 students and one teacher dead. More than 20 others were injured. Learn more about the Columbine shooting in Chapter 14. In Texas, seven people died and seven others were wounded at a Christian music festival when a lone gunman named Larry Ashbrook opened fire at the Wedgwood Baptist Church. Ashbrook, who was 47 at the time of the shooting, took careful aim at worshipers as he fired as many as 24 rounds from a .38-caliber revolver and a 9mm semiautomatic handgun, holding one weapon in each hand. Two video cameras were rolling as Ashbrook fired over a two-minute period, and authorities were later able to watch his methodical movements and to count the number of shots fired.[14] Ashbrook took his own life after a 19-year-old church member, Jeremiah Neitz, talked to him about religion.[15] Six unused clips of bullets remained in his pockets.

On May 22, 2000, Texas Judge Bill Harmon sentenced convicted "railway killer" Angel Maturino Resendiz (aka Rafael Resendez-Ramirez), 40, to die by lethal injection after Houston jurors returned a death penalty recommendation following two hours of deliberation.[16] Resendiz, an illegal immigrant from Mexico, was dubbed the "railway killer" because he killed people near train tracks. Resendiz, it turns out, was a drifter who had been jumping trains since the 1970s. Although he admitted killing at least

A family mourning the loss of Columbine High School students at a makeshift memorial near Littleton, Colorado. Fourteen students and a teacher died and 20 others were injured when 18-year-old Eric Harris and 17-year-old Dylan Klebold, both students at the school, carried out a planned attack on their classmates and teachers on April 20, 1999.

Ed Andrieski, AP/Wide World Photos

eight other people in a cross-country bloodbath (and is suspected of having committed many more murders, both in the United States and in Mexico[17]), Resendiz was convicted only of the 1998 murder of Dr. Claudia Benton. Benton, a pediatric geneticist, had lived in the Houston area. The Resendiz case is discussed in more detail in Chapters 2 and 4.

The twenty-first century[18] opened with the sad story of 14-year-old Nathaniel Brazill, of Lake Worth, Florida. Brazill, a former honor student with no criminal record, was convicted on May 16, 2001, of second-degree murder for shooting his favorite middle school English teacher, Barry Grunow, in the head one day before summer vacation was set to begin. Brazill, who was 13 at the time of the killing, was tried as an adult and was sentenced to 28 years in prison. His case fed a national debate over trying juveniles as adults.

Later that same year, Andrea Yates, a 36-year-old Texas mother, was charged with capital murder in the systematic drowning of her five young children in a bathtub.[19] The children ranged in age from six months to seven years. Yates, who was undergoing psychiatric care prior to the killings, had previously attempted suicide but had been taken off of antipsychotic medication. She admitted killing the children but blamed her actions on severe postpartum depression. In March 2002, a Texas court found her guilty of capital murder in the death of her children, and she was sentenced to life in prison.

Also in 2001, 27-year-old Ukrainian immigrant Nikolay Soltys became one of the FBI's "Ten Most Wanted" criminals following the brutal murders of six of his relatives near Sacramento, California. Following his arrest, Soltys confessed to police, saying that he had stabbed and slashed the throats of family members in a killing spree that lasted several hours because he believed that they were trying to poison him.[20] The dead included Lyubov Soltys, the killer's 23-year-old pregnant wife; their three-year-old son, Sergey; Soltys' nine-year-old nephew and niece; and his aunt and uncle. Soltys was caught as he tried to enter his brother's home, which police had staked out.[21] Soltys committed suicide in jail in early 2002. Learn more about Nikolay Soltys and the special problems that crimes committed by recent immigrants pose for the justice system in the CJ Today News box near the end of this chapter.

Crime can take many different forms. On February 11, 2000, for example, former telephone repairman Andrew Burnett, 27, of San Jose, California, grabbed a small dog named Leo from its owner's lap and flung it to its death in expressway traffic.[22] The dog's owner, Sara McBurnett, a real estate agent from Incline Village, Nevada, had just rear-ended Burnett's car near San Jose International Airport. A witness later testified that after both vehicles stopped, Burnett "approached McBurnett's car yelling and screaming, reached both hands inside, pulled Leo out and threw him into traffic."[23] California is among the 31 states that make intentional abuse of an animal a felony. On July 13, 2001, California Judge Kevin Murphy sentenced Burnett to three years in prison. Courtroom observers erupted in applause as the sentence was announced.[24]

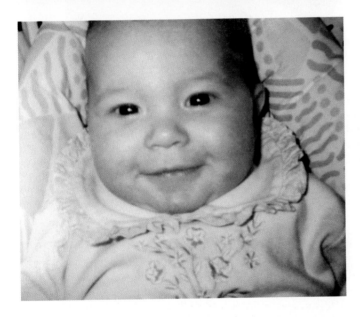

Andrea Pia Yates, the Texas mother, convicted in 2002 of capital murder in the drowning deaths of her five young children in the family's bathtub. The children, Luke, 2, Paul, 3, John, 5, Noah, 7, and Mary, 6 months, are shown above and to the left. Yates was sentenced to life in prison, and will have to serve 40 years before parole eligibility. At trial, Yates lawyers claimed that she suffered from severe postpartum depression and was insane at the time of the killings.

© AFP Photo, Steve Ueckert, CORBIS; Reuters, TimePix

Finally, as we discussed at the start of this chapter, a series of highly destructive and well-coordinated terrorist attacks on New York City and Washington, D.C., on September 11, 2001, resulted in the collapse and total destruction of the twin 110-story towers of the World Trade Center and a devastating explosion at the Pentagon. Terrorism is discussed in more detail in Chapter 17. As that chapter points out, terrorism is a criminal act, and preventing terrorism and investigating terrorist incidents after they occur is a highly important role for local, state, and federal law enforcement agencies.

While not every high-visibility crime can be reported in this introductory material, a check of local or national newspapers, TV news shows, or news-oriented websites will show that crimes, including shocking, violent, personal, and seemingly random crimes, continue unabated. Violent crimes punctuated with seemingly random cruelty (including terrorism) have changed the mood of the American public or, perhaps more accurately, have accelerated what was an already changing mood. A growing national frustration with the apparent inability of our society and its justice system to prevent crimes and to consistently hold offenders who are identified and then arrested to heartfelt standards of right and wrong has led to increased conservatism in the public-policy arena. That conservative tendency, which was given new life by the World Trade Center attacks, was already firmly rooted in the public consciousness by the time of the 1994 congressional elections, where "get tough on crime" policies won the day. Since that time, numerous other public officials have

> If you break the law,
> we're going to hold you
> accountable, and there
> will be tough consequences
> for your actions.
>
> —North Carolina Governor
> Jim Hunt[i]

Sara McBurnett holding a photograph of her dog, Leo. Leo was thrown to his death on a San Jose freeway by Andrew Burnett during a road rage incident in 2000. Burnett received a three-year prison sentence for killing the dog.

AP/Wide World Photos

joined the "get tough" bandwagon. Many have stopped asking what society can do to protect individuals accused of crimes and instead demand to know how offenders can better be held accountable for violations of the criminal law. As we set off into the twenty-first century, public perspectives have largely shifted away from seeing the criminal as an unfortunate victim of poor social and personal circumstances, to seeing him or her as a dangerous social predator. For a detailed look at crimes that have shaped the twentieth century, see **Web Extra! 1–2** at cjtoday.com.

A man coated with ash and debris from the collapse of the World Trade Center's south tower recovering near City Hall in lower Manhattan on September 11, 2001. The criminal acts that led to the eventual collapse of both towers were planned and committed by international terrorists.

AP/Wide World Photos

Darrel Frank, the founder of Dead Serious, Incorporated, standing next to the organization's official vehicle. Reflecting the "get tough on crime and criminals" attitude now so prevalent in American society, Dead Serious offers a $5,000 reward to members who legally kill a criminal.

Fort Worth Star-Telegram

The Themes of This Book

This book, which is about the American system of criminal justice and the agencies and processes that constitute it, builds upon a theme that we think is especially valuable for studying criminal justice today. That theme, *individual rights versus public order,* draws upon historical developments that have shaped our legal system and our understandings of crime and justice. It remains one of the primary determinants of the nature of contemporary criminal justice—including criminal law, police practice, sentencing, and corrections. For many years, the dominant philosophy in American criminal justice focused on guaranteeing the rights of criminal defendants while seeking to understand the root causes of crime and violence. However, during the last decade or two, a growing conservative emphasis has concerned itself with the interests of an ordered society, with public safety, and with the rights of crime victims. Conservative sentiments continue to influence today's public policy and were given new life by highly destructive terrorist attacks on the World Trade Center and Pentagon in 2001. Following the attacks, U.S. House of Representatives Democratic leader Richard Gephardt said that Congress should move quickly to open debate on security measures such as a national ID card. "We are in a new world," Gephardt said. "This event will change the balance between freedom and security."[25]

In recent years, events such as the WTC disaster have called into question some of the fundamental premises upon which the American justice system rests. A few weeks after the terrorist attacks, for example, U.S. Supreme Court Justice Sandra Day O'Connor told an audience at New York University that as a result of the nation's heightened need for security, "we're likely to experience more restrictions on our personal freedom than has ever been the case in our country."[26]

This book's underlying theme can be stated as follows:

There is widespread recognition in contemporary society of the need to balance (1) the freedoms and privileges of our nation's citizens and the respect accorded the rights of individuals faced with criminal prosecution against (2) the valid interests that society has in preventing future crimes, in public safety, and in reducing the harm caused by criminal activity. While the personal freedoms guaranteed to law-abiding citizens as well as to criminal suspects by the Constitution, as interpreted by the U.S. Supreme Court, must be closely guarded, so too the urgent social needs of local communities for controlling unacceptable behavior and protecting law-abiding citizens from harm must be recognized. Still to be adequately addressed are the needs and interests of victims and the fear of crime so prevalent in the minds of many law-abiding citizens.

Figure 1–1 represents our theme. The figure shows that most people today who intelligently consider the criminal justice system assume one of two viewpoints. In keeping with our first theme, we shall refer to those who seek to protect personal freedoms and civil rights within society, and especially within the criminal justice process, as **individual-rights advocates**. Those who suggest that under certain circumstances involving criminal threats to public safety, the interests of society (especially crime control and social order) should take precedence over individual rights will be called **public-order advocates**. Justice O'Connor, in a 2001 address at New York University, summed up the differences between these two perspectives by asking, "At what point does the cost to civil liberties from legislation designed to prevent terrorism [and crime] outweigh the added security that that legislation provides?"[27] In this book, we seek to look at ways that the individual-rights and public-order perspectives can be balanced to serve both sets of needs. Hence you will find our first theme discussed throughout this text, including Individual Rights versus Public Order boxes, as well as highlighted in many of the Web Quest! sections at the end of each chapter.

This book also builds upon two subthemes:

- The future of crime and justice, including social issues and changing technology
- The impact of multiculturalism and social diversity upon the contemporary practice of criminal justice, and especially the role of the police

The first of these subthemes, *the future of crime and justice*, explores the potential impact of emerging social issues on the justice field while describing developing technologies that could significantly alter the nature of crime and the practice of criminal justice in the near future. This subtheme can be stated as follows:

Social change and technological advances have had a significant impact on the nature and extent of crime in American society over the past century and will continue to do so in the future, most likely with increasing rapidity. Today's criminal justice agencies are increasingly challenged by the growing implementation of new and emerging technologies in the commission of crime and by changing social values which have contributed to a redefinition of the nature of crime and illegal activity. If they are to be effective, social policy initiatives and criminal justice agencies that seek to address the crime problem in America must recognize the changing nature of crime and especially the impact that emerging technologies and changing values are having on crime and the criminal law.

Learn more about the changing nature of crime in the United States via **Library Extra!1–2** at cjtoday.com.

The important relationship between emerging technology and potentially new and highly destructive forms of criminality cannot be overstated. Following the appointment of Tom Ridge as Director of the new federal Office of Homeland Security in 2001, for example, Senator Joseph Lieberman, Chairman of the Senate's Committee on Governmental Affairs, called for the addition of anti-cyberterrorism to the list of duties with which the office was to be

individual-rights advocate

One who seeks to protect personal freedoms within the process of criminal justice.

public-order advocate

One who suggests that under certain circumstances involving a criminal threat to public safety, the interests of society should take precedence over individual rights.

> Crime does more than expose the weakness in social relationships; it undermines the social order itself, by destroying the assumptions on which it is based.
>
> —James Q. Wilson, UCLA[ii]

> We must not defeat our liberties in trying to defend them.
>
> —Former National Security Adviser Anthony Lake[iii]

FIGURE 1–1

The theme of this book: balancing the concern for individual rights with the need for public order through the administration of criminal justice.

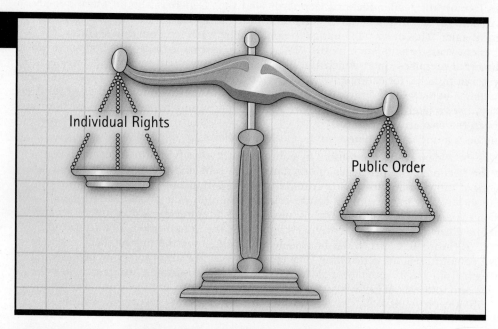

Individual Rights

Public Order

charged. "So much of our lives, commerce, and society are on the Internet," said Lieberman, "that we've created a new form of vulnerability."[28] The relationship between technology and criminality will be explored in CJ Futures boxes throughout this book. A focused overview of emerging technologies affecting criminal justice practice can be found in Chapter 17.

Our second subtheme, *the impact of multiculturalism and social diversity upon the contemporary practice of criminal justice,* is one of the most widespread and important issues facing the justice system today. It can be stated as follows:

> American society is culturally and socially diverse and shows signs of becoming increasingly so. Cultural and social diversity, which often flow from racial, ethnic, gender, religious, economic, and lifestyle differences, represent a special challenge to today's criminal justice system. Justice agencies and their representatives must become aware of and sensitive to the diverse beliefs, traditions, values, and routine practices of many different groups in order to effectively combat crime in the United States today.

Multiculturalism and diversity are discussed in many chapters throughout this text, including this chapter and Chapters 2, 4, 6, 7, and 9. Most materials related to multiculturalism and diversity appear as boxed items within these chapters.

The themes around which this textbook is written are intended to (1) describe in detail the American criminal justice system (with frequent comparisons to international practice); (2) help students develop an appreciation for the delicacy of the balancing act now facing the criminal justice system; (3) enhance students' appreciation for multicultural issues and diversity issues, especially as they affect police departments, the courts, prisons, victims, and the practices of probation and parole; and (4) provide readers with insight into the impact that emerging technologies and new social issues are likely to have on the everyday practice of criminal justice in the near future.

As you read this book, you will see that all three thematic issues are interwoven, and you will come to recognize that each has implications for the others. Changing technology, for example, can increase surveillance opportunities among justice agencies and can enhance methods of **social control**. The first CJ Today News box in this chapter discusses the growing use of face-recognition technology and surveillance cameras in public areas to alert police officers to the presence of fugitives. Some, however, claim that this kind of technology has a negative impact on individual rights. A later chapter (Chapter 6) describes new thermal imaging equipment that is able to "see" inside of a building and is used to detect the presence of fugitives and drug-manufacturing operations. Such technology also has an impact on individual rights (and its use, as Chapter 6 discusses, usually requires a search warrant). As we shall also see, the demands and expectations placed on justice agencies in multicultural societies involve a similar dilemma: how to protect the rights of individuals to self-expression while ensuring social control and the safety and security of the public.

Social Justice

On September 20, 2001, in the immediate aftermath of the World Trade Center destruction, President George W. Bush delivered a televised address to the American people. In his rallying cry to a nation about to embark on a war against world terrorism, Bush said, "We will bring our enemies to justice; or we will bring justice to our enemies."[29] The word *justice* is powerful, and the president's choice of words spoke to all Americans.

Bush's call to arms, however inspiring it may have been, was made all the more difficult by the fact that in fighting terrorism worldwide, no one seemed to be sure of just what *justice* might mean and what form it might eventually take. The trouble, of course, is that *justice* means different things to different people—even to those living within the same society. Just as *justice* can be an elusive term for politicians, even in times of war, it is not always clear exactly how justice can be achieved in the criminal justice system. We might ask ourselves, for example, if "justice for all" is a reasonable expectation of today's system of criminal justice—or of tomorrow's. That question is complicated because individual interests and social needs sometimes diverge and sometimes parallel one another. As a consequence, justice can look very different when seen from the perspective of a society or an entire nation than it does when seen from the viewpoint of an individual or a small group of people. Hence it is to the nature of justice that we now turn our attention.

The well-known British philosopher and statesman Benjamin Disraeli (1804–1881) once defined **justice** as "truth in action." One popular dictionary definition of *justice* says that it is "the principle of moral rightness, or conformity to truth."[30]

Of special concern to anyone seeking to enact "justice" are **criminal justice** and **civil justice**—both of which are aspects of a wider form of equity termed **social justice**.

> Criminal justice cannot be achieved in the absence of social justice.
>
> —American Friends' Service Committee, *Struggle for Justice*

social control

The use of sanctions and rewards within a group to influence and shape the behavior of individual members of that group. Social control is a primary concern of social groups and communities, and it is their interest in the exercise of social control that leads to the creation of both criminal and civil statutes.

justice

The principle of fairness; the ideal of moral equity.

criminal justice

In the strictest sense, the criminal (penal) law, the law of criminal procedure, and the array of procedures and activities having to do with the enforcement of this body of law. Criminal justice cannot be separated from social justice because the kind of justice enacted in our nation's criminal courts is a reflection of basic American understandings of right and wrong.

civil justice

The civil law, the law of civil procedure, and the array of procedures and activities having to do with private rights and remedies sought by civil action. Civil justice cannot be separated from social justice because the kind of justice enacted in our nation's civil courts is a reflection of basic American understandings of right and wrong.

social justice

An ideal that embraces all aspects of civilized life and that is linked to fundamental notions of fairness and to cultural beliefs about right and wrong.

[a]s this chapter points out, the central theme of this textbook is that of *individual rights versus public order*. This theme examines the legal rights of criminal suspects as they face police investigation and possible later processing by the criminal justice system. It contrasts those rights (and their accompanying social consequences) with the interests that both individual communities and society as a whole have in crime control, social and legal predictability, social order, and public safety.

An emphasis on individual rights rose to ascendancy in America during the 1960s and 1970s, a period known as the *civil rights era*. The civil rights era led to the recognition of fundamental personal rights that had illegally been denied to many people on the basis of race, ethnicity, gender, sexual preference, and disability. The rights movement soon expanded to include the rights of many other groups, including criminal suspects, parolees and probationers, trial participants, prison and jail inmates, and victims. As the emphasis on civil rights grew, new laws and court decisions broadened the rights available to many.

National sentiments, however, have historically been somewhat akin to the swings of a pendulum. Hence, beginning in the 1980s, the emphasis on the individual rights of criminal suspects was largely eclipsed by calls for social control and individual responsibility. The public-order perspective, still dominant today, was given an added boost by the 2001 terrorist attacks on the World Trade Center and the Pentagon. At the same time, the public-order perspective has shown signs of weakening in the face of claimed inequities that many think continue to characterize the American justice system. Nationally publicized police officer misconduct, televised trials in which fairness doesn't seem to matter, and the continued enforcement of certain far-reaching laws (that is, drug laws, which have resulted in the imprisonment of many young African-American men, a fact that is perceived as "unjust" by some members of society) have led to a crisis of legitimacy for the justice system as a whole.

Nonetheless, the tension between the individual-rights and public-order perspectives still forms the basis for most policy-making activity in the criminal justice arena. Individual-rights advocates continue to carry on the fight for an expansion of civil and criminal rights, seeing both as necessary to an equitable and just social order. The treatment of the accused, they argue, mirrors basic cultural values. The purpose of any civilized society, they say, should be to secure rights and freedoms for each of its citizens—including the criminally accused. Rights advocates fear unnecessarily restrictive government action and view it as an assault upon basic human dignity and individual liberty. In defense of their principles, criminal-rights activists tend to recognize that it is sometimes necessary to sacrifice some degree of public safety and predictability to guarantee basic freedoms. Hence rights advocates are content with a justice system that limits police powers and that holds justice agencies accountable to the highest procedural standards.

An example of the kind of criminal justice outcome feared by individual-rights advocates can be seen in the case of James Richardson, who served 21 years in a Florida prison for a crime that he did not commit.[1] Following perjured testimony, Richardson was convicted in 1968 of the poisoning deaths of his seven children. He was released many years later after a baby-sitter confessed to poisoning the children's last meal because of personal jealousies. The criminal-rights perspective holds that it is probably necessary to allow some guilty people to go free to reduce the likelihood of convicting the innocent.

In the present environment, however, calls for system accountability are often tempered with new demands to unfetter the criminal justice system to make arrests easier and punishments swift and harsh. Advocates of law and order, wanting ever-greater police powers, have mounted a seemingly effective drive to abandon some of the gains made in support of the rights of criminal defendants during the civil rights period. Citing high rates of recidivism, uncertain punishments, and an inefficient courtroom maze, they claim that the criminal justice system has coddled offenders and encouraged continued law violation. Society, they say, if it is to survive in an organized fashion, can no longer afford to accord too many rights to the individual or to place the interests of any one person over that of the group.

As we move through the first decade of the twenty-first century, the trick, it seems, is to balance individual rights and personal freedoms with public order and respect for legitimate authority. Years ago, during the height of what was then a powerful movement to win back control of our nation's cities and to reign in skyrocketing crime rates, the *New York Post* sponsored a conference on crime and civil rights. The keynote speaker at that conference was New York City Mayor Rudolph W. Giuliani. In his speech, Giuliani identified the tension between personal freedoms and individual responsibilities as the crux of the crime problems then facing his city and the nation. We mistakenly look to government and elected officials, Giuliani said, to assume responsibility for solving the problem of crime when, instead, it is each individual citizen who must become accountable for fixing what is wrong with our society. In the mayor's words, "We only see the oppressive side of authority. . . . What we don't see is that freedom is not a concept in which people can do anything they want, be anything they can be. Freedom is about authority. Freedom is about the willingness of every single human being to cede to lawful authority a great deal of discretion about what you do."[2]

? DISCUSSION QUESTIONS

1. What are the major differences between the individual-rights perspective and the public-order perspective? Which perspective appeals to you the most? Why?
2. How can we, as a society, best "balance individual rights and personal freedoms with social control and respect for legitimate authority"?
3. This box cites Mayor Giuliani as saying, "What we don't see is that freedom is not a concept in which people can do anything they want, be anything they can be." What did Giuliani mean by this?

[1]"A Free Man," *USA Today*, April 27, 1989, p. 13A.
[2]Philip Taylor, "Civil Libertarians: Giuliani's Efforts Threaten First Amendment," Freedom Forum Online. Web posted at http://www.freedomforum.org. Accessed November 9, 2001.

Social justice is a concept that embraces all aspects of civilized life. It is linked to notions of fairness and to cultural beliefs about right and wrong. Questions of social justice can arise about relationships between individuals and between parties (such as corporations and agencies of government), between the rich and the poor, between the sexes, between ethnic groups and minorities, and about social linkages of all sorts. In the abstract, the concept of social justice embodies the highest personal and cultural ideals.

Civil justice, one component of social justice, concerns itself with fairness in relationships between citizens, government agencies, and businesses in private matters, such as those involving contractual obligations, business dealings, hiring, and equality of treatment. Criminal justice, on the other hand, refers to the aspects of social justice which concern violations of the criminal law. As mentioned earlier, community interests in the criminal justice sphere demand the apprehension and punishment of law violators. At the same time, criminal justice ideals extend to the protection of the innocent, the fair treatment of offenders, and fair play by the agencies of law enforcement, including courts and correctional institutions. Criminal justice, ideally speaking, is "truth in action" within the process that we call *the administration of justice.* It is therefore vital to remember that justice, in the truest and most satisfying sense of the word, is the ultimate goal of criminal justice—and of the day-to-day practices and challenges which characterize the American criminal justice system. Reality, unfortunately, typically falls short of the ideal and is severely complicated by the fact that justice seems to wear different guises when viewed from diverse social vantage points. To many people, the criminal justice system and criminal justice agencies often seem biased in favor of the powerful. The laws they enforce seem to emanate more from well-financed, organized, and vocal interest groups than they do from any idealized sense of social justice. As a consequence, disenfranchised groups, those that do not feel as though they share in the political and economic power of society, are often wary of the agencies of justice, seeing them more as enemies than as benefactors.

On the other hand, justice practitioners, including police officers, prosecutors, judges, and correctional officials, frequently complain of unfair criticism of their efforts to uphold the law. The realities of law enforcement and of justice itself, they say, are often overlooked by critics of the system who have little experience in dealing with offenders and victims. We must recognize, practitioners often tell us, that those accused of violating the criminal law face an elaborate process built around numerous legislative, administrative, and organizational concerns. Viewed realistically, the criminal justice process, while it can be fine-tuned to take into consideration the interests of ever-wider numbers of people, rarely pleases everyone. The outcome of the criminal justice process in any particular case is a social product, and like any product that is the result of group effort, it must inevitably be a patchwork quilt of human emotions, reasoning, and concerns.

A criminal defense attorney making a point to the jury. The primary goal of the criminal justice system is to reach a just and fair outcome in each and every case it processes. Justice, however, has many aspects and can mean different things to different people—especially in a multicultural and diverse society like ours.

Jeff Cadge, Getty Images, Inc.

["Big Brother" Cameras on Watch for Criminals]

TAMPA—In spirited family groupings and knots of raucous collegians, as many as 35,000 visitors stroll the blocked-off avenues of Tampa's historic Ybor City entertainment district on a busy Saturday night.

As the revelers canvass the neon-lit storefronts for an appealing disco, bar or restaurant, they walk past curbside warning signs reading "Area Under Video Monitoring." And if their glances wander to tall poles placed every block or so, the visitors can see 36 surveillance cameras swiveling silently.

At a nearby command post, police officers viewing 10 video screens are doing more than watching for street fracases. They are using sophisticated face-recognition technology to scan the crowds for wanted criminals. The practice is fueling a nationwide debate over whether Big Brother is behind the camera.

Since June 29, 2001, surveillance cameras have been linked to a computer that randomly compares pedestrians' faces with 1,000 database images of known felons and teenage runaways.

Critics say the identification technique erodes privacy rights and raises the specter of government tracking individuals' movements. The American Civil Liberties Union is in rare alliance with conservative House Republican leader Dick Armey in saying that the software should be banned.

But surveillance advocates say the face-recognition software enhances public safety. "If it is Big Brother, it's Big Brother watching out for you," says Virginia Beach, Va., Police Chief Jay Jacocks, who is lobbying city officials to install a Tampa-style system in his city.

Like fingerprinting and DNA analysis, face-recognition technology is a form of biometrics, the science of identifying people by unique physical characteristics. The automated software measures 80 facial features, converts them to a mathematical formula and searches the database for a match.

To privacy watchdogs, the digitized facial inspections being done by police lengthen a list of high-technology threats to anonymity:

■ Employers and the FBI are monitoring e-mail and Web browsing.
■ Car-rental companies are using global positioning satellites to detect and fine speeders.
■ In 40 cities, automatic cameras trigger citations for running red lights.

In Tampa, "merely by walking down the street, a person is in essence put into an electronic police lineup without even knowing it," ACLU Associate Director Gregory Nojeim says. "If this isn't Big Brother, I don't know what is."

Four times so far in Ybor (pronounced EE-bore) City, the computer has sounded an alarm signaling an apparent match, but police viewing a monitor have decided the faces were different. Police have not detained anyone.

Tampa is getting a free, 1-year trial of the FaceIt software made by Visionics Corp. of New Jersey. The City Council, which approved the deal in May, 2001, without a hearing, has been having second thoughts amid a public uproar. Two weeks ago, the council deadlocked 3-3 over asking Mayor Dick Greco to scrap the contract. Another vote is scheduled for today. However the advisory vote goes, Greco says he'll continue the experiment.

In a second weekend of protests, 25 activists from the Green Party and other groups marched Saturday night on Ybor City's Seventh Avenue and chanted, "Big Bro, hell, no." One demonstrator was costumed as a computer monitor with Greco's face onscreen. Public opinion in Ybor City is deeply split over the technology, which as configured here prevents wholesale tracking by deleting images that don't match mug shots.

"Safety was the intent, and safety is exactly what it did: keep the troublemakers off the streets," says Jason Fernandez, managing partner of a restaurant in Ybor City.

"If it can help parents find out that their missing child is alive, then it's fine," says Mary Thurston, 34, a computer technician. "If you have something to hide, you shouldn't be out in public, right?"

But Jonathan Kish, 22, a stage technician visiting from Atlanta, says, "I don't want these people spying on me."

Nora Lee Smith, 41, a Tampa sales rep, says, "The cameras are not effective. They should use the money for more police patrol."

In 1998, British officials combined FaceIt with 300 surveillance cameras in London's gritty borough of Newham. Friday, London police chasing down a computer match arrested a man on a warrant for street crime, one of "less than 10" such arrests locally, says Bob Lack, Newham security director. Similar surveillance is under way in Birmingham, England, along Israel's Gaza boundary and at 80 U.S. casinos. The airport near Reykjavik, Iceland, is installing it.

Using another company's software, Tampa first tried face-scanning in January, 2001, at Super Bowl XXXV and in Ybor City before the game. The ACLU dubbed the event the Snooper Bowl. Checking 100,000 faces at stadium turnstiles against 1,700 criminals in the database, the system registered 19 hits. Supervisors considered only one resemblance worth dispatching an officer to find the suspect, an alleged ticket scalper, who vanished.

Untested legally, face-recognition surveillance probably would withstand Supreme Court scrutiny, says Erwin Chemerinsky, a law professor at the University of Southern California. "We have no reasonable expectation of privacy in a public place—that we're not going to be seen, or that our picture won't be taken," he says.

On June 11, 2001, the Supreme Court weighed high-tech searches in *Kyllo vs. United States,* a 5-4 opinion written by Justice Antonin Scalia. The ruling: Police must obtain a search warrant before employing imaging techniques not readily available to the public to snoop inside a home.

Left open was the question of using advanced technology on public streets. "Whether or not it's illegal, it's deeply troubling," says Jeffrey Rosen, a George Washington University law professor and author of *The Unwanted Gaze: The Destruction of Privacy in America.*

Federal agents in the *Kyllo* arrest in 1992 used an infrared imager to detect heat from lamps used to grow marijuana indoors. As Scalia noted, the government now is financing development of far more advanced snooping methods.

The Pentagon's Defense Advanced Research Projects Agency is administering a $50 million program, HumanID, to improve face-recognition capability. The goal is to guard U.S. embassies and military installations overseas from would-be terrorists.

For several years, law enforcement has used facial databases unattached to surveillance cameras as an investigative tool. Most often, an unidentified suspect's photo is run against digitized libraries of jail booking shots.

In 1997, Los Angeles County sheriff's deputies scored a match from a police sketch and arrested a man who later pleaded guilty to carjacking. Others using the technique: police in Orlando; Indianapolis; and Santa Ana, Calif.; and sheriffs in Arizona.

Police aren't getting a blank check. When they pushed to explore the vast photo databases of state motor-vehicle departments, they hit a backlash.

Recently, angry reaction erupted after Colorado Gov. Bill Owens signed a bill authorizing the Department of Motor Vehicles to buy and share with police a three-dimensional, digitized library of drivers. Owens, a Republican, says he'll try to amend the law in January to restrict police use to "reasonable suspicion" of a particular person.

Last week, Visionics President-CEO Joseph Atick joined a chorus of calls for federal legislation regulating face-recognition technology. He says databases should be restricted to criminals, runaways and missing persons. "It's a question of making sure there is no room for abuse down the line."

For the latest in crime and justice news, visit the Talk Justice news feed at http://www.crimenews.info.

Source: Martin Kasindorf, " 'Big Brother' Cameras on Watch for Criminals: High-Tech Face-Recognition Software Sparks Public Safety versus Privacy Debate across USA," *USA Today*, August 2, 2001, page 3A. © 2001, *USA Today.* Reprinted with permission.

Whichever side we choose in the ongoing debate over the nature and quality of criminal justice in America, it is vital that we recognize the plethora of pragmatic issues involved in the administration of justice while also keeping a clear focus on the justice ideal.[31] Was justice done, for example, in the criminal trial of O. J. Simpson or in the trials of the Los Angeles police officers accused of beating Rodney King? While answers to such questions may reveal a great deal about the American criminal justice system, they also have much to say about the perspective of those who provide them.

American Criminal Justice: The System

The Consensus Model

So far, we have described a **criminal justice system**[32] consisting of the agencies of police, courts, and corrections. Each of these agencies can, in turn, be described in terms of its subsystems. Corrections, for example, includes jails, prisons, community-based treatment programs like halfway houses, and programs for probation and parole. Each subsystem contains still more components. Prisons, for example, can be described in terms of custody levels, inmate programs, health care, security procedures, and so on. Some prisons operate as "boot camp" facilities designed to "shock" offenders into quick rehabilitation, while others are long-term confinement facilities designed for the hard-core criminals who are likely to return to crime quickly if released. Students of corrections also study the process of sentencing, through which an offender's fate is decided by the justice system, and examine the role of jails in holding prisoners prior to conviction and sentencing.

The systems model of criminal justice is characterized primarily by its assumption that the various parts of the justice system work together by design to achieve the wider purpose we have been calling *justice*. Hence the systems perspective on criminal justice generally encompasses a point of view called the **consensus model**. The consensus model assumes that each of the component parts of the criminal justice system strives toward a common goal and that the movement of cases and people through the system is smooth due to cooperation between the various components of the system.

The systems model of criminal justice, however, is more an analytic tool than a reality. An analytic model, whether in the hard sciences or in the social sciences, is simply a convention chosen for its explanatory power. By explaining the actions of criminal justice officials (such as arrest, prosecution, and sentencing) as though they were systematically related, we are able to envision a fairly smooth and predictable process (which is described in more detail later in this chapter).

The systems model has been criticized for implying a greater level of organization and cooperation among the various agencies of justice than actually exists. The word *system* calls to mind a near-perfect form of social organization. The modern mind associates the idea of a system with machinelike precision in which the problems of wasted effort, redundancy, and conflicting actions are quickly corrected. The justice system has nowhere near this level of perfection, and the systems model is admittedly an oversimplification that is

criminal justice system

The aggregate of all operating and administrative or technical support agencies that perform criminal justice functions. The basic divisions of the operational aspects of criminal justice are law enforcement, courts, and corrections.

consensus model

A criminal justice perspective that assumes that the system's components work together harmoniously to achieve the social product we call *justice*.

primarily useful for analytic purposes. Conflicts among and within agencies are rife; immediate goals are often not shared by individual actors within the system; and the system may move in different directions depending upon political currents, informal arrangements, and personal discretionary decisions.

The Conflict Model

conflict model

A criminal justice perspective that assumes that the system's components function primarily to serve their own interests. According to this theoretical framework, justice is more a product of conflicts among agencies within the system than it is the result of cooperation among component agencies.

The **conflict model** provides another approach to the study of American criminal justice. The conflict model says that the interests of the criminal justice agencies tend to make actors within the system self-serving. According to this model, pressures for success, promotion, pay increases, and general accountability fragment the efforts of the system as a whole, leading to a criminal justice *non*system.[33]

A classic study of clearance rates by Jerome H. Skolnick provides support for the idea of a criminal justice nonsystem.[34] Clearance rates are a measure of crimes solved by the police. The more crimes the police can show they have solved, the better they look to the public they serve. Skolnick discovered an instance in which a burglar was caught red-handed during the commission of a burglary. After his arrest, the police suggested that he confess to many unsolved burglaries which they knew he had not committed. In effect they said, "Help us out, and we will try to help you out!" The burglar did confess—to over 400 other burglaries. Following the confession, the police were satisfied because they could say they had "solved" many burglaries, and the suspect was pleased as well because the police had agreed to speak on his behalf before the judge.

Both models have something to tell us. Agencies of justice with a diversity of functions (police, courts, and corrections) and at all levels (federal, state, and local) are linked closely enough for the term *system* to be meaningfully applied to them. On the other hand, the very size of the criminal justice undertaking makes effective cooperation between component agencies difficult. The police, for example, have an interest in seeing offenders put behind bars. Prison officials, on the other hand, are often working with extremely overcrowded facilities. They may favor early-release programs for certain categories of offenders, such as those who are judged to be nonviolent. Who wins out in the long run could be just a matter of internal politics. Everyone should be concerned, however, when the goal of justice is affected, and sometimes even sacrificed, because of conflicts within the system.

American Criminal Justice: The Process

Structurally, as we have discussed, the criminal justice system can be described in terms of its component agencies: police, courts, and corrections. Functionally, the components of the "system" may work together well, or they may be in conflict. Whether part of a system or a nonsystem, however, the agencies of criminal justice must process the cases which come before them. An analysis of case processing within the system provides both a useful guide to this book and a "road map" to the criminal justice system itself. Beginning with the investigation of reported crimes, Figure 1–2 illustrates the processing of a criminal case through the federal justice system. The process in most state systems is similar. See **Web Extra! 1–3** at cjtoday.com for more information about the process shown in Figure 1–2.

Investigation and Arrest

The modern justice process begins with investigation. When a crime has been committed, it is often discovered and reported to the police. On occasion, a police officer on routine patrol discovers the crime while it is still in progress. Evidence is gathered at the scene when possible, and a follow-up investigation attempts to reconstruct the likely sequence of activities. A few offenders are arrested at the scene of the crime, and some are apprehended only after an extensive investigation. In such cases, an arrest

warrant

In criminal proceedings, a writ issued by a judicial officer directing a law enforcement officer to perform a specified act and affording the officer protection from damages if he or she performs it.

warrant issued by a magistrate or another judge provides the legal basis for an apprehension by police.

An arrest, in which a person is taken into custody, limits the arrestee's freedom. Arrest is a serious step in the process of justice and involves a discretionary decision made by the police seeking to bring criminal sanctions to bear. Most arrests are made peacefully, but some involve force when the suspect tries to resist. Only about 50% of all people arrested are eventually convicted, and of those, only about 25% are sentenced to a year or more in prison.

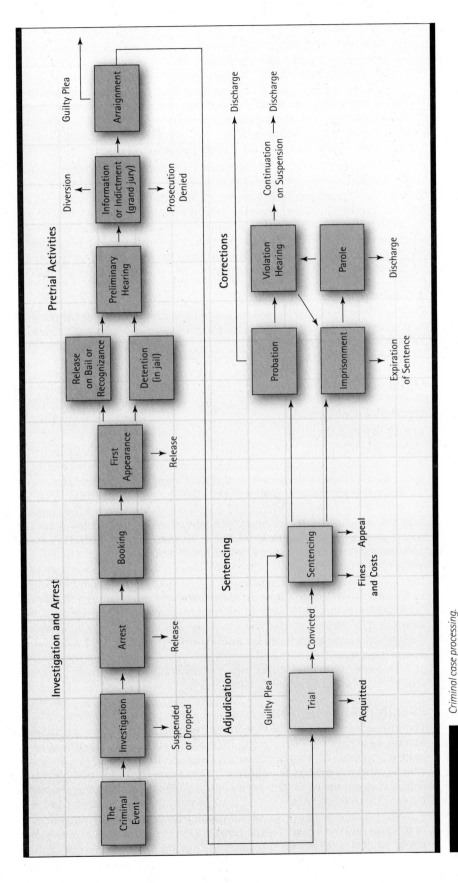

FIGURE 1-2

Criminal case processing.

Source: Adapted from U.S. Department of Justice, *Compendium of Federal Justice Statistics, 1989* (Washington, D.C.: Bureau of Justice Statistics, 1992), p. 3.

During arrest and prior to questioning, defendants are usually advised of their constitutional rights as enumerated in the famous Supreme Court decision of *Miranda* v. *Arizona*.[35] Defendants are told:

(1) "You have the right to remain silent." (2) "Anything you say can and will be used against you in court." (3) "You have the right to talk to a lawyer for advice before we ask you any questions, and to have him with you during questioning." (4) "If you cannot afford a lawyer, one will be appointed for you before any questioning if you wish." (5) "If you decide to answer questions now without a lawyer present, you will still have the right to stop answering at any time. You also have the right to stop answering at any time and may talk with a lawyer before deciding to speak again." (6) "Do you wish to talk or not?" and (7) "Do you want a lawyer?"[36]

It is important to realize that although popular television programs almost always show a rights advisement at the time of arrest, the *Miranda* decision requires only that police advise a person of his or her rights prior to questioning. An arrest without questioning can occur in the absence of any warning. When an officer interrupts a crime in progress, public-safety considerations may make it reasonable for the officer to ask a few questions prior to a rights advisement. Many officers, however, feel they are on sound legal ground only by immediately following an arrest with an advisement of rights.

Investigation and arrest are discussed in detail in Chapter 7, "Policing: Legal Aspects."

BOOKING

During the arrest process, suspects are booked. Pictures are taken, fingerprints are made, and personal information, such as address, date of birth, weight, and height, is gathered. Details of the charges are recorded, and an administrative record of the arrest is created.

During **booking**, suspects are again advised of their rights and are asked to sign a form on which each right is written. The written form generally contains a statement acknowledging the advisement of rights and attesting to the fact that the suspect understands them.

Pretrial Activities

FIRST APPEARANCE

Within hours of arrest, suspects must be brought before a magistrate (a judicial officer) for a first (or initial) appearance. The judge will tell them of the charges against them, will again advise them of their rights, and may sometimes provide the opportunity for **bail**.

Most defendants are released on recognizance (into their own care or the care of another) or are given the chance to post a bond during their first appearance. A bond may take the form of a cash deposit or a property bond in which a house or other property serves as collateral against flight. Those who flee may be ordered to forfeit the posted cash or property. Suspects who are not afforded the opportunity for bail because their crimes are very serious or who do not have the needed financial resources are taken to jail to await the next stage in the justice process.

If a defendant doesn't have a lawyer, one will be appointed at the first appearance. The defendant may actually have to demonstrate financial hardship or be ordered to pay for counsel. The names of assigned lawyers are usually drawn off the roster of practicing defense attorneys in the county. Some jurisdictions use public defenders to represent indigent defendants.

All aspects of the first appearance, including bail bonds and appointed counsel, are discussed in detail in Chapter 8, "The Courts."

PRELIMINARY HEARING

The primary purpose of a **preliminary hearing**, also sometimes called a *preliminary examination*, is to establish whether sufficient evidence exists against a person to continue the justice process. At the preliminary hearing, the hearing judge will seek to determine whether there is **probable cause** to believe that (1) a crime has been committed and (2) the defendant committed it. The decision is a judicial one, but the process provides the prosecutor with an opportunity to test the strength of the evidence at his or her disposal.

The preliminary hearing also allows defense counsel the chance to assess the strength of the prosecution's case. As the prosecution presents evidence, the defense is said to "discover" what it is. Hence the preliminary hearing serves a discovery function for the defense. If the defense attorney thinks the evidence is strong, he or she may suggest that a plea bargain be arranged. Indigent defendants have a right to be represented by counsel at the preliminary hearing.

---

booking

A law enforcement or correctional administrative process officially recording an entry into detention after arrest and identifying the person, the place, the time, the reason for the arrest, and the arresting authority.

bail

The money or property pledged to the court or actually deposited with the court to effect the release of a person from legal custody.

preliminary hearing

A proceeding before a judicial officer in which three matters must be decided: (1) whether a crime was committed, (2) whether the crime occurred within the territorial jurisdiction of the court, and (3) whether there are reasonable grounds to believe that the defendant committed the crime.

probable cause

A set of facts and circumstances that would induce a reasonably intelligent and prudent person to believe that a particular other person has committed a specific crime. Also, reasonable grounds to make or believe an accusation. Probable cause refers to the necessary level of belief that would allow for police seizures (arrests) of individuals and full searches of dwellings, vehicles, and possessions.

INFORMATION OR INDICTMENT

In some states, the prosecutor may seek to continue the case against a defendant by filing an information with the court. An information, which is a formal written accusation, is filed on the basis of the outcome of the preliminary hearing.

Other states require that an **indictment** be returned by a **grand jury** before prosecution can proceed. The grand jury hears evidence from the prosecutor and decides whether a case should go to trial. In effect, the grand jury is the formal indicting authority. It determines whether probable cause exists to charge a defendant formally with a crime. Grand juries can return an indictment on less than a unanimous vote.

The grand jury system has been criticized because it is one-sided. The defense has no opportunity to present evidence; the grand jury is led only by the prosecutor, often through an appeal to emotions or in ways which would not be permitted in a trial. At the same time, the grand jury is less bound by specific rules than a trial jury. For example, one member of a grand jury told the author that a rape case had been dismissed because the man had taken the woman to dinner first. Personal ignorance and subcultural biases are far more likely to be decisive in grand jury hearings than in criminal trials.

In defense of the grand jury, however, we should recognize that defendants who are clearly innocent will likely not be indicted. A refusal to indict can save considerable time and money by diverting poorly prepared cases from further processing by the system.

ARRAIGNMENT

The **arraignment** is "the first appearance of the defendant before the court that has the authority to conduct a trial."[37] At arraignment, the accused stands before a judge and hears the information, or indictment, against him or her as it is read. Defendants are again notified of their rights and are asked to enter a plea. Acceptable pleas generally include (1) not guilty, (2) guilty, and (3) no contest *(nolo contendere)*, which may result in conviction but which can't be used later as an admission of guilt in civil proceedings. Civil proceedings, while not covered in detail in this book, provide an additional avenue of relief for victims or their survivors. Convicted offenders increasingly find themselves facing suits brought against them by victims seeking to collect monetary damages.

The Federal Rules of Criminal Procedure specify that "arraignment shall be conducted in open court and shall consist of reading the indictment or information to the defendant or stating to him the substance of the charge and calling on him to plead thereto. He shall be given a copy of the indictment or information before he is called upon to plead."[38]

Guilty pleas are not always accepted by the judge. If the judge feels a guilty plea was made under duress or because of a lack of knowledge on the part of the defendant, the plea will be rejected and a plea of "not guilty" will be substituted for it. Sometimes defendants "stand mute"; that is, they refuse to speak or to enter a plea of any kind. In that case, the judge will enter a plea of "not guilty" on their behalf.

The arraignment process, including pretrial motions made by the defense, is discussed in detail in Chapter 8, "The Courts."

Adjudication

Every criminal defendant has a right under the Sixth Amendment to the U.S. Constitution to a **trial** by jury. The U.S. Supreme Court, however, has held that petty offenses are not covered by the Sixth Amendment guarantee and that the seriousness of a case is determined by the way in which "society regards the offense." For the most part, "offenses for which the maximum period of incarceration is six months or less are presumptively petty."[39] In *Blanton* v. *City of North Las Vegas* (1989), the Court held that "a defendant can overcome this presumption and become entitled to a jury trial, only by showing that . . . additional penalties [such as fines and community service] viewed together with the maximum prison term, are so severe that the legislature clearly determined that the offense is a serious one."[40] The *Blanton* decision was further reinforced in the case of *U.S.* v. *Nachtigal* (1993).[41]

In most jurisdictions, many criminal cases never come to trial. The majority are "pleaded out" (that is, dispensed of as the result of a bargained plea) or dismissed for a variety of reasons. Studies have found that as many as 82% of all sentences are imposed in criminal cases because of guilty pleas rather than trials.[42]

In cases which do come to trial, the procedures governing the submission of evidence are tightly controlled by procedural law and precedent. Procedural law specifies the type of evidence that may be submitted, the credentials of those allowed to represent the state or the defendant, and what a jury is allowed to hear.

---

indictment

A formal, written accusation submitted to the court by a grand jury, alleging that a specified person has committed a specified offense, usually a felony.

grand jury

A group of jurors who have been selected according to law and have been sworn to hear the evidence and to determine whether there is sufficient evidence to bring the accused person to trial, to investigate criminal activity generally, or to investigate the conduct of a public agency or official.

arraignment

Strictly, the hearing before a court having jurisdiction in a criminal case, in which the identity of the defendant is established, the defendant is informed of the charge and of his or her rights, and the defendant is required to enter a plea. Also, in some usages, any appearance in court prior to trial in criminal proceedings.

trial

In criminal proceedings, the examination in a court of the issues of fact and law in a case for the purpose of reaching a judgment of conviction or acquittal of the defendant.

Precedent refers to understandings built up through common usage and also to decisions rendered by courts in previous cases. Precedent in the courtroom, for example, requires that lawyers request permission from the judge before approaching a witness. It also can mean that excessively gruesome items of evidence may not be used or must be altered in some way so that their factual value is not lost in the strong emotional reactions they may create.

Some states allow trials for less serious offenses to occur before a judge if defendants waive their right to a trial by jury. This is called a *bench trial.* Other states require a jury trial for all serious criminal offenses.

Trials are expensive and time-consuming. They pit defense attorneys against prosecutors. Regulated conflict is the rule, and jurors are required to decide the facts and apply the law as the judge explains it to them. In some cases, however, a jury may be unable to decide. In such cases, it is said to be "deadlocked," and the judge declares a mistrial. The defendant may be tried again when a new jury is impaneled.

The criminal trial and its participants are described fully in Chapter 9, "The Courtroom Work Group and the Criminal Trial."

Sentencing

Once a person is convicted, it becomes the responsibility of the judge to impose some form of punishment. The sentence may take the form of supervised probation in the community, a fine, a prison term, or some combination of these. Defendants will often be ordered to pay the costs of court or of their own defense if they are able.

Prior to sentencing, a sentencing hearing may be held in which lawyers on both sides present information concerning the defendant. The judge may also request that a presentence report be compiled by a probation or parole officer. The report will contain information on the defendant's family and business situation, emotional state, social background, and criminal history. It will be used to assist the judge in making an appropriate sentencing decision.

Judges traditionally have had considerable discretion in sentencing, although new state and federal laws now place limits on judicial discretion in some cases, requiring that a sentence "presumed" by law be imposed. Judges still retain enormous discretion, however, in specifying whether sentences on multiple charges are to run consecutively or concurrently. Offenders found guilty of more than one charge may be ordered to serve one sentence after another is completed (a **consecutive sentence**) or may be told that their sentences will run at the same time (a **concurrent sentence**).

Many convictions are appealed. The appeals process can be complex, involving both state and federal judiciaries. An appeal is based upon the defendant's claim that rules of procedure were not followed properly at some earlier stage in the justice process or that the defendant was denied the rights accorded him or her by the U.S. Constitution.

Chapter 10, "Sentencing," outlines modern sentencing practices and describes the many modern alternatives to imprisonment.

Corrections

Once an offender has been sentenced, the corrections stage begins. Some offenders are sentenced to prison, where they "do time" for their crimes. Once in the correctional system, they are classified according to local procedures and are assigned to confinement facilities and treatment programs. Newer prisons today bear little resemblance to the massive bastions of the past, which isolated offenders from society behind huge stone walls. Many modern prisons, however, still suffer from a "lock psychosis" (a preoccupation with security) among top- and mid-level administrators as well as a lack of significant rehabilitation programs.

Chapter 12, "Prisons and Jails," discusses the philosophy behind prisons and sketches their historical development. Chapter 13, "Prison Life," portrays life on the inside and delineates the social structures which develop as a response to the pains of imprisonment.

PROBATION AND PAROLE

Not everyone who is convicted of a crime and sentenced ends up in prison. Some offenders are ordered to prison only to have their sentences suspended and a probationary term imposed. They may also be ordered to perform community-service activities as a condition of their probation. During the term of probation, these offenders are required to submit to

consecutive sentence

One of two or more sentences imposed at the same time, after conviction for more than one offense, and served in sequence with the other sentence. Also, a new sentence for a new conviction, imposed upon a person already under sentence for a previous offense, which is added to the previous sentence, thus increasing the maximum time the offender may be confined or under supervision.

concurrent sentence

One of two or more sentences imposed at the same time, after conviction for more than one offense, and served at the same time. Also, a new sentence for a new conviction, imposed upon a person already under sentence for a previous offense, served at the same time as the previous sentence.

supervision by a probation officer and to meet other conditions set by the court. Failure to do so results in revocation of probation and imposition of the original prison sentence.

Offenders who have served a portion of their prison sentences may be freed on parole. They are supervised by a parole officer and assisted in their readjustment to society. As in the case of probation, failure to meet the conditions of parole may result in parole revocation and a return to prison.

Chapter 10, "Sentencing," and Chapter 11, "Probation, Parole, and Community Corrections," deal with the practice of probation and parole and with the issues surrounding it. Learn more about the criminal justice process at **Library Extra! 1–3** at cjtoday.com.

Due Process and Individual Rights

Imposed upon criminal justice case processing is the constitutional requirement of fairness and equity. Guaranteed by the Fifth, Sixth, and Fourteenth Amendments to the U.S. Constitution, this requirement is referred to as **due process**. Simply put, *due process* is a term that means procedural fairness.[43] The due process clause of the U.S. Constitution is succinctly stated in the Fifth Amendment, which reads, "No person shall be . . . deprived of life, liberty, or property, without due process of law." The constitutional requirement of due process mandates the recognition of individual rights in the processing of criminal defendants facing prosecution by the states or the federal government. Not only is the guarantee of due process found in the Fifth Amendment, but it underlies the first ten amendments to the U.S. Constitution, which are collectively known as the *Bill of Rights.* The Fourteenth Amendment is of special importance, however, for it makes due process binding upon the states; that is, it requires individual states in the union to respect the due process rights of U.S. citizens who come under their jurisdiction.

The fundamental guarantees of the Bill of Rights have been interpreted and clarified by courts (especially the U.S. Supreme Court) over time. The due process standard became reality following a number of far-reaching Supreme Court decisions affecting criminal procedure which were made during the 1960s. That period was the era of the Warren Court (1953–1969), led by Chief Justice Earl Warren, a Supreme Court which is remembered for its concern with protecting the innocent against the massive power of the state in criminal proceedings.[44] As a result of the tireless efforts of the Warren Court to institutionalize the Bill of Rights, the daily practice of modern American criminal justice is now set squarely upon the due process standard. Due process requires that agencies of justice recognize individual rights in their enforcement of the law, and under the due process standard, rights violations may become the basis for the dismissal of evidence or of criminal charges, especially at the appellate level. Table 1–1 outlines the basic rights to which defendants in criminal proceedings are generally entitled.

due process

A right guaranteed by the Fifth, Sixth, and Fourteenth Amendments of the U.S. Constitution and generally understood, in legal contexts, to mean the due course of legal proceedings according to the rules and forms established for the protection of individual rights. Due process of law, in criminal proceedings, is generally understood to include the following basic elements: a law creating and defining the offense, an impartial tribunal having jurisdictional authority over the case, accusation in proper form, notice and opportunity to defend, trial according to established procedure, and discharge from all restraints or obligations unless convicted.

INDIVIDUAL RIGHTS GUARANTEED BY THE BILL OF RIGHTS*	TABLE 1–1

A right to be assumed innocent until proven guilty
A right against unreasonable searches of person and place of residence
A right against arrest without probable cause
A right against unreasonable seizure of personal property
A right against self-incrimination
A right to fair questioning by the police
A right to protection from physical harm throughout the justice process
A right to an attorney
A right to trial by jury

A right to know the charges
A right to cross-examine prosecution witnesses
A right to speak and present witnesses
A right not to be tried twice for the same crime
A right against cruel or unusual punishment
A right to due process
A right to a speedy trial
A right against excessive bail
A right against excessive fines
A right to be treated the same as others, regardless of race, sex, religious preference, and other personal attributes

*As interpreted by the U.S. Supreme Court.

The Role of the Courts in Defining Rights

Although the Constitution deals with many issues, what we have been calling *rights* are open to interpretation. Many modern rights, although written into the Constitution, would not exist in practice were it not for the fact that the U.S. Supreme Court decided, at some point in history, to recognize them in cases brought before it. The well-known Supreme Court case of *Gideon* v. *Wainwright* (1963),[45] for example (which is discussed in detail in Chapter 9), found the Court embracing the Sixth Amendment guarantee of a right to a lawyer for all criminal defendants and mandating that states provide lawyers for defendants who are unable to pay for them. Prior to *Gideon*, court-appointed attorneys for defendants unable to afford their own counsel were practically unknown, except in capital cases and in some federal courts. After the *Gideon* decision, court-appointed counsel became commonplace, and measures were instituted in jurisdictions across the nation to select attorneys fairly for indigent defendants. It is important to note, however, that while the Sixth Amendment specifically says, among other things, that "[i]n all criminal prosecutions, the accused shall enjoy the right . . . to have the Assistance of Counsel for his defense," it does *not* say, in so many words, that the state is *required* to provide counsel. It is the U.S. Supreme Court which, interpreting the Constitution, has said that.

Unlike the high courts of many other nations, the U.S. Supreme Court is very powerful, and its decisions often have far-reaching consequences. The decisions rendered by the justices in cases like *Gideon* become, in effect, the law of the land. For all practical purposes, such decisions often carry as much weight as legislative action. For this reason, some writers speak of "judge-made law" (rather than legislated law) in describing judicial precedents which affect the process of justice.

Rights which have been recognized by Court decision are often subject to continual refinement. New interpretations may broaden or narrow the scope of applicability accorded to constitutional guarantees. Although the process of change is usually very slow, we should recognize that any right is subject to continual interpretation by the courts—and especially by the U.S. Supreme Court.

Crime Control through Due Process

Two primary goals were identified in our discussion of this book's theme: (1) the need to enforce the law and to maintain public order and (2) the need to protect individuals from injustice—especially at the hands of the criminal justice system. The first of these principles values the efficient arrest and conviction of criminal offenders. It is often referred to as the **crime-control model** of justice. The crime-control model was first brought to the attention of the academic community in Herbert Packer's cogent analysis of the state of criminal justice in the late 1960s.[46] For that reason, it is sometimes referred to as *Packer's crime-control model.*

The second principle is called the **due process model** because of its emphasis on individual rights. Due process is a central and necessary part of American criminal justice. It requires a careful and informed consideration of the facts of each individual case. Under the model, police are required to recognize the rights of suspects during arrest, questioning, and handling. Prosecutors and judges must recognize constitutional and other guarantees during trial and the presentation of evidence. Due process is intended to ensure that innocent people are not convicted of crimes.

Up until now, we have suggested that the dual goals of crime control and due process are in constant and unavoidable opposition to one another. Some critics of American criminal justice have argued that the practice of justice is too often concerned with crime control at the expense of due process. Other conservative analysts of the American scene maintain that our type of justice coddles offenders and does too little to protect the innocent.

While it is impossible to avoid ideological conflicts such as these, it is also realistic to think of the American system of justice as representative of *crime control through due process;* that is, as a system of social control that is fair to those whom it processes. It is this model of law enforcement, infused with the recognition of individual rights, which provides a workable conceptual framework for understanding the American system of criminal justice—both now and in the future.

crime-control model
—————————————
A criminal justice perspective that emphasizes the efficient arrest and conviction of criminal offenders.

due process model
—————————————
A criminal justice perspective that emphasizes individual rights at all stages of justice system processing.

Criminal Justice and Criminology

The study of criminal justice as an academic discipline began in this country in the late 1920s, when August Vollmer (1876–1955), the former Police Chief of the Los Angeles Police Department (LAPD), persuaded the University of California to offer courses on the subject.[47] Vollmer was joined by his former student Orlando W. Wilson (1900–1972) and by William H. Parker (who later served as Chief of the LAPD from 1950 to 1966) in calling for increased professionalism in police work through better training.[48] Largely as a result of Vollmer's influence, early criminal justice education was practice oriented; it was a kind of extension of on-the-job training for working practitioners. Hence in the early days of the discipline, criminal justice students were primarily focused on the application of general management principles to the administration of police agencies. Criminal justice came to be seen as a practical field of study concerned largely with issues of organizational effectiveness.

While criminal justice has historically been viewed as a technically oriented field of study, it has recently taken its place alongside other academic disciplines in the social sciences. Criminology, on the other hand, has long had a firm academic base. **Criminology** is the interdisciplinary study of the causes of crime and of criminal motivation. It combines the academic disciplines of sociology, psychology, biology, economics, and political science in an effort to explore the mind of the offender and the social and economic conditions which give rise to criminality. The study of criminology is central to the criminal justice discipline, and courses in criminology are almost always found in criminal justice programs. Victimology is a subfield of criminology which seeks answers to the question of why some people are victimized while others are not.

As a separate field of study, criminal justice had fewer than 1,000 students before 1950.[49] The turbulent 1960s and 1970s brought an increasing concern with social issues and, in particular, justice. Drug use, social protests, and dramatically increasing crime rates turned the nation's attention to the criminal justice system. During that period, Congress passed two significant pieces of legislation: (1) the Law Enforcement Assistance Act of 1965, which created the Law Enforcement Assistance Administration (LEAA), and (2) the Omnibus Crime Control and Safe Streets Act of 1968. Through LEAA, vast amounts of money were funneled into fighting crime. Students interested in the study of criminal justice were often eligible for financial help under LEAA's Law Enforcement Education Program (LEEP). LEEP monies funded a rapid growth in criminal justice offerings nationwide. By 1975, more than 100,000 students were studying criminal justice at 1,065 schools with assistance from LEEP.[50]

LEEP funding began to decline in 1979. Meanwhile, criminal justice programs nationwide were undergoing considerable self-examination. The direction of justice studies and the future of the discipline were open to debate. The resultant clarification of criminal justice as a discipline, combined with the resurgence of federal funding initiatives through the Violent Crime Control and Law Enforcement Act of 1994 and the "block grants" and other programs it and later legislation provided, has made the field stronger and more professional than ever before. **Web Extra! 1–4** at cjtoday.com contains the full text of the 1994 legislation.

To meet the growing needs of police officers for college-level training, the International Association of Police Professors (IAPP) was formed in 1963. The IAPP later changed its name to the Academy of Criminal Justice Sciences (ACJS) and widened its focus to include all aspects of criminal justice education. Today, ACJS and its sister organization, the American Society of Criminology (ASC), are the two largest associations of community college–based and university-based criminal justice trainers and educators in the world.[51] Learn more about ACJS and ASC via **Web Extras! 1–5** and **1–6** at cjtoday.com.

Today, criminal justice is well established as an academic discipline and is offered as a major course of study in well over 1,000 colleges and universities across the country. Freda Adler, a well-known criminal justice academic, notes that "from an obscure discipline scorned by most academics with only two small doctoral programs as recently as 1970, criminal justice has exploded to 350,000 undergraduate majors at colleges and universities."[52]

The largest criminal justice program in the United States is offered at the John Jay College of Criminal Justice in New York City. John Jay, as the school is called, serves over

criminology

The scientific study of the causes and prevention of crime and the rehabilitation and punishment of offenders.

10,000 students studying in the criminal justice area and conducts research in criminal justice organization, law enforcement, and forensic science. Other well-known criminal justice programs can be found at Sam Houston State University, the University of Illinois at Chicago, Rutgers (New Jersey), Florida State University, the State University of New York at Albany, Michigan State University, the University of Louisville, the University of Maryland, the University of Illinois, the Ohio State University, East Tennessee State University, and the University of California at Irvine.[53] In addition to campus-based programs, distance learning and Web-based criminal justice programs are quickly becoming popular. Schools of special note that now offer criminal justice undergraduate degrees online include the University of Phoenix and the Kaplan Colleges. Many other colleges and universities are moving courses online. Learn more about such programs via **Web Extra! 1–7** at cjtoday.com.

Research and Professionalism

By the 1960s, students of criminal justice were beginning to apply the techniques of social scientific research—many of them borrowed from sister disciplines like criminology, sociology, psychology, and political science—to the study of all aspects of the justice system. Scientific research into the operation of the criminal justice system was encouraged by the 1967 President's Commission on Law Enforcement and Administration of Justice, which influenced passage of the Safe Streets and Crime Control Act of 1968. The Safe Streets Act led to the creation of the National Institute of Law Enforcement and Criminal Justice, which later became the National Institute of Justice (NIJ). As a central part of its mission, NIJ continues to support research in the criminal justice field through substantial funding for scientific explorations into all aspects of the discipline, and it funnels much of the $3 billion spent annually by the Department of Justice to help local communities fight crime.

Many early government-funded scientific studies in the criminal justice field focused on police management practices; they are discussed in more detail in Chapter 5. Scientific research has since become characteristic of the entire criminal justice discipline, with studies of all aspects of criminal justice administration, practice, and ideology now routinely undertaken as well as reported at academic conferences and professional meetings and in journals focusing on the profession. Such research has become a major element in the increasing professionalization of criminal justice, both as a career field and as a field of study, and can be expected to play an ever-wider role in the twenty-first century.

While space doesn't permit discussion of most scientific studies in the justice field, a report by Lawrence W. Sherman and his colleagues at the University of Maryland stands out as one of the most definitive criminal justice studies of the last decade.[54] The *New York Times* calls the Sherman report "the most comprehensive study ever" of the criminal justice system in this country.[55] The Sherman study, which may set the tone for research for years to come, is a meta-analysis—or a study of other studies. Conducted at the request of the U.S. Congress and released in 1997, the report analyzed the results of hundreds of other criminal justice studies conducted over the past few decades. Entitled *Preventing Crime: What Works, What Doesn't, What's Promising*, the massive survey examined independent studies of more than 500 local crime-prevention programs throughout the country in an effort to determine which programs and practices are effective at preventing or reducing crime. The study surveyed literature on gang violence prevention programs, community-based mentoring programs, after-school recreational programs, family-based crime-prevention programs, school-based programs, policing programs such as neighborhood watches and community policing, drug-treatment programs, and "get tough" sentencing initiatives like prison boot camps, home confinement, and electronic monitoring (all of which are discussed later in this book).

The report concluded that some of the most popular programs then in widespread use, including prison boot camps, midnight basketball, neighborhood watches, and drug-education classes, had little impact on crime rates in the United States. The study did find some promising results for certain programs, especially intensified police patrols in high-crime areas, drug treatment in prisons, and home visits by nurses, social workers, and others for infants in troubled families.

The most important finding of the study, however, was its conclusion: that it remains difficult to assess federally funded crime-prevention programs because there is far too little ongoing rigorous, scientific evaluation of such programs. As the study's lead author says, "The most important finding is that we really can't tell how a majority of funding is affecting crime." The major reason for that problem, Sherman says, is that Congress has never insisted on the same kind of scientific evaluation of crime-prevention programs as it

It is commonly assumed that these three components—law enforcement (police, sheriffs, marshals), the judicial process (judges, prosecutors, defense lawyers), and corrections (prison officials, probation, and parole officers)—add up to a "system" of criminal justice. A system implies some unity of purpose and organized interrelationship among component parts. In the typical American city and state, and under federal jurisdiction as well, no such relationship exists. There is, instead, a reasonably well-defined criminal process, a continuum through which each accused offender may pass: from the hands of the police, to the jurisdiction of the courts, behind the walls of a prison, then back onto the street. The inefficiency, fall-out, and failure of purpose during this process is notorious.

—National Commission on the Causes and Prevention of Violence

I hope somewhere down the road I will be forgotten . . . that I will just be able to live the life I had before jail, a quiet life unknown to the world, and I'll be satisfied with that.

—Long Island shooter Colin Ferguson, commenting before sentencing

---

CJ Futures

[The National Law Enforcement and Corrections Technology Center]

You will encounter a number of CJ Futures boxes in this book. These boxes illustrate the first subtheme of your textbook: the future of crime and justice, including social issues and changing technology.

A major source of information about the impact of technology on the criminal justice system is the National Law Enforcement and Corrections Technology Center (NLECTC), located in Rockville, Maryland. NLECTC maintains branch offices in Rome, New York; North Charleston, South Carolina; Denver, Colorado; and El Segundo, California.

The NLECTC system also includes the Border Research and Technology Center in San Diego, California; the Office of Law Enforcement Standards in Gaithersburg, Maryland; the Office of Law Enforcement Technology Commercialization in Wheeling, West Virginia; and the National Center for Forensic Science in Orlando, Florida.

NLECTC is supported by the National Institute of Justice (NIJ), an arm of the U.S. Department of Justice. It is overseen by the Office of Science and Technology within NIJ.

David G. Boyd, director of the NIJ's Office of Science and Technology, is convinced of the important role that technology will continue to play in the fight against crime. According to Boyd, "The technological revolution that has swept society as a whole in recent years has also affected the criminal justice system. Some technologies that not long ago seemed advanced—vests that can stop bullets and electronic monitoring of probationers—today seem commonplace. But the revolution continues apace, with ever more spectacular advances now being made, or in the testing stages, or on the drawing board."

NLECTC provides a wealth of online information for anyone interested in technology assessment as applied to criminal justice. The agency's free newsletter, *TechBeat,* is published four times each year, both on paper and in electronic format. To request a subscription, e-mail asknlectc@nlectc.org. You can visit NLECTC on the Web via **Web Extra! 1–8.**

Source: Adapted from *TechBeat* (the online newsletter of the National Law Enforcement and Corrections Technology Center, a program of the National Institute of Justice), Spring 2001.

---

does, for example, in testing new drugs before they are approved for public consumption. The Sherman report is available in its entirety at **Library Extra! 1–4** at cjtoday.com.

Multiculturalism and Diversity in Criminal Justice

In late 2001, Tom Green, a 52-year-old Mormon with five wives, another five former wives, and 29 known children, was sentenced to five years in a Utah prison after being convicted of four counts of polygamy.[56] The Church of Jesus Christ of Latter-Day Saints brought plural marriage to Utah in the early nineteenth century, but the state legislature banned the practice more than 100 years ago, and now the church officially excommunicates polygamists. Green's case was unusual because he was the first polygamist prosecuted in Utah in 50 years. The last major prosecution occurred in 1953, when the federal government raided the polygamous town of Short Creek, on the Utah–Arizona border. Images of children being torn away from their parents led to a public relations fiasco. Since then, the government has mostly ignored practitioners. Green's supporters claimed that the 2002 Winter Olympics in Salt Lake City led to a roundup of polygamists, including Green. Two years before the Olympics, the Utah legislature appropriated monies for the hiring of a specialist in polygamy prosecutions. The "polygamy czar" was supposed to assist the state's counties in ferreting out crimes in small towns and "closed societies." While the exact number of polygamists in Utah and elsewhere is unknown, the existence of such alternative family lifestyles is but one indicator of the fact that the United States is a multicultural and diverse society.

Multiculturalism (a term that is akin to *cultural pluralism*) refers to a society that is home to a multitude of different cultures, each with its own set of norms, values, and routine behaviors. American society today is a true multicultural society, encompassing a wide variety of racial and ethnic heritages, diverse religions, incongruous values, disparate traditions, and distinct languages.

Multiculturalism in America is not new. The Western Hemisphere was multicultural long before the Europeans arrived. For thousands of years, groups of Native Americans

E Pluribus Unum (Out of Many, One)

multiculturalism

The existence within one society of diverse groups that maintain unique cultural identities while frequently accepting and participating in the larger society's legal and political system.[iv] *Multiculturalism* is usually used in conjunction with the term *diversity* to identify many distinctions of social significance.

Utah polygamist Tom Green posing with his five wives and 29 known children. In 2001, Green was sentenced to consecutive five-year prison terms on each of four counts of bigamy and one charge of failure to pay child support. Green, who said he had no money, was also ordered to pay $78,000 in restitution to the state.
© AFP Photo/CORBIS

each spoke their own language, were bound to customs that differed significantly between tribal nations, and practiced a wide range of religions. Some nations were warlike; others were peaceful. Some were settled permanently, farmed the land, and lived in adobe-style dwellings; others were nomadic, lived in tents (tepees) that could be quickly disassembled and moved, and practiced a hunter-gatherer lifestyle.

European immigration, which began in earnest in the seventeenth century, led to greater diversity still. Successive waves of immigrants, along with the slave trade of the early and mid-nineteenth century, brought a diversity of values, beliefs, and routinized patterns of behavior to American shores that frequently conflicted with prevailing cultures. Differences in languages and traditions fed the American melting pot of the late nineteenth and early twentieth centuries, and made effective communications between groups difficult.

The face of multiculturalism in America today is quite different than it was in the past, due largely to relatively high birth rates among some minority populations and the huge but relatively recent immigration of Spanish-speaking people from Mexico, Cuba, Latin America, and South America. Part of that influx consists of substantial numbers of undocumented immigrants who have entered the country illegally and who may have a special fear of police authority and a general distrust for the law. Such fears make members of this group hesitant to report being victimized, and their undocumented status makes them easy prey for illegal scams like extortion, blackmail, and documentation crimes. Learn more about immigration and crime via **Library Extra! 1–5** at cjtoday.com.

Diversity characterizes both immigrant and U.S.-born individuals. U.S. Census Bureau statistics show that people identifying themselves as white account for 71% of the U.S. population—a percentage that has been dropping steadily for at least the past 40 years. People of Hispanic origin constitute approximately 12% of the population and are the fastest-growing group in the country. Individuals identifying themselves as African-American make up another 12% of the population, and people of Asian and Pacific Island origin make up almost 4% of the total. Native Americans, including American Indians, Eskimos, and Aleuts, account for slightly less than 1% of all Americans.[57] Statistics like these, however, are only estimates, and their interpretation is complicated by the fact that surveyed individuals may be of mixed race. Nonetheless, it is clear that American society today is ethnically and racially quite diverse.

It is important to realize, however, that *race* and *ethnicity* are only buzzwords that people often use when they talk about multiculturalism. After all, neither race nor ethnicity determines a person's values, attitudes, or behavior. Just as there is no uniquely identifiable "white culture" in American society, it is a mistake to think that all African-Americans share the same values or that everyone of Hispanic descent honors the same traditions or even speaks Spanish.

Multiculturalism, as the term is used today, is but one form of *diversity*. Taken together, these two concepts—multiculturalism and diversity—encompass many distinctions of social

African-American men comprise less than 6% of the U.S. population and almost one half of its criminal prisoners.

—Bureau of Justice Statistics

significance. The broad brush of contemporary multiculturalism and social diversity draws attention to variety along racial, ethnic, subcultural, generational, faith, economic and gender lines. Lifestyle diversity is also important. The fact that influential elements of the wider society are less accepting of some lifestyles than others doesn't mean that such lifestyles aren't recognized from the viewpoint of multiculturalism. It simply means that at least for now, some lifestyles are accorded less official acceptability than others. As a result, certain lifestyle choices, even within a multicultural society that generally respects and encourages diversity, may still be criminalized (as with the case of polygamy that opened this section).

Multiculturalism and diversity will be discussed in various chapters throughout this textbook. For now, it is sufficient to recognize that the diverse values, perspectives, and behaviors characteristic of various groups within our society have a significant impact on the justice system. Whether it is the confusion that arises from a police officer's commands to a non-English-speaking suspect, the need for interpreters in the courtroom, a deep-seated distrust of the police in some minority communities, a lack of willingness among some immigrants to report crime, the underrepresentation of women in criminal justice agencies, or the continued existence of gangs like the "Mexican Mafia" in our nation's prisons, diversity and multiculturalism present special challenges to the everyday practice of criminal justice in America.

> America, known the world over as the land of the free, was founded on the principle of liberty and justice for all.... Yet, at the same time, some 2 million of our citizens are denied their freedom.... At some point we must ask ourselves: What is the moral price we pay as a nation for locking up our youth rather than lifting them up?
>
> —Reverend Jesse L. Jackson, Sr.[v]

CJ Today News

[Immigrants Pose Cultural Challenges to the Criminal Justice System]

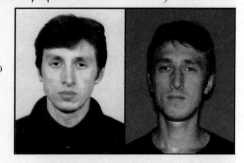

РАЗЫСКИВАЕТСЯ ЧЕЛОВЕК
ВОЗНАГРАЖДЕНИЕ $70,000

Описание Подозреваемого:

Дата:	20 августа 2001 г.
Номер дела:	01-69534
Имя:	НИКОЛАЙ СОЛТЫС
Адрес:	Mills Station Road
	Rancho Cordova, CA 95670
Рост:	1м 83 см
Вес:	75 кг
Возраст:	27 лет
Пол:	Мужской
Глаза:	Голубые
Волосы:	Светлые
Цвет кожи:	Белый
Дата Рожд.:	19 мая 1974

Автомобиль Подозреваемого:

Форд Эксплорер, гг. выпуска – 90-ые.

Зеленый цвет двух тонов с серебрянной полосой внизу.

Дверь, открывающаяся сзади (см. стрелку на рисунке), покрашена в зеленый цвет другого оттенка, чем бока автомобиля.

Back of vehicle has a different shade of green than the sides.

Николай Солтыс разыскивается в связи с шестью смертями в пределах Округа Сакраменто. В настоящее время неизвестно во что он одет. Он украинец.

Мы полагаем, что этот человек вооружен и опасен. Не пытайтесь вступить в контакт с этим человеком. Если вы знаете, где он, сообщите в отдел Шерифа.

Этот случай убийств расследуется Отделом Убийств Шерифа Округа Сакраменто. Специальные номера телефонов для информации, работающие 24 часа:

916-874-5321
916-874-5414
1-800-AA-CRIME / 1-800-222-7463

A Russian-language wanted poster showing Nikolay Soltys, the 27-year-old Ukrainian immigrant who confessed to the brutal murders of six of his relatives in 2001. Soltys allegedly slashed the throats of his family members in a killing spree that lasted several hours and led police on a gruesome search for victims throughout the Sacramento, California area. He later committed suicide while in jail. An English version of the poster was also printed and disseminated before Soltys was apprehended.

AP/Wide World Photos

CITRUS HEIGHTS, CALIF.—Police nearly missed capturing a Ukrainian immigrant suspected of brutally killing six relatives because they couldn't speak the language.

Most everyone they talked to spoke Russian or Ukrainian, forcing investigators to abandon the usual rules. And when the crucial call came in to 911, it took police several minutes to find a Ukrainian translator and learn from the caller that Nikolay Soltys was hiding in the back yard of his mother's house in the Sacramento suburb of Citrus Heights.

It's a phenomenon that is happening nationwide as law enforcement agencies cope with new immigrant communities.

About 11 percent of the nation—30 million people—is now foreign-born, up from less than 5 percent in 1970, according to the 2000 census.

Minority enclaves are increasingly appearing outside the traditional entry points of California, Florida and New York. The Center for Immigration Studies found states with fast-growing populations like Colorado, North Carolina and Nevada each

(continued)

experienced jumps in foreign-born residents of more than 180 percent since 1990.

"The U.S. may be the most diverse country in the world. It means the community no longer has the shared understanding of what acceptable and unacceptable behavior is," said Northwestern University law professor Paul H. Robinson, who helped develop criminal codes for Ukraine and Belarus.

Columbus, Ohio, police carry language identifier booklets to figure out which translator can help with the 30 to 40 language groups in central Ohio.

"It's certainly intensified over the last 10 years," Columbus Sgt. Earl Smith said. "And law enforcement has to always be in a process of adapting."

It's not just language that challenges police. Deep-seated cultural differences also have an effect.

For instance, Hmong women who have been raped rarely come forward because of the extreme stigma imported from their homeland in the mountains of Southeast Asia.

"They're really abandoned by their families. They're seen as damaged goods," said Michael Jordan, a spokesman for St. Paul, Minn., police.

Police there also have run into cultural differences on what constitutes domestic violence.

"'You're charging me with hitting my wife? She's mine. I paid for her,'" Jordan said, paraphrasing one argument. "In that culture they often pay a dowry, so they feel they own her."

Detroit police have had a tough time persuading members of the Bangladeshi community to testify against a countryman suspected of harassing fellow immigrants.

"They want to take care of it their way," and can't understand American concepts such as due process, Lt. Paul Janness said. "Luckily it's been minor stuff. Nobody's killed anybody."

That's not the case in Sacramento, where investigators say distrust of authority and other cultural differences hampered an investigation conducted largely within the region's growing community of 75,000 Russians and Ukrainians.

Police had so little cooperation that Senior Pastor Adam Bondaruk of Bethany Slavic Missionary Church had to plead at the victims' funerals for his countrymen to put aside the fear of police they brought with them from the former Soviet Union.

Soltys was eventually captured . . . after his brother alerted police when he spotted the 27-year-old fugitive hiding in his back yard.

Immigrants often distrust even institutions such as banks and motor vehicle departments, said Marouf Jwanmery of the National Crime Prevention Council in Washington.

That distrust made tracking Soltys difficult: He had no known credit cards, and his vehicle was unregistered so police didn't know his license plate number.

Cultural differences facing police also can involve seemingly mundane issues.

It's all about respect and dignity, said Sharon Rummery of the U.S. Immigration and Naturalization Service.

"A little patience, a little humor, and it's remarkable what you can accomplish," Columbus' Smith said.

For the latest in crime and justice news, visit the Talk Justice news feed at http://www.crimenews.info.

Source: Don Thompson, "Immigrants Pose Cultural Challenges," Associated Press wire service, September 2, 2001. Reprinted with permission of the Associated Press.

Things to Come: An Overview of This Book

This textbook is divided into five parts. Part 1, entitled "Crime in America," provides a general introduction to the study of criminal justice, including crime statistics (Chapter 2), the causes of crime (Chapter 3), and criminal law (Chapter 4).

Part 2 is called "Policing." Its three chapters focus on the activities of law enforcement agencies. The law enforcement field is described in Chapters 5 and 6, where historical developments are combined with modern studies to depict a dynamic profession. Precedent-setting court cases are introduced in Chapter 7, along with more recent decisions which have refined earlier ones.

Part 3, "Adjudication," includes chapters on the courts (Chapters 8 and 9) and sentencing (Chapter 10).

Special attention is given throughout Part 4, "Corrections," to the legal issues surrounding correctional institutions and various forms of criminal punishment. Prisons and jails (Chapter 12) and prison life (Chapter 13) are discussed, along with probation, parole, and community corrections (Chapter 11).

The final section, Part 5, "Special Issues," looks at problems facing the justice system today. Included are juvenile justice (Chapter 14) and victimless crimes and drug abuse (Chapter 15). Chapter 16 provides an overview of criminal justice systems in other nations and points out the need for international understanding. Finally, the challenges and opportunities which the future holds for the practice of American criminal justice, including computer crime and emerging investigative technologies, are discussed in the last chapter (Chapter 17).

Although this book covers many issues, its overall structure is sequential. Consecutive chapters provide a tour of criminal justice agencies and practices as they exist in the United

> The current crisis in criminal and juvenile justice is fueled by the public's conviction that the system no longer represents an effective response to the problem of crime.
>
> —The Reinventing Probation Council

States today. The tour begins in Part 1 with an explanation of how criminal law is created and ends in Part 4 with a discussion of problems facing criminal justice in the future.

Summary

In this chapter, the process of American criminal justice has been described as a system with three major components: police, courts, and corrections. As we have warned, however, such a viewpoint is useful primarily for the reduction in complexity it provides. A more realistic approach to understanding criminal justice may be the nonsystem approach. As a nonsystem, criminal justice is depicted as a fragmented activity in which individuals and agencies within the process have interests and goals which at times coincide but often conflict.

Defendants processed by the justice system come into contact with numerous workers whose duty it is to enforce the law but who also have a stake in the agencies employing them and who hold their own personal interests and values. As defendants wend their way through the system, they may be held accountable to the law, but in the process they will also be buffeted by the personal whims of "officials" as well as by the practical needs of the system itself. A complete view of American criminal justice must recognize that the final outcome of any encounter with the criminal justice system will be a consequence of decisions made not just at the legislative level, but in the day-to-day activities undertaken by everyone involved in the system. Hence in a very real sense, justice is a product whose quality depends just as much upon practical considerations predicated upon justice system exigencies, as it does upon idealistic notions of right and wrong. Multiculturalism, an idea that was introduced near the end of this chapter, complicates the practice of American criminal justice still further since there is rarely universal agreement in our society about what is right or wrong or about what constitutes "justice."

An alternative way of viewing the practice of criminal justice is in terms of its two goals: crime control and due process. The crime-control perspective urges rapid and effective enforcement of the law and calls for the stiff punishment of lawbreakers. Due process, on the other hand, requires a recognition of the defendant's rights and holds the agents of justice accountable for any actions which might contravene those rights. The goals of crime control and due process are often in conflict. Popular opinion may even see them as mutually exclusive. As we describe the agencies of justice in the chapters which follow, the goals of crime control and due process will appear again and again. They will often be phrased in terms of the overall theme of this book, which contrasts the need to balance the rights of individuals against other valid social interests, especially the need for public order. Twin subthemes focus on (1) advancing technology as it affects both crime and the practice of criminal justice and (2) the impact of multiculturalism and social diversity upon contemporary American criminal justice agencies.

Our central theme is represented by two opposing groups: individual-rights advocates and public-order advocates. As we shall see, however, the most fundamental challenge facing the practice of American criminal justice is achieving efficient enforcement of the laws while recognizing and supporting the legal rights of suspects and the legitimate personal differences and prerogatives of individuals. This goal is made all the more difficult by changing social values and by rapid advances in the kinds of technology available to criminals. Nonetheless, this mandate of crime control through due process ensures that criminal justice will remain an exciting and ever-evolving undertaking well into the twenty-first century and beyond.

Discussion Questions

1. What are the themes upon which this textbook is built? How do they relate to the study of criminal justice? How do they interrelate?
2. This chapter describes two models of the criminal justice system. What are they, and how do they differ? Which model do you think is more useful? Which is more accurate? Why?
3. What have we suggested are the primary goals of the criminal justice system? Do you think that any one goal is more important than the others? If so, which one? Why?

4. What do we mean when we say that the "primary purpose of law is the maintenance of order"? Why is public order necessary? What would life be like without it?
5. Do we have too many criminal laws? Too few? Do we have enough public order or too little? How can we tell? How can we improve on the present situation, if at all?
6. What might a large, complex society like ours be like without laws? Without a system of criminal justice? Would you want to live in such a society? Explain.
7. What do we, as individuals, have to give up to facilitate public order? Do we ever give up too much in the interest of public order? If so, when?
8. What is multiculturalism? What is diversity? What impact do multiculturalism and diversity have on the practice of criminal justice in contemporary American society?

To participate in an online discussion on these topics and others, go to the Global Town Meeting electronic message board for Chapter 1 on the *Criminal Justice Today* Companion Website at cjtoday.com.

Web Quest!

Familiarize yourself with the *Criminal Justice Today* Companion Website and with its many features. To get there, point your browser to http://cjtoday.com. Once you've opened the site, you'll be able to read the latest crime and justice news, explore student-oriented message boards, join the *Criminal Justice Today* e-mail discussion list, and sign up to receive announcements of late-breaking crime stories. You can learn about your textbook's chapter objectives, practice with online review questions, preview chapter summaries, submit electronic homework to your instructor, and enjoy many Web-based criminal justice projects. (If your instructor decides to use the electronic homework feature of the site, it's always a good idea to keep a copy of any materials that you submit.) The site also allows you to listen to the author introduce each chapter.

Unique Web Extras! and book-specific Library Extras! substantially enhance the learning opportunities your text offers. Web Extras! bring the justice system to life by providing a wealth of links to relevant and informative sites. Library Extras! help you learn more about important topics in the justice field via the *Criminal Justice Today* electronic library. Library Extras! include the latest reports and bulletins from the Bureau of Justice Statistics, the National Institute of Justice, the Bureau of Justice Assistance, the FBI, and other agencies. Each report has been selected by the author to complement the textbook and to enhance your learning experience.

One *Criminal Justice Today* Web resource of special importance is Dr. Frank Schmalleger's Cybrary of Criminal Justice links (*Cybrary* means "cyber-library"). Known to justice professionals as "the world's crime and justice directory," Dr. Schmalleger's Cybrary contains annotated links to more than 12,000 crime and justice sites throughout the nation and around the world. Because it is continually updated and fully searchable, the Cybrary can be an invaluable tool as you write term papers or do Web-based research on crime and justice. You can reach the Cybrary directly by going to http://www.cybrary.info.

To complete this Web Quest! online, go to the Web Quest! module in Chapter 1 of the *Criminal Justice Today* Companion Website at cjtoday.com.

Library Extras!

Library Extras! may be accessed on the Web at cjtoday.com. Many, but certainly not all, of the Library Extras! found in this textbook contain articles from the National Institute of Justice's four-volume series, *Criminal Justice 2000*. All *Criminal Justice 2000* files are in PDF format, and you will need to have Adobe Acrobat Reader or Adobe Acrobat installed on your computer in order to read them.

More than 60 criminal justice professionals contributed material for NIJ's four-volume series, which was designed to reflect on criminal justice research accomplishments and to analyze current and emerging trends in crime and criminal justice practice in the United

States.[58] The series examines how research has influenced today's criminal justice policies and practices and how future policies and practices can build on the current state of knowledge in the justice field. Topics include criminology, drugs and crime, juvenile justice, immigration and crime, domestic violence, community justice, mental illness and the criminal justice system, community policing, sentencing reform, information technology, fear of crime, and court performance. The volumes are titled as follows:

Criminal Justice 2000, Volume 1: The Nature of Crime—Continuity and Change (NIJ, 2000).

Criminal Justice 2000, Volume 2: Boundary Changes in Criminal Justice Organizations (NIJ, 2000).

Criminal Justice 2000, Volume 3: Policies, Processes, and Decisions of the Criminal Justice System (NIJ, 2000).

Criminal Justice 2000, Volume 4: Measurement and Analysis of Crime and Justice (NIJ, 2000).

You will find the entire series online at cjtoday.com/series.htm.

Library Extras! of special relevance to this chapter are shown below.

Library Extra! 1–1   *Fear of Crime in the United States* (NIJ, 2000).
Library Extra! 1–2   *The Changing Nature of Crime in America* (NIJ, 2000).
Library Extra! 1–3   *Policies, Processes, and Decisions of the Criminal Justice System* (NIJ, 2000).
Library Extra! 1–4   *Preventing Crime: What Works, What Doesn't, What's Promising* (NIJ, 1997).
Library Extra! 1–5   *On Immigration and Crime* (NIJ, 2000).

To explore these resources online, go to the Library Extras! area of the *Criminal Justice Today* Companion Website at cjtoday.com. You should also check the author's "Late Picks" online for newly released documents and updated Library Extras! You can find Late Picks at http://cjtoday.com/latepicks.htm.

Marginal Notes

[i] Quoted in *Criminal Justice Newsletter,* September 16, 1997, p. 1.

[ii] Quoted in Charles E. Silberman, *Criminal Violence, Criminal Justice* (New York: Random House, 1978), p. 12.

[iii] ABC News, September 11, 2001.

[iv] Adapted from Robert M. Shusta et al., *Multicultural Law Enforcement,* 2d ed. (Upper Saddle River, NJ: Prentice Hall, 2002), p. 443.

[v] Reverend Jesse L. Jackson, Sr., "Liberty and Justice for Some: Mass Incarceration Comes at a Moral Cost to Every American," July 10, 2001. Web posted at http://www.motherjones.com/prisons/print_liberty.html. Accessed January 22, 2002.

Notes

1. American Civil Liberties Union website at http://www.aclu.org/issues/criminal/iscj.html. Accessed January 22, 2002.

2. ABC News, September 11, 2001. Christopher was repeating a phrase generally attributed to former U.S. Supreme Court Justice Arthur Goldberg.

3. See "Remarks of U.S. Attorney General John Ashcroft, September 20, 2001," on the U.S. Department of Justice's website at http://www.usdoj.gov/ag/agcrisisremarks9_20.htm. Accessed September 25, 2001.

4. See Kevin Johnson, "Ashcroft Says 'Serious Threat' of More Terror," *USA Today,* October 1, 2001, p. 1A; and Mitchel Maddux, "U.S. Hunts Hidden Terror Cells," *The Record,* September 23, 2001. Web posted at http://www.bergen.com/news/probefeds200109232.htm. Accessed October 1, 2001.

5. Joby Warrick et al., "FBI Ill-Equipped to Predict Terror Attacks," *Washington Post,* September 24, 2001.

6. Ibid.

7. Web posted at http://www.fbi.gov. Accessed October 2, 2001.

8. Public Law 107-56.

9. For a thorough discussion of immigration as it relates to crime, see Ramiro Martinez, Jr., and Matthew T. Lee, "On Immigration and Crime," in National Institute of Justice, *Criminal Justice 2000, Volume 1: The Nature of Crime—Continuity and Change* (Washington, D.C.: U.S. Department of Justice, Office of Justice Programs, 2000).

10. See "Cries of Relief," *Time,* April 26, 1993, p. 18; and "King II: What Made the Difference?" *Newsweek,* April 26, 1993, p. 26.
11. "Cries of Relief."
12. "FBI: Definitely a Bomb," *USA Today,* March 1, 1993, p. 1A.
13. "Gay Victim Was Tortured for Information," APB Online, November 19, 1998. Web posted at http://www.apbonline.com/911/1998/11/19/gay1119_1.html. Accessed November 8, 2001.
14. Karin Kelly, "Church Massacre Captured on Videotape," WFAA.com, September 17, 1999. Web posted at http://www.wfaa.com/wfaa/articledisplay2/1,1053,2954,00.html. Accessed January 22, 2002.
15. "Teen Tried Reasoning with Gunman," Associated Press wire service, September 18, 1999.
16. See Mark Babineck, "Railroad Killer Gets Death Penalty," Associated Press wire service, May 22, 2000, from which some of the information in this paragraph and the next is taken. Web posted at http://cnews.tribune.com/news/tribune/story/0,1235, tribune-nation-37649,00.html. Accessed March 3, 2002.
17. "Railway Killer Leads Authorities to Remains," Associated Press wire service, July 16, 2000. Web posted at http://enquirer.com/editions/2000/07/16/loc_railway_killer_leads.html. Accessed January 17, 2002.
18. Technically, the twenty-first century began on January 1, 2001.
19. See Charisse Jones, "Kids' Dad Defends His Wife," *USA Today,* June 22–24, 2001, p. 1A.
20. Sam Stanton, Ralph Montaño, and Ted Bell, "Soltys Captured: Sources Say He Admits to Six Killings," *Sacramento Bee,* August 31, 2001. Web posted at http://www.sacbee.com/news/news/local01_20010831.html. Accessed September 4, 2001.
21. Roxanne Stites, "Patience Was Murder Suspect's Ally: Eluding Capture, Man Stayed in Abandoned House, Traveled on Foot, *San Jose Mercury News,* August 31, 2001. Web posted at http://www0.mercurycenter.com/partners/docs/001168.htm. Accessed September 3, 2001.
22. John Rittner, "Man Guilty in Dog-Flinging Case Killed Pet after Traffic Altercation," *USA Today* Online, June 20, 2001. Web posted at http://www.usatoday.com/usatonline/20010620/3415750s.htm. Accessed August 21, 2001.
23. Ibid.
24. "Man Gets Three Years for Throwing Dog in Traffic," CNN.com Lawcenter, July 13, 2001. Web posted at http://www.cnn.com/2001/LAW/07/13/roadrage.dog/index.html. Accessed September 10, 2001.
25. *The Drudge Report,* September 23, 2001. Web posted at http://www.drudgereport.com/id.htm. Accessed October 1, 2001.
26. Linda Greenhouse, "O'Connor Foresees Limits on Freedom," *New York Times,* September 29, 2001.
27. Ibid.
28. Cara Garretson, "Senator Says New Office Should Cover Cyberterrorism," IDG News Service (Washington Bureau), September 21, 2001. Web posted at http://www.idg.net/spc_697783_190_9-10025.html. Accessed September 27, 2001.
29. George W. Bush, "Presidential Address to the Nation," September 20, 2001.
30. *The American Heritage Dictionary on CD-ROM* (Boston: Houghton Mifflin, 1991).
31. For a good overview of the issues involved, see Judge Harold J. Rothwax, *Guilty: The Collapse of Criminal Justice* (New York: Random House, 1996).
32. The systems model of criminal justice is often attributed to the frequent use of the term *system* by the 1967 Presidential Commission in its report, *The Challenge of Crime in a Free Society* (Washington, D.C.: U.S. Government Printing Office, 1967).
33. One of the first published works to use the nonsystems approach to criminal justice was the American Bar Association's *New Perspective on Urban Crime* (Washington, D.C.: ABA Special Committee on Crime Prevention and Control, 1972).
34. Jerome H. Skolnick, *Justice without Trial* (New York: John Wiley, 1966), p. 179.
35. *Miranda* v. *Arizona,* 384 U.S. 436, 86 S.Ct. 1602, 16 L. Ed. 2d 694 (1966).
36. North Carolina Justice Academy, *Miranda Warning Card* (Salemburg, NC).
37. John M. Scheb and John M. Scheb II, *American Criminal Law* (St. Paul, MN: West, 1996), p. 32.
38. Federal Rules of Criminal Procedure, 10.
39. *Blanton* v. *City of North Las Vegas,* 489 U.S. 538, 103 L. Ed. 2d 550, 109 S.Ct. 1289 (1989).
40. Ibid.
41. *U.S.* v. *Nachtigal,* 122 L. Ed. 2d 374, 113 S.Ct. 1072, 1073 (1993), *per curiam.*
42. Barbara Borland and Ronald Sones, *Prosecution of Felony Arrests* (Washington, D.C.: Bureau of Justice Statistics, 1991).
43. "The Defendants' Rights at a Criminal Trial." Web posted at http://www.mycounsel.com/content/arrests/court/rights.html. Accessed February 10, 2002.
44. For a complete and now-classic analysis of the impact of decisions made by the Warren Court, see Fred P. Graham, *The Due Process Revolution: The Warren Court's Impact on Criminal Law* (New York: Hayden Press, 1970).
45. *Gideon* v. *Wainwright,* 372 U.S. 353 (1963).
46. Herbert Packer, *The Limits of the Criminal Sanction* (Stanford, CA: Stanford University Press, 1968).
47. For an excellent history of policing in the United States, see Edward A. Farris, "Five Decades of American Policing: 1932–1982," *Police Chief,* November 1982, pp. 30–36.
48. Gene Edward Carte, "August Vollmer and the Origins of Police Professionalism," *Journal of Police Science and Administration,* Vol. 1, No. 1 (1973), pp. 274–281.
49. Larry L. Gaines, "Criminal Justice Education Marches On!" in Roslyn Muraskin, ed., *The Future of Criminal Justice Education* (New York: Criminal Justice Institute, Long Island University, C. W. Post Campus, 1987).
50. Ibid.
51. For more information, contact ACJS at Suite C, 7319 Hanover Parkway, Greenbelt, MD 20770 (800-757-ACJS), or ASC at 1314 Kinnear Rd., Suite 212, Columbus, OH 43212. Visit Dr. Frank Schmalleger's Cybrary at http://talkjustice.com/cybrary.asp for links to these and other professional organizations in the criminal justice field.
52. Fox Butterfield, "A Newcomer Breaks into the Liberal Arts," *New York Times,* December 5, 1998.
53. This list includes schools that are well known for producing graduate students specializing in either criminal justice or criminology. Because of the liberal arts emphasis at many of the schools in the list, however,

programs may be officially designated as Criminology or even Sociology rather than Criminal Justice. One (at the University of California at Irvine) is housed within the Program in Social Ecology.

54. Lawrence W. Sherman et al., *Preventing Crime: What Works, What Doesn't, What's Promising—A Report to the United States Congress* (Washington, D.C.: National Institute of Justice, 1997).

55. Fox Butterfield, *New York Times* wire service, April 16, 1997.

56. See Patrick O'Driscoll, "Utah Steps Up Prosecutions of Polygamists," *USA Today,* May 14, 2001, p. 5A, from which some of the wording in this paragraph is adapted.

57. U.S. Census Bureau website at http://www.census.gov. Accessed March 22, 2002. Population statistics are estimates because race is a difficult concept to define, and Census Bureau interviewers allow individuals to choose more than one race when completing census forms.

58. This paragraph is adapted from National Institute of Justice, "Publications and Products." Web posted at http://www.ojp.usdoj.gov/nij/pubs-sum/cj2000.htm. Accessed January 2, 2002.

The Crime Picture

LEARNING OBJECTIVES

After reading this chapter you should be able to

- Name and describe the two major national crime data-gathering programs in the United States today

- Describe some of the limitations inherent in statistical reports of crime

- Differentiate between the two data-gathering programs

- List the eight major crimes found in the Uniform Crime Reports

- Discuss the meaning of the term *clearance rate*

- Describe the difference between the UCR's Part I and Part II Offenses

- Explain how the National Incident-Based Reporting System operates and how it differs from the traditional Uniform Crime Reporting Program

- Define *hate crime*

chapter 2

Key Concepts

[Terms]

aggravated assault	forcible rape	Part II offenses
arson	hate crime	property crime
assault	larceny-theft	rape
Bureau of Justice Statistics (BJS)	motor vehicle theft	robbery
burglary	murder	sexual battery
clearance rate	National Crime Victimization Survey (NCVS)	stranger violence
Crime Index	National Incident-Based Reporting System	superpredator
dark figure of crime	(NIBRS)	Uniform Crime Reports (UCR)
date rape	Part I offenses	violent crime

[Cases]

Capital Square Review and Advisory Board v. *Pinette*	*Forsyth County, Ga.* v. *Nationalist Movement*	*Wisconsin* v. *Mitchell*
	R.A.V. v. *City of St. Paul*	

Hear the author discuss this chapter at **cjtoday.com**

Introduction

On a hot July afternoon in 1999, Atlanta's Buckhead financial district was shaken by a workplace shooting that ultimately left 13 dead and 13 others injured.[2] The alleged killer, 44-year-old Mark O. Barton, reportedly walked into the office of Momentum Securities, a brokerage house used by day-traders (people who buy and sell stock throughout the day as a way of making a living). Barton was heard to say, "I hope this doesn't ruin your trading day,"[3] before he pulled out two powerful handguns and started shooting. Within minutes, four people lay dead. Barton then walked across a busy six-lane highway and into the offices of All-Tech Investment Group, another day-trading firm. Five people died there. Witnesses to the gunfire said that Barton told his victims that he had been distressed over heavy trading losses. Media reports later said that he had lost $105,000 trading stocks in the two months preceding the rampage.[4] After the shootings, Barton fled in a green minivan, taking the time to buckle himself in before driving off.

A college graduate, Barton seemed an unlikely killer. His career included work as a chemist and salesman, and he had recently moved back in with his second wife, 27-year-old Leigh Ann. The two had been legally separated only months before. Barton had custody of his two young children from a former marriage—Elizabeth Mychelle, 7, and Matthew, 11. When officers went to the Barton residence, they found the dead bodies of Barton's wife and children. All three had suffered hammer blows to the head, and the children had been placed face down in a filled bathtub to prevent any chance of their reviving.

Soon after Barton fled, investigators learned that he had been the primary suspect in the 1993 murders of his first wife, 36-year-old Deborah Spivey Barton, and her mother, Eloise Powell Spivey, 59.[5] The bodies of both women were found beaten to death at Riverside Campground on Weiss Lake in northeastern Alabama. They had been spending Labor Day weekend in a camper at the lake with Barton. The camper showed no signs of forced entry, and no one was ever arrested in the killings. Barton had taken out a $600,000 life insurance policy on his first wife shortly before her death.

Four hours after the Atlanta shootings, Georgia officers spotted Barton's vehicle in Acworth, a town 30 miles northwest of Atlanta. Police corralled the vehicle at a service station. The incident ended when Barton shot and killed himself. He had left four notes at his apartment for investigators to read. You can view their contents by visiting **Web Extra! 2–1** at cjtoday.com.

As this book goes to press, thirteen civil suits are being brought by survivors and relatives of those murdered by Barton. They name as defendants the day-trading firms where

The Barton family. Left to right: daughter, Elizabeth Mychelle (7), Leigh Ann Barton, Mark Barton, and son Matthew (11). In 1999, Barton killed his wife and children before going on a shooting spree that claimed the lives of ten people and injured 13 others.

Henry County Police, AP/Wide World Photos.

Barton had traded, as well as the building owners and property managers of the office complex.[6] The suits claim that the defendants contributed to the conditions that led to the shootings and should have foreseen the incident and prevented it. The plaintiffs are seeking compensation for lives lost in the tragedy and for suffering and lost productivity. (To learn more about civil lawsuits and how they differ from criminal proceedings, see Chapter 4.)

This chapter provides a statistical picture of crime in America today. It does so by examining information on reported crimes from the Federal Bureau of Investigation's **Uniform Crime Reports (UCR)**, as well as data from the door-to-door **National Crime Victimization Survey (NCVS)** conducted by the Bureau of Justice Statistics. Not all crimes are as newsworthy as the Atlanta killings. While reading this chapter, however, it is important to keep in mind that statistical aggregates of reported crime, whatever their source, do not readily reveal the lost lives, human suffering, lessened productivity, and reduced quality of life that crime causes. Although all murder victims, like the people killed by Mark Barton, led intricate lives and had families, dreams, and desires, their deaths at the hands of other people are routinely recorded only as a numerical count in statistical reports. Such information does not contain details on the personal lives of crime victims, but merely represents a numerical compilation of reported law violations.

Crime Data and Social Policy

Crime statistics provide an overview of crime in this country. If used properly, they can provide one of the most powerful tools for creating social policy. Decision makers at all levels, including legislators, elected public officials, and administrators throughout the criminal justice system, rely on crime data to analyze and evaluate existing programs, fashion and design new crime-control initiatives, develop funding requests, and plan new laws and crime-control legislation. The "get tough" policies described in the previous chapter, for example, are in large part based upon the public's fear of criminal victimization and the measured ineffectiveness of existing programs to reduce the incidence of repeat offending.

Some, however, question just how objective—and therefore how useful—crime statistics are. Social events, including crime, are complex and difficult to quantify. Even the decision of which crimes should be included in statistical reports, and which excluded, is itself a judgment reflecting the interests and biases of policymakers.

Moreover, public opinion about crime is not always realistic, nor is it always based on a careful consideration of statistics. As well-known criminologist Norval Morris points out, the news media does more to influence public perceptions of crime than any official data.[7] Between 1991 and 1995, for example, the frequency of crime stories reported in the

Uniform Crime Reports (UCR)

An annual FBI publication that summarizes the incidence and rate of reported crimes throughout the United States.

National Crime Victimization Survey (NCVS)

An annual survey of selected American households conducted by the Bureau of Justice Statistics to determine the extent of criminal victimization—especially unreported victimization—in the United States.

national media increased by a factor of 4. From 1993 to 1995, crime was at the top of the list in subject matter covered in news stories at both the local and national levels. "Please note," says Morris, that "the grossly increasing preoccupation with crime stories came at a time of steadily declining crime and violence." However, as Morris adds, "Aided and abetted by this flood of misinformation, the politicians, federal and state and local, fostered the view that the public demands our present 'get tough' policies."

The Collection of Crime Data

Nationally, crime statistics come from two major sources: (1) the Uniform Crime Reporting Program of the Federal Bureau of Investigation (FBI) and (2) the National Crime Victimization Survey of the **Bureau of Justice Statistics (BJS)**. The most widely quoted numbers purporting to describe crime in America today probably come from the FBI's Uniform Crime Reports and are based upon reports to the police by victims of crime. One problem with such summaries is that citizens do not always make official reports, sometimes because they are afraid to contact the police or perhaps because they don't think the police can do anything about the offense. Even when reports are made, they are filtered through a number of bureaucratic levels. As noted methodologist Frank Hagan points out, "The government is very keen on amassing statistics. They collect them, add to them, raise them to the nth power, take the cube root, and prepare wonderful diagrams. But what you must never forget is that every one of these figures comes in the first instance from the *chowty dar* [village watchman], who puts down what he damn pleases."[8]

Another problem with the UCR is that certain kinds of crimes are rarely reported, if at all. These include "victimless crimes," or crimes which, by their nature, involve willing participants. Victimless crimes (also known as *social-order offenses*) include such things as drug use, prostitution, and gambling. Similarly, white-collar and high-technology offenses, such as embezzlement, computer crime, and corporate misdeeds, probably only rarely enter the official statistics. Hence, a relatively large amount of criminal activity in the United States likely remains unreported in the UCR, while the types of crimes that are reported may paint a misleading picture of the true nature of criminal activity by virtue of the publicity accorded to them.

A second data-collection format is typified by the BJS's National Crime Victimization Survey. The NCVS relies upon personal interpretations of what may or may not have been criminal events and upon quasi-confidential surveys which may selectively include data from people most willing to answer the interviewer's questions. Unfortunately, the survey tends to exclude information from less gregarious and more reclusive respondents.

The NCVS suffers from other shortcomings, as well. Some victims are afraid to report crimes, even to nonpolice interviewers. Others may inaccurately interpret their own experiences or may be tempted to invent victimizations for the sake of the interviewer. As the first page of the NCVS report admits, "Details about the crimes come directly from the victims, and no attempt is made to validate the information against police records or any other source."[9]

Another source of crime data is offender self-reports based upon surveys that ask respondents to reveal any illegal activity in which they have been involved. Offender self-reports are not discussed in detail in this chapter since surveys utilizing them are not national in scope. Offenders are often reluctant to accurately report ongoing or recent criminal involvement, making information derived from such surveys somewhat unreliable and less than current. Where information from such surveys is available, however, it tends to show that criminal activity is more widespread than most "official" surveys show.

Finally, although the FBI's UCR and the BJS's NCVS are the country's major sources of crime data, other regular publications contribute to our knowledge of crime patterns throughout the nation. Available yearly is the *Sourcebook of Criminal Justice Statistics*, a compilation of national information on crime and on the criminal justice system. The *Sourcebook* is published by the BJS through support provided by the Justice System Improvement Act of 1979. A Web-based version of the *Sourcebook* is continually updated as data become available. The National Institute of Justice (NIJ), which is the primary research arm of the U.S. Department of Justice, the Office of Juvenile Justice and Delinquency Prevention (OJJDP), the Federal Justice Research Program, and the National Victim's Resource Center provide still more information on crime patterns. Visit **Web Extra! 2–2** at cjtoday.com for an overview of the many sources of crime data. See **Library Extra! 2–1** at cjtoday.com to learn more about the measurement and analysis of crime.

Bureau of Justice Statistics (BJS)

A U.S. Department of Justice agency responsible for the collection of criminal justice data, including the annual National Crime Victimization Survey.

The Uniform Crime Reports

Development of the UCR Program

In 1930, Congress authorized the U.S. attorney general to survey crime in America, and the FBI was designated to implement the program. The bureau quickly built upon earlier efforts by the International Association of Chiefs of Police (IACP) to create a national system of uniform crime statistics. As a practical measure, IACP recommendations had used readily available information, and so it was that citizens' reports of crimes to the police became the basis of the FBIs plan.[10]

During its first year of operation, the FBI's Uniform Crime Reporting Program received reports from 400 cities in 43 states. Twenty million people were covered by that first comprehensive survey. Today, approximately 16,000 law enforcement agencies provide crime information for the program, with data coming from city, county, and state departments. To ensure uniformity in reporting, the FBI has developed standardized definitions of offenses and terminologies used in the program. A number of publications, including the *Uniform Crime Reporting Handbook* and the *Manual of Law Enforcement Records,* are supplied to participating agencies, and training for effective reporting is made available through FBI-sponsored seminars and instructional literature.

Following IACP recommendations, the original UCR Program was designed to permit comparisons over time through construction of a **Crime Index**. The index summed the occurrences of seven major offenses—murder, forcible rape, robbery, aggravated assault, burglary, larceny-theft, and motor vehicle theft—and expressed the result as a crime rate based on population. In 1979, by congressional mandate, an eighth offense—arson—was added to the index. Although UCR categories today parallel statutory definitions of criminal behavior, they are not legal classifications, only conveniences created for statistical-reporting purposes. Because many of the definitions of crime used in this textbook are derived from official UCR terminology, it is important to remember that UCR terminology may differ from statutory definitions of crime.

Historical Trends

Most UCR information is reported as a rate of crime. Rates are computed as the number of crimes *per* some unit of population. National reports generally make use of large units of population, such as 100,000 people. Hence, the rate of rape reported by the UCR for 2000 was 32 forcible rapes per every 100,000 inhabitants of the United States.[11] Rates allow for a meaningful comparison over areas and across time. The rate of reported rape for 1960, for example, was only about 10 per 100,000. We expect the number of crimes to increase as population grows, but rate increases are cause for concern because they indicate that crimes are increasing faster than the population is growing. Rates, however, require interpretation. Since the FBI definition of rape includes only female victims, for example, the rate of victimization might be more meaningfully expressed in terms of every 100,000 female inhabitants. Similarly, although there is a tendency to judge an individual's risk of victimization based upon rates, such judgments tend to be inaccurate since they are based purely on averages and do not take into consideration individual life circumstances, such as place of residence, wealth, and educational level. While rates may tell us about aggregate conditions and trends, we must be very careful in applying them to individual cases.

Since the UCR Program began, there have been two major shifts in crime rates—and we are in the middle of what is now a third. The first occurred during the early 1940s, when crime decreased sharply due to the large number of young men who entered military service during World War II. Young males make up the most "crime-prone" segment of the population, and their removal to the European and Pacific theaters of war did much to lower crime rates at home. From 1933 to 1941, the Crime Index declined from 770 to 508 offenses per every 100,000 members of the American population.[12]

The second noteworthy shift in offense statistics—a dramatic increase in most forms of crime between 1960 and the early 1990s—also had a link to World War II. With the end of the war and the return of millions of young men to civilian life, birthrates skyrocketed between 1945 and 1955, creating a postwar baby boom. By 1960, baby boomers were entering their teenage years. A disproportionate number of young people produced a dramatic increase in most major crimes as the baby-boom generation swelled the proportion of the American population in the crime-prone age range.

Other factors contributed to the increase in reported crime during the same period. Modified reporting requirements, which made it less stressful for victims to file police

---

Crime Index

An inclusive measure of the violent and property crime categories, or Part I offenses, of the Uniform Crime Reports. The Crime Index has been a useful tool for geographic (state-to-state) and historical (year-to-year) comparisons because it employs the concept of a crime rate (the number of crimes per unit of population). However, the addition of arson as an eighth index offense and the new requirements with regard to the gathering of hate-crime statistics could result in new Crime Index measurements which provide less-than-ideal comparisons.

reports, and the publicity associated with the rise in crime sensitized victims to the importance of reporting. Crimes which may have gone undetected in the past began to figure more prominently in official statistics. Similarly, the growing professionalization of some police departments resulted in greater and more accurate data collection, making some of the most progressive departments appear to be associated with the largest crime increases.[13]

The 1960s were tumultuous years. The Vietnam War, a vibrant civil rights struggle, the heady growth of secularism, a dramatic increase in the divorce rate, diverse forms of "liberation," and the influx of psychedelic and other drugs all combined to fragment existing institutions. Social norms were blurred, and group control over individual behavior declined substantially. The "normless" quality of American society in the 1960s contributed greatly to the rise in crime. From 1960 to 1980, crime rates rose from 1,887 to 5,950 offenses per every 100,000 U.S. residents.

Crime rates continued their upward swing, with a brief respite in the early 1980s when postwar boomers began to age out of the crime-prone years and American society emerged from the cultural drift which had characterized the previous 20 years. About the same time, however, an increase in drug-related criminal activity led crime rates to soar once again, especially in the area of violent crime. Crime rates peaked during the early 1990s.

We have since experienced a third major shift, with significant declines in the rate of most major crimes being reported. Between 1991 and 2000, the Crime Index dropped from 5,897 to 4,124 offenses per every 100,000 citizens—sending it down to levels not seen since 1975. Various reasons for the decline have been suggested.[14]

- A coordinated, collaborative, and well-funded national effort to combat crime, beginning with the Safe Streets Act of 1968 and continuing through the USA PATRIOT Act of 2000
- Stronger, better-prepared criminal justice agencies, resulting from increased spending by federal and state governments on crime-control programs
- Growth in the popularity of innovative police programs, such as community policing (discussed in detail in Chapter 6)
- An aggressive approach to gun control, including the Brady Handgun Violence Prevention Act (discussed later in this chapter)
- A strong victims' movement and enactment of the 1984 federal Victims of Crime Act (see Chapter 10) and the 1994 Violence Against Women Act (discussed later in this chapter), which established the Office for Victims of Crime in the U.S. Department of Justice
- Sentencing reform, including various "get tough on crime" initiatives (see Chapter 10)
- A movement to eliminate inequities in the justice system (see Chapter 4 for a discussion of what equitable justice might mean)
- The "War on Drugs," begun in the 1970s has resulted in stiff penalties for drug dealers and repeat drug offenders
- Increased use of the death penalty (see Chapter 10)
- A substantial growth in the use of incarceration (see Chapter 12) due to changes in sentencing law practice (see Chapter 10)
- Advances in forensic science and enforcement technology, including the increased use of real-time communications, the growth of the Internet (see Chapter 17), and the advent of DNA evidence (see Chapters 10 and 17)

Recent decreases in crime, however, while they are noteworthy, do not even begin to bring the overall rate of crime in this country anywhere close to the low crime rates characteristic of the early 1940s and 1950s. From a long-term perspective, even with recent declines, crime rates in this country remain more than eight times what they were in 1940. See **Library Extra! 2–2** at cjtoday.com to learn more about why crime rates have recently backed off from what had been record levels.

A fourth shift may be discernible on the horizon as the size of an increasingly violent teenage population is anticipated to grow over the next decade or two. In the mid-1990s, John J. DiIulio, Jr., warned of a coming generation of **superpredators**—young violent offenders bereft of any moral sense and steeped in violent traditions. Superpredators, said DiIulio, are juveniles "who are coming of age in actual and 'moral poverty' without the benefits of parents, teachers, coaches, or clergy to teach them right from wrong and show them 'unconditional love.'"[15]

Although the idea of a coming generation of youthful superpredators has recently fallen into disfavor within the academic criminal justice community, others think that the idea

> We talk about the criminal justice system, but rarely does it perform as a system.
>
> —Samuel F. Saxton, Director, Prince George's County (Maryland) Department of Corrections

superpredator

A juvenile who is coming of age in actual and "moral poverty" without the benefit of parents, teachers, coaches, or clergy to teach right and wrong, and who turns to criminal activity. The term is often applied to inner-city youth, socialized in violent settings without the benefit of wholesome life experiences, who hold considerable potential for violence.[i]

has been unfairly discounted. James Alan Fox of Northeastern University notes that the number of teens aged 14 to 17 is about to increase significantly, with the largest increase among blacks in this age group.[16] Such an observation, says Fox, is especially worrisome because black males aged 14 to 24, although making up only 1% of the population, "now constitute 17% of the victims of homicide and over 30% of the perpetrators." Also, says Fox, "the differential trends by age of offender observed for homicide generalize to other violent offenses." Writers like DiIulio and Fox have predicted that the coming crime wave will peak around 2010.[17] Figure 2–1 shows historical rates of crime and projected rates through 2010. Keep in mind that official crime rates are based upon the FBI's eight major crimes and do not include drug offenses. As we will see in Chapter 15, while official rates of crime appear to be down, drug offenses continue to increase, accounting for much of the growth in prison populations our country has experienced over the past two decades.

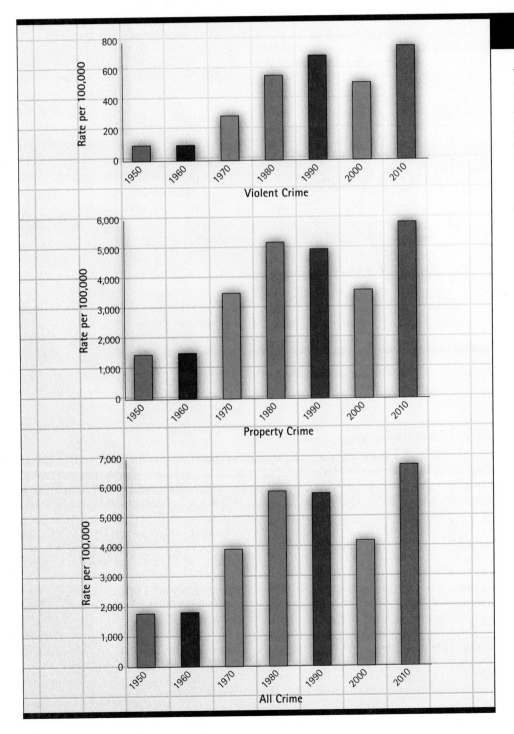

FIGURE 2–1

Actual and projected rates of crime in the United States per 100,000 inhabitants, 1950–2010.

Source: Federal Bureau of Investigation, *Crime in the United States* (Washington, D.C.: U.S. Government Printing Office, various years); and James Alan Fox, *Trends in Juvenile Violence: A Report to the United States Attorney General on Current and Future Rates of Offending* (Washington, D.C.: Bureau of Justice Statistics, 1996).

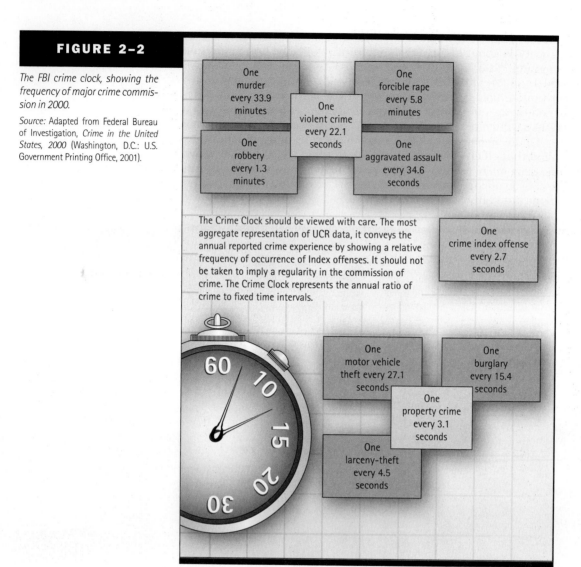

FIGURE 2-2

The FBI crime clock, showing the frequency of major crime commission in 2000.

Source: Adapted from Federal Bureau of Investigation, *Crime in the United States, 2000* (Washington, D.C.: U.S. Government Printing Office, 2001).

One murder every 33.9 minutes

One forcible rape every 5.8 minutes

One violent crime every 22.1 seconds

One robbery every 1.3 minutes

One aggravated assault every 34.6 seconds

The Crime Clock should be viewed with care. The most aggregate representation of UCR data, it conveys the annual reported crime experience by showing a relative frequency of occurrence of Index offenses. It should not be taken to imply a regularity in the commission of crime. The Crime Clock represents the annual ratio of crime to fixed time intervals.

One crime index offense every 2.7 seconds

One motor vehicle theft every 27.1 seconds

One burglary every 15.4 seconds

One property crime every 3.1 seconds

One larceny-theft every 4.5 seconds

UCR Terminology

Figure 2–2 shows the FBI crime clock, which is calculated yearly as a shorthand way of diagramming crime frequency in the United States. It is important to remember that crime clock data imply a regularity to crime that, in reality, does not exist.[18] Also, although the crime clock is a useful diagrammatic tool, it is not a rate-based measure of criminal activity and does not allow easy comparisons over time. Seven Part I offenses, or major crimes, are listed on the right-hand side of the figure. The Part I offenses are (1) murder, (2) forcible rape, (3) robbery, (4) aggravated assault, (5) burglary, (6) larceny-theft, and (7) motor vehicle theft. The sum total of all Part I offenses, divided by the nation's population, comprises the UCR's widely reported Crime Index, which facilitates comparisons of crime rates over time, as noted earlier. Arson, however, which was added as a Part I offense relatively late in the history of the UCR Program, is sometimes excluded from official Crime Index calculations— as it is from the crime clock.

The crime clock distinguishes between two categories of Part I offenses: **violent crime** and **property crime**. Violent, or personal, crimes include murder, forcible rape, robbery, and aggravated assault. Property crimes, as the figure shows, are burglary, motor vehicle theft, and larceny-theft. Other than the use of this simple dichotomy, UCR data do not provide a clear measure of the severity of the crimes they cover.

violent crime

A UCR offense category that includes murder, rape, robbery, and aggravated assault.

property crime

A UCR offense category that includes burglary, larceny-theft, motor vehicle theft, and arson.

Crime clock data are based, as are most UCR statistics, upon crimes reported to (or discovered by) the police. For a few offenses, the numbers reported are probably close to the numbers which actually occur. Murder, for example, is a crime that is difficult to conceal because of its seriousness. Even where the crime is not immediately discovered, the victim is often quickly missed by family members, friends, and associates, and someone files a "missing persons" report with the police. Auto theft is another crime that is reported in numbers similar to its actual rate of occurrence, probably because insurance companies require that the victim file a police report before the claim will be paid.

Built into the UCR's traditional reporting system is the hierarchy rule, which is a way of "counting" crime reports such that only the most serious out of a series of events is scored. If a man and woman go on a picnic, for example, and their party is set upon by a criminal who kills the man, rapes the woman, steals the couple's car, and later burns the vehicle, the hierarchy rule dictates that only one crime will be reported in official statistics—the murder. The offender, if apprehended, may later be charged with each of the offenses listed, but only one report of murder will appear in UCR data.

A commonly used term in today's UCRs is **clearance rate**, which refers to the proportion of reported crimes which have been "solved." Clearances are judged primarily on the basis of arrests and do not involve judicial disposition. Once an arrest has been made, a crime is regarded as "cleared" for reporting purposes. Exceptional clearances (sometimes called *clearances by exceptional means*) can result when law enforcement authorities believe they know who the perpetrator of a crime is but cannot make an arrest. The perpetrator may have fled the country, committed suicide, or died, for example.

For data-gathering and reporting purposes, the UCR Program divides the country into four geographic regions: Northeast, West, South, and Midwest. Unfortunately, no real attempt has been made to create divisions with nearly equal populations or similar demographic characteristics, and it is difficult to meaningfully compare one region of the country to another. Table 2–1 summarizes UCR statistics for 2000. For a detailed overview of the most recent UCR data, see **Web Extra! 2–3** at cjtoday.com.

clearance rate

A traditional measure of investigative effectiveness that compares the number of crimes reported or discovered to the number of crimes solved through arrest or other means (such as the death of the suspect).

MAJOR CRIMES KNOWN TO THE POLICE, 2000 (UCR PART I OFFENSES)				**TABLE 2–1**

Offense	Number	Rate per 100,000	Clearance Rate
Personal/Violent Crimes			
Murder	15,517	5.5	63.1%
Forcible rape	90,186	32.0	46.9
Robbery	407,842	144.9	25.7
Aggravated assault	910,744	323.6	56.9
Property Crimes			
Burglary	2,049,946	728.4	13.4
Larceny-theft	6,965,957	2,475.3	18.2
Motor vehicle theft	1,165,559	414.2	14.1
Arson[1]	78,280	36.9	16.5
U.S. total	11,684,031	4,124.0	20.5

[1]Arson can be classified as either a property crime or a violent crime, depending upon whether personal injury or loss of life results from its commission. It is generally classified as a property crime, however. Arson statistics are incomplete for 2000 and do not enter in the "total" tabulations.

Source: Adapted from Federal Bureau of Investigation, *Crime in the United States, 2000* (Washington, D.C.: U.S. Government Printing Office, 2001).

Part I Offenses
MURDER

murder

The unlawful killing of a human being. Murder is a generic term which in common usage may include first- and second-degree murder, manslaughter, involuntary manslaughter, and other similar offenses.

Part I offenses

A set of UCR categories used to report murder, rape, robbery, aggravated assault, burglary, larceny-theft, motor vehicle theft, and arson, as defined under the FBI's Uniform Crime Reporting Program.

Murder is the unlawful killing of one human being by another.[19] UCR statistics on murder describe the yearly incidence of all willful and unlawful homicides within the United States. Included in the count are all cases of nonnegligent manslaughter which have been reported or discovered by the police. Not included in the count are suicides, justifiable homicides (that is, those committed in self-defense), deaths caused by negligence or accident, and murder attempts. In 2000, some 15,517 murders came to the attention of police departments across the United States.[20] First-degree murder is a criminal homicide which is planned or which involves premeditation. Second-degree murder is an intentional and unlawful killing but one which is generally unplanned and which may happen "in the heat of passion."

Murder is the smallest numerical category in the **Part I offenses**. The 2000 murder rate was 5.5 homicides for every 100,000 persons in the country—a small decrease over the previous year. Murder rates tend to peak annually in the warmest months. In many years, July and August show the highest number of homicides. As is typical, in 2000 the greatest number of murders occurred in July.

Geographically, murder is most common in the southern states. However, because they are also the most populous, a meaningful comparison across regions of the country is difficult.

Age is no barrier to murder. Statistics for 2000 reveal that 217 infants (under the age of one) were victims of homicide, as were 265 people aged 75 and over.[21] Young adults between 20 and 24 were the most likely to be murdered. Murder perpetrators were also most common in this age group.

Firearms are the weapon of choice in most murders. Guns accounted for 65.6% of all killings in 2000. Handguns outnumbered shotguns almost 15 to 1 in the murder statistics, while rifles were a distant third. Knives were used in approximately 13% of all murders. Other weapons included explosives, poison, narcotics overdose, blunt objects like clubs, hands, feet, and fists.

Few murders are committed by strangers. Only 13% of all murders in 2000 were perpetrated by offenders classified as "strangers." In 42.6% of all killings, the relationship between the parties had not yet been determined. The largest category of killers was officially listed as "acquaintances," which probably includes a large number of former friends. Arguments cause most murders (29.4%), but murders also occur during the commission of other crimes, such as robbery, rape, and burglary. Homicides which follow from other crimes are more likely to be impulsive rather than planned.

Murders may occur in sprees, which "involve killings at two or more locations with almost no time break between murders."[22] Andrew Cunanan, who killed fashion designer Gianni Versace in 1997, provides an example of a spree killer. Cunanan's killing spree lasted three months and claimed five victims.[23] He was put on the FBI's "Ten Most Wanted" list before committing suicide aboard a Miami yacht where he had hidden.

In contrast to spree killing, mass murder entails "the killing of four or more victims at one location, within one event."[24] Recent mass murderers have included the likes of Timothy McVeigh (the anti-government Oklahoma City bomber) and Mohammed Atta and the terrorists whom he led in the September 11, 2001, attacks against American targets.

Yet another kind of murder, serial murder, happens over time and is officially defined to "involve the killing of several victims in three or more separate events."[25] In cases of serial murder, days, months, or even years may elapse between killings. Serial killers have frequently been portrayed in the media.[26] Some of the more infamous serial killers of recent years are Jeffrey Dahmer, who received 936 years in prison for the homosexual dismemberment murders of 15 young men (and who was himself later murdered in prison); Ted Bundy, who killed many college-aged women; Henry Lee Lucas, now in a Texas prison, who confessed to 600 murders but later recanted (yet was convicted of 11 murders and linked to at least 140 others);[27] Ottis Toole, Lucas's partner in crime; Charles Manson, still serving time for ordering followers to kill seven Californians, including famed actress Sharon Tate; Andrei Chikatilo, the Russian "Hannibal Lecter," who killed 52 people, mostly schoolchildren;[28] David Berkowitz, also known as the "Son of Sam," who killed six people and wounded seven on lover's lanes around New York City; Theodore Kaczynski, the Unabomber, who perpetrated a series of bomb attacks on "establishment" figures (see Chapter 17); Seattle's Green River Killer, who killed as many as 49 women (mostly prostitutes and runaways) during the 1980s (a suspect in the killings was arrested in December 2001 and was still being interrogated by police as this book went to press); and "railroad killer" Angel Maturino Resendiz, whose crimes were discussed in Chapter 1. Although he was convicted of only one murder—that of Dr. Claudia Benton, which occurred in 1998—Resendiz is suspected of many more.[29]

Because murder is such a serious crime, it consumes substantial police resources. Consequently, over the years the offense has shown the highest clearance rate of any index crime. Sixty-three percent of all homicides were cleared in 2000. Figure 2–3 shows clearance rates for all Part I offenses.

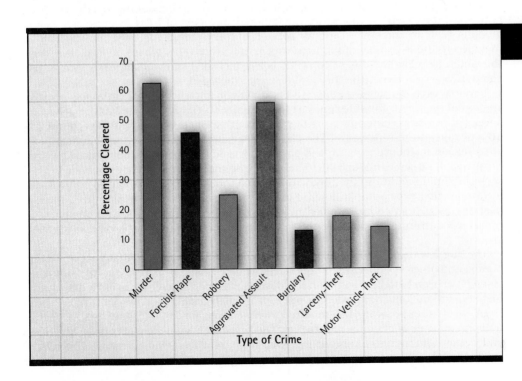

FIGURE 2–3

Crimes cleared by arrest, 2000.

Source: Federal Bureau of Investigation, *Crime in the United States, 2000* (Washington, D.C.: U.S. Government Printing Office, 2001).

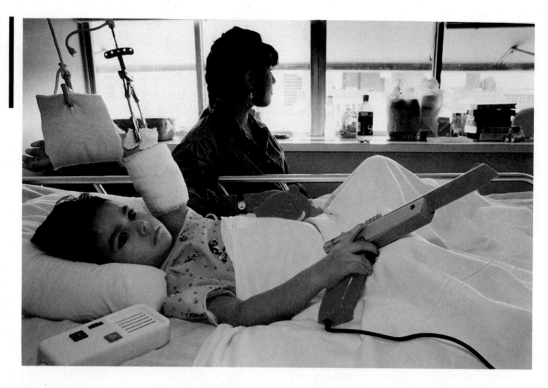

A three-year-old in San Antonio's Santa Rosa Children's Hospital recovering after becoming the victim of a drive-by shooting. Personal violence is the type of crime that engenders the greatest fear.

Rick Hunter, CORBIS/Sygma

rape

Unlawful sexual intercourse, achieved through force and without consent. Broadly speaking, the term *rape* has been applied to a wide variety of sexual attacks and may include same-sex rape and the rape of a male by a female. Some jurisdictions refer to same-sex rape as *sexual battery.*

forcible rape (UCR)

The carnal knowledge of a female forcibly and against her will. For statistical reporting purposes, the FBI defines *forcible rape* as "unlawful sexual intercourse with a female, by force and against her will, or without legal or factual consent." Statutory rape differs from forcible rape in that it generally involves nonforcible sexual intercourse with a minor. Date rape, or acquaintance rape, is a subcategory of rape which is of special concern today.

sexual battery

Intentional and wrongful physical contact with a person, without his or her consent, that entails a sexual component or purpose.

FORCIBLE RAPE

Broadly speaking, the term **rape** has been applied to a wide variety of sexual attacks and, in popular terminology, may include same-sex rape and the rape of a male by a female. For statistical-reporting purposes, however, the term **forcible rape** has a specific and somewhat different meaning. The Uniform Crime Reports defines *forcible rape* as "the carnal knowledge of a female forcibly and against her will."[30] By definition, rapes reported under the UCR Program are always of females. In contrast to what may be emerging social convention, in which male rape is a recognized form of sexual assault, the *Uniform Crime Reporting Handbook,* which serves as a statistical-reporting guide for law enforcement agencies, says, "Sex attacks on males are excluded [from the crime of forcible rape] and should be classified as assaults or 'other sex offenses,' depending on the nature of the crime and the extent of the injury."[31] Although not part of UCR terminology, some jurisdictions refer to same-sex rape as **sexual battery**. Incidents of sexual battery are not included in the UCR tally of reported rapes. Statutory rape, where no force is involved but the victim is below the age of consent, is not included in rape statistics, but attempts to commit rape by force or the threat of force are included.

Forcible rape is the least reported of all violent crimes. Typical estimates are that only one out of every four forcible rapes which actually occur are reported to the police. An even lower figure was reported by a 1992 government-sponsored study, which found that only 16% of rapes were reported.[32] The victim's fear of embarrassment is the most commonly cited reason for nonreports. In the past, reports of rape were usually taken by seemingly hardened desk sergeants or male detectives who may not have been sensitive to the needs of the victim. In addition, the physical examination which victims had to endure was often a traumatizing experience in itself. Finally, many states routinely permitted the woman's past sexual history to be revealed in detail in the courtroom if a trial ensued. All these practices contributed to a considerable hesitancy on the part of rape victims to report their crime.

The last few decades have seen many changes designed to facilitate accurate reporting of rape and other sex offenses. Trained female detectives often interview the victims, physicians have been better educated in handling the psychological needs of victims, and sexual histories are no longer regarded as relevant in most trials.

UCR statistics show 90,186 reported forcible rapes for 2000 (Figure 2–4), a 1% decrease over the number of offenses reported for the previous year. Rape is a crime which has generally shown an increase in reporting, even in years when other personal crimes have been on the decline.

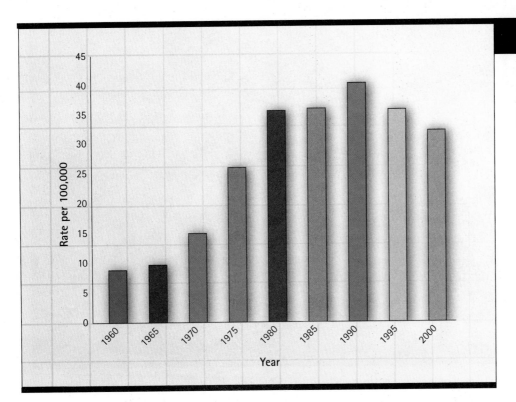

FIGURE 2-4

Rate of reported rape, 1960–2000.

Source: Federal Bureau of Investigation, *Crime in the United States* (Washington, D.C.: U.S. Government Printing Office, various years).

The offense of rape follows homicide in its seasonal variation. The greatest number of forcible rapes in 2000 were reported in the hot summer months, while January, February, November, and December recorded the lowest number of reports.

Rape is frequently committed by a man known to the victim, as in the case of date rape. Victims may be held captive and subjected to repeated assaults.[33] In the crime of heterosexual rape, any female—regardless of age, appearance, or occupation—is a potential victim. Through personal violation, humiliation, and physical battering, rapists seek a sense of personal aggrandizement and dominance. In contrast, victims of rape often experience a lessened sense of personal worth; increased feelings of despair, helplessness, and vulnerability; a misplaced sense of guilt; and a lack of control over their personal lives.

Contemporary wisdom holds that forcible rape is often a planned violent crime which serves the offender's need for power rather than sexual gratification.[34] The "power thesis" has its origins in the writings of Susan Brownmiller, who argued in 1975 that the primary motivation leading to rape is the male desire to "keep women in their place" and to preserve sexual role inequality through violence.[35] Although many writers on the subject of forcible rape have generally accepted the power thesis, recent studies have caused some to rethink it. In a 1995 survey of the motives of serial rapists, for example, Dennis J. Stevens found that 41% of imprisoned rapists—the largest category of all—reported that "lust" was "the primary motive for predatory rape."[36]

Statistically speaking, however, most rapes are committed by acquaintances of the victims and often betray a trust or friendship. **Date rape**, which falls into this category, appears to be far more common than previously believed. Recently, the growing number of rapes perpetrated with the use of the "date rape drug" Rohypnol have alarmed law enforcement personnel. Rohypnol, which is discussed in more detail in Chapters 4 and 15, is an illegal pharmaceutical substance that is virtually tasteless. Available on the black market, it dissolves easily in drinks and can leave anyone who unknowingly consumes it unconscious for hours, making them vulnerable to sexual assault.

Rape within marriage, which has not always been recognized as a crime, is a growing area of concern in American criminal justice, and many laws have been enacted over the past few decades to deter it. Similarly, even though UCR statistics report only the rape or attempted rape of females,[37] some state statutes, by definition, allow for the rape of a male by a female. Such an offense, when it occurs, however, is typically of the statutory variety. In 1997, for example, sixth-grade schoolteacher Mary Kay LeTourneau, a 35-year-old married mother of four, pleaded guilty in Burien, Washington, to second-degree child rape after having a child by one of her students, a 13-year-old boy named Vili Fualuaau. LeTourneau had known the

date rape

Unlawful forced sexual intercourse with a female against her will that occurs within the context of a dating relationship.

boy since he was in the second grade. "When the sexual relationship started," she told reporters, "it seemed natural. What didn't seem natural was that there was a law forbidding such a natural thing."[38] She was sentenced to six months in jail and banned from seeing the boy or their child. Following her release after a brief jail stay, LeTourneau became known as "America's most famous pedophile" after she had a second child by her teenage lover. In 1998, she was sentenced to a seven and a half year prison term for violating probation.[39] Learn more about the crime of rape and about what women can do to protect themselves at **Web Extra! 2–4** at cjtoday.com. Read about statistical measures relating to the sexual victimization of women at **Library Extra! 2–3** at cjtoday.com.

ROBBERY

robbery (UCR)

The unlawful taking or attempted taking of property that is in the immediate possession of another by force or violence and/or by putting the victim in fear. Armed robbery differs from unarmed or strong-arm robbery with regard to the presence of a weapon. Contrary to popular conceptions, highway robbery does not necessarily occur on a street—and rarely in a vehicle. The term *highway robbery* applies to any form of robbery which occurs outdoors in a public place.

Robbery, which should not be confused with burglary, is a personal crime and involves a face-to-face confrontation between victim and perpetrator. Weapons may be used, or strong-arm robbery may occur through intimidation, especially where gangs threaten victims by their sheer number. Purse snatching and pocket picking are not classified as robbery by the UCR Program but are included under the category of larceny-theft.

In 2000, individuals were the most common target of robbers. Banks, gas stations, convenience stores, and other businesses were the second most common target, with residential robberies accounting for only 12.2% of the total. In 2000, 407,842 robberies were reported to the police, and 46% of them were highway robberies (meaning that they occurred outdoors, probably as the victim was walking), or muggings. Strong-arm robberies accounted for 40.4% of the total robberies reported. Guns were used in 40.9% of all robberies, and knives in 8.4%.

Armed robbers are dangerous. Guns are actually discharged in 20% of all robberies.[40] Whenever a robbery occurs, the UCR Program scores the event as one robbery, even when a number of victims were robbed during the event. With the move toward incident-driven reporting (discussed later in this chapter), however, the UCR will soon make data available on the number of individuals robbed in each incident. Because statistics on crime show only the most serious offense which occurred during a particular episode, robberies are often hidden when they occur in conjunction with other, more serious, crimes. For example, 3% of robbery victims are also raped, and a large number of homicide victims are robbed.[41]

Robbery is primarily an urban offense, and most arrestees are young males who are members of minority groups. The robbery rate in large cities in 2000 was 440.2 per every 100,000 inhabitants, while it was only 15.5 in rural areas. Ninety percent of those arrested for robbery in 2000 were male, 63% were under the age of 25, and 56% were minorities.[42]

Multiculturalism and Diversity in America

[Investigating Crime in a Multicultural Setting]

In the mid-1990s, the Washington, D.C.-based National Crime Prevention Council (NCPC) published an important guide for American law enforcement officers who work with multicultural groups. The principles it contains can be applied equally to most foreign-born individuals living in the United States and are especially important to both patrol officers and criminal investigators.

The NCPC guide points out that it is important for well-intentioned newcomers to this country to learn that the law enforcement system in the United States is not a national police force but a series of local, regional, and state agencies that take seriously their obligation to "serve and protect" law-abiding residents. Newcomers need to know that police can teach them how to protect themselves and their families from crime. Many immigrants, especially political refugees, come from countries in which the criminal justice system is based upon tyranny, repression, and fear.

The NCPC suggests that law enforcement officers and other members of the criminal justice system can help ease this transition by working not only to communicate with immigrants, but also to understand them and the complexities of their native cultures. The mere absence of conflict in a neighborhood, says NCPC, does not mean that residents of different cultures have found harmony and a cooperative working relationship. True multicultural integration occurs when various cultures reach a comfortable day-to-day interaction marked by respect, interest, and caring.

Communities in which immigrants and law enforcement have established close positive ties benefit considerably, according to the NCPC. Immigrants gain greater access to police and other services,

such as youth programs, victim assistance, parenting classes, medical assistance programs, business networking, and neighborhood groups. Crime decreases in communities where law enforcement officers help immigrants learn to protect themselves against crime.

For police officers working in communities in which "language is a serious barrier between cultures," the NCPC suggests the following pointers for communicating more effectively:

- Be patient when speaking with someone who does not clearly understand your language. Speak slowly and distinctly. Be willing to repeat words or phrases if necessary. Remember that shouting never helps a nonnative speaker understand better.
- Be careful with your choice of words, selecting those that are clear, straightforward, and simple to understand. Avoid colloquialisms and slang.
- Allow extra time for investigation when the people involved have not mastered English.
- Be sure that anyone who serves as an interpreter is fully qualified and has had experience. Interpreting under pressure is a difficult task; lack of training can lead to mistakes.
- Be candid about your ability to speak or understand a language. Trying to "fake it" just leads to confusion, misunderstanding, and misspent time.
- Never assume that someone is less intelligent just because he or she doesn't speak English well.

Visit the National Crime Prevention Council via **Web Extra! 2–5** at cjtoday.com.

Web EXTRA!

Source: Adapted from National Crime Prevention Council, *Building and Crossing Bridges: Refugees and Law Enforcement Working Together* (Washington, D.C.: NCPC, 1994).

AGGRAVATED ASSAULT

On November 14, 2001, a county judge found 22–year-old Maryland resident Lee P. McPhatter guilty of assaulting Cookie Monster during a June brawl at the Sesame Place theme park in Middletown, Pennsylvania.[43] McPhatter, who became angry when his three-year-old daughter was seemingly pushed aside while trying to get her picture taken with the Monster, was sentenced to one year's probation and was ordered to complete 25 hours of community service as well as anger-management counseling. Jennie McNelis, the 22–year-old woman who was wearing the furry blue monster suit during the attack, suffered bruises and a strained neck. Witnesses testified that McPhatter punched McNelis through the mouth of the costume, then kicked her in the ribs and legs when she fell to the ground. The beating occurred in full view of a crowd of stunned children and parents.

Assaults are of two types: aggravated and simple. For statistical-reporting purposes, simple assaults may involve pushing and shoving or even fistfights (although, technically speaking, the correct legal term used to describe such incidents is *battery*). **Aggravated assaults** are distinguished from simple assaults in that either they include the use of a weapon or the assault victim requires medical assistance. When a deadly weapon is employed, even if no injury results, an aggravated assault may be charged as attempted murder.[44] Hence, because of their potentially serious consequences, the UCR Program scores some cases of attempted assault as aggravated assault.

In 2000, 910,744 cases of aggravated assault were reported to law enforcement agencies in the United States. The summer months had the greatest frequency of assault, while

assault (UCR)

An unlawful attack by one person upon another. Historically, *assault* meant only the attempt to inflict injury on another person; a completed act constituted the separate offense of battery. Under modern statistical usage, however, attempted and completed acts are grouped together under the generic term *assault*.

aggravated assault

The unlawful, intentional inflicting, or attempted or threatened inflicting, of serious injury upon the person of another. While *aggravated assault* and *simple assault* are standard terms for reporting purposes, most state penal codes use labels like *first-degree* and *second-degree* to make such distinctions.

FIGURE 2–5

Weapons used in aggravated assaults, 2000.

Source: Federal Bureau of Investigation, *Crime in the United States, 2000* (Washington, D.C.: U.S. Government Printing Office, 2001).

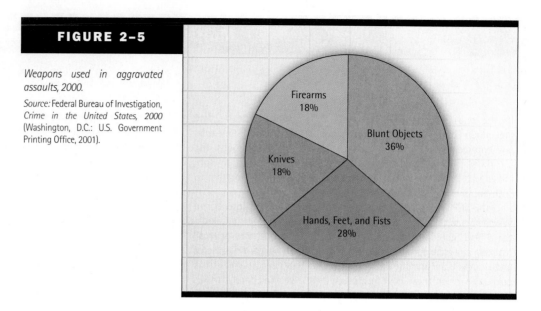

February, November, and December were the months with the lowest number of reports. Most aggravated assaults were committed with blunt objects or objects near at hand (36%), while hands, feet, and fists were also commonly used (28%). Less frequent were knives and firearms (18% each), as Figure 2–5 shows. Because those who commit assaults are often known to their victims, aggravated assaults are relatively easy to solve. Fifty-seven percent of all aggravated assaults reported to the police in 2000 were cleared by arrest.

BURGLARY

burglary (UCR)

The unlawful entry of a structure to commit a felony or a theft (excludes tents, trailers, and other mobile units used for recreational purposes). For the UCR, the crime of burglary can be reported if (1) an unlawful entry of an unlocked structure has occurred, (2) a breaking and entering (of a secured structure) has taken place, or (3) a burglary has been attempted.

Although it may involve personal and even violent confrontation, **burglary** is primarily a property crime. Burglars are interested in financial gain and usually fence (that is, illegally sell) stolen items to recover a fraction of their cash value. About 2 million burglaries were reported to the police in 2000. Dollar losses to burglary victims totaled nearly $3 billion, with an average loss per offense of $1,462.

Many people fear nighttime burglary of their residence. They imagine themselves asleep in bed as a stranger breaks into their home, and they conjure up visions of a violent confrontation. While such scenarios do occur, daytime burglary is more common. Many families now have two or more breadwinners, and since children are in school during the day, some homes—and even entire neighborhoods—are unoccupied during daylight hours. This shift in patterns of social activity has led to a growing burglary threat against residences during daytime.

The UCR Program employs three classifications of burglary: (1) forcible entry, (2) unlawful entry where no force is used, and (3) attempted forcible entry. In most jurisdictions, force need not be employed for a crime to be classified as burglary. Unlocked doors and open windows are invitations to burglars, and the crime of burglary consists not so much of a forcible entry as it does of the intent to trespass and steal. In 2000, 63.7% of all burglaries were forcible entries, 29.5% were unlawful entries, and 6.8% were attempted forcible entries.[45] The most dangerous burglaries were those in which a household member was home (about 10% of all burglaries).[46] Residents who were home during a burglary suffered a greater than 30% chance of becoming the victim of a violent crime.[47]

Property crimes generally involve low rates of clearance. Burglary is no exception. The clearance rate for burglary in 2000 was only 13.4%. Burglars are usually unknown to their victims, and even if known, they conceal their identity by committing their crime when the victim is not present.

LARCENY-THEFT

larceny-theft (UCR)

The unlawful taking or attempted taking, carrying, leading, or riding away of property, from the possession or constructive possession of another (including attempts). Motor vehicles are excluded. Larceny is the most common of the eight major offenses, although probably only a small percentage of all larcenies are actually reported to the police because of the small dollar amounts involved.

Larceny is another name for theft, and the UCR uses the term **larceny-theft** to describe these kinds of offenses. Some states distinguish between simple larceny and grand larceny. Grand larceny is usually defined as theft of valuables in excess of a certain set dollar amount, such as $200. Categorizing the crime by dollar amount, however, can present unique problems, as during the 1970s, when legislatures found themselves unable to enact statutory revisions fast enough to keep pace with inflation.

Larceny-theft, as defined by the UCR Program, includes theft of valuables of any dollar amount. The reports specifically list the following offenses as types of larceny (listed here in order of declining frequency):

- Thefts from motor vehicles
- Shoplifting
- Thefts of motor vehicle parts and accessories
- Thefts from buildings
- Bicycle thefts
- Pocket picking
- Purse snatching
- Thefts from coin-operated machines

Thefts of farm animals (known as *rustling*) and thefts of most types of farm machinery also fall into the larceny category. In fact, larceny is such a broad category that it serves as a kind of catchall in the UCR. In 1995, for example, Yale University officials filed larceny charges against 25-year-old student Lon Grammer, claiming that he had fraudulently obtained university funds.[48] The university maintained that Grammer stole his education by forging college and high-school transcripts and concocting letters of recommendation prior to admission. Grammer's alleged misdeeds, which Yale University officials said misled them into thinking that Grammer, a poor student before attending Yale, had an exceptional scholastic record, permitted him to receive $61,475 in grants and loans during the time he attended the school. Grammer was expelled.

Reported thefts can involve a wide diversity of materials with values that range anywhere from pocket change to the stealing of a $100 million aircraft. Specifically excluded from the count of larceny for reporting purposes are crimes of embezzlement, con games, forgery, and worthless checks. Larceny has been traditionally thought of as a crime which requires physical possession of the item appropriated. Hence, most computer crimes, including thefts engineered through online access or thefts of software and information

Motor vehicle theft or larceny? Even members of the FBI's Education and Training Services Unit in Washington, D.C., were unsure of how to classify the 1995 theft of this M-60 tank by Shawn Nelson, a former Army tank operator. Nelson drove the tank through the streets of San Diego before being shot and killed by police, who jumped on the tank and cut the hatch open with bolt cutters. In this photo, Nelson's body is being removed from the tank shortly after he was shot.

David McNew, CORBIS/Sygma

itself, have typically not been scored as larcenies unless electronic circuitry, disks, or computer equipment was actually stolen. On the other hand, the crime of larceny may cover other types of high-technology thefts. In 1995, for example, Dr. Ricardo Asch, a world-renowned fertility doctor working at the University of California–Irvine's Center for Reproductive Health, was accused of stealing frozen human embryos and implanting them into infertile women. After fleeing to Mexico, Asch gave a videotaped deposition from a Tijuana hotel room, where he testified that he never stopped to determine if legal consent to donate had been given when he transferred eggs and embryos from one woman to another.[49] He was soon indicted on 35 counts of criminal activity, including using the mail to steal from insurance companies through the filing of false claims. The center at which Asch had worked closed after more than 50 suits were filed against it.

Reports to the police in 2000 showed 6,965,957 larcenies nationwide, with the total value of property stolen placed at $5.1 billion. The most common form of larceny in recent years has been theft of motor vehicle parts, accessories, and contents. Tires, wheels, hubcaps, radar detectors, stereos, CD players, cassette tapes, compact discs, and cellular phones account for many of the items reported stolen.

Larceny-theft is the most frequently reported major crime, according to the UCR. It may also be the UCR's most underreported crime category because small thefts rarely come to the attention of the police. The average value of items reported stolen in 2000 was about $735.

MOTOR VEHICLE THEFT

For record-keeping purposes, the UCR Program defines *motor vehicles* as self-propelled vehicles which run on the ground and not on rails. Included in the definition are automobiles, motorcycles, motor scooters, trucks, buses, and snowmobiles. Excluded are trains, airplanes, bulldozers, most farm and construction machinery, ships, boats, and spacecraft; the theft of these would be scored as larceny-theft.[50] Vehicles that are temporarily taken by individuals who have lawful access to them are not thefts. Hence, spouses who jointly own all property may drive the family car, even though one spouse may think of the vehicle as his or her exclusive personal property.

> **motor vehicle theft (UCR)**
>
> The theft or attempted theft of a motor vehicle. *Motor vehicle* is defined as a self-propelled road vehicle that runs on land surface and not on rails. The stealing of trains, planes, boats, construction equipment, and most farm machinery is classified as larceny under the UCR Program, not as motor vehicle theft.

As mentioned earlier, most occurrences of **motor vehicle theft** are reported to law enforcement agencies. Insurance companies require police reports before they will reimburse car owners for their losses. Some reports of motor vehicle thefts, however, may be false. People who have damaged their own vehicles in solitary crashes or who have been unable to sell them may try to force insurance companies to "buy" them through reports of theft.

In 2000, 1,165,559 motor vehicles were reported stolen. The average value per vehicle stolen was $6,682, making motor vehicle theft a $7.8 billion crime. The clearance rate for motor vehicle theft was only 14% in 2000. City agencies reported the lowest rates of clearance (9%), while rural counties had the highest rate (29.3%). Many stolen vehicles are quickly disassembled in chop shops, and the parts are resold. Auto parts are, of course, much more difficult to identify and trace than are intact vehicles. In some parts of the country, chop shops operate like big businesses, and one shop may strip a dozen or more cars per day.

Motor vehicle theft can turn violent, as in cases of carjacking—a crime in which offenders usually force the car's occupants onto the street before stealing the vehicle. In 2000, for example, Christy Robel watched helplessly as her six-year-old son, Jake, was dragged to his death after a man jumped behind the wheel of her car and sped off.[51] Robel had left the car running with the boy inside as she made a brief stop at a Kansas City sandwich shop. The carjacker, 35-year-old Kim L. Davis, tried to push Jake from the car as he made his escape, but the boy became entangled in his seat belt and was dragged for five miles at speeds of more than 80 mph. In October 2001, Davis was convicted of murder and sentenced to spend the rest of his life in prison without possibility of parole.[52] The FBI estimates that carjackings account for slightly more than 1% of all motor vehicle thefts.

Arrest reports for motor vehicle theft show that the typical offender is a young male. Sixty-seven percent of all arrestees in 2000 were under the age of 25, and 84.2% were male.

ARSON

> **arson (UCR)**
>
> The burning or attempted burning of property, with or without the intent to defraud. Some instances of arson result from malicious mischief, some involve attempts to claim insurance monies, and some are committed in an effort to disguise other crimes, such as murder, burglary, or larceny.

The UCR Program received crime reports from more than 16,000 law enforcement agencies in 2000.[53] Of these, only 12,011 submitted arson data. Even fewer agencies provided complete data as to the type of **arson** (the nature of the property burned), the estimated monetary value of the property, the ownership, and so on.

Arson data include only those fires which, through investigation, are determined to have been willfully or maliciously set. Fires of unknown or suspicious origin are excluded from arson statistics.[54]

The intentional and unlawful burning of structures (houses, storage buildings, manufacturing facilities, and so on) was the type of arson reported most often in 2000 (30,116 instances). The arson of vehicles was the second most common category, with 20,396 such burnings reported. The average dollar loss per instance of arson in 2000 was $11,042, and total nationwide property damage was placed at close to $1 billion.[55] As with most property crimes, the clearance rate for arson was low—only 16.5% nationally.

The crime of arson exists in a kind of statistical limbo. In 1979, Congress ordered that it be added as an eighth index offense. To date, however, the UCR Program has been unable to integrate statistics on arson successfully into the yearly Crime Index. The problem is twofold: (1) Many law enforcement agencies have not yet begun making regular reports to the FBI on arson offenses which occur in their jurisdiction, and (2) any change in the index offenses produces a Crime Index which will not permit meaningful comparisons. The Crime Index will allow useful comparisons over time and between jurisdictions only as long as it retains definitional consistency. Adding another offense to the index, or substantially changing the definition of any of its categories, still provides a measure of crime, but it changes the meaning of the term.

Some of these difficulties have been resolved through the Special Arson Program, authorized by Congress in 1982. The FBI, in conjunction with the National Fire Data Center, now operates a Special Arson Reporting System, which focuses upon fire departments across the nation. The reporting system is designed to provide data which supplement yearly UCR arson tabulations.[56]

Part II Offenses

The Uniform Crime Reports also include information on what the FBI calls **Part II offenses**. Part II offenses, which are generally less serious than those that make up the Crime Index, include a number of social-order, or so-called victimless, crimes. The statistics on Part II offenses are for recorded arrests, not for crimes reported to the police. The logic inherent in this form of scoring is that most Part II offenses would never come to the attention of the police were it not for arrests. Part II offenses are shown in Table 2–2 with the number of estimated arrests made in each category for 2000.

Part II offenses

A set of UCR categories used to report arrests for less serious offenses.

UCR PART II OFFENSES, 2000		TABLE 2-2
Offense Category	**Number of Arrests**	
Simple assault	1,312,169	
Forgery and counterfeiting	108,654	
Fraud	345,732	
Embezzlement	18,952	
Stolen property (receiving, etc.)	118,641	
Vandalism	281,305	
Weapons (carrying, etc.)	159,181	
Prostitution and related offenses	87,620	
Sex offenses (statutory rape, etc.)	93,399	
Drug-law violations	1,579,566	
Gambling	10,842	
Offenses against the family (nonsupport, etc.)	147,663	
Driving under the influence	1,471,289	
Liquor-law violations	683,124	
Public drunkenness	637,554	
Disorderly conduct	638,740	
Vagrancy	32,542	
Curfew violation/loitering	154,711	
Runaways	141,975	
Total	8,023,659	

Source: Adapted from Federal Bureau of Investigation, *Crime in the United States, 2000* (Washington, D.C.: U.S. Government Printing Office, 2001).

A Part II arrest is counted each time a person is taken into custody. As a result, the statistics in Table 2–2 do not measure the number of suspects arrested, but rather the number of arrests made. Some suspects were arrested more than once.

NIBRS: The New UCR

The Uniform Crime Reports are undergoing significant changes in the way in which data are gathered and reported. Whereas the original UCR system was "summary based," the newly enhanced UCR, called the **National Incident-Based Reporting System (NIBRS)**, is incident driven (Table 2–3). Under NIBRS, city, county, state, and federal law enforcement agencies throughout the country furnish detailed data on crime and arrest activities at the incident level to either the individual state incident-based reporting programs or directly to the federal NIBRS program.

The goals of NIBRS are to enhance the quantity, quality, and timeliness of crime data collection by law enforcement and to improve the methodology used for compiling, analyzing, auditing, and publishing the collected data. A major advantage of NIBRS, beyond the increase in data collected, is the ability to break down and combine crime offense data into specific information.[57]

The old UCR system depended upon statistical tabulations of crime data which were often little more than frequency counts. Under the new system, many details are being gathered about each criminal incident. Included among them are information on place of occurrence, weapon used, type and value of property damaged or stolen, the personal characteristics of the offender and the victim, the nature of any relationship between the two, the nature of the disposition of the complaint, and so on (Table 2–4).

The new reporting system replaces the old Part I and Part II offenses with 22 general offenses: arson, assault, bribery, burglary, counterfeiting, embezzlement, extortion, forcible sex offenses, fraud, gambling, homicide, kidnapping, larceny, motor vehicle theft, narcotics offenses, nonforcible sex offenses, pornography, prostitution, receiving stolen property, robbery, vandalism, and weapons violations. Other offenses on which NIBRS data are being gathered include bad checks, vagrancy, disorderly conduct, driving under the influence, drunkenness, nonviolent family offenses, liquor law violations, "Peeping Tom" activity, runaways, trespass, and a general category of all "other" criminal law violations.

NIBRS also eliminates the need for the hierarchy rule (because multiple types of crimes can be reported within a single incident) and collects an expanded array of attributes

National Incident-Based Reporting System (NIBRS)

An incident-based reporting system that collects data on every single crime occurrence. NIBRS data will soon supersede the kinds of traditional data provided by the FBI's Uniform Crime Reports.

TABLE 2–3	**DIFFERENCES BETWEEN THE UCR AND NIBRS**
The Uniform Crime Reports	**National Incident-Based Reporting System**
Consists of monthly aggregate crime counts for eight index crimes	Consists of individual incident records for the eight index crimes and 38 other offenses, with details on offense, victim, offender and property involved
Records one offense per incident as determined by hierarchy rule; hierarchy rule suppresses counts of lesser offenses in multiple-offense incidents	Records each offense occurring in an incident
Does not distinguish between attempted and completed crimes	Distinguishes between attempted and completed crimes
Records rape of females only	Records rape of males and females
Collects assault information in five categories	Restructures definition of assault
Collects weapon information for murder, robbery, and aggravated assault	Collects weapon information for all violent offenses
Provides counts on arrests for the eight index crimes and 21 other offenses	Provides details on arrests for the eight index crimes and 49 other offenses

Source: Adapted from *Effects of NIBRS on Crime Statistics,* BJS Special Report (Washington, D.C.: Bureau of Justice Statistics, 2000), p. 1.

INFORMATION THAT NIBRS RECORDS ON EACH CRIMINAL INCIDENT · TABLE 2-4

Administrative Segment	Victim Segment
ORI number[1]	Victim number
Incident number	Victim UCR offense code
Incident date/hour	Type of victim
Exceptional clearance indicator	Age of victim
Exceptional clearance date	Sex of victim
	Race of victim
	Ethnicity of victim
	Resident status of victim
	Homicide/assault circumstances
	Justifiable homicide circumstances
	Type of injury
	Related offender number
	Relationship of victim to offender

Offense Segment	Property Segment
UCR offense code	Type of property loss
Attempted/completed code	Property description
Alcohol/drug use by offender	Property value
Type of location	Recovery date
Number of premises entered	Number of stolen motor vehicles
Method of entry	Number of recovered motor vehicles
Type of criminal activity	Suspected drug type
Type of weapon/force used	Estimated drug quantity
Bias crime code	Drug measurement unit

Offender Segment	Arrestee Segment
Offender number	Arrestee number
Age of offender	Transaction number
Sex of offender	Arrest date
Race of offender	Type of arrest
	Multiple clearance indicator
	UCR arrest offense code
	Arrestee armed indicator
	Age of arrestee
	Sex of arrestee
	Race of arrestee
	Ethnicity of arrestee
	Resident status of arrestee
	Disposition of arrestee under 18

[1]ORI, or "originating agency identifier," refers to the reporting agency's unique identification number.
Source: Effects of NIBRS on Crime Statistics, BJS Special Report (Washington, D.C.: Bureau of Justice Statistics, 2000), p. 4.

involved in the commission of offenses, including whether the offender is suspected of using alcohol, drugs or narcotics, or a computer in the commission of the offense.

The FBI began accepting crime data in NIBRS format in January 1989. Although NIBRS was intended to be fully in place by 1999, delays have been routine. By 2001, 21 state crime-reporting programs had been certified for NIBRS participation, and an additional 15 states were nearing completion of the certification process. The remaining states were continuing to report crime incident data under the old format.[58] A study by the National Consortium for

Justice Information and Statistics (SEARCH) concluded that for many law enforcement agencies, "the costs of implementing changes in reporting practices to make their systems NIBRS-compliant (for example, revising offense reporting forms, department-wide training, and software reprogramming), compounded by concerns over the impact NIBRS will have on the department's reported crime rate and a lack of understanding on how the data will be used at state and federal levels, create formidable impediments to NIBRS implementation."[59]

A sample of NIBRS data can be viewed at **Web Extra! 2–6** at cjtoday.com. To learn more about the effects of NIBRS on crime statistics—including comparisons of UCR data and NIBRS data—see **Web Extra! 2–7** at cjtoday.com. Finally, the Bureau of Justice Statistics provides a NIBRS information website, which can be accessed via **Web Extra! 2–8** at cjtoday.com.

In addition to NIBRS, other changes in crime reporting occurred during the 1990s. The 1990 Crime Awareness and Campus Security Act, for example, required college campuses to commence publishing annual security reports, beginning in September 1992. Most campuses share crime data with the FBI, increasing the reported national incidence of a variety of offenses. The U.S. Department of Education reported that 395 murders and 3,982 forcible sex offenses occurred on and around college campuses in 2000. Another 12,894 robberies, 18,761 aggravated assaults, 68,486 burglaries, and 31,056 motor vehicle thefts were also reported.[60] For the latest campus crime statistics, see **Web Extra! 2–9** at cjtoday.com. **Library Extra! 2–4** at cjtoday.com provides statistical information on the sexual victimization of college women.

Hate Crimes

hate crime

A criminal offense in which the motive is "hatred, bias, or prejudice, based on the actual or perceived race, color, religion, national origin, ethnicity, gender, or sexual orientation of another individual or group of individuals."[ii]

A final change in reporting practices followed from the Hate Crime Statistics Act,[61] signed into law by President George Bush in 1990. The act mandates a statistical tally of **hate crimes**, and data collection under the law began in 1991. Congress defined *hate crimes* as offenses "in which the defendant's conduct was motivated by hatred, bias, or prejudice, based on the actual or perceived race, color, religion, national origin, ethnicity, gender, or sexual orientation of another individual or group of individuals."[62] In 2000, police agencies reported a total of 8,152 hate-crime incidents, including 19 murders, across the country. Sixteen percent of the incidents were motivated by religious bias, while 54.8% were caused by racial hatred. Another 16% of all hate crimes were based on sexual orientation, and most of those were committed against males believed by their victimizers to be homosexuals.[63] Most hate crimes consisted of intimidation, although vandalism, simple assault, and aggravated assault also accounted for a fair number of hate-crime offenses. Notable in recent years has been a spate of arsons throughout the South of predominantly African-American churches. A few robberies and rapes were also classified under the hate-crime umbrella in 2000.

One particularly heinous and widely publicized hate crime culminated in death sentences for white Jasper County, Texas, residents John William King, 24, and Lawrence Russell Brewer, 32.[64] In 1999, King and Brewer were found guilty in separate trials of first-degree murder for lashing James Byrd, Jr., a 49-year-old black man, to a pickup truck with a chain and dragging him to his death over three miles of rural Texas asphalt. Byrd, who was tied by his ankles, died after his right arm and head were severed when his body struck the edge of a culvert. If executed, King or Brewer will become only the second white person ever put to death in Texas for killing a black person. A third white supremacist, 24-year-old Shawn Allen Berry, was found guilty of participating in the crime and was sentenced to life in prison.

Although hate crimes are popularly conceived of as crimes motivated by racial enmity, the Violent Crime Control and Law Enforcement Act of 1994 created a new definitional category of "crimes of violence motivated by gender." Congress defined this crime to mean "a crime of violence committed because of gender or on the basis of gender, and due, at least in part, to an animus based on the victim's gender." The 1994 act did not establish separate penalties for gender-motivated crimes, anticipating that they would be prosecuted as felonies under existing laws. The 1994 act also mandated the addition to the hate-crimes category of crimes motivated by biases against people with disabilities.

Hate crimes are sometimes called *bias crimes.* One form of bias crime that bears special mention is homophobic homicide. This term refers to the murder of homosexuals by those opposed to their lifestyles. A 1997 movie, *Licensed to Kill,* by producer-director Arthur Dong, for example, tells a harrowing story about homophobia and murder using police interrogation videos, crime-scene photos, and courtroom footage of real-life events. Included in the movie is a detailed description of how former U.S. Army Sergeant Kenneth French, Jr., randomly killed four people in a Fayetteville, North Carolina, restaurant in response to President Clinton's decision to allow gays into the military. According to witnesses, French shouted, "I'll show you, Clinton, about letting gays into the army," as he fired at patrons and the restaurant's owner.[65]

Even more worrisome to many enforcement agencies is the continued growth of separatist groups with their own vision of a future America. Some, like the White Aryan Resistance (WAR), hope for the start of RAHOWA, or racial holy war. In 1999, for example, Buford Oneal Furrow, Jr., a 37-year-old mechanic, was charged with multiple counts of attempted murder in an armed attack on a day-care facility in Los Angeles run by the North Valley Jewish Community Center. The attack injured three little boys, a counselor, and a receptionist. Furrow, a member of the supremacist group known as Aryan Nations, was also charged with the murder of a postal employee. A year earlier he had told police, "I am a white separatist." The declaration came as Furrow waved a knife in a Seattle-area psychiatric hospital where he tried to have himself committed.

Other supremacist groups include the White Patriot Party; Posse Comitatus; the Covenant, the Sword, and the Arm of the Lord; the Ku Klux Klan; the Order; and umbrella organizations like the Christian Conservative Church. Described variously as the *radical right, neo-Nazis, skinheads, white supremacists,* and *racial hate groups,* these groups appear to be organized, well financed, and extremely well armed. John R. Harrell, leader of the Christian Conservative Church, preaches that the nation is on the eve of destruction. According to some authorities, Christian patriots are exhorted to stand ready to seize control of the nation before leadership can fall into "the wrong hands."[66] Such extremist groups adhere to identity theology, a religion which claims that members of the white race are God's chosen people. Identity theology envisions an America ruled exclusively by white people under "God's law."[67] Figure 2–6 shows the location of various supremacist and survivalist groups in the United States.

Whatever we may think of them, the activities of supremacist groups may be constitutionally protected, at least in some instances. Some authors suggest, for example, that statutes intended to control hate crimes may run afoul of constitutional considerations insofar as they (1) are too vague, (2) criminalize thought more than action, (3) attempt to control what would otherwise be free speech, and (4) deny equal protection of the laws to those who wish to express their personal biases.[68] The U.S. Supreme Court would seem to agree. In the 1992 case of *R.A.V.* v. *City of St. Paul,*[69] which involved a burning cross on the front lawn of a black family, the Court struck down a city ordinance designed to prevent the bias-motivated display of symbols or objects, such as Nazi swastikas or burning crosses. In the same year, in the case of *Forsyth County, Ga.* v. *Nationalist Movement,*[70] the Court held that a county requirement regulating parades was

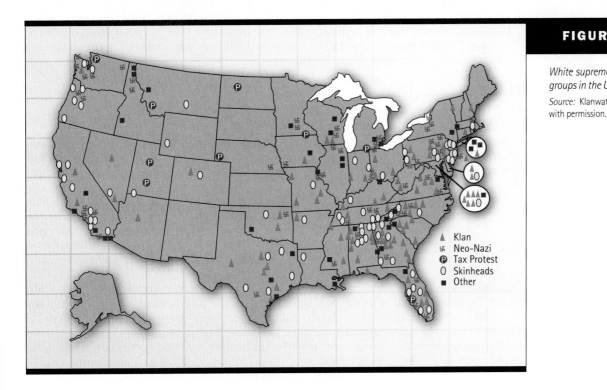

FIGURE 2-6

White supremacist and survivalist groups in the United States.

Source: Klanwatch Project. Reprinted with permission.

▲ Klan
ᛋᛋ Neo-Nazi
🅟 Tax Protest
O Skinheads
■ Other

Convicted killer John William King (left photo) being escorted from the Jasper County (Texas) Courthouse in 1999. King, along with two other men, was convicted of the pick-up truck dragging death of James Byrd, Jr. (right), and received the death penalty.

David J. Phillip, AP/Wide World Photos; Buck Kelly, Getty Images, Inc.

unconstitutional because it regulated freedom of speech—in this case, a plan by an affiliate of the Ku Klux Klan (KKK) to parade in opposition to a Martin Luther King birthday celebration. In 1995, in the case of *Capitol Square Review and Advisory Board* v. *Pinette*,[71] the Court reiterated its position, saying that KKK organizers in Ohio could legitimately erect an unattended cross on the Statehouse Plaza in Columbus's Capitol Square. Some laws intended to reduce the incidence of hate crimes appear to pass Supreme Court muster, however. In 1993, in the case of *Wisconsin* v. *Mitchell*,[72] for example, the Court held that Mitchell, a black man whose severe beating of a white boy was racially motivated, could be punished with additional severity as permitted by Wisconsin law because he acted out of race hatred. The Court called the assault "conduct unprotected by the First Amendment" and upheld the Wisconsin statute, saying, "[since] the statute has no 'chilling effect' on free speech, it is not unconstitutionally overboard." Learn more about hate crimes and what can be done to address them via **Library Extras! 2–5** and **2–6** at cjtoday.com.

The National Crime Victimization Survey

As mentioned earlier, a second major source of statistical data about crime in the United States is the National Crime Victimization Survey, which is based on victim self-reports rather than on police reports. The NCVS is designed to estimate the occurrence of all crimes, whether reported or not.[73] The NCVS began operation in 1972. It built upon efforts in the late 1960s by both the National Opinion Research Center and the President's Commission on Law Enforcement and the Administration of Justice to uncover what some had been calling the **dark figure of crime**. This term refers to those crimes that are not reported to the police and that remain unknown to officials. Prior to the development of the NCVS, little was known about such unreported and undiscovered offenses.

Early data from the NCVS changed the way criminologists thought about crime in the United States. The use of victim self-reports led to the discovery that crimes of all types were more prevalent than UCR statistics indicated. Many cities were shown to have victimization rates more than twice the rate of reported offenses. Others, like Saint Louis, Missouri, and Newark, New Jersey, were found to have rates of victimization which very nearly approximated reported crime. New York, often thought of as a high-crime city, was discovered to have one of the lowest rates of self-reported victimization.

dark figure of crime

Crime that is not reported to the police and that remains unknown to officials.

NCVS data are gathered by the Bureau of Justice Statistics through a cooperative arrangement with the U.S. Census Bureau.[74] NCVS interviewers work with a national sample of more than 50,000 households which are interviewed twice each year. Household lists are completely revised at the end of every three-year period. BJS statistics are published in an annual report entitled *Criminal Victimization*.

Using definitions similar to those used by the UCR Program (Table 2–5), the NCVS includes data on the national incidence of rape, sexual assault, robbery, assault, burglary, personal and household larceny, and motor vehicle theft. Not included are murder,

		OFFENSE DEFINITIONS BY REPORTING PROGRAM	TABLE 2–5
Offense	**Uniform Crime Reports**	**National Incident-Based Reporting System**	**National Crime Victimization Survey**
Murder and nonnegligent manslaughter	The unlawful killing of a human being.	The willful (nonnegligent) killing of one human being by another.	NA
Forcible sex offense	NA	Any sexual act directed against another person, forcibly and/or against that person's will; or not forcibly or against the person's will where the victim is incapable of giving consent. Forcible rape, forcible sodomy, sexual assault with an object, and forcible fondling are included in this category.	NA
Forcible rape	The carnal knowledge of a female, forcibly and against her will.	The carnal knowledge of a person, forcibly and/or against that person's will; or not forcibly or against the person's will where the victim is incapable of giving consent because of his/her temporary or permanent mental or physical incapacity or because of his/her youth.	Carnal knowledge through the use of force or threat of force, including attempts. Rape includes victimization of both males and females.
Sexual assault	NA	NA	A wide range of victimizations, separate from rape or attempted rape. These crimes include attacks or attempted attacks generally involving unwanted sexual contact between victim and offender. Sexual assaults may or may not involve force and include such things as grabbing or fondling. Sexual assault also includes verbal threats.
Robbery	The unlawful taking or attempted taking of property that is in the immediate possession of another by force or threat of force or violence and/or by putting the victim in fear.	The taking, or attempting to take, anything of value under confrontational circumstances from the control, custody, or care of another person by force or threat of force or violence and/or by putting the victim in fear of immediate harm.	Completed or attempted theft, directly from a person, of property or cash by force or threat of force, with or without a weapon.

(continued)

TABLE 2–5		OFFENSE DEFINITIONS BY REPORTING PROGRAM (*continued*)

Offense	Uniform Crime Reports	National Incident-Based Reporting System	National Crime Victimization Survey
Assault	An unlawful attack by one person upon another.	An unlawful attack by one person upon another.	An unlawful physical attack, whether aggravated or simple, on a person. It includes attempted assaults with or without a weapon, but excludes rape, attempted rape, and attacks involving theft or attempted theft (which are classified as robbery).
Aggravated assault	The unlawful, intentional inflicting, or attempted or threatened inflicting, of serious injury upon the person of another.	An unlawful attack by one person upon another wherein the offender uses a weapon or displays it in a threatening manner, or the victim suffers obvious severe or aggravated bodily injury involving apparent broken bones, loss of teeth, possible internal injury, severe laceration, or loss of consciousness. This also includes assault with disease (as in cases when the offender is aware that he/she is infected with a deadly disease and deliberately attempts to inflict the disease by biting, spitting, etc.).	Unlawful or forcible entry or attempted entry of a residence, garage, shed, or other structure on the premises, usually but not always involving theft.
Burglary	The unlawful entry of a structure to commit a felony or a theft (excludes tents, trailers, and other mobile units used for recreational purposes).	The unlawful entry of a structure to commit a felony or a theft (excludes tents, trailers, and other mobile units used for recreational purposes).	Unlawful or forcible entry or attempted entry of a residence, garage, shed, or other structure on the premises, usually but not always involving theft.
Larceny-theft	The unlawful taking or attempted taking, carrying, leading, or riding away of property from the possession or constructive possession of another (including attempts). Motor vehicles are excluded.	The unlawful taking, carrying, leading, or riding away of property from the possession or constructive possession of another (including attempts). Motor vehicles are excluded.	Completed or attempted theft of property or cash without personal contact.
Motor vehicle theft	The theft or attempted theft of a motor vehicle. Motor vehicle is defined as a self-propelled vehicle that runs on land surface and not on rails. This offense category includes the stealing of automobiles, trucks, buses, motorcycles, motor scooters, snowmobiles, etc. It does not include farm equipment, bulldozers, airplanes, construction equipment, or motorboats.	The theft or attempted theft of a motor vehicle. Motor vehicle is defined as a self-propelled vehicle that runs on land surface and not on rails. This offense category includes the stealing of automobiles, trucks, buses, motorcycles, motor scooters, snowmobiles, etc. It does not include farm equipment, bulldozers, airplanes, construction equipment, or motorboats.	Stealing or unauthorized taking of a motor vehicle, including attempted thefts.
Arson	The burning or attempted burning of property, with or without the intent to defraud.	NA	NA

NA = not applicable.

kidnapping, and victimless crimes. Commercial robbery and the burglary of businesses were dropped from NCVS reports in 1977. The NCVS employs a hierarchical counting system similar to that of the pre-NIBRS system: It counts only the most "serious" incident in any series of criminal events perpetrated against the same individual. Both completed and attempted offenses are counted, although only people 12 years of age and older are included in household surveys.

Highlights of NCVS statistics for the 1990s reveal the following:

■ Approximately 25% of American households are touched by crime every year.

■ Nearly 26 million victimizations are reported to the NCVS per year.

■ City residents are about twice as likely as rural residents to be victims of crime.

■ About half of all violent crimes, and slightly more than one-third of all property crimes, are reported to police.[75]

■ The total "personal cost" of crime to victims is about $13 billion per year for the United States as a whole.

■ Victims of crime are more often men than women.

■ Younger people are more likely than the elderly to be victims of crime.

■ Blacks are more likely than whites or members of other racial groups to be victims of violent crimes.

■ Violent victimization rates are highest among people in lower-income families.

■ Young males have the highest violent victimization rates; elderly females the lowest.

■ The chance of violent criminal victimization is much higher for young black males than for any other segment of the population. (The life chances of murder run from a high of 1 in 21 for a black male to a low of 1 in 369 for a white female.)[76]

A report by the Bureau of Justice Statistics found that in 2000, NCVS crime rates had reached their lowest level since the survey began.[77] Declines began in the mid-1990s, with violent crime rates dropping 46.2% between 1994 and 2000.[78] In 1999 alone, the rate of violent crime declined 10%, with another 15% drop in 2000. The report showed that estimates of surveyed property crimes decreased 42.6% in 2000. As the statistics show, declining crime rates are a recent phenomenon. UCR statistics, which go back almost another 40 years, show that today's crime rate is still many times what it was in the early and middle years of the 20th century, however.[79]

A comparison of UCR and NCVS data for 2000 can be found in Table 2–6. Explore the latest NCVS data via **Web Extra! 2–10** at cjtoday.com.

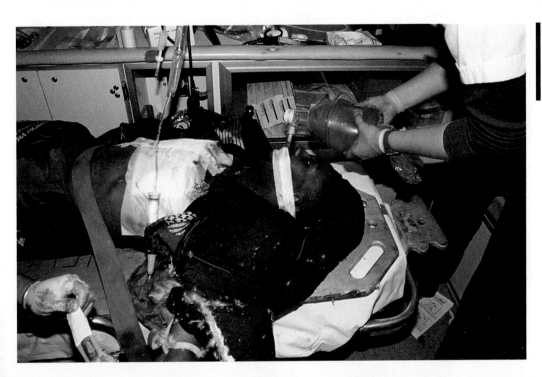

A shooting victim receiving emergency help from paramedics. Young black males are more likely to be victims of violent crime than are members of any other group.

P. Cahuvel, CORBIS/Sygma

TABLE 2-6	COMPARISON OF UCR AND NCVS DATA, 2000

Offense	Uniform Crime Reports	National Crime Victimization Survey[1]
Personal/Violent Crimes		
Homicide[2]	15,517	—
Forcible rape[3]	90,186	261,000
Robbery	407,842	732,000
Aggravated assault	910,744	1,293,000
Property Crimes		
Burglary[4]	2,049,946	3,444,000
Larceny	6,965,957	14,916,000
Motor vehicle theft	1,165,559	937,000
Arson[5]	78,280	—
Total of all crimes recorded[6]	11,684,031	25,893,000

[1]NCVS data covers "households touched by crime," not absolute numbers of crime occurrences. More than one victimization may occur per household, but only the number of households in which victimizations occur enters the tabulations.

[2]Homicide statistics are not reported by the NCVS.

[3]NCVS statistics include both rape and sexual assault.

[4]NCVS statistics include only household burglary and attempts.

[5]Arson data are incomplete in the UCR and are not reported by the NCVS.

[6]The NCVS total includes other crimes not shown in this table.

Source: Compiled from U.S. Department of Justice, *Criminal Victimization, 2000* (Washington, D.C.: Bureau of Justice Statistics, 2001); and Federal Bureau of Investigation, *Crime in the United States, 2000* (Washington, D.C.: U.S. Government Printing Office, 2001).

Because most researchers believe that self-reports provide a more accurate gauge of criminal incidents than do police reports, many tend to accept NCVS data over that provided by the UCR Program. Learn more about the use of self-report surveys in the measurement of crime and delinquency via **Library Extras! 2–7** and **2–8** at cjtoday.com.

Comparisons of the UCR and the NCVS

Table 2–7 summarizes the differences between the UCR and the NCVS. Both provide estimates of crime in America. Both are limited by the type of crimes they choose to measure and those they exclude and by the methods they use to gather crime data.

Crime statistics from the UCR and the NCVS are often used in devising explanations for criminal behavior. Unfortunately, however, researchers too often forget that statistics which are merely descriptive can be weak in explanatory power. For example, NCVS data show that "household crime rates" are highest for households (1) headed by blacks, (2) headed by younger people, (3) with six or more members, (4) headed by renters, and (5) located in central cities.[80] Such findings, combined with statistics which show that most crime occurs among members of the same race, have led some researchers to conclude that values among certain black subcultural group members both propel them into crime and make them targets of criminal victimization. The truth may be, however, that crime is more a function of inner-city location than of culture. From simple descriptive statistics, it is difficult to know which is the case. Learn more about how the UCR and the NCVS compare by viewing **Web Extra! 2–11** at cjtoday.com.

	Uniform Crime Reports	National Crime Victimization Survey
HOW THE UCR AND THE NCVS COMPARE		**TABLE 2-7**
Offenses Measured	Homicide Rape Robbery (personal and commercial) Assault (aggravated) Burglary (commercial and household) Larceny (commercial and household) Motor vehicle theft Arson	Rape Robbery (personal) Assault (aggravated and simple) Burglary (household) Larceny (personal and household) Motor vehicle theft
Scope	Crimes reported to police in most jurisdictions	Crimes both reported and not reported to police; all data are available for a few large geographic areas
Collection Method	Police departments report to FBI or to centralized state agencies that then report to FBI	Survey interviews; periodically measures the total number of crimes committed by asking a national sample of 50,000 households encompassing more than 100,000 persons aged 12 and over about their experiences as victims of crime during a specified period
Kinds of Information	In addition to offense counts, provides information on crime clearances, persons arrested, persons charged, law enforcement officers killed and assaulted, and characteristics of homicide victims	Provides details about victims (such as age, race, sex, education, income, and whether the victim and offender were related to each other) and about crimes (such as time and place of occurrence, whether reported to police, use of weapons, occurrence of injury, and economic consequences)
Sponsor	U.S. Department of Justice; Federal Bureau of Investigation	U.S. Department of Justice; Bureau of Justice Statistics

Source: Bureau of Justice Statistics, *Report to the Nation on Crime and Justice,* 2d ed. (Washington, D.C.: U.S. Department of Justice, 1988), p. 11.

Guns, Crime, and Gun Control

The Second Amendment to the U.S. Constitution reads, "A well regulated Militia, being necessary to the security of a free State, the right of the people to keep and bear Arms, shall not be infringed." Constitutional guarantees have combined with historical circumstances to make ours a well-armed society. In a typical year, approximately 10,000 murders are committed in the United States with firearms—most with handguns. Handguns

> If people here were not getting killed on the job in homicides, we would have quite a low rate of fatalities.
>
> —Samuel Ehrenhalt, former Labor Department official, commenting on findings that show murder to be the top cause of on-the-job deaths in New York City

are also used in many other crimes. Approximately 1 million serious violations of the law in which a handgun is used—including homicide, rape, robbery, and assault—occur each year. A 2001 report by the Bureau of Justice Statistics found that 18% of state prison inmates and 15% of federal inmates were armed at the time they committed the crime for which they were imprisoned.[81]

A 1999 Pew Research Center poll found that two-thirds of all Americans—including three out of four women—believe that increasing restrictions on guns will prevent crime and that this goal is more important than protecting the rights of people to own guns.[82]

Gun-Control Legislation

The federal government and the states have already responded to growing public concern over the easy availability of handguns. In 1994, the U.S. Congress passed the Brady Handgun Violence Prevention Act, which President Bill Clinton signed into law. The law was named for former Press Secretary James Brady, who was shot and severely wounded in an attempt on President Ronald Reagan's life on March 30, 1981. The law provides for a five-day waiting period before the purchase of a handgun, and it established a national instant criminal background check system that firearms dealers must use before the transfer of any firearm. Applications must be checked to determine whether the applicant's receipt or possession of a handgun would be in violation of federal, state, or local law.[83] Under the system, licensed importers, manufacturers, and dealers are required to verify the identity of a firearm purchaser, using a valid photo ID (such as a driver's license), and must contact the system to receive a unique identification number authorizing the purchase before they transfer the handgun. While the Brady law may limit retail purchases of handguns by felons, a 2001 BJS study found that most offenders obtained weapons from friends, family members, or "on the street"—without attempting to purchase them at retail establishments.[84] Moreover, according to the study, an ever-growing number of violent criminals are now carrying handguns.

The Violent Crime Control and Law Enforcement Act of 1994 regulates the sale of firearms within the United States, banning the manufacture of 19 military-style assault weapons, including those with specific combat features, such as high-capacity ammunition clips capable of holding more than ten rounds. The 1994 law also prohibits the sale or transfer of a gun to a juvenile, as well as the possession of a gun by a juvenile, and it prohibits gun sales to, and possession by, people subject to family violence restraining orders.

The 1996 Domestic Violence Offender Gun Ban[85] is a relatively new tool in the federal gun control arsenal. The ban prohibits individuals convicted of misdemeanor domestic violence offenses from owning or using firearms. Soon after the law was passed, however, it became embroiled in controversy when hundreds of police officers across the country who had been convicted of domestic violence offenses were found to be in violation of the ban.

Police buying a handgun from an unidentified man under San Francisco's Gun Amnesty Program. Residents receive up to $100 for each gun turned in. The program is one of many police-sponsored programs across the country that attempt to remove guns from the streets.

S. Kermani, Getty Images, Inc.

A number of officers lost their jobs, while others were placed in positions that did not require them to carry firearms. Beth Weaver, a spokeswoman for the National Association of Police Organizations, noted that "the [ban] is causing more chaos than almost anything I've ever seen in law enforcement."[86] While some legislators pushed to exempt police officers and military personnel from the ban's provisions, others argued that they should be included. Feminist Majority President Eleanor Smeal was angered. "Rather than trying to seek an exemption for police officers and military personnel who are abusers, we should be concerned with why we are recruiting so many abusers for these positions," she said.[87]

Following the 1999 Columbine High School shooting, a number of states moved to tighten controls over handguns and assault weapons. The California legislature, for example, restricted gun purchases to one per month and tightened a ten-year-old ban on assault weapons. Similarly, Illinois passed a law requiring that gun owners lock their weapons away from anyone under 14. Learn more about gun control, and lawsuits against gun manufacturers in Chapter 4 and at **Web Extra! 2–12** at cjtoday.com. For the latest information on gun violence and gun laws, visit the Brady Center to Prevent Gun Violence via **Web Extra! 2–13**.

Support for Gun Ownership

Not everyone agrees that gun sales and gun ownership should be subject to additional regulation. The National Rifle Association (NRA), the Citizen's Committee for the Right to Keep and Bear Arms, and other pro-gun-ownership groups have filed lawsuits to derail enforcement of the Brady Act and the assault weapons provisions of the Violent Crime Control and Law Enforcement Act. In the combined cases of *Printz* v. *U.S.* (1997)[88] and *Mack* v. *U.S.* (1997),[89] for example, the U.S. Supreme Court held that state officials could not be required to perform background checks on gun buyers under *federal* law (a requirement originally imposed by the Brady Act). The NRA continues to maintain that many existing gun-control laws violate the Constitution's Second Amendment. Similarly, the NRA criticizes a federally proposed ban on guns in housing projects, arguing that the ban would be "discriminatory" and would disarm and "single out low-income citizens."

Prior to the recent spate of high school shootings around the country, the U.S. Supreme Court, in the case of *U.S.* v. *Alfonso Lopez, Jr.* (1995),[90] upheld a lower court ruling dismissing charges against a twelfth-grade student who had carried a concealed .38-caliber handgun and five bullets into Edison High School in San Antonio, Texas. The student was charged with violating the federal Gun-Free School Zones Act of 1990, which forbids "any individual knowingly to possess a firearm at a place that [he or she] knows . . . is a school zone." The law had been passed to assuage parents' concerns that their children might be in mortal danger due to the presence of guns in the hands of school-aged children and interlopers on school property. The Court ruled that education and the administration of educational facilities were a local and not a national function, effectively invalidating the law.

Emerging Patterns of Criminal Activity

As both the NCVS and the UCR reflect, patterns of criminal activity in the United States are changing. In the late 1980s, Georgette Bennett termed the shift in crime patterns *crimewarps*.[91] Crimewarps, said Bennett, represent major changes in what society considers criminal and in who future criminal offenders will be. Bennett predicted that changes would include (1) the decline of street crime, (2) the growth of white-collar crime, (3) increased female involvement in crime, (4) increased crime commission by the elderly, (5) a shift in high crime rates from the Frost Belt to the Sun Belt, (6) safer cities, with increasing criminal activity in rural areas, and (7) the growth of high-technology crimes.[92]

Bennett's predictions have been quite accurate. Now, however, some experts are predicting that declining crime rates may soon be a thing of the past. While crime rates are down, prisons are bulging, and the steady flow of convicted offenders back into society may contribute to a future increase in crime rates. Similarly, some predict that economic prosperity—a characteristic of the mid- to late-1990s—reduces crime. Not surprisingly, as the U.S. economy began to falter in 2000, early indicators showed that crime rates started to level off[93] and that violent crimes were likely to experience a resurgence.[94] If the American economy continues to worsen, crime rates are likely to rise as more and more people find themselves without jobs. The economy also affects tax revenues, and police and other services may need to be cut soon, creating the potential for further rate increases.

> The public is properly obsessed with safety. Of industrialized countries, the U.S. has the highest rate of violent crime.
>
> —Bob Moffitt, Heritage Foundation

The anticipated growth of the superpredator population, mentioned earlier in this chapter, may also hold considerable significance for future crime rates and for the types of crime that might be committed. If a superpredator population truly develops, as some suggest, we can expect to see a dramatic rise in both violent and property crimes by 2010.

The Fear of Crime

Although we may read in newspapers or in books that violent street crime is decreasing, we may not fully believe it. In fact, we may be just as afraid as ever. As some authors point out, the fear of crime is often out of proportion to the likelihood of criminal victimization.[95] Table 2–8 compares the rate of death from homicide with other causes of death for Americans aged 15 to 24. For most people, regardless of age, the chance of accidental death is far greater than the chance of being murdered.

The Bureau of Justice Statistics says that "fear of crime affects many people, including some who have never been victims of crime."[96] Sources of fear are diverse. Some flow from personal experience with victimization, but most people fear crime because of dramatizations of criminal activity on television and in movies and because of frequent news reports of crime. Feelings of vulnerability may result from learning that a friend has been victimized or from hearing that a neighbor's home has been burglarized.

Speaking to a session of the American Psychiatric Association in 1999, following the Columbine High School shootings, Kathleen M. Fisher of Pennsylvania State University said that schools are much safer today than they were ten years ago. "Schools are safe, that is the reality," said Fisher. Still, she noted, the fear generated by school shootings makes parents everywhere afraid for the safety of their children and contributes to the general perception in American society that violent crime is out of control.[97]

One social commentator suggests that fear of crime is directly related to the amount and type of crime presented by the news media. *Boston Globe* columnist A. R. Indira Lakshmanan says, "How about this for a theory: crime news is a product. Like all manufacturers, the makers of crime news strive to constantly broaden their market. They try to diversify their product line, increase public awareness of its existence, raise its quality, and increase its quantity."[98] Lakshmanan's perspective received support from a study published in 2000 that found that the amount of time that people spend watching local news shows (which include coverage of crimes in the viewers' area) is directly related to the amount of crime fear they report experiencing.[99] According to the study,

TABLE 2-8	DEATHS AND DEATH RATES FOR THE TEN LEADING CAUSES OF DEATH FOR AMERICANS AGED 15–24		
Cause of Death		**Number of Deaths**	**Rate per 100,000**
Accident (except motor vehicle)		17,120	47.3
Motor vehicle accident		10,624	29.3
Homicide		6,548	18.1
Suicide		4,369	12.1
Cancer		1,642	4.5
Heart disease		920	2.5
HIV/AIDS		420	1.2
Congenital anomaly		387	1.1
Lung disease/asthma		230	0.6
Pneumonia and influenza		197	0.5
Stroke/brain hemorrhage		174	0.5
All other causes		3,940	10.9
Total		46,571	128.6

Source: National Center for Health Statistics, *Annual Report* (Washington, D.C.: U.S. Government Printing Office, 2000).

local television news coverage has a much greater impact on viewers' fear of crime than national news coverage. Fears were found to be highest among frequent viewers of local news who lived in high-crime areas.

It may be that what people fear the most is the chance of becoming the victim of a random act of violence. Random violence is often associated with **stranger violence**. Stranger violence occurs when seemingly random violence, perpetrated by offenders unknown to their victims, unexpectedly injures or kills innocent people going about their daily routines. Such crimes—which include most school shootings, road rage incidents, carjackings, acts of terrorism, street robberies, and a fair number of sexual assaults— have shaken confidence in the American criminal justice system and have contributed to a gnawing fear of personal victimization, which persists even in the midst of today's falling official crime rates.

Interestingly, the groups at highest risk of becoming crime victims are not the ones who experience the greatest fear. The elderly and women report the greatest fear of victimization, even though they are among the lowest-risk groups for violent crimes. Young males, on the other hand, who stand the greatest statistical risk of victimization, often report feeling the least fear.[100] For current public opinion poll data on crime issues, view **Web Extra! 2–14** at cjtoday.com.

stranger violence

Seemingly random violence perpetrated by assailants who were previously unknown to their victims. Stranger violence often results from rage, opportunity, or insanity.

Women and Crime

FEMALE VICTIMS

Women are victimized less frequently than men in every major personal crime category other than rape.[101] The overall U.S. rate of violent victimization is about 56 per 1,000 males age 12 or older, and 39 per 1,000 females.[102] When women become victims of violent crime, however, they are more likely than men to be injured (29% versus 22%, respectively).[103] Moreover, a larger proportion of women than men make modifications in the way they live because of the threat of crime.[104] Women, especially those living in cities, have become increasingly careful about where they travel and the time of day they leave their homes—particularly if unaccompanied—and are often wary of unfamiliar males in a diversity of settings.

Very real concerns reflected in movies, television programs, and newspaper editorial pages have identified date rape, familial incest, spouse abuse, and the exploitation of women through social-order offenses such as prostitution and pornography as major issues facing American society today. Testimony before Congress has tagged domestic violence as the largest cause of injury to American women,[105] and former Surgeon General C. Everett Koop once identified violence against women by their partners as the number one health problem facing women in America.[106] Several years ago, the 1995 murder trial of O. J. Simpson focused national concerns on issues of spousal abuse and on the victimization of women by spouses and ex-husbands.

Findings from the National Violence Against Women Survey (NVAWS), published in 2000, revealed the following:[107]

■ Physical assault is widespread among American women. Fifty-two percent of surveyed women said that they had been physically assaulted as a child or as an adult.

■ Approximately 1.9 million women are physically assaulted in the United States each year.

■ Eighteen percent of women experienced a completed or attempted rape at some time in their life.

■ Of those reporting rape, 22% were under 12 years old, and 32% were between 12 and 17 years old when they were first raped.

■ Native American and Alaska Native women were most likely to report rape and physical assault, while Asian/Pacific Islander women were least likely to report such victimization. Hispanic women were also less likely to report rape than non-Hispanic women.

■ Women report significantly more partner violence than do men. Twenty-five percent of surveyed women, and only 8% of surveyed men, said they had been raped or physically assaulted by a current or former spouse, cohabiting partner, or date.

■ Violence against women is primarily partner violence. Seventy-six percent of the women who had been raped or physically assaulted since age 18 were assaulted by a current or former husband, cohabiting partner, or date, compared with 18% of the men.

> The typical mass murderer is extraordinarily ordinary.
>
> —James Alan Fox

■ Women are significantly more likely than men to be injured during an *assault.* Thirty-two percent of the women and 16% of the men who had been raped since age 18 were injured during their most recent rape; 39% of the women and 25% of the men who were physically assaulted since age 18 were injured during their most recent physical assault.

■ Stalking is more prevalent than previously thought. Eight percent of surveyed women and 2% of surveyed men said they had been stalked at some time in their life. According to survey estimates, approximately 1 million women and 371,000 men are stalked annually in the United States.

A detailed BJS analysis found that women who are victims of violent crime are twice as likely to be victimized by strangers as by people whom they know.[108] However, they are far more likely than men to be victimized by individuals with whom they are (or have been) in an intimate relationship. When the perpetrators are known to them, women are most likely to be violently victimized by ex-husbands, boyfriends, and spouses (in descending order of incidence). The BJS study also found that separated or divorced women are six times more likely to be victims of violent crime than widows, four and a half times more likely than married women, and three times more likely than widowers and married men. Other findings indicated that (1) women living in central-city areas are considerably more likely to be victimized than women residing in the suburbs; (2) suburban women, in turn, are more likely to be victimized than women living in rural areas; (3) women from low-income families experience the highest amount of violent crime; (4) the victimization of women falls as family income rises; (5) unemployed women, female students, and those in the armed forces are the most likely of all women to experience violent victimization; (6) black women are victims of violent crimes more frequently than are women of any other race; (7) Hispanic women find themselves victimized more frequently than white women; and (8) women in the age range of 20 to 24 are most at risk for violent victimization, while those aged 16 to 19 make up the second most likely group of victims. Learn more about violence against women via **Library Extra! 2–9** at cjtoday.com.

Library EXTRA!

Survey findings, such as those discussed here, show that greater emphasis needs to be placed on alleviating the social conditions that victimize women. Suggestions already under consideration call for expansion in the number of federal and state laws designed to control domestic violence, a broadening of the federal Family Violence Prevention and Services Act, federal help in setting up state advocacy offices for battered women, increased funding for battered women's shelters, and additional funds for prosecutors and courts to develop spouse-abuse units. The federal Violent Crime Control and Law Enforcement Act of 1994 was designed to meet many of these needs through a subsection entitled the Violence Against Women Act (VAWA). That act allocated $1.6 billion to fight violence against women.

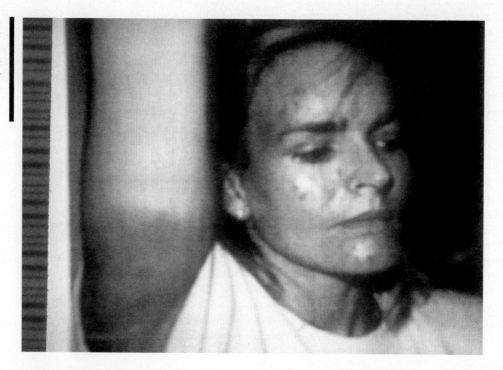

A bruised Nicole Brown Simpson after one of many alleged attacks by her husband, O. J. Simpson. According to sociologists, violence against women is perpetuated by social conditions which devalue families.

CORBIS/Sygma

Multiculturalism and Diversity in America

[Gender Issues]

The Violent Crime Control and Law Enforcement Act of 1994 included significant provisions intended to enhance gender equality throughout the criminal justice system. Title IV of the Violent Crime Control and Law Enforcement Act known as the Violence Against Women Act (VAWA) of 1994, contains the Safe Streets for Women Act. This act increases federal penalties for repeat sex offenders and requires mandatory restitution for sex crimes, including costs related to medical services (including physical, psychiatric, and psychological care); physical and occupational therapy or rehabilitation; necessary transportation, temporary housing, and child-care expenses; lost income; attorneys' fees, plus any costs incurred in obtaining a civil protection order; and any other losses suffered by the victim as a result of the offense. The act also requires that compliance with a restitution order be made a condition of probation or supervised release (if such a sentence is imposed by the court) and provides that violation of the order will result in the offender's imprisonment.

Chapter 2 of the Violence Against Women Act provides funds for grants to combat violent crimes against women. The purpose of funding is to assist states and local governments "develop and strengthen effective law enforcement and prosecution strategies to combat violent crimes against women, and to develop and strengthen victim services in cases involving violent crimes against women." The law also provides funds for the "training of law enforcement officers and prosecutors to more effectively identify and respond to violent crimes against women, including the crimes of sexual assault and domestic violence"; for "developing, installing, or expanding data collection and communication systems, including computerized systems, linking police, prosecutors, and courts or for the purpose of identifying and tracking arrests, protection orders, violations of protection orders, prosecutions, and convictions for violent crimes against women, including the crimes of sexual assault and domestic violence"; and for developing and strengthening "victim services programs, including sexual assault and domestic violence programs." The act also creates the crime of crossing state lines in violation of a protection order and

the crime of crossing state lines to commit assault on a domestic partner, and it sets out federal penalties for the latter offense of up to life in prison in cases where death results.

Chapter 3 of the Violence Against Women Act provides funds to increase the "safety for women in public transit and public parks." It authorizes up to $10 million in grants through the Department of Transportation to enhance lighting, camera surveillance, and security telephones in public transportation systems used by women.

Chapter 5 of the Violence Against Women Act provides for the creation of hot lines, educational seminars, informational materials, and training programs for professionals who provide assistance to victims of sexual assault. Another portion of the law, titled the Safe Homes for Women Act, increases grants for battered women's shelters, encourages arrest in cases of domestic violence, and provides for the creation of a national domestic violence hot line to provide counseling, information, and assistance to victims of domestic violence. The act also orders that any protection order issued by a state court must be recognized by the other states and by the federal government and must be enforced "as if it were the order of the enforcing state."

Section 40401, known as the Equal Justice for Women in the Courts Act of 1994, provides funds "for the purpose of developing, testing, presenting, and disseminating model programs" to be used by states in training judges and court personnel in the laws "on rape, sexual assault, domestic violence, and other crimes of violence motivated by the victim's gender." The goal of the training is to help participants recognize the underreporting of rape, sexual assault, and child sexual abuse; the physical, psychological, and economic impact of rape and sexual assault on the victim; and the psychology of sex offenders, their high rate of recidivism, and implications for sentencing.

In 2000, VAWA was reauthorized by Congress, which provided $3.3 billion in additional funding over a five-year period. Much of the money was earmarked for programs that coordinate the work of victims' advocates, police, and prosecutors in the fight against domestic violence.

Included are funds to (1) educate police, prosecutors, and judges about the special needs of female victims, (2) encourage pro-arrest policies in cases of domestic abuse, (3) provide specialized services for female victims of crime, (4) fund battered women's shelters across the country, and (5) support rape education in a variety of settings nationwide. The law also extends "rape shield law" protections to civil cases and to all criminal cases in order to bar irrelevant inquiries into a victim's sexual history. VAWA was reauthorized by Congress in 2000. Read the text of the original VAWA legislation at **Web Extra! 2–15** at cjtoday.com.

FEMALE OFFENDERS

In 1999, Susan Eubanks, a 35-year-old mother, was convicted in Vista, California, of shooting her four sons to death at their home. Authorities found the body of 14-year-old Brandon Armstrong, a well-liked football player at the local junior high, lying facedown on the living room floor with two bullets in his head. Spilled breakfast cereal was next to his body. In a nearby bedroom, Brandon's seven-year-old brother, Austin, was found sitting upright on the top level of his bunk bed, dead from two shots to the head. Two younger brothers, six-year-old Brigham and four-year-old Matthew, were found on the bottom bunk—also dead from gunshot wounds to the head.[109] Eubanks shot her sons after an argument with her boyfriend. She stopped once to reload the .38-caliber revolver she was using, and then she shot herself in the stomach. Police found her crying on a bedroom floor. At trial, prosecutors argued that Eubanks deliberately plotted to kill her sons to torment her boyfriend and the boy's fathers (two ex-husbands).

In 1992, Aileen Carol Wuornos, a 35-year-old former prostitute, received multiple death sentences in Florida after confessing to a string of seven murders. Wuornos, labeled by the FBI as the "first textbook female serial killer,"[110] preyed upon men who offered her rides as she hitchhiked. Property belonging to all seven victims—most of whom were robbed, killed, and left naked—was found in a storage unit rented by Wuornos. One victim was a former police chief, another a security guard. All were white, middle-aged men who were traveling alone. Each was killed with a small-caliber handgun.[111] In 1996, the U.S. Supreme Court turned down an appeal by Wuornos, who argued that her claims that she killed the men in self-defense when they became violent, raped her, and did not pay for sexual services, were not given sufficient weight before sentencing.[112]

In 1995, another woman, Susan Smith of Union, South Carolina, gained notoriety nationwide after she confessed to the drowning murders of her two young sons, one-year-old Alex and three-year-old Michael. The boys died after their mother rolled their car off the end of a pier and into a lake, leaving her sons strapped in their safety seats. Smith's confession came after investigators found a letter from Smith's adulterous lover, suggesting that he felt unable to continue the relationship because of the children.

The crimes committed by Eubanks, Wuornos, and Smith, ghastly as they are, fall outside what we know to be the pattern for female criminality. Although the popular media has sometimes portrayed female criminals as similar to their male counterparts in motivation and behavior, that image is misleading. Similarly, the academic study of women's criminality has been fraught with misconceptions.

One of the first writers to attempt a definitive explanation of the criminality of women was Otto Pollak. Pollak's book, *The Criminality of Women*,[113] written in 1950, suggested that women commit the same number of offenses as men but that most of their criminality is hidden. Pollak claimed that women's roles (at the time, primarily those of homemaker and mother) served to disguise their criminal undertakings. He also proposed that chivalrous treatment by a male-dominated justice system acted to bias every stage of criminal justice processing in favor of women. Hence, according to Pollak, although women are just as criminal as men, they are rarely arrested, tried, or imprisoned. In fact, while the criminality of women may approach or exceed that of men in selected offense categories, it is safe to say today that Pollak was incorrect in his assessment of the degree of female criminality.

Recent perspectives on female criminality stress the fact "that a key to understanding and responding to women as offenders is understanding their status as crime victims."[114] Psychologist Cathy Spatz Widom, for example, examines the life cycle of female offenders, looking for links between childhood abuse and neglect and later criminality. Widom suggests that the successful socialization of girls can be "derailed" by early victimization through mechanisms such as "running away, deficits in cognitive ability and achievement, growing up without traditional social controls, engaging in relationships with deviant or delinquent individuals, and failing to learn the social and psychological skills necessary for successful adult development."[115]

Contemporary statistics tell us that although females make up 51% of the population of the United States, they are arrested for only 17.4% of all violent crimes and 29.9% of property crimes. The relatively limited involvement of women in the FBI's eight major crimes can be seen in Table 2–9. The number of women committing crimes appears to be increasing faster than the number of male offenders, however. Between 1970 and 2000, the number of crimes committed by men grew by 46%, while crimes committed by women increased 144%. Violent crimes by men increased 82% during the period; by women, 260%. Property crimes perpetrated by men grew by 3%; by women, 85%.[116]

Relative increases in the FBI's Part II offenses tell a similar story. Arrests of women for embezzlement, for example, increased by more than 228% between 1970 and 2000, versus only 8.5% for men—reflecting women's increased entry into areas of financial responsibility. Arrests of women for drug abuse grew by 289%, and liquor-law violations by women increased 285% (versus 96% for men).[117] In two officially reported categories—prostitution and runaways—women outnumber men in the volume of offenses committed.[118] Other crimes in which significant numbers of women (relative

MALE AND FEMALE INVOLVEMENT IN CRIME: OFFENSE PATTERNS

TABLE 2-9

UCR Index Crime	Percentage of All Arrests	
	Males	Females
Murder and nonnegligent manslaughter	89.4%	10.6%
Rape	98.9	1.1
Robbery	89.9	10.1
Aggravated assault	79.9	20.1
Burglary	86.7	13.3
Larceny-theft	64.1	35.9
Motor vehicle theft	84.2	15.8
Arson	84.9	15.1

Gender Differences

- Men are more likely than women to be arrested for serious crimes, such as murder, rape, robbery, and burglary.
- Arrest, jail, and prison data all suggest that more women than men who commit crimes are involved in property crimes, such as larceny, forgery, fraud, and embezzlement, and in drug offenses.

Source: Federal Bureau of Investigation, *Crime in the United States, 2000* (Washington, D.C.: U.S. Government Printing Office, 2001), p. 233.

CJ Today News

[Law Enforcers Report Spike in Cybercrime]

SAN FRANCISCO—Cybercrime cases are rising in high-tech regions, say U.S. law-enforcement officials.

Prosecutors and investigators are seeing more cases related to computer hacking, theft of trade secrets and hardware, and other tech crimes.

In Silicon Valley, the Santa Clara District Attorney's Office is tackling almost 30 tech-related cases this year—twice as many as last year, investigator John McMullen says. In Boston, federal prosecutor John Grossman's high-tech unit is juggling 10 cybercrime cases—"a marked increase" from last year. In Austin, Texas, incidents of tech crime have "skyrocketed," says Detective Paul Brick of the Austin Police Department. Its cases are up 30%, to 84, for the first 8 months of this year from last year.

As the global tech economy grows, so does the value of stolen tech goods and intellectual property. Last year, 273 firms surveyed by the Computer Security Institute said they lost $266 million to tech crime. The $80 billion software industry estimates it lost $12 billion in revenue last year due to piracy.

Why the spike in cases?

■ *Tight budgets.* With attorneys and security consultants charging $200 to $300 an hour, cash-strapped firms are more reluctant during the economic downturn to spend on lengthy cybercrime investigations, law-enforcement officials say. So, they are referring more cases to government prosecutors. Says investigator

McMullen: "It costs a small fortune for companies to hire outside law firms and investigative firms. But we're free."

■ *Businesses go on the offensive.* Many companies shy away from pursuing criminal cases because they don't want the negative publicity. Now, more companies are reporting incidents—even if it means going to court.

Last winter, for instance, three large retailers turned immediately to the FBI when a former Office Depot employee allegedly tried to sell confidential business information over the Internet to rivals OfficeMax and Staples. Aubrey J. Fisher, 28, was charged with mail fraud.

■ *More cooperation.* The dozens of tech crime units that have sprung up in recent years are working more closely with companies. Police and prosecutors in Texas, which boasts the largest high-tech economy outside of Silicon Valley, team with IBM, Applied Materials, Advanced Micro Devices and others. Microsoft and federal officials are stepping up action against software piracy. In Boston, Assistant U.S. Attorney Allison Burroughs says prosecutors meet with companies to discuss possible cases—giving them the option to walk away.

"Clearly, there's a more heightened focus on reporting, investigating and prosecuting these crimes," says IBM security manager Rick Wagner in Austin.

For the latest in crime and justice news, visit the Talk Justice news feed at http://crimenews.info.

Source: Edward Iwata, "Law Enforcers Report Spike in Cybercrime: High-Tech Cities See 'a Marked Increase,'" *USA Today,* August 31, 2001, p. 1B. Copyright 2001. *USA Today.* Reprinted with permission.

to men) are involved include larceny-theft (where 35.9% of reported crimes are committed by women), forgery and counterfeiting (39%), fraud (44.9%), and embezzlement (50%).[119] Nonetheless, as Table 2–9 shows, female offenders still account for only a small proportion of all reported crimes. Statistics on female criminality are difficult to interpret since reports of increasing female criminality may reflect more the greater equality of treatment accorded women in contemporary society than they do actual increases in criminal activity. In the past, when women committed crimes, they were dealt with less officiously than is likely to be the case today.

When women do commit serious crimes, they are more often followers than leaders. A 1996 study of women in correctional settings, for example, found that women are far more likely to assume "secondary follower rules during criminal events" than "dominant leadership roles."[120] Only 14% of women surveyed played primary roles, but those that did "felt that men had little influence in initiating or leading them into crime." African-American women were found to be more likely to play "primary and equal crime roles" with men or with female accomplices than were white or Hispanic women. Statistics such as these dispel the myth that the female criminal in America has taken her place alongside the male offender—in terms of either leadership roles or the absolute number of crimes committed. Learn more about female offenders and the changing rates of crime as they relate to gender at **Library Extra! 2–10** at cjtoday.com.

The Economic Cost of Crime

The national costs of crime are difficult to measure. The Bureau of Justice Statistics estimates the personal cost of crime (direct dollar losses to individuals, not including criminal justice system costs) at around $17.6 billion per year.[121] Robberies cost the nation about $500 million annually, burglaries nearly $4 billion, and larceny-thefts account for another $4 billion. Not included in the bureau's figures are the costs to crime victims of lost work, medical treatment, and the expense of new security measures they may implement. Lost work time, for example, was reported in 12% of aggravated assaults and 17% of rapes.

In 1996, the National Institute of Justice attempted to calculate both the direct and indirect costs of criminal victimization. NIJ researchers concluded that when crimes of all types are counted, "victimizations generate $105 billion annually in property and productivity losses and outlays for medical expenses. This amounts to an annual 'crime tax' of roughly $425 per man, woman, and child in the United States. When the values of pain, long-term emotional trauma, disability, and risk of death are put in dollar terms, the costs rise to $450 billion annually (or $1,800 per person)."[122] Overall, said the study authors, "rape is the costliest crime: With annual victim costs at $127 billion, it exacts a higher price than murder."[123]

The economic impact of crime is different for different groups. Households reporting an annual family income of less than $7,500, for example, suffer from almost twice the rate of burglary as do households reporting incomes of over $35,000. In fact, as family income rises, the rate of reported burglaries steadily declines. The opposite is true of auto theft; rates of auto theft rise in direct proportion to household income.[124]

The commercial costs of crime are substantial as well. Losses from commercial robberies (including bank robberies) and business burglaries have been put at $1.2 billion per year.[125] Frauds perpetrated against financial institutions in 1999 numbered 8,799 discovered cases with an associated dollar loss running into the billions.[126] Financial institution fraud includes crimes like money-laundering; check fraud; counterfeit negotiable instruments; counterfeit cash; stolen and counterfeit corporate checks; fraudulent money orders, payroll checks, and credit and debit cards; and counterfeit U.S. Treasury checks.

The costs to businesses of white-collar crime are not known but are thought to be substantial. To guard against crimes by employees and by members of the public, private businesses spend in excess of $21 billion per year for alarms, surveillance, and private security operations.[127]

Costs to the government for the apprehension, prosecution, and disposition of offenders, including crime-prevention efforts by the police, far outstrip the known dollar losses resulting from all non-drug-related crimes. Federal criminal justice expenditures for fiscal year 1999 were in excess of $27 billion,[128] and combined federal, state, and local expenditures totaled over $147 billion.[129] Nonetheless, government spending on criminal justice services amounts to only about 5% of all governmental expenditures. State and local governments absorb most of the costs of criminal justice–related activity.

Isolated criminal events can produce staggering crime costs. The September 11, 2001, attacks on the World Trade Center and the Pentagon, for example, resulted in direct property losses of around $100 billion—a figure based on clean-up and replacement costs of the buildings and the airplanes that were destroyed. Not included in that figure is the cost of lost productivity by those killed or injured in the attack, the loss of economic opportunity suffered by related businesses (especially airlines), infrastructure-related costs (including the destruction of emergency vehicles, damage to public streets, and the repairs required to things like sewer lines, gas pipes, and fiber-optic and copper cable serving the area), and fear-fed declines in U.S. stock markets. In late 2001, David Anderson, an economist at Davidson College, included estimates of such costs in an elaborate economic assessment of the terrorist attacks.[130] Anderson concluded that when stock market losses were figured in, the September 11 attacks cost the American economy nearly $2 trillion.

Peter Navarro, an economist in the Graduate School of Management at the University of California, Irvine, predicts that terrorism-related costs associated with increased use of private security and deterrence, enhancements in public security (such as airport security), and the cost of lifestyle changes (that is, fewer airline passengers, decreased occupancy at vacation destinations, and the like), combined with more "traditional" crime costs, will produce a post–September 11 annual net burden of crime costs totaling around $2 trillion.[131] Learn more about the costs and benefits of both crime and justice via **Library Extra! 2–11** at cjtoday.com.

Drugs and Crime

Drug-law violations do not figure into Crime Index calculations. Unlike index crimes, however, they mostly continue to increase, lending support to those who feel that this country is experiencing more crime than traditional index tabulations show. The relentless increase in drug violations largely accounts for the fact that America's prison populations have continued to grow, even when official crime rates (that is, index offenses) are declining. Figure 2–7 shows the number of suspects arrested for drug-law violations in the United States between 1975 and 2000. Compare Figure 2–7 with Figure 2–1 to see how drug arrests show a far different pattern over time than do index offenses. Note, however, that while Figure 2–1 depicts the *rate* of crime, Figure 2–7 shows only the raw number of arrests for given years. Even so, when rates are

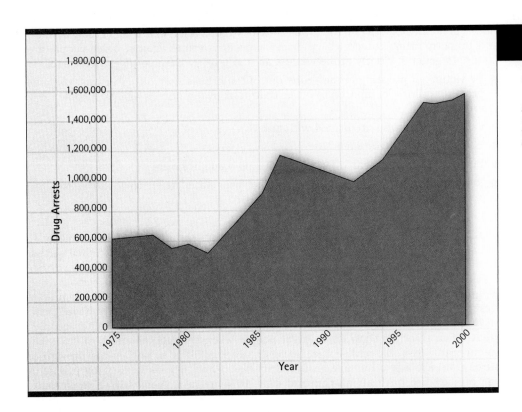

FIGURE 2-7

Drug arrests in the United States, 1975–2000.

Source: Federal Bureau of Investigation, *Crime in the United States* (Washington, D.C.: U.S. Government Printing Office, various years).

computed, it is easy to see that the number of drug crimes per 100,000 Americans has more than doubled since 1975.

Drugs and other forms of crime are often found together. Drug-law violations are themselves criminal, but more and more studies are linking drug abuse to other serious crimes. A study by the RAND Corporation found that most of the "violent predators" among prisoners had extensive histories of heroin abuse, often in combination with alcohol and other drugs.[132] Some cities report that a large percentage of their homicides are drug related.[133] Many property crimes are committed to sustain "habits," and the numbers of both violent and property crimes committed by drug users have been shown to be directly related to the level at which the offenders use drugs.[134] Substance abuse may well be the most expensive of all illegal activities. The social cost of drug abuse has been estimated at nearly $60 billion per year, with half of that amount due to lost job productivity.[135] Drunk driving alone is thought to cost over $13 billion in property losses and medical expenses yearly.[136] Chapter 15 will examine the drug-crime link in considerable detail. Suffice it to say here that the link appears strong and shows few signs of abating.

The Elderly and Crime

Relative to other age groups, older offenders rarely appear in the crime statistics. Criminality seems to decline with age, suggesting that a burnout factor applies to criminal behavior as it does to many other areas of life.

Still, some older people do commit crime—even serious violent crime. In 2000, for example, 80-year-old career bank robber Forest "Woody" Tucker was sentenced to 13 years in a Florida prison after he pleaded guilty to one count of bank robbery. Tucker needed a walker to get around, but his holdup of a bank in Jupiter, Florida, netted him $5,600.[137]

In 2000, people aged sixty-five and over accounted for less than 1% of all arrests.[138] The type and number of crimes committed by older people, however, appear to be changing. According to the UCR, arrests of the elderly for serious crimes decreased slightly between 1975 and 2000.[139] Overall, arrests of people sixty-five and older for all crimes declined by about 30% during the period.[140] On the other hand, when elderly people are sent to prison, it is usually for violent crimes, though violent crimes account for far less than 50% of prison admissions among younger people.

The elderly are also victims of crime. Victimization data pertaining to older people comes mostly from the NCVS, which, for such purposes, looks at people sixty-five and older. The elderly generally experience the lowest rate of victimization of any age group in both violent and property crime categories.[141] Some aspects of crime against older people are worth noting. In general, elderly crime victims are more likely than younger victims to

- Be victims of property crime—nine out of ten crimes committed against the elderly are property crimes, compared to fewer than four in ten crimes against people between 12 and 24
- Face offenders who are armed with guns
- Be victimized by strangers
- Be victimized in or near their homes during daylight hours
- Report their victimization to the police, especially when they fall victim to violent crime
- Be physically injured

In addition, elderly people are less likely to attempt to protect themselves when they are victims of violent crimes. Only 49% of elderly victims attempt to protect themselves versus 70% of young victims.

Elderly people are victimized disproportionately if they fall into certain categories. Relative to their numbers in the elderly population, black men are overrepresented as victims. Similarly, separated or divorced people and urban residents have higher rates of victimization than do other elderly people. As observed earlier, older people live in greater fear of crime than do younger people, even though their risk of victimization is considerably less. Elderly people, however, are less likely to take crime-prevention measures than are any other age group. Only 6% of households headed by people over the age of sixty-five have an alarm, and only 16% engrave their valuables (versus a 25% national average).

[Race and the Criminal Justice System]

Several years ago, Professor Lani Guinier of the University of Pennsylvania School of Law was interviewed on *Think Tank,* a public television show. Guinier was asked by Ben Wattenberg, the program's moderator, "When we talk about crime, crime, crime, are we really using a code for black, black, black?" Guinier responded this way: "To a great extent, yes, and I think that's a problem, not because we shouldn't deal with the disproportionate number of crimes that young black men may be committing, but because if we can't talk about race, then when we talk about crime, we're really talking about other things, and it means that we're not being honest in terms of acknowledging what the problem is and then trying to deal with it."[1]

Crimes, of course, are committed by individuals of all races. The link between crime—especially violent, street, and predatory crimes—and race, however, shows a pattern that is striking. In most crime categories, arrests of black offenders equal or exceed arrests of whites. In any given year, arrests of blacks account for more than 50% of all arrests for violent crimes. Blacks, however, comprise only 12% of the U.S. population, and when *rates* (which are based upon the relative proportion of racial groups) are examined, the statistics are even more striking. The murder rate among blacks, for example, is ten times that of whites. Similar rate comparisons, when calculated for other violent crimes, show that far more blacks than whites are involved in other street crimes, such as assault, burglary, and robbery. Related studies show that 30% of all the young black men in America are under correctional supervision on any given *day*—far greater percentage than members of any other race in the country.[2]

The real question for anyone interested in the justice system is how to explain such huge racial disparities. Some authors maintain that racial differences in arrests and in rates of imprisonment are due to the differential treatment of blacks at the hands of a discriminatory criminal justice system. Marvin D. Free, Jr., for example, says that the fact that blacks are underrepresented as criminal justice professionals results in their being overrepresented in arrest and confinement statistics.[3] Some police officers, says Free, more prone to arrest blacks than whites, frequently arrest blacks without sufficient evidence to support criminal charges, and overcharge in criminal cases involving black defendants—leading to misleading statistical tabulations which depict blacks as responsible for a greater proportion of crime than is, in fact, the case.

Other writers disagree. In *The Myth of a Racist Criminal Justice System,* for example, William Wilbanks claims that while the practice of American criminal justice may have been significantly racist in the past, and while some vestiges of racism may indeed remain, the system today is by and large objective in its processing of criminal defendants.[4] Using statistical data, Wilbanks shows that "at every point from arrest to parole there is little or no evidence of an overall racial effect, in that the percentage outcomes for blacks and whites are not very different."[5] Wilbanks claims to have reviewed "all the available studies that have examined the possible existence of racial discrimination from arrest to parole." In essence, he says, "this examination of the available evidence indicates that support for the 'discrimination thesis' is sparse, inconsistent, and frequently contradictory."

Wilbanks is careful to counter arguments advanced by those who continue to suggest the system is racist. He writes, for example, "perhaps the black/white gap at arrest is a product of racial bias by the police in that the police are more likely to select and arrest black than white offenders. The best evidence on this question comes from the National Crime Survey which interviews 130,000 Americans each year about crime victimization. . . . The percent of offenders described by victims as being black is generally consistent with the percent of offenders who are black according to arrest figures."

A fundamental critique of Wilbanks's thesis comes from Coramae Richey Mann, who says that his overreliance on quantitative or statistical data fails to capture the reality of racial discrimination within the justice system.[6] White victims, says Mann, tend to overreport being victimized by black offenders because they often misperceive Hispanic and other minority offenders as black. Similarly, black victims are sometimes reluctant to report victimization—especially at the hands of whites. Moreover, statistics on specific crimes, such as rape, may include false accusations by white women to hide their involvement with black lovers. And finally, a greater integration of black neighborhoods (in the sense that whites are less reluctant to enter black neighborhoods than blacks are to enter white neighborhoods) may result in a disproportionate but misleading number of reports by white victims.

Mann's arguments are discounted by those who point out that the statistics appear to be overwhelming. *If* they are accurate, then another question emerges: Why do blacks commit more crimes? Wilbanks says, "The assertion that the criminal justice system is not racist does not address the reasons why blacks appear to offend at higher rates than whites before coming into contact with the criminal justice system. . . . It may be that racial discrimination in American society has been responsible for conditions (for example, discrimination in employment, housing, and education) that lead to higher rates of offending by blacks."

Marvin Free, Jr., suggests that blacks are still systematically denied equal access to societal resources which would allow for full participation in American society—resulting in a higher rate of law violation. In a work that considers such issues in great detail, John Hagan and Ruth D. Peterson acknowledge the reality of higher crime rates among ethnic minorities and attribute them to (1) concentrated poverty, (2) joblessness, (3) family disruption, and (4) racial segregation.[7]

The question of *actual* fairness of the justice system can be quite different from one of *perceived* fairness. As University of Maryland Professor Katheryn K. Russell points out, "Study after study has shown that blacks and whites hold contrary views on the fairness of the criminal justice system's operation; blacks tend to be more cautious in their praise and frequently view the system as unfair and racially biased; by contrast whites have a favorable impression of the justice system. . . . The point is not that whites are completely satisfied with the justice system, but rather that, relative to blacks, they have faith in the system."[8] One reason for such differences may be that blacks are more likely to be victims of police harassment and brutality or may know someone who has been. Even if blacks do

(*continued*)

Multiculturalism and Diversity in America (*continued*)

engage in more criminal activity than whites, says one author, higher rates of offending may be due, at least in part, to their perception that members of their group have historically been treated unfairly by agents of social control—resulting in anger and defiance which express themselves in criminal activity.[9] From this vantage point, crime—at least crime committed by minority group members—becomes a kind of protest against a system which is perceived as fundamentally unfair.

According to Russell, inequities in the existing system may propel blacks into crime and combine with stereotypical images in the popular media to perpetuate what she calls the *criminalblackman myth.* The criminalblackman myth, says Russell, is a stereotypical portrayal of black men as *inherently* more sinister, evil, and dangerous than their white counterparts. The myth of the criminalblackman, adds Russell, is self-perpetuating, resulting in continued frustration, more crime, and growing alienation among black Americans.

[1]Quoted in "For the Record," *Washington Post* wire service, March 3, 1994.
[2]Marvin D. Free, Jr., *African-Americans and the Criminal Justice System* (New York: Garland, 1996).
[3]Ibid.
[4]William Wilbanks, *The Myth of a Racist Criminal Justice System* (Monterey, CA: Brooks/Cole, 1987).
[5]William Wilbanks, "The Myth of a Racist Criminal Justice System," *Criminal Justice Research Bulletin,* Vol. 3, No. 5 (Huntsville, TX: Sam Houston State University, 1987), p. 2.
[6]Coramae Richey Mann, "The Reality of a Racist Criminal Justice System," in Barry W. Hancock and Paul M. Sharp, eds., *Criminal Justice in America: Theory, Practice, and Policy* (Upper Saddle River, NJ: Prentice Hall, 1996), pp. 51–59.
[7]John Hagan and Ruth D. Peterson, *Crime and Inequality* (Stanford, CA: Stanford University Press, 1995).
[8]Katheryn K. Russell, "The Racial Hoax as Crime: The Law as Affirmation," *Indiana Law Journal,* Vol. 71 (1996), pp. 593–621.
[9]Thomas J. Bernard, "Angry Aggression among the 'Truly Disadvantaged,'" *Criminology,* Vol. 28, No. 1 (1990), pp. 73–96.

Summary

Two comprehensive national programs gather crime statistics in the United States today: the FBI's Uniform Crime Reporting Program and the National Institute of Justice's National Crime Victimization Survey. These programs provide a picture of victim characteristics through self-reports (the NCVS) and reports to the police (the UCR) and allow for a tabulation of the dollar costs of crime. Both programs also permit historical comparisons in crime rates and allow for some degree of predictability as to trends in crime. It is important to realize, however, that all statistics, including crime statistics, are inherently limited by the way in which they are gathered. Statistics can only portray the extent of crime according to the categories they are designed to measure and in terms understood by those whose responses they include.

Lacking in most of the crime statistics that are gathered today is any realistic appraisal of the human costs of crime, although some recent efforts by researchers at the National Institute of Justice have attempted to address this shortcoming. The trauma suffered by victims and survivors, the lowered sense of security experienced after victimization, the loss of productivity, and the reduced quality of life caused by crime are still difficult to gauge.

On the other side of the balance sheet, statistics fail to adequately identify the social costs suffered by offenders and their families. The social deprivation which may lead to crime, the fragmentation of private lives following conviction, and the loss of individuality which comes with confinement are all costs in which society must share, just as they are the culturally imposed consequences of crime and failure. Except for numbers on crimes committed, arrests made, and offenders incarcerated, today's data-gathering strategies fall far short of gauging the human suffering and wasted human potential which both cause and follow crime.

Even reports that do provide victim-impact measures may still fail to assess some of the dollar costs of crime, including lowered property values in high-crime areas and inflated prices for consumer purchases caused by the underground economy in stolen goods. White-collar crimes in particular are often well hidden and difficult to measure, yet many produce the largest direct dollar losses of any type of criminal activity. Hence, although modern crime statistics are useful, they do not provide the whole picture. Students of criminal justice need to be continually aware of aspects of the crime picture that fall outside official data.

Discussion Questions

1. What are the two major sources of crime statistics for the United States? How do they differ? How are they alike?

2. What can crime statistics tell us about the crime picture in America? How has that picture changed over time?

3. What are the potential sources of error in the major reports on crime? Can you think of some popular usage of those statistics that might be especially misleading?

4. What is the Crime Index? What crimes make up the Crime Index? How is it computed? Why is it difficult to add offenses to (or remove them from) the index without lessening its value as a comparative tool?

5. Why are many crime statistics expressed as a rate? How does the use of crime rates instead of simple numerical tabulation improve the reporting of crime data?

6. What are the two major crime categories in Part I offenses? Do some property crimes have a violent aspect? Are there any personal crimes that could be nonviolent? If so, what might they be?

7. What is the hierarchy rule in crime-reporting programs? What purpose does it serve? What do you think of modifications in the hierarchy rule now occurring under NIBRS?

8. What does it mean to say that a crime has been "cleared"? In what ways can a crime be cleared?

To participate in an online discussion on these topics and others, go to the Global Town Meeting electronic message board for Chapter 2 on the *Criminal Justice Today* Companion Website at cjtoday.com.

Web Quest!

Visit Dr. Frank Schmalleger's Cybrary of Criminal Justice Links on the Web at http://www.cybrary.info, and familiarize yourself with the Cybrary's features. Note that a number of general categories are listed on the home page. (Click "Show All Categories" at the bottom of the page to see more.) The power of the Cybrary lies in its advanced search capabilities. Practice using the Cybrary's search feature. Once you have become familiar with how the search feature works, use it to find links to the Uniform Crime Reports (hint: look for the FBI's home page), the *Sourcebook of Criminal Justice Statistics,* and the Bureau of Justice Statistics. Visit all three sites to gather information on the crime of rape.

Compare the availability of information on the crime of rape at these three sites. What are the similarities and the differences? What are some of the other differences between these sites? Which do you find most useful? Why?

Submit the answers to these questions to your instructor if asked to do so.

To complete this Web Quest! online, go to the Web Quest! module in Chapter 2 of the *Criminal Justice Today* Companion Website at cjtoday.com.

Library Extras!

Library Extra! 2–1 *Measurement and Analysis of Crime and Justice* (NIJ, 2000).
Library Extra! 2–2 *Crime's Decline—Why?* (NIJ, 1998).
Library Extra! 2–3 *Measuring the Sexual Victimization of Women* (NIJ, 2000).
Library Extra! 2–4 *The Sexual Victimization of College Women* (NIJ, 2000).
Library Extra! 2–5 *Addressing Hate Crimes: Six Initiatives That Are Enhancing the Efforts of Criminal Justice Practitioners* (BJA, 2000).
Library Extra! 2–6 *Hate Crimes Reported in NIBRS, 1997–99* (BJS, 2001).
Library Extra! 2–7 *The Self-Report Method for Measuring Delinquency and Crime* (NIJ, 2000).

Library Extra! **2–8** *Self-Report Surveys as Measures of Crime and Criminal Victimization* (NIJ, 2000).

Library Extra! **2–9** *Full Report of the Prevalence, Incidence, and Consequences of Violence against Women* (NIJ, 2000).

Library Extra! **2–10** *Changes in the Gender Gap in Crime and Women's Economic Marginalization* (NIJ, 2000).

Library Extra! **2–11** *Measuring the Costs and Benefits of Crime and Justice* (NIJ, 2000).

To explore these resources online, go to the Library Extras! area of the *Criminal Justice Today* Companion Website at cjtoday.com. You should also check the author's "Late Picks" online for newly released documents and updated Library Extras! You can find Late Picks at http://cjtoday.com/latepicks.htm.

Marginal Notes

i. The term *superpredator* is generally attributed to John J. DiIulio, Jr. See John J. DiIulio, Jr., "The Question of Black Crime," *Public Interest* (fall 1994), pp. 3–12.

ii. H. R. 4797, 102d Cong. 2d Sess. (1992).

Notes

1. John Q. Wilson, "Point of View," *Chronicle of Higher Education,* June 10, 1992, p. A40.
2. The dead included the shooter and three members of his family.
3. Laura Parker, Gary Fields, and Scott Bowles, "Average Neighbor Lived with a Dark Past," *USA Today,* July 30, 1999, p. 1A.
4. Mark Krantz, "Even for Day Trader, Killer Lost Big Money, *USA Today,* August 1, 1999, p. 1A.
5. "Gunman Was Suspect in 1993 Murder," *USA Today,* July 30, 1999, p. 1A.
6. Trisha Renaud, "Victims of Day-Trader Rampage Say Industry Itself to Blame," *Fulton County (Ga.) Daily Report,* November 30, 2001. Web posted at law.com. Accessed November 30, 2001.
7. Norval Morris, "Crime, the Media, and Our Public Discourse," National Institute of Justice, Perspectives on Crime and Justice video series, recorded May 13, 1997.
8. Frank Hagan, *Research Methods in Criminal Justice and Criminology* (New York: Macmillan, 1982), p. 89.
9. Bureau of Justice Statistics, *Criminal Victimization in the United States, 1985* (Washington, D.C.: U.S. Government Printing Office, 1987), p. 1.
10. Federal Bureau of Investigation, *Crime in the United States, 1987* (Washington, D.C.: U.S. Government Printing Office, 1988), p. 1.
11. Federal Bureau of Investigation, *Crime in the United States, 2000* (Washington, D.C.: U.S. Government Printing Office, 2001), available online at http://www.fbi.gov/ucr.htm.
12. The President's Commission on Law Enforcement and Administration of Justice, *The Challenge of Crime in a Free Society* (Washington, D.C.: U.S. Government Printing Office, 1967). The commission relied on Uniform Crime Reports data. The other crime statistics reported in this section come from Uniform Crime Reports for various years.
13. Hagan, *Research Methods in Criminal Justice and Criminology.*
14. U.S. Department of Justice, *Fiscal Years 2000–2005 Strategic Plan* (Washington, D.C.: U.S. Government Printing Office, 2000).
15. John J. DiIulio, Jr., "The Question of Black Crime," *Public Interest* (fall 1994), pp. 3–12.
16. James Alan Fox, *Trends in Juvenile Violence: A Report to the United States Attorney General on Current and Future Rates of Juvenile Offending* (Washington, D.C.: Bureau of Justice Statistics, 1996).
17. See also David G. Savage, "Urban Crime Resurges After Decade Drop," *Los Angeles Times,* November 25, 2001, in which Fox continues to predict a rise in crime.
18. That is, while crime clock data may imply that one murder occurs every half hour or so, most murders actually occur during the evening, and only a very few around sunrise.
19. Most offense definitions in this chapter are derived from those used by the UCR Program and are taken from the FBI's *Crime in the United States, 2000* or from Bureau of Justice Statistics, *Criminal Justice Data Terminology,* 2d ed. (Washington, D.C.: Bureau of Justice Statistics, 1981).
20. FBI, *Crime in the United States, 2000.*
21. These and other statistics in this chapter are derived primarily from the FBI's *Crime in the United States, 2000.*
22. Bureau of Justice Statistics, *Report to the Nation on Crime and Justice,* 2d ed. (Washington, D.C.: U.S. Government Printing Office, 1988), p. 4.
23. There is no definitive "line" between serial killing and spree killing in terms of time. Cunanan's three-month spree might qualify him as a serial killer in the minds of some criminologists. Nonetheless, renowned homicide investigators Robert Ressler (a former FBI criminal

profiler) and Vernon Geberth (a retired New York commander of homicide investigations and a noted forensic expert) both classify him as a spree killer. (See Michael Grunwald, "Cunanan Leaves Experts at Loss," *Boston Globe* via Simon & Schuster Newslink e-mail service, July 28, 1997.)

24. Ibid.

25. Ibid.

26. For excellent coverage of serial killers, see Steven Egger, *The Killers among Us: An Examination of Serial Murder and Its Investigation* (Upper Saddle River, NJ: Prentice Hall, 1998); Steven A. Egger, *Serial Murder: An Elusive Phenomenon* (Westport, CT: Praeger, 1990); and Stephen J. Giannangelo, *The Psychopathology of Serial Murder: A Theory of Violence* (New York: Praeger, 1996).

27. A few years ago, Lucas recanted all of his confessions, saying he never killed anyone—except possibly his mother (a killing which he said he didn't remember). See "Condemned Killer Admits Lying, Denies Slayings," *Washington Post*, October 1, 1995.

28. Chikatilo was executed in 1994.

29. See Mark Babineck, "Railroad Killer Gets Death Penalty," Associated Press wire service, May 22, 2000, from which some of the information in this paragraph and the next are taken. Web posted at http://cnews.tribune.com/news/tribune/story/0,1235,tribune-nation-37649,00.html. Accessed March 3, 2002.

30. FBI, *Crime in the United States, 2000.*

31. Federal Bureau of Investigation, *Uniform Crime Reporting Handbook* (Washington, D.C.: FBI, 1984), p. 10.

32. "Study: Rape Vastly Underreported," Associated Press wire service, April 26, 1992.

33. Ronald Barri Flowers, *Women and Criminality: The Woman as Victim, Offender, and Practitioner* (Westport, CT: Greenwood Press, 1987), p. 36.

34. A. Nichols Groth, *Men Who Rape: The Psychology of the Offender* (New York: Plenum Press, 1979).

35. Susan Brownmiller, *Against Our Will: Men, Women, and Rape* (New York: Simon & Schuster, 1975).

36. Dennis J. Stevens, "Motives of Social Rapists," *Free Inquiry in Creative Sociology,* Vol. 23, No. 2 (November 1995), pp. 117–126.

37. The latest edition of the *Uniform Crime Reporting Handbook,* which serves as a statistical reporting guide for law enforcement agencies, says, for example, "By definition, sex attacks on males are excluded and should be classified as assaults or 'other sex offenses,' depending on the nature of the crime and the extent of the injury." FBI, *Uniform Crime Reporting Handbook,* p. 10.

38. "Teen: Teacher's Pregnancy Planned," Associated Press wire service, August 22, 1997.

39. *Washington* v. *LeTourneau,* Court TV Online, March 18, 1998. Web posted at http://www.courttv.com/trials/letourneau/031898.html. Accessed February 20, 2000.

40. BJS, *Report to the Nation on Crime and Justice,* p. 5.

41. Ibid.

42. FBI, *Crime in the United States, 2000.* For UCR reporting purposes, "minorities" are defined as blacks, Native Americans, Asians, Pacific Islanders, and Alaskan Natives.

43. The material for this story comes from Laurie Mason, "Cookie Monster Attacker Guilty," *Bucks County (Pa.) Courier Times,* November 15, 2001. McPhatter was convicted of simple assault, disorderly conduct, and harassment under Pennsylvania law.

44. This offense is sometimes called *assault with a deadly weapon with intent to kill* (AWDWWIK).

45. FBI, *Crime in the United States, 2000.*

46. BJS, *Report to the Nation on Crime and Justice,* p. 6.

47. Ibid.

48. "Yale Says Student Stole His Education," *USA Today,* April 12, 1995, p. 3A.

49. Jim Mulvaney and Susan Kelleher, "Doctor Continues Deposition," *Orange County (Calif.) Register* Online. Web posted at http://www.ocregister.com/clinic/tlr/0121dep.htm. Accessed May 20, 1999.

50. FBI, *Uniform Crime Reporting Handbook,* p. 28.

51. Matt Stearns and Donald Bradley, "Boy's Last Moments of Life are Frozen in Mother's Memory," *Kansas City Star,* February 23, 2000.

52. "Jury Recommends Life Term in Dragging Death Wednesday," Associated Press wire service, October 3, 2001.

53. FBI, *Crime in the United States, 2000.*

54. As indicated in the UCR definition of *arson.* See FBI, *Crime in the United States, 1998.*

55. FBI, *Crime in the United States, 2000.*

56. Ibid.

57. See the FBI's UCR/NIBRS website at http://www.fbi.gov/hq/cjisd/ucr.htm. Accessed March 2, 2002.

58. FBI, *Crime in the United States, 2000,* p. 3.

59. *NIBRS Overview,* SEARCH Project website, http://www.nibrs.search.org. Accessed February 10, 2000.

60. Security on Campus, "College and University Campus Crime Statistics, 1998–2000." Web posted at http://campussafety.org/crimestats/2010.html. Accessed March 1, 2002.

61. Public Law 101-275.

62. H.R. 4797, 102d Cong. 2d Sess. (1992).

63. FBI, *Crime in the United States, 2000.*

64. "Dragging Death Still Haunts Family," APB News, June 7, 1999. Web posted at http://www.apbnews.com/newscenter/breakingnews/1999/06/07/byrd0607 01.html. Accessed January 2, 2000.

65. "Grim Portraits of Homophobic Killers," *Boston Globe* Online, May 10, 1997.

66. Michael E. Wiggins, "Societal Changes and Right Wing Membership," paper presented at the annual meeting of the Academy of Criminal Justice Sciences, San Francisco, April 1988.

67. Richard Holden, "God's Law: Criminal Process and Right Wing Extremism in America," paper presented at the annual meeting of the Academy of Criminal Justice Sciences, San Francisco, April 1988.

68. See, for example, John Kleinig, "Penalty Enhancements for Hate Crimes," *Criminal Justice Ethics* (summer/fall 1992), pp. 3–6.

69. *R.A.V.* v. *City of St. Paul, Minn.,* 112 S.Ct. 2538 (1992).

70. *Forsyth County, Ga.* v. *Nationalist Movement,* 112 S.Ct. 2395 (1992).

71. *Capitol Square Review and Advisory Board* v. *Pinette,* 515 U.S. 753 (1995).

72. *Wisconsin* v. *Mitchell,* 508 U.S. 47 (1993).

73. "Trends in Crime and Victimization," *Criminal Justice Research Reports,* Vol. 2, No. 6 (July/August 2001), p. 83.

74. For additional information, see Bureau of Justice Statistics, *Criminal Victimization, 2000: Changes 1999–2000 with Trends, 1993–2000* (Washington, D.C.: BJS, 2001).

75. Ibid.

76. BJS, *Criminal Victimization, 2000.*

77. Ibid.

78. Ibid., p. 11.

79. See, for example, President's Commission on Law Enforcement and Administration of Justice, *The Challenge of Crime in a Free Society*, pp. 22–23.

80. BJS, *Report to the Nation on Crime and Justice*, p. 27.

81. Caroline Wolf Harlow, *Firearm Use by Offenders* (Washington, D.C.: Bureau of Justice Statistics, 2001).

82. "Two-thirds of Americans Support Gun Control," APB Online, May 20, 1999. Web posted at http://www.apbonline.com/911/1999/05/20/gunpoll0520_01.html. Accessed January 20, 2000.

83. 18 U.S.C., Section 922(q)(1)(A).

84. Harlow, *Firearm Use by Offenders.*

85. PL 104–208. An amendment to Section 921(a) of Title 18, U.S.C. Also known as the Lautenberg Amendment.

86. Jacob R. Clark, "Police Careers May Take a Beating from Fed Domestic-Violence Law," *Law Enforcement News*, Vol. 23, No. 461 (February 14, 1997), p. 1.

87. Ibid.

88. *Printz v. U.S.*, 521 U.S. 98 (1997).

89. *Mack v. U.S.* (1997), 521 U.S. 98 (1997).

90. *U.S. v. Alfonso Lopez, Jr.*, 115 S.Ct. 1624, 131 L. Ed. 2d 626 (1995).

91. Georgette Bennett, *Crimewarps: The Future of Crime in America* (Garden City, NY: Anchor/Doubleday, 1987).

92. Ibid.

93. Fox Butterfield, "Data Hint Crime Plunge May Be Leveling Off," *New York Times*, December 19, 2000. Web posted at http://www.nytimes.com/2000/12/19/national/19CRIM.html. Accessed October 12, 2000.

94. David G. Savage, "Urban Crime Resurges after Decade Drop," *Los Angeles Times*, November 25, 2001.

95. Bennett, *Crimewarps*, p. xiv.

96. BJS, *Report to the Nation on Crime and Justice*, p. 24.

97. "School Killings Drop, But Gang Activity Rises," APB Online, May 19, 1999. Web posted at http://www.apbonline.com/911/1999/05/19/schools0519_01.html. Accessed May 20, 1999.

98. Indira A. R. Lakshmanan, "Fear Goes Up as Crime Goes Down," *Boston Globe* Online, August 18, 1994. Web posted at http://world.std.com/jlr/comment/crime.htm. Accessed May 20, 1999.

99. Ted Chicoros et al., "Fear, TV News, and the Reality of Crime," *Criminology*, Vol. 38, No. 3 (2000), pp. 755–785.

100. BJS, *Report to the Nation on Crime and Justice*, p. 32.

101. The definition of *rape* employed by the UCR, however, automatically excludes crimes of homosexual rape such as might occur in prisons and jails. As a consequence, the rape of males is excluded from the official count for crimes of rape.

102. Thomas Simon, et al., *Injuries from Violent Crime, 1992–98* (Washington, D.C.: BJS, 2001), p. 5.

103. Ibid.

104. See, for example, Elizabeth Stanko, "When Precaution Is Normal: A Feminist Critique of Crime Prevention," in Loraine Gelsthorpe and Allison Morris, eds., *Feminist Perspectives in Criminology* (Philadelphia: Open University Press, 1990).

105. For more information, see Eve S. Buzawa and Carl G. Buzawa, *Domestic Violence: The Criminal Justice Response* (Thousand Oaks, CA: Sage, 1996).

106. "Battered Women Tell Their Stories to the Senate," *Charlotte* (N.C.) *Observer*, July 10, 1991, p. 3A.

107. Patricia Tjaden and Nancy Thoennes, *Full Report of the Prevalence, Incidence, and Consequences of Violence against Women: Findings from the National Violence Against Women Survey* (Washington, D.C.: National Institute of Justice, 2000).

108. Caroline Wolf Harlow, *Female Victims of Violent Crime* (Washington, D.C.: Bureau of Justice Statistics, 1991).

109. "Woman Convicted of Murdering Four Sons," APB Online, August 19, 1999. Web posted at http://www.apbonline.com/911/1999/08/19/foursons0819_01.html. Accessed January 2, 2000.

110. "Florida Woman Sentenced to Death," *USA Today*, February 1, 1992, p. 3A.

111. "Fla. Slayings: Men Beware," *USA Today*, December 17, 1990, p. 3A.

112. *Wuornos v. Florida*, No. 96-5766.

113. Otto Pollak, *The Criminality of Women* (Philadelphia: University of Pennsylvania Press, 1950).

114. Cathy Spatz Widom, "Childhood Victimization and the Derailment of Girls and Women to the Criminal Justice System," in Beth E. Richie et al., eds., *Research on Women and Girls in the Justice System* (Washington, D.C.: National Institute of Justice, 2000), p. iii.

115. Ibid., pp. 27–36.

116. FBI, *Crime in the United States, 1970* and *2000.*

117. Ibid.

118. FBI, *Crime in the United States, 2000.*

119. Ibid., p. 233.

120. Leanne Fiftal Alarid et al., "Women's Roles in Serious Offenses: A Study of Adult Felons," *Justice Quarterly*, Vol. 13, No. 3 (September 1996), pp. 432–454.

121. Patsy A. Klaus, *The Costs of Crime to Victims*, a Bureau of Justice Statistics Crime Data Brief (Washington, D.C.: Bureau of Justice Statistics, 1994).

122. Ted R. Miller, Mark A. Cohen, and Brian Wiersema, *Victim Costs and Consequences: A New Look* (Washington, D.C.: National Institute of Justice, 1996).

123. Ibid.

124. BJS, *Criminal Victimization, 2000.*

125. BJS, *Report to the Nation on Crime and Justice.*

126. Federal Bureau of Investigation, *Financial Institution Fraud and Failure Report* (Washington, D.C.: U.S. Department of Justice, no date). Web posted at http://www.fbi.gov/publications/financial/1998fif.pdf. Accessed January 22, 2002.

127. BJS, *Report to the Nation on Crime and Justice*, p. 114.

128. Justice Expenditure and Employment in the United States, 1999 (Washington, D.C.: Bureau of Justice Statistics, 2002).

129. Ibid.

130. David Anderson, "The Aggregate Burden of Crime," *Journal of Law and Economics*, forthcoming. Web posted at http://www.davidson.edu/administrative/newsevnt/99.10anderson.html. Accessed January 30, 2002.

131. Peter Navarro and Aron Spencer, "September 11, 2001: Assessing the Costs of Terrorism," *Milken Institute Review* (fourth quarter, 2001), pp. 16–31.

132. J. M. Chaiken and M. R. Chaiken, *Varieties of Criminal Behavior* (Santa Monica, CA: RAND Corporation, 1982).

133. D. McBride, "Trends in Drugs and Death," paper presented at the annual meeting of the American Society of Criminology, Denver, 1983.

134. B. Johnson et al., *Taking Care of Business: The Economics of Crime by Heroin Abusers* (Lexington, MA: Lexington Books, 1985). See also Bernard A. Grooper, *Research in Brief: Probing the Links between Drugs and Crime* (Washington, D.C.: National Institute of Justice, 1985).

135. BJS, *Report to the Nation on Crime and Justice,* p. 114.

136. Ibid.

137. "80-Year-Old Bank Robber Gets 13 Years in Fla.," APB News, October 23, 2000. Web posted at http://apbnews. com/newscenter/breakingnews/2000/10/23/ bankrobber1023_01.html. Accessed March 12, 2002.

138. FBI, *Crime in the United States, 2000.*

139. FBI, *Crime in the United States, 1975* and *2000.*

140. Ibid.

141. Much of the data in this section comes from Bureau of Justice Statistics, *Crimes against Persons Age 65 or Older, 1992–97* (Rockville, MD: BJS, 2000); and Bureau of Justice Statistics, *Elderly Crime Victims* (Rockville, MD: BJS, 1994).

The Search for Causes

LEARNING OBJECTIVES

After reading this chapter, you should be able to

- List the various categories of theoretical approaches used to explain crime

- Describe the basic features of biological theories of crime causation

- Describe the basic features of psychological explanations for crime

- Describe the basic features of sociological theories of crime causation

- Identify two emergent theories of crime causation

chapter 3

Key Concepts

[Terms]

anomie	interdisciplinary theory	radical criminology
atavism	labeling theory	rational choice theory
behavioral conditioning	life course perspective	reaction formation
Biological School	moral enterprise	research
broken windows thesis	neoclassical criminology	routine activities theory
Chicago School	peacemaking criminology	schizophrenic
Classical School	phenomenological criminology	social development theory
conflict perspective	phrenology	social disorganization
constitutive criminology	Positivist School	social learning theory
containment	postmodern criminology	social-psychological theory
dangerousness	psychoanalysis	somatotyping
deconstructionist theory	psychological profiling	subculture of violence
defensible space theory	Psychological School	supermale
deviance	psychopath	theory
feminist criminology	psychopathology	
hypothesis	psychosis	

[Names]

Freda Adler	Sigmund Freud	Robert Park
Cesare Beccaria	Franz Joseph Gall	Harold Pepinsky
Howard Becker	Stuart Henry	Richard Quinney
Jeremy Bentham	Richard Herrnstein	Walter Reckless
Ernest Burgess	John H. Laub	Robert J. Sampson
Meda Chesney-Lind	Cesare Lombroso	Clifford Shaw
Hervey Cleckley	Henry McKay	William Sheldon
Albert Cohen	Sarnoff Mednick	Rita Simon
Lawrence Cohen	Robert Merton	Edwin Sutherland
Kathleen Daly	Walter Miller	James Q. Wilson
Marcus Felson	Dragan Milovanovic	Marvin Wolfgang

Introduction

Hear the author discuss this chapter at **cjtoday.com**

In 1994, rapper Keith Murray burst on the music scene with the hit CD *The Most Beautifullest Thing in the World,* which soon "went gold."[3] Murray's next release, *Enigma,* was well-received in 1996. In 1998, however, Murray was arrested and charged with assault following a brawl at a Connecticut nightclub. He was convicted of the charges and served 33 months behind bars. Murray's arrest and incarceration captured headlines in newspapers and on television news shows across the country. What no one seemed able to answer was why Murray, a rising star with a bright future, would get involved in criminal activity.

Fundamental questions about crime causation have concerned criminologists for years: Why do people commit crime? Why are they deviant? What are the root causes of violence and aggression? Are people basically good, or are they motivated only by self-interest? More precisely, we might ask, "Why does a particular person commit a particular crime on a given occasion and under specific circumstances?" No discussion of crime and of the criminal justice system would be complete without giving some consideration to the causes of crime and **deviance**. That is the purpose of this chapter.

deviance

A violation of social norms defining appropriate or proper behavior under a particular set of circumstances. Deviance often includes criminal acts.

Hip-hop artist Keith Murray (left) arriving at the Source Hip-Hop Awards in Miami Beach, Florida, in 2001. Murray, who spent 33 months in prison for assaulting a teenager with a bar stool, was released from confinement a few months before the awards ceremony. In the photo at right, rapper J. T. Money mugs for photographers at the Billboard Music Awards in Las Vegas, Nevada, where he won the award for Rap Artist of the Year. Some people think that violent crimes are glorified and encouraged by certain kinds of rap music, especially "gangsta rap," and by some forms of hip-hop.

© Steve Marcus/Reuters New Media, Inc. CORBIS (right); Joe Raedle, Getty Images, Inc. (left)

Before we begin, however, some brief definitions are in order. *Crime*, as noted in Chapter 1, is a violation of the criminal law without acceptable legal justification,[4] while *deviant behavior* is a violation of social norms specifying appropriate or proper behavior under a particular set of circumstances. Deviant behavior is a broad category which often includes crime.

Many different kinds of theories have been advanced to explain all sorts of rule-violating behavior. Some observers of the contemporary scene, for example, find explanations for modern-day violence and seemingly increased rates of criminal victimization in the now widespread and commonplace episodes of violence in the American media—especially on television, in music, and in film. Experts who study the media estimate that the average American child watches 8,000 murders and 100,000 acts of violence while growing up.[5] At an international conference, Suzanne Stutman, President of the Institute for Mental Health Initiatives, a nonprofit organization in Washington, reported that studies consistently show that the extent of exposure to television violence in childhood is a good predictor of future criminal behavior.[6]

Robert Brown, Executive Director of the Washington, D.C., Children's Trust Neighborhood Initiative, tends to lay much of the blame for contemporary violence on rap music, especially "gangsta rap" and some forms of hip-hop. "So many of our young men," says Brown, "have accepted false icons of manhood for themselves . . . because the popular culture of videos and rap—Snoop Doggy Dogg and the rest—reinforces that this is the correct way to be. Guys . . . try to exude an aura that says, 'I am so bad that I am not afraid to take your life or to offer mine up in the process.'"[7]

An African-American critic of gangsta rap puts it this way: "The key element is aggression—in rappers' body language, tone, and witty rhymes—that often leaves listeners hyped, on edge, angry about . . . something. Perhaps the most important element in gangsta rap is its messages, which center largely around these ideas: that women are no more than 'bitches and hos,' disposable playthings who exist merely for men's abusive delight; that it's cool to use any means necessary to get the material things you want; and most importantly, it's admirable to be cold-blooded and hard."[8] The Reverend Arthur L. Cribbs, Jr., an African-American social critic, agrees. Cribbs, writing in a national editorial, calls gangsta rap "nothing but modern-day violence and vulgarity wrapped and packaged in blackface."[9]

The political right believes that the root cause of violent crime is bad genes or bad morals. Not so, says the left. The root cause of violent crime is bad housing or dead-end jobs. And I tell you that while doing something about the causes of violence surely requires a political ideology, the only way we can determine what those causes are in the first place is to check our ideologies at the door and to try to keep our minds open as wide, and for as long, as we can bear.

—John Monahan, speaking at the U.S. Sentencing Commission's Inaugural Symposium on Crime and Punishment

Cesare Lombroso (left), who has been dubbed "the father of modern criminology," posing with friend Louis Lombard in a rare surviving photograph from 1909.

Culver Pictures, Inc.

The public tends to agree. In fact, according to one recent survey, "57% of the public thinks violence in the media is a major factor in real-life violence" of all kinds.[10]

But whether violence in the media and aggressive themes in popular music are indeed a cause of crime, as many believe, or merely a reflection of the social conditions that exist in many American communities today is less than clear. Hence, getting legislators to address the issue of violence in the media is difficult. A proposed labeling system for video games and other forms of entertainment was advanced in mid-1999 by Representatives Zach Wamp (R-Tenn.) and Bart Stupak (D-Mich.). Both argued that the government requires warning labels on food, alcohol, and tobacco and should do likewise on sources of violence. The proposal was voted down by a count of 266–161.[11]

Criminological Theory

It is important to recognize that focusing on songwriters, recording companies, and broadcasters reflects just one way of explaining crime and criminal violence. Explanations of this sort are persuasive because they emphasize the role of economics, greed, and financial irresponsibility on the part of the nation's business leaders. Many other types of explanations for crime can also be offered, such as genetic abnormalities which may predispose people to crime and violence or other explanations which look to individual psychological differences or variations in patterns of early socialization. Likewise, social institutions like the family, schools, and churches can be examined for their role in reducing or enhancing the likelihood of criminality among young people.

Regardless of the particular mode of explanation chosen, there is probably no single cause of crime. Crime appears rooted in a diversity of causal factors and takes a variety of forms, depending upon the situation in which it occurs. Nonetheless, some theories of human behavior help us understand why certain people engage in acts which society defines as criminal or deviant, while others do not.

A **theory** is a kind of model. Theories posit relationships, often of a causal sort, between events and things under study. So it is not unusual to hear someone suggest that "rap music causes crime." However, while everyone may have his or her own pet theory about crime, the word *theory* takes on a special meaning in the social sciences and in the study of criminal justice. Formally, a complete theory is said to consist of a series of interrelated

theory

A set of interrelated propositions that attempt to describe, explain, predict, and ultimately control some class of events. A theory gains explanatory power from inherent logical consistency and is "tested" by how well it describes and predicts reality.

propositions which attempt to describe, explain, predict, and ultimately control some class of events. A theory's explanatory power derives primarily from its inherent logical consistency, and theories are tested by how well they describe and predict reality. In other words, a good theory provides relatively complete understanding of the phenomenon under study, and carefully made observations support predictions based upon the theory. A good theory fits the facts, and it stands up to continued scrutiny. Figure 3–1 diagrams the important aspects of theory creation in the social sciences, using the well-known association between poverty and crime as an example.

History is rife with theories purporting to explain rule-violating behavior. An old Roman theory, for example, based on ancient observations that more crime and deviance seem to occur on nights with a full moon, proposed that the moon causes a kind of temporary insanity—hence the term *lunacy*. According to the lunacy theory, human behavior isn't just random, but ebbs and flows in cadence with the lunar cycle. As a consequence, crime and deviance could be directly explained as due to the influence of the moon. In fact, although modern statisticians have noted an apparent association between phases of the moon and crime rates, the precise mechanism by which the moon influences behavior—if it does—has never been adequately explained.

A complete theory attempts to flesh out all the causal linkages between phenomena which are associated, or said to be "correlated." Hence, a comprehensive theory of lunacy might suggest, as some do, that light from the full moon stimulates the reticular activating system (RAS) in the limbic portion of the human brain, leading to easy excitement and hyperactivity—and then to deviance and crime. Others have suggested, quite simply, that people commit more crimes when the moon is full because it is easier to see.

Theories, once created, must still be tested to determine whether they are valid. As a consequence, modern criminology has become increasingly scientific.[12] Generally accepted research designs—coupled with careful data-gathering strategies and statistical techniques for data analysis—have yielded considerable confidence in certain explanations for crime, while at the same time tending to disprove others. Theory testing usually involves the development of **hypotheses** based upon what the theory under scrutiny would predict. A theory of lunacy, for example, might be tested in a variety of ways, including (1) observing rates of crime and deviance on nights when the light of the full moon is obscured by clouds (we would expect no rise in crime rates if the RAS or visibility explanations are correct); and (2) examining city crime rates on full-moon nights—especially in well-lighted city areas where the light of the moon hardly increases visibility. If the predictions made by a theory are validated by careful observation, the theory gains greater acceptability.

Sadly, many contemporary theories of deviant and criminal behavior are far from complete, offering only limited ideas rather than complete explanations for the behavior in question. Other theories are difficult to test. Moreover, when we consider the wide range of behaviors regarded as criminal—from murder to drug use to white-collar crime—it seems difficult to imagine a theory that can explain them all. Yet many past theoretical approaches to crime causation were unicausal and all-inclusive. That is, they posited a single, identifiable source for all serious deviant and criminal behavior.

Theories of crime causation which have met rigorous scientific tests for acceptability give policymakers the intellectual basis they need to create informed crime-control strategies. The ultimate goal of **research** and theory building in criminology is to provide models that permit a better understanding of criminal behavior and that enhance the development of strategies intended to address the problem of crime.

While we will use the word *theory* in describing various explanations for crime throughout this chapter, it should be recognized that the word is only loosely applicable to some of the perspectives we will discuss. As noted, many social scientists insist that to be considered "theories," explanations must consist of sets of clearly stated, logically interrelated, and measurable propositions. The fact that few of the "theories" which follow rise above the level of organized conjecture, and that many others are not readily amenable to objective scrutiny through scientific testing, is one of the greatest failures of social science today.

For our purposes, explanations of criminal behavior fall into nine general categories:

■ Classical

■ Biological

■ Psychobiological

hypothesis

An explanation that accounts for a set of facts and that can be tested by further investigation. Also, something that is taken to be true for the purpose of argument or investigation.[i]

research

The use of standardized, systematic procedures in the search for knowledge.

Steps in criminal justice theory building and social policy creation.

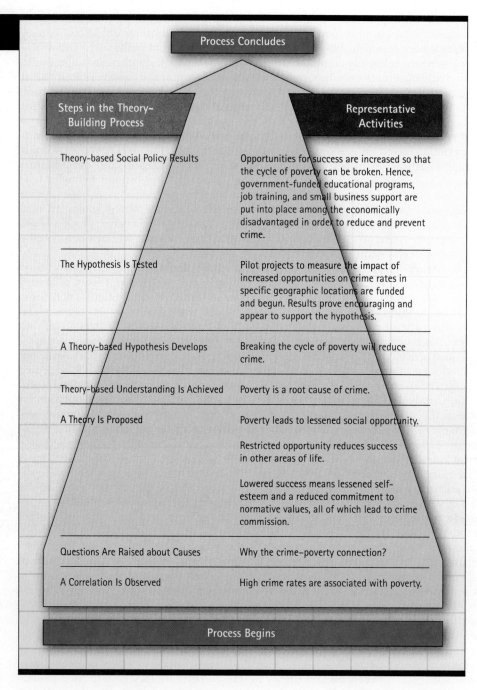

Steps in the Theory-Building Process	Representative Activities
Process Concludes	
Theory-based Social Policy Results	Opportunities for success are increased so that the cycle of poverty can be broken. Hence, government-funded educational programs, job training, and small business support are put into place among the economically disadvantaged in order to reduce and prevent crime.
The Hypothesis Is Tested	Pilot projects to measure the impact of increased opportunities on crime rates in specific geographic locations are funded and begun. Results prove encouraging and appear to support the hypothesis.
A Theory-based Hypothesis Develops	Breaking the cycle of poverty will reduce crime.
Theory-based Understanding Is Achieved	Poverty is a root cause of crime.
A Theory Is Proposed	Poverty leads to lessened social opportunity. Restricted opportunity reduces success in other areas of life. Lowered success means lessened self-esteem and a reduced commitment to normative values, all of which lead to crime commission.
Questions Are Raised about Causes	Why the crime–poverty connection?
A Correlation Is Observed	High crime rates are associated with poverty.
Process Begins	

- Psychological
- Sociological
- Social-psychological
- Conflict
- Phenomenological
- Emergent

interdisciplinary theory

An approach that integrates a variety of theoretical viewpoints in an attempt to explain crime and violence.

The differences among these approaches are summarized in Table 3–1. A tenth category might be that of **interdisciplinary theories**, or approaches that integrate a variety of theoretical viewpoints in an attempt to explain crime and violence. One of the more interesting ongoing interdisciplinary studies of crime causation is Harvard University's Project on

TYPES OF CRIMINOLOGICAL THEORY · TABLE 3-1

Type	Theorists	Characteristics
Classical and Neoclassical		
Free will theories	Beccaria	Crime is caused by the individual exercise of free will. Prevention is possible through swift and certain punishment that offsets any gains to be had through criminal behavior.
Hedonistic calculus	Bentham	
Rational choice theory	Cohen	
Routine activities theory	Felson	
Biological		
Phrenology	Gall	"Criminal genes" cause deviant behavior. Criminals are identifiable through physical characteristics or genetic makeup. Treatment is generally ineffective, but aggression may be usefully redirected.
Atavism	Lombroso	
Criminal families	Dugdale	
	Goddard	
Somatotypes	Sheldon	
Psychobiological		
Chromosome theory	Jacobs	Human DNA, environmental contaminants, nutrition, hormones, physical trauma, and body chemistry play important and interwoven roles in producing human cognition, feeling, and behavior—including crime.
Biochemical approaches		
Heredity	Mednick	
	Wilson	
	Herrnstein	
Psychological		
Behavioral conditioning	Pavlov	Crime is the result of inappropriate behavioral conditioning or a diseased mind. Treatment necessitates extensive behavioral therapy.
Psychoanalysis	Freud	
Psychopathology	Cleckley	
Sociological		
Social disorganization	Park	The structure of society and its relative degree of organization or disorganization are important factors contributing to the prevalence of criminal behavior. Group dynamics, group organization, and subgroup relationships form the causal nexus out of which crime develops. Effective social policy may require basic changes in patterns of socialization and an increase in accepted opportunities for success.
Anomie	Durkheim	
	Merton	
Subcultures	Cohen	
Focal concerns	Burgess	
	McKay	
	Miller	
	Wolfgang	
	Ferracuti	
Social development theory		
Life course perspective	Sampson	
	Laub	
Social-Psychological		
Differential association	Sutherland	Crime results from the failure of self-direction, inadequate social roles, or association with defective others. Social policy places responsibility for change upon the offender.
Social learning	Burgess	
	Akers	
Containment	Reckless	
Social control	Hirschi	
Neutralization	Sykes	
	Matza	

(continued)

TABLE 3-1	TYPES OF CRIMINOLOGICAL THEORY (*continued*)		
	Type	**Theorists**	**Characteristics**
	Conflict		
	Radical criminology	Turk Vold Chambliss	Conflict is fundamental to social life. Crime is a natural consequence of social, political, and economic inequities. Fundamental changes to the structure of society are needed for crime to disappear.
	Peacemaking criminology	Pepinsky Quinney	
	Phenomenological		
	Symbolic interaction Labeling	Mead Becker	The source of criminal behavior is unknown, but an understanding of crime requires recognition that the definition of crime is imposed upon behavior by the wider society. Individuals defined as "criminal" may be excluded by society from "normal" opportunities. Therapy requires a total reorientation of the offender.
	Emergent		
	Feminist criminology	Adler Simon Daly Chesney-Lind	Feminist criminology, which is representative of other new and emerging theories, emphasizes the need for gender awareness in the criminological enterprise.
	Postmodern criminology	Henry Milovanovic	Deconstructionist approaches challenge existing theories in order to replace them with perspectives more relevant to the modern era.

Human Development in Chicago Neighborhoods. Described in more detail later in this chapter, the Harvard project has been examining the role of personality, school, and community features as they contribute to juvenile delinquency and criminal behavior. See **Web Extra! 3–1** at cjtoday.com for more information on the project. **Web Extra! 3–2** at cjtoday.com leads you to more information on the general categories of criminological theory mentioned here, and **Library Extra! 3–1** at cjtoday.com discusses recent theoretical developments in the field of criminological theorizing.

The Classical School

Classical School

An eighteenth-century approach to crime causation and criminal responsibility that grew out of the Enlightenment and that emphasized the role of free will and reasonable punishments. Classical thinkers believed that punishment, if it is to be an effective deterrent, had to outweigh the potential pleasure derived from criminal behavior.

Theories of the **Classical School** of crime causation dominated criminological thought for much of the late eighteenth and early nineteenth centuries. Most classical theories of crime causation, both old and new, make certain basic assumptions. Among them are these:

■ Crime is caused by the individual exercise of free will. Human beings are fundamentally rational, and most human behavior is the result of free will coupled with rational choice.

■ Pain and pleasure are the two central determinants of human behavior.

■ Crime disparages the quality of the bond which exists between individuals and society and is therefore an immoral form of behavior.

■ Punishment, a necessary evil, is sometimes required to deter law violators and to serve as an example to others who would also violate the law.

■ Crime prevention is possible through swift and certain punishment which offsets any gains to be had through criminal behavior.

Cesare Beccaria: Crime and Punishment

In 1764, Cesare Beccaria (1738–1794) published his *Essays on Crimes and Punishment*. The book was an immediate success and stirred a hornet's nest of controversy over the treatment of criminal offenders. Beccaria proposed basic changes in the criminal laws of his day which would make them more "humanitarian." He called for abolition of physical punishment and an end to the death penalty. Beccaria believed in the thoughtful exercise of free will and is best remembered for his suggestion that punishment should be just strong enough to offset the tendency toward crime. Punishment, he said, should be sufficient to deter, but never excessive. Because Beccaria's writings stimulated many other thinkers throughout the eighteenth and early nineteenth century, he is referred to today as the founder of the Classical School of criminology.

Jeremy Bentham: Hedonistic Calculus

Among those influenced by Beccaria was the Englishman Jeremy Bentham (1748–1832). Bentham devised a "hedonistic calculus" in keeping with the idea that the individual exercise of free will would lead people to avoid crime where the benefit to be derived from committing crime was outweighed by the pain of punishment. Bentham termed his philosophy of social control *utilitarianism*. Both Bentham and Beccaria agreed that punishment had to be "swift and certain"—as well as just—to be effective.

The Classical School of criminology represented a noteworthy advance over previous thinking about crime because it moved beyond superstition and mysticism as explanations for deviance. A product of the Enlightenment then sweeping through Europe, the Classical School demanded recognition of rationality and made possible the exercise of informed choice in human social life. Thinkers who were to follow, however, wasted little time in subjugating free will to a secondary role in the search for causal factors in crime commission. As noted criminologist Stephen Schafer puts it, "In the eighteenth-century individualistic orientation of criminal law, the act was judged and the man made responsible. In the next scene in the historic drama of crime, the man is judged and the search is on for finding the responsible factor."[13] Learn more about Jeremy Bentham at **Web Extra! 3–3** at cjtoday.com.

The Neoclassical Perspective

Neoclassical criminology is a contemporary perspective that owes much to the early classical thinkers. Although classical criminology focuses primarily on pleasure and pain as motivators of human behavior, neoclassical criminology places greater emphasis on rationality and cognition. Central to such perspectives is **rational choice theory**, a point of view which holds that criminality is largely the result of conscious choices that people make. According to the theory, offenders choose to violate the law when the benefits of doing so appear to outweigh the costs.

Rational choice theory is represented by a somewhat narrower perspective called **routine activities theory**. Routine activities theory was first proposed by Lawrence Cohen and Marcus Felson in 1979.[14] Cohen and Felson argued that lifestyles contribute significantly to both the volume and type of crime found in any society, and they noted that "the risk of criminal victimization varies dramatically among the circumstances and locations in which people place themselves and their property."[15] For example, a person who routinely uses an automated teller machine late at night in an isolated location is far more likely to be preyed upon by robbers than is someone who stays home after dark. Lifestyles that contribute to criminal opportunities are likely to result in crime because they increase the risk of potential victimization.[16] Rational choice theorists concentrate on "the decision-making process of offenders confronted with specific contexts" and have shifted "the focus of the effort to prevent crime . . . from broad social programs to target hardening, environmental design or any impediment that would [dissuade] a motivated offender from offending."[17]

Central to the routine activities approach is the claim that crime is likely to occur when a motivated offender and a suitable target come together in the absence of a capable guardian. Capable guardians are those who effectively discourage crime and prevent it from occurring. Capable guardians do not necessarily have to confront would-be offenders directly, but might, for example, be people who have completed classes in crime prevention and who have taken steps to reduce their chances of victimization.

neoclassical criminology

A contemporary version of classical criminology which emphasizes deterrence and retribution and which holds that human beings are essentially free to make choices in favor of crime and deviance or conformity.

rational choice theory

A perspective on crime causation which holds that criminality is the result of conscious choice and which predicts that individuals choose to commit crime when the benefits of doing so outweigh the costs of disobeying the law.

routine activities theory

A neoclassical perspective which suggests that lifestyles contribute significantly to both the volume and the type of crime found in any society.

Social Policy and Classical Theories

Much of the practice of criminal justice in America today is built around a conceptual basis provided by Classical School theorists. Many contemporary programs designed to prevent crime have their philosophical roots in the classical axioms of deterrence and punishment. Modern heirs of the Classical School see punishment as a necessary central tenet of criminal justice policy and believe it to be a natural and deserved consequence of criminal activity. Such thinkers call for greater prison capacity and new prison construction. They use evidence of high crime rates to argue that punishment is a necessary crime preventive. In Chapter 1, we used the term *public-order advocates,* and it can be applied to modern-day proponents of classical theory who frequently seek stiffer criminal laws and enhanced penalties for criminal activity. The emphasis on punishment, however, as an appropriate response to crime, whether founded on principles of deterrence or revenge, has left many contemporary criminal justice policy initiatives foundering in overcrowded prisons and courtrooms packed into near paralysis.

Biological Theories

Biological School

A perspective on criminological thought that holds that criminal behavior has a physiological basis.

Most early theories of the **Biological School** of crime causation, which built upon inherited or bodily characteristics and features, made certain fundamental assumptions. Among them are these:

- The basic determinants of human behavior, including criminal tendencies, are, to a considerable degree, constitutionally or genetically based.

- The basic determinants of human behavior, including criminality, may be passed on from generation to generation. In other words, a penchant for crime may be inherited.

- At least some human behavior is the result of biological propensities inherited from more primitive developmental stages in the evolutionary process. Some human beings may be further along the evolutionary ladder than others, and their behavior may reflect it.

Franz Joseph Gall: Phrenology

The idea that the quality of a person can be judged by a study of the person's face is as old as antiquity. Even today, we often judge people on their looks, saying, "He has an honest face" or "She has tender eyes." Horror movies have played upon unspoken cultural themes as to how a "maniac" might look. Jack Nicholson's portrayal of a crazed killer in *The Shining* and Anthony Hopkins's role as a serial killer in *Silence of the Lambs* turned that look into a fortune at the box office.

Franz Joseph Gall (1758–1828) was one of the first thinkers to present systematically the idea that bodily constitution might reflect personality. Gall was writing at a time when it was thought that organs throughout the body determined one's mental state and behavior. People were said to be "hard-hearted" or to have a "bad spleen" which filled them with bile. Gall focused on the head and the brain and called his approach *cranioscopy.* It can be summarized in four propositions:

- The brain is the organ of the mind.
- The brain consists of localized faculties or functions.
- The shape of the skull reveals the underlying development (or corresponding lack of it) of areas within the brain.
- The personality can be revealed by a study of the skull.

phrenology

The study of the shape of the head to determine anatomical correlates of human behavior.

Gall never systematically "tested" his theory in a way that would meet contemporary scientific standards. Even so, his approach to predicting behavior, which came to be known as **phrenology**, quickly spread through Europe. Gall's student, Johann Gaspar Spurzheim (1776–1853), brought phrenology to America in a series of lectures and publications on the subject. By 1825, 29 phrenological journals were being produced in the United States and Britain.[18] Phrenology remained popular in America in some circles until the turn of the twentieth century, where it could still be found in some diagnostic schemes used to classify new prisoners.

Phrenology remains a part of popular culture today. Movies of the fictional Sherlock Holmes depict the great investigator making use of skulls inked with phrenological maps, and personality readings based upon liberal interpretations of Gall's theory are available at some county fairs, church socials, and fortune-telling booths.[19]

Cesare Lombroso: Atavism

Gall's theory was "deterministic" in the sense that it left little room for choice. What a person did depended more upon the shape of the skull than upon any exercise of free will. Other biological theories were soon to build upon that premise. One of the best known is that created by the Italian psychologist Cesare Lombroso (1835–1909).

Lombroso began his criminal anthropology with a postmortem evaluation of famous criminals, including one by the name of Vilella. Lombroso had the opportunity to interview Vilella on a number of occasions. After the man's death, he correlated earlier observations of personality traits with measurable physical abnormalities. As a result of this and other studies, Lombroso concluded that criminals were atavistic human beings—throwbacks to earlier stages of evolution who were not sufficiently mentally advanced for successful life in the modern world. **Atavism** was identifiable in suspicious individuals, Lombroso suggested, through measures designed to reveal "primitive" physical characteristics.

In the late nineteenth century, Charles Darwin's theory of evolution was rapidly being applied to a diversity of fields. It was not surprising, therefore, that Lombroso would make the link between evolution and criminality. What separated Lombroso from his predecessors, however, was his continual refinement of his theory through ongoing observation. Based upon studies of known offenders, whom he compared to conformists, Lombroso identified a large number of atavistic traits, which, he claimed, seemed to characterize criminals. Among them were long arms, large lips, crooked noses, an abnormally large amount of body hair, prominent cheekbones, eyes of different colors, and ears which lacked clearly defined lobes.

Atavism implies the notion of born criminals. Throughout his life Lombroso grappled with the task of identifying the proportion of born criminals from among the total population of offenders. His estimates ranged at different times between 70% and 90%. Career criminals and criminals of opportunity without atavistic features he termed *criminaloids,* and he recognized the potential causative roles of greed, passion, and circumstance in their behavior.

Today, Lombroso is known as the founder of the **Positivist School** of criminology because of the role observation played in the formulation of his theories. Stephen Schafer calls Lombroso "the father of modern criminology,"[20] since most contemporary criminologists follow in the tradition that Lombroso began—scientific observation and a comparison of theory with fact.

atavism

A condition characterized by the existence of features thought to be common in earlier stages of human evolution.

Positivist School

An approach to criminal justice theory that stresses the application of scientific techniques to the study of crime and criminals.

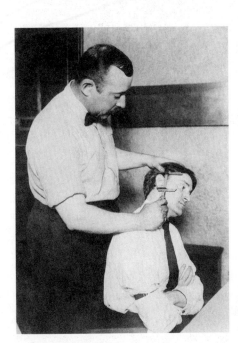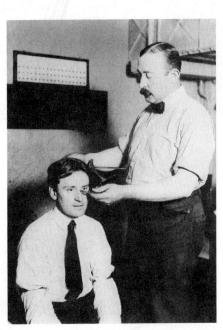

The Bertillion system of identification being applied to a subject in the years prior to the development of fingerprinting. The theory of atavism, based upon the ideas of Charles Darwin, supported the use of physical anthropology in the identification of offenders.

Courtesy of the Library of Congress

THE EVIDENCE FOR AND AGAINST ATAVISM

After Lombroso died, two English physicians, Charles Goring and Karl Pearson, decided to conduct a test of atavism. Goring and Pearson studied more than 3,000 prisoners and compared them along physiological criteria to an army detachment known as the Royal Engineers. No significant differences were found between the two groups, and Lombroso's ideas rapidly began to fall into disrepute.

A further study of atavism was published in 1939 by Ernest A. Hooton, a distinguished Harvard University anthropologist. Hooton had spent 12 years constructing anthropometric profiles of 13,873 male convicts in ten different American states. He measured each inmate in 107 different ways and compared them to 3,203 volunteers from National Guard units, firehouses, beaches, and hospitals. Surprisingly, Hooton did find some basis for Lombroso's beliefs, and he concluded that the inmate population in his study demonstrated a decided physical "inferiority."

Hooton never did recognize the fact, however, that the prisoners he studied were only a subgroup of the population of all offenders throughout the country. They were, in fact, the least successful offenders—the ones who had been caught and imprisoned. Other criminals—the ones who had avoided capture—may have unknowingly been measured by Hooton among his "conformist" population. Hence, the "inferiority" Hooton observed may have been an artificial product of a process of selection (arrest) by the justice system.

Criminal Families

The concept of biological inheritance has been applied to "criminal families" as well as to individuals. The idea of mental degeneration as an inherited contributor to crime was first explored by Richard Dugdale.[21] Dugdale used the family tree method to study a family he called the Jukes, publishing his findings in 1877. The Juke lineage had its beginning in America with "Max" (whose last name is unknown), a descendant of Dutch immigrants to New Amsterdam in the early eighteenth century. Two of Max's sons married into the notorious "Juke family of girls," six sisters, all of whom were illegitimate. Male Jukes were reputed to have been "vicious," while one of the women, named Ada, had an especially bad reputation and eventually came to be known as "the mother of criminals."

Dugdale found that, over the next 75 years, Ada's heirs included 1,200 people, most of whom were "social degenerates." Only a handful of socially productive progeny could be identified. In 1915, Dugdale's study of the Jukes was continued by Arthur A. Estabrook, who extended the line to include 2,094 descendants and found just as few conformists.

A similar study was published by Henry Goddard in 1912.[22] Goddard examined the Kallikak family, which contained two clear lines of descent. One emanated from an affair which Martin Kallikak, a Revolutionary War soldier, had with a "feebleminded" barmaid. She bore a son, and the line eventually produced 480 identifiable descendants. After the war, Kallikak returned home and married a "virtuous" Quaker woman in Philadelphia. This legitimate line produced 496 offspring by 1912, of whom only three were abnormal; none was criminal. The illegitimate group, however, contained over half "feebleminded" or deviant progeny.

The theme which runs through these studies is that crime is an outlet for degenerate urges, produced and propagated through the social group by bad genetic material. Lacking is any recognition of the roles socialization and life circumstances play in the development of criminal behavior.

William Sheldon: Somatotypes

somatotyping

The classification of human beings into types according to body build and other physical characteristics.

The last of the famous constitutional[23] theorists was William Sheldon (1893–1977), who developed the idea of **somatotyping**. Sheldon studied 200 juvenile delinquents between the ages of 15 and 21 at the Hayden Goodwill Institute in Boston, Massachusetts, and decided that the young men possessed one of three somatotypes (or body types). The types of bodies described by Sheldon were (in his words):

- *Mesomorphs* with a relative predominance of muscle, bone, and connective tissue
- *Endomorphs* with a soft roundness throughout the various regions of the body; short tapering limbs; small bones; and soft, smooth, velvety skin
- *Ectomorphs* characterized by thinness, fragility, and delicacy of body

Sheldon developed a system of measurements by which an individual's physique could be expressed as a combination of three numbers, such as 4.0–4.0–3.5 (the representation of an average male). The numbers represented the degree of mesomorphy, endomorphy, and ectomorphy present in the individual on a scale of 0 to 7, where 0 indicates a complete lack of features of one category. American females were said to average 5.0–3.0–3.5 on the scale. Although he wrote that each somatotype was possessed of a characteristic personality, Sheldon believed that predominantly mesomorphic individuals were most prone to aggression, violence, and delinquency.[24]

Social Policy and Biological Theories

Because traditional biological theories of crime causation attribute the cause of crime to fundamental physical characteristics which are not easily modified, they tend to suggest the need for extreme social policies. During the 1920s and early 1930s, for example, biological theories of crime causation, especially those which focused on inherited mental degeneration, led to the eugenics movement, under which mentally handicapped women were sometimes sterilized to prevent their bearing offspring. The eugenics movement was institutionalized by the 1927 U.S. Supreme Court case of *Buck* v. *Bell*,[25] in which Justice Oliver Wendell Holmes, Jr., writing in support of a Virginia statute permitting sterilization, said, "It is better for all the world, if instead of waiting to execute degenerate offspring for crime, or to let them starve for their imbecility, society can prevent those persons who are manifestly unfit from continuing their kind." Visit **Web Extra! 3–4** at cjtoday.com to learn more about biological theories of crime and violence.

Psychobiological Theories

Over the past few decades, a sophisticated approach to biological theorizing about crime causation has arisen. Contemporary biochemical and physiological perspectives are sometimes termed *psychobiology.* The psychobiology of crime highlights the role of human DNA, environmental contaminants, nutrition, hormones, physical trauma (especially to the brain), and body chemistry in human cognition, feeling, and behavior.

Chromosome Theory

The ongoing mapping of human DNA and recent advances in the field of recombinant DNA have rekindled interest in genetic correlates of deviant behavior. More sophisticated than their historical counterparts, the biological theories of today often draw upon the latest medical advances or build upon popular health concerns.

Chromosome theory became an explanation for criminal behavior in the 1960s. A normal female has a chromosome structure often diagrammed as "XX" because of how the sex-determining gene pair looks in an electron microscope. A male has a Y chromosome in place of the second X, for a typical male XY pattern. Although it had been known for some time that a few people had abnormal patterns which included "extra" chromosomes (such as XXX females, XXY males with Klinefelter's syndrome, and XXYY "double males"), it wasn't until the early 1960s that linkages between chromosome patterns and crime were explored. In 1965, the respected English journal *Nature* reported on the work of Patricia Jacobs, who had identified **supermales**—men with an extra Y chromosome. Jacobs found that supermales were more common in prisons than in the general population.[26]

Other early studies claimed that the XYY male was more aggressive than other males and that he possessed a number of specific physical and psychological traits, such as height (over 6′1″), thinness, acne, a tendency toward homosexuality, a somewhat low IQ, and "a marked tendency to commit a succession of apparently motiveless property crimes."[27] Later studies disputed many of these findings, and the significance of the XYY pattern for behavioral prediction is today in doubt.

supermale

A human male displaying the XYY chromosome structure.

Biochemical Factors and Imbalances

Research in the area of nutrition has produced some limited evidence that the old maxim "You are what you eat!" may contain more than a grain of truth. Biocriminology is a field of study which has made some strides in linking violent or disruptive behavior to eating habits, vitamin deficiencies, genetics, inheritance, and other conditions which impact body tissues.

One of the first studies to focus on chemical imbalances in the body as a cause of crime was reported in the British medical journal *Lancet* in 1943.[28] Authors of the study linked murder to hypoglycemia, or low blood sugar. Low blood sugar, produced by too much insulin in the blood or by near-starvation diets, was said to reduce the mind's capacity to reason effectively or to judge the long-term consequences of behavior.

Allergic reactions to common foods have been reported as the cause of violence and homicide in a number of studies.[29] Foods said to produce allergic reactions in sensitive individuals, leading to a swelling of the brain and brain stem, include milk, citrus fruit, chocolate, corn, wheat, and eggs. Involvement of the central nervous system in such allergies, it has been suggested, reduces the amount of learning which occurs during childhood and may contribute to delinquency as well as to adult criminal behavior. Some studies have implicated food additives, such as monosodium glutamate, dyes, and artificial flavorings, in producing criminal behavior.[30]

Other research has found that the amount of coffee and sugar consumed by inmates is considerably greater than in the outside population.[31] Theorists have suggested that high blood levels of caffeine and sugar produce antisocial behavior.[32] It is unclear whether inmates consume more coffee through boredom or whether "excitable" personalities feel a need for the kind of stimulation available through coffee drinking. On the other hand, habitual coffee drinkers in nonprison populations have not been linked to crime, and other studies, such as that conducted by Mortimer Gross of the University of Illinois, show no link between the amount of sugar consumed and hyperactivity.[33] Similarly, studies "have not yielded evidence that a change in diet will result in [a] significant reduction in aggressive or antisocial behavior" among inmate populations.[34] Nonetheless, some prison programs have limited the intake of dietary stimulants through nutritional management and the substitution of artificial sweeteners for refined sugar.

Vitamins have also been examined for their impact on delinquency. Abram Hoffer found that disruptive children consumed far less than the optimum levels of vitamins B_3 and B_6 than did nonproblem youths.[35] He claimed that the addition of these vitamins to the diets of children who were deficient in them could control unruly behavior and improve school performance.

The role of food and diet in producing criminal behavior, however, has not been well established. The American Dietetic Association and the National Council against Health Fraud have concluded that no convincing scientific relationship between crime and diet has yet been demonstrated.[36] Both groups are becoming concerned that poor nutrition may result from programs intended to have behavioral impacts and that reduce or modify diets in prisons or elsewhere.

Hormones have also come under scrutiny as potential behavioral determinants. The male sex hormone, testosterone, has been linked to aggressiveness in males. Some studies of blood-serum levels of testosterone have shown a direct relationship[37] between the amount of chemical present and the degree of violence used by sex offenders,[38] and steroid abuse among bodybuilders has been linked to destructive urges and psychosis.[39] One 1998 study found that high levels of testosterone, especially when combined with low socioeconomic status, produced antisocial personalities, resulting in deviance and criminality.[40]

Some studies of brain chemistry have led researchers to conclude that low levels of certain neurotransmitters, especially serotonin, are directly related to a person's inability to control aggressive impulses.[41] The presence of adequate serotonin levels in the human brain seems to buffer irritating experiences which might otherwise result in anger and aggression. Low serotonin levels may result from the ingestion of toxic pollutants, such as the metals lead and manganese, according to one 1997 study.[42] Reduced serotonin levels, say other researchers, may also be found in men with an extra Y chromosome.[43]

A malfunctioning endocrine system has also been implicated by researchers as a cause of physical abuse, antisocial behavior, and psychopathology. A Swedish study published in 1999 focused on variations in blood-serum levels of two thyroid hormones: triiodothyronine (T3) and thyroxine (FT4).[44] Researchers found that elevated T3 levels were related to alcoholism and criminality. Serum levels of FT4 were found to be negatively correlated to such behavior.

Heredity and Environment

As in the 1998 testosterone study, some contemporary biological theorists have identified an environmental linkage. Sarnoff Mednick, for example, has found some basis for the claim that the autonomic nervous system (ANS) predisposes certain individuals toward criminality by limiting their ability to learn quickly.[45] Those with a slow ANS are thought to be unable to inhibit antisocial behavior quickly enough to avoid punishment and stigmatization.[46] Also, physical trauma, especially brain injury, has been shown to be capable of inducing severe personality changes, including aggression and violent behavior in people with a previous behavioral history of neither.[47] Similarly, people born with certain abnormalities of the brain, especially frontal lobe dysfunction, may display a penchant for violence.[48] Frontal lobe dysfunction is sometimes caused by reduced cerebral blood flow.

Studies of children adopted at birth have shown a tendency for the criminality of biological parents to be reflected in the behavior of their children, independent of the environment in which the children were raised.[49] Identical twins seem to exhibit a greater similarity in behavior than do nonidentical (or "fraternal") twins, and a number of studies have shown that identical twins are more alike in patterns and degree of criminal involvement than are fraternal twins.[50]

Perhaps the best known of modern-day biological perspectives on crime was proposed by James Q. Wilson and Richard Herrnstein in their book *Crime and Human Nature,* published in 1985.[51] Wilson and Herrnstein argue that inherited traits, such as maleness, aggressiveness, mesomorphic body type, and low intelligence, combine with environmental influences, including poor schools and strained family life, to produce crime. Although the authors reject a firm determinism, asserting that it is the interaction between genetics and environment that determines behavior, they do claim that children who will eventually grow up to be criminals can sometimes be identified early in their lives. The most important factor in the diversion of potential offenders from lives of crime, according to Wilson and Herrnstein, is a healthy family life in which affection for others and conscience can develop.[52] Wilson and Herrnstein also use cross-cultural data from Japan, where crime rates are very low, to suggest that inherited tendencies toward introversion among the Japanese result in fewer serious crimes than in the United States. The Wilson-Herrnstein thesis has been criticized for failing to explain crime that extends beyond "traditional lower-class street crime" and for failing to recognize the political nature of criminal definitions.[53]

Social Policy and Psychobiological Theories

Psychobiological theories tend to suggest modifying body chemistry to produce desirable behavioral changes. Hence, just as researchers working with recombinant DNA techniques seek to create a "magic bullet" which might target defective chromosomes in the human immune system which allow for the growth of cancerous tissue, others envision the day when similar techniques might be applied to the prevention and control of crime. If a gene for crime can be found, such researchers suggest, it might be turned off. In the meantime, psychobiologists have to be content with medicinal approaches to the treatment of crime and violence, employing tranquilizers, antipsychotics, mood-altering substances, and other drugs.

While drug treatments fashioned after psychobiological perspectives may appear to control aggressive and criminal behavior, at least temporarily, there is little evidence to suggest that they produce lasting results. In 1993, all biologically based theories of crime and violence were called into question by the National Academy of Sciences, whose review of hundreds of studies on the relationship among biology, violence, and crime concluded that "no patterns precise enough to be considered reliable biological markers for violent behavior have yet been identified."[54] The study did, however, find what it called "promising leads for future research."

Psychological Theories

Theories of the **Psychological School** of crime causation have an increasingly significant place in the criminological literature. Most psychological theories of crime make certain fundamental assumptions. Among them are these:

- The individual is the primary unit of analysis.
- Personality is the major motivational element within individuals, since it is the seat of drives and the source of motives.

> When internal cultures conflict, it can be as destructive as a collision between an iceberg and an ocean liner. Misunderstanding between two cultural groups can lead to conflict and, taken to the extreme, physical confrontations.
>
> —Sherman Block, Los Angeles County Sheriff

Psychological School

A perspective on criminological thought that views offensive and deviant behavior as the product of dysfunctional personalities. Psychological thinkers identify the conscious, and especially the subconscious, contents of the human psyche as major determinants of behavior.

- Crimes result from inappropriately conditioned behavior *or* from abnormal, dysfunctional, or inappropriate mental processes within the personality.

- Defective or abnormal mental processes may have a variety of causes, including a diseased mind and inappropriate learning or improper conditioning—often occurring in early childhood.

Behavioral Conditioning

behavioral conditioning

A psychological principle that holds that the frequency of any behavior can be increased or decreased through reward, punishment, and association with other stimuli.

A twin thread was woven through early psychological theories. One emphasized **behavioral conditioning**, while the other focused mostly on personality disturbances and diseases of the mind. Taken together, these two foci constituted the early field of psychological criminology. Conditioning is a psychological principle which holds that the frequency of any behavior, including criminal or deviant behavior, can be increased or decreased through reward, punishment, and association with other stimuli. The concept of conditioned behavior was popularized through the work of the Russian physiologist Ivan Pavlov (1849–1936), whose work with dogs won him the Nobel Prize in physiology and medicine in 1904. Similarly, behavioral psychologists suggest that criminal behavior, which may be inherently rewarding under many circumstances, tends to be more common in those who are able to avoid punishment when involved in rule-breaking behavior.

Freudian Psychoanalysis

psychoanalysis

A theory of human behavior, based upon the writings of Sigmund Freud, that sees personality as a complex composite of interacting mental entities.

The name most widely associated with the field of psychology is that of Sigmund Freud (1856–1939). Freudian theory posits the existence of an id, an ego, and a superego within the personality.[55] The id is the source of drives, which are seen as primarily sexual. The ego is a rational mental entity, which outlines paths through which the desires of the id can be fulfilled. It has often been called the *reality principle* because of the belief that it relates desires to practical behavioral alternatives. The superego is a guiding principle, often compared to conscience, which judges the quality of the alternatives presented by the ego according to the standards of right and wrong acquired by the personality of which it is a part. Freud wrote very little about crime, but his followers, who developed the school of Freudian **psychoanalysis**, believed that crime could result from at least three conditions.

The first possible source of criminal behavior is a weak superego, which cannot responsibly control the drives which emanate from the id. Sex crimes, crimes of passion, murder, and other violent crimes are thought to follow inadequate superego development. People

A battered woman turning away from her husband. When a woman is victimized, it is often at the hands of an "intimate other," such as a spouse or a boyfriend. Sigmund Freud suggested that a male perpetrator of spousal violence may be symbolically acting out a deep-seated resentment toward women that resulted from his relationship with his mother when he was a child. This kind of theoretical perspective, however, is rarely given credence by criminologists today.

SuperStock, Inc.

Charles Manson, one of the most photographed criminal offenders of all time, 20 years after he and his "family" shocked the world with their gruesome crimes.

Grey Villet, Black Star

who lack fully developed superegos are often called *psychopaths* or *sociopaths* to indicate that they cannot see beyond their own interests. Freudian psychologists would probably agree with Canadian criminologist Gwynn Nettler, who has observed that "civilization is paid for through development of a sense of guilt."[56]

Freud also created the concept of sublimation to explain the process by which one thing is symbolically substituted for another. He believed that sublimation was necessary when the direct pursuit of one's desires was not possible. Freud suggested, for example, that many children learned to sublimate negative feelings about their mothers. In the society in which Freud developed his theories, mothers closely controlled the lives of their children, and Freud saw the developing child as continually frustrated in seeking freedom to act on his or her own. The strain produced by this conflict could not be directly expressed by the child because the mother also controlled rewards and punishments. Hence, dislike for one's mother (which Freud thought was especially strong in boys) might show itself symbolically later in life. Crimes against women could then be explained as being committed by men expressing a symbolic hatred.

A final Freudian explanation for criminality is based upon the death wish, or Thanatos, which Freud believed each of us carries. Thanatos is the often unrecognized desire of animate matter to return to the inanimate. Potentially self-destructive activities, including smoking, speeding, skydiving, bad diets, "picking fights," and so on, can be explained by Thanatos. The self-destructive wish may also motivate offenders to commit crimes which are themselves dangerous or self-destructive—such as burglary, assault, murder, prostitution, and drug use—or it may result in unconscious efforts to be caught. Criminals who leave evidence behind, sometimes even items of personal identification like a driver's license, may be responding to some basic need for apprehension and punishment.

Psychopathology and Crime

From a psychiatric point of view, crime might also occur because of a diseased mind or a disordered personality—conditions which may collectively be referred to as *psychopathy*. (The study of psychopathic mental conditions is called **psychopathology**.) The role of a disordered personality in crime causation was central to early psychiatric theorizing. In 1944, for example, the well-known psychiatrist David Abrahamsen wrote, "When we seek to explain the riddle of human conduct in general and of antisocial behavior in particular, the solution must be sought in the personality."[57] In later years, some psychiatrists went so far as to claim that criminal behavior itself is only a symptom of a more fundamental psychiatric disorder.[58]

psychopathology

The study of pathological mental conditions—that is, mental illness.

By the 1950s, psychiatrists had developed the concept of a psychopathic personality. The **psychopath**, also called a *sociopath*, is seen as perversely cruel—often without thought or feeling for his or her victims. The concept of a psychopathic personality, which by its very definition is asocial, was fully developed by Hervey Cleckley in his 1964 book, *The Mask of Sanity*.[59] Cleckley described the psychopath as a "moral idiot," or as one who does not feel empathy with others even though the person may be fully cognizant of what is objectively happening around him or her. The central defining characteristic of a psychopath is poverty of affect, or the inability to accurately imagine how others think and feel. Hence, it becomes possible for a psychopath to inflict pain and engage in cruelty without appreciation for the victim's suffering. Charles Manson, for example, whom some have called a psychopath, once told a television reporter, "I could take this book and beat you to death with it, and I wouldn't feel a thing. It'd be just like walking to the drugstore." According to Cleckley, psychopathic indicators appear early in life, often in the teenage years. They include lying, fighting, stealing, and vandalism. Even earlier signs may be found, according to some authors, in bed-wetting, cruelty to animals, sleepwalking, and fire setting.[60]

While the terms *psychopath* and *criminal* are not synonymous, individuals manifesting characteristics of a psychopathic personality are likely, sooner or later, to run afoul of the law. As one writer says, "The impulsivity and aggression, the selfishness in achieving one's own immediate needs, and the disregard for society's rules and laws bring these people to the attention of the criminal justice system."[61]

Although much studied, the causes of psychopathology are unclear. Somatogenic causes, or those which are based upon physiological aspects of the human organism, are said to include (1) a malfunctioning central nervous system characterized by a low state of arousal, which drives the sufferer to seek excitement, and (2) brain abnormalities, which may be present in most psychopaths from birth. Psychogenic causes, or those rooted in early interpersonal experiences, are thought to include the inability to form attachments to parents or other caregivers early in life, sudden separation from the mother during the first six months of life, and other forms of insecurity during the first few years of life. In short, a lack of love or the sensed inability to unconditionally depend upon one central loving figure (typically the mother in most psychological literature) immediately following birth is often posited as a major psychogenic factor contributing to psychopathic development. Learn more about psychopathology and crime at **Library Extra! 3–2** at cjtoday.com. Read more about the Manson murders at **Web Extra! 3–5** at cjtoday.com.

The Psychotic Offender

Another form of mental disorder is called **psychosis**. Psychotic people, according to psychiatric definitions, are out of touch with reality in some fundamental way. They may suffer from hallucinations, delusions, or other breaks with reality. The classic psychotic thinks he or she is Napoleon or sees spiders covering what others perceive as a bare wall. Psychoses may be either organic (that is, caused by physical damage to, or abnormalities in, the brain) or functional (that is, with no known physical cause). Psychotic people have also been classified as schizophrenic or paranoid schizophrenic. **Schizophrenics** are said to be characterized by disordered or disjointed thinking, in which the types of logical associations they make are atypical of other people. Paranoid schizophrenics suffer from delusions and hallucinations.

Psychoses may lead to crime in a number of ways. Following the Vietnam War, for example, a number of instances were reported in which former American soldiers suffering from a kind of battlefield psychosis killed friends and family members, thinking they were enemy soldiers. These men, who had been traumatized by battlefield experiences in Southeast Asia, relived their past on American streets.

Psychological Profiling

Psychological profiling is the attempt to derive a composite picture of an offender's social and psychological characteristics from the crime he or she committed and from the manner in which it was committed. Psychological profiling began during World War II as an effort by William Langer (1896–1977), a government psychiatrist hired by the Office of Strategic Services, to predict Adolf Hitler's actions.[62] Profiling in criminal investigations is

psychopath

A person with a personality disorder, especially one manifested in aggressively antisocial behavior, which is often said to be the result of a poorly developed superego.

psychosis

A form of mental illness in which sufferers are said to be out of touch with reality.

schizophrenic

A mentally ill individual who suffers from disjointed thinking and possibly from delusions and hallucinations.

psychological profiling

The attempt to categorize, understand, and predict the behavior of certain types of offenders based upon behavioral clues they provide.

Jeffrey Dahmer, accused in the dismemberment slayings of more than a dozen young men, listening as the charges against him are read. The crimes of some law violators seem to defy explanation. Dahmer, ordered to serve multiple life sentences, was killed in prison by another inmate.

Allan Fredrikson, Reuters, CORBIS

based upon the belief that criminality, because it is a form of behavior, can be viewed as symptomatic of the offender's personality. Psychological evaluations of crime scenes, including the analysis of evidence, are used to re-create the offender's frame of mind during the commission of the crime. A profile of the offender is then constructed to help in the investigation of suspects.

During the 1980s, the Federal Bureau of Investigation led the movement toward psychological profiling[63] through its focus on violent sex offenses[64] and arson.[65] FBI profilers described what they termed *lust murderers* and serial arsonists. Often depicted as loners with an aversion to casual social contact, lust murderers were shown rarely to arouse suspicions in neighbors or employers. Other personality characteristics became the focus of police efforts to arrest such offenders through a prediction of what they might do next.

In the mid-1990s, caregivers who suffer from a disorder called *Munchausen syndrome by proxy* (MSBP) became the subject of profilers. MSBP, which has not yet been accepted by the courts as a defense to criminal charges, involves "subject[s] (who) injure or induce illnesses in their children in order to gain attention and sympathy for themselves."[66] Most perpetrators are women, and the majority make their own children sick so that they themselves can receive attention from relatives, doctors, and health treatment personnel. Profilers have found that MSBP is a serial offense, although in families with multiple children only one child is usually affected at a time. Most MSBP offenders have been found to possess the following characteristics: a history of self-inflicted injuries (called *Munchausen syndrome,* but involving no "proxy"); past psychiatric treatment; a history of attempted suicides; an upper-class or upper-middle-class background; a good education; and a medical background or medical education of some sort. MSBP sufferers also remain uncharacteristically calm, welcome medical tests that are painful for the child, praise medical staffs excessively, appear knowledgeable about the victim's illness, shelter the victim from school and other outside activities, allow only selected people close to their children, stay very attentive to the victim, and find emotional satisfaction when the child is hospitalized.

Other new areas for psychological profiling include hostage negotiation[67] and international terrorism.[68] Right-wing terrorist groups in the United States have also been the subject of profiling efforts.

A television cameraman pointing his lens toward a poster of Osama bin Laden during an event in Washington in late 2001 to showcase the FBI's new "Most Wanted" list of international terrorists. Some criminal offenders are motivated by "causes"—whether real or imaginary.

© REUTERS NewMedia, Inc./Kevin Lamarque/CORBIS

dangerousness

The likelihood that a given individual will later harm society or others. Dangerousness is often measured in terms of recidivism, or as the likelihood of additional crime commission within five years following arrest or release from confinement.

Chicago School

A sociological approach which emphasizes demographics (the characteristics of population groups) and geographics (the mapped location of such groups relative to one another) and which sees the social disorganization that characterizes delinquency areas as a major cause of criminality and victimization.

Social Policy and Psychological Theories

Like psychological theories themselves, crime-control policies based upon psychological perspectives tend to be primarily individualistic. They are oriented toward individualized treatment, characteristically exposing the individual offender to various forms of therapy intended to overcome the person's penchant for criminality.

One special emphasis of most crime-control strategies based upon psychological theories is the attempt to assess personal **dangerousness**, a process which involves psychological testing and other efforts intended to identify personality-based characterics which predict interpersonal aggression. Although the ability to accurately predict future dangerousness is of great concern to today's policymakers, definitions of dangerousness are fraught with difficulty. As some authors have pointed out, "Dangerousness is not an objective quality like obesity or brown eyes, rather it is an ascribed quality like trustworthiness."[69] Hence, dangerousness is not necessarily a personality trait which is stable or easily identifiable. Even if it were, some studies of criminal careers seem to show that involvement in crime decreases with age.[70] As one author puts it, if "criminality declines more or less uniformly with age, then many offenders will be 'over the hill' by the time they are old enough to be plausible candidates for preventive incarceration."[71]

Before crime-control policies can be based upon present understandings of dangerousness, we need to ask, Can past behavior predict future behavior? Do former instances of criminality presage additional ones? Are there other, identifiable, characteristics which violent offenders might manifest which could serve as warning signs to criminal justice decision makers faced with the dilemma of whether to release convicted felons? This, like many other areas, is one in which criminologists are still learning.

Sociological Theories

Sociological theories are largely an American contribution to the study of crime causation. In the 1920s and 1930s, the famous **Chicago School** of sociology explained criminality as a product of society's impact upon the individual. The structure of prevailing social arrangements, the interaction between individuals and groups, and the social environment were all seen as major determinants of criminal behavior.

Sociological perspectives on crime causation are quite diverse. Most such perspectives, however, build upon certain fundamental assumptions. Among them are these:

- Social groups, social institutions, the arrangements of society, and social roles all provide the proper focus for criminological study.
- Group dynamics, group organization, and subgroup relationships form the causal nexus out of which crime develops.
- The structure of society and the relative degree of social organization or **social disorganization** are important factors contributing to the prevalence of criminal behavior.

All sociological perspectives on crime share the foregoing characteristics, but particular theories may give greater or lesser weight to the following aspects of social life:

- The clash of norms and values among variously socialized groups
- Socialization and the process of association between individuals
- The existence of subcultures and varying types of opportunities

social disorganization

A condition said to exist when a group is faced with social change, uneven development of culture, maladaptiveness, disharmony, conflict, and lack of consensus.

Social Ecology Theory

In the 1920s, during the early days of sociological theorizing, the University of Chicago brought together such thinkers as Robert Park,[72] Ernest Burgess, Clifford Shaw, and Henry McKay.[73] Park and Burgess recognized that Chicago, like most cities, could be mapped according to its social characteristics. Their map resembled a target with a bull's-eye in the center. Shaw and McKay adapted these concentric zones to the study of crime when they realized that the zones nearest the center of the city had the highest crime rates. In particular, zone 2 (one removed from the center) consistently showed the highest crime rate over time, regardless of the groups or nationalities inhabiting it. This "zone of transition" (so called because new immigrant groups moved into it as earlier ones became integrated into American culture and moved out) demonstrated that crime was dependent to a considerable extent upon aspects of the social structure of the city itself. Structural elements identified by Shaw and McKay included poverty, illiteracy, lack of schooling, unemployment, and illegitimacy. In combination, these elements were seen to lead to social disorganization, which in turn produced crime.

Anomie Theory

The French word **anomie** has been loosely translated as a condition of "normlessness." Anomie entered the literature as a sociological concept with the writings of Émile Durkheim (1858–1917) in the late nineteenth century.[74] Robert Merton (1910–) applied anomie to criminology in 1938 when he used the term to describe a disjunction between socially acceptable goals and means in American society.[75]

anomie

A socially pervasive condition of normlessness. Also, a disjunction between approved goals and means.

Merton believed that while the same goals and means are held out by society as desirable for everyone to participate in, they are not equally available to all. Socially approved goals in American society, for example, include wealth, status, and political power. The acceptable means to achieve these goals are education, wise investment, and hard work. Unfortunately, however, opportunities are not equally distributed throughout society, and some people turn to illegitimate means to achieve the goals they are pressured to reach. Still others reject both the acceptable goals and the legitimate means to reach them.

Merton represented his theory with a chart, shown in Table 3–2, in which conformists are seen to accept both the goals and means which society holds out as legitimate, while innovators accept the goals but reject the means. It is innovators whom Merton identified as criminal. (They are not *inventors,* as invention is a legitimate path to success, but rather *innovators* in the use of illegal means to gain money, power, and success.) The inherent logic of the model led Merton to posit other social types. Ritualists are said to be those who reject success goals but still perform their daily tasks in conformity with social expectations. They might hold regular jobs, but without the desire to advance in life. Retreatists reject both the goals and the means and usually drop out of society by becoming derelicts, drug users, or the like. Rebels constitute a special category—in which the existence of both "pluses" and "minuses" indicate their desire to replace the existing system of socially approved goals and means with some other system more to their liking. They are the revolutionaries of the theory.

CJ Futures

[The Physical Environment and Crime]

Social ecology theory, an outgrowth of the Chicago School of sociological thought which flourished during the 1920s and 1930s, posited a link between physical location and crime. A modern perspective, called *crime prevention through environmental design* (CPTED), bears a strong resemblance to earlier ecological theories. CPTED, which was first formulated in the 1960s and 1970s, focuses on the settings in which crimes occur and on techniques for reducing vulnerability within those settings. Because defensible space concepts are being increasingly applied to the design of physical facilities, including housing, parking garages, public buildings, and even entire neighborhoods, it is highly likely that applications of CPTED will accelerate throughout the twenty-first century.

Second-generation **defensible space theory,** upon which contemporary CPTED is built, developed around 1980 and considered more carefully how the impact of physical features on fear and victimizations depends upon other social and cultural features in the setting. Second-generation defensible space theory employed the **broken windows thesis,** which holds that physical deterioration and an increase in unrepaired buildings lead to increased concerns for personal safety among area residents. Heightened concerns, in turn, lead to further decreases in maintenance and repair and to increased delinquency, vandalism, and crime among local residents—which spawns even further deterioration in both a sense of safety and in the physical environment. Offenders from other neighborhoods are then increasingly attracted by the area's perceived vulnerability.

Research on CPTED has shown environmental design to be effective in lowering crime and crime-related public-order problems. Effective use of CPTED to alter features of the physical environment can affect potential offenders' perceptions about a possible crime site, their evaluations of the opportunities associated with that site, and the availability and visibility of one or more natural guardians at or near the site. CPTED is based upon the belief that offenders decide whether to commit a crime in a particular location after they evaluate the area's features, including (1) the ease of entry to the area, (2) the visibility of the target to others—that is, the chance of being seen, (3) the attractiveness or vulnerability of the target, (4) the likelihood that criminal behavior will be challenged or thwarted if discovered, and (5) the ease of egress (that is, the ability to quickly and easily leave the area once the crime has been committed).

According to the National Institute of Justice, CPTED suggests four approaches to making a location more resistant to crime and to crime-related public-order problems:

■ *Housing design or block layout*—making it more difficult to commit crimes by (1) reducing the availability of crime targets, (2) removing barriers that prevent easy detection of potential offenders or of an offense in progress, and (3) increasing physical obstacles to committing a crime.

■ *Land use and circulation patterns*—creating safer use of neighborhood space by reducing routine exposure of potential offenders to crime targets. This can be accomplished through careful attention to walkways, paths, streets, traffic patterns, and location and hours of operation of public spaces and facilities. Street closings or revised traffic patterns that decrease vehicular volume may, under some conditions, encourage residents to better maintain the sidewalks and streets in front of their houses.

A run-down city street. To explain crime, criminologists sometimes use the "broken windows" approach, which says that neighborhood deterioration leads to rising crime rates. Similarly, poverty, unemployment, a relative lack of formal education, and low skill levels, which often characterize inner-city populations, seem to be linked to criminality.

Peter Byron, PhotoEdit

■ *Territorial features*—encouraging the use of territorial markers or fostering conditions that will lead to more extensive marking to indicate that the block or site is occupied by vigilant residents. Sponsoring cleanup and beautification contests and creating controllable, semiprivate outdoor locations may encourage such activities. This strategy focuses on small-scale, private, and semi-public sites, usually within predominantly residential locales. It is most relevant at the street-block level and below. It enhances the chances that residents themselves will generate semifixed features that demonstrate their involvement in and watchfulness over a particular delimited location.

■ *Physical maintenance*—controlling physical deterioration to reduce offenders' perceptions that areas are vulnerable to crime and that residents are so fearful they would do nothing to stop a crime. Physical improvements may reduce the signals of vulnerability and increase commitment to joint protective activities.

Physical deterioration, in all probability, not only influences the cognition and behavior of potential offenders, but also shapes how residents behave and what they think about other residents.

For additional information on CPTED via the Crime Mapping Research Center, see **Web Extra! 3-6** at cjtoday.com.

❓ DISCUSSION QUESTIONS

1. Consider the area that surrounds your campus. (If you are a distance-learning student, you might examine the area around your home.) How might it be made safer by employing CPTED principles? How might your campus be made safer?

2. Someone has to pay for the physical changes and improvements required to implement defensible space concepts. How can needed renovations be made in poor neighborhoods? Who would pay the bill?

Sources: Oscar Newman, *Defensible Space* (New York: Macmillan, 1972); Oscar Newman, *Creating Defensible Space* (Washington, D.C.: Office of Housing and Urban Development, 1996); James Q. Wilson and George Kelling, "Broken Windows," *Atlantic Monthly*, March 1982; Dan Fleissner and Fred Heinzelmann, *Crime Prevention through Environmental Design and Community Policing* (Washington, D.C.: National Institute of Justice, 1996); Ralph B. Taylor and Adele V. Harrell, *Physical Environment and Crime* (Washington, D.C.: National Institute of Justice, 1996); Mary S. Smith, *Crime Prevention through Environmental Design in Parking Facilities* (Washington, D.C.: National Institute of Justice, 1996); and Corey L. Gordon and William Brill, *The Expanding Role of Crime Prevention through Environmental Design in Premises Liability* (Washington, D.C.: National Institute of Justice, 1996).

---

defensible space theory

The belief that an area's physical features may be modified and structured so as to reduce crime rates in that area and to lower the fear of victimization which residents experience.

broken windows thesis

A perspective on crime causation which holds that physical deterioration in an area leads to increased concerns for personal safety among residents and to higher crime rates.

Merton believed that categories are not intentionally selected by the individuals who occupied them, but rather are imposed on people by structural aspects of society. Such factors as where people live, how wealthy their family is, and what ethnic background they come from are all thought to be significant determinants of the "box" into which people are placed.

Modern writers on anomie have come to recognize that normlessness is not likely to be expressed as criminality unless people who experience it also feel that they are capable of doing something to change their lives. As Catherine Ross and John Mirowsky put it, "A person who has high levels of normlessness and powerlessness is less likely to get in trouble with the law than a person who has a high level of normlessness and a high level of instrumentalism."[76]

MERTON'S ANOMIE THEORY AND IMPLIED TYPES OF CRIMINALITY			**TABLE 3-2**

Category	Goals	Means	Examples
Conformist	+	+	Law-abiding behavior
Innovator	+	−	Property offenses
			White-collar crimes
Retreatist	−	−	Drug use/addiction, vagrancy, some "victimless" crimes
Ritualist	−	+	A repetitive and mundane lifestyle
Rebel	±	±	Political crime (for example, environmental activists who violate the law, violence-prone antiabortionists)

Source: Adapted with the permission of the Free Press, a Division of Simon & Schuster, Inc., from *Social Theory and Social Structure*, 1968 Enlarged Edition by Robert K. Merton. Copyright © 1967, 1968 by Robert K. Merton.

Merton's anomie theory drew attention to the lack of equality of opportunity which existed in society at the time he was writing. An honest appraisal would probably recognize that while considerable efforts have been made to eradicate it, some of that same inequality continues today.

Subcultural Theory

Another sociological contribution to criminological theory is the idea of a subculture. A subculture is composed of a group of people who participate in a shared system of values and norms which are at variance with those in the larger culture. Subcultural explanations of crime posit the existence of group values supportive of criminal behavior. Subcultures were first recognized in the enclaves formed by immigrants who came to America during the early part of the twentieth century. Statistics have shown that certain immigrant groups had low crime rates.[77] Among them were the Scandinavians, Chinese, Dutch, Germans, and Japanese. Other immigrant groups, including Italians, Mexicans, Puerto Ricans, and Africans, demonstrated a significantly greater propensity for involvement in crime.[78]

Albert Cohen (1918–) coined the term **reaction formation** to encompass the rejection of middle-class values by status-seeking lower-class youths who find they are not permitted access to approved opportunities for success.[79] In Cohen's eyes, reaction formation leads to the development of gangs and perpetuates the existence of subcultures. Walter Miller described the focal concerns of subcultural participants in terms of "trouble," "toughness," "excitement," "smartness," "fate," and "autonomy."[80] It is a focus on such concerns, Miller suggested, that leads members of criminal subcultures into violations of the law. Richard Cloward and Lloyd Ohlin proposed the existence of an illegitimate opportunity structure that permits delinquent youths to achieve in ways which are outside of legitimate avenues to success.[81]

During the 1950s, Marvin Wolfgang and Franco Ferracuti examined homicide rates in Philadelphia and found that murder was a way of life among certain groups.[82] They discovered a "wholesale" and a "retail" price for murder—which depended upon who was killed and who did the killing. Killings which occurred within violent subgroups were more likely to be partially excused than were those that happened elsewhere. The term **subculture of violence** has come to be associated with their work and has since been applied to other locations across the country.

Critiques of subcultural theory have been numerous. A major difficulty for these theories lies in the fact that studies involving self-reports of crime commission have shown that much violence and crime occur outside of "criminal" subcultures. It appears that many middle- and upper-class lawbreakers are able to avoid the justice system and therefore do not enter the "official" crime statistics. Hence, criminal subcultures may be those in which crime is more visible rather than more prevalent.

The Life Course Perspective

Some of the most recent perspectives on crime causation belong to a subcategory of sociological thought called **social development theory**. According to the social development perspective, human development occurs on many levels simultaneously, including psychological, biological, familial, interpersonal, cultural, societal, and ecological. Hence, social development theories tend to be integrated theories—that is, theories that combine various points of view on the process of development. Theories that fall into this category, however, tend to highlight the process of interaction between individuals and society as the root cause of criminal behavior. In particular, they emphasize that a critical period of transition occurs in a person's life as he or she moves from childhood to adulthood.

One social development perspective of special significance is the **life course perspective**. According to Robert Sampson and John Laub,[83] who named the life course perspective in 1993, criminal behavior tends to follow an identifiable pattern throughout a person's life cycle. In the lives of those who eventually become criminal, crimelike or deviant behavior is relatively rare during early childhood, tends to begin as sporadic instances during early adolescence, becomes more common during the late-teen and early-adult years, and then gradually diminishes as the person gets older.

Sampson and Laub also used the idea of *transitions* in the life course, or turning points that identify significant events in a person's life and represent the opportunity for people

---

reaction formation

The process whereby a person openly rejects that which he or she wants or aspires to but cannot obtain or achieve.

subculture of violence

A cultural setting in which violence is a traditional and often accepted method of dispute resolution.

social development theory

An integrated view of human development that points to the process of interaction among and between individuals and society as the root cause of criminal behavior.

life course perspective

An approach to explaining crime and deviance that investigates developments and turning points in the course of a person's life over time.

to turn either away from, or toward, deviance and crime. An employer who gives an employee a second chance, for example, may provide a unique opportunity that helps determine the future course of that person's life. Similarly, the principle of *linked lives*, also common to life course theories, highlights the fact that no one lives in isolation. Events in the life course are constantly being influenced by family members, friends, acquaintances, employers, teachers, and so on. Not only may such influences determine the life course of any given individual, but also they are active throughout the life course. Figure 3–2 diagrams some of the life course influences experienced by most adolescents. Also shown in the diagram are positive and negative indicators of development, and desired outcomes.

In 1986, the federal Office of Juvenile Justice and Delinquency Prevention (OJJDP) began funding a study of life pathways as they lead to criminality. The study, which is known as the Program of Research on the Causes and Correlates of Delinquency, continues to produce results.[84] Researchers have been examining how delinquency, violence, and drug use develop within and are related to various social contexts, including the family, peer groups, schools, and the surrounding community. To date, the study has identified three distinct pathways to delinquency, which are shown in Figure 3–3. These pathways are not mutually exclusive and can sometimes converge:

- *The authority conflict pathway*, along which children begin to move during their early years (as early as three or four years old), involves stubborn behavior and resistance to parental authority. Defiance of authority begins around age 11, and authority avoidance (that is, truancy, running away) begins about the same time.

- *The covert pathway*, which starts with minor covert acts like shoplifting and lying around age 10, quickly progresses to acts of vandalism involving property damage. Moderate to severe delinquency frequently begins a year or two later.

- *The overt pathway* is marked by minor aggression, such as bullying, that develops around age 11 or 12. The overt pathway leads to fighting and physical violence during the teenage years and tends to eventuate in serious violent criminality that may include rape, robbery, and assault.

A similar study is under way at the Project on Human Development in Chicago Neighborhoods (PHDCN), mentioned earlier in this chapter. PHDCN researchers are "tracing how criminal behavior develops from birth to age 32."[85] Participating researchers come from a variety of scientific backgrounds and include psychiatrists, developmental psychologists, sociologists, criminologists, physicians, educators, statisticians, and public health officials. The study focuses on the influence of communities, peers, families, and health-related, cognitive, and emotional factors to decipher the lines along which crime and delinquency are likely to develop. Learn more about the Causes and Correlates study via **Web Extra! 3–7**. Find out more about the PHDCN project via **Web Extra! 3–1** and **Library Extra! 3–3** at cjtoday.com.

Social Policy and Sociological Theories

Theoretical approaches which fault the social environment as the root cause of crime point in the direction of social action as a panacea. A contemporary example of intervention efforts based upon sociological theories can be found in Targeted Outreach,[86] a program now being operated by Boys and Girls Clubs of America. The club program had its origins in the 1972 implementation of a youth-development strategy based upon studies undertaken at the University of Colorado which showed that at-risk youths could be effectively diverted from the juvenile justice system through the provision of positive alternatives. Utilizing a referral network comprised of local schools, police departments, and various youth-service agencies, club officials work to end what they call the "inappropriate detention of juveniles." The program, in its current form, recruits at-risk youngsters—many as young as seven years old—and diverts them into activities which are intended to promote a sense of belonging, competence, usefulness, and power. Belonging is fostered through clubs which provide familiar settings where individuals are accepted. Competence and usefulness are developed through the provision of opportunities for meaningful activities which young people in the club program can successfully undertake. Finally, Targeted Outreach provides its youthful participants with a chance to be heard and, consequently, with the opportunity to influence decisions affecting their future (empowerment). Targeted Outreach is typical of the kinds of

> If we are ever to reduce the tragic toll of crime in society, we must compare the measured benefits of incarceration to less costly and more productive crime prevention strategies—especially those programs aimed at helping high-risk families and young people escape the hopelessness that surrounds their lives.
>
> —Barry Krisberg, President, National Council on Crime and Delinquency

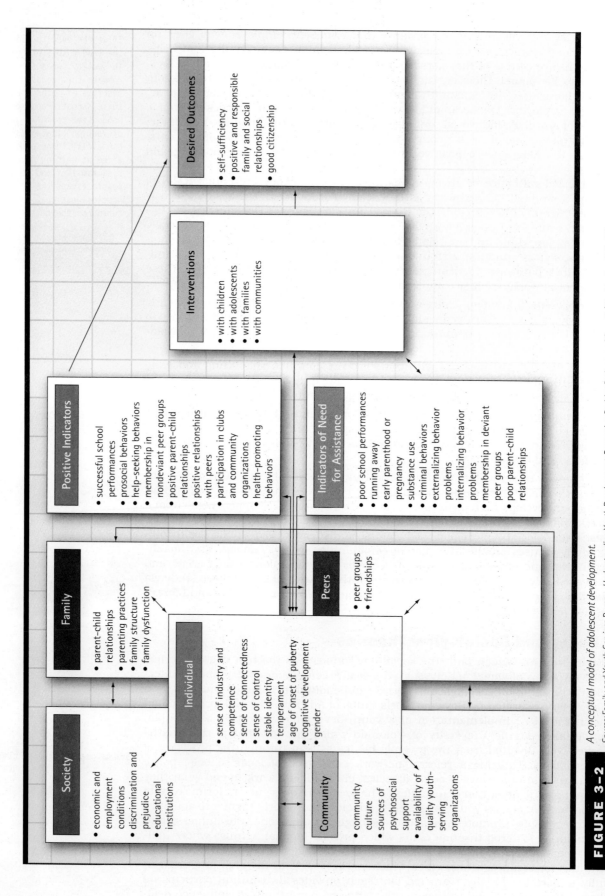

FIGURE 3-2

A conceptual model of adolescent development.

Source: Family and Youth Services Bureau, *Understanding Youth Development: Promoting Positive Pathways of Growth* (Washington, D.C.: U.S. Department of Health and Human Services, 2000).

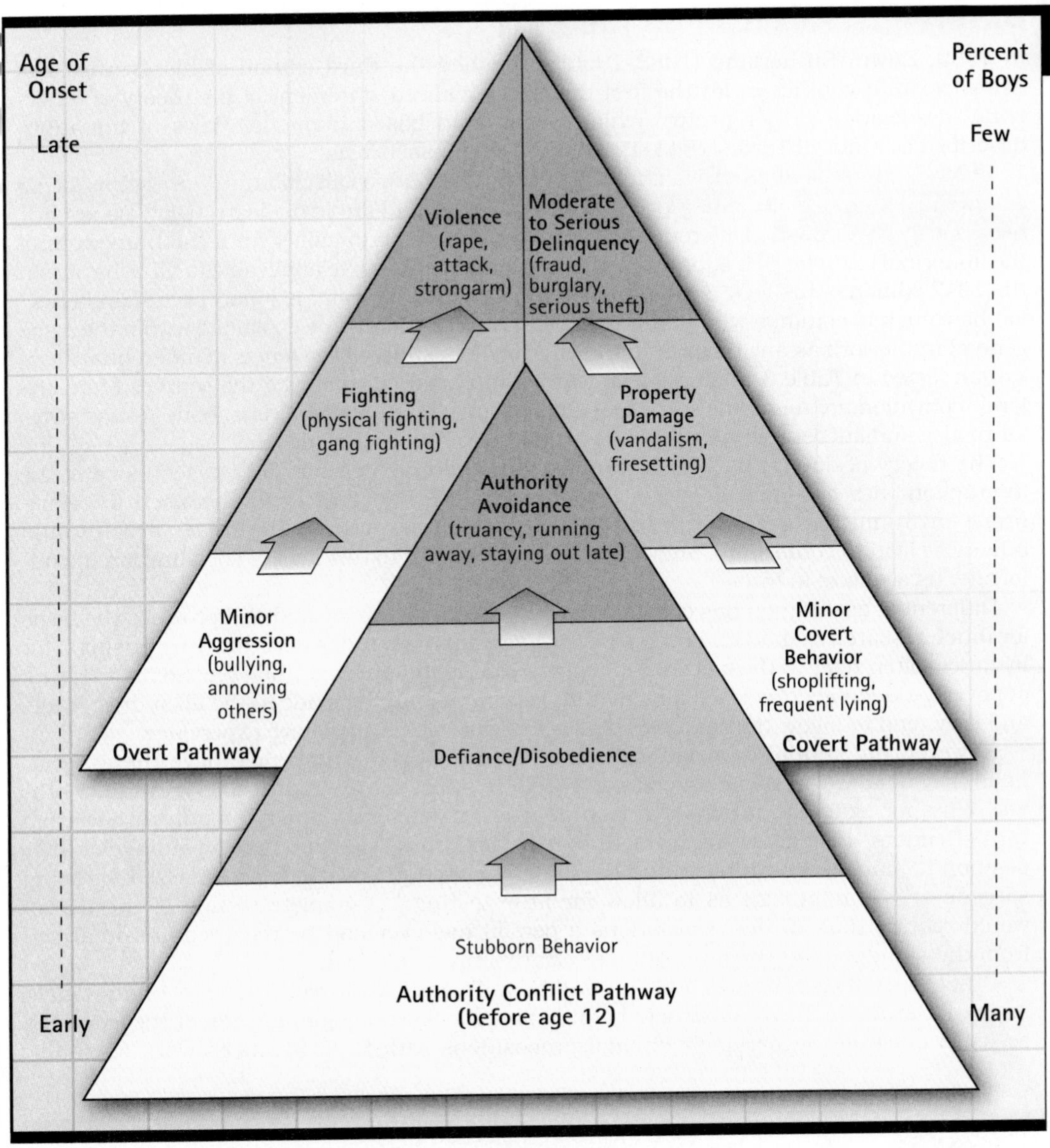

FIGURE 3-3

Three pathways to disruptive behavior and delinquency.

Source: Developmental Pathways in Boys' Disruptive and Delinquent Behavior (Washington, D.C.: Office of Juvenile Justice and Delinquency Prevention, 1997).

programs which theorists who focus on the social environment typically seek to implement. Social programs of this sort are intended to change the cultural conditions and societal arrangements which are thought to lead people into crime.

Social–Psychological Theories

While psychological approaches to crime causation uncover aspects of the personality hidden even from the mind in which they reside, and sociological theories look to institutional arrangements in the social world to explain crime, social-psychological approaches attempt to explain deviant behavior by relating it to the cultural environment in which the individual matures. **Social-psychological theories** add to the more structural analysis of sociological theories by including individual behavior and chosen responses to the social world.

Many social-psychological theories highlight the role of social learning. They build upon the premise that behavior—both "good" and "bad"—is learned and suggest that "bad" behavior can be unlearned. Social-psychological theories are probably the most attractive to contemporary policymakers because they demand that responsibility be placed upon the offender for actively participating in rehabilitation efforts and because they are consistent with popular cultural and religious values centered on teaching right from wrong.

social-psychological theory

A perspective on criminological thought that highlights the role played in crime causation by weakened self-esteem and meaningless social roles. Social-psychological thinkers stress the relationship of the individual to the social group as the underlying cause of behavior.

Differential Association Theory

In 1939, Edwin Sutherland (1883–1950) published the third edition of his *Principles of Criminology*. It contained, for the first time, a formalized statement of his theory of differential association, a perspective which Sutherland based upon the "laws of imitation" described by Gabriel Tarde (1843–1904), the French sociologist.

Differential association views crime as the product of socialization and sees it as being acquired by criminals according to the same principles that guide the learning of law-abiding behavior in conformists. Differential association removes criminality from the framework of the abnormal and places it squarely within a general perspective applicable to all behavior. In the 1947 edition of his text, Sutherland wrote, "Criminal behavior is a part of human behavior, has much in common with non-criminal behavior, and must be explained within the same general framework as any other human behavior."[87] A study of the tenets of differential association (listed in Table 3–3) shows that Sutherland believed that even the sources of behavioral motivation are much the same for conformists and criminals; that is, both groups strive for money and success but choose different paths to the same goal.

The theory of differential association explained crime as a natural consequence of the interaction with criminal lifestyles. Sutherland suggested that children raised in crime-prone environments were often isolated and unable to experience the values which would otherwise lead to conformity. Some modern writers refer to this lack of socialization in conformity as a *failure to train*.[88]

Differential association has considerable relevance even today and still provides the basis for much research in modern criminology.[89] Even popular stories of young drug pushers, for instance, often refer to the fact that inner-city youths imitate what they see. Some residents of poverty-ridden ghettos learn quickly that fast money can be made in the illicit drug trade, and they tend to follow the examples of success with which they have experience.

However, differential association theory fails to explain why people have the associations they do and why some associations seem to affect certain individuals more than others. Why, for example, are most prison guards unaffected by their constant association with offenders, while a few are brought over to the inmate side and take advantage of their position to smuggle contraband and the like? The theory has also been criticized for being so general and imprecise as to allow for little testing.[90] Complete testing of the theory would require that all the associations a person has ever had be recorded and analyzed from the standpoint of the individual—a clearly impossible task.

Other theorists continue to build on Sutherland's early work. Robert Burgess and Ronald Akers, for example, have constructed a differential association–reinforcement theory which seeks to integrate Sutherland's original propositions with B. F. Skinner's work on condi-

TABLE 3–3	**SUTHERLAND'S PRINCIPLES OF DIFFERENTIAL ASSOCIATION**

1. Criminal behavior is learned.
2. Criminal behavior is learned in interaction with others in a process of communication.
3. The principal part of the learning of criminal behavior occurs within intimate personal groups.
4. When criminal behavior is learned, the learning includes (a) techniques of committing the crime, which are sometimes very complicated, sometimes very simple, and (b) the specific direction of motives, drives, rationalizations, and attitudes.
5. The specific direction of motives and drives is learned from definitions of the legal codes as favorable or unfavorable.
6. A person becomes delinquent because of an excess of definitions favorable to violations of law over definitions unfavorable to violations of law.
7. Differential associations may vary in frequency, duration, priority, and intensity.
8. The process of learning criminal behavior by association with criminal and anticriminal patterns involves all the mechanisms that are involved in any other learning.
9. While criminal behavior is an expression of general needs and values, it is not explained by those general needs and values since noncriminal behavior is an expression of the same needs and values.

Source: Edwin Sutherland, *Principles of Criminology*, 4th ed. (Chicago: J. B. Lippincott, 1947), pp. 6–7.

tioning.[91] Burgess and Akers suggest that although values and behavior patterns are learned in association with others, the primary mechanism through which such learning occurs is operant conditioning. Reinforcement is the key, they say, to understanding any social learning as it takes place. The name **social learning theory** has been widely applied to the work of Burgess and Akers. It is somewhat a misnomer, however, since the term can easily encompass a wide range of approaches and should not be limited to one specific combination of the ideas found in differential association and reinforcement theory.

Restraint Theories

As we have seen throughout this chapter, most criminological theories posit a cause of crime.[92] Some theories, however, focus less on causes than on constraints. They are called *restraint theories.*

CONTAINMENT THEORY

Walter Reckless's (1899–1988) containment theory, a type of restraint theory, assumes that all of us are subject to inducements to crime.[93] Some of us resist these "pushes" toward criminal behavior, while others do not. The difference, according to Reckless, can be found in forces which contain behavior.

Reckless described two types of **containment:** inner and outer. Outer containment depends upon social roles and the norms and expectations which apply to them. People who occupy significant roles in society find themselves insulated from deviant tendencies. A corporate executive, for example, is probably less apt to hold up a liquor store than is a drifter. The difference, according to Reckless, is not due solely to income, but to the pressure to conform that the "successful" role exerts upon its occupant.

Inner containment involves a number of factors, including conscience, a positive self-image, a tolerance for frustration, and aspirations which are in line with reality. Reckless saw inner containment as more powerful than outer containment. Inner containment functions even in secret. An inner-directed person, for example, may come across a lost purse and feel compelled to locate its rightful owner and return it. If theft or greed cross the mind of the inner-directed, they will say to themselves, "I'm not that kind of person. That would be wrong."

Reckless studied small, close-knit societies—including the Hutterites, Mennonites, and Amish—in developing his theory. He realized that the "containment of behavior . . . is . . . maximized under conditions of isolation and homogeneity of culture, class, and population."[94] Hence, its applicability to modern American society, with its considerable heterogeneity of values and perspectives, is questionable.

social learning theory

A psychological perspective that says that people learn how to behave by modeling themselves after others whom they have the opportunity to observe.

containment

The aspects of the social bond and of the personality which act to prevent individuals from committing crimes and which keep them from engaging in deviance.

SOCIAL CONTROL THEORY

Travis Hirschi emphasized the bond between individuals and society as the primary operative mechanism in his social control theory.[95] Hirschi identified four components of that bond: (1) emotional attachments to significant others, (2) a commitment to appropriate lifestyles, (3) involvement or immersion in conventional values, and (4) a belief in the "correctness" of social obligations and the rules of the larger society. These components act as social controls on deviant and criminal behavior; as they weaken, social control suffers, and the likelihood of crime and deviance increases. Using self-reports of delinquency from high school students in California, Hirschi concluded that youngsters who were less attached to teachers and parents and who had few positive attitudes about their own accomplishments were more likely to engage in crime and deviance than were others.[96]

Restraint theories provide only one-half of the causal picture. Since they focus primarily on why people do *not* break the law, they are especially weak in identifying the social-structural sources of motivations to commit crimes.[97] Similarly, the ways in which bonds with different institutions interact with one another and with personal attributes, as well as the variety of bonds operative throughout the life cycle, have yet to be clarified.[98]

NEUTRALIZATION TECHNIQUES

Complementing restraint theory is the neutralization approach of Gresham Sykes and David Matza.[99] Sykes and Matza believed that most people drift into and out of criminal behavior but would not commit crime unless they had available to them techniques of neutralization. Such techniques are actually rationalizations which allow offenders to shed feelings of guilt and any sense of responsibility for their behavior. Sykes and Matza's study primarily concerned juveniles in whom, they suggested, neutralization techniques provided only a temporary respite from guilt. That respite, however, lasted long enough to avoid the twinges of conscience while a crime was being committed. Neutralization techniques include the following:

- Denial of responsibility ("I'm a product of my background.")
- Denial of injury ("No one was really hurt.")
- Denial of the victim ("They deserved it.")
- Condemnation of the condemners ("The cops are corrupt.")
- Appeal to higher loyalties ("I did it for my friends.")

Like containment theory, restraint theories tend to depend upon a general agreement as to values, or they assume that offenders are simply conformists who suffer temporary lapses. Neutralization techniques, by definition, are only needed when the delinquent has been socialized into middle-class values or where conscience is well developed. Even so, neutralization techniques do not in themselves explain crime. Such techniques are available to us all, if we make only a slight effort to conjure them up. The real question is why some people readily allow proffered neutralizations to affect their behavior, while others discount them seemingly out of hand.

Conflict Theories

Basic to the **conflict perspective** is the belief that conflict is a fundamental aspect of social life itself and can never be fully resolved. At best, according to this perspective, formal agencies of social control merely coerce the unempowered or the disenfranchised to comply with the rules established by those in power. From the conflict point of view, laws become a tool of the powerful, useful in keeping others from wresting control over important social institutions. Social order, rather than being the result of any consensus or process of dispute resolution, rests upon the exercise of power through law. The conflict perspective can be described in terms of four key elements:[100]

- Society is composed of diverse social groups, and diversity is based upon distinctions which people hold to be significant, such as gender, sexual orientation, social class, and so on.
- Conflict among groups is unavoidable because of differing interests and differing values. Hence, conflict is inherent in social life.
- The fundamental nature of group conflict centers on the exercise of political power. Political power is the key to the accumulation of wealth and to other forms of power.

> The word needs to go out on the street. We have had it with violence. We have had it with violent people. We're tired of being told to try to understand their childhood or understand their past.
>
> —Newt Gingrich, former Speaker of the House[ii]

WHAT WOULD YOU DO?

The CD-ROM scenario for Chapter 3 builds on the Bill of Rights and constitutional guarantees against illegal searches and seizures. In doing so, it prepares you for chapters that are to come. Use the CD-ROM in the back of your textbook to work through this scenario.

---

conflict perspective

A theoretical approach that holds that crime is the natural consequence of economic and other social inequities. Conflict theorists highlight the stresses which arise among and within social groups as they compete with one another for resources and for survival. The social forces that result are viewed as major determinants of group and individual behavior, including crime.

■ Law is a tool of power and furthers the interests of those powerful enough to make it. Laws allow those in control to gain what they define (through the law) as legitimate access to scarce resources and to deny (through the law) such access to the politically disenfranchised.

Radical Criminology

Criminological theory took a new direction during the 1960s and 1970s, brought about in part by the turmoil which characterized American society during that period. **Radical criminology** was born and, like so many other perspectives of the time, placed the blame for criminality and deviant behavior squarely upon officially sanctioned cultural and economic arrangements. The distribution of wealth and power in society was held to be the primary cause of criminal behavior, especially among those who were disenfranchised—or left out of the American dream. Poverty and discrimination were seen to lead to frustration and pent-up hostilities that expressed themselves in murder, rape, theft, and other crimes.

Radical criminology had its roots in earlier conflict theories and in the thought of Dutch criminologist Willem Bonger. Some authors have distinguished between conflict theory and radical criminology by naming them "conservative conflict theory" and "radical conflict theory."[101] The difference, however, is mostly to be found in the rhetoric of the times. Early theories saw conflict as a natural part of any society and believed that struggles for power and control would always occur. "Losers" would tend to be defined as "criminal," and constraints on their behavior would be legislated. Characteristic of this perspective are the approaches of Austin Turk[102] (1934–) and George Vold (1896–1967). An even earlier conflict perspective can be found in the culture conflict notions of Thorsten Sellin, who was concerned with the clash of immigrant values and traditions with those of established American culture.[103]

Radical criminology went a step farther. It recognized that the struggle to control resources is central to society, and it encompassed the notion that the law itself is a tool of the powerful. The focus of radical criminology, however, was capitalism and the evils which capitalism was believed to entail. The ideas of Karl Marx (1818–1883) decisively entered the field of criminology through the writings of William Chambliss[104] (1933–) and Richard Quinney[105] (1934–). Marxist thought assumed that the lower classes are always exploited by the "owners" in society. According to Marx, the labor of the lower classes provides the basis for the accumulated wealth of the upper classes. Marx saw the working classes as suffering under the consequences of a "false class consciousness" perpetrated by the powerful. The poor were trained to believe that capitalism was in their best interests, and according to Marx, only when the exploited workers realized their exploitation would they rebel and change society for the better.

American radical criminology built upon the ideals of the 1960s and charged that the "establishment," controlled by the upper classes, perverted justice through the unequal application of judicial sanctions. As David Greenberg has observed, "Many researchers attributed the overrepresentation of blacks and persons from impoverished family backgrounds in arrest and conviction statistics to the discriminatory practices of the enforcement agencies. It was not that the poor stole more, but rather that when they did, the police were more likely to arrest them."[106]

Conflict theories of criminality face the difficulty of realistic implementation. Radical criminology in particular is flawed by its narrow-sighted emphasis on capitalist societies. It fails to recognize adequately the role of human nature in the creation of social classes and in the perpetuation of the struggle for control of resources. Radical criminology seems to imply that some sort of utopian social arrangements—perhaps communism—would eliminate most crime. Such a belief is contrary to historical experience: A close look at any contemporary communist society will reveal both social conflict and crime.

Peacemaking Criminology

Peacemaking criminology, which some theorists see as a mature expression of earlier conflict theories, holds that crime-control agencies and the citizens they serve should work together to alleviate social problems and human suffering and thus reduce crime.[107] Criminology as peacemaking has its roots in ancient Christian and Eastern philosophies, as well as in traditional conflict theory. Peacemaking criminology, which includes the notion of service and has also been called *compassionate criminology*, suggests that "compassion, wisdom, and love are essential for understanding the suffering of which we are all a part, and

radical criminology

A conflict perspective that sees crime as engendered by the unequal distribution of wealth, power, and other resources, which adherents believe is especially characteristic of capitalist societies.

peacemaking criminology

A perspective which holds that crime-control agencies and the citizens they serve should work together to alleviate social problems and human suffering and thus reduce crime.

> An honest and fully professional police community would acknowledge in its police education the root causes of crime—poverty, unemployment, underemployment, racism, poor health care, bad housing, weak schools, mental illness, alcoholism, addiction, single-parent families, teenage pregnancy, and a society of selfishness and greed.
>
> —Patrick V. Murphy, former New York City Police Commissioner

for practicing a criminology of nonviolence."[108] Peacemaking criminology also holds that official agents of social control need to work with both the victimized and the victimizers to achieve a new world order which is more just and fair to all who live in it. In a fundamental sense, peacemaking criminologists exhort their colleagues to transcend personal dichotomies to end the political and ideological divisiveness which separates people. "If we ourselves cannot know peace . . . how will our acts disarm hatred and violence?" they ask.[109]

Peacemaking criminology was popularized by the works of Harold Pepinsky[110] and Richard Quinney[111] beginning in 1986. Both Pepinsky and Quinney restate the problem of crime control from one of "how to stop crime" to one of "how to make peace" within society and among citizens and criminal justice agencies. Peacemaking criminology draws attention to many issues, among them the perpetuation of violence through the continuation of social policies based upon dominant forms of criminological theory, the role of education in peacemaking, "commonsense theories of crime," crime control as human rights enforcement, and conflict resolution within community settings.[112]

Social Policy and Conflict Theories

Because radical and conflict criminologists see crime as being caused by social inequality, many such theorists have suggested that the only way to achieve real change in the rate of crime is through revolution. Revolution—because it holds the promise of greater equality for underrepresented groups and because it mandates a redistribution of wealth and power—was thought necessary for any lasting reduction in crime.

Some contemporary writers on radical criminology, however, have attempted to address the issue of what can be done under our current system, probably because they recognize that a sudden and total reversal of existing political arrangements within the United States is highly unlikely. Hence, they have begun to focus on promoting "middle-range policy alternatives" to the present system, including "equal justice in the bail system, the abolition of mandatory sentences, prosecution of corporate crimes, increased employment opportunities, and promoting community alternatives to imprisonment."[113] Likewise, programs to reduce prison overcrowding, efforts to highlight injustices within the current system, the elimination of racism and other forms of inequality in the handling of both victims and offenders, growing equality in criminal justice system employment, and the like are all frequently mentioned as mid-range strategies for bringing about a justice system which is more fair and closer to the radical ideal.

Raymond Michalowski summarizes the policy directions envisioned by today's radical criminologists when he says, "We cannot be free from the crimes of the poor until there are no more poor; we cannot be free from domination of the powerful until we reduce the inequalities that make domination possible; and we cannot live in harmony with others until we begin to limit the competition for material advantage over others that alienates us from one another."[114]

The Phenomenological School

phenomenological criminology

A perspective on crime causation that holds that the significance of criminal behavior is ultimately knowable only to those who participate in it. Central to this school of thought is the belief that social actors endow their behavior with meaning and purpose. Hence, a crime might mean one thing to the person who commits it, quite another to the victim, and something far different still to professional participants in the justice system.

Phenomenological criminology built upon the ideas of George Herbert Mead[115] (1863–1931), William Thomas[116] (1863–1947), and the German philosopher Alfred Schutz[117] (1899–1959). Mead propounded a theory called *symbolic interaction*, in which he demonstrated how people give meaning to the things around them and to their lives. Thomas explained that the significance of any human behavior is relative to the intentions behind it and to the situation in which it is interpreted. Hence, behavior which, in one place or at one time, is taken for granted may, in another place or time, be perceived as deviant or even criminal. From this viewpoint, crime, like any other social phenomenon, is more a definition imposed by society upon a particular type of activity than it is a quality inherent in the behavior itself. As a consequence, crime may mean different things to different people and is, no doubt, variously interpreted by the offender, by the victim, and by agents of social control. Phenomenological criminology is a perspective on crime causation which holds that the significance of criminal behavior depends upon one's interests in the crime and one's point of view and is ultimately knowable only to those who participate in it. Central to this school of thought are the following principles:

■ The significance of any behavior depends upon a social consensus about what that behavior "means."

■ Crime is the product of an active process of interpretation and social definition.

■ Continued criminal activity may be more a consequence of limited opportunities for acceptable behavior which are imposed upon individuals defined as "criminal" than it is a product of choice.

Stuart Henry and Dragan Milovanovic, two contemporary proponents of phenomenological criminology, use the term **constitutive criminology** to refer to the process by which human beings create "an ideology of crime that sustains it as a concrete reality."[118] A central feature of constitutive criminology is its assertion that individuals shape their world while also being shaped by it. Constitutive criminology claims that crime and crime control are not "object-like entities," but constructions produced through a social process in which offender, victim, and society are all involved.[119] "We are concerned," write Henry and Milovanovic, "with the ways in which human agents actively coproduce that which they take to be crime." For Henry and Milovanovic, the idea of crime itself is a social construction, and researchers, they say, should recognize that criminals and victims are also "emergent realities." In short, constitutive criminology focuses on the social process by which crime and criminology become cultural realities.[120]

Labeling Theory

As we saw earlier in this chapter, the worth of any theory of behavior is proved by how well it reflects the reality of the social world. In practice, however, theoretical perspectives find acceptance in the academic environment via a number of considerations. Labeling theory, for example, became fashionable in the 1960s. Its popularity, however, may have been due more to the cultural environment into which it was introduced rather than to any inherent quality of the theory itself.

In fact, labeling theory had been introduced by Frank Tannenbaum (1893–1969) in 1938 under the rubric of *tagging*.[121] He wrote, "The young delinquent becomes bad because he is defined as bad and because he is not believed if he is good." He went on to say, "The process of making the criminal, therefore, is a process of tagging. . . . It becomes a way of stimulating . . . and evolving the very traits that are complained of. . . . The person becomes the thing he is described as being."[122] Tannenbaum focused on society's power to *define* an act or an individual as bad and drew attention to the group need for a scapegoat in explaining crime. The search for causes inherent in individuals was not yet exhausted, however, and Tannenbaum's theory fell mostly on deaf ears.

By the 1960s, the social and academic environments in America had changed, and the issue of responsibility was seen more in terms of the group than the individual. In 1963, Howard Becker pointed out in his book *Outsiders* that criminality is not a quality inherent in an act or in a person. Crime, said Becker, results from a social definition, through law, of unacceptable behavior. That definition arises through **moral enterprise**, by which groups on both sides of an issue debate and eventually legislate their notion of what is moral and what is not. Becker wrote, "The central fact about deviance [is that] it is created by society. . . . Social groups create deviance by making the rules whose infraction constitutes deviance."[123]

The criminal label, however, produces consequences for labeled individuals which may necessitate continued criminality. In describing the criminal career, Becker wrote, "To be labeled a criminal one need only commit a single criminal offense. . . . Yet the word carries a number of connotations specifying auxiliary traits characteristic of anyone bearing the label."[124] The first time a person commits a crime, the behavior is called *primary deviance* and may be a merely transitory form of behavior.

However, in the popular mind, a "known" criminal is not to be trusted, should not be hired because of the potential for crimes on the job, and would not be a good candidate for the military, marriage, or any position requiring responsibility. Society's tendency toward such thinking, Becker suggested, closes legitimate opportunities, ensuring that the only new behavioral alternatives available to the labeled criminal are deviant ones. Succeeding episodes of criminal behavior are seen as a form of secondary deviance, which eventually become stabilized in the behavioral repertoire and self-concept of the labeled person.[125]

Labeling theory, like phenomenological approaches in general, can be critiqued along a number of dimensions. First, it is not really a "theory" in that labeling does not uncover the genesis of criminal behavior. It is more useful in describing how such behavior continues than in explaining how it originates. Second, labeling theory does not recognize the possibility that the labeled individual may make successful attempts at reform and may shed the negative label. Finally, the theory does not provide an effective way of dealing with

constitutive criminology

The study of the process by which human beings create an ideology of crime that sustains the notion of crime as a concrete reality.

moral enterprise

The process undertaken by an advocacy group to have its values legitimated and embodied in law.

labeling theory

An interactionist perspective that sees continued crime as a consequence of the limited opportunities for acceptable behavior which follow from the negative responses of society to those defined as offenders.

offenders. Should people who commit crimes not be arrested and tried, so as to avoid the consequences of negative labels? It would be exceedingly naive to suggest that all repeat criminal behavior would cease, as labeling theory might predict, if people who commit crimes are not officially "handled" by the system.

Emergent Theories

A number of new and exciting theories of criminology hold promise for the future. Although space does not permit discussion of them all, **feminist criminology** provides a useful example of the kind of emergent thought characterizing these perspectives.[126]

As some writers in the developing field of feminist criminology have observed, "Women have been virtually invisible in criminological analysis until recently and much theorizing has proceeded as though criminality is restricted to men."[127] Others put it this way: "[Traditional] criminological theory assumes a woman is like a man."[128] Feminist criminologists are now working to change long-cherished notions of crime and of criminal justice so that the role of women in both crime causation and crime control might be better appreciated.

Early works in the field of feminist criminology include Freda Adler's *Sisters in Crime*[129] and Rita Simon's *Women and Crime*.[130] Both books were published in 1975, and in them the authors attempted to explain existing divergences in crime rates between men and women as due primarily to socialization rather than biology. Women, claimed these authors, were taught to believe in personal limitations, faced reduced socioeconomic opportunities, and, as a result, suffered from lowered aspirations. As gender equality increased, they said, it could be expected that male and female criminality would take on similar characteristics. More recent researchers, however, have not found this to be true, with substantial differences between the criminality of men and women remaining, even as gender equality grows.[131]

Contemporary feminist thinking in criminology is represented by the works of writers like Kathleen Daly and Meda Chesney-Lind.[132] Daly and Chesney-Lind emphasize the need for a "gender-aware" criminology and stress the usefulness of applying feminist thinking to criminological analysis. Gender, say these writers, is a central organizing principle of contemporary life. As a way of seeing the world, especially the criminal world, they suggest, it holds much promise. As a consequence, feminist thought, at least for the time being, may be more important for the way it informs and challenges existing criminology than for the new theories it offers.

In fact, much feminist thought within contemporary criminology emphasizes the need for gender awareness. Theories of crime causation and prevention, it is suggested, must include women, and more research on gender-related issues in the field is badly needed. Additionally, some authors say, "Criminologists should begin to appreciate that their discipline and its questions are a product of white, economically privileged men's experiences."[133] They suggest that rates of female criminality, which are lower than those of males, may show that criminal behavior is not as "normal" as once thought. Because modern-day criminological perspectives were mostly developed by white middle-class males, the propositions and theories they advance fail to take into consideration women's "ways of knowing."[134] Hence, the fundamental challenge posed by feminist criminology is this: Do existing theories of crime causation apply as well to women as they do to men? Or, as Daly and Chesney-Lind put it, given the current situation in theory development, "Do theories of men's crime apply to women?"[135] Read some of Chesney-Lind's recent work via **Library Extra! 3–4** at cjtoday.com.

Before concluding this chapter, it is important to note that **postmodern criminology** is a term applied to a wide variety of novel perspectives which have developed over the past decade or two and which include evolving paradigms with such intriguing names as *chaos theory, discourse analysis, topology theory, critical theory, realist criminology, constitutive theory,* and *anarchic criminology*.[136] Postmodern criminology builds upon the belief that past criminological approaches have failed to realistically assess the true causes of crime and have therefore failed to offer workable solutions for crime control—or if they have, that such theories and solutions may have been appropriate at one time but no longer apply to the postmodern era. Because postmodern criminology challenges and debunks existing perspectives, it is referred to as *deconstructionist,* and such theories are sometimes called **deconstructionist theories**. Two especially

feminist criminology

A developing intellectual approach that emphasizes gender issues in criminology.

postmodern criminology

A brand of criminology that developed after World War II and which builds upon the tenets inherent in postmodern social thought.

deconstructionist theory

One of the emerging approaches which challenge existing criminological perspectives to debunk them and which work toward replacing them with concepts more applicable to the postmodern era.

notable authors in the field of postmodern criminology are Stuart Henry and Dragan Milovanovic,[137] whose work in the area of constitutive criminology was discussed earlier in this chapter. Read some of Milovanovic's work via **Library Extra! 3–5** at cjtoday.com.

Summary

This chapter describes theoretical explanations for crime. Most of the perspectives discussed are grounded in biology, psychology, or sociology. Biological theories posit a genetic or a physiological basis for deviant and criminal behavior. The notion of a "weak" gene which might predispose certain individuals toward criminal activity has recently been expanded to include the impact of environmental contaminants, poor nutrition, and food additives on behavior. Studies of fraternal twins and chromosome structure have helped to lead biological theories into the modern day.

Psychological explanations of crime are individualistic. Some psychoanalytical theories see offenders as sick; others claim merely that criminal behavior is a type of conditioned response. The stimulus-response model depicts criminal behavior as the consequence of a conditioning process which extends over the entire life span of an individual.

Sociological theories, which hold that the individual is a product of the environment, constitute today's perspective of choice. These theories emphasize the role of social structure, inequality, and socialization in generating criminality. The danger of most sociological approaches, however, is that they tend to deny the significance of any influences beyond those which are mediated through social interaction.

An integrated perspective which recognizes that human behavior results from a mix of biology, mental processes, and acquired traits holds much future promise. As a consequence, our understanding of crime causation seems headed toward the day when a unified theory of conduct will draw upon many types of explanations to interpret the whole range of human behavior—including crime.

Discussion Questions

1. What is a theory? Can you name or describe any theories that you use in making decisions in your daily life?
2. What is the purpose of criminological theory? Do any of the theories described in this chapter fill that purpose especially well? If so, which ones?
3. What do we mean when we say that most theories are unicausal? What would a multicausal theory be like?
4. Describe the major groups of criminological theories discussed in this chapter. What are the shortcomings of each? Which group do you think has the most explanatory power? Why?
5. Which of the major types of theories discussed in this chapter is probably the most accepted today? What dangers do you see in accepting any one type of theory over any other?
6. How do restraint theories differ from other kinds of explanations of crime causation? What do restraint theories assume is true about most of us? Are they correct?
7. Why are social policy initiatives often based upon specific criminological theories? What kinds of social policy or what form of "treatment" might be predicated upon phenomenological theories of crime?
8. How do radical criminologists explain crime? What form of "treatment" might be predicated upon radical theories of crime? What kinds of social policies might be derived from radical theories?

To participate in an online discussion on these topics and others, go to the Global Town Meeting electronic message board for Chapter 3 on the *Criminal Justice Today* Companion Website at cjtoday.com.

Web Quest!

One of the most informative criminal justice–related sites on the Web is the Justice Information Center (JIC), run by the National Criminal Justice Reference Service (NCJRS). Visit the JIC at ncjrs.org, or use the Cybrary to locate the NCJRS. Once you have found the JIC, explore each of the major informational categories it provides: Corrections, Courts, Crime Prevention, Criminal Justice Statistics, Drugs and Crime, International, Juvenile Justice, Law Enforcement, Research and Evaluation, and Victims.

Visit each category, and make a note of the features available. View at least three sample documents from each category. Write a summary of each document (you should have a total of 30), and submit the summaries to your instructor if asked to do so.

Reenter each JIC category, and make a note of the Web sites referenced there. Visit at least three sites under each category, and write a brief description of each site (you should have a total of 30). Submit the descriptions to your instructor if asked to do so.

To complete this Web Quest! online, go to the Web Quest! module in Chapter 3 of the *Criminal Justice Today* Companion Website at cjtoday.com.

Library Extras!

Library Extra! 3–1 *Theoretical Developments in Criminology* (NIJ, 2000).
Library Extra! 3–2 *Can Criminal Psychopaths Be Identified?* (Correctional Service of Canada, 1999).
Library Extra! 3–3 *Project on Human Development in Chicago Neighborhoods* (NIJ, 1997).
Library Extra! 3–4 *Critical Criminology: Toward a Feminist Praxis* (University of Hawaii at Manoa, no date).
Library Extra! 3–5 *Dueling Paradigms: Modernist versus Postmodernist Thought* (Northeastern Illinois University, no date).

To explore these resources online, go to the Library Extras! area of the *Criminal Justice Today* Companion Website at cjtoday.com. You should also check the author's "Late Picks" online for newly released documents and updated Library Extras! You can find Late Picks at http://cjtoday.com/latepicks.htm.

Marginal Notes

i. *The American Heritage Dictionary and Electronic Thesaurus on CD-ROM* (Boston: Houghton Mifflin, 1987).

ii. "Gingrich Says Felons Should Be Tracked by Satellite," Reuters wire service, March 4, 1995.

Notes

1. "Remarks by the President on Project Safe Neighborhoods," Pennsylvania Convention Center, Philadelphia, Pennsylvania, May 14, 2001. Web posted at http://www.whitehouse.gov/news/releases/2001/05/200 10514-1.html. Accessed April 2, 2002.
2. Quoted in Gwynn Nettler, *Killing One Another* (Cincinnati: Anderson, 1982), p. 194.
3. Information for this story comes from Steve Jones, "Out of Prison, Rapper Reflects on Life's Value," *USA Today,* May 23, 2001.
4. As we shall see in Chapter 4, behavior that violates the criminal law may not be "crime" if accompanied by acceptable legal justification or excuse. Justifications and excuses that are recognized by the law may serve as defenses to a criminal charge.
5. This and many of the statistics in these opening paragraphs come from Jonathan Wright, "Media Are Mixed Blessing, Criminologists Say," Reuters wire service, May 2, 1995.
6. See "Comments of James T. Hamilton before the Federal Communications Commission, in the Matter of Industry Proposal for Rating Video Programming," May 23, 1997, citing Suzanne Stutman, Joanne Cantor, and Victoria Duran, *What Parents Want in a Television Rating System: Results of a National Survey* (Madison: University of Wisconsin Communications Arts, 1996); and Wes Shipley and Gary Cavender, "Murder and Mayhem at the Movies," *Journal of Criminal Justice and Popular Culture,* Vol. 9, No. 1 (2001), pp. 1–14.
7. Wright, "Media Are Mixed Blessing, Criminologists Say."

8. Nathan McCall, "My Rap against Rap," *Washington Post* wire services, November 14, 1993.

9. Arthur L. Cribbs, Jr., "Gangsta Rappers Sing White Racists' Tune," *USA Today,* December 27, 1993, p. 9A.

10. *U.S. News/*UCLA Survey on the Media and Violence, reported in "Hollywood: Right Face," *U.S. News and World Report,* May 15, 1995, p. 71.

11. See "Congress Hopes Ten Commandments Curb Violence," APB Online, June 17, 1999. Web posted at http://www.apbonline.com/911/1999/06/17/congress0617_01.html. Accessed March 1, 2000.

12. The word *scientific* is used here to refer to the application of generally accepted research strategies designed to reject explanations which rival the one under study.

13. Stephen Schafer, *Theories in Criminology* (New York: Random House, 1969), p. 109.

14. L. E. Cohen and Marcus Felson, "Social Change and Crime Rate Trends: A Routine Activity Approach," *American Sociological Review,* Vol. 44, No. 4 (August 1979), pp. 588–608. Also see Marcus Felson and L. E. Cohen, "Human Ecology and Crime: A Routine Activity Approach," *Human Ecology,* Vol. 8, No. 4 (1980), pp. 389–406; Marcus Felson, "Linking Criminal Choices, Routine Activities, Informal Control, and Criminal Outcomes," in Derek B. Cornish and Ronald V. Clarke, eds., *The Reasoning Criminal: Rational Choice Perspectives on Offending* (New York: Springer-Verlag, 1986), pp. 119–128; and Ronald V. Clarke and Marcus Felson, eds., *Advances in Criminological Theory: Routine Activity and Rational Choice* (New Brunswick, NJ: Transaction, 1993).

15. Lawrence E. Cohen and Marcus Felson, "Social Change and Crime Rate Trends," p. 595.

16. For a test of routine activities theory as an explanation for victimization in the workplace, see John D. Wooldredge, Francis T. Cullen, and Edward J. Latessa, "Victimization in the Workplace: A Test of Routine Activities Theory," *Justice Quarterly,* Vol. 9, No. 2 (June 1992), pp. 325–335.

17. Werner Einstadter and Stuart Henry, *Criminological Theory: An Analysis of Its Underlying Assumptions* (Fort Worth: Harcourt Brace, 1995), p. 70.

18. For a modern reprint of a widely read nineteenth-century work on phrenology, see Orson Squire Fowler and Lorenzo Niles Fowler, *Phrenology: A Practical Guide to Your Head* (New York: Chelsea House, 1980).

19. Ibid.

20. Schafer, *Theories in Criminology,* p. 123.

21. Richard Louis Dugdale, *The Jukes: A Study in Crime, Pauperism, Disease, and Heredity,* 3d ed. (New York: G. P. Putnam's Sons, 1985).

22. Henry Herbert Goddard, *The Kallikak Family: A Study in the Heredity of Feeblemindedness* (New York: Macmillan, 1912).

23. "Constitutional" theories of crime causation refer to the *physical constitution,* or bodily characteristics, of the offenders and have nothing to do with the Constitution of the United States.

24. For more information, see Richard Herrnstein, "Crime File: Biology and Crime," a study guide (Washington, D.C.: National Institute of Justice, no date).

25. *Buck* v. *Bell,* 274 U.S. 200, 207 (1927).

26. Patricia Jacobs et al., "Aggressive Behavior, Mental Subnormality, and the XYY Male," *Nature,* Vol. 208 (1965), pp. 1351–1352.

27. Schafer, *Theories in Criminology,* p. 193.

28. D. Hill and W. Sargent, "A Case of Matricide," *Lancet,* Vol. 244 (1943), pp. 526–527.

29. See, for example, A. R. Mawson and K. J. Jacobs, "Corn Consumption, Tryptophan, and Cross-National Homicide Rates," *Journal of Orthomolecular Psychiatry,* Vol. 7 (1978), pp. 227–230; and A. Hoffer, "The Relation of Crime to Nutrition," *Humanist in Canada,* Vol. 8 (1975), p. 8.

30. See, for example, C. Hawley and R. E. Buckley, "Food Dyes and Hyperkinetic Children," *Academy Therapy,* Vol. 10 (1974), pp. 27–32; and Alexander Schauss, *Diet, Crime and Delinquency* (Berkeley, CA: Parker House, 1980).

31. "Special Report: Measuring Your Life with Coffee Spoons," *Tufts University Diet and Nutrition Letter,* Vol. 2, No. 2 (April 1984), pp. 3–6.

32. See, for example, "Special Report: Does What You Eat Affect Your Mood and Actions?" *Tufts University Diet and Nutrition Letter,* Vol. 2, No. 12 (February 1985), pp. 4–6.

33. See *Tufts University Diet and Nutrition Letter,* Vol. 2, No. 11 (January 1985), p. 2; and "Special Report: Why Sugar Continues to Concern Nutritionists," *Tufts University Diet and Nutrition Letter,* Vol. 3, No. 3 (May 1985), pp. 3–6.

34. Diana H. Fishbein and Susan E. Pease, "Diet, Nutrition, and Aggression," in Marc Hillbrand and Nathaniel J. Pallone, eds., *The Psychobiology of Aggression: Engines, Measurement, Control* (New York: Haworth Press, 1994), pp. 114–117.

35. A. Hoffer, "Children with Learning and Behavioral Disorders," *Journal of Orthomolecular Psychiatry,* Vol. 5 (1976), p. 229.

36. "Special Report: Does What You Eat Affect Your Mood and Actions?" p. 4.

37. See, for example, R. T. Rada, D. R. Laws, and R. Kellner, "Plasma Testosterone Levels in the Rapist," *Psychomatic Medicine,* Vol. 38 (1976), pp. 257–268.

38. Later studies, however, have been less than clear. See, for example, J. M. Dabbs, Jr., "Testosterone Measurements in Social and Clinical Psychology," *Journal of Social and Clinical Psychology,* Vol. 11 (1992), pp. 302–321.

39. "The Insanity of Steroid Abuse," *Newsweek,* May 23, 1988, p. 75.

40. E. G. Stalenheim et al., "Testosterone as a Biological Marker in Psychopathy and Alcoholism," *Psychiatry Research,* Vol. 77, No. 2 (February 1998), pp. 79–88.

41. For a summary of such studies, see Serena-Lynn Brown, Alexander Botsis, and Herman M. Van Praag, "Serotonin and Aggression," in Marc Hillbrand and Nathaniel J. Pallone, eds., *The Psychobiology of Aggression: Engines, Measurement, Control* (New York: Haworth Press, 1994), pp. 28–39.

42. Roger D. Masters, Brian Hone, and Anil Doshi, "Environmental Pollution, Neurotoxicity, and Criminal Violence," in J. Rose, ed., *Environmental Toxicology* (London and New York: Gordon and Breach, 1997).

43. B. Bioulac et al., "Serotonergic Functions in the XYY Syndrome," *Biological Psychiatry,* Vol. 15 (1980), pp. 917–923.

44. E. G. Stalenheim, L. von Knorring, and L. Wide, "Serum Levels of Thyroid Hormones as Biological Markers in a Swedish Forensic Psychiatric Population," *Biological Psychiatry,* Vol. 43, No. 10 (May 15, 1998), pp. 755–761.

45. Sarnoff Mednick and Jan Volavka, "Biology and Crime," in Norval Morris and Michael Tonry, eds., *Crime and Justice* (Chicago: University of Chicago Press, 1980), pp. 85–159.

46. Sarnoff Mednick and S. Gloria Shaham, eds., *New Paths in Criminology* (Lexington, MA: D. C. Heath, 1979).

47. For a good survey of studies in this area, see Laurence Miller, "Traumatic Brain Injury and Aggression," in Marc Hillbrand and Nathaniel J. Pallone, eds., *The*

Psychobiology of Aggression: Engines, Measurement, Control (New York: Haworth Press, 1994), pp. 91–103.

48. For an excellent overview of such studies, see Shari Mills and Arian Raine, "Neuroimaging and Aggression," in Marc Hillbrand and Nathaniel J. Pallone, eds., *The Psychobiology of Aggression: Engines, Measurement, Control* (New York: Haworth Press, 1994), pp. 145–158.

49. R. B. Cattell, *The Inheritance of Personality and Ability: Research Methods and Findings* (New York: Academic Press, 1982).

50. Karl Christiansen, "A Preliminary Study of Criminality among Twins," in Sarnoff Mednick and Karl O. Christiansen, eds., *Biosocial Bases of Criminal Behavior* (New York: Gardner Press, 1977).

51. James Q. Wilson and Richard J. Herrnstein, *Crime and Human Nature* (New York: Simon & Schuster, 1985).

52. "Criminals Born and Bred," *Newsweek*, September 16, 1985, p. 69.

53. William J. Chambliss, *Exploring Criminology* (New York: Macmillan, 1988), p. 202.

54. A. Reiss and J. Roth, eds., *Understanding and Preventing Violence* (Washington, D.C.: National Academy Press, 1993).

55. Sigmund Freud, *A General Introduction to Psychoanalysis* (New York: Boni and Liveright, 1920).

56. Nettler, *Killing One Another*, p. 79.

57. David Abrahamsen, *Crime and the Human Mind* (reprint, Montclair, NJ: Patterson Smith, 1969), p. 23.

58. See Adrian Raine, *The Psychopathology of Crime: Criminal Behavior as a Clinical Disorder* (Orlando, FL: Academic Press, 1993).

59. Hervey M. Cleckley, *The Mask of Sanity*, 4th ed. (St. Louis, MO: Mosby, 1964).

60. Nettler, *Killing One Another*, p. 179.

61. Albert I. Rabin, "The Antisocial Personality— Psychopathy and Sociopathy," in Hans Toch, *Psychology of Crime and Criminal Justice* (Prospect Heights, IL: Waveland, 1979), p. 330.

62. Richard L. Ault and James T. Reese, "A Psychological Assessment of Crime Profiling," *FBI Law Enforcement Bulletin* (March 1980), pp. 22–25.

63. John E. Douglas and Alan E. Burgess, "Criminal Profiling: A Viable Investigative Tool against Violent Crime," *FBI Law Enforcement Bulletin* (December 1986), pp. 9–13.

64. Robert R. Hazelwood and John E. Douglass, "The Lust Murderer," *FBI Law Enforcement Bulletin* (April 1980), pp. 18–22.

65. A. O. Rider, "The Firesetter—A Psychological Profile," *FBI Law Enforcement Bulletin*, (June 1980), pp. 4–11.

66. Kathryn A. Artingstall, "Munchausen Syndrome by Proxy," *FBI Law Enforcement Bulletin*, (August 1995), pp. 5–11.

67. M. Reiser, "Crime-Specific Psychological Consultation," *The Police Chief* (March 1982), pp. 53–56.

68. Thomas Strentz, "A Terrorist Psychosocial Profile: Past and Present," *FBI Law Enforcement Bulletin* (April 1988), pp. 13–19.

69. Jill Peay, "Dangerousness—Ascription or Description," in M. P. Feldman, ed., *Violence*, Vol. 2 of *Developments in the Study of Criminal Behavior* (New York: John Wiley, 1982), p. 211, citing N. Walker, "Dangerous People," *International Journal of Law and Psychiatry*, Vol. 1 (1978), pp. 37–50.

70. See, for example, Michael Gottfredson and Travis Hirschi, *A General Theory of Crime* (Stanford, CA: Stanford University Press, 1990); and Travis Hirschi and Michael Gottfredson, "Age and the Explanation of Crime," *American Journal of Sociology*, Vol. 89 (1983), pp. 552–584.

71. David F. Greenberg, "Modeling Criminal Careers," *Criminology*, Vol. 29, No. 1 (1991), p. 39.

72. Robert E. Park and Ernest Burgess, *Introduction to the Science of Sociology*, 2d ed. (Chicago: University of Chicago Press, 1924); and Robert E. Park, ed., *The City* (Chicago: University of Chicago Press, 1925).

73. Clifford R. Shaw and Henry D. McKay, "Social Factors in Juvenile Delinquency," in Vol. 2 of the *Report on the Causes of Crime*, National Commission on Law Observance and Enforcement Report No. 13 (Washington, D.C.: U.S. Government Printing Office, 1931); and Clifford R. Shaw, *Juvenile Delinquency in Urban Areas* (Chicago: University of Chicago Press, 1942).

74. Émile Durkheim, *Suicide* (reprint, New York: Free Press, 1951).

75. Robert K. Merton, "Social Structure and Anomie," *American Sociological Review*, Vol. 3 (1938), pp. 672–682.

76. Catherine E. Ross and John Mirowsky, "Normlessness, Powerlessness, and Trouble with the Law," *Criminology*, Vol. 25, No. 2 (May 1987), p. 257.

77. See Nettler, *Killing One Another*, p. 58.

78. This is not to say that all members of these groups engaged in criminal behavior, but rather that statistics indicated higher average crime rates for these groups than for certain others immediately after immigration to the United States.

79. Albert K. Cohen, *Delinquent Boys: The Culture of the Gang* (Glencoe, IL: Free Press, 1958).

80. Walter B. Miller, "Lower Class Culture as a Generating Milieu of Gang Delinquency," *Journal of Social Issues*, Vol. 14 (1958), pp. 5–19.

81. Richard Cloward and Lloyd Ohlin, *Delinquency and Opportunity: A Theory of Delinquent Gangs* (New York: Free Press, 1960).

82. Marvin Wolfgang, *Patterns in Criminal Homicide* (Philadelphia: University of Pennsylvania Press, 1958). See also Marvin Wolfgang and Franco Ferracuti, *The Subculture of Violence: Toward an Integrated Theory in Criminology* (London: Tavistock, 1967).

83. Robert J. Sampson and John H. Laub, *Crime in the Making: Pathways and Turning Points through the Life Course* (Cambridge, MA: Harvard University Press, 1993).

84. Katharine Browning et al., "Causes and Correlates of Delinquency Program," *OJJPD Fact Sheet* (Washington, D.C.: U.S. Department of Justice, April 1999).

85. MacArthur Foundation, "The Project on Human Development in Chicago Neighborhoods." Web posted at http://www.macfound.org/research/hcd/hcd_5.htm. Accessed January 5, 2001.

86. "Gang Prevention through Targeted Outreach—Boys and Girls Clubs of America." Web posted at http://ojjdp.ncjrs.org/pubs/gun_violence/sect08-k.html. Accessed April 10, 2002.

87. Edwin Sutherland, *Principles of Criminology*, 4th ed. (Chicago: J. B. Lippincott, 1947), p. 4.

88. Nettler, *Killing One Another*.

89. See, for example, James D. Orcutt, "Differential Association and Marijuana Use: A Closer Look at Sutherland (with a Little Help from Becker)," *Criminology*, Vol. 25, No. 2 (1987), pp. 341–358.

90. John E. Conklin, *Criminology*, 3d ed. (New York: Macmillan, 1989), p. 278.

91. Robert L. Burgess and Ronald L. Akers, "A Differential Association–Reinforcement Theory of Criminal Behavior," *Social Problems*, Vol. 14 (fall 1996), pp. 128–147.

92. Some theories are multicausal and provide explanations for criminal behavior which include a diversity of "causes."

93. Walter C. Reckless, *The Crime Problem,* 4th ed. (New York: Appleton-Century-Crofts, 1961).

94. Ibid., p. 472.

95. Travis Hirschi, *Causes of Delinquency* (Berkeley: University of California Press, 1969).

96. Ibid., p. 472.

97. For a more elaborate criticism of this sort, see Conklin, *Criminology,* p. 260.

98. Ibid.

99. Gresham Sykes and David Matza, "Techniques of Neutralization: A Theory of Delinquency," *American Sociological Review,* Vol. 22 (1957), pp. 664–670.

100. Adapted from Raymond Michalowski, "Perspectives and Paradigm: Structuring Criminological Thought," in Robert F. Meier, ed., *Theory in Criminology* (Beverly Hills, CA: Sage, 1977).

101. See George B. Vold, *Theoretical Criminology* (New York: Oxford University Press, 1986).

102. Austin T. Turk, *Criminality and the Legal Order* (Chicago: Rand McNally, 1969).

103. Thorsten Sellin, *Culture Conflict and Crime* (New York: Social Science Research Council, 1938).

104. William J. Chambliss and Robert B. Seidman, *Law, Order, and Power* (Reading, MA: Addison-Wesley, 1971).

105. Richard Quinney, *The Social Reality of Crime* (Boston: Little, Brown, 1970).

106. David F. Greenberg, *Crime and Capitalism* (Palo Alto, CA: Mayfield, 1981), p. 3.

107. For examples of how this might be accomplished, see F. H. Knopp, "Community Solutions to Sexual Violence: Feminist/Abolitionist Perspectives," in Harold E. Pepinsky and Richard Quinney, eds., *Criminology as Peacemaking* (Bloomington: Indiana University Press, 1991), pp. 181–193; and S. Caringella-MacDonald and D. Humphries, "Sexual Assault, Women, and the Community: Organizing to Prevent Sexual Violence," in Harold E. Pepinsky and Richard Quinney, eds., *Criminology as Peacemaking,* pp. 98–113.

108. Richard Quinney, "Life of Crime: Criminology and Public Policy as Peacemaking," *Journal of Crime and Justice,* Vol. 16, No. 2 (1993), pp. 3–9.

109. Ram Dass and P. Gorman, *How Can I Help? Stories and Reflections on Service* (New York: Alfred A. Knopf, 1985), p. 165, as cited in Richard Quinney and John Wildeman, *The Problem of Crime: A Peace and Social Justice Perspective,* 3d ed. (Mayfield, CA: Mountain View Press, 1991), p. 116, originally published as *The Problem of Crime: A Critical Introduction to Criminology* (New York: Bantam, 1977).

110. See, for example, Harold E. Pepinsky, "This Can't Be Peace: A Pessimist Looks at Punishment," in W. B. Groves and G. Newman, eds., *Punishment and Privilege* (Albany, NY: Harrow and Heston, 1986); Harold E. Pepinsky, "Violence as Unresponsiveness: Toward a New Conception of Crime," *Justice Quarterly,* Vol. 5 (1988), pp. 539–563; and Harold E. Pepinsky and Richard Quinney, eds., *Criminology as Peacemaking* (Bloomington: University of Indiana Press, 1991).

111. See, for example, Richard Quinney, "Crime, Suffering, Service: Toward a Criminology of Peacemaking," *Quest,* Vol. 1 (1988), pp. 66–75; Richard Quinney, "The Theory and Practice of Peacemaking in the Development of Radical Criminology," *Critical Criminologist,* Vol. 1, No. 5 (1989), p. 5; and Quinney and Wildeman, *The Problem of Crime.*

112. All of these themes are addressed, for example, in Pepinsky and Quinney, eds., *Criminology as Peacemaking.*

113. Michael J. Lynch and W. Byron Groves, *A Primer in Radical Criminology,* 2d ed. (Albany, NY: Harrow and Heston, 1989), p. 128.

114. Raymond J. Michalowski, *Order, Law, and Crime: An Introduction to Criminology* (New York: Random House, 1985), p. 410.

115. George Herbert Mead and Charles W. Morris, eds., *Mind, Self, and Society* (Chicago: University of Chicago Press, 1934).

116. William I. Thomas and Florian Znaniecki, *The Polish Peasant in Europe and America* (Chicago: University of Chicago Press, 1918).

117. Alfred Schutz, *The Phenomenology of the Social World* (Evanston, IL: Northwestern University Press, 1967).

118. Stuart Henry and Dragan Milovanovic, "Constitutive Criminology: The Maturation of Critical Theory," *Criminology,* Vol. 29, No. 2 (May 1991), p. 293.

119. Dragan Milovanovic, *Postmodern Criminology* (Hamden, CT: Garland, 1997).

120. See also Stuart Henry and Dragan Milovanovic, *Constitutive Criminology: Beyond Postmodernism* (London: Sage, 1996).

121. Many of the concepts used by Howard Becker in explicating his theory of labeling were, in fact, used previously not only by Frank Tannenbaum, but also by Edwin M. Lemert. Lemert wrote of "societal reaction" and "primary" and "secondary deviance" and even used the word *labeling* in his book *Social Pathology* (New York: McGraw-Hill, 1951).

122. Frank Tannenbaum, *Crime and the Community* (Boston: Ginn, 1938), pp. 19–20.

123. Howard Becker, *Outsiders: Studies in the Sociology of Deviance* (New York: Free Press, 1963), pp. 8–9.

124. Ibid.

125. Ibid., p. 33.

126. For an excellent overview of feminist theory in criminology and for a comprehensive review of research regarding female offenders, see Joanne Belknap, *The Invisible Woman: Gender Crime and Justice* (Belmont, CA: Wadsworth, 1996).

127. Don C. Gibbons, *Talking about Crime and Criminals: Problems and Issues in Theory Development in Criminology* (Englewood Cliffs, NJ: Prentice Hall, 1994), p. 165, citing Loraine Gelsthorpe and Alison Morris, "Feminism and Criminology in Britain," *British Journal of Criminology,* Vol. 110.

128. Sally S. Simpson, "Feminist Theory, Crime and Justice," *Criminology,* Vol. 27, No. 4 (1989), p. 605.

129. Freda Adler, *Sisters in Crime: The Rise of the New Female Criminal* (New York: McGraw-Hill, 1975).

130. Rita J. Simon, *Women and Crime* (Lexington, MA: Lexington Books, 1975).

131. See, for example, Darrell J. Steffensmeir, "Sex Differences in Patterns of Adult Crime, 1965–1977: A Review and Assessment," *Social Forces,* Vol. 58 (1980), pp. 1098–1099.

132. See, for example, Kathleen Daly and Meda Chesney-Lind, "Feminism and Criminology," *Justice Quarterly,* Vol. 5, No. 5 (December 1988), pp. 497–535.

133. Ibid., p. 506.

134. Ibid.

135. Ibid., p. 514.

136. For an excellent and detailed discussion of many of these approaches, see Milovanovic, *Postmodern Criminology.*

137. See, for example, Henry and Milovanovic, *Constitutive Criminology*; and Milovanovic, *Postmodern Criminology.*

Criminal Law

LEARNING OBJECTIVES

After reading this chapter, you should be able to

■ Discuss the history, nature, and purposes of the criminal law

■ Explain the concept of natural law, and differentiate between *mala in se* and *mala prohibita* offenses

■ Understand the nature of the rule of law and its purpose in Western democratic societies

■ Identify the various categories or types of law and the purpose of each

■ List five categories of criminal law violations

■ List the eight general features of crime

■ Explain the concept of *corpus delicti*

■ Discuss the four broad categories of defenses to crime that our legal system recognizes

■ Name at least five new and emerging innovative defenses

chapter 4

[
Law is the art of the good and the fair.
]

—Ulpian, Roman judge (circa A.D. 200)

[
Every law is an infraction of liberty.
]

—Jeremy Bentham (1748–1832)

[
Law should be like death, which spares no one.
]

—Montesquieu (1689–1755)

Key Concepts

[Terms]

actus reus	element (of a crime)	M'Naghten rule
alibi	entrapment	motive
alter ego rule	espionage	natural law
attendant circumstances	excuse	offense
battered women's syndrome (BWS)	felony	penal code
case law	gross negligence	precedent
civil law	guilty but mentally ill (GBMI)	procedural defense
class-action lawsuit	inchoate offense	procedural law
codification	incompetent to stand trial	punitive damages
common law	infraction	reasonable force
compensatory damages	insanity defense	reckless behavior
concurrence	jural postulates	rule of law
concurring opinion	jurisprudence	self-defense
corpus delicti	justification	*stare decisis*
criminal law	law	statutory law
criminal negligence	legal cause	strict liability
cultural defense	*mala in se*	substantive criminal law
defense (to a criminal charge)	*mala prohibita*	tort
diminished capacity	*mens rea*	treason
double jeopardy	misdemeanor	

[Names]

Oliver Wendell Holmes	John Stuart Mill	Roscoe Pound
Karl Marx	Daniel M'Naghten	Nigel Walker

[Cases]

Ake v. *Oklahoma*	*Ford* v. *Wainwright*	*U.S.* v. *Brawner*
The Crown v. *Dudly & Stephens*	*Foucha* v. *Louisiana*	*U.S.* v. *Felix*
Durham v. *United States*		

Introduction

Hear the author discuss this chapter at **cjtoday.com**

Twenty years ago, as South American jungles were being cleared to make way for farmers and other settlers, a group of mercenaries brutally attacked and wiped out a small tribe of local Indians. About two dozen native men, women, and children were either hacked to death with machetes or shot. The Indians had refused to give up their land and would not move. At their arrest, the killers uttered something that, to our ears, sounds frightening: "How can you arrest us?" they said. "We didn't know it was illegal to kill Indians!"

These men killed many people. But, they claimed, they were ignorant of the fact that the law forbade such a thing. In this case, these killers didn't consider their victims to be human. It may seem obvious to us that what they had done was commit murder, but to them it was something else. Nevertheless, their ignorance of the law was rejected as a defense at their trial, and they were convicted of murder. All received lengthy prison sentences.

The men in this story were hardly literate, with almost no formal education. They knew very little about the law and, apparently, even less about basic moral principles. We, on the other hand, living in a modern society with highly developed means of communication, much formal schooling, and a large workforce of professionals skilled in interpreting the law, usually know what the law *says*. But do we really know what the law *is?* The job of this chapter is to discuss the law both as a product of rule creation and as a guide for behavior. We will also examine criminal law in some detail, and we will discuss defenses commonly used by defendants charged with violations of the criminal law.

The Nature of Law

Practically speaking, **laws** regulate relationships between people and also between parties (such as agencies of government and individuals). Most of us would probably agree that the law is whatever legislators, through the exercise of their politically sanctioned wisdom, tell us it is. If we hold to that belief, we would expect to be able to find the law unambiguously specified in a set of books or codes. As we shall see, however, such is not always the case.

The laws of our nation, or of a state, are found in statutory provisions and constitutional enactments,[1] as well as in hundreds of years of rulings by courts at all levels. According to the authoritative *Black's Law Dictionary*, the word *law* "generally contemplates both **statutory and case law**."[2] If "the law" could be found entirely ensconced in written legal codes, it would be plain to nearly everyone, and we would need far fewer lawyers than we find practicing today. But some laws (in the sense of precedents established by courts) do not exist "on the books," and even those that do are open to interpretation.

The Development of Law

Modern law is the result of a long evolution of legal principles (Table 4–1). A complete and accurate understanding of today's criminal law can only be had by someone who is informed as to both its history and its philosophical foundation. Before discussing further the nature of law, it will be useful to examine some of the historical sources of contemporary law. It is to such sources that our attention now turns.

The Code of Hammurabi

The Code of Hammurabi, the earliest known **codification** of laws, is also one of the oldest bodies of law to survive and be available for study today. King Hammurabi ruled the ancient city of Babylon around the year 1750 B.C. The Code of Hammurabi is a set of laws, engraved on stone tablets, that were intended to establish property and other rights. Babylon was a commercial center, and the right of private property formed a crucial basis for prosperous growth. Hammurabi's laws spoke to issues of theft, ownership, sexual relationships, and interpersonal violence. Even though Hammurabi's code specified a variety of corporal punishments—even death for a number of offenses—it routinized the practice of justice in Babylonian society by lending predictability to punishments. Prior to the code, captured offenders often faced the most barbarous and capricious of punishments, frequently at the hands of revenge-seeking victims, no matter how minor their offenses had been. As renowned criminologist Marvin Wolfgang has observed, "In its day, 1700 B.C., the Hammurabi Code, with its emphasis on retribution, amounted to a brilliant advance in penal philosophy mainly because it represented an attempt to keep cruelty within bounds."[3] See **Web Extras! 4–1** and **4–2** at cjtoday.com to learn more about the Code of Hammurabi.

law

A rule of conduct, generally found enacted in the form of a statute, that proscribes or mandates certain forms of behavior. Statutory law is often the result of moral enterprise by interest groups that, through the exercise of political power, are successful in seeing their valued perspectives enacted into law.

statutory law

Written or codified law; the "law on the books," as enacted by a government body or agency having the power to make laws.

case law

The body of judicial precedent, historically built upon legal reasoning and past interpretations of statutory laws, that serves as a guide to decision making, especially in the courts.

codification

The act or process of rendering laws in written form.

SOURCES OF THE LAW	**TABLE 4–1**

Historical Sources of the Law	Modern Sources of American Law
Natural law	The U.S. Constitution
Early Roman law	The Declaration of Independence
Common law	Statutes
The Old and New Testaments	Case law
The Magna Carta	
Religious belief and practice	

The Code of Hammurabi, one of the oldest judicial codes known. It was discovered inscribed on this stone obelisk, which dates from 1750 B.C. Figures at the top of the stone (a portion of which is shown here) depict King Hammurabi receiving the law from the Babylonian sun god.

CORBIS

Early Roman Law

The Code of Hammurabi is primarily of archaeological importance. Of considerable significance for our own legal tradition, however, is early Roman law. Roman legions under the Emperor Claudius conquered England in the middle of the first century. Roman authority over Britannia was consolidated by later rulers, who built walls and fortifications to keep out the still-hostile Scots. Roman customs, law, and language were forced upon the English population during the succeeding three centuries under the Pax Romana—a peace imposed by the military of Rome.[4]

Roman law derived from the Twelve Tables, written about 450 B.C. The Twelve Tables were a collection of basic rules related to family, religious, and economic life. The tables appear to have been based upon common and fair practices generally accepted among early tribes, which existed prior to the establishment of the Roman Republic. Unfortunately, only fragments of the tables survive today.

The best-known legal period of Roman history occurred under the rule of the Emperor Justinian I, who ruled between A.D. 527 and 565. By the sixth century, the Roman Empire had declined substantially in size and influence and was near the end of its life. In what may have been an effort to preserve Roman values and traditions, Justinian undertook the laborious process of distilling Roman laws into a set of writings. The Justinian Code actually consisted of three lengthy legal documents: (1) the Institutes, (2) the Digest, and (3) the code itself. Justinian's code distinguished between two major legal categories: public and private laws. Public laws dealt with the organization of the Roman state, its senate, and governmental offices. Private law concerned itself with contracts, personal possessions, the legal status of various types of people (citizens, free people, slaves, freedmen, guardians, husbands and wives, and so on), and injuries to citizens. It contained elements of both our modern civil and criminal law and, no doubt, influenced Western legal thought through the Middle Ages.

Common Law

Common law forms the basis of much of our modern statutory and case law. It has often been called the major source of modern criminal law in the United States.

Common law had its origins in early English society. The term *common law* refers to a traditional body of early unwritten legal precedents created from everyday English social customs, rules, and practices that were supported by judicial decisions during the Middle Ages. As novel situations arose and were dealt with by British justices, their reasoning and recorded declarations provided a basis for deciding similar cases in the future. These decisions generally incorporated the customs of society as they existed at the time. Eventually, this growing body of judicial pronouncements congealed into a set of legal rules that were widely accepted as a kind of national law and were commonly applied throughout England—and common law was born. During this early stage of legal development, judges often took it upon themselves to formally criminalize actions that had previously been regarded as the basis for private disputes. Hence, many acts which we call *crimes* today, such as murder, rape, arson, and burglary, might have remained in the private sphere had

common law

Law originating from usage and custom rather than from written statutes. The term refers to an unwritten body of judicial opinion, originally developed by English courts, that is based upon nonstatutory customs, traditions, and precedents that help guide judicial decision making.

it not been for such common law developments. As Howard Abadinsky, professor of criminal justice at Saint Xavier University in Chicago said, "Common law involved the transformation of community rules into a national legal system. The controlling element [was] precedent."[5]

Common law was given considerable legitimacy in England upon the official declaration that it was the law of the land by King Edward the Confessor in the eleventh century. The authority of common law was further reinforced by the decision of William the Conqueror to use popular customs as the basis for judicial action following his subjugation of Britain in A.D. 1066. Eventually, court decisions were recorded and made available to barristers (the English name for trial lawyers) and judges throughout England and much of the British empire.

English common law has had a substantial impact upon the development of law in the United States since the early colonial period. Like the rest of the British empire at the time, the colonies fashioned their budding judicial systems out of principles inherent in the common law. Today, common law has been largely supplanted in all U.S. jurisdictions by statutory (written) law. Nonetheless, common law principles still serve as powerful interpreters of legal issues which frequently arise around the need to clarify terminology found in state codes, as well as the dictates of state law. Hence, it is not uncommon to hear of jurisdictions within the United States referred to as "common law jurisdictions" or "common law states." Learn more about common law at **Web Extra! 4–3** at cjtoday.com.

The Magna Carta

The Magna Carta (literally, "great charter") is another important source of modern laws and legal procedure. The Magna Carta was signed on June 15, 1215, by King John of England at Runnymede, under pressure from British barons who took advantage of John's military defeats at the hands of Pope Innocent III and King Philip Augustus of France. The barons demanded a pledge from the king to respect their traditional rights, and they forced the king to agree to be bound by law.

At the time of its signing, the Magna Carta, although 63 chapters in length, was little more than a feudal document[6] listing specific royal concessions. Its wording, however, was later interpreted during a judicial revolt in 1613 to support individual rights. Sir Edward Coke, Chief Justice under James I, held that the Magna Carta guaranteed basic liberties for all British citizens and ruled that any acts of Parliament which contravened common law would be void. There is some evidence that this famous ruling served as a model for the U.S. Supreme Court, with its power to nullify laws enacted by Congress.[7] Similarly, one specific provision of the Magna Carta, designed originally to prohibit the king from prosecuting the barons without just cause, was expanded into the concept of due process of law, a cornerstone of modern legal procedure. Because of these later interpretations, the Magna Carta has been called "the foundation stone of our present liberties."[8]

The U.S. Constitution

The U.S. Constitution is one of the most significant and enduring wellsprings of our modern criminal law. The Constitution was created through a long process of debate by the federal Constitutional Convention, which met in Philadelphia in 1787. The Constitution is the final authority in all questions pertaining to the rights of individuals, the power of the federal government and the states to create laws and to prosecute offenders, and the limits of punishments which can be imposed for law violations.

Although the Constitution does not itself contain many specific prohibitions on behavior, it is the final authority in deciding whether new and existing laws are acceptable according to the ideals upon which our country was founded. Historically, under the principle of due process (discussed in more detail in Chapter 1), embodied in the Fifth, Sixth, and Fourteenth Amendments, it has also served to guide justices in gauging the merits of citizens' claims concerning the handling of their cases by the agencies of justice.

> No State shall make or enforce any law which shall abridge the privileges or immunities of citizens of the United States; nor shall any State deprive any person of life, liberty, or property, without due process of law; nor deny to any person within its jurisdiction the equal protection of the laws.
>
> —Fourteenth Amendment to the U.S. Constitution

Natural Law

Some people believe that the basis for many of our criminal laws can be found in immutable moral principles or in some identifiable aspect of the natural order. The Ten Commandments, "inborn tendencies," the idea of sin, and perceptions of various forms of order in the universe and in the social world have all provided a basis for the assertion that a "natural law" exists. **Natural law** comes from outside the social group and is thought to be knowable through some form of revelation, intuition, reason, or prophecy.

natural law

Rules of conduct inherent in human nature and in the natural order that are thought to be knowable through intuition, inspiration, and the exercise of reason, without the need for reference to created laws.

Natural law was used by the early Christian church as a powerful argument in support of its interests. Secular rulers were pressed to reinforce church doctrine in any laws they decreed. Thomas Aquinas (1225–1274) wrote in his *Summa Theologica* that any man-made law which contradicts natural law is corrupt in the eyes of God.[9] Religious practice, which strongly reflected natural law conceptions, was central to the life of early British society. Hence, natural law, as it was understood at the time, was incorporated into English common law throughout the Middle Ages.

The U.S. Declaration of Independence is built around natural law, as understood by Thomas Jefferson and other signers of that important document. When Jefferson wrote of inalienable rights to "Life, Liberty, and the pursuit of Happiness," he referred to the natural due of all men and women. Truths which are held to be "self-evident" can only be such if they are somehow available to us all through reasoning or the promptings of conscience.

Students of natural law have set for themselves the task of uncovering just what that law encompasses. The modern debate over abortion is an example of the use of natural law arguments to support both sides in the dispute. Antiabortion forces, frequently called *pro-lifers,* claim that the unborn fetus is a person and that he or she is entitled to all the protections that we could reasonably and ethically be expected to give to any other living human being. Such protection, they suggest, is basic and humane and lies in the natural relationship of one human being to another. They are striving for passage of a law or a reinterpretation of past Supreme Court precedent that would support their position.

Proponents of the present court-supported standard (which allows abortion upon request under certain conditions) maintain that abortion is a right of any pregnant woman because she is the one in control of her body. Such pro-choice groups also claim that the legal system must address the abortion question, but only by way of offering protection to this natural right of women. Keep in mind, however, that what we refer to as "the present law" is not so much a law "on the books," but rather a consequence of a decision rendered by the U.S. Supreme Court in the 1973 case of *Roe* v. *Wade.*[10]

Natural law advocates may well find supporters in high places. Natural law became an issue, for example, in the confirmation hearings conducted for U.S. Supreme Court judicial nominee Clarence Thomas in 1991. Because Judge Thomas had mentioned natural law and natural rights in speeches given prior to his nomination to the Court, Senate Judiciary Committee Chairman Joseph Biden grilled him about the concept. Biden suggested that natural law was a defunct philosophical perspective, no longer worthy of serious legal consideration, and said that the duty of a U.S. Supreme Court justice was to follow the U.S. Constitution. Thomas responded by pointing out that natural law concepts contributed greatly to the principles underlying the Constitution. It was the natural law writings of John Locke, Thomas suggested, that inspired the framers to declare: "All men are created equal."

MALA IN SE AND *MALA PROHIBITA*

mala in se
————————————
Acts that are regarded, by tradition and convention, as wrong in themselves.

Natural law lends credence to the belief that certain actions are wrong in themselves. These behaviors are called **mala in se,** a Latin term which generally includes crimes against humanity (such as the planned extermination of much of the Jewish population in parts of Nazi-controlled Europe during World War II) and serious personal crimes, including murder, rape, assault, and other crimes of violence. Years ago, based at least partially on natural law arguments, some states legislated a special offense category called *crime against nature.* Crimes against nature, as specified in laws which have been handed down from those times, mostly encompass sexual deviance, which is regarded as "contrary to the order of nature." Homosexuality, bestiality, and oral copulation may be prosecuted under such statutes and can carry with them quite severe potential punishments—even though large segments of the contemporary American population have experienced a shift in values. Today, relatively few forms of personal choice in the sexual arena (outside of those which directly victimize nonwilling participants) are inherently condemned or seen as "unnatural."

It is easy to imagine that members of primitive societies, without a system of codified statutes, would still understand that some forms of behavior are wrong. This intuitive recognition of deviance lends support to the idea of natural law and to the classification of certain offenses as *mala in se.*

mala prohibita
————————————
Acts that are considered wrong only because there is a law against them.

Crimes which fall outside of the "natural" category are called **mala prohibita,** meaning that they are wrong only because they are prohibited by the law (*malum prohibitum* is the term that refers to one such crime). Poaching on the king's land is an example of what was a *mala prohibita* crime under English common law. Most crimes which fall under the heading of "morals offenses" today might be called *mala prohibita*. Such offenses include prostitution, gambling, and illicit drug use.

The distinction between *mala in se* and *mala prohibita* offenses derives from common law and was an important consideration in deciding sentences in early England. *Mala prohibita* crimes were tried by justices of the peace and carried penalties which were generally far less severe than those for *mala in se* crimes.

> The greatest happiness of the greatest number is the foundation of morals and legislation.
>
> —Jeremy Bentham

The Rule of Law

The social, economic, and political stability of any society depends largely upon the development and institutionalization of a predictable system of laws. Western democratic societies adhere to the **rule of law**, which is sometimes also referred to as the *supremacy of law.*

The rule of law concept centers around the belief that an orderly society must be governed by established principles and known codes which are applied uniformly and fairly to all of its members. Under the rule of law, no one is above the law, and those who enforce the law must abide by it.

The rule of law has been called the greatest political achievement of our culture. Without it, few other human achievements—especially those which require the efforts of a large number of people working together in coordinated fashion—would be possible.

President John F. Kennedy eloquently explained the rule of law, saying, "Americans are free to disagree with the law, but not to disobey it; for [in] a government of laws and not of men, no man, however prominent and powerful, no mob, however unruly or boisterous, is entitled to defy a court of law."[11]

The American Bar Association notes that the rule of law includes these elements:

- Freedom from private lawlessness provided by the legal system of a politically organized society
- A relatively high degree of objectivity in the formulation of legal norms and a like degree of evenhandedness in their application
- Legal ideas and juristic devices for the attainment of individual and group objectives within the bounds of ordered liberty
- Substantive and procedural limitations on governmental power in the interest of the individual for the enforcement of which there are appropriate legal institutions and machinery[12]

To learn more about the rule of law, visit **Web Extra! 4–4** at cjtoday.com.

rule of law

The maxim that an orderly society must be governed by established principles and known codes that are applied uniformly and fairly to all of its members.

Purposes of the Law

Imagine a society without laws. People would not know what to expect from one another (an area controlled by the law of contracts) nor would they be able to plan for the future with any degree of certainty (administrative law); they wouldn't feel safe (criminal law), knowing that the more powerful or better armed could take what they wanted from the less powerful; and they might not be able to exercise basic rights which would otherwise be available to them as citizens of a free nation (constitutional law). In short, laws channel human behavior while they simultaneously constrain it, and they empower individuals while contributing to public order.

A few years ago, the author encountered the results of a survey of attitudes among college-aged males from across the country. One of the most surprising of the survey's findings was this: Nearly 90% of the young men questioned said they would probably rape a woman if there were no laws against forced sexual behavior. These men were admitting to strong sexual drives, which they conceded they would attempt to gratify if the threat of legislated sanctions could not be applied to them. While the honesty of those responding to the questionnaire is to be appreciated, this single finding highlights the need for formal rules which put limits on the behavior of all those who make up any society. Laws, and criminal laws in particular, are needed to prevent the victimization of innocents by those seeking purely selfish pleasures. The truth of this assertion is borne out by the lawlessness experienced in war zones, where the number of crimes of all sorts—especially rape and looting—tends to rise dramatically (as happened in Kuwait after Iraqi forces overran the country in 1991, as well as during the more recent wars in Bosnia, Serbia, and Croatia).

Max Weber (1864–1920), an eminent sociologist of the early twentieth century, said the primary purpose of law is to regulate the flow of human interaction.[13] By creating enforceable rules, laws make the behavior of others predictable. This first, and most significant, purpose of the law can be simply stated: Laws support public order.

Laws also serve a variety of other purposes. They ensure that the philosophical, moral, and economic perspectives of their creators are protected and made credible. They maintain values and uphold established patterns of social privilege. They sustain existing power relationships, and finally, they support a system for the punishment and rehabilitation of offenders (see Table 4–2). Modifications of the law, when gradually induced, promote orderly change in the rest of society.

The question of *what the law does* is quite different from the question of *what the law should do.* Writing in the mid-1800s, for example, John Stuart Mill (1806–1873) questioned the liberal use of the criminal law as a tool for social reform.[14] Mill objected strongly to the use of law as a "way of compulsion and control" for any purpose other than to prevent harm to others. Behavior which might be thought morally wrong should not be contravened by law, said Mill, unless it is also harmful to others. In similar fashion, Nigel Walker, a British criminologist of this century, applied what he called "a sociological eye" to the criminal codes of Western nations and concluded that criminal statutes are not appropriate when they seek to contravene behavior which lacks a clear and immediate harm to others; nor, he said, should laws be created for the purpose of compelling people to act in their own good.[15]

In reality, few legal codes live up to the Walker-Mill criteria. Most are influenced strongly by cultural conceptions of right and wrong. Throughout American criminal law, for example, Judeo-Christian principles hold considerable sway. Concepts such as sin and atonement provide for a view of men and women as willful actors in a world of personal and sensual temptations. Such ideas have made possible both the legal notion of guilt and corrections-based punishment, and encompass many behaviors which are not immediately and directly harmful to anyone but those who choose to be involved with them. These illegal activities, often called *victimless crimes,* include drug abuse, certain forms of "deviant" sexuality, gambling, and various other legally proscribed consensual deeds. Advocates of legislation designed to curb these activities suggest that while such behavior is not always directly harmful to others, it may erode social cohesiveness and ruin the lives of those who engage in it.

Standing in strong opposition to the Walker-Mill perspective are legislators and theorists who purposefully use the law as a tool to facilitate social change. Modifications in the legal structure of a society can quickly and dramatically produce changes in the behavior of entire groups. A change in the tax laws, for example, typically sends people scrambling to their accountants to devise spending and investment strategies which take advantage of the change. Our legal system not only condemns interpersonal violence and enforces tax codes, it also serves to support the dominant economic order (capitalism) and to protect the powerful and the wealthy (through an emphasis on private property and the rights which attach to property).

The realization that laws respond to the needs and interests of society at any given time was put into words by the famed jurist Oliver Wendell Holmes (1841–1935) in an address he gave at Harvard University in 1881. Holmes said, "The life of the law has not been logic; it has been experience. The felt necessities of the time, the prevalent moral and political theories, institutions of public policy, avowed or unconscious, even the prejudices which judges share with their fellowmen have had a good deal more to do than the syllogism in

TABLE 4–2	**WHAT DO LAWS DO?**
• Laws maintain order in society.	• Laws promote orderly social change.
• Laws regulate human interaction.	• Laws sustain individual rights.
• Laws enforce moral beliefs.	• Laws redress wrongs.
• Laws define the economic environment.	• Laws identify wrongdoers.
• Laws enhance predictability.	• Laws mandate punishment and retribution.
• Laws support the powerful.	

determining the rules by which men should be governed."[16] The "syllogism," as Holmes used the term, referred to abstract theorizing as the basis for law. The importance of such "theorizing" he thoroughly discounted.

Once law has been created, it is generally slow to change because it is built upon years of tradition. The law can be thought of as a force which supports public order but which is opposed to rapid social change. When law facilitates change, that change usually proceeds in an orderly and deliberate fashion. Revolutions, on the other hand, produce near-instantaneous legal changes but bring with them massive social disorder.

Social Engineering

One of the greatest legal scholars of the twentieth century was Roscoe Pound (1870–1964), Dean of the Harvard Law School from 1916 to 1936. Pound built the rule of law principle to describe law as a useful tool for intentional social engineering.[17] The law can be used as a tool, Pound said, to meet the demands of men and women living together in society. Pound believed that the law must be able to change with the times and to reflect new needs as they arise. Intentional changes in the law, said Pound, can result in predictable and planned changes in the structure and functioning of society.

Pound distilled his ideas into a set of **jural postulates**. Such postulates, claimed Pound, form the basis of all law because they reflect shared needs. In 1942, Pound published his postulates in the form of five propositions.[18] Visit **Web Extra! 4–5** at cjtoday.com to learn more about Roscoe Pound's jural postulates.

Pound's postulates form a theory of "consensus" about the origins of law—both civil and criminal. They suggest that most laws are the product of shared social needs experienced by the majority of members in the society where they arise. However, a number of writers have criticized Pound for failing to recognize the diversity of society. How, they ask, can the law address common needs in society when society consists of many different groups, each with its own set of interests and needs? As a consequence of such criticism, Pound modified his theory to include a "jurisprudence of interest." Whereas the concept of **jurisprudence** refers simply to the philosophy of law or to the science and study of the law, the concept of a jurisprudence of interest holds that one of the basic purposes of law is to satisfy "as many claims or demands of as many people as possible."[19] Learn more about structuring criminal codes to perform specific functions via **Library Extra! 4–1.**

Social Conflict

Opposed to Pound's theory of consensus is William Chambliss's view of law as a tool of powerful individuals and groups acting in their own interests—and often in conflict with one another.[20] Conflict theory has its roots in the writings of Karl Marx (1818–1883), who explained all of social history as the result of an ongoing conflict between the haves and the have-nots.

Chambliss believes we should not see the agencies of criminal justice as "neutral." Rather, he says, government is "a weapon of the dominant classes or interest groups in society."[21] Putting it more directly, Chambliss writes, "In one way or another, the laws which are passed, implemented, and incorporated into the legal system reflect the interests of those groups capable of having their views incorporated into the official (that is legal) views of the society."[22]

Types of Law

Criminal and civil law are the best-known types of modern law. However, scholars and philosophers have drawn numerous distinctions between categories of law which rest upon their source, intent, and application. Laws in modern societies can be usefully described in terms of the following groups:

- Criminal law
- Civil law
- Administrative law
- Case law
- Procedural law

This typology is helpful in understanding and thinking about the law, and we will now discuss each type of law in some detail.

jural postulates

Propositions developed by the famous jurist Roscoe Pound that hold that the law reflects shared needs without which members of society could not coexist. Pound's jural postulates are often linked to the idea that the law can be used to engineer the social structure to ensure certain kinds of outcomes. (In capitalist societies, for example, the law of theft protects property rights.)

jurisprudence

The philosophy of law. Also, the science and study of the law.

Criminal Law

criminal law

The branch of modern law that concerns itself with offenses committed against society, its members, their property, and the social order.

Fundamental to the concept of **criminal law** is the assumption that criminal acts injure not just individuals, but society as a whole. Hence we can define *criminal law* as the body of rules and regulations that define and specify punishments for offenses of a public nature or for wrongs committed against the state or society. Criminal law is also called *penal law.*

Public order, as reflected in the values supported by statute, is reduced to some degree whenever a criminal act occurs. In old England (from which much of American legal tradition devolves), offenders were said to have violated the "king's peace" when they committed a crime. They not only offended their victims, but contravened the peaceful order established under the rule of the monarch. For this reason, in criminal cases the state, as the injured party, begins the official process of bringing the offender to justice. Even if the victim is dead and has no one to speak on his or her behalf, the agencies of justice will investigate the crime and file charges against the offender. Because crimes injure the fabric of society, the state, not the individual victim, becomes the plaintiff in criminal proceedings. Cases in criminal court reflect this fact by being cited as follows: *State of New York* v. *Smith* (where state law has been violated) or *U.S.* v. *Smith* (where the federal government is the injured party).

Violations of the criminal law result in the imposition of punishment. Punishment is philosophically justified by the fact that the criminal *intended* the harm and is responsible for it. Punishment serves a variety of purposes, which we will discuss in Chapter 10. When punishment is imposed in a criminal case, however, it is for one basic reason: to express society's fundamental displeasure with the offensive behavior and to hold the offender accountable for it.

penal code

The written, organized, and compiled form of the criminal laws of a jurisdiction.

Criminal law, which is built upon constitutional principles and which operates within an established set of procedures applicable to the criminal justice system, is composed of both statutory and case law. Statutory law is the "law on the books." It is the result of legislative action and is often thought of as the "law of the land." Written laws exist in both criminal and civil areas and are called *codes.* Once laws have been written down in organized fashion, they are said to be *codified.* Federal statutes are compiled in the U.S. Code (U.S.C.). State codes and municipal ordinances are also readily available in written, or statutory, form. The written form of the criminal law is called the **penal code**.

substantive criminal law

The part of the law that defines crimes and specifies punishments.

Written law is of two types: substantive and procedural. Substantive law deals directly with specifying the nature of, and appropriate punishment for, particular offenses. For example, every state in our country has laws against murder, rape, robbery, and assault. Differences in the law among these various jurisdictions can be studied in detail because each offense and the punishments associated with it are available in written form in the **substantive criminal law**. Procedural laws, on the other hand, specify acceptable methods for dealing with violations of substantive laws, especially within the context of a judicial setting. Learn more about the criminal law via **Library Extras! 4–2, 4–3,** and **4–4.**

Civil Law

civil law

The branch of modern law that governs relationships between parties.

Civil law provides a formal means for regulating noncriminal relationships between and among people, businesses and other organizations, and agencies of government. In contrast to the criminal law, whose violation is an offense against the state or against the nation, civil law governs relationships between parties. Civil law contains rules for contracts, divorce, child support and custody, the creation of wills, property transfers, negligence, libel, unfair practices in hiring, the manufacture and sale of consumer goods with hidden hazards for the user, and many other contractual and social obligations. When the civil law is violated, a civil suit may follow.

tort

A wrongful act, damage, or injury not involving a breach of contract. Also, a private or civil wrong or injury.

Civil suits seek not punishment, but compensation, usually in the form of property or monetary damages. They may also be filed to achieve an injunction, or a kind of judicial cease-and-desist order. A violation of the civil law may be a **tort** (a wrongful act, damage, or injury not involving a breach of contract) or a contract violation, but it is not a crime. A tort involving, say, an automobile accident may give rise to civil liability under which the injured party may sue the person or entity who caused the injury and ask that the offending party be ordered to pay damages directly to them. Because a tort is a personal wrong, however, it is left to the aggrieved individual to set the machinery of the court in motion— that is, to bring a suit.

Civil law is more concerned with assessing liability than it is with intent. Civil suits arising from automobile crashes, for example, do not allege that the driver intended to inflict bodily harm. Nor do they claim that it was the intent of the driver to damage either vehicle.

However, when someone is injured, or property damage occurs, even in an accident, civil procedures make it possible to gauge responsibility and to assign liability to one party or the other. The parties to a civil suit are referred to as the *plaintiff* (who seeks relief) and the *defendant* (against whom relief is sought).

In 1999, for example, jurors in Pontiac, Michigan, decided that the producers of the Jenny Jones television talk show would have to pay more than $25 million in damages associated with the slaying of a guest who had appeared on the show. Scott Amedure was killed by Jonathan Schmitz after revealing on national television that he had a crush on Schmitz. Jurors found the producers liable because they created the situation which led to Amedure's death and because they misled Schmitz into thinking he was about to meet a woman. Amedure's family was ordered to receive $5 million in damages for the suffering Amedure endured before his death, $10 million for the loss of a loved one's companionship, and another $10 million for the loss of money Amedure would have earned during his lifetime.[23]

Compensatory damages are awarded to compensate the victim or his or her survivors for actual losses and for the dollar amount that can be ascribed to pain, suffering, lost quality of life, and so on.

Currently, many states award **punitive damages** (which are often intended to compensate for mental anguish, degradation, shame, or hurt feelings suffered by the plaintiff) when jurors determine that the chances were better than 50% that the defendant acted with **gross negligence**. Punitive damage awards can be huge. In 1996, for example, an Alabama jury awarded 37-year-old Alex Hardy $50 million in compensatory damages and $100 million in punitive damages after he was left partially paralyzed in the crash of his Chevrolet Blazer. Jurors found that door latches on the vehicle were defective, causing Hardy to be thrown from the vehicle.[24]

That amount pales, however, beside the $4.9 billion civil judgment against General Motors awarded to six people by a Los Angeles jury in 1999. The case, which resulted in the biggest personal-injury award in U.S. history, involved an exploding gas tank on a 1979 Chevrolet Malibu, a problem which General Motors apparently knew about but refused to fix. Only $107 million of the judgment was awarded for compensatory damages in the 1993 accident. The other $4.8 billion consisted of punitive damages. Los Angeles Superior Court Judge Ernest Williams later reduced the punitive damage award to $1.1 billion. General Motors is continuing to appeal the judgment as this book goes to press.[25]

Another huge product liability award was made in 1994 when a judge agreed to accept a $4.2 billion financial settlement between Dow Corning and other makers of silicone breast implants and members of a class-action suit that had been brought against the

compensatory damages

Damages recovered in payment for an actual injury or economic loss.

punitive damages

Damages requested and/or awarded in a civil lawsuit when the defendant's willful acts were malicious, violent, oppressive, fraudulent, wanton, or grossly reckless.[i]

gross negligence

The intentional failure to perform a manifest duty in reckless disregard of the consequences as affecting the life or property of another."[ii]

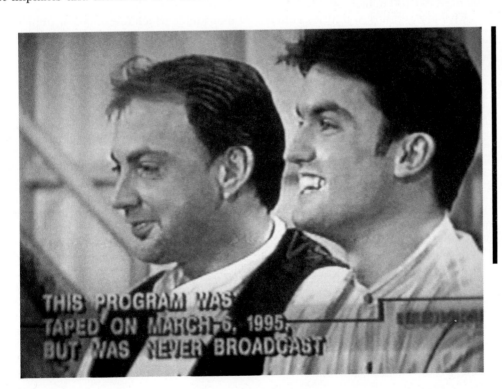

Jonathan Schmitz (right) sitting next to Scott Amedure in this image taken from video shown to jurors in Schmitz's first-degree murder trial in Pontiac, Michigan, in 1996. Schmitz was convicted of killing Amedure after Amedure revealed during a taping of the Jenny Jones show that he had a crush on Schmitz. In 1999, Schmitz was sentenced to 25 to 50 years in prison for the murder. In a civil suit decided a few months earlier, Warner Brothers, the corporate parent of the Jenny Jones show, was ordered to pay more than $25 million to Amedure's family.

Court TV, AP/Wide World Photos

Patricia Anderson posing with her daughter, Alisha Parker, at their attorney's office. In 1999, Anderson, her four children, and a family friend were awarded $4.9 billion by a Los Angeles civil jury in a suit against General Motors. The suit stemmed from a 1993 Beverly Hills accident in which the plaintiffs were burned when the gas tank of their 1979 Chevrolet Malibu exploded in flames. The huge personal-injury award was the largest in U.S. history. Upon appeal, it was reduced to $1.1 billion.

Fred Prouser, Reuters, Getty Images, Inc.

manufacturers. Dow Corning later reorganized its operations under bankruptcy protection. To date, the largest civil settlement (reached prior to trial), however, is the $206 billion that American tobacco companies agreed to pay in late 1998 to compensate states for the cost of caring for patients with cancer caused by smoking and to help finance antismoking research and education programs. The amount is to be paid over a 25-year period.

Lawsuits against tobacco companies continue. In July 2000, jurors in Dade County, Florida, awarded $145 billion to plaintiffs in a **class-action lawsuit** against five of the nation's largest tobacco companies. The judgment, if it stands up to appeals, will benefit 700,000 Floridians who became sick as the result of smoking (or their survivors). In 2001, a Los Angeles jury ordered Philip Morris, Inc., to pay more than $3 billion to sick smoker Richard Boeken, 56, of Topanga, California. Later that same year, however, the award was reduced to $100 million by a Los Angeles Superior Court judge.[26]

Civil law pertains to injuries suffered by individuals which are unfair or unjust according to the standards operative in the social group. Breaches of contract, unfair practices in hiring, the manufacture and sale of consumer goods with hidden hazards for the user, and slanderous comments made about others have all been grounds for civil suits. Suits may, on occasion, arise as extensions of criminal action. Monetary compensation may be sought through our system of civil laws by a victim of a criminal assault after a criminal conviction has been obtained.

In a 1993 civil case, for example, a Florida jury found Kmart liable for selling a gun to a drunken man. The buyer, Thomas W. Knapp, used the weapon a half hour later to shoot his girlfriend, Deborah Kitchen, in the neck, leaving her permanently paralyzed. Knapp had consumed 24 beers and nearly 25 shots of whiskey prior to purchasing the weapon. He was convicted of attempted first-degree murder and is serving a 40-year prison term. Following a civil suit brought by Kitchen, Kmart was ordered to pay her $12 million, sending a message to gun retailers across the nation. In 1997, the Florida Supreme Court upheld the award.[27]

In a precedent-setting 1995 case, a San Francisco Superior Court judge ruled that a lawsuit against a gun maker brought by the widow of a man slain by gunfire was based upon solid legal principles and could proceed.[28] At issue was whether the handgun maker, Miami-based Navegar, Inc., could be sued under a legal theory that holds manufacturers liable for injuries caused by their products. In this case, Michelle Scully sued the gun manufacturer after her husband, John, was killed by an assailant who opened fire on workers in a California law office in 1993. As the shooting started, John Scully threw himself over his wife and shielded her with his body. The gunman, Gian Luigi Ferri, used three weapons, including two TEC-9 military-style assault pistols made by Navegar. The TEC-9s were equipped with high-capacity ammunition magazines and fitted with "Hell-Fire" triggers—

class-action lawsuit

A lawsuit filed by one or more people on behalf of themselves and a larger group of people "who are similarly situated."[iii]

devices designed to make them fire faster than they normally would.[29] Ferri killed eight people and wounded seven more before taking his own life. Although the number of killed and wounded was high, some criticized the judge's ruling against the manufacturer, saying that it opened a Pandora's box of potential suits against manufacturers of all kinds of products. Lawsuits targeting products which are not defective and which function precisely as intended, they pointed out, might result in suits against automobile manufacturers; makers of alcohol, insecticides, and high-cholesterol foods; and even against companies that make knives, gasoline, candles, cigarette lighters, and flammable materials when irresponsible individuals choose to use those products to harm others. Nonetheless, in 1999, the California Court of Appeals agreed with the lower court judge and ruled that Navegar could be held liable for damages caused by its products.[30] In August 2001, however, the suit against Navegar finally ended when the California Supreme Court dismissed the case,[31] holding that gun manufacturers are protected against certain types of lawsuits by a state law enacted in the early 1980s.[32] The California law says that, as a matter of public policy, a gun manufacturer may not be held liable "[i]n a products liability action . . . on the basis that the benefits of [its] product do not outweigh the risk of injury posed by [the product's] potential to cause serious injury, damage, or death when discharged."[33] Nonetheless, Navegar, Inc. went out of business in mid-2001. Read the California Supreme Court's opinion, which includes extracts from relevant state law, at **Web Extra! 4–6** at cjtoday.com.

Outside California, suits against gun manufacturers continued to proliferate. In 1999 and 2000, a number of cities, including Atlanta, Miami, Bridgeport, New Orleans, Chicago, Cleveland, and Boston, sued the firearms industry to recoup municipal monies spent on gun crime. The suits sought to recover costs for city-supported services utilized in instances of gun crime. Expenses for emergency medical personnel and equipment,

> If a married woman shall be caught lying with another man, both shall be bound and thrown into the river.
>
> —Code of Hammurabi

CJ Today News

[Makers Can't Be Sued for Gun Misuse]

LOS ANGELES—Reversing a lower court's landmark decision, the California Supreme Court ruled Monday that crime victims cannot sue gunmakers for damages on grounds of negligence when criminals misuse firearms.

The 5-1 decision invalidated a 1999 opinion that had marked a rare victory for plaintiffs in a wave of suits against the gun industry by individuals and local governments.

The case stems from a 1993 massacre in a San Francisco office tower. Gian Ferri, a man with a grudge against lawyers, carried two TEC-DC9 assault pistols and a third gun into the office of a law firm. Firing in rapid bursts, Ferri killed eight people and wounded six before fatally shooting himself.

A state appeals court had held that a jury could consider whether Miami-based Navegar breached a duty to the public by allegedly advertising its low-priced, fast-firing TEC-DC9 in ways that enticed criminals. Monday's ruling, a narrowly worded opinion with little direct bearing on lawsuits in other states, said that a 1983 California law exempts gun manufacturers from most product-liability suits.

"We are not insensitive to the terrible tragedy that occurred on July 1, 1993," Justice Ming Chin wrote for the Supreme Court majority. "But . . . the Legislature has set California's public policy regarding a gun manufacturer's liability under these circumstances."

In 1989, California banned sales of the TEC-DC9. (Ferri bought his guns legally in Nevada.) In 1994, Congress banned future manufacture of the pistol but allowed existing TEC-DC9s to stay in circulation. The two teenage perpetrators of the Columbine High School killings in Colorado in April 1999 used a TEC-DC9 and other weapons.

Lawrence Keane, vice president and general counsel of the National Shooting Sports Foundation, an association of gunmakers, welcomed the decision. The ruling "is just the most recent in a series of appellate court decisions repeatedly stating that you can't sue the manufacturer of a legal, non-defective product for criminal misuse of firearms," Keane said.

The New York State Court of Appeals ruled recently that a Brooklyn jury had no legal basis for finding three manufacturers liable for gun deaths in a suit the NAACP brought on behalf of several individuals. About 15 other suits by individuals have lost on appeal.

But on June 27, [2001,] a New Mexico appeals court revived a lawsuit against a handgun manufacturer and a distributor, saying they could be held liable for the injuries of a teenager accidentally shot by a friend.

Since 1998, nearly 40 municipalities have sued gun sellers on a variety of legal theories. Dismissals of suits in Cincinnati, Atlanta, New Orleans and Miami have been upheld on appeal.

Dennis Henigan, an attorney for the Washington-based Center to Prevent Handgun Violence, said Monday's decision would not derail lawsuits by 11 California cities and counties. Many of those suits allege unfair trade practices and other grounds not involving negligence.

For the latest in crime and justice news, visit the Talk Justice news feed at http://www.crimenews.info.

Source: Martin Kasindorf, "Makers Can't Be Sued for Gun Misuse: Court Says California Ruling Reverses Rare Victory for Crime Victims," *USA Today*, August 7, 2001. © 2001, *USA Today*. Reprinted with permission.

city-run hospitals, and police investigations were all covered by the suits. To date, such suits have met with only limited success, although a number are still ongoing as this book goes to press. See Chapter 2 for a more detailed discussion of gun crime and lawsuits against gun manufacturers.

Not all suits against gun makers seek monetary damages. In 1999, for example, the National Association for the Advancement of Colored People (NAACP) announced that it would sue more than a hundred handgun manufacturers, distributors, and importers in a bid to impose restrictions on the marketing and sale of firearms.[34] The NAACP's goal is to keep guns out of the hands of criminals. In place of money, the suit seeks court orders that would force gun manufacturers to monitor where the guns they produce are distributed. Another portion of the suit would place limits on multiple handgun purchases by the same individual.

Criminal action, not otherwise excusable, may even be grounds for a civil suit by the offender. In 1992, for example, a civil jury awarded $2.15 million to convicted murderer William Freeman and his family. Freeman, a former assistant chief of police from Fort Stockton, Texas, is serving a life sentence for killing his friend, Donnie Hazelwood. A jury agreed with Freeman's claim that a sleeping pill, Halcion, altered his personality and caused him to kill Hazelwood.[35] It found that the drug's manufacturer, the Upjohn Company (now known as Pharmacia Corporation, following a corporate merger), had been grossly negligent in dispensing Halcion. The jury also found, however, that Freeman did not suffer any actual injury because of Upjohn's negligence or its product. On the basis of the jury's second finding, the multimillion dollar award was later denied by the Fifth District Texas Court of Appeals, which held that damages could not be legally awarded unless actual damages to the plaintiff could be demonstrated.[36]

In June 2001, drugmaker GlaxoSmith-Kline, Inc., found itself on the losing end of a civil suit when a U.S. District Court panel in Wyoming awarded $8 million to the surviving family of an oil field worker who went on a murderous rampage in 1998 after taking the antidepressant Paxil.[37] Donald Schell killed his wife, daughter, infant granddaughter, and himself almost immediately after beginning therapy involving the drug. The court apparently accepted the plaintiff's claim that the drug can trigger inner turmoil and agitation called *akathisia*, leading to violence.

Some claim that civil suits seeking monetary damages have taken on the characteristics of a lottery, offering instant riches to those "lucky" enough to win them. In a typical year, 100 million lawsuits are filed in this country—approximately one for every three living Americans. While most of these suits, which may involve divorces, wills, and bad debts, are legitimate, some are simply shots in the dark, taken by lawsuit-happy citizens hoping to win at least some limited type of fame or fortune through the courts. It is becoming increasingly clear to critics of the current system that American civil courts can unwittingly serve the get-rich-quick schemes of the greedy who feign injury.

The largest civil suit ever filed, for example, was brought by Allen and Kathy Wilson in 1994.[38] The Wilsons filed suit in Carson City, Nevada, asking the state to pay them $657 trillion—the amount the couple said they were owed on a $1,000 state-issued bond purchased in 1865. The Wilsons bought the bond in 1992 from a widow who had inherited it from her husband. They calculated the amount they claimed they were owed by compounding interest at an annual rate of 24% for 130 years. The state of Nevada successfully maintained that time had run out for redeeming the bond.

In 1996, the U.S. Congress passed legislation which would have limited punitive damage claims in civil suits brought in federal and state courts to a maximum of $250,000, or three times the plaintiff's economic damages from such things as lost income and medical expenses—whichever was greater. Under this legislation, known as the Civil Justice Fairness Act, compensatory damages would have been awarded only for the amount of damages the plaintiff could prove were actually incurred.[39] The act, however, was vetoed by President Bill Clinton, and an attempted override of the presidential veto failed. Opponents of the congressional initiative argued that limits on punitive damages are inherently unfair and claimed that federal restrictions on suits filed in state courts illegally preempt state authority over such matters.

A short time later, however, the U.S. Supreme Court ruled that the U.S. Constitution does not permit "grossly excessive" damage awards in civil suits. The 1996 case involved Dr. Ira Gore, Jr., who sued Bavarian Motor Works after learning that a new BMW he had bought in 1990 had been repainted before he took delivery of the car.[40] Dr. Gore's vehicle had been damaged by acid rain during shipment to the United States from a manufacturing facility in Germany, and BMW repainted portions of the car when it arrived in the

United States—without telling Dr. Gore that it had done so before selling the vehicle to him. When Gore sued, a state jury awarded him $4,000 in compensatory damages and $4 million in punitive damages. The state's supreme court reduced the award to $2 million. In overturning the large award, the U.S. Supreme Court ruled that "the due process (fair hearing) clause of the 14th Amendment prohibits a state from imposing a 'grossly excessive' punishment on a [civil wrongdoer]." The wrongdoing in this case, said the Court, "involved a decision by a national distributor of automobiles [BMW] not to advise its dealers, and hence their customers, of predelivery damage to new cars when the cost of repair amounted to less than 3 percent of the car's suggested retail price." In wording that may hold considerable significance for future civil suits seeking large punitive damages, the Court's majority wrote, "Elementary notions of fairness enshrined in our constitutional jurisprudence dictate that a person receive fair notice not only of the conduct that will subject him to punishment but also of the severity of the penalty that a state may impose." Since the amount of punitive damages awarded in the Gore case was hundreds of times the amount of the actual damage done to the vehicle, the Court reasoned, BMW could never have anticipated having to pay such massive damages for such a relatively minor transgression. The case was sent back to the Alabama Supreme Court for a new hearing and was concluded in 1997 when that court ordered BMW to pay Dr. Gore $50,000.[41]

In 2001, the U.S. Supreme Court ruled that appellate courts must use "searching scrutiny" to determine whether a jury's punitive damages award is excessive. The case, *Cooper Industries, Inc.* v. *Leatherman Tool Group, Inc.*,[42] concerned an unfair competition claim in which the plaintiff was awarded $50,000 in compensatory damages and another $4.5 million in punitive damages. "Searching scrutiny" refers to a *de novo* judicial standard which means that appellate judges who are asked to review a trial court's determination of punitive damages must conduct their own independent examination rather than merely defer to the lower court's finding. Writing for the majority, Justice John Paul Stevens noted that while a jury's determination of compensatory damages is "essentially a factual determination" (which should, therefore, not be reexamined by an appellate court in the absence of the jury's "abuse of discretion"), an award of punitive damages is merely "an expression of [the jury's] moral condemnation." Stevens also noted that the Court's decision in *Cooper Industries* was consistent with the Eighth Amendment's prohibition against "excessive fines."

Administrative Law

Administrative law refers to the body of regulations which have been created by governments to control the activities of industry, business, and individuals. Tax laws, health codes, restrictions on pollution and waste disposal, vehicle registration, building codes, and the like are examples of administrative law. Other administrative laws cover practices in the areas of customs (imports and exports), immigration, agriculture, product safety, and most areas of manufacturing.

Administrative agencies will sometimes arrange settlements which fall short of court action but which are considered binding on individuals or groups that have not lived up to the intent of federal or state regulations. Education, environmental protection, and discriminatory hiring practices are all areas in which such settlements have been employed.

Although the criminal law is, for the most part, separate from administrative regulations, the two may overlap. For instance, the rise in organized criminal activity in the area of toxic waste disposal—an area covered by many administrative regulations—has led to criminal prosecutions in several states. The intentional and systematic denial of civil rights in areas generally thought to be administrative in nature, such as hiring, employment, job compensation, and so forth, may also lead to criminal sanctions through the federal system of laws.

Case Law

Case law (which comes from judicial decisions) is also referred to as the law of **precedent**. It represents the accumulated wisdom of trial and appellate courts (those which hear appeals) in criminal, civil, and administrative law cases over the years. Once a court decision is rendered, it is written down. At the appellate level, the reasoning behind the decision is recorded as well. Under the rule of precedent, this reasoning should then be taken into consideration by other courts in settling similar future cases.

precedent

A legal principle that ensures that previous judicial decisions are authoritatively considered and incorporated into future cases.

Appellate courts have considerable power to influence new court decisions at the trial level. The court with the greatest influence, of course, is the U.S. Supreme Court. The precedents it establishes are incorporated as guidelines into the process of legal reasoning by which lower courts reach conclusions.

The principle of recognizing previous decisions as precedents to guide future deliberations, called ***stare decisis,*** forms the basis for our modern "law of precedent." Lief H. Carter, professor of political science at Colorado College, has pointed out that precedent operates along two dimensions.[43] He calls them the *vertical* and the *horizontal*. A vertical rule requires that decisions made by a higher court be taken into consideration by lower courts in their deliberations. Under this rule, state appellate courts, for example, should be expected to follow the spirit of decisions rendered by the state supreme court.

The horizontal dimension means that courts on the same level should be consistent in their interpretation of the law. The U.S. Supreme Court, operating under the horizontal rule, for example, should not be expected to change its ruling in cases similar to those it has already decided.

Stare decisis makes for predictability in the law. Defendants walking into a modern courtroom are represented by lawyers who are trained in legal precedents as well as procedure. As a consequence, defendants have a good idea of what to expect about the manner in which their trial will proceed.

Procedural Law

Procedural law is another kind of statutory law. It is a body of rules that regulate the processing of an offender by the criminal justice system. **Procedural law**, for example, specifies in most jurisdictions that the testimony of one party to certain "victimless crimes" cannot be used as the sole evidence against the other party. General rules of evidence, search and seizure, procedures to be followed in an arrest, and other specified processes by which the justice system operates are also contained in procedural law.

As a great jurist once said, however, the law is like a living thing. It changes and evolves over time. Legislatures enact new statutory laws, and justices set new precedents, sometimes overruling established ones. Many jurisdictions today, for example, because of the changed role of women in society, now allow wives to bring charges of rape against their husbands—something not permitted under the laws of most states as little as a decade or two ago. Similarly, in many states, wives may now testify against their husbands in certain cases, even though such action is contrary to years of previously acknowledged precedent.

General Categories of Crime

Violations of the criminal law can be of many different types and can vary in severity. Five categories of violation will be discussed in the pages which follow:

- Felonies
- Misdemeanors
- Offenses
- Treason and espionage
- Inchoate offenses

Felonies

Violations of the criminal law can be more or less serious. **Felonies** are serious crimes. The felony category includes crimes such as murder, rape, aggravated assault, robbery, burglary, and arson. Under common law, felons could be sentenced to death, could have their property confiscated, or both. Today, many felons receive prison sentences, although the potential range of penalties includes anything from probation and a fine to capital punishment in many jurisdictions. Following common law tradition, people who are today convicted of felonies usually lose certain privileges. Some states, for example, make a felony conviction and incarceration grounds for uncontested divorce. Others prohibit offenders from running for public office or owning a firearm and exclude them from some professions, such as medicine, law, and police work.

The federal government and many states have moved to a scheme of classifying the seriousness of felonies, using a number or letter designation. The federal system, for example, for purposes of criminal sentencing, assigns a score of 43 to first-degree murder, while the crime of theft is only rated a "base offense level" of 4.[44] Attendant circumstances and the criminal history of the offender are also taken into consideration in sentencing decisions.

Because of differences among the states, a crime classified as a felony in one part of the country may be a misdemeanor in another, while in still other areas it may not even be a crime at all! This is especially true of some drug-law violations and of certain other public-order offenses, such as homosexuality, prostitution, and gambling, which in a number of jurisdictions are perfectly legal (although such activity may still be subject to certain administrative regulations).

Misdemeanors

Misdemeanors are relatively minor crimes, consisting of offenses such as petty theft (the theft of items of little worth), simple assault (in which the victim suffers no serious injury and in which none was intended), breaking and entering, the possession of burglary tools, disorderly conduct, disturbing the peace, filing a false crime report, and writing bad checks (although the amount for which the check is written may determine the classification of this offense).

In general, misdemeanors can be thought of as any crime punishable by a year or less in prison. In fact, most misdemeanants receive suspended sentences involving a fine and supervised probation. If an "active sentence" is received for a misdemeanor violation of the law, it probably will involve time to be spent in a local jail, perhaps on weekends, rather than imprisonment in a long-term confinement facility. Alternatively, some misdemeanants are sentenced to community service activities, requiring them to do such things as wash school buses, paint local government buildings, or clean parks and other public areas.

Normally, a police officer cannot arrest a person for a misdemeanor unless the crime was committed in the officer's presence. If this requirement is not met, the officer will need to seek an arrest warrant from a magistrate or other judicial officer. Once a warrant has been issued, the officer may then proceed with the arrest.

Offenses

A third category of crime is the **offense**. Although, strictly speaking, all violations of the law can be called *criminal offenses*, the term *offense* is sometimes used specifically to refer to minor violations of the law which are less serious than misdemeanors. When the term is used in that sense, it refers to such things as jaywalking, spitting on the sidewalk, littering, and certain traffic violations, including the failure to wear a seat belt. Another word used to describe such minor law violations is **infraction**. People committing infractions are typically ticketed and released, usually upon a promise to appear later in court. Court appearances may often be waived through payment of a small fine, which is often mailed in.

Treason and Espionage

Felonies, misdemeanors, offenses, and the people who commit them constitute the daily work of the justice system. Special categories of crime, however, exist and should be recognized. They include treason and espionage, two crimes that are often regarded as the most serious of felonies. **Treason** has been defined as "a U.S. citizen's actions to help a foreign government overthrow, make war against, or seriously injure the United States."[45] Treason, in addition to being a federal offense, is also a crime under the laws of most states. Hence treason can be more generally defined as the attempt to overthrow the government of the society of which one is a member. Some states, like California, have legislatively created the crime of treason, and in other states, the crime is constitutionally defined. Florida's constitution, for example, which mirrors wording in the U.S. Constitution, says that "[t]reason against the state shall consist only in levying war against it, adhering to its enemies, or giving them aid and comfort, and no person shall be convicted of treason except on the testimony of two witnesses to the same overt act or on confession in open court."[46]

Espionage, an offense akin to treason, refers to the "gathering, transmitting, or losing"[47] of information related to the national defense in such a manner that the information becomes available to enemies of the United States and may be used to their advantage. Espionage against the United States did not end with the cold war. In July 2001, for example, 56-year-old former Federal Bureau of Investigation (FBI) agent Robert Hanssen pleaded guilty in U.S. District Court in Alexandria, Virginia, to 15 counts of espionage and conspiracy against the United States.[48] Hanssen admitted having passed U.S. secrets to Moscow from about 1979. His activities ended only when he was arrested in February 2001, after undercover investigators caught him leaving a package under a wooden footbridge in a Virginia park for his Russian handlers to retrieve. The 25-year veteran FBI

misdemeanor

An offense punishable by incarceration, usually in a local confinement facility, for a period whose upper limit is prescribed by statute in a given jurisdiction, typically one year or less.

offense

A violation of the criminal law. Also, in some jurisdictions, a minor crime, such as jaywalking, that is sometimes described as *ticketable*.

infraction

A minor violation of state statute or local ordinance punishable by a fine or other penalty or by a specified, usually limited, term of incarceration.

treason

A U.S. citizen's actions to help a foreign government overthrow, make war against, or seriously injure the United States.[iv] Also, the attempt to overthrow the government of the society of which one is a member.

espionage

The "gathering, transmitting, or losing"[v] of information related to the national defense in such a manner that the information becomes available to enemies of the United States and may be used to their advantage.

Self-confessed FBI spy Robert Hanssen being arraigned before U.S. Magistrate Judge Theresa Buchanan. From left are Assistant U.S. Attorney Randy Bellows, defense attorney Plato Cacheris, Robert Hanssen, and defense attorney Preston Burton.

AP/Wide World Photos

agent had accepted over $1.4 million in cash and diamonds from the Russians in return for disclosing secret and highly sensitive information, including U.S. nuclear warfare plans, advanced eavesdropping technology, and the identities of U.S. spies working in Russia. Government officials feared that the information Hanssen provided had resulted in the deaths of a number of U.S. agents working in Russia. Prosecutors described the damage done to national security by Hanssen's spying as extremely grave. In return for his full cooperation in assessing the damage he had caused, however, Hanssen was spared the death penalty but was sentenced to life in prison without possibility of parole. Learn more about Robert Hanssen and the crimes he committed at **Web Extra! 4–7** at cjtoday.com.

In 1999, one of the most significant espionage cases ever came to light. It involved the theft of highly classified American nuclear weapons secrets by spies working for the People's Republic of China. Over at least three decades, beginning in the 1960s, Chinese spies apparently stole enough weapons-related information to advance China's nuclear weapons program into the modern era. Were it not for the missile and bomb information gathered by the spies, congressional officials said, China's nuclear weapons technology might still be where America's was in the 1950s. See **Web Extra! 4–8** and **Library Extra! 4–5** at cjtoday.com for additional information on this very serious incident.

Inchoate Offenses

Another special category of crime is called *inchoate*. The word *inchoate* means "incomplete or partial," and **inchoate offenses** are those which have not yet been fully carried out. Conspiracies are an example. When a person conspires to commit a crime, any action undertaken in furtherance of the conspiracy is generally regarded as a sufficient basis for arrest and prosecution. For instance, a woman who intends to kill her husband may make a phone call to find a hit man to carry out her plan. The call itself is evidence of her intent and can result in her imprisonment for conspiring to murder.

Another type of inchoate offense is the attempt. Sometimes an offender is not able to complete the crime. Homeowners may arrive just as a burglar is beginning to enter their residence. The burglar may drop his tools and run. Even so, in most jurisdictions, this frustrated burglar can be arrested and charged with attempted burglary.

inchoate offense
- - - - - - - - - - - - - - -
An offense not yet completed. Also, an offense that consists of an action or conduct that is a step toward the intended commission of another offense.

General Features of Crime

From the perspective of Western jurisprudence, all crimes can be said to share certain features, and the notion of crime itself can be said to rest upon such general principles. Taken together, these features, which are described in this section, make up the legal essence of the concept of crime. Conventional legal wisdom holds that the essence of crime consists of three conjoined elements: (1) the criminal act (which in legal parlance is termed the *actus reus*), (2) a culpable mental state *(mens rea)*, and (3) a concurrence of the two. Hence as we shall see in the following pages, the essence of criminal conduct consists of a concurrence of a criminal act with a culpable mental state.

The Criminal Act (*Actus Reus*)

A necessary first feature of any crime is some act in violation of the law. Such an act is termed the **actus reus** of a crime. The term means "guilty act." Generally, a person must commit some voluntary act before he or she is subject to criminal sanctions. Someone who admits (perhaps on a TV talk show) that he is a drug user, for example, cannot be arrested on that basis. To *be something* is not a crime; to *do something* may be. In the case of the admitted drug user, police who heard the admission might begin gathering evidence to prove some specific law violation in that person's past, or perhaps they might watch that individual for future behavior in violation of the law. An arrest might then occur. If it did, it would be based upon a specific action in violation of the law pertaining to controlled substances.

Vagrancy laws, popular in the early part of the twentieth century, have generally been invalidated by the courts because they did not specify what act violated the law. In fact, the *less* a person did, the more vagrant he or she was.

An omission to act, however, may be criminal where the person in question is required by law to do something. Child-neglect laws, for example, focus on parents and child guardians who do not live up to their responsibilities for caring for their children.

Threatening to act can itself be a criminal offense. Telling someone, "I'm going to kill you," might result in an arrest based upon the offense of communicating threats. Threatening the president of the United States is taken seriously by the Secret Service, and individuals are regularly arrested for boasting about planned violence to be directed at the president.

Attempted criminal activity is also illegal. An attempt to murder or rape, for example, is a serious crime, even when the planned act is not accomplished.

Conspiracies were mentioned earlier in this chapter. When a conspiracy unfolds, the ultimate act that it aims to bring about does not have to occur for the parties to the conspiracy to be arrested. When people plan to bomb a public building, for example, they can be legally stopped before the bombing. As soon as they take steps to "further" their plan, they have met the requirement for an act. Buying explosives, telephoning one another, or drawing plans of the building may all be actions in "furtherance of the conspiracy."

Not all conspiracy statutes require actions in furtherance of the "target crime" before an arrest can be made. Technically speaking, crimes of conspiracy can be seen as entirely distinct from the crimes which are contemplated by the conspiracy. For example, in 1994 the U.S. Supreme Court upheld the drug-related conviction of Reshat Shabani when it ruled that in the case of certain antidrug laws,[49] "it is presumed that Congress intended to adopt the common law definition of conspiracy, which does not make the doing of any act other than the act of conspiring a condition of liability."[50] Hence according to the Court, "the criminal agreement itself," even in the absence of actions directed toward realizing the target crime, can be grounds for arrest and prosecution.

Similar to conspiracy statutes are many newly enacted antistalking laws. Antistalking statutes are intended to prevent harassment and intimidation, even when no physical harm occurs. Over the course of a typical year, it is estimated that about 1 million women and nearly 400,000 men are stalked in the United States.[51] It is estimated that half of those being stalked are celebrities. Stalkers often strike after their victims have unsuccessfully complained to authorities about stalking-related activities, such as harassing phone calls and letters. Antistalking statutes, however, still face a constitutional hurdle of attempting to prevent people not otherwise involved in criminal activity from walking and standing where they wish and from speaking freely. Ultimately, the U.S. Supreme Court will probably have to decide the legitimacy of such statutes.

A Guilty Mind (*Mens Rea*)

Mens rea is the second general component of crime. The term, which literally means "guilty mind," refers to the defendant's specific mental state at the time the behavior in question occurred. The importance of *mens rea* as a component of crime cannot be overemphasized. It can be seen in the fact that some courts have held that "[a]ll crime exists primarily in the mind."[52] The extent to which a person can be held criminally

actus reus

An act in violation of the law. Also, a guilty act.

EQUAL JUSTICE UNDER LAW

—Words inscribed above the entrance to the U.S. Supreme Court building

mens rea

The state of mind that accompanies a criminal act. Also, a guilty mind.

responsible for his or her actions generally depends upon the nature of the mental state under which he or she was laboring at the time of the offense.

Four levels, or types, of *mens rea* can be distinguished: (1) purposeful (or intentional), (2) knowing, (3) reckless, and (4) negligent. *Mens rea* is most clearly present when a person acts purposefully and knowingly, but *mens rea* sufficient for criminal prosecution may also result from reckless or negligent behavior. However, pure accident, which involves no recklessness or negligence, cannot serve as the basis for either criminal or civil liability. "Even a dog," the famous Supreme Court Justice Oliver Wendell Holmes once wrote, "distinguishes between being stumbled over and being kicked."[53]

Purposeful or intentional action is that which is undertaken to achieve some goal. Sometimes the harm that results from intentional action may be quite unintended—and yet fail to reduce criminal liability. The doctrine of transferred intent, for example, which operates in all U.S. jurisdictions, would hold a person guilty of murder even if he took aim and shot at an intended victim but missed, killing another person instead. The philosophical notion behind the concept of transferred intent is that the killer's intent to kill, which existed at the time of the crime, transferred from the intended victim to the person who was struck by the bullet and died.

Knowing behavior is action undertaken with awareness. Hence, a person who acts purposefully always acts knowingly, although a person may act in a knowingly criminal way but for another purpose. An airline captain, for example, who allows a flight attendant to transport cocaine aboard an airplane may do so to gain sexual favors from the attendant—but without having the purpose of drug smuggling in mind. Knowing behavior involves near certainty. Hence if the flight attendant in this example carries cocaine aboard the airplane, it *will* be transported. In another example, if an HIV-infected individual has unprotected sexual intercourse with another person, the partner *will* be exposed to the virus.

Reckless behavior, in contrast, is activity which increases the risk of harm. Although knowledge may be a part of such behavior, it exists more in the form of probability than certainty. So, for example, an Elton John song about Marilyn Monroe (and later, dedicated to Princess Diana) says, "You lived your life like a candle in the wind." The wind is, of course, a risky place to keep a lighted candle, and doing so increases the likelihood that its flame will be extinguished. But there is no certainty that the flame will be blown out or, if so, when it might happen. As a practical example, reckless driving is a frequent charge in many jurisdictions; it is generally brought when a driver engages in risky activity which endangers others.

Nonetheless, *mens rea* is said to be present when a person *should have known better*, even if the person did not directly intend the consequences of his or her action. A person who acts negligently and thereby endangers others may be found guilty of **criminal negligence** when harm occurs, even though no negative consequences were intended. For example, a mother who leaves her 12-month-old child alone in the tub can later be prosecuted for negligent homicide if the child drowns.[54] It should be emphasized, however, that negligence in and of itself is not a crime. Negligent conduct can be evidence of crime only when it falls below some acceptable standard of care. That standard is today applied in criminal courts through the fictional creation of a *reasonable person*. The question to be asked in a given case is whether a reasonable person, in the same situation, would have known better and acted differently than the defendant. The reasonable person criterion provides a yardstick for juries faced with thorny issues of guilt or innocence.

Mens rea is a thorny concept. Not only is it philosophically and legally complex, but a person's state of mind during the commission of an offense can rarely be known directly unless the person confesses. Hence, *mens rea* must generally be inferred from a person's actions and from all the circumstances which surround those actions. It is also important to note that *mens rea*, even in the sense of intent, is not the same thing as motive. A **motive** refers to a person's reason for committing a crime. While evidence of motive may be admissible during a criminal trial to help prove a crime, motive itself is not an essential element of a crime. As a result, we cannot say that a bad or immoral motive makes an act a crime.

STRICT LIABILITY AND *MENS REA*

A special category of crimes, called **strict liability** offenses, requires no culpable mental state and presents a significant exception to the principle that all crimes require a concurrence of *actus reus* and *mens rea*. Strict liability offenses (also called *absolute liability offenses*) make it a crime simply to *do* something, even if the offender has no intention of violating the law. Strict liability is philosophically based upon the presumption that causing harm is in itself blameworthy, regardless of the actor's intent.

reckless behavior

Activity that increases the risk of harm.

criminal negligence

Behavior in which a person fails to reasonably perceive substantial and unjustifiable risks of dangerous consequences.

motive

A person's reason for committing a crime.

strict liability

Liability without fault or intention. Strict liability offenses do not require *mens rea*.

Routine traffic offenses are generally considered strict liability offenses. They do not require intent and may be committed by drivers who are unaware of what they are doing. Drivers commit minor violations of the state motor vehicle code simply by doing that which is forbidden. Hence, driving 65 miles per hour in a 55-mile-per-hour zone is a violation of the law, even though the driver may be listening to music, thinking, or simply going with the flow of traffic, entirely unaware that his or her vehicle is exceeding the posted speed limit.

Statutory rape provides another example of the concept of strict liability.[55] The crime of statutory rape generally occurs between two consenting individuals and requires only that the offender have sexual intercourse with a person under the age of legal consent. Statutes describing the crime routinely avoid any mention of a culpable mental state. In many jurisdictions, it matters little whether the "perpetrator" knew the exact age of the "victim" or whether the "victim" lied about his or her age or had given consent, since such laws are "an attempt to prevent the sexual exploitation of persons deemed legally incapable of giving consent."[56]

Concurrence

The concurrence of an unlawful act and a culpable mental state provides the third basic component of crime. **Concurrence** requires that the act and the mental state occur together in order for a crime to take place. If one precedes the other, the requirements of the criminal law have not been met. A person may intend to kill a rival, for example. As he drives to the intended victim's house, gun in hand, fantasizing about how he will commit the murder, the victim is crossing the street on the way home from grocery shopping. If the two accidentally collide and the intended victim dies, there has been no concurrence of act and intent.

concurrence

The coexistence of (1) an act in violation of the law and (2) a culpable mental state.

Other Features of Crime

Some scholars contend that the three features of crime which we have just outlined—*actus reus, mens rea,* and concurrence—are sufficient to constitute the essence of the legal concept of crime. Other scholars, however, see modern Western law as more complex. They argue that recognition of five additional principles is necessary to fully appreciate contemporary understandings of crime. These five principles are (1) causation, (2) a resulting harm, (3) the principle of legality, (4) the principle of punishment, and (5) necessary attendant circumstances. We will now discuss each of these additional features in turn.

CAUSATION

Causation refers to the fact that the concurrence of a guilty mind and a criminal act may produce, or cause, harm. While some statutes criminalize only conduct, others subsume the notion of concurrence under causality and specify that a causality relationship is a necessary element of a given crime. Such laws require that the offender *cause* a particular result before criminal liability can be incurred. Sometimes, however, a causal link is anything but clear. A classic example of this principle involves assault with a deadly weapon with intent to kill. If a person shoots another, but the victim is seriously injured and not killed, the victim might survive for a long time in a hospital. Death may occur, perhaps a year or more later, because pneumonia sets in or because blood clots form in the injured person from lack of activity. In such cases, defense attorneys would likely argue that the defendant did not cause the death, but rather that the death occurred because of disease. If a jury agrees with the defense's claim, the shooter may go free or be found guilty of a lesser charge, such as assault.

To clarify the issue of causation, the American Law Institute suggests use of the term **legal cause** to emphasize the notion of a legally recognizable cause and to preclude any assumption that such a cause must be close in time and space to the result it produces. Legal causes can be distinguished from those causes which may have produced the result in question but which may not provide the basis for a criminal prosecution because they are too complex, too indistinguishable from other causes, not knowable, or not provable in a court of law.

legal cause

A legally recognizable cause. A legal cause must be demonstrated in court in order to hold an individual criminally liable for causing harm.

HARM

A harm occurs in any crime, although not all harms are crimes. When a person is murdered or raped, harm can clearly be identified. Some crimes, however, have come to be called *victimless*. Perpetrators maintain that they are not harming anyone in committing such crimes. Rather, they say, the crime is pleasurable. Prostitution, gambling, "crimes against nature" (sexual deviance), and drug use are commonly classified as "victimless." People involved in such crimes argue that if anyone is being hurt, it is only themselves. What these offenders fail to recognize, say legal theorists, is the social harm caused by their behavior. In areas afflicted with chronic prostitution, drug use, sexual deviance, and illegal gambling, property values fall, family life disintegrates, and other, more traditional crimes increase as money is sought to support the "victimless" activities. Law-abiding citizens will flee the area.

In a criminal prosecution, however, it is rarely necessary to prove harm as a separate element of a crime, since it is subsumed under the notion of a guilty act. In the crime of murder, for example, the "killing of a human being" brings about a harm but is, properly speaking, an act. When committed with the requisite *mens rea*, it becomes a crime. A similar type of reasoning applies to the criminalization of attempts, and some writers have used the example of throwing rocks at blind people to illustrate that behavior need not actually produce harm for it to be criminal. One could imagine a scenario in which vandals decide to throw rocks at visually impaired individuals but, because of bad aim, the rocks never hit anyone and the intended targets remain blissfully unaware that anyone is trying to harm them. In such a case, shouldn't throwing rocks provide a basis for criminal liability? As one authority on the subject observes, "Criticism of the principle of harm has . . . been based on the view that the harm actually caused may be a matter of sheer accident and that the rational thing to do is to base the punishment on the *mens rea*, and the action, disregarding any actual harm or lack of harm or its degree."[57] This observation also shows why we have said that the essence of crime consists only of three things: (1) *actus reus*, (2) *mens rea*, and (3) the concurrence of an illegal act and a culpable mental state.

LEGALITY

The principle of legality is concerned with the fact that a behavior cannot be criminal if no law exists which defines it as such. It is all right to drink beer if you are of drinking age because there is no statute on the books prohibiting it. During Prohibition, of course, the situation was quite different. (In fact, some parts of the United States are still "dry," and the purchase or public consumption of alcohol can be a law violation regardless of age.) The principle of legality also includes the notion that a law cannot be created tomorrow which will hold a person legally responsible for something he or she does today. These are called *ex post facto* laws. Laws are binding only from the date of their creation or from some future date at which they are specified as taking effect.[58]

PUNISHMENT

The principle of punishment says that no crime can be said to occur where punishment has not been specified in the law. Larceny, for example, would not be a crime if the law simply said, "It is illegal to steal." Punishment needs to be specified so that if a person is found guilty of violating the law, sanctions can be lawfully imposed.

NECESSARY ATTENDANT CIRCUMSTANCES

attendant circumstances

The facts surrounding an event.

Finally, statutes defining some crimes specify that additional elements, called **attendant circumstances**, be present for a conviction to be obtained. Attendant circumstances refer to the "facts surrounding an event"[59] and include such things as time and place. Attendant circumstances, specified by law as necessary elements of an offense, are sometimes referred to as *necessary attendant circumstances*. This indicates that the existence of such circumstances is necessary, along with the other elements included in the relevant statute, for a crime to have been committed.

Florida law, for example, makes it a crime to "[k]nowingly commit any lewd or lascivious act in the presence of any child under the age of 16 years."[60] In this case, the behavior in question might not be a crime if committed in the presence of persons older than 16. Curfew violations are being increasingly criminalized by states that are shifting liability for a minor's behavior to his or her parents. To violate a curfew, it is necessary that a juvenile be in a public place between specified times (such as 11 P.M. and 5 A.M.). In those states which hold parents liable for the behavior of their children, parents can be jailed or fined when such violations occur.

Sometimes attendant circumstances increase the degree, or level of seriousness, of an offense. Under Texas law, for example, the crime of burglary has two degrees, defined by state law as follows: Burglary is a "(1) state jail felony if committed in a building other than a habitation; or (2) felony of the second degree [that is, a more serious crime] if committed in a habitation." Hence, the degree of the offense of burglary changes depending upon the nature of the place burglarized.

Circumstances surrounding a crime can also be classified as aggravating or mitigating and may, by law, increase or lessen the penalty that can be imposed upon a convicted offender. Aggravating and mitigating circumstances are not elements of an offense, since they are primarily relevant at the sentencing stage of a criminal prosecution. They are discussed in Chapter 10.

Elements of a Specific Criminal Offense

We have just identified the principles which constitute the *general* notion of crime. We can now examine individual statutes to see what particular statutory **elements** constitute a *specific* crime. Written laws specify exactly what conditions are necessary for a person to be charged in a given instance of criminal activity, and they do so for every particular offense. Hence, elements of a crime are specific legal aspects of a criminal offense which must be proved by the prosecution in order to obtain a conviction. In almost every jurisdiction in the United States, for example, the crime of first-degree murder involves four quite distinct elements:

element (of a crime)

In a specific crime, one of the essential features of that crime as specified by law or statute.

1. An unlawful killing
2. Of a human being
3. Intentionally
4. With planning (or "malice aforethought")

The elements of any specific crime are the statutory minimum without which that crime cannot be said to have occurred. In any case that goes to trial, the task of the prosecution is to prove that all the elements were indeed present and that the accused was ultimately responsible for producing them. Since statutes differ between jurisdictions, the specific elements of a particular crime may vary. To convict a defendant of a particular crime, prosecutors must prove to a judge or jury that all the required statutory elements are present.[61] If even one element of an offense cannot be established beyond a reasonable doubt, criminal liability will not have been demonstrated, and the defendant will be found not guilty.

The Example of Murder

Every statutory element in a given instance of crime serves some purpose and is necessary. As mentioned, the crime of first-degree murder includes *an unlawful killing* as one of its required elements. Even if all the other elements of first-degree murder are present, the act will still not be first-degree murder if the initial element has not been met. In a wartime situation, for instance, killings of human beings occur. They are committed with planning and sometimes with "malice." They are certainly intentional. Yet killing in war is not unlawful as long as the belligerents wage war according to international conventions.

The second element of first-degree murder specifies that the killing must be *of a human being*. People kill all the time. They kill animals for meat, they hunt, and they practice euthanasia upon aged and injured pets. Even if the killing of an animal is planned and involves malice (perhaps a vendetta against a neighborhood dog that overturns trash cans), it does not constitute first-degree murder. Such a killing, however, may violate statutes pertaining to cruelty to animals.

The third element of first-degree murder, *intentionality*, is the basis for the defense of accident. An unintentional or nonpurposeful killing is not first-degree murder, although it may violate some other statute.

Finally, murder has not been committed unless *malice* is involved. There are different kinds of malice. Second-degree murder involves malice in the sense of hatred or spite. A more extreme form of malice is necessary for a finding of first-degree murder. Sometimes the phrase used to describe this type of feeling is *malice aforethought*. This extreme kind of malice can be demonstrated by showing that planning was involved in the commission of the murder. Often, first-degree murder is described as "lying in wait," a practice which shows that thought and planning went into the illegal killing.

Whether any particular behavior meets the specific statutory minimums to qualify as a crime may be open to debate. Ten years ago, for example, Adam Brown, 30, of Roseburg, Oregon, was charged with attempted first-degree murder for having knowingly exposed five children to the acquired immunodeficiency syndrome (AIDS) virus when he allegedly had unprotected sex with them. Brown, a lay minister, was informed that he had tested positive for the AIDS virus more than a year prior to the incidents. Some questioned just what form of malice characterized Brown's behavior.[62]

A charge of second-degree murder in most jurisdictions would necessitate proving that a voluntary (or intentional) killing of a human being took place—although a "crime of passion" may have been committed without the degree of malice necessary for it to be classified as first degree. Manslaughter, another type of homicide, can be defined simply as the unlawful killing of a human being. Not only is malice lacking in third-degree murder cases, but the killer may not have even intended that any harm come to the victim. Manslaughter statutes, however, frequently necessitate some degree of negligence on the part of the killer. A charge of negligent homicide may result from an automobile accident in which the driver did not exercise due care. When legally defined "gross negligence" (involving a wanton disregard for human life) is present, however, some jurisdictions permit the offender to be charged with a more serious count of murder.

In 1995, for example, in the case of Karin Smith, a grand jury returned a homicide indictment against a laboratory doctor and a technician for a fatal misdiagnosis.[63] The laboratory workers had misread Pap smears performed on Smith, returning a clean bill of health to the doctor in charge of her care. Smith died on March 8, 1995, at age 29 from cervical cancer that had spread throughout her body. Experts testifying before a grand jury said that evidence of the presence of cancer was "unequivocal" in slides from Pap smears done on Smith in 1988 and 1989 but that the laboratory which received the sample tissue had misread the test results. The prosecutor in the case claimed that laboratory personnel had demonstrated a wanton disregard for human life when they "failed to install random controls to check the quality of the Pap smear analysis; and showed indifference toward professional standards and the need for continuing education."[64]

Although most people think that homicide charges are brought primarily against those who intend to kill, the trend seen in the mid-1990s, of charging negligent medical personnel with homicide is evidence that the machinery of the criminal justice system can be applied outside its traditional sphere. About the time of the Smith case, for example, Denver anesthesiologist Dr. Joseph J. Verbrugge, Sr., was charged with manslaughter in the death of an eight-year-old boy undergoing ear surgery.[65] Police investigators said the doctor had fallen asleep during the surgery, allowing the boy to receive a lethal dose of anesthetic. In a similar case, Dr. Gerald Einaugler of New York was ordered to spend 52 weekends in jail for causing the death of a nursing home patient when he mistook a dialysis tube for a feeding tube and pumped food into the patient's kidneys.[66] Dr. David Benjamin of New York faced a possible life prison sentence after being convicted of murder in the death of a woman who went to him for an abortion. Upon his 1995 conviction, Dr. Benjamin became the first doctor in New York State to be found guilty of murder for the medical mistreatment of a patient.[67] The patient, Guadalupe Negron, bled to death following a bungled abortion in the doctor's storefront clinic.

Finally, the 1997 manslaughter convictions of three young adults in Tampa, Florida, who pulled up stop signs at rural intersections near Lithia, Florida, provides another clear example that criminal liability in such crimes does not require an intent to cause death. Defendants Christopher Cole, 20, Nissa Baillie, 21, and Thomas Miller, 20, were each sentenced to 30 years in prison for causing the deaths of three 18-year-olds who were returning home from an evening of bowling. The victims were killed by an eight-ton truck hauling fertilizer as they crossed through an intersection where a stop sign had been removed. At sentencing, Florida Circuit Judge Bob Mitchum told the defendants, "I don't believe for one minute that you . . . pulled these signs up with the intent of causing the death of anyone."[68] Cole, Baillie, and Miller will be eligible for parole after 13 years.[69]

The *Corpus Delicti* of a Crime

corpus delicti

The facts that show that a crime has occurred. The term literally means "the body of the crime."

The term **corpus delicti** literally means "the body of the crime." The term is often confused with the statutory elements of a crime. Sometimes the concept is mistakenly thought to mean the body of a murder victim or some other physical result of criminal activity. It actually means something quite different.

One way to understand the concept of *corpus delicti* is to realize that a person cannot be tried for a crime unless it can first be shown that the offense has, in fact, occurred. In other words, to establish the *corpus delicti* of a crime, the state has to demonstrate that a criminal law has been violated and that someone violated it. Hence, there are only two aspects to the *corpus delicti* of an offense: (1) that a certain result has been produced and (2) that a person is criminally responsible for its production. As one court said, "*Corpus delicti* consists of a showing of (1) the occurrence of the specific kind of injury, and (2) someone's criminal act as the cause of the injury."[70] So, for example, the crime of larceny requires proof that the property of another has been stolen—that is, unlawfully taken by someone whose intent it was to permanently deprive the owner of its possession.[71] Hence, evidence offered to prove the *corpus delicti* in a trial for larceny is insufficient if it fails to prove that any property has been stolen or if property found in a defendant's possession cannot be identified as having been stolen. Similarly, "[i]n an arson case, the *corpus delicti* consists of (1) a burned building or other property, and (2) some criminal agency which caused the burning. . . . In other words, the *corpus delicti* includes not only the fact of burning, but it must also appear that the burning was by the willful act of some person, and not as a result of a natural or accidental cause."[72]

To the requirement to establish the *corpus delicti* of a crime before a successful prosecution can occur we might add the observation that the identity of the perpetrator is not an element of the *corpus delicti* of an offense. Hence, the fact that a crime has occurred can be established without having any idea who committed it or even why it was committed. This principle was clearly enunciated in a Montana case when the state's supreme court held that "the identity of the perpetrator is not an element of the *corpus delicti*." In *State* v. *Kindle* (1924),[73] the court continued, "we stated that '[i]n a prosecution for murder, proof of the *corpus delicti* does not necessarily carry with it the identity of the slain nor of the slayer.' . . . The essential elements of the *corpus delicti* are . . . establishing the death and the fact that the death was caused by a criminal agency, nothing more." *Black's Law Dictionary* puts it another way: "The *corpus delicti* [of a crime] is the fact of its having been actually committed."[74]

Types of Defenses to a Criminal Charge

When a person is charged with a crime, he or she typically offers some defense. A **defense** consists of evidence and arguments offered by a defendant and his or her attorneys to show why that person should not be held liable for a criminal charge. Our legal system generally recognizes four broad categories of defenses: (1) **alibi**, (2) **justifications**, (3) **excuses**, and (4) **procedural defenses**. An alibi, if shown to be valid, means that the defendant could not have committed the crime in question because he or she was somewhere else (and generally with someone else) at the time of the crime. When a defendant offers a justification as a defense, he or she admits committing the act in question but claims that it was necessary to avoid some greater evil. A defendant who offers an excuse as a defense, on the other hand, claims that some personal condition or circumstance at the time of the act was such that he or she should not be held accountable under the criminal law. Procedural defenses make the claim that the defendant was in some significant way discriminated against in the justice process or that some important aspect of official procedure was not properly followed in the investigation or prosecution of the crime charged. Finally, a number of innovative defense strategies have emerged in recent years and will be discussed as a fifth category—although, technically speaking, each of these innovative defenses could be classified as a justification or an excuse. Table 4–3 lists the types of defenses which fall into our five categories. Each will be discussed in the pages that follow.

Alibi

A reference book for criminal trial lawyers says, "Alibi is different from all of the other defenses . . . because . . . it is based upon the premise that the defendant is truly innocent."[75] The defense of alibi denies that the defendant committed the act in question. All of the other defenses we are about to discuss grant that the defendant committed the act, but they deny that he or she should be held criminally responsible. While justifications and excuses may produce findings of "not guilty," the defense of alibi claims outright innocence.

Alibi is best supported by witnesses and documentation. A person charged with a crime can use the defense of alibi to show that he or she was not present at the scene when the crime was alleged to have occurred. Hotel receipts, eyewitness identification, and participation in social events have all been used to prove alibis.

Justifications

As defenses, justifications claim a kind of moral high ground. Justifications may be offered by people who find themselves facing a choice between a "lesser of two evils." Generally speaking, conduct which a person believes is necessary to avoid a harm or evil to

defense (to a criminal charge)

Evidence and arguments offered by a defendant and his or her attorney to show why that person should not be held liable for a criminal charge.

alibi

A statement or contention by an individual charged with a crime that he or she was so distant when the crime was committed, or so engaged in other provable activities, that his or her participation in the commission of that crime was impossible.

justification

A legal defense in which the defendant admits to committing the act in question but claims it was necessary in order to avoid some greater evil.

excuse

A legal defense in which the defendant claims that some personal condition or circumstance at the time of the act was such that he or she should not be held accountable under the criminal law.

procedural defense

A defense that claims that the defendant was in some significant way discriminated against in the justice process or that some important aspect of official procedure was not properly followed in the investigation or prosecution of the crime charged.

TABLE 4-3	**TYPES OF DEFENSES**			
Alibi	**Justifications**	**Excuses**	**Procedural Defenses**	**Innovative Defenses**
A claim of alibi	Self-defense	Duress	Entrapment	Abuse defense
	Defense of others	Age	Double jeopardy	Premenstrual syndrome
	Defense of home and property	Mistake	*Collateral estoppel*	Other biological defenses
	Necessity	Involuntary intoxication	Selective prosecution	Black rage
	Consent	Unconsciousness	Denial of a speedy trial	Urban survival syndrome
	Resisting unlawful arrest	Provocation	Prosecutorial misconduct	Cultural defenses
		Insanity	Police fraud	
		Diminished capacity		
		Mental incompetence		

him- or herself or to avoid harm to another is justifiable if the harm or evil to be avoided is greater than that which the law defining the offense seeks to avoid. For example, a firefighter might set a controlled fire to create a firebreak to head off a conflagration threatening a community. While intentionally setting a fire may constitute arson, doing so to save a town may be justifiable behavior in the eyes of the community *and* in the eyes of the law. Included under the broad category of justifications are (1) self-defense, (2) defense of others, (3) defense of home and property, (4) necessity, (5) consent, and (6) resisting unlawful arrest.

SELF-DEFENSE

self-defense

The protection of oneself or of one's property from unlawful injury or from the immediate risk of unlawful injury. Also, the justification that the person who committed an act that would otherwise constitute an offense reasonably believed that the act was necessary to protect self or property from immediate danger.

reasonable force

A degree of force that is appropriate in a given situation and is not excessive. Also, the minimum degree of force necessary to protect oneself, one's property, a third party, or the property of another in the face of a substantial threat.

Self-defense is probably the best known of the justifications. This defense strategy makes the claim that it was necessary to inflict some harm on another to ensure one's own safety in the face of near-certain injury or death. A person who harms an attacker can generally use this defense. However, the courts have held that where a "path of retreat" exists for a person being attacked, it should be taken. In other words, the safest use of self-defense is only when cornered, with no path of escape.

The amount of defensive force used must be proportional to the amount of force or the perceived degree of threat that one is seeking to defend against. Hence, **reasonable force** is the degree of force that is appropriate in a given situation and that is not excessive. Reasonable force can also be thought of as the minimum degree of force necessary to protect oneself, one's property, a third party, or the property of another in the face of a substantial threat. Deadly force, the highest degree of force, is considered reasonable only when used to counter an immediate threat of death or great bodily harm. Deadly force cannot be used against nondeadly force.

Force, as the term is used within the context of self-defense, means physical force and does not extend to emotional, psychological, economic, psychic, or other forms of coercion. A person who turns the tables on a robber and assaults him during a robbery attempt, for example, may be able to claim self-defense, but a businessperson who physically assaults a financial rival to prevent a hostile takeover of her company will have no such recourse.

Self-defense has been used in killings by wives of their abusive spouses. A killing which occurs while the physical abuse is in process, especially where a history of such abuse can be shown, is likely to be accepted by a jury as justified. On the other hand, wives who suffer repeated abuse but coldly plan the killing of their husbands have not fared well in court.

DEFENSE OF OTHERS

The use of force to defend oneself has generally been extended to permit the use of reasonable force to defend others who are or who appear to be in imminent danger. The defense of others, sometimes called *defense of a third person,* is circumscribed in some jurisdic-

alter ego rule

In some jurisdictions, a rule of law that holds that a person can only defend a third party under circumstances and only to the degree that the third party could act on his or her own behalf.

tions by the **alter ego rule**. The alter ego rule holds that a person can only defend a third party under circumstances and only to the degree that the third party could act. In other words, a person who aids a person whom he sees being attacked may become criminally liable if that person initiated the attack or if the assault is a lawful one—for example, an assault made by a law enforcement officer conducting a lawful arrest of a person who is resisting. A few jurisdictions, however, do not recognize the alter ego rule and allow a person to act in defense of another if the actor reasonably believes that his or her intervention is immediately necessary to protect the third person.

Defense of others cannot be claimed by an individual who joins an illegal fight merely to assist a friend or family member. Likewise, one who intentionally aids an offender in an assault, even though the tables have turned and the offender is losing the battle, cannot claim defense of others. Under the law, defense of a third person always requires that the defender be free from fault and that he or she act to aid an innocent person who is in the process of being victimized. The same restrictions that apply to self-defense also apply to the defense of a third party. Hence, a defender may act only in the face of an immediate threat to another person, cannot use deadly force against nondeadly force, and must only act to the extent and use only the degree of force needed to repel the attack.

DEFENSE OF HOME AND PROPERTY

In most jurisdictions, the owner of property can justifiably use reasonable, *nondeadly* force to prevent others from unlawfully taking or damaging it. As a general rule, the preservation of human life outweighs the protection of property, and the use of deadly force to protect property is not justified unless the perpetrator of the illegal act may intend to commit, or is in the act of committing, a violent act against another human being. A person who shoots an unarmed trespasser, for example, could not claim "defense of property" to avoid criminal liability. However, a person who shoots and kills an armed robber while being robbed can. The difference is that a person facing an armed robber has a right to protect his or her property but is also in danger of death or serious bodily harm. An unarmed trespasser represents no such serious threat.[76]

The use of mechanical devices to protect property is a special area of law. Since, generally speaking, deadly force is not permitted in defense of property, the setting of booby traps, such as spring-loaded shotguns, electrified gates, explosive devices, and the like, is generally not permitted to protect property which is unattended and unoccupied. If an individual is injured as a result of a mechanical device intended to cause death or injury in the protection of property, criminal charges may be brought against the person who set the device.

On the other hand, acts which would otherwise be criminal may carry no criminal liability if undertaken to protect one's home. For purposes of the law, one's home is one's dwelling, whether owned, rented, or merely borrowed. Hotel rooms, rooms aboard vessels, and rented rooms in houses belonging to others are all considered, for purposes of the law, one's home. The retreat rule, referred to earlier, which requires a person under attack to retreat when possible before resorting to deadly force, is subject to what some call the *castle exception*. The castle exception can be traced to the writings of the sixteenth-century English jurist Sir Edward Coke, who said, "A man's house is his castle—for where shall a man be safe if it be not in his house?"[77] The castle exception generally recognizes that a person has a fundamental right to be in his or her home and that the home is a final and inviolable place of retreat (that is, the home offers a place of retreat from which a person can be expected to retreat no further). Hence, it is not necessary for one to retreat from one's home in the face of an immediate threat, even where such retreat is possible, before resorting to deadly force in protection of the home. A number of court decisions have extended the castle exception to include one's place of business, such as a store or an office.

NECESSITY

Necessity, or the claim that some illegal action was needed to prevent an even greater harm, is a useful defense in cases which do not involve serious bodily harm. One of the most famous uses of this defense occurred in *The Crown* v. *Dudly & Stephens* in the late nineteenth century.[78] This British case involved a shipwreck in which three sailors and a cabin boy were set adrift in a lifeboat. After a number of days at sea without food, two of the sailors decided to kill and eat the cabin boy. At their trial, they argued that it was necessary to do so, or none of them would have survived. The court, however, reasoned that the cabin boy was not a direct threat to the survival of the men and rejected this defense.

Convicted of murder, they were sentenced to death, although they were spared the gallows by royal intervention. Although cannibalism is usually against the law, courts have sometimes recognized the necessity of consuming human flesh where survival was at issue. Those cases, however, involved only "victims" who had already died of natural causes.

CONSENT

The defense of consent claims that whatever harm was done occurred only after the injured person gave his or her permission for the behavior in question. During the 1980s, for example, Robert Chambers pleaded guilty to first-degree manslaughter in the killing of 18-year-old Jennifer Levin. In what was dubbed the "Preppy Murder Case,"[79] Chambers had claimed that Levin died as a result of "rough sex" during which she had tied his hands behind his back and injured his testicles. Other cases, some involving sexual asphyxia (partial suffocation designed to heighten erotic pleasures) and bondage, culminated in a headline in *Time* heralding the era of the "rough-sex defense."[80] The magazine suggested that such a defense works best with a good-looking defendant who appears remorseful; a "hardened type of character," it said, could not effectively use the defense.[81]

In the "Condom Rapist Case," Joel Valdez was found guilty of rape in 1993 after a jury in Austin, Texas, rejected his claim that the act became consensual once he complied with his victim's request to use a condom. Valdez, who was drunk and armed with a knife at the time of the offense, claimed that his victim's request was a consent to sex. After that, he said, "we were making love."[82]

RESISTING UNLAWFUL ARREST

All jurisdictions consider resistance in the face of an unlawful arrest justifiable. Some have statutory provisions detailing the limits imposed on such resistance and the conditions under which it can be used. Such laws generally state that a person may use a reasonable amount of force, other than deadly force, to resist an unlawful arrest or an unlawful search by a law enforcement officer if the officer uses or attempts to use greater force than necessary to make the arrest or search. Such laws are inapplicable in cases where the defendant is the first to resort to force. Deadly force to resist arrest is not justified unless the law enforcement officer resorts to deadly force when it is not called for.

Excuses

An excuse, in contrast to a justification, does not claim that the conduct in question is justified by the situation or that it is moral. An excuse claims, rather, that the actor who engaged in the unlawful behavior was, at the time, not legally responsible for his or her actions and should not be held accountable under the law. So, for example, a person who assaults a police officer thinking that the officer is really a disguised space alien who has come to abduct him may be found "not guilty" of the charge of assault and battery by reason of insanity. Actions for which excuses are offered do not morally outweigh the wrong committed, but criminal liability may still be negated on the basis of some personal disability of the actor or because of some special circumstances that characterize the situation. Excuses recognized by the law include (1) duress, (2) age, (3) mistake, (4) involuntary intoxication, (5) unconsciousness, (6) provocation, (7) insanity, (8) diminished capacity, and (9) mental incompetence.

DURESS

Duress is a defense which depends upon an understanding of the situation. Duress has been defined as "any unlawful threat or coercion used by a person to induce another to act (or to refrain from acting) in a manner he or she otherwise would not (or would)."[83] A person may act under duress if, for example, he or she steals an employer's payroll to meet a ransom demand for kidnappers holding the person's children. Should the person later be arrested for larceny or embezzlement, the person can claim that he or she felt compelled to commit the crime to help ensure the safety of the children. Duress is generally not a useful defense when the crime committed involves serious physical harm, since the harm committed may outweigh the coercive influence in the minds of jurors and judges. The defense of duress is sometimes also called *coercion*.

AGE

Age offers another kind of excuse in the face of a criminal charge, and the defense of "infancy"—as it is sometimes known in legal jargon—has its roots in the ancient belief that children cannot reason logically until around the age of seven. Early doctrine in the Christian church sanctioned that belief by declaring that rationality develops around the age of seven. As a consequence, only children past that age could be held responsible for their crimes.

The defense of infancy today has been expanded to include people well beyond the age of seven. Many states set the sixteenth birthday as the age at which a person becomes an adult for purposes of criminal prosecution. Others use the age of 17, and still others 18. When a person below the age required for adult prosecution commits a "crime," it is termed a *juvenile offense*. He or she is not guilty of a criminal violation of the law by virtue of youth.

In most jurisdictions, children below the age of seven cannot be charged even with juvenile offenses, no matter how serious their actions may appear to others. However, in a rather amazing 1994 case, prosecutors in Cincinnati, Ohio, charged a 12-year-old girl with murder after she confessed to drowning her toddler cousin ten years previously. The cousin, 13-month-old Lamar Howell, drowned in 1984 in a bucket of bleach mixed with water. Howell's drowning had been ruled an accidental death until his cousin came forward. In discussing the charges with the media, Hamilton (Ohio) County Prosecutor Joe Deters admitted that the girl could not be prosecuted successfully. "Frankly," he said, "anything under seven cannot be an age where you form criminal intent."[84] The prosecution's goal, claimed one of Deters's associates, was simply to "make sure she gets the counseling she needs."

MISTAKE

Two types of mistake may serve as a defense. One is mistake of law, and the other is mistake of fact. Rarely is the defense of mistake of law acceptable. Most people realize that it is their responsibility to know the law as it applies to them. "Ignorance of the law is no excuse" is an old dictum still heard today. On occasion, however, humorous cases do arise in which such a defense is accepted by authorities—for example, the instance of the elderly woman who raised marijuana plants because they could be used to make a tea which relieved her arthritis. When her garden was discovered, she was not arrested but was advised as to how the law applied to her.

Mistake of fact is a much more useful form of the mistake defense. In 2000, for example, the statutory rape conviction of 39-year-old Charles Ballinger of Bradley County, Tennessee, was reversed by Tennessee's Court of Criminal Appeals at Knoxville on a mistake of fact claim.[85] Ballinger admitted that he had sex with his 15-year-old female neighbor, who was under the age of legal consent at the time of the act in 1998. In his defense, however, Ballinger claimed that he had had good reason to mistake the girl's age.

INVOLUNTARY INTOXICATION

The claim of involuntary intoxication may form the basis for another excuse defense. Either drugs or alcohol may produce intoxication. Voluntary intoxication itself is rarely a defense to a criminal charge because it is a self-induced condition. It is widely recognized in our legal tradition that an altered mental condition which is the product of voluntary activity cannot be used to exonerate guilty actions which follow from it. Some state statutes formalize this general principle of law and specifically state that voluntary intoxication cannot be offered as a defense to a charge of criminal behavior.[86]

Involuntary intoxication, however, is another matter. On occasion, a person may be tricked into consuming an intoxicating substance. Secretly "spiked" punch, popular aphrodisiacs, or LSD-laced desserts all might be ingested unknowingly. In the mid-1990s, for example, the Drug Enforcement Administration reported that a powerful sedative manufactured by Hoffmann-LaRoche Pharmaceuticals and sold under the brand name Rohypnol had become popular with college students and with "young men [who] put doses of Rohypnol in women's drinks without their consent in order to lower their inhibitions."[87] What other behavioral effects the pills, known variously as *roples, roche, ruffles, roofies,* and *rophies* on the street, might have is unknown.

Because the effects and taste of alcohol are so widely known in our society, the defense of involuntary intoxication due to alcohol consumption can be difficult to demonstrate. A more unusual situation results from a disease caused by the yeast *Candida albicans,* occasionally found living in human intestines. A Japanese physician was the first to identify this disease, in which a person's digestive processes ferment the food they eat. Fermentation turns a portion of the food into alcohol, and people with this condition become intoxicated whenever they eat. First recognized about twenty years ago, the disease has not yet been used successfully in this country to support the defense of involuntary intoxication.

UNCONSCIOUSNESS

A very rarely used excuse is that of unconsciousness. An individual cannot be held responsible for anything he or she does while unconscious. Because unconscious people rarely do anything at all, this defense is almost never seen in the courts. However, cases of sleepwalking, epileptic seizure, and neurological dysfunction may result in injurious, although unintentional, actions by people so afflicted. Under such circumstances, a defense of unconsciousness might be argued with success.

PROVOCATION

Provocation recognizes that a person can be emotionally enraged by another who intends to elicit just such a reaction. Should the person then strike out at the tormentor, some courts have held, he or she may not be guilty of criminality or may be guilty of a lesser degree of criminality than might otherwise be the case. The defense of provocation is commonly used in barroom brawls where a person's parentage may have been called into question, although most states don't look favorably upon verbal provocation alone. This defense has also been used in some recent spectacular cases where wives have killed their husbands, or children their fathers, citing years of verbal and physical abuse. In these latter instances, perhaps because the degree of physical harm inflicted appears to be out of proportion to the claimed provocation, the defense of provocation has not been readily accepted by the courts. As a rule, the defense of provocation is generally more acceptable in minor offenses than in serious violations of the law.

INSANITY

insanity defense

A legal defense based on claims of mental illness or mental incapacity.

Chapter 1 briefly mentioned the case of 40-year-old Angel Maturino Resendiz, an illegal immigrant convicted in 2000 of murdering Dr. Claudia Benton, a pediatric geneticist. Dr. Benton had been surprised by Resendiz as she arrived home after work at the Baylor College of Medicine. Resendiz, known as the "railway killer" because his killings occurred near train tracks, was also discussed in the serial killers section of Chapter 2. He appears to have been responsible for as many as 27 deaths throughout the United States and Mexico.[88]

Although Resendiz was ultimately convicted of Dr. Benton's murder and was sentenced to die, defense efforts to mount an **insanity defense** on his behalf captured widespread

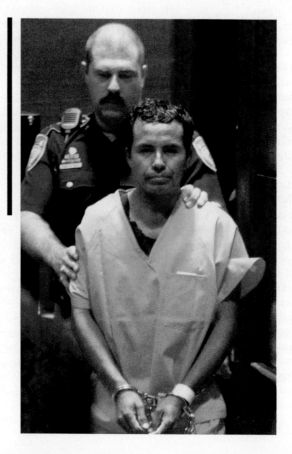

Itinerant worker Angel Maturino Resendiz being escorted into court in Harris County, Texas. Resendiz was convicted in 2000 of one murder but has confessed to killing eight others and is suspected in as many as 27 deaths in the United States and Mexico. During the trial, lawyers representing Resendiz used an insanity defense, claiming that he thought he was being guided by God to kill. Jurors did not believe the claim, and Resendiz was sentenced to die.

AP/Wide World Photos

A handwritten letter from Resendiz to his pastor. The defense in Resendiz's murder trial argued that this letter was evidence of insanity.
Rev. Rick Downey

attention during the trial. One of the first defense witnesses called to testify on behalf of Resendiz was his mother, Virginia Maturino Resendiz. She told the court that her son had suffered a serious head injury when he was born and that he later experienced additional episodes of head trauma during his early teen years.

Also testifying for the defense was neuropsychologist Dr. Larry Pollock. Pollock said that Resendiz was "a paranoid schizophrenic who suffered from severe delusions that were magnified by his fervent belief that his perceptions were real."[89] According to Pollock, who spent 10 hours examining Resendiz, a history of head injuries and heavy drug abuse, including glue sniffing, seriously damaged his ability to separate fact from fiction.

Another defense witness, forensic psychologist Dr. Robert Cohen, testified to his belief that Resendiz suffered from delusions brought on by paranoid schizophrenia and that Resendiz thought that by killing he was doing God's work.[90] Cohen claimed that Resendiz simply did not know that his conduct was wrong. Mental delusion, said Cohen, had Resendiz believing that his victims were evil and that he "was justified in his behaviors."

Additional evidence portrayed a defendant who saw himself as an "angel of wrath," able to cause floods and earthquakes, and able to evade police by becoming invisible. Resendiz, defense experts said, had come to believe that he had developed a sense for detecting evil and felt drawn to his victims. During the Benton killing, defense attorneys said, Resendiz imagined he saw pictures of fetuses on the doctor's computer screen, and he jumped to the conclusion that she was performing evil experiments on babies.

Family members testified that Resendiz would often rant about his interpretations of Old Testament beliefs and said that he offered bizarre mathematical formulas predicting the end of the world. He told his brothers and his pastor that he had a mandate from God to kill those who were evil.[91] Resendiz himself said that he used a statue found in the house to bludgeon Dr. Benton to death because he thought it meant that she worshiped idols and it seemed an appropriate tool of punishment.

Dr. Ramon Laval, a psychiatrist testifying for the prosecution, agreed that while Resendiz had unhealthy views of people and of women in particular, he "knew what he was doing" when he killed Dr. Benton. Prosecutors also called convicted bank robber Mitchell Rollins, 43, to the stand. Rollins, who had been a cellmate of Resendiz's in the early 1990s at the Marianna Federal Corrections Institute in Florida, testified that the two of them had often counseled fellow inmates on how to plead insanity. "We ordered some books and read up on it," Rollins said.

In closing arguments, prosecutors told jurors, "The defendant does suffer from one delusion, and the delusion he has is that he will be able to convince one of you he's insane."[92] See a handwritten letter from Resendiz to his priest on page 159 and at **Web Extra! 4–9** on cjtoday.com.

The insanity defense has received much attention from the popular media; movies and shows highlighting this defense are commonplace. In practice, however, the defense of insanity is rarely raised. According to an eight-state study, funded by the National Institute of Mental Health and reported in the *Bulletin of the American Academy of Psychiatry and the Law,* the insanity defense was used in less than 1% of the cases that came before county-level courts.[93] The study showed that only 26% of all insanity pleas were argued successfully and that 90% of those who employed the defense had been previously diagnosed with a mental illness. As the American Bar Association says, "The best evidence suggests that the mental nonresponsibility defense is raised in less than one percent of all felony cases in the United States and is successful in about a fourth of these."[94]

It is important to realize that for purposes of the criminal law, *insanity* has a legal definition and not a medical one. Legal definitions of *insanity* often have very little to do with psychological or psychiatric understandings of mental illness. Legal insanity is a concept developed over time to meet the needs of the judicial system in assigning guilt or innocence to particular defendants. It is not primarily concerned with understanding the origins of mental pathology or with its treatment, as is the case in psychiatry. As a consequence, medical conceptions of mental illness do not always fit well into the legal categories created by courts and legislatures to deal with the phenomenon. The differences between psychiatric and legal conceptualizations of insanity often lead to disagreements among expert witnesses who, in criminal court, may appear to provide conflicting testimony as to the sanity of a defendant.

The M'Naghten Rule Prior to the nineteenth century, the insanity defense, as we know it today, was nonexistent. Insane people who committed crimes were punished in the same way as other law violators. It was Daniel M'Naghten (sometimes spelled McNaughten or M'Naughten), a woodworker from Glasgow, Scotland, who, in 1844, became the first person to be found not guilty of a crime by reason of insanity. M'Naghten had tried to assassinate Sir Robert Peel, the British prime minister. He mistook Edward Drummond, Peel's secretary, for Peel himself, and killed Drummond instead. At his trial, defense attorneys argued that M'Naghten suffered from vague delusions centered on the idea that the Tories, a British political party, were persecuting him. Medical testimony at the trial agreed with the assertion of M'Naghten's lawyers that he didn't know what he was doing at the time of the shooting. The jury accepted M'Naghten's claim, and the insanity defense was born. The **M'Naghten rule**, as it has come to be called, was not so much a product of M'Naghten's trial, however, as it was of a later convocation of English judges assembled by the leadership of the House of Lords to define the criteria necessary for a finding of insanity.

M'Naghten rule

A rule for determining insanity, which asks whether the defendant knew what he or she was doing or whether the defendant knew that what he or she was doing was wrong.

The M'Naghten rule holds that *a person is not guilty of a crime if, at the time of the crime, the person either didn't know what he or she was doing or didn't know that what he or she was doing was wrong.* The inability to distinguish right from wrong must be the result of some mental defect or disability. The M'Naghten rule is still followed in many U.S. jurisdictions today. However, in most states, the burden of proving insanity falls upon the defendant. Just as defendants are assumed to be innocent, they are also assumed to be sane at the outset of any criminal trial.

Irresistible Impulse The M'Naghten rule worked well for a time. Eventually, however, some cases arose in which defendants clearly knew what they were doing, and they knew it was wrong. Even so, they argued in their defense that they couldn't stop doing what they knew was wrong. Such people are said to suffer from an irresistible impulse, and they may be found not guilty by reason of that particular brand of insanity in 18 states. Some states which do not use the irresistible-impulse test in determining insanity may still allow the successful demonstration of such an impulse to be considered in sentencing decisions.

Lorena Bobbitt, acquitted in 1994 of charges of malicious wounding after she admitted to cutting off her husband's penis with a kitchen knife as he slept. Bobbitt's attorneys successfully employed the irresistible-impulse defense.

Stephen Jaffe, Reuters, CORBIS

In a spectacular 1994 Virginia trial, Lorena Bobbitt successfully employed the irresistible-impulse defense against charges of malicious wounding stemming from an incident in which she cut off her husband's penis with a kitchen knife as he slept. In the case, which made headlines around the world, Bobbitt's defense attorney told the jury, "What we have is Lorena Bobbitt's life juxtaposed against John Wayne Bobbitt's penis. The evidence will show that in her mind it was his penis from which she could not escape, that caused her the most pain, the most fear, the most humiliation."[95] The impulse to sever the organ, said the lawyer, became irresistible.

The irresistible-impulse test has been criticized on a number of grounds. Primary among them is the belief that all of us suffer from compulsions. Most of us, however, learn to control them. If we give in to a compulsion, the critique goes, then why not just say it was unavoidable so as to escape any legal consequences?

The Durham Rule Another rule for gauging insanity is called the *Durham rule*. It was originally created in 1871 by a New Hampshire court and was later adopted by Judge David Bazelon in 1954 as he decided the case of *Durham* v. *United States* for the Court of Appeals in the District of Columbia.[96] The Durham rule states that *a person is not criminally responsible for his or her behavior if the person's illegal actions were the result of some mental disease or defect.*

Courts which follow the Durham rule typically hear from an array of psychiatric specialists as to the mental state of the defendant. Their testimony is inevitably clouded by the need to address the question of cause. A successful defense under the Durham rule necessitates that jurors be able to see the criminal activity in question as the *product* of mental deficiencies harbored by the defendant. And yet, many people who suffer from mental diseases or defects never commit crimes. In fact, low IQ, mental retardation, and lack of general mental capacity are not allowable excuses for criminal behavior. Because the Durham rule is especially vague, it provides fertile ground for conflicting claims.

The Substantial Capacity Test Nineteen states follow another guideline—the substantial capacity test—as found in the Model Penal Code (MPC) of the American Law Institute (ALI).[97] Also called the *ALI rule* or the *MPC rule*, it suggests that insanity should be defined as the lack of a substantial capacity to control one's behavior. This test requires a judgment to the effect that the defendant either had, or lacked, "the mental capacity needed to understand the wrongfulness of his act or to conform his behavior to the requirements of the law."[98] The substantial capacity test is a blending of the M'Naghten rule with the irresistible-impulse standard. "Substantial capacity" does not require total mental incompetence, nor does the rule require the behavior in question to live up to the criterion of total irresistibility. The problem, however, of establishing just what constitutes "substantial mental capacity" has plagued this rule from its conception.

The Brawner Rule Judge Bazelon, apparently dissatisfied with the application of the Durham rule, created a new criterion for gauging insanity in the 1972 case of *U.S.* v. *Brawner*.[99] The Brawner rule, as it has come to be called, places responsibility for deciding insanity squarely with the jury. Bazelon suggested that the jury should be concerned with whether the defendant could be *justly* held responsible for the criminal act in the face of any claims of insanity. Under this proposal, juries are left with few rules to guide them other than their own sense of fairness.

Insanity and Social Reality The insanity defense originated as a means of recognizing the social reality of mental disease. Unfortunately, the history of this defense has been rife with change, contradiction, and uncertainty. Psychiatric testimony is expensive; a medical specialist might charge thousands of dollars per day. Still worse is the fact that one "expert" is commonly contradicted by another.

Public dissatisfaction with the jumble of rules defining legal insanity peaked in 1982, when John Hinckley was acquitted of trying to assassinate then-President Ronald Reagan. At his trial, Hinckley's lawyers claimed that a series of delusions brought about by a history of schizophrenia left him unable to control his behavior. Government prosecutors were unable to counter defense contentions of insanity. The resulting acquittal shocked the nation and resulted in calls for a review of the insanity defense.

One response has been to ban the insanity defense from use at trial. A ruling by the U.S. Supreme Court in support of a Montana law allows states to prohibit defendants from claiming that they were insane at the time they committed their crimes. In 1994, without comment, the high court let stand a Montana Supreme Court ruling which held that eliminating the insanity defense does not violate the U.S. Constitution. Currently, only three states—Montana, Idaho, and Utah—bar use of the insanity defense.[100]

Guilty but Mentally Ill In 1997, Pennsylvania multimillionaire John E. du Pont was found **guilty but mentally ill (GBMI)** in the shooting death of former Olympic gold medalist David Schultz during a delusional episode. Although defense attorneys were able to show that du Pont sometimes saw Nazis in his trees, heard the walls talking, and had cut off pieces of his skin to remove bugs from outer space, he was held criminally liable for Schultz's death and was sentenced to 13 to 30 years in confinement.

The guilty but mentally ill verdict (in a few states the finding is "guilty but insane") is now possible in at least 11 states. It is one form of response to public frustration with the insanity issue. A GBMI verdict means that a person can be held responsible for a specific criminal act even though a degree of mental incompetence may be present in his or her personality. In most GBMI jurisdictions, a jury must return a finding of "guilty but mentally ill" if (1) every element necessary for a conviction has been proved beyond a reasonable doubt, (2) the defendant is found to have been *mentally ill* at the time the crime was committed, and (3) the defendant was *not* found to have been *legally insane* at the time the crime was committed. The difference between mental illness and legal insanity is a crucial one, since a defendant can be mentally ill by standards of the medical profession but sane for purposes of the law.

Upon return of a GBMI verdict, a judge may impose any sentence possible under the law for the crime in question. Mandated psychiatric treatment, however, is often part of the commitment order. The offender, once cured, is usually placed in the general prison population to serve any remaining sentence.

As some authors have observed, the "guilty but mentally ill" finding has three purposes: "first, to protect society; second, to hold some offenders who were mentally ill accountable for their criminal acts; [and] third, to make treatment available to convicted offenders suffering from some form of mental illness."[101]

The U.S. Supreme Court case of *Ford* v. *Wainwright* recognized an issue of a different sort.[102] The 1986 decision specified that prisoners who become insane while incarcerated cannot be executed. Hence although insanity may not always be a successful defense to criminal prosecution, it can later become a block to the ultimate punishment.

guilty but mentally ill (GBMI)

A verdict, equivalent to a finding of "guilty," that establishes that the defendant, although mentally ill, was in sufficient possession of his or her faculties to be morally blameworthy for his or her acts.

Multimillionaire eccentric John E. du Pont being taken into custody by special weapons and tactics (SWAT) team members at his Newton Square, Pennsylvania, estate in 1996. Du Pont shot and killed former Olympic gold medalist David Schultz during a delusional episode, and insanity became an issue at his 1997 murder trial. He was found guilty but mentally ill and was sentenced to serve 13 to 30 years in confinement.

Jim Graham, AP/Wide World Photos

Temporary Insanity Temporary insanity is another possible defense against a criminal charge. Widely used in the 1940s and 1950s, temporary insanity meant that the offender claimed to be insane only at the time of the commission of the offense. If a jury agreed, the defendant went free. The suspect was not guilty of the criminal action by virtue of having been insane at the time, yet he or she could not be ordered to undergo psychiatric counseling or treatment because the insanity was no longer present. This type of plea has become less popular as legislatures have regulated the circumstances under which it can be made.

The Insanity Defense under Federal Law In 1984, the U.S. Congress passed the federal Insanity Defense Reform Act (IDRA). The act created major revisions in the federal insanity defense. Insanity under the law is now defined as a condition in which the defendant can be shown to have been suffering under a "severe mental disease or defect" and, as a result, "was unable to appreciate the nature and quality or the wrongfulness of his acts."[103] This definition of insanity comes close to that set forth in the old M'Naghten rule.

The act also places the burden of proving the insanity defense squarely on the defendant—a provision which has been challenged a number of times since the act was passed. The Supreme Court supported such a requirement prior to the act's passage. In 1983, in the case of *Jones* v. *U.S.*[104] the Court ruled that defendants can be required to prove their insanity when it becomes an issue in their defense. Shortly after the act became law, the Court, in *Ake* v. *Oklahoma* (1985),[105] held that the government must ensure access to a competent psychiatrist whenever a defendant indicates that insanity will be an issue at trial.

Consequences of an Insanity Ruling The insanity defense today is not an "easy way out" of criminal prosecution, as some people assume. Once a verdict of "not guilty by reason of insanity" is returned, the judge may order the defendant to undergo psychiatric treatment until cured. Because psychiatrists are reluctant to declare any potential criminal "cured," such a sentence may result in more time spent in an institution than would have been spent in a prison. In *Foucha* v. *Louisiana* (1992),[106] however, the U.S. Supreme Court held that a defendant found not guilty by reason of insanity in a criminal trial could not thereafter be institutionalized indefinitely without a showing that he or she was either dangerous or mentally ill.

DIMINISHED CAPACITY

diminished capacity

A defense based upon claims of a mental condition that may be insufficient to exonerate the defendant of guilt but that may be relevant to specific mental elements of certain crimes or degrees of crime.

The defense of **diminished capacity**, also called *diminished responsibility*, is available in some jurisdictions. However, "the terms 'diminished responsibility' and 'diminished capacity' do not have a clearly accepted meaning in the courts."[107] Some defendants who offer diminished capacity defenses do so in recognition of the fact that such claims may be based on a mental condition which would not qualify as mental disease or mental defect nor be sufficient to support the defense of insanity, but which might still lower criminal culpability. According to Peter Arenella, professor of law at UCLA, "the defense [of diminished capacity] was first recognized by Scottish common law courts to reduce the punishment of the 'partially insane' from murder to culpable homicide, a non-capital offense."[108]

The diminished capacity defense is similar to the defense of insanity in that it depends upon a showing that the defendant's mental state was impaired at the time of the crime. As a defense, diminished capacity is most useful where it can be shown that because of some defect of reason or mental shortcoming, the defendant's capacity to form the *mens rea* required by a specific crime was impaired. Unlike an insanity defense, however, which can result in a finding of "not guilty," a diminished capacity defense is built upon the recognition that "[m]ental condition, though insufficient to exonerate, may be relevant to specific mental elements of certain crimes or degrees of crime."[109] For example, a defendant might present evidence of mental abnormality in an effort to reduce first-degree murder to second-degree murder, or second-degree murder to manslaughter, when a killing occurs under extreme emotional disturbance. Similarly, in some jurisdictions, very low intelligence will, if proved, serve to reduce first-degree murder to manslaughter.[110]

As is the case with the insanity defense, some jurisdictions have entirely eliminated the diminished capacity defense. The California Penal Code, for example, states, "The defense of diminished capacity is hereby abolished,"[111] adding that "[a]s a matter of public policy there shall be no defense of diminished capacity, diminished responsibility, or irresistible impulse in a criminal action or juvenile adjudication hearing."[112]

MENTAL INCOMPETENCE

incompetent to stand trial

In criminal proceedings, a finding by a court that as a result of mental illness, defect, or disability, a defendant is incapable of understanding the nature of the charges and proceedings against him or her, of consulting with an attorney, and of aiding in his or her own defense.

In July 2001, Jefferson County (Alabama) Circuit Court Judge James Garrett ended the prosecution of 72-year-old Bobby Frank Cherry, declaring him mentally **incompetent to stand trial**.[113] Cherry, a former Ku Klux Klansman, was the last living defendant in the bombing of a black church in Birmingham, Alabama, in 1963. Four African-American children were killed in the basement of the church, which was known as the 16th Street Baptist Church, when the bomb went off. Cherry had been suspected of involvement in the bombing since shortly after the explosion. A Birmingham jury convicted a codefendant, 62-year-old former Klansman Thomas E. Blanton, only two months before Cherry was found incompetent. Following six rounds of psychiatric evaluations, Judge Garrett determined that Cherry's dementia was too severe for him to help his lawyers. The case involving Cherry was strongly influenced by Alabama law, which requires the prosecution to show "clear, unequivocal and convincing evidence" that a defendant is competent to stand trial once the defendant has shown that he or she is incompetent. In Cherry's case, both a defense psychologist and a court-appointed psychiatrist had determined that he was incompetent after brain scans indicated that he suffered from vascular dementia, a physical deterioration of the brain caused by a series of small strokes. In contrast to Alabama law, federal law requires a much lower level of proof of competency, one that depends upon a mere preponderance of the evidence. While insanity refers to an assessment of the offender's mental condition at the time the crime was committed, mental incompetence refers to his or her condition immediately prior to prosecution.

Procedural Defenses

No person shall be . . . twice put in jeopardy of life or limb.

—Fifth Amendment to the U.S. Constitution

Procedural defenses make the claim that the defendant was in some manner discriminated against in the justice process or that some important aspect of official procedure was not properly followed and that, as a result, the defendant should be released from any criminal liability. The procedural defenses we shall discuss here are (1) entrapment, (2) double jeop-

Former Ku Klux Klansmen Thomas E. Blanton (left) and Bobby Frank Cherry appearing in court. In 2001, Jefferson County (Alabama) Circuit Court Judge James Garrett ended the prosecution of the 72-year-old Cherry, declaring him mentally incompetent to stand trial. Cherry was the last living defendant in the bombing of an African-American church in Birmingham, Alabama, in 1963 in which four young girls were killed. His codefendant, 62-year-old Blanton, was convicted of murder and was sentenced to life in prison.

Charles Nesbitt, Birmingham News, CORBIS/Sygma

ardy, (3) *collateral estoppel,* (4) selective prosecution, (5) denial of a speedy trial, (6) prosecutorial misconduct, and (7) police fraud.

ENTRAPMENT

Entrapment, which can be defined as an improper or illegal inducement to crime by enforcement agents, is a defense which limits the enthusiasm with which police officers may enforce the law. Entrapment defenses argue that enforcement agents effectively created a crime where there would otherwise have been none. For entrapment to have occurred, the idea for the criminal activity must have originated with official agents of the criminal justice system. Entrapment can also result when overzealous undercover police officers convince a defendant that the contemplated law-violating behavior is not a crime. To avoid claims of entrapment, officers must not engage in activity that would cause a person to commit a crime that he or she would not otherwise commit. Merely providing an opportunity for a willing offender to commit a crime, however, is *not* entrapment.

Entrapment was claimed in the case of automaker John DeLorean. DeLorean was arrested in 1982 by federal agents near the Los Angeles airport.[114] An FBI videotape, secretly made at the scene, showed him allegedly "dealing" with undercover agents and holding packets of cocaine, which he said were "better than gold." DeLorean was charged with narcotics smuggling violations involving a large amount of drugs.

At his 1984 trial, DeLorean claimed that he had been set up by the police to commit a crime which he would not have been involved in were it not for their urging. DeLorean's auto company had fallen on hard times, and he was facing heavy debts. Federal agents, acting undercover, proposed to DeLorean a plan whereby he could make a great deal of money through drugs. Because the idea originated with the police, not with DeLorean, and because DeLorean was able to demonstrate successfully that he was repeatedly threatened by a police informant not to pull out of the deal, the jury returned a "not guilty" verdict.

The concept of entrapment is well summarized in a statement made by DeLorean's defense attorney to *Time* before the trial: "This is a fictitious crime. Without the Government there would be no crime. This is one of the most insidious and misguided law-enforcement operations in history."[115]

DOUBLE JEOPARDY

The Fifth Amendment to the U.S. Constitution makes it clear that no person may be tried twice for the same offense. People who have been acquitted or found innocent may not again be "put in jeopardy of life or limb" for the same crime. The same is true of those who

entrapment

An improper or illegal inducement to crime by agents of enforcement. Also, a defense that may be raised when such inducements occur.

Members of the New York City Police Department's Street Crimes Unit preparing for a day's work. Entrapment will likely not be an effective defense for muggers who attack these decoys.

Courtesy of the New York City Police Department

have been convicted: They cannot be tried again for the same offense. Cases that are dismissed for a lack of evidence also come under the double jeopardy rule and cannot result in a new trial. The U.S. Supreme Court has ruled that "the Double Jeopardy Clause protects against three distinct abuses: a second prosecution for the same offense after acquittal; a second prosecution for the same offense after conviction; and multiple punishments for the same offense."[116]

double jeopardy

A common law and constitutional prohibition against a second trial for the same offense.

Double jeopardy does not apply in cases of trial error. Hence, convictions which are set aside because of some error in proceedings at a lower court level (for example, inappropriate instructions to the jury by the trial court judge) will permit a retrial on the same charges. Similarly, when a defendant's motion for a mistrial is successful, or when members of the jury cannot agree upon a verdict (resulting in a "hung jury"), a second trial may be held.

Defendants, however, may be tried in both federal and state courts without necessarily violating the principle of double jeopardy. For example, 33-year-old Rufina Canedo pleaded guilty to possession of 50 kilograms of cocaine in 1991 and received a six-year prison sentence from a California court.[117] Federal prosecutors, however, indicted her again—this time under a federal law—for the same offense. They offered her a deal: Testify against your husband, or face federal prosecution and the possibility of 20 years in a federal prison. Because state and federal statutes emanate from different jurisdictions, the Supreme Court has held this kind of dual prosecution to be constitutional. To prevent abuse, the U.S. Justice Department acted in 1960 to restrict federal prosecution in such cases to situations involving a "compelling federal interest," such as civil rights violations. However, in the face of soaring drug-law violations in recent years, the restriction has been relaxed.

In 1992, in another drug case, the Supreme Court ruled that the double jeopardy clause of the U.S. Constitution "only prevents duplicative prosecution for the same offense" but that "a substantive offense and a conspiracy to commit that offense are not the same offense for double jeopardy purposes." In that case, *U.S. v. Felix* (1992),[118] a Missouri man was convicted in that state of manufacturing methamphetamine and was then convicted again in Oklahoma of the "separate crime" of conspiracy to manufacture a controlled substance—in part based upon his activities in Missouri.

Generally, because civil and criminal law differ as to purpose, it is possible to try someone in civil court to collect damages for a possible violation of civil law, even if they were found "not guilty" in criminal court, without violating the principle of double jeopardy. The well-known 1997 California civil trial of O. J. Simpson on grounds of wrongful death resulted in widespread publicity of just such a possibility. In cases where civil penalties are "so punitive in form and effect as to render them criminal,"[119] however, a person sanctioned by a court in a civil case may not be tried in criminal court.

COLLATERAL ESTOPPEL
Collateral estoppel is similar to double jeopardy, but it applies to facts that have been determined by a "valid and final judgment."[120] Such facts cannot become the object of new litigation. For example, if a defendant has been acquitted of a murder charge by virtue of an alibi, it would not be permissible to try that person again for the murder of a second person killed along with the first.

SELECTIVE PROSECUTION
The procedural defense of selective prosecution is based upon the Fourteenth Amendment's guarantee of "equal protection of the laws." This defense may be available where two or more individuals are suspected of criminal involvement, but not all are actively prosecuted. Selective prosecution based fairly upon the strength of available evidence is not the object of this defense. But when prosecution proceeds unfairly on the basis of some arbitrary and discriminatory attribute, such as race, sex, friendship, age, or religious preference, this defense may offer protection. In 1996, however, in a case that reaffirmed reasonable limits on claims of selective prosecution, the U.S. Supreme Court ruled that for a defendant to successfully "claim that he was singled out for prosecution on the basis of his race, he must make a . . . showing that the Government declined to prosecute similarly situated suspects of other races."[121]

DENIAL OF A SPEEDY TRIAL
The Sixth Amendment to the Constitution guarantees a right to a speedy trial. The purpose of the guarantee is to prevent unconvicted and potentially innocent people from languishing in jail. The federal government[122] and most states have laws (generally referred to as *speedy trial acts*) that define the time limit necessary for a trial to be "speedy." They generally set a reasonable period, such as 90 or 120 days following arrest. Excluded from the total number of days are delays which result from requests by the defense to prepare the defendant's case. If the limit set by law is exceeded, the defendant must be set free, and no trial can occur.

> In all criminal prosecutions, the accused shall enjoy the right to a speedy and public trial, by an impartial jury.
>
> —Sixth Amendment to the U.S. Constitution

Speedy trial claims were raised unsuccessfully by defense attorneys in the case of Byron De La Beckwith, the unrepentant 75-year-old white supremacist who was convicted in 1994 of the murder of black civil rights leader Medgar Evers in Mississippi. The killing took place in 1963. More than 30 years after the murder, Beckwith was sentenced to life in prison, but only after two previous trials had ended in hung juries. In 1998, the Mississippi Supreme Court denied a request that Beckwith's case be reviewed.

PROSECUTORIAL MISCONDUCT
Another procedural defense is prosecutorial misconduct. Generally speaking, legal scholars use the term *prosecutorial misconduct* to describe actions undertaken by prosecutors which give the government an unfair advantage or that prejudice the rights of a defendant or a witness. Prosecutors are expected to uphold the highest ethical standards in the performance of their roles. When they knowingly permit false testimony, when they hide information that would clearly help the defense, or when they make unduly biased statements to the jury in closing arguments, the defense of prosecutorial misconduct may be available to the defendant.

The most famous instance of prosecutorial misconduct may have occurred during a convoluted 17-year-long federal case against former Cleveland autoworker John Demjanjuk. Demjanjuk, who was accused of committing war crimes as the notorious Nazi guard "Ivan the Terrible," was extradited in 1986 by the federal government to Israel to face charges there. In late 1993, however, the Sixth U.S. Circuit Court of Appeals in Cincinnati,

Ohio, ruled that federal prosecutors, working under what the court called a "win-at-any-cost" attitude, had intentionally withheld evidence which might have exonerated Demjanjuk (who was stripped of his U.S. citizenship when extradited but later returned to the United States after the Supreme Court of Israel overturned his sentence there).[123]

POLICE FRAUD

During the 1995 double-murder trial of O. J. Simpson, defense attorneys suggested that evidence against Simpson had been concocted and planted by police officers with a personal dislike of the defendant. In particular, defense attorneys pointed a finger at Los Angeles Police Detective Mark Fuhrman, suggesting that he had planted a bloody glove at the Simpson estate and had tampered with bloodstain evidence taken from Simpson's white Ford Bronco. To support allegations that Fuhrman was motivated by racist leanings, defense attorneys subpoenaed tapes Fuhrman made over a ten-year period with a North Carolina screenwriter who had been documenting life within the Los Angeles Police Department.

As one observer put it, however, the defense of police fraud builds upon extreme paranoia about the government and police agencies. This type of defense, said Francis Fukuyama, carries "to extremes a distrust of government and the belief that public authorities are in a vast conspiracy to violate the rights of individuals."[124] It can also be extremely unfair to innocent people, for a strategy of this sort subjects otherwise well-meaning public servants to intense public scrutiny, effectively shifting attention away from criminal defendants and onto the police officers—sometimes with disastrous personal results. Anthony Pellicano, a private investigator hired by Fuhrman's lawyers, put it this way: "[Fuhrman's] life right now is in the toilet. He has no job, no future. People think he's a racist. He can't do anything to help himself. He's been ordered not to talk. His family and friends, he's told them not to get involved. . . . Mark Fuhrman's life is ruined. For what? Because he found a key piece of evidence."[125] The 43-year-old Furhman retired from police work before the Simpson trial concluded and has since written two books.

Innovative Defenses

In recent years, some innovative defense strategies have been employed, with varying degrees of success, in criminal cases—and it is to these that we now turn our attention. Technically speaking, the defenses listed here can be properly subsumed under the broader categories of justifications or excuses. They are discussed as a separate group, however, because each is virtually new and relatively untried. The unique and emerging character of these novel defenses makes discussing them worthwhile. The innovative defenses discussed in the next few pages include (1) the abuse defense, (2) premenstrual syndrome, (3) other biological defenses, (4) black rage, (5) urban survival syndrome, and (6) cultural defenses.

THE ABUSE DEFENSE

One innovative defense which seems to be gaining in popularity with defense attorneys today, especially in murder cases, is the abuse defense. Actually, the abuse defense is not new, having evolved from domestic abuse cases in the 1970s, which emphasized the inability of some battered women to escape from the demeaning situation surrounding them. **Battered women's syndrome (BWS)**, involving long-term abuse, was said to effectively prevent women from seeking divorce and, in some cases, to drive women temporarily insane, leading them to kill their abusive spouse. BWS, sometimes also referred to as *battered spouse syndrome* or *battered person's syndrome*, entered public awareness with the 1979 publication of Lenore E. Walker's book, *The Battered Woman*.[126] Defense attorneys were quick to use Walker's slogan of "learned helplessness" to explain why battered women were unable to leave an abusive situation and why they sometimes found it necessary to resort to violence to free themselves from it. Early versions of the abuse defense depended upon its link to the more traditional defenses of insanity and self-defense. As judges and juries increasingly accepted abuse defenses, however, "attorneys began to use similar arguments to defend not only wives, but also homosexual lovers, and then children, husbands, and a slew of other accused criminals."[127]

The abuse defense attempts to turn the tables on criminal prosecutors by claiming that chronic abuse sufferers may have to defend themselves at times when their abusers are most vulnerable—such as when they are asleep or otherwise distracted. This kind of argument is more frequently offered where the "victim" is weaker than the abuser, as in the case of women and children said to be abused by men.

battered women's syndrome (BWS)

I. A series of common characteristics that appear in women who are abused physically and psychologically over an extended period of time by the dominant male figure in their lives. II. A pattern of psychological symptoms that develops after somebody has lived in a battering relationship. III. A pattern of responses and perceptions presumed to be characteristic of women who have been subjected to continuous physical abuse by their mates.[vi]

Aspects of the abuse defense could be seen in the trials of Lorena Bobbitt and Lyle and Erik Menendez. Bobbit, whose case is discussed earlier in this chapter, was acquitted on charges of malicious wounding after admitting she severed her husband's penis with a kitchen knife. The Menendez brothers were charged with murdering their parents. Their first trial ended in hung juries after their attorneys claimed the boys' actions were the result of a lifetime of sexual abuse at the hands of their father. In 1996, in a second trial, however, the Menendez brothers were convicted of the murders of their parents and were sentenced to life imprisonment without parole.[128]

Some observers of the American scene say that jurors are especially sympathetic to abuse victims who act out their frustrations through crime. New York attorney Ronald L. Kuby says, for example, "One of the salutary effects of the pop psychology boom of the 1970s is that people increasingly ask, 'How did I end up like this and what can I do about it.'"[129] Popular television talk shows have also played a part in sensitizing people to the role of personal and family tragedies in people's lives. As a consequence, people everywhere may be ready to excuse criminal culpability if they can be shown its roots in a given situation. Southwestern University Law School Professor Robert Pugsley puts it this way: "We are entering the age of the empathetic or sympathetic jury that is willing to turn the courtroom into the Oprah [Winfrey] . . . show."[130]

Not everyone is enamored with the willingness of juries to consider the abuse defense, however. Los Angeles Deputy District Attorney Kathleen Cady, for example, saw Moosa Hanoukai convicted of voluntary manslaughter rather than first-degree murder as Cady had hoped. Hanoukai had beaten his wife to death with a wrench, but his attorneys claimed that he killed her because she made him sleep on the floor, called him names, and paid him a small allowance for work he did around the house. Jurors were told that Hanoukai, whose Jewish background prevented divorce, had been psychologically emasculated by his overbearing wife. But, as Cady puts it, "Every single murderer has a reason why they killed someone. . . . I think it sends a very frightening message to the rest of society that all you have to do is come up with some kind of excuse when you commit a crime."[131] Even a history of abuse, others say, should not be a license to kill.

Even so, the long-term trend may favor those with an abuse defense available to them. James Blatt, the attorney who defended Hanoukai, says, "I think the trend is, if you can show legitimate psychological abuse over a prolonged period of time, then be prepared for a jury's reaction to that. . . . Whether a lot of people like it or not, it may become an inherent part of American jurisprudence."[132]

PREMENSTRUAL SYNDROME

The use of premenstrual syndrome (PMS) as a defense against criminal charges demonstrates how changing social conceptions and advancing technology can modify the way in which courts view illegal behavior. In 1980, British courts heard the case of Christine English, who killed her live-in lover when he threatened to leave her. An expert witness at the trial testified that English had suffered from PMS for more than a decade. The witness, Dr. Katharina Dalton, advanced the claim that PMS had rendered Ms. English "irritable, aggressive . . . and confused, with loss of self-control."[133] The jury, apparently accepting the claim, returned a verdict of "not guilty."

PMS is not an officially acceptable defense in American criminal courts. However, in 1991, a Fairfax, Virginia, judge dismissed drunk-driving charges against a woman who cited the role PMS played in her behavior.[134] Dr. Geraldine Richter, an orthopedic surgeon, admitted to drinking four glasses of wine and allegedly kicked and cursed a state trooper who stopped her car because it was weaving down the road. A Breathalyzer test showed a blood-alcohol level of 0.13%—higher than the 0.10% needed to meet the requirement for drunk driving under Virginia law. But a gynecologist who testified on Dr. Richter's behalf said that the behavior she exhibited is characteristic of PMS. "I guess this is a new trend," said the state's attorney in commenting on the judge's ruling.

OTHER BIOLOGICAL DEFENSES

Modern nutritional science may be on the verge of establishing a category of defense related to "chemical imbalances" in the human body produced by eating habits. Vitamin deficiencies, food allergies, the consumption of stimulants (including coffee and nicotine), and the excessive ingestion of sugar may all soon be advanced by attorneys in defense of their clients.

The case of Dan White helped begin the development of innovative defenses.[135] In 1978, White, a former police officer, walked into the office of San Francisco Mayor George Moscone and shot both the mayor and City Councilman Harvey Milk to death. White was arrested and charged with murder. It was established at the trial that White had spent the night before the killings drinking Coca-Cola and eating Twinkies, a packaged pastry. Expert witnesses testified that the huge amounts of sugar consumed by White prior to the crime substantially altered his judgment and his ability to control his behavior. The jury, influenced by the expert testimony, convicted White of a lesser charge, and he served a short prison sentence.

The strategy used by White's lawyers came to be known as the "Twinkie defense." It may well have set the tone for many of the innovative defense strategies that were later used in cases across the nation.

BLACK RAGE

The defense of "black rage" originated with the multiple-murder trial of Colin Ferguson, who was charged with killing six passengers and wounding 19 others in what authorities described as "a racially motivated attack" aboard a Long Island Rail Road commuter train in December 1993. In preparation for trial, Ferguson's original attorneys, William Kunstler and Ronald Kuby, had planned to argue that Ferguson, who is black, was overcome by rage resulting from society-wide mistreatment of blacks by whites. (All the victims in Ferguson's shooting spree were either white or Asian-American.)

Kunstler suggested that the black rage defense is fundamentally a claim of insanity. "We are mounting a traditional insanity defense, long recognized in our law, with 'black rage' triggering last December's massacre," Kunstler and Kuby wrote in a letter to the *New York Times*.[136] "Without a psychiatric defense, Colin has no defense," Kunstler was quoted as saying.[137] "There was no doubt that he was there, that he fired the weapon, that he would have fired it more if he had not been wrestled to the ground. There is no doubt that Colin Ferguson, if sane, was guilty," said Kunstler.

Ferguson eventually rejected the recommendation of Kunstler and Kuby that he plead not guilty by reason of insanity caused by black rage at racial injustice. After conducting his own defense, in what some called a mockery of an accused's right to act as his own attorney, Ferguson was convicted of all the charges against him. He had maintained his innocence throughout the trial, despite being identified by more than a dozen eyewitnesses, including some of his victims.

Colin Ferguson conducting his own defense. Ferguson, who rejected attorneys' recommendations that he employ an innovative "black rage" defense, was convicted in 1995 of killing six people and wounding 19 others in a racially motivated shooting aboard a Long Island Rail Road commuter train.

AP/Wide World Photos

URBAN SURVIVAL SYNDROME

Several years ago, in a Fort Worth, Texas, murder case, a mistrial was declared after jurors deadlocked over lawyers' claims that their client, 18-year-old Daimion Osby, had killed two men because he suffered from "urban survival syndrome." Although Osby admitted to shooting both unarmed men in the head in a downtown parking lot, his attorneys told jurors that he had simply staged a preemptive strike against vicious people who had been threatening him for a year.

Jurors in Osby's trial heard defense attorneys argue that urban survival syndrome is a predilection to engage in violence to prevent oneself from being victimized—a kind of "shoot first, ask questions later" response to the growing violence now so characteristic of many American inner cities. Lawyers described the syndrome as "a sort of mind fix that comes over a young black male living in an urban neighborhood when he's been threatened with deadly force by another black male."[138] "For young blacks to take into account what they see happening in their own neighborhoods is not being racist," said David Bays, one of Osby's lawyers. "It's being realistic." Osby, said his lawyers, had been scared into a state of "hypervigilance," convinced that he had no alternative but to kill to ensure his own survival. Later, however, Osby was tried again. This time jurors rejected urban survival syndrome as a defense. Osby was convicted and sentenced to life in prison.[139]

As one commentator on the new defense put it, "I certainly don't like the idea of using some syndrome to get someone off a murder beef. But I've met enough people who use bathtubs as bulletproof beds to know that urban survival syndrome is real. How long can people live in fear before they snap?"[140]

A similar defense, that of "urban fear syndrome," was used in the 1995 murder trial of Nathaniel Hurt. Hurt, 62, fired a .357 Magnum revolver at teenagers, killing a 13-year-old, after young people had repeatedly trashed his yard and thrown rocks at his car. His attorneys claimed that Hurt snapped under the strain of constant harassment from inner-city thugs and that his murderous reaction was excusable because he lived in constant fear. Hurt was convicted of lesser charges after the judge in the case limited application of the defense by ruling that the syndrome claimed by Hurt's lawyers was not "medically recognized."[141]

CULTURAL DEFENSES

A defense to a criminal charge in which a defendant's culture is taken into account in assessing his or her culpability is called a **cultural defense**. According to attorney Kari Converse, a former state and federal public defender, "the concept of 'melting pot' has just begun to reach criminal law." Immigrants "who are only minutes 'off the boat,'" says Converse, "are held to the same level of knowledge of our laws. If an immigrant does something that in his country is legal but in the United States is a crime, the traditional response has been, 'too bad, ignorance of the law is no excuse.'"[142]

Cultural defenses are rarely used but are not without merit. Legal scholars say that "a cultural defense will negate or mitigate criminal responsibility where acts are committed under a reasonable good-faith belief in their propriety, based upon the actor's cultural heritage or tradition."[143]

One well-known case in which a cultural defense was used is that of *People* v. *Chen* (1989).[144] The case involved a Chinese immigrant named Dong Lu Chen, who killed his adulterous wife, Jian Wan Chen, with a claw hammer. The killing took place in New York City. At trial, an expert in Chinese culture testified that in Chen's community of origin, it was considered culturally appropriate for a husband who learns of his wife's infidelity to assert publicly that he will kill her. According to this anthropologist, the custom requires the community to act to save the wife from the husband who has set out to kill her, thereby sparing her while restoring the husband's dignity. The community's intervention allows the husband to say that he would have killed his wife but was prevented from doing so by others. Unfortunately, in New York City, the traditional community that the expert described did not exist, and Mrs. Chen was not saved.[145] Testimony by the anthropologist appeared to sway the court in favor of leniency. Although Chen might have been convicted of first-degree murder, he was found guilty only of second-degree manslaughter and was sentenced to five years' probation.

Conduct that may be intended as merely friendly, or even a style of dress that to a person of the dominant U.S. culture may be considered a matter of comfort (for example, a tank top and shorts in the hot summer), may be taken as interest in or consent to sexual intercourse by people from other cultures. In the case of *State* v. *Curbello-Rodriguez*

cultural defense

A defense to a criminal charge in which the defendant's culture is taken into account in judging his or her culpability.

(1984),[146] two young women agreed late at night to accompany a Cuban man to an apartment that he shared with several other Cuban males. The young women, dressed in tank tops and shorts, said later that they had only gone to the apartment to borrow a dollar. While there, they smoked marijuana with the men and had sex with them. One of the women later charged one of the men, Lazaro Curbello-Rodriguez, with rape. At trial, Curbello-Rodriguez said he thought that the woman had consented to sex, signaling her interest by the way she was dressed and had behaved. Nonetheless, he was convicted on three counts of first-degree sexual assault and another six counts of first-degree sexual assault as an aider and abettor. He received consecutive sentences totaling 80 years in prison. The Wisconsin Court of Appeals eventually reviewed the case and upheld both the conviction and the sentence. Nonetheless, in a **concurring opinion**, Judge Martha J. Bablitch stated her belief that culture could be relevant to sentencing. She wrote,

> [T]his court is powerless to remedy a sentence which shocks its conscience unless the trial court seriously falters in employing the familiar checklist of discretionary factors relevant to its decision. . . . The defendant in this case, a recent immigrant from Cuba, has no prior criminal record. He did not set forth to seek sexual adventure on the night in question. He said he believed the girls (or "women" as he called them) were "available" when they came to the apartment about midnight, looking for a dollar and some marijuana, and stayed to talk and smoke marijuana with a group of men they did not know, whose language they did not share. Perhaps, in his culture, such conduct at such an hour would be widely interpreted as an invitation to sexual games by willing players familiar with the possible consequences. Perhaps he proceeded on that assumption, however loathsome such an assumption is rightly regarded as being in this culture, in this day.
>
> [We] do not suggest that cultural factors or a "macho" world-view excuse these crimes. They do not. But eighty years of a person's life is a high price to exact for acts which may have been set in motion by misjudgment about the mores of a new culture, and misreading the signals of its women.

Many other criminal cases in which culture played a role can be cited, including California's *People* v. *Kimura* (1985),[147] in which a woman, shamed by her husband's infidelity, attempted the Japanese practice of honorable suicide known as *oyaku shinju*. She waded into the Pacific Ocean with her two children, attempting to kill herself and, like a proper mother, not leave her children alone on earth without a mother. The three were seen, but rescue efforts saved only the mother. Her children drowned. The prosecutor in the case accepted evidence of the mother's cultural beliefs and allowed her to plead guilty to voluntary manslaughter rather than prosecuting her for a higher degree of murder.

Another case involving a cultural defense is *People* v. *Kong Moua* (1985),[148] in which a Hmong tribesman from Laos who was living in California was charged with kidnapping and rape after practicing the Laotian tribal marriage ritual known as *zij poj niam*. The ritual involves what is supposed to appear as a forceful abduction of a bride by her future husband. The bride is expected to cry out and to weep and moan as a way of demonstrating her virtue. The suitor is expected to consummate the marriage in the face of such protest.[149] In *Kong Moua*, the prosecutor dropped rape and kidnapping charges and allowed the defendant to plead guilty to a misdemeanor charge of false imprisonment. The judge, after reviewing a doctoral dissertation on Hmong marriage customs and hearing testimony about the practice, reduced Moua's sentence from six months in jail to only three.

In practice, one problem for cultural defenses is that crimes that are considered to be among the most serious in this country are also likely to be violations of the criminal law in the offender's country of origin. See **Web Extra! 4–10** at cjtoday.com to learn more about cultural defenses.

THE FUTURE OF INNOVATIVE DEFENSES

Future years will no doubt hold many surprises for students of the criminal law as defense attorneys become ever more willing to experiment with innovative tactics. As David Rosenhan, a professor of law and psychology at Stanford University, explains it, "We're getting to see some very, very interesting things, and obviously some long shots. . . . There are a terrific number of them."[150] To make his case, Rosenhan points to a number of situations where people who didn't file income taxes escaped IRS prosecution by arguing that traumatic life experiences gave them an aversion to forms—a condition their legal counselors termed *failure to file syndrome*. Another claimed psychological condition came to light in 2001, when a panel of special masters recommended that Los Angeles Superior Court

concurring opinion

An opinion written by a judge who agrees with the conclusion reached by the majority of judges hearing a case but whose reasons for reaching that conclusion differ. Concurring opinions, which typically stem from an appellate review, are written to identify issues of precedent, logic, or emphasis that are important to the concurring judge but that were not identified by the court's majority opinion.

[Legal Authority and the Criminal Law]

Multiculturalism and social diversity affect American criminal law in a number of important ways. They help determine the content of legislative initiatives, influence the kinds of laws that are enacted, reshape existing statutes, contribute to the elimination of laws that are unfair, and form the basis for innovative defenses to a criminal charge. Earlier in this chapter, we discussed innovative strategies based on cultural defenses. Cultural defenses are predicated upon the fact that multicultural societies sometimes criminalize practices regarded as both traditional and acceptable in an offender's native culture. Hence they raise the claim that to hold immigrants, especially recent ones, to the same standards expected of long-term U.S. residents is not just.

In Chapter 3, we discussed moral enterprise, a process whereby politically influential groups with differing interests—sometimes formed around varying cultural traditions and values—each strive to have their particular point of view enacted into law. Moral enterprise is an ongoing process, as constituencies with common interests continually band together and work to elect political candidates who are likely to legislate their perspectives into law.

Multiculturalism and diversity, however, are important for yet another reason: their potential for contributing to the acceptance or nonacceptance of legal authority. Disenfranchised groups, especially those whose members do not believe that American law reflects their way of thinking, their sense of morality, or their needs, are likely to remain uncommitted to the enforcement of existing laws and will sometimes intentionally ignore the law. Survivalist and antigovernment groups, for example, some of whom have established their own small fortresslike communities in sparsely populated states such as Montana and Idaho, may comprise members who reject "official" laws. Such groups may declare their independence from the United States, insist that U.S. law does not apply to them, refuse to pay local, state, and federal taxes, drive without licenses, and possess weapons classified as illegal under federal law—including fully automatic assault rifles and weapons of mass destruction. Members of such groups often see federal and state governments and their representatives as "the enemy."

Antigovernment groups, however, provide an extreme example because they tend to reject the entire U.S. legal system. Nonetheless, they highlight the potential challenge of establishing and maintaining legal authority in diverse societies. As was pointed out in Chapter 1, when we discussed the importance of individual rights and personal freedoms in the face of social obligations and the need for public order, adherence to the law—and especially to criminal laws—is essential if society is to remain organized and if personal safety is to be at least partially ensured.

In contrast to extreme antigovernment factions, many culturally diverse groups within our society disagree only with aspects of existing laws. As this chapter points out, present-day law is the product of a long and complex evolutionary process built largely upon Western traditions. Hence cultural groups who do not share in those traditions may have a difficult time accepting the legitimacy of today's laws.

One recent study that includes a thorough overview of past research on the acceptability of laws in a culturally diverse society was published by Tom R. Tyler in 2000.[1] Tyler, who is a faculty member at New York University School of Law, not only was interested in studying acceptance of the law, but also wanted to know "whether deference to the law is constant across different subgroups."[2] According to Tyler, studies have shown that (1) the threat of punishment "has little empirical support as a behavioral change agent or inhibitor"[3] and (2) voluntary compliance with the law is a necessary feature of any democratic society.

Spectators lining the street at a Macy's Thanksgiving Day parade in New York City. These revelers illustrate the diversity of ethnicity, age, gender, and cultural heritage that characterize American society. Researchers have long wondered how a broad base of support for the criminal law can be maintained in a diverse society like ours.

© Joseph Sohm, ChromoSohm, Inc./CORBIS

(continued)

Multiculturalism and Diversity in America (*continued*)

Tyler found that "people are more inclined to follow laws they believe are right and which are administered by governing agencies in which they have respect and trust."[4] He also notes that officials in multicultural societies must treat all people with "dignity and respect" if their actions are to be perceived as fair. Tyler concludes that "if authorities make decisions in fair ways, their decisions are generally accepted among citizens."[5] Of special relevance to the criminal justice system and the criminal law is Tyler's finding that "people will accept decisions, regardless of whether they personally are helped or disadvantaged by them, if these decisions are reached fairly."[6] The implication is that members of most, if not all, cultural groups share something of a common understanding as to what is right, fair, and just (and what isn't). If so, then it will be increasingly important—as the growth of multicultural populations continues throughout the United States—for justice system personnel to explore the idea of fairness in the decision-making process and to apply what they learn to on-the-job encounters.

[1]Tom R. Tyler, "Multiculturalism and the Willingness of Citizens to Defer to Law and to Legal Authorities," *Law and Social Inquiry,* Vol. 25, No. 4 (2000), p. 983.

[2]Some of the material in this section is adapted from "Study Presents Optimistic View of Acceptance of Legal Authority in Multicultural Society," *Criminal Justice Research Reports,* Vol. 2, No. 4 (March–April 2001), pp. 55 and 63.

[3]Ibid., p. 55.

[4]Ibid.

[5]Tyler, "Multiculturalism and the Willingness of Citizens to Defer to Law and to Legal Authorities."

[6]"Study Presents Optimistic View of Acceptance of Legal Authority in Multicultural Society," p. 55.

Judge Patrick Couwenberg be removed from the bench for lying about his background. While under consideration for a judicial appointment, Couwenberg apparently fabricated stories about serving in Vietnam, working for the CIA, holding a law degree from Loyola Law School, and earning a master's degree in psychology. Couwenberg's attorney defended his client, saying that the judge had been diagnosed with a condition known as *pseudologia fantastica,* or compulsive lying, under which he felt compelled to "tell tales and mix fantasy with facts." The panel rejected the attorney's arguments, however, finding that "a judicial applicant who gets appointed after submitting falsified qualifications brings the judiciary into disrepute."[151]

Some defenses to even very serious charges seem to border on the ludicrous. In 1995, for example, the state of Texas executed John Fearance, Jr., 40, for stabbing a man 19 times during a burglary, killing him while the man's spouse watched. In his defense, Fearance had claimed that he was temporarily insane at the time of the burglary-murder, explaining that his wife had baked a meat casserole for dinner on the night of the crimes, and he "likes his meat served separately."[152]

The number of new and innovative defenses being tried on juries and judges today is staggering. Some attribute the phenomenon to what they call "creative lawyering." Others, like Kent Scheidegger of the Criminal Justice Legal Foundation, call most such defenses "outrageous." They're the tactics of lawyers "who have nothing left to argue," Scheidegger says.[153] He includes defenses like those of 37-year-old Michael Ricksgers, a Pennsylvania man who argued that sleep apnea (a disorder that causes irregular breathing during sleep) led him to pick up a .357-caliber Magnum and kill his wife; and Edward Kelly, who entered a plea of not guilty to a charge of rape because the crime was supposedly committed by one of his 30 personalities and not by him.

In an insightful article, Stephen Morse, an expert in psychiatry and the law, says that American criminal justice is now caught in the grips of a "new syndrome excuse syndrome"—meaning that new excuses are being offered on an almost daily basis for criminal activity.[154] Many of these "excuses" are documented in the psychiatric literature as syndromes or conditions, and they include antisocial personality disorder, posttraumatic stress disorder, intermittent explosive disorder, kleptomania, pathological gambling, postconcussional disorder, caffeine withdrawal, and premenstrual dysphoric disorder (also known as premenstrual syndrome). All these conditions are listed in the American Psychiatric Association's authoritative *Diagnostic and Statistical Manual of Mental Disorders.*[155] Emerging defenses, says Morse, include battered women's syndrome, Vietnam syndrome, child sexual abuse syndrome, Holocaust survivor syndrome, urban survival syndrome, rotten social background syndrome, and adopted child syndrome. "Courts," says Morse, "are increasingly inundated with claims that syndromes old and new, validated and unvalidated, should be the basis for two types of legal change": (1) the creation of new defenses to a criminal charge; and (2) "the expansion of old defenses: for example, loosening objective standards for justifications such as self-defense." Morse says that the new syndromes tend to work as defenses because they describe personal abnormalities, and most people are willing to accept abnormalities as "excusing conditions that bear on the accused's responsibility." The mistake, says Morse, is to think "that if we identify a cause for conduct, including mental or physical disorders, then the conduct is necessarily excused." "Causation," he cautions, "is not an excuse," only an explanation for the behavior.

Even so, attempts to offer novel defenses which are intended to convince jurors that even admitted criminal offenders should not be held responsible for their actions are becoming increasingly characteristic of the American way of justice. Whether such strategies will ultimately provide effective defenses may depend more upon finding juries sympathetic to them than it will upon the inherent quality of the defenses themselves.

Summary

Laws regulate relationships between people and also between parties. Hence, one of the primary functions of the law is the maintenance of public order. Generally speaking, laws reflect the values held by the society that created them, and legal systems throughout the world reflect the experience of the society of which they are a part. The emphasis placed by any law upon individual rights, personal property, and criminal reformation and punishment can tell us much about the cultural and philosophical basis of the society that created it.

Although various kinds of laws can be identified, this chapter concerns itself primarily with criminal law—or the form of the law which defines and specifies punishments for offenses of a public nature or for wrongs committed against the state or the society. American criminal law developed out of a long tradition of legal reasoning, extending back to the Code of Hammurabi, the earliest known codification of laws. One especially important source of modern criminal law is English common law. Common law, which grew out of the customs and daily practices of English citizens during the Middle Ages, provides the basis for much of contemporary American legal practice. True to its heritage, modern criminal law generally distinguishes between serious crimes (felonies) and those which are less grave (misdemeanors). Guilt can be demonstrated, and criminal offenders convicted, only if all of the statutory elements of a particular crime can be proved in court.

Our legal system recognizes a number of defenses to a criminal charge. Primary among them are justifications and excuses. One form of excuse, the insanity defense, has recently met with considerable criticism, and efforts to reduce its application have been under way for more than a decade. Even as limits are placed on some traditional defenses, however, new and innovative defenses are emerging.

Discussion Questions

1. Name and describe some of the historical sources of modern law.
2. What is common law? Can aspects of the common law still be found in American criminal law today? If so, where?
3. Do you think there is a "natural" basis for laws? If so, upon what basis do you think it would be appropriate to build a system of laws? Do any of our modern laws appear to have a foundation in natural law?
4. What is the difference between *mala in se* and *mala prohibita* offenses? Do you think such a difference is practical or only theoretical? Why?
5. What kinds of concerns have influenced the development of the criminal law? How are social values and power arrangements in society represented in today's laws?
6. What is meant by the *corpus delicti* of a crime? How does the *corpus delicti* of a crime differ from the statutory elements that must be proved to convict a particular defendant of committing that crime?
7. Does the insanity defense serve a useful function today? If you could create your own rules for determining insanity in criminal trials, what would they be? How would they differ from existing rules?

8. What is a cultural defense? Do you think that cultural defenses should be available? If so, under what circumstances should they be used? If not, why not?

9. Near the end of this chapter, Stephen Morse describes many emerging defenses, saying that an explanation for behavior is not the same thing as an excuse. What does Morse mean? Might an explanation be an excuse under some circumstances? If so, when?

To participate in an online discussion on these topics and others, go to the Global Town Meeting electronic message board for Chapter 4 on the *Criminal Justice Today* Companion Website at cjtoday.com.

Web Quest!

Use the Cybrary (http://www.cybrary.info) to locate websites containing state criminal codes. Choose a state, and locate the statutes pertaining to the FBI's eight major crimes. (Remember that the terminology may be different. Whereas the FBI may use the term *rape*, for example, the state you've selected may use *sexual assault*.) After studying the statutes, describe the *corpus delicti* of each major offense. That is, list the elements of each offense that a prosecutor must prove in court to obtain a conviction.

Now choose a second state, preferably from a different geographic region of the country. Again, list the elements of each major offense. Compare the way in which those elements are described with the terminology used by the first state you chose. What differences, if any, exist? Submit your findings to your instructor if asked to do so.

To complete this Web Quest! online, go to the Web Quest! module in Chapter 4 of the *Criminal Justice Today* Companion Website at cjtoday.com.

Library Extras!

Library Extra! 4–1 Paul H. Robinson, *Structuring Criminal Codes to Perform Their Function.*
Library Extra! 4–2 *American Criminal Law Review.*
Library Extra! 4–3 *Buffalo Criminal Law Review.*
Library Extra! 4–4 *California Criminal Law Review.*
Library Extra! 4–5 *The Cox Report on Chinese Spying.*

To explore these resources online, go to the Library Extras! area of the *Criminal Justice Today* Companion Website at cjtoday.com. You should also check the author's "Late Picks" online for newly released documents and updated Library Extras! You can find Late Picks at http://cjtoday.com/latepicks.htm.

Marginal Notes

i. Gerald Hill and Kathleen Hill, *The Real Life Dictionary of the Law* (Santa Monica, CA: General Publishing Group, 2000). Online version Web posted at http://dictionary.law.com/lookup2.asp. Accessed February 21, 2001.

ii. Henry Campbell Black, Joseph R. Nolan, and Jacqueline M. Nolan-Haley, *Black's Law Dictionary*, 6th ed. (St. Paul, MN: West, 1990), p. 1003.

iii. Hill and Hill, *The Real Life Dictionary of the Law.* Accessed February 21, 2002.

iv. Daniel Oran, *Oran's Dictionary of the Law* (St. Paul, MN: West, 1983), p. 306.

v. Black, Nolan, and Nolan-Haley, *Black's Law Dictionary*, 6th ed., p. 24.

vi. *People v. Romero*, 8 Cal.4th 728, 735 (1994).

Notes

1. Henry Campbell Black, Joseph R. Nolan, and Jacqueline M. Nolan-Haley, *Black's Law Dictionary,* 6th ed. (St. Paul, MN: West, 1990), p. 884.

2. Ibid.

3. Marvin Wolfgang, *The Key Reporter* (Phi Beta Kappa), Vol. 52, No. 1.

4. Roman influence in England had ended by A.D. 442, according to Robin W. Winks, Crane Brinton, John B. Christopher, and Robert L. Wolff, eds., *A History of Civilization* (Upper Saddle River, NJ: Prentice Hall, 1996).

5. Howard Abadinsky, *Law and Justice* (Chicago: Nelson-Hall, 1988), p. 6.

6. Edward McNall Burns, *Western Civilization,* 7th ed. (New York: W. W. Norton, 1969), p. 339.

7. Ibid., p. 533.

8. Winks, Brinton, Christopher, and Wolff, eds., *A History of Civilization.*

9. Thomas Aquinas, *Summa Theologica* (Notre Dame, IN: University of Notre Dame Press, 1983).

10. *Roe* v. *Wade,* 410 U.S. 113 (1973).

11. John F. Kennedy, *Profiles in Courage* (New York: Harper and Row, 1956).

12. American Bar Association Section of International and Comparative Law, *The Rule of Law in the United States* (Chicago: ABA, 1958).

13. Max Rheinstein, ed., *Max Weber on Law in Economy and Society* (Cambridge: Harvard University Press, 1954).

14. John Stuart Mill, *On Liberty* (London: Parker, 1859).

15. Nigel Walker, *Punishment, Danger, and Stigma: The Morality of Criminal Justice* (Totowa, NJ: Barnes and Noble, 1980).

16. O. W. Holmes, *The Common Law* (Boston: Little, Brown, 1881).

17. Roscoe Pound, *Social Control through Law* (Hamden, CT: Archon, 1968), pp. 64-65.

18. Ibid.

19. As found in William Chambliss and Robert Seidman, *Law, Order, and Power* (Reading, MA: Addison-Wesley, 1971), p. 140.

20. Ibid.

21. Ibid., p. 51.

22. Ibid.

23. "Jury Finds 'Jenny Jones Show' Negligent," APB News Online, May 7, 1999. Web posted at http://www.apbnews.com/newscenter/breakingnews/1999/05/07/jones0507_01.html. Accessed January 10, 2000.

24. Carrie Dowling, "Jury Awards $150 Million in Blazer Crash," *USA Today,* June 4, 1996, p. 3A.

25. "Jury Awards $4.9 Billion in Suit against GM," *USA Today* Online, July 7, 1999. Web posted at http://www.usatoday.com/hlead.htm. Accessed July 9, 1999.

26. "Cancer Patient Accepts Reduced $100 Million Award in Los Angeles Tobacco Case," Associated Press wire service, August 23, 2001.

27. While the state supreme court ruled in favor of Kitchen on the general issue of liability for gun sales, it agreed with a lower court that the case should be retried because of a procedural error.

28. San Francisco County Superior Court, No. 959-316.

29. This sentence, and some of the information in this paragraph, is adapted from the Brady Center, "Brady Center Decries California Supreme Court Ruling" (news release), August 6, 2001. Web posted at http://www.gunlawsuits.org/features/press/release.asp?Record=325. Accessed January 5, 2002.

30. *Merrill* v. *Navegar, Inc.,* No. A0079863 (Cal. App. Dist. 1 10/25/1999).

31. *Merrill* v. *Navegar, Inc.,* No. S083466 (Cal. 08/06/2001).

32. California Civil Code, §1714.4, subd. (a).

33. Majority opinion, *Merrill* v. *Navegar, Inc.,* No. S083466 (Cal. 08/06/2001).

34. Paul Shepard, "NAACP to Sue Gun Industry," Associated Press wire service, July 11, 1999. Web posted at http://search.washingtonpost.com/wp-srv/WAPO/19990711/V000281-071199-idx.html. Accessed July 13, 1999. See also "Brady Center to Prevent Gun Violence Legal Action Project" page at http://www.gunlawsuits.org/features/index.asp. Accessed January 22, 2002.

35. "Jury Says Halcion Led to Murder, Awards $2.15 Million," Associated Press wire service, November 13, 1992.

36. *Upjohn Company* v. *William R. Freeman,* 885 S.W.2d 538 (1994).

37. See Emily Heller, "Paxil Maker Hit with $8 Million Verdict," *National Law Journal* (June 2001).

38. "Part-Time Carpenter Seeks $657 Trillion Payment," Reuters wire service, June 13, 1994.

39. See Liz Spayd, "America, the Plaintiff: In Seeking Perfect Equity, We've Made a Legal Lottery," *Washington Post* wire services, March 5, 1995.

40. *BMW of North America, Inc.* v. *Gore,* 116 S.Ct. 1589 (1996).

41. Phillip Rawls, "BMW Paint-Liability," Associated Press wire service, May 9, 1997.

42. *Cooper Industries, Inc.* v. *Leatherman Tool Group, Inc.,* No. 99-2035 (U.S. Supreme Court, decided May 14, 2001).

43. Lief H. Carter, *Reason in Law,* 4th ed. (New York: Harper Collins, 1994).

44. U.S. Sentencing Commission, *Federal Sentencing Guidelines Manual* (St. Paul, MN: West, 1987).

45. Daniel Oran, *Oran's Dictionary of the Law* (St. Paul, MN: West, 1983), p. 306.

46. Florida Constitution, Section 20.

47. Black, Nolan, and Nolan-Haley, *Black's Law Dictionary,* p. 24.

48. Much of the information in this paragraph and the next comes from "Hanssen Pleads Guilty to Spying for Moscow," CNN.com Law Center, July 8, 2001. Web posted at http://www.cnn.com/2001/LAW/07/06/hanssen/index.html. Accessed September 22, 2001.

49. Specifically, 21 U.S.C. §846.

50. *United States* v. *Shabani,* No. 93-981 (1994).

51. Patricia T. Jaden and Nancy Thoeness, *Stalking in America: Findings From the National Violence Against Women Survey* (Washington, D.C.: NIJ, 1998).

52. *Gordon* v. *State,* 52 Ala. 3008, 23 Am. Rep. 575 (1875).

53. Holmes, *The Common Law,* Vol. 3.

54. But not for more serious degrees of homicide, since leaving a young child alone in a tub of water, even if

intentional, does not necessarily mean that the person who so acts intends the child to drown.

55. There is disagreement among some jurists as to whether the crime of statutory rape is a strict liability offense. Some jurisdictions treat it as such and will not accept a reasonable mistake about the victim's age. Others, however, do accept such a mistake as a defense.

56. *State* v. *Stiffler,* 763 P.2d. 308 (Idaho App. 1988).

57. John S. Baker, Jr., et al., *Hall's Criminal Law,* 5th ed. (Charlottesville, VA: Michie, 1993), p. 138.

58. The same is not true for procedures within the criminal justice system, which can be modified even after a person has been sentenced and, hence, become retroactive. See, for example, the U.S. Supreme Court case of *California Department of Corrections* v. *Morales,* 514 U.S. 499 (1995), which approved of changes in the length of time between parole hearings, even though those changes applied to offenders already sentenced.

59. Black, Nolan, and Nolan-Haley, *Black's Law Dictionary,* p. 127.

60. The statute also says, "A mother's breastfeeding of her baby does not under any circumstance violate this section."

61. Common law crimes, of course, are not based upon statutory elements.

62. "Murder Attempt Charged in AIDS Exposure Case," Associated Press wire service, November 16, 1992.

63. James A. Carlson, "Cancer Inquest," Associated Press wire service, April 10, 1995.

64. Ibid.

65. Ibid.

66. Ibid.

67. Lynette Holloway, "Doctor Found Guilty of Murder in Botched Abortion," *New York Times* wire service, August 8, 1995.

68. "Three Get 15 Years in Prison," Associated Press wire service, June 21, 1997; and Deborah Sharp, "Missing Stop Sign, Lost Lives," *USA Today,* June 19, 1997, p. 3A.

69. The judge suspended half of each 30-year sentence, resulting in a 13-year parole eligibility date.

70. *Willoughby* v. *State* (1990), Ind., 552 N.E.2d 462, 466.

71. See *Maughs* v. *Commonwealth,* 181 Va. 117, 120, 23 S.E.2d 784, 786 (1943).

72. *State* v. *Stephenson,* Opinion No. 24403 (South Carolina, 1996). See also *State* v. *Blocker,* 205 S.C. 303, 31 S.E.2d 908 (1944).

73. *State* v. *Kindle* (1924), 71 Mont. 58, 64, 227.

74. Black, Nolan, and Nolan-Haley, *Black's Law Dictionary,* p. 343.

75. Patrick L. McCloskey and Ronald L. Schoenberg, *Criminal Law Deskbook* (New York: Matthew Bender, 1988), Section 20.03[13].

76. The exception, of course, is that of a trespasser who trespasses in order to commit a more serious crime.

77. Sir Edward Coke, 3 *Institute,* 162.

78. *The Crown* v. *Dudly & Stephens,* 14 Q.B.D. 273, 286, 15 Cox C. C. 624, 636 (1884).

79. "The Rough-Sex Defense," *Time,* May 23, 1988, p. 55.

80. Ibid.

81. "The Preppie Killer Cops a Plea," *Time,* April 4, 1988, p. 22.

82. "Jury Convicts Condom Rapist," *USA Today,* May 14, 1993, p. 3A.

83. Black, Nolan, and Nolan-Haley, *Black's Law Dictionary,* p. 504.

84. "Girl Charged," Associated Press wire service, northern edition, February 28, 1994.

85. *State of Tennessee* v. *Charles Arnold Ballinger,* No. E2000-01339-CCA-R3-CD (Tenn.Crim.App. 01/09/2000).

86. See, for example, *Montana* v. *Egelhoff,* 116 S.Ct. 2013, 135 L. Ed. 2d 361 (1996).

87. "'Rophies' Reported Spreading Quickly throughout the South," *Drug Enforcement Report,* June 23, 1995, pp. 1-5.

88. Ellen Y. Chang, "Rail Killer Convicted of Capital Murder," APB News, May 18, 2000. Web posted at http://www.apbnews.com/crimesolvers/serialkiller/2000/05/18/resendiz0518_01.html. Accessed January 17, 2002.

89. "Second Psychologist in Resendiz's Trial to Help Mount Insanity Defense," Associated Press wire service, April 21, 2000. Web posted at http://www.khou.com/news/stories/2423.html. Accessed January 10, 2002.

90. "Psychiatrist to Take Stand Again," Associated Press wire service, March 18, 2002. Web posted at http://www.khou.com/news/stories/2433.html. Accessed January 17, 2002.

91. The information in this section comes from various news reports provided by CNN and the Associated Press, including "Maturino Resendiz Convicted of Murder in Railway Killings," CNN, May 18, 2000. Web posted at www.cnn.com/2000/LAW/05/18/railway.killer.verdict.02. Accessed January 17, 2002.

92. Lisa Teachey, "Rail Killer Trial Jury Is Sequestered after Deliberating Case Eight Hours," *Houston Chronicle,* May 17, 2000. Web posted at http://www.chron.com/cs/CDA/story.hts/special/rrr/555651. Accessed January 17, 2002.

93. L. A. Callahan, et al., "The Volume and Characteristics of Insanity Defense Pleas: An Eight-State Study," *Bulletin of the American Academy of Psychiatry and the Law,* Vol. 19, No. 4 (1991), pp. 331-8.

94. American Bar Association Standing Committee on Association Standards for Criminal Justice, *Proposed Criminal Justice Mental Health Standards* (Chicago: ABA, 1984).

95. "Mrs. Bobbitt's Defense 'Life Worth More Than Penis,'" Reuters world wire service, January 10, 1994.

96. *Durham* v. *United States,* 214 F.2d 867, 875 (D.C. Cir. 1954).

97. American Law Institute, *Model Penal Code: Official Draft and Explanatory Notes* (Philadelphia: American Law Institute, 1985).

98. Ibid.

99. *U.S.* v. *Brawner,* 471 F.2d 969, 973 (D.C. Cir. 1972).

100. See Joan Biskupic, "Insanity Defense: Not a Right; In Montana Case, Justices Give States Option to Prohibit Claim," *Washington Post* wire service, March 29, 1994.

101. Biskupic, "Insanity Defense: Not a Right."

102. *Ford* v. *Wainwright,* 477 U.S. 399, 106 S.Ct. 2595, 91 L. Ed. 2d 335 (1986).

103. 18 U.S.C. §401.

104. *Jones* v. *U.S.,* U.S. Sup. Ct. (1983), 33 CrL 3233.

105. *Ake* v. *Oklahoma,* 470 U.S. 68, 105 S.Ct. 1087, 84 L. Ed. 2d 53 (1985).

106. *Foucha* v. *Louisiana,* 504 U.S. 71 (1992).

107. *U.S.* v. *Pohlot,* 827 F.2d 889 (1987).

108. Peter Arenella, "The Diminished Capacity and Diminished Responsibility Defenses: Two Children of a Doomed Marriage," *Columbia Law Review,* Vol. 77 (1977), p. 830.

109. *U.S.* v. *Brawner,* 471 F.2d 969 (1972).

110. Black, Nolan, and Nolan-Haley, *Black's Law Dictionary,* p. 458.
111. California Penal Code, Section 25 (a).
112. California Penal Code, Section 28 (b).
113. Kevin Sack, "Church Bombing Figure Found to Be Incompetent," *New York Times,* July 17, 2001.
114. *Time,* March 19, 1984, p. 26.
115. Ibid.
116. *U.S.* v. *Halper,* 490 U.S. 435 (1989).
117. "Dual Prosecution Can Give One Crime Two Punishments," *USA Today,* March 29, 1993, p. 10A.
118. *U.S.* v. *Felix,* 112 S.Ct. 1377 (1992).
119. See, for example, *Hudson* v. *U.S.,* 18 S.Ct. 488 (1997); and *United States* v. *Ursery,* 518 U.S. 267 (1996).
120. McCloskey and Schoenberg, *Criminal Law Deskbook,* Section 20.02[4].
121. *U.S.* v. *Armstrong,* 116 S.Ct. 1480, 134 L. Ed. 2d 687 (1996).
122. Speedy Trial Act, 18 U.S.C. §3161. Significant cases involving the U.S. Speedy Trial Act are those of *U.S.* v. *Carter,* 476 U.S. 1138, 106 S.Ct. 2241, 90 L. Ed. 2d 688 (1986); and *Henderson* v. *U.S.,* 476 U.S. 321, 106 S.Ct. 1871, 90 L. Ed. 2d 299 (1986).
123. See Jim McGee, "Judges Increasingly Question U.S. Prosecutors' Conduct," *Washington Post* wire service, November 23, 1993.
124. Francis Fukuyama, "Extreme Paranoia about Government Abounds," *USA Today,* August 24, 1995, p. 17A.
125. Lorraine Adams, "Simpson Trial Focus Shifts to Detective with Troubling Past," *Washington Post* wire service, August 22, 1995.
126. Lenore E. Walker, *The Battered Woman* (New York: Harper Collins, 1979).
127. Niko Price, "Abuse Defenses," Associated Press wire service, May 29, 1994.
128. "Menendez Brothers Get Life without Parole," CNN Interactive, July 2, 1996.
129. Price, "Abuse Defenses."
130. "In S.C. Case, Reports of Abuse," *USA Today,* April 12, 1995, p. 3A.
131. Price, "Abuse Defenses."
132. Ibid.
133. As reported in Arnold Binder, *Juvenile Delinquency: Historical, Cultural, Legal Perspectives* (New York: Macmillan, 1988), p. 494.
134. "Drunk Driving Charge Dismissed: PMS Cited," Associated Press wire service, June 7, 1991.
135. *Facts on File,* 1978 (New York: Facts on File, 1979).
136. Price, "Abuse Defenses."
137. "Train Shooting," Associated Press wire service, August 12, 1994.
138. Courtland Milloy, "Self-Defense Goes Insane in the City," *Washington Post* wire service, May 18, 1994.
139. Robert Davis, "We Live in Age of Exotic Defenses," *USA Today,* November 22, 1994, p. 1A.
140. Ibid.
141. "Murder Acquittal in 'Urban Fear' Trial," *USA Today,* April 12, 1995, p. 3A.
142. Kari Converse, "Cultural Issues in Defense: How Culture Can Affect Culpability, Sentence and Client Communications," *Indigent Defense,* November–December 1999. Web posted at http://www.nlada.org/indig/ novdec99/cultural.htm. Accessed February 12, 2002.
143. John Lyman, "Cultural Defense: Viable Doctrine or Wishful Thinking?" *Journal of Criminal Justice,* Vol. 9 (1986), pp. 87–88.
144. *People* v. *Chen,* No. 7774/87 (N.Y. Super. Ct. 1989).
145. This paragraph is partially adapted from Doriane Lambelet Coleman, "Immigrant Crime and the Cultural Defense," unpublished manuscript, Duke University School of Law. Web posted at http://www.law.duke.edu/alumni/news/for97Imm. htm. Accessed December 12, 2001.
146. *State* v. *Curbello-Rodriguez,* 351 N.W.2d 758 (Wis. 1984).
147. *People* v. *Kimura,* No. A-091133 (Santa Monica Super. Ct. 1985).
148. *People* v. *Kong Moua,* No. 315972-0 (Cal. Super. Ct. Feb. 7, 1985).
149. Taryn Goldstein, "Cultural Conflicts in Court: Should the American Criminal Justice System Formally Recognize a 'Cultural Defense'?" 99 *Dick. Law Rev.* 141, 149 (1994).
150. "Murder Acquittal in 'Urban Fear' Trial."
151. See Sonia Giordani, "'Pseudologia Fantastica' Won't Fly," *The Recorder,* May 18, 2001.
152. "Nationline: Execution," *USA Today,* June 21, 1995, p. 3A.
153. Davis, "We Live in Age of Exotic Defenses."
154. Stephen J. Morse, "The 'New Syndrome Excuse Syndrome,'" *Criminal Justice Ethics* (winter–spring, 1995), pp. 3-15.
155. American Psychiatric Association, *Diagnostic and Statistical Manual of Mental Disorders,* 4th ed. (Washington, D.C.: APA, 1994).

part two

Individual Rights versus Public Order Concerns

■ Rights of the Accused under Investigation

Common law, constitutional, statutory, and humanitarian rights of the accused:

- A right against unreasonable searches
- A right against unreasonable arrest
- A right against unreasonable seizures of property
- A right to fair questioning by authorities
- A right to protection from personal harm

These individual rights must be effectively balanced against these community concerns:

- The efficient apprehension of offenders
- The prevention of crimes

How does our system of justice work toward balance?

Policing

To Protect and to Serve

Famed police administrator and former New York City Police Commissioner Patrick V. Murphy once said, "It is a privilege to be a police officer in a democratic society." While Murphy's words still ring true, many of today's law enforcement officers might hear in them only the echo of a long-dead ideal, unrealistic for today's times.

America's police officers form the front line in the unending battle against crime—a battle which seems to get more sinister and more demanding with each passing day. It is the police who are called when a crime is in progress or when one has been committed. The police are expected to objectively and impartially investigate law violations, gather evidence, solve crimes, and make arrests resulting in the successful prosecution of suspects—all the while adhering to strict due process standards set forth in the Constitution and enforced by the courts. The chapters in this section of *Criminal Justice Today* provide an overview of the historical development of policing; describe law enforcement agencies at the federal, state, and local levels; explore issues related to police administration; and discuss the due process and legal environments surrounding police activity.

As you will see, while the police are ultimately charged with protecting the public, they often believe that members of the public do not accord them the respect they deserve, and they feel that the distance between the police and the public is not easily bridged. Within the last few decades, however, an image of policing has emerged which may do much to heal that divide. This model, known as *community policing,* goes well beyond traditional conceptions of the police as mere law enforcers and encompasses the idea that police agencies should take counsel from the communities they serve. Under this model, the police are expected to prevent crime, as well as solve it, and to help members of the community deal with other pressing social issues.

Policing: History and Structure

LEARNING OBJECTIVES

After reading this chapter, you should be able to

■ Explain the basic purposes of policing in democratic societies

■ Provide an overview of the historical development of the police in this country, including the impact of the Prohibition era on American policing

■ Describe the nature of scientific police studies, and explain the significance they hold for law enforcement practice today

■ List and describe the three major levels of public law enforcement in the United States today

■ Describe the nature and extent of private protective services in the United States today, and explain what role such services may play in the future

■ Explain the relationship of the private security industry in this country to public policing.

chapter 5

The purpose of the police service is to uphold the law fairly and firmly; to prevent crime; to pursue and bring to justice those who break the law; to keep the . . . peace; to protect, help and reassure the community; and to be seen to do this with integrity, common sense and sound judgment.

—United Kingdom Police Service,
Statement of Common Purpose

Unlike the soldier fighting a war on foreign soil, police officers, who provide for our safety at home, have never been given the honor that was their due.

—Hubert Williams, President, The Police Foundation[1]

Key Concepts

[Terms]

bobbies
Bow Street Runners
comes stabuli
directed patrol
Exemplary Projects Program
Kansas City experiment

Law Enforcement Assistance
  Administration (LEAA)
new police
night watch
private protective services
scientific police management

sheriff
Statute of Winchester
vigilantism
Wickersham Commission

[Names]

Henry Fielding
Richard Mayne

Patrick V. Murphy
Robert Peel

Charles Rowan

Hear the author
discuss this chapter
at **cjtoday.com**

Introduction

Many of the techniques used by today's police differ quite a bit from those employed in days gone by. Listen to how a policeman, writing two hundred years ago, describes the way pickpockets were caught in London around 1800: "I walked forth the day after my arrival, rigged out as the very model of a gentleman farmer, and with eyes, mouth, and pockets wide open, and a stout gold-headed cane in my hand, strolled leisurely through the fashionable thoroughfares, the pump-rooms, and the assembly-rooms, like a fat goose waiting to be plucked. I wore a pair of yellow gloves well wadded, to save me from falling, through a moment's inadvertency, into my own snare, which consisted of about fifty fish-hooks, large black hackles, firmly sewn barb downward, into each of the pockets of my brand new leather breeches. The most blundering 'prig' alive might have easily got his hand to the bottom of my pockets, but to get it out again, without tearing every particle of flesh from the bones, was a sheer impossibility. . . . I took care never to see any of my old customers until the convulsive tug at one or other of the pockets announced the capture of a thief. I then coolly linked my arm in that of the prisoner, [and] told him in a confidential whisper who I was."[2]

Police tactics and strategy have changed substantially since historical times, and many different kinds of police agencies—some of them highly specialized—function within the modern criminal justice system. Even so, the basic purposes of policing in democratic societies remain the same: (1) to prevent and investigate crimes, (2) to apprehend offenders, (3) to help ensure domestic peace and tranquillity, and (4) to enforce and support the laws (especially the criminal laws) of the society of which the police are a part. Simply put, as Sir Robert Peel, founder of the British system of policing, explained it in 1822: "The basic mission for which the police exist is to reduce crime and disorder."[3]

Historical Development of the Police

This chapter describes the development of organized policing in Western culture and discusses contemporary American police forces as they function at the federal, state, and local levels. Agency examples are given at each level, and training, professionalism, and employment issues are all summarized. Finally, the promise held by private protective services, the recent rapid growth of private security organizations, and the quasi-private system of justice are discussed.

English Roots

The rise of the police as an organized force in the Western world coincided with the evolution of strong centralized governments. Although police forces have developed throughout the world, often in isolation from one another, the historical growth of the English police is of special significance to students of criminal justice in America, for it was upon the British model that much of early American policing was based.

Records indicate that efforts at law enforcement in early Britain, except for military intervention in the pursuit of bandits and habitual thieves, were not well organized until around the year A.D. 1200.[4] When a person committed an offense and could be identified, he or she was usually pursued by an organized posse. All able-bodied men who were in a position to hear the hue and cry raised by the victim were obligated to join the posse in a common effort to apprehend the offender. The posse was led by the shire reeve (the leader of the county) or by a mounted officer (the **comes stabuli**). Our modern words *sheriff* and *constable* are derived from these early terms. The *comites stabuli* (the plural form of the term) were not uniformed, nor were they numerous enough to perform all the tasks we associate today with law enforcement. This early system, employing a small number of mounted officers, depended for its effectiveness upon the ability to organize and direct the efforts of citizens toward criminal apprehension.

The offender, cognizant of a near-certain end at the hands of the posse, often sought protection from trusted friends and family. As a consequence, feuds developed among organized groups of citizens, some seeking revenge and some siding with the offender. Suspects who lacked the shelter of a sympathetic group might flee into a church and invoke the time-honored custom of sanctuary. Sanctuary was rarely an ideal escape, however, as pursuers could surround the church and wait out the offender, while preventing food and water from being carried inside. The offender, once caught, became the victim. Guilt was usually assumed, and trials were rare. Public executions, often involving torture, typified this early justice and served to provide a sense of communal solidarity as well as group retribution.

The development of law enforcement in English cities and towns grew out of an early reliance on bailiffs, or watchmen. Bailiffs were assigned the task of maintaining a **night watch**, primarily to detect fires and thieves. They were few in number but only served to rouse the sleeping population, which could then deal with whatever crisis was at hand. Larger cities expanded the idea of bailiffs by creating both a night watch and a day ward.

British police practices became codified in the **Statute of Winchester**, written in 1285. The statute (1) specified the creation of the watch and the ward in cities and towns; (2) mandated the draft of eligible males to serve those forces; (3) institutionalized the use of the hue and cry, making citizens who disregarded this call for help subject to criminal penalties; and (4) required that citizens maintain weapons in their home for answering the call to arms.

Some authors have attributed the growth of modern police forces to the gin riots which plagued London and other European cities in the eighteenth and nineteenth centuries. The invention of gin around 1720 provided, for the first time, a potent and inexpensive alcoholic drink readily available to the massed populations gathered in the early industrial ghettos of eighteenth-century cities. Seeking to drown their troubles, huge numbers of people, far beyond the ability of the bailiffs to control, began binges of drinking and rioting. Over the next hundred years, these gin riots created an immense social problem for British authorities. By this time, the bailiff system was staffed by a group of woefully inadequate substitutes, hired to perform their duties in place of the original—and far more capable—draftees. Incompetent and unable to depend upon the citizenry for help in enforcing the laws, bailiffs became targets of mob violence and were often attacked and beaten for sport.

THE BOW STREET RUNNERS

The early eighteenth century saw the emergence in London of a large criminal organization led by Jonathan Wild. Wild ran a type of fencing operation built around a group of loosely organized robbers, thieves, and burglars who would turn their plunder over to him. Wild would then negotiate with the legitimate owners for a ransom of their possessions.

The police response to Wild was limited by disinterest and corruption. However, when Henry Fielding, a well-known writer, became the magistrate of the Bow Street region of London, changes began to occur. Fielding attracted a force of dedicated officers, dubbed the **Bow Street Runners**, who soon stood out as the best and most disciplined enforcement agents that London had to offer. Fielding's personal inspiration and his ability to communicate what he saw as the social needs of the period may have accounted for his success.

In February 1725, Wild was arrested and arraigned on the following charges: "(1) that for many years past he had been a confederate with great numbers of highwaymen, pick-

comes stabuli

A nonuniformed mounted law enforcement officer of medieval England. Early police forces were small and relatively unorganized but made effective use of local resources in the formation of posses, the pursuit of offenders, and the like.

night watch

An early form of police patrol in English cities and towns.

Statute of Winchester

A law, written in 1285, that created a watch and ward system in English cities and towns and that codified early police practices.

> If you want the present to be different from the past, study the past.
>
> —Baruch Spinoza (1632–1677)

Bow Street Runners

An early English police unit formed under the leadership of Henry Fielding, magistrate of the Bow Street region of London.

pockets, housebreakers, shop-lifters, and other thieves, (2) that he had formed a kind of corporation of thieves, of which he was the head or director . . . , (3) that he had divided the town and country into so many districts, and appointed distinct gangs for each, who regularly accounted with him for their robberies . . . , (4) that the persons employed by him were for the most part felon convicts . . . , (5) that he had, under his care and direction, several warehouses for receiving and concealing stolen goods, and also a ship for carrying off jewels, watches, and other valuable goods, to Holland, where he had a superannuated thief for his benefactor, and (6) that he kept in his pay several artists to make alterations, and transform watches, seals, snuff-boxes, rings, and other valuable things, that they might not be known."[5] Convicted of these and other crimes, Wild attempted suicide by drinking a large amount of laudanum, an opium compound. The drug merely rendered him senseless, and he was hanged the following morning, having only partially recovered from its effects.

In 1754, Henry Fielding died. His brother John took over his work and occupied the position of Bow Street magistrate for another 25 years. The Bow Street Runners remain famous to this day for quality police work.

THE NEW POLICE

In 1829, Sir Robert Peel, who later became prime minister of England, formed what many have hailed as the world's first modern police force. Passage of the Metropolitan Police Act that same year allocated the resources for Peel's force of 1,000 uniformed, handpicked men. The London Metropolitan Police Force, also known simply as the **new police**, soon became a model for police forces around the world.

Members of the Metropolitan Police were quickly dubbed **bobbies**, after their founder. London's bobbies were organized around two principles: the belief that it was possible to discourage crime and the practice of preventive patrol. Peel's police patrolled the streets, walking beats. Their predecessors, the watchmen, had occupied fixed posts throughout the city, awaiting a public outcry. The new police were uniformed, resembling a military organization, and adopted a military administrative style.

London's first two police commissioners were Colonel Charles Rowan, a career military officer, and Richard Mayne, a lawyer. Rowan brought to law enforcement the belief that mutual respect between the police and the citizenry would be crucial to the success of the new force. As a consequence, early bobbies were chosen for their ability to reflect and inspire the highest personal ideals among young men in early-nineteenth-century Britain.

Unfortunately, the new police were not well received immediately. Some elements of the population saw them as an occupying army, and open battles between the police and the citizenry ensued. The tide of sentiment turned, however, when an officer was viciously killed in the Cold Bath Fields riot of 1833. A jury, considering a murder charge against the killer, returned a verdict of "not guilty," inspiring a groundswell of public support for the much-maligned force.

The Early American Experience

Early American law enforcement efforts were based to some degree upon the British experience. Towns and cities in colonial America depended upon modified versions of the night watch and the day ward, but citizens intent on evading their duty dramatically reduced the quality of police service.

The unique experience of the American colonies, however, quickly differentiated the needs of colonists from those of the masses remaining in Europe. Huge expanses of uncharted territory, vast wealth, a widely dispersed population engaged mostly in agriculture, and a sometimes ferocious frontier all combined to mold American law enforcement in a distinctive way. Recent writers on the history of the American police have observed that policing in America was originally "decentralized," "geographically dispersed," "idiosyncratic," and "highly personalized."[6]

THE FRONTIER

One of the major factors determining the development of American law enforcement was the frontier, which remained vast and wild until late in the nineteenth century. The backwoods areas provided a natural haven for outlaws and bandits. Henry Berry Lowery (the "popular outlaw" of the Carolinas), the James Gang, and many lesser-known desperadoes felt at home in the unclaimed swamps and forests.

new police

A police force formed in 1829 under the command of Sir Robert Peel, which became the model for modern-day police forces throughout the Western world.

bobbies

The popular British name given to members of Sir Robert (Bob) Peel's Metropolitan Police Force.

Only the boldest of settlers tried to police the frontier. Early among them was Charles Lynch, a Virginia farmer of the late eighteenth century. Lynch and his associates tracked and punished offenders, often according to the dictates of the still well-known lynch law, or vigilante justice, which they originated. Citizen posses and vigilante groups were often the only law available to settlers on the Western frontier. Judge Roy Bean ("the Law West of the Pecos"), "Wild Bill" Hickok, Bat Masterson, Wyatt Earp, and Pat Garrett were other popular figures of the nineteenth century who took it upon themselves, sometimes in semi-official capacities, to enforce the law on the books, along with standards of common decency.

Although **vigilantism** has today taken on a negative connotation, most of the original vigilantes of the American West were honest men and women trying to forge an organized and predictable lifestyle out of the challenging situations that they encountered. Often faced with unscrupulous, money-hungry desperadoes, they did what they could to bring the standards of civilization, as they understood them, to bear in their communities.

vigilantism

The act of taking the law into one's own hands.

POLICING AMERICA'S EARLY CITIES

Small-scale, organized law enforcement came into being quite early in America's larger cities. In 1658, paid watchmen were hired by the city of New York to replace drafted citizens.[7] By 1693, the first uniformed officer was employed by the city, and in 1731, the first neighborhood, or precinct, station was constructed. Boston, Cincinnati, and New Orleans were among the American communities which followed the New York model and hired a force of watchmen in the early nineteenth century.

Peel's new police were closely studied by American leaders, and one year after its creation, Stephen Girard, a wealthy manufacturer, donated a considerable amount of money to the city of Philadelphia to create a capable police force. The city hired 120 men to staff a night watch and 24 to perform similar duties during the day.

In 1844, New York's separate day and night forces were combined into the New York City Police Department. Boston followed suit in 1855. Further advances in American policing were precluded by the Civil War. Southern cities captured in the war found themselves under martial law and subject to policing by the military.

The coming of the twentieth century, coinciding as it did with numerous technological advances and significant social changes, brought a flood of reform. The International Association of Chiefs of Police (IACP) was formed in 1902 and immediately moved to create a nationwide clearinghouse for criminal identification. In 1915, the Fraternal Order of Police (FOP) initiated operations, patterning itself after labor unions but prohibiting strikes and accepting personnel of all ranks, from patrol officer to chief. In 1910, Alice Stebbins Wells became the first policewoman in the world, serving with the Los Angeles Police Department.[8] Prior to Wells's appointment, women had served as jail matrons, and widows had sometimes been carried on police department payrolls after their officer-husbands had died in the line of duty, but they had not been fully "sworn" with carrying out the duties of a police officer.

Judge Roy Bean (seated on barrel) holding court in Langtry, Texas, circa 1900.

Culver Pictures, Inc.

> The most fundamental weakness in crime control is the failure of federal and state governments to create a framework for local policing. Much of what is wrong with the police is the result of the absurd, fragmented, unworkable nonsystem of more than 17,000 local departments.
>
> —Patrick V. Murphy, Former New York City Police Commissioner

Wells became an outspoken advocate for the hiring of more policewomen, and police departments across the country began to hire female officers, especially to provide police services to children and to women and to "protect male officers from delicate and troublesome situations"[9]—such as the need to physically restrain female offenders. In 1915, the U.S. Census reported that 25 cities employed policewomen. In that year, coinciding with the creation of the FOP, the International Association of Policewomen (now the International Association of Women Police) was formed in the city of Baltimore. In 1918, Ellen O'Grady became the first woman to hold a high administrative post in a major police organization when she was promoted to the rank of deputy police commissioner for the city of New York. As Dorothy Moses Schulz, a contemporary commentator on women's entry into policing, has observed, "The Policewomen's movement was not an isolated phenomenon, but was part of women's movement into other newly created or newly professionalized fields."[10]

During the early twentieth century, telephones, automobiles, and radios all had their impact on the American police. Teddy Roosevelt, the twenty-sixth president of the United States, began his career by serving as a police commissioner in New York City from 1895 to 1897. While there, he promoted the use of a call box system of telephones, which allowed citizens to report crimes rapidly and made it possible for officers to call quickly for assistance. As president, Roosevelt later helped to organize the Bureau of Investigation, which later became the Federal Bureau of Investigation (FBI). Federal law enforcement already existed in the form of U.S. marshals, created by an act of Congress in 1789, and in the form of postal inspectors, authorized by the U.S. Postal Act of 1829. The FBI became a national investigative service designed to quickly identify and apprehend offenders charged with a growing list of federal offenses.

Automobiles created an era of affordable, rapid transportation and gave police forces far-reaching powers and high mobility. Telephones and radios provided the ability to maintain constant communication with central authorities. State police agencies arose to counter the threat of the mobile offender, with Massachusetts and Pennsylvania leading the way to statewide forces.

PROHIBITION AND POLICE CORRUPTION

A dark period for American law enforcement agencies began in 1920 with the passage of a constitutional prohibition against all forms of alcoholic beverages. Until Prohibition was repealed in 1933, most parts of the country were rife with criminal activity, much of it supporting the trade in bootlegged liquor. Bootleggers earned huge sums of money, and some of them became quite wealthy. Massive wealth in the hands of law violators greatly increased the potential for corruption among police officials, some of whom were "paid off" to support bootlegging operations.

A New York City police officer "mugging" a prisoner in the early days of police photography.
Courtesy of the Library of Congress

In 1931, the **Wickersham Commission**, officially called the National Commission on Law Observance and Enforcement, recognized that Prohibition was unenforceable and reported that it carried a great potential for police corruption.[11] The commission also established guidelines for enforcement agencies which directed many aspects of American law enforcement until the 1970s.

The Last Half Century

The 1960s and 1970s were a time of cultural reflection in America which forever altered the legal and social environment in which the police must work. During that period, in conjunction with a burgeoning civil rights movement, the U.S. Supreme Court frequently enumerated constitutionally based personal rights for those facing arrest, investigation, and criminal prosecution. Although a "chipping away" at those rights, which some say is continuing today, may have begun in the 1980s, the earlier emphasis placed upon the rights of defendants undergoing criminal investigation and prosecution will have a substantial impact on law enforcement activities for many years to come.

The 1960s and 1970s were also a period of intense examination of police operations, from day-to-day enforcement decisions to administrative organization and police-community relations. In 1967, the President's Commission on Law Enforcement and Administration of Justice issued its report, *The Challenge of Crime in a Free Society*, which found that the police were often isolated from the communities they served.[12] In 1969, the **Law Enforcement Assistance Administration (LEAA)** was formed to assist police forces across the nation in acquiring the latest in technology and in adopting new enforcement methods. In 1973, the National Advisory Commission on Criminal Justice Standards and Goals issued a comprehensive report detailing strategies for combating and preventing crime and for improving the quality of law enforcement efforts at all levels.[13] Included in the report was a call for greater participation in police work by women and ethnic minorities and the recommendation that a college degree be made a basic prerequisite for police employment by the 1980s. The creation of a third major commission, the National Commission on Crime Prevention and Control, was authorized by the federal Violent Crime Control and Law Enforcement Act of 1994, but the commission never saw the light of day. Read about the crime commission that never was at **Web Extra! 5–1** at cjtoday.com.

SCIENTIFIC POLICE MANAGEMENT

In 1969, with the passage of the Omnibus Crime Control and Safe Streets Act, the U.S. Congress created the Law Enforcement Assistance Administration. LEAA was charged with combating crime via the expenditure of huge amounts of money in support of crime-prevention and crime-reduction programs. Some have compared the philosophy establishing LEAA to that which supported the American space program's goal of landing people on the moon: Put enough money into any problem, and it will be solved! Unfortunately, the crime problem was more difficult to address than the challenge of a moon landing; even after the expenditure of nearly $8 billion, LEAA had not come close to its goal. In 1982, LEAA expired when Congress refused it further funding.

The legacy of LEAA is an important one for police managers, however. The research-rich years of 1969 to 1982, supported largely through LEAA funding, have left a plethora of scientific findings of relevance to police administration and, more importantly, have established a tradition of program evaluation within police management circles. This tradition, which is known as **scientific police management**, is a natural outgrowth of LEAA's insistence that every funded program contain a plan for its evaluation. *Scientific police management* refers to the application of social science techniques to the study of police administration for the purpose of increasing effectiveness, reducing the frequency of citizen complaints, and enhancing the efficient use of available resources. The heyday of scientific police management occurred in the 1970s, when federal monies were far more readily available to support such studies than they are today.

LEAA was not alone in funding police research during the 1970s. On July 1, 1970, the Ford Foundation announced the establishment of a Police Development Fund totaling $30 million, to be spent over the next five years to support major crime-fighting strategies of police departments. This funding led to the establishment of the Police Foundation, which continues to exist today with the mission of "foster[ing] improvement and innovation in American policing."[14] Police Foundation—sponsored studies over the past 20 years have added to the growing body of scientific knowledge about policing.

Wickersham Commission

Officially called the National Commission on Law Observance and Enforcement, this body issued a report in 1931 stating that Prohibition was unenforceable and carried a great potential for police corruption.

Law Enforcement Assistance Administration (LEAA)

A now-defunct federal agency established under Title I of the Omnibus Crime Control and Safe Streets Act of 1967 to funnel federal funding to state and local law enforcement agencies.

scientific police management

The application of social science techniques to the study of police administration for the purpose of increasing effectiveness, reducing the frequency of citizen complaints, and enhancing the efficient use of available resources.

Federal support for criminal justice research and evaluation continues today under the National Institute of Justice (NIJ) and the Bureau of Justice Statistics (BJS), both part of the Office of Justice Assistance, Research, and Statistics (OJARS). OJARS, created by Congress in 1980, functions primarily as a clearinghouse for criminal justice statistics and information. The National Criminal Justice Reference Service (NCJRS), a part of NIJ, assists researchers nationwide in locating information applicable to their research projects. "Custom searches" of the NCJRS computer database can be done online and can yield voluminous information in most criminal justice subject areas. NIJ also publishes a series of informative reports every month *(NIJ Reports)*, which serve to keep criminal justice practitioners and researchers informed about recent findings.

EXEMPLARY PROJECTS

In 1973, LEAA established the **Exemplary Projects Program**, which was designed to recognize outstanding innovative efforts to combat crime and to provide assistance to crime victims, so that such initiatives might serve as models for the nation. One project which won exemplary status early in the program was the Street Crimes Unit (SCU) of the New York City Police Department. The SCU disguised officers as potential mugging victims and put them in areas where they were most likely to be attacked. In its first year, the SCU made nearly 4,000 arrests and averaged a successful conviction rate of around 80%. Perhaps the most telling statistic was the "average officer days per arrest." The SCU invested only 8.2 days in each arrest, whereas the department average for all uniformed officers was 167 days.[15]

Many other programs were supported and evaluated. The Hidden Cameras Project in Seattle, Washington, was one of those. The project utilized cameras hidden in convenience stores, which were triggered when a "trip" bill located in the cash register drawer was removed. The clearance rate for robberies of businesses with hidden cameras was twice that of other similar businesses. The conviction rate for photographed robbers was shown to be more than twice that of suspects arrested for robbing stores without cameras. Commercial robbery in Seattle decreased by 38% in the first year of the project.

THE KANSAS CITY EXPERIMENT

By far the most famous application of social research principles to police management was the Kansas City Preventive Patrol Experiment.[16] Sponsored by the Police Foundation, the results of the year-long **Kansas City experiment** were published in 1974. The study divided the southern part of Kansas City into 15 areas. Five of these "beats" were patrolled in the usual fashion. Another five beats experienced a doubling of patrol activities and had twice the normal number of patrol officers assigned to them. The final third of the beats received a novel "treatment" indeed: No patrols were assigned to them, and no uniformed officers entered that part of the city unless they were called. The program was kept secret, and citizens were unaware of the difference between the patrolled and unpatrolled parts of the city.

The results of the Kansas City experiment were surprising. Records of "preventable crimes," those toward which the activities of patrol were oriented—like burglary, robbery, auto theft, larceny, and vandalism—showed no significant differences in rate of occurrence among the three experimental beats. Similarly, citizens didn't seem to notice the change in patrol patterns in the two areas where patrol frequency was changed. Surveys conducted at the conclusion of the experiment showed no difference among citizens in the three areas as to their fear of crime before and after the study.

The 1974 study can be summed up in the words of the author of the final report: "The whole idea of riding around in cars to create a feeling of omnipresence just hasn't worked. . . . Good people with good intentions tried something that logically should have worked, but didn't."[17]

A second Kansas City study focused on "response time."[18] It found that even consistently fast police response to citizen reports of crime had little effect on citizen satisfaction with the police or on the arrest of suspects. The study uncovered the fact that most reports made to the police came only after a considerable amount of time had passed. Hence, the police were initially handicapped by the timing of the report, and even the fastest police response was not especially effective.

The original Kansas City study has been credited with beginning the now-established tradition of scientific studies of policing. Scientific studies of special significance to law enforcement are summarized in Table 5–1.

Exemplary Projects Program

An initiative, sponsored by the Law Enforcement Assistance Administration, designed to recognize outstanding innovative efforts to combat crime and to provide assistance to crime victims.

Kansas City experiment

The first large-scale scientific study of law enforcement practices. Sponsored by the Police Foundation, it focused on the practice of preventive patrol.

	SELECTED SCIENTIFIC STUDIES IN LAW ENFORCEMENT		**TABLE 5-1**
Year	**Study Name**	**Focus**	
2001	Boston's Operation Ceasefire Evaluation	City-wide efforts to reduce gun violence, especially gang-related homicides	
1999	National Evaluation of Weed and Seed programs	"Weed and seed" programs in eight states	
1998	Community Policing in Action (Indianapolis)	Police and citizen cooperation and neighborhood security	
1994	The Kansas City Gun Experiment	Supplemental police patrol to reduce gun crime	
1992	The New York City Police Department's Cadet Corps Study	Level of education among officers and hiring of minority officers	
1992	Metro-Dade Spouse Abuse Experiment Replication (Florida)	Replication of the 1984 Minneapolis study	
1991	Quality Policing in Madison, Wisconsin	Community policing and participatory police management	
1990	Minneapolis "Hot Spot" Patrolling	Intensive patrol of problem areas	
1987	Newport News (Virginia) Problem-Oriented Policing	Police solutions to community crime problems	
1986	Crime Stoppers: A National Evaluation	Media crime-reduction programs	
1986	Reducing Fear of Crime in Houston and Newark	Strategies for fear reduction among urban populations	
1984	Minneapolis Domestic Violence Experiment	Effective police action in domestic violence situations	
1981	Newark Foot Patrol Experiment	Costs versus benefits of foot patrol	
1977	Cincinnati Team Policing Experiment	Team versus traditional policing	
1977	Patrol Staffing in San Diego	One- versus two-officer units	
1976	Police Response Time (Kansas City)	Citizen satisfaction with police response	
1976	The Police and Interpersonal Conflict	Police intervention in domestic and other disputes	
1976	Managing Investigations	Detective/patrol officer teams	
1976	Kansas City Peer Review Panel	Improving police behavior	
1974	Kansas City Preventive Patrol Experiment	Effectiveness of police patrol	

EFFECTS OF THE KANSAS CITY STUDIES

The Kansas City studies greatly affected managerial assumptions about the role of preventive patrol and traditional strategies for responding to citizen calls for assistance. As Joseph Lewis, then Director of Evaluation at the Police Foundation, said, "I think that now almost everyone would agree that almost anything you do is better than random patrol."[19]

While some basic assumptions about patrol were called into question by the Kansas City studies, patrol remains the backbone of police work. New patrol strategies for the effective utilization of human resources have led to various kinds of **directed patrol** activities. One form of directed patrol varies the number of officers involved in patrolling according to the time of day or the frequency of reported crimes within the areas. The idea is to put the most officers where and when crime is most prevalent.

Other cities have prioritized calls for service,[20] ordering a quick police response only when crimes are in progress or when serious crimes have occurred. Less significant offenses, such as minor larcenies and certain citizen complaints, are handled through the mail or by having citizens come to the police station to make a report. Wilmington, Delaware, was one of the first cities to make use of split-force patrol, in which only a part of the patrol force performs routine patrol.[21] The remainder respond to calls for service, take reports, and conduct investigations.

directed patrol

A police management strategy designed to increase the productivity of patrol officers through the scientific analysis and evaluation of patrol techniques.

RECENT STUDIES

Early scientific studies of policing, such as the Kansas City patrol experiment, were designed to identify and probe some of the basic, and often taken for granted, assumptions that guided police work throughout the twentieth century. The initial response to many such studies was, "Why should we study that? Everybody knows the answer already!" As in the case of the Kansas City experiment, however, it soon became obvious that conventional wisdom was not always correct. The value of applying evaluative techniques to police work can also be seen in the following, more recent, examples:

- The 2001 evaluation of Boston's gun project, known as Operation Ceasefire. The project, a problem-oriented policing initiative targeting homicide victimization among the city's youths, was found to be successful in its implementation.[22]

- The 1999 National Evaluation of Weed and Seed Programs focused on programs in eight states. It found that the effectiveness of the "weed and seed" philosophy varied considerably. ("Weed and seed" is a community-based anticrime approach that links intensified geographically targeted law enforcement efforts by police and prosecutors with local neighborhood improvement initiatives and human service programs.) The programs that worked best were those that relied on bottom-up, participatory decision-making approaches, especially when combined with efforts to build capacity and partnerships among local organizations.[23] Learn more about the national "weed and seed" evaluation at **Library Extra! 5–1**. You can also read about neighborhood attitudes toward crime and how they affect the police at **Library Extra! 5–2**.

- The 1994 Kansas City Gun Experiment was designed to "learn whether vigorous enforcement of existing gun laws could reduce gun crime." The Kansas City Police Department's "weed and seed" program targeted areas designated as "hot spots" within the city. These were locations identified by computer analysis as having the most gun-related crimes within the metropolitan area. A special gun-detection unit was assigned to the area, and guns were removed from citizens following searches incident to arrest for other (non-gun-related) crimes, at traffic stops, and as the result of other legal stop-and-frisk activities. While the program was in operation, gun crimes declined by 49% in the target area, while they increased slightly in a comparison area. Drive-by shootings, which dropped from seven (in the six months prior to the program) to only one following implementation of the program, were particularly affected.[24] Learn more about the

  Kansas City Gun Experiment at **Library Extra! 5–3.**

- The 1984 Minneapolis Domestic Violence Experiment was the first scientifically engineered social experiment to test the impact of the use of arrest (versus alternative forms of disposition) upon crime.[25] In this case, the crime in focus was violence in the home. Investigators found that offenders who were arrested were less likely to commit repeat offenses than were those who were handled in some other fashion. A Police Foundation–sponsored study of domestic violence in the Metro-Dade (Florida) area in 1992 reinforced the Minneapolis findings but found that the positive effect of arrest applied almost solely to those who were employed.

- Another example of scientific police management comes from Newport News, Virginia.[26] In the late 1980s, the police in Newport News decided to test traditional incident-driven policing against a new approach called *problem-oriented policing*. Incident-driven policing mobilizes police forces to respond to complaints and offenses reported by citizens. It is what the Newport News police called "the standard method for delivering police services." Problem-oriented policing, on the other hand, was developed in Newport News to identify critical crime problems in the community and to address effectively the underlying causes of crime. For example, one identified problem involved thefts from vehicles parked in the Newport News shipbuilding yard. As many as 36,000 cars were parked in those lots during the day. Applying the principles of problem-oriented policing, Newport News officers sought to explore the dimensions of the problem. After identifying theft-prone lots and a small group of frequent offenders, officers arrested one suspect in the act of breaking into a vehicle. That suspect provided the information police were seeking: It turned out that drugs were the real target of the car thieves. "Muscle cars," rock music bumper stickers, and other indicators were used by the thieves as clues to which cars had the highest potential for yielding drugs. The police learned that what seemed to be a simple problem of thefts from automobiles was really a search for drugs by a small group of hard-core offenders. Strategies to address the problem were developed, including wider efforts to reduce illicit drug use throughout the city.

These and other studies have established a sound basis for the use of scientific evaluation in police work today. The accumulated wisdom of police management studies can be summed up in the words of Patrick V. Murphy, who, near retirement as Director of the Police Foundation, stated five tenets for guiding American policing in the future:[27]

1. Neighborhood policing programs of all kinds need to be developed, improved, and expanded.

2. More police officers need college- and graduate-level education.

3. Police departments should hire more civilians. Civilian specialists can add to department operations and release sworn officers for police duties.

4. Departments must continue to become more representative of the communities they serve by recruiting more women and minorities.

5. Restraint in the use of force, especially deadly force, must be increased.

American Law Enforcement Today: From the Federal to the Local Level

The organization of American law enforcement has been called the most complex in the world. Three major legislative and judicial jurisdictions exist in the United States—federal, state, and local—and each has created a variety of police agencies to enforce its laws. Unfortunately, there has been little uniformity among jurisdictions as to the naming, function, or authority of enforcement agencies. The matter is complicated still more by the rapid growth of private security firms, which operate on a profit basis and provide services that have traditionally been regarded as law enforcement activities.

Federal Law Enforcement Agencies

There are 21 separate federal law enforcement agencies distributed among eight U.S. government services (Table 5–2). In addition to the enforcement agencies listed in the table, dozens of other federal government offices are involved in enforcement activities through inspection, regulation, and control activities. The FBI, one of the best-known federal law enforcement agencies, is described in the paragraphs that follow.

Visit the home pages of many federal law enforcement agencies via **Web Extra! 5–2** at cjtoday.com. Learn more about staffing levels of federal criminal justice agencies at **Library Extra! 5–4**.

THE FEDERAL BUREAU OF INVESTIGATION

The Federal Bureau of Investigation may be the most famous law enforcement agency in the country and in the world. Today, when mention is made of the FBI, many people immediately think of the Fox Network television show *The X-Files*. Long before there was an *X-Files*, however, the Federal Bureau of Investigation was fighting crime across America. The FBI is held in high regard by many citizens, who think of it as an example of what a law enforcement organization should be and who believe that FBI agents are exemplary police officers. William Webster, former Director of the FBI, reflected this sentiment when he said, "Over the years the American people have come to expect the most professional law enforcement from the FBI. Although we use the most modern forms of management and technology in the fight against crime, our strength is in our people—in the character of the men and women of the FBI. For that reason we seek only those who have demonstrated that they can perform as professional people who can, and will, carry on our tradition of fidelity, bravery, and integrity."[28]

History of the FBI The FBI has a history which spans almost 100 years. It began in 1908 as the Bureau of Investigation, when it was designed to serve as the investigative arm of the U.S. Department of Justice. The creation of the FBI was motivated, at least in part, by the inability of other agencies to stem the rising tide of American political and business corruption.[29]

The bureau began as a small organization, 35 agents originally hired to investigate crimes such as antitrust violations and bankruptcy fraud and to pursue federal fugitives. However, the bureau grew quickly as passage of the White Slave Traffic Act in 1910 necessitated a

TABLE 5-2	AMERICAN POLICING: FEDERAL LAW ENFORCEMENT AGENCIES

Department of the Treasury	**Department of Defense**
Bureau of Alcohol, Tobacco, and Firearms	Criminal Investigation Division
Internal Revenue Service	Office of Special Investigations
U.S. Customs Service	Naval Investigative Service
U.S. Secret Service	Defense Criminal Investigator Service
Federal Law Enforcement Training Center	
	Department of Transportation
Department of Justice	U.S. Coast Guard
Bureau of Prisons	
Drug Enforcement Administration	**General Services Administration**
Federal Bureau of Investigation	Federal Protective Services
U.S. Marshals Service	
Immigration and Naturalization Service	**U.S. Postal Service**
	Postal Inspections Service
Department of the Interior	
Fish and Wildlife Service	**Washington, D.C.**
National Park Service	Metropolitan Police Department
U.S. Park Police	

coordinated interstate law enforcement effort to fight organized prostitution. Incidents of sabotage and espionage on American soil during World War I also contributed to the rapid growth of the FBI, and the Espionage Act of 1917 provided a legal basis for the bureau's investigation into subversive activities.

In 1924, J. Edgar Hoover was appointed to direct the FBI. He immediately initiated a plan to increase professionalism among agents. New agents were hired only from among college graduates, and lawyers and accountants were especially sought after. Training was thorough, and assignments were made on a national basis.

On July 1, 1924, the bureau opened its Identification Division to serve as a national clearinghouse for information on criminals who, with the popular availability of the automobile, were becoming increasingly mobile. The division began operations with 810,188 fingerprint cards received from the Federal Penitentiary at Leavenworth, Kansas, and from the International Association of Chiefs of Police.

In 1932, the bureau opened its fledgling Crime Laboratory with a borrowed microscope. Before the laboratory had completed its first year of operations, 963 analyses had been performed, mostly ballistics testing for homicide cases and handwriting examinations for fraud cases.

During the late 1920s and early 1930s, the combination of Prohibition and organized criminal cartels propelled the bureau into a "war" with well-armed and violent groups. Famous gangsters of the period who made the FBI's "Ten Most Wanted" list include "Baby Face" Nelson, Clyde Barrow, Bonnie Parker, "Ma" Barker, John Dillinger, "Pretty Boy" Floyd, "Machine Gun" Kelly, and Alvin Karpis. It was during this period of its development that the bureau's trustworthy image and the popular conception of the tough G-man entranced the nation.

In 1935, the Bureau of Investigation officially changed its name to the Federal Bureau of Investigation. In 1936, President Franklin Roosevelt directed the FBI to collect information on radical groups within American borders, including Communist and extremist organizations. During World War II, the FBI proved highly effective in combating the efforts of Nazi and Japanese saboteurs. Following the war, FBI attention focused on Soviet spy rings, which were attempting to steal defense secrets, including techniques for the manufacture of atomic bombs.

During the 1960s, at the direction of Attorney General Robert F. Kennedy, the FBI became increasingly involved in investigations of civil rights violations. Some critics have charged that the FBI's image was tarnished during this era, since FBI investigations of rights activists were as common as those of antirights groups.[30] Learn more about the recent history of the FBI at **Web Extra! 5–3** at cjtoday.com.

> Fidelity, bravery, and integrity.
>
> —Motto of the Federal Bureau of Investigation

The FBI Today The official purpose of today's FBI can be found succinctly stated in the agency's mission statement: "The Mission of the FBI is to uphold the law through the investigation of violations of federal criminal law; to protect the United States from foreign intelligence and terrorist activities; to provide leadership and law enforcement assistance to federal, state, local, and international agencies; and to perform these responsibilities in a manner that is responsive to the needs of the public and is faithful to the Constitution of the United States."[31] This mission is further divided into five functional areas: criminal law enforcement; law enforcement services; foreign counterintelligence; investigative and operational support; and direction, control, and administration.

Each function within the mission statement is further defined. For example, the criminal law enforcement function requires the agency to "investigate violations of the laws of the United States within FBI jurisdiction, collect evidence in domestic and international cases in which the United States is or may be a party of interest, conduct personnel investigations, and perform other duties imposed by law or Executive Order. Major investigative programs supporting this function include: organized crime/drugs, violent crimes, and white-collar crime."

The law enforcement services function mandates that the FBI "provide forensic, identification, information, and training services to law enforcement personnel and agencies outside the FBI. Programs supporting this function include: general law enforcement training, forensic services, non-federal fingerprint identification, as well as criminal justice data and statistics services through the National Crime Information Center (NCIC) and the Uniform Crime Reports (UCR) programs."

The FBI's foreign counterintelligence function is becoming increasingly important as acts of international terrorism committed within the United States—such as the 2001 terrorist attacks on the World Trade Center and the Pentagon—hold the potential for greater loss of life than ever before. The foreign counterintelligence function specifies that the FBI is to "conduct investigations to collect, analyze, and exploit information to identify and neutralize the activities of foreign powers and their agents that adversely affect U.S. national security through counterintelligence, counterterrorism, and security countermeasures."

Major administrative divisions within the FBI are the Administrative Services Division; the Counterterrorism Division; the Criminal Investigative Division; the Criminal Justice Information Services Division; the Finance Division; the Information Resources Division; the Inspection Division; the Investigative Services Division; the Laboratory Division; the National Security Division; and the Training Division. While space does not permit a detailed portrayal of each division, a few are briefly described in the following paragraphs.

The Counterterrorism Division consolidates all FBI counterterrorism initiatives. The National Infrastructure Protection Center (NIPC) and the National Domestic Preparedness Office (NDPO) are assigned to this division. The NIPC serves as the U.S. government's focal point for threat assessment, warning, investigation, and response for threats or attacks against critical components of the U.S. infrastructure. The NDPO coordinates all federal efforts to assist state and local first responders with planning, training, and equipment needs necessary to respond to incidents involving conventional or unconventional weapons of mass destruction. The FBI's counterterrorism efforts became especially important following the September 11, 2001, attacks on the World Trade Center in New York City and the Pentagon. Two months after the attacks, U.S. Attorney General John Ashcroft announced a major "reorganization and mobilization" of the FBI and other federal agencies, such as the Immigration and Naturalization Service. Speaking at a press conference in Washington, D.C., Ashcroft said, "Our strategic plan mandates fundamental change in several of the most critical components of American justice and law enforcement, starting with the organization that is at the center of our counterterrorism effort, the Federal Bureau of Investigation. In its history, the FBI has been many things: the protector of our institutions when they were under assault from organized crime; the keeper of our security when it was threatened by international espionage; and the defender of our civil rights when they were denied to some Americans on the basis of their race, color or creed. Today the American people call upon the Federal Bureau of Investigation to put prevention of terrorism at the center of its law-enforcement and national-security efforts."[32]

The FBI's Criminal Investigative Division (CID) coordinates investigations into organized crime, including drugs, racketeering, and money laundering; investigations into violent crimes, including wanted fugitives, escaped federal prisoners, unlawful flight to avoid prosecution, violent gangs, serial murders, kidnappings, bank robberies, violent crimes and property crimes of an interstate nature, crime on Indian reservations, crimes against U.S.

> The attacks of September 11 [2001] have redefined the mission of the Department of Justice. Defending our nation and defending the citizens of America against terrorist attacks is now our first and overriding priority. To fulfill this mission, we are devoting all the resources necessary to eliminate terrorist networks, to prevent terrorist attacks and to bring to justice those who kill Americans in the name of murderous ideologies. We are engaged in an aggressive arrest and detention campaign of lawbreakers with a single objective: to get terrorists off the street before they can harm more Americans.
>
> —U.S. Attorney General John Ashcroft

Everyday [as a police officer] you get to be a different person. In that regard it is the best job in the world. You get to play many roles: rabbi, lawyer, social worker, psychiatrist.

—New York Police Officer
Salvatore Maniscalco

citizens overseas, and theft of government property; investigations into white-collar crime, fraud against the government, corruption of public officials, health care fraud, election law violations, business and economic frauds, and corruption crimes; and investigations into civil rights violations. The division contains eight sections, including the Asset Forfeiture Program, the Financial Crimes Section, and the Internet Fraud Complaint Center.

Headquartered in Clarksburg, West Virginia, the Criminal Justice Information Services (CJIS) Division serves as the central repository for criminal justice information services in the FBI. The FBI describes the division as "a customer-driven organization providing state-of-the-art identification and information services to local, state, federal, and international criminal justice communities." In support of these activities, CJIS has developed an advisory process that involves sharing management and policy-making decisions with local, state, and federal criminal justice agencies. The CJIS Division includes the Fingerprint Identification Program, National Crime Information Center (NCIC) Program, Uniform Crime Reporting Program, and the Integrated Automated Fingerprint Identification System (IAFIS)—a computer-based system that can store, process, analyze, and retrieve millions of fingerprints in a relatively short period of time.

The FBI Laboratory Division operates one of the largest and most comprehensive crime laboratories in the world. It provides services related to the scientific solution and prosecution of crimes throughout the country. It is also the only full-service federal forensic laboratory in the United States. Laboratory activities include crime-scene searches, special surveillance photography, latent-fingerprint examinations, forensic examinations of evidence (including DNA testing), court testimony by laboratory personnel, and other scientific and technical services. The FBI offers laboratory services, free of charge, to all law enforcement agencies in the United States. Learn more about the FBI's administrative divisions, including the activities of each, via **Web Extra! 5–4** at cjtoday.com.

The FBI also runs a National Academy Program, which is part of its Training Division. The program offered its first class in 1935 and had 23 students. It was then known as the FBI National Police Training School. In 1940, the school moved from Washington, D.C., to the U.S. Marine Amphibious Base at Quantico, Virginia. In 1972, the facility expanded to 334 acres, and the FBI Academy, as we know it today, officially opened.[33] According to the most recent statistics available, the academy program has produced 32,121 graduates since it began operations. This includes 1,860 graduates from foreign countries and 305 graduates from U.S. territories and possessions, making a grand total of 2,165 graduates from outside the United States. Nearly 200 sessions have been offered since inception of the training program. Visit the FBI Academy on the Web via **Web Extra! 5–5** at cjtoday.com.

The FBI operates 56 field offices located throughout the United States and in Puerto Rico and employs more than 27,800 people, including 11,400 special agents. Many special

The FBI crime laboratory—often regarded as a model of quality forensic analysis.

Courtesy of the Federal Bureau of Investigation

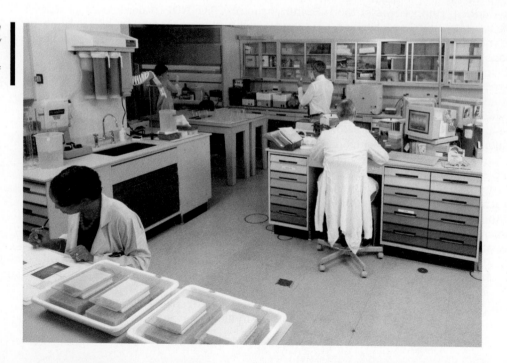

agents are women, and in 1992 Burdena "Birdie" Pasenelli became the first woman to head an FBI field office. With a budget of around $3.5 billion per year, the FBI's jurisdiction extends to more than 200 specific crimes and certain broad areas of criminal activity.[34]

The FBI also operates "legal attaché offices" in a number of major cities around the world, including London and Paris. Such offices permit the international coordination of enforcement activities and facilitate the flow of law enforcement–related information between the FBI and police agencies in host countries. In 1995, a few years after the end of the cold war, the FBI opened a legal attaché office in Moscow. The Moscow office assists Russian police agencies in the growing battle against organized crime in that country and helps American officials track suspected Russian criminals operating in the United States. Also in 1995, an Eastern European version of the FBI Academy, known as the International Law Enforcement Academy (ILEA), opened in Budapest, Hungary. Its purpose is to train police administrators from all of Eastern Europe in the latest crime-fighting techniques.[35]

A little over a decade ago, the FBI formed the National Computer Crime Squad (NCCS) to investigate violations of the federal Counterfeit Access Device and Computer Fraud and Abuse Act of 1984, the Computer Fraud and Abuse Act of 1986 (CFAA),[36] and other federal

CJ Futures

[NCIC 2000]

The FBI's National Crime Information Center (NCIC) 2000 is a nationwide information system dedicated to serving and supporting local, state, and federal criminal justice agencies in their mission to uphold the law and to protect the public. NCIC 2000's predecessor, the original NCIC, was established in 1967. NCIC 2000, which began operations in July 1999, serves criminal justice agencies in all 50 states, the District of Columbia, the Commonwealth of Puerto Rico, the U.S. Virgin Islands, and Canada, as well as federal law enforcement agencies. NCIC 2000 provides improved services and extends these services down to the patrol car and mobile officer. NCIC 2000's capabilities focus on immediate, on-the-scene suspect identification and include[1]

- *Enhanced name search (ENS).* ENS uses the New York State Identification and Intelligence System (NYSIIS) to phonetically return similar names when inquiries are made by law enforcement officers (for example, Marko-Marco, Knowles-Nowles, and derivatives of names such as William, Willie, and Bill).
- *Fingerprint searches.* This digital service, designed to identify wanted and missing persons, stores and searches the right index fingerprint of everyone on file.
- *Probation/parole.* NCIC 2000's Convicted Persons or Supervised Release File contains detailed records of people under supervised release.
- *Online manuals.* State Control Terminal Agencies (CTAs) can download training and other law enforcement-related manuals and make them available to users online.
- *Improved data quality.* Using an automated point-of-entry check for errors, NCIC 2000 validates keyboarded data (e.g., VINs) to verify that it has been entered correctly. It also checks that data is entered in all mandatory fields; it links text and image information; and expands miscellaneous fields so that they can hold additional types of information.

- *Information linking.* NCIC 2000 uses sophisticated computer equipment to connect records so that an inquiry on one record automatically retrieves related records.
- *Mug shots.* NCIC 2000 accepts digitized mug shot records, as well as digitized fingerprints, signatures, and up to 10 other identifying images, such as scars, marks, and tattoos.
- *Other images.* Other types of images that NCIC 2000 is designed to handle include pictures of written materials, vehicles, boats, and vehicle or boat parts. A file of generic images (for example, a picture of a 1989 Ford Mustang) is maintained by the system.
- *Convicted sex offender registry.* The NCIC registry contains nationwide records of convicted sexual offenders and violent sexual predators.
- *SENTRY file.* NCIC maintains a descriptive index of individuals who are incarcerated in the federal prison system.
- *Delayed inquiry.* Requests for information are checked against an inquiry log, providing the entering and inquiring agencies with a response if any other agency inquired on the subject within the past five days.
- *Online ad hoc inquiry.* Users can search active databases and access the system's historical data.

Law enforcement administrators say that NCIC 2000's enhanced ability to deliver information to on-the-scene patrol officers, including the availability of photographic images and single fingerprint technology that can provide immediate positive identification, will ensure increased officer safety while minimizing the risk of improperly detaining the wrong individual.

To take advantage of all of the features of NCIC 2000, police agencies need a computerized workstation at a centralized site and specially equipped patrol cars. Workstation equipment standards include a flatbed scanner, a "livescan" fingerprint-imaging device, an image printer, and two-way radio equipment. Patrol cars must be equipped with a mobile display, a keyboard, a one-finger "livescan" imaging device, a radio interface, and a video or digital camera.

[1]Information in this section is adapted from the NCIC home page at http://www.fbi.gov/hq/cjisd/ncic.htm. Accessed December 2, 2001.

computer crime laws. NCCS focused on computer crimes such as (1) intrusions of public switched networks (telephone company networks), (2) major computer network intrusions, (3) network integrity violations, (4) privacy violations, (5) industrial espionage, (6) pirated computer software, and (7) other crimes in which a computer is centrally involved. In recent years, the FBI has created individual computer crime investigation teams in each of its field offices within the United States.

The FBI also operates the Combined DNA Index System (CODIS), a computerized forensic database of DNA "profiles" of offenders convicted of serious crimes (such as rape, other sexual assaults, murder, and certain crimes against children), as well as DNA profiles from unknown offenders.[37] CODIS, now a part of the National DNA Index System (NDIS), was formally authorized by the federal DNA Identification Act of 1994.[38] It is being enhanced daily through the work of federal, state, and local law enforcement agencies who take DNA samples from biological evidence gathered at crime scenes and from offenders themselves. The computerized CODIS system can rapidly identify a perpetrator when it finds a match between an evidence sample and a stored profile. By 1998, every state had enacted legislation establishing a CODIS database and requiring that DNA from offenders convicted of certain serious crimes be entered into the system. Today, the CODIS database contains about 400,000 DNA profiles, and the number is growing quickly.

State-Level Agencies

Most state police agencies were created in the late nineteenth or early twentieth century to meet specific needs. The Texas Rangers, created in 1835 before Texas attained statehood, functioned as a military organization responsible for patrolling the republic's borders. The apprehension of Mexican cattle rustlers was one of the main concerns.[39] Massachusetts, targeting vice control, was the second state to create a law enforcement agency. The Pennsylvania Constabulary, known today as the Pennsylvania State Police, has been called the "first modern state police agency,"[40] since it was formed to meet a variety of law enforcement needs at the state level. Today, a wide diversity of state policing agencies exists. Table 5–3 provides a list of typical state-sponsored law enforcement agencies.

State law enforcement agencies are usually organized after one of two models. In the first, a centralized model, the tasks of major criminal investigations are combined with the patrol of state highways. Centralized state police agencies generally do the following:

■ Assist local law enforcement departments in criminal investigations when asked to do so

■ Operate identification bureaus

■ Maintain a centralized criminal records repository

■ Patrol the state's highways

■ Provide select training for municipal and county officers

The Pennsylvania State Police was the first modern force to combine these duties and has served as a model to many states. Michigan, New Jersey, New York, Vermont, and Delaware are a few of the states which patterned their state-level enforcement activities after the Pennsylvania model.

The second state model, the decentralized model of police organization, tends to characterize operations in the southern United States but is found as well in the Midwest and in some western states. The model draws a clear distinction between traffic enforcement on state highways and other state-level law enforcement functions by creating at least two separate agencies. North Carolina, South Carolina, and Georgia are a few of the many states which employ both a highway patrol and a state bureau of investigation. The names of the respective agencies may vary, however, even though their functions are largely the same. In North Carolina, for example, the two major state-level law enforcement agencies are the North Carolina Highway Patrol and the State Bureau of Investigation. Georgia fields

TABLE 5–3	AMERICAN POLICING: STATE LAW ENFORCEMENT AGENCIES

Highway patrol	State police	State bureaus of investigation
Fish and wildlife agencies	State park services	Weigh station operations
Alcohol law enforcement agencies	State university police	Port authorities

Texas Ranger Drew Carter at a ceremony recognizing the Rangers for their work in the apprehension of serial killer Angel Maturino Resendiz. The Texas Rangers have long been held in high regard among state police agencies.

AP/Wide World Photos

a highway patrol and the Georgia Bureau of Investigation, and South Carolina operates a highway patrol and the South Carolina Law Enforcement Division.

States which use the decentralized model usually have a number of other adjunct state-level law enforcement agencies. North Carolina, for example, has created a State Wildlife Commission with enforcement powers, a Board of Alcohol Beverage Control with additional agents, and a separate Enforcement and Theft Bureau for enforcing certain motor vehicle and theft laws. Learn more about state-level law enforcement agencies by visiting **Web Extra 5–6!** at cjtoday.com.

Local Agencies

The term *local police* encompasses agencies of wide variety. Municipal departments, rural sheriff's departments, and specialized groups like campus police and transit police can all be grouped under the "local" rubric. Local police agencies employ approximately 730,000, people (of whom approximately 420,000 are sworn) throughout the United States today.[41] Large municipal departments are highly visible because of their vast size, huge budgets, and innovative programs. The nation's largest law enforcement agency, the New York City Police Department, for example, has about 44,000 full-time employees, including about 37,000 full-time sworn officers.[42]

Far greater in number, however, are small-town and county sheriff's departments. There are approximately 13,580 municipal police departments and 3,100 sheriff's departments in the United States.[43] Every incorporated municipality in the country has the authority to create its own police force. Some very small communities hire only one officer, who fills the roles of chief, investigator, and night watch—as well as everything in between. The majority of local agencies employ fewer than ten full-time officers, and about three in eight agencies (more than 7,000 in all) employ fewer than five full-time officers. These smaller agencies include 2,245 (or 12%) with just one full-time officer and 1,164 (or 6%) with only part-time officers.[44] A few communities contract with private security firms for police services, and still others have no active police force at all, depending instead upon local sheriff's departments to deal with law violators.

City police chiefs are typically appointed by the mayor or selected by the city council. Their departments' jurisdictions are limited by convention to the geographic boundaries of their communities. **Sheriffs**, on the other hand, are elected public officials whose agencies

sheriff

The elected chief officer of a county law enforcement agency. The sheriff is usually responsible for law enforcement in unincorporated areas and for the operation of the county jail.

TABLE 5-4	AMERICAN POLICING: LOCAL LAW ENFORCEMENT AGENCIES		
Municipal police departments	Housing authority agencies	Marine patrol agencies
Campus police	City/county agencies	Sheriff's departments
Coroners or medical examiners	Constables	Transit police

are responsible for law enforcement throughout the counties in which they function. Sheriff's deputies mostly patrol the "unincorporated" areas of the county, or those which lie between municipalities. They do, however, have jurisdiction throughout the county, and in some areas they routinely work alongside municipal police to enforce laws within towns and cities.

Sheriff's departments are generally responsible for serving court papers, including civil summonses, and for maintaining security within state courtrooms. Sheriffs also run county jails and are responsible for more detainees awaiting trial than any other type of law enforcement department in the country. For example, the Los Angeles (L.A.) County Jail System, operated by the L.A. County Sheriff's Department, is the largest in the world.[45] In 2001, with nine separate facilities, it had an average daily population of 19,136 inmates—considerably larger than the number of inmates held in many state prison systems. Over 2,200 uniformed officers and 1,265 civilian employees work in the Custody Division of the L.A. County Sheriff's Department, and that division alone operates with a yearly budget in excess of $205 million.[46]

Sheriff's departments remain strong across most of the country, although in parts of New England, deputies mostly function as court agents with limited law enforcement duties. One report found that most sheriff's departments are small, with nearly two-thirds of them employing fewer than 25 sworn officers.[47] Only 12 departments employ more than 1,000 officers. Even so, southern and western sheriffs are still considered the "chief law enforcement officers" in their counties. A list of conventional police agencies found at the local level is shown in Table 5-4. For information on selected local law enforcement agencies, view **Web Extra! 5-7** at cjtoday.com. Visit **Library Extras! 5-5** and **5-6** at cjtoday.com to learn more about staffing levels at local and state police agencies.

Private Protective Services

Private protective services constitute a fourth level of enforcement activity in the United States today. Private security has been defined as "those self-employed individuals and privately funded business entities and organizations providing security-related services to specific clientele for a fee, for the individual or entity that retains or employs them, or for themselves, in order to protect their persons, private property, or interests from various hazards."[48] Public police are employed by the government and enforce public laws. Private security personnel work for corporate employers and secure private interests. In 2002, for example, $212.7 million was spent for security arrangements at the Salt Lake City, Utah, Olympic winter games—leading to the employment of more than 40,000 private security personnel in association with the event.[49]

According to the *Hallcrest Report II*, a major government-sponsored analysis of the private security industry, more people are employed in private security than in all local, state, and federal police agencies combined.[50] Nearly two million people are estimated to be working in private security today, while slightly less than half that number are engaged in public law enforcement activities.[51] Employment in the field of private security is anticipated to continue to expand by around 4% per year, while public police agencies are expected to grow by only 2.8% per year for the foreseeable future. Still faster growth is predicted in private security industry revenues—anticipated to increase about 7% per year, a growth rate almost three times greater than that projected for the gross national product (GNP). Table 5-5 lists the ten largest private security agencies in business today and some of the services they offer.

Private agencies provide tailored policing funded by the guarded organization rather than through the expenditure of public monies. Experts estimate that private security services cost American industries an astounding $64.5 billion, while monies spent on public policing total only $40 billion.[52] Contributing to this vast expenditure is the federal gov-

| AMERICAN POLICING: PRIVATE SECURITY AGENCIES | **TABLE 5–5** |

The Largest Private Security Agencies in the United States

Security Bureau, Inc.	Globe Security	Pinkerton's, Inc.
Wackenhut Corp.	Wells Fargo Guard Services	Allied Security, Inc.
Guardsmark, Inc.	Advance Security, Inc.	Burns International Security Services
American Protective Services		

Private Security Services

Bank guards	Airport security	Hospital security
Company guards	Automated teller machine services	Nuclear facility security
Loss-prevention specialists	Computer/information security	School security
Railroad detectives	Executive protection	Store/mall security

Source: Adapted from William C. Cunningham, John J. Strauchs, and Clifford W. Van Meter, *The Hallcrest Report II: Private Security Trends, 1970–2000* (McLean, VA: Hallcrest Systems, 1990).

ernment, which is itself a major employer of private security personnel, contracting for services which range from guards to highly specialized electronic snooping and computerized countermeasures at military installations and embassies throughout the world.

Major reasons for the quick growth of the American proprietary security sector include "(1) an increase in crimes in the workplace, (2) an increase in fear (real or perceived) of crime, (3) the fiscal crises of the states, [which have] limited public protection, and (4) an increased public and business awareness and use of . . . more cost-effective private security products and services."[53]

The Development of Private Policing

Private policing in America has a long and rich history. The first security firms began operation in the mid-nineteenth century, hired mostly by the railroad companies which were laying tracks to support the burgeoning westward expansion of our nation. Company shipments of supplies, guns, and money, as well as engineers and company officials, all needed protection from Native Americans, outlaws, and assorted desperadoes.

Allan Pinkerton opened his Pinkerton National Detective Agency in 1851 with the motto "We Never Sleep."[54] Pinkerton's agency specialized in railroad security and would protect shipments as well as hunt down thieves who had gotten away. The Pinkerton service emblazoned an open eye, to signify constant vigilance, on its office doors and stationery. The term *private eye* is thought to have evolved from the use of this logo.

Henry Wells and William Fargo began their still-famous Wells Fargo Company in 1852. Wells Fargo supplied detectives and protective services to areas west of Missouri.

The early days of private security services led quickly to abuses by untrained and poorly disciplined agents. No licensing standards applied to the private security field, and security personnel sometimes became private "goons," responding only to the wishes of their employers. To cope with the situation, Pinkerton developed an elaborate code of ethics for his employees. Pinkerton's code prohibited his men and women from accepting rewards, from working for one political party against another, and from handling divorce cases (which are a primary source of revenue for private detectives today).

The year 1859 was an important one for private security. The Brinks Company began as a general package delivery service in 1859 and grew to a fleet of 85 armored wagons by 1900, and also in 1859, Edwin Holmes began the first electronic burglar alarm firm in Boston, Massachusetts.

Former law enforcement administrators began to get into the private security field in 1909, when a former director of the Bureau of Investigation formed the William J. Burns International Detective Agency. In 1954, George R. Wackenhut, a former FBI special agent, formed the Wackenhut Security Corporation, which has become one of the largest private security firms today.

> Law enforcement can ill afford to continue its traditional policy of isolating and even ignoring the activities of private security.
>
> —National Institute of Justice, *Crime and Protection in America*

Much has changed since the early days of private policing. Modern security firms provide services for hospitals, manufacturing plants, communications industries, retirement homes, hotels, casinos, exclusive communities and clubs, nuclear storage facilities and reactors, and many other types of businesses. Physical security, loss prevention, information security, and the protection of personnel are all service areas for private security organizations.

Private security agencies have been praised for their ability to adapt to new situations and technology. Although most security personnel are poorly paid and perform typical "watchman" roles, the security industry is able to contract with experts in almost any area. Specially assembled teams, hired on a subcontractual basis, have allowed some firms to move successfully into information and technology security. As financial opportunities continue to build in high-tech security, the industry is seeing the creation of a well-educated and highly specialized cadre of workers able to meet the most complex security needs of today's large and multinational corporations. The ability of private agents to work across state lines, and even across international boundaries, is an added benefit of private security for many employers.

Security personnel sometimes work undercover among company employees to learn who is pilfering inventories or selling business secrets to competitors. According to the Society of Competitor Intelligence Professionals, over 80% of the *Fortune* 1000 companies have regular in-house "snoops" on the payroll.[55] Companies everywhere are becoming concerned with "spookproofing" their files and corporate secrets.[56]

Bodyguards, another area of private security activity, are commonplace among wealthy business executives, media stars, and successful musicians. One of the most successful executive protection programs in the world is offered by Executive Security International (ESI) in Aspen, Colorado. ESI was incorporated in 1981, and its founder, Bob Duggan, a martial arts expert and trainer built terrorist-simulation exercises into most training courses.[57] In the late 1980s, Richard W. Kobetz, a former Chicago police lieutenant, began the Executive Protection Institute, a threat management program at its North Mountain Pines Training Center in Berryville, Virginia.[58] Training at EPI includes "offensive and escort driving techniques," threat-assessment education, searches, alarms, weapons, communications, protocol, legal issues, and firearms and defensive techniques. Activities focus on "low-profile" protection utilizing limited personnel and resources, in contrast to the use of very expensive "high-profile" security as a deterrent technique, which agencies like the Secret Service are able to use.[59] EPI offers "certification" as a Personal Protection Specialist (PPS) following successful completion of its training.

An early contingent of Pinkerton Guards posing outside the Kenilworth Park Race Track in Buffalo, New York, in 1907. Today, private security personnel outnumber public police officers by a ratio of two to one.

Culver Pictures, Inc.

The Private System of Justice

Security agencies work for paying clients, while law enforcement agencies are government entities. Differences between the roles of private and public agencies were revealed in a survey sponsored by the National Institute of Justice which showed that security executives order their managerial priorities as follows: (1) the protection of lives and property, (2) crime prevention, (3) loss prevention, (4) fire prevention, and (5) access control. In contrast, public law enforcement officials list a somewhat different set of priorities: (1) the protection of lives and property, (2) the arrest and prosecution of suspects, (3) the investigation of criminal incidents, (4) the maintenance of public order, and (5) crime prevention.[60]

This difference in priorities, combined with the fact that hired security operatives serve the interests of corporate employers rather than the public, has led to charges that a private justice system operates next to the official government-sponsored justice system. The private system may see behavior which public police agencies would interpret as a violation of the criminal law as merely misguided employee activity. Within the private justice system, conflict resolution, economic sanctions, or retraining sometimes supplant criminal prosecution as the most effective method of dealing with offenders. According to the NIJ survey, "Security managers in all sectors . . . report that the most frequently investigated crime is employee theft, and nearly half of them resolve such incidents within their own organizations."[61]

One reason why white-collar and business crimes are substantially underreported in official crime statistics is that unofficial resolutions, based upon investigations by proprietary security forces, are often the preferred method of handling such offenses. As some writers have observed, the public justice system may find itself increasingly bypassed by proprietary security operations that generally find in the courts "an unsympathetic attitude . . . concerning business losses due to crime."[62] The *Hallcrest Report* points out that not only has a "fundamental shift in protection resources . . . occurred from public policing to the private sector," but that "this shift has also been accompanied by a shift in the character of social control."[63] According to the report, "Private security defines deviance in instrumental rather than moral terms: protecting corporate interests becomes more important than fighting crime, and sanctions are applied more often against those who *create* opportunities for loss rather than those who *capitalize* on the opportunity—the traditional offenders."[64]

The *Hallcrest Report* identified the growth of the private justice system as a major source of friction between private security and public law enforcement. According to the report, "Law enforcement agencies have enjoyed a dominant position in providing protective services to their communities but now foresee an erosion of their 'turf' to private security."[65] Other sources of friction between the two include (1) "moonlighting" for private agencies by public officers, (2) the fact that "cases brought by private security are usually well developed, putting the law enforcement agency in the thankless position of being an information processor for the prosecutor's office,"[66] and (3) the fact that many cases developed by private security agencies are disposed of through "plea bargaining, which police officers may not understand or support, but which may suit the purposes of a company interested in [deterrence]."[67] Moonlighting by public officers is a source of conflict because (1) police authority may be seen as being used for personal gain, (2) officers who moonlight long hours may not be fit for their official duties due to exhaustion, and (3) public police departments may be legally liable for the actions of their uniformed officers even though they are temporarily working for private employers.

The Professionalization of Private Security

An issue facing lawmakers across the country today is the extent of authority and the degree of force that security guards can legitimately use. Courts have generally held that private security personnel derive their legitimacy from the same basic authority that an employer would have in protecting his or her own property. In other words, if I have the legal right to use force to protect my home or business, then so do the guards I have hired to act in my place. According to some courts, private security personnel, because their authority is simply an extension of private rights, are not directly bound by the legal strictures which govern the use of force, the gathering of evidence, and so on by sworn police officers. Other courts, however, have ruled that private security personnel should be bound by the same procedural rules as sworn officers because they are *perceived* by the

CJ Today News

[FBI Joins Private Companies to Fight Espionage]

WASHINGTON—The FBI is investigating at least five economic espionage cases based on information from an unprecedented program in which it communicates regularly with businesses.

In most of those cases, companies contacted the FBI after seeing news reports in January [1998] about a man pleading guilty to stealing secrets about Gillette's Mach3 razor. That case was prompted by a call from Gillette to an FBI agent serving as a liaison to businesses.

The FBI won't discuss the investigations. But officials say they are communicating directly with more U.S. businesses now than during the Cold War. Why? Businesses are more fearful of corporate spies—both foreign and domestic—and the FBI is more focused on economic espionage.

"The last real battlefield is the economic battlefield," says David Howard of the American Society of Industrial Security, which represents corporate security officers. "The technologies necessary for doing business have made companies much more susceptible. It's critical for us to pool our resources with the FBI."

The FBI sends regular fax and e-mail advisories on security threats to 30,000 corporate security officers. And it often arranges for top executives to get clearance so they can receive classified information.

"By releasing certain information, we hope upper management will keep security in mind when making decisions," says FBI agent Larry Watson, who heads the Awareness of National Security Issues and Responses program.

In January [1998], the FBI put out an advisory on an Islamic militant who had urged attacks on U.S. citizens and facilities. In March [1998], an advisory warned of attacks on computer systems [that could produce the so-called] "Blue Screen of Death" at government agencies and universities.

The FBI also has designated an agent in each of its 56 field offices to serve as a corporate liaison. Calls to FBI liaisons have led to two major cases:

Steven Davis, who worked for Gillette subcontractor Wright Industries, was sentenced to 27 months in prison for trying to pass secrets about the Mach3 to Warner-Lambert, Bic and American Safety Razor. Davis said he did it because he was angry at his boss.

Two brothers pleaded guilty in 1997 to conspiring to steal secrets from paint, glass and chemicals company PPG Industries and sell them to competitor Owens-Corning. Owens alerted PPG.

"The FBI is realizing the nature of threats has changed. It's about competitive intelligence now," says Regis Becker, PPG's security director.

For the latest in crime and justice news visit the Talk Justice news feed at http://www.crimenews.info.

Source: Tom Lowry, "FBI Joins Private Companies to Fight Espionage," *USA Today,* May 28, 1998, p. 1B. Copyright 1998, *USA Today.* Reprinted with permission.

public as wielding the authority of public law enforcement officers.[68] The situation is complicated by the fact that, as previously discussed, some police officers moonlight as private guards when they are off duty.

To ensure at least a minimal degree of competence among private security personnel, a number of states have moved to a licensing process for officers, although a few still require little other than an application and a small fee.[69] Twenty-three states mandate training if the security officer is to be armed, but only 14 require any training for unarmed guards.[70] Most of the training which does occur is relatively simplistic. Topics typically covered include (1) fire prevention, (2) first aid, (3) building safety, (4) equipment use, (5) report writing, and (6) the legal powers of private security personnel.[71] Reflecting on training and licensing requirements, one specialist has warned, "We have a vast private police force largely untrained, with few restraints, with the power to use force to take liberty and life."[72]

Most private security firms today depend upon their own training programs to prevent actionable mistakes by their employees. Training in private security operations is also available from a number of schools and agencies. One is the International Foundation for Protection Officers, with offices in Cochrane, Alberta (Canada), and Midvale, Utah. Following the successful completion of a home-study course, students are accorded the status of Certified Protection Officer (CPO). In an effort to increase the professional status of the private security industry, the 32,000-member American Society for Industrial Security (ASIS), established in 1955, administers a comprehensive examination periodically in various locations across the country. Applicants who pass the examination earn the coveted title of Certified Protection Professional (CPP). CPP examinations are thorough and usually require a combination of experience and study to earn a passing grade.

Examination subject areas include (1) security management, (2) physical security, (3) loss prevention, (4) investigation, (5) internal/external relations, (6) protection of sensitive information, (7) personnel security, (8) emergency planning, (9) legal aspects of security, and (10) substance abuse. In addition, candidates are allowed to select from a mandated group of specialized topic areas (such as nuclear power security, public utility security, retail security, and computer security) which pertain to the fields in which they plan to work.[73]

ASIS also functions as a professional association, with yearly meetings held to address the latest in security techniques and equipment. ASIS Online, sponsored by ASIS, provides subscribers with daily security news, up-to-date international travel briefings, and a searchable security news database. In its efforts to heighten professionalism throughout the industry, ASIS has developed a private security code of ethics for its members. The code of ethics is reproduced in the CJ Today Exhibit box in this chapter. Visit ASIS Online via **Web Extra! 5–8** at cjtoday.com.

Another sign of increased professionalization in private security is the number of publications offered in the area. The *Journal of Security Administration*, published in Miami, Florida; ASIS's *Security Management* magazine; the *Security Management* newsletter, published semimonthly by the National Foremen's Institute in Waterford, Connecticut; and the older journal *Security World* serve the field as major sources of up-to-date information. Learn more about the privatization of American policing at **Library Extra! 5–7** at cjtoday.com.

Integrating Public and Private Security

As the private security field grows, its relationship to public law enforcement continues to evolve. Although competition between the sectors remains, many experts now recognize that each can help the other. A government-sponsored report makes the following policy recommendations designed to maximize the cooperative crime-fighting potential of existing private and public security resources:[74]

1. The resources of proprietary and contract security should be brought to bear in cooperative, community-based crime prevention and security awareness programs.

2. An assessment should be made of (1) the basic police services the public is willing to support financially, (2) the types of police services most acceptable to police administrators and the public for transfer to the private sector, and (3) which services

Allan Pinkerton (seated, right), founder of the Pinkerton Detective Agency, shown with Secret Service men at U.S. Army headquarters on the Potomac River in 1862. The link between public and private police agencies has a long history.

Corbis

CJ Today Exhibit 5-1

[American Society for Industrial Security—Code of Ethics]

Preamble

Aware that the quality of professional security activity ultimately depends upon the willingness of practitioners to observe special standards of conduct and to manifest good faith in professional relationships, the American Society for Industrial Security adopts the following Code of Ethics and mandates its conscientious observance as a binding condition of membership in or affiliation with the Society:

Code of Ethics

I. A member shall perform professional duties in accordance with the law and the highest moral principles.

II. A member shall observe the precepts of truthfulness, honesty, and integrity.

III. A member shall be faithful and diligent in discharging professional responsibilities.

IV. A member shall be competent in discharging professional responsibilities.

V. A member shall safeguard confidential information and exercise due care to prevent its improper disclosure.

VI. A member shall not maliciously injure the professional reputation or practice of colleagues, clients, or employers.

ARTICLE I

A member shall perform professional duties in accordance with the law and the highest moral principles.

Ethical Considerations

I-1 A member shall abide by the law of the land in which the services are rendered and perform all duties in an honorable manner.

I-2 A member shall not knowingly become associated in responsibility for work with colleagues who do not conform to the law and these ethical standards.

I-3 A member shall be just and respect the rights of others in performing professional responsibilities.

ARTICLE II

A member shall observe the precepts of truthfulness, honesty, and integrity.

Ethical Considerations

II-1 A member shall disclose all relevant information to those having the right to know.

II-2 A right to know is a legally enforceable claim or demand by a person for disclosure of information by a member. Such a right does not depend upon prior knowledge by the person of the existence of the information to be disclosed.

II-3 A member shall not knowingly release misleading information nor encourage or otherwise participate in the release of such information.

ARTICLE III

A member shall be faithful and diligent in discharging professional responsibilities.

Ethical Considerations

III-1 A member is faithful when fair and steadfast in adherence to promises and commitments.

III-2 A member is diligent when employing best efforts in an assignment.

III-3 A member shall not act in matters involving conflicts of interest without appropriate disclosure and approval.

III-4 A member shall represent services or products fairly and truthfully.

ARTICLE IV

A member shall be competent in discharging professional responsibilities.

Ethical Considerations

IV-1 A member is competent who possesses and applies the skills and knowledge required for the task.

IV-2 A member shall not accept a task beyond the member's competence nor shall competence be claimed when not possessed.

ARTICLE V

A member shall safeguard confidential information and exercise due care to prevent its improper disclosure.

Ethical Considerations

V-1 Confidential information is nonpublic information, the disclosure of which is restricted.

V-2 Due care requires that the professional must not knowingly reveal confidential information, or use a confidence to the disadvantage of the principal or to the advantage of the member or a third person, unless the principal consents after full disclosure of all the facts. This confidentiality continues after the business relationship between the member and his principal has terminated.

V-3 A member who receives information and has not agreed to be bound by confidentiality is not bound from disclosing it. A member is not bound by confidential disclosures made of acts or omissions which constitute a violation of the law.

V-4 Confidential disclosures made by a principal to a member are not recognized by law as privileged in a legal proceeding. The member may be required to testify in a legal proceeding to the information received in confidence from his principal over the objection of his principal's counsel.

V-5 A member shall not disclose confidential information for personal gain without appropriate authorization.

ARTICLE VI

A member shall not maliciously injure the professional reputation or practice of colleagues, clients, or employers.

Ethical Considerations

VI-1 A member shall not comment falsely and with malice concerning a colleague's competence, performance, or professional capabilities.

VI-2 A member who knows, or has reasonable grounds to believe, that another member has failed to conform to the Society's Code of Ethics shall present such information to the Ethical Standards Committee in accordance with Article VIII of the Society's bylaws.

Source: American Society for Industrial Security. Reprinted with permission.

Private security officers significantly outnumber sworn law enforcement officers in the United States. Cooperation among private security agencies and public law enforcement offices can help solve and prevent crimes.

Michael Newman, PhotoEdit

might be performed for a lower unit cost by the private sector with the same level of community satisfaction.

3. With special police powers, security personnel could resolve many or most minor criminal incidents prior to police involvement. State statutes providing such powers could also provide for standardized training and certification requirements, thus assuring uniformity and precluding abuses. . . . Ideally, licensing and regulatory requirements would be the same for all states, with reciprocity for firms licensed elsewhere.

4. Law enforcement agencies should be included in the crisis-management planning of private organizations. . . . Similarly, private security should be consulted when law enforcement agencies are developing SWAT [special weapons and tactics] and hostage-negotiation teams. The federal government should provide channels of communication with private security with respect to terrorist activities and threats.

5. States should enact legislation permitting private security firms access to criminal history records in order to improve the selection process for security personnel and also to enable businesses to assess the integrity of key employees.

6. Research should . . . attempt to delineate the characteristics of the private justice system; identify the crimes most frequently resolved; assess the types and amount of unreported crime in organizations; quantify the redirection of [the] public criminal justice workload . . . and examine [the] . . . relationships between private security and . . . components of the criminal justice system.

7. A federal tax credit for security expenditures, similar to the energy tax credit, might be a cost-effective way to reduce police workloads.

Summary

Today's police departments owe a considerable historical legacy to Sir Robert Peel and the London Metropolitan Police Force. The "Met," begun in 1829 under Peel's leadership, was the world's first modern police force. It was organized around the practice of preventive patrol by uniformed officers.

American police agencies function to enforce the statutes created by lawmaking bodies, and differing types and levels of legislative authority are reflected in the diversity of police forces which we have in our country today. As a consequence, American policing presents a complex picture which is structured along federal, state, and local lines. Each federal agency empowered by Congress to enforce specific statutes has its own enforcement arm, and tasks deemed especially significant by state legislatures, such as patrol of the highways, have resulted in the creation of specialized law enforcement agencies under state jurisdiction. For many of today's local law enforcement agencies, patrol retains a central role—with investigation, interrogation, and numerous support roles rounding out an increasingly specialized profession.

Studies sponsored by the Police Foundation and the Law Enforcement Assistance Administration during the 1970s and 1980s brought scientific scrutiny to bear on many of the guiding assumptions of police work.

Private policing, represented by the recent tremendous growth of for-hire security agencies, adds another dimension to American policing. Private security is now undergoing many of the changes which have already occurred in other law enforcement areas. Heightened training requirements, legislative regulation, court-mandated changes, and college-level educational programs in private security are all leading to increased professionalism within the security profession. Recognizing the pervasiveness of today's private security operations, many municipal departments have begun concerted efforts to involve security organizations in their crime-detection and crime-prevention efforts.

Discussion Questions

1. What assumptions about police work did scientific studies of law enforcement call into question? What other assumptions are made about police work today which might be similarly questioned or studied?
2. What are the three levels of law enforcement described in this chapter? Why do we have so many different types of enforcement agencies in the United States? What problems, if any, do you think are created by such a diversity of agencies?
3. What do you think will be the role of private protective services in the United States in the future? How can the quality of such services be ensured?

To participate in an online discussion on these topics and others, go to the Global Town Meeting electronic message board for Chapter 5 on the *Criminal Justice Today* Companion Website at cjtoday.com.

Web Quest!

Visit at least four of the federal law enforcement agencies listed under Web Extra! 5–2 at cjtoday.com. Use the online information that each site provides to describe each agency in terms of its history, organization, and mission. Do the same with at least four of the state-level law enforcement agencies listed under Web Extra! 5–6 and with at least four of the local-level law enforcement agencies listed under Web Extra! 5–7. If you would like to use federal, state, or local agencies other than those listed at cjtoday.com, you can find many such sites in the Cybrary at http://www.cybrary.info.

Assemble a notebook (or disk) containing the information you have gathered, organized by level and by agency. Submit the material to your instructor if asked to do so.

To complete this Web Quest! online, go to the Web Quest! module in Chapter 5 of the *Criminal Justice Today* Companion Website at cjtoday.com.

Library Extras!

Library Extra! **5–1**   *National Evaluation of Weed and Seed: Cross-Site Analysis* (NIJ, 1999).
Library Extra! **5–2**   *Attitudes toward Crime, the Police, and the Law: Individual and Neighborhood Differences* (NIJ, June 1999).
Library Extra! **5–3**   *The Kansas City Gun Experiment* (NIJ, 1995).
Library Extra! **5–4**   *Federal Law Enforcement Officers* (BJS, current volume).
Library Extra! **5–5**   *Census of State and Local Law Enforcement Agencies* (BJS, current volume).
Library Extra! **5–6**   *Law Enforcement Management and Administrative Statistics* (BJS, current volume).
Library Extra! **5–7**   *The Privatization and Civilianization of Policing* (NIJ, 2000).

To explore these resources online, go to the Library Extras! area of the *Criminal Justice Today* Companion Website at cjtoday.com. You should also check the author's "Late Picks" online for newly released documents and updated Library Extras! You can find Late Picks at http://cjtoday.com/latepicks.htm.

Notes

1. Police Foundation, *Annual Report 1991* (Washington, D.C.: Police Foundation, 1992).
2. "A Reminiscence of a Bow-Street Officer," *Harper's New Monthly Magazine*, Vol. 5, No. 28 (September 1852), p. 484.
3. Andrew P. Sutor, *Police Operations: Tactical Approaches to Crimes in Progress* (St. Paul, MN: West, 1976), p. 68, citing Peel.
4. For a good discussion of the development of the modern police, see Sue Titus Reid, *Criminal Justice: Procedures and Issues* (St. Paul, MN: West, 1987), pp. 110–115; and Henry M. Wrobleski and Karen M. Hess, *Introduction to Law Enforcement and Criminal Justice*, 4th ed. (St. Paul, MN: West, 1993), pp. 3–51.
5. Camdem Pelham, *Chronicles of Crime*, Vol. 1 (London: T. Miles, 1887), p. 59.
6. Gary Sykes, "Street Justice: A Moral Defense of Order Maintenance Policing," *Justice Quarterly*, Vol. 3, No. 4 (December 1986), p. 504.
7. Law Enforcement Assistance Administration, *Two Hundred Years of American Criminal Justice: An LEAA Bicentennial Study* (Washington, D.C.: U.S. Government Printing Office, 1976), p. 15.
8. For an excellent discussion of the history of policewomen in the United States, see Dorothy Moses Schulz, *From Social Worker to Crimefighter: Women in United States Municipal Policing* (Westport, CT: Praeger, 1995); and Dorothy Moses Schulz, "Invisible No More: A Social History of Women in U.S. Policing," in Barbara R. Price and Natalie J. Sokoloff, eds., *The Criminal Justice System and Women: Offender, Victim, Worker*, 2d ed. (New York: McGraw Hill, 1995), pp. 372–382.
9. Schulz, *From Social Worker to Crimefighter*, p. 25.
10. Ibid., p. 27.
11. National Commission on Law Observance and Enforcement, *Wickersham Commission Reports*, 14 vols. (Washington, D.C.: U.S. Government Printing Office, 1931).
12. President's Commission on Law Enforcement and Administration of Justice, *The Challenge of Crime in a Free Society* (Washington, D.C.: U.S. Government Printing Office, 1967).
13. National Advisory Commission on Criminal Justice Standards and Goals, *A National Strategy to Reduce Crime* (Washington, D.C.: U.S. Government Printing Office, 1973).
14. Thomas J. Deakin, "The Police Foundation: A Special Report," *FBI Law Enforcement Bulletin* (November 1986), p. 2.
15. National Institute of Justice, *The Exemplary Projects Program* (Washington, D.C.: U.S. Government Printing Office, 1982), p. 11.
16. George L. Kelling et al., *The Kansas City Patrol Experiment* (Washington, D.C.: Police Foundation, 1974).
17. Kevin Krajick, "Does Patrol Prevent Crime?" *Police Magazine* (September 1978), quoting Dr. George Kelling.
18. William Bieck and David Kessler, *Response Time Analysis* (Kansas City, MO: Board of Police Commissioners,

1977). See also J. Thomas McEwen et al., *Evaluation of the Differential Police Response Field Test: Executive Summary* (Alexandria, VA: Research Management Associates, 1984); and Lawrence Sherman, "Policing Communities: What Works?" in Michael Tonry and Norval Morris, eds., *Crime and Justice: An Annual Review of Research*, Vol. 8 (Chicago: University of Chicago Press, 1986).
19. Krajick, "Does Patrol Prevent Crime?"
20. Ibid.
21. Ibid.
22. David M. Kennedy, et al., *Reducing Gun Violence: The Boston Gun Project's Operation Ceasefire* (Washington, D.C.: National Institute of Justice, 2001).
23. Terence Dunworth and Gregory Mills, *National Evaluation of Weed and Seed* (Washington, D.C.: National Institute of Justice, 1999).
24. Lawrence W. Sherman, Dennis P. Rogan, and James W. Shaw, "The Kansas City Gun Experiment—NIJ Update," *Research in Brief*, November 1994.
25. Lawrence W. Sherman and Richard A. Berk, *Minneapolis Domestic Violence Experiment*, Police Foundation Report 1 (Washington, D.C.: Police Foundation, April 1984).
26. National Institute of Justice, *Newport News Tests Problem-Oriented Policing*, National Institute of Justice Reports (Washington, D.C.: U.S. Government Printing Office, January–February 1987).
27. Adapted from Deakin, "The Police Foundation."
28. U.S. Department of Justice, *A Proud History . . . a Bright Future: Careers with the FBI*, pamphlet (October 1986), p. 1.
29. Much of the information in this section comes from U.S. Department of Justice, *The FBI: The First 75 Years* (Washington, D.C.: U.S. Government Printing Office, 1986).
30. Howard Abadinsky, *Crime and Justice: An Introduction* (Chicago: Nelson-Hall, 1987), p. 262.
31. Federal Bureau of Investigation's website at www.fbi.gov/yourfbi/facts/fbimission.html. Accessed February 20, 2002.
32. "Attorney General Ashcroft and Deputy Attorney General Thompson Announce Reorganization and Mobilization of the Nation's Justice and Law Enforcement Resources," U.S. Department of Justice press release, November 8, 2001.
33. Much of the information in this paragraph comes from the FBI Academy website at http://www.fbi.gov/hq/td/academy/academy.htm. Accessed March 3, 2002.
34. Statistical information in this section comes from the FBI's website at http://www.fbi.gov. Accessed February 20, 2002.
35. Telephone conversation with FBI officials, April 21, 1995.
36. Public Laws 98–473 and 99–474.
37. Information in this section comes from Christopher H. Asplen, "National Commission Explores Its Future," *NIJ Journal* (January 1999), pp. 17–24.

38. The DNA Identification Act is Section 210301 of the Violent Crime Control and Law Enforcement Act of 1994.

39. Wrobleski and Hess, *Introduction to Law Enforcement and Criminal Justice*, p. 34.

40. Ibid., p. 35.

41. Bureau of Labor Statistics, *Occupational Outlook Handbook, 2000–01 Edition* (Washington, D.C.: BLS, 2000); and Brian A. Reaves and Timothy C. Hart, *Law Enforcement Management and Administrative Statistics, 1999: Data for Individual State and Local Agencies with 100 or More Officers* (Washington, D.C.: Bureau of Justice Statistics, 2000). Note that LEMAS, which only includes data from approximately 700 state and local law enforcement agencies that employ 100 or more full-time sworn personnel and assign 50 or more of these officers to respond to calls for service, reports finding 402,000 full-time sworn personnel among those departments in its 1999 survey. BLS data are more comprehensive and include part-time personnel.

42. Ibid.

43. Reaves and Hart, *Law Enforcement Management and Administrative Statistics, 1999*.

44. Ibid.

45. Note, however, that New York City jails may have average daily populations which, on a given day, exceed those of Los Angeles County.

46. Telephone communication with Deputy Ethan Marquez, L.A. County Sheriff's Department, Custodial Division, January 24, 2002.

47. Brian A. Reaves, "Sheriffs' Departments, 1990," *Bureau of Justice Statistics Bulletin* (Washington, D.C.: U.S. Department of Justice, 1992).

48. *Private Security: Report of the Task Force on Private Security* (Washington, D.C.: U.S. Government Printing Office, 1976), p. 4.

49. "Olympic Committee to Review Salt Lake Security in Wake of Terror Attacks," Associated Press, September 17, 2001.

50. William C. Cunningham, John J. Strauchs, and Clifford W. Van Meter, *The Hallcrest Report II: Private Security Trends, 1970–2000* (McLean, VA: Hallcrest Systems, 1990).

51. Includes full-time employees working for local police, sheriff's departments, special police, and state police. See Brian A. Reaves and Andrew L. Goldberg, *Census of State and Local Law Enforcement Agencies, 1996* (Washington, D.C.: Bureau of Justice Statistics, 1998);

Reaves and Hart, *Law Enforcement Management and Administrative Statistics, 1999;* and Bureau of Labor Statistics, *Occupational Outlook Handbook, 2000–01 Edition.*

52. The Security Industry Association website at http://www.siaonline.org/wp_size.html. Accessed January 20, 2000.

53. Cunningham, Strauchs, and Van Meter, *The Hallcrest Report II*, p. 236.

54. Dae H. Chang and James A. Fagin, eds., *Introduction to Criminal Justice: Theory and Application*, 2d ed. (Geneva, IL: Paladin House, 1985), pp. 275–277.

55. "George Smiley Joins the Firm," *Newsweek,* May 2, 1988, pp. 46–47.

56. Ibid.

57. For more information on Executive Services International, visit the ESI website at http: www.esi-lifeforce.com. Accessed March 25, 2002.

58. "More Than a Bodyguard," *Security Management,* February 10, 1986.

59. "A School for Guards of Rich, Powerful," *Akron (Ohio) Beacon Journal,* April 21, 1986.

60. National Institute of Justice, *Crime and Protection in America: A Study of Private Security and Law Enforcement Resources and Relationships—Executive Summary* (Washington, D.C.: U.S. Department of Justice, 1985), p. 42.

61. Ibid., p. 60.

62. Cunningham, Strauchs, and Van Meter, *The Hallcrest Report II*, p. 299.

63. Ibid., p. 301.

64. Ibid. (italics added).

65. Ibid., p. 117.

66. NIJ, *Crime and Protection in America*, p. 12.

67. Ibid., p. 12.

68. *People* v. *Zelinski*, 594 P.2d 1000 (1979).

69. For additional information, see *Police and Private Security: What the Future Holds,* Proceedings of the Police Futures Group National Conference (November 27–30, 1999).

70. Cunningham, Strauchs, and Van Meter, *The Hallcrest Report II*, p. 147.

71. NIJ, *Crime and Protection in America*, p. 37.

72. Richter Moore, "Private Police: The Use of Force and State Regulation," unpublished manuscript.

73. "The Mark of Professionalism," *Security Management,* 35th Anniversary Supplement, 1990, pp. 97–104.

74. NIJ, *Crime and Protection in America*, pp. 59–72.

Police Management

LEARNING OBJECTIVES

After reading this chapter, you should be able to

- Identify three styles of policing, and discuss differences in these approaches

- Identify factors that influence police use of discretion

- Describe different types of police corruption

- Explain civil liability issues in policing

- Describe efforts to professionalize the police

chapter 6

[*Respect and appreciation for diversity relating to gender, race, victims, and people with special needs are central to recognizing human rights. Police agencies that understand and value diverse communities create structures and systems that reach outward, enjoining and empowering police officers and citizens to collaborate in problem-solving on issues of crime and disorder.*]

—Police Executive Research Forum[1]

Key Concepts

[Terms]

1983 lawsuit	Peace Officer Standards and Training (POST)	police use of force
Bivens action	program	police working personality
community policing	police-community relations (PCR)	problem police officer
deadly force	police corruption	problem-solving policing
internal affairs	police discretion	racial profiling
Knapp Commission	police ethics	service style
learning organization	police management	team policing
legalistic style	police professionalism	watchman style
less-than-lethal weapons	police subculture	

[Cases]

Biscoe v. *Arlington County*	*Graham* v. *Connor*	*Malley* v. *Briggs*
Bivens v. *Six Unknown Federal Agents*	*Hunter* v. *Bryant*	*Maurice Turner* v. *Fraternal Order of Police*
City of Canton, Ohio v. *Harris*	*Idaho* v. *Horiuchi*	*Tennessee* v. *Garner*

Hear the author discuss this chapter at **cjtoday.com**

Introduction

Several years ago,[2] members of the special weapons and tactics (SWAT) team of Stanislaus County, California, wearing ski masks and acting on a tip that an illegal methamphetamine lab was in operation, kicked down the doors of the Oakdale home of Marian and William Hauselmann.[3] Once inside, they handcuffed Mrs. Hauselmann, put a pillowcase over her head, and wrestled her to the floor. Her 64-year-old husband, who suffers from a heart condition, was shouted into silence. His face was cut, and officers stepped on his back after throwing him down. No illegal drugs were found. Police soon realized that they had been misled by their informant and apologized to the Hauselmanns. Then they borrowed a knife from the couple's kitchen to cut the plastic handcuffs from their wrists. The county sheriff offered to pay for the broken doors. Following the incident, the Hauselmanns reported being unable to sleep.

A few months prior to the Hauselmanns' ordeal, multimillionaire rancher Donald Scott was fatally shot during a drug raid gone terribly wrong. His Malibu, California, property, the target of a police attack, yielded no drugs, and Scott appears to have been trying to protect himself from what he thought were intruders when he was shot.

Both these cases highlight the potentially disastrous consequences of improper police action. Effective **police management**, through which laws are enforced while the rights of suspects and of innocent people are protected, may be the single most important issue facing the criminal justice system in the twenty-first century. As Dorothy Ehrlich of northern California's American Civil Liberties Union (ACLU) says, efficient enforcement of the laws is necessary, "but terrorizing innocent people is a price no one should have to pay."[4]

Police Administration

Police management refers to the administrative activities of controlling, directing, and coordinating police personnel, resources, and activities in the service of crime prevention, the apprehension of criminals, the recovery of stolen property, and the performance of a variety of regulatory and helping services.[5] Police managers include any "sworn" law enforcement personnel with administrative authority, from the rank of sergeant to captain, chief, or sheriff, and civilian personnel such as police commissioners, attorneys general, state secretaries of crime control, and public safety directors.

police management

The administrative activities of controlling, directing, and coordinating police personnel, resources, and activities in the service of crime prevention, the apprehension of criminals, the recovery of stolen property, and the performance of a variety of regulatory and helping services.

The history of American policing can be divided into three different eras.[6] Each era can be distinguished from the others by the relative dominance of a particular administrative approach to police operations. The first period, the political era, was characterized by close ties between police and public officials. It began in the 1840s and ended around 1930. Throughout the period, American police agencies tended to serve the interests of powerful politicians and their cronies, while providing public-order maintenance services almost as an afterthought. The second period, the reform era, began in the 1930s and lasted until the 1970s. The reform era was characterized by pride in professional crime fighting. Police departments during this period focused most of their resources on solving "traditional" crimes, such as murder, rape, and burglary, and on capturing offenders. The final era, which is still developing, is the era of community problem solving. The problem-solving approach to police work stresses the service role of police officers and envisions a partnership between police agencies and their communities.

Styles of Policing

The influence of each historical phase survives today in what James Q. Wilson called "policing styles."[7] Simply put, a style of policing describes how a particular police agency sees its purpose and identifies the methods and techniques it uses to fulfill that purpose. Wilson's three types of policing—which he did not identify with a particular historical era—are (1) the watchman style (characteristic of the Harvard symposium's political era), (2) the legalistic style (professional crime fighting of the reform era), and (3) the service style (which is becoming more commonplace today). These three styles characterize nearly all municipal law enforcement agencies now operating in this country, although some departments are a mixture of two or more styles.

THE WATCHMAN STYLE OF POLICING

Police departments marked by the **watchman style** of policing are primarily concerned with achieving a goal that Wilson called "order maintenance." They see their job as controlling illegal and disruptive behavior. The watchman style makes considerable use of discretion compared to the legalistic style. Order in watchman-style communities may be arrived at through informal police intervention, including persuasion and threats, or even by "roughing up" a few disruptive people from time to time. Some authors have condemned this style of policing, suggesting that it is unfairly found in lower-class or lower-middle-class communities, especially where interpersonal relations include a fair amount of violence or physical abuse.

watchman style

A style of policing marked by a concern for order maintenance. Watchman policing is characteristic of lower-class communities where informal police intervention into the lives of residents is employed in the service of keeping the peace.

Police officers removing protesters at an antiabortion protest in Austin, Texas. The maintenance of social order is a police function closely akin to the watchman style of policing.

Bob Daemmrich, Stock Boston

The watchman style of policing appears to have been in use in Los Angeles, California, at the time of the now-historic Rodney King beating (see Chapter 7 for details). Following the riots that ensued, the Independent Commission on the Los Angeles Police Department (the Christopher Commission) determined that the Los Angeles police "placed greater emphasis on crime control over crime prevention, a policy that distanced cops from the people they serve."[8]

THE LEGALISTIC STYLE OF POLICING

legalistic style

A style of policing marked by a strict concern with enforcing the precise letter of the law. Legalistic departments may take a hands-off approach to disruptive or problematic behavior that does not violate the criminal law.

Departments operating under the **legalistic style** are committed to enforcing the letter of the law. The speed limit on some interstate highways in the United States, for example, is 70 mph. An officer who stops and tickets a person going 71 mph may be enforcing the law, but he or she is clearly an adherent of the legalistic style of policing.

Conversely, legalistically oriented departments can be expected to routinely avoid involvement in community disputes arising from violations of social norms which do not break the law. Police expert Gary Sykes calls this enforcement style "laissez-faire policing" in recognition of its hands-off approach to behaviors which are simply bothersome or inconsiderate of community principles.[9]

THE SERVICE STYLE OF POLICING

service style

A style of policing marked by a concern with helping rather than strict enforcement. Service-oriented police agencies are more likely to take advantage of community resources, such as drug-treatment programs, than are other types of agencies.

Departments which stress the goal of service reflect the felt needs of the community. In service-oriented departments, the police see themselves more as helpers than as embattled participants in a war against crime. Such departments work hand in hand with social services and other agencies to provide counseling for minor offenders and to assist community groups in preventing crimes and solving problems. Prosecutors may support the **service style** of policing by agreeing not to prosecute law violators who seek psychiatric help or who voluntarily participate in programs like Alcoholics Anonymous, family counseling, drug treatment, and the like. The service style is supported in part by citizen attitudes which seek to avoid the personal embarrassment which might result from a public airing of personal problems. Such attitudes reduce the number of criminal complaints filed, especially in minor disputes.

The following excerpt from the Bradley County (Tennessee) Sheriff's Office mission statement illustrates some of the principles characteristic of a service style of policing:[10]

The Declaration of Independence explains that people form governments to secure their rights. Governments pass laws in order to carry out this responsibility. The law is therefore intended to be a servant to the people, and not their master. As agents of government charged with responsibility of enforcing the law, we must be mindful of our obligation to use the law, and our power to enforce it, not as an end in itself but rather as a means to maintaining public order and creating a safer society. When responding to criminal incidents and while working in partnership with our communities to identify and solve problems, we must put law enforcement in its proper place as just one tool with which we achieve the desired results. The law must always be enforced with a view to achieving justice and "keeping the peace." Enforcing the letter of the law can easily become oppressive. The careful use of discretion in enforcing the spirit of the law must be prudently practiced, and consistently monitored, modeled, and reinforced by conscientious supervision.

Police-Community Relations

police-community relations (PCR)

An area of police activity that stresses the need for the community and the police to work together effectively and that emphasizes the notion that the police derive their legitimacy from the community they serve. PCR began to be of concern to many police agencies in the 1960s and 1970s.

In the 1960s, the legalistic style of policing, so common in America until then, began to yield to the newer service-oriented policing. The decade of the 1960s was one of unrest, fraught with riots and student activism. The war in Vietnam, civil rights concerns, and other burgeoning social movements produced large demonstrations and marches. The police, who were generally inexperienced in crowd control, all too often found themselves embroiled in tumultuous encounters with citizen groups. The police came to be seen by many as agents of "the establishment," and pitched battles between the police and the citizenry sometimes occurred.

As social disorganization increased, police departments across the nation sought ways to understand and deal better with the problems they faced. The **police-community relations (PCR)** programs which many departments created were a significant outgrowth of this effort.

PCR represented a movement away from an exclusive police emphasis on the apprehension of law violators and meant increasing the level of positive police-citizen interaction. At the height of the PCR movement, city police departments across the country opened store-

front centers where citizens could air complaints and easily interact with police representatives. As Egon Bittner recognized in 1976, for PCR programs to be truly effective, they need to reach to "the grassroots of discontent," where citizen dissatisfaction with the police exists.[11]

Many contemporary PCR programs involve public-relations officers appointed to provide an array of services to the community. "Neighborhood watch" programs, drug-awareness workshops, "Project ID"—which uses police equipment and expertise to mark valuables for identification in the event of theft—and police-sponsored victim's assistance programs are all examples of services embodying the spirit of PCR. Modern PCR programs, however, often fail to achieve their goal of increased community satisfaction with police services because they focus on providing services to groups who already are well satisfied with the police. PCR initiatives which do reach disaffected community groups are difficult to manage and may even alienate participating officers. Thus, as Bittner noted, "while the first approach fails because it leaves out those groups to which the program is primarily directed, the second fails because it leaves out the police department."

TEAM POLICING

During the 1960s and 1970s, a number of communities began to experiment with the concept of **team policing**, an idea thought to have originated in Aberdeen, Scotland.[12] Team policing rapidly became an extension of the PCR movement. Some authors have called team policing a "technique to deliver total police services to a neighborhood."[13] Others, however, have dismissed it as "little more than an attempt to return to the style of policing that was prevalent in the United States over a century ago."[14]

With team policing, officers were assigned semipermanently to particular neighborhoods, where it was expected they would become familiar with the inhabitants and with their problems and concerns. Patrol officers were given considerable authority in processing complaints from receipt through resolution. Crimes were investigated and solved at the local level, with specialists called in only if the resources needed to continue an investigation were not available locally.

COMMUNITY POLICING

In recent years, the police-community relations concept has undergone a substantial shift in emphasis. The old PCR model was built around the unfortunate self-image of many police administrators as enforcers of the law who were isolated from, and often in

team policing

— — — — — — — — — —

The reorganization of conventional patrol strategies into "an integrated and versatile police team assigned to a fixed district."[i]

opposition to, the communities they policed. Under such jaded administrators, PCR easily became a shallowly disguised and insecure effort to overcome public suspicion and community hostility.

In contrast, an increasing number of law enforcement administrators today are embracing the role of service provider. Modern police departments are frequently called upon to help citizens resolve a vast array of personal problems, many of which involve no law-breaking activity. Officers might be asked to help a sick child or a distraught person, open a car with the keys locked inside, organize a community crime-prevention effort, investigate a domestic dispute, regulate traffic, or give a talk to a class of young people on the dangers of drug abuse. Today, calls for service far exceed calls which directly relate to law violations. As a consequence, the referral function of the police is crucial in producing effective law enforcement. Officers may make referrals, rather than arrests, for interpersonal problems to agencies as diverse as Alcoholics Anonymous, social services, domestic violence centers, drug-rehabilitation programs, and psychiatric clinics.

In contemporary America, according to Harvard University's Executive Session on Policing, police departments function a lot like business corporations. According to the session, three generic kinds of "corporate strategies" guide American policing: (1) strategic policing, (2) problem-solving policing, and (3) community policing.[15]

The first, strategic policing, is something of a holdover from the reform era of the mid-twentieth century. **Strategic policing** "emphasizes an increased capacity to deal with crimes that are not well controlled by traditional methods."[16] Strategic policing retains the traditional police goal of professional crime fighting but enlarges the enforcement target to include nontraditional kinds of criminals, such as serial offenders, gangs and criminal associations, drug-distribution networks, and sophisticated white-collar and computer criminals. To meet its goals, strategic policing generally makes use of innovative enforcement techniques, including intelligence operations, undercover stings, electronic surveillance, and sophisticated forensic methods.

The other two strategies give greater recognition to the service style described by James Q. Wilson. **Problem-solving** (or problem-oriented) **policing** takes the view that many crimes are caused by existing social conditions in the communities served by the police. To control crime, problem-oriented police managers attempt to uncover and effectively address underlying social problems. Problem-solving policing makes thorough use of community resources, such as counseling centers, welfare programs, and job-training facilities. It also attempts to involve citizens in crime prevention through education, negotiation, and conflict management. Residents of poorly maintained housing areas, for example, might be asked to clean up litter, install better lighting, and provide security devices for their houses and apartments in the belief that clean, well-lighted, secure areas are a deterrent to criminal activity.

The third, and newest, police strategy **community policing** (sometimes called *community-oriented policing*), goes a step beyond the other two. Community policing has been described as "a philosophy based on forging a partnership between the police and the community, so that they can work together on solving problems of crime, [and] fear of crime and disorder, thereby enhancing the overall quality of life in their neighborhoods."[17] The community policing approach to law enforcement seeks to address the causes of crime and reduce the fear of crime and social disorder through problem-solving strategies and police-community partnerships.

Community policing is a concept which evolved out of the early work of George Kelling and Robert Trojanowicz, who conducted studies of foot-patrol programs in Newark, New Jersey,[18] and Flint, Michigan.[19] Their studies showed that "police could develop more positive attitudes toward community members and could promote positive attitudes toward police if they spent time on foot in their neighborhoods."[20] The definitive work on this topic may well be Trojanowicz's *Community Policing*, published in 1990.[21]

Community policing attempts to actively involve the community with the police in the task of crime control by creating an effective working partnership between the community and the police.[22] Under the community-policing ideal, community members and the police are expected to share responsibility for establishing and maintaining peaceful neighborhoods.[23] As a consequence, community policing permits members of the community to participate more fully than ever before in defining the police role. In the words of police expert Jerome Skolnick, community policing is "grounded on the notion that, together, police and public are more effective and more humane coproducers of safety and public order than are the police alone."[24] According to Skolnick, community policing involves at

---

strategic policing

A type of policing that retains the traditional police goal of professional crime fighting but enlarges the enforcement target to include nontraditional kinds of criminals, such as serial offenders, gangs and criminal associations, drug-distribution networks, and sophisticated white-collar and computer criminals. Strategic policing generally makes use of innovative enforcement techniques, including intelligence operations, undercover stings, electronic surveillance, and sophisticated forensic methods.

problem-solving policing

A type of policing that assumes that many crimes are caused by existing social conditions within the community and that crimes can be controlled by uncovering and effectively addressing underlying social problems. Problem-solving policing makes use of community resources, such as counseling centers, welfare programs, and job-training facilities. It also attempts to involve citizens in crime prevention through education, negotiation, and conflict management.

community policing

"A collaborative effort between the police and the community that identifies problems of crime and disorder and involves all elements of the community in the search for solutions to these problems."[ii]

least one of four elements: (1) community-based crime prevention, (2) the reorientation of patrol activities to emphasize the importance of nonemergency services, (3) increased police accountability to the public, and (4) a decentralization of command, including a greater use of civilians at all levels of police decision making.[25] As one writer explains it, "Community policing seeks to integrate what was traditionally seen as the different law enforcement, order maintenance and social service roles of the police. Central to the integration of these roles is a working partnership with the community in determining what neighborhood problems are to be addressed, and how."[26] Table 6–1 highlights the differences between traditional and community policing.

Community policing is a two-way street. It not only requires the police to be aware of community needs, it also mandates both involvement and crime-fighting action on the part of citizens themselves. As Detective Tracie Harrison of the Denver Police Department explains, "When the neighborhood takes stock in their community and they're serious they don't want crime, then you start to see crime go down. . . . They're basically fed up and know the police can't do it alone."[27]

Creative approaches to policing have produced a number of innovative programs over the past few decades. In the early 1980s, for example, Houston's Directed Area Responsibility Teams (DART) Program emphasized problem-oriented policing; the Baltimore County Police Department began Project COPE (Citizen Oriented Police Enforcement); and Denver initiated its Community Service Bureau, one of the first major community-policing programs. By the late 1980s, Jerome Skolnick and David Bayley's study of six American cities, entitled *The New Blue Line: Police Innovation in Six American Cities*,[28] documented the growing strength of police-community cooperation throughout the nation, giving further credence to the continuing evolution of service-oriented styles of policing.

Police departments throughout the country continue to join the community-policing bandwagon. A 2001 report by the Bureau of Justice Statistics (BJS) showed that state and local law enforcement agencies across the United States had nearly 113,000 full-time sworn personnel regularly engaged in community-policing activities.[29] BJS noted that only about 21,000 officers would have been so categorized in 1997. At the time of the report, 64% of local police departments serving 86% of all residents had full-time officers engaged in some form of community-policing activity, compared to 34% of departments serving 62% of all residents in 1997.

Typical of many departments, the Chicago Police Department launched its comprehensive community-policing program in 1993. It was called Chicago's Alternative Policing Strategy (CAPS). Chicago Mayor Richard M. Daley played a significant role in the

Police officers serving food during an anticrime rally to encourage citizen involvement in crime fighting. Activities like this help foster the community-policing ideal through which law enforcement officers and members of the public become partners in controlling crime and keeping communities safe.

Dale Stockton

TABLE 6-1		TRADITIONAL VERSUS COMMUNITY POLICING	
Question		**Traditional Policing**	**Community Policing**
Who are the police?		The police are a government agency principally responsible for law enforcement.	The police are the public, and the public are the police. Police officers are paid to give full-time attention to the duties of every citizen.
What is the relationship of the police force to other public-service departments?		Priorities often conflict.	The police are one department among many responsible for improving the quality of life.
What is the role of the police?		To solve crimes.	To solve problems.
How is police efficiency measured?		By detection and arrest rates.	By the absence of crime and disorder.
What are the highest priorities?		Crimes that are high value (for example, bank robberies) and those involving violence.	Whatever problems disturb the community most.
What do police deal with?		Incidents.	Citizens' problems and concerns.
What determines the effectiveness of police?		Response times.	Public cooperation.
What view do police take of service calls?		They deal with them only if there is no real police work to do.	They view them as a vital function and a great opportunity.
What is police professionalism?		Providing a swift, effective response to serious crime.	Keeping close to the community.
What kind of intelligence is most important?		Crime intelligence (study of particular crimes or series of crimes).	Criminal intelligence (information about the activities of individuals or groups).
What is the essential nature of police accountability?		Highly centralized; governed by rules, regulations, and policy directives; accountable to the law.	Local accountability to community needs.
What is the role of headquarters?		To provide the necessary rules and policy directives.	To preach organizational values.
What is the role of the press liaison department?		To keep the "heat" off operational officers so they can get on with the job.	To coordinate an essential channel of communication with the community.
How do the police regard prosecutions?		As an important goal.	As one tool among many.

Source: William R. Parks II, "Community Policing: A Foundation for Restorative Justice." Web posted at http://www.realjustice.org/Pages/t2000papers/t2000_wparks.html. Accessed March 5, 2002. Originally printed in Malcolm K. Sparrow, *Implementing Community Policing* (Washington, D.C.: National Institute of Justice, 1988), pp. 8–9.

development of a strategic plan for "reinventing the Chicago Police Department," which led to the development of CAPS. Daley noted that community policing "means doing more than responding to calls for service and solving crimes. It means transforming the Department to support a new, proactive approach to preventing crimes before they occur. It means forging new partnerships among residents, business owners, community leaders, the police, and City services to solve long-range community problems."[30] Read the mayor's original report, written in conjunction with the Chicago Police Department, at **Library Extra! 6–1** at cjtoday.com.

Today, CAPS is a department-wide initiative functioning throughout Chicago. The Chicago plan uses rapid-response teams composed of roving officers to handle emergencies, while many other officers have been put on permanent beats throughout the city where they are highly visible, with the avowed goal of maintaining and heightening citizen's perceptions of a police presence in their neighborhoods. Central to the CAPS program are monthly "beat meetings" between patrol officers and local residents. District Neighborhood Relations Offices provide an additional channel for communications between the police department and the public. The department's Joint Community Police Training (JCPT) project offers residents of all 279 beats the opportunity to learn about CAPS and how to work with the police in solving neighborhood crime problems. The JCPT project teams police officers with community trainers who go out into city neighborhoods to offer a brief orientation class and a series of problem-solving sessions to interested residents.

CAPS actively brings other city agencies into the process of public-order maintenance, tearing down deserted buildings, towing away abandoned cars, erasing graffiti, improving street lighting, and removing pay phones frequented by drug dealers. "Most of all," says Chicago Mayor Richard M. Daley, "we've enlisted the active participation of the people of Chicago. We have formed citizen advisory councils to track court cases and address other community issues that contribute to crime. . . . CAPS only works when people get involved."[31]

Ongoing evaluations of CAPS[32] have found that the program has "improved the lives of residents in virtually every area."[33] Survey-based measures show crime-related problems declining after CAPS implementation, and official crime statistics continue to show a steady decline in major crimes committed in Chicago.[34] Residents also report that street drug dealing, shootings, violence by gangs, and robbery victimization have all declined since CAPS was implemented, although it is difficult to conclude from the evaluations that the decline has been entirely due to CAPS. At least one study did report conclusively, however, that city residents have experienced a significant increase in optimism about police services since CAPS began, especially in the area of police responsiveness to neighborhood concerns.[35] Learn more about CAPS via **WebExtra! 6–1** at cjtoday.com. A review of Chicago's experience with community policing is available at **Library Extra! 6–2** at cjtoday.com.

Although community-policing programs began in the nation's metropolitan areas, the spirit of these programs, which center on community engagement and problem solving, has since spread to rural areas. Sheriff's departments that operate community-policing programs sometimes refer to them as "neighborhood-oriented policing" in recognition of the decentralized nature of rural communities. A report on neighborhood-oriented policing by the Bureau of Justice Assistance (BJA) notes that "the stereotypical view is that police officers in rural areas naturally work more closely with the public than do officers in metropolitan areas."[36] This view, warns the BJA, may not be entirely accurate, and rural departments would do well "to recognize that considerable diversity exists among rural communities and rural law enforcement agencies." Hence, as in metropolitan areas, effective community policing requires the involvement of all members of the community in identifying and solving problems.

The emphasis on community policing continues to grow. Title I of the Violent Crime Control and Law Enforcement Act of 1994, known as the Public Safety Partnership and Community Policing Act of 1994, highlighted the role of community policing in combating crime nationwide and made funding available for (among other things) "increas[ing] the number of law enforcement officers involved in activities that are focused on interaction with members of the community on proactive crime control and prevention by redeploying officers to such activities." The avowed purposes of the Community Policing Act were (1) to substantially increase the number of law enforcement officers interacting directly with members of the community (through a funded program known as Cops on the Beat); (2) to provide additional and more effective training to law enforcement officers to enhance their problem solving, service, and other skills needed in interacting with members of the community; (3) to encourage the development and implementation of innovative programs to permit members of the community to assist local law enforcement agencies in the prevention of crime in the community; and (4) to encourage the development of new technologies to assist local law enforcement agencies in reorienting the emphasis of their activities from reacting to crime to preventing crime.

In response to the 1994 law, the U.S. Department of Justice created the Office of Community Oriented Policing Services (COPS). The COPS Office administered the funds necessary to add 100,000 community-policing officers to our nation's streets—the number originally targeted by law. In 1999, the U.S. Department of Justice and COPS reached an

> Crime is a community problem and stands today as one of the most serious challenges of our generation. Our citizens must . . . recognize their responsibilities in its suppression.
>
> —O. W. Wilson

> The police in the United States are not separate from the people. They draw their authority from the will and consent of the people, and they recruit their officers from them. The police are the instrument of the people to achieve and maintain order; their efforts are founded on principles of public service and ultimate responsibility to the public.
>
> —National Advisory Commission on Criminal Justice Standards and Goals

important milestone by funding the 100,000th officer ahead of schedule and under budget. Although the Community Policing Act originally provided COPS funding only through 2000, Congress has continued to fund COPS—making another $500 million available for the hiring of an additional 50,000 officers.[37]

About the same time that the Violent Crime Control and Law Enforcement Act was passed, the Community Policing Consortium, based in Washington, D.C., began operations. The consortium, which is administered and funded by the U.S. Department of Justice's Bureau of Justice Assistance, provides a forum for training and information exchange in the area of community policing. Members of the consortium include the International Association of Chiefs of Police, the National Sheriff's Association, the Police Executive Research Forum, the Police Foundation, and the National Organization of Black Law Enforcement Executives. Visit the Community Policing Consortium via **WebExtra! 6–2** at cjtoday.com.

CRITIQUE OF COMMUNITY POLICING

As some authors have noted, "Community policing has become the dominant theme of contemporary police reform in America."[38] Nonetheless, problems have plagued the community-policing movement since its inception, and many of them still remain.[39] For one thing, the range, complexity, and evolving nature of community-policing programs have made their effectiveness difficult to measure.[40] Moreover, "citizen satisfaction" with police performance can be difficult to conceptualize and quantify. Most early studies of citizen satisfaction examined the attitudes of citizens developed through face-to-face interaction with individual police officers. They generally found a far higher level of dissatisfaction with the police among African-Americans than among most other groups. Recent findings, like those of years past, continue to show that, in general, the attitudes of African-Americans toward the police are quite poor. Given the wider reach of these studies, however, evaluators have discovered that overall quality of life and type of neighborhood may form the primary roots of such dissatisfaction.[41] Since, on average, African-Americans continue to experience a lower quality of life than most other U.S. citizens, and because they tend to live in neighborhoods characterized by economic problems, drug trafficking, and street crime, recent studies conclude that it is these conditions of life, rather than race, which are most predictive of citizen dissatisfaction with the police.

Those who study community policing have often been stymied by ambiguity surrounding the concept of community.[42] Sociologists, who sometimes define a community as "any area in which members of a common culture share common interests,"[43] tend to deny that a community needs to be limited geographically. Police departments, on the other hand, tend to define communities "within jurisdictional, district or precinct lines, or within the confines of public or private housing developments."[44] The well-known police researcher Robert Trojanowicz cautions police planners that "the impact of mass transit, mass communications and mass media have widened the rift between a sense of community based on geography and one [based] on interest."[45]

Researchers who follow the police definition of *community* have come to recognize that there may not be a high degree of consensus within and between members of a local community about community problems and appropriate solutions. Robert Bohm and colleagues at the University of Central Florida have found, for example, that while there may be some "consensus about social problems and their solutions . . . the consensus may not be community-wide." It may, in fact, exist only among "a relatively small group of 'active' stakeholders who differ significantly about the seriousness of most of the problems and the utility of some solutions."[46]

Finally, there is continuing evidence that not all police officers or police managers are ready to accept nontraditional images of police work. One reason is that the goals of community policing frequently conflict with standard police performance criteria (such as arrests), leading to a perception among officers that community-policing programs are inefficient at best and, at worst, a waste of time.[47] Similarly, many officers are loathe to take on new responsibilities as service providers whose role is increasingly defined by community needs and less by strict interpretation of the law. As one writer, a police sergeant with a Ph.D. in sociology, puts it, "It is an unrealistic leap of faith to presume that the police institution has the resources or capability to carry on all that its newly defined function will demand of it. . . . There is no valid reason for the police to take on all of these responsibilities other than what appears to be a tacit argument that the agency of last resort is the only one that can be held strictly accountable to the public."[48] In this writer's

A successful community policing program . . . requires officers to be well versed in cultural diversity and competent to perform tasks needed to accomplish their duties. This, obviously, requires considerable training for officers at all levels of the department.

—Samuel D. Pratcher, Chief of Police, Wilmington, Delaware

It shall be the mission of the Bradley County Sheriff's Office to consistently meet the public safety needs of all the people we serve, with integrity, respect, and fairness, within the resources allocated to us for this purpose. We shall strive to meet or exceed the expectations of those we serve, while enforcing the spirit of the law, and by always doing what is right.

—Mission statement, Bradley County (Tennessee) Sheriff's Office[iii]

view, the police, once their role is broadly defined by community needs, become a kind of catchall agency, or "agency of last resort," required to deal with problems ranging from handling the homeless to "worrying about the small mountains of trash on the all-too-many empty lots that once housed people and businesses."

A New York City police officer offers yet another criticism: "If we make the goals of community policing impossible to achieve, we doom the undertaking to failure. If we overwhelm police administrators with the enormity and vagueness of their proposed function, they will resist all attempts at reform."[49] He adds, "The notion of allowing the 'community' to participate in defining the police role is ill-conceived, and the most potentially explosive idea associated with community policing. . . . If we follow the proposal that the police function is now anything the community defines it to be, it will become virtually impossible for police departments to accomplish any goals."[50]

Some authors have warned that **police subculture** is so committed to a traditional view of police work, which is focused almost exclusively on crime fighting, that efforts to promote community policing can demoralize an entire department, rendering it ineffective at its basic tasks.[51] As the Independent Commission on the Los Angeles Police Department (the Christopher Commission) found following the "Rodney King riots," "Too many . . . patrol officers view citizens with resentment and hostility; too many treat the public with rudeness and disrespect."[52] Some analysts warn that only when the formal values espoused by today's innovative police administrators begin to match those of rank-and-file officers can any police organization begin to be high performing in terms of the goals espoused by community-policing reformers.[53]

Nor have all public officials been ready to accept community policing. Ten years ago, for example, New York City Mayor Rudolph W. Giuliani criticized the police department's Community Police Officer Program (CPOP), saying that it "has resulted in officers doing too much social work and making too few arrests."[54] Similarly, many citizens are not ready to accept a greater involvement of the police in their personal lives. Although the turbulent protest-prone years of the 1960s and early 1970s are long gone, some groups remain suspicious of the police. No matter how inclusive community-policing programs become, it is doubtful that the gap between the police and the public will ever be entirely bridged. The police role of restraining behavior which violates the law will always produce friction between police departments and some segments of the community.

Interestingly, as American police departments have outwardly embraced the community-policing model, they have also steadily increased their paramilitary capabilities. While only about 59% of police departments had SWAT teams in 1982, for example, approximately 90% had them by 1995. Moreover, a 1997 survey of police departments nationwide showed that 20% of departments without a SWAT team said they were planning to establish one. Hence, as the survey authors observe, "these findings reflect the aggressive turn many law enforcement agencies are assuming behind the rhetoric of community and problem-oriented policing reforms."[55] Learn more about measures of police effectiveness, including those related to community policing, at **Library Extra! 6-3** at cjtoday.com.

police subculture

A particular set of values, beliefs, and acceptable forms of behavior characteristic of American police with which the police profession strives to imbue new recruits. Socialization into the police subculture commences with recruit training and continues thereafter.

Discretion and the Individual Officer

Regardless of the "official" policing style espoused by a department, individual officers retain considerable discretion in what they do. **Police discretion** refers to the exercise of choice by law enforcement officers in the decision to investigate or apprehend, the disposition of suspects, the carrying out of official duties, and the application of sanctions. As one author has observed, "Police authority can be, at once, highly specific and exceedingly vague."[56] Decisions to stop and question someone, to arrest a suspect, and to perform many other police tasks are made solely by individual officers. Kenneth Culp Davis, who pioneered the study of police discretion says, "The police make policy about what law to enforce, how much to enforce it, against whom, and on what occasions."[57] To the individual who has contact with the police, the discretionary authority exercised by individual law enforcement officers is of potentially greater significance than all the department manuals and official policy statements combined.

Patrolling officers often decide against a strict enforcement of the law, preferring instead to handle situations informally. Minor law violations, crimes committed out of the officer's presence where the victim refuses to file a complaint, and certain violations of the criminal law where the officer suspects that sufficient evidence to guarantee a conviction is lacking may all lead to discretionary action short of arrest. Although the widest exercise of discretion

police discretion

The opportunity of law enforcement officers to exercise choice in their daily activities.

is more likely in routine situations involving relatively less serious violations of the law, serious and clear-cut criminal behavior may occasionally result in discretionary decisions not to make an arrest. Drunk driving, possession of controlled substances, and assault are but a few examples of crimes in which on-the-scene officers may decide warnings or referrals are more appropriate than arrest.

Studies of police discretion have found that a number of factors influence the discretionary decisions of individual officers. Here are some of these factors:

■ *Background of the officer.* Law enforcement officers bring to the job all of their previous life experiences. Values shaped through early socialization in the family, as well as attitudes acquired from ongoing socialization, influence the decisions an officer will make. If the officer has learned prejudice against certain ethnic groups, it is likely that this prejudice will manifest itself in enforcement decisions. Officers who place a high value on the nuclear family may handle spouse abuse, child abuse, and domestic disputes in predetermined ways.

■ *Characteristics of the suspect.* Some officers treat men and women differently. A police friend of the author's has voiced the belief that women "are not generally bad . . . but when they do go bad, they go very bad." His official treatment of women has been tempered by this belief. Very rarely will this officer arrest a woman, but when he does, he spares no effort to see her incarcerated. Other characteristics of the suspect which may influence police decisions include demeanor, style of dress, and grooming.[58] Belligerent suspects are often seen as "asking for it" and as challenging police authority. Well-dressed suspects are likely to be treated with deference, but poorly groomed suspects can expect less respectful treatment. Suspects sporting personal styles with a message—biker's attire, unkempt beards, outlandish haircuts, and other nonconformist styles—are more likely to be arrested than are others.

■ *Department policy.* Discretion, while not entirely subject to control by official policy, can be influenced by it. If a department has targeted certain kinds of offenses, or if supervisors adhere to strict enforcement guidelines and closely monitor dispatches and other communications, the discretionary release of suspects will be quite rare.

■ *Community interest.* Public attitudes toward certain crimes will increase the likelihood of arrest for suspected offenders. Contemporary attitudes toward crimes involving children—including child sex abuse, the sale of drugs to minors, domestic violence involving children, and child pornography—have all led to increased and strict enforcement of laws governing such offenses across the nation. Communities may identify particular problems affecting them and ask law enforcement to respond. Fayetteville, North Carolina, adjacent to a major military base, was plagued some years ago by a downtown area notorious for prostitution and massage parlors. Once the community voiced its concern over the problem and clarified its economic impact on the city, the police responded with a series of highly effective arrests, which eliminated massage parlors within the city limits. Departments which require officers to live in the areas they police recognize that community interests affect citizens and officers alike.

■ *Pressure from victims.* Victims who refuse to file a complaint are commonly associated with certain crimes, such as spouse abuse, the "robbery" of drug merchants, and assaults on customers of prostitutes. When victims refuse to cooperate with the police, there is often little that can be done. On the other hand, some victims are very vocal in insisting that their victimization be recognized and dealt with. Victim's assistance groups, such as People Assisting Victims, the Victim's Assistance Network, and others, have sought to keep pressure on police departments and individual investigators to ensure the arrest and prosecution of suspects.

■ *Disagreement with the law.* Some laws lack a popular consensus. Among them are laws relating to many "victimless" offenses, such as gambling, homosexuality, lesbianism, prostitution, drug use, pornography, and some crimes involving alcohol. Not all of these behaviors are even crimes in certain jurisdictions. Gambling is legal in Atlantic City, New Jersey, aboard cruise ships, and in parts of Nevada. Many states have now legalized homosexuality, lesbianism, and most forms of sexual behavior between consenting adults. Prostitution is officially sanctioned in portions of Nevada, and some drug offenses have been "decriminalized," with offenders being ticketed rather than arrested. Unpopular laws are not likely to bring much attention from law enforcement officers. Sometimes such crimes are regarded as just "part of the landscape" or as the conse-

Effective police work in the emerging society will depend less on the holster and more on the head.

—Alvin Toffler

quence of laws which have not kept pace with a changing society. When arrests do occur, it may be because individuals investigated for more serious offenses were caught in the act of violating an unpopular statute. For example, drug offenders arrested in the middle of the night may be "caught in the act" of an illegal sexual performance when the police break in. Charges may then include "crime against nature," as well as possession or sale of drugs.

On the other hand, certain behaviors which are not law violations and which may even be protected by guarantees of free speech may be annoying, offensive, or disruptive according to the normative standards of a community or the personal standards of an officer. Where the law has been violated and the guilty party is known to the officer, the evidence necessary for a conviction in court may be "tainted" or in other ways not usable. Gary Sykes, in recognizing these possibilities, says, "One of the major ambiguities of the police task is that officers are caught between two profoundly compelling moral systems: justice as due process . . . and conversely, justice as righting a wrong as part of defining and maintaining community norms."[59] In such cases, discretionary police activity may take the form of "street justice" and may approach vigilantism.

- *Available alternatives.* Police discretion can be influenced by the officer's awareness of alternatives to arrest. Community treatment programs, including outpatient drug and alcohol counseling, psychiatric or psychological services, and domestic dispute–resolution centers, may all be considered by officers looking for a way out of official action.
- *Personal practices of the officer.* Some officers view the violation of particular laws less seriously than do other officers. The police officer who has an occasional marijuana cigarette with friends at a party may be inclined to deal less harshly with minor drug offenders than nonuser officers. The officer who routinely exceeds speed limits while driving the family car may be lenient with speeders encountered while on duty.

Issues and Challenges in Contemporary Policing

A number of issues hold special interest for today's police administrators and officers. Some concerns, such as on-the-job dangers, officer stress, and the use of deadly force, derive from the very nature of police work. Others have arisen over the years due to commonplace practice, characteristic police values, public expectations about the enforcement of laws, and ongoing societal change. Policing a multicultural society, which is discussed in a box in this section, has become one of the most significant challenges facing American police departments and their officers today.

Police Personality and Culture

In the 1960s, Jerome Skolnick described what he called the "working personality" of police officers.[60] Skolnick's description was consistent with William Westley's classic study of the Gary, Indiana, Police Department, in which he found a police culture with its own "customs, laws, and morality,"[61] and with Arthur Niederhoffer's observation that cynicism was pervasive among officers in New York City.[62] More recent authors have claimed that the "big curtain of secrecy" surrounding much of police work shields knowledge of the nature of the police personality from outsiders.[63]

Skolnick found that a process of informal socialization, through which officers learn what is appropriate police behavior, occurs when new officers begin to work with seasoned veterans. Such informal socialization is often far more important than formal police academy training in determining how rookies will see police work. In everyday life, formal socialization occurs through schooling, church activities, job training, and so on. Informal socialization is acquired primarily from one's peers in less institutionalized settings and provides an introduction to value-laden subcultures. The information that passes between officers in the locker room, in a squad car, over a cup of coffee, or in many other relatively private moments produces a shared view of the world that can best be described as "streetwise." The streetwise cop may know what official department policy is, but he or she also knows the most efficient way to get a job done. By the time they become streetwise, rookie officers will know just how acceptable various informal means of accomplishing the job will be to other officers. The police subculture creates few real mavericks, but it also produces few officers who view their jobs exclusively in terms of public mandates and official dictums.

> To introduce and implement new police ideas is not easy, but it is possible. More than that, it is essential if we are to achieve elementary public safety in American cities and confidence in the police by those who are being policed.
>
> —Jerome H. Skolnick and David H. Bayley[iv]

[Policing a Multicultural Society]

Members of some culturally diverse groups have backgrounds, values, and perspectives that, while not directly supportive of lawbreaking, contrast sharply with those of many police officials. Robert M. Shustra, a well-known writer on multicultural law enforcement, says that police officers "need to recognize the fact of poor police-minority relations historically, including *unequal* treatment under the law."[1] Moreover, says Shustra, "many officers and citizens are defensive with each other because their contact is tinged with negative historical 'baggage.'"

In other words, even though discrimination in the enforcement of the criminal law may not be commonplace today, it *was* in the past—and perceptions built upon past experience are often difficult to change. Moreover, if the function of law enforcement is to "protect and serve" law-abiding citizens from all backgrounds, then it becomes vital for officers to understand and respect differences in habits, customs, beliefs, patterns of thought, and traditions.[2] Hence, as Shustra says, "The acts of approaching, communicating, questioning, assisting, and establishing trust with members of different groups require special knowledge and skills that have nothing to do with the fact that 'the law is the law' and must be enforced equally. Acquiring sensitivity, knowledge, and skills leads to [an increased appreciation for the position of others] that will contribute to improved communications with members of all groups."[3]

How can police officers acquire greater sensitivity to the issues involved in policing a diverse multicultural society? Some researchers suggest that law enforcement officers of *all* backgrounds begin by exploring their own prejudices. Prejudices, which are judgments or opinions formed before facts are known and which usually involve negative or unfavorable thoughts about groups of people, can lead to discrimination. Hence, most citizens, including police officers, should

be able to reduce their tendency to discriminate against those who are different by exploring and uprooting their own personal prejudices.

One technique for identifying prejudices is cultural awareness training. As practiced in some police departments today, cultural awareness training explores the impact of culture on human behavior—and especially law-breaking behavior. Cultural awareness training generally involves four stages:[4]

- *Clarifying the relationship between cultural awareness and police professionalism.* As Shustra explains it, "The more professional a peace officer is, the more sophisticated he or she is in responding to people of all backgrounds and the more successful he or she is in cross-cultural contact."[5]
- *Recognizing personal prejudices.* In the second stage of cultural awareness training, participating officers are asked to recognize and identify their own personal prejudices and biases. Once prejudices have been identified, trainers strive to show how they can affect daily behavior.
- *Acquiring sensitivity to police-community relations.* In this stage of training, participating officers learn about historical and existing community perceptions of the police. Training can often be enhanced through the use of carefully chosen and well-qualified guest speakers or participants from minority communities.
- *Developing interpersonal relations skills.* The goal of this last stage of training is to assist with the development of positive verbal and nonverbal communications skills necessary for successful interaction with community members. Many trainers believe that basic skills training will result in the continuing development of such skills because officers will quickly begin to see the benefits (in terms of lessened interpersonal conflict) of effective interpersonal skills.

[1]Robert M. Shusta et al., *Multicultural Law Enforcement: Strategies for Peacekeeping in a Diverse Society*, 2d ed. (Upper Saddle River, N.J.: Prentice Hall, 2002), p. 4.
[2]Ibid., p. 16.
[3]Ibid., p. 4.
[4]Ibid., pp. 104–106.
[5]Ibid., p. 4.

police working personality

All aspects of the traditional values and patterns of behavior evidenced by police officers who have been effectively socialized into the police subculture. Characteristics of the police personality often extend to the personal lives of law enforcement personnel.

Skolnick says that the **police working personality** has at least six recognizable characteristics. Additional writers have identified others.[64] Taken in concert, they create the picture of the police personality shown in Table 6–2.

Some components of the police working personality are essential for survival and effectiveness. Officers are exposed daily to situations which are charged with emotions and can be potentially threatening. The need to quickly gain control over belligerent people leads to the development of authoritarian strategies for handling people. Eventually, such strategies become second nature, and the cornerstone of the police personality is firmly set. Cynicism evolves from a constant flow of experiences which demonstrate that people and events are not always what they seem to be. The natural tendency of most suspects, even when they are clearly guilty in the eyes of the police, is denial. Repeated attempts to mislead the police in the performance of their duty creates suspicion and cynicism in the minds of most officers.

The police personality has at least two sources. On the one hand, some aspects of the worldview that comprises that personality can be attributed to the socialization which occurs

THE POLICE PERSONALITY			TABLE 6–2
Authoritarian	Cynical	Conservative	Dogmatic
Suspicious	Hostile	Individualistic	
Insecure	Loyal	Efficient	
Honorable	Secret	Prejudiced	

when rookie officers are inducted into police ranks. On the other, it may be that components of the police personality already exist in some individuals and lead them into police work.[65] Supporting the latter view are studies which indicate that police officers who come from conservative backgrounds view themselves as defenders of middle-class morality.[66]

Socialization into police subculture appears to be an ongoing process. The term *police subculture* was defined earlier in this chapter. It can also be thought of as "the set of informal values which characterize the police force as a distinct community with a common identity."[67] Police subculture exists because it eases the life of working police officers. Police subculture is more concerned with the "way one actually gets things done,"[68] than with official policies, administrative procedures, or even laws. In what some may find surprising, police subculture appears to be relatively homogeneous throughout many parts of the world. A study of police subculture in South Africa, for example, found "seven key elements," including "a sense of 'mission'; a combination of suspicion and paranoia; representation of the police as a separate community; resistance to change; a gender-based chauvinism which reinforces the belief in force as a means of problem solving; bigoted views about black people and women; and an emphasis on realism and pragmatism above respect for the law."[69] Similar elements have been reported by researchers who have examined police subculture in the United States. Researchers have concluded that like all cultures, police subculture may change over time but that it is a relatively stable collection of beliefs and values that is unlikely to change from within. Police subculture may, however, be changed through external pressures, such as new hiring practices, investigations into police corruption or misuse of authority, and commission reports that create pressures for police reform.[70]

Corruption and Integrity

The police role carries both power and authority. Officers are expected to act fairly and to exercise a well-informed discretion in all of their activities. The combination of power, authority, and discretion in police work produces great potential for abuse.

Police corruption has been a problem in American society since the early days of policing. It is probably an ancient and natural tendency of human beings to attempt to placate or "win over" those in positions of authority over them. This tendency is complicated in today's materialistic society by greed and by the personal and financial benefits to be derived from evading the law. The temptations toward illegality offered to police range all the way from a free cup of coffee given by a small restaurant owner in the thought that one day it may be necessary to call upon the goodwill of the officer, perhaps for something as simple as a traffic ticket, to huge monetary bribes arranged by drug dealers to guarantee that the police will look the other way as an important shipment of contraband arrives. As noted criminologist Carl B. Klockars says, policing, by its very nature, "is an occupation that is rife with opportunities for misconduct. Policing is a highly discretionary, coercive activity that routinely takes place in private settings, out of the sight of supervisors, and in the presence of witnesses who are often regarded as unreliable."[71]

The effects of **police corruption** can be far-reaching. As Michael Palmiotto of Wichita State University notes, "Not only does misconduct committed by an officer personally affect that officer, it also affects the community, the police department that employs the officer and every police department and police officer in America. Frequently, negative police actions caused by inappropriate police behavior reach every corner of the nation, and at times, the world."[72]

Ethicists say that police corruption ranges from minor offenses to serious violations of the law. Exactly what constitutes corruption, however, is not always clear. In recognition of what some have called corruption's "slippery slope,"[73] most police departments now explicitly prohibit even the acceptance of minor gratuities. The slippery slope perspective holds

police corruption

The abuse of police authority for personal or organizational gain.[v]

The Los Angeles Police Department's Rampart Station office, where a corruption scandal occurred in 2000 and 2001. A number of officers assigned to the Rampart division were investigated on charges ranging from falsifying evidence to the theft and sale of illegal drugs. In what some call "the biggest police scandal case in Los Angeles history," many cases against criminal defendants had to be dismissed.

David McNew, Newsmakers, Liason, Getty Images, Inc.

> Nearly all men can stand adversity, but if you want to test a man's character, give him power.
>
> —Abraham Lincoln[vi]

Knapp Commission

A committee that investigated police corruption in New York City in the early 1970s.

that even small thank-you's which are accepted from members of the public can lead to a more ready acceptance of larger bribes. An officer who begins to accept, and then expect, gratuities may soon find that his or her practice of policing becomes influenced by such gifts and that larger ones soon follow. At that point, the officer may easily slide to the bottom of the moral slope, which was made slippery by previous small concessions.

Another useful distinction is made by Thomas Barker and David Carter, who distinguish between "occupational deviance" and "abuse of authority."[74] Occupational deviance, they say, is motivated by the desire for personal benefit. Abuse of authority, however, occurs most often to further the organizational goals of law enforcement, including arrest, ticketing, and the successful conviction of suspects.

FBI Special Agent Frank Perry, former chief of the bureau's ethics unit, distinguishes between police deviance and police corruption.[75] Although Perry doesn't define the term *police deviance*, he says that the concept is useful because it "best captures the nature of the precursory signs of corruption, as opposed to actual corruption."[76] Police deviance, according to Perry, is a precursor of individual and organizational corruption. It may eventually lead to outright corruption unless police supervisors and internal affairs units are alert to the warning signs and actively intervene to prevent corruption from developing. Perry says that police deviance consists of "unprofessional on- and off-duty misconduct, isolated instances of misuse of position, improper relationships with informants or criminals, sexual harassment, disparaging racial or sexual comments, embellished/falsified reporting, time and attendance abuse, insubordination, nepotism, cronyism, and non-criminal unauthorized disclosure of information."[77]

Examples of police corruption, ranked in what this author judges to be an increasing level of severity, are shown in Figure 6–1. Not everyone would agree with this ranking. For example, a survey of 6,982 New York City police officers found that 65% did not classify excessive force as corrupt behavior.[78] Likewise, 71% of responding officers said that accepting a free meal is not a corrupt practice. Another 15% said that personal use of illegal drugs by law enforcement officers should not be considered corruption.

In the early 1970s, Frank Serpico made headlines as he testified before the **Knapp Commission** on police corruption in New York City.[79] Serpico, an undercover operative within the police department, revealed a complex web of corruption in which money and services routinely changed hands in "protection rackets" created by unethical officers. The Knapp Commission report distinguished between two types of corrupt officers, which they termed "grass eaters" and "meat eaters."[80] "Grass eating," the most common form of police corruption, was described as illegitimate activity which occurs from time to time in the normal course of police work. It involves mostly small bribes or relatively minor services

FIGURE 6-1

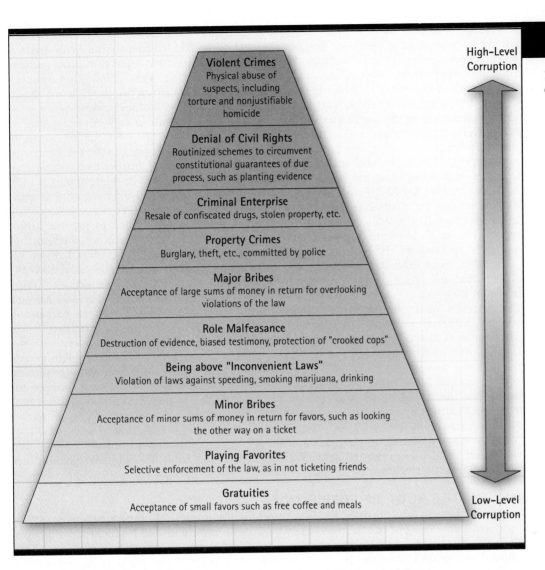

High-Level
Corruption

Low-Level
Corruption

Types and examples of police corruption.

offered by citizens seeking to avoid arrest and prosecution. "Meat eating" is a much more serious form of corruption, involving as it does the active seeking of illicit money-making opportunities by officers. Meat eaters solicit bribes through threat or intimidation, whereas grass eaters make the simpler mistake of not refusing bribes which are offered.

In 1993, during 11 days of corruption hearings reminiscent of the Knapp Commission era, a parade of crooked New York police officers testified before a commission headed by former judge and deputy mayor Milton Mollen. Among the many revelations, officers spoke of dealing drugs, stealing confiscated drug funds, stifling investigations, and beating innocent people. Officer Michael Dowd, for example, told the commission that he had run a cocaine ring out of his station house in Brooklyn and had bought three homes on Long Island and a Corvette with the money he made. Most shocking of all, however, were allegations that high-level police officials attempted to hide embarrassing incidents in a "phantom file" and that many officials may have condoned unprofessional and even criminal practices by the officers under their command. Honest officers, including internal affairs investigators, described how their efforts to end corruption among their fellows had been defused and resisted by higher authorities.

Some experts say that the New York City Police Department actually has corruption under better control than most other large-city departments and that the few cases of corruption identified by the Mollen Commission were trivial relative to the size of the department. Even so, the hearings did seem to show that corruption is nearly impossible to stamp out completely and that it reemerges with each new generation of officers.

Corruption, of course, is not unique to New York. In mid-2000, for example, the Los Angeles Police Department became embroiled in a far-reaching corruption scandal centered around the antigang unit of the department's Rampart Subdivision.[81] Many of the unit's officers were accused of operating like a criminal organization in order to frame hundreds of people through threats and beatings, by planting evidence, and by committing perjury. They and other officers were alleged to be running a drug ring, while eliminating competition from civilian dealers by framing them and seeing them sent to prison.[82] Seven shootings and at least two killings, said to be perpetrated by police officers, were among the illegal activities allegedly committed by officers. The scandal came to light after Los Angeles Police Department (LAPD) officer Rafael Perez was caught stealing $1 million worth of cocaine from an evidence room. In exchange for an offer of leniency, Perez turned informant and cooperated with prosecutors. Perez, who was also accused of murder by a former girlfriend, provided investigators with details about ongoing corruption in the Rampart area.[83] As events unfolded, LAPD Police Chief Bernard Parks was accused by prosecutors of withholding critical information needed to build a case against the accused officers. According to prosecutors, the LAPD, under the direction of Chief Parks, "failed to provide arrest reports, witness statements and background information." The prosecutors claimed that "on several occasions, the LAPD . . . actually hindered the progress of the investigation."[84]

By 2001, more than 100 falsely obtained convictions had been thrown out, and 20 LAPD officers had left active duty. Another three officers were convicted of conspiring to frame innocent people and are facing sentencing as this book goes to press.[85] The Los Angeles City Attorney agreed to pay $10.9 million to settle lawsuits stemming from the corruption scandal, although pending cases may eventually raise that figure to $125 million.[86] The department is now operating under a consent decree, a legally binding agreement with the U.S. Department of Justice, that calls for major reforms within the LAPD. The decree requires the department to install a computer system to track complaints and disciplinary actions against LAPD officers; to collect data on the racial makeup of citizens stopped for traffic violations; and to create a special unit within the department to investigate shootings and beatings by police officers to determine whether excess force was used.[87] Rafael Perez, sentenced to five years in prison, warned young officers as he was sentenced that "whoever chases monsters must see that he not become a monster himself."[88] Repercussions and continuing criminal and civil trials resulting from the Rampart scandal are expected to last for years.

MONEY—THE ROOT OF POLICE EVIL?

The police personality provides fertile ground for the growth of corrupt practices. Police "cynicism" develops out of continued association with criminals and problem-laden people. The cop who is "streetwise" is also ripe for corrupt influences to take root. Years ago, Edwin Sutherland applied the concept of differential association to the study of deviant behavior.[89] You may recall from our discussion in Chapter 3 in connection with the causes of crime that Sutherland suggested that frequent, continued association with one type of person would make the associates similar.

Of course, Sutherland was talking about criminals, not police officers. Consider, however, the dilemma of the average officer: A typical day is spent running down petty thieves, issuing traffic citations to citizens who try to talk their way out of a ticket, dealing with prostitutes who feel hassled by the police presence, and arresting drug users who think it should be their right to do what they want as long as it "doesn't hurt anyone." The officer encounters personal hostility and experiences a constant, and often quite vocal, rejection of society's formalized norms. Bring into this environment low pay and the resulting sense that police work is not really valued, and it is easy to understand how an officer might develop a jaded attitude about the double standards of the civilization he or she is sworn to protect.

In fact, low pay may be a critical ingredient of the corruption mix. Salaries paid to police officers in this country have been notoriously low when compared to that of other professions involving personal dedication, extensive training, high stress, and the risk of bodily harm. As police professionalism increases, many police administrators hope that salaries will rise. No matter how much police pay grows, however, it will never be able to compete with the staggering amounts of money to be made through dealing in contraband.

Working hand in hand with monetary pressures toward corruption are the moral dilemmas produced by unenforceable laws which provide the basis for criminal profit. During the Prohibition era, the Wickersham Commission warned of the potential for official corruption inherent in the legislative taboos on alcohol. The immense demand for drink called into question the wisdom of the law while simultaneously providing vast resources

> It is practically an article of faith among young, black males that they are more likely than whites to be stopped, frisked, spread-eagled, and arrested by the police, often on the flimsiest of charges.
>
> —Hutchinson Report, July 2001

designed to circumvent it. Today's drug scene bears some similarities to the Prohibition era. As long as many people are willing to make large financial and other sacrifices to feed the drug trade, the pressures on the police to embrace corruption will remain substantial.

BUILDING POLICE INTEGRITY

The difficulties of controlling corruption can be traced to several factors, including the reluctance of police officers to report corrupt activities by their fellow officers, the reluctance of police administrators to acknowledge the existence of corruption in their agencies, the benefits of corrupt transactions to the parties involved, and the lack of immediate victims willing to report corruption. High moral standards, however, embedded into the principles of the police profession and effectively communicated to individual officers through formal training and peer-group socialization, can raise the level of integrity in any department. There are, of course, many officers of great personal integrity who hold to the highest of professional ideals. There is evidence that law enforcement training programs are becoming increasingly concerned with instruction designed to reinforce the high ideals many recruits bring to police work. As one Federal Bureau of Investigation (FBI) article explains it, "Ethics training must become an integral part of academy and in-service training for new and experienced officers alike."[90]

Ethics training is part of a "reframing" strategy targeting police corruption that emphasizes *integrity.* In 1997, for example, the National Institute of Justice (NIJ) released a report entitled *Police Integrity: Public Service with Honor.*[91] The report, based upon recommendations made by participants in a national symposium on police integrity, suggested (1) integrating ethics training into the programs offered by newly funded Regional Community Policing Institutes throughout the country, (2) broadening research activities in the area of ethics through NIJ-awarded grants for research on police integrity, and (3) conducting case studies of departments that have an excellent track record in the area of police integrity.

The NIJ report was followed in 2001 by a U.S. Department of Justice document entitled *Principles for Promoting Police Integrity.*[92] The foreword states, "For community policing to be successful, and crime reduction efforts to be effective, citizens must have trust in the police. All of us must work together to address the problems of excessive use of force and racial profiling, and—equally important—the perceptions of many minority residents that law enforcement treats them unfairly, if we are to build the confidence in law enforcement necessary for continued progress. Our goal must be professional law enforcement that gives all citizens of our country the feeling that they are being treated fairly, equally and with respect." The report covered such topics as the use of force; complaints and misconduct investigations; accountability and effective management; training; nondiscriminatory policing; and recruitment, hiring, and retention. Read the full report, which provides examples of promising police practices and policies in support of increased integrity, at **Library Extra! 6–4** at cjtoday.com.

Most large law enforcement agencies have their own **internal affairs** divisions, which are empowered to investigate charges of wrongdoing made against officers. Where necessary, state police agencies may be called upon to examine reported incidents. Federal agencies, including the FBI and the Drug Enforcement Administration (DEA), involve themselves when corruption goes far enough to violate federal statutes. The U.S. Department of Justice (DOJ), through various investigative offices, has the authority to examine possible violations of civil rights which may result from the misuse of police authority. The DOJ is often supported in these endeavors by the American Civil Liberties Union, the National Association for the Advancement of Colored People (NAACP), and other watchdog groups.

DRUG TESTING OF POLICE EMPLOYEES

On November 17, 2000, the U.S. Court of Appeals for the Fourth Circuit, found that the chief of police in Westminster, Maryland, had acted properly in asking a doctor to test an officer's urine for the presence of heroin without the officer's knowledge.[93] Westminster police officer Eric Carroll had gone to the local hospital complaining of tightness in his chest and fatigue. The doctor who examined him diagnosed Carroll as suffering from high blood pressure. Carroll was placed on a disability leave for three days. While Carroll was gone the police chief received a call from someone who said that Carroll was using heroin. The chief verified the caller's identity, then called the department doctor and asked him to test Carroll for drugs—but directed that Carroll not be informed of the test. When Carroll returned to the physician for a follow-up visit, the doctor took a urine sample, saying that

> We must strive to eliminate any racial, ethnic, or cultural bias that may exist among our ranks.
>
> —Sherman Block,
> Los Angeles County Sheriff

internal affairs

The branch of a police organization tasked with investigating charges of wrongdoing involving members of the department.

it was to test for the presence of blood. Although no blood was found in Carroll's urine, it did test positive for heroin. As a consequence, Officer Carroll's employment with the department was terminated. He then sued in federal court alleging conspiracy, defamation, and violations of his constitutional rights. The Fourth Circuit Court of Appeals, however, determined that the chief's actions were reasonable because, among other things, Carroll had signed a pre-employment waiver that permitted the department to conduct drug tests at any time, with or without cause.[94]

The widespread potential for police corruption created by illicit drugs has led to focused efforts to combat drug use by officers. Drug-testing programs in local police departments are an example of such efforts. In 1986, when concern was at its highest, the National Institute of Justice conducted a telephone survey of 33 large police departments across the nation to determine what measures were being taken to identify officers and civilian employees who were using drugs.[95] The NIJ learned that almost all departments had written procedures to test employees who were reasonably suspected of drug abuse. Applicants for police positions were being tested by 73% of the departments surveyed, and 21% of the departments were actively considering testing all officers. In what some people found a surprisingly low figure, 21% reported that they might offer treatment to identified violators rather than dismiss them, depending upon their personal circumstances.

The International Association of Chiefs of Police makes available to police managers a Model Drug Testing Policy. The policy, designed to meet the needs of local departments, suggests the following:[96]

- Testing all applicants and recruits for drug or narcotics use

- Testing current employees when performance difficulties or documentation indicate a potential drug problem

- Testing current employees when they are involved in the use of excessive force or suffer or cause on-duty injury

- Routine testing of all employees assigned to special "high-risk" areas, such as narcotics and vice

The courts have supported drug testing based upon a reasonable suspicion that drug abuse has been or is occurring (*Maurice Turner* v. *Fraternal Order of Police,* 1985),[97] although random testing of officers was banned by the New York State Supreme Court in the case of *Philip Caruso, President of P.B.A.* v. *Benjamin Ward, Police Commissioner* (1986).[98] Citing overriding public interests, a 1989 decision by the U.S. Supreme Court upheld the testing of U.S. Customs personnel applying for transfer into positions involving drug-law enforcement or carrying a firearm.[99] Many legal issues surrounding employee drug testing, however, remain to be resolved in court.

Complicating the situation is the fact that drug and alcohol addictions are "handicaps" protected by the Federal Rehabilitation Act of 1973. As such, federal law enforcement employees, as well as those working for agencies with federal contracts, are entitled to counseling and treatment before action toward termination can be taken.

The issue of employee drug testing in police departments, as in many other agencies, is a sensitive one. Some claim that existing tests for drug use are inaccurate, yielding a significant number of "false positives." Repeated testing and high threshold levels for narcotic substances in the blood may eliminate many of these concerns. Less easy to address, however, is the belief that drug testing intrudes upon the personal rights and professional dignity of individual employees.

Learn more about corruption and the continuing drive toward police integrity with **Library Extras! 6–5** and **6–6** at cjtoday.com.

The Dangers of Police Work

On October 15, 1991, the National Law Enforcement Officers' Memorial was unveiled in Washington, D.C. The memorial contained the names of 12,561 law enforcement officers killed in the line of duty, including U.S. Marshals Service Officer Robert Forsyth, who in 1794 became the nation's first law enforcement officer ever killed. Nearly 2,500 names have been added since opening day.[100] At the memorial, an interactive video system provides visitors with brief biographies and photographs of officers who have died. Tour the memorial by visiting **WebExtra! 6–3** at cjtoday.com.

As the memorial shows, police work is, by its very nature, dangerous. Although many officers never once fire their weapons in the line of duty, it is also plain that some officers

meet death while performing their jobs. On-the-job police deaths occur from stress, training accidents, and auto crashes. However, it is violent death at the hands of criminal offenders that police officers and their families fear most.

VIOLENCE IN THE LINE OF DUTY

In February 1997, two heavily armed men bungled a daytime bank robbery attempt in North Hollywood, California. The men were wearing full body armor and carrying automatic weapons. LAPD Lieutenant Greg Meyer described the scene this way: "Imagine yourself working uniformed patrol at 9:15 A.M. on a warm sunny day and you suddenly find yourself in Beirut, Bosnia, or back in the Mekong Delta. You go from thinking about where you'll stop for that next cup of coffee, to having your black-and-white shot up with full-automatic AK-47 rounds. Within the next few minutes, officers and civilians all about you are shot down in the street by bank robbers who look like Ninja Turtles dressed to kill. And unlike the usual 'gunbattle' that lasts a few seconds, this time the shooting just keeps going, and going, and going."[101]

The robbers didn't run when police arrived; instead, they stood their ground and fired bursts of armor-piercing rounds from 100-clip magazines. Covered from head to toe in full body armor, the men took numerous hits from police small-arms fire without seeming to notice. Detective Gordon Hagge, one of the first officers on the scene of the shoot-out, later told reporters for the *Los Angeles Times* that he started thinking, "I'm in the wrong place with the wrong gun."[102] Then reality set in, said Meyer, and officers soon realized that they had "brought cap guns to World War III."[103]

Courageous officers succeeded in blocking the robbers' escape route long enough for the LAPD SWAT team's armored personnel carrier to arrive. Both would-be robbers, Larry Eugene Philips, Jr., and Emil Mataasarenanu, were finally killed in the massive exchange of gunfire that ensued. The firefight lasted nearly 20 minutes and was televised by a news helicopter hovering over the scene. By the time the incident ended, 18 civilians and officers had been injured.[104]

Although running gun battles are a relative rarity in police work, they appear to be occurring with greater regularity. Unlike the North Hollywood incident, however, most officers who are shot are killed by lone suspects armed with a single weapon. In 2001, for example, 35-year-old Whitehall (Ohio) Police Officer Terry McDowell was shot and killed as he and his partner attempted to serve a traffic citation.[105] Earlier that day, a woman had driven to the police station to pick up her husband, who had been arrested on a charge of driving under the influence. When officers discovered that she did not have a driver's license, the woman and her intoxicated husband were told that they would have to walk home.

A short time later, McDowell and his partner arrived at the woman's home. As the officers knocked on the door, the woman's husband fired a .357-caliber handgun through the door without warning. The bullet struck McDowell in the chest above his bulletproof vest. The husband then immediately fired a second time, striking McDowell's partner in the face, seriously wounding him. As the injured officer retreated and called for assistance, the suspect stood over McDowell's body and shot him several more times. The suspect then walked to the backyard of his home, where he committed suicide after backup officers arrived. The weapon used by the suspect was later found to have been stolen from a neighbor who had been murdered. Officer McDowell had been with the Whitehall Police Department for 12 years and was survived by his wife and two children.

In 2000, 150 American law enforcement officers were killed in the line of duty.[106] Figure 6–2 shows the number of officers killed in different types of incidents. Although the statistics on the number of officers killed in 2001 are still being compiled as this book goes to press, the new category of "Terrorist Attack" will be included in official compilations. Initial figures show that in 2001, 71 officers were killed by terrorist attacks, bringing the total number of officers killed in the line of duty for that year to well over 200.[107] All of the police officers who fell victim to terrorism in 2001 were killed in the September 11 attacks on the World Trade Center.

A study by the FBI found that slain officers appeared to be good-natured and conservative in the use of physical force, "as compared to other law enforcement officers in similar situations. They were also perceived as being well-liked by the community and the department, friendly to everyone, laid back, and easy going."[108] Finally, the study, which was published before the September 11, 2001, terrorist attacks, also found that most officers who were killed failed to wear protective vests.

For statistics on police killings to have meaning beyond the personal tragedy they entail, however, it is necessary to place them within a larger framework. As Chapter 5 notes, there are approximately 730,000 state and local police employees in this country[109] and another 88,000 federal agents nationwide.[110] Such numbers demonstrate that the rate of violent death among law enforcement officers in the line of duty is small indeed.

RISK OF DISEASE AND INFECTED EVIDENCE

Not all of the dangers facing law enforcement officers are as direct as outright violence and assault. The increasing incidence of serious diseases capable of being transmitted by blood and other bodily fluids, combined with the fact that crime and accident scenes are inherently dangerous, has made *caution* a necessary byword among investigators and "first on the scene" officers. The potential for minor cuts and abrasions abounds in the broken glass and torn metal of a wrecked car, in the sharp edges of knives found at the scene of an assault or murder, and in drug implements like razor blades and hypodermic needles secreted in vehicles, homes, and pockets. Such minor injuries, previously shrugged off by many police personnel, have become a focal point for warnings about the dangers of

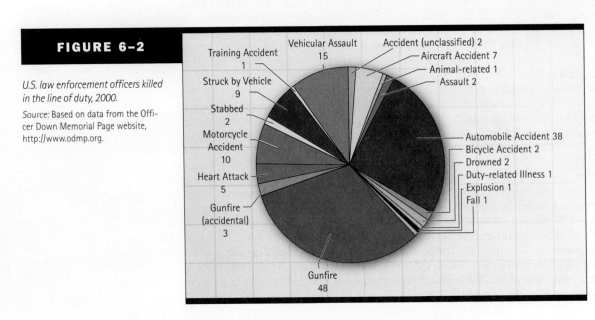

FIGURE 6–2

U.S. law enforcement officers killed in the line of duty, 2000.

Source: Based on data from the Officer Down Memorial Page website, http://www.odmp.org.

Training Accident 1
Vehicular Assault 15
Accident (unclassified) 2
Aircraft Accident 7
Animal-related 1
Assault 2
Struck by Vehicle 9
Stabbed 2
Motorcycle Accident 10
Heart Attack 5
Gunfire (accidental) 3
Automobile Accident 38
Bicycle Accident 2
Drowned 2
Duty-related Illness 1
Explosion 1
Fall 1
Gunfire 48

acquired immunodeficiency syndrome (AIDS), hepatitis B, tuberculosis, and other diseases spread through contact with infected blood.

In 1988, in Sonoma County, California, Sheriff Dick Michaelson became the first law enforcement supervisor to announce a clear-cut case of AIDS infection in an officer caused by interaction with a suspect. A deputy in Michaelson's department apparently contracted AIDS a few years earlier when he was pricked by a hypodermic needle during a pat-down search.[111]

Understandably, there is much concern among officers as to how to deal with the threat of AIDS and other bloodborne diseases. However, as a publication of the New York City Police Department reminds its officers, "Police officers have a professional responsibility to render assistance to those who are in need of our services. We cannot refuse to help. Persons with infectious diseases must be treated with the care and dignity we show all citizens."[112]

The FBI has also become concerned with the use of breath alcohol instruments on infected persons, the handling of evidence of all types, seemingly innocuous implements such as staples, the emergency delivery of babies in squad cars, and the risk of attack (especially bites) by infected individuals who are being questioned or who are in custody. The following are among the 16 recommendations made by the FBI as "defenses against exposure" to infectious substances (others are listed in Table 6–3):[113]

1. The first line of defense against infection at the crime scene is protecting your hands and keeping them away from your eyes, mouth, and nose.
2. If you have a cut, an abrasion, or any other break in the skin on your hands, do not handle blood or other body fluids without protection.
3. Use gloves, and replace them whenever you leave the crime scene. Wash hands thoroughly.
4. Never smoke, eat, drink, or apply makeup at the crime scene.

AIDS-RELATED LAW ENFORCEMENT CONCERNS	**TABLE 6-3**

Concern	Precaution and Response
Human bites	Person who bites usually receives the victim's blood; viral transmission through saliva is highly unlikely. If bitten by anyone, milk wound to make it bleed, wash the area thoroughly, and seek medical attention.
Spitting	Viral transmission through saliva is highly unlikely.
Urine/feces	Virus isolated in only very low concentrations in urine, not at all in feces. No cases of AIDS or AIDS-virus infection associated with either urine or feces.
Cuts/puncture wounds	Use caution in handling sharp objects and searching areas hidden from view. Needle-stick studies show risk of infection is very low.
CPR/first aid	To eliminate the already minimal risk associated with CPR, use masks/air ways. Avoid blood-to-blood contact by keeping open wounds covered and wearing gloves when in contact with bleeding wounds.
Body removal	Observe crime-scene rules; do not touch anything. Those who must come into contact with blood or other bodily fluids should wear gloves.
Casual contact	No cases of AIDS or AIDS-virus infection attributed to casual contact.
Any contact with blood or body fluids	Wear gloves if contact with blood or body fluids is considered likely. If contact occurs, wash thoroughly with soap and water; clean up spills with one part water to nine parts household bleach.
Contact with dried blood	No cases of infection have been traced to exposure to dried blood. The drying process itself appears to inactivate the virus. Despite low risk, however, caution dictates wearing gloves, a mask, and protective shoe coverings if exposure to dried blood particles is likely (for example, crime-scene investigation).

Source: Massachusetts Administrative Office of the Trial Court, *Personnel Policies and Procedures Manual,* Section 24.000 ("Statement of Policy and Procedures on AIDS"). Web posted at http://www.state.ma.us/courts/admin/hr/tableofcontents.html. Accessed January 5, 2002.

5. Use the utmost care when handling knives, razors, broken glass, nails, and the like to prevent a puncture of the skin.

6. If a puncture of the skin does occur, cleanse it thoroughly with rubbing alcohol, and wash with soap and water. Then seek immediate medical assistance.

7. When possible, use disposable items at the crime scene, such as pencils, gloves, and throwaway masks. These items should be incinerated after use.

8. Decontaminate nondisposable items, such as cameras and notebooks, using bleach mixed with water.

The National Institute of Justice adds to this list the recommendations that suspects should be asked to empty their own pockets when possible and that a puncture wound should be "milked," as in the case of a snakebite, to help flush infectious agents from the wound.[114]

To better combat the threat of infectious diseases among public-safety employees and health-care professionals, the federal Bloodborne Pathogens Act of 1991[115] requires that police officers receive proper training in how to prevent contamination by bloodborne infectious agents. The act also requires that police officers undergo an annual refresher course on the topic.

Police departments will face an increasing number of legal challenges in the years to come in cases involving infectious diseases like AIDS. Some predictable areas of concern will involve (1) the need to educate officers and other police employees relative to AIDS and other serious infectious diseases, (2) the responsibility of police departments to prevent the spread of AIDS in police lockups, and (3) the necessity of effective and nondiscriminatory enforcement activities and life-saving measures by police officers in AIDS environments. With regard to nondiscriminatory activities, the National Institute of Justice has suggested that legal claims in support of an officer's refusal to render assistance to people with AIDS would probably not be effective in court.[116] The reason is twofold: The officer has a basic duty to render assistance to individuals in need of it, and the possibility of AIDS transmission by casual contact has been scientifically established as extremely remote. A final issue of growing concern involves activities by police officers infected with the AIDS virus. Few statistics are currently available on the number of officers with AIDS, but public reaction to those officers may be a developing problem which police managers will soon need to address.

STRESS AND FATIGUE AMONG POLICE OFFICERS

Perhaps the most insidious and least visible of all threats facing law enforcement personnel today is debilitating stress. While some degree of stress can be a positive motivator, serious stress, over long periods of time, is generally regarded as destructive, even life threatening. For example, police detectives who worked around the clock in 1994 searching for two missing South Carolina boys whose mother first reported them as kidnapped found the case especially stressful since it brought to mind many emotions. "I feel like I aged 10 years in 10 days," said Union County Sheriff Howard Wells, after Susan Smith confessed to her sons' murders.[117]

Stress is a natural component of police work.[118] The American Institute of Stress, based in Yonkers, New York, ranks policing among the top ten stress-producing jobs in the country.[119] Danger, frustration, paperwork, the daily demands of the job, and a lack of understanding from family members and friends contribute to the negative stress officers experience. The Bureau of Justice Statistics points out that "exposure to violence, suffering, and death is inherent to the profession of the law enforcement officer. There are other sources of stress as well. Officers who deal with offenders on a daily basis may view some sentences as too lenient; they may perceive the public's opinion of police performance to be unfavorable; they often are required to work mandatory, rotating shifts; and they may not have enough time to spend with their families. Police officers also face unusual, often highly disturbing, situations, such as dealing with a child homicide victim or the survivors of vehicle crashes."[120]

Some of the stressors in police work are particularly destructive. One is frustration brought on by the inability to be effective, regardless of the amount of personal effort expended. From the point of view of the individual officer, the police mandate is to bring about some change in society for the better. The crux of police work involves making arrests based upon thorough investigations which lead to convictions and the removal of individuals who are damaging to the social fabric of the community—all under the umbrella of the criminal law. Unfortunately, reality is often far from the ideal. Arrests may not lead to convictions. Evidence which is available to the officer may not be allowed in court. Sentences which are imposed may seem too "light" to the arresting officer. The feelings of powerlessness and frustration which come from seeing repeat offenders back on the streets and from witnessing numerous injustices worked upon seemingly innocent victims may greatly stress police officers and cause them to question the purpose of their professional lives. It may also lead to desperate attempts to find relief. As one researcher observes, "The suicide rate of police officers is more than twice that of the general population."[121]

Another source of stress—that of living with constant danger—is incomprehensible to most of us, even to the family members of many officers. As one officer says, "I kick in a door and I've gotta talk some guy into putting a gun down. . . . And I go home, and my wife's upset because the lawn isn't cut and the kids have been bad. Now, to her that's a real problem."[122]

Stress is not unique to the police profession, but because of the "macho" attitude that has traditionally been associated with police work, denial of the stress may be found more often among police officers than in other occupational groups. Certain types of individuals are probably more susceptible to the negative effects of stress than are others. The type A personality, popularized thirty years ago, is most likely to perceive life in terms of pressure and performance. Type B people are more laid back and less likely to suffer from the negative effects of stress. Police ranks, drawn as they are from the general population, are filled with both stress-sensitive and stress-resistant personalities.

Stress Reduction It is natural to try to reduce and control stress.[123] Humor helps, even if it's somewhat cynical. Health-care professionals, for example, are noted for their ability to joke around patients who are seriously ill or even dying. Police officers may similarly use humor to defuse their reactions to dark or threatening situations. Keeping an emotional distance from stressful events is another way of coping with them, although such distance is not always easy to maintain. Police officers who have had to deal with serious cases of child abuse have often reported on the emotional turmoil they experienced as a consequence of what they saw.

The support of family and friends can be crucial in developing other strategies for handling stress. Exercise, meditation, abdominal breathing, biofeedback, self-hypnosis, guided imaging, induced relaxation, subliminal conditioning, music, prayer, and diet have all been cited as useful techniques for stress reduction. Devices to measure stress levels are available in the form of handheld heart-rate monitors, blood pressure devices, "biodots" (which change color according to the amount of blood flow in the extremities), and psychological inventories.

A new approach to dealing with stress among police officers holds that the amount of stress an officer experiences is directly related to his or her reactions to potentially stressful situations.[124] Officers who can filter out extraneous stimuli and who can distinguish between truly threatening situations and those that are benign are much less likely to report job-related stressors than those lacking these abilities. Because stress-filtering abilities are often closely linked to innate personality characteristics, some researchers suggest careful psychological screening of police applicants to better identify those who have a natural ability to cope with situations that others might perceive as stressful.[125]

The family members of police officers often report feelings of stress that are directly related to the officer's work. The Bureau of Justice Statistics has identified six important sources of family stress: (1) shift work and overtime, (2) concern over the officer's inability or unwillingness to express feelings at home; (3) fear that the spouse will be killed in the line of duty, (4) presence of a gun in the home, (5) the officer's 24-hour role as a law enforcer; and (6) avoidance, teasing, or harassment of the officer's children by other children because of the parent's job.[126] In recent years, police departments nationwide have begun to realize that family problems and stress can negatively affect the quality of a police officer's work and the overall performance of police departments. As a result, some departments have developed innovative programs to allay family stress. The Collier County (Florida) Spousal Academy, for example, is a family support program that offers training to spouses and other domestic partners of deputies and recruits who are enrolled in the department's training academy. The ten-hour program deals directly with issues that are likely to produce stress and informs participants of department and community resources that are available to help them. Peer-support programs for spouses and life partners and for the adolescent children of officers are also beginning to operate nationwide. **Library Extra! 6–7** at cjtoday.com provides a comprehensive overview of issues related to police officer stress.

Officer Fatigue Like stress, fatigue can affect a police officer's performance. As criminologist Bryan Vila points out, "Tired, urban street cops are a national icon. Weary from overtime assignments, shift work, night school, endless hours spent waiting to testify, and the emotional and physical demands of the job, not to mention trying to patch together a family and social life during irregular islands of off-duty time, they fend off fatigue with coffee and hard-bitten humor."[127] Vila found levels of police officer fatigue to be six times as high as those of shift workers in industrial and mining jobs.[128] As Vila notes, few departments set work-hour standards, and fatigue associated with the pattern and length of work hours may be expected to contribute to police accidents, injuries, and misconduct. Vila suggests controlling the work hours of police officers, "just as we control the working hours of many other occupational groups."[129]

Police Civil Liability

In 1996, 51-year-old Richard Kelley filed suit in federal court against the Massachusetts State Police and the Weymouth (Massachusetts) Police Department.[130] The suit resulted from an incident during which, Kelley alleged, state troopers and Weymouth police officers treated him as a drunk, rather than recognizing that he had just suffered a stroke while driving. According to Kelley, following a minor traffic accident caused by the stroke, officers pulled him from his car, handcuffed him, dragged him along the ground, and ignored his pleas for help—forcing him to stay at a state police barracks for seven hours before taking him for medical treatment. Drunk-driving charges against Kelley were dropped after medical tests failed to reveal the presence of any intoxicating substances in his body.

> Citizens are coproducers of justice.
>
> —Bureau of Justice Statistics, Princeton Project

Civil suits brought against law enforcement personnel are of two types: state and federal. Suits brought in state courts have generally been the most common form of civil litigation involving police officers. In recent years, however, an increasing number of suits have been brought in federal courts on the basis of the legal rationale that the civil rights of the plaintiff, as guaranteed by federal law, have been denied.

COMMON SOURCES OF CIVIL SUITS

As the Kelley case demonstrates, police officers may become involved in a variety of situations which could result in civil suits against the officers, their superiors, and their departments. Major sources of police civil liability are listed in Table 6–4. Charles Swanson, an expert in police procedure, says that the most common source of lawsuits against the police involve "assault, battery, false imprisonment, and malicious prosecution."[131]

A female police recruit learning how to restrain a suspect without injuring him. Adequate training can offset claims of liability.

Bonnie Kamin, Comstock Images

MAJOR SOURCES OF POLICE CIVIL LIABILITY	TABLE 6-4

Failure to protect property in police custody
Negligence in the care of suspects in police custody
Failure to render proper emergency medical assistance
Failure to prevent a foreseeable crime
Failure to aid private citizens
Lack of due regard for the safety of others
False arrest
False imprisonment
Inappropriate use of deadly force
Unnecessary assault or battery
Malicious prosecution
Violations of constitutional rights
Patterns of unfair and inequitable treatment
Racial profiling

Of all complaints brought against the police, assault charges are the best known, being, as they are, subject to high media visibility. Less visible, but not uncommon, are civil suits charging the police with false arrest or false imprisonment. In the 1986 case of *Malley* v. *Briggs*,[132] the U.S. Supreme Court held that a police officer who effects an arrest or conducts a search on the basis of an improperly issued warrant may be liable for monetary damages when a reasonably well-trained officer, under the same circumstances, "would have known that his affidavit failed to establish probable cause and that he should not have applied for the warrant." Significantly, the Court ruled that an officer "cannot excuse his own default by pointing to the greater incompetence of the magistrate."[133] That is, the officer, rather than the judge who issued the warrant, is ultimately responsible for establishing the basis for pursuing the arrest or search.

When an officer makes an arrest without just cause, or simply impedes an individual's right to leave the scene without good reason, he or she may also be liable for the charge of false arrest. Officers who enjoy "throwing their weight around" are especially subject to this type of suit, grounded as it is on the abuse of police authority. Because employers may generally be sued for the negligent or malicious actions of their employees, many police departments are finding themselves named as codefendants in lawsuits today.

Negligent actions by officers also provide a basis for civil suits. High-speed chases are especially dangerous because of the potential for injury to innocent bystanders. Flashing blue or red lights (the color of police vehicle lights varies by state) legally only *request* the right-of-way on a highway; they do not demand it. Officers who drive in such a way as to place others in danger may find themselves the subject of suits. In the case of *Biscoe* v. *Arlington County* (1984),[134] for example, Alvin Biscoe was awarded $5 million after he lost both legs as a consequence of a high-speed chase while he was waiting to cross the street. Biscoe, an innocent bystander, was struck by a police car which went out of control. The officer driving the car had violated department policies prohibiting high-speed chases, and the court found that he had not been properly trained. Departments may protect themselves to some degree through training combined with regulations limiting the authority of their personnel. One year after the *Biscoe* case was decided, for example, a Louisiana police department was not held liable in an accident which occurred during a high-speed chase because of its policy limiting emergency driving to no more than 20 miles per hour over the posted speed limit and because officers were trained in that policy. The officer, who drove 75 mph in a 40-mph zone, was found to be negligent and was held liable for damages.[135]

Law enforcement supervisors may find themselves the object of lawsuits by virtue of the fact that they are responsible for the actions of their officers. If it can be shown that supervisors were negligent in hiring (as when someone with a history of alcoholism, mental problems, sexual deviance, or drug abuse is employed), or if supervisors failed in their responsibility to properly train officers before arming and deploying them, they may be found liable for damages.

WHAT WOULD YOU DO?

The CD-ROM scenario for Chapter 6 builds on concepts of sovereign immunity and police civil liability. It is derived from a real-life incident involving a police officer's high speed chase of a bank robbery suspect. The actual case eventually found its way to the U.S. Supreme Court, with unfavorable consequences for the on-the-scene officer and his department. Use the CD-ROM found in the back of your textbook to work through this scenario, and see if you can make better decisions than the responding officer did.

In the 1989 case of the *City of Canton, Ohio v. Harris*,[136] the U.S. Supreme Court ruled that a "failure to train" can become the basis for legal liability on the part of a municipality where the "failure to train amounts to deliberate indifference to the rights of persons with whom the police come in contact."[137] In that case, Geraldine Harris was arrested and taken to the Canton, Ohio, police station. While at the station she slumped to the floor several times. Officers decided to leave her on the floor and never called for qualified medical assistance. Upon release, Harris was taken by family members to a local hospital, where she was found to be suffering from several emotional ailments. Harris was hospitalized for a week and received follow-up outpatient treatment for the next year.

In the 1997 case of *Board of the County Commissioners of Bryan County, Oklahoma v. Brown*,[138] however, the Supreme Court ruled that to establish liability, plaintiffs must show that "the municipal action in question was not simply negligent, but was taken with 'deliberate indifference' as to its known or obvious consequences." In *Brown*, a deputy named Burns was hired by the sheriff of Bryan County, Oklahoma. Burns later used excessive force in arresting a woman, and the woman sued the county for damages, claiming that Deputy Burns had been hired in spite of his criminal record. In fact, some years earlier, Burns had pleaded guilty to various driving infractions and other misdemeanors, including assault and battery—a charge which resulted from a college fight. At trial, a spokesperson for the sheriff's department admitted to receiving Burns's driving and criminal records but said he had not reviewed either in detail before the decision to hire Burns was made. Nonetheless, the Supreme Court held that deliberate indifference on the part of the county had not been established because the plaintiff had not demonstrated that "Burns' background made his use of excessive force in making an arrest a plainly obvious consequence of the hiring decision." According to the Court, "Only where adequate scrutiny of the applicant's background would lead a reasonable policymaker to conclude that the plainly obvious consequence of the decision to hire the applicant would be the deprivation of a third party's federally protected right can the official's failure to adequately scrutinize the applicant's background constitute 'deliberate indifference.'" In other words, according to this decision, a municipality (in this case, a county) may not be held liable solely because it employs a person with an arrest record.

FEDERAL LAWSUITS

Civil suits alleging police misconduct that are filed in federal courts are often called **1983 lawsuits** because they are based upon Section 1983 of Title 42 of the U.S. Code—an act passed by Congress in 1871 to ensure the civil rights of men and women of all races. That act requires due process of law before any person can be deprived of life, liberty, or property and specifically provides redress for the denial of these constitutional rights by officials acting under color of state law. It reads as follows:

> Every person who, under color of any statute, ordinance, regulation, custom, or usage, of any State or Territory, subjects, or causes to be subjected, any citizen of the United States or other person within the jurisdiction thereof to the deprivation of any rights, privileges, or immunities secured by the Constitution and laws, shall be liable to the party injured in an action at law, suit in equity, or other proper proceeding for redress.[139]

A 1983 suit may be brought, for example, against officers who shoot suspects under questionable circumstances, thereby denying them their right to life without due process. Similarly, an officer who makes an arrest based on accusations that he or she knows to be untrue may be subject to a 1983 lawsuit.

Another type of liability action, this one directed specifically at federal officials or enforcement agents, is called a ***Bivens* action**. The case of *Bivens v. Six Unknown Federal Agents* (1971)[140] established a path for legal action against agents enforcing federal laws, which is similar to that found in a 1983 suit. *Bivens* actions may be addressed against individuals but not against the United States or its agencies.[141] Federal officers have generally been granted a court-created qualified immunity and have been protected from suits where they were found to have acted in the belief that their action was consistent with federal law.[142]

In the past, the doctrine of sovereign immunity barred legal actions against state and local governments. Sovereign immunity was a legal theory which held that a governing body could not be sued because it made the law and therefore could not be bound by it. Immunity is a much more complex issue today. Some states have officially abandoned any

CJ Today News

["De-policing" a Response to Community's Criticism]

CINCINNATI—Four months ago, riots broke out here for four days after a white police officer shot and killed an unarmed black man.

In a frenzy of community reaction, police were accused by politicians, the media and key black leaders of using excessive force—not just in that instance, but also in previous shootings. The federal government opened two civil rights investigations into allegations of racial bias in police practices, which police deny.

In response to the criticism, the police simply backed off. It's a practice known as "de-policing."

When a police department has been accused of some sort of misconduct, officers sometimes quit routine patrolling and respond only to 911 emergency calls.

That happened in Cincinnati in the wake of the riots. It also has happened in Seattle and Prince George's County, Md., in the suburbs of Washington, D.C. Both those police forces also face allegations of excessive use of force.

After passive police work in Cincinnati, there was a decline in arrests and a corresponding increase in crime. From April 16 through July 22, [2001,] arrests fell by nearly half. The number of shooting incidents in the city this year has climbed past 60. They left 82 people wounded and seven dead.

In Prince George's County, where police are being investigated in connection with excessive use of force, there have been 61 homicides since January. That's just 10 fewer than all of last year. According to *The Washington Post,* carjackings have doubled, and robberies are up 37%. The slowdown, and the increase in homicides, comes after a series of controversies, including the shooting death of Prince Jones Jr., an unarmed black man, by a county officer last Sept. 1. Federal authorities have also opened an investigation.

In Seattle, where police have been accused of racial profiling, officers readily admit to passively patrolling the city. But the police chief denies that and released statistics last week to show that crime appears to remain unchanged.

As 17-year Seattle patrolman Eric Michl told *The Seattle Times:* "Parking under a shady tree to work a crossword puzzle is a great alternative to being labeled a racist and being dragged through an inquest, a review board, an FBI and a U.S. attorney's investigation and a lawsuit."

Police union officials are careful to say de-policing is not an official job action, which might be illegal. They say it's a predictable response to tremendous pressure.

"It's symptomatic of a shell-shocked police department without any (community) support," says Keith Fangman, president of the police union in Cincinnati.

Counters James Fyfe, a criminologist at Temple University in Philadelphia: "If the police have a problem with criticism, they need to find a different way to deal with it. I don't think it's fair to shortchange taxpayers in one of the most critical jobs they pay for."

For the latest in crime and justice news, visit the Talk Justice news feed at http://www.crimenews.info.

Cincinnati police officers in riot gear stand guard as firefighters put out a fire started by vandals in downtown Cincinnati in April 2001. Protests over the fatal police shooting of an unarmed black man turned violent as demonstrators broke store windows and started fires.
AP/Wide World Photos

Source: Debbie Howlett, "'De-policing' a Response to Community's Criticism," *USA Today,* August 8, 2001, p. 4A.
Copyright 2001, *USA Today.* Reprinted with permission.

pretext of immunity through legislative action. New York State, for example, has declared that public agencies are equally as liable as private agencies for violations of constitutional rights. Other states, like California, have enacted statutory provisions which define and limit governmental liability.[143] A number of state immunity statutes have been struck down by court decision. In general, states are moving in the direction of setting dollar limits on liability and adopting federal immunity principles to protect individual officers, including "good faith" and "reasonable belief" rules.

At the federal level, the concept of sovereign immunity is embodied in the Federal Tort Claims Act (FTCA),[144] which grants broad immunity to federal government agencies engaged in discretionary activities. When a federal employee is sued for a wrongful or negligent act, the Federal Employees Liability Reform and Tort Compensation Act of 1988, commonly known as the Westfall Act, empowers the attorney general to certify that the employee was acting within the scope of his or her office or employment at the time of the incident. Upon certification, the employee is dismissed from the action, and the United States is substituted as defendant. The case then falls under the governance of the FTCA.

In 1995, in a case involving the FTCA, a Miami federal judge ordered the federal government to pay out more than $1 million to five crew members and a passenger aboard an airplane from Belize which was scheduled to stop in Miami after taking on additional passengers in Honduras. Testimony revealed that DEA agents had planted cocaine on the plane at its point of origin and had planned to arrest Miami dealers when they retrieved the drugs. The DEA agents had failed to notify Honduran authorities of the planted drugs, however, and when the plane landed in Honduras, it was searched. Honduran police then arrested the six men—beating them with rubber hoses and kicking them down stairs in an effort to get confessions.[145] The judge hearing the suit against the government ruled that although the FTCA gives broad immunity to government agencies whose officials exercise discretion in everyday activities, it was not the intent of Congress to extend immunity to government agencies when the actions of their employees fail to comply with established regulations. In effect, the judge said, the failure by DEA agents to notify Honduran police of the "sting" in progress constituted a failure to perform an official duty.

For its part, the U.S. Supreme Court has supported a type of "qualified immunity" for individual officers (as opposed to the agencies for which they work) which "shields law enforcement officers from constitutional lawsuits if reasonable officers believe their actions to be lawful in light of clearly established law and the information the officers possess." The Supreme Court has also described qualified immunity as a defense "which shields public officials from actions for damages unless their conduct was unreasonable in light of clearly established law."[146] According to the Court, "[T]he qualified immunity doctrine's central objective is to protect public officials from undue interference with their duties and from potentially disabling threats of liability."[147] In the context of a warrantless arrest, the Court said in *Hunter* v. *Bryant* (1991),[148] "[E]ven law enforcement officials who reasonably but mistakenly conclude that probable cause is present are entitled to immunity."[149]

Criminal charges can also be brought against officers who appear to overstep boundaries, or who act in violation of set standards. In 2001, for example, in the case of *Idaho* v. *Horiuchi*,[150] the Ninth U.S. Circuit Court of Appeals ruled that federal law enforcement officers are not immune from state prosecution where their actions violate state law "either through malice or excessive zeal." The case involved FBI sharpshooter Lon Horiuchi, who was charged with negligent manslaughter by prosecutors in Boundary County, Idaho, following a 1992 incident at Ruby Ridge, Idaho.

The incident began when federal agents attempted to arrest Randy Weaver, a self-proclaimed separatist, on weapons charges. Following an initial confrontation and a gun battle in which a deputy U.S. Marshal was killed, a standoff between federal officers and the Weaver family ensued. Agents surrounded the isolated Weaver cabin, a small dwelling in which Weaver's young children had taken shelter along with Randy Weaver, his wife Vickie, and an unknown number of armed supporters. Horiuchi, operating under rules of engagement developed by his FBI supervisors, fired at an armed man who, while outside the cabin, seemed to be taking aim at an approaching FBI helicopter. As his target sought cover, Horiuchi again fired at him just as the man entered the Weaver cabin. The bullet struck Vickie Weaver in the head, then went on to find its intended target. Mrs. Weaver died instantly, holding her baby in her arms as she fell. Although Horiuchi later argued that he was attempting to protect the helicopter and that his actions had therefore been reasonable, the appellate court justices questioned his story and decided that the helicopter had never been in any real danger. Not only should Horiuchi have known that, they concluded, but he fired into the cabin in violation of the FBI's established rules of engagement, which had been designed to protect the Weaver children. The appellate court's decision opened the door to Horiuchi's prosecution by Idaho authorities on state manslaughter charges.

By the time of the appellate court's decision, however, a new Boundary County district attorney had been elected. He declined to indict Horiuchi, saying that too much time had passed for an effective case to be made.[151] Although Randy Weaver served 16 months in a federal prison following the incident, surviving members of the Weaver family were awarded $3 million in a suit they brought against the federal government.[152]

Today, most police departments at both state and federal levels carry liability insurance to protect themselves against the severe financial damage which can result from the loss of a large civil suit. Some officers also acquire private policies which provide coverage in the event they are named as individuals in a civil suit. Both types of insurance policies generally cover legal fees up to a certain amount, regardless of the outcome of the case. Police departments that face civil prosecution because of the actions of an officer may find that legal and financial liability extends to supervisors, city managers, and the community itself. Where insurance coverage does not exist or is inadequate, city coffers may be nearly drained to meet the damages awarded.[153]

In one five-year period, for example, the city of Los Angeles, California, paid out $23 million to people who brought suits against the LAPD for civil rights violations.[154] Former Los Angeles Chief of Police Daryl Gates, in commenting on the prevalence of lawsuits against police officers, observed that although California cities are allowed to pay damage awards for individual officers, they do not have to. Gates continued, "Think about the chilling factor in that. [It says] 'Hey, Chief, you're on your own. We're not gonna pay anything.' Think what that does. It says, 'Hey Chief, don't open your mouth—Don't tell the public anything. Don't let them know what the real facts are in this case. Don't tell the truth.' And what does it tell the police officers? 'Don't do your work, because you're liable to wind up in court, being sued.' That, to me, is probably the most frightening thing that's happening in the United States today."[155]

Recent research shows that Gates may be right. A 2001 study of a large sample of police chiefs throughout Texas found that most believed that lawsuits or the threat of civil litigation against the police makes it harder for individual officers to do their jobs. Most of the chiefs espoused the idea that adequate training, better screening of applicants, close supervision of officers, and "treating people fairly" all reduced the likelihood of lawsuits.[156]

Racial Profiling

One area of civil liability that burst upon the national scene in the late 1990s involves the alleged use by police of so-called **racial profiling**. Racial profiling is quite different from psychological profiling, which was discussed in Chapter 3. Many law enforcement professionals are loathe to use the word *profiling* in conjunction with enforcement practices that are often viewed as unfair. News agencies, however, have popularized the term, and it is now part of popular culture.

Racial profiling has sometimes been derisively called "driving while black" or "driving while brown," although it may also apply to situations other than those involving the use of a motor vehicle. Racial profiling came to the attention of the public when police in New Jersey and Maryland were accused of the unfair treatment of black motorists and admitted that race was a factor in traffic stops.

A 1999 report by the attorney general of New Jersey concluded that New Jersey state troopers *had* engaged in racial profiling along the New Jersey Turnpike.[157] The report, which tracked the racial breakdowns of traffic stops between 1997 and 1998, found that people of color constituted 40.6% of the stops made on the turnpike. Although few stops resulted in a search, 77.2% of individuals searched were people of color. An analysis of the productivity of these searches indicated that 10.5% of the searches that involved white motorists, and 13.5% of the searches involving black motorists, resulted in arrest or seizure.[158] An earlier racial profiling report, which had been compiled in support of a lawsuit against the state of New Jersey, showed that blacks comprised 13.5% of New Jersey Turnpike users, and 15% of drivers who were speeding.[159] At the same time, blacks represented 35% of those stopped and 73.2% of those arrested. The lawsuit resulted in the suppression of evidence in many criminal cases involving black motorists who had been arrested on the turnpike.

Police actions based on racial profiling may take a number of forms. Minority accounts of disparate treatment at the hands of police officers include being stopped for being "in

racial profiling

"Any police-initiated action that relies on the race, ethnicity, or national origin rather than [1] the behavior of an individual, or [2] on information that leads the police to a particular individual who has been identified as being, or having been, engaged in criminal activity."[vii]

> The calculus of reasonableness must embody allowance for the fact that police officers are often forced to make split-second judgments—in circumstances that are tense, uncertain, and rapidly evolving—about the amount of force that is necessary in a particular situation.
>
> —*Graham v. Connor*, 490 U.S. 386, 396–397 (1989)

the wrong car" (for example, a police stop of an African-American youth driving an expensive late-model BMW); being stopped and questioned for being in the wrong neighborhood (that is, police stops of members of minority groups driving through traditionally white residential neighborhoods); and perceived harassment at the hands of police officers for petty traffic violations like underinflated tires, failure to signal properly before switching lanes, vehicle equipment failures, speeding less than 10 miles per hour above the speed limit, or having an illegible license plate.[160]

Profiling, as the term is understood within the context of racial profiling by the police, was originally intended to help catch drug couriers attempting to enter the country. The U.S. Customs Service and the Drug Enforcement Administration developed a number of "personal indicators" which seemed, from the agency's day-to-day enforcement experiences, to be associated with increased likelihood of law violation. Among the indicators were these: speaking Spanish; entering the United States on flights originating in Colombia, Ecuador, Mexico, and certain other Central and South American countries; being young (between 18 and 32); being male; having purchased tickets for cash; and having a short planned stay (often of only a day or two) in the United States. Federal agents frequently used these criteria in deciding which airline passengers to search and which bags to inspect. Many young Hispanics coming into the United States from South America claimed that they were targeted and harassed. Most complaints, however, fell on deaf ears.

Those who defend the use of racial profiling by the police argue that it is not a bigoted practice when based on facts (as when a police department decides to increase patrols in a particular area because of exceptionally high crime rates) or when significant criminal potential exists among even a few members of a group. An example of the latter is the widespread public suspicions that focused on Arab-Americans (and other Arabs living in the United States or traveling through the country) following the terrorist attacks on the United States in 2001. As soon as it was publicly announced that the hijackers had been of Middle Eastern origin, some flight crews demanded that Arab-looking passengers be removed from their airplanes before takeoff, and passengers refused to fly with people who looked like Arabs onboard.[161] A CNN/*USA Today*/Gallup poll conducted a few days after the terrorist attacks found[162]

- 58% of Americans backed more intensive security checks for Arab airplane passengers
- 49% supported special IDs that Arabs—even U.S. citizens—should have to carry
- 35% said they now trusted Arabs living here less than they had before
- 32% said that Arabs living in the United States should be put under special surveillance as Japanese-Americans were following Pearl Harbor

None of this is to say, of course, that race or ethnicity somehow inherently *cause* crime (or that they somehow cause poverty or increase the risk of victimization). If anything, race and ethnicity may simply display a significant correlation with certain types of crime, as they do with certain kinds of victimization. Hence, although the *real* causes of criminality may be socialization into criminal subcultures, economically deprived neighborhoods, a lack of salable job skills, and intergenerational poverty, and not race per se, race has seemed to some law enforcement agencies to provide one more indicator of the likelihood of criminality. David Cole, a professor at Georgetown University's Law Center, for example, notes that in the minds of many police officials, "racial and ethnic disparities reflect not discrimination [or bigotry] but higher rates of offenses among minorities."[163] "Nationwide," says Cole, "blacks are 13 times more likely to be sent to state prisons for drug convictions than are whites, so it would seem rational for police to assume that all other things being equal, a black driver is more likely than a white driver to be carrying drugs." Statistics like this, of course, may further enhance police focus on minorities and may result in even more arrests, thereby reinforcing the beliefs upon which racial profiling by enforcement agents is based. Such observations led esteemed sociologist Amitai Etzioni to declare in 2001 that racial profiling is not necessarily racist.[164] Moreover, warned Etzioni, an end to racial profiling "would penalize those African-American communities with high incidences of violent crime" because they would lose the levels of policing that they need to remain relatively secure.

Regardless of arguments in support of racial profiling, the practice has been widely condemned as being contrary to basic ethical principles. National public opinion polls conducted by the Gallup Organization in 1999, for example, showed that 81% of respondents were morally opposed to the practice of racial profiling by the police.[165] Those participating in the survey generally felt that profiling is wrong because it is a form of race-based discrimination. Findings from the poll might be interpreted to mean that most people believe that racial discrimination of any kind is inherently unethical and not permissible in a free society based upon principles of equality and due process. Moreover, as Christopher Stone, known for his writings on racial justice, explains, "Most people of all races and ethnic groups are never convicted of a crime, but stereotypes can work to brand all members of some groups with suspicion . . . putting an undue burden on innocent members of these groups."[166]

From a more pragmatic viewpoint, however, racial profiling is unacceptable because it weakens the public's confidence in the police, thereby decreasing police-citizen trust and cooperation. As some authors explain, "Truly effective policing will only be achieved when police both protect their neighborhoods from crime and respect the civil liberties of all residents. When law enforcement practices are perceived to be biased, unfair, or disrespectful, communities of color are less willing to trust and confide in police officers, report crimes, participate in problem-solving activities, be witnesses at trials, or serve on juries."[167] These authors summarize the current situation with regard to racial profiling this way: "The challenge that confronts American police organizations is how to sustain the historic decline in rates of criminal activity while enhancing police legitimacy in the eyes of the communities they serve. Appropriately addressing allegations of racial profiling is central to this new mission."[168] Learn more about racial profiling and police management via **Library Extra! 6–8** at cjtoday.com.

Racially Biased Policing

In 2001, the Police Executive Research Forum (PERF) released a detailed report entitled *Racially Biased Policing: A Principled Response.*[169] PERF researchers surveyed more than 1,000 police executives, analyzed material from over 250 law enforcement agencies, and sought input from law enforcement agency personnel, community activists, and civil rights leaders about racial bias in policing. Researchers concluded that "the vast majority of law enforcement officers—of all ranks, nationwide—are dedicated men and women committed to serving all citizens with fairness and dignity."[170] Most police officers, said the report, share an intolerance for racially biased policing. The report's authors noted that some police behaviors may be misinterpreted as biased when, in fact, the officer is just doing his or her job. "The good officer continually scans the environment for anomalies to normalcy—for conditions, people and behavior that are unusual for that environment," they said. "In learning and practicing their craft, officers quickly develop a sense for what is normal and expected, and conversely, for what is not."[171] Hence, for officers of any race to take special notice of unknown young white males who unexpectedly appear in a traditionally African-American neighborhood, for example, might be nothing other than routine police procedure. Such an observation, however, is not in itself sufficient for an investigatory stop but might be used in conjunction with other trustworthy and relevant information already in the officer's possession—such as the officer's prior knowledge that young white men have been routinely visiting a particular apartment complex in the neighborhood to purchase drugs—to justify such a stop.

The PERF report describes the qualities of an unbiased police officer as follows:

> Good police officers carry out their duties with fairness, integrity, diligence and impartiality. They respect basic human rights and civil liberties. They know how to communicate effectively and respectfully to people of any race, culture or background. They make the effort to understand the culture, language, mores, and customs of whatever population they are policing, and to get others to understand their own perspective. They look for ways to resolve disputes and address chronic community problems without creating or aggravating racial tension. . . . They reject racial and cultural stereotypes, recognizing how unfair, inadequate and even dangerous they are to effective policing. They have the self-confidence and courage that is sometimes needed to reject the biased attitudes and behavior they occasionally find among fellow police officers. These qualities are essential to reducing racial bias in policing.

Finally, the PERF report provides an extensive antibiased policing policy for law enforcement agencies to adopt. The report also provides many specific recommendations to help police departments be free of bias. One recommendation, for example, says that "Supervisors should monitor activity reports for evidence of improper practices and patterns. They should conduct spot-checks and regular sampling of in-car videotapes, radio transmissions, and in-car computer and central communications records to determine if both for-

CJ Today News

[Once Appalled by Race Profiling, Many Find Themselves Doing It]

SEATTLE—Ron Arnold understands racial profiling. "I'm a black American, and I've been racially profiled all my life," said Mr. Arnold, a 43-year-old security officer here, "and it's wrong."

But Mr. Arnold admits that he is engaging in some racial profiling himself these days, casting a wary eye on men who look to be of Middle Eastern descent. If he saw a small knot of such men boarding a plane on which he was about to fly, he said: "Yes, I'd be aware of them. I'd be nervous. It sickens me that I feel that way, but it's the real world."

Adrian Estala, 27, a risk-management consultant in Houston who is Hispanic, is struggling with the same emotions. Mr. Estala is "absolutely against" racial profiling, he said, because it is one of the most fundamental violations of liberty he can think of. But asked the same question about sharing an airplane flight with Arab-looking men, he said he would be anxious.

"Absolutely I have to be honest," Mr. Estala said. "Yes, it would make me second-guess. Anybody that says no, they're a better man than I am, or a better woman. I would feel nervous. I mean, who wouldn't?"

On the other side of the divide, Arab-Americans are also feeling new discomfort about attitudes toward them. Nadeem Salem, head of the Association of Arab-Americans in Toledo, Ohio, said such views were extremely offensive. "Think what it really means," said Mr. Salem, a second-generation American-born citizen. "People's civil liberties are being tarnished, compromised. That's not what this country is all about."

For many Americans who say they have deeply believed that it was wrong for law enforcement officers to single out members of minorities for special interrogation or searches, the terrorist attacks on Sept. 11 [2001] have prompted a painful confrontation with the sudden anxieties they acknowledge feeling in the presence of one minority in particular. With all of the roughly 20 hijackers involved in the attacks believed to have Arab backgrounds, these Americans say, the police and the Federal Bureau of Investigation have ample reason to zero in on that group. "It's not right," said Virginia Hawthorne, a retired accountant from Bremerton, Wash., "but it's justified."

Such sentiments seem to have been in play on Thursday in Minneapolis when three Middle Eastern–looking men were denied permission to board a Northwest Airlines flight to their homes in Salt Lake City after several passengers complained of their presence, an airline spokesman said. The men were later permitted to take a Delta flight.

While expressing regret at what they portrayed as the need for more detailed interrogations of people of Arab background, many people said the subjects of such extra attention should understand and accept the reasons for it.

"They shouldn't be offended," said Leslie Brenaman, a retired Boeing graphics designer, who is white. "They shouldn't take it personally after what's happened." . . .

In interviews around the country, many people expressed revulsion at the spate of attacks on Muslims, as well as on Hindus and Sikhs, and the vandalism at mosques. Those interviewed spoke of national ideals of colorblindness—but in nearly the same breath they said that for the sake of national safety, the police should single out Arab-looking men for questioning.

Kathy Komlance, 43, who was wearing an American flag T-shirt as she worked at a taffy stand at the Mid-South Fair in Memphis, said she favored checking their credentials. "I think a person who is Arab should be questioned if they get on a bus or plane or go in a government building," Ms. Komlance said. "You don't want to be afraid of Arabs, Iranians or other foreign people. But how do you differentiate and figure out which one is the bad one from those who love freedom and our country?"

Kareem Alasady (center) describing the ordeal that he, his brother Akram Alasady (left), and Raheem Alkinani went through ten days after the September 11, 2001, terrorist attacks on the World Trade Center and the Pentagon. The Iraqi men, two of whom are U.S. citizens, were denied passage on the second leg of their Northwest Airlines flight from Minneapolis to their homes in Salt Lake City after airline officials apparently became suspicious of their nationality.

AP/Wide World Photos

A CNN/USA Today/Gallup poll taken a few days after the attacks showed that Americans were supporting special measures intended for those of Arab descent. In the survey, 58 percent backed more intensive security checks for Arabs, including those who are United States citizens, compared with other travelers; 49 percent favored special identification cards for such people, and 32 percent backed "special surveillance" for them.

Many people who belong to minorities said they felt especially torn by their newfound acceptance of at least one form of racial profiling.

"I've seen prejudice all my life, with me growing up as an African-American male," said Jermaine Johnson, 19, a business management student at Southwest Tennessee Community College in Memphis. "I try not to judge."

But Mr. Johnson added: "I would not feel comfortable at all if an Arab-looking person sat next to me on a plane. I would be nervous, I mean right now it could be anyone and that's not good if they sit next to you on a plane. I don't feel comfortable with the ones I don't know. It's hard to know who to trust."

Others said they were consciously trying to put aside any snap judgments they were making about others based on their race.

"I think it's just wrong to do anything like that, even with what's happened," said Viridiana Chaveste, 18, a cleaner at Seattle's Safeco Field who is Hispanic.

Her friend Karen Calderon, 20, agreed. "Honestly, thoughts would go through my head," she said when asked how she would react to seeing a group of Arab men on the street or at an airport departure gate. "But I wouldn't do anything about it. I wouldn't treat them any differently."

For the latest in crime and justice news, visit the Talk Justice news feed at http://www.crimenews.info.

Source: Sam Howe Verhovek, "Once Appalled by Race Profiling, Many Find Themselves Doing It," *New York Times,* September 23, 2001.

---

mal and informal communications are professional and free from racial bias and other disrespect."[172] Read the entire PERF report at **Library Extra! 6–9** at cjtoday.com.

Police Use of Force

Police use of force can be defined as the use of physical restraint by a police officer when dealing with a member of the public.[173] Law enforcement officers are, of course, authorized to use the amount of force that is reasonable and necessary given the circumstances. Most officers are trained in the use of force and typically encounter numerous situations during their careers when the use of force is appropriate—for example, when making some arrests, restraining unruly combatants, or controlling a disruptive demonstration. Force may involve hitting; holding or restraining; pushing; choking; threatening with a flashlight, baton, or chemical or pepper spray; restraining with a police dog; or threatening with a gun. Some definitions of police use of force include handcuffing.

The Bureau of Justice Statistics estimates that nearly 45 million people nationwide have face-to-face contact with the police over a typical 12-month period and that approximately 1%, or about 500,000 of these people, become subject to the use of force or the threat of force.[174] When handcuffing is included in the definition of force, the number of people subjected to force increases to 1.2 million, or slightly more than 2.5% of those having contact with the police. Other studies show that police use weaponless tactics in approximately 80% of use-of-force incidents, and that half of all use-of-force incidents involve merely grabbing or holding the suspect.[175]

Studies show that police use force in less than 20% of adult custody arrests (see Figure 6–3). Even in instances where force is used, the police primarily use weaponless tactics, such as grabbing or holding (see Figure 6–4).

The National Institute of Justice says that research conducted in the field has revealed six things about police use of force:[176]

- Only a small percentage of police-public encounters involve force.

- Use of force typically occurs when police are trying to make an arrest and the suspect is resisting.

- Use of force appears to be unrelated to an officer's personal characteristics, such as age, gender, and ethnicity.

- Use of force is most likely to occur when the police are dealing with suspects under the influence of alcohol or drugs or with mentally ill individuals.

- When injuries occur as a result of the use of force, they are likely to be minor. In one study, researchers found that the most common injury to a suspect was a bruise or abrasion (48%).

- A small proportion of officers are disproportionately involved in use-of-force incidents.

Library EXTRA!

police use of force

The use of physical restraint by a police officer when dealing with a member of the public.[viii]

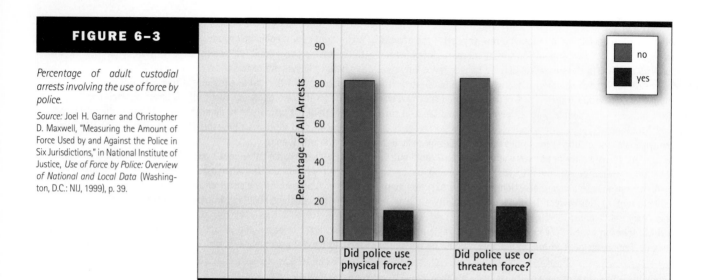

FIGURE 6-3

Percentage of adult custodial arrests involving the use of force by police.

Source: Joel H. Garner and Christopher D. Maxwell, "Measuring the Amount of Force Used by and Against the Police in Six Jurisdictions," in National Institute of Justice, *Use of Force by Police: Overview of National and Local Data* (Washington, D.C.: NIJ, 1999), p. 39.

NIJ notes that "from a police administrator's point of view, these findings are predictable. Officers are trained to use force progressively along a continuum, and policy requires that officers use the least amount of force necessary to accomplish their goals."[177]

More problematic than the simple use of force is the use of *excessive* force. Force is excessive when it exceeds the level considered justifiable under the circumstances.[178] When excessive force is employed, the activities of the police often come under public scrutiny and receive attention from the media and legislators. The use of excessive force by police officers can also result in lawsuits by members of the public who feel that they have been treated unfairly. Whether the use of excessive force is aberrant behavior on the part of an individual officer or is a practice of an entire law enforcement agency, both the law and public opinion generally condemn it.

Kenneth Adams, Chair of the Criminal Justice Faculty at Indiana University at Indianapolis and an expert in the use of force by police, notes that there is an important difference between the terms *excessive force* (such as shoving or pushing when simply grabbing a suspect would be adequate) and the *excessive use of force,* which refers to

FIGURE 6-4

Types of force used by police in adult custodial arrests.

Source: Joel H. Garner and Christopher D. Maxwell, "Measuring the Amount of Force Used by and Against the Police in Six Jurisdictions," in National Institute of Justice, *Use of Force by Police: Overview of National and Local Data* (Washington, D.C.: NIJ, 1999), p. 40.

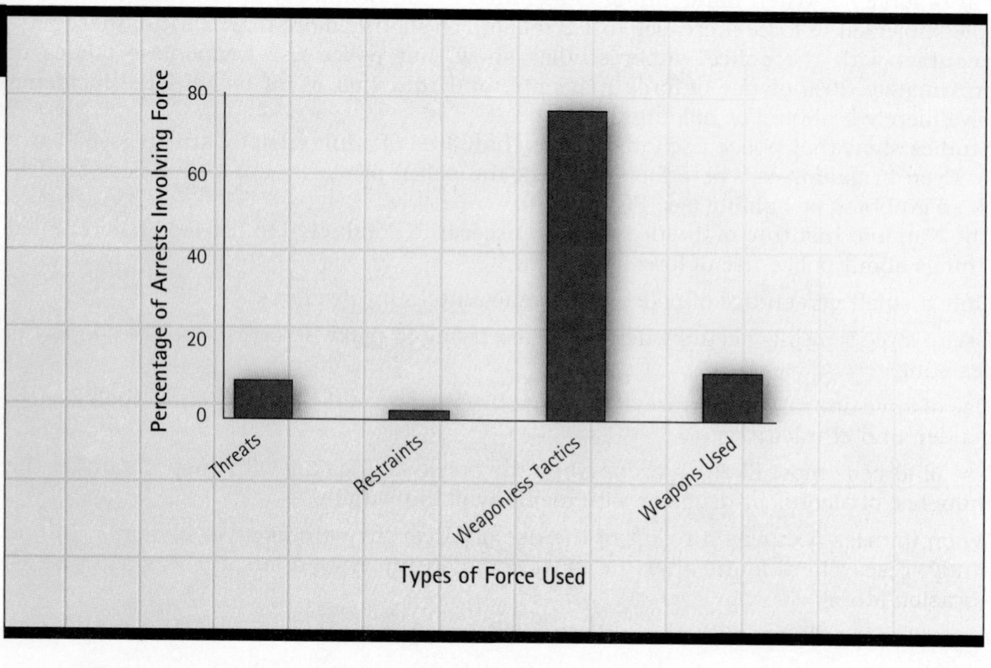

unacceptably high amounts of force on a department-wide basis. According to Adams, "Excessive use of force refers to high rates of force, which suggest that police are using force too freely when viewed in the aggregate." The term, says Adams, "deals with relative comparisons among police agencies, and there are no established criteria for judgment." The use of excessive force and the excessive use of force may be distinguished from the *illegal use of force*, which refers to situations in which use of force by police violates a law or statute.[179]

In a study reported in 2001, Geoffrey Alpert and Roger Dunham found that the "force factor"—the level of force used by the police relative to the suspect's level of resistance—is a key element to consider in attempting to reduce injuries to both the police and suspects.[180] The force factor is calculated by measuring both the suspect's level of resistance and the officer's level of force on an equivalent scale and by then subtracting the level of resistance from the level of police force used. Results from the Alpert and Dunham study indicate that, on average, the level of force used by officers is closely related to the type of training emphasized by their departments.

Excessive force can also be symptomatic of **problem police officers**. Problem police officers are those who exhibit problem behavior, as indicated by high rates of citizen complaints and use-of-force incidents and by other evidence.[181] The Christopher Commission, which studied the structure and operation of the LAPD in the wake of the Rodney King beating, found a number of "repeat offenders" on the LAPD force.[182] According to the commission, approximately 1,800 LAPD officers were alleged to have used excessive force or improper tactics between 1986 and 1990. Of these officers, more than 1,400 had only one or two allegations against them. Another 183 officers had four or more allegations, 44 had six or more, 16 had eight or more, and one had 16 such allegations. The commission also found that, generally speaking, the 44 officers with six complaints or more had received positive performance evaluations that failed to record "sustained" complaints or to discuss their significance.

Recent studies have found that problem police officers do not differ significantly in race or ethnicity from nonproblem officers, although they tend to be male and have disciplinary records that are more serious than those of other officers. Some departments are developing early warning systems to allow police managers to identify potentially problematic officers and to reduce problem police officer behavior. Learn more about police use of force, as well as force used against the police, via **Library Extras! 6–10** and **6–11** at cjtoday.com.

DEADLY FORCE

Generally speaking, **deadly force** is likely to cause death or great bodily harm. The FBI defines *deadly force* as "the intentional use of a firearm or other instrument resulting in a high probability of death."[183] According to a report released by the Bureau of Justice Statistics in 2001, the number of justifiable homicides by police averages "nearly 400 felons each year."[184]

The use of deadly force by police officers, especially when it is *not* considered justifiable, as in the *Horiuchi* case discussed earlier in this chapter, is one area of potential civil liability that has received considerable attention in recent years. Historically, the "fleeing felon rule" applied to most U.S. jurisdictions. It held that officers could use deadly force to prevent the escape of a suspected felon, even when that person represented no immediate threat to the officer or to the public. The fleeing felon rule probably stemmed from early common law punishments, which specified death for a large number of crimes. Today, however, the death penalty is far less frequently applied, and the fleeing felon rule has been called into question in a number of courts.

The 1985 U.S. Supreme Court case of *Tennessee* v. *Garner*[185] specified the conditions under which deadly force could be used in the apprehension of suspected felons. Edward Garner, a 15-year-old suspected burglar, was shot to death by Memphis police after he refused their order to halt and attempted to climb over a chain-link fence. In an action initiated by Garner's father, who claimed that his son's constitutional rights had been violated, the Court held that the use of deadly force by the police to prevent the escape of a fleeing felon could be justified only where the suspect could reasonably be thought to represent a significant threat of serious injury or death to the public or to the officer and where deadly force is necessary to effect the arrest. In reaching its decision, the Court declared that "[t]he use of deadly force to prevent the escape of *all* felony suspects, whatever the circumstances, is constitutionally unreasonable."

problem police officer

A law enforcement officer who exhibits problem behavior, as indicated by high rates of citizen complaints and use-of-force incidents and by other evidence.[ix]

deadly force

Force likely to cause death or great bodily harm. Also, "the intentional use of a firearm or other instrument resulting in a high probability of death."[x]

In 1989, in the case of *Graham* v. *Connor,*[186] the Court established the standard of "objective reasonableness" under which an officer's use of deadly force could be assessed in terms of "reasonableness at the moment." In other words, whether deadly force has been used appropriately should be judged, the Court said, from the perspective of a reasonable officer on the scene and not with the benefit of "20/20 hindsight." The justices wrote, "The calculus of reasonableness must embody allowance for the fact that police officers are often forced to make split-second judgments—in circumstances that are tense, uncertain, and rapidly evolving—about the amount of force that is necessary in a particular situation."

In 1995, following investigations into the actions of federal agents at the deadly siege of the Branch Davidian compound at Waco, Texas, and the tragic deaths associated with a 1992 FBI assault on antigovernment separatists in Ruby Ridge, Idaho, the federal government announced that it was adopting an "imminent danger" standard for the use of deadly force by federal agents. The "imminent danger" standard restricts the use of deadly force to those situations in which the lives of agents or others are in danger. As the new standard was announced, federal agencies were criticized for taking so long to adopt them. The federal deadly force policy, as adopted by the FBI, contains the following elements:[187]

- *Defense of life.* Agents may use deadly force only when necessary—that is, only when they have probable cause to believe that the subject poses an imminent danger of death or serious physical injury to the agents or to others.

- *Fleeing subject.* Deadly force may be used to prevent the escape of a fleeing subject if there is probable cause to believe that the subject has committed a felony involving the infliction or threatened infliction of serious physical injury or death and that the subject's escape would pose an imminent danger of death or serious physical injury to the agents or to others.

- *Verbal warnings.* If feasible, and if doing so would not increase the danger to the agent or to others, a verbal warning to submit to the authority of the agent should be given prior to the use of deadly force.

- *Warning shots.* Agents may not fire warning shots.

- *Vehicles.* Agents may not fire weapons solely to disable moving vehicles. Weapons may be fired at the driver or other occupant of a moving motor vehicle only when the agents have probable cause to believe that the subject poses an imminent danger of death or serious physical injury to the agents or to others and when the use of deadly force does not create a danger to the public that outweighs the likely benefits of its use.

Studies of killings by the police have often focused on claims of discrimination—that is, that black and minority suspects are more likely to be shot than whites. Research has not provided solid support for such claims. While individuals shot by police are more likely to be minorities, an early study by James Fyfe found that police officers will generally respond with deadly force when mortally threatened and that minorities are considerably more likely to use weapons in assaults on officers than are whites.[188] Complicating the picture further, Fyfe's study showed that minority officers are involved in the shootings of suspects more often than other officers, a finding that may be due to the assignment of minority officers to inner-city and ghetto areas. However, a later study by Fyfe, which analyzed police shootings in Memphis, Tennessee, found that black property offenders were twice as likely as whites to be shot by police.[189]

Although relatively few police officers ever fire their weapons at suspects during the course of their careers, those who do may find themselves embroiled in a web of social, legal, and personal complications. It is estimated that in an average year, 600 suspects are killed by public police in America, while another 1,200 are shot and wounded, and 1,800 are shot at and missed.[190] The personal side of police shootings is well summarized in the title of an article that appeared in *Police Magazine.* The article, "I've Killed That Man Ten Thousand Times," demonstrated how police officers who have to use their weapons may be haunted by years of depression and despair.[191] Not long ago, according to author Anne Cohen, all departments did to help officers who had shot someone was to "give him enough bullets to reload his gun." The stress and trauma that result from police shootings are only now being realized, and many departments have yet to develop mechanisms for adequately dealing with them.[192]

The Case of Bernard McCummings

[a] 1993 U.S. Supreme Court decision that drew wide outrage allowed convicted subway mugger Bernard McCummings to keep the $4.3 million he was awarded in a suit he brought against the city of New York. McCummings was shot twice in the back in 1984 by Transit Authority Officer Manuel Rodriguez as he attempted to flee a subway platform after beating and robbing a 71-year-old man. At the time of the crime, McCummings had just gotten out of prison for robbery. Since the shooting, McCummings, who was 23 years old when he was injured, has been paralyzed from the chest down. After pleading guilty to the mugging, he was sentenced to prison, where he served two years. When McCummings brought suit against the city, however, a jury and appeals court found that officers had used excessive force. Before paying the award, the city appealed to the U.S. Supreme Court. In upholding the cash award to McCummings, the Court reiterated earlier rulings that police officers cannot use deadly force against unarmed fleeing suspects who pose no apparent threat to officers or to the public.

McCummings's victim, Jerome Sandusky, who was carrying less than $30 when he was attacked, decried the ruling, saying, "It's justice turned upside down . . . and it sends a terrible message . . . that crime *does* pay." Said Sandusky, "Ordinarily I would be sorry for anyone that was made a cripple. But he was made a cripple because of his own action." Gerald Arenberg of the National Association of Chiefs of Police sided with Sandusky. "The criminal is very well protected by the Supreme Court," Arenberg said in a national interview.

Lawyers for the city were disappointed. "The message is," said one, "it's probably wiser for a police officer to do nothing, in terms of civil liability," when faced with a fleeing suspect.

Opinions on the case were, however, varied. "It was the right decision," said David Breibart, McCummings's lawyer. "It gives me great faith in the system." A *Washington Post* editorial, on the other hand, suggested that police should not be bound by the rules of fair play when criminals are not. "What if felons knew that cops could shoot them if they fled?" the editorial asked. "More of them would likely freeze and put up their hands. . . . Criminal behavior should not be treated as if it were some sort of quasi-legitimate enterprise, governed by the laws of negligence." The editorial concluded, "McCummings was as much a victim of his own criminality as he was of a violation of the rules regarding the use of deadly force. Once he chose to break the law he wasn't entitled to be compensated by it." McCummings's victim agreed. Sandusky filed suit against McCummings, seeking to get the $4.3 million award. Sandusky brought suit under New York's modified "Son of Sam" law, which is intended to prevent criminals from profiting from their crimes.

❓ DISCUSSION QUESTIONS

1. Do you feel that McCummings should have been compensated for his injuries? Explain. If so, might there have been some way of compensating him that did not involve money?

2. Do you agree with the assertion that police officers should not be bound by the rules of fair play when criminals are not? Explain.

3. Whose rights seem more important here: the rights of the criminal, the victim, the police, or society? How can you tell?

Sources: "Mugger Shot by Cop to Keep $4.3 million," *USA Today*, November 30, 1993, p. 1A; "Mugging Lawsuit," Associated Press wire service, December 15, 1993; "Compensation for a Criminal," *Washington Post* wire service, December 2, 1993; and "Scotus—Excessive Force," Associated Press wire service, November 30, 1993.

Especially difficult to deal with are instances of "suicide by cop," in which individuals bent on dying engage in behavior that causes responding officers to resort to deadly force. In 1997, for example, 19-year-old Moshe "Moe" Pergament, a well-mannered college student, was shot to death by Nassau County, New York, police officers after he pulled a $1.79 toy revolver from his waistband and pointed it at the officers during a traffic stop. Pergament apparently wanted to be shot by law enforcement personnel and had planned his death. In a note found after his death and addressed to "the officer who shot me," Pergament apologized for what he had planned. "Officer," the note read, "it was a plan. I'm sorry to get you involved. I just needed to die."[193] Pergament had also written good-bye messages to friends and family members. He was apparently depressed over a $6,000 gambling debt. A 1998 study of fatal shootings by Los Angeles police officers found that an astonishingly large number—over 10%—could be classified as "suicide by cop."[194] Recently, researchers have identified three main "suicide by cop" categories": direct confrontations, in which suicidal subjects instigate attacks on police officers for the purpose of dying; disturbed interventions, in which potentially suicidal subjects take advantage of police intervention in their suicide attempt in order to die; and criminal interventions, in which criminal suspects prefer death to capture and arrest.[195]

LESS-THAN-LETHAL WEAPONS

Less-than-lethal-weapons offer what may be a problem-specific solution to potential incidents of "suicide by cop," as well as a generic solution to at least some charges of use of

less-than-lethal weapon

A weapon that is designed to disable, capture, or immobilize—but not kill—a suspect. Occasional deaths do result from the use of such weapons, however, and they are sometimes referred to as *less-lethal* weapons.

A South Carolina SWAT team preparing for action during an inmate uprising at the Broad River Correctional Institution near Columbia. Deadly force can only be used in situations involving extreme and imminent danger.

AP/Wide World Photos

excessive force. Less-than-lethal weapons are those that are designed to disable, capture, or immobilize a suspect rather than kill him or her. Efforts to provide law enforcement officers with less-than-lethal weapons began in 1987.[196] Stun guns, Tasers, rubber bullets, beanbag projectiles, and pepper spray are examples of such weapons that are currently in use. More exotic types of less-than-lethal weapons, however, are on the horizon. They include snare nets fired from shotguns, disabling sticky foam that can be sprayed from a distance, microwave beams that heat the tissue of people exposed to them until they desist in their illegal or threatening behavior or lose consciousness, and high-tech guns that fire bolts of electromagnetic energy at a target, causing painful sensory overload and violent muscle spasms. The National Institute of Justice says that it is "moving forward with research development and evaluation of devices for use by line patrol officers under a wide variety of circumstances. . . . The goal is to give line officers effective and safe alternatives to lethal force."[197]

A photo promotion showing the effects of Taser International's Advanced Taser.® This less-than-lethal weapon, intended for use in law enforcement and private security, incapacitates potential attackers by delivering an electrical shock to the person's nervous system. The technology is intended to reduce injury rates to both suspects and officers.

TASER International

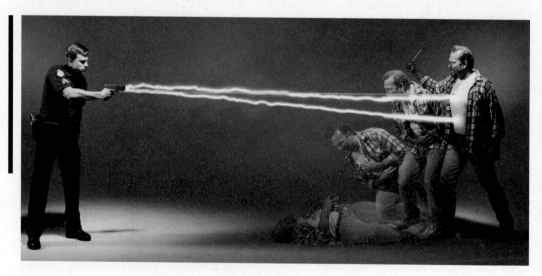

CJ Today Exhibit 6-1

[The Law Enforcement Code of Ethics]

As a Law Enforcement Officer, my fundamental duty is to serve mankind; to safeguard lives and property; to protect the innocent against deception, the weak against oppression or intimidation, and the peaceful against violence or disorder; and to respect the Constitutional rights of all men to liberty, equality, and justice.

I will keep my private life unsullied as an example to all; maintain courageous calm in the face of danger, scorn, or ridicule; develop self-restraint; and be constantly mindful of the welfare of others. Honest in thought and deed in both my personal and official life, I will be exemplary in obeying the laws of the land and the regulations of my department. Whatever I see or hear of a confidential nature or that is confided to me in my official capacity will be kept secret unless revelation is necessary in the performance of my duty.

I will never act officiously or permit personal feelings, prejudices, animosities, or friendships to influence my decisions. With no compromise for crime and with relentless prosecution of criminals, I will enforce the law courteously and appropriately without fear or favor, malice or ill will, never employing unnecessary force or violence and never accepting gratuities.

I recognize the badge of my office as a symbol of public faith, and I accept it as a public trust to be held so long as I am true to the ethics of the police service. I will constantly strive to achieve these objectives and ideals, dedicating myself before God to my chosen profession . . . law enforcement.

Source: International Association of Chiefs of Police. Reprinted with permission.

Professionalism and Ethics

Police administrators have responded in a variety of ways to issues of corruption, danger, and liability. Among the most significant responses have been calls for increased **police professionalism** at all levels of policing. A profession is an organized undertaking characterized by a body of specialized knowledge acquired through extensive education[198] and by a well-considered set of internal standards and ethical guidelines which hold members of the profession accountable to one another and to society. Associations of like-minded practitioners generally serve to create and disseminate standards for the profession as a whole.

Contemporary policing evidences many of the attributes of a profession. Specialized knowledge in policing includes a close familiarity with criminal law, laws of procedure, constitutional guarantees, and relevant Supreme Court decisions; a working knowledge of weapons and hand-to-hand tactics, driving skills, and vehicle maintenance; a knowledge of radio communications; report-writing abilities; interviewing techniques, and media and human-relations skills. Other specialized knowledge may include Breathalyzer operation, special weapons skills, polygraph operation, conflict resolution, and hostage negotiation. Supervisory personnel require an even wider range of skills, including general and personnel administrative skills, management techniques, and strategies for optimum utilization of human and physical resources.

Police work is guided by an ethical code developed in 1956 by the Peace Officer's Research Association of California (PORAC) in conjunction with Dr. Douglas M. Kelley of Berkeley's School of Criminology.[199] The Law Enforcement Code of Ethics is reproduced in CJ Today Exhibit 6-1. Ethics training is still not well integrated into most basic law enforcement training programs, but a movement in that direction has begun, and calls for expanded training in **police ethics** are increasing.

Professional associations abound in police work. The Fraternal Order of Police (FOP) is one of the best-known organizations of public service workers in the United States. The International Association of Chiefs of Police has done much to raise professional standards in policing and continually strives for improvements in law enforcement nationwide.

Accreditation provides another path toward police professionalism. The Commission on Accreditation for Law Enforcement Agencies (CALEA) was formed in 1979. Police departments wishing to apply for accreditation through the commission must meet hundreds of standards relating to areas as diverse as day-to-day operations, administration, review of

police professionalism

The increasing formalization of police work and the accompanying rise in public acceptance of the police.

police ethics

The special responsibility to adhere to moral duty and obligation that is inherent in police work.

incidents involving the use of a weapon by officers, and evaluation and promotion of personnel. To date, relatively few police agencies are accredited, although a number are currently undergoing the accreditation process. Although accreditation makes possible the identification of high-quality police departments, it is often undervalued because it carries few incentives. Accreditation does not guarantee a department any rewards beyond that of peer recognition. As of January 1, 2000, nearly 470 U.S. law enforcement agencies were accredited by CALEA, but that number represents only 2.5% of the nation's 18,769 police agencies.[200] Visit CALEA online via **WebExtra! 6–4** at cjtoday.com.

Education and Training

Basic law enforcement training requirements were begun in the 1950s by the state of New York and through a voluntary **Peace Officer Standards and Training (POST) program** in California. (Additional information on California's POST standards can be accessed via **WebExtra! 6–5** at cjtoday.com.) Today, POST-like requirements are mandated by law in every jurisdiction in the nation, although they vary considerably from region to region. Modern police education generally involves training in subject areas as diverse as human relations, firearms and weapons, communications, legal aspects of policing, patrol, criminal investigations, administration, report writing, and criminal justice systems. According to a 1999 Bureau of Justice Statistics report, the median number of hours of classroom training required of new officers is highest in state police agencies (823) and lowest in sheriff's departments (448).[201] The requirements for county and municipal police are 760 and 640 hours, respectively. Standards continue to be modified. In 2002, for example, the California Commission on POST responded to statewide concerns over racial profiling by adding material to the police training curriculum to ensure that all California law enforcement officers receive training "that reinforces the fact that racial profiling has a profound negative impact on communities and cannot be tolerated."[202]

Federal law enforcement agents receive schooling at the Federal Law Enforcement Training Center (FLETC) in Glynco, Georgia. The center provides training for about 60 federal law enforcement agencies, excluding the FBI and the DEA, which have their own training academies in Quantico, Virginia. The center also offers advanced training to state and local police organizations through the National Center for State and Local Law Enforcement Training, located on the FLETC campus. Specialized schools, such as Northwestern University's Traffic Institute, have also been credited with raising the level of police practice from purely operational concerns to a more professional level.

As the concern for quality policing builds, increasing emphasis is also being placed on the formal education of police officers. As early as 1931, the National Commission on Law Observance and Enforcement (the Wickersham Commission) highlighted the importance of a well-educated police force by calling for "educationally sound" officers.[203] In 1967, the President's Commission on Law Enforcement and Administration of Justice voiced the belief that "the ultimate aim of all police departments should be that all personnel with general enforcement powers have baccalaureate degrees."[204] At the time, the average educational level of police officers in the United States was 12.4 years—slightly beyond a high-school degree. In 1973, the National Advisory Commission on Criminal Justice Standards and Goals made the following rather specific recommendation: "Every police agency should, no later than 1982, require as a condition of initial employment the completion of at least four years of education . . . at an accredited college or university."[205]

Recommendations, of course, do not always translate into practice. A 1999 Bureau of Justice Statistics report found that 16% of state police agencies require a two-year college degree, and 4% require a four-year degree. County police are the next most likely to require either a two-year (13%) or four-year (3%) degree.[206] Among large municipal police agencies, 9% have a degree requirement, with 2% requiring a four-year degree. Among sheriff's departments, 6% require a degree, including 1% with a four-year degree requirement.

A survey of 699 police departments by the Police Executive Research Forum found that the average level of educational achievement among both black and white officers was 14 years of schooling, nearly the equivalent of an associate's degree from a two-year or community college.[207] Female officers (with an average level of educational achievement of 14.6 years) tend to be better educated than their male counterparts (who report an average attainment level of 13.6 years). Only 3.3% of male officers hold graduate degrees, while almost one-third (30.2%) of female officers hold such degrees. On the downside, 34.8% of male officers have no college experience, and 24.1% of female officers have none. The PERF

Peace Officer Standards and Training (POST) program

The official program of a state or legislative jurisdiction through which standards for the training of law enforcement officers are set. All states set such standards, although not all use the term *POST.*

The ability of the police to fulfill their sacred trust will improve as a lucid sense of ethical standards is developed.

—Patrick V. Murphy, Former Commissioner, New York City Police Department

report explained the difference between male and female educational achievement by saying that "women tend to rely on higher education more than men as a springboard for a law enforcement career . . . [and] police departments may utilize higher standards—consciously or unconsciously—for selecting women officers."[208]

The PERF report also stressed the need for educated police officers, citing the following benefits which accrue to police agencies from the hiring of educated officers:[209] (1) better written reports, (2) enhanced communications with the public, (3) more effective job performance, (4) fewer citizen complaints, (5) greater initiative, (6) a wiser use of discretion, (7) a heightened sensitivity to racial and ethnic issues, and (8) fewer disciplinary problems. On the other hand, the greater likelihood that educated officers will leave police work and their tendency to question orders and to request reassignment with relative frequency are some education-related drawbacks.

A growing number of agencies now require the completion of at least some college-level work for officers seeking promotion. The San Diego Police Department, for example, requires two years of college work for promotion to the rank of sergeant.[210] The Sacramento (California) Police Department requires a four-year college degree for promotion to lieutenant, and the New York City Police Department requires at least 64 college credits for promotion to supervisory ranks. At the state level, a variety of plans exist for integrating college work into police careers. Minnesota now requires a college degree for new candidates taking the Peace Officer Standards and Training Board's licensing examination. Successful completion of all POST requirements permits employment as a fully certified law enforcement officer in the state of Minnesota. The state of New York set 60 semester hours of college-level work as a mandated minimum for hiring by the New York State Police. Finally, many federal agencies require college degrees for entry-level positions. Among them are the FBI, the DEA, the Bureau of Alcohol, Tobacco, and Firearms (ATF), the Secret Service, the U.S. Customs Service, and the Immigration and Naturalization Service.

Recruitment and Selection

All professions need informed, dedicated, and competent personnel. When the National Advisory Commission on Criminal Justice Standards and Goals issued its 1973 report on the police, it bemoaned the fact that "many college students are unaware of the varied, interesting, and challenging assignments and career opportunities that exist within the police service."[211] In the intervening years, the efforts made by police departments to correct such misconceptions have had a considerable effect. Today, police organizations actively recruit new officers from two- and four-year colleges and universities, technical institutions, and professional organizations. Education is an important criterion in selecting today's police recruits. As mentioned earlier, some departments require a minimum number of college credits for entry-level work. A policy of the Dallas Police Department[212] requiring a minimum of 45 semester hours of successful college-level study for new recruits was upheld in 1985 by the Fifth U.S. Circuit Court of Appeals in the case of *Davis v. Dallas*.[213]

The national commission report stressed the setting of high standards for police recruits and recommended a strong emphasis on minority recruitment, an elimination of residence requirements (which required officers to live in the area they were hired to serve) for new officers, a decentralized application and testing procedure, and various recruiting incentives.

Effective policing, however, may depend more upon personal qualities than it does upon educational attainment. O. W. Wilson once enumerated some of the "desirable personal qualities of patrol officers."[214] They include (1) initiative, (2) the capacity for responsibility, (3) the ability to deal alone with emergencies, (4) the capacity to communicate effectively with people from diverse social, cultural, and ethnic backgrounds, (5) the ability to learn a variety of tasks quickly, (6) the attitude and ability necessary to adapt to technological changes, (7) the desire to help people in need, (8) an understanding of others, (9) emotional maturity, and (10) sufficient physical strength and endurance.

Standard procedures employed by modern departments in selecting trainees usually include basic skills tests, physical agility measurements, interviews, physical examinations, eye tests, psychological evaluations, and background investigations into the personal character of applicants. After training, successful applicants are typically placed on probation for one year. The probationary period in police work has been called the "first true job-related test . . . in the selection procedure,"[215] providing the opportunity for supervisors to gauge the new officer's response to real-life situations.

> Community policing, or variations of it, has become the national mantra of the American police.
>
> —Jack R. Green, Northeastern University[xi]

Police Departments as Learning Organizations

Enhanced police professionalism is rapidly becoming an important tool in the effort to reduce corruption, on-the-job danger, and police civil liability. Another promising approach is the management of police departments as learning organizations. A **learning organization** is "an organization skilled at creating, acquiring, and transferring knowledge and at modifying its behavior to reflect new knowledge and insights"[216] A learning organization challenges, in fundamental ways, the dominant 'bureaucratic' paradigm which has prevailed at the core of western civilization for some 200 years."[217] Learning organizations employ teamwork as a way of operating, give employees decision-making responsibility and accountability, assume a problem-solving approach as "the way to do business," encourage new ideas and innovation, support employee development, work to actively apply new skills and knowledge, and share their knowledge and information systems with others.[218]

Police departments that have become effective learning organizations are sometimes said to embody the concept of "knowledge-led policing." They have become expert at adaptive learning—that is, at learning how best to respond to their environment while serving the law enforcement and crime-control agendas with which they are charged. Such departments value information from many sources, including the community, police officers at all ranks, civilian employees, national and local surveys about crime and public opinion, crime-mapping data, and internal and external research studies. Some of the information these departments process has already been analyzed, while other information must be internally processed and evaluated.

Learning organizations can be contrasted with the traditional kinds of organizations that emerged following the Industrial Revolution and which have characterized Western society for the past few hundred years. Traditional organizations utilize multilayered management structures designed to ensure accurate compliance by employees with plans and orders formulated and transmitted from the top. They react to problems rather than anticipating them, and they accept change only when it is made inescapable by outside events. Traditional organizations often require obedience from employees and give employees few opportunities to contribute to the development of the organization itself.[219] The qualities of a traditional organization were well articulated by Peter Drucker over four decades ago and are often associated with "management by objectives" (MBO) and similar management techniques.[220] Many police department administrators were well schooled in the MBO tradition and have yet to make the shift to newer organizational models.

William Walsh, Director of the Southern Police Institute at the University of Louisville, says that if the police are to remain viable within the society they serve, they must adapt their methods and their strategies to the political, social, and economic trends of emerging postindustrial society. Moreover, says Walsh, "policing has reached an important crossroads with organizational managers dividing their support between traditional [and] community/problem solving operational models."[221] Others agree. Captain Andrew Harvey of the Covina (California) Police Department, for example, suggests that "to deal with the rapidly changing environment in the twenty-first century, law enforcement's paramilitary hierarchy, with rigid controls and strict chains of command, must give way to a structure that emphasizes network-type communication and flexibility. The traditional organizational pyramid, with the chief at the top and line officers at the bottom, must become inverted."[222] Says Harvey, "The community must sit at the top of the pyramid, followed by line officers, then supervisors, and finally the chief." Effective police administrators of the future, he says, "will be consensus builders and agents of change." These leaders will look to the future, "anticipating trends while they perform day-to-day tasks."

Although learning organizations are proving far more capable than traditional organizations at adapting to and taking full advantage of the knowledge revolution now occurring, many police departments are still mired in the traditional bureaucratic stage of organizational development. Attorney William Geller, a consultant who specializes in reorienting public safety organizations to successfully participate in the knowledge revolution, calls such departments "learning disabled."[223] Many departments remain learning disabled, according to Geller, for six reasons: (1) They are skeptical about what they see as "ivory tower research" and its applicability to everyday issues; (2) they adhere to the myth that encouraging critical thinking among rank-and-file members of the department will undermine necessary paramilitary discipline; (3) the indoctrination process of most police departments inhibits employees from contributing meaningfully to organizational self-appraisal; (4) officers, supervisors, and administrators are reluctant to have cherished views challenged; (5) there is simply not enough time for officers to reflect on their work, and there is no time for them to conduct research of their own about department or community problems; and most important of all, (6) people fear change.

Geller suggests that police departments can begin to become effective learning organizations by (1) creating research and development units that actually *do* research and that have respectable research budgets; (2) implementing crime-analysis units that span precincts and even jurisdictional boundaries in order to track crime problems and changes in the nature of criminal offending over time and from place to place; (3) fostering an interest in active learning by organizing police work around problem-solving efforts; (4) "priming the pump" of critical thinking within the department by developing institutional methods to challenge established forms of "groupthink"; (5) inventing an employee suggestion program that really works; and (6) expanding police-researcher partnerships such as those sponsored by the National Institute of Justice. Learn more about police departments as learning organizations from **Library Extra! 6–12** at cjtoday.com.

CJ Futures

[Police Learning Organizations and Technology]

As this chapter discusses, law enforcement agencies across the country are transforming themselves into learning organizations. Learning organizations continually process knowledge and information in an effort to operate more effectively. A number of new technologies that are becoming available for use in the justice system are designed to enhance information collection and data analysis. Here are a few of those technologies:

- *Speech enhancement.* Developed by the U.S. Air Force to clarify pilot communications, speech enhancement technology can automatically identify and eliminate audio interference from many different sources. Speech enhancement technology is being used to add intelligibility to law enforcement patrol communications, suspect interviews, conversations originating with body wire equipment, monitored surveillance recordings, and interrogation recordings. The enhanced audio signal also reduces listener fatigue and communication errors.

- *Speaker recognition.* Speaker recognition technology identifies a speaker from a live or recorded fragment of his or her speech. Given a speech sample from an unknown speaker and a database of speech samples from known speakers, the technology compares the unknown speaker against the database to find the closest match. The technology operates independently of the speaker's language, accent, and choice of words. Identifications can be made with as little as one word (approximately one-third of a second of speech). Law enforcement agencies are using speaker recognition technology to identify telephone callers in sexual harassment cases, false reports of fires, and other illegal activities.

- *Timeline analysis.* Timeline analysis renders events as graphic icons on a computer screen to show event patterns and to predict possible future events. Some especially interesting timeline analysis technology, Web-based timeline analysis system (WEBTAS), allows a user to plot and analyze criminal events along a timeline. Behavior patterns can be modeled from past events to show future probabilities of occurrence.

- *Information extraction.* Converting paper documents to an electronic form, automatically extracting information, and then presenting the information in meaningful ways that capture patterns is the idea behind information extraction technology. The process involves identifying words and word sequences in a document and then categorizing them by their meanings. These words and word sequences are called *named entities.* Recently, in conjunction with an Arizona law enforcement agency, The Law Enforcement Analysis Facility (LEAF), of the National Law Enforcement and Corrections Technology Center (NLECTC), demonstrated that information extraction is feasible even when applied to 6,600 seized documents related to a money-laundering investigation.

- *Automatic gisting.* Automatic "gisting" is the capability of a computer to monitor human speech for the presence of keywords or keyword patterns that may indicate criminal activity. Gisting produces a synopsis of the information in the communications. Automatic gisting of conversations may someday be useful for law enforcement and corrections surveillance. Because the gist of conversations can be acquired by a computer without a human listener, conversations could be monitored for indications of illegal activities with little manpower and (possibly) without interfering with basic privacy rights.

- *Automatic spoken language translation.* Automatic spoken language translation (ASLT) is the computer translation of human speech from one language to another. A user speaks into a device that translates the speech into another language, and then outputs (speaks) the translation. Originally used by the U.S. military in field interrogations, this device allows civilian law enforcement and corrections personnel to communicate with non-English speakers in their own languages, eliminating the time needed to locate an interpreter. It also makes the collection of critical information at crime scenes more efficient and makes interrogation easier and less costly.

Source: Adapted from *Tech Beat* (the online newsletter of the National Law Enforcement and Corrections Technology Center, a program of the National Institute of Justice), spring 2001.

Ethnic and Gender Diversity in Policing

In 1967, the National Advisory Commission on Civil Disorders conducted a survey of supervisory personnel in police departments.[224] They found a marked disparity between the number of black and white officers in leadership positions. One of every 26 black police officers had been promoted to the rank of sergeant, while the ratio among whites was one in 12. Only one of every 114 black officers had become a lieutenant, while among whites the ratio was one in 26. At the level of captain, the disparity was even greater: One out of every 235 black officers had achieved the rank of captain, while one of every 53 whites had climbed to that rank.

Since then, the emphasis placed upon minority recruitment by task forces, civil rights groups, courts, and society in general has done much to rectify the situation. In 1979, for example, one of the first affirmative action disputes involving a police department was settled out of court. The settlement required the San Francisco Police Department to ensure that over the next ten years minorities would receive 50% of all promotions and that 20% of all new officers hired would be women.[225]

Today, many departments, through dedicated recruitment efforts, have dramatically increased their complement of officers from underrepresented groups. The Metropolitan Detroit Police Department, for example, now has a force that is more than 30% black. According to a recent report by the Bureau of Justice Statistics, blacks make up 11.8% of all sworn officers nationwide, while other ethnic minorities constitute over 8% of all sworn personnel (Figure 6–5).[226]

Although ethnic minorities are now employed in policing in numbers that approach their representation in the American population, women are still significantly underrepresented (Figure 6–6). The 2000 Status of Women in Policing Survey, conducted by the National Center for Women and Policing (NCWP), found that women fill only 13% of all sworn law enforcement positions nationwide.[227] On the other hand, the NCWP notes that women account for 46.5% of employed persons over the age of 16 nationwide, meaning that they are "strikingly under-represented within the field of sworn law enforcement."[228] Key findings from the survey show that[229]

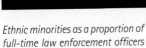

FIGURE 6-5

Ethnic minorities as a proportion of full-time law enforcement officers and as a proportion of the U.S. population.

Source: Adapted from Kathleen Maguire and Ann L. Pastore, eds., *Sourcebook of Criminal Justice Statistics* [online] (Washington, D.C.: Bureau of Justice Statistics), accessed January 30, 2002; and U.S. Census Bureau, "Estimates of the United States by Sex, Race, and Hispanic Origin" (Washington, D.C.: U.S. Census Bureau, 2001).

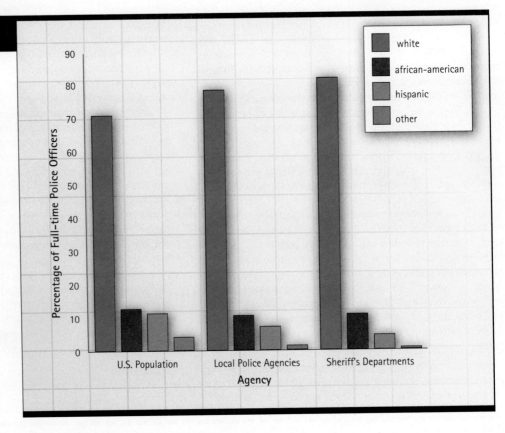

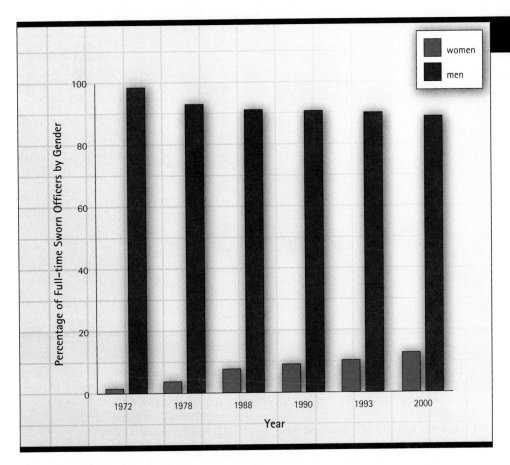

FIGURE 6-6

Full-time sworn law enforcement officers by gender, 1972–2000.

Source: National Center for Women and Policing, *Equity Denied: The Status of Women in Policing, 2000* (Los Angeles, NCWP, 2001), p. 4.

- Women currently fill about 13% of all sworn law enforcement positions among municipal, county, and state agencies in the United States with 100 or more sworn officers. Women of color hold 4.9% of these positions.

- Between 1990 and 2000, the representation of women in sworn law enforcement ranks has increased from 9% to 13%—a gain of only 4%, or less than 0.5% each year.

- If the slow growth rate of women in policing holds, women will not achieve equal representation within the police profession for another 70 years, and many experts caution that time alone may not be sufficient to substantially increase the number of female officers.

- Women hold 7.3% of sworn top command law enforcement positions, 10.3% of supervisory positions, and 13.7% of line operation positions (Figure 6–7). Women of color hold 1.7% of sworn top command law enforcement positions, 3.2% of supervisory positions, and 5.3% of line operation positions.

- Fifty-seven percent of the agencies surveyed reported no women in top command positions, and 88% of the agencies reported no women of color in their highest ranks.

- State agencies trail municipal and county agencies by a wide margin in hiring and promoting women. Specifically, 6.8% of the sworn law enforcement officers in state agencies are women, which is significantly lower than the percentage reported by municipal agencies (14.5%) and county agencies (13.5%).

- Consent decrees mandating the hiring and promotion of women and minorities are a significant factor in the gains women have made in law enforcement. Of the 25 agencies with the highest percentage of sworn women, ten are subject to this type of consent decree. In sharp contrast, only four of the 25 agencies with the lowest percentage of sworn women operate under a consent decree.

- On average, in agencies without a consent decree mandating the hiring and promotion of women and minorities, women comprise 9.7% of sworn personnel, whereas those agencies with a consent decree in force average 14.0% women in their ranks. The percentage of women of color is 6.3% in agencies without a consent decree and 11.7% in agencies operating under one.

When a woman makes a mistake, the men can't wait to jump on the bandwagon, but if a man makes a mistake, it is covered up.

—Police Sergeant C. Lee Bennett, citing interviews with female police officers

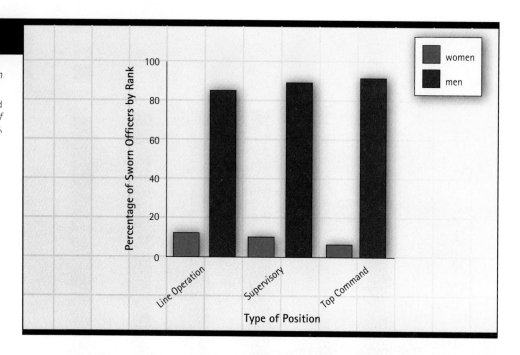

FIGURE 6-7

Women as a percentage of sworn law enforcement officers by rank.

Source: National Center for Women and Policing, *Equity Denied: The Status of Women in Policing, 2000* (Los Angeles, NCWP, 2001), p. 5.

It is unclear, of course, just how many women actually *want* to work in policing. Nonetheless, many police departments continue to make substantial efforts to recruit and retain women because they realize the benefits of having more women among the ranks of sworn officers. Benefits stem from the fact that female police officers tend to use less physical force than male officers and are less likely to be accused of using excessive force; female officers are better at defusing and deescalating potentially violent confrontations with citizens; female officers often possess better communication skills than their male counterparts; and they are better able to facilitate the cooperation and trust required to implement a community policing model. Moreover, the NCWP says that "female officers often respond more effectively to incidents of violence against women—crimes that represent one of the largest categories of calls to police departments. Increasing the representation of women on the force is also likely to address another costly problem for police administrators—the pervasive problem of sex discrimination and sexual harassment—by changing the climate of modern law enforcement agencies."[230] Finally, "because women frequently have different life experiences than men, they approach policing with a different perspective, and the very presence of women in the field will often bring about changes in policies and procedures that benefit both male and female officers."[231] For additional information on how police departments can recruit and retain female officers, see **Library Extra! 6-13** at cjtoday.com.

Women as Effective Police Officers

One research report on female police officers in Massachusetts found that female officers (1) are "extremely devoted to their work," (2) "see themselves as women first, and then police officers," and (3) are more satisfied when working in nonuniformed capacities.[232] The researcher identified two groups of female officers: (1) those who felt themselves to be well integrated into their departments and were confident in their jobs and (2) those who experienced strain and on-the-job isolation. The officers' children were cited as a significant influence on their self-perceptions and on the way in which they viewed their jobs. The demands which attend child rearing in contemporary society were found to be a major factor contributing to the resignation of female officers. The study also found that the longer female officers stayed on the job, the greater the stress and frustration they tended to experience, primarily as a consequence of the noncooperative attitudes of male officers. Some of the female officers interviewed identified networking as a potential solution to the stresses encountered by female officers but also said that when women get together to solve problems, they are seen as "crybabies" rather than professionals. Said one of the women in the study, "We've lost a lot of good women who never should have left the job. If we had helped each other maybe they wouldn't have left."[233]

Lieutenant Gail Marsh of the Redmond (Washington) Police Department. Women in uniform have become a common sight throughout our nation's cities and towns.

Therese Frare, Black Star

Some studies have found that female officers are often underutilized and that many departments are hesitant to assign women to patrol and to other potentially dangerous field activities.[234] As a consequence, some women in police work experience frustrations and a lack of satisfaction with their jobs. An analysis of the genderization of the criminal justice workplace by Susan Ehrlich Martin and Nancy Jurik, for example, points out that gender inequality is part of a historical pattern of entrenched forms of gender interaction relating to the division of labor, power, and culture.[235] According to Martin and Jurik, women working in the justice system are viewed in terms of such historically developed filters, causing them to be judged and treated according to normative standards developed for men rather than for women. As a consequence, formal and informal social controls continue to disenfranchise women who wish to work in the system and make it difficult to recognize the specific contributions that they make as women.

What Can Be Done?

In an effort to increase the representation of ethnic minorities and women in police work, the Police Foundation recommends (1) involving underrepresented groups in affirmative action and long-term planning programs which are undertaken by police departments, (2) encouraging the development of an open system of promotions whereby women can feel free to apply for promotion and in which qualified individuals of any race or gender will face equity in the promotion process, and (3) using periodic audits to ensure that female officers are not being underutilized by being ineffectively tracked into clerical and support positions.[236]

Networking is quickly taking root among the nation's female police officers, as attested to by the growth of organizations like the International Association of Women Police, based in New York City. Networks offer support to female officers and help them deal with the dilemmas of their job. Mentoring is another method for introducing women to police work.[237] Mentoring creates semiformal relationships between experienced female officers and rookies. Through this relationship, problems can be addressed as they arise, and the experienced officer can guide her junior partner through the maze of formal and informal expectations which surround the job of policing.

Barriers to diversity continue to fall. In 1979, for example, San Francisco became the first city in the world to actively recruit homosexuals for its police force. That action

> Pressures—from the community, from peers, from the circumstances in which police find themselves—are intense.
>
> —James Q. Wilson, former Chairman of the Board, the Police Foundation

Black and Hispanic police officers in Los Angeles. Ethnic minorities, while still underrepresented in the criminal justice field, have many opportunities for employment throughout the system.

David R. Frazier Photolibrary, Photo Researchers, Inc.

reduced the fear of reporting crimes among many homosexuals, who for years had been victims of organized assaults by bikers and street gangs. During the Clinton administration, Attorney General Janet Reno ordered all Justice Department agencies to end hiring discrimination based on sexual orientation.

In another important area of change, women have begun to enter the ranks of police administration. The 2,000-member International Association of Women Police estimates, for example, that there are more than 100 female chiefs of police throughout the country. Another growing organization, the Women's Police Chief Association, offers networking opportunities to women seeking and holding high rank within police departments nationwide.[238] The National Center for Women and Policing, which is a project of the Feminist Majority Foundation, provides a nationwide resource for law enforcement agencies, community leaders, and public officials seeking to increase the numbers of female police officers in their communities.

Summary

Three styles of policing are identified in this chapter: (1) the watchman style, (2) the legalistic style, and (3) the service style. The style of policing that characterizes a community tends to flow from the lifestyles of those who live there. While the watchman style of policing, with its emphasis on order maintenance, was widespread during the mid-twentieth century, the service style, which finds embodiment in the community policing model, is becoming commonplace today.

Police discretion refers to the exercise of choice by law enforcement officers in the decision to investigate or apprehend, the disposition of suspects, the carrying out of official duties, and the application of sanctions. Police work today is characterized by the opportunity for individual officers to exercise considerable discretion, by a powerful subculture which communicates select values in support of a police personality, and by the very real possibility of corruption and deviance. As defined in this chapter, police corruption refers to the abuse of police authority for personal or organizational gain.

Opposed to the illegitimate use of police authority, however, are increased calls for integrity and ethical awareness in police work and for continuing growth of professionalism. Professionalism, with its emphasis on education, training, high ethical values, and personal accountability, should soon lead to greater public recognition of the significance of police work and to higher salaries for career police personnel. Increased salaries and a clear public appreciation for the work done by police officers and other police department employees should, in turn, do much to decrease corruption and deviance in law enforcement ranks.

Civil liability issues are of great importance in policing. They may arise from the fact that law enforcement personnel and the agencies they serve have the power to inappropriately curtail the civil and due process rights of criminal suspects. Allegations of assault provide what may be the most visible instances of potential police civil liability today, since such incidents are often widely publicized by the media. Both police departments and individual police officers can become the targets of civil lawsuits. Supervisors can be named as defendants in lawsuits as a result of claimed failures to properly train those whom they are responsible for managing.

Federal suits based on claims that officers acted with disregard for an individual's right to due process are called *1983 lawsuits* because they are based upon Section 1983 of Title 42 of the U.S. Code, an act passed by Congress in 1871 to ensure the civil rights of men and women of all races, including constitutional rights to life, liberty, and property. Another type of civil suit that can be brought specifically against federal agents is known as a *Bivens* action. Although the doctrine of sovereign immunity barred legal action against state and local governments in the past, recent court cases and legislative activity have restricted the opportunity for law enforcement agencies and their officers to exercise claims of immunity.

As the environment surrounding the individual officer changes, so too will societal expectations for the police profession. The movement away from policing as order maintenance and a new emphasis on community policing presage continued shifts in the police role which will likely continue well into the twenty-first century.

Discussion Questions

1. Do you think police officers exercise too much discretion in the performance of their duties? Explain. If you think it would be desirable to limit discretion, how would you do it?
2. How is the police role in America affected by the fact that police officers work within a multicultural society?
3. What are the central features of the police working personality? How does the police working personality develop? What programs might be initiated to shape the police personality in a more desirable way?
4. What themes run through the findings of the Knapp Commission and the Wickersham Commission? What innovative steps might police departments take to reduce or eliminate corruption among their officers?
5. Is police work a profession? Explain. What advantages are there to viewing policing as a profession? How do you think most police officers today see their work—as a profession or as just a job?
6. Reread the Law Enforcement Code of Ethics (found in CJ Today Exhibit 6–1). Do you think most police officers make conscious efforts to apply the code in the performance of their duties? How might ethics training in police departments be improved?

To participate in an online discussion on these topics and others, go to the Global Town Meeting electronic message board for Chapter 6 on the *Criminal Justice Today* Companion Website at cjtoday.com.

Web Quest!

Visit the National Criminal Justice Reference Service (NCJRS) at http://www.ncjrs.org. Click on the "Keyword Search" option, then on "Help Text" to view tips on performing effective searches, modifying search queries, and interpreting search results. Write a description of the search techniques available under "Keyword Search," including wild-card, proximity, concept, Boolean, and pattern searching. What does the help text suggest you do if you find too much in your search? If you find too little?

Return to the "Keyword Search" page, and click "Advanced Searches." What kinds of advanced searches are available? How can you search for a whole phrase?

Revisit the NCJRS home page, and click on "Abstracts Database." What is the Abstracts Database? How does it differ from the NCJRS full-text collection?

After you have familiarized yourself with searching techniques, put your skills to use by conducting a search of the NCJRS site to identify documents on community policing. (Note: You may have to develop your own search strategy using other keywords in combination with "community policing" to narrow down the results of your search.) What kinds of documents did you find? What conclusions, if any, did you come to about community policing after reading these documents? Would you recommend that every law enforcement agency have a community-policing program? Explain.

To complete this Web Quest! online, go to the Web Quest! module in Chapter 6 of the *Criminal Justice Today* Companion Website at cjtoday.com.

Library Extras!

Library Extra! **6–1**	*Together We Can: A Strategic Plan for Reinventing the Chicago Police Department* (Chicago Police Department, 1993).
Library Extra! **6–2**	*Public Involvement: Community Policing in Chicago* (NIJ, 2000).
Library Extra! **6–3**	*Measuring What Matters: Developing Measures of What the Police Do* (NIJ, 1997).
Library Extra! **6–4**	*Principles for Promoting Police Integrity* (USDOJ, 2001).
Library Extra! **6–5**	*Noble Cause Corruption and the Police Ethic* (FBI, 1999).
Library Extra! **6–6**	*The Measurement of Police Integrity* (NIJ, 2000).
Library Extra! **6–7**	*On-the-Job Stress in Policing: Reducing It, Preventing It* (NIJ, 2000).
Library Extra! **6–8**	*Racially Biased Policing: A Principled Response* (PERF, 2001).
Library Extra! **6–9**	*A Resource Guide on Racial Profiling Data Collection Systems* (USDOJ, 2000).
Library Extra! **6–10**	*Use of Force by Police: Overview of National and Local Data* (BJS, 1999).
Library Extra! **6–11**	*Understanding the Use of Force by and against the Police* (NIJ, 1996).
Library Extra! **6–12**	*Suppose We Were Really Serious about Police Departments Becoming "Learning Organizations"?* (NIJ, 1997).
Library Extra! **6–13**	*Recruiting and Retaining Women: A Self-Assessment Guide for Law Enforcement* (Center for Women and Policing, 2001).

To explore these resources online, go to the Library Extras! area of the *Criminal Justice Today* Companion Website at cjtoday.com. You should also check the author's "Late Picks" online for newly released documents and updated Library Extras! You can find Late Picks at http://cjtoday.com/latepicks.htm.

Marginal Notes

i. Sam S. Souryal, *Police Administration and Management* (St. Paul, MN: West, 1977), p. 261.

ii. Community Policing Consortium, *What Is Community Policing?* (Washington, D.C.: Community Policing Consortium, 1995).

iii. Jim Hodgson, "Living the Bradley County Sheriff's Mission Statement." Web posted at http://www.bradleysheriff.com/majorthoughts.htm. Accessed February 22, 2002.

iv. Jerome H. Skolnick and David H. Bayley, *The New Blue Line: Police Innovation in Six American Cities* (New York: Free Press, 1986), p. 229.

v. Carl B. Klockars et al., *The Measurement of Police Integrity,* National Institute of Justice Research in Brief (Washington, D.C.: NIJ, 2000), p. 1.

vi. Karyn S. Hunttings, *Quotation World.* Web posted at http://s-2000.com/quoteworld/character.html. Accessed March 20, 2002.

vii. Deborah Ramierz, Jack McDevitt, and Amy Farrell, *A Resource Guide on Racial Profiling Data Collection Systems: Promising Practices and Lessons Learned* (Washington, D.C.: Department of Justice, 2000), p. 3.

viii. National Institute of Justice, *Use of Force by Police: Overview of National and Local Data* (Washington, D.C.: NIJ, 1999).

ix. Samuel Walker, Geoffrey P. Albert, and Dennis J. Kenney, *Responding to the Problem Police Officer: A National Study of Early Warning Systems* (Washington, D.C.: National Institute of Justice, 2000).

x. Sam W. Lathrop, "Reviewing Use of Force: A Systematic Approach," *FBI Law Enforcement Bulletin,* October 2000, p. 18.

xi. Jack R. Greene, "Community Policing in America: Changing the Nature, Structure, and Function of the Police," in Julie Horney, ed., *Criminal Justice 2000,* Vol. 3 (Washington, D.C.: Department of Justice, 2000), p. 301.

xii. David A. Garvin, "Building a Learning Organization," *Harvard Business Review* (1993), pp. 78–91.

Notes

1. Lorie Fridell et al., *Racially Biased Policing: A Principled Response* (Washington, D.C.: Police Executive Research Forum, 2001), p. 41.

2. It happened in 1992. To learn more about similar drug busts gone wrong, including some with serious consequences, visit http://mojo.calyx.com/~umacrc/library/misfires.

3. "Bust 180 Degrees Wrong," *USA Today,* December 1, 1992, p. 3A.

4. Ibid.

5. The elements of this definition draw upon the now-classic work by O. W. Wilson, *Police Administration* (New York: McGraw-Hill, 1950), pp. 2–3.

6. For a history of these three categories, see: Francis X. Hartmann, "Debating the Evolution of American Policing," *Perspectives on Policing,* No. 5 (Washington, D.C.: National Institute of Justice, 1988).

7. James Q. Wilson, *Varieties of Police Behavior: The Management of Law and Order in Eight Communities* (Cambridge, MA: Harvard University Press, 1968).

8. Independent Commission on the Los Angeles Police Department, *Report of the Independent Commission on the Los Angeles Police Department* (Los Angeles: The Commission, 1991).

9. Gary W. Sykes, "Street Justice: A Moral Defense of Order Maintenance Policing," *Justice Quarterly,* Vol. 3, No. 4 (December 1986), p. 505.

10. Jim Hodgson, "Living the Bradley County Sheriff's Mission Statement." Web posted at http://www.bradleysheriff.com/majorthoughts.htm. Accessed February 22, 2002.

11. Egon Bittner, "Community Relations," in Alvin W. Cohn and Emilio C. Viano, eds., *Police Community Relations: Images, Roles, Realities* (Philadelphia: J. B. Lippincott, 1976), pp. 77–82.

12. Charles Hale, *Police Patrol: Operations and Management* (New York: John Wiley, 1981), p. 112.

13. Paul B. Weston, *Police Organization and Management* (Pacific Palisades, CA: Goodyear, 1976), p. 159.

14. Hale, *Police Patrol.*

15. Mark H. Moore and Robert C. Trojanowicz, "Corporate Strategies for Policing," *Perspectives on Policing,* No. 6 (Washington, D.C.: National Institute of Justice, 1988).

16. Ibid., p. 6.

17. Community Policing Consortium, *Community Policing Is Alive and Well* (Washington, D.C.: Community Policing Consortium, 1995), p. 1.

18. George L. Kelling, *The Newark Foot Patrol Experiment* (Washington, D.C.: Police Foundation, 1981).

19. Robert C. Trojanowicz, "An Evaluation of a Neighborhood Foot Patrol Program," *Journal of Police Science and Administration,* Vol. 11 (1983).

20. Bureau of Justice Assistance, *Understanding Community Policing: A Framework for Action* (Washington, D.C.: Bureau of Justice Statistics, 1994), p. 10.

21. Robert C. Trojanowicz and Bonnie Bucqueroux, *Community Policing* (Cincinnati, OH: Anderson, 1990).

22. Moore and Trojanowicz, "Corporate Strategies for Policing," p. 8.

23. S. M. Hartnett and W. G. Skogan, "Community Policing: Chicago's Experience," *National Institute of Justice Journal,* (April 1999), pp. 2–11.

24. Jerome H. Skolnick and David H. Bayley, *Community Policing: Issues and Practices around the World* (Washington, D.C.: National Institute of Justice, 1988).

25. Ibid.

26. William L. Goodbody, "What Do We Expect New-Age Cops to Do?" *Law Enforcement News,* April 30, 1995, pp. 14, 18.

27. Sam Vincent Meddis and Desda Moss, "Many 'Fed-Up' Communities Cornering Crime," *USA Today,* May 22, 1995, p. 8A.

28. Jerome H. Skolnick and David H. Bayley, *The New Blue Line: Police Innovation in Six American Cities* (New York: Free Press, 1986).

29. Matthew J. Hickman and Brian A. Reaves, *Community Policing in Local Police Departments, 1997 and 1999,* Bureau of Justice Statistics Special Report (Washington, D.C.: Department of Justice, 2001).

30. Richard M. Daley and Matt L. Rodriguez, *Together We Can: A Strategic Plan for Reinventing the Chicago Police Department* (Chicago: Chicago Police Department, 1993). Web posted at http://www.ci.chi.il.us/CommunityPolicing/Statistics/Reports/TWC.pdf. Accessed March 5, 2002.

31. Richard M. Daley, "A Message from the Mayor," Chicago Police Department's website, http://www.ci.chi.il.us/CommunityPolicing/Welcome/Mayor.html. Accessed June 9, 2001.

32. Chicago Community Policing Evaluation Consortium, *Community Policing in Chicago: Year Three Evaluation* (Chicago: Illinois Criminal Justice Information Authority, 1996).

33. Chicago Community Policing Evaluation Consortium, *Community Policing in Chicago, Year Two: An Interim Report* (Chicago: Illinois Criminal Justice Information Authority, 1995).

34. For the latest statistics, visit the CAPS program on the World Wide Web at http://www.ci.chi.il.us/CommunityPolicing.

35. Chicago Community Policing Evaluation Consortium, *Community Policing in Chicago: Year Three Evaluation.*

36. Bureau of Justice Assistance, *Neighborhood-Oriented Policing in Rural Communities: A Program Planning Guide* (Washington, D.C.: Bureau of Justice Statistics, 1994), p. 4.

37. See the COPS Office website at http://www.usdoj.gov/cops. Accessed January 22, 2000.

38. Jihong Zhao, Nicholas P. Lovrich, and Quint Thurman, "The Status of Community Policing in American Cities: Facilitators and Impediments Revisited," *Policing,* Vol. 22, No. 1 (1999), p. 74.

39. For a good critique and overview of community policing, see Geoffrey P. Alpert et al., *Community Policing: Contemporary Readings* (Prospect Heights, IL: Waveland Press, 1998).

40. Jack R. Greene, "Community Policing in America: Changing the Nature, Structure, and Function of the Police," in U.S. Department of Justice, *Criminal Justice 2000*, Vol. 3 (Washington, D.C.: USDOJ, 2000).

41. Michael D. Reisig and Roger B. Parks, "Experience, Quality of Life, and Neighborhood Context: A Hierarchical Analysis of Satisfaction with Police," *Justice Quarterly*, Vol. 17, No. 3 (2000), p. 607.

42. Mark E. Correla, "The Conceptual Ambiguity of Community in Community Policing: Filtering the Muddy Waters," *Policing*, Vol. 23, No. 2 (2000), pp. 218–233.

43. Adapted from Donald R. Fessler, *Facilitating Community Change: A Basic Guide* (San Diego, CA: San Diego State University, 1976), p. 7.

44. Daniel W. Flynn, *Defining the "Community" in Community Policing* (Washington, D.C.: Police Executive Research Forum, 1998).

45. Robert C. Trojanowicz and Mark H. Moore, *The Meaning of Community in Community Policing* (East Lansing: Michigan State University's National Neighborhood Foot Patrol Center, 1988).

46. Robert M. Bohm, K. Michael Reynolds, and Stephen T. Holms, "Perceptions of Neighborhood Problems and Their Solutions: Implications for Community Policing," *Policing*, Vol. 23, No. 4 (2000), p. 439.

47. Ibid., p. 442.

48. Goodbody, "What Do We Expect New-Age Cops to Do?"

49. Ibid.

50. Ibid.

51. Malcolm K. Sparrow, "Implementing Community Policing," *Perspectives on Policing*, No. 9 (Washington, D.C.: National Institute of Justice, 1988).

52. "L.A. Police Chief: Treat People Like Customers," *USA Today*, March 29, 1993, p. 13A.

53. Robert Wasserman and Mark H. Moore, "Values in Policing," *Perspectives in Policing*, No. 8 (Washington, D.C.: National Institute of Justice, 1988), p. 7.

54. "New York City Mayor Sparks Debate on Community Policing," *Criminal Justice Newsletter*, Vol. 25, No. 2 (January 18, 1994), p. 1.

55. Peter B. Kraska and Victor E. Kappeler, "Militarizing American Police: The Rise and Normalization of Paramilitary Units," *Social Problems*, Vol. 44, No. 1 (February 1997), pp. 1–18.

56. Howard Cohen, "Overstepping Police Authority," *Criminal Justice Ethics* (summer/fall 1987), pp. 52–60.

57. Kenneth Culp Davis, *Police Discretion* (St. Paul, MN: West, 1975).

58. See, for example, Robert Shepard Engel, James J. Sobol, and Robert E. Worden, "Further Exploration of the Demeanor Hypothesis: The Interaction of Effects of Suspects' Characteristics and Demeanor on Police Behavior," *Justice Quarterly*, Vol. 17, No. 2 (2000), p. 235.

59. Sykes, "Street Justice," p. 505.

60. Jerome H. Skolnick, *Justice without Trial: Law Enforcement in a Democratic Society* (New York: John Wiley, 1966).

61. William A. Westley, *Violence and the Police: A Sociological Study of Law, Custom, and Morality* (Cambridge, MA: MIT Press, 1970); and William A. Westley, "Violence and the Police," *American Journal of Sociology*, Vol. 49 (1953), pp. 34–41.

62. Arthur Niederhoffer, *Behind the Shield: The Police in Urban Society* (Garden City, NY: Anchor Press, 1967).

63. Thomas Barker and David L. Carter, *Police Deviance* (Cincinnati, OH: Anderson, 1986). See also Christopher P. Wilson, *Cop Knowledge: Police Power and Cultural Narrative in Twentieth-Century America* (Chicago: University of Chicago Press, 2000).

64. See, for example, Michael Brown, *Working the Street: Police Discretion and the Dilemmas of Reform* (New York: Russell Sage Foundation, 1981); and Wilson, *Cop Knowledge*. Wilson's book is about the production and influence of cultural knowledge about American policing.

65. Richard Bennett and Theodore Greenstein, "The Police Personality: A Test of the Predispositional Model," *Journal of Police Science and Administration*, Vol. 3 (1975), pp. 439–445.

66. James Teevan and Bernard Dolnick, "The Values of the Police: A Reconsideration and Interpretation," *Journal of Police Science and Administration* (1973), pp. 366–369.

67. Janine Rauch and Etienne Marasis, "Contextualizing the Waddington Report," Web posted at http://www.wits.ac.za/csvr/papers/papwadd.html. Accessed January 5, 2002.

68. Ibid.

69. Ibid.

70. Ibid.

71. Carl B. Klockars et al., "The Measurement of Police Integrity," *National Institute of Justice Research in Brief* (Washington, D.C.: NIJ, 2000), p. 1.

72. Michael J. Palmiotto, ed., *Police Misconduct: A Reader for the Twenty-first Century* (Upper Saddle River, NJ: Prentice Hall, 2001), preface.

73. Tim Prenzler and Peta Mackay, "Police Gratuities: What the Public Thinks," *Criminal Justice Ethics* (winter/spring 1995), pp. 15–25.

74. Thomas Barker and David L. Carter, *Police Deviance* (Cincinnati, OH: Anderson, 1986). For a detailed overview of the issues involved in police corruption, see Victor E. Kappeler, Richard D. Sluder, and Geoffrey P. Alpert, *Forces of Deviance: Understanding the Dark Side of Policing*, 2d ed. (Prospect Heights, IL: Waveland Press, 1998); Dean J. Champion, *Police Misconduct in America: A Reference Handbook* (Santa Barbara, CA: Abo-Clio, 2002); and Kim Michelle Lersch, ed., *Policing and Misconduct* (Upper Saddle River, NJ: Prentice Hall, 2002).

75. Frank L. Perry, "Repairing Broken Windows: Preventing Corruption within Our Ranks," *FBI Law Enforcement Bulletin*, February 2001, pp. 23–26.

76. Ibid., p. 23.

77. Ibid.

78. "Nationline: NYC Cops—Excess Force Not Corruption," *USA Today*, June 16, 1995, p. 3A.

79. *Knapp Commission Report on Police Corruption* (New York: George Braziller, 1973).

80. Ibid.

81. See Erwin Chemerinsky, *An Independent Analysis of the Los Angeles Police Department's Board of Inquiry Report on the Rampart Scandal*, September 11, 2000. Web posted at http://www.usc.edu/dept/law/faculty/chemerinsky/rampart_finalrep.html. Accessed January 10, 2002.

82. Linda Deutsch, "Appeals Court Intercedes in LAPD Corruption Trial," Associated Press, October 12, 2000. Web posted at http://www.newstimes.com/archive2000/oct12/nah.htm. Accessed January 20, 2002.

83. "Three LAPD Officers Convicted," *USA Today* online edition, November 15, 2000. Accessed July 16, 2001.

84. "Prosecutors: LAPD Hindering Police Corruption Trial," Associated Press, October 6, 2000. Web posted at http://www.newstimes.com/archive2000/oct06/nac.htm. Accessed February 2, 2002.

85. "Three LAPD Officers Convicted."

86. Ibid.

87. Tina Daunt and Jim Newton, "Council OKs Police Reform Pact with Justice Department," *Los Angeles Times* online edition, November 3, 2000. Accessed May 20, 2001.

88. Scott Glover and Matt Lait, "A Tearful Perez Gets five Years," *Los Angeles Times* online edition, February 26, 2000. Accessed August 28, 2001.

89. Edwin H. Sutherland and Donald Cressey, *Principles of Criminology,* 8th ed. (Philadelphia: J. B. Lippincott, 1970).

90. Tim R. Jones, Compton Owens, and Melissa A. Smith, "Police Ethics Training: A Three-Tiered Approach," *FBI Law Enforcement Bulletin,* June 1995, pp. 22–26.

91. Stephen J. Gaffigan and Phyllis P. McDonald, *Police Integrity: Public Service with Honor* (Washington, D.C.: National Institute of Justice, 1997).

92. U.S. Department of Justice, *Principles for Promoting Police Integrity: Examples of Promising Police Practices* (Washington, D.C.: DOJ, 2001).

93. *Carroll* v. *City of Westminster,* 4th Cir. No. 99-1556, November 17, 2000.

94. The material in this paragraph is adapted from Sharon Burrell, "Random Drug Testing of Police Officers Upheld," Legal Views—A Resource from Montgomery County's (Maryland) Office of the County Attorney, Vol. 6, No. 2 (February 2001), p. 4.

95. See National Institute of Justice, *Employee Drug Testing Policies in Police Departments,* National Institute of Justice Research in Brief (Washington, D.C.: Department of Justice, 1986).

96. Ibid.

97. *Maurice Turner* v. *Fraternal Order of Police,* 500 A.2d 1005 (D.C. 1985).

98. *Philip Caruso, President of P.B.A.* v. *Benjamin Ward, Police Commissioner,* New York State Supreme Court, Pat. 37, Index no. 12632-86, 1986.

99. *National Treasury Employees Union* v. *Von Raab,* 489 U.S. 656, 659 (1989).

100. National Law Enforcement Officers' Memorial Fund website, http://www.nleomf.com. Accessed January 20, 2002.

101. Greg Meyer, "LAPD Faces Urban Warfare in North Hollywood Bank Shoot-Out," *Police* (April 1997), pp. 20–23.

102. Ibid.

103. Ibid.

104. Nine police officers and two civilians were wounded by gunfire. Seven other people were injured, including a police officer and a civilian involved in a car crash. For a definitive accounting of injuries in the incident, see Greg Meyer, "40 Minutes in North Hollywood," *Police* (June 1997), pp. 27–37.

105. From the Officer Down Memorial Page on the Web, http://odmp.org/officer.php?oid=15754. Accessed February 22, 2002.

106. Officer Down Memorial Page on the Web, http://odmp.org. Accessed October 22, 2001.

107. Ibid., http://www.odmp.org/yeardisp.php?year=2001. Accessed January 16, 2001.

108. Anthony J. Pinizzotto and Edward F. Davis, "Cop Killers and Their Victims," *FBI Law Enforcement Bulletin,* December 1992, p. 10.

109. Bureau of Labor Statistics, *Occupational Outlook Handbook, 2000–01 Edition* (Washington, D.C.: BLS, 2000); and Brian A. Reaves and Timothy C. Hart, *Law Enforcement Management and Administrative Statistics, 1999: Data for Individual State and Local Agencies with 100 or More Officers* (Washington, D.C.: Bureau of Justice Statistics, 2000). Note that LEMAS only includes data from approximately 700 state and local law enforcement agencies that employ 100 or more full-time sworn personnel and that assign 50 or more of these officers to respond to calls for service. LEMAS reports finding 402,000 full-time sworn personnel among those departments in its 1999 survey. BLS data are more comprehensive and include part-time personnel.

110. Brian A. Reaves and Timothy C. Hart, *Federal Law Enforcement Officers, 2000* (Washington, D.C.: Bureau of Justice Statistics, 2001).

111. As reported by the Headline News Network, April 26, 1988.

112. *AIDS and Our Workplace,* New York City Police Department pamphlet, November 1987.

113. "Collecting and Handling Evidence Infected with Human Disease-Causing Organisms," *FBI Law Enforcement Bulletin,* July 1987.

114. Theodore M. Hammett, "Precautionary Measures and Protective Equipment: Developing a Reasonable Response," *National Institute of Justice Bulletin* (Washington, D.C.: U.S. Government Printing Office, 1988).

115. See Occupational Safety and Health Administration, OSHA Bloodborne Pathogens Act of 1991 (29 CFR 1910.1030).

116. *National Institute of Justice Reports,* No. 206 (November/December 1987).

117. "Drowned Boys Case Takes Toll on Officers, Clergy," *Florida Times-Union* (Jacksonville), November 10, 1994, p. A6.

118. See "On-the-Job Stress in Policing: Reducing It, Preventing It," *National Institute of Justice Journal* (January 2000), pp. 18–24.

119. "Stress on the Job," *Newsweek,* April 25, 1988, p. 43.

120. "On-the-Job Stress in Policing," p. 19.

121. Kevin Barrett, "Police Suicide: Is Anyone Listening?" *Journal of Safe Management of Disruptive and Assaultive Behavior* (spring 1997), pp. 6–9.

122. Ibid.

123. For an excellent review of coping strategies among police officers, see Robin N. Haarr and Merry Morash, "Gender, Race, and Strategies of Coping with Occupational Stress in Policing," *Justice Quarterly,* Vol. 16, No. 2 (June 1999), pp. 303–336.

124. Mark H. Anshel, "A Conceptual Model and Implications for Coping with Stressful Events in Police Work," *Criminal Justice and Behavior,* Vol. 27, No. 3 (2000), p. 375.

125. Ibid.

126. "On-the-Job Stress in Policing," p. 20.

127. Bryan Vila, "Tired Cops: Probable Connections between Fatigue and the Performance, Health, and Safety of Patrol Officers," *American Journal of Police,* Vol. 15, No. 2 (1996), pp. 51–92.

128. Bryan Vila et al., *Evaluating the Effects of Fatigue on Police Patrol Officers: Final Report* (Washington, D.C.: National Institute of Justice, 2000).

129. Bryan Vila and Erik Y. Taiji, "Fatigue and Police Officer Performance," paper presented at the annual meeting of the American Society of Criminology, Chicago, 1996.

130. "Stroke Victim Sues State over Arrest," Associated Press wire service, April 24, 1996.

131. Charles R. Swanson, Leonard Territo, and Robert W. Taylor, *Police Administration: Structures, Processes, and Behavior,* 2d ed. (New York: Macmillan, 1988).

132. *Malley* v. *Briggs,* 475 U.S. 335, 106 S.Ct. 1092 (1986).

133. Ibid., at 4246.

134. *Biscoe* v. *Arlington County,* 238 U.S. App. D.C. 206, 738 F.2d 1352, 1362 (1984). See also, 738 F.2d 1352 (D.C. Cir. 1984), cert denied; 469 U.S. 1159; and 105 S.Ct. 909, 83 L.E.2d 923 (1985).

135. *Kaplan* v. *Lloyd's Insurance Co.,* 479 So. 2d 961 (La. App. 1985).

136. *City of Canton, Ohio* v. *Harris,* U.S. 109 S.Ct. 1197 (1989).

137. Ibid., at 1204.

138. *Board of the County Commissioners of Bryan County, Oklahoma* v. *Brown,* 520 U.S. 397 (1997).

139. Title 42, U.S. Code, Section 1983.

140. *Bivens* v. *Six Unknown Federal Agents,* 403 U.S. 388 (1971).

141. See *F.D.I.C.* v. *Meyer,* 510 U.S. 471 (1994), in which the U.S. Supreme Court reiterated its ruling under *Bivens,* stating that only government employees and not government agencies can be sued.

142. *Wyler* v. *U.S.,* 725 F.2d 157 (2d Cir. 1983).

143. California Government Code, § 818.

144. Federal Tort Claims Act, 28 U.S.C. 1346(b), 2671–2680.

145. "Victims of Failed DEA Sting Win More Than $1 Million Judgment," *Drug Enforcement Report,* March 23, 1995, pp. 1–2.

146. *Elder* v. *Holloway,* 114 S.Ct. 1019, 127 L. Ed. 2d 344 (1994).

147. Ibid.

148. *Hunter* v. *Bryant,* 112 S.Ct. 534 (1991).

149. William U. McCormack, "Supreme Court Cases: 1991–1992 Term," *FBI Law Enforcement Bulletin,* November 1992, p. 30.

150. *State of Idaho* v. *Horiuchi,* No. 98-30149 (9th Cir. 06/05/2001).

151. See John Bacon, "FBI Sharpshooter Won't Be Prosecuted," *USA Today* online edition, June 15, 2001.

152. Kevin Johnson, "Court Says Idaho Can Prosecute FBI Agent," *USA Today,* June 6, 2001, p. 3A.

153. For more information on police liability, see Daniel L. Schofield, "Legal Issues of Pursuit Driving," *FBI Law Enforcement Bulletin,* May 1988, pp. 23–29.

154. "Playboy Interview: Daryl Gates," *Playboy,* August 1991, p. 60.

155. Ibid., p. 63.

156. Michael S. Vaughn, Tab W. Cooper, and Rolando V. del Carmen, "Assessing Legal Liabilities in Law Enforcement: Police Chiefs' Views," *Crime and Delinquency,* Vol. 47, No. 1 (2001), p. 3.

157. Peter Verniero and Paul Zoubek, *New Jersey Attorney General's Interim Report of the State Police Review Team Regarding Allegations of Racial Profiling* (Trenton, NJ: Office of the New Jersey Attorney General, 1999).

158. This paragraph is adapted from Ramirez, McDevitt, and Farrell, *A Resource Guide on Racial Profiling Data Collection Systems,* pp. 7–8.

159. *State of New Jersey* v. *Pedro Soto et al.,* Superior Court of New Jersey, 734 A.2d 350, 1996.

160. David Harris, *Driving While Black: Racial Profiling on Our Nation's Highways* (Washington, DC: American Civil Liberties Union, 1999).

161. Blaine Harden and Somini Sengupta, "Some Passengers Singled Out for Exclusion by Flight Crew," *New York Times,* September 22, 2001.

162. Gallup Organization, "Attack on America: Review of Public Opinion," September 17, 2001. Web posted at http://www.gallup.com/poll/Releases/Pr010917.asp. Accessed September 28, 2001.

163. David Cole and John Lambreth, "The Fallacy of Racial Profiling," *New York Times* online, May 13, 2001. Posted at http://college1.nytimes.com/buests/articles/2001/05/13/846196.xml. Accessed August 28, 2001.

164. Amitai Etzioni, "Another Side of Racial Profiling," *USA Today,* May 21, 2001, p. 15A.

165. Gallup Organization, *Racial Profiling Is Seen as Widespread, Particularly Among Young Black Men* (Princeton, NJ: Gallup Poll Organization, December 9, 1999), p. 1.

166. Christopher Stone, "Race, Crime, and the Administration of Justice," *National Institute of Justice Journal* (April 1999), p. 28.

167. Ramirez, McDevitt, and Farrell, *A Resource Guide on Racial Profiling Data Collection Systems,* p. 3.

168. Ibid., p. 55.

169. Police Executive Research Forum, *Racially Biased Policing: A Principled Response* (Washington, D.C.: PERF, 2001).

170. Ibid., foreword.

171. Ibid., p. 39.

172. Ibid., p. 47.

173. Some of the material in this section is adapted or derived from National Institute of Justice, *Use of Force by Police: Overview of National and Local Data* (Washington, D.C.: NIJ, 1999).

174. Lawrence A. Greenfeld, Patrick A. Langan, and Steven K. Smith, "Revising and Fielding the Police-Public Contact Survey," in National Institute of Justice, *Use of Force by Police: Overview of National and Local Data* (Washington, D.C.: NIJ, 1999).

175. Joel H. Garner and Christopher D. Maxwell, "Measuring the Amount of Force Used by and against the Police in Six Jurisdictions," in National Institute of Justice, *Use of Force by Police: Overview of National and Local Data* (Washington, D.C.: NIJ, 1999), p. 41.

176. Geoffrey P. Alpert and Roger G. Dunham, "The Force Factor: Measuring and Assessing Police Use of Force and Suspect Resistance," in National Institute of Justice, *Use of Force by Police: Overview of National and Local Data* (Washington, D.C.: NIJ, 1999).

177. Ibid., p. vii.

178. Kenneth Adams, "What We Know about Police Use of Force," in National Institute of Justice, *Use of Force by Police: Overview of National and Local Data* (Washington, D.C.: NIJ, 1999), p. 4.

179. Ibid.

180. Geoffrey P. Alpert and Roger G. Dunham, *The Force Factor: Measuring Police Use of Force Relative to Suspect Resistance—A Final Report* (Washington, D.C.: National Institute of Justice, 2001).

181. Samuel Walker, Geoffrey P. Alpert, and Dennis J. Kenney, *Responding to the Problem Police Officer: A National Study of Early Warning Systems* (Washington, D.C.: National Institute of Justice, 2000).

182. See Human Rights Watch, "The Christopher Commission Report," from which some of the wording in the paragraph is adapted. Web posted at http://www.hrw.org/reports98/police/uspo73.htm. Accessed March 30, 2002.

183. Lathrop, "Reviewing Use of Force," p. 18.

184. Jodi M. Brown and Patrick A. Langan, *Policing and Homicide, 1976–98: Justifiable Homicide by Police, Police Officers Murdered by Felons* (Washington, D.C.: Bureau of Justice Statistics, 2001), p. iii.

185. *Tennessee* v. *Garner*, 471 U.S. 1 (1985).

186. *Graham* v. *Connor*, 490 U.S. 386, 396–397 (1989).

187. John C. Hall, "FBI Training on the New Federal Deadly Force Policy," *FBI Law Enforcement Bulletin,* April 1996, pp. 25–32.

188. James Fyfe, *Shots Fired: An Examination of New York City Police Firearms Discharges* (Ann Arbor, MI: University Microfilms, 1978).

189. James Fyfe, "Blind Justice? Police Shootings in Memphis," paper presented at the annual meeting of the Academy of Criminal Justice Sciences, Philadelphia, March 1981.

190. It is estimated that American police shoot at approximately 3,600 people every year. See William Geller, *Deadly Force* study guide, Crime File Series (Washington, D.C.: National Institute of Justice, no date).

191. Anne Cohen, "I've Killed That Man Ten Thousand Times," *Police Magazine,* July 1980.

192. For more information, see Joe Auten, "When Police Shoot," *North Carolina Criminal Justice Today,* Vol. 4, No. 4 (summer 1986), pp. 9–14.

193. "Man Attracts Police Gunfire to Commit Suicide," Associated Press wire service, November 17, 1997.

194. "Ten Percent of Police Shootings Found to Be 'Suicide by Cop,'" *Criminal Justice Newsletter,* September 1, 1998, pp. 1–2.

195. Robert J. Homant and Daniel B. Kennedy, "Suicide by Police: A Proposed Typology of Law Enforcement Officer–Assisted Suicide," *Policing: An International Journal of Police Strategies and Management,* Vol. 23, No. 3 (2000), pp 339–355.

196. David W. Hayeslip and Alan Preszler, "NIJ Initiative on Less-than-Lethal Weapons," *NIJ Research in Brief* (Washington, D.C.: National Institute of Justice, 1993).

197. Ibid.

198. Michael Siegfried, "Notes on the Professionalization of Private Security," *Justice Professional* (spring 1989).

199. See Edward A. Farris, "Five Decades of American Policing, 1932–1982: The Path to Professionalism," *Police Chief* (November 1982), p. 34.

200. Commission on Accreditation for Law Enforcement Agencies (CALEA) website, http://www.calea.org. Accessed January 10, 2000. Agency estimates are from Brian A. Reaves and Andrew L. Goldberg, *Census of State and Local Law Enforcement Agencies, 1996* (Washington, D.C.: Bureau of Justice Statistics, 1998).

201. Brian A. Reaves and Andrew L. Goldberg, *Law Enforcement Management and Administrative Statistics, 1997: Data for Individual State and Local Law Enforcement Agencies with 100 or More Officers* (Washington, D.C.: Bureau of Justice Statistics, 1999).

202. California Commission on POST, "California Responds to Racial Profiling." Web posted at http://www.post.ca.gov/surveys/racialprofile.htm. Accessed March 3, 2002.

203. National Commission on Law Observance and Enforcement, *Report on Police* (Washington, D.C.: U.S. Government Printing Office, 1931).

204. President's Commission on Law Enforcement and Administration of Justice, *The Challenge of Crime in a Free Society* (Washington, D.C.: USGPO, 1967).

205. National Advisory Commission on Criminal Justice Standards and Goals, *Report on the Police* (Washington, D.C.: U.S. Government Printing Office, 1973).

206. Reaves and Goldberg, *Law Enforcement Management and Administrative Statistics, 1997.*

207. David L. Carter, Allen D. Sapp, and Darrel W. Stephens, *The State of Police Education: Policy Direction for the Twenty-first Century* (Washington, D.C.: Police Executive Research Forum, 1989).

208. Ibid., p. xiv.

209. Ibid., pp. xxii–xxiii.

210. Brian A. Reaves, *Local Police Departments, 1993* (Washington, D.C.: Bureau of Justice Statistics, April 1996), p. 84.

211. National Advisory Commission on Criminal Justice Standards and Goals, *Report on the Police,* p. 238.

212. "Dallas PD College Rule Gets Final OK," *Law Enforcement News,* July 7, 1986, pp. 1, 13.

213. *Davis* v. *Dallas,* 777 F.2d 205 (5th Cir. 1985).

214. O. W. Wilson and Roy Clinton McLaren, *Police Administration,* 4th ed. (New York: McGraw-Hill, 1977), p. 259.

215. Ibid., p. 270.

216. David A. Garvin, "Building a Learning Organization," *Harvard Business Review* (1993), pp. 78–91.

217. Barry Sugarman, "Learning, Working, Managing, Sharing: The New Paradigm of the 'Learning Organization.'" *Journal of Pedagogy, Pluralism, and Practice,* Vol. 1, No. 2 (fall 1997). Web posted at http://www.lesley.edu/journals/jppp/2/sugarman.html. Accessed March 14, 2002.

218. Adapted from Garvin, "Building a Learning Organization."

219. Independent Committee of Inquiry into the Role and Responsibilities of the Police, *Police Performance and Accountability* p. 46. Web posted at http://www.psi.org.uk/publications/archivepdfs/Role 20pol/INDPOL-0.F.pdf. Accessed January 21, 2002.

220. See, for example, Peter F. Drucker, *Management: Tasks, Responsibilities, Practices* (New York: Harper and Row, 1973).

221. William F. Walsh, "Policing at the Crossroads: Changing Directions for the New Millennium," paper presented at the annual meeting of the Academy of Criminal Justice Sciences, Louisville, Kentucky, March 1997.

222. Andrew J. Harvey, "Building an Organizational Foundation for the Future," *FBI Law Enforcement Bulletin,* November 1996, pp. 12–17.

223. See William A. Geller, "Suppose We Were Really Serious About Police Departments Becoming 'Learning Organizations'?" *National Institute of Justice Journal* (1997), pp. 2–8, from which much of the information in this paragraph and the next is taken.

224. *Report of the National Advisory Commission on Civil Disorders* (New York: E. P. Dutton, 1968), p. 332.

225. As reported in Charles Swanson and Leonard Territo, *Police Administration: Structures, Processes, and Behavior* (New York: Macmillan, 1983), p. 203, from *Affirmative Action Monthly* (February 1979), p. 22.

226. Kathleen Maguire and Ann L. Pastore, *Sourcebook of Criminal Justice Statistics 2000* (Washington, D.C.: USGPO, 2001).

227. National Center for Women and Policing, *Equality Denied: The Status of Women in Policing, 2000* (Los Angeles: NCWP, 2001), p. 1.

228. Ibid.

229. Ibid., p. 3, from which some of the wording in the list is taken.

230. National Center for Women and Policing, *Recruiting and Retaining Women: A Self-Assessment Guide for Law Enforcement* (Los Angeles: NCWP, 2001), p. 22.

231. Ibid.

232. C. Lee Bennett, "Interviews with Female Police Officers in Western Massachusetts," paper presented at the annual meeting of the Academy of Criminal Justice Sciences, Nashville, Tennessee, March 1991.

233. Ibid., p. 9.

234. Carole G. Garrison, Nancy K. Grant, and Kenneth L. J. McCormick, "Utilization of Police Women," unpublished manuscript.

235. Susan Ehrlich Martin and Nancy C. Jurik, *Doing Justice, Doing Gender: Women in Law and Criminal Justice Occupations* (Thousand Oaks, CA: Sage, 1996).

236. Police Foundation, *On the Move: The Status of Women in Policing* (Washington, D.C.: Police Foundation, 1990).

237. See, for example, Pearl Jacobs, "Suggestions for the Greater Integration of Women into Policing," paper presented at the annual meeting of the Academy of Criminal Justice Sciences, Nashville, Tennessee, March 1991; and Cynthia Fuchs Epstein, *Deceptive Distinctions: Sex, Gender, and the Social Order* (New Haven, CT: Yale University Press, 1988).

238. See Sara Roen, "The Longest Climb," *Police* (October 1996), pp. 44–46, 66.

Policing: Legal Aspects

LEARNING OBJECTIVES

After reading this chapter, you should be able to

■ Explain how the Bill of Rights and democratically inspired legal restraints upon the police help to ensure personal freedoms in our society and prevent the development of a police state in America

■ Describe the nature of due process and the specific constitutional amendments upon which due process guarantees are based

■ Explain the importance of the exclusionary rule and the fruit of the poisoned tree doctrine

■ Identify the major differences between the Warren, Burger, and Rehnquist Courts

■ Define *arrest,* and describe how popular depictions of arrest by the police may not be consistent with legal understandings of the term

■ Describe the circumstances under which police officers may search vehicles and the extent to which such searches are permissible

■ Explain how the need to ensure public safety may justify suspicionless searches

■ Recite the *Miranda* warnings, and describe in detail recent U.S. Supreme Court cases that have affected *Miranda* warning requirements

chapter 7

[*"Yeah," the detective mumbled. "Fifteen guys. You might want to think about that. Only two of us . . . " He shook his head. "Sneaking a bunch of cops into a neighborhood like this is going to be like trying to sneak the sun past a rooster. . . ." As he started up the stairs, Angelo reached not for his gun but for his wallet. He took out a Chase Manhattan calendar printed on a supple but firm slip of plastic. He flicked the card at Rand. "I'll open the door with this. You step in and freeze them."*

"Jesus Christ, Angelo," the agent almost gasped. "We can't do that. We haven't got a warrant."

"Don't worry about it, kid," Angelo said, drawing up to the second door on the right on the second floor. "It ain't a perfect world."]

—Larry Collins and Dominique Lapierre[1]

Key Concepts

[Terms]

arrest	fruit of the poisoned tree doctrine	plain view
Bill of Rights	good-faith exception	probable cause
compelling interest	illegally seized evidence	psychological manipulation
Electronic Communications Privacy Act (ECPA)	inherent coercion	reasonable suspicion
electronic evidence	interrogation	search incident to an arrest
emergency search	landmark case	"sneak and peek" search
exclusionary rule	latent evidence	suspicionless search
fleeting targets exception	*Miranda* triggers	writ of *certiorari*
	Miranda warnings	

[Cases]

Alabama v. *White*	*Florida* v. *Bostick*	*Richards* v. *Wisconsin*
Arizona v. *Fulminante*	*Horton* v. *California*	*Silverthorne Lumber Co.* v. *U.S.*
Brecht v. *Abrahamson*	*Illinois* v. *Perkins*	*Smith* v. *Ohio*
Brown v. *Mississippi*	*Indianapolis* v. *Edmond*	*Terry* v. *Ohio*
California v. *Hodari D.*	*Kyllo* v. *U.S.*	*U.S.* v. *Robinson*
Carroll v. *U.S.*	*Mapp* v. *Ohio*	*U.S. Dept. of Justice* v. *Landano*
Chimel v. *California*	*Minnick* v. *Mississippi*	*Weeks* v. *U.S.*
Dickerson v. *U.S.*	*Miranda* v. *Arizona*	*Wilson* v. *Arkansas*
Escobedo v. *Illinois*	*Nix* v. *Williams*	

Introduction

Hear the author discuss this chapter at **cjtoday.com**

What some people believe was a hate crime committed by New York City police officers made national headlines in 1999. During the incident, four white officers unleashed a barrage of 41 bullets at Amadou Diallo, a 22-year-old West African immigrant.[2] Diallo, who was black, was struck by 19 of the 41 bullets and died at the scene. The incident began when officers of a special New York Police Department (NYPD) street crimes unit were searching for a rape suspect in a Bronx neighborhood. They came across Diallo standing in the doorway of his apartment building. Although accounts of what happened next vary, attorneys for the officers told reporters that Diallo resembled the suspect they were looking for. When the officers yelled "Freeze," Diallo apparently did not comply, but instead reached into his pocket. The officers later indicated that they fired because they thought he was reaching for a gun. Diallo's shocked friends, however, later said that he spoke little English and may have been reaching for identification. The seemingly excessive use of firepower resulted in charges of second-degree murder being brought against the officers involved. In February 2000, a state jury found the officers innocent of any criminal wrongdoing. In 2001, the U.S. Department of Justice declined to file federal charges against the officers after deciding that they could not prove that Diallo's rights had been violated.[3] A $61 million civil suit, brought by Diallo's family against the city of New York, is still pending as this book goes to press.[4] Read more about the Diallo case at **Web Extra! 7–1** at cjtoday.com.

The Abuse of Police Power

In August 1997, almost two years before the Diallo incident, a storm of protest swirled around NYPD officers serving Brooklyn's 70th Precinct. In the midst of the storm stood four officers accused of savagely beating and sexually assaulting Abner Louima, a 30-year-

old Haitian immigrant, in a station house bathroom. Louima, a black man who worked as a security guard, had been arrested on charges of assaulting a police officer following an early morning scuffle outside a nightclub. He claimed that after his arrival at the station house, a white officer, Justin Volpe, beat him nearly senseless, then sodomized him with the handle of a toilet plunger while another white officer, Charles Schwarz, held him down. Louima underwent surgery to repair a torn rectum and injured gallbladder and was hospitalized for weeks following the incident.[5] In 1999, Volpe, the lead defendant in the case, pleaded guilty to charges stemming from the beating. Schwarz was convicted separately in a federal trial of violating Louima's civil rights; and officers Thomas Wiese and Thomas Bruder were convicted of conspiracy to obstruct justice and sentenced to five years in prison. In 2002, however, a federal appeals court overturned the convictions of all the officers involved except Volpe.[6]

National publicity surrounding the Louima incident was considerably less intense than that which centered on the 1991 videotaped beating of motorist Rodney King by Los Angeles Police Department (LAPD) officers. King, an unemployed 25-year-old black man, was stopped by LAPD officers for an alleged violation of motor vehicle laws. Police said King had been speeding and had refused to stop for a pursuing patrol car. Officers claimed to have clocked King's 1988 Hyundai at 115 miles per hour (mph) on suburban Los Angeles's Foothill Freeway—even though the car's manufacturer later said the vehicle was not capable of speeds over 100 mph.

Eventually King did stop, but then officers of the LAPD attacked him, shocking him twice with electronic stun guns and striking him with nightsticks and fists. Kicked in the stomach, face, and back, he was left with 11 skull fractures, missing teeth, a crushed cheekbone, and a broken ankle. A witness told reporters she heard King begging officers to stop the beating but that they "were all laughing, like they just had a party."[7] King eventually underwent surgery for brain injuries. Twenty-five police officers—21 from the LAPD, two California Highway Patrol officers, and two school district officers—were involved in the incident. Four of them, who were later indicted, beat King as the other 21 watched.

The entire incident was captured on videotape by an amateur photographer on a nearby balcony who was trying out his new night-sensitive video camera. The two-minute videotape was repeatedly broadcast over national television and was picked up by hundreds of local TV stations. The furor that erupted over the tape led to the ouster of LAPD Chief Daryl Gates and initiated a Justice Department review of law enforcement practices across the country.[8] Some people defended the police officers, citing the "war zone" mentality of today's inner-city crime fighters as fostering a violent mind-set. Officers involved in the beating claimed that King, at 6 feet 3 inches and 225 pounds, appeared strung out on PCP and that he and his two companions made the officers feel threatened.[9]

In 1992, a California jury found the four police defendants not guilty—a verdict that resulted in days of rioting across Los Angeles. A year later, however, in the spring of 1993, two of the officers, Sergeant Stacey Koon and Officer Laurence Powell, were found guilty by a jury in federal court of denying King his constitutional right "not to be deprived of liberty without due process of law, including the right to be . . . free from the intentional use of unreasonable force."[10] Later that year, both were sentenced to two and a half years in prison, far less than might have been expected under federal sentencing guidelines. They were released from prison in December of 1995, and a three-year court battle over whether federal sentencing guideline provisions were violated was resolved in the officers' favor in 1996. Officers Theodore Briseno and Timothy Wind were exonerated at the federal level.

In 1994, King settled a civil suit against the city of Los Angeles for a reported $3.8 million. Observers later concluded that King himself was not a model citizen. At the time of the beating, he was on parole after having served time in prison for robbery. Following the beating, he came under investigation for another robbery and was arrested again three months after his release from the hospital for allegedly picking up a male prostitute dressed as a woman and for trying to run over police who confronted him.[11] He was sentenced in 1996 to 90 days in jail on charges of assault with a deadly weapon for trying to run over his wife during a domestic dispute,[12] and a month later he was fined $1,436 and ordered to serve 30 days on a highway cleanup crew for violating probation on a drunk-driving conviction.[13] In 1999, King was again arrested and charged with spousal battery, child abuse, and vandalism for allegedly beating an ex-wife and her 16-year-old daughter.[14] He pleaded guilty to misdemeanor spousal abuse and received no jail time. In 2001, King again pleaded guilty—this time to three counts of being under the influence of PCP and one count of indecent exposure.[15] He was sentenced to spend a year at a live-in drug-treatment center. Regardless of what has happened to Rodney King over the past decade, his 1991 beating continues to serve as a rallying point for individual-rights activists concerned with ensuring that citizens remain protected from the abuse of police power in an increasingly conservative society. Learn more about the Rodney King incident and its ramifications at **Web Extra! 7–2** at cjtoday.com.

This chapter shows how the police, like everyone else, are not above the law. It describes the legal environment surrounding police activities—from search and seizure through arrest and the interrogation of suspects. As we shall see throughout, democratically inspired legal restraints upon the police help ensure individual freedoms in our society and prevent the development of a police state in America. Like anything else, however, the rules by which the police are expected to operate are in constant flux, and their continuing development forms the meat of this chapter.

The beating of Rodney King by Los Angeles police officers, captured here by a man trying out a new video camera. The 1991 incident raised many questions about police integrity while highlighting the power of new technology to uncover police abuses.

CORBIS/Sygma

A Changing Legal Climate

The Constitution of the United States is designed—especially in the **Bill of Rights**—to protect citizens against abuses of police power (Table 7–1). However, the legal environment surrounding the police in modern America is much more complex than it was just 40 years ago. Up until that time, the Bill of Rights was largely given only lip service in criminal justice proceedings around the country. In practice, law enforcement, especially on the state and local level, revolved around tried-and-true methods of search, arrest, and interrogation that sometimes left little room for recognition of individual rights. Police operations during that period were often far more informal than they are today, and investigating officers frequently assumed that they could come and go as they pleased, even to the extent of invading someone's personal space without a search warrant. Interrogations could quickly turn violent, and the infamous "rubber hose," which was reputed to leave few marks on the body, was probably more widely used during the questioning of suspects than many would like to believe. Similarly, "doing things by the book" could mean the use of thick telephone books for beating suspects, since the books spread out the force of blows and left few visible bruises. Although such abuses were not necessarily day-to-day practices in all police agencies, and while they probably did not characterize more than a relatively small proportion of all officers, such conduct pointed to the need for greater control over police activities so that even the potential for abuse might be curtailed.

It was during the 1960s that the U.S. Supreme Court, under the direction of Chief Justice Earl Warren (1891–1974), accelerated the process of guaranteeing individual rights in the face of criminal prosecution. Warren Court rulings bound the police to strict procedural requirements in the areas of investigation, arrest, and interrogation. Later rulings scrutinized trial court procedure and enforced humanitarian standards in sentencing and punishment. The Warren Court also seized upon the Fourteenth Amendment and made it a basis for judicial mandates requiring that both state and federal criminal justice agencies adhere to the Court's interpretation of the Constitution. The apex of the individual-rights emphasis in Supreme Court decisions was reached in the 1966 case of *Miranda* v. *Arizona*,[16] which established the famous requirement of a police "rights advisement" of suspects. In wielding its brand of idealism, the Warren Court (which held sway from 1953 until 1969) accepted the fact that a few guilty people would go free in order that the rights of the majority of Americans would be protected.

Supreme Court decisions of the last few decades—the product of a new conservative Court philosophy—have begun what some call a "reversal" of Warren-era advances in the area of individual rights. By creating exceptions to some of the Warren Court's rules and

Bill of Rights

- - - - - - - - - - - - - -

The popular name given to the first ten amendments to the U.S. Constitution, which are considered especially important in the processing of criminal defendants.

CONSTITUTIONAL AMENDMENTS OF SPECIAL SIGNIFICANCE TO THE AMERICAN SYSTEM OF JUSTICE	TABLE 7–1

This Right Is Guaranteed	By This Amendment
The right against unreasonable searches and seizures	Fourth
The right against arrest without probable cause	Fourth
The right against self-incrimination	Fifth
The right against "double jeopardy"	Fifth
The right to due process of law	Fifth, Sixth, Fourteenth
The right to a speedy trial	Sixth
The right to a jury trial	Sixth
The right to know the charges	Sixth
The right to cross-examine witnesses	Sixth
The right to a lawyer	Sixth
The right to compel witnesses on one's behalf	Sixth
The right to reasonable bail	Eighth
The right against excessive fines	Eighth
The right against cruel and unusual punishments	Eighth
The applicability of constitutional rights to all citizens, regardless of state law or procedure	Fourteenth

restraints and in allowing for the emergency questioning of suspects before they are read their rights, a changed Supreme Court has recognized the realities attending day-to-day police work and the need to ensure public safety. This practical approach to justice, which came into vogue during the Reagan-Bush political era and is still with us, is all the more interesting because it must struggle to emerge from within the confines of earlier Supreme Court decisions.

Individual Rights

The Constitution of the United States provides for a system of checks and balances among the legislative, judicial, and executive (presidential) branches of government. By this we mean that one branch of government is always held accountable to the other branches. The system is designed to ensure that no *one* individual or agency can become powerful enough to usurp the rights and freedoms guaranteed under the Constitution. Without accountability, it is possible to imagine a police state in which the power of law enforcement is absolute and is related more to political considerations and personal vendettas than to objective considerations of guilt or innocence.

Under our system of government, courts become the arena for dispute resolution, not just between individuals, but between citizens and the agencies of government. After handling by the justice system, people who feel they have not received the respect and dignity due them under the law can appeal to the courts for redress. Such appeals are usually based upon procedural issues and are independent of more narrow considerations of guilt or innocence.

In this chapter, we spend a great deal of time on cases that are important for having clarified constitutional guarantees concerning individual liberties within the criminal justice arena. They involve issues which most of us have come to call *rights*. It is common to hear arrestees today say, "You can't do that! I know my rights!" Rights are concerned with procedure, that is, with how police and other actors in the criminal justice system handle each part of the process of dealing with suspects. Rights violations have often become the basis for the dismissal of charges, the acquittal of defendants, or the release of convicted offenders after an appeal to a higher court.

Due Process Requirements

As you may recall from Chapter 1, due process is a requirement of the Fifth, Sixth, and Fourteenth Amendments to the U.S. Constitution, which mandates that justice system officials respect the rights of accused individuals throughout the criminal justice process. Most due process requirements of relevance to the police pertain to three major areas: (1) evidence and investigation (often called *search and seizure*), (2) arrest, and (3) interro-

An officer questions a suspect. The legal environment surrounding the police helps ensure proper official conduct. In a stop like this, inappropriate behavior on the part of the officer can later become the basis for civil or criminal action against the officer and the police department.

Courtesy of the New York City Police Department

gation. Each of these areas has been addressed by a plethora of landmark U.S. Supreme Court decisions. **Landmark cases** produce substantial changes in both the understanding of the requirements of due process and in the practical day-to-day operations of the justice system. Another way to think of landmark cases is that they help significantly in clarifying the "rules of the game"—the procedural guidelines by which the police and the rest of the justice system must abide.

The three areas we are about to discuss have been well defined by decades of court precedent. Keep in mind, however, that judicial interpretations of the constitutional requirement of due process are constantly evolving. As new decisions are rendered and as the composition of the Court itself changes, additional refinements (and even major changes) may occur.

Search and Seizure

The U.S. Constitution declares that people must be secure in their homes and in their persons against unreasonable searches and seizures. This right is asserted by the Fourth Amendment, which reads, "The right of the people to be secure in their persons, houses, papers, and effects, against unreasonable searches and seizures, shall not be violated, and no Warrants shall issue, but upon probable cause, supported by Oath or affirmation, and particularly describing the place to be searched, and the persons or things to be seized." This amendment, a part of the Bill of Rights, was adopted by Congress and became effective on December 15, 1791.

The language of the Fourth Amendment is familiar to all of us. "Warrants," "probable cause," and other phrases from the amendment are frequently cited in editorials, TV news shows, and daily conversation about **illegally seized evidence**. It is the interpretation of these phrases over time by the U.S. Supreme Court, however, which has given them the impact they have on the justice system today.

The Exclusionary Rule

The first landmark case concerning search and seizure was that of *Weeks* v. *U.S.* (1914).[17] Freemont Weeks was suspected of using the U.S. mail to sell lottery tickets, a federal crime. Weeks was arrested, and federal agents went to his home to conduct a search. They had no search warrant, since at the time investigators did not routinely use warrants. They confiscated many incriminating items of evidence, as well as some of the suspect's personal possessions, including clothes, papers, books, and even candy.

Prior to trial, Weeks's attorney asked that the personal items be returned, claiming that they had been illegally seized under Fourth Amendment guarantees. A judge agreed and ordered the materials returned. On the basis of the evidence that was retained, however, Weeks was convicted in federal court and was sentenced to prison. He appealed his conviction through other courts, and his case eventually reached the U.S. Supreme Court. There, his lawyer reasoned that if some of his client's belongings had been illegally seized, then the remainder of them were also taken improperly. The Court agreed and overturned Weeks's earlier conviction.

The *Weeks* case forms the basis of what is now called the **exclusionary rule**. The exclusionary rule holds that evidence illegally seized by the police cannot be used in a trial. The rule acts as a control over police behavior and specifically focuses upon the failure of officers to obtain warrants authorizing them either to conduct searches or to effect arrests (especially where arrest may lead to the acquisition of incriminating statements or to the seizure of physical evidence).

It is important to note, incidentally, that Freemont Weeks could have been retried on the original charges following the Supreme Court decision in his case. He would not have faced double jeopardy because he was in fact not *finally* convicted on the earlier charges. His conviction was nullified on appeal, resulting in neither a conviction nor an acquittal. Double jeopardy becomes an issue only when a defendant faces retrial on the same charges following acquittal at his or her original trial or when the defendant is retried after having been convicted.

It is also important to recognize that the decision of the Supreme Court in the *Weeks* case was binding, at the time, only upon federal officers, because it was federal agents who were involved in the illegal seizure. Read the *Weeks* decision in its entirety at **Library Extra! 7–1** at cjtoday.com.

landmark case

A precedent-setting court decision that produces substantial changes in both the understanding of the requirements of due process and in the practical day-to-day operations of the justice system.

illegally seized evidence

Evidence seized without regard to the principles of due process as described by the Bill of Rights. Most illegally seized evidence is the result of police searches conducted without a proper warrant or of improperly conducted interrogations.

exclusionary rule

The understanding, based on Supreme Court precedent, that incriminating information must be seized according to constitutional specifications of due process or it will not be allowed as evidence in a criminal trial.

PROBLEMS WITH PRECEDENT

The *Weeks* case demonstrates the power of the Supreme Court in enforcing what we have called the "rules of the game." It also lays bare the much more significant role that the Court plays in rule creation. Until the *Weeks* case was decided, federal law enforcement officers had little reason to think they were acting in violation of due process. Common practice had not required that they obtain a warrant before conducting searches. The rule which resulted from *Weeks* was new, and it would forever alter the enforcement activities of federal officers. Yet the *Weeks* case was also retroactive, in the sense that it was applied to Weeks himself.

There is a problem in the way in which our system generates and applies principles of due process, which may be obvious from our discussion of the *Weeks* case. The problem is that the present appeals system, focusing as it does upon the "rules of the game," presents a ready-made channel for the guilty to go free. There can be little doubt that Freemont Weeks had violated federal law. A jury had convicted him. Yet he escaped punishment because of the illegal behavior of the police—behavior which, until the Court ruled, had not been regarded as anything but legitimate.

Even if the police knowingly violate the principles of due process, which they sometimes do, our sense of justice is compromised when the guilty go free. Famed Supreme Court Justice Benjamin Cardozo (1870–1938) once complained, "The criminal is to go free because the constable has blundered."

Students of criminal justice have long considered three possible solutions to this problem. The first solution suggests that rules of due process, especially when newly articulated by the courts, should be applied only to future cases, not to the initial case in which they are stated. The justices in the *Weeks* case, for example, might have said, "We are creating the 'exclusionary rule' based upon our realization in this case. Law enforcement officers are obligated to use it as a guide in all future searches. However, insofar as the guilt of Mr. Weeks was decided by a jury under rules of evidence existing at the time, we will let that decision stand."

A second solution would punish police officers or other actors in the criminal justice system who act illegally but would not allow the guilty defendant to escape punishment. This solution would be useful in applying established precedent where officers and officials had the benefit of clearly articulated rules and should have known better. Under this arrangement, any officer today who intentionally violates due process guarantees might be suspended, be reduced in rank, lose pay, or be fired. Some authors have suggested that decertification might serve as "an alternative to traditional remedies for police misconduct."[18] Departments which employed the decertification process would punish violators by removing their certification as police officers. Because, as we discussed in Chapter 6, officers in every state except Hawaii[19] must meet the certification requirements of state boards in order to hold employment, some authors argue that decertification would have a much more personal (and therefore more effective) impact on individual officers than the exclusionary rule ever could.[20]

A third possibility would allow the Supreme Court to address theoretical questions involving issues of due process. Concerned supervisors and officials could ask how the Court would rule "if . . ." As things now work, the Court can only address real cases and does so on a **writ of *certiorari*,** in which the Court orders the record of a lower court case to be prepared for review.

The obvious difficulty with these solutions, however, is that they would substantially reduce the potential benefits available to defendants through the appeals process. Hence, they would effectively eliminate the process itself.

THE FRUIT OF THE POISONED TREE DOCTRINE

The Court further built upon the rules concerning evidence with its ruling in *Silverthorne Lumber Co. v. U.S.* (1920).[21] In 1918, Frederick Silverthorne and his sons operated a lumber company and were accused of avoiding payment of federal taxes. When asked to turn over the company's books to federal investigators, the Silverthornes refused, citing their Fifth Amendment privilege against self-incrimination.

Shortly thereafter, federal agents descended on the lumber company and, without a search warrant, seized the company's books. The Silverthornes' lawyer appeared in court and asked that the materials be returned, citing the need for a search warrant, as had been established in the *Weeks* case. The prosecutor agreed, and the books were returned to the Silverthornes.

The Silverthornes came to trial thinking they would be acquitted because the evidence against them was no longer in the hands of prosecutors. In a surprise move, however, the prosecution introduced photographic copies of incriminating evidence which they had made

writ of *certiorari*

A writ issued from an appellate court for the purpose of obtaining from a lower court the record of its proceedings in a particular case. In some states, this writ is the mechanism for discretionary reviews. A request for review is made by petitioning for a writ of *certiorari*, and the granting of review is indicated by the issuance of the writ.

from the returned books. The Silverthornes were convicted in federal court. Their appeal eventually reached the U.S. Supreme Court. The Court ruled that just as illegally seized evidence cannot be used in a trial, neither can evidence be used which *derives* from an illegal seizure.[22] The conviction of the Silverthornes was overturned, and they were set free.

The *Silverthorne* case articulated a new principle of due process that today we call the **fruit of the poisoned tree doctrine**. This doctrine is potentially far-reaching. Complex cases developed after years of police investigative effort may be ruined if defense attorneys are able to demonstrate that the prosecution's case was originally based upon a search or seizure which violated due process. In such cases, it is likely that all evidence will be declared "tainted" and will become useless. You can read the full text of the Court's opinion in the *Silverthorne* case at **Library Extra! 7–2** at cjtoday.com.

The Warren Court (1953–1969)

Before the 1960s, the U.S. Supreme Court intruded only infrequently upon the overall operation of the criminal justice system at the state and local levels. As one author has observed, however, the 1960s were a time of youthful idealism, and "without the distraction of a depression or world war, individual liberties were examined at all levels of society."[23] Hence, while the exclusionary rule became an overriding consideration in federal law enforcement from the time that it was first defined by the Supreme Court in the *Weeks* case in 1914, it was not until 1961 that the Court, under Chief Justice Earl Warren, decided a case that was to change the face of American law enforcement forever. That case, *Mapp* v. *Ohio* (1961),[24] made the exclusionary rule applicable to criminal prosecutions at the state level. Beginning with the now-famous *Mapp* case, the Warren Court set out to chart a course which would guarantee nationwide recognition of individual rights, as it understood them, by agencies at all levels of the criminal justice system.

APPLICATION OF THE EXCLUSIONARY RULE TO THE STATES

The *Mapp* case began like many others during the protest-prone 1960s. Dolree Mapp was suspected of harboring a fugitive wanted in a bombing. When Ohio police officers arrived at her house, she refused to admit them. Eventually, they forced their way in. During the search which ensued, pornographic materials, including photographs, were uncovered. Mapp was arrested and eventually convicted under a state law which made possession of such materials illegal.

Prior decisions by the U.S. Supreme Court, including *Wolf* v. *Colorado* (1949),[25] had led officers to expect that the exclusionary rule did not apply to agents of state and local law enforcement. Nonetheless, in a wide-reaching and precedent-setting decision, Mapp's conviction was overturned upon appeal by a majority of Warren Court justices who decided that the U.S. Constitution, under the Fourteenth Amendment's due process guarantee, mandates that state and local law enforcement officers must be held to the same standards of accountability as federal officers. There could be little doubt, said the justices, that the evidence against Mapp had been illegally obtained and therefore could not be used against her in any court of law in the United States. The precedent established in *Mapp* v. *Ohio* firmly applied the principles developed in *Weeks* and *Silverthorne* to trials in state courts, making police officers at all levels accountable to the rule of law, which, as embodied in the words of the Fourteenth Amendment, reads, "No State shall . . . deprive any person of life, liberty, or property, without due process of law; nor deny to any person within its jurisdiction the equal protection of the laws." The full text of the Court's opinion in *Mapp* v. *Ohio* is available at **Library Extra! 7–3** at cjtoday.com.

Another important Warren-era case, that of *Chimel* v. *California* (1969),[26] involved both arrest and search activities by local law enforcement officers. Ted Chimel was convicted of the burglary of a coin shop based upon evidence gathered at the scene of his arrest—his home. Officers, armed with an arrest warrant but not a search warrant, had taken Chimel into custody when they arrived at his residence and had proceeded with a search of his entire three-bedroom house, including the attic, a small workshop, and the garage. Although officers realized that the search might be challenged in court, they justified it by claiming that it was conducted not so much to uncover evidence, but as part of the arrest process. Searches which are conducted incidental to arrest, they argued, are necessary for the officers' protection and should not require a search warrant. Coins taken from the burglarized coin shop were found in various places in Chimel's residence, including the garage, and were presented as evidence against him at trial.

fruit of the poisoned tree doctrine

A legal principle that excludes from introduction at trial any evidence later developed as a result of an illegal search or seizure.

Chimel's appeal eventually reached the U.S. Supreme Court, which ruled that the search of Chimel's residence, although incidental to arrest, became invalid when it went beyond the person arrested and the area subject to that person's "immediate control." The thrust of the Court's decision was that searches during arrest can be made to protect arresting officers, but that without a search warrant, their scope must be strongly circumscribed. Legal implications of *Chimel* v. *California* are summarized in Table 7–2.

The decision in the case of Ted Chimel was predicated upon earlier reasoning by the Court in the case of *U.S.* v. *Rabinowitz* (1950).[27] Rabinowitz, a stamp collector, had been arrested and charged by federal agents with selling altered postage stamps in order to defraud other collectors. Employing a valid arrest warrant, officers arrested Rabinowitz at his place of employment and then proceeded to search his desk, file cabinets, and safe. They did not have a search warrant, but his office was small—only one room—and the officers conducted the search with a specific object in mind, the illegal stamps. Eventually, 573 altered postage stamps were seized in the search, and Rabinowitz was convicted in federal court of charges related to selling altered stamps.

Rabinowitz's appeal to the U.S. Supreme Court, based upon the claim that the warrantless search of his business was illegal, was denied. The Court ruled that the Fourth Amendment provides protection against *unreasonable* searches but that the search in this case followed legally from the arrest of the suspect. In the language used by the Court, "It is not disputed that there may be reasonable searches, incident to arrest, without a search warrant. Upon acceptance of this established rule that some authority to search follows from lawfully taking the person into custody, it becomes apparent that such searches turn upon the reasonableness under all the circumstances and not upon the practicability of procuring a search warrant, for the warrant is not required."

Since the early days of the exclusionary rule, other court decisions have highlighted the fact that "the Fourth Amendment protects people, not places."[28] In other words, although the commonly heard claim that "a person's home is his or her castle" has a great deal of validity within the context of constitutional law, people can have a reasonable expectation to privacy in "homes" of many descriptions. Apartments, duplex dwellings, motel rooms—even the cardboard boxes or makeshift tents of the homeless—can all become protected places under the Fourth Amendment. In *Minnesota* v. *Olson* (1990),[29] for example, the U.S. Supreme Court extended the protection against warrantless searches to overnight guests residing in the home of another. The capacity to claim the protection of the Fourth Amendment, said the Court, depends upon whether the *person* who makes that claim has a legitimate expectation of privacy in the place searched.

Finally, in 1998, in the case of *Minnesota* v. *Carter*,[30] the Court held that for a defendant to be entitled to Fourth Amendment protection, "he must demonstrate that he personally

| IMPLICATIONS OF *CHIMEL* V. *CALIFORNIA* (1969) | **TABLE 7-2** |

What Arresting Officers May Search
- The defendant
- The physical area within easy reach of the defendant

Valid Reasons for Conducting a Search
- To protect the arresting officers
- To prevent evidence from being destroyed
- To keep the defendant from escaping

When a Search Becomes Illegal
- When it goes beyond the defendant and the area within the defendant's immediate control
- When it is conducted for other than a valid reason

has an expectation of privacy in the place searched, and that his expectation is reasonable." The Court noted that "the extent to which the Amendment protects people may depend upon where those people are. While an overnight guest may have a legitimate expectation of privacy in someone else's home . . . one who is merely present with the consent of the householder may not."

The Burger (1969–1986) and Rehnquist (1986–Present) Courts

The swing toward conservatism which our country experienced during the 1980s and early 1990s gave rise to a renewed concern with protecting the financial and other interests of those who live within the law. The Reagan-Bush years, and the popularity of two presidents in whom many saw the embodiment of "old-fashioned" values, reflected the tenor of a nation seeking a return to simpler times.

Throughout the late 1980s, the U.S. Supreme Court mirrored the nation's conservative tenor by distancing itself from certain earlier decisions of the Warren Court. The underlying theme of the new Court, under Chief Justice Warren E. Burger, was its adherence to the principle that criminal defendants, in claiming violations of their due process rights, need to bear most of the responsibility of showing that police went beyond the law in the performance of their duties. That trend continues today under the Rehnquist Court, led by Chief Justice William H. Rehnquist.

GOOD-FAITH EXCEPTIONS TO THE EXCLUSIONARY RULE

The Burger Court, which held sway from 1969 until 1986, began a "chipping away" at the strict application of the exclusionary rule originally set forth in the *Weeks* and *Silverthorne* cases. In the case of *Illinois* v. *Gates* (1983),[31] the Court was asked to modify the exclusionary rule to permit the use of evidence in court which had been seized in "reasonable good faith" by officers, even though the search was later ruled illegal. The Court, however, chose not to address the issue at that time.

But only a year later, in the 1984 case of *U.S.* v. *Leon*,[32] the Court recognized what has come to be called the **good-faith exception** to the exclusionary rule. The *Leon* case involved the Burbank (California) Police Department and its investigation of a drug-trafficking suspect. The suspect, Alberto Leon, was placed under surveillance following a tip from a confidential informant. Investigators applied for a search warrant based upon information gleaned from the surveillance. They believed that they were in compliance with the Fourth Amendment requirement that "no Warrants shall issue, but upon probable cause." **Probable cause**, a tricky but important concept, is a legal criterion residing in a set of facts and circumstances which would cause a reasonable person to believe that a particular other person has committed a specific crime. Probable cause must be satisfactorily demonstrated by police officers in a written affidavit to a magistrate before a search warrant can be issued. Magistrates[33] are low-level judges and act to ensure that the police have established the probable cause needed for warrants to be obtained.

In *U.S.* v. *Leon*, the affidavit submitted by police to a magistrate requesting a search warrant was reviewed by numerous deputy district attorneys, and the magistrate decided to issue the warrant. A search of Leon's three residences yielded a large amount of drugs

good-faith exception

An exception to the exclusionary rule. Law enforcement officers who conduct a search, or who seize evidence, on the basis of good faith (that is, when they believe they are operating according to the dictates of the law) and who later discover that a mistake was made (perhaps in the format of the application for a search warrant) may still use the seized evidence in court.

probable cause

A set of facts and circumstances that would induce a reasonably intelligent and prudent person to believe that a particular other person has committed a specific crime. Also, reasonable grounds to make or believe an accusation. Probable cause refers to the necessary level of belief that would allow for police seizures (arrests) of individuals and full searches of dwellings, vehicles, and possessions. Upon a demonstration of probable cause, magistrates will issue warrants authorizing law enforcement officers to effect arrests and conduct searches.

and other evidence. Although Leon was convicted of drug trafficking, a later ruling in a federal district court resulted in the suppression of evidence against him on the basis that the original affidavit prepared by the police had not, in the opinion of the court, been sufficient to establish probable cause.

The government petitioned the U.S. Supreme Court to consider whether evidence gathered by officers acting in good faith as to the validity of a warrant should fairly be excluded at trial. The impending modification of the exclusionary rule was presaged in the first sentences of the Court's written decision: "This case presents the question whether the Fourth Amendment exclusionary rule should be modified so as not to bar the use in the prosecution's case-in-chief of evidence obtained by officers acting in reasonable reliance on a search warrant issued by a detached and neutral magistrate but ultimately found to be unsupported by probable cause." The Court continued, "When law enforcement officers have acted in objective good faith or their transgressions have been minor, the magnitude of the benefit conferred on such guilty defendants offends basic concepts of the criminal justice system." Reflecting the renewed conservatism of the Burger Court, the justices found for the government and reinstated Leon's conviction.

In that same year, the Supreme Court case of *Massachusetts* v. *Sheppard* (1984)[34] further reinforced the concept of good faith. In the *Sheppard* case, officers executed a search warrant which failed to describe accurately the property to be seized. Although they were aware of the error, they had been assured by a magistrate that the warrant was valid. After the seizure was complete and a conviction had been obtained, the Massachusetts Supreme Judicial Court reversed the finding of the trial court. Upon appeal, the U.S. Supreme Court reiterated the good-faith exception and reinstated the original conviction.

The cases of *Leon* and *Sheppard* represented a clear reversal of the Warren Court's philosophy, and the trend continued with the 1987 case of *Illinois* v. *Krull*.[35] In *Krull*, the Court, now under the leadership of Chief Justice William H. Rehnquist, held that the good-faith exception applied to a warrantless search supported by state law even though the state statute was later found to violate the Fourth Amendment. Similarly, another 1987 Supreme Court case, *Maryland* v. *Garrison*,[36] supported the use of evidence obtained with a search warrant which was inaccurate in its specifics. In *Garrison*, officers had procured a warrant to search an apartment, believing it was the only dwelling on the building's third

---

CJ Futures

[The "Computer Errors Exception" to the Exclusionary Rule]

Over the past few decades, criminal justice agencies have become increasingly dependent upon computer technology for records management and other purposes. As we begin the twenty-first century, the use of such technology will continue to grow, further affecting the daily activities of criminal justice agencies and bringing with it the increased likelihood of computer-generated or computer-based mistakes.

In 1995, in the case of *Arizona* v. *Evans,*[1] the U.S. Supreme Court created a "computer errors exception" to the exclusionary rule, holding that a traffic stop which led to the seizure of marijuana was legal even though officers conducted the stop based upon an arrest warrant improperly stored in their computer. The case began in 1991, when Isaac Evans was stopped in Phoenix, Arizona, for driving the wrong way on a one-way street in front of a police station. A routine computer check reported an outstanding arrest warrant for Evans, and he was taken into custody. Police found marijuana in the car Evans had been driving, and he was eventually convicted on charges of possessing a controlled substance. After his arrest, however, police learned

that the arrest warrant reported to them by their computer had actually been quashed a few weeks earlier but, through the clerical oversight of a court employee, had never been removed from the computer.

In upholding Evans's conviction, the high court reasoned that officers could not be held responsible for a clerical error made by a court worker and concluded that the arresting officers were acting in good faith based upon the information available to them at the time of the arrest. In addition, the majority opinion said that "the rule excluding evidence obtained without a warrant was intended to deter police misconduct, not mistakes by court employees."

In what may have been a warning to police administrators not to depend upon the excuse of computer error, however, Justice Sandra Day O'Connor, in a concurring opinion, wrote, "The police, of course, are entitled to enjoy the substantial advantages [computer] technology confers. . . . They may not, however, rely on it blindly. With the benefits of more efficient law enforcement mechanisms comes the burden of corresponding constitutional responsibilities."

[1] *Arizona* v. *Evans,* 115 S.Ct. 1185, 131 L.Ed. 2d 34 (1995).

floor. After searching the entire floor, they discovered that it housed more than one apartment. Even so, evidence acquired in the search was held to be admissible based upon the reasonable mistake of the officers.

The 1990 case of *Illinois* v. *Rodriguez*[37] further diminished the scope of the exclusionary rule. In *Rodriguez*, a badly beaten woman named Gail Fischer complained to police that she had been assaulted in a Chicago apartment. Fischer led police to the apartment—which she indicated she shared with the defendant—produced a key, and opened the door to the dwelling. Inside, investigators found the defendant, Edward Rodriguez, asleep on a bed, with drug paraphernalia and cocaine spread around him. Rodriguez was arrested and charged with assault and possession of a controlled substance.

Upon appeal, Rodriguez demonstrated that Fischer had not lived with him for at least a month and argued that she could no longer be said to have legal control over the apartment. Hence, the defense claimed, Fischer had no authority to provide investigators with access to the dwelling. According to arguments made by the defense, the evidence, which had been obtained without a warrant, had not been properly seized. The Supreme Court disagreed, ruling that "even if Fischer did not possess common authority over the premises, there was no Fourth Amendment violation if the police *reasonably believed* at the time of their entry that Fischer possessed the authority to consent."

Legal scholars have suggested that the exclusionary rule may undergo even further modification in the near future. Some analysts of the contemporary scene point to the fact that "the [Rehnquist] Court's majority is [now] clearly committed to the idea that the exclusionary rule is not directly part of the Fourth Amendment (and Fourteenth Amendment due process), but instead is an evidentiary device instituted by the Court to effectuate it."[38] In other words, if the Court should be persuaded that the rule is no longer effective or that some other strategy could better achieve the aim of protecting individual rights, the rule could be abandoned entirely. A general listing of established exceptions to the exclusionary rule is provided in Table 7–3, including three which we will now discuss.

THE PLAIN-VIEW DOCTRINE

Police officers have the opportunity to begin investigations or to confiscate evidence, without a warrant, based upon what they find in **plain view** and open to public inspection. The plain-view doctrine was succinctly stated in the U.S. Supreme Court case of *Harris* v. *U.S.* (1968),[39] in which a police officer inventorying an impounded vehicle discovered evidence of a robbery.[40] In the *Harris* case, the Court ruled that "objects falling in the plain view of an officer who has a right to be in the position to have that view are subject to seizure and may be introduced in evidence."[41] Read the full text of the *Harris* opinion at **Library Extra! 7–4** at cjtoday.com.

Common situations in which the plain-view doctrine is applicable include crimes in progress, fires, accidents, and other emergencies. A police officer responding to a call for assistance, for example, might enter a residence intending to provide aid to an injured person and find drugs or other contraband in plain view. If so, the officer would be within his or her legitimate authority to confiscate the materials and to effect an arrest if the owner of the substance can be identified.

The plain-view doctrine applies only to sightings by the police under legal circumstances—that is, in places where the police have a legitimate right to be and, typically, only if the sighting was coincidental. Similarly, the incriminating nature of the evidence seized must have been "immediately apparent" to the officers making the seizure.[42] If officers conspired to avoid the necessity for a search warrant by helping to create a plain-view situation through surveillance, duplicity, or other means, the doctrine likely would not apply.

The plain-view doctrine was restricted by later federal court decisions. In the 1982 case of *U.S.* v. *Irizarry*,[43] the First Circuit Court of Appeals held that officers could not move objects to gain a view of evidence otherwise hidden from view. In that case, agents had arrested a number of men in a motel room in Isla Verde, Puerto Rico. A valid arrest warrant formed the legal basis for the arrest, and some quantities of plainly visible drugs were seized from the room. An agent, looking through a window into the room prior to the arrest, had seen one of the defendants with a gun. After the arrest was complete, and no gun had been found on the suspects, another officer noticed a bathroom ceiling panel out of place. The logical conclusion was that a weapon had been secreted there. Upon inspection, a substantial quantity of cocaine and various firearms were found hidden in the ceiling. The court, however, refused to allow these weapons and drugs to be used as evidence because, it said, "the items of evidence found above the ceiling panel were not plainly visible to the agents standing in the room."[44]

plain view

A legal term describing the ready visibility of objects that might be seized as evidence during a search by police in the absence of a search warrant specifying the seizure of those objects. To lawfully seize evidence in plain view, officers must have a legal right to be in the viewing area and must have cause to believe that the evidence is somehow associated with criminal activity.

TABLE 7-3	ESTABLISHED EXCEPTIONS TO THE EXCLUSIONARY RULE	
This Police Power		**Is Supported By**
Stop and frisk		*Terry* v. *Ohio* (1968)
Warrantless search incident to a lawful arrest		*U.S.* v. *Rabinowitz* (1950)
Seizure of evidence in good faith, even in the face of some exclusionary rule violations		*U.S.* v. *Leon* (1984) *Illinois* v. *Krull* (1987)
Warrantless vehicle search where probable cause exists to believe that the vehicle contains contraband and/or that the occupants have been lawfully arrested		*Carroll* v. *U.S.* (1925) *New York* v. *Belton* (1981) *U.S.* v. *Ross* (1982) *California* v. *Carney* (1985) *California* v. *Acevedo* (1991) *Ornelas* v. *U.S.* (1996)
Gathering of incriminating evidence during interrogation in noncustodial circumstances		*Beckwith* v. *U.S.* (1976)
Authority to search incidental to arrest and/or to conduct a protective sweep in conjunction with an in-home arrest		*Chimel* v. *California* (1969) *U.S.* v. *Edwards* (1974) *Maryland* v. *Buie* (1990)
Authority to enter and/or search an "open field" without a warrant		*Hester* v. *U.S.* (1924) *Oliver* v. *U.S.* (1984) *U.S.* v. *Dunn* (1987)
Warrantless naked-eye aerial observation of open areas and/or greenhouses		*California* v. *Ciraolo* (1986) *Florida* v. *Riley* (1989)
Warrantless seizure of abandoned materials and refuse		*California* v. *Greenwood* (1988)
Prompt action in the face of threat to public or personal safety		*Warden* v. *Hayden* (1967) *New York* v. *Quarles* (1984) *Borchardt* v. *U.S.* (1987)
Seizure of evidence in plain view		*Harris* v. *U.S.* (1968) *Coolidge* v. *New Hampshire* (1971) *Horton* v. *California* (1990)
Use of police informants in jail cells		*Kuhlmann* v. *Wilson* (1986) *Illinois* v. *Perkins* (1990) *Arizona* v. *Fulminante* (1991)
Arrest based upon computer error made by clerk		*Arizona* v. *Evans* (1995)

The right of the people to be secure in their persons, houses, papers, and effects, against unreasonable searches and seizures, shall not be violated, and no Warrants shall issue, but upon probable cause, supported by Oath or affirmation, and particularly describing the place to be searched, and the persons or things to be seized.

—Fourth Amendment to the U.S. Constitution

In the Supreme Court case of *Arizona* v. *Hicks* (1987),[45] the requirement that evidence be in plain view, without requiring officers to move or dislodge objects, was reiterated. In the *Hicks* case, officers responded to a shooting in an apartment. A bullet had been fired in a second-floor apartment and had gone through the floor, injuring a man in the apartment below. The quarters of James Hicks were found to be in considerable disarray when investigating officers entered. As officers looked for the person who might have fired the weapon, they discovered and confiscated a number of guns and a stocking mask, such as might be used in robberies. In one corner, officers noticed two expensive stereo sets. One of the officers, suspecting that the stereos were stolen, went over to the equipment and was able to read the serial numbers of one of the components from where it rested. Some of the serial numbers, however, were not clearly visible, and the investigating officer moved some of the equipment in order to read the numbers. When he called the numbers in to headquarters, he was told that the stereos indeed had been stolen. They were seized, and James Hicks was arrested. Hicks was eventually convicted on a charge of armed robbery, based upon the evidence seized.

Upon appeal, the *Hicks* case reached the U.S. Supreme Court, which ruled that the officer's behavior had become illegal when he moved the stereo equipment to record the serial

Although the concept of plain view is difficult to define, Latasha Smith (shown here sitting on a curb) provides a personal example of the concept. After Dallas narcotics officers searched the house behind her for crack cocaine, they turned their attention to Smith, who was arrested for failing to appear in court for a previous misdemeanor violation.

AP/Wide World Photos

numbers. The Court held that persons have a "reasonable expectation to privacy,"[46] which means that officers lacking a search warrant, even when invited into a residence, must act more like guests than inquisitors.

Most evidence seized under the plain-view doctrine is discovered "inadvertently"— that is, by accident.[47] However, in 1990, the U.S. Supreme Court ruled in the case of *Horton* v. *California*[48] that "even though inadvertence *is* a characteristic of most legitimate 'plain view' seizures, it *is not* a necessary condition."[49] In the *Horton* case, a warrant was issued authorizing the search of Terry Brice Horton's home for stolen jewelry. The affidavit, completed by the officer who requested the warrant, alluded to an Uzi submachine gun and a stun gun—weapons purportedly used in the jewelry robbery. It did not request that those weapons be listed on the search warrant. Officers searched the defendant's home but did not find the stolen jewelry. They did, however, seize a number of weapons, among them an Uzi, two stun guns, and a .38-caliber revolver. Horton was convicted of robbery in a trial in which the seized weapons were introduced into evidence. He appealed his conviction, claiming that officers had reason to believe that the weapons were in his home at the time of the search and were therefore not seized inadvertently. His appeal was rejected by the Court. As a result of the *Horton* case, inadvertence is no longer considered a condition necessary to ensure the legitimacy of a seizure which results when evidence other than that listed in a search warrant is discovered.

CJ Today Exhibit 7-1

[Plain-View Requirements]

Following the opinion of the U.S. Supreme Court in the case of *Horton* v. *California* (1990), items seized under the plain-view doctrine may be admissible as evidence in a court of law if both of the following conditions are met:

1. The officer who seized the evidence was lawfully in the viewing area.
2. The officer had probable cause to believe that the evidence was somehow associated with criminal activity.

EMERGENCY SEARCHES OF PROPERTY

Certain emergencies may justify a police officer in searching premises, even without a warrant. Decisions by U.S. appeals courts have resulted in such activities being termed *exigent circumstances searches* (**emergency searches**). According to the Legal Counsel Division of the Federal Bureau of Investigation (FBI), there are three threats which "provide justification for emergency warrantless action."[50] They are clear dangers (1) to life, (2) of escape, and (3) of the removal or destruction of evidence. Any one of these situations may create an exception to the Fourth Amendment's requirement of a search warrant. When emergencies necessitate a quick search of premises, however, law enforcement officers are responsible for demonstrating that a dire situation existed that justified their actions. Failure to do so successfully in court will, of course, taint any seized evidence and make it unusable.

The need for emergency searches was first recognized by the U.S. Supreme Court in 1967 in the case of *Warden* v. *Hayden*.[51] In that case, the Court approved the warrantless search of a residence following reports that an armed robber had fled into the building. In *Mincey* v. *Arizona* (1978),[52] the Supreme Court held that "the Fourth Amendment does not require police officers to delay in the course of an investigation if to do so would gravely endanger their lives or the lives of others."[53]

A 1990 decision, rendered in the case of *Maryland* v. *Buie*,[54] extended the authority of police to search locations in a house where a potentially dangerous person could hide while an arrest warrant is being served. The *Buie* decision was meant primarily to protect investigators from potential danger and can apply even when officers lack a warrant, probable cause, or even reasonable suspicion.

In 1995, in the case of *Wilson* v. *Arkansas*,[55] the U.S. Supreme Court ruled that police officers generally must knock and announce their identity before entering a dwelling or other premises, even when armed with a search warrant. Under certain emergency circumstances, however, exceptions may be made, and officers may not need to knock or identify themselves prior to entering.[56] In *Wilson*, the Court added that the Fourth Amendment requirement that searches be reasonable "should not be read to mandate a rigid rule of announcement that ignores countervailing law enforcement interests." Hence, officers need not announce themselves, the Court said, when suspects may be in the process of destroying evidence, officers are pursuing a recently escaped arrestee, or officers' lives may be endangered by such an announcement. Because the *Wilson* case involved an appeal from a drug dealer who was apprehended by police officers who entered her unlocked house while she was flushing marijuana down a toilet, some say that it establishes a "drug-law exception" to the knock-and-announce requirement.

In 1997, however, in *Richards* v. *Wisconsin*,[57] the Supreme Court clarified its position on "no knock" exceptions, saying that individual courts have the duty in each case to "determine whether the facts and circumstances of the particular entry justified dispensing with the requirement." The Court went on to say that "[a] 'no knock' entry is justified when the police have a reasonable suspicion that knocking and announcing their presence, under the particular circumstances, would be dangerous or futile, or that it would inhibit the effective investigation of the crime. This standard strikes the appropriate balance," said the Court, "between the legitimate law enforcement concerns at issue in the execution of search warrants and the individual privacy interests affected by no knock entries."

Finally, in 2001, in the case of *Illinois* v. *McArthur*,[58] the U.S. Supreme Court ruled that police officers with probable cause to believe that a home contains contraband or evidence of criminal activity may reasonably prevent a suspect found outside the home from reentering it while they apply for a search warrant. The case involved Charles McArthur, an Illinois resident, who was convicted of drug charges after his wife, Tera, called police officers to the couple's mobile home. She wanted them to keep the peace while she removed her belongings from the residence. After emerging with her possessions, she spoke to an officer who was on the porch. Tera McArthur suggested that officers should check the trailer because "Chuck had dope in there." She added that she had seen her husband hide some marijuana underneath the couch. The officer requested permission from Charles McArthur to search the trailer, but he refused. Another officer was then sent to get a search warrant, and McArthur, who had exited the residence, was informed that he would have to remain on the porch and could not reenter the trailer unless a police officer accompanied him. When the warrant arrived, officers on the scene secured the trailer and searched it. The search uncovered a small amount of marijuana, a pipe used for smoking marijuana, and some other marijuana paraphernalia.

---

emergency search

A search conducted by the police without a warrant, which is justified on the basis of some immediate and overriding need, such as public safety, the likely escape of a dangerous suspect, or the removal or destruction of evidence.

While every person is entitled to stand silent, it is more virtuous for the wrongdoer to admit his offense and accept the punishment he deserves. . . . It is wrong, and subtly corrosive of our criminal justice system, to regard an honest confession as a mistake.

—Justice Antonin Scalia, dissenting in *Minnick* v. *Mississippi*, 498 U.S. 146 (1990)

Arrest

Officers seize not only property, but people as well—a process referred to as *arrest*. Most people think of arrest in terms of what they see on popular TV crime shows. The suspect is chased, subdued, and "cuffed" after committing some loathsome act in view of the camera. Some arrests do occur that way. In reality, however, most instances of arrest are far more mundane.

In technical terms, an **arrest** occurs whenever a law enforcement officer restricts a person's freedom to leave. There may be no yelling "You're under arrest!" No *Miranda* warnings may be offered, and in fact, the suspect may not even consider himself or herself to be in custody. Such arrests, and the decision to enforce them, evolve as the situation between the officer and the suspect develops. They usually begin with polite conversation and a request by the officer for information. Only when the suspect tries to leave and tests the limits of the police response may the suspect discover that he or she is really in custody. In the 1980 case of *U.S. v. Mendenhall*,[59] Justice Potter Stewart set forth the "free to leave" test for determining whether a person has been arrested. Stewart wrote, "A person has been 'seized' within the meaning of the Fourth Amendment only if in view of all the circumstances surrounding the incident, a reasonable person would have believed that he was not free to leave." The "free to leave" test "has been repeatedly adopted by the Court as the test for a seizure."[60] In 1994, in the case of *Stansbury v. California*,[61] the Court once again used such a test in determining the point at which an arrest had been made. In *Stansbury*, where the focus was on the interrogation of a suspected child molester and murderer, the Court ruled, "In determining whether an individual was in custody, a court must examine all of the circumstances surrounding the interrogation, but the ultimate inquiry is simply whether there [was] a formal arrest or restraint on freedom of movement of the degree associated with a formal arrest."

Arrests which follow the questioning of a suspect are probably the most common type. When the decision to arrest is reached, the officer has come to the conclusion that a crime has been committed and that the suspect is probably the one who committed it. The presence of these elements constitutes the probable cause needed for an arrest. Probable cause is the basic minimum necessary for an arrest under any circumstances.

Arrests may also occur when the officer comes upon a crime in progress. Such situations often require apprehension of the offender to ensure the safety of the public. Most arrests made during crimes in progress, however, are for misdemeanors rather than felonies. In fact, many states do not allow arrest for a misdemeanor unless it is committed in the presence of an officer, since visible crimes in progress clearly provide the probable cause necessary for an arrest. In 2001, in a case that made headlines nationwide,[62] the U.S. Supreme Court upheld a warrantless arrest made by Largo Vista, Texas, patrolman Bart Turek for a seatbelt violation. In what many saw as an unfair exercise of discretion, Turek stopped, then arrested, Gail Atwater, a young local woman whom he observed driving a pickup truck in which she and her two small children (ages three and five) were unbelted. Facts in the case showed that Turek verbally berated the woman after stopping her vehicle, that he handcuffed her, placed her in his squad car, and drove her to the local police station, where she was made to remove her shoes, jewelry, and eyeglasses and empty her pockets. Officers took her "mug shot" and placed her alone in a jail cell for about an hour, after which she was taken before a magistrate and released on $310 bond. Atwater was charged with a misdemeanor violation of Texas seatbelt law. She later pleaded no contest and paid a $50 fine. Soon afterward, she and her husband filed a Section 1983 lawsuit against the officer, his department, and the police chief, alleging that the actions of the officer violated Atwater's Fourth Amendment right to be free from unreasonable seizures. The Court, however, concluded that "the Fourth Amendment does not forbid a warrantless arrest for a minor criminal offense, such as a misdemeanor seatbelt violation punishable only by a fine." The Court added, "[T]he arrest and booking were inconvenient and embarrassing to Atwater, but not so extraordinary as to violate the Fourth Amendment."

Most jurisdictions allow arrest for a felony without a warrant when a crime is not in progress, as long as probable cause can be established.[63] Some, however, require a warrant. In the case of *Payton v. New York* (1980),[64] the U.S. Supreme Court ruled that unless the suspect gives consent or an emergency exists, an arrest warrant is necessary if an arrest requires entry into a suspect's private residence.[65] Arrest warrants are issued by magistrates when police officers can demonstrate probable cause. Magistrates will usually require that the officers seeking an arrest warrant submit a written affidavit outlining their reason for the arrest.

arrest

The act of taking an adult or juvenile into physical custody by authority of law for the purpose of charging the person with a criminal offense, a delinquent act, or a status offense, terminating with the recording of a specific offense. Technically, an arrest occurs whenever a law enforcement officer curtails a person's freedom to leave.

> There is more law at the end of the policeman's nightstick than in all the decisions of the Supreme Court.
>
> —Alexander "Clubber" Williams, late-nineteenth-century New York police officer

CJ Today News

[High Court Upholds Mom's Arrest in Seatbelt Violation—Cuffs, Jail Allowed in Minor Offenses]

A divided Supreme Court ruled Tuesday that people stopped for minor traffic offenses, such as not using seatbelts or driving with expired plates, can be subject to a full-scale police arrest including handcuffs, booking and jail.

The ruling, in the case of a Texas mother who was stopped while driving home with her children after soccer practice, could have wide consequences for the nation's 187 million drivers. [The case, *Atwater* v. *Lago Vista*, was decided on April 24, 2001.]

Dissenting justices raised the specter of police using minor offenses as an excuse to harass racial minorities. "As the recent debate over racial profiling demonstrates all too clearly, a relatively minor traffic infraction may often serve as an excuse for stopping . . . an individual," Justice Sandra Day O'Connor said.

By an unusual 5-4 split, with Justice David Souter writing the majority opinion, the Court said Fourth Amendment protection against unreasonable seizures does not cover Gail Atwater, who was ordered out of her pickup in 1997 for not using seatbelts for herself and her young children.

Atwater said she had let her daughter, 5, and son, 3, out of their belts as they were driving in Lago Vista so that they could better look for a toy that had dropped outside of the truck.

Bart Turek, the arresting officer, said Atwater told him she also did not have her license and insurance information, as required by Texas law, because her purse had been stolen the day before.

Turek cuffed Atwater, put her in a squad car and took her to jail, where she was forced to remove her shoes and empty her pockets and a "mug shot" was taken. Souter acknowledged that the officer engaged in "gratuitous humiliations." However, he said the law has long allowed police to arrest people if they believe a crime is being committed, no matter how small.

Reviewing centuries of common law practice, Souter rejected Atwater's plea for a rule that would forbid arrests when the penalty for an offense carries no jail time. The fine for not wearing a seatbelt was $50.

"Neither . . . history . . . nor subsequent legal development indicates that the Fourth Amendment was originally understood, or has traditionally been read, to embrace Atwater's position," said Souter, who noted that statutes in all 50 states permit arrests for such misdemeanors.

He also said it was important for police, who may not know the penalties for various crimes, to have a clear rule.

A liberal on this court, Souter was joined in rejecting Atwater's claim against Lago Vista by the traditional conservatives: Chief Justice William Rehnquist and Justices Antonin Scalia, Anthony Kennedy and Clarence Thomas.

In a blistering dissent, O'Connor wrote that the "rule that the court creates has potentially serious consequences for the everyday lives of Americans." She was joined by Justices John Paul Stevens, Ruth Bader Ginsburg and Stephen Breyer.

Atwater said she was saddened by the ruling: "I remember . . . how terrifying it was for the kids."

James George, representing Lago Vista, praised the ruling as clear guidance for police.

For the latest in crime and justice news, visit the Talk Justice news feed at http://www.crimenews.info.

Gail Atwater, the Texas mother who was ordered out of her pickup by a police officer in 1997 and arrested for not using seatbelts for herself and her young children. In 2001, the U.S. Supreme Court ruled that Atwater's warrantless arrest had been perfectly legal.

AP/Wide World Photos

Source: Joan Biskupic, "High Court Upholds Mom's Arrest in Seatbelt Violation—Cuffs, Jail Allowed in Minor Offenses," *USA Today*, April 25, 2001. Copyright 2001, *USA Today*. Reprinted with permission.

Arresting officers patting down a drug suspect. The courts have generally held that to protect themselves and the public, officers have the authority to search suspects being arrested.

Craig Filipacchi, Getty Images, Inc.

Searches Incident to Arrest

The U.S. Supreme Court has established a clear rule that police officers have the right to conduct a search of a person being arrested and to search the area under the arrestee's immediate control to protect themselves from attack. This is true even if the officer and the arrestee are of different sexes.

This "rule of the game" regarding **search incident to an arrest** was created in the *Rabinowitz* and *Chimel* cases discussed earlier. It became firmly established in other cases involving personal searches, such as the 1973 case of *U.S.* v. *Robinson*.[66] Robinson was stopped for a traffic violation when it was learned that his driver's license had expired. He was arrested for operating a vehicle without a valid license. Officers subsequently searched the defendant to be sure he wasn't carrying a weapon and discovered a substance which later proved to be heroin. He was convicted of drug possession but appealed. When Robinson's appeal reached the U.S. Supreme Court, the Court upheld the officer's right to conduct a search without a warrant for purposes of personal protection and to use the fruits of the search when it turns up contraband. In the words of the Court, "A custodial arrest of a suspect based upon probable cause is a reasonable intrusion under the Fourth Amendment; that intrusion being lawful, a search incident to the arrest requires no additional jurisdiction."[67]

The Court's decision in *Robinson* reinforced an earlier ruling in *Terry* v. *Ohio* (1968),[68] involving a seasoned officer who conducted a pat-down search of two men whom he suspected were casing a store, about to commit a robbery. The arresting officer was a 39-year veteran of police work who testified that the men "did not look right." When he approached them, he suspected they might be armed. Fearing for his life, he quickly spun the men around, put them up against a wall, patted down their clothing, and found a gun on one of the men. The man, Terry, was later convicted in Ohio courts of carrying a concealed weapon.

Terry's appeal was based upon the argument that the suspicious officer had no probable cause to arrest him and therefore no cause to search him. The search, he argued, was illegal, and the evidence obtained should not have been used against him. The Supreme Court disagreed, saying, "In view of these facts, we cannot blind ourselves to the need for law enforcement officers to protect themselves and other prospective victims of violence in situations where they may lack probable cause for an arrest."

search incident to an arrest

A warrantless search of an arrested individual conducted to ensure the safety of the arresting officer. Because individuals placed under arrest may be in possession of weapons, courts have recognized the need for arresting officers to protect themselves by conducting an immediate search of arrestees without obtaining a warrant.

The *Terry* case set the standard for a brief stop and frisk based upon reasonable suspicion. Attorneys refer to such brief encounters as *Terry-type stops*. **Reasonable suspicion** can be defined as a belief, based upon a consideration of the facts at hand and upon reasonable inferences drawn from those facts, that would induce an ordinarily prudent and cautious person under the same circumstances to conclude that criminal activity is taking place or that criminal activity has recently occurred. It is the level of suspicion needed to justify an officer in making further inquiry or in conducting further investigation. Reasonable suspicion, which is a *general* and reasonable belief that a crime is in progress or has occurred, should be differentiated from probable cause. Probable cause, as noted earlier, is a reasonable belief that a *particular* person has committed a *specific* crime. It is important to note that the *Terry* case, for all the authority it conferred on officers, also made it clear that officers must have reasonable grounds for any stop and frisk that they conduct. Read the full text of the Court's opinion in *Terry* at **Library Extra! 7–5** at cjtoday.com.

In 1989, the Supreme Court, in the case of *U.S.* v. *Sokolow*,[69] clarified the basis upon which law enforcement officers, lacking probable cause to believe that a crime has occurred, may stop and briefly detain a person for investigative purposes. In *Sokolow*, the Court ruled that the legitimacy of such a stop must be evaluated according to a "totality of circumstances" criterion—in which all aspects of the defendant's behavior, taken in concert, may provide the basis for a legitimate stop based upon reasonable suspicion. In this case, the defendant, Andrew Sokolow, appeared suspicious to police because, while traveling under an alias from Honolulu, he had paid $2,100 in $20 bills (from a large roll of money) for two airplane tickets after spending a surprisingly small amount of time in Miami. In addition, the defendant was obviously nervous and checked no luggage. A warrantless airport investigation by Drug Enforcement Administration (DEA) agents uncovered more than a 1,000 grams of cocaine in the defendant's belongings. The Court, in upholding Sokolow's conviction, ruled that although no single behavior was proof of illegal activity, taken together they created circumstances under which suspicion of illegal activity was justified.

In 1993, however, in the case of *Minnesota* v. *Dickerson*,[70] the U.S. Supreme Court placed new limits on an officer's ability to seize evidence discovered during a pat-down search conducted for protective reasons when the search itself was based merely upon suspicion and failed to immediately reveal the presence of a weapon. In this case, Timothy Dickerson, who was observed leaving a building known for cocaine trafficking, was stopped by Minneapolis police officers after they noticed him acting suspiciously. The officers decided to investigate further and ordered Dickerson to submit to a pat-down search. The search revealed no weapons, but the officer conducting it testified that he felt a small lump in Dickerson's jacket pocket, believed it to be a lump of crack cocaine upon examining it with his fingers, and then reached into Dickerson's pocket and retrieved a small bag of cocaine. Dickerson was arrested, tried, and convicted of possession of a controlled substance. His appeal, which claimed that the pat-down search had been illegal, eventually made its way to the U.S. Supreme Court. The high court ruled that "if an officer lawfully pats down a suspect's outer clothing and feels an object whose contour or mass makes its identity immediately apparent, there has been no invasion of the suspect's privacy beyond that already authorized by the officer's search for weapons." However, in *Dickerson*, the justices ruled, "the officer never thought that the lump was a weapon, but did not immediately recognize it as cocaine." The lump was determined to be cocaine only after the officer "squeezed, slid, and otherwise manipulated the pocket's contents." Hence, the Court held, the officer's actions in this case did not qualify under what might be called a "plain feel" exception. In any case, said the Court, the search in *Dickerson* went far beyond what is permissible under *Terry*, where officer safety was the crucial issue. The Court summed up its ruling in *Dickerson* this way: "While *Terry* entitled [the officer] to place his hands on respondent's jacket and to feel the lump in the pocket, his continued exploration of the pocket after he concluded that it contained no weapon was unrelated to the sole justification for the search under *Terry*" and was therefore illegal.

Just as arrest must be based upon probable cause, officers may not stop and question an unwilling citizen whom they have no reason to suspect of a crime. In the case of *Brown* v. *Texas* (1979),[71] two Texas law enforcement officers stopped the defendant and asked for identification. Ed Brown, they later testified, had not been acting suspiciously, nor did they think he might have a weapon. The stop was made simply because officers wanted to know who he was. Brown was arrested under a Texas statute that required a person to identify himself properly and accurately when asked to do so by peace officers. Eventually, his appeal reached the U.S. Supreme Court, which ruled that under the circumstances of the *Brown* case, a person "may not be punished for refusing to identify himself."

In *Smith* v. *Ohio* (1990),[72] the Court held that an individual has the right to protect his or her belongings from unwarranted police inspection. In *Smith,* the defendant was approached by two officers in plain clothes who observed that he was carrying a brown paper bag. The officers asked him to "come here a minute" and, when he kept walking, identified themselves as police officers. The defendant threw the bag onto the hood of his car and attempted to protect it from the officers' intrusion. Marijuana was found inside the bag, and the defendant was arrested. Since there was little reason to stop the suspect in this case and because control over the bag was not thought necessary for the officer's protection, the Court found that the Fourth Amendment protects both "the traveler who carries a toothbrush and a few articles of clothing in a paper bag" and "the sophisticated executive with the locked attaché case."[73]

The following year, however, in what some Court observers saw as a turnabout, the Court ruled in *California* v. *Hodari D.* (1991)[74] that suspects who flee from the police and throw away evidence as they retreat may later be arrested based upon the incriminating nature of the abandoned evidence. The case centered on the behavior of a group of juveniles who had been standing around a parked car. Two Oakland, California, police officers, driving an unmarked car but wearing jackets with the word *Police* emblazoned in large letters on them, approached the youths. As they came close, the juveniles apparently panicked and fled. One of them tossed away a "rock" of crack cocaine, which the officers retrieved. The juvenile was later arrested and convicted of the possession of a controlled substance, but the California Court of Appeals reversed his conviction, reasoning that the officers did not have sufficient reasonable suspicion to make a *Terry*-type stop. The U.S. Supreme Court, in reversing the finding of the California court, found that reasonable suspicion was not needed, since no "stop" was made. The suspects had not been "seized" by the police, the Court ruled. Therefore, the evidence taken was not the result of an illegal seizure within the meaning of the Fourth Amendment. The significance of *Hodari* for future police action was highlighted by California prosecutors who pointed out that cases like *Hodari* occur "almost every day in this nation's urban areas."[75]

Finally, in 2000, the Court decided the case of William Wardlow.[76] Wardlow had fled upon seeing a caravan of police vehicles converge on an area of Chicago known for narcotics trafficking. Officers caught him, however, and conducted a pat-down search of his clothing for weapons, revealing a handgun. The officers arrested Wardlow on weapons charges, but his lawyer argued that police had acted illegally in stopping him since they did not have reasonable suspicion that he had committed an offense. The Illinois Supreme Court agreed with Wardlow's attorney, holding that "sudden flight in a high crime area does not create a reasonable suspicion justifying a *Terry* stop because flight may simply be an exercise of the right to 'go on one's way.'"[77] The case eventually reached the U.S. Supreme Court, which overturned the Illinois court, finding, instead, that the officers' actions did not violate the Fourth Amendment. In the words of the Court, "This case, involving a brief encounter between a citizen and a police officer on a public street, is governed by *Terry,* under which an officer who has a reasonable, articulable suspicion that criminal activity is afoot may conduct a brief, investigatory stop. While 'reasonable suspicion' is a less demanding standard than probable cause, there must be at least a minimal level of objective justification for the stop. An individual's presence in a 'high crime area,' standing alone, is not enough to support a reasonable, particularized suspicion of criminal activity, but a location's characteristics are relevant in determining whether the circumstances are sufficiently suspicious to warrant further investigation. . . . In this case, moreover, it was also Wardlow's unprovoked flight that aroused the officers' suspicions. Nervous, evasive behavior is another pertinent factor in determining reasonable suspicion. . . and headlong flight is the consummate act of evasion."[78]

> In terms that apply equally to seizures of property and to seizures of persons, the Fourth Amendment has drawn a firm line at the entrance to the house. Absent exigent circumstances, that threshold may not reasonably be crossed without a warrant.
>
> —*Payton* v. *New York*, 445 U.S. 573, 590 (1980)

Emergency Searches of Persons

It is possible to imagine emergency situations in which officers may have to search people based upon quick decisions: a person who matches the description of an armed robber, a woman who is found lying unconscious, a man who has what appears to be blood on his shoes. Such searches can save lives by disarming fleeing felons or by uncovering a medical reason for an emergency situation. They may also prevent criminals from escaping or destroying evidence.

Emergency searches of persons, like those of premises, fall under the exigent circumstances exception to the warrant requirement of the Fourth Amendment. In the 1979 case of *Arkansas* v. *Sanders*,[79] the Supreme Court recognized the need for such searches "where the societal costs of obtaining a warrant, such as danger to law officers or the risk of loss or destruction of evidence, outweigh the reasons for prior recourse to a neutral magistrate."[80]

The 1987 case of *U.S.* v. *Borchardt*,[81] decided by the Fifth Circuit Court of Appeals, held that Ira Eugene Borchardt could be prosecuted for heroin uncovered during medical treatment, even though the defendant had objected to the treatment. Borchardt was a federal inmate when he was found unconscious in his cell. He was taken to a hospital, where tests revealed heroin in his blood. His heart stopped, and he was revived using cardiopulmonary resuscitation (CPR). Borchardt was given three doses of Narcan, a drug used to counteract the effects of heroin, and he improved, regaining consciousness. The patient refused requests to pump his stomach but began to become lethargic, indicating the need for additional Narcan. Eventually, he vomited nine plastic bags full of heroin, along with two bags which had burst. The heroin was turned over to federal officers, and Borchardt was eventually convicted of heroin possession. Attempts to exclude the heroin from evidence were unsuccessful, and the appeals court ruled that the necessity of the emergency situation overruled the defendant's objections to search his person.

The Legal Counsel Division of the FBI provides the following guidelines for conducting emergency warrantless searches of individuals, where the possible destruction of evidence is at issue. (Keep in mind that there may be no probable cause to *arrest* the individual being searched.) All four conditions must apply:[82]

1. There was probable cause at the time of the search to believe that there was evidence concealed on the person searched.

2. There was probable cause to believe an emergency threat of destruction of evidence existed at the time of the search.

3. The officer had no prior opportunity to obtain a warrant authorizing the search.

4. The action was no greater than necessary to eliminate the threat of destruction of evidence.

> [The police] are not perfect; we don't sign them up on some far-off planet and bring them into police service. They are products of society, and let me tell you, the human product today often is pretty weak.
>
> —Former Los Angeles Police Chief Daryl Gates

Vehicle Searches

Vehicles present a special law enforcement problem. They are highly mobile, and when an arrest of a driver or an occupant occurs, the need to search them may be immediate.

The first significant Supreme Court case involving an automobile was that of *Carroll* v. *U.S.*[83] in 1925. In the *Carroll* case, a divided Court ruled that a warrantless search of an automobile or other vehicle is valid if it is based upon a reasonable belief that contraband is present. In 1964, however, in the case of *Preston* v. *U.S.*,[84] the limits of warrantless vehicle searches were defined. Preston was arrested for vagrancy and taken to jail. His vehicle was impounded, towed to the police garage, and later searched. Two revolvers were uncovered in the glove compartment, and more incriminating evidence was found in the trunk. Preston was convicted on weapons possession and other charges and eventually appealed to the U.S. Supreme Court. The Court held that the warrantless search of Preston's vehicle had occurred while the automobile was in secure custody and had therefore been illegal. Time and circumstances would have permitted acquisition of a warrant to conduct the search, the Court reasoned.

When the search of a vehicle occurs after it has been impounded, however, that search may be legitimate if it is undertaken for routine and reasonable purposes. In the case of *South Dakota* v. *Opperman* (1976),[85] for example, the Court held that a warrantless search undertaken for purposes of inventorying and safekeeping the personal possessions of the car's owner was not illegal, even though it turned up marijuana. The intent of the search had not been to discover contraband, but to secure the owner's belongings from possible theft. Again, in *Colorado* v. *Bertine* (1987),[86] the Court reinforced the idea that officers may open closed containers found in a vehicle while conducting a routine search for inventorying purposes. In the words of the Court, such searches are "now a well-defined exception in the warrant requirement." In 1990, however, in the precedent-setting case of *Florida* v. *Wells*,[87] the Court agreed with a lower court's suppression of marijuana discovered in a locked suitcase in the trunk of a defendant's impounded vehicle. In *Wells*, the Court held that standardized criteria authorizing the search of a vehicle for inventorying purposes were necessary before such a discovery could be legitimate. Standardized

> The public safety exception [to the exclusionary rule] was intended to protect the police, as well as the public, from danger.
>
> —*U.S.* v. *Brady*, 819 F.2d 884 (1987)

criteria, said the Court, might take the form of department policies, written general orders, or established routines.

Generally speaking, where vehicles are concerned, an investigatory stop is permissible under the Fourth Amendment if supported by reasonable suspicion,[88] and a warrantless search of a stopped car is valid if it is based on probable cause.[89] Reasonable suspicion can expand into probable cause when the facts in a given situation so warrant. In the 1996 case of *Ornelas* v. *U.S.*,[90] for example, two experienced police officers stopped a car driven by two men who were known or suspected drug traffickers. One of the officers noticed a loose panel above an armrest in the vehicle's backseat and then searched the car. A package of cocaine was found beneath the panel. Following conviction, the defendants appealed to the U.S. Supreme Court, claiming that no probable cause to search the car existed at the time of the stop. The majority opinion, however, noted that in the view of the court which originally heard the case, "the model, age, and source-State origin of the car, and the fact that two men traveling together checked into a motel at 4 o'clock in the morning without reservations, formed a drug-courier profile and . . . this profile together with the [computer] reports gave rise to a reasonable suspicion of drug-trafficking activity. . . . [I]n the court's view, reasonable suspicion became probable cause when [the deputy] found the loose panel."[91] Probable cause permits a warrantless search of a vehicle under what has been called the **fleeting targets exception** to the exclusionary rule.[92]

Warrantless vehicle searches may extend to any area of the vehicle and may include sealed containers, the trunk, and the glove compartment if officers have probable cause to conduct a purposeful search or if officers have been given permission to search the vehicle. In the 1991 case of *Florida* v. *Jimeno*,[93] arresting officers stopped a motorist who gave them permission to search his car. The defendant was later convicted on a drug charge when a bag on the floor of the car was found to contain cocaine. Upon appeal to the U.S. Supreme Court, however, he argued that the permission given to search his car did not extend to bags and other items within the car. In a decision which may have implications beyond vehicle searches, the Court held that "[a] criminal suspect's Fourth Amendment right to be free from unreasonable searches is not violated when, after he gives police permission to search his car, they open a closed container found within the car that might reasonably hold the object of the search. The amendment is satisfied when, under the circumstances, it is objectively reasonable for the police to believe that the scope of the suspect's consent permitted them to open the particular container."[94]

In *U.S.* v. *Ross* (1982),[95] the Court found that officers had not exceeded their authority in opening a bag in the defendant's trunk which was found to contain heroin. The search was held to be justifiable on the basis of information developed from a search of the passenger compartment. The Court said, "If probable cause justifies the search of a lawfully stopped vehicle, it justifies the search of every part of the vehicle and its contents that may conceal the object of the search."[96] Moreover, according to the 1996 U.S. Supreme Court decision in *Whren* v. *U.S.*,[97] officers may stop a vehicle being driven suspiciously and then search it once probable cause has developed, even if their primary assignment centers on duties other than traffic enforcement *or* "if a reasonable officer would not have stopped the motorist absent some additional law enforcement objective" (which in the case of *Whren* was drug enforcement). Motorists[98] and their passengers may be ordered out of stopped vehicles in the interest of officer safety, and any evidence developed as a result of such a procedure may be used in court. In 1997, for example, in the case of *Maryland* v. *Wilson*,[99] the U.S. Supreme Court overturned a decision by a Maryland court which held that crack cocaine found during a traffic stop was seized illegally when it fell from the lap of a passenger ordered out of a stopped vehicle by a Maryland state trooper. The Maryland court reasoned that the police should not have authority to order seemingly innocent passengers out of vehicles—even vehicles which have been stopped for legitimate reasons. The Supreme Court cited concerns for officer safety in overturning the Maryland court's ruling and held that the activities of passengers are subject to police control.

In 1998, however, the U.S. Supreme Court placed clear limits on warrantless vehicle searches. In the case of *Knowles* v. *Iowa*,[100] an Iowa policeman stopped Patrick Knowles for speeding, issued him a citation but did not make a custodial arrest. The officer then conducted a full search of his car without Knowles's consent and without probable cause. Marijuana was found, and Knowles was arrested. At the time, Iowa state law gave officers authority to conduct full-blown automobile searches when issuing only a citation. The Supreme Court found, however, that while concern for officer safety during a routine traffic stop may justify the minimal intrusion of ordering a driver and passengers out of a car,

fleeting targets exception

An exception to the exclusionary rule that permits law enforcement officers to search a motor vehicle based upon probable cause but without a warrant. The fleeting targets exception is predicated upon the fact that vehicles can quickly leave the jurisdiction of a law enforcement agency.

A police officer searching a vehicle in San Diego, California. Warrantless vehicle searches, where the driver is suspected of a crime, have generally been justified by the fact that vehicles are highly mobile and can quickly leave police jurisdiction.

David R. Frazier, Photolibrary, Inc.

it does not by itself justify what it called "the considerably greater intrusion attending a full field-type search." Hence, while a search incident to arrest may be justifiable in the eyes of the Court, a search incident to citation clearly is not.

Finally, in the 1999 case of *Wyoming* v. *Houghton*,[101] the Court ruled that police officers with probable cause to search a car may inspect passengers' belongings found in the car that are capable of concealing the object of the search.

ROADBLOCKS AND MOTOR VEHICLE CHECKPOINTS

> Our police officers are high-school graduates; they are not lawyers; they are not judges.
>
> —U.S. Representative Chuck Douglas

The Fourth and Fourteenth Amendments to the U.S. Constitution guarantee liberty and personal security to all people residing within the United States. Courts have generally held that police officers have no legitimate authority to detain or arrest people who are going about their business in a peaceful manner, when probable cause is lacking to believe that a crime has been committed. In a number of instances, however, the U.S. Supreme Court has decided that community interests may necessitate a temporary suspension of personal liberty, even when probable cause is lacking. One such case is that of *Michigan Dept. of State Police* v. *Sitz* (1990),[102] which involved the legality of highway sobriety checkpoints, including those at which nonsuspicious drivers are subjected to scrutiny. In *Sitz*, the Court ruled that such stops are reasonable insofar as they are essential to the welfare of the community as a whole. That the Court reached its conclusion based upon pragmatic social interests is clear from the words used by Chief Justice Rehnquist: "No one can seriously dispute the magnitude of the drunken driving problem or the States' interest in eradicating it. Media reports of alcohol-related death and mutilation on the Nation's roads are legion. Drunk drivers cause an annual death toll of over 25,000 and in the same time span cause nearly one million personal injuries and more than five billion dollars in property damage. . . . [T]he balance of the State's interest in preventing drunken driving, the extent to which this system can reasonably be said to advance that interest, and the degree of intrusion upon individual motorists who are briefly stopped, weighs in favor of the state program."[103]

In a second case, *U.S.* v. *Martinea-Fuerte* (1976),[104] the Court upheld brief, suspicionless seizures at a fixed international checkpoint designed to intercept illegal aliens. The Court noted that "to require that such stops always be based on reasonable suspicion would be impractical because the flow of traffic tends to be too heavy to allow the particularized study of a given car necessary to identify it as a possible carrier of illegal aliens. Such a requirement also would largely eliminate any deterrent to the conduct of well-disguised smuggling operations, even though smugglers are known to use these highways regularly."[105]

In 2000, however, in what some people saw as a change in direction, the Court struck down a narcotics checkpoint program established by the Indianapolis Police Department in 1998. Under the program, stopped drivers were told that they were at a drug checkpoint, and officers examined each driver's license and registration while visually assessing the driver for signs of impairment. Drug-sniffing dogs were then walked around the vehicle's exterior. On average, motorists were stopped for three minutes. In ruling the program illegal, the justices held that the Fourth Amendment prohibits even a brief "seizure" of a motorist "under a program whose primary purpose is ultimately indistinguishable from the general interest in crime control." The Court's written opinion in *Indianapolis* v. *Edmond*[106] indicated that similar programs with the purpose of verifying driver's licenses and vehicle registrations would continue to be permissible because they were not intended to "detect evidence of ordinary criminal wrongdoing."

WATERCRAFT AND MOTOR HOMES

The 1983 case of *U.S.* v. *Villamonte-Marquez*[107] widened the *Carroll* decision (discussed earlier) to include watercraft. The case involved an anchored sailboat occupied by Villamonte-Marquez, which was searched by a U.S. Customs officer after one of the crew members appeared unresponsive to being hailed. The officer thought he smelled burning marijuana after boarding the vessel and, through an open hatch, saw burlap bales which he suspected might be contraband. A search proved him correct, and the ship's occupants were arrested. Their conviction was overturned upon appeal, but the U.S. Supreme Court reversed the appellate court. The Court reasoned that a vehicle on the water can easily leave the jurisdiction of enforcement officials, just as a car or truck can.

In *California* v. *Carney* (1985),[108] the Court extended police authority to conduct warrantless searches of vehicles to include motor homes. Earlier arguments had been advanced that a motor home, because it is more like a permanent residence, should not be considered a vehicle for purposes of search and seizure. In a 6-3 decision, the Court rejected those arguments, reasoning that a vehicle's appointments and size do not alter its basic function of providing transportation.

Houseboats were brought under the automobile exception to the Fourth Amendment warrant requirement in the 1988 Tenth Circuit Court case of *U.S.* v. *Hill*.[109] In the *Hill* case, Drug Enforcement Administration agents developed evidence which led them to believe that methamphetamine was being manufactured aboard a houseboat traversing Lake Texoma in Oklahoma. Because a storm warning had been issued for the area, agents decided to board

INDIVIDUAL RIGHTS VERSUS PUBLIC ORDER

Fairness in Policing

[t]his chapter builds upon the following theme: For police action to be "just," it must recognize the rights of individuals while holding them accountable to the social obligations defined by law. It is important to realize that many democratically inspired legal restraints upon the police stem from the Bill of Rights, which comprises the first ten amendments to the U.S. Constitution. Such restraints help ensure individual freedoms in our society and prevent the development of a "police state" in America.

In police work and elsewhere, the principles of individual liberty and social justice are cornerstones upon which the American way of life rests. Ideally, the work of police agencies, as well as the American system of criminal justice, is to ensure justice while guarding liberty. The liberty-justice issue is the dual thread which holds the tapestry of the justice system together—from the simplest daily activities of police on the beat to the often complex and lengthy renderings of the U.S. Supreme Court.

For the criminal justice system as a whole, the question becomes, How can individual liberties be maintained in the face of the need for official action, including arrest, interrogation, incarceration, and the like? The answer is far from simple, but it begins with the recognition that liberty is a double-edged sword, entailing obligations as well as rights.

❓ DISCUSSION QUESTIONS

1. What does it mean to say that "for police action to be 'just,' it must recognize the rights of individuals while holding them accountable to the social obligations defined by law"? How can police agencies accomplish this? What can individual officers do to help their agencies in this regard?

2. This box asks, "How can individual liberties be maintained in the face of the need for official action, including arrest, interrogation, incarceration, and the like?" What's your answer?

3. What does it mean to say, as this box does, that "liberty is a double-edged sword, entailing obligations as well as rights"?

and to search the boat prior to obtaining a warrant. During the search, an operating amphetamine laboratory was discovered, and the boat was seized. In an appeal, the defendants argued that the houseboat search had been illegal because agents lacked a warrant to search their home. The appellate court, however, in rejecting the claims of the defendants, ruled that a houseboat, because it is readily mobile, may be searched without a warrant when probable cause exists to believe that a crime has been or is being committed.

Suspicionless Searches

In two 1989 decisions, the U.S. Supreme Court ruled for the first time in its history that there may be instances when the need to ensure public safety provides a **compelling interest** which negates the rights of any individual to privacy, permitting **suspicionless searches**—those that occur when a person is not suspected of a crime. In the case of *National Treasury Employees Union* v. *Von Raab* (1989),[110] the Court, by a 5-4 vote, upheld a program of the U.S. Customs Service which required mandatory drug testing for all workers seeking promotions or job transfers involving drug interdiction and the carrying of firearms. The Court's majority opinion read, "We think the government's need to conduct the suspicionless searches required by the Customs program outweighs the privacy interest of employees engaged directly in drug interdiction, and of those who otherwise are required to carry firearms."

The second case, *Skinner* v. *Railway Labor Executives' Association* (1989),[111] was decided on the same day. In *Skinner*, the justices voted 7 to 2 to permit the mandatory testing of railway crews for the presence of drugs or alcohol following serious train accidents. The *Skinner* case involved evidence of drugs in a 1987 train wreck outside of Baltimore, Maryland, in which 16 people were killed and hundreds were injured.

The 1991 Supreme Court case of *Florida* v. *Bostick*,[112] which permitted warrantless "sweeps" of intercity buses, moved the Court deeply into conservative territory. The *Bostick* case came to the attention of the Court as a result of the Broward County (Florida) Sheriff's Department's routine practice of boarding buses at scheduled stops and asking passengers for permission to search their bags. Terrance Bostick, a passenger on one of the buses, gave police permission to search his luggage, which was found to contain cocaine. Bostick was arrested and eventually pleaded guilty to charges of drug trafficking. The Florida Supreme Court, however, found merit in Bostick's appeal, which was based upon a Fourth Amendment claim that the search of his luggage had been unreasonable. The Florida court held that "a reasonable passenger in [Bostick's] situation would not have felt free to leave the bus to avoid questioning by the police," and it overturned the conviction.

The state appealed to the U.S. Supreme Court, which held that the Florida Supreme Court had erred in interpreting Bostick's *feelings* that he was not free to leave the bus. In the words of the Court, "Bostick was a passenger on a bus that was scheduled to depart. He would not have felt free to leave the bus even if the police had not been present. Bostick's movements were 'confined' in a sense, but this was the natural result of his decision to take the bus." In other words, Bostick was constrained not so much by police action as by his own feelings that he might miss the bus were he to get off. Following this line of reasoning, the Court concluded that warrantless, suspicionless "sweeps" of buses, "trains, planes, and city streets" are permissible as long as officers (1) ask individual passengers for permission before searching their possessions, (2) do not coerce passengers to consent to a search, and (3) do not convey the message that citizen compliance with the search request is mandatory. Passenger compliance with police searches must be voluntary for the searches to be legal.

In contrast to the tone of Court decisions more than two decades earlier, the justices did not require officers to inform passengers that they were free to leave nor that they had the right to deny officers the opportunity to search (although Bostick himself was so advised by Florida officers). Any reasonable person, the Court ruled, should feel free to deny the police request. In the words of the Court, "The appropriate test is whether, taking into account all of the circumstances surrounding the encounter, a reasonable passenger would feel free to decline the officers' requests or otherwise terminate the encounter." The Court continued, "Rejected, however, is Bostick's argument that he must have been seized because no reasonable person would freely consent to a search of luggage containing drugs, since the 'reasonable person' test presumes an innocent person."

Critics of the decision saw it as creating new "gestapo-like" police powers in the face of which citizens on public transportation will feel compelled to comply with police requests for search authority. Dissenting Justices Blackmun, Stevens, and Marshall held that "the bus sweep at issue in this case violates the core values of the Fourth Amendment." However, in words which may presage a significant change of direction for other Fourth Amendment issues, the Court's majority defended its ruling by writing, "[T]he Fourth Amendment proscribes unreasonable searches and seizures; it does not proscribe voluntary cooperation."

In mid-2000, however, in the case of *Bond* v. *U.S.*,[113] the Court ruled that physical manipulation of a carry-on bag in the possession of a bus passenger without the owner's consent violates the Fourth Amendment's proscription against unreasonable searches. In *Bond*, a Border Patrol agent boarded a bus in Texas to check the immigration status of its passengers. As he walked off the bus, he squeezed the soft luggage which passengers had placed in the overhead storage space. As he squeezed a canvas bag above one seat, he noticed that it contained a "bricklike" object. After a passenger admitted owning the bag and only then consented to its search, the agent opened the bag and found a "brick" of methamphetamine. The bag's owner was indicted on federal drug charges, but his attorney moved to suppress the drugs as evidence, arguing that the agent conducted an illegal search of the bag. The passenger was convicted, and his appeal reached the U.S. Supreme Court. The Court held that the Border Patrol agent's physical manipulation of the suspect's carry-on bag went beyond mere viewing and violated the Fourth Amendment's proscription against unreasonable searches.

High-Technology Searches

The burgeoning use of high technology to investigate crime and to uncover what might otherwise remain undiscovered violations of the criminal law is forcing courts throughout the nation to evaluate the applicability of constitutional guarantees in light of high-tech searches and seizures. In 1996, the California appellate court decision in *People* v. *Deutsch*[114] presaged the kinds of issues that are likely to be encountered as American law enforcement expands its use of cutting-edge technology. In *Deutsch*, judges faced the question of whether a warrantless scan made with a thermal imaging device of a private dwelling constitutes an unreasonable search within the meaning of the Fourth Amendment. A thermal imaging device identifies and can record differential temperatures associated with various parts of a dwelling without requiring officers to enter the structure. The California court defined a thermal imaging device as "a passive, non-intrusive system which detects differences in temperature at surface levels." Such devices (also called *forward-looking infrared [FLIR] systems*)

A photo created by a thermal imaging device. The photo shows "hot spots" in a suspected marijuana grower's home that might be produced by lights used to grow the plants indoors. In Kyllo v. U.S. *(2001), the U.S. Supreme Court held that the police may not use such devices without a search warrant.*

Image compliments of SPi-www. x20.org.

The USA PATRIOT Act of 2001

[O]n October 26, 2001, President George W. Bush signed into law the USA PATRIOT Act, also known as the Uniting and Strengthening America by Providing Appropriate Tools Required to Intercept and Obstruct Terrorism Act. The law, which was drafted in response to the September 11, 2001, terrorist attacks on the World Trade Center and the Pentagon, substantially increased the investigatory authority of federal, state, and local police agencies. The act permits longer jail terms for certain suspects arrested without a warrant, broadens **"sneak and peek" search** authority (searches conducted without prior notice and in the absence of the suspect), and enhances the power of prosecutors. The law also increases the ability of federal authorities to tap phones (including wireless devices), share intelligence information, track Internet usage, crack down on money laundering, and protect U.S. borders. Many of the new crime-fighting powers created under the legislation are not limited to acts of terrorism, but apply to many different kinds of criminal offenses. (Some of the act's other provisions are discussed in boxes like this one in Chapters 15 and 17.)

The new law has led individual-rights advocates to question whether the government unfairly expanded police powers at the expense of civil liberties. Immediately after signing the legislation, President Bush assured the nation that such was not the case. "Today, we take an essential step in defeating terrorism while protecting the constitutional rights of all Americans," Bush declared.[1] Prior to passage, the legislation had been questioned by the American Civil Liberties Union (ACLU), which feared that it would substantially reduce the constitutional rights of individuals facing processing by the justice system. After the bill became law, the ACLU pledged to work with the Bush administration and law enforcement agencies across the country "to ensure that civil liberties in America are not eroded." Anthony D. Romero, Executive Director of the ACLU, avowed, "The passage of this broad legislation is by no means the end of the story. . . . The ACLU remains firm in our belief that we can be both safe and free."[2]

Major provisions of the law relevant to law enforcement investigations in general are shown in this box. Some of the new law's provisions (although none of the ones shown here) will "sunset," or expire, at the end of 2005. Nonetheless, those provisions and other parts of the law will undoubtedly be challenged in U.S. courts in the months and years to come.

One Hundred Seventh Congress
of the
United States of America
AT THE FIRST SESSION
Begun and held at the City of Washington on Wednesday, the third day of January, two thousand and one
An Act
To deter and punish terrorist acts in the United States and around the world, to enhance law enforcement investigatory tools, and for other purposes.
Be it enacted by the Senate and House of Representatives of the United States of America in Congress assembled,

Section 1. Short Title and Table of Contents.

(a) SHORT TITLE.—This Act may be cited as the "Uniting and Strengthening America by Providing Appropriate Tools Required to Intercept and Obstruct Terrorism (USA PATRIOT Act) Act of 2001".

Title II—Enhanced Surveillance Procedures Sec. 203. Authority to Share Criminal Investigative Information.

(b) AUTHORITY TO SHARE ELECTRONIC, WIRE, AND ORAL INTERCEPTION INFORMATION.—
(1) LAW ENFORCEMENT.—Section 2517 of title 18, United States Code, is amended by inserting at the end the following:
"(6) Any investigative or law enforcement officer, or attorney for the Government, who by any means authorized by this chapter, has obtained knowledge of the contents of any wire, oral, or electronic communication, or evidence derived therefrom, may disclose such contents to any other Federal law enforcement, intelligence, protective, immigration, national defense, or national security official to the extent that such contents include foreign intelligence or counterintelligence (as defined in section 3 of the National Security Act of 1947 (50 U.S.C. 401a)), or foreign intelligence information (as defined in subsection 19 of section 2510 of this title), to assist the official who is to receive that information in the performance of his official duties. Any Federal official who receives information pursuant to this provision may use that information only as necessary in the conduct of that person's official duties subject to any limitations on the unauthorized disclosure of such information."

Sec. 213. Authority for Delaying Notice of the Exectuion of a Warrant.

Section 3103a of title 18, United States Code, is amended—
(1) by inserting "(a) IN GENERAL.—" before "In addition"; and (2) by adding at the end the following:
"(b) DELAY.—With respect to the issuance of any warrant or court order under this section, or any other rule of law, to search for and seize any property or material that constitutes evidence of a criminal offense in violation of the laws of the United States, any notice required, or that may be required, to be given may be delayed if—"(1) the court finds reasonable cause to believe that providing immediate notification of the execution of the warrant may have an adverse result (as defined in section 2705); "(2) the warrant prohibits the seizure of any tangible property, any wire or electronic communication (as defined in section 2510), or, except as expressly provided in chapter 121, any stored wire or electronic information, except where the court finds reasonable necessity for the seizure; and "(3) the warrant provides for the giving of such notice within a reasonable period of its execution, which period may thereafter be extended by the court for good cause shown."

What This Means

Prior to enactment of the USA PATRIOT Act, government agents already had the authority, in limited situations, to delay notification for searches of some forms of electronic communications that were in the custody of a third party. (Delayed notification searches are sometimes called "sneak and peek" searches.) Previous law, according to the U.S.

Department of Justice,[3] was a mix of inconsistent rules, practices, and court decisions varying widely from jurisdiction to jurisdiction across the country. The lack of uniformity was said to have hindered the investigation of terrorism cases and other nationwide investigations.

The USA PATRIOT Act attempts to resolve this problem by amending Title 18, Section 3103, of the U.S. Code to create a uniform standard authorizing courts to delay the provision of required notice if the court finds "reasonable cause" to believe that providing immediate notification of the execution of the warrant may have an "adverse result" (such as endangering the life or physical safety of an individual, flight from prosecution, evidence tampering, or witness intimidation) or might otherwise seriously jeopardize an investigation or unduly delay a trial. This section of the USA PATRIOT Act is primarily designed to authorize delayed notice of *searches,* rather than delayed notice of *seizures.*

Sec. 216. Modifiction of Authorities Relating to Use of Pen Registers and Trap and Trace Devices.

(b) ISSUANCE OF ORDERS.—
(1) IN GENERAL.—Section 3123(a) of title 18, United States Code, is amended to read as follows:
"(a) IN GENERAL.—
"(1) ATTORNEY FOR THE GOVERNMENT.—Upon an application made under section 3122(a)(1), the court shall enter an *ex parte* order authorizing the installation and use of a pen register or trap and trace device anywhere within the United States, if the court finds that the attorney for the Government has certified to the court that the information likely to be obtained by such installation and use is relevant to an ongoing criminal investigation."

What This Means

Although Congress enacted a pen/trap statute in 1986 (which made possible the collection of noncontent traffic information associated with communications, such as the phone number dialed from a particular telephone), it could not anticipate the dramatic expansion in electronic communications that would occur in the next 15 years. Thus, the 1986 statute (18 U.S.C. § 3127) contained certain language that appeared to apply to telephone communications and that did not unambiguously encompass communications over computer networks.

Section 216 of the USA PATRIOT Act updates the pen/trap statute in three important ways: (1) The amendments clarify that law enforcement may use pen/trap orders to trace communications on the Internet and other computer networks; (2) pen/trap orders issued by federal courts now have nationwide effect; and (3) law enforcement authorities must file a special report with the court whenever they use a pen/trap order to install their own monitoring device on computers belonging to a public provider.

Sec. 219. Single-Jurisdiction Search Warrants for Terrorism.

Rule 41(a) of the Federal Rules of Criminal Procedure is amended by inserting after "executed" the following: "and (3) in an investigation of domestic terrorism or international terrorism (as defined in section 2331 of title 18, United States Code), by a Federal magistrate judge in any district in which activities related to the terrorism may have occurred, for a search of property or for a person within or outside the district."

What This Means

Under prior law, Rule 41(a) of the Federal Rules of Criminal Procedure required that a search warrant be obtained within a district for searches within that district. The only exception was for cases in which property or a person within the district might leave the district prior to execution of the warrant. The rule created what some saw as unnecessary delays and burdens in the investigation of terrorist activities and networks that spanned a number of districts, since warrants had to be obtained separately in each district. Section 219 purports to solve that problem by providing that, in domestic or international terrorism cases, a search warrant may be issued by a magistrate judge in any district in which activities related to the terrorism have occurred for a search of property or persons located within or outside of the district.

Sec. 224. Sunset.

(a) IN GENERAL.—Except as provided in subsection (b), this title and the amendments made by this title (other than sections 203(a), 203(c), 205, 208, 210, 211, 213, 216, 219, 221, and 222, and the amendments made by those sections) shall cease to have effect on December 31, 2005.

What This Means

None of the provisions shown in this box are slated to expire in 2005.

Civil Rights Implications

While many aspects of the USA PATRIOT Act have been criticized as potentially unconstitutional, Section 213, which authorizes delaying notice of the execution of a warrant, may be most subject to challenge. The ACLU maintains that under this section, law enforcement agents could enter a house, apartment, or office with a search warrant while the occupant is away, search through his or her property, and take photographs without having to tell the suspect about the search until later.[4] The ACLU says that this provision will "mark a sea change in the way search warrants are executed in the United States." The ACLU also believes that the new provision is likely to be illegal because the Fourth Amendment to the Constitution protects against unreasonable searches and seizures and requires the government to both obtain a warrant and to give notice to the person whose property will be searched before conducting the search. The notice requirement enables the suspect to assert his or her Fourth Amendment rights. A person with notice, for example, might be able to point out irregularities in the warrant, such as the fact that the police are at the wrong address or that because the warrant is limited to a search for a stolen car, the police have no authority to be looking in dresser drawers. In a covert search warrant, there are often no clear limitations on what can be searched. According to the ACLU, Section 213 has taken what had previously been an extremely limited authority and expanded it so that it is now available in any kind of search (physical or electronic) and in any kind of criminal case.

The ACLU also questions the constitutionality of Section 216, "Modification of Authorities Relating to Use of Pen Registers and Trap and Trace Devices."[5] That section essentially says that courts *shall* issue search warrants whenever a qualified prosecuting attorney, acting in an official capacity, certifies that the warrant is needed. This requirement effectively eliminates judicial oversight in the issuance of such warrants and mandates that courts issue warrants under specified circumstances rather than assess the lawfulness of warrant requests.

(continued)

INDIVIDUAL RIGHTS VERSUS PUBLIC ORDER (continued)

The Supreme Court has yet to rule on the constitutionality of "sneak and peek" searches or on Section 213 requirements.

Follow-up

Within weeks of the USA PATRIOT Act's becoming law, U.S. Attorney General John Ashcroft announced that he was using the authority of his office to allow federal corrections officials and select others to listen in on certain telephone communications between jailed suspects accused of terrorism and their lawyers—without obtaining prior approval by a judge. The Justice Department said that communications between inmates and their lawyers would be monitored when "reasonable suspicion exists to believe that a particular inmate may use communications with attorneys or their agents to further or facilitate acts of terrorism."[6]

Ashcroft's decision, which raised questions in Congress, effectively ended the long-standing tradition of lawyer-client confidentiality for telephone conversations with federal prisoners. The decision was criticized by many individual-rights advocates, including New York lawyer Benito Romano, who asked, "How far

do you want to go in sacrificing civil liberties for the purpose of furthering an investigation?"[7] Irwin H. Schwartz, President of the National Association of Criminal Defense Lawyers, condemned the decision, saying, "We call ourselves a nation of laws, and the test of a nation of laws is whether it adheres to them in times of stress."[8]

Following Ashcroft's announcement, President George W. Bush signed an executive order allowing secret military tribunals to try foreign terrorism suspects at home or abroad, without many of the constitutional protections given to defendants in the federal court system. The president's order effectively removed suspected foreign terrorists from the jurisdiction of the federal court system. Bush said that the order was required to avoid having to prosecute accused terrorists under court rules that might result in the disclosure of state secrets or make the United States more vulnerable to terrorism.[9]

Read the entire USA PATRIOT Act of 2001 via **Web Extra! 7–3** at cjtoday.com. Title 18 of the U.S. Code is available at **Web Extra! 7–4** at cjtoday.com.

Sources: U.S. Department of Justice, *Field Guidance on Authorities (Redacted) Enacted in the 2001 Anti-Terrorism Legislation* (Washington, D.C.: DOJ, no date), Web posted at http://www.epic.org/terrorism/DOJ_guidance.pdf; USA PATRIOT Act, 2001 (Public Law 107-56); American Civil Liberties Union, *How the Anti-Terrorism Bill Expands Law Enforcement "Sneak and Peek" Warrants,* Web posted at http://www.aclu.org/congress/1102301b.html; and American Civil Liberties Union, *How the Anti-Terrorism Bill Limits Judicial Oversight of Telephone and Internet Surveillance,* Web posted at http://www.aclu.org/congress/1102301g.html.

[1]"Bush Signs Anti-Terror Legislation," Reuters wire service, October 26, 2001.

[2]Stefanie Olsen, "PATRIOT Act Draws Privacy Concerns," CNET News.com, October 26, 2001. Web posted at http://news.cnet.com/news/0-1005-200-7671240.html?tag=rltdnws. Accessed November 3, 2001.

[3]All references to the Department of Justice in this box are derived from U.S. Department of Justice, *Field Guidance on Authorities (Redacted) Enacted in the 2001 Anti-Terrorism Legislation* (Washington, D.C.: DOJ, no date). Web posted at http://www.epic.org/terrorism/DOJ_guidance.pdf. Accessed February 10, 2002.

[4]Much of the information in this paragraph is taken from American Civil Liberties Union, *How the Anti-Terrorism Bill Expands Law Enforcement "Sneak and Peek" Warrants.* Web posted at http://www.aclu.org/congress/1102301b.html. Accessed February 12, 2002.

[5]American Civil Liberties Union, *How the Anti-Terrorism Bill Limits Judicial Oversight of Telephone and Internet Surveillance.* Web posted at http://www.aclu.org/congress/1102301g.html. Accessed February 12, 2002.

[6]William Glaberson, "Experts Divided on New Antiterror Policy That Scuttles Lawyer-Client Confidentiality," *New York Times,* November 13, 2001. Web posted at http://www.nytimes.com/2001/11/13/national/13LEGA.html. Accessed November 15, 2001.

[7]Ibid.

[8]Ibid.

[9]Joan Biskupic, "Terrorist Tribunals Allowed: Bush Order Approves Secret Military Trials for Foreign Suspects," *USA Today,* November 14, 2001, p. 1A.

"sneak and peek" search

A search that occurs in the suspect's absence and without his or her prior knowledge.

measure radiant energy in the radiant heat portion of the electromagnetic spectrum[115] and display their readings as thermographs. Thermographs, which look something like photographs, show areas which are relatively cold as nearly black, warmer areas in shades of gray, and hot areas as white. The "heat picture" that a thermal imager produces can be used, as it was in the case of Dorian Deutsch, to reveal unusually warm areas or rooms that might be associated with the cultivation of drug-bearing plants, such as marijuana. Two-hundred cannabis plants, which were being grown hydroponically under high-wattage lights in two walled-off portions of Deutsch's home, were seized following a thermal scan of her home by a police officer who drove by the residence at 1:30 in the morning. Because no entry of the house was anticipated during the search, the officer had acted without a search warrant. The California court ruled that the scan was an illegal search because "society accepts a reasonable expectation of privacy" surrounding "nondisclosed activities within the home."[116]

Multiculturalism and Diversity in America

[The USA PATRIOT Act of 2001]

The impact of the USA PATRIOT Act of 2001 on law enforcement powers is described in a box in this chapter. The law was enacted to give police and prosecutors greater power in combating terrorism, and the legislation was signed at a time when the country was facing the threat of continued terrorism originating in the Middle East. Nonetheless, the statute contained a "sense of Congress" provision recognizing the important contributions of Muslims and Arabs to social order and economic development in America. That provision called for criminal punishments to be imposed upon anyone victimizing Muslim Americans or persons of Arab origin living peacefully in this country. The relevant section of the law is reprinted below.

Sec. 102. Sense of Congress Condemning Discrimination Against Arab and Muslim Americans.

(a) FINDINGS.—Congress makes the following findings:

(1) Arab Americans, Muslim Americans, and Americans from South Asia play a vital role in our Nation and are entitled to nothing less than the full rights of every American.

(2) The acts of violence that have been taken against Arab and Muslim Americans since the September 11, 2001, attacks against the United States should be and are condemned by all Americans who value freedom.

(3) The concept of individual responsibility for wrongdoing is sacrosanct in American society, and applies equally to all religious, racial, and ethnic groups.

(4) When American citizens commit acts of violence against those who are, or are perceived to be, of Arab or Muslim descent, they should be punished to the full extent of the law.

(5) Muslim Americans have become so fearful of harassment that many Muslim women are changing the way they dress to avoid becoming targets.

(6) Many Arab Americans and Muslim Americans have acted heroically during the attacks on the United States, including Mohammed Salman Hamdani, a 23-year-old New Yorker of Pakistani descent, who is believed to have gone to the World Trade Center to offer rescue assistance and is now missing.

(b) SENSE OF CONGRESS.—It is the sense of Congress that—

(1) the civil rights and civil liberties of all Americans, including Arab Americans, Muslim Americans, and Americans from South Asia, must be protected, and that every effort must be taken to preserve their safety;

(2) any acts of violence or discrimination against any Americans [must] be condemned; and

(3) the Nation is called upon to recognize the patriotism of fellow citizens from all ethnic, racial, and religious backgrounds.

In a separate but similar case, *Kyllo* v. *U.S* (2001),[117] the U.S. Supreme Court reached much the same conclusion. Based on the results of a warrantless search conducted by officers using a thermal imaging device, investigators applied for a search warrant of Kyllo's home. The subsequent search uncovered more than 100 marijuana plants that were being grown under bright lights. In overturning Kyllo's conviction on drug-manufacturing charges, the Court held, "Where, as here, the Government uses a device that is not in general public use, to explore details of a private home that would previously have been unknowable without physical intrusion, the surveillance is a Fourth Amendment 'search,' and is presumptively unreasonable without a warrant."[118] Learn more about the issues surrounding search and seizure at **Web Extra! 7–5** at cjtoday.com.

The Intelligence Function

The police role encompasses the need to gather information by questioning both suspects and informants. Even more often, the need for information leads police investigators to question potentially knowledgeable citizens who may have been witnesses or victims. Data gathering is a crucial form of intelligence, without which enforcement agencies would be virtually powerless to plan and effect arrests.

The importance of gathering information in police work cannot be overstressed. Studies have found that the one factor most likely to lead to arrest in serious crimes is the presence of a witness who can provide information to the police. Undercover operations, neighborhood watch programs, "crime stopper" groups, and organized detective work all contribute information to the police.

Informants

Information gathering is a complex process, and many ethical questions have been raised about the techniques police use to gather information. The use of paid informants, for example, is an area of concern to ethicists who believe that informants are often paid to get away with crimes. The police practice (endorsed by some prosecutors) of agreeing not to charge one offender out of a group if he or she will "talk" and testify against others is another concern.

As we have seen, probable cause is an important aspect of both police searches and legal arrests. The Fourth Amendment specifies, "[N]o Warrants shall issue, but upon probable cause." As a consequence, the successful use of informants in supporting requests for a warrant depends upon the demonstrable reliability of their information. The case of *Aguilar* v. *Texas* (1964)[119] clarified the use of informants and established a two-pronged test. The U.S. Supreme Court ruled that informant information could establish probable cause if both of the following criteria are met:

- The source of the informant's information is made clear.
- The police officer has a reasonable belief that the informant is reliable.

The two-pronged test of *Aguilar* v. *Texas* was intended to prevent the issuance of warrants on the basis of false or fabricated information. Two later cases provided exceptions to the two-pronged test. *Harris* v. *U.S.* (1971)[120] recognized the fact that when an informant provided information that was damaging to him or her, it was probably true. In *Harris*, an informant told police that he had purchased non-tax-paid whiskey from another person. Since the information also implicated the informant in a crime, it was held to be accurate, even though it could not meet the second prong of the *Aguilar* test. The 1969 Supreme Court case of *Spinelli* v. *U.S.*[121] created an exception to the requirements of the first prong. In *Spinelli*, the Court held that some information can be so highly specific that it must be accurate, even if its source is not revealed.

In 1983, in the case of *Illinois* v. *Gates*,[122] the Court adopted a totality-of-circumstances approach, which held that sufficient probable cause for issuing a warrant exists where an informant can be reasonably believed on the basis of everything that is known by the police. The *Gates* case involved an anonymous informant who provided incriminating information about another person through a letter to the police. Although the source of the information was not stated and the police were unable to say whether the informant was reliable, the overall sense of things, given what was already known to police, was that the information supplied was probably valid.

In the 1990 case of *Alabama* v. *White*,[123] the Supreme Court ruled that an anonymous tip, even in the absence of other corroborating information about a suspect, could form the basis for an investigatory stop if the informant accurately predicted the *future* behavior of the suspect. The Court reasoned that the ability to predict a suspect's behavior demonstrates a significant degree of familiarity with the suspect's affairs. In the words of the Court, "Because only a small number of people are generally privy to an individual's itinerary, it is reasonable for the police to believe that a person with access to such information is likely to also have access to reliable information about that individual's illegal activities."[124]

In 2000, in the case of *Florida* v. *J.L.*, the Court held that an anonymous tip that a person is carrying a gun does not, without more, justify a police officer's stop and frisk of that person. Ruling that such a search is invalid under the Fourth Amendment, the Court rejected the suggestion of a firearm exception to the general stop and frisk rule.[125]

The identity of informants may be kept secret only if sources have been explicitly assured of confidentiality by investigating officers or if a reasonably implied assurance of confidentiality has been made. In *U.S. Dept. of Justice* v. *Landano* (1993),[126] the U.S. Supreme Court required that an informant's identity be revealed through a request made under the federal Freedom of Information Act. In that case, the FBI had not specifically assured the informant of confidentiality, and the Court ruled that "the government is not entitled to a presumption that all sources supplying information to the FBI in the course of a criminal investigation are confidential sources."

Police Interrogation

Several years ago, Richard Jewell, a former campus security guard, became the primary suspect in the pipe-bombing attack that took place in Atlanta's Centennial Park during the 1996 Olympics. FBI investigators were apparently convinced that Jewell was guilty and, according to Jewell, used a ruse to try to trick him into confessing.[127] Jewell claimed that agents asked him to sign a waiver of his *Miranda* rights, even before he knew he was a suspect, by telling him that the waiver document was a prop in a training film. Agents told Jewell that they were making a film about how to interrogate suspects and that Jewell was chosen for the starring role because of his heroic activities at the time of the bombing. Later, when authorities dropped their investigation of Jewell, he sued CNN, the *Atlanta Journal-Constitution*, and his former college employer for libel and character defamation—and threatened a suit against the FBI. FBI Director Louis Freeh later admitted that agents had made a "major error in judgment" when they tried to trick Jewell.[128] As the Jewell investigation was to show, police interrogators must remember that not all suspects are guilty and that everyone is entitled to constitutional rights during investigation and interrogation.

Interrogation has been defined by the U.S. Supreme Court as any behaviors by the police "that the police should know are reasonably likely to elicit an incriminating response from the suspect."[129] Hence, interrogation may involve activities which go well beyond mere verbal questioning, and the Court has held that interrogation may include "staged lineups, reverse lineups, positing guilt, minimizing the moral seriousness of crime, and casting blame on the victim or society." It is noteworthy that the Court has also held that "police words or actions normally attendant to arrest and custody do not constitute interrogation" unless they involve pointed or directed questions. Hence, an arresting officer may instruct a suspect on what to do and may chitchat with him or her without engaging in interrogation within the meaning of the law. Once police officers make inquiries intended to elicit information about the crime in question, however, interrogation has begun. The interrogation of suspects, like other areas of police activity, is subject to constitutional limits as interpreted by the courts, and a series of landmark decisions by the U.S. Supreme Court has focused on police interrogation.

> **interrogation**
>
> The information-gathering activities of police officers that involve the direct questioning of suspects.

PHYSICAL ABUSE

The first in a series of significant cases was that of *Brown* v. *Mississippi*,[130] decided in 1936. The *Brown* case began with the robbery of a white store owner in Mississippi in 1934. During the robbery, the victim was killed. A posse formed and went to the home of a local black man rumored to have been one of the perpetrators. They dragged the suspect from his home, put a rope around his neck, and hoisted him into a tree. They repeated this process a number of times, hoping to get a confession from the man, but failing. The posse was headed by a deputy sheriff who then arrested other suspects in the case and laid them over chairs in the local jail and whipped them with belts and buckles until they "confessed." These confessions were used in the trial which followed, and all three defendants were convicted of murder. Their convictions were upheld by the Mississippi Supreme Court. In 1936, however, the case was reviewed by the U.S. Supreme Court, which overturned all of the convictions, saying that it was difficult to imagine techniques of interrogation more "revolting" to the sense of justice than those used in this case. Read the full text of the Court's opinion in *Brown* v. *Mississippi* at **Library Extra! 7–6** on cjtoday.com.

INHERENT COERCION

Interrogation need not involve physical abuse for it to be contrary to constitutional principles. In the case of *Ashcraft* v. *Tennessee* (1944),[131] the U.S. Supreme Court found that interrogation involving **inherent coercion** was not acceptable. Ashcraft had been charged with the murder of his wife, Zelma. He was arrested on a Saturday night and interrogated by relays of skilled interrogators until Monday morning, when he purportedly made a statement implicating himself in the murder. During questioning he had faced a blinding light but was not physically mistreated. Investigators later testified that when the suspect requested cigarettes, food, or water, they "kindly" provided them. The Court's ruling, which reversed Ashcraft's conviction, made it plain that the Fifth Amendment guarantee against self-incrimination excludes any form of official coercion or pressure during interrogation.

A similar case, *Chambers* v. *Florida*, had occurred in 1940.[132] In that case, four black men were arrested without warrants as suspects in the robbery and murder of an aged white man. After several days of questioning in a hostile atmosphere, the men confessed to the murder. The confessions were used as the primary evidence against them at the trial which ensued, and all four were sentenced to die. Upon appeal, the U.S. Supreme Court held that "the very circumstances surrounding their confinement and their questioning without any formal charges having been brought, were such as to fill petitioners with terror and frightful misgivings."[133]

> **inherent coercion**
>
> The tactics used by police interviewers that fall short of physical abuse but that nonetheless pressure suspects to divulge information.

PSYCHOLOGICAL MANIPULATION

Not only must interrogation be free of coercion and hostility, but also it cannot involve sophisticated trickery designed to ferret out a confession. While interrogators do not necessarily have to be scrupulously honest in confronting suspects, and while the expert opinions of medical and psychiatric practitioners may be sought in investigations, the use of professionals skilled in **psychological manipulation** to gain confessions was banned by the Court in the case of *Leyra* v. *Denno*[134] in 1954.

The early 1950s were the heyday of psychiatric perspectives on criminal behavior. In the *Leyra* case, detectives employed a psychiatrist to question Camilo Leyra, who had been charged with the hammer slayings of his parents. Leyra had been led to believe that the medical doctor to whom he was introduced in an interrogation room had actually been sent to help him with a sinus problem. Following a period of questioning, including subtle suggestions by the psychiatrist that he would feel better if he confessed to the murders, Leyra did indeed confess.

The Supreme Court, on appeal, ruled that the defendant had been effectively and improperly duped by the police. In the words of the Court, "Instead of giving petitioner the medical advice and treatment he expected, the psychiatrist by subtle and suggestive questions simply continued the police effort of the past days and nights to induce petitioner to admit his guilt. For an hour and a half or more the techniques of a highly trained psychiatrist were used to break petitioner's will in order to get him to say he had murdered his parents."[135]

In 1991, in the case of *Arizona* v. *Fulminante*,[136] the U.S. Supreme Court threw an even more dampening blanket of uncertainty over the use of sophisticated techniques to gain a confession. Oreste Fulminante was an inmate in a federal prison when he was approached secretly by a fellow inmate who was an FBI informant. The informant told Fulminante that other inmates were plotting to kill him because of a rumor that he had killed a child. He offered to protect Fulminante if he was told the details of the crime. Fulminante then described his role in the murder of his 11-year-old stepdaughter. Fulminante was arrested for that murder, tried, and convicted. Upon appeal to the U.S. Supreme Court, his lawyers argued that Fulminante's confession had been coerced because of the threat of violence communicated by the informant. The Court agreed that the confession had been coerced and ordered a new trial at which the confession could not be admitted into evidence. Simultaneously, however, the Court found that the admission of a coerced confession should be considered a harmless "trial error" which need not necessarily result in reversal of a conviction if other evidence still proves guilt. The decision was especially significant because it partially reversed the Court's earlier ruling, in *Chapman* v. *California* (1967),[137] where it was held that forced confessions were such a basic form of constitutional error that they automatically invalidated any conviction to which they related.

The Right to a Lawyer at Interrogation

In 1964, in the case of *Escobedo* v. *Illinois*,[138] the right to have legal counsel present during police interrogation was recognized. Danny Escobedo was arrested without a warrant for the murder of his brother-in-law, made no statement during his interrogation, and was released the same day. A few weeks later, another person identified Escobedo as the killer. Escobedo was rearrested and taken back to the police station. During the interrogation which followed, officers told him that they "had him cold" and that he should confess. Escobedo asked to see his lawyer but was told that an interrogation was in progress and that he couldn't just go out and see his lawyer. Soon the lawyer arrived and asked to see Escobedo. Police told him that his client was being questioned and could be seen after questioning concluded. Escobedo later claimed that while he repeatedly asked for his lawyer, he was told, "Your lawyer doesn't want to see you."

Eventually, Escobedo confessed and was convicted at trial on the basis of his confession. Upon appeal, the U.S. Supreme Court overturned Escobedo's conviction, ruling that counsel is necessary at police interrogations to protect the rights of the defendant and should be provided when the defendant desires.

In 1981, the case of *Edwards* v. *Arizona*[139] established a "bright-line rule" (that is, specified a criterion that cannot be violated) for investigators to use in interpreting a suspect's right to counsel. In *Edwards*, the Supreme Court reiterated its *Miranda* concern that once a suspect who is in custody and is being questioned has requested the assistance of counsel, all questioning must cease until an attorney is present. In 1990, the Court refined the rule in *Minnick* v. *Mississippi*,[140] when it held that interrogation may *not* resume after the suspect has had an opportunity to consult his or her lawyer when the lawyer is no longer present. Similarly, according to *Arizona* v. *Roberson* (1988),[141] the police may not avoid the suspect's request for a lawyer by beginning a new line of questioning, even if it is about an unrelated offense. In 1994, however, in the case of *Davis* v. *U.S.*,[142] the Court "put the burden on custodial suspects to make unequivocal invocations of the right to counsel." In the *Davis* case, a man being interrogated in the death of a sailor waived his *Miranda* rights but later said, "Maybe I should talk to a lawyer." Investigators asked the suspect clarifying questions, and he responded, "No, I don't want a lawyer." Upon conviction he appealed, claiming that interrogation should have ceased when he mentioned a lawyer. The Court, in affirming the conviction, stated that "it will often be good police practice for the interviewing officers to clarify whether or not [the suspect] actually wants an attorney."

Suspect Rights: The *Miranda* Decision

In the area of suspect rights, no case is as famous as that of *Miranda* v. *Arizona* (1966),[143] which established the well-known **Miranda warnings**. Many people regard *Miranda* as the centerpiece of the Warren Court due process rulings.

The case involved Ernesto Miranda, who was arrested in Phoenix, Arizona, and was accused of having kidnapped and raped a young woman. At police headquarters, he was identified by the victim. After being interrogated for two hours, Miranda signed a confession that formed the basis of his later conviction on the charges.

Upon eventual appeal to the U.S. Supreme Court, the Court rendered what some regard as the most far-reaching opinion to have affected criminal justice in the last few decades. The Court ruled that Miranda's conviction was unconstitutional because "[t]he entire aura and atmosphere of police interrogation without notification of rights and an offer of assistance of counsel tends to subjugate the individual to the will of his examiner."

The Court continued, saying that the suspect "must be warned prior to any questioning that he has the right to remain silent, that anything he says can be used against him in a court of law, that he has the right to the presence of an attorney, and that if he cannot afford an attorney one will be appointed for him prior to any questioning if he so desires. Opportunity to exercise these rights must be afforded to him throughout the interrogation. After such warnings have been given, and such opportunity afforded him, the individual may knowingly and intelligently waive these rights and agree to answer the questions or make a statement. But unless and until such warnings and waiver are demonstrated by the prosecution at the trial, no evidence obtained as a result of interrogation can be used against him."

Miranda warnings

The advisement of rights due criminal suspects by the police prior to the beginning of questioning. *Miranda* warnings were first set forth by the Supreme Court in the 1966 case of *Miranda* v. *Arizona*.

CJ Today Exhibit 7-2

[The *Miranda* Warnings]

Adult Rights Warning

Persons 18 years old or older who are in custody must be given this advice of rights before any questioning.

1. You have the right to remain silent.
2. Anything you say can be used against you in a court of law.
3. You have the right to talk to a lawyer and to have a lawyer present while you are being questioned.
4. If you want a lawyer before or during questioning but cannot afford to hire a lawyer, one will be appointed to represent you at no cost before any questioning.
5. If you answer questions now without a lawyer here, you still have the right to stop answering questions at any time.

Waiver of Rights

After reading and explaining the rights of a person in custody, an officer must also ask for a waiver of those rights before any questioning. The following waiver questions must be answered affirmatively, either by express answer or by clear implication. Silence alone is not a waiver.

1. Do you understand each of these rights I have explained to you? (Answer must be YES.)
2. Having these rights in mind, do you now wish to answer questions? (Answer must be YES.)
3. Do you now wish to answer questions without a lawyer present? (Answer must be YES.)

For juveniles age 14, 15, 16, and 17, the following question must be asked:

4. Do you now wish to answer questions without your parents, guardians, or custodians present? (Answer must be YES.)

⍰ DISCUSSION QUESTIONS

1. Are there any other "rights" that you would add to those listed here? If so, which ones?
2. Are there any "rights" that you would remove from those listed here? If so, which ones?

Source: North Carolina Justice Academy. Reprinted with permission.

Ernesto Miranda, shown here after a jury convicted him for a second time. Miranda's conviction on rape and kidnapping charges after arresting officers failed to advise him of his rights led to the now-famous Miranda *warnings.*

AP/Wide World Photos

To ensure that proper advice is given to suspects at the time of their arrest, the now-famous *Miranda* rights are read before any questioning begins. These rights, as they appear on a *Miranda* warning card commonly used by police agencies, appear in CJ Today Exhibit 7–2.

Once suspects have been advised of their *Miranda* rights, they are commonly asked to sign a paper which lists each right, in order to confirm that they were advised of their rights and that they understand each right. Questioning may then begin, but only if suspects waive the right not to talk or to have a lawyer present during interrogation.

When the *Miranda* decision was handed down, some hailed it as ensuring the protection of individual rights guaranteed under the Constitution. To guarantee those rights, they suggested, no better agency is available than the police themselves, since the police are present at the initial stages of the criminal justice process. Critics of *Miranda*, however, argued that the decision put police agencies in the uncomfortable and contradictory position not only of enforcing the law, but also of having to offer defendants advice on how they might circumvent conviction and punishment. Under *Miranda*, the police partially assume the role of legal adviser to the accused.

During the last years of the Reagan administration, then-Attorney General Edwin Meese called the *Miranda* decision the "antithesis of law and order." He pledged the resources of his office to an assault upon the *Miranda* rules to eliminate what he saw as the frequent release of guilty parties on the basis of "technicalities." Meese was unsuccessful, and later administrations vigorously defended the *Miranda* decision.

In 1999, however, in the case of *U.S.* v. *Dickerson*,[144] the Fourth Circuit U.S. Court of Appeals upheld an almost-forgotten law that Congress had passed in 1968 with the intention of overturning *Miranda*. That law, Section 3501 of Chapter 223, Part II of Title 18 of the U.S. Code, says that "a confession . . . shall be admissible in evidence if it is voluntarily given." In determining the voluntariness of the confession, the trial judge is to

"take into consideration all the circumstances surrounding the giving of the confession, including (1) the time elapsing between arrest and arraignment of the defendant making the confession, if it was made after arrest and before arraignment; (2) whether such defendant knew the nature of the offense with which he was charged or of which he was suspected at the time of making the confession; (3) whether or not such defendant was advised or knew that he was not required to make any statement and that any such statement could be used against him; (4) whether or not such defendant had been advised prior to questioning of his right

A suspect being read his Miranda rights immediately after arrest. Officers often read Miranda rights from a card to preclude the possibility of mistake.

Bob Daemmrich, Stock Boston

to the assistance of counsel; and (5) whether or not such defendant was without the assistance of counsel when questioned and when giving such confession."

Upon appeal in 2000, the U.S. Supreme Court upheld its original *Miranda* ruling by a 7 to 2 vote and found that *Miranda* is a constitutional rule (that is, a fundamental right inherent in the U.S. Constitution) that cannot be dismissed by an act of Congress. "*Miranda* and its progeny," the majority wrote in *Dickerson* v. *U.S.*, will continue to "govern the admissibility of statements made during custodial interrogation in both state and federal courts."[145] Individual-rights advocates saw the decision as a good one. Deanne Maynard, a Washington attorney and author of the friend-of-the-court brief filed by the National Association of Criminal Defense Lawyers, applauded the decision, saying, "It's an important victory for individual liberties given the inherently coercive nature of interrogation while in custody."[146] Dissenting Justices Scalia and Thomas, on the other hand, were appalled by what they saw as the Court's illegal denial of completely legitimate congressional action. In a scathing dissenting opinion, the justices wrote that the *Miranda* requirements can be found nowhere in the Constitution. "The only thing that [this decision] can possibly mean," they said, "is that the Court has the power, not merely to apply the Constitution but to expand it, imposing what it regards as useful 'prophylactic' restrictions

---

CJ Today Exhibit 7-3

[The *Miranda* Triggers]

■ Custody
■ Interrogation[1]

[1]Custodial interrogation triggers the need for *Miranda* warnings.

upon the Congress and the States. This is an immense and frightening and antidemocratic power, and it does not exist." Read the full text of the original *Miranda* decision, the text of Section 3501 of the U.S. Code, the Fourth Circuit Court's 1999 opinion in *Dickerson*, and the final U.S. Supreme Court majority and dissenting opinions at the "*Miranda* Revisited" site via **Web Extra! 7–6** at cjtoday.com.

WAIVER OF *MIRANDA* RIGHTS BY SUSPECTS

Suspects in police custody may legally waive their *Miranda* rights through a *voluntary* "knowing and intelligent" waiver. A *knowing waiver* can only be made if a suspect has been advised of his or her rights and was in a condition to understand the advisement. A rights advisement made in English, for example, to a Spanish-speaking suspect cannot produce a knowing waiver. Likewise, an *intelligent waiver* of rights requires that the defendant be able to understand the consequences of not invoking the *Miranda* rights. In the case of *Moran* v. *Burbine* (1986),[147] the U.S. Supreme Court defined an intelligent and knowing waiver as one "made with a full awareness both of the nature of the right being abandoned and the consequences of the decision to abandon it." Similarly, in *Colorado* v. *Spring* (1987),[148] the Court held that an intelligent and knowing waiver can be made even though a suspect has not been informed of all the alleged offenses about which he or she is about to be questioned.

In 1992, *Miranda* rights were effectively extended to illegal immigrants living in the United States. In a settlement of a class-action lawsuit reached in Los Angeles with the Immigration and Naturalization Service, U.S. District Court Judge William Byrne, Jr., approved the printing of millions of notices in several languages to be given to arrestees. The approximately 1.5 million illegal aliens arrested each year must be told they may (1) talk with a lawyer, (2) make a phone call, (3) request a list of available legal services, (4) seek a hearing before an immigration judge, (5) possibly obtain release on bond, and (6) contact a diplomatic officer representing their country. This kind of thing was "long overdue," said Roberto Martinez of the American Friends Service Committee's Mexico-U.S. border program. "Up to now, we've had total mistreatment of civil rights of undocumented people."[149]

INEVITABLE-DISCOVERY EXCEPTION TO *MIRANDA*

A good example of the change in Supreme Court philosophy, alluded to earlier in this chapter as a movement away from an individual-rights perspective and toward a public-order perspective, is the case of Robert Anthony Williams. The case epitomizes what some have called a "nibbling away" at the advances in defendant rights which reached their apex in *Miranda*. The case had its beginnings in 1969, at the close of the Warren Court era, when Williams was convicted of murdering a ten-year-old girl, Pamela Powers, around Christmastime. Although Williams had been advised of his rights, detectives searching for the girl's body were riding in a car with the defendant when one of them made what has since come to be known as the "Christian burial speech." The detective told Williams that, since Christmas was almost upon them, it would be "the Christian thing to do" to see to it that Pamela could have a decent burial rather than having to lay in a field somewhere. Williams relented and led detectives to the body. However, because Williams had not been reminded of his right to have a lawyer present during his conversation with the detective, the Supreme Court in *Brewer* v. *Williams* (1977)[150] overturned Williams's conviction, saying that the detective's remarks were "a deliberate eliciting of incriminating evidence from an accused in the absence of his lawyer."

In 1977, Williams was retried for the murder, but his remarks in leading detectives to the body were not entered into evidence. The discovery of the body was itself used, however, prompting another appeal to the Supreme Court based upon the argument that the body should not have been used as evidence since it was discovered due to the illegally gathered statements. This time, in *Nix* v. *Williams* (1984),[151] the Supreme Court affirmed Williams's second conviction, holding that the body would have been found anyway, since detectives were searching in the direction where it lay when Williams revealed its location. That ruling came during the heyday of the Burger Court and clearly demonstrates a tilt by the Court away from suspect's rights and an accommodation with the imperfect world of police procedure. The *Williams* case, as it was finally resolved, is said to have created the *inevitable-discovery exception* to the *Miranda* requirements.

PUBLIC-SAFETY EXCEPTION TO *MIRANDA*

In 1984, the U.S. Supreme Court also established what has come to be known as the *public-safety exception* to the *Miranda* rule. The case of *New York* v. *Quarles*[152] centered upon a rape in which the victim told police her assailant had fled, with a gun, into a nearby A & P supermarket. Two police officers entered the store and apprehended the suspect. One officer immediately noticed that the man was wearing an empty shoulder holster and, apparently fearing that a child might find the discarded weapon, quickly asked, "Where's the gun?"

Quarles was convicted of rape but appealed his conviction, requesting that the weapon be suppressed as evidence because officers had not advised him of his *Miranda* rights before asking him about it. The Supreme Court disagreed, stating that considerations of public safety were overriding and negated the need for rights advisement prior to limited questioning which focused on the need to prevent further harm.

Where the police have not been coercive and have issued *Miranda* warnings, the U.S. Supreme Court has held that even a later demonstration that a person may have been suffering from mental problems will not necessarily negate a confession. *Colorado* v. *Connelly* (1986)[153] involved a man who approached a Denver police officer and said he wanted to confess to the murder of a young girl. The officer immediately informed him of his *Miranda* rights, but the man waived them and continued to talk. When a detective arrived, the man was again advised of his rights and again waived them. After being taken to the local jail, the man began to hear "voices" and later claimed that it was these voices which had made him confess. At the trial, the defense moved to have the earlier confession negated on the basis that it was not voluntarily or freely given because of the defendant's mental condition. Upon appeal, the U.S. Supreme Court disagreed, saying that "no coercive government conduct occurred in this case." Hence, "self-coercion," be it through the agency of a guilty conscience or faulty thought processes, does not appear to bar prosecution based on information revealed willingly by a suspect.

In a final refinement of *Miranda*, the lawful ability of a police informant placed in a jail cell along with a defendant to gather information for later use at trial was upheld in the 1986 case of *Kuhlmann* v. *Wilson*.[154] The passive gathering of information was judged to be acceptable, provided that the informant did not make attempts to elicit information.

In the case of *Illinois* v. *Perkins* (1990),[155] the Court expanded its position to say that under appropriate circumstances, even the active questioning of a suspect by an undercover officer posing as a fellow inmate does not require *Miranda* warnings. In *Perkins*, the Court found that, lacking other forms of coercion, the fact that the suspect was not aware of the questioner's identity as a law enforcement officer ensured that his statements were freely given. In the words of the Court, "The essential ingredients of a 'police-dominated atmosphere' and compulsion are not present when an incarcerated person speaks freely to someone that he believes to be a fellow inmate."

MIRANDA AND THE MEANING OF INTERROGATION

Modern interpretations of the applicability of *Miranda* warnings turn upon an understanding of *interrogation*. The *Miranda* decision, as originally rendered, specifically recognized the necessity for police investigators to make inquiries at crime scenes to determine facts or to establish identities. So long as the individual questioned is not yet in custody and so long as probable cause is lacking in the investigator's mind, such questioning can proceed without the need for *Miranda* warnings. In such cases, interrogation, within the meaning of *Miranda*, has not yet begun.

The case of *Rock* v. *Zimmerman* (1982)[156] provides a different sort of example—one in which a suspect willingly made statements to the police before interrogation began. The suspect had burned his own house and shot and killed a neighbor. When the fire department arrived, he began shooting again and killed the fire chief. Cornered later in a field, the defendant, gun in hand, spontaneously shouted at police, "How many people did I kill, how many people are dead?"[157] This spontaneous statement was held to be admissible evidence at the suspect's trial.

It is also important to recognize that the Supreme Court, in the *Miranda* decision, required that officers provide warnings only in those situations involving *both* arrest and custodial interrogation—what some call the **Miranda triggers**. In other words, it is generally permissible for officers to take a suspect into custody and listen without asking questions while he or she tells a story. Similarly, they may ask questions without providing a *Miranda* warning, even within the confines of a police station house, as long as the person questioned is not a suspect and is not under arrest.[158] Warnings are required only when officers begin to actively solicit responses from the defendant.

Officers were found to have acted properly in the case of *South Dakota* v. *Neville* (1983)[159] in informing a man suspected of driving while intoxicated (DWI), without reading

Miranda triggers

The dual principles of custody and interrogation, both of which are necessary before an advisement of rights is required.

him his rights, that he would stand to lose his driver's license if he did not submit to a Breathalyzer test. When the driver responded, "I'm too drunk. I won't pass the test," his answer became evidence of his condition and was permitted at trial.

A third-party conversation recorded by the police after a suspect has invoked the *Miranda* right to remain silent may be used as evidence, according to a 1987 ruling in *Arizona* v. *Mauro*.[160] In *Mauro,* a man who willingly conversed with his wife in the presence of a police tape recorder, even after invoking his right to keep silent, was held to have effectively abandoned that right.

When a waiver is not made, however, in-court references to a defendant's silence following the issuing of *Miranda* warnings are unconstitutional. In the 1976 case of *Doyle* v. *Ohio*,[161] the U.S. Supreme Court definitively ruled that "a suspect's [post-*Miranda*] silence will not be used against him." Even so, according to the Court in *Brecht* v. *Abrahamson* (1993),[162] prosecution efforts to use such silence against a defendant may not invalidate a finding of guilt by a jury unless the "error had substantial and injurious effect or influence in determining the jury's verdict."[163]

Gathering Special Kinds of Nontestimonial Evidence

The role of law enforcement is complicated by the fact that suspects are often privy to special evidence of a nontestimonial sort. Nontestimonial evidence is generally physical evidence, and most physical evidence is subject to normal procedures of search and seizure. A special category of nontestimonial evidence, however, includes very personal items, which may be within or part of a person's body, such as ingested drugs, blood cells, foreign objects, medical implants, and human DNA. Also included in this category might be fingerprints and other kinds of biological residue. The gathering of such special kinds of nontestimonial evidence is a complex area rich in precedent. The Fourth Amendment guarantee that people be secure in their homes and in their persons has generally been interpreted by the courts to mean that the improper seizure of physical evidence of any kind is illegal and will result in exclusion of that evidence at trial. When very personal kinds of nontestimonial evidence are considered, however, the issue becomes more complicated still.

THE RIGHT TO PRIVACY

Two 1985 cases, *Hayes* v. *Florida*[164] and *Winston* v. *Lee*,[165] are examples of limits the courts have placed upon the seizure of very personal forms of nontestimonial evidence. The *Hayes* case established the right of suspects to refuse to be fingerprinted when probable cause necessary to effect an arrest does not exist. *Winston* demonstrated the inviolability of the body against surgical and other substantially invasive techniques which might be ordered by authorities against a suspect's will.

In the *Winston* case, Rudolph Lee, Jr., was found a few blocks from the scene of a robbery with a gunshot wound in his chest. The robbery had involved an exchange of gunshots by a store owner and the robber, with the owner noting that the robber had apparently been hit by a bullet. At the hospital, the store owner identified Lee as the robber. The prosecution sought to have Lee submit to surgery to remove the bullet in his chest, arguing that the bullet would provide physical evidence linking him to the crime. Lee refused the surgery, and in *Winston* v. *Lee*, the U.S. Supreme Court ruled that Lee could not be ordered to undergo surgery because such a magnitude of intrusion into his body was unacceptable under the right to privacy guaranteed by the Fourth Amendment. The *Winston* case was based upon precedent established in *Schmerber* v. *California* (1966).[166] The *Schmerber* case turned upon the extraction against the defendant's will of a blood sample to be measured for alcohol content. In *Schmerber,* the Court ruled that warrants must be obtained for bodily intrusions unless fast action is necessary to prevent the destruction of evidence by natural physiological processes.

BODY CAVITY SEARCHES

Body cavity searches are among the most problematic types of searches for police today. "Strip" searches of convicts in prison, including the search of body cavities, have generally been held permissible.

The 1985 Supreme Court case of *U.S.* v. *Montoya de Hernandez*[167] focused on the issue of "alimentary canal smuggling," in which the offender typically swallows condoms filled with cocaine or heroin and waits for nature to take its course to recover the substance. In the *Montoya* case, a woman known to be a "balloon swallower" arrived in the

United States on a flight from Colombia. She was detained by customs officials and given a pat-down search by a female agent. The agent reported that the woman's abdomen was firm and suggested that X rays be taken. The suspect refused and was given the choice of submitting to further tests or taking the next flight back to Colombia. No flight was immediately available, however, and the suspect was placed in a room for 16 hours, where she refused all food and drink. Finally, a court order for an X ray was obtained. The procedure revealed "balloons," and the woman was detained another four days, during which time she passed numerous cocaine-filled plastic condoms. The Court ruled that the woman's confinement was not unreasonable, based as it was upon the supportable suspicion that she was "body-packing" cocaine. Any discomfort she experienced, the court ruled, "resulted solely from the method that she chose to smuggle illicit drugs."[168]

Electronic Eavesdropping

Modern technology makes possible increasingly complex forms of communication. From fiber-optic phone lines, microwave and cellular transmissions, and fax machines to computer communications involving modems and databases, today's global village is a close-knit weave of flowing information.

One of the first and best known of the Supreme Court decisions involving electronic communications was the 1928 case of *Olmstead* v. *U.S.*[169] In *Olmstead*, bootleggers used their personal telephones to discuss and transact business. Agents tapped the lines and based their investigation and ensuing arrests upon conversations they overheard. The defendants were convicted and eventually appealed to the high court, arguing that the agents had in effect seized information illegally without a search warrant in violation of the defendants' Fourth Amendment right to be secure in their homes. The Court ruled, however, that telephone lines were not an extension of the defendant's home and therefore were not protected by the constitutional guarantee of security. Subsequent federal statutes (discussed shortly) have substantially modified the significance of *Olmstead*.

Recording devices carried on the body of an undercover agent or an informant were ruled to produce admissible evidence in *On Lee* v. *U.S.* (1952)[170] and *Lopez* v. *U.S.* (1963).[171] The 1967 case of *Berger* v. *New York*[172] permitted wiretaps and "bugs" in instances where state law provided for the use of such devices and where officers obtained a warrant based upon probable cause.

The Court appeared to undertake a significant change of direction in the area of electronic eavesdropping when, in 1967, it decided the case of *Katz* v. *U.S.*[173] Federal agents had monitored a number of Katz's telephone calls from a public phone using a device separate from the phone lines and attached to the glass of the phone booth. The Court, in this case, stated that what a person makes an effort to keep private, even in a public place, requires a judicial decision, in the form of a warrant issued upon probable cause, to unveil. In the words of the Court, "The government's activities in electronically listening to and recording the petitioner's words violated the privacy upon which he justifiably relied while using the telephone booth and thus constituted a 'search and seizure' within the meaning of the Fourth Amendment."

In 1968, with the case of *Lee* v. *Florida*,[174] the Court applied the Federal Communications Act[175] to telephone conversations which may be the object of police investigation and held that evidence obtained without a warrant could not be used in state proceedings if it resulted from a wiretap. The only person who has the authority to permit eavesdropping, according to that act, is the sender of the message.

The Federal Communications Act, originally passed in 1934, does not specifically mention the potential interest of law enforcement agencies in monitoring communications. Title III of the Omnibus Crime Control and Safe Streets Act of 1968, however, mostly prohibits wiretaps but does allow officers to listen to electronic communications when (1) an officer is one of the parties involved in the communication, (2) one of the parties is not the officer but willingly decides to share the communication with the officer, or (3) officers obtain a warrant based upon probable cause. In the 1971 case of *U.S.* v. *White*,[176] the Court held that law enforcement officers may intercept electronic information when one of the parties involved in the communication gives his or her consent, even without a warrant.

In 1984, the Supreme Court decided the case of *U.S.* v. *Karo*,[177] in which DEA agents had arrested James Karo for cocaine importation. Officers had placed a radio transmitter inside a 50-gallon drum of ether purchased by Karo for use in processing the cocaine. The transmitter was placed inside the drum with the consent of the seller of the ether but without a search warrant. The shipment of ether was followed to the Karo house, and Karo was arrested and convicted of cocaine trafficking charges. Karo appealed to the U.S. Supreme Court, claiming that the radio beeper had violated his reasonable expectation of privacy inside his premises and that, without a warrant, the evidence it produced was tainted. The Court agreed and overturned his conviction.

MINIMIZATION REQUIREMENT FOR ELECTRONIC SURVEILLANCE

The Supreme Court established a minimization requirement pertinent to electronic surveillance in the 1978 case of *U.S. v. Scott.*[178] *Minimization* means that officers must make every reasonable effort to monitor only those conversations, through the use of phone taps, body bugs, and the like, which are specifically related to the criminal activity under investigation. As soon as it becomes obvious that a conversation is innocent, then the monitoring personnel are required to cease their invasion of privacy. Problems arise if the conversation occurs in a foreign language, if it is "coded," or if it is ambiguous. It has been suggested that investigators involved in electronic surveillance maintain log books of their activities which specifically show monitored conversations, as well as efforts made at minimization.[179]

Electronic Communications Privacy Act (ECPA)

A law passed by Congress in 1986 governing the requirements necessary for law enforcement officers to intercept wire communications.

THE ELECTRONIC COMMUNICATIONS PRIVACY ACT OF 1986

Passed by Congress in 1986, the **Electronic Communications Privacy Act (ECPA)**[180] brought major changes in the requirements law enforcement officers must meet to intercept *wire* communications (those involving the human voice). The ECPA deals specifically with three areas of communication: (1) wiretaps and bugs, (2) pen registers (which record the numbers dialed from a telephone), and (3) tracing devices which determine the number from which a call emanates. The act also addresses the procedures to be followed by officers in obtaining records relating to communications services, and it establishes requirements for gaining access to stored electronic communications and records of those communications. The ECPA basically requires that investigating officers must obtain wiretap-type court orders to eavesdrop on *ongoing communications*. The use of pen registers and recording devices, however, is specifically excluded by the law from court order requirements.[181]

A related measure, the Communications Assistance for Law Enforcement Act of 1994,[182] appropriated $500 million to modify the U.S. phone system to allow for continued wiretapping by law enforcement agencies. The law also specifies a standard-setting process for the redesign of existing equipment which would permit effective wiretapping in the face of coming technological advances. In the words of the FBI's Telecommunications Industry Liaison Unit, "This law requires telecommunications carriers, as defined in the Act, to ensure law enforcement's ability, pursuant to court order or other lawful authorization, to intercept communications notwithstanding advanced telecommunications technologies."[183] In the year 2000, 1,190 wiretap requests were approved by federal and state judges, and approximately 2.1 million conversations were intercepted by law enforcement agencies throughout the country.[184]

THE TELECOMMUNICATIONS ACT OF 1996

Title V of the Telecommunications Act of 1996[185] made it a federal offense for anyone engaged in interstate or international communications to knowingly use a telecommunications device "to create, solicit, or initiate the transmission of any comment, request, suggestion, proposal, image, or other communication which is obscene, lewd, lascivious, filthy, or indecent, with intent to annoy, abuse, threaten, or harass another person." The law also provided special penalties for anyone who "makes a telephone call . . . without disclosing his identity and with intent to annoy, abuse, threaten, or harass any person at the called number or who receives the communication" or who "makes or causes the telephone of another repeatedly or continuously to ring, with intent to harass any person at the called number; or makes repeated telephone calls" for the purpose of harassing a person at the called number.

A section of the law, known as the Communications Decency Act (CDA)[186] criminalized the transmission to minors of "patently offensive" obscene materials over the Internet or other computer telecommunications services. The CDA, portions of which were invalidated by the U.S. Supreme Court in the case of *Reno* v. *ACLU* (1997),[187] is discussed in greater detail in Chapter 17.

THE USA PATRIOT ACT OF 2001

The USA PATRIOT Act of 2001, which is also discussed in a box in this chapter, made it easier for police investigators to intercept many forms of electronic communication. Under previous federal law, for example, investigators could not obtain a wiretap order to intercept *wire* communications for violations of the Computer Fraud and Abuse Act.[188] In several well-known investigations, however, hackers had stolen teleconferencing services from telephone companies and then used those services to plan and execute hacking attacks.

The USA PATRIOT Act[189] added felony violations of the Computer Fraud and Abuse Act to Section 2516(1) of Title 18 of the U.S. Code—the portion of federal law that lists specific types of crimes for which investigators may obtain a wiretap order for wire communications. The change is only a temporary one, however, and unless renewed by Congress, the provision will expire on December 31, 2005.

The USA PATRIOT Act of 2001 also modified that portion of the ECPA that governs law enforcement access to stored electronic communications (such as e-mail) to include stored wire communications (such as voice mail). Prior to the modification, law enforcement officers needed to obtain a wiretap order (rather than a search warrant) to obtain unopened voice communications. Because today's e-mail messages may contain digitized voice "attachments," investigators were sometimes required to obtain both a search warrant and a wiretap order to learn the contents of a specific message. Under the act, the same rules now apply to both stored wire communications and stored electronic communications. Wiretap orders, which are often much more difficult to obtain than search warrants, are now only required to intercept real-time telephone conversations. This provision will also expire on December 31, 2005, unless renewed.

Prior to passage of the USA PATRIOT Act, federal law allowed investigators to use an administrative subpoena (that is, a subpoena authorized by a federal or state statute or by a federal or state grand jury or trial court) to compel Internet service providers to provide a limited class of information, such as a customer's name, address, length of service, and means of payment. Also under previous law, investigators could not subpoena certain records, including credit card numbers or details about other forms of payment for Internet service. Such information, however, can be highly relevant in determining a suspect's true identity because, in many cases, users register with Internet service providers using false names.

Previous federal law[190] was also technology-specific, relating primarily to telephone communications. Local and long-distance telephone billing records, for example, could be subpoenaed, but not billing information for Internet communications or records of Internet session times and durations. Similarly, previous law allowed the government to use a subpoena to obtain the customer's "telephone number or other subscriber number or identity" but did not define what that phrase meant in the context of Internet communications.

The USA PATRIOT Act amended portions of this federal law[191] to update and expand the type of records that law enforcement authorities may obtain with a subpoena. "Records of session times and durations," as well as "any temporarily assigned network address" may now be gathered. Such changes should make the process of identifying computer criminals and tracing their Internet communications faster and easier. This section of the Act is not subject to sunset provisions.

Learn more about electronic surveillance and wiretapping in criminal cases via **Web Extra! 7–7** at cjtoday.com.

GATHERING ELECTRONIC EVIDENCE

The Internet, computer networks, and automated data systems present an enormous new opportunity for committing criminal activity.[192] Computers and other electronic devices are increasingly being used to commit, enable, or support crimes perpetrated against people, organizations, and property. Whether the crime involves attacks such as against computer systems or the information they contain or more traditional offenses such as murder, money laundering, trafficking, or fraud, **electronic evidence** is increasingly involved.

Electronic evidence is "information and data of investigative value that is stored in or transmitted by an electronic device."[193] Such evidence is often acquired when physical items, such as computers, removable disks, CDs, DVDs, magnetic tape, flash memory chips, cellular telephones, personal digital assistants, and other electronic devices are collected from a crime scene or are obtained from a suspect.

electronic evidence

Information and data of investigative value that are stored in or transmitted by an electronic device.[i]

Electronic evidence has special characteristics. (1) It is latent. (2) It can transcend national and state borders quickly and easily. (3) It is fragile and can easily be altered, damaged, compromised, or destroyed by improper handling or improper examination. (4) It may be time-sensitive. Like DNA or fingerprints, electronic evidence is **latent evidence** because it is not readily visible to the human eye under normal conditions. Special equipment and software are required to "see" and evaluate electronic evidence. In the courtroom, expert testimony may be needed to explain the acquisition of electronic evidence and the examination process used to interpret it.

In 2001, in recognition of the special challenges posed by electronic evidence, the International Association of Chiefs of Police, in conjunction with the U.S. Secret Service, released a brief manual entitled *Best Practices for Seizing Electronic Evidence.*[194] The manual can be accessed via **Library Extra! 7–7** at cjtoday.com.

About the same time, the Technical Working Group for Electronic Crime Scene Investigation (TWGECSI) released a much more detailed guide for law enforcement officers to use in gathering electronic evidence. The manual, *Electronic Crime Scene Investigation: A Guide for First Responders,*[195] grew out of a partnership formed in 1998 between the National Cybercrime Training Partnership, the Office of Law Enforcement Standards, and the National Institute of Justice. The working group was asked to identify, define, and establish basic criteria to assist federal and state agencies in handling electronic investigations and related prosecutions.

TWGECSI guidelines say that law enforcement must take special precautions when documenting, collecting, preserving, and examining electronic evidence to maintain its integrity. The guidelines also note that the first law enforcement officer on the scene (commonly called the *first responder*) should take steps to ensure the safety of everyone at the scene and to protect the integrity of all evidence, both traditional and electronic. When dealing with electronic evidence, say the TWGECSI guidelines, the following general forensic and procedural principles should be applied:

- Actions taken to secure and collect electronic evidence should not change that evidence.

- Investigators who examine electronic evidence should be trained for that purpose.

- All activity relating to the seizure, examination, storage, and transfer of electronic evidence should be fully documented, preserved, and available for review.

Specific TWGECSI guidelines tell on-the-scene investigators to

- Follow jurisdictional policy for securing the crime scene. This includes ensuring that everyone is removed from the immediate area from which evidence is to be collected. At this point in the investigation, the condition of any electronic devices should not be altered: If it is off, leave it off. If it is on, leave it on.

- Protect perishable data physically and electronically. Perishable data may be found on pagers, caller ID boxes, electronic organizers, cell phones, and other similar devices. The first responder should always keep in mind that any device containing perishable data should be immediately secured, documented, and/or photographed.

- Identify telephone lines attached to devices such as modems and caller ID boxes. Document, disconnect, and label each telephone line from the wall rather than the device, when possible. There may also be other communications lines present for LAN/Ethernet connections.

- Preserve any latent fingerprints or other physical evidence on keyboards, the computer mouse, diskettes, CDs, or other electronic components. Chemicals used in processing latent prints can damage equipment and data. Therefore, latent prints should be collected after electronic evidence recovery is complete.

- Take care when recovering and preserving nonelectronic evidence, which can be crucial in the investigation of electronic crime. Items relevant to subsequent examination of electronic evidence may exist in other forms (for example, handwritten passwords and other notes, blank pads of paper with indented writing, hardware and software manuals, calendars, literature, text or graphical computer printouts, and photographs) and should be secured and preserved for future analysis.

The entire TWGECSI guide, which includes many other practical instructions for investigators working with electronic evidence, is available as **Library Extra! 7–8** at cjtoday.com. Chapter 17 contains additional information on crimes committed with modern technology.

Summary

This chapter describes the legal environment surrounding police activities, from search and seizure through the arrest and interrogation of suspects. The Constitution of the United States—especially the Bill of Rights—is designed to protect citizens against abuses of police power. It does so by guaranteeing due process of law for every suspect and by ensuring the availability of constitutional rights to all citizens, regardless of state law or procedure. Within the context of criminal case processing, due process requirements mandate that justice system officials respect the rights of accused individuals throughout the criminal justice process.

From 1953 to 1969, the U.S. Supreme Court was known as the Warren Court because it was presided over by Chief Justice Earl Warren. The Warren Court was instrumental in expanding due process requirements so that they applied to the states as well as to the federal government. The Burger Court (1969–1986), headed by Chief Justice Warren E. Burger, began a movement away from Warren-era precedents and adhered to the principle that criminal defendants who claim violations of their due process rights need to bear most of the responsibility of showing that the police acted outside of the law. The trend begun by the Warren Court continues today.

Discussion Questions

1. Which Supreme Court decisions discussed in this chapter do you see as most important? Why? Do you disagree with any Supreme Court decisions discussed in this chapter? If so, which ones? Why do you disagree?
2. Do you agree that for police action to be "just," it must recognize the rights of individuals while holding them accountable to the social obligations defined by law? Support your position.
3. What does the term *due process environment* mean to you? Can we ensure due process in our legal system without substantially increasing the risk of criminal activity?
4. Justice Benjamin Cardozo once complained, "The criminal is to go free because the constable has blundered." Can we afford to let some guilty people go free to ensure that the rights of the rest of us are protected? Is there some better way to achieve this goal?
5. What is electronic evidence? How should it be handled by first-on-the-scene law enforcement personnel?

To participate in an online discussion on these topics and others, go to the Global Town Meeting message board for Chapter 7 on the *Criminal Justice Today* Companion Website at cjtoday.com.

Web Quest!

Create a list of every U.S. Supreme Court decision discussed in this chapter. Group the cases by subject (that is, vehicle searches, searches following arrest, interrogation, and so on), and list them in order by year of decision. Use the Web to collect full-text opinions from the Court for as many of these cases as you can find. (Hint: Visit the Legal Information Institute at Cornell University at http://www.law.cornell.edu for some of the best Supreme Court information available anywhere.) Submit the materials you find to your instructor if asked to do so.

Note: This is a large project, and your instructor may ask that you work with just one area (such as vehicle searches) or may assign the entire project to your class, asking individual students or groups of students to be responsible for separate subjects.

To complete this Web Quest! online, go to the Web Quest! module in Chapter 7 of the *Criminal Justice Today* Companion Website at cjtoday.com.

Library Extras!

Library Extra! **7–1** *Weeks* v. *U.S.* (1914).
Library Extra! **7–2** *Silverthorne Lumber Co.* v. *U.S.* (1920).
Library Extra! **7–3** *Mapp* v. *Ohio* (1961).
Library Extra! **7–4** *Harris* v. *U.S.* (1968).
Library Extra! **7–5** *Terry* v. *Ohio* (1968).
Library Extra! **7–6** *Brown* v. *Mississippi* (1936).
Library Extra! **7–7** *Best Practices for Seizing Electronic Evidence* (IACP and USSS, 2001).
Library Extra! **7–8** *Electronic Crime Scene Investigation* (TWGECSI, 2001).

To explore these resources online, go to the Library Extras! area of the *Criminal Justice Today* Companion Website at cjtoday.com. You should also check the author's "Late Picks" online for newly released documents and updated Library Extras! You can find Late Picks at http://cjtoday.com/latepicks.htm.

Marginal Note

i. Adapted from Technical Working Group for Electronic Crime Scene Investigation, *Electronic Crime Scene Inves-* *tigation: A Guide for First Responders* (Washington, D.C.: National Institute of Justice, 2001), p. 2.

Notes

1. Larry Collins and Dominique Lapierre, *The Fifth Horseman* (New York: Simon & Schuster, 1980).
2. Michelle Gotthelf, "41 Shots Heard around the World," APB Online. Web posted at http://www.apbonline.com/majorcases/diallo/background.html. Accessed January 5, 2000.
3. Pat Milton, "Feds Decline to File Charges against Police in Diallo Case," Associated Press Online, January 31, 2001. Accessed March 5, 2002.
4. Ibid.
5. "One Cop Convicted in NYC Torture Case," APB Online, June 8, 1999. Web posted at http://www.apbonline.com/911/1999/06/08/louima0608_01.html. Accessed January 10, 2000.
6. David Stout, "Three Convictions Overturned in Louima Toture Case," *The New York Times*, February 28, 2002.
7. "Police Brutality!" *Time*, March 25, 1991, p. 18.
8. Ibid., pp. 16–19.
9. "Police Charged in Beating Case Say They Feared for Their Lives," *Boston Globe*, May 22, 1991, p. 22.
10. "Cries of Relief," *Time*, April 26, 1993, p. 18.
11. "Rodney King's Run-ins," *USA Today*, May 30, 1991, p. 2A.
12. "Rodney King Gets Jail Time," Associated Press Online, August 22, 1996. See also Erica Werner, "King Became Civil Rights Symbol but Never Acted the Part," Associated Press Online, March 3, 2001.
13. "Rodney King to Clean Streets," Associated Press Online, September 15, 1996.
14. "Rodney King Arrested for Allegedly Beating Daughter, Her Mother," *Dodge City Daily Globe*, March 6, 1999. Web posted at http://www.dodgeglobe.com/stories/030699/fea_0306990023.shtml. Accessed May 25, 2001.
15. "King Pleads Guilty in Drug Case," Associated Press wire service, October 26, 2001.
16. *Miranda* v. *Arizona*, 384 U.S. 436 (1966).
17. *Weeks* v. *U.S.*, 232 U.S. 383 (1914).
18. Roger Goldman and Steven Puro, "Decertification of Police: An Alternative to Traditional Remedies for Police Misconduct," *Hastings Constitutional Law Quarterly*, Vol. 15 (1988), pp. 45–80.
19. Hawaii police departments set their own training requirements. The Honolulu Police Department, for example, requires six and a half months of student officer training and another 14 weeks of postgraduation field training. See the Honolulu Police Department's website at http://www.honolulupd.org/main/index.html. Accessed March 27, 2000.
20. Goldman and Puro, "Decertification of Police."
21. *Silverthorne Lumber Co.* v. *U.S.*, 251 U.S. 385 (1920).
22. Ibid.
23. Clemmens Bartollas, *American Criminal Justice* (New York: Macmillan, 1988), p. 186.
24. *Mapp* v. *Ohio*, 367 U.S. 643 (1961).
25. *Wolf* v. *Colorado*, 338 U.S. 25 (1949).
26. *Chimel* v. *California*, 395 U.S. 752 (1969).
27. *U.S.* v. *Rabinowitz*, 339 U.S. 56 (1950).
28. *Katz* v. *U.S.*, 389 U.S. 347, 88 S.Ct. 507 (1967).
29. *Minnesota* v. *Olson*, 110 S.Ct. 1684 (1990).
30. *Minnesota* v. *Carter*, 525 U.S. 83 (1998).
31. *Illinois* v. *Gates*, 426 U.S. 213 (1983).
32. *U.S.* v. *Leon*, 468 U.S. 897, 104 S.Ct. 3405, 82 L.Ed. 2d 677, 52 U.S.L.W. 5155 (1984).
33. Judicial titles vary between jurisdictions. Many lower-level state judicial officers are called *magistrates*. Federal magistrates, however, are generally regarded as functioning at a significantly higher level of judicial authority.
34. *Massachusetts* v. *Sheppard*, 104 S.Ct. 3424 (1984).
35. *Illinois* v. *Krull*, 107 S.Ct. 1160 (1987).

36. *Maryland* v. *Garrison,* 107 S.Ct. 1013 (1987).

37. *Illinois* v. *Rodriguez,* 110 S.Ct. 2793 (1990).

38. William H. Erickson, William D. Neighbors, and B. J. George, Jr., *United States Supreme Court Cases and Comments* (New York: Matthew Bender, 1987), Section 1.13 [7].

39. *Harris* v. *U.S.,* 390 U.S. 234 (1968).

40. The legality of plain-view seizures was also confirmed in earlier cases, including *Ker* v. *California,* 374 U.S. 23, 42–43 (1963); *U.S.* v. *Lee,* 274 U.S. 559 (1927); *U.S.* v. *Lefkowitz,* 285 U.S. 452, 465 (1932); and *Hester* v. *U.S.,* 265 U.S. 57 (1924).

41. As cited in Kimberly A. Kingston, "Look but Don't Touch: The Plain View Doctrine," *FBI Law Enforcement Bulletin,* December 1987, p. 18.

42. *Horton* v. *California,* 110 S.Ct. 2301, 47 CrL. 2135 (1990).

43. *U.S.* v. *Irizarry,* 673 F.2d 554, 556–67 (1st Cir. 1982).

44. Kingston, "Look but Don't Touch," p. 20.

45. *Arizona* v. *Hicks,* 107 S.Ct. 1149 (1987).

46. See *Criminal Justice Today,* North Carolina Justice Academy (Fall 1987), p. 24.

47. Inadvertence, as a requirement of legitimate plain-view seizures, was first cited in the U.S. Supreme Court case of *Coolidge* v. *New Hampshire,* 403 U.S. 443, 91 S.Ct. 2022 (1971).

48. *Horton* v. *California,* 110 S.Ct. 2301, 47 CrL. 2135 (1990).

49. Ibid.

50. John Gales Sauls, "Emergency Searches of Premises," Part 1, *FBI Law Enforcement Bulletin,* March 1987, p. 23.

51. *Warden* v. *Hayden,* 387 U.S. 294 (1967).

52. *Mincey* v. *Arizona,* 437 U.S. 385, 392 (1978).

53. Sauls, "Emergency Searches of Premises," p. 25.

54. *Maryland* v. *Buie,* 110 S.Ct. 1093 (1990).

55. *Wilson* v. *Arkansas,* 115 S.Ct. 1914 (1995).

56. For additional information, see Michael J. Bulzomi, "Knock and Announce: A Fourth Amendment Standard," *FBI Law Enforcement Bulletin,* May 1997, pp. 27–31.

57. *Richards* v. *Wisconsin,* 117 S.Ct. 1416 (1997), syllabus.

58. *Illinois* v. *McArthur,* 531 U.S. _____ (2001).

59. *U.S.* v. *Mendenhall,* 446 U.S. 544 (1980).

60. A. Louis DiPietro, "Voluntary Encounters or Fourth Amendment Seizures," *FBI Law Enforcement Bulletin,* January 1992, pp. 28–32 at note 6.

61. *Stansbury* v. *California,* 114 S.Ct. 1526, 1529, 128 L.Ed. 2d 293 (1994).

62. *Atwater* v. *Lago Vista,* 532 U.S. _____ (2001).

63. In 1976, in the case of *Watson* v. *U.S.* (432 U.S. 411), the U.S. Supreme Court refused to impose a warrant requirement for felony arrests that occur in public places.

64. *Payton* v. *New York,* 445 U.S. 573 (1980).

65. In 1981, in the case of *U.S.* v. *Steagald* (451 U.S. 204), the Court ruled that a search warrant is also necessary when the planned arrest involves entry into a third party's premises.

66. *U.S.* v. *Robinson,* 414 U.S. 218 (1973).

67. Ibid.

68. *Terry* v. *Ohio,* 392 U.S. 1 (1968).

69. *U.S.* v. *Sokolow,* 109 S.Ct. 1581 (1989).

70. *Minnesota* v. *Dickerson,* 113 S.Ct. 2130, 124 L.Ed. 2d 334 (1993).

71. *Brown* v. *Texas,* 443 U.S. 47 (1979).

72. *Smith* v. *Ohio,* 110 S.Ct. 1288 (1990).

73. Ibid., at 1289.

74. *California* v. *Hodari D.,* 111 S.Ct. 1547 (1991).

75. *Criminal Justice Newsletter,* May 1, 1991, p. 2.

76. *Illinois* v. *Wardlow,* 528 U.S. 119 (2000).

77. Ibid., syllabus. Web posted at http://supct.law.cornell.edu/supct/html/98-1036.ZS.html. Accessed April 1, 2002.

78. Ibid.

79. *Arkansas* v. *Sanders,* 442 U.S. 753 (1979).

80. Ibid.

81. *U.S.* v. *Borchardt,* 809 F.2d 1115 (5th Cir. 1987).

82. *FBI Law Enforcement Bulletin,* January 1988, p. 28.

83. *Carroll* v. *U.S.,* 267 U.S. 132 (1925).

84. *Preston* v. *U.S.,* 376 U.S. 364 (1964).

85. *South Dakota* v. *Opperman,* 428 U.S. 364 (1976).

86. *Colorado* v. *Bertine,* 479 U.S. 367, 107 S.Ct. 741 (1987).

87. *Florida* v. *Wells,* 110 S.Ct. 1632 (1990).

88. *Terry* v. *Ohio,* 392 U.S. 1 (1968).

89. *California* v. *Acevedo,* 500 U.S. 565 (1991).

90. *Ornelas* v. *U.S.,* 517 U.S. 690 (1996).

91. Ibid.

92. The phrase is usually attributed to the 1991 U.S. Supreme Court case of *California* v. *Acevedo* (498 U.S. 807 [1990]). See Devallis Rutledge, "Taking an Inventory," *Police,* November 1995, pp. 8–9.

93. *Florida* v. *Jimeno,* 111 S.Ct. 1801 (1991).

94. *Florida* v. *Jimeno,* syllabus. Web posted at http://laws.findlaw.com/us/500/248.html. Accessed March 2, 2002.

95. *U.S.* v. *Ross,* 456 U.S. 798 (1982).

96. Ibid.

97. *Whren* v. *U.S.,* 517 U.S. 806 (1996).

98. See *Pennsylvania* v. *Mimms,* 434 U.S. 106 (1977).

99. *Maryland* v. *Wilson,* 117 S.Ct. 882 (1997).

100. *Knowles* v. *Iowa,* 525 U.S. 113 (1998).

101. *Wyoming* v. *Houghton,* 526 U.S. 295 (1999).

102. *Michigan Dept. of State Police* v. *Sitz,* 110 S.Ct. 2481 (1990).

103. Ibid.

104. *U.S.* v. *Martinea-Fuerte,* 428 U.S. 543 (1976).

105. Ibid., syllabus.

106. *Indianapolis* v. *Edmond,* 531 U.S. 32 (2000). Web posted at http://supct. law.cornell.edu/supct/html/99-1030.ZS.html. Accessed April 2, 2002.

107. *U.S.* v. *Villamonte-Marquez,* 462 U.S. 579 (1983).

108. *California* v. *Carney,* 471 U.S. 386, 105 S.Ct. 2066, 85 L.Ed. 2d 406, 53 U.S.L.W. 4521 (1985).

109. *U.S.* v. *Hill,* 855 F.2d 664 (10th Cir. 1988).

110. *National Treasury Employees Union* v. *Von Raab,* 489 U.S. 656 (1989).

111. *Skinner* v. *Railway Labor Executives' Association,* 489 U.S. 602 (1989).

112. *Florida* v. *Bostick,* 111 S.Ct. 2382 (1991).

113. *Bond* v. *U.S.,* 529 U.S. 334 (2000). Web posted at http://supct.law.cornell.edu/supct/html/98-9349.ZS.html. Accessed January 10, 2002.

114. *People* v. *Deutsch,* 96 C.D.O.S. 2827 (1996).

115. The thermal imager differs from infrared devices (such as night-vision goggles) in that infrared devices amplify the infrared spectrum of light, whereas thermal imagers register solely the portion of the infrared spectrum that we call *heat.*

116. *People* v. *Deutsch,* 96 C.D.O.S. 2827 (1996).

117. *Kyllo* v. *U.S.,* 533 U.S. 27 (2001).

118. Ibid.

119. *Aguilar* v. *Texas,* 378 U.S. 108 (1964).

120. *Harris* v. *U.S.,* 403 U.S. 573 (1971).

121. *Spinelli* v. *U.S.,* 393 U.S. 410 (1969).

122. *Illinois* v. *Gates,* 426 U.S. 213 (1983).

123. *Alabama* v. *White,* 110 S.Ct. 2412 (1990).

124. Ibid., at 2417.

125. Some of the wording in this paragraph is adapted from the *LIIBulletin*, "End of Term Wrap-Up," June 29, 2000 (e-mail bulletin of the Legal Information Institute, Cornell University School of Law).

126. *U.S. Dept. of Justice v. Landano*, 113 S.Ct. 2014, 124 L.Ed. 2d 84 (1993).

127. Kevin Johnson and Gary Fields, "Jewell Investigation Unmasks FBI 'Tricks,'" *USA Today*, November 8, 1996, p. 13A.

128. Gary Fields, "FBI Admits Mistake in Jewell Case," *USA Today*, April 9, 1997, p. 2A.

129. *South Dakota v. Neville*, 103 S.Ct. 916 (1983).

130. *Brown v. Mississippi*, 297 U.S. 278 (1936).

131. *Ashcraft v. Tennessee*, 322 U.S. 143 (1944).

132. *Chambers v. Florida*, 309 U.S. 227 (1940).

133. Ibid.

134. *Leyra v. Denno*, 347 U.S. 556 (1954).

135. Ibid.

136. *Arizona v. Fulminante*, 111 S.Ct. 1246 (1991).

137. *Chapman v. California*, 386 U.S. 18 (1967).

138. *Escobedo v. Illinois*, 378 U.S. 478 (1964).

139. *Edwards v. Arizona*, 451 U.S. 477, 101 S.Ct. 1880, 68 L.Ed. 2d 378 (1981).

140. *Minnick v. Mississippi*, 498 U.S. 146 (1990).

141. *Arizona v. Roberson*, 486 U.S. 675, 108 S.Ct. 2093 (1988).

142. *Davis v. U.S.*, 114 S.Ct. 2350 (1994).

143. *Miranda v. Arizona*, 384 U.S. 436 (1966).

144. *U.S. v. Dickerson*, 166 F.3d 667.

145. *Dickerson v. U.S.*, 530 U.S. 428 (2000). Web posted at http://supct.law.cornell.edu/supct/html/99-5525.ZS.html. Accessed May 10, 2002.

146. Amy Worden, "Miranda Decision Sparks Debate," APB News, June 26, 2000.

147. *Moran v. Burbine*, 475 U.S. 412, 421 (1986).

148. *Colorado v. Spring*, 479 U.S. 564, 107 S.Ct. 851 (1987).

149. "Immigrants Get Civil Rights," *USA Today*, June 11, 1992, p. 1A.

150. *Brewer v. Williams*, 430 U.S. 387 (1977).

151. *Nix v. Williams*, 104 S.Ct. 2501 (1984).

152. *New York v. Quarles*, 104 S.Ct. 2626, 81 L.Ed. 2d 550 (1984).

153. *Colorado v. Connelly*, 107 S.Ct. 515, 93 L.Ed. 2d 473 (1986).

154. *Kuhlmann v. Wilson*, 477 U.S. 436 (1986).

155. *Illinois v. Perkins*, 495 U.S. 292 (1990).

156. *Rock v. Zimmerman*, 543 F. Supp. 179 (M.D. Pa. 1982).

157. Ibid.

158. See *Oregon v. Mathiason*, 429 U.S. 492, 97 S.Ct. 711 (1977).

159. *South Dakota v. Neville*, 103 S.Ct. 916 (1983).

160. *Arizona v. Mauro*, 107 S.Ct. 1931, 95 L.Ed. 2d 458 (1987).

161. *Doyle v. Ohio*, 426 U.S. 610 (1976).

162. *Brecht v. Abrahamson*, 113 S.Ct. 1710, 123 L.Ed. 2d 353 (1993).

163. Citing *Kotteakos v. U.S.*, 328 U.S. 750 (1946).

164. *Hayes v. Florida*, 470 U.S. 811, 105 S.Ct. 1643 (1985).

165. *Winston v. Lee*, 470 U.S. 753, 105 S.Ct. 1611 (1985).

166. *Schmerber v. California*, 384 U.S. 757 (1966).

167. *U.S. v. Montoya de Hernandez*, 473 U.S. 531, 105 S.Ct. 3304 (1985).

168. Ibid.

169. *Olmstead v. U.S.*, 277 U.S. 438 (1928).

170. *On Lee v. U.S.*, 343 U.S. 747 (1952).

171. *Lopez v. U.S.*, 373 U.S. 427 (1963).

172. *Berger v. New York*, 388 U.S. 41 (1967).

173. *Katz v. U.S.*, 389 U.S. 347 (1967).

174. *Lee v. Florida*, 392 U.S. 378 (1968).

175. Federal Communications Act of 1934, 47 U.S.C. 151.

176. *U.S. v. White*, 401 U.S. 745 (1971).

177. *U.S. v. Karo*, 468 U.S. 705 (1984).

178. *U.S. v. Scott*, 436 U.S. 128 (1978).

179. For more information, see *FBI Law Enforcement Bulletin*, June 1987, p. 25.

180. Electronic Communications Privacy Act of 1986, Public Law 99-508.

181. For more information on the ECPA, see Robert A. Fiatal, "The Electronic Communications Privacy Act: Addressing Today's Technology," *FBI Law Enforcement Bulletin*, April 1988, pp. 24–30.

182. Communications Assistance for Law Enforcement Act of 1994, Public Law 103-414.

183. Federal Bureau of Investigation, "Notice: Implementation of the Communications Assistance for Law Enforcement Act," February 23, 1995.

184. The Center for Democracy and Technology, "The Nature and Scope of Governmental Electronic Surveillance Activity," May 8, 2001. Web posted at http://www.cdt.org/digi_tele/wiretap_overview.html. Accessed March 11, 2002.

185. Telecommunications Act of 1996, Public Law 104, 110 Statute 56.

186. Title 47, U.S.C.A., Section 223(a)(1)(B)(ii) (Supp. 1997).

187. *Reno v. ACLU*, 117 S.Ct. 2329 (1997).

188. 18 U.S.C. §1030.

189. Section 202.

190. 18 U.S.C. §2703(c).

191. Ibid.

192. Adapted from Technical Working Group for Electronic Crime Scene Investigation, *Electronic Crime Scene Investigation: A Guide for First Responders* (Washington, D.C.: National Institute of Justice, 2001), from which much of the information in this section is taken.

193. Technical Working Group, *Electronic Crime Scene Investigation*, p. 2.

194. International Association of Chiefs of Police and the U.S. Secret Service, *Best Practices for Seizing Electronic Evidence*. Web posted at http://www.treas.gov/usss/index.htm?electronic_evidence.htm. Accessed September 29, 2001.

195. Ibid.

part three
....

■ Rights of the Accused before the Court

Common law, constitutional, statutory, and humanitarian rights of the accused:

- The right to a speedy trial
- The right to legal counsel
- The right against self-incrimination
- The right not to be tried twice for the same offense
- The right to know the charges
- The right to cross-examine witnesses
- The right against excessive bail

These individual rights must be effectively balanced against these community concerns:

- Conviction of the guilty
- Exoneration of the innocent
- The imposition of appropriate punishment
- The protection of society
- Efficient and cost-effective procedures
- Seeing justice done

How does our system of justice work toward balance?

POLICE LINE: DO NOT CROSS

Adjudication

Equal Justice Under Law

Well-known British philosopher and statesman Benjamin Disraeli (1804–1881) once defined justice as "truth in action." The study of criminal case processing by courts at all levels provides perhaps the best opportunity available to us from within the criminal justice system to observe what should ideally be "truth in action." The courtroom search for truth, which is characteristic of criminal trials, pits the resources of the accused against those of the state. The ultimate outcome of such procedures, say advocates of our adversarial-based system of trial practice, should be both truth and justice.

Others are not so sure. British novelist William McIlvanney (1936–) once wrote, "Who thinks the law has anything to do with justice? It's what we have because we can't have justice." Indeed, many critics of the present system claim that courts at all levels have become so concerned with procedure and with sets of formalized rules that they have lost sight of the truth.

The chapters that make up this section of *Criminal Justice Today* provide an overview of American courts, including their history and present structure, and examine the multifaceted roles played by both professional and lay courtroom participants. Sentencing—the practice whereby juries recommend and judges impose sanctions on convicted offenders—is covered in the concluding chapter of this section. Whether American courts routinely uncover truth and therefore dispense justice, or whether they are merely locked into a pattern of hollow procedure which does little other than mock the justice ideal, will be for you to decide.

The Courts

LEARNING OBJECTIVES

After reading this chapter, you should be able to

■ Describe the unique characteristics of American court history

■ Explain the differences between the federal and state court systems

■ List and explain the steps typically taken during pretrial activities

chapter 8

[Courts are one of the few institutions of American government that have outperformed our expectations. We've come to look at them as the ultimate safeguard of our rights.]

—New York University law professor Burt Neuborne[1]

[No person shall be held to answer for a capital, or otherwise infamous crime, unless on a presentment or indictment of a Grand Jury . . . ; nor shall any person be subject for the same offence to be twice put in jeopardy of life or limb; nor shall be compelled in any criminal case to be a witness against himself, nor be deprived of life, liberty, or property, without due process of law.]

—Fifth Amendment to the U.S. Constitution

Key Concepts

[Terms]

appeal
appellate jurisdiction
bail bond
community court
competent to stand trial
court of last resort
danger law
dispute-resolution center

federal court system
first appearance
judicial review
jurisdiction
nolo contendere
original jurisdiction
plea
plea bargaining

pretrial release
property bond
release on recognizance (ROR)
state court administrator
state court system
trial *de novo*

[Cases]

County of Riverside v. *McLaughlin*
Herrera v. *Collins*
Keeney v. *Tamayo-Reyes*

Marbury v. *Madison*
McNabb v. *U.S.*
Santobello v. *New York*

U.S. v. *Montalvo-Murillo*

Hear the author
discuss this chapter
at **cjtoday.com**

> There is no such thing as justice—in or out of court.
>
> —Clarence Darrow (1857–1938)

Introduction

Just before dawn on a January morning in 1997, two dynamite bombs exploded in downtown Vallejo, California, a small city of slightly more than 100,000 people located at the mouth of the Napa River in Solano County. One bomb damaged automated teller machines at a Wells Fargo bank, while the other blew a hole in the side of the Solano County courthouse. About the same time, authorities found 30 sticks of dynamite in a backpack lying against the wall of a public library where some police evidence was kept. A few days later, police arrested Kevin Lee Robinson, 29, an ex-convict who was scheduled to be tried on drug-related charges. Police accused Robinson and five other men of the bombings. According to investigators, Robinson planned the bombings to derail the county's criminal justice system. Bombing the courthouse, said detectives, was an attempt by Robinson to prevent his case from being tried under the state's three-strikes-and-you're-out law—which could have meant a sentence of life in prison for the already twice-convicted Robinson.[2] According to Police Chief Robert Nichelini, Robinson's "thought process was this would somehow stop the trial."[3] Following Robinson's arrest, police confiscated 500 pounds of dynamite. In 1998, Robinson was sent to prison for 110 years.

The bombings highlight the central role played by our nation's courts in the criminal justice process. Without courts to decide issues of guilt or innocence and to impose sentence on those convicted of crimes, the activities of law enforcement officials would become meaningless, and the nation's correctional facilities would serve little purpose.

There are many different kinds of courts in the United States. But courts at all levels dispense justice daily and work to ensure that all official actors in the justice system carry out their duties in recognition of the rule of law. At many points in this textbook and in three specific chapters (Chapter 7, "Policing: Legal Aspects"; Chapter 11, "Probation, Parole, and Community Corrections"; and Chapter 12, "Prisons and Jails"), we take a close look at court precedents which have defined the legality of enforcement efforts and correctional action. In Chapter 4, "Criminal Law," we explored the lawmaking function of courts. To provide a picture of how courts work, this chapter will describe the American court system at both the state and the federal levels. Then in Chapter 9, we will look at the roles of courtroom actors—from attorneys to victims and from jurors to judges—and we will examine each of the steps in a criminal trial.

American Court History

Two types of courts function within the American criminal justice system: (1) state courts and (2) federal courts. Figure 8–1 outlines the structure of today's **federal court system**, and Figure 8–2 diagrams a typical **state court system**. This dual-court system is the result of general agreement among the nation's founders about the need for individual states to retain significant legislative authority and judicial autonomy separate from federal control. Under this concept, the United States developed as a relatively loose federation of semi-independent provinces. New states joining the union were assured of limited federal intervention into local affairs. Under this arrangement, state legislatures were free to create laws, and state court systems were needed to hear cases in which violations of those laws occurred. The last 200 years have seen a slow ebbing of states' rights relative to the power of the federal government. Even today, however, state courts do not hear cases involving alleged violations of federal law, nor do federal courts involve themselves in deciding issues of state law unless there is a conflict between local or state statutes and federal constitutional guarantees. When that happens, claimed violations of federal due process guarantees—especially those found in the Bill of Rights—can provide the basis for appeals made to federal courts by offenders convicted in state court systems.

This chapter describes both federal and state court systems in terms of their historical development, **jurisdiction**, and current structure. Because it is within state courts that the large majority of criminal cases originate, we turn our attention first to them.

State Court Development

Each of the original American colonies had its own court system for resolving disputes, both civil and criminal. As early as 1629, the Massachusetts Bay Colony had created a General Court, composed of the governor, his deputy, 18 assistants, and 118 elected officials. The General Court was a combined legislature and court that made laws, held trials, and imposed sentences.[4] By 1639, as the colony grew, county courts were created, and the General Court took on the hearing of appeals as its primary job, retaining original jurisdiction only in cases involving "tryalls of life, limm, or banishment" and divorce.[5]

Pennsylvania began its colonial existence with the belief that "every man could serve as his own lawyer."[6] The Pennsylvania system utilized "common peacemakers" who served as

federal court system

The three-tiered structure of federal courts, comprising U.S. district courts, U.S. courts of appeals, and the U.S. Supreme Court.

state court system

A state judicial structure. Most states have at least three court levels: generally, trial courts, appellate courts, and a state supreme court.

jurisdiction

The territory, subject matter, or people over which a court or other justice agency may exercise lawful authority, as determined by statute or constitution.

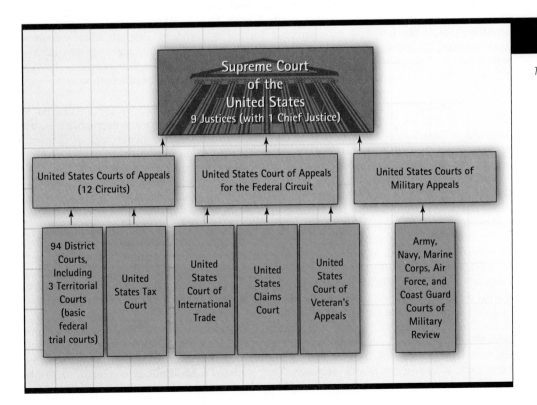

FIGURE 8–1

The structure of the federal courts.

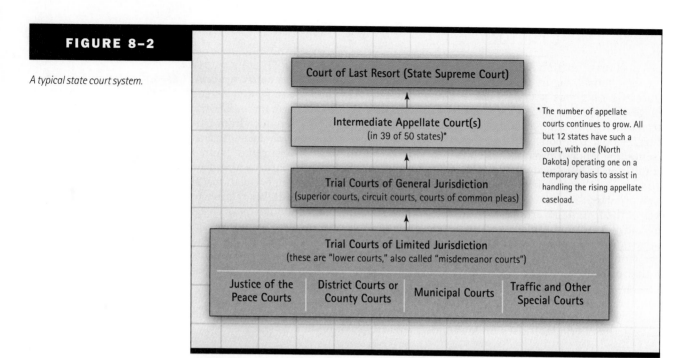

FIGURE 8-2

A typical state court system.

Court of Last Resort (State Supreme Court)

Intermediate Appellate Court(s)
(in 39 of 50 states)*

Trial Courts of General Jurisdiction
(superior courts, circuit courts, courts of common pleas)

Trial Courts of Limited Jurisdiction
(these are "lower courts," also called "misdemeanor courts")

| Justice of the Peace Courts | District Courts or County Courts | Municipal Courts | Traffic and Other Special Courts |

* The number of appellate courts continues to grow. All but 12 states have such a court, with one (North Dakota) operating one on a temporary basis to assist in handling the rising appellate caseload.

referees in disputes. Parties to a dispute, including criminal suspects, could plead their case before a common peacemaker they had chosen. The decision of the peacemaker was binding upon the parties. Although the Pennsylvania referee system ended in 1766, lower-level judges, called *magistrates* in many other jurisdictions, are still referred to as *justices of the peace* in Pennsylvania and a few other states.

Prior to 1776, all of the American colonies had established fully functioning court systems. The practice of law, however, was substantially inhibited by a lack of trained lawyers. A number of the early colonies even displayed a strong reluctance to recognize the practice of law as a profession. A Virginia statute enacted in 1645, for example, provided for the removal of "mercenary attorneys" from office and prohibited the practice of law for a fee. Most other colonies retained strict control over the number of authorized barristers (another name for lawyers) by requiring formal training in English law schools and appointment by the governor. New York, which provided for the appointment of "counselors at law," permitted a total of only 41 lawyers to practice law between 1695 and 1769[7]—in large part due to the distrust of formally trained attorneys which was then widespread.

The tenuous status of lawyers in the colonies was highlighted by the 1735 New York trial of John Zenger. Zenger was the editor of the *New York Journal*, a newspaper, and was accused of slandering Governor William Cosby. When Cosby threatened to disbar any lawyer who defended Zenger, the editor hired Pennsylvania lawyer Andrew Hamilton, who was immune to the governor's threats because he was from out of state.[8]

Following the American Revolution, colonial courts provided the organizational basis for the growth of fledgling state court systems. Since there had been considerable diversity in the structure of colonial courts, state courts were anything but uniform. Initially, most states made no distinction between **original jurisdiction** (which can be defined as the lawful authority of a court to hear cases which arise within a specified geographic area or which involve particular kinds of law violations) and **appellate jurisdiction** (that is, the lawful authority of a court to review a decision made by a lower court). Many, in fact, had no provisions for appeal. Delaware, for example, did not allow appeals in criminal cases until 1897. States which did permit appeals often lacked any established appellate courts and sometimes used state legislatures for that purpose.

By the late nineteenth century, a dramatic increase in population, growing urbanization, the settlement of the West, and other far-reaching changes in the American way of life led to a tremendous increase in civil litigation and criminal arrests. Legislatures tried to keep pace with the rising tide of cases. They created a multiplicity of courts at the trial, appellate, and supreme court levels, calling them by a diversity of names and assigning

original jurisdiction

The lawful authority of a court to hear or act upon a case from its beginning and to pass judgment on the law and the facts. The authority may be over a specific geographic area or over particular types of cases.

appellate jurisdiction

The lawful authority of a court to review a decision made by a lower court.

An engraving from the time of the Spanish Inquisition showing a "suspect" undergoing fire torture on "the wheel" while being questioned about alleged heretical activities. Although often criticized, today's criminal trial courts provide a civilized forum for exploring a variety of conflicting claims about guilt and innocence.
CORBIS

them functions which sometimes bore little resemblance to those of similarly named courts in neighboring states. City courts, which were limited in their jurisdiction by community boundaries, arose to handle the special problems of urban life, such as disorderly conduct, property disputes, and the enforcement of restrictive and regulatory ordinances. Other tribunals, such as juvenile courts, developed to handle special kinds of problems or special clients. Some, like magistrates' or small-claims courts, handled only petty disputes and minor law violations. Still others, like traffic courts, were very narrow in focus. The result was a patchwork quilt of hearing bodies, some only vaguely resembling modern notions of a trial court.

State court systems did, however, have several models to follow during their development. One was the New York State Field Code of 1848, which was eventually copied by most other states. The Field Code clarified jurisdictional claims and specified matters of court procedure, but it was later amended so extensively that its usefulness as a model dissolved. Another court system model was provided by the federal Judiciary Act of 1789 and later by the federal Reorganization Act of 1801. States which followed the federal model developed a three-tiered structure of (1) trial courts of limited jurisdiction, (2) trial courts of general jurisdiction, and (3) appellate courts.

State Court Systems Today

The three-tiered federal model was far from a panacea, however. Within the structure it provided, many local and specialized courts proliferated. Traffic courts, magistrate's courts, municipal courts, recorder's courts, probate courts, and courts held by justices of the peace were but a few which functioned at the lower levels. A movement toward simplification of state court structures, led primarily by the American Bar Association and the American Judicature Society, began in the early twentieth century. Proponents of state court reform sought to unify redundant courts which held overlapping jurisdictions. Most reformers suggested a uniform model for states everywhere which would build upon (1) a centralized court structure composed of a clear hierarchy of trial and appellate courts, (2) the consolidation of numerous lower-level courts with overlapping jurisdictions, and (3) a centralized state court authority which would be responsible for budgeting, financing, and management of all courts within a state.

The court reform movement is still in evidence today. Although reformers have made a substantial number of inroads in many states, there are still many differences between and among state court systems. Reform states, which early on embraced the reform

A criminal trial in progress. Courts have often been called "the fulcrum of the criminal justice system."

Peter Bryon, PhotoEdit

movement, are now characterized by streamlined judicial systems consisting of precisely conceived trial courts of limited and general jurisdiction, supplemented by one or two appellate court levels. Nonreform, or traditional, states retain judicial systems which are a conglomeration of multilevel and sometimes redundant courts with poorly defined jurisdictions. Even in nonreform states, however, most criminal courts can be classified within the three-tiered structure of two trial court echelons and an appellate tier.

STATE TRIAL COURTS

Trial courts are where criminal cases begin. The trial court conducts arraignments, sets bail, takes pleas, and conducts trials. (We will discuss these separate functions in more depth later in this chapter and in the next.) If the defendant is found guilty (or pleads guilty), the trial court imposes sentence. Trial courts of limited, or special, jurisdiction are also called *lower courts*. Lower courts are authorized to hear only less serious criminal cases, usually involving misdemeanors, or to hear special types of cases, such as traffic violations, family disputes, small claims, and so on. Courts of limited jurisdiction, which are depicted in TV shows such as *Judge Judy* and *Joe Brown,* rarely hold jury trials, depending instead on the hearing judge to make determinations of both fact and law. At the lower-court level, a detailed record of the proceedings is not maintained. Case files will only include information on the charge, the plea, the finding of the court, and the sentence. All but six of the United States make use of trial courts of limited jurisdiction.[9]

Lower courts are much less formal than are courts of general jurisdiction. In an intriguing analysis of court characteristics, Thomas Henderson, Director of the National Center for State Courts, found that misdemeanor courts process cases according to a "decisional model."[10] The decisional model, said Henderson, is informal, personal, and decisive. It depends upon the quick resolution of relatively uncomplicated issues of law and fact.

Trial courts of general jurisdiction—called variously *high courts, circuit courts,* or *superior courts*—are authorized to hear any criminal case. In many states, they also provide the first appellate level for courts of limited jurisdiction. In most cases, superior courts offer defendants whose cases originated in lower courts the chance for a new trial instead of a review of the record of the earlier hearing. When a new trial is held, it is referred to as **trial de novo**.

Henderson describes courts of general jurisdiction according to a "procedural model."[11] Such courts, he says, make full use of juries, prosecutors, defense attorneys, witnesses, and all the other actors we usually associate with American courtrooms. The procedural model, which is far more formal than the decisional model, is fraught with numerous court appearances to ensure that all of a defendant's due process rights are protected. The procedural model makes for a long, expensive, relatively impersonal, and highly formal series of legal maneuvers involving many professional participants—a fact clearly seen in the widely televised 1995 double-murder trial of famed athlete and television personality O. J. Simpson.

Trial courts of general jurisdiction operate within a fact-finding framework called the *adversarial process.* That process pits the interests of the state, represented by prosecu-

trial *de novo*

Literally, "new trial." The term is applied to cases that are retried on appeal, as opposed to those that are simply reviewed on the record.

tors, against the professional skills and abilities of defense attorneys. The adversarial process is not a free-for-all; rather, it is constrained by procedural rules specified in law and sustained through tradition.

STATE APPELLATE COURTS

Most states today have an appellate division, consisting of an intermediate appellate court (often called the *court of appeals*) and a high-level appellate court (generally termed the *state supreme court*). High-level appellate courts are referred to as **courts of last resort**, indicating that no other appellate route remains to a defendant within the state court system once the high court rules on a case. All states have supreme courts, although only 39 have intermediate appellate courts.[12]

An **appeal** by a convicted defendant asks that a higher court review the actions of a lower court. Courts within the appellate division, once they accept an appeal, do not conduct a new trial. Instead, they review the case on the record. In other words, appellate courts examine the written transcript of lower-court hearings to ensure that those proceedings were carried out fairly and in accordance with proper procedure and state law. They may also allow brief oral arguments to be made by attorneys for both sides and will generally consider other briefs or information filed by the appellant (the party initiating the appeal) or the appellee (the side opposed to the appeal). State statutes generally require that sentences of death or life imprisonment be automatically reviewed by the state supreme court.

Most convictions are affirmed upon appeal. Occasionally, however, an appellate court will determine that the trial court erred in allowing certain kinds of evidence to be heard, that it failed to interpret properly the significance of a relevant statute, or that some other impropriety occurred. When that happens, the verdict of the trial court will be reversed, and the case may be remanded, or sent back for a new trial. When a conviction is overturned by an appellate court because of constitutional issues or when a statute is determined to be invalid, the state usually has recourse to the state supreme court or the U.S. Supreme Court (when an issue of federal law is involved, as when a state court has ruled a federal law unconstitutional).

Defendants who are not satisfied with the resolution of their case within a state court system may attempt an appeal to the U.S. Supreme Court. For such an appeal to have any chance of being heard, it must be based upon claimed violations of the defendant's rights, as guaranteed under federal law or the U.S. Constitution. Under certain circumstances, federal district courts may also provide a path of relief for state defendants who can show that their federal constitutional rights were violated. However, in the 1993 case of *Keeney* v. *Tamayo-Reyes*,[13] the U.S. Supreme Court ruled that a "respondent is entitled to a federal evidentiary hearing [only] if he can show cause for his failure to develop the facts in the state-court proceedings and actual prejudice resulting from that failure, or if he can show that a fundamental miscarriage of justice would result from failure to hold such a hearing." Justice Byron White, writing for the Court, said, "It is hardly a good use of scarce judicial resources to duplicate fact-finding in federal court merely because a petitioner has negligently failed to take advantage of opportunities in state court proceedings." Likewise, in *Herrera* v. *Collins* (1993),[14] the Court ruled that new evidence of innocence is no reason for a federal court to order a new state trial if constitutional grounds are lacking. In *Herrera*, where the defendant was under a Texas death sentence for the murder of two police officers, the Court said, "Where a defendant has been afforded a fair trial and convicted of the offense for which he was charged, the constitutional presumption of innocence disappears. . . . Thus, claims of actual innocence based on newly discovered evidence have never been held [to be] grounds for relief, absent an independent constitutional violation occurring in the course of the underlying state criminal proceedings. To allow a federal court to grant relief . . . would in effect require a new trial 10 years after the first trial, not because of any constitutional violation at the first trial, but simply because of a belief that in light of his new found evidence a jury might find him not guilty at a second trial." The *Keeney* and *Herrera* decisions have severely limited access by state defendants to federal courts. See **Library Extra! 8–1** at cjtoday.com for additional information on challenging state court criminal convictions within the federal court system.

THE FLORIDA COURT SYSTEM: AN EXAMPLE

Florida provides an example of a reform state which has streamlined the structure of its courts. Prior to a 1973 reorganization, Florida had more different kinds of trial courts than

court of last resort

The court authorized by law to hear the final appeal on a matter.

appeal

Generally, the request that a court with appellate jurisdiction review the judgment, decision, or order of a lower court and set it aside (reverse it) or modify it.

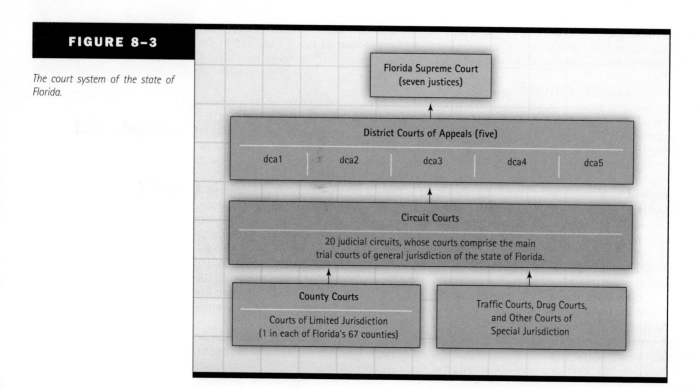

FIGURE 8-3

The court system of the state of Florida.

any state except New York.[15] Today, the Florida system, which is diagrammed in Figure 8–3, consists of one state supreme court, five district courts of appeals, trial courts of general jurisdiction called circuit courts, and county courts of limited jurisdiction which hear cases involving petty offenses and civil disputes involving $15,000 or less. County courts are often called *people's courts* in Florida.

Florida's supreme court, headquartered in the Supreme Court Building in Tallahassee, is composed of seven justices, at least four of whom must agree on a decision in each case. By a majority vote of the justices, one of the justices is elected to serve as chief justice (an office which is rotated every two years). The supreme court must review final orders imposing death sentences, district court decisions declaring a state statute or a provision of the state constitution invalid, and actions of statewide agencies relating to public utilities. At its discretion, the court may also review any decision of a district court of appeals that declares invalid a state statute, interprets a provision of the state or federal constitution, affects a class of state officers, or directly conflicts with a decision of another district court or of the state supreme court on a question of law.

Most of the trial court decisions which are appealed are never heard by the supreme court. Rather, they are reviewed by three-judge panels of the district courts of appeals. Florida's constitution provides that the legislature shall divide the state into appellate court districts and that there shall be a district court of appeals (DCA) serving each district. There are five such districts, which are headquartered in Tallahassee, Lakeland, Miami, West Palm Beach, and Daytona Beach. Fifteen judges serve in the first DCA, 14 in the second, 11 in the third, 12 in the fourth, and nine in the fifth. Like supreme court justices, district court judges serve terms of six years and are eligible for successive terms under a merit retention vote of the electors in their districts. In each district court, a chief judge, who is selected by other district court judges, is responsible for the administrative duties of the court.

The jurisdiction of the district courts of appeals extends to appeals from judgments or orders of trial courts and to the review of certain nonfinal orders. By law, district courts in Florida have been granted the power to review most actions taken by state agencies. As a general rule, decisions of the district courts of appeals represent the final appellate review of litigated cases. A person who is displeased with a district court's express decision may ask for review in the Florida Supreme Court or in the U.S. Supreme Court, but neither tribunal is required to accept the case for further hearing.

The majority of jury trials in Florida take place before one judge sitting as judge of a circuit court. The circuit courts are sometimes referred to as *courts of general jurisdiction*, in

> I have tried to minimize what I feel is one of the less desirable aspects of the job . . . that judges can become isolated from the people whose lives their decisions affect.
>
> —U.S. Supreme Court Justice Stephen Breyer

recognition of the fact that most criminal and civil cases originate at this level. Florida's constitution provides that a circuit court shall be established to serve each judicial circuit established by the legislature, of which there are 20. Within each circuit, there may be any number of judges, depending upon the population and caseload of the particular area. To be eligible for the office of circuit judge, a person must be a resident elector of Florida and must have been admitted to the practice of law in the state for the preceding five years. Circuit court judges are elected by the voters of the various circuits. Circuit court judges serve six-year terms and are subject to the same disciplinary standards and procedures as Florida Supreme Court justices and district court judges. A chief judge is chosen from among the circuit judges in each judicial circuit to carry out administrative responsibilities for all trial courts (both circuit and county courts) within the circuit.

Circuit courts have general trial jurisdiction over matters not assigned by statute to the county courts, and they also hear appeals from county court cases. Thus, circuit courts are simultaneously the highest trial courts and the lowest appellate courts in Florida's judicial system. The trial jurisdiction of circuit courts includes, among other matters, original jurisdiction over civil disputes involving more than $15,000; controversies involving the estates of decedents, minors, and people adjudicated to be incompetent; cases relating to juveniles; criminal prosecutions for all felonies; tax disputes; and actions to determine the title and boundaries of real property.

County courts represent the lowest trial court level in Florida. State constitution establishes a county court in each of Florida's 67 counties. The number of judges in each county court varies with the population and caseload of the county. To be eligible for the office of county judge, a person must be a resident of the county and must have been a member of the Florida Bar for five years; in counties with a population of 40,000 or less, a person must only be a member of the Florida Bar. County judges serve four-year terms, and they are subject to the same disciplinary standards as all other judicial officers. The trial jurisdiction of county courts is established by statute and extends to civil disputes involving $15,000 or less. The majority of nonjury trials in Florida take place before one judge sitting as a judge of the county court. The county courts are sometimes referred to as the *people's courts,* probably because a large part of the court's work involves high-volume citizen disputes, such as traffic offenses, less serious criminal matters (misdemeanors), and relatively small monetary disputes.

Other, special-purpose, courts do exist in the state. In 1989, for example, the Florida legislature authorized the establishment of a Civil Traffic Infraction Hearing Officer Program to free up county judges for other county court work and for circuit court assignments. Initially, participation in the program was limited to those counties with a civil traffic infraction caseload of 20,000 hearings, but the threshold was subsequently lowered to 15,000. The 1990–1991 legislature expanded the magistrate's jurisdiction to include accidents resulting in property damage (not bodily injury). At the end of the year-long pilot project, the Florida Supreme Court recommended, and the legislature approved, that the program be continued on a local-option basis.

STATE COURT ADMINISTRATION

To function efficiently, courts require uninterrupted funding, adequate staffing, trained support personnel, a well-managed case flow, and coordination between levels and among jurisdictions. To oversee these and other aspects of judicial management, every state today has its own mechanism for court administration. Most make use of **state court administrators** who manage these operational functions.

The first state court administrator was appointed in New Jersey in 1948.[16] Although other states were initially slow to follow New Jersey's lead, increased federal funding for criminal justice administration during the 1970s and a growing realization that some form of coordinated management was necessary for effective court operation eventually led most states to create similar administrative offices.

Florida created its Office of the State Courts Administrator (OSCA) in 1972. Florida's OSCA is divided into three sections, with a deputy state court administrator heading each one. The Information Systems and Program Support section includes Research, Planning and Court Services, Alternative Dispute Resolution, and Information Systems Services. The Administrative Services section includes Finance and Accounting, Budget, Personnel Services, and General Services. The Legal Affairs and Education section includes Legal Affairs, Judiciary Education Services, and various commissions and committees authorized by the legislature and the court. As in many other states, the state court administrator in Florida serves as the

state court administrator

A coordinator who assists with case-flow management, operating funds budgeting, and court docket administration.

liaison between the court system and the legislative branch, the executive branch, the auxiliary agencies of the court, and national court research and planning agencies.

The following tasks are typical of state court administrators across the country:[17]

■ The preparation, presentation, and monitoring of a budget for the state court system

■ The analysis of case flows and backlogs to determine where additional personnel, such as judges, prosecutors, and others, are needed

■ The collection and publication of statistics describing the operation of state courts

■ Efforts to streamline the flow of cases through individual courts and the system as a whole

■ Service as a liaison between state legislatures and the court system

■ The development or coordination of requests for federal and other outside funding

■ The management of state court personnel, including promotions for support staff and the handling of retirement and other benefits packages for court employees

■ The creation and coordination of plans for the training of judges and other court personnel (in conjunction with local chief judges and supreme court justices)

■ The assignment of judges to judicial districts (especially in states that use rotating judgeships)

■ The administrative review of payments to legal counsel for indigent defendants

State court administrators can receive assistance from the National Center for State Courts (NCSC) in Williamsburg, Virginia. The NCSC is an independent, nonprofit organization dedicated to the improvement of the American court system. It was founded in 1971 at the behest of Chief Justice Warren E. Burger. The NCSC provides services to state courts, which include helping to

■ Develop policies to enhance state courts

■ Advance state courts' interests within the federal government

■ Secure sufficient resources for state courts

■ Strengthen state court leadership

■ Facilitate state court collaboration

■ Provide a model for organizational administration

You can visit the National Center for State Courts via **Web Extra! 8–1** at cjtoday.com.

At the federal level, the federal court system is administered by the Administrative Office of the United States Courts (AO), located in Washington, D.C. The AO, created by Congress in 1939, prepares the budget and legislative agenda for federal courts. It also performs audits of court accounts, manages funds for the operation of federal courts, compiles and publishes statistics on the volume and type of business conducted by the courts, and recommends plans and strategies to efficiently manage court business. You can visit the Administrative Office of the United States Courts via **Web Extra! 8–2** at cjtoday.com.

DISPUTE-RESOLUTION CENTERS AND COMMUNITY COURTS

dispute-resolution center

An informal hearing place designed to mediate interpersonal disputes without resorting to the more formal arrangements of criminal trial courts.

Some communities recognize that it is possible to resolve most minor disputes without a formal court hearing. **Dispute-resolution centers**, which hear victim's claims of minor wrongs, such as passing bad checks, trespassing, shoplifting, and petty theft, function today in over 200 locations throughout the country.[18] Frequently staffed by volunteer mediators, such programs work to resolve disagreements (in which minor criminal offenses might otherwise be charged) without the need to assign blame. Dispute-resolution programs began in the early 1970s, with the earliest being the Community Assistance Project in Chester, Pennsylvania; the Columbus, Ohio, Night Prosecutor Program; and the Arbitration as an Alternative Program in Rochester, New York. Following the lead of these programs, the U.S. Department of Justice helped promote the development of three experimental Neighborhood Justice Centers in Los Angeles, Kansas City, and Atlanta. Each center accepted both minor civil and criminal cases.

Mediation centers are often closely integrated with the formal criminal justice process and may substantially reduce the caseload of lower-level courts. Some centers are, in fact, run by the courts and work only with court-ordered referrals. Others are semiautonomous but may be dependent upon courts for endorsement of their decisions; others function with complete autonomy. Rarely, however, do dispute-resolution programs entirely supplant the formal criminal justice mechanism, and defendants who appear before a community mediator may later be charged with a crime. Community mediation programs have become a central feature of today's restorative-justice movement (discussed in more detail in Chapter 10).

Recently, the community court movement has led to the creation of innovative low-level courts in certain parts of the country. Unlike dispute-resolution centers, **community courts** are always *official* components of the formal justice system. As a consequence, they can hand down sentences, including fines and jail time, without further court review. Like dispute-resolution centers, community courts focus on quality-of-life crimes that erode a neighborhood's morale, emphasize problem-solving rather than punishment, and build upon restorative principles like community service and restitution. The Midtown Community Court in New York City, which is profiled in the Individual Rights versus Public Order box in this chapter, provides an example of how community courts work.

Both mediation centers and community courts have been criticized because they typically work only with minor offenders, thereby denying the opportunity for mediation to victims and offenders in more serious cases. They have also come under criticism because defendants may see them as just another form of criminal sanction, rather than as a true alternative to processing by the criminal justice system.[19] Dispute-resolution centers, in particular, have been criticized for doing little more than providing a forum for shouting matches between the parties involved. Learn more about problem-solving courts via **Library Extra! 8–2** at cjtoday.com.

> **community court**
>
> A low-level court that focuses on quality-of-life crimes that erode a neighborhood's morale, that emphasizes problem-solving rather than punishment, and that builds upon restorative principles like community service and restitution.

The Rise of the Federal Courts

As we have seen, state courts had their origins in early colonial arrangements. Federal courts, however, were created by the U.S. Constitution. Article III, Section 1, of the Constitution provides for the establishment of "one supreme Court, and . . . such inferior Courts as the Congress may from time to time ordain and establish." Article III, Section 2, specifies that such courts are to have jurisdiction over cases arising under the Constitution, federal laws, and treaties. Federal courts are also to settle disputes between states and to have jurisdiction in cases where one of the parties is a state.

Today's federal court system represents the culmination of a series of congressional mandates which have expanded the federal judicial infrastructure so that it can continue to carry out the duties envisioned by the Constitution. Notable federal statutes which have contributed to the present structure of the federal court system include the Judiciary Act of 1789, the Judiciary Act of 1925, and the Magistrate's Act of 1968.

As a result of constitutional mandates, congressional action, and other historical developments, today's federal judiciary consists of three levels: (1) U.S. district courts, (2) U.S. courts of appeals, and (3) the U.S. Supreme Court. Each is described in turn in the following sections.

U.S. DISTRICT COURTS

The U.S. district courts are the trial courts of the federal court system.[20] Within limits set by Congress and the Constitution, the district courts have jurisdiction to hear nearly all categories of federal cases, including both civil and criminal matters. There are 94 federal judicial districts, including at least one district in each state, the District of Columbia, and Puerto Rico. Each district includes a U.S. bankruptcy court as a unit of the district court. Three territories of the United States—the Virgin Islands, Guam, and the Northern Mariana Islands—have district courts that hear federal cases, including bankruptcy cases. There are two special trial courts that have nationwide jurisdiction over certain types of cases. The Court of International Trade addresses cases involving international trade and customs issues. The U.S. Court of Federal Claims has jurisdiction over most claims for money damages against the United States, disputes over federal contracts, unlawful "takings" of private property by the federal government, and a variety of other claims against the United States.

Federal district courts have original jurisdiction over all cases involving alleged violations of federal statutes. Each state has at least one U.S. district court, and some, like New York and California, have as many as four. A district may itself be divided into divisions and may have several places where the court hears cases. District courts were first authorized by

Community Justice and the Courts

Introduction

[f]or many years, an important element has been missing from the criminal justice system. Although courts, police, and prosecutors have become increasingly modernized in recent years, they still often fail to meet the needs of the justice system's primary consumers: the neighborhoods that experience crime and its consequences every day. This problem was first recognized by advocates of community policing, who argued that police officers could address neighborhood crime and disorder more effectively if they established a close relationship with community residents and neighborhood groups. The idea of community justice has since spread to other branches of the justice system, including courts, probation departments, prosecutors, and corrections offices. What is community justice? The concept takes many practical forms, but at its core are partnership and problem solving. Community justice is about creating new relationships both within the justice system and with stakeholders in the community, such as residents, merchants, churches, and schools. It's also about testing new and aggressive approaches to public safety rather than merely responding to crime.

One important aspect of the community justice movement is community courts. Community courts often begin as grassroots movements by community residents and local organizations seeking to build confidence in the way offenders are handled for less serious offenses. Community courts commonly sentence convicted offenders to work within the community, "where neighbors can see what they are doing."[1]

Using the Midtown Community Court in New York City as a case study, this box presents a set of common principles for community courts that researchers have developed.

Creating a Community Court in New York City

New York City's Midtown Community Court, which opened in October 1993, was born of a profound frustration with quality-of-life crime in the neighborhood, particularly prostitution, vandalism, and low-level drug offenses. The Community Court differs dramatically from the way that lower courts have operated in the city for many years. Nevertheless, it reflects a return to an old idea.

In 1962, New York City closed a network of neighborhood magistrate's courts that had handled intake for the city's court system. These courts had arraigned defendants and disposed of low-level offenses that did not need to be forwarded to a higher tribunal. When the magistrate's courts were closed, intake and arraignment duties were shifted to lower-court judges in centralized courthouses serving each of the city's five boroughs. While this change increased efficiency to an extent, its cost was remoteness: The new centralized courts were removed from the communities they served. As caseloads increased, felony cases naturally began to claim more and more attention. Fewer resources were devoted to quality-of-life misdemeanors like shoplifting, prostitution, and subway fare cheating, and judges were under tremendous pressure to dispose of such cases quickly. All too often, defendants arrested for low-level offenses were released after being sentenced to either "time served" while awaiting their court appearance, a fine that might or might not be paid, or community service that might or might not be performed.

Mindful of these problems, Midtown Community Court planners sought to re-create neighborhood-based intake and arraignment along the lines of the magistrate's courts, but with innovations to meet current needs. It was hoped that the court could focus on the quality-of-life crimes that erode a community's morale. This return to a concern about crimes that affect neighborhood life coincided with the New York City Police Department's growing emphasis on community policing, as well as with a growing interest in community-oriented justice on the part of prosecutors, probation offices, and corrections agencies nationwide. Planning for the Midtown project lasted from 1991 to 1993.

With the help of the local community board—the smallest unit of government in New York City—planners found a location for the court near Times Square on the West Side of Manhattan, an area teeming with quality-of-life crimes. The 1896 building, which was once a magistrate's court, was renovated and now has clean, bright holding rooms secured with glass panels—a sharp contrast to New York's squalid downtown holding pens. The newly designed courthouse includes an entire floor of office space for social workers to assist offenders referred by the judge in the courtroom a few floors below. Additionally, the court's offices are wired to accommodate a computer system that allows the judge, attorneys, and social service workers to communicate with one another and to access defendants' records at the click of a mouse.

The court's location, architecture, and technology are part of a larger strategy to honor the idea of community by making justice restorative. Offenders are sentenced to make restitution to the community through work projects in the neighborhood. Such work includes caring for trees lining the streets, removing graffiti, cleaning subway stations, and sorting cans and bottles for recycling. At the same time, the court uses its legal leverage to link offenders with drug-treatment programs, health care facilities, educational institutions, and social service agencies.

By the summer of 1996, Midtown had become one of the busiest courts in the city, arraigning an average of 65 cases per day for an annual total of more than 16,000 cases. Offenders sentenced by the court perform the equivalent of $175,000 worth of community service work per year. Midtown's emphasis on immediate restitution (offenders must report to the court's community service or social service center immediately after sentencing) has improved compliance rates. Nearly 75% of offenders processed through Midtown complete their community service sentences as mandated; this is the highest rate in the city. The court's success has stirred the interest of prosecutors, judges, court administrators, and neighborhood groups across the country who hope to make courts responsive to community needs and more effective in dealing with quality-of-life offenses. Learn more about community courts at **Web Extra! 8-3**.

Web EXTRA!

❓ DISCUSSION QUESTIONS

1. Are community courts a true twenty-first-century innovation, or do they merely reflect America's early courtrooms?
2. What does the term *community justice* mean to you?
3. How do community courts contribute to a sense of community justice?
4. What kinds of cases should community courts handle?

[1]"Bridging the Gap between Communities and Courts." Web posted at http://www.communityjustice.org. Accessed November 22, 2001.
Source: John Feinblatt and Greg Berman, "Creating a Community Court," *Bureau of Justice Assistance Bulletin* (Washington, D.C.: BJA, February 2001).

Congress through the Judiciary Act of 1789, which allocated one federal court to each state. Because of population increases over the years, new courts have been added in a number of states.

Nearly 650 district court judges staff federal district courts. Because some courts are much busier than others, the number of district court judges varies from a low of two in some jurisdictions to a high of 27 in others. District court judges are appointed by the president and confirmed by the Senate, and they serve for life. An additional 369 full-time and 110 part-time magistrate judges (referred to as *U.S. magistrates* prior to 1990) serve the district court system and assist the federal judges. Magistrate judges have the power to conduct arraignments and may set bail, issue warrants, and try minor offenders.

U.S. district courts handle thousands of criminal cases per year. In 2000, for example, 62,745 criminal cases[21] and 259,517 civil cases[22] were filed in U.S. district courts. Drug prosecution, especially in courts located close to the U.S.-Mexican border, have led to considerable growth in the number of cases filed. Federal drug prosecutions in border states (including California, Arizona, New Mexico, and Texas) more than doubled between 1994 and 2000, from 2,864 to 6,116, and immigration prosecutions increased more than sevenfold, from 1,056 to 7,613.[23] During the past 20 years, the number of cases handled by the entire federal district court system has grown exponentially. The hiring of new judges and the creation of new courtroom facilities have not kept pace with the increase in caseload, and questions persist as to the quality of justice that overworked judges can deliver.

One of the most pressing issues facing district court judges is the fact that their pay, which at $145,100 in mid-2000[24] placed them in the top 1% of income-earning Americans, is small compared to what most could earn in private practice. Since 1993, the salaries of federal judges have remained relatively stagnant, leading many judges to leave the bench. Learn more about the federal courts via **Library Extra! 8-3** at cjtoday.com.

U.S. COURTS OF APPEALS

The 94 judicial districts are organized into 12 regional circuits, each of which has a U.S. court of appeals.[25] A court of appeals hears appeals from the district courts located within its circuit, as well as appeals from decisions of federal administrative agencies. In addition, the Court of Appeals for the Federal Circuit has nationwide jurisdiction to hear appeals in special cases, such as those involving patent laws and cases decided by the Court of International Trade and the Court of Federal Claims.

The U.S. Court of Appeals for the Federal Circuit and the 12 regional courts of appeals are often referred to as *circuit courts*. That is because early in the nation's history, the judges of the first courts of appeals visited each of the courts in one region in a particular sequence, traveling by horseback and riding the "circuit." Today, the regional courts of appeals review matters from the district courts of their geographic regions, from the U.S. Tax Court, and from certain federal administrative agencies. A disappointed party in a district court usually has the right to have the case reviewed in the court of appeals for the circuit. The First through Eleventh Circuits each include three or more states, as illustrated by Figure 8–4.

Each court of appeals consists of six or more judges, depending on the caseload of the court. Circuit court judges are appointed for life by the president with the advice and consent of the Senate. The judge who has served on the court the longest and who is under 65 years of age is designated as the chief judge and performs administrative duties in addition to hearing cases. The chief judge serves for a maximum term of seven years. There are 167 judges on the 12 regional courts of appeals.

The U.S. Court of Appeals for the District of Columbia, which is often called the Twelfth Circuit, hears cases arising in the District of Columbia and has appellate jurisdiction assigned by Congress in legislation concerning many departments of the federal government. The U.S. Court of Appeals for the Federal Circuit (in effect, the Thirteenth Circuit) was created in 1982 by the merging of the U.S. Court of Claims and the U.S. Court of Customs and Patent Appeals. The court hears appeals in cases from the U.S. Court of Federal Claims, the U.S. Court of International Trade, the U.S. Court of Veterans Appeals, the International Trade Commission, the Board of Contract Appeals, the Patent and Trademark Office, and the Merit Systems Protection Board. The Federal Circuit Court also hears appeals from certain decisions of the secretaries of the Department of Agriculture and the

FIGURE 8-4

The 13 federal judicial circuits.

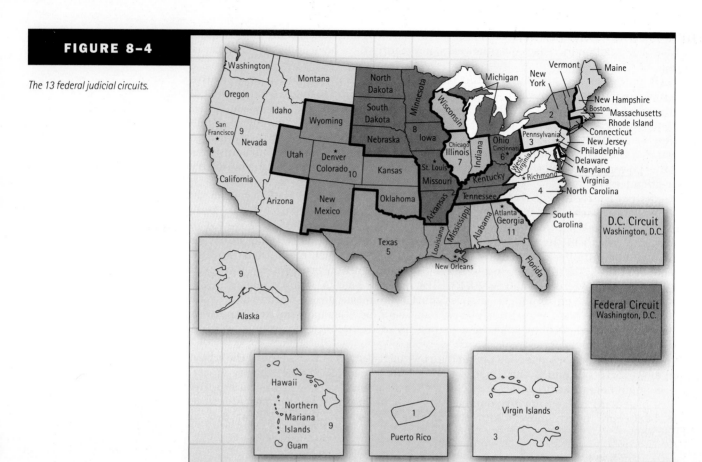

Department of Commerce and cases from district courts involving patents and minor claims against the federal government.

Federal appellate courts have mandatory jurisdiction over the decisions of district courts within their circuits. Mandatory jurisdiction means that U.S. courts of appeals are required to hear the cases brought to them. Criminal appeals from federal district courts are usually heard by panels of three judges sitting on a court of appeals rather than by all the judges of each circuit.

Federal appellate courts operate under the *Federal Rules of Appellate Procedure*, although each has also created its own separate Local Rules. Local Rules may mean that one circuit, such as the Second, will depend heavily upon oral arguments, while others may substitute written summary depositions in their place. Appeals generally fall into one of three categories: (1) frivolous appeals, which have little substance, raise no significant new issues, and are generally disposed of quickly; (2) ritualistic appeals, which are brought primarily because of the demands of litigants, even though the probability of reversal is negligible; and (3) nonconsensual appeals, which entail major questions of law and policy and on which there is considerable professional disagreement among the courts and within the legal profession.[26] The probability of reversal is, of course, highest in the case of nonconsensual appeals.

Because the Constitution guarantees a right to an appeal, federal circuit courts face an ever-increasing workload. Almost all appeals from federal district courts go to the court of appeals serving the circuit in which the case was first heard. A defendant's right to appeal, however, has been interpreted to mean the right to one appeal. Hence, the U.S. Supreme Court need not necessarily hear the appeals of defendants who are dissatisfied with the decision of a federal appeals court. Learn more about criminal appeals in federal courts via **Library Extra! 8-4** at cjtoday.com.

THE U.S. SUPREME COURT

At the apex of the federal court system stands the U.S. Supreme Court. The Supreme Court is located in Washington, D.C., across the street from the U.S. Capitol. The Court consists of nine justices, eight of whom are associate justices. The ninth presides over the Court as the chief justice of the United States (Table 8–1). Supreme Court justices are nominated by the president, are confirmed by the Senate, and serve for life. Lengthy terms of service are a tradition among justices. One of the earliest chief justices, John Marshall, served the Court for 34 years, from 1801 to 1835. The same was true of Justice Stephen J. Field, who sat on the bench between 1863 and 1897. Justice Hugo Black passed the 34-year milestone, serving an additional month, before he retired in 1971. Justice William O. Douglas set a record for longevity on the bench, retiring in 1975 after 36 and a half years of service. You may view the biographies of today's Supreme Court justices via **Web Extra! 8–4** at cjtoday.com.

The Supreme Court of the United States wields immense power. The Court's greatest authority lies in its capacity for **judicial review** of lower-court decisions and state and federal statutes. By exercising its power of judicial review, the Court decides what laws and lower-court decisions are in keeping with the intent of the U.S. Constitution. The power of judicial review is not explicit in the Constitution but was anticipated by its framers. In the *Federalist Papers*, which urged adoption of the Constitution, Alexander Hamilton wrote that through the practice of judicial review, the Court would ensure that "the will of the whole people," as grounded in the Constitution, would be supreme over the "will of the legislature," which might be subject to temporary whims.[27] It was not until 1803, however, that the Court forcefully asserted its power of judicial review. In an opinion written for the case of *Marbury* v. *Madison* (1803),[28] Chief Justice John Marshall established the Court's authority as final interpreter of the U.S. Constitution, declaring, "It is emphatically the province of the judicial department to say what the law is."

Increasing Complexity and the Supreme Court

The evolution of the U.S. Supreme Court provides one of the most dramatic examples of institutional development in American history. Sparsely described in the Constitution, the Court has grown from a handful of circuit-riding justices into a modern organization that wields tremendous legal power over all aspects of American life. Much of the Court's growth has been due to its increasing willingness to mediate fundamental issues of law and to act as a resort from arbitrary and capricious processing by the justice systems of the states and the national government.

The *Marbury* decision established the Court as a mighty force in federal government by virtue of the power of judicial review. As we discussed in Chapter 7, the Court began to apply that power during the 1960s to issues of crime and justice at the state and local

judicial review

The power of a court to review actions and decisions made by other agencies of government.

Oyez, oyez, oyez! All persons having business before the honorable, the Supreme Court of the United States, are admonished to draw near and give their attention, for the Court is now sitting. God save the United States and this honorable Court.

—Marshal's cry at the opening of public sessions of the U.S. Supreme Court

---

Justice	Entered Duty	Views
JUSTICES OF THE U.S. SUPREME COURT		**TABLE 8-1**
Chief Justice		
William H. Rehnquist*	January 1972	Very conservative
Associate Justices		
John Paul Stevens	December 1975	Moderate to liberal
Sandra Day O'Connor	September 1981	Moderate to conservative
Antonin Scalia	September 1986	Very conservative
Anthony Kennedy	February 1988	Conservative
David Souter	October 1990	Conservative
Clarence Thomas	October 1991	Conservative
Ruth Bader Ginsburg	August 1993	Moderate
Stephen Breyer	August 1994	Moderate

*Appointed Chief Justice in September 1986.

The chambers of the U.S. Supreme Court in Washington, D.C.
AP/Wide World Photos

> When we have examined in detail the organization of the Supreme Court, and the entire prerogatives which it exercises, we shall readily admit that a more imposing judicial power was never constituted by any people.
>
> —Alexis de Tocqueville, *Democracy in America* (1835)

levels. You may recall that the Court signaled its change in orientation in 1961 with the case of *Mapp* v. *Ohio,*[29] which extended the exclusionary rule to the states. Such extension, combined with the near-simultaneous end of the hands-off doctrine which had previously exempted state prison systems from Court scrutiny, placed the authority of the Court squarely over the activities of state criminal justice systems. From that time forward, the Court's workload became increasingly heavy and today shows few signs of abatement.

The Supreme Court Today   The Supreme Court has limited original jurisdiction and does not conduct trials except in disputes between states and some cases of attorney disbarment. Instead, the Court reviews the decisions of lower courts and may accept cases from both U.S. courts of appeals and from state supreme courts. For a case to be heard, at least four justices must vote in favor of a hearing. When the Court agrees to hear a case, it will issue a writ of *certiorari* to a lower court, ordering it to send the records of the case forward for review. Once having granted *certiorari,* the justices can revoke the decision. In such cases, a writ is dismissed by ruling it improvidently granted.

The U.S. Supreme Court may review any decision appealed to it which it decides is worthy of review. In fact, however, the Court elects to review only cases which involve a substantial federal question. Of approximately 5,000 requests for review received by the Court yearly, only about 200 are actually heard.

A term of the Supreme Court begins, by statute, on the first Monday in October and lasts until early July. The term is divided among sittings, when cases will be heard, and time for the writing and delivering of opinions. Between 22 and 24 cases are heard at each sitting, with each side allotted 30 minutes for arguments before the justices. Intervening recesses allow justices time to study arguments and supporting documentation and to work on their opinions.

Decisions rendered by the Supreme Court are rarely unanimous. Instead, the opinion that a majority of the Court's justices agree upon becomes the judgment of the Court. Justices who agree with the Court's judgment write concurring opinions if they agree for a different reason or if they feel that they have some new light to shed on a legal issue involved in the case. Justices who do not agree with the decision of the Court write dissenting opinions. Those dissenting opinions may offer new possibilities for successful appeals made at a later date. Visit the U.S. Supreme Court via **Web Extra! 8–5** at cjtoday.com, and learn more about the federal judiciary via **Library Extra! 8–5** at cjtoday.com.

Ideas for Change   Increasing caseloads at the federal appellate court level, combined with the many requests for Supreme Court review, have led to proposals to restructure the federal appellate court system. In 1973, a study group appointed by Chief Justice Burger suggested the creation of a National Court of Appeals, which would serve as a kind of "mini Supreme Court."[30] Under the proposal, the National Court of Appeals would be staffed on a rotating basis by judges who now serve the various circuit courts of appeals. The study group suggested that the new court review cases awaiting hearings before the Supreme Court so that the high court's workload might be reduced.

The U.S. Supreme Court justices. From front left, Antonin Scalia, John Paul Stevens, Chief Justice William H. Rehnquist, Sandra Day O'Connor, and Anthony Kennedy. From back left, Ruth Bader Ginsburg, David Souter, Clarence Thomas, and Stephen Breyer.

Markel, Getty Images, Inc.

A similar National Court of Appeals was proposed in 1975 by the Congressional Commission on Revision of the Federal Court Appellate System. The National Court proposed by the commission would have heard cases sent to it via transfer jurisdiction (from lower appellate courts) and through reference jurisdiction (when the Supreme Court decided to forward cases to it). In a similar idea, the Senate Judiciary Committee suggested the creation of a mini Supreme Court in 1986, calling it the Intercircuit Tribunal of the U.S. Courts of Appeals. To date, however, no legislation to establish such a court has passed both houses of Congress.

The most recent suggestions for change in the federal appellate structure came from the Commission on Structural Alternatives for the Federal Courts of Appeals, which submitted its final report to the president and Congress in 1998. Chief Justice Rehnquist appointed the commission in late 1997, after Congress called for its creation and tasked it with studying the federal appellate system, with particular emphasis to be placed on the overworked Ninth Circuit.[31] The five-member commission, chaired by retired Justice Byron White, recommended several measures to "equip the courts of appeals with an ability, structurally and procedurally, to accommodate continued caseload growth into the indefinite future, while maintaining the quality of the appellate process and delivering consistent decisions—assuming, of course, that the system has the necessary number of judges and other resources." Read the commission's full report at **Library Extra! 8–6**.

Pretrial Activities

In the next chapter, we will discuss typical stages in a criminal trial and will describe the many roles assumed by courtroom participants such as judges, prosecutors, defense attorneys, victims, and suspects. A number of court-related activities, however, routinely take place *before* trial can begin. Although such activities (as well as the names given to them) vary among jurisdictions, they are described generally in the pages that follow.

The First Appearance

first appearance

An appearance before a magistrate during which the legality of the defendant's arrest is initially assessed and the defendant is informed of the charges on which he or she is being held. At this stage in the criminal justice process, bail may be set or pretrial release arranged.

Following arrest, most defendants do not come into contact with an officer of the court until their **first appearance** before a magistrate or a lower-court judge.[32] A first appearance, sometimes called an *initial appearance* or *magistrate's review,* occurs when defendants are brought before a judge to be (1) given formal notice of the charges against them, (2) advised of their rights, (3) given the opportunity to retain a lawyer or to have one appointed to represent them, and (4) perhaps afforded the opportunity for bail.

According to the procedural rules of all jurisdictions, defendants who have been taken into custody must be offered an in-court appearance before a magistrate "without unnecessary delay." The 1943 U.S. Supreme Court case of *McNabb* v. *U.S.*[33] established that any unreasonable delay in an initial court appearance would make confessions inadmissible if interrogating officers obtained them during the delay. Based upon the *McNabb* decision, 48 hours following arrest became the standard maximum time by which a first appearance should be held.

The first appearance may also involve a probable cause hearing, although such hearings may be held separately (or, in some jurisdictions, may be combined with the preliminary hearing) since they do not require the defendant's presence. Probable cause hearings are necessary when arrests are made without a warrant because such arrests do not require a prior judicial determination of probable cause. During a probable cause hearing, also called a *probable cause determination,* a judicial officer will review police documents and reports to ensure that probable cause supported the arrest. The review of the arrest proceeds in a relatively informal fashion, with the judge seeking to decide whether, at the time of apprehension, the arresting officer had reason to believe both (1) that a crime had been or was being committed and (2) that the defendant was the person who committed it. Most of the evidence presented to the judge comes either from the arresting officer or from the victim. If probable cause is not found to exist, the suspect will be released.

In 1991, the U.S. Supreme Court, in a class-action suit entitled *County of Riverside* v. *McLaughlin,*[34] imposed a promptness requirement upon probable cause determinations for in-custody arrestees. The Court held that "a jurisdiction that provides judicial determinations of probable cause within 48 hours of arrest will, as a general matter, comply with the promptness requirement." The Court specified, however, that weekends and holidays could not be excluded from the 48-hour requirement (as they had been in Riverside County, California) and that, depending upon the specifics of the case, delays of fewer than two days may still be unreasonable.

Thurgood Marshall (1908–1993), the nation's first African-American U.S. Supreme Court justice.

John Ficara, Woodfin Camp & Associates

During a first appearance, the suspect is not given an opportunity to present evidence, although the U.S. Supreme Court has held that defendants are entitled to representation by counsel at their first appearance.[35] Following a reading of the charges and an advisement of rights, counsel may be appointed to represent indigent defendants, and proceedings may be adjourned until counsel can be obtained. In cases where a suspect is unruly, intoxicated, or uncooperative, a judicial review may occur in his or her absence.

Some states waive a first appearance and proceed directly to arraignment (discussed later), especially when the defendant has been arrested on a warrant. In states which move directly to arraignment, the procedures undertaken to obtain a warrant are regarded as sufficient to demonstrate a basis for detention prior to arraignment.

PRETRIAL RELEASE AND BAIL

A highly significant aspect of the first appearance hearing is the consideration of **pretrial release**. Defendants charged with very serious crimes, or those thought likely to escape or injure others, are usually held in jail until trial. Such a practice is called *pretrial detention*. The majority of defendants, however, are afforded the opportunity for release. Many jurisdictions make use of pretrial services programs, which may also be called *early intervention programs*.[36] Such programs, which are typically funded by the states or by individual counties, perform two critical functions: (1) They gather and present information about newly arrested defendants and about available release options for use by judicial officers in deciding what (if any) conditions are to be set for a defendant's release prior to trial, and (2) they supervise defendants released from custody during the pretrial period by monitoring their compliance with release conditions and by helping to ensure that they appear for scheduled court events (see Figure 8–5). Learn more about pretrial services via **Library Extra! 8–7** at cjtoday.com.

The initial pretrial release/detention decision is usually made by a judicial officer or by a specially appointed hearing officer after considering the background information provided by the pretrial service program, along with the representations made by the prosecutor and the defense attorney. In making this decision, judicial officers are concerned about two types of risk: (1) the risk of flight or nonappearance for scheduled court appearances and (2) the risk to public safety. In assessing these risks, judicial officers tend to focus on four key factors:

- The seriousness of the current charge, as set forth in the complaint and the representations of the prosecutor

- The defendant's prior criminal record, which is widely viewed as relevant to assessing the risk to public safety that would be posed by a decision to release or to set a relatively low money bond amount

- Information about the defendant, including community and family ties; employment status; housing; existence and nature of any substance-abuse problems; and (if the defendant had been arrested before) record of compliance with conditions of release set on previous occasions, including any failures to appear

- Information about available supervisory options if the defendant is released

pretrial release

The release of an accused person from custody, for all or part of the time before or during prosecution, upon his or her promise to appear in court when required.

Library EXTRA!

FIGURE 8-5

Prototype operations: early intervention pretrial services programs.

Source: Barry Mahoney et al., *Pretrial Services Programs: Responsibilities and Potential* (Washington, D.C.: National Institute of Justice, 2001), p. 10.

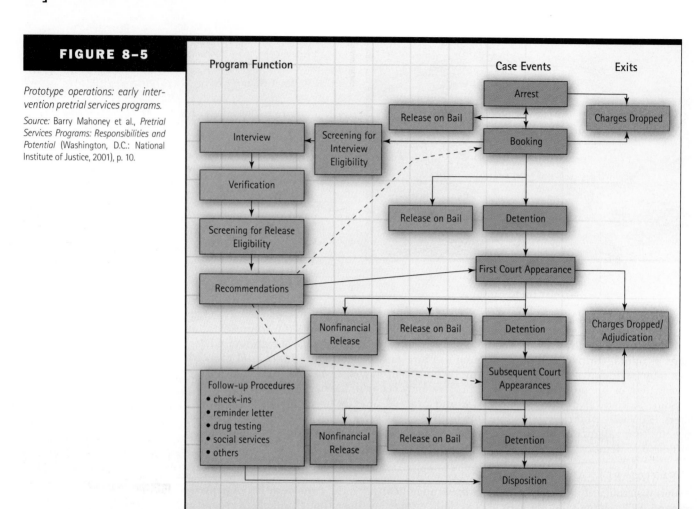

Bail continues to be the most common mechanism for release/detention decision making in most American courts. Bail serves two purposes: (1) It helps ensure reappearance of the accused, and (2) it prevents unconvicted persons from suffering imprisonment unnecessarily.

Bail involves the posting of a bond as a pledge that the accused will return for further hearings. **Bail bonds** usually involve cash deposits but may be based on property or other valuables. A fully secured bond requires the defendant to post the full amount of bail set by the court. The usual practice, however, is for a defendant to seek privately secured bail through the services of a professional bail bondsman. The bondsman will assess a percentage (usually 10–15%) of the required bond as a fee, which the defendant will have to pay up front. Those who "skip bail" by hiding or fleeing will sometimes find their bond ordered forfeit by the court. Forfeiture hearings must be held before a bond can be taken, and most courts will not order bail forfeited unless it appears that the defendant intends to avoid prosecution permanently. Bail forfeiture will often be reversed if the defendant later willingly appears to stand trial.

In many states, bondsmen are empowered to hunt down and bring back defendants who have fled. In some jurisdictions, bondsmen hold virtually unlimited powers and have been permitted by courts to pursue, arrest, and forcibly extradite their charges from foreign jurisdictions without concern for the due process considerations or statutory limitations which apply to law enforcement officers.[37] Recently, however, a number of states have enacted laws which eliminate for-profit bail bond businesses, replacing them instead with state-operated pretrial service agencies. Visit the Professional Bail Agents of the United States via **Web Extra! 8–6** at cjtoday.com to learn more about the job of bail bondsman and to view the group's code of ethics.

bail bond

A document guaranteeing the appearance of a defendant in court as required and recording the pledge of money or property to be paid to the court if he or she does not appear, which is signed by the person to be released and anyone else acting in his or her behalf.

CJ Today Exhibit 8-1

[Nonjudicial Pretrial Release Decisions]

In most American jurisdictions, judicial officers decide whether an arrested person will be detained or released. Some jurisdictions, however, allow others to make that decision. Some observers argue that the critical issue is not whether the decision maker is a judge, but whether there are clear and appropriate criteria for making the decision, whether the decision maker has adequate information, and whether he or she has been well trained in pretrial release/detention decision making. Nonjudicial decision makers and release/detention mechanisms include the following:

- *Police officers and desk appearance tickets.* Desk appearance tickets, or citations, are summonses given to defendants at the police station, usually for petty offenses or misdemeanor charges. The tickets can greatly reduce the use of pretrial detention and can save the court system a great deal of time by avoiding initial pretrial release or bail hearings in minor cases. However, because they are typically based only on the current charge (and sometimes on a computer search to check for outstanding warrants), high-risk defendants could be released without supervision or monitoring. As computerized access to criminal history information becomes more available, enabling rapid identification of individuals with prior records who pose a risk to the community, desk appearance tickets may become more widely used.

- *Jail administrators.* In many jurisdictions, jail officials have the authority to release (or to refuse to book into jail) arrestees who meet certain criteria. In some localities, jail officials exercise this authority pursuant to a court order that specifies priorities with respect to the categories of defendants who can be admitted to the jail and those who are to be released when the jail population exceeds a court-imposed ceiling. The "automatic release" approach helps minimize jail crowding, but it does so at the risk of releasing some defendants who pose a high risk of becoming fugitives or committing criminal acts. To help minimize these risks, some sheriffs and jail administrators have developed their own pretrial services or "release on recognizance" units with staff who conduct risk assessments based on interviews with arrestees, information from references, and criminal history checks.

- *Bail schedules.* These predetermined schedules set levels of bail (from release on recognizance to amounts of surety bond) based solely on the offense charged. Depending on local practices, release pursuant to a bail schedule may take place at a police station, at the local jail, or at court. This practice saves time for judicial officers and allows rapid release of defendants who can afford to post the bail amount. However, release determinations based solely on the current charge are of dubious value because there is no proven relationship between a particular charge and risk of flight or subsequent crime. Release pursuant to a bail schedule depends simply on the defendant's ability to post the amount of the bond. Moreover, when a defendant is released by posting bond, there is generally no procedure for supervision to minimize the risks of nonappearance and subsequent crime.

- *Bail bondsmen.* When a judicial officer sets the amount of bond that a defendant must produce to be released, or when bond is set mechanically on the basis of a bail schedule, the real decision makers are often the surety bail bondsmen. If no bondsman will offer bond, the defendant without other sources of money remains in jail. The defendant's ability to pay a bondsman the 10% fee (and sometimes to post collateral) often bears no relationship to his or her risk of flight or danger to the community.

- *Pretrial services agencies.* In some jurisdictions, pretrial services agencies have authority to release certain categories of defendants. The authority is usually limited to relatively minor cases, although agencies in a few jurisdictions can release some categories of felony defendants. Because the pretrial services agency can obtain information about the defendant's prior record, community ties, and other pending charges, its decision to release or detain is based on more extensive information and criteria than when the decision is based on a bail schedule. However, because these programs lack the independence of judicial officers, they can be targets of political and public pressure.

Source: Adapted from Barry Mahoney et al., *Pretrial Services Programs: Responsibilities and Potential* (Washington, D.C.: National Institute of Justice, 2001).

ALTERNATIVES TO BAIL

The Eighth Amendment to the U.S. Constitution does not guarantee the opportunity for bail but does state that "[e]xcessive bail shall not be required." Some studies, however, have found that many defendants who are offered the opportunity for bail are unable to raise the money. Years ago, a report by the National Advisory Commission on Criminal Justice Standards and Goals found that as many as 93% of felony defendants in some jurisdictions were unable to make bail.[38]

To extend the opportunity for pretrial release to a greater proportion of nondangerous arrestees, a number of states and the federal government now make available various alternatives to the cash bond system. Alternatives include (1) release on recognizance, (2) property bond, (3) deposit bail, (4) conditional release, (5) third-party custody, (6) unsecured bond, and (7) signature bond.

A typical bail bond office. Bail bond offices like this one are usually found near courthouses where criminal trials are held.

Mark Richards

release on recognizance (ROR)

The pretrial release of a criminal defendant on his or her written promise to appear in court as required. No cash or property bond is required.

property bond

The setting of bail in the form of land, houses, stocks, or other tangible property. In the event that the defendant absconds prior to trial, the bond becomes the property of the court.

Release on Recognizance (ROR) involves no cash bond, requiring as a guarantee only that the defendant agree in writing to return for further hearings as specified by the court. As an alternative to cash bond, release on recognizance was tested during the 1960s in a social experiment called the Manhattan Bail Project.[39] In the experiment, not all defendants were eligible for release on their own recognizance. Those arrested for serious crimes, including murder, rape, and robbery, and defendants with extensive prior criminal records were excluded from participating in the project. The rest of the defendants were scored and categorized according to a number of "ideal" criteria used as indicators of both dangerousness and the likelihood of pretrial flight. Criteria included (1) no previous convictions, (2) residential stability, and (3) a good employment record. Those likely to flee were not released.

Studies of the bail project revealed that it released four times as many defendants prior to trial as had been freed under the traditional cash bond system.[40] Even more surprising was the finding that only 1% of those released fled from prosecution—a figure which was the same as for those set free on cash bond.[41] Later studies, however, were unclear as to the effectiveness of release on recognizance, with some finding a no-show rate as high as 12%.[42]

Property Bonds substitute other items of value in place of cash. Land, houses, automobiles, stocks, and so on may be consigned to the court as collateral against pretrial flight.

Deposit Bail is an alternative form of cash bond available in some jurisdictions. Deposit bail places the court in the role of the bondsman, allowing the defendant to post a percentage of the full bail with the court. Unlike private bail bondsmen, court-run deposit bail programs usually return the amount of the deposit except for a small (perhaps 1%) administrative fee. If the defendant fails to appear for court, the entire amount of court-ordered bail is forfeited.

Conditional Release imposes a set of requirements upon the defendant. Requirements might include participation in a drug-treatment program; staying away from specified others, such as potential witnesses; and attendance at a regular job. Release under supervision is similar to conditional release but adds the stipulation that defendants report to an officer of the court or to a police officer at designated times.

Third-Party Custody is a bail bond alternative that assigns custody of the defendant to an individual or agency which promises to ensure his or her later appearance in court.[43] Some pretrial release programs allow attorneys to assume responsibility for their clients in this fashion. If clients fail to appear, however, the attorney's privilege to participate in the program may be ended.

Unsecured Bonds are based upon a court-determined dollar amount of bail. Like a credit contract, it requires no monetary deposit with the court. The defendant agrees in writing that failure to appear will result in forfeiture of the entire amount of the bond, which might then be taken in seizures of land, personal property, bank accounts, and so on.

Signature Bonds allow release based upon the defendant's written promise to appear. Signature bonds involve no particular assessment of the defendant's dangerousness or likelihood of later appearance in court. They are used only in cases of minor offenses like traffic law violations and some petty drug-law violations. Signature bonds may be issued by the arresting officer acting on behalf of the court.

PRETRIAL RELEASE AND PUBLIC SAFETY

Pretrial release is common practice. Approximately 63% of all state-level felony criminal defendants[44] and 66% of all federal felony defendants[45] are released prior to trial (Figure 8–6). A growing movement, arguing that defendants released prior to trial may be dangerous to themselves or to others, seeks to reduce the number of defendants released under any conditions. Advocates of this conservative policy cite a number of studies documenting crimes committed by defendants released on bond. One such study found that 16% of defendants released before trial were rearrested, and of those, 30% were arrested more than once.[46] Another determined that as many as 41% of those released prior to trial for serious crimes, such as rape and robbery, were rearrested before their trial date.[47] Not surprisingly, such studies generally find that the longer the time spent on bail prior to trial, the greater the likelihood of misconduct.

In response to findings like these, some states have enacted **danger laws**, which limit the right to bail to certain kinds of offenders.[48] Other states, including Arizona, California, Colorado, Florida, and Illinois, have approved constitutional amendments restricting the use of bail.[49] Most such provisions exclude defendants charged with certain crimes from being eligible for bail and demand that other defendants being considered for bail meet stringent conditions. Some states combine these strictures with tough release conditions designed to keep close control over defendants prior to trial.

The 1984 federal Bail Reform Act allows federal judges to assess the danger of an accused to the community and to deny bail to defendants who are thought to be dangerous. In the words of the act, a suspect held in pretrial custody on federal criminal charges must be detained if "after a hearing . . . he is found to pose a risk of flight and a danger to others or the community and if no condition of release can give reasonable assurances

danger law

A law intended to prevent the pretrial release of criminal defendants judged to represent a danger to others in the community.

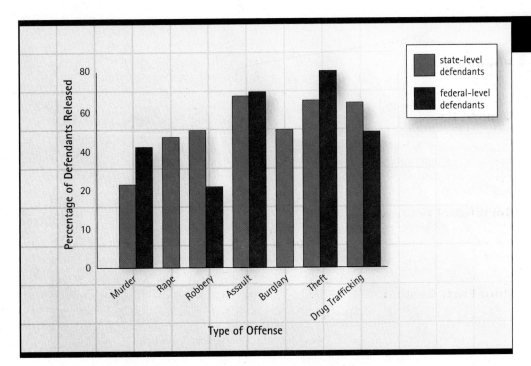

FIGURE 8–6

Proportion of state and federal felony defendants released prior to trial.

Sources: Timothy C. Hart and Brian A. Reaves, *Felony Defendants in Large Urban Counties, 1996* (Washington, D.C.: Bureau of Justice Statistics, 1999); Brian A. Reaves and Jacob Perez, *Pretrial Release of Felony Defendants, 1992* (Washington, D.C.: Bureau of Justice Statistics, 1994); and John Scalia, *Federal Pretrial Release and Detention, 1996* (Washington, D.C.: Bureau of Justice Statistics, 1999). Note: Federal pretrial release statistics are not available for the crimes of rape and burglary.

against these contingencies."[50] Defendants seeking bail are faced with the necessity of demonstrating a high likelihood of later court appearance. The act also requires that a defendant have a speedy first appearance and, if he or she is to be detained, that a detention hearing be held together with the initial appearance.

In the 1990 case of *U.S.* v. *Montalvo-Murillo*,[51] however, a defendant who was not provided with a detention hearing at the time of his first appearance and was subsequently released by an appeals court was found to have no "right" to freedom because of this "minor" statutory violation. The Supreme Court held that "unless it has a substantial influence on the outcome of the proceedings . . . failure to comply with the Act's prompt hearing provision does not require release of a person who should otherwise be detained" because "[a]utomatic release contravenes the statutory purpose of providing fair bail procedures while protecting the public's safety and assuring a defendant's appearance at trial."[52]

Court challenges to the constitutionality of pretrial detention legislation have not met with much success. The U.S. Supreme Court case of *U.S.* v. *Hazzard* (1984),[53] decided only a few months after enactment of federal bail reform, held that Congress was justified in providing for denial of bail to offenders who represent a danger to the community. Later cases have supported the presumption of flight, which federal law presupposes for certain types of defendants.[54]

The Grand Jury

The federal government and about half of the states use grand juries as part of the pretrial process. Grand juries comprise private citizens (often 23 in number) who hear evidence presented by the prosecution. Grand juries serve primarily as filters to eliminate from further processing cases for which there is not sufficient evidence.

In early times, grand juries served a far different purpose. The grand jury system began in England in 1166 as a way of identifying law violators. Lacking a law enforcement agency with investigative authority, the government looked to the grand jury as a source of information on criminal activity in the community. Even today, grand juries in most jurisdictions may initiate prosecution independently of the prosecutor, although they rarely do.

Grand jury hearings are held in secret, and the defendant is generally not afforded the opportunity to appear before the grand jury.[55] Similarly, the defense has no opportunity to cross-examine prosecution witnesses. Grand juries have the power to subpoena witnesses and to mandate a review of books, records, and other documents crucial to their investigation.

After hearing the evidence, the grand jury votes on the indictment presented to it by the prosecution. The indictment is a formal listing of proposed charges. If the majority of grand

A grand jury in action. Grand jury proceedings are generally very informal, as this picture shows.

David Young-Wolff, Getty Images, Inc.

jury members agree to forward the indictment to the trial court, it becomes a "true bill" upon which further prosecution will turn.

The Preliminary Hearing

States that do not use grand juries rely instead upon a preliminary hearing "for charging defendants in a fashion that is less cumbersome and arguably more protective of the innocent."[56] In these jurisdictions, the prosecutor files an accusatorial document called an *information*, or complaint, against the accused. A preliminary hearing is then held to determine whether there is probable cause to hold the defendant for trial. A few states, notably Tennessee and Georgia, use both the grand jury mechanism and a preliminary hearing as a "double check against the possibility of unwarranted prosecution."[57]

Although the preliminary hearing is not nearly as elaborate as a criminal trial, it has many of the same characteristics. The defendant is taken before a lower-court judge who summarizes the charges and reviews the rights to which all criminal defendants are entitled. The prosecution may present witnesses and will offer evidence in support of the complaint. The defendant is afforded the right to testify and may also call witnesses.

The primary purpose of the preliminary hearing is to give the defendant an opportunity to challenge the legal basis for his or her detention. At this point, defendants who appear to be or claim to be mentally incompetent may be ordered to undergo further evaluation to determine whether they are **competent to stand trial**. Competence to stand trial, which was briefly discussed in Chapter 4, may become an issue when a defendant appears to be incapable of understanding the proceedings or is unable to assist in his or her own defense due to mental disease or defect. In 1996, for example, lawyers for multimillionaire chemical heir John E. du Pont successfully argued at a pretrial hearing that their client was psychotic and unable to work effectively with lawyers in preparing a defense to murder charges. Du Pont had been accused of shooting and killing David Schultz, an Olympic wrestler and 1984 gold medalist who had trained on du Pont's estate near Philadelphia. At the hearing, du Pont was declared schizophrenic, and his delusions of being the Dalai Lama, Jesus, and "heir to the Third Reich" were publicized in national media.[58]

Barring a finding of mental incompetence, all that is required for the wheels of justice to grind forward is a demonstration "sufficient to justify a prudent man's belief that the suspect has committed or was committing an offense" within the jurisdiction of the court.[59] If the magistrate finds enough evidence to justify a trial, the defendant is bound over to the grand jury—or sent directly to the trial court in those states which do not require grand jury review. If the complaint against the defendant cannot be substantiated, the defendant is released. A release is not a bar to further prosecution, however, and the defendant may be rearrested if further evidence comes to light.

Arraignment and the Plea

Once an indictment has been returned, or an information filed, the accused will be formally arraigned. Arraignment is "the first appearance of the defendant before the court that has the authority to conduct a trial."[60] Arraignment is generally a brief process with two purposes: (1) to once again inform the defendant of the specific charges against him or her and (2) to allow the defendant to enter a **plea**. The Federal Rules of Criminal Procedure allow for one of three types of pleas to be entered: guilty, not guilty, and *nolo contendere*. A no-contest **(nolo contendere)** plea is much the same as a guilty plea. A defendant who pleads no contest is immediately convicted and may be sentenced just as though he or she had pleaded guilty. A no-contest plea, however, is not an admission of guilt and provides one major advantage to defendants: It may not be used later as a basis for civil proceedings which seek monetary or other damages against the defendant.

Some defendants refuse to enter any plea and are said to "stand mute." Standing mute is a defense strategy that is rarely employed. Defendants who choose this alternative simply do not answer the request for a plea. However, for procedural purposes, a defendant who stands mute is considered to have entered a plea of not guilty.

PLEA BARGAINING

Guilty pleas often are not as straightforward as they might seem and are typically arrived at only after complex negotiations known as *plea bargaining*. **Plea bargaining** is a process of negotiation which usually involves the defendant, the prosecutor, and the defense counsel. It is founded upon the mutual interests of all involved. Defense attorneys and their clients

---

The judicial Power of the United States shall be vested in one supreme Court, and in such inferior Courts as the Congress may from time to time ordain and establish.

—Article III, U.S. Constitution

competent to stand trial

A finding by a court, when the defendant's sanity at the time of trial is at issue, that the defendant has sufficient present ability to consult with his or her attorney with a reasonable degree of rational understanding and that the defendant has a rational as well as factual understanding of the proceedings against him or her.

plea

In criminal proceedings, the defendant's formal answer in court to the charge contained in a complaint, information, or indictment that he or she is guilty of the offense charged, is not guilty of the offense charged, or does not contest the charge.

nolo contendere

A plea of "no contest." A no-contest plea is used when the defendant does not wish to contest conviction. Because the plea does not admit guilt, however, it cannot provide the basis for later civil suits that might follow upon the heels of a criminal conviction.

plea bargaining

The process of negotiating an agreement among the defendant, the prosecutor, and the court as to an appropriate plea and associated sentence in a given case. Plea bargaining circumvents the trial process and dramatically reduces the time required for the resolution of a criminal case.

will agree to a plea of guilty when they are unsure of their ability to win acquittal at trial. Prosecutors may be willing to bargain because the evidence they have against the defendant is weaker than they would like it to be. From the prosecutorial perspective, plea bargaining results in a quick conviction without the need to commit the time and resources necessary for trial. Benefits to the accused include the possibility of reduced or combined charges, lessened defense costs, and a lower sentence than might otherwise be anticipated.

The U.S. Supreme Court has held that a guilty plea constitutes conviction.[61] To validate the conviction, negotiated pleas require judicial consent. Judges often accept pleas which are the result of a bargaining process because such pleas reduce the workload of the court. Although few judges are willing to guarantee a sentence before a plea is entered, most prosecutors and criminal trial lawyers know what sentences to expect from typical pleas.

In the past, plea bargaining, though apparently common, was often veiled in secrecy. Judicial thinking held that, for pleas to be valid, they had to be given freely. Pleas struck as the result of bargains seemed to depend upon the state's coercive power to encourage the defendant's cooperation. The 1973 National Advisory Commission on Criminal Justice Standards and Goals recommended abolishing the practice of plea negotiation.[62] That recommendation came in the midst of a national debate over the virtues of trading a plea for a reduction in sentence. However, in 1970, even before the commission's recommendation, the U.S. Supreme Court had given its consent to the informal decision-making processes of bargained pleas. In the case of *Brady* v. *U.S.*,[63] the Court reasoned that such pleas were acceptable if voluntarily and knowingly made. A year later, in *Santobello* v. *New York* (1971),[64] the high court forcefully ruled that plea bargaining is an important and necessary component of the American system of justice. In the words of the Court, "The disposition of criminal charges by agreement between the prosecutor and the accused, sometimes loosely called 'plea bargaining,' is an essential component of the administration of justice. Properly administered, it is to be encouraged. If every criminal charge were subjected to a full-scale trial, the States and the Federal Government would need to multiply by many times the number of judges and court facilities."[65]

Bargained pleas are commonplace. Some surveys have found that 90% of all criminal cases prepared for trial are eventually resolved through a negotiated plea.[66] In a study of 37 big-city prosecutors, the Bureau of Justice Statistics found that for every 100 adults arrested on a felony charge, half were eventually convicted of either a felony or a misdemeanor.[67] Of all convictions, fully 94% were the result of a plea. Only 6% of convictions were the result of a criminal trial.

After a guilty plea has been entered, it may be withdrawn with the consent of the court. In the case of *Henderson* v. *Morgan* (1976),[68] for example, the U.S. Supreme Court permitted a defendant to withdraw a plea of guilty nine years after it had been given. In *Henderson*, the defendant had originally entered a plea of guilty to second-degree murder but attempted to withdraw it before trial. Reasons for wanting to withdraw the plea included the defendant's belief that he had not been completely advised as to the nature of the charge or the sentence he might receive as a result of the plea.

Some Supreme Court decisions, however, have enhanced the prosecutor's authority in the bargaining process by declaring that negotiated pleas cannot be capriciously withdrawn by defendants.[69] Other rulings have supported discretionary actions by prosecutors in which sentencing recommendations were retracted even after bargains had been struck.[70] Some lower-court cases have upheld the government's authority to withdraw from a negotiated plea when the defendant fails to live up to certain conditions.[71] Conditions may include requiring the defendant to provide information on other criminals, criminal cartels, the activities of smugglers, and so on.

Because it is a process of negotiation involving many interests, plea bargaining may have unintended consequences. For example, while it is generally agreed that bargained pleas should relate in some way to the original charge, actual practice may not adhere to such expectations. Many plea negotiations turn on the acceptability of the anticipated sentence rather than on a close relationship between the charge and the plea. Entered pleas may be chosen for the punishments likely to be associated with them rather than for their accuracy in describing the criminal offense in which the defendant was involved.[72] This is especially true when the defendant is concerned with minimizing the socially stigmatizing impact of the offense. A charge of indecent liberties, for example, in which the defendant is accused of sexual misconduct, may be pleaded out as assault. Such a plea, which takes advantage of the fact that indecent liberties can be thought of as a form of sexual assault, would effectively disguise the true nature of the offense.

Even though plea bargaining has been endorsed by the Supreme Court, the public continues to view it suspiciously. Law-and-order advocates, who generally favor harsh punishments and long jail terms, claim that plea bargaining results in unjustifiably light sentences. As a consequence, prosecutors who regularly engage in the practice rarely advertise it. Often unrealized is the fact that plea bargaining can be a powerful prosecutorial tool.

Power carries with it, however, the potential for misuse. Because they circumvent the trial process, plea bargains could be abused by prosecutors and defense attorneys who are more interested in the speedy resolution of cases than they are in seeing justice done. Carried to the extreme, plea bargaining may result in defendants being convicted of crimes they did not commit. Although it probably happens only rarely, it is conceivable that innocent defendants (especially those with prior criminal records) who—for whatever reason— think a jury will convict them, may plead guilty to lessened charges to avoid a trial. In an effort to protect defendants against hastily arranged pleas, the Federal Rules of Criminal Procedure require judges to (1) inform the defendant of the various rights he or she is surrendering by pleading guilty, (2) determine that the plea is voluntary, (3) require disclosure of any plea agreements, and (4) make sufficient inquiry to ensure there is a factual basis for the plea.[73]

Bargained pleas can take many forms and be quite inventive. The case of Jeffrey Morse illustrates an unusual attempt at a bargained plea. In 1998, Morse, a convicted sex offender, petitioned courts in Illinois for permission to leave jail prior to sentencing for sexual assaults on two young girls so that he could undergo surgical castration. A judge agreed, and he was surgically castrated in a 45-minute outpatient procedure. Morse's mother noted that the surgery was done in an effort to avoid a long prison sentence. "He will cut whatever bodily part he has to be able to reduce his sentence," she said.[74] Two months later, however, Kane County Judge Donald C. Hudson refused to show leniency for Morse. Instead, Hudson sentenced Morse to 26 years in prison, saying that he wouldn't "place a seal of approval on trading body parts for a lesser sentence."[75]

WHAT WOULD YOU DO?

The CD-ROM scenario for Chapter 8 follows state court administrators as they attempt to create a prerelease policy for state magistrates to follow. The scenario is based upon actual guidelines created by the U.S. Supreme Court. Work through the scenario using the CD-ROM found in the back of your textbook to learn what those guidelines are.

Summary

Throughout the United States, there are two judicial systems. One consists of state and local courts established under the authority of state governments. The other is the federal court system, created by Congress under the authority of the Constitution of the United States.

State courts have virtually unlimited power to decide nearly every type of case, subject only to the limitations of the U.S. Constitution, their own state constitutions, and state law. State and local courts, located in almost every town and county across the nation, are the courts with which citizens usually have contact. These courts handle most criminal matters and the great bulk of legal business concerning wills and inheritance, estates, marital disputes, real estate and land dealings, commercial and personal contracts, and other day-to-day matters.

State criminal courts present an intriguing contrast. On the one hand, they exude an aura of highly formalized judicial procedure, while on the other they demonstrate a surprising lack of organizational uniformity. Courts in one state may bear little resemblance to those in another. Court reform has not had an equal impact on all areas of the country and has, in some instances, exacerbated the differences between state court systems.

Federal courts, located principally in larger cities, decide only those cases over which the Constitution gives them authority. The highest federal court, the U.S. Supreme Court, is located in Washington, D.C., and hears cases only on appeal from lower courts.

This chapter also described pretrial practices in preparation for a detailed consideration of trial-related activities in the next chapter. Prior to trial, courts often act to shield the accused from the punitive power of the state through the use of pretrial release. In doing so, they must balance the rights of the unconvicted defendant against the potential for future harm which that person may represent. A significant issue facing pretrial decision makers is how to ensure that all defendants, rich and poor, black and white, male and female, are afforded the same degree of protection.

I left [the Supreme Court] . . . perfectly convinced that . . . a system so defective . . . would not obtain the energy, weight, and dignity which are essential to its affording due support to the national government, nor acquire the public confidence and respect which, as the last resort of the justice of the nation, it should possess.

—John Jay, first chief justice of the United States, in a letter to John Adams, 1801

Discussion Questions

1. What is the dual-court system? Why do we have a dual-court system in America? Could the drive toward court unification eventually lead to a monolithic court system? Would such a system be effective?
2. This chapter says that 90% of all criminal cases carried beyond the initial stages are finally resolved through plea bargaining. What are some of the problems associated with plea bargaining? Given those problems, do you believe that plea bargaining is an acceptable practice in today's criminal justice system? Explain.
3. People who are accused of crimes are often granted pretrial release. Do you think all defendants accused of crimes should be released before trial? If not, what types of defendants would you keep in jail? Why?
4. What inequities exist in today's system of pretrial release? How might the system be improved?

To participate in an online discussion on these topics and others, go to the Global Town Meeting electronic message board for Chapter 8 on the *Criminal Justice Today* Companion Website at cjtoday.com.

Web Quest!

Visit the Federal Judiciary website run by the Administrative Office of the United States Courts at http://www.uscourts.gov. After visiting the site, describe the purpose and history of the Administrative Office, the courts it serves, and the nature of the services it provides.

Also visit the National Center for State Courts at http://ncsconline.org. What is the mission of the NCSC? What are the divisions of the NCSC? What does each division do? What "affiliated associations" are listed on the NCSC home page? What is the purpose of each of these associations?

Write down and submit what you have learned to your instructor if asked to do so.

To complete this Web Quest! online, go to the Web Quest! module in Chapter 8 of the *Criminal Justice Today* Companion Website at cjtoday.com.

Library Extras!

Library Extra! 8–1 *Federal Habeas Corpus Review: Challenging State Court Criminal Convictions* (DOJ, 1995).
Library Extra! 8–2 *Therapeutic Jurisprudence and the Emergence of Problem-Solving Courts* (NIJ, 1999).
Library Extra! 8–3 *Understanding the Federal Courts* (AO, 2000).
Library Extra! 8–4 *Federal Criminal Appeals* (BJS, 2001).
Library Extra! 8–5 *Report to Congress on the Optimal Utilization of Judicial Resources* (AO, 2001).
Library Extra! 8–6 Commission on Structural Alternatives for the Federal Courts of Appeals, *Final Report* (USGPO, 1998).
Library Extra! 8–7 *Pretrial Services Programs: Responsibilities and Potential* (NIJ, 2001).

To explore these resources online, go to the Library Extras! area of the *Criminal Justice Today* Companion Website at cjtoday.com. You should also check the author's "Late Picks" online for newly released documents and updated Library Extras! You can find Late Picks at http://cjtoday.com/latepicks.htm.

Notes

1. In Joan Biskupic, "Courts Can't Unravel All Election Snags," *USA Today,* September 17, 2000.

2. Debbie Howlett and Gary Fields, "Cluster of Bombings Touches Off Concerns," *USA Today,* February 4, 1997, p. 3A.

3. Ann Bancroft, "Police Arrest Six Men in California Bombings," Associated Press wire service, February 4, 1997. Web posted at http://www.newstimes.com/ archive97/feb0497/nad.htm. Accessed February 12, 2002.

4. Law Enforcement Assistance Administration, *Two Hundred Years of American Criminal Justice* (Washington, D.C.: U.S. Government Printing Office, 1976), p. 31.

5. Ibid.

6. Ibid.

7. Ibid., p. 32.

8. Ibid.

9. David B. Rottman, Carol R. Flango, and R. Shedine Lockley, *State Court Organization, 1993* (Washington, D.C.: Bureau of Justice Statistics, 1995), p. 11.

10. Thomas A. Henderson et al., *The Significance of Judicial Structure: The Effects of Unification on Trial Court Operations* (Washington, D.C.: National Institute of Justice, 1984).

11. Ibid.

12. In 1957, only 13 states had permanent intermediate appellate courts. Now, all but 12 states have these courts, and North Dakota is operating one on a temporary basis to assist in handling the rising appellate caseload in that state. See Rottman, Flango, and Lockley, *State Court Organization, 1993*, p. 5.

13. *Keeney, Superintendent, Oregon State Penitentiary* v. *Tamayo-Reyes,* 113 S.Ct. 853, 122 L.Ed. 2d 203 (1993).

14. *Herrera* v. *Collins,* 113 S.Ct. 853, 122 L.Ed. 2d 203 (1993).

15. Some of the wording in this section is taken from "Overview of the Florida State Courts System," on the Florida court system's website, http://www.flcourts. org/pubinfo/system2.html. Accessed January 26, 2001.

16. H. Ted Rubin, *The Courts: Fulcrum of the Justice System* (Pacific Palisades, CA: Goodyear, 1976), p. 200.

17. Ibid., p. 198.

18. Martin Wright, *Justice for Victims and Offenders* (Bristol, PA: Open University Press, 1991), p. 56.

19. Ibid., pp. 104 and 106.

20. Most of the information and some of the wording in this section comes from Administrative Office of the U.S. Courts, *Understanding the Federal Courts.* Web posted at http://www.uscourts.gov/UFC99.pdf. Accessed April 2, 2002.

21. Administrative Office of the U.S. Courts, "U.S. District Courts—Criminal Cases Commenced, Terminated, and Pending during the 12-Month Periods Ending September 30, 1999 and 2000." Web posted at http://www. uscourts.gov/judbus2000/appendices/d00sep00.pdf. Accessed March 11, 2002.

22. Administrative Office of the U.S. Courts, "U.S. District Courts—Civil Cases Commenced, Terminated, and Pending during the 12-Month Periods Ending September 30, 1999 and 2000." Web posted at http://www. uscourts.gov/judbus2000/appendices/c00sep00.pdf. Accessed March 11, 2002.

23. Administrative Office of the U.S. Courts, "U.S. District Courts—Criminal Cases Commenced, Terminated, and Pending."

24. Ibid.

25. Much of the information and some of the wording in this section comes from Administrative Office of the U.S. Courts, "About the Federal Courts." Web posted at www.uscourts.gov/about.html. Accessed October 4, 2001.

26. Stephen L. Wasby, *The Supreme Court in the Federal Judicial System,* 3d ed. (Chicago: Nelson-Hall, 1988), p. 58.

27. *The Supreme Court of the United States* (Washington, D.C.: U.S. Government Printing Office, no date), p. 4.

28. *Marbury* v. *Madison,* 1 Cranch 137 (1803).

29. *Mapp* v. *Ohio,* 367 U.S. 643 (1961).

30. Wasby, *The Supreme Court,* pp. 58–59.

31. See Public Law 105-119, signed November 26, 1997.

32. *Arraignment* is also a term used to describe an initial appearance, although we will reserve use of that word to describe a later court appearance following the defendant's indictment by a grand jury or the filing of an information by the prosecutor.

33. *McNabb* v. *U.S.,* 318 U.S. 332 (1943).

34. *County of Riverside* v. *McLaughlin,* 111 S.Ct. 1661 (1991).

35. *White* v. *Maryland,* 373 U.S. 59 (1963).

36. Much of the information in this section comes from Barry Mahoney et al., *Pretrial Services Programs: Responsibilities and Potential* (Washington, D.C.: National Institute of Justice, 2001).

37. *Taylor* v. *Taintor,* 83 U.S. 66 (1873).

38. National Advisory Commission on Criminal Justice Standards and Goals, *The Courts* (Washington, D.C.: U.S. Government Printing Office, 1973), p. 37.

39. C. Ares, A. Rankin, and H. Sturz, "The Manhattan Bail Project: An Interim Report on the Use of Pre-Trial Parole," *New York University Law Review,* Vol. 38 (January 1963), pp. 68–95.

40. H. Zeisel, "Bail Revisited," *American Bar Foundation Research Journal,* Vol. 4 (1979), pp. 769–789.

41. Ibid.

42. "12% of Those Freed on Low Bail Fail to Appear," *New York Times,* December 2, 1983, p. 1.

43. Bureau of Justice Statistics, *Report to the Nation on Crime and Justice,* 2d ed. (Washington, D.C.: U.S. Department of Justice, 1988), p. 76.

44. See Timothy C. Hart and Brian A. Reaves, *Felony Defendants in Large Urban Counties, 1996* (Washington, D.C.: Bureau of Justice Statistics, 1999), p. 16. Web posted at http://www.ojp.usdoj.gov/bjs/pub/pdf/fdluc96.pdf. Accessed January 25, 2002.

45. John Scalia, *Federal Pretrial Release and Detention, 1996* (Washington, D.C.: Bureau of Justice Statistics, 1999), p. 1. Web posted at http://www.ojp.usdoj.gov/bjs/ pub/pdf/fprd96.pdf. Accessed January 25, 2002.

46. Donald E. Pryor and Walter F. Smith, "Significant Research Findings Concerning Pretrial Release," *Pretrial Issues,* Vol. 4, No. 1 (Washington, D.C.: Pretrial Services Resource Center, February 1982). See also the Pretrial Services Resource Center on the Web at http://www.pretrial.org/mainpage.htm.

47. BJS, *Report to the Nation on Crime and Justice,* p. 77.

48. According to Joseph B. Vaughn and Victor E. Kappeler, the first such legislation was the 1970 District of Columbia Court Reform and Criminal Procedure Act. See Vaughn and Kappeler, "The Denial of Bail: Pre-Trial Preventive Detention," *Criminal Justice Research Bulletin,* Vol. 3, No. 6 (Huntsville, TX: Sam Houston State University, 1987), p. 1.

49. Ibid.

50. Bail Reform Act of 1984, 18 U.S.C. 3142(e).

51. *U.S.* v. *Montalvo-Murillo,* 495 U.S. 711 (1990).

52. *U.S.* v. *Montalvo-Murillo* (1990), syllabus.

53. *U.S.* v. *Hazzard,* 35 CrL 2217 (1984).

54. See, for example, *U.S.* v. *Motamedi,* 37 CrL 2394, CA 9 (1985).

55. A few states now have laws that permit the defendant to appear before the grand jury.

56. John M. Scheb and John M. Scheb II, *American Criminal Law* (St. Paul, MN: West, 1996), p. 31.

57. Ibid.

58. In February 1997, following six months of treatment with antipsychotic drugs, du Pont was found guilty of third-degree murder in the killing of Schultz and was sentenced to 13 to 30 years in confinement.

59. *Federal Rules of Criminal Procedure* 5.1(a).

60. Scheb and Scheb, *American Criminal Law,* p. 32.

61. *Kercheval* v. *U.S.,* 274 U.S. 220, 223, 47 S.Ct. 582, 583 (1927); *Boykin* v. *Alabama,* 395 U.S. 238 (1969); and *Dickerson* v. *New Banner Institute, Inc.,* 460 U.S. 103 (1983).

62. The National Advisory Commission on Criminal Justice Standards and Goals, *Courts* (Washington, D.C.: U.S. Government Printing Office, 1973), p. 46.

63. *Brady* v. *U.S.,* 397 U.S. 742 (1970).

64. *Santobello* v. *New York,* 404 U.S. 257 (1971).

65. Ibid.

66. Bureau of Justice Statistics, *The Prosecution of Felony Arrests* (Washington, D.C.: U.S. Government Printing Office, 1983).

67. Barbara Boland et al., *The Prosecution of Felony Arrests, 1987* (Washington, D.C.: U.S. Government Printing Office, May 1990).

68. *Henderson* v. *Morgan,* 426 U.S. 637 (1976).

69. *Santobello* v. *New York* (1971).

70. *Mabry* v. *Johnson,* 467 U.S. 504 (1984).

71. *U.S.* v. *Baldacchino,* 762 F.2d 170 (1st Cir. 1985); *U.S.* v. *Reardon,* 787 F.2d 512 (10th Cir. 1986); and *U.S.* v. *Donahey,* 529 F.2d 831 (11th Cir. 1976).

72. For a classic discussion of such considerations, see David Sudnow, "Normal Crimes: Sociological Features of the Penal Code in a Public Defender Office," *Social Problems,* Vol. 123, No. 3 (Winter, 1965), p. 255.

73. *Federal Rules of Criminal Procedure,* No. 11.

74. "A Desperate Act," *Prime Time Live,* ABCNews.com, January 28, 1998. Web posted at http://archive. abcnews.go.com/onair/PTL/html–files/transcripts/ ptl0128c.html. Accessed July 21, 1999.

75. Dan Rozek, "Castration Doesn't Gain Leniency for Pedophile," *Chicago Sun-Times,* March 4, 1998.

The Courtroom Work Group and the Criminal Trial

LEARNING OBJECTIVES

After reading this chapter, you should be able to

- Identify and explain the roles of the various professional members of the courtroom work group

- Identify and explain the roles of the various nonprofessional courtroom participants

- Describe the various stages in a criminal trial

- Describe methods that have been suggested for improving the adjudication process

POLICE LINE: DO NOT CROSS

chapter 9

—D. Graham Burnett, Jury Foreman[1]

Key Concepts

[Terms]

adversarial system	hearsay rule	real evidence
bailiff	judge	rules of evidence
change of venue	juror	scientific jury selection
circumstantial evidence	jury selection	sequestered jury
closing argument	lay witness	Speedy Trial Act
courtroom work group	opening statement	subpoena
defense counsel	peremptory challenge	testimony
direct evidence	perjury	verdict
evidence	prosecutor	victim-assistance program
expert witness	prosecutorial discretion	
hearsay	public defender	

[Cases]

Burns v. *Reed*	*Fex* v. *Michigan*	*Michigan* v. *Lucas*
Coy v. *Iowa*	*Georgia* v. *McCollum*	*Mu'Min* v. *Virginia*
Crosby v. *U.S.*	*Gideon* v. *Wainwright*	*Powers* v. *Ohio*
Demarest v. *Manspeaker et al.*	*Idaho* v. *Wright*	*White* v. *Illinois*
Doggett v. *U.S.*	*Imbler* v. *Pachtman*	*Zafiro* v. *U.S.*
Edmonson v. *Leesville Concrete Co., Inc.*	*Maryland* v. *Craig*	

Introduction

Hear the author discuss this chapter at **cjtoday.com**

"Every day, as he ambles through the cobwebbed halls of the New Orleans criminal court building, public defender Richard Tessier feels he violates his clients' constitutional rights" to legal counsel.[2] Tessier, an attorney who is paid just $18,500 per year by the state of Louisiana, has so many clients and so few resources that he believes he can't possibly do them all justice. Several years ago, in an effort to bring his plight before the public, Tessier filed suit against his own office. A local judge agreed, finding Louisiana's system of indigent defense unconstitutional. Former Louisiana Governor Edwin Edwards, commenting on the ruling, said that underfunding of public defenders is not limited to New Orleans but is "a state problem and a national problem."[3]

The Courtroom Work Group: Professional Courtroom Actors

Were it not for people like Richard Tessier, few would be aware of the problems facing our nation's courts. To the public eye, criminal trials generally appear to be well managed and even dramatic events. Like plays on a stage, they involve many participants playing many different roles. Parties to the event can be divided into two categories: professionals and outsiders. The professionals are the official courtroom actors, well versed in criminal trial practice, who set the stage for and conduct the business of the court. Judges, prosecuting attorneys, defense attorneys, public defenders, and others who earn a living serving the court fall into this category. Professional courtroom actors are also called the **courtroom work group**. Some writers have pointed out that aside from statutory requirements and ethical considerations, courtroom interaction among professionals involves an implicit recognition of informal rules of civility, cooperation, and shared goals.[4] Hence, even within the adversarial framework of a criminal trial, the courtroom work group is dedicated to bringing the procedure to a successful close.[5]

courtroom work group

The professional courtroom actors, including judges, prosecuting attorneys, defense attorneys, public defenders, and others who earn a living serving the court.

In contrast, "outsiders" are generally unfamiliar with courtroom organization and trial procedure. Most outsiders visit the court temporarily to provide information or to serve as members of the jury. Similarly, because of their temporary involvement with the court, defendants and victims are also outsiders, even though they may have more of a personal investment in the outcome of the trial than anyone else.

This chapter continues to examine trial court activities, building upon the pretrial process described in the last chapter. To place the trial process within its human context, however, the various roles of the many participants in a criminal trial are discussed first.

> To hear patiently, to weigh deliberately and dispassionately, and to decide impartially; these are the chief duties of a judge.
>
> —Albert Pike (1809–1891)

The Judge
THE ROLE OF THE JUDGE

The trial **judge** is probably the figure most closely associated with a criminal trial. The judge has the primary duty of ensuring justice. The American Bar Association's *Standards for Criminal Justice* describes the duties of the trial judge as follows: "The trial judge has the responsibility for safeguarding both the rights of the accused and the interests of the public in the administration of criminal justice. . . . The only purpose of a criminal trial is to determine whether the prosecution has established the guilt of the accused as required by law, and the trial judge should not allow the proceedings to be used for any other purpose."[6]

In the courtroom, the judge holds ultimate authority, ruling on matters of law, weighing objections from both sides, deciding on the admissibility of evidence, and disciplining anyone who challenges the order of the court. In most jurisdictions, judges also sentence offenders after a verdict has been returned; in some states, judges serve to decide guilt or innocence for defendants who waive a jury trial.

Most state jurisdictions have a chief judge who, besides serving on the bench as a trial judge, must also manage the court system. Management includes hiring staff, scheduling sessions of court, ensuring the adequate training of subordinate judges, and coordinating activities with other courtroom actors. Chief judges usually assume their position by virtue of seniority and rarely have any formal training in management. Hence, the managerial effectiveness of a chief judge is often a matter of personality and dedication more than anything else.

judge

An elected or appointed public official who presides over a court of law and who is authorized to hear and sometimes to decide cases and to conduct trials.

JUDICIAL SELECTION

As we discussed in Chapter 8, judges at the federal level are nominated by the president of the United States and take their place on the bench only after confirmation by the Senate. At the state level, things work somewhat differently. Depending upon the jurisdiction, state judgeships are won through either popular election or political (usually gubernatorial) appointment. The processes involved in judicial selection at the state level are set by law.

Both judicial election and appointment have been criticized because each system allows politics to enter the judicial arena—although in somewhat different ways. Under the election system, judicial candidates must receive the endorsement of their parties, generate contributions, and manage an effective campaign. Under the appointment system, judicial hopefuls must be in favor with incumbent politicians to receive appointments. Because partisan politics plays a role in both systems, critics have claimed that sitting judges can rarely be as neutral as they should be. They carry to the bench with them campaign promises, personal indebtedness, and possible political agendas.

To counter some of these problems, a number of states have adopted what has come to be called the Missouri Plan (or the Missouri Bar Plan) for judicial selection.[7] The Missouri Plan combines elements of both election and appointment. It requires candidates for judicial vacancies to undergo screening by a nonpartisan state judicial nominating committee. Candidates selected by the committee are reviewed by an arm of the governor's office, which selects a final list of names for appointment. Incumbent judges must face the electorate after a specified term in office. They then run unopposed in nonpartisan elections in which only their records may be considered. Voters have the choice of allowing a judge to continue in office or asking that another be appointed to take his or her place. Because the Missouri Plan provides for periodic public review of judicial performance, it is also called the *merit plan of judicial selection.*

QUALIFICATIONS OF JUDGES

A few decades ago, many states did not require any special training, education, or other qualifications for judges. Anyone (even someone without a law degree) who won election or was appointed could assume a judgeship. Today, however, almost all states require that judges in general jurisdiction and appellate courts hold a law degree, be a licensed attorney, and be a member of their state bar association. Many states also require newly elected judges to attend state-sponsored training sessions dealing with such subjects as courtroom procedure, evidence, dispute resolution, judicial writing, administrative record keeping, and ethics.

While most states provide instruction to meet the needs of trial judges, other organizations also provide specialized training. The National Judicial College, located on the campus of the University of Nevada at Reno, is one such institution. The National Judicial College was established in 1963 by the Joint Committee for the Effective Administration of Justice, chaired by Justice Tom C. Clark of the U.S. Supreme Court.[8] More than 32,000 judges have enrolled in courses since the college began operation.[9] Visit the National Judicial College via **Web Extra! 9–1** at cjtoday.com.

In some parts of the United States, lower-court judges, such as justices of the peace, local magistrates, and "district" court judges, may still be elected without educational and other professional requirements. Today, in 43 states, some 1,300 nonlawyer judges are serving in mostly rural courts of limited jurisdiction.[10] In New York, for example, of the 3,300 judges in the state's unified court system, approximately 65% are part-time town or village justices. Approximately 80% of town and village justices are not lawyers.[11] The majority of cases which come before New York lay judges involve alleged traffic violations, although they may also include misdemeanors, small-claims actions, and some civil cases (of up to $3,000).

Some authors have defended lay judges as being closer to the citizenry in their understanding of justice.[12] Even so, in most jurisdictions, the number of lay judges appears to be declining. States which continue to use lay judges in lower courts do require that candidates for judgeships not have criminal records, and most states require that they attend special training sessions if elected.

JUDICIAL MISCONDUCT

In June 1997, a bond hearing in West Virginia took a turn for the worse when Pleasant County Circuit Judge Joseph Troisi allegedly bit defendant Bill Whittens on the nose.[13] The bite, said Whittens, was inflicted after he directed a derogatory remark at the judge. Whittens's nose required medical treatment at a local hospital. Judge Troisi had no comment, and the Federal Bureau of Investigation (FBI) was called in to investigate.

While most judges are highly professional in and out of the courtroom, some judges occasionally overstep the limits of their authority. Poor judgment may result from bad taste or archaic attitudes, as in the case of a male lower-court judge who repeatedly told a female defense counselor that she was too pretty to be a lawyer and that she should be at home having children. Other sexist comments resulted in calls for that judge's dismissal. Sexist behavior hasn't been confined to male judges. In 1996, for example, Cleveland Judge Shirley Strickland Saffold caused an outcry among Ohio voters when she told a woman being sentenced for misusing a credit card to "dump your boyfriend, show your legs, and marry a doctor." The judge, who is herself married to a physician, continued, "You can go sit in the bus stop, put on a short skirt, cross your legs, and pick up 25 [men]. Ten of them will give you their money."[14]

All states provide mechanisms for administratively dealing with complaints about judicial conduct. In 1995, for example, Pennsylvania District Justice Bradford C. Timbers was suspended by the state's Judicial Conduct Board after being charged with "trying to fix a friend's speeding ticket, slapping a female co-worker's buttocks, and drinking alcohol on the job."[15] In 1997, the chief justice of the Alaska Supreme Court, Allen I. Compton, 59, stepped down from his position after being admonished for sexual harassment. Compton resigned his post as chief justice after receiving a private rebuke from the Alaska Commission on Judicial Conduct, which said that his conduct on two occasions in 1995 and 1996, with two different female court employees, constituted sexual harassment.[16] Also in 1997, 62-year-old James D. Heiple was forced to resign his position as chief justice of the Illinois Supreme Court after admitting that he used his office in attempts to evade traffic tickets.[17] Although he remains on the court, the Illinois Courts Commission officially censured Heiple for "conduct that is prejudicial to the administration of justice and conduct that brings the judicial office into disrepute."

At the federal level, the Judicial Councils Reform and Judicial Conduct and Disability Act, passed by Congress in 1980, specifies the procedures necessary to register complaints against federal judges and, in serious cases, to begin the process of impeachment, or forced removal from the bench.

James D. Heiple, former Chief Justice of the Illinois Supreme Court, being "mugged" by the Pekin (Illinois) Police Department. Heiple was forced to resign his position after admitting that he used his office in attempts to evade traffic tickets. Most judges are highly respected members of the criminal justice system, but some overstep the boundaries of judicial propriety and can be disciplined.

AP/Wide World Photos

The Prosecuting Attorney

The **prosecutor**—called variously the *solicitor, district attorney, state's attorney, county attorney,* or *commonwealth attorney*—is responsible for presenting the state's case against the defendant. Technically speaking, the prosecuting attorney is the primary representative of the people by virtue of the belief that violations of the criminal law are an affront to the public. Except for federal prosecutors (called *U.S. attorneys*) and solicitors in five states, prosecutors are elected and generally serve four-year terms with the possibility of continuing reelection.[18] Widespread criminal conspiracies, whether they involve government officials or private citizens, may require the services of a special prosecutor whose office can spend the time and resources needed for efficient prosecution.[19]

In many jurisdictions, because the job of prosecutor entails too many duties for one person to handle, most prosecutors supervise a staff of assistant district attorneys who do most in-court work. Assistants are trained attorneys, usually hired directly by the chief prosecutor and licensed to practice law in the state where they work. Approximately 2,300 chief prosecutors, assisted by 24,000 deputy attorneys, serve the nation's counties and independent cities.[20]

Another prosecutorial role has traditionally been that of quasi-legal adviser to local police departments. Because prosecutors are sensitive to the kinds of information needed for conviction, they may help guide police investigations and will exhort detectives to identify credible witnesses, uncover additional evidence, and the like. This role is limited, however. Police departments are independent of the administrative authority of the prosecutor, and cooperation between them, although based on the common goal of conviction, is purely voluntary. Moreover, close cooperation between prosecutors and police may not always be legal. A 1998 federal law known as the McDade law,[21] for example, requires that federal prosecutors abide by all state bar ethics rules. In late 2000, in a reflection of the federal sentiment, the Oregon Supreme Court effectively ended police-prosecutor collaboration in that state in instances involving potential deception by law enforcement officers.[22] The court, ruling in the Oregon State Bar disciplinary case of *In re Gatti*,[23] held that all lawyers within the state, including government prosecutors overseeing organized crime, child pornography, and narcotics cases, must abide by the Oregon State Bar's strictures against dishonesty, fraud, deceit, and misrepresentation.[24] Under the court's ruling, a prosecutor in Oregon who encourages an undercover officer or an informant to misrepresent himself or

prosecutor

An attorney whose official duty is to conduct criminal proceedings on behalf of the state or the people against those accused of having committed criminal offenses.

> I don't know if I ever want to try another case. I don't know if I ever want to practice law again.
>
> —Christopher Darden, Los Angeles County Assistant Prosecutor, expressing frustration over the O. J. Simpson case

herself could be disbarred and prohibited from practicing law. As a result of the highly controversial ruling, the FBI and the Drug Enforcement Administration ended all big undercover operations in Oregon, and local police departments canceled many ongoing investigations. Immediately after the decision, Ed Herdin, President of the Oregon State Bar, observed that "everyone agrees that lawyers should not misrepresent themselves as something other than what they are. But [given the court's ruling] how do we provide the police with meaningful advice as to how to act in a legal manner?" As this book goes to press, the U.S. Justice Department is suing the Oregon State Bar, arguing that its prohibitions "encroach upon the authority of the federal government to engage in covert law enforcement activities that necessarily involve deceit or misrepresentation."[25] The Oregon State Bar is meeting in an attempt to redraft relevant provisions in its code of ethics. Deep philosophical divisions among the participants have, however, prevented any action to date.

There is no debate over the fact that once a trial begins, the job of the prosecutor is to vigorously present the state's case against the defendant. Prosecutors introduce evidence against the accused, steer the testimony of witnesses "for the people," and argue in favor of conviction. Since defendants are presumed innocent until proven guilty, the burden of demonstrating guilt beyond a reasonable doubt rests with the prosecutor.

PROSECUTORIAL DISCRETION

In August 2001, Miami prosecutors decided to drop domestic violence charges against Mayor Joe Carollo.[26] Carollo, who allegedly hit his wife, Ledon, on the head with a cardboard tea box during an argument at their home, had been arrested after one of the couple's daughters called 911 and reported, "My dad's hurting my mom." Charges against the mayor were dropped after he completed a counseling program for first-time domestic violence offenders. At a news conference held after the charges were dropped, Carollo told reporters, "The bottom line was that there was no crime committed. . . . It was an accident, and that is behind us now."

Whether or not Carollo's assertion about no crime having occurred is true, his case highlights the fact that American prosecutors occupy a unique position in the nation's criminal justice system by virtue of the considerable **prosecutorial discretion** they exercise. As U.S. Supreme Court Justice Robert H. Jackson noted in 1940, "The prosecutor has more control over life, liberty, and reputation than any other person in America."[27] Before a case comes to trial, the prosecutor may decide to accept a plea bargain, divert the suspect to a public or private social service agency, ask the suspect to seek counseling, or dismiss the case entirely for lack of evidence or for a variety of other reasons. Studies have found that from one-third to one-half of all felony cases are dismissed by the prosecution prior to trial or before a plea bargain is made.[28] Prosecutors also play a significant role before grand juries. States which use the grand jury system depend upon prosecutors to bring evidence before the grand jury and to be effective in seeing indictments returned against suspects.

In preparation for trial, the prosecutor decides what charges are to be brought against the defendant, examines the strength of the incriminating evidence, and decides which witnesses to call. Two important U.S. Supreme Court decisions have held that it is the duty of prosecutors to, in effect, assist the defense in building its case by making available any evidence in their possession. The first case, *Brady* v. *Maryland*,[29] was decided in 1963. In *Brady*, the Court held that the prosecution is required to disclose to the defense evidence that directly relates to claims of either guilt or innocence. The second and more recent case is that of *U.S.* v. *Bagley*,[30] decided in 1985. In *Bagley*, the Court ruled that the prosecution must disclose any evidence that the defense requests. The Court reasoned that to withhold evidence, even when it does not relate directly to issues of guilt or innocence, may mislead the defense into thinking that such evidence does not exist.

One special decision the prosecutor makes concerns the filing of separate or multiple charges. The decision to try a defendant simultaneously on multiple charges allows for the presentation of a considerable amount of evidence and permits an in-court demonstration of a complete sequence of criminal events. This strategy has a practical side as well; it saves time and money by substituting one trial for what might otherwise be a number of trials if each charge were to be brought separately before the court. From the prosecutor's point of view, however, trying the charges one at a time carries the advantage of allowing for another trial on a new charge if a "not guilty" verdict is returned.

The activities of the prosecutor do not end with a finding of guilt or innocence. Following conviction, prosecutors are usually allowed to make sentencing recommendations to

---

prosecutorial discretion

The decision-making power of prosecutors, based upon the wide range of choices available to them, in the handling of criminal defendants, the scheduling of cases for trial, the acceptance of bargained pleas, and so on. The most important form of prosecutorial discretion lies in the power to charge, or not to charge, a person with an offense.

the judge. They can be expected to argue that aggravating factors (which we will discuss in Chapter 10), prior criminal record, or especially heinous qualities of the offense in question call for strict punishment. When a convicted defendant appeals, prosecutors may need to defend their own actions and to argue, in briefs filed with appellate courts, that the conviction was properly obtained. Most jurisdictions also allow prosecutors to make recommendations when defendants they have convicted are being considered for parole or for early release from prison.

Until relatively recently, it has generally been held that prosecutors enjoyed much the same kind of immunity against liability in the exercise of their official duties that judges do. The 1976 Supreme Court case of *Imbler v. Pachtman*[31] provided the basis for such thinking with its ruling that "state prosecutors are absolutely immune from liability . . . for their conduct in initiating a prosecution and in presenting the State's case." However, in the 1991 case of *Burns v. Reed*,[32] the Court held that "[a] state prosecuting attorney is absolutely immune from liability for damages . . . for participating in a probable cause hearing, but not for giving legal advice to the police." The *Burns* case involved Cathy Burns of Muncie, Indiana, who allegedly shot her sleeping sons while laboring under a multiple personality disorder. To explore the possibility of multiple personality further, the police asked the prosecuting attorney if it would be appropriate for them to hypnotize the defendant. The prosecutor agreed that hypnosis would be a permissible avenue for investigation, and the suspect confessed to the murders while hypnotized. She later alleged in her complaint to the Supreme Court "that [the prosecuting attorney] knew or should have known that hypnotically induced testimony was inadmissible" at trial.[33]

THE ABUSE OF DISCRETION

Because of the large amount of discretion prosecutors wield, there is considerable potential for abuse. Discretionary decisions not to prosecute friends or political cronies or to accept guilty pleas to drastically reduced charges for personal considerations are always inappropriate and potentially dangerous possibilities. On the other hand, overzealous prosecution by district attorneys seeking heightened visibility to support grand political ambitions can be another source of abuse. Administrative decisions, such as case scheduling, which can wreak havoc with the personal lives of defendants and the professional lives of defense attorneys, can also be used by prosecutors to harass defendants into pleading guilty. Some forms of abuse may be unconscious. At least one study suggests that some prosecutors have an inherent tendency toward leniency where female defendants are concerned and tend to discriminate against minorities when deciding whether to prosecute.[34]

Although the electorate are the final authority to which prosecutors must answer, gross misconduct by prosecutors may be addressed by the state supreme court or by the state attorney general's office. Short of addressing *criminal* misconduct, however, most of the options available to the court and to the attorney general are limited.

THE PROSECUTOR'S PROFESSIONAL RESPONSIBILITY

As members of the legal profession, prosecutors are subject to the American Bar Association (ABA) Code of Professional Responsibility. Serious violations of the code may result in a prosecutor's being disbarred from the practice of law. The ABA Standard for Criminal Justice 3-1.1 describes the prosecutor's duty this way: "The duty of the prosecutor is to seek justice, not merely to convict." Hence, prosecutors are barred by the standards of the legal profession from advocating any fact or position which they know is untrue. Prosecutors have a voice in influencing public policy affecting the safety of America's communities through the National District Attorneys Association (NDAA). Visit the NDAA via **Web Extra! 9–2** at cjtoday.com.

The Defense Counsel

THE ROLE OF THE DEFENSE COUNSEL

The **defense counsel** is a trained lawyer who may specialize in the practice of criminal law. The task of the defense attorney is to represent the accused as soon as possible after arrest and to ensure that the defendant's civil rights are not violated during processing by the criminal justice system. Other duties of the defense counsel include testing the strength of the prosecution's case, taking part in plea negotiations, and preparing an adequate defense to be used at trial. In the preparation of a defense, criminal lawyers may enlist private detectives, experts, witnesses to the crime, and character witnesses. Some lawyers perform aspects of the role of private detective or of investigator themselves. Defense attorneys also review relevant court precedents to identify the best defense strategy.

> From the moment you walk into the courtroom, you are the defendant's only friend.
>
> —Austin defense attorney
> Michael E. Tigar

Web EXTRA!

defense counsel

A licensed trial lawyer, hired or appointed to conduct the legal defense of a person accused of a crime and to represent him or her before a court of law.

Defense preparation may involve intense communications between lawyer and defendant. Such discussions are recognized as privileged communications protected under the umbrella of lawyer-client confidentiality. In other words, lawyers cannot be compelled to reveal information which their clients have confided to them.[35]

If a client is found guilty, defense attorneys will be involved in arguments at sentencing, may be asked to file an appeal, and will probably counsel the defendant and the defendant's family as to what civil matters (payment of debts, release from contractual obligations, and so on) may need to be arranged after sentence is imposed. Hence, the work of the defense attorney encompasses many roles, including attorney, negotiator, investigator, confidant, family and personal counselor, social worker, and, as we shall see, bill collector.

THE CRIMINAL LAWYER

Three major categories of defense attorneys assist criminal defendants in the United States: (1) private attorneys, usually referred to as *criminal lawyers* or *retained counsel;* (2) *court-appointed counsel;* and (3) *public defenders.*

Private attorneys either have their own legal practices or work for law firms in which they are partners or employees. As those who have had to hire defense attorneys know, the fees of private attorneys can be high. Most privately retained criminal lawyers charge in the range of $100 to $200 per hour. Included in their bill is the time it takes to prepare for a case, as well as time spent in the courtroom. "High-powered" criminal defense attorneys who have established a regional or national reputation for successfully defending their clients can be far more expensive. A few such attorneys, such as Alan Dershowitz, Robert Shapiro, F. Lee Bailey, Johnnie Cochran (who was catapulted to fame during the widely televised O. J. Simpson criminal trial), the late civil rights attorney William Kunstler, and Stephen Jones (who defended Timothy McVeigh), have become household names by virtue of their association with famous defendants and well-publicized trials. Fees charged by famous criminal defense attorneys can run into the hundreds of thousands of dollars—and sometimes exceed $1 million—for handling just one case!

No less an authority than William H. Rehnquist, Chief Justice of the U.S. Supreme Court, has complained that the profit motive has turned the practice of law into a business, leaving many lawyers dissatisfied and perhaps less trusted by their clients than was true in the past. Speaking to Catholic University's graduating law students, Rehnquist noted that "market capitalism has come to dominate the legal profession in a way that it did not a generation ago. . . . Today, the profit margin seems to be writ large in a way that it was not in the past."[36] He continued, "The practice of law is today a business where once it was a profession." Even so, the chief justice concluded, practicing law is still "the most satisfying way of making a living that I know of."

Although there are many high-priced criminal defense attorneys in the country, Rehnquist's comments were meant to apply mostly to civil attorneys who take a large portion of the monetary awards they win for their clients. Few law students actually choose to specialize in criminal law, even though the job of a criminal lawyer may appear glamorous. Those who do often begin their careers immediately following law school, while others seek to gain experience working as assistant district attorneys or assistant public defenders for a number of years before going into private practice. The collection of fees can be a significant source of difficulty for many defense attorneys. Most defendants are poor. Those who aren't are often reluctant to pay what may seem to them to be an exorbitant fee, and woe be it to the defense attorney whose client is convicted before the fee has been paid! Visit the National Association of Criminal Defense Lawyers (NACDL) via **Web Extra! 9–3** and the Association of Federal Defense Attorneys (AFDA) via **Web Extra! 9–4** to learn more about the practice of criminal law.

CRIMINAL DEFENSE OF THE POOR

A series of U.S. Supreme Court decisions has guaranteed that defendants unable to pay for private criminal defense attorneys will receive adequate representation at all stages of criminal justice processing. In *Powell* v. *Alabama* (1932),[37] the Court held that the Fourteenth Amendment requires state courts to appoint counsel for defendants in capital cases who are unable to afford their own. In 1938, in *Johnson* v. *Zerbst,*[38] the Court overturned the conviction of an indigent federal inmate, holding that his Sixth Amendment due process right to counsel had been violated. The Court declared, "If the accused . . . is not represented by counsel and has not competently and intelligently waived his constitutional right, the Sixth Amendment stands as a jurisdictional bar to a valid conviction and sentence depriving him of his life or his liberty." The decision established the right of indigent defendants to receive the assistance of appointed counsel in all criminal proceedings in federal courts. The 1963 case of *Gideon* v. *Wainwright*[39] extended the right to appointed counsel to all indigent defendants charged with a felony in state courts. *Argersinger* v. *Hamlin* (1972)[40] saw the Court require adequate legal representation for anyone facing a potential sentence of imprisonment. Juveniles charged with delinquent acts were granted the right to appointed counsel in the case of *In re Gault* (1967),[41] which is discussed in detail in Chapter 14.

States have responded to the federal mandate for indigent defense in a number of ways. Most now use one of three systems to deliver legal services to criminal defendants who are unable to afford their own: (1) court-appointed counsel, (2) public defenders, and (3) contractual arrangements. Most such systems are administered at the county level, although funding arrangements may involve state, county, and municipal monies—as well as federal grants and court fees.

Court-appointed defense attorneys, whose fees are paid at a rate set by the state or local government, are also called *assigned counsel*. They are usually drawn from a roster of all practicing criminal attorneys within the jurisdiction of the trial court.

One problem with appointed counsel concerns degree of effort. Although most attorneys assigned by the court to indigent defense probably take their jobs seriously, some feel only a loose commitment to their clients. Paying clients, in their eyes, deserve better service and are apt to get it. In 2001, for example, New York's court-appointed attorneys were paid only $25 per hour for out-of-court preparation time and $40 an hour for time spent in the courtroom—a rate of pay that is 10–20 times *less* than what they normally earn.[42]

The second type of indigent defense, the **public defender** program (such as the one described in the opening paragraph of this chapter), depends upon full-time salaried staff. Staff members include defense attorneys, defense investigators, and office personnel. Defense investigators gather information in support of the defense effort. They may interview friends, family members, and employers of the accused, with an eye toward effective defense. Public defender programs have become popular in recent years, with approximately 64% of counties nationwide now funding them.[43] A 1996 Bureau of Justice Statistics report found that a public defender system is the primary method used to provide indigent counsel for criminal defendants and that 28% of state jurisdictions nationwide use public defender programs exclusively to provide indigent defense.[44] Critics charge that public defenders, because they are government employees, are not sufficiently independent from prosecutors and judges. For the same reason, clients may be suspicious of public defenders, viewing them as state functionaries. Finally, the huge caseloads typical of public defenders' offices create pressures toward an excessive use of plea bargaining.

Through a third type of indigent defense, contract attorney programs, county and state officials arrange with local criminal lawyers to provide for indigent defense on a contractual basis. Individual attorneys, local bar associations, and multipartner law firms may all be tapped to provide services. Contract defense programs are the least widely used form of indigent defense at present, although their numbers are growing.

Critics of the current system of indigent defense point out that the system is woefully underfunded. Findings from the most recent National Survey of Indigent Defense Systems (NSIDS) were published in 2001.[45] The survey found that states spent a total of $662,590,139 on indigent criminal defense in 1999. Most of the money ($337 million) went to fund public defender programs, while assigned counsel programs cost $191 million, and contract attorney fees totaled $53 million. New Jersey, the most populous of the states covered by the survey, spent the most money ($73 million) on indigent criminal defense. While these figures may seem quite large, they total only about one-third the amount that states spend every year to prosecute criminal defendants. As a result, the report of the National Symposium on Indigent Defense proclaimed in 2000, "Indigent defense today, in terms of funding, caseloads, and quality, is in a chronic state of crisis."[46] Some question the quality of services available through public defender systems due to the fact that entry-level public defenders are paid poorly in comparison to what new attorneys entering private law firms might earn. In 1999, for example, entry-level assistant public defenders in Massachusetts earned $28,600, while new public defenders in New Mexico earned $28,941, and those in Vermont were paid $29,500. Moreover, the cost to the states for representing an indigent defendant averages around $490, while private attorney fees are generally much higher.[47]

public defender

An attorney employed by a government agency or subagency, or by a private organization under contract to a government body, for the purpose of providing defense services to indigents, or an attorney who has volunteered such service.

As a consequence of such limited funding, many public defender's offices are said to employ what critics call a "plead-'em-and-speed-'em through" strategy, often involving a heavy use of plea bargaining and initial meetings with clients in courtrooms as trials are about to begin. Mary Broderick of the National Legal Aid and Defender Association says, "We aren't being given the same weapons. . . . It's like trying to deal with smart bombs when all you've got is a couple of cap pistols."[48] Proposed enhancements to indigent defense systems are offered by the National Legal Aid and Defender Association (NLADA). You can visit the NLADA via **Web Extra! 9–5** at cjtoday.com.

The entire 200-page report of the National Symposium on Indigent Defense is available as **Library Extra! 9–1** at cjtoday.com; and the Bureau of Justice Statistics' 2001 overview of the National Survey of Indigent Defense Systems can be found at **Library Extra! 9–2**. **Library Extra! 9–3** provides an overview of indigent defense services that are state funded.

Although state indigent defense services may sometimes be woefully underfunded, the same is not true of the federal system. The defense of indigent Oklahoma City bomber Timothy McVeigh, for example, cost taxpayers an estimated $13.8 million—which doesn't include the cost of his appeal or execution. McVeigh's expenses included $6.7 million for attorneys, $2 million for investigators, $3 million for expert witnesses, and approximately $1.4 million for office rent and secretarial assistance.[49]

In 2000, the Bureau of Justice Statistics (BJS) reported data on publicly financed counsel nationwide in two research reports that appear to conflict with the conclusions reached by the National Survey of Indigent Defense Systems.[50] BJS statisticians found that court-appointed defense attorneys represent 66% of federal felony defendants, as well as 82% of felony defendants in the nation's 75 most populous counties. The study also found that conviction rates for indigent defendants and those with their own lawyers were about the same in both federal and state courts. About 90% of the federal defendants and 75% of defendants in the most populous counties were found guilty regardless of the type of attorney they had. However, the study showed that those found guilty and represented by publicly financed attorneys were incarcerated at a higher rate than those defendants who paid for their own legal representation—88% compared to 77% in federal courts and 71% compared to 54% in the most populous counties. On average, however, prison sentences for defendants with publicly financed attorneys were shorter than were those with hired counsel. In federal district court, convicted defendants who had publicly financed attorneys were sentenced to less than five years on average, and those with private attorneys to just over five years. In large counties, those with publicly financed attorneys were sentenced to an average of two and one-half years, and those with private attorneys to three years.

Of course, defendants need not accept any assigned counsel. Defendants may waive their right to an attorney and undertake their own defense—a right held to be inherent in the Sixth Amendment to the U.S. Constitution by the U.S. Supreme Court in the 1975 case of *Faretta* v. *California*.[51] Self-representation is uncommon, however, and only 1% of federal inmates and 3% of state inmates report having represented themselves.[52] Two famous and relatively recent instances of self-representation can be found in the 1995 trial of Long Island Rail Road commuter train shooter Colin Ferguson, which is discussed later in this chapter, and the 1999 trial of Dr. Jack Kevorkian.

Defendants who are not pleased with the lawyer appointed to defend them are in a somewhat different situation. They may request, through the court, that a new lawyer be assigned to represent them, as Timothy McVeigh did following his conviction and death sentence in the Oklahoma City bombing case. However, unless there is clear reason for reassignment, such as an obvious personality conflict between defendant and attorney, few judges are likely to honor a request of this sort. Short of obvious difficulties, most judges will trust in the professionalism of appointed counselors.

State-supported indigent defense systems may also be called upon to provide representation for clients upon appeal. An attorney who is appointed to represent an indigent defendant on appeal, however, may conclude that an appeal would be frivolous. If so, he or she may request that the appellate court allow him or her to withdraw from the case or that the court dispose of the case without requiring the attorney to file a brief arguing the merits of the appeal. In 1967, in the case of *Anders* v. *California*,[53] the U.S. Supreme Court found that in order to protect a defendant's constitutional right to appellate counsel, appellate courts must safeguard against the risk of accepting an attorney's negative assessment of a case where an appeal is not actually frivolous. The Court also found California's existing procedure for evaluating such requests inadequate, and set forth an acceptable procedure. In 1979, in the case of *People* v. *Wende*,[54] the state of California adopted a new standardized procedure which, although not the same as that put forth in *Anders*, was designed to protect the right of a criminal defendant to appeal.

The *Wende* standard was put to the test in the 2000 case of *Smith* v. *Robbins*.[55] The case began when convicted California murderer Lee Robbins told his court-appointed counsel that he wanted to file an appeal. His attorney, however, concluded that the appeal would be frivolous and filed a brief with the state court of appeals to that effect. The court agreed with the attorney's assessment, and the appeal was not heard. The California Supreme Court denied further review of the case. After exhausting his state postconviction remedies, Robbins appealed to the federal courts, arguing that he had been denied effective assistance of appellate counsel because his counsel's brief did not comply with one of the requirements in *Anders*—specifically, the requirement that the brief must mention "anything in the record that might arguably support the appeal." A federal district court agreed, concluding that there were at least two issues that might have supported Robbins's appeal and finding that his counsel's failure to include them in his brief deviated from the *Anders* procedure and thus amounted to deficient performance by counsel. The Ninth Circuit Court agreed, concluding that *Anders* established a mandatory procedure as a standard against which the performance of appointed counsel could be assessed. When the case finally reached the U.S. Supreme Court, the justices held that the *Anders* procedure is only one method of satisfying the Constitution's requirements for indigent criminal appeals and that the states are free to adopt different procedures as long as those procedures adequately safeguard a defendant's right to appellate counsel.

Finally, in 2001, in the case of *Texas* v. *Cobb*,[56] the Court ruled that the Sixth Amendment right to counsel is "offense specific" and applies only to the offense with which a defendant is charged, and not to other offenses even if they may be factually related to the charged offense. The case originated with the arrest of Raymond Cobb on charges of burglary. A woman and her 16-month-old daughter had disappeared from a house that had been burglarized, although it was unclear to investigators if the burglary and the disappearance were related. Counsel was appointed to represent Cobb, who then confessed to

A heated exchange between prosecutor Marcia Clark and defense attorney F. Lee Bailey during the O. J. Simpson trial. "I do not appreciate being called a liar in any court!" Bailey told the judge. The Simpson trial gave the public a close-up look at the adversarial nature of our criminal justice system.

Agence France Press (AFP)

CJ Today Exhibit 9-1

[Gideon v. Wainwright and Indigent Defense]

Today, about three-fourths of state-level criminal defendants and one-half of federal defendants are represented in court by publicly funded counsel.[1] As recently as 40 years ago, however, the practice of publicly funded indigent defense was uncommon. That changed in 1963 when, in the case of *Gideon* v. *Wainwright*,[2] the U.S. Supreme Court extended the right to legal counsel to indigent defendants charged with a criminal offense. The reasoning of the Court is well summarized in this excerpt from the majority opinion written by Justice Hugo Black:

> Governments, both state and federal, quite properly spend vast sums of money to establish machinery to try defendants accused of crime. Lawyers to prosecute are everywhere deemed essential to protect the public's interest in an orderly society. Similarly, there are few defendants charged with crime, few indeed, who fail to hire the best lawyers they can get to prepare and present their defenses. That government hires lawyers to prosecute and defendants who have the money hire lawyers to defend are the strongest indications of the widespread belief that lawyers in criminal courts are necessities, not luxuries. The right of one charged with crime to counsel may not be deemed fundamental and essential to fair trials in some countries, but it is in ours. From the very beginning, our state and national constitutions and laws have laid great emphasis on procedural and substantive safeguards designed to assure fair trials before impartial tribunals in which every defendant stands equal before the law. This noble ideal cannot be realized if the poor man charged with crime has to face his accusers without a lawyer to assist him.

? DISCUSSION QUESTIONS

1. Do you agree with the Court that all indigent defendants should have the opportunity to have counsel appointed to represent them? Why or why not?
2. What would our system of criminal justice be like if poor defendants had no access to court-appointed attorneys?

[1]Steven K. Smith and Carol J. DeFrances, *Indigent Defense* (Washington, D.C.: Bureau of Justice Statistics, 1996).
[2]*Gideon* v. *Wainwright*, 372 U.S. 335 (1963).

the burglary but denied knowledge of the disappearance of the woman and child from the home. While free on bond on the burglary charge, he confessed to his father that he had killed the woman and child. His father then contacted the police, and Cobb was arrested. While in custody, Cobb waived his *Miranda* rights and confessed to the murders. He was later convicted of capital murder and was sentenced to death. On appeal to the Texas Court of Criminal Appeals, he argued that his confession should not have been admitted into evidence at his trial because it was obtained in violation of his Sixth Amendment right to counsel. That right, he claimed, stemmed from the fact that counsel had been appointed for him in the burglary case. The Texas court agreed with Cobb and reversed his conviction, finding that once the right to counsel attaches to the offense charged, it also attaches to any other offense that is very closely related factually to the offense charged. When the case reached the U.S. Supreme Court, however, the justices overturned the Texas court's ruling and held that the Sixth Amendment right to counsel is "offense specific" and does *not* necessarily extend to offenses that are "factually related" to those that have actually been charged.

THE ETHICS OF DEFENSE

In November 2000, criminal defense attorney David B. Smith made a career-ending disclosure to officials at the Charlotte-based offices of the North Carolina Center for Death Penalty Litigation.[57] Smith admitted that he had betrayed his own client, death row inmate Russell Tucker, while handling the man's appeal, because of a *feeling* he had that Tucker deserved to die. Tucker had been convicted of the cold-blooded killing of Kmart security guard Maurice Travone Williams in 1994, after stealing a pair of boots and a coat from the store in which Williams worked. As the unarmed security officer approached him, Tucker pulled out a handgun and killed the guard as he attempted to flee. When Smith, a former federal prosecutor, met Tucker, he immediately disliked him. All he could think of, he said, were the gruesome autopsy photographs of Williams that were in Tucker's file. Smith signed an affidavit stating that although he had been appointed by the court to handle Tucker's appeal, he had "passively sabotaged" the procedure. Although Smith's honesty in admitting to mishandling Tucker's case because of personal emotions is admirable, the job

of defense counsel, as we have already mentioned, is to prepare and offer a vigorous defense on behalf of the accused at trial and to appeal cases that have merit.

A proper defense at trial often involves the presentation of evidence and the examination of witnesses, all of which require careful thought and planning. Good attorneys, like Smith is reputed to have been during most of his career, may find themselves emotionally committed to the outcome of trials in which they are involved. Beyond the immediacy of a particular trial, however, many attorneys realize that their reputations can be influenced by lay perceptions of their performance and that their careers and personal financial success depend upon consistently "winning" in the courtroom.

The nature of the adversarial process, fed by the emotions of the participants, combined with the often privileged and extensive knowledge that defense attorneys have about their cases, is enough to tempt the professional ethics of some counselors. Because the defense counsel may often know more about the guilt or innocence of the defendant than anyone else prior to trial, the defense role is carefully prescribed by ethical and procedural considerations. Attorneys violate both law and the standards of their profession if they knowingly misrepresent themselves or their clients.

To help attorneys understand what is expected of them, ethical standards abound. Four main groups of standards, each drafted by the American Bar Association (which you can visit via **Web Extra! 9–6** at cjtoday.com), are especially applicable to defense attorneys:

- Canons of Professional Ethics
- Model Code of Professional Responsibility
- Model Rules of Professional Conduct
- Standards for Criminal Justice

Each set of standards is revised periodically. The ABA Standard for Criminal Justice, Number 4–1.2, reads, in part,

> (e) Defense counsel, in common with all members of the bar, is subject to standards of conduct stated in statutes, rules, decisions of courts, and codes, canons, or other standards of professional conduct. Defense counsel has no duty to execute any directive of the accused which does not comport with law or such standards. Defense counsel is the professional representative of the accused, not the accused's alter ego.
> (f) Defense counsel should not intentionally misrepresent matters of fact or law to the court.
> (g) Defense counsel should disclose to the tribunal legal authority in the controlling jurisdiction [information] known to defense counsel to be directly adverse to the position of the accused and not disclosed by the prosecutor.

> If O. J. is so innocent, why are they trying to suppress all the evidence?
>
> —Denise Brown, Nicole Brown Simpson's sister, commenting on defense efforts to exclude evidence at the murder trial of O. J. Simpson

(h) It is the duty of every lawyer to know and be guided by the standards of professional conduct as defined in codes and canons of the legal profession applicable in defense counsel's jurisdiction. Once representation has been undertaken, the functions and duties of defense counsel are the same whether defense counsel is assigned, privately retained, or serving in a legal aid or defender program.

Even with these directives, however, defense attorneys are under no obligation to reveal information *obtained from a client* without the client's permission. Sometimes, however, they may go too far. In 1992, Minneapolis multimillionaire Russell Lund, Jr., was arrested and charged with the murder of his estranged wife and her boyfriend, a former Iowa state senator. Following the murder, attention shifted to the activities of Lund's attorneys who, police claim, waited until the day after the killings before reporting the shooting, hired a private detective who may have destroyed some evidence, and checked Mr. Lund into a private psychiatric facility under a different name without telling police where he was—all activities which may have been both unethical and illegal.[58]

In 1986, the U.S. Supreme Court case of *Nix* v. *Whiteside*[59] clarified the duty of lawyers to reveal known instances of client perjury. The *Nix* case came to the Court upon the complaint of the defendant, Whiteside, who claimed that he was deprived of the assistance of effective counsel during a murder trial because his lawyer would not allow him to testify untruthfully. Whiteside wanted to testify that he had seen a gun or something metallic in his victim's hand before killing him. Before trial, however, Whiteside admitted to his lawyer that he had actually seen no weapon, but he believed that to testify to the truth would result in his conviction. The lawyer told Whiteside that, as a professional counselor, he would be forced to challenge Whiteside's false testimony if it occurred and to explain to the court the facts as he knew them. On the stand, Whiteside said only that he thought the victim was reaching for a gun but did not claim to have seen one. He was found guilty of second-degree murder and appealed to the Supreme Court on the claim of inadequate representation.

The Court, recounting the development of ethical codes in the legal profession, held that a lawyer's duty to a client "is limited to legitimate, lawful conduct compatible with the very nature of a trial as a search for truth. . . . Counsel is precluded from taking steps or in any way assisting the client in presenting false evidence or otherwise violating the law."[60]

Finally, in 2001, the American Bar Association eased its secrecy rules surrounding lawyer-client relationships.[61] Previously, criminal defense attorneys had been permitted to disclose incriminating information about a client only in order to prevent imminent death or substantial bodily harm. The new rule dispenses with the word *imminent,* and attorneys are now allowed to reveal clients' secrets in order to stop future deaths or to prevent substantial bodily harm.

CJ Today Exhibit 9-2

[American Bar Association Code of Professional Responsibility]

For most criminal trial lawyers, the intense effort of advocacy results in an emotional and personal investment in the outcome of a case. To strike a balance between zealous and effective advocacy, on the one hand, and just professional conduct within the bounds of the law, on the other, the American Bar Association has developed a Code of Professional Responsibility. It reads, in part,

In his representation of a client, a lawyer shall not:

■ File a suit, assert a position, conduct a defense, delay a trial, or take other action on behalf of his client when he knows or when it is obvious that such action would serve merely to harass or maliciously injure another.

■ Knowingly advance a claim or defense that is unwarranted under existing law. . . .

■ Conceal or knowingly fail to disclose that which he is required by law to reveal.

■ Knowingly use perjured testimony or false evidence.

■ Knowingly make a false statement of law or fact.

■ Participate in the creation or preservation of evidence when he knows or it is obvious that the evidence is false.

■ Counsel or assist his client in conduct that the lawyer knows to be illegal or fraudulent.

Source: Excerpted from American Bar Association, *Code of Professional Responsibility,* Disciplinary Rule 7–102. Reprinted by permission of the American Bar Association. All rights reserved. Copies of this publication are available from Service Center, ABA, 750 N. Lakeshore Dr., Chicago, IL 60611; 800-285-2221.

The Bailiff

The **bailiff**, another member of the professional courtroom work group, is usually an armed law enforcement officer. The job of the bailiff, also called a *court officer*, is to ensure order in the courtroom, to announce the judge's entry into the courtroom, to call witnesses, and to prevent the escape of the accused (if the accused has not been released on bond). The bailiff also supervises the jury when it is sequestered and controls public and media access to jury members. Bailiffs in federal courtrooms are deputy U.S. marshals.

Courtrooms can be dangerous places. In 1993, George Lott was sentenced to die for a courtroom shooting in Tarrant County, Texas, which left two lawyers dead and three other people injured.[62] Lott said he was frustrated by the court's handling of his divorce and by child molestation charges filed against him by his ex-wife. In a similar case in 1992, a man opened fire with two pistols in a St. Louis courtroom during divorce proceedings, killing his wife and wounding her two lawyers and a security officer. The same day, a presiding judge in Grand Forks, North Dakota, was shot to death by a man accused of failing to pay child support.[63] In 1997, a hooded man walked into an Urbana, Illinois, courtroom and lobbed a firebomb at a judge. The gas-filled bottle bounced off the judge's head and burst against a wall, setting the courtroom on fire. Three people were injured, and the judge suffered a cut on his head. "There's no court security in our building," explained Champaign County (Illinois) Sheriff Dave Madigan.[64] Following such incidents, most courts initiated the use of metal detectors, and many now require visitors to leave packages, cellular phones, and objects that might conceal weapons in lockers or to check them with personnel before entering the courtroom.

Local Court Administrators

Many states now employ trial court administrators whose job is to facilitate the smooth functioning of courts in particular judicial districts or areas. A major impetus toward the hiring of local court administrators came from the 1967 President's Commission on Law Enforcement and Administration of Justice. Examining state courts, the report found "a system that treats defendants who are charged with minor offenses with less dignity and consideration than it treats those who are charged with serious crimes."[65] A few years later, the National Advisory Commission on Criminal Justice Standards and Goals recommended that all courts with five or more judges create the position of trial court administrator.[66]

Court administrators provide uniform court management, assuming many of the duties previously performed by chief judges, prosecutors, and court clerks. Where court administrators operate, the ultimate authority for running the court still rests with the chief judge. Administrators, however, are able to relieve the judge of many routine and repetitive tasks, such as record keeping, scheduling, case-flow analysis, personnel administration, space utilization, facilities planning, and budget management. They may also take the minutes at meetings of judges and their committees.

Juror management is another area in which trial court administrators are becoming increasingly involved. Juror utilization studies can identify problems such as the overselection of citizens for the jury pool and the reasons for excessive requests to be excused from jury service. They can also suggest ways to reduce the time jurors waste waiting to be called or impaneled.

Effective court administrators are able to track lengthy cases and identify bottlenecks in court processing. They then suggest strategies to make the administration of justice more efficient for courtroom professionals and more humane for lay participants.

The Court Recorder

The role of the court recorder (also called the *court stenographer* or *court reporter*) is to create a record of all that occurs during a trial. Accurate records are very important in criminal trial courts because appeals may be based entirely upon what went on in the courtroom. Especially significant are all verbal comments made in the courtroom, including testimony, objections, the judge's rulings, the judge's instructions to the jury, arguments made by attorneys, and the results of conferences between the attorneys and the judge. Occasionally, the judge will rule that a statement should be "stricken from the record" because it is inappropriate or unfounded. The official trial record, often taken on a stenotype machine or an audio recorder, may later be transcribed in manuscript form and will become the basis for any appellate review of the trial. Today's court stenographers often employ computer-aided transcription (CAT) software, which translates typed stenographic shorthand into complete and

bailiff

The court officer whose duties are to keep order in the courtroom and to maintain physical custody of the jury.

> The American criminal justice system is theater to the world.
>
> —Harvard University law professor Alan Dershowitz

readable transcripts. Court reporters may be members of the National Court Reporters Association, the United States Court Reporters Association, or the Association of Legal Administrators—all of which support the activities of these professionals. You can visit the National Court Reporters Association via **Web Extra! 9–7** at cjtoday.com.

The Clerk of Court

The duties of the clerk of court (also known as the *county clerk*) extend beyond the courtroom. The clerk maintains all records of criminal cases, including all pleas and motions made both before and after the actual trial. The clerk also prepares a jury pool, issues jury summonses, and subpoenas witnesses for both the prosecution and the defense. During the trial, the clerk (or an assistant) marks physical evidence for identification as instructed by the judge and maintains custody of that evidence. The clerk also swears in witnesses and performs other functions as the judge directs.

Some states allow the clerk limited judicial duties, such as the power to issue warrants, to handle certain matters relating to individuals declared mentally incompetent,[67] and to serve as judge of probate—overseeing wills and the administration of estates.

The Expert Witness

Most of the "insiders" we've talked about so far are either employees of the state or have ongoing professional relationships with the court (as in the case of defense counsel). **Expert witnesses**, however, may not have that kind of status, although some do. Expert witnesses are recognized as having specialized skills and knowledge in an established profession or technical area. They must demonstrate their expertise through education, work experience, publications, and awards. Their testimony at trial provides an effective way of introducing scientific evidence in such areas as medicine, psychology, ballistics, crime-scene analysis, photography, and many other disciplines. Expert witnesses, like the other courtroom actors described in this chapter, are generally paid professionals. And, like all other witnesses, they are subject to cross-examination. Unlike lay witnesses, they are allowed to express opinions and to draw conclusions, but only within their particular area of expertise.

Expert witnesses have played significant roles in many well-known cases. The 1995 criminal trial of O. J. Simpson, for example, became a stage for a battle between experts in the analysis of human DNA, while expert testimony in the 1982 trial of John Hinckley resulted in a finding of "not guilty by reason of insanity" for the man accused of shooting President Ronald Reagan. Similarly, the highly publicized 1995 trial of Susan Smith, the South Carolina mother who confessed to drowning her two young children, relied heavily upon the testimony of psychiatric experts and social workers. An important U.S. Supreme Court case addressing the admissibility of expert witness testimony is *Daubert* v. *Merrell Dow Pharmaceuticals, Inc.* (1993),[68] which is discussed in greater detail in Chapter 17.

Some authors have called attention to the difficulties surrounding expert testimony. One of the difficulties with expert testimony is that it can be confusing to the jury. Sometimes the trouble is due to the nature of the subject matter and sometimes to disagreements between the experts themselves. Often, however, it arises from the strict interpretation given to expert testimony by procedural requirements. The difference between medical and legal definitions of insanity, for example, points to a divergence in both history and purpose between the law and science. Courts which attempt to apply criteria like the M'Naghten rule (discussed in Chapter 4) in deciding claims of "insanity" often find themselves faced with the testimony of psychiatric experts who refuse even to recognize the word. Such experts may prefer, instead, to speak in terms of *psychosis* and *neurosis*—words which have no place in judicial jargon. Because of the uncertainties they create, legal requirements may pit experts against one another and may confuse the jury.

Even so, most authorities agree that expert testimony is usually viewed by jurors as more trustworthy than other forms of evidence. In a study of scientific evidence, one prosecutor commented that if he had to choose between presenting a fingerprint or an eyewitness at trial, he would always go with the fingerprint.[69] As a consequence of the effectiveness of scientific evidence, the National Institute of Justice recommends that "prosecutors consider the potential utility of such information in all cases where such evidence is available."[70]

---

expert witness

A person who has special knowledge and skills recognized by the court as relevant to the determination of guilt or innocence. Unlike lay witnesses, expert witnesses may express opinions or draw conclusions in their testimony.

CJ Today News

[Secret-Telling Sparks Some Ethical Conflicts]

Defense attorneys fire a psychiatrist for convicted FBI spy Robert Hanssen for going public with a theory that "demons" led Hanssen to betray the bureau.

A New York priest hears a teenager admit to committing a murder in 1987 for which two others were convicted, and keeps the secret—until the confessor dies. A judge frees the wrongly convicted men after the priest testifies about his talk with the teen.

The circumstances under which psychiatrist Alen Salerian and the Rev. Joseph Towle revealed information told to them in confidence could not have been more different. But analysts say the cases vividly illustrate questions that straddle matters of law and ethics for doctors, ministers, and others to whom secrets often are told: What obligation to society does the recipient of such information have? Where do professional ethics and the demands of the law meet? Can anyone keep a secret anymore?

For much of U.S. history, doctors have been governed by tradition and codes of ethics that encouraged confidentiality. In recent decades, such relations have been recognized by law. The sanctity of confessions to clergy is entrenched in statutes and case law.

The American Psychiatric Association's policy for therapist confidentiality requires mental-health professionals to take actions that might violate confidentiality if a patient explicitly threatens to kill or seriously injure someone. The laws differ from state to state.

That wasn't the situation in the Hanssen case, however. Salerian maintains that Hanssen, who spied for Moscow for more than 15 years, allowed the psychiatrist to speak publicly about their conversations. The implication was that Hanssen might have wanted to signal to prosecutors that he was prepared to claim he had a diminished mental capacity to try to avoid a death sentence. (Hanssen received a life sentence in a plea deal.)

After going public, Salerian was widely criticized by his peers and fired by Hanssen's attorneys, who said they had not endorsed the release of personal information.

"That is not something (Salerian) should have done," said Paul Appelbaum, chairman of the psychiatry department at the University of Massachusetts Medical School. "Most forensic psychiatrists would agree that one owes an obligation to the attorney who hired you . . . and not to the media."

For priest and penitent, confidentiality protections are part of case law. Even so, conflicts arise.

In 1996, a prosecutor ordered the jailhouse taping of discussions between a homicide suspect and a Roman Catholic priest in Eugene, Oregon. The request was dropped after local Catholics protested.

The case involving Towle has generated some debate among legal analysts and ethicists over when a clergy member becomes obligated to break a secret.

Towle says he merely repeated the substance of a discussion he had with the young man and did not reveal a confession. He is backed by his archdiocese, which said Towle's talk with the teen did not amount to a sacramental confession. That gave the priest more latitude under church policy to go to authorities.

Meanwhile, there has been little inclination among the states or in Washington to pierce secret conversations between clergy and church members. Rep. Pete King, R-N.Y., has offered bills that would give priests ironclad legal protection in keeping confessors' secrets. "There are tough moments when a guilty person may go free," he says. "But society has a greater need for protection of religious freedom."

For the latest in crime and justice news, visit the Talk Justice news feed at http://www.crimenews.info.

Father Joseph Towle, the Catholic priest whose testimony in 2001 helped free a man convicted of murder in 1988.
AP/Wide World Photos

Source: Donna Leinwand, "Secret-Telling Sparks Some Ethical Conflicts," *USA Today,* July 30, 2001, p. A4. Copyright 2001, *USA Today.* Reprinted with permission.

Expert witnesses may be veterans of many trials. Some well-known expert witnesses traverse the country and earn very high fees by testifying at trial. DNA specialist John Gerdes, for example, was paid $100 per hour for his work in support of the defense in the 1995 O. J. Simpson criminal trial, and New York forensic pathologist Michael Baden charged $1,500 per day for time spent working for Simpson in Los Angeles. Baden billed Simpson more than $100,000, and the laboratory for which Gerdes worked received more than $30,000 from Simpson's defense attorneys.[71]

Outsiders: Nonprofessional Courtroom Participants

Many people become either unwilling or inadvertent participants in criminal trials. Into this category fall defendants, victims, and most witnesses. Although they are "outsiders" who lack the status of paid professional participants, these are precisely the people who provide the grist for the judicial mill. Without them, trials could not occur, and the professional roles described earlier would be rendered meaningless.

Lay Witnesses

lay witness

An eyewitness, character witness, or other person called upon to testify who is not considered an expert. Lay witnesses must testify to facts alone and may not draw conclusions or express opinions.

subpoena

A written order issued by a judicial officer or grand jury requiring an individual to appear in court and to give testimony or to bring material to be used as evidence. Some subpoenas mandate that books, papers, and other items be surrendered to the court.

Nonexpert witnesses, also known as **lay witnesses**, may be called to testify by either the prosecution or the defense. Lay witnesses may be eyewitnesses who saw the crime being committed or who came upon the crime scene shortly after the crime had occurred. Another type of lay witness is the character witness, who frequently provides information about the personality, family life, business acumen, and so on of the defendant in an effort to show that this is not the kind of person who would commit the crime he or she is charged with. Of course, the victim may also be a witness, providing detailed and sometimes lengthy testimony about the defendant and the crime.

Witnesses are officially notified that they are to appear in court to testify by a written document called a **subpoena**. Subpoenas are generally "served" by an officer of the court or by a police officer, though they are sometimes mailed. Both sides in a criminal case may subpoena witnesses and might ask that individuals called to testify bring with them books, papers, photographs, videotapes, or other forms of physical evidence. Witnesses who fail to appear when summoned may face contempt-of-court charges.

The job of a witness is to provide accurate testimony concerning only those things of which he or she has direct knowledge. Normally, witnesses are not allowed to repeat things told to them by others unless it is necessary to do so to account for certain actions of their own. Since few witnesses are familiar with courtroom procedure, the task of testifying is fraught with uncertainty and can be traumatizing.

Everyone who testifies in a criminal trial must do so under oath, in which some reference to God is made, or after affirmation,[72] a pledge to tell the truth used by those who find either swearing or a reference to God objectionable.

All witnesses are subject to cross-examination, a process that will be discussed in detail later in this chapter. Lay witnesses may be surprised to find that cross-examination can force them to defend their personal and moral integrity. A cross-examiner may question a witness about past vicious, criminal, or immoral acts, even when such matters have never been the subject of a criminal proceeding.[73] As long as the intent of such questions is to demonstrate to the jury that the witness is not credible, they will normally be permitted by the judge.

Witnesses have traditionally been shortchanged by the judicial process. Subpoenaed to attend court, they have often suffered from frequent and unannounced changes in trial dates. A witness who promptly responds to a summons to appear may find that legal maneuvering has resulted in unanticipated delays. Strategic changes by either side may make the testimony of some witnesses entirely unnecessary, and people who have prepared themselves for the psychological rigors of testifying often experience an emotional letdown.

To compensate witnesses for their time and to make up for lost income, many states pay witnesses for each day that they spend in court. Payments range from $5 to $30 per day,[74] although some states pay nothing at all. In the case of *Demarest* v. *Manspeaker et al.* (1991)[75] the U.S. Supreme Court held that federal prisoners subpoenaed to testify are entitled to witness fees just as nonincarcerated witnesses would be.

In another move to make the job of witnesses less onerous, 39 states and the federal government have laws or guidelines requiring that witnesses be notified of scheduling changes and cancellations in criminal proceedings.[76] In 1982, Congress passed the Victim and Witness Protection Act, which required the U.S. attorney general to develop guidelines to assist victims and witnesses in meeting the demands placed upon them by the justice system. A number of **victim-assistance programs** (also called *victim/witness assistance programs*) have also taken up a call for the rights of witnesses and are working to make the courtroom experience more manageable.

victim-assistance program

An organized program that offers services to victims of crime in the areas of crisis intervention and follow-up counseling and that helps victims secure their rights under the law.

Jurors

Article III of the U.S. Constitution requires that "[t]he trial of all crimes . . . shall be by jury." States have the authority to determine the size of criminal trial juries. Most states use juries composed of 12 people and one or two alternates designated to fill in for **jurors** who are unable to continue due to accident, illness, or personal emergency. Some states allow for juries smaller than 12, and juries with as few as six members have survived Supreme Court scrutiny.[77]

Jury duty is regarded as a responsibility of citizenship. Other than juveniles and people in certain occupations, such as police personnel, physicians, members of the armed services on active duty, and emergency services workers, those who are called for jury duty must serve unless they can convince a judge that they should be excused for overriding reasons. Aliens, convicted felons, and citizens who have served on a jury within the past two years are excluded from jury service in most jurisdictions.

The names of prospective jurors are often gathered from the tax register, motor vehicle records, or voter registration rolls of a county or municipality. Minimum qualifications for jury service include adulthood, a basic command of spoken English, citizenship, "ordinary intelligence," and local residency. Jurors are also expected to possess their "natural faculties," meaning that they should be able to hear, speak, see, move, and so forth. Some jurisdictions have recently allowed physically disabled people to serve as jurors, although the nature of the evidence to be presented in a case may preclude people with certain kinds of disabilities from serving.

Ideally, the jury should be a microcosm of society, reflecting the values, rationality, and common sense of the average person. The U.S. Supreme Court has held that criminal defendants have a right to have their cases heard before a jury of their peers.[78] Peer juries are those composed of a representative cross section of the community in which the alleged crime occurred and where the trial is to be held. The idea of a peer jury stems from the Magna Carta's original guarantee of jury trials for "freemen." Freemen in England during the thirteenth century, however, were more likely to be of similar mind than is a cross section of Americans today. Hence, although the duty of the jury is to deliberate upon the evidence and, ultimately, to determine guilt or innocence, social dynamics may play just as great a role in jury verdicts as do the facts of a case.

In a 1945 case, *Thiel* v. *Southern Pacific Co.*,[79] the Supreme Court clarified the concept of a "jury of one's peers" by noting that while it is not necessary for every jury to contain representatives of every conceivable racial, ethnic, religious, gender, and economic group in the community, court officials may not systematically and intentionally exclude any juror solely because of his or her social characteristics. Learn more about what it's like to serve on a jury in a criminal trial at **Web Extra! 9–8**.

The Victim

Not all crimes have clearly identifiable victims. Some, such as murder, do not have victims who survive. Where there is an identifiable surviving victim, however, he or she is often one of the most forgotten people in the courtroom. Although the victim may have been profoundly affected by the crime itself and is often emotionally committed to the proceedings and trial outcome, he or she may not even be permitted to participate directly in the trial process. Although a powerful movement to recognize the interests of victims is in full swing in this country, it is still not unusual for crime victims to be totally unaware of the final outcome of a case which intimately concerns them.[80]

Hundreds of years ago, the situation surrounding victims was far different. During the early Middle Ages in much of Europe, victims or their survivors routinely played a central role in trial proceedings and in sentencing decisions. They testified, examined witnesses, challenged defense contentions, and pleaded with the judge or jury for justice, honor, and often revenge. Sometimes they were even expected to carry out the sentence of the court, by flogging the offender or by releasing the trapdoor used for hangings. This "golden age" of the victim ended with the consolidation of power into the hands of monarchs who declared that vengeance was theirs alone.

Today, victims, like witnesses, experience many hardships as they participate in the criminal court process. These are a few of the rigors they endure:

- Uncertainties as to their role in the criminal justice process
- A general lack of knowledge about the criminal justice system, courtroom procedure, and legal issues
- Trial delays which result in frequent travel, missed work, and wasted time
- Fear of the defendant or of retaliation from the defendant's associates
- The trauma of testifying and of cross-examination

juror

A member of a trial or grand jury, selected for jury duty and required to serve as an arbiter of the facts in a court of law. Jurors are expected to render verdicts of *guilty* or *not guilty* as to the charges brought against the accused, although they may sometimes fail to do so (as in the case of a hung jury).

> The beauty of the jury is their morality. Tap into it.
>
> —San Francisco defense attorney Tony Serra

> I do not know whether the jury is useful to those who are in litigation; but I am certain it is highly beneficial to those who decide the litigation; and I look upon it as one of the most efficacious means for the education of the people which society can employ.
>
> —Alexis de Tocqueville

The defendant's role can be crucial to the outcome of any trial, especially if he or she takes the stand. Shown here is 19-year-old Louise Woodward, the British nanny convicted of second-degree murder in the death of Matthew Eappen, an eight-month-old Massachusetts infant in her care. Woodward was originally sentenced to 15 years in prison after a jury did not believe her testimony, but Judge Hiller Zobel ordered her conviction reduced to involuntary manslaughter and resentenced her to the time she had already served in jail. She eventually returned to her home in England.

Jim Bourg, Getty Images, Inc.

> From what I see in my courtroom every day, many American juries might as well be using Ouija boards.
>
> —Judge Harold J. Rothwax

The trial process itself can make for a bitter experience. If victims take the stand, defense attorneys may test their memory, challenge their veracity, or even suggest that they were somehow responsible for their own victimization. After enduring cross-examination, some victims report feeling as though they, and not the offender, were portrayed as the criminal to the jury. The difficulties encountered by victims have been compared to a second victimization at the hands of the criminal justice system. Additional information on victims and victim's issues, including victim-assistance programs, is provided in the next chapter.

The Defendant

Generally, defendants must be present at their trials. Federal rules of criminal procedure, like state rules, require that a defendant "must be present at every stage of a trial . . . [except that a defendant who] is initially present may . . . be voluntarily absent after the trial has commenced." In *Crosby* v. *U.S.* (1993),[81] the U.S. Supreme Court held that a defendant may not be tried in absentia, even if he or she was present at the beginning of a trial, if his or her absence is due to escape or failure to appear. In a related issue, *Zafiro* v. *U.S.* (1993),[82] the justices held that, at least in federal courts, defendants charged with similar or related offenses may be tried together, even when their defenses differ substantially.

The majority of criminal defendants are poor, uneducated, and often alienated from the philosophy which undergirds the American justice system. A common view of the defendant in a criminal trial is that of a relatively powerless person at the mercy of judicial mechanisms. Some defendants are just that. However, this image is often far from the truth. Defendants, especially those who seek an active role in their own defense, choreograph many courtroom activities. Experienced defendants, notably those who are career offenders, may be well versed in courtroom demeanor.

Defendants in criminal trials have a right to represent themselves and need not retain counsel nor accept the assistance of court-appointed attorneys. Such a choice, however, may not be in their best interests. The most famous instance of self-representation in recent years was probably the 1995 trial of Long Island Rail Road commuter train shooter Colin Ferguson. Ferguson, who rejected both legal advice and in-court assistance from defense attorneys and who chose to represent himself during trial, was convicted of killing six passengers and wounding 19 others during a racially motivated shooting rampage in 1993. Some observers said that Ferguson's performance as defendant-turned-defense-attorney "distressed his court-appointed lawyer-advisers, exacerbated the pain of the victims' family members and turned the courtroom of Nassau County Judge Donald E. Belfi into a theater of the bizarre."[83] Others called it a "sham" and a "circus," but astute observers noted that it set the stage for a successful appeal. Following conviction, Ferguson reportedly asked famed defense attorney William M. Kunstler, one of his original lawyers, to file an appeal, focusing on whether Ferguson was mentally fit to represent himself and whether the judge erred in allowing him to do so.[84]

Even without self-representation, every defendant who chooses to do so can substantially influence events in the courtroom. Defendants exercise choice in (1) deciding whether to testify personally, (2) selecting and retaining counsel, (3) planning a defense strategy in coordination with their attorney, (4) deciding what information to provide to (or withhold from) the defense team, (5) deciding what plea to enter, and (6) determining whether to file an appeal if convicted.

Nevertheless, even the most active defendants suffer from a number of disadvantages. One is the tendency of others to assume that anyone on trial must be guilty. Although a person is "innocent until proven guilty," the very fact that he or she is accused of an offense casts a shadow of suspicion that may foster biases in the minds of jurors and other courtroom actors. Another disadvantage lies in the often-substantial social and cultural differences which separate the offender from the professional courtroom staff. While lawyers and judges tend to identify with upper-middle-class values and lifestyles, few offenders do. The consequences of such a gap between defendant and courtroom staff may be insidious and far-reaching.

The Press

Often overlooked, because they do not have an official role in courtroom proceedings, are spectators and the press. At any trial, both spectators and media representatives may be present in large numbers. Spectators include members of the families of both victim and defendant, friends of either side, and curious onlookers—some of whom are avocational court watchers.

Journalists, TV reporters, and other members of the press are apt to be present at "spectacular" trials (those involving some especially gruesome aspect or famous personality) and at those in which there is a great deal of community interest. The right of reporters and spectators to be present at a criminal trial is supported by the Sixth Amendment's requirement of a public trial.

Press reports at all stages of a criminal investigation and trial often create problems for the justice system. Significant pretrial publicity about a case may make it difficult to find jurors who have not already formed an opinion as to the guilt or innocence of the defendant. News

An artist's depiction of a portion of the 1995 South Carolina murder trial of Susan Smith. Federal courts and some state jurisdictions still restrict the use of cameras in the courtroom. Smith was convicted of drowning her two young children by rolling the car in which they were strapped into a lake. She was sentenced to life in prison.
Yvonne Hemsey, Getty Images, Inc.

reports from the courtroom may influence or confuse nonsequestered jurors who hear them, especially when they contain information brought to the bench but not heard by the jury.

In the 1976 case of *Nebraska Press Association* v. *Stuart*,[85] the U.S. Supreme Court ruled that trial court judges could not legitimately issue gag orders preventing the pretrial publication of information about a criminal case, as long as the defendant's right to a fair trial and an impartial jury could be ensured by traditional means.[86] These means include (1) a **change of venue**, whereby the trial is moved to another jurisdiction less likely to have been exposed to the publicity; (2) trial postponement, which would allow for memories to fade and emotions to cool; and (3) jury selection and screening to eliminate biased people from the jury pool. In 1986, the Court extended press access to preliminary hearings, which it said are "sufficiently like a trial to require public access."[87] In 1993, in the case of *Caribbean International News Corporation* v. *Puerto Rico*,[88] the Court effectively applied that requirement to territories under U.S. control.

Today, members of the press and their video, television, and still cameras are allowed into most state courtrooms. Forty-two states specifically allow cameras at most criminal trials,[89] although the majority require that permission be obtained from the judge before filming begins. Most states also impose restrictions on certain kinds of recording—of jurors or of juveniles, for example, or of conferences between an attorney and the defendant, or between an attorney and the judge—although most states allow the filming of such proceedings without audio pickup. Only a few states ban television or video cameras outright. Indiana, Maryland, Mississippi, Nebraska, and Utah all prohibit audiovisual coverage of criminal trials. The District of Columbia prohibits cameras at trials and at appellate hearings.[90]

The U.S. Supreme Court has been far less favorably disposed to television coverage than have most state courts. In 1981, a Florida defendant appealed his burglary conviction to the Supreme Court,[91] arguing that the presence of television cameras at his trial had turned the court into a circus for attorneys and made the proceedings more a sideshow than a trial. The Supreme Court, recognizing that television cameras have an untoward effect upon many people, found in favor of the defendant. In the words of the Court, "Trial courts must be especially vigilant to guard against any impairment of the defendant's right to a verdict based solely upon the evidence and the relevant law."

Cameras of all kinds have been prohibited in all federal district criminal proceedings since 1946 by Rule 53 of the Federal Rules of Criminal Procedure. In 1972, the Judicial Conference of the United States, the primary policy-making arm of the federal courts, adopted a policy opposing broadcast of civil proceedings in district courts, and that policy was incorporated into the Code of Conduct for United States Judges. Nonetheless, some district courts have local rules that allow photographs and filming during selected proceedings.

A three-year pilot project that allowed television cameras into six U.S. district courts and two appeals courts closed on December 31, 1994, when the Judicial Conference voted to end the project. Conference members expressed concerns that cameras were a distracting influence and were having a "negative impact on jurors [and] witnesses"[92] by exposing them to possible harm by revealing their identities. Hence, under current policy, television and radio coverage of federal criminal and civil proceedings at both the trial and appellate level is effectively banned.

Changes may be in the offing, however. As this book goes to press, new legislation is pending that would authorize the presiding judge of a U.S. appellate or district court to permit the photographing, electronic recording, broadcasting, or televising to the public of court proceedings over which that judge presides.[93] The bill would also permit witnesses to request to have their faces obscured and their voices disguised.

The Criminal Trial

From arrest through sentencing, the criminal justice process is carefully choreographed. Arresting officers must follow proper procedure in the gathering of evidence and in the arrest and questioning of suspects. Magistrates, prosecutors, jailers, and prison officials are all subject to their own strictures. Nowhere, however, is the criminal justice process more closely circumscribed than it is at the criminal trial.

Procedures in a modern courtroom are highly formalized. **Rules of evidence**, which govern the admissibility of evidence, and other procedural guidelines determine the course of a criminal hearing and trial. Rules of evidence are partially based upon tradition. All U.S. jurisdictions, however, have formalized rules of evidence in written form. Criminal trials at the federal level generally adhere to the requirements of the Federal Rules of Evidence.

---

change of venue

The movement of a suit or trial from one jurisdiction to another or from one location to another within the same jurisdiction. A change of venue may be made in a criminal case to ensure that the defendant receives a fair trial.

WHAT WOULD YOU DO?

The CD-ROM scenario for Chapter 9 is built around a computer database error that results in a person's arrest. The scenario is based upon an actual U.S. Supreme Court case. Work through the scenario using the CD-ROM found in the back of your textbook to learn how computer errors may affect the work of both the police and the courts.

---

rules of evidence

Rules of court that govern the admissibility of evidence at a criminal hearing and trial.

Trials are also circumscribed by informal rules and professional expectations. An important component of law school education is the teaching of rules which structure and define appropriate courtroom demeanor. In addition to statutory rules, law students are thoroughly exposed to the ethical standards of their profession as found in American Bar Association standards and other writings.

In the remainder of this chapter, we will describe the chronology of a criminal trial and will comment on some of the widely accepted rules of criminal procedure. Before we begin the description, however, it is good to keep two points in mind. One is that the primary purpose of any criminal trial is the determination of the defendant's guilt or innocence. In this regard, it is important to recognize the crucial distinction that scholars make between factual guilt and legal guilt. Factual guilt deals with the issue of whether the defendant is actually responsible for the crime of which he or she stands accused. If the defendant did it, then he or she is, in fact, guilty. Legal guilt is not as clear. Legal guilt is established only when the prosecutor presents evidence which is sufficient to convince the judge (where the judge determines the verdict) or the jury that the defendant is guilty as charged. The distinction between factual guilt and legal guilt is crucial because it points to the fact that the burden of proof rests with the prosecution, and it indicates the possibility that guilty defendants may, nonetheless, be found "not guilty."

The second point to remember is that criminal trials under our system of justice are built around an **adversarial system** and that central to this system is the advocacy model. Participating in the adversarial system are advocates for the state (the prosecution or the district attorney) and for the defendant (defense counsel, public defender, and so on). The philosophy behind the adversarial system is that the greatest number of just resolutions in criminal trials will occur when both sides are allowed to argue their cases effectively and vociferously before a fair and impartial jury. The system requires that advocates for both sides do their utmost, within the boundaries set by law and professional ethics, to protect and advance the interests of their clients (that is, the defendant and the state). The advocacy model makes clear that it is not the job of the defense attorney or the prosecution to determine the guilt of any defendant. Hence, even defense attorneys who are convinced that their client is guilty are still exhorted to offer the best possible defense and to counsel their client as effectively as possible.

The adversarial system has been criticized by some thinkers who point to fundamental differences between law and science in the way the search for truth is conducted.[94] While proponents of traditional legal procedure accept the belief that truth can best be uncovered through an adversarial process, scientists adhere to a painstaking process of research and replication to acquire knowledge. Most of us would agree that scientific advances in recent years may have made factual issues less difficult to ascertain. For example, some of the new scientific techniques in evidence analysis, such as DNA fingerprinting (discussed in detail in Chapter 17), can now unequivocally link suspects to criminal activity. Whether scientific findings should continue to serve a subservient role to the adversarial process itself is a question now being raised. The ultimate answer will probably be determined by the results the two processes are able to produce. If the adversarial model results in the acquittal of too many demonstrably guilty people because of legal "technicalities," or if the scientific approach identifies too many suspects inaccurately, either could be restricted.

We turn now to a discussion of the steps in a criminal trial. As Figure 9–1 shows, trial chronology consists of eight stages:

1. Trial initiation
2. Jury selection
3. Opening statements
4. The presentation of evidence
5. Closing arguments
6. The judge's charge to the jury
7. Jury deliberations
8. The verdict

Jury deliberations and the verdict are discussed jointly. If the defendant is found guilty, a sentence is imposed by the judge at the conclusion of the trial. Sentencing is discussed in the next chapter.

> A jury consists of 12 persons chosen to decide who has the better lawyer.
>
> —Robert Frost (1874–1963)

adversarial system

The two-sided structure under which American criminal trial courts operate that pits the prosecution against the defense. In theory, justice is done when the most effective adversary is able to convince the judge or jury that his or her perspective on the case is the correct one.

FIGURE 9-1

Stages in a criminal trial.

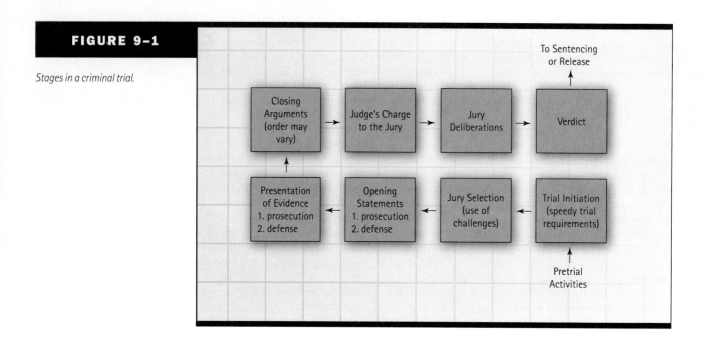

Trial Initiation: The Speedy Trial Act

As we mentioned in Chapter 8, the Sixth Amendment to the U.S. Constitution guarantees that "[i]n all criminal prosecutions, the accused shall enjoy the right to a speedy and public trial." Clogged court calendars, limited judicial resources, and general inefficiency, however, often combine to produce what appears to many to be unreasonable delays in trial initiation. The attention of the U.S. Supreme Court was brought to bear on trial delays in three precedent-setting cases: *Klopfer* v. *North Carolina* (1967),[95] *Barker* v. *Wingo* (1972),[96] and *Strunk* v. *U.S.* (1973).[97] The *Klopfer* case involved a Duke University professor and focused on civil disobedience in a protest against segregated facilities. In ruling on Klopfer's long-delayed trial, the Court asserted that the right to a speedy trial is a fundamental guarantee of the Constitution. In the *Baker* case, the Court held that Sixth Amendment guarantees to a quick trial could be illegally violated even in cases where the accused did not explicitly object to delays. In *Strunk*, it found that the denial of a speedy trial should result in the dismissal of all charges.

In 1974, against the advice of the Justice Department, the U.S. Congress passed the federal **Speedy Trial Act**.[98] The act, which was phased in gradually and became fully effective in 1980, allows for the dismissal of federal criminal charges in cases where the prosecution does not seek an indictment or information within 30 days of arrest (a 30-day extension is granted when the grand jury is not in session) or where a trial does not begin within 70 working days after indictment for defendants who plead not guilty. If a defendant is not available for trial, or if witnesses cannot be called within the 70-day limit, the period may be extended up to 180 days. Delays brought about by the defendant, through requests for a continuance or because of escape, are not counted in the specified time periods. The Speedy Trial Act has been condemned by some as shortsighted. One federal judge, for example, wrote, "The ability of the criminal justice system to operate effectively and efficiently has been severely impeded by the Speedy Trial Act. Resources are misdirected, unnecessary severances required, cases proceed to trial inadequately prepared, and in some indeterminate number of cases, indictments against guilty persons are dismissed."[99]

In an important 1988 decision, *U.S.* v. *Taylor*,[100] the U.S. Supreme Court applied the requirements of the Speedy Trial Act to the case of a drug defendant who had escaped following arrest. The Court made it clear that trial delays that derive from the willful actions of the defendant do not apply to the 70-day period. The Court also held that trial delays, even when they result from government action, do not necessarily provide grounds for dismissal if they occur "without prejudice." Delays without prejudice are those which are due to circumstances beyond the control of criminal justice agencies.

In 1993, an Indiana prisoner, William Fex, appealed a Michigan conviction on armed robbery and attempted murder charges, claiming that he had to wait 196 days after sub-

Speedy Trial Act

A 1974 federal law requiring that proceedings against a defendant in a criminal case begin within a specified period of time, such as 70 working days after indictment. Some states also have speedy trial requirements.

mitting a request to Indiana prison authorities for his Michigan trial to commence. In *Fex v. Michigan* (1993),[101] the U.S. Supreme Court ruled that "common sense compel[s] the conclusion that the 180-day period does not commence until the prisoner's disposition request has actually been delivered to the court and prosecutor of the jurisdiction that lodged the detainer against him." In Fex's case, Indiana authorities had taken 22 days to forward his request to Michigan.

However, in a 1992 case, *Doggett* v. *U.S.*,[102] the Court held that a delay of eight and a half years violated speedy trial provisions because it resulted from government negligence. In *Doggett*, the defendant was indicted on a drug charge in 1980 but left the country for Panama, where he lived until 1982, when he reentered the United States. He lived openly in the United States until 1988, when a credit check revealed him to authorities. He was arrested, tried, and convicted of federal drug charges stemming from his 1980 indictment. In overturning his conviction, the U.S. Supreme Court ruled, "[E]ven delay occasioned by the Government's negligence creates prejudice that compounds over time, and at some point, as here, becomes intolerable."[103]

The federal Speedy Trial Act is applicable only to federal courts. However, the *Klopfer* case effectively made constitutional guarantees of a speedy trial applicable to state courts. In keeping with the trend toward reduced delays, many states have since enacted their own speedy trial legislation. Most state legislation sets a limit of 90 or 120 days as a reasonable period of time for a trial to commence.

> In suits at common law, . . . the right of trial by jury shall be preserved, and no fact tried by a jury, shall be otherwise reexamined in any Court of the United States, than according to the rules of the common law.
>
> —Seventh Amendment to the U.S. Constitution

Jury Selection

As we mentioned in our discussion of the role of the jury in a criminal trial, the Sixth Amendment guarantees the right to an impartial jury. An impartial jury is not necessarily an ignorant one. In other words, potential jurors will not always be excused from service on a jury if they have some knowledge of the case which is before them.[104] However, candidates who have already formed an opinion as to the guilt or innocence of a defendant are likely to be excused.

Anyone who has ever been called as a juror knows that some prospective jurors *try* to get excused, while others who would *like* to serve are excused because they are not judged to be suitable. Prosecution and defense attorneys use challenges to ensure the impartiality of the jury which is being impaneled. Three types of challenges are recognized in criminal courts: (1) challenges to the array, (2) challenges for cause, and (3) **peremptory challenges**.

Challenges to the array signify the belief, generally by the defense attorney, that the pool from which potential jurors are to be selected is not representative of the community or is biased in some significant way. A challenge to the array is argued before the hearing judge before **jury selection** begins.

During jury selection, both prosecution and defense attorneys question potential jurors in a process known as *voir dire* examination. Jurors are expected to be unbiased and free of preconceived notions of guilt or innocence. Challenges for cause, which may arise during *voir dire* examination, make the claim that an individual juror cannot be fair or impartial. One special issue of juror objectivity has concerned the U.S. Supreme Court. It is whether jurors with philosophical opposition to the death penalty should be excluded from juries whose decisions might result in the imposition of capital punishment. In the case of *Witherspoon* v. *Illinois* (1968),[105] the Court ruled that a juror opposed to the death penalty could be excluded from such juries if it were shown that (1) the juror would automatically vote against conviction without regard to the evidence or (2) the juror's philosophical orientation would prevent an objective consideration of the evidence. The *Witherspoon* case left unresolved a number of issues, among them the concern that it is difficult to demonstrate how a juror would automatically vote, a fact which might not even be known to the juror before trial begins.

Another area of concern that the Supreme Court has addressed involves the potential that jurors could be influenced by pretrial news stories. Such concerns provided an especially tricky issue for Judge Lance Ito during the double-murder trial of O. J. Simpson as Ito supervised the process of jury selection. A similar but far less well-known case which was reviewed by the Court is that of *Mu'Min* v. *Virginia* (1991).[106] Dawud Majud Mu'Min was a Virginia inmate who was serving time for first-degree murder. While accompanying a work detail outside the prison, he committed another murder. At the ensuing trial, eight of the 12 jurors who were seated admitted that they had heard or read something about the case, although none indicated that he or she had formed an opinion in advance as to Mu'Min's guilt or innocence. Following his conviction, Mu'Min appealed to the Supreme

peremptory challenge

The right to challenge a potential juror without disclosing the reason for the challenge. Prosecutors and defense attorneys routinely use peremptory challenges to eliminate from juries individuals who, although they express no obvious bias, are thought to hold the potential to sway the jury in an undesirable direction.

jury selection

The process whereby, according to law and precedent, members of a particular trial jury are chosen.

Court, claiming that his right to a fair trial had been denied due to pretrial publicity. The Court disagreed and upheld his conviction, citing the jurors' claim not be biased.

The third kind of challenge, the peremptory challenge, allows attorneys to remove potential jurors without having to give a reason. Peremptory challenges, used by both the prosecution and the defense, are limited in number. Federal courts allow each side up to 20 peremptory challenges in capital cases and as few as three in minor criminal cases.[107] States vary as to the number of peremptory challenges they permit.

A developing field which seeks to take advantage of peremptory challenges is **scientific jury selection**. Scientific jury selection uses correlational techniques from the social sciences to gauge the likelihood that a potential juror will vote for conviction or acquittal. It makes predictions based on the economic, ethnic, and other personal and social characteristics of each member of the juror pool. Intentional jury selection techniques appeared to play a significant role in the outcome of the trial of Larry Davis. Davis, who is black, was charged with the 1986 shooting of seven white New York City police officers as they attempted to arrest the heavily armed defendant for the alleged murder of four drug dealers.[108] None of the officers died, and Davis was later apprehended. At the trial, defense attorney William Kunstler assembled a jury of ten blacks and two Hispanics. On two previous occasions, Judge Bernard Fried had dismissed previous juries before the trial could begin, saying that Kunstler was packing the panel with blacks.[109] Although many of the wounded officers testified against Davis, and no one seriously disputed the contention that Davis was the triggerman in the shooting of the officers, the jury found him not guilty. The finding prompted one of the injured policemen to claim, "It was a racist verdict."[110] Explaining the jury's decision another way, a spokesperson for the National Association for the Advancement of Colored People's Legal Defense Fund said after the trial, "The experience of blacks in the criminal justice system may make them less prone to accept the word of a police officer."[111] Interestingly, Davis was also acquitted of charges that he murdered the four drug dealers, although he was later convicted of the murder of another dealer and of weapons charges. Davis is now serving a sentence of 30 years to life in a state prison in Sullivan County, New York, and has changed his name to Adam Abdul Hakeem.[112]

Criticisms of jury selection techniques have focused on the end result of the process. Such techniques generally remove potential jurors who have any knowledge or opinions about the case to be tried. Also removed are people who have been trained in the law or in criminal justice. Anyone working for a criminal justice agency or anyone who has a family member working for such an agency or for a defense attorney will likely be dismissed through peremptory challenges on the chance that they may be biased in favor of one side or the other. Scientific jury selection techniques may result in the additional dismissal of educated or professionally successful individuals to eliminate the possibility of such individuals exercising undue control over jury deliberations. Critics charge that the end result of the jury selection process is a jury composed of people who are uneducated, uninformed, and generally inexperienced at making any type of well-considered decision. Some jurors may not understand the charges against the defendant or comprehend what is required for a finding of guilt or innocence. Likewise, some may not even possess the attention span needed to hear all the testimony that will be offered in a case. As a consequence, decisions rendered by such a jury may be based more upon emotion than upon findings of fact, critics say.

JURY SELECTION AND RACE

Juries intentionally selected so that they are racially unbalanced may soon be a thing of the past. As long ago as 1880, the U.S. Supreme Court held that "a statute barring blacks from service on grand or petit juries denied equal protection of the laws to a black man convicted of murder by an all-white jury."[113] Even so, peremptory challenges continued to tend to lead to racial imbalance. In 1965, for example, a black defendant in Alabama was convicted of rape by an all-white jury. The local prosecutor had used his peremptory challenges to exclude blacks from the jury. The case eventually reached the Supreme Court, where the conviction was upheld.[114] At that time, the Court refused to limit the practice of peremptory challenges, reasoning that to do so would place them under the same judicial scrutiny as challenges for cause.

However, in 1986, following what many claimed were widespread abuses of peremptory challenges by prosecution and defense alike, the Supreme Court was forced to overrule its earlier decision. It did so in the case of *Batson v. Kentucky*.[115] Batson, a black

---

scientific jury selection

The use of correlational techniques from the social sciences to gauge the likelihood that potential jurors will vote for conviction or acquittal.

No citizen possessing all other qualifications which are or may be prescribed by law shall be disqualified for service as grand or petit juror in any court of the United States, or of any State on account of race, color, or previous condition of servitude.

—18 U.S.C. 243

man, had been convicted of second-degree burglary and other offenses by an all-white jury. The prosecutor had used his peremptory challenges to remove all blacks from jury service at the trial. The Court agreed that the use of peremptory challenges for apparently purposeful discrimination constitutes a violation of the defendant's right to an impartial jury.

The *Batson* decision laid out the requirements which defendants must prove when seeking to establish the discriminatory use of peremptory challenges. They include the need to prove that the defendant is a member of a recognized racial group which has been intentionally excluded from the jury and the need to raise a reasonable suspicion that the prosecutor used peremptory challenges in a discriminatory manner. Justice Thurgood Marshall, writing a concurring opinion in *Batson,* presaged what was to come: "The inherent potential of peremptory challenges to destroy the jury process," he wrote, "by permitting the exclusion of jurors on racial grounds should ideally lead the Court to ban them entirely from the criminal justice system."

A few years later, in *Ford* v. *Georgia* (1991),[116] the Court moved much closer to Justice Marshall's position when it remanded a case for a new trial because the prosecutor had misused peremptory challenges. The prosecutor had used nine of the ten peremptory challenges available under Georgia law to eliminate prospective black jurors. Following his conviction on charges of kidnapping, raping, and murdering a white woman, the black defendant, James Ford, argued that the prosecutor had demonstrated a systematic racial bias in other cases as well as his own. Specifically, Ford argued that his Sixth Amendment right to an impartial jury had been violated by the prosecutor's racially based method of jury selection. His appeal to the Supreme Court claimed that "the exclusion of members of the black race in the jury when a black accused is being tried is done in order that the accused will receive excessive punishment if found guilty, or to inject racial prejudice into the fact finding process of the jury."[117] While the Court did not find a basis for such a Sixth Amendment claim, it did determine that the civil rights of the jurors themselves had been violated under the Fourteenth Amendment due to a pattern of discrimination based on race.

In another 1991 case, *Powers* v. *Ohio*[118] (see CJ Today Exhibit 9–3), the Court found in favor of a white defendant who claimed that his constitutional rights had been violated by the intentional exclusion of blacks from his jury through the use of peremptory challenges. In *Powers,* the Court held that "[a]lthough an individual juror does not have the right to sit on any particular petit jury, he or she does possess the right not to be excluded from one on account of race."

In *Edmonson* v. *Leesville Concrete Co., Inc.* (1991),[119] a civil case with significance for the criminal justice system, the Court held that peremptory challenges in *civil* suits were not acceptable if based upon race: "The importance of [*Edmonson*] lies in the Court's significant expansion of the scope of state action—the traditionally held doctrine that private attorneys are immune to constitutional requirements because they do not represent the government." Justice Anthony Kennedy, writing for the majority, said that race-based juror exclusions are forbidden in civil lawsuits because jury selection is a "unique governmental function delegated to private litigants" in a public courtroom.

In the 1992 case of *Georgia* v. *McCollum,*[120] the Court barred defendants and their attorneys from using peremptory challenges to exclude potential jurors on the basis of race. In *McCollum,* Justice Harry Blackmun, writing for the majority, said, "Be it at the hands of the state or defense, if a court allows jurors to be excluded because of group bias, it is a willing participant in a scheme that could only undermine the very foundation of our system of justice—our citizen's confidence in it." Soon thereafter, peremptory challenges based upon gender were similarly restricted (*J.E.B.* v. *Alabama,* 1994[121]), although at the time of this writing the Court has refused to ban peremptory challenges which exclude jurors because of religious or sexual orientation.[122] Also, in 1996, the Court refused to review "whether potential jurors can be stricken from a trial panel because they are too fat."[123] The case involved Luis Santiago-Martinez, a drug defendant whose lawyer objected to the prosecution's use of peremptory challenges "because the government," he said, "had used such strikes to discriminate against the handicapped, specifically the obese." The attorney, who was himself obese, claimed that thin jurors might have been unfairly biased against his arguments.

Finally, in the 1998 case of *Campbell* v. *Louisiana,*[124] the Court held that a white criminal defendant can raise equal protection and due process objections to discrimination against blacks in the selection of grand jurors. Terry Campbell, who was white, objected to an apparent pattern of discrimination in the selection of grand jury forepersons.

> Ninety-five percent of the time, the only black thing a black defendant sees in the courtroom is the judge's robe.
>
> —Delano Stewart, former Chairman, Florida chapter of the National Bar Association

A pen-and-ink drawing, circa 1867, depicting one of the first jury trials on which both blacks and whites served.

Courtesy of the Library of Congress

The foreperson of the Evangeline Parish, Louisiana, grand jury that heard second-degree murder charges against him (in the killing of another white man) was white, as had been all such forepersons for the last 16 years. The Supreme Court reasoned that "regardless of skin color, an accused suffers a significant 'injury in fact' when the grand jury's composition is tainted by racial discrimination." The court also said, "The integrity of the body's decisions depends on the integrity of the process used to select the grand jurors."

After wrangling over jury selection has run its course, the jury is sworn in, and alternates are selected. At this point, the judge will decide whether the jury is to be sequestered during the trial. Members of **sequestered juries**, like those in the O. J. Simpson criminal trial, are not permitted to have contact with the public and are often housed in a motel or hotel until completion of the trial. Anyone who attempts to contact a sequestered jury or to influence members of a nonsequestered jury may be held accountable for jury tampering. Following jury selection, the stage is set for opening arguments[125] to begin.

Opening Statements

The presentation of information to the jury begins with **opening statements** made by the prosecution and the defense. The purpose of opening statements is to advise the jury of what the attorneys intend to prove and to describe how such proof will be offered. Evidence is not offered during opening statements. Eventually, however, the jury will have to weigh the evidence presented during the trial and decide which side made the most effective arguments. When a defendant has little evidence to present, the main job of the defense attorney will be to dispute the veracity of the prosecution's version of the facts. Under such circumstances, defense attorneys may choose not to present any evidence or testimony at all, focusing instead on the burden of proof requirement facing the prosecution. Such plans will generally be made clear during opening statements. At this time, the defense attorney is also likely to stress the human qualities of the defendant and to remind jurors of the awesome significance of their task.

Lawyers for both sides are bound by a "good-faith" ethical requirement in their opening statements. Attorneys may mention only the evidence which they actually believe can and will be presented as the trial progresses. Allusions to evidence which an attorney has no intention of offering are regarded as unprofessional and have been defined by the U.S. Supreme Court as "professional misconduct."[126] When material alluded to in an opening statement cannot, for whatever reason, later be presented in court, it offers opposing counsel an opportunity to discredit the other side.

sequestered jury

A jury that is isolated from the public during the course of a trial and throughout the deliberation process.

opening statement

The initial statement of an attorney (or of a defendant representing himself or herself) made in a court of law to a judge, or to a judge and jury, describing the facts that he or she intends to present during trial to prove the case.

My experience was like being in prison.

—Tracy Hampton, who was excused from the Simpson criminal jury after four months of sequestration

CJ Today Exhibit 9-3

[Peremptory Challenges and Race]

A "peremptory challenge to a juror means that one side in a trial has been given the right to throw out a certain number of possible jurors before the trial without giving any reasons."[1]

As the definition—borrowed from a legal dictionary—indicates, attorneys were once able to remove unwanted potential jurors from a criminal case during jury-selection procedures through the use of a limited number of peremptory challenges without having to provide any reason whatsoever for the choices they made. (Challenges for cause, on the other hand, although not limited in number, require an acceptable rationale for juror removal.) The understanding of peremptory challenges was changed by the 1991 landmark U.S. Supreme Court case of *Powers* v. *Ohio*.[2] The *Powers* case dealt with a white defendant's desire to ensure a racially balanced jury. In *Powers*, the Supreme Court identified three reasons why peremptory challenges may not be issued if based on race:[3]

First, the discriminatory use of peremptory challenges causes the defendant cognizable injury, and he or she has a concrete interest in challenging the practice, because racial discrimination in jury selection casts doubt on the integrity of the judicial process and places the fairness of the criminal proceeding in doubt.

Second, the relationship between the defendant and the excluded jurors is such that . . . both have a common interest in eliminating racial discrimination from the courtroom. . . .

Third, it is unlikely that a juror dismissed because of race will possess sufficient incentive to set in motion the arduous process needed to vindicate his or her own rights.

The Court continued:

The very fact that [members of a particular race] are singled out and expressly denied . . . all right to participate in the administration of the law, as jurors, because of their color, though they are citizens, and may be in other respects fully qualified, is practically a brand upon them, affixed by the law, an assertion of their inferiority, and a stimulant to that race prejudice which is an impediment to securing to individuals of that race equal justice which the law aims to secure to all others.

In a move that surprised many court watchers, the Supreme Court, near the end of its 1991 term, extended its ban on racially motivated peremptory challenges to civil cases. In *Edmonson* v. *Leesville Concrete Co., Inc.*,[4] the Court ruled,

The harms we recognized in Powers *are not limited to the criminal sphere. A civil proceeding often implicates significant rights and interests. Civil juries, no less than their criminal counterparts, must follow the law and act as impartial fact-finders. And, as we have observed, their verdicts, no less than those of their criminal counterparts, become binding judgments of the court. Racial discrimination has no place in the courtroom, whether the proceeding is civil or criminal.*

Following *Powers* and *Edmonson*, it is clear that neither prosecuting nor civil attorneys in the future will be able to exclude minority jurors consistently unless they are able to articulate clearly credible race-neutral rationales for their actions.

Even so, recent dissenting opinions indicate that considerable sentiment may exist among the justices which could lead to the return of a broader use of peremptory challenges. In a dissenting opinion in *J.E.B.* v. *Alabama* (1994),[5] Justices Antonin Scalia, William H. Rehnquist, and Clarence Thomas wrote, "[T]he core of the Court's reasoning [banning peremptory challenges based upon gender] is that peremptory challenges on the basis of any group characteristic subject to heightened scrutiny are inconsistent with the guarantee of the Equal Protection Clause. . . . Since all groups are subject to the peremptory challenge . . . it is hard to see how any group is denied equal protection."

Read **Library Extra! 9–4** at cjtoday.com to learn more about the role of race in America's courtrooms today.

Library EXTRA!

? DISCUSSION QUESTIONS

1. Do you agree with the Court's reasoning in *Powers* that peremptory challenges based upon race should not be permitted in the selection of criminal trial juries? Explain your position.
2. Review the Bill of Rights, reprinted at the back of this book. What support do you find in the Bill of Rights for the *Powers* ruling? Be as specific as possible.

[1]Daniel Oran, *Oran's Dictionary of the Law* (St. Paul, MN: West, 1983), p. 312.

[2]*Powers* v. *Ohio*, 499 U.S. 400 (1991).

[3]Ibid.

[4]*Edmonson* v. *Leesville Concrete Co., Inc.*, 500 U.S. 614, 111 S.Ct. 2077, 114 L.Ed. 2d 660 (1991).

[5]*J.E.B.* v. *Alabama*, 114 S.Ct. 1419, 128 L.Ed. 2d 89 (1994).

The Presentation of Evidence

The crux of the criminal trial is the presentation of evidence. First the state is given the opportunity to present evidence intended to prove the defendant's guilt. After prosecutors have rested their case, the defense is afforded the opportunity to provide evidence favorable to the defendant.

CJ Today Exhibit 9-4

[Pretrial and Posttrial Motions]

A *motion* is "an oral or written request made to a court at any time before, during, or after court proceedings, asking the court to make a specified finding, decision, or order."[1] Written motions are called *petitions.* This exhibit lists the most common motions made by both sides in a criminal case before and after trial.

Motion for Discovery

A motion for discovery, filed by the defense, asks the court to allow the defendant's lawyers to view the evidence which the prosecution intends to present at trial. Physical evidence, lists of witnesses, documents, photographs, and so on, which the prosecution plans to introduce in court, are usually made available to the defense as a result of a motion for discovery.

Motion to Suppress Evidence

The defense may file a motion to suppress evidence if it learns, in the preliminary hearing or through pretrial discovery, of evidence that it believes to have been unlawfully acquired.

Motion to Dismiss Charges

A variety of circumstances may result in the filing of a motion to dismiss charges. They include (1) an opinion, by defense counsel, that the indictment or information is not sound; (2) violations of speedy trial legislation; (3) a plea bargain with the defendant, which may require testimony against codefendants; (4) the death of an important witness or the destruction or disappearance of necessary evidence; (5) the confession, by a supposed victim, that the facts in the case were fabricated; and (6) the success of a motion to suppress evidence which effectively eliminates the prosecution's case.

Motion for Continuance

This motion seeks a delay in the start of the trial. Defense motions for continuance are often based upon an inability to locate important witnesses, the illness of the defendant, or a change in defense counsel immediately prior to trial.

Motion for Change of Venue

In well-known cases, pretrial publicity may lessen the opportunity for a case to be tried before an unbiased jury. A motion for a change in venue asks that the trial be moved to some other area where prejudice against the defendant is less likely to exist.

Motion for Severance of Offenses

Defendants charged with a number of crimes may ask to be tried separately on all or some of the charges. Although consolidating charges

for trial saves time and money, some defendants may think that it is more likely to make them appear guilty.

Motion for Severance of Defendants

This request asks the court to try the accused separately from any codefendants. Motions for severance are likely to be filed when the defendant believes that the jury may be prejudiced against him or her by evidence applicable only to other defendants.

Motion to Determine Present Sanity

A lack of "present sanity," even though it may be no defense against the criminal charge, can delay trial. A person cannot be tried, sentenced, or punished while insane. If a defendant is insane at the time a trial is to begin, this motion may halt the proceedings until treatment can be arranged.

Motion for a Bill of Particulars

This motion asks the court to order the prosecutor to provide detailed information about the charges which the defendant will be facing in court. Defendants charged with a number of offenses, or with a number of counts of the same offense, may make such a motion. They may, for example, seek to learn which alleged instances of an offense will become the basis for prosecution or which specific items of contraband allegedly found in their possession are held to violate the law.

Motion for a Mistrial

A mistrial may be declared at any time, and a motion for mistrial may be made by either side. Mistrials are likely to be declared in cases in which highly prejudicial comments are made by either attorney. Defense motions for a mistrial do not provide grounds for a later claim of double jeopardy.

Motion for Arrest of Judgment

After the verdict of the jury has been announced, but before sentencing, the defendant may make a motion for arrest of judgment. With this motion, the defendant asserts that some legally acceptable reason exists as to why sentencing should not occur. Defendants who are seriously ill, who are hospitalized, or who have gone insane prior to judgment being imposed may file such a motion.

Motion for a New Trial

After a jury has returned a guilty verdict, the court may entertain a defense motion for a new trial. Acceptance of such a motion is most often based upon the discovery of new evidence which is of significant benefit to the defense and which will set aside the conviction.

[1]U.S. Department of Justice, *Dictionary of Criminal Justice Data Terminology,* 2d ed. (Washington, D.C.: U.S. Government Printing Office, 1982).

Evidence can be either direct or circumstantial. **Direct evidence**, if believed, proves a fact without requiring the judge or jury to draw inferences. For example, direct evidence may consist of the information contained in a photograph or videotape. It might also consist of testimonial evidence provided by a witness on the stand. A straightforward statement by a witness, such as "I saw him do it!" is a form of direct evidence.

Circumstantial evidence is indirect. It requires the judge or jury to make inferences and to draw conclusions. At a murder trial, for example, a person who heard gunshots and moments later saw someone run by with a smoking gun in hand might testify to those facts. Even without an eyewitness to the actual homicide, the jury might later conclude that the person seen with the gun was the one who pulled the trigger and committed the crime. Contrary to popular belief, circumstantial evidence is sufficient to produce a verdict and conviction in a criminal trial. In fact, some prosecuting attorneys claim to prefer working entirely with circumstantial evidence, weaving a tapestry of the criminal act in their arguments to the jury.

Real evidence, which may be either direct or circumstantial, consists of physical material or traces of physical activity. Weapons, tire tracks, ransom notes, and fingerprints all fall into the category of real evidence. Real, or physical, evidence is introduced in the trial by means of exhibits. Exhibits are objects or displays which, once formally accepted as evidence by the judge, may be shown to members of the jury. Documentary evidence, one type of real evidence, includes writings such as business records, journals, written confessions, and letters. Documentary evidence can extend beyond paper and ink to include data on magnetic and optical storage devices used in computer operations and video and voice recordings.

One of the most significant decisions a trial court judge makes is deciding which evidence can be presented to the jury. In making that decision, judges will examine the relevance of the evidence to the case at hand. Relevant evidence has a bearing on the facts at issue. For example, a decade or two ago, it was not unusual for a woman's sexual history to be brought out in rape trials. Under "rape shield statutes," most states today will not allow such a practice, recognizing that these details often have no bearing on the case. Rape shield statutes have been strengthened by recent U.S. Supreme Court decisions, including the 1991 case of *Michigan* v. *Lucas*.[127] In this case, the defendant, Nolan K. Lucas, had been charged with criminal sexual conduct involving his former girlfriend. Lucas had forced the woman into his apartment at knifepoint, beat her, and forced her to engage in several nonconsensual sex acts. At his trial, Lucas asked to have evidence introduced demonstrating that a prior sexual relationship had existed between the two. At the time, however, Michigan law required that a written motion to use such information had to be made within ten days following arraignment—a condition Lucas failed to meet. Lucas was convicted and was sentenced to a term of from 44 to 180 months in prison, but he appealed his conviction, claiming that the Sixth Amendment to the U.S. Constitution guaranteed him the right to confront the witnesses against him. The U.S. Supreme Court disagreed, however, and ruled that the Sixth Amendment guarantee does not necessarily extend to evidence of a prior sexual relationship between a rape victim and a criminal defendant.

In evaluating evidence, judges must also weigh the probative value of an item of evidence against its potential inflammatory or prejudicial qualities. Evidence has probative value when it is useful and relevant. Even useful evidence, however, may unduly bias a jury if it is exceptionally gruesome or is presented in such a way as to imply guilt. For example, gory photographs, especially color photographs, may be withheld from the jury's eyes. In one recent case, a new trial was ordered when 35mm slides of the crime scene were projected on a wall over the head of the defendant as he sat in the courtroom. An appellate court found the presentation to have prejudiced the jury.

On occasion, some evidence is found to have only limited admissibility. This means that the evidence can be used for a specific purpose but that it might not be accurate in other details. Photographs, for example, may be admitted as evidence for the narrow purpose of showing spatial relationships between objects under discussion, even though the photographs themselves may have been taken under conditions that did not exist (such as daylight) when the offense was committed.

When judges err in allowing the use of evidence that may have been illegally or unconstitutionally gathered, grounds may be created for a later appeal if the trial concludes with a "guilty" verdict. Even when evidence is improperly introduced at trial, however, a number of Supreme Court decisions[128] have held that there may be no grounds for an effective

evidence

Anything useful to a judge or jury in deciding the facts of a case. Evidence may take the form of witness testimony, written documents, videotapes, magnetic media, photographs, physical objects, and so on.

direct evidence

Evidence that, if believed, directly proves a fact. Eyewitness testimony and videotaped documentation account for the majority of all direct evidence heard in the criminal courtroom.

circumstantial evidence

Evidence that requires interpretation or that requires a judge or jury to reach a conclusion based upon what the evidence indicates. From the close proximity of a smoking gun to the defendant, for example, the jury might conclude that she pulled the trigger.

real evidence

Evidence consisting of physical material or traces of physical activity.

CJ Today Exhibit 9-5

["Pleading the Fifth"]

The Fifth Amendment to the U.S. Constitution is one of the best-known portions of the Bill of Rights. Movies, television shows, and crime novels have popularized the phrases "pleading the Fifth" and "taking the Fifth." As the popular media recognize, the Fifth Amendment is a powerful ally of any criminal defendant. When, upon the advice of counsel, the accused decides to invoke the Fifth Amendment right against self-incrimination, the state cannot require the defendant to testify. In the past, defendants who refused to take the stand were often denigrated by comments the prosecution made to the jury. In 1965, the U.S. Supreme Court, in the case of *Griffin* v. *California*,[1] ruled that the defendant's unwillingness to testify could not be interpreted as a sign of guilt. The Court reasoned that such interpretations forced the defendant to testify and effectively negated Fifth Amendment guarantees. Defendants who choose to testify, however, but who fail to adequately answer the questions put to them, may lawfully find themselves the target of a prosecutorial attack during cross-examination.

In 2001, in the case of *Ohio* v. *Reiner*,[2] the U.S. Supreme Court extended Fifth Amendment protections to witnesses who deny any and all guilt in association with a crime for which another person is being prosecuted. *Reiner* involved the death of a two-month-old boy named Alex Reiner. Death was caused by "shaken baby syndrome," a form of child abuse. Immediately before the child died, he had been in the care of his father, Matthew Reiner. In the preceding three hours, however, the child had been alone with a babysitter, Susan Batt. After a police investigation, Reiner was arrested and charged with involuntary manslaughter. Batt was called to testify in Reiner's trial. However, she informed the court in advance of testifying that she intended to

assert her Fifth Amendment privilege. At the state's request, the trial court granted her immunity from prosecution and ordered her to testify. Batt then testified that she had done nothing wrong. She denied any involvement in Alex's death and specifically denied shaking him. Batt also testified that she had demanded immunity only on the advice of her attorney. At the conclusion of the trial, a jury found Reiner guilty of involuntary manslaughter. His conviction was later overturned, however, by the Ohio Supreme Court, which held that Batt had no valid Fifth Amendment privilege and that the trial court's grant of immunity was therefore unlawful.[3] The court reasoned that Batt's testimony could not have incriminated her because she denied any involvement in the abuse. The wrongful grant of immunity, the court held, effectively told the jury that Batt did not cause Alex's injuries and led them to conclude that Reiner must have been responsible for his son's death.

The case made its way to the U.S. Supreme Court, which reinstated Reiner's conviction. The Court reasoned that "Batt had 'reasonable cause' to apprehend danger from her answers if questioned at [Reiner's] trial."[4] According to the Court, reasonable cause rested on the fact that (1) Batt had spent extended periods of time alone with Alex in the weeks immediately preceding his death and the discovery of his injuries, (2) Batt was with Alex within the potential time frame of the fatal trauma, and (3) the defense's theory of the case was that Batt, not Reiner, was responsible for Alex's death. "In this setting," said the Court, "it was reasonable for Batt to fear that answers to possible questions might tend to incriminate her. Batt therefore had a valid Fifth Amendment privilege against self-incrimination."

[1]*Griffin* v. *California*, 380 U.S. 609 (1965).
[2]*Ohio* v. *Reiner*, U.S. Supreme Court, No. 00-1028 (*per curiam;* March 19, 2001).
[3]*State* v. *Reiner*, 89 Ohio St. 3d 342, 358, 731 N.E.2d 662, 677 (2000).
[4]*Ohio* v. *Reiner*, U.S. Supreme Court, No. 00-1028 (*per curiam;* March 19, 2001).

appeal unless such introduction "had substantial and injurious effect or influence in determining the jury's verdict."[129] Called the *harmless error rule*, this standard does place the burden upon the prosecution to show that the jury's decision would most likely have been the same even in the absence of the inappropriate evidence. The rule is not applicable when a defendant's constitutional guarantees are violated by "structural defects in the constitution of the trial mechanism" itself[130]—as when a judge gives constitutionally improper instructions to a jury. (We'll discuss those instructions later in this chapter.)

THE TESTIMONY OF WITNESSES

testimony

Oral evidence offered by a sworn witness on the witness stand during a criminal trial.

Witness **testimony** is generally the chief means by which evidence is introduced at trial. Witnesses may include victims, police officers, the defendant, specialists in recognized fields, and others with useful information to provide. Some of these witnesses may have been present during the commission of the offense, while most will have had only a later opportunity to investigate the situation or to analyze evidence.

Before a witness will be allowed to testify to any fact, the questioning attorney must establish the person's competence. Competence to testify requires that witnesses have personal knowledge of the information they will discuss and that they understand their duty to tell the truth.

One of the defense attorney's most critical decisions is whether to put the defendant on the stand. Defendants have a Fifth Amendment right to remain silent and to refuse to testify. In the precedent-setting case of *Griffin* v. *California* (1965),[131] the U.S. Supreme Court declared that if a defendant refuses to testify, prosecutors and judges are enjoined from even commenting on this fact, although the judge should instruct the jury that such a failure cannot be held to indicate guilt. Griffin was originally arrested for the beating death of a woman whose body was found in an alley. Charged with first-degree murder, he declined to take the stand when his case came to trial. At the time of the trial, Article I, Section 13, of the California Constitution provided, in part, "[I]n any criminal case, whether the defendant testifies or not, his failure to explain or to deny by his testimony any evidence or facts in the case against him may be commented upon by the court and by counsel, and may be considered by the court or the jury." The prosecutor, remarking on the evidence in closing arguments to the jury, declared, "These things he has not seen fit to take the stand and deny or explain. . . . Essie Mae is dead, she can't tell you her side of the story. The defendant won't." The judge then instructed the jury that they might infer from the defendant's silence his inability to deny the evidence which had been presented against him. Griffin was convicted of first-degree murder, and his appeal reached the Supreme Court. The Court ruled that the Fifth Amendment, which the Fourteenth Amendment made applicable to the states, protected the defendant from any inferences of guilt based upon a failure to testify. The verdict of the trial court was voided.

Direct examination of a witness takes place when a witness is first called to the stand. If the prosecutor calls the witness, the witness is referred to as a *witness for the prosecution.* Where the direct examiner is a defense attorney, the witness is called a *witness for the defense.*

The direct examiner may ask questions which require a "yes" or "no" answer but can also employ narrative questions which allow the witness to tell a story in his or her own words. During direct examination, courts generally prohibit the use of leading questions, or those which suggest answers to the witness.[132]

Cross-examination refers to the examination of a witness by someone other than the direct examiner. Anyone who offers testimony in a criminal court has the duty to submit to cross-examination.[133] The purpose of cross-examination is to test the credibility and the memory of the witness.

Most states and the federal government restrict the scope of cross-examination to material covered during direct examination. Questions about other matters, even though they may relate to the case before the court, are not allowed. A small number of states allow the cross-examiner to raise any issue as long as the court deems it relevant. Leading questions, generally disallowed in direct examination, are regarded as the mainstay of cross-examination. Such questions allow for a concise restatement of testimony which has already been offered and serve to focus efficiently on potential problems that the cross-examiner seeks to address.

Some witnesses commit **perjury**, or make statements which they know to be untrue. Reasons for perjured testimony vary, but most witnesses who lie on the stand probably do so in an effort to help friends accused of crimes. Witnesses who perjure themselves are subject to impeachment, in which either the defense or the prosecution demonstrates that a witness has intentionally offered false testimony. For example, previous statements made by the witness may be shown to be at odds with more recent declarations. When it can be demonstrated that a witness has offered inaccurate or false testimony, the witness has been effectively impeached. Perjury is a serious offense in its own right, and dishonest witnesses may face fines or jail time.

perjury

The intentional making of a false statement as part of the testimony by a sworn witness in a judicial proceeding on a matter relevant to the case at hand.

At the conclusion of the cross-examination, the direct examiner may again question the witness. This procedure is called *redirect examination* and may be followed by a *recross-examination* and so on, until both sides are satisfied that they have exhausted fruitful lines of questioning.

CHILDREN AS WITNESSES

An area of special concern involves the use of children as witnesses in a criminal trial, especially when the children are also victims. Currently, in an effort to avoid what may be traumatizing direct confrontations between child witnesses and the accused, 37 states allow the use of videotaped testimony in criminal courtrooms, and 32 permit the use of closed-circuit television, which allows the child to testify out of the presence of the defendant. In 1988, however, in the case of *Coy* v. *Iowa,*[134] the U.S. Supreme Court ruled that a courtroom screen, used to shield child witnesses from visual confrontation with a defendant in a child sex abuse case, had violated the confrontation clause of the Constitution.

On the other hand, in the 1990 case of *Maryland* v. *Craig*,[135] the Court upheld the use of closed-circuit television to shield children who testify in criminal courts. The Court's decision was partially based upon the realization that "a significant majority of States have enacted statutes to protect child witnesses from the trauma of giving testimony in child-abuse cases . . . [which] attests to the widespread belief in the importance of such a policy." The case involved Sandra Craig, a former preschool owner and administrator in Clarksville, Maryland, who had been found guilty by a trial court of 53 counts of child abuse, assault, and perverted sexual practices, which she had allegedly performed on the children under her care. During the trial, four young children, none past the age of six, had testified against Craig while separated from her in the judge's chambers. Questioned by the district attorney, the children related stories of torture, burying alive, and sexual assault with a screwdriver.[136] Craig and the jury watched the children reply over a television monitor set up in the courtroom. Following the trial, Craig appealed, arguing that her ability to communicate with her lawyer (who had been in the judge's chambers and not in the courtroom during the questioning of the children) had been impeded and that her right to a fair trial under the Sixth Amendment to the U.S. Constitution had been denied since she was not given the opportunity to be "confronted with the witnesses" against her. In finding against Craig, Justice Sandra Day O'Connor, writing for the Court's majority, stated, "[I]f the State makes an adequate showing of necessity, the State interest in protecting child witnesses from the trauma of testifying in a child-abuse case is sufficiently important to justify the use of a special procedure that permits a child witness in such cases to testify . . . in the absence of face-to-face confrontation with the defendant."[137]

Although a face-to-face confrontation with a child victim may not be necessary in the courtroom, until 1992 the Supreme Court had been reluctant to allow into evidence descriptions of abuse and other statements made by children, even to child-care professionals, when those statements were made outside the courtroom. In *Idaho* v. *Wright* (1990),[138] the Court reasoned that such "statements [are] fraught with the dangers of unreliability which the Confrontation Clause is designed to highlight and obviate."

However, in *White* v. *Illinois* (1992),[139] the Court seemed to reverse its stance, ruling that in-court testimony provided by a medical provider and the child's baby-sitter, which repeated what the child had said to them concerning White's sexually abusive behavior, was permissible. The Court rejected White's claim that out-of-court statements should be admissible only when the witness is unavailable to testify at trial, saying instead, "A finding of unavailability of an out-of-court declarant is necessary only if the out-of-court statement was made at a prior judicial proceeding." Placing *White* within the context of generally established exceptions, the Court declared, "A statement that has been offered in a moment of excitement—without the opportunity to reflect on the consequences of one's exclamation—may justifiably carry more weight with a trier of fact than a similar statement offered in the relative calm of the courtroom. Similarly, a statement made in the course of procuring medical services, where the declarant knows that a false statement may cause misdiagnosis or mistreatment, carries special guarantees of credibility that a trier of fact may not think replicated by courtroom testimony."

THE HEARSAY RULE

One aspect of witness testimony bears special mention. **Hearsay** is anything not based upon the personal knowledge of a witness. A witness may say, for example, "John told me that Fred did it!" Such a witness becomes a hearsay declarant, and following a likely objection by counsel, the trial judge will have to decide whether the witness's statement will be allowed to stand as evidence. In most cases, the judge will instruct the jury to disregard such comments from the witness, thereby enforcing the **hearsay rule**, which prohibits the use of "secondhand evidence."

There are some exceptions to the hearsay rule that have been established by both precedent and tradition. One is the dying declaration. A dying declaration is a statement made by a person who is about to die. When heard by a second party, it may usually be repeated in court, provided that certain conditions have been met. A dying declaration is generally a valid exception to the hearsay rule when it is made by someone who knows that he or she is about to die and when the statement made relates to the cause and circumstances of the impending death.

hearsay

Something that is not based upon the personal knowledge of a witness. Witnesses who testify about something they have heard, for example, are offering hearsay by repeating information about a matter of which they have no direct knowledge.

hearsay rule

The long-standing precedent that hearsay cannot be used in American courtrooms. Rather than accepting testimony based upon hearsay, the court will ask that the person who was the original source of the hearsay information be brought in to be questioned and cross-examined. Exceptions to the hearsay rule may occur when the person with direct knowledge is dead or is otherwise unable to testify.

Spontaneous statements provide another exception to the hearsay rule. A statement is considered spontaneous when it is made in the heat of excitement before the person has time to make it up. For example, a defendant who is just regaining consciousness following a crime may make an utterance which could later be repeated in court by those who heard it.

Out-of-court statements made by a witness, especially when they were recorded in writing or by some other means, may also become exceptions to the hearsay rule. The use of such statements usually requires the witness to testify that the statements were accurate at the time they were made. This "past recollection recorded" exception to the hearsay rule is especially useful in drawn-out court proceedings which occur long after the crime. Under such circumstances, witnesses may no longer remember the details of an event. Their earlier statements to authorities, however, can be introduced into evidence as past recollection recorded.

Closing Arguments

At the conclusion of a criminal trial, both sides have the opportunity for a final narrative presentation to the jury in the form of a **closing argument**. This summation provides a review and analysis of the evidence. Its purpose is to persuade the jury to draw a conclusion favorable to the presenter. Testimony can be quoted, exhibits referred to, and attention drawn to inconsistencies in the evidence presented by the other side.

States vary as to the order of closing arguments. Nearly all allow the defense attorney to speak to the jury before the prosecution makes its final points. A few permit the prosecutor the first opportunity for summation. Some jurisdictions and the Federal Rules of Criminal Procedure[140] authorize a defense rebuttal. A rebuttal is a response to the closing argument of the other side.

Some specific issues may need to be addressed during summation. If, for example, the defendant has not taken the stand during the trial, the defense attorney's closing argument will inevitably stress that this failure to testify cannot be regarded as indicating guilt. Where the prosecution's case rests entirely upon circumstantial evidence, the defense can be expected to stress the lack of any direct proof, and the prosecutor is likely to argue that circumstantial evidence can be stronger than direct evidence, since it is not as easily affected by human error or false testimony.

closing argument

An oral summation of a case presented to a judge, or to a judge and jury, by the prosecution or by the defense in a criminal trial.

The Judge's Charge to the Jury

After closing arguments, the judge charges the jury to "retire and select one of your number as a foreman . . . and deliberate upon the evidence which has been presented until you have reached a verdict." The words of the charge vary somewhat between jurisdictions and among judges, but all judges will remind members of the jury of their duty to consider objectively only the evidence which has been presented and of the need for impartiality. Most judges also remind jury members of the statutory elements of the alleged offense, of the burden of proof which rests upon the prosecution, and of the need for the prosecution to have proved the defendant's guilt beyond a reasonable doubt before the jury can return a guilty verdict.

In their charge, many judges also provide a summary of the evidence presented, usually from notes they have taken during the trial, as a means of refreshing the jurors' memories of events. About half of all the states allow judges the freedom to express their own views as to the credibility of witnesses and the significance of evidence. Other states only permit judges to summarize the evidence in an objective and impartial manner.

Following the charge, the jury is removed from the courtroom and is permitted to begin its deliberations. In the absence of the jury, defense attorneys may choose to challenge portions of the judge's charge. If they feel that some oversight has occurred in the original charge, they may also request that the judge provide the jury with additional instructions or information. Such objections, if denied by the judge, often become the basis for appeals when a conviction is returned.

> The highest act of citizenship is jury service.
>
> —Abraham Lincoln

Jury Deliberations and the Verdict

In cases in which the evidence is either very clear or very weak, jury deliberations may be brief, lasting only a matter of hours or even minutes. Some juries, however, deliberate days or sometimes weeks, carefully weighing all the nuances of the evidence they have seen and heard. Many jurisdictions require that juries reach a unanimous **verdict**, although the U.S.

verdict

The decision of the jury in a jury trial or of a judicial officer in a nonjury trial.

The first trial of Lyle and Erik Menendez, on charges of killing their parents after a lifetime of alleged sexual abuse, resulted in hung juries. At a retrial in 1996, both were convicted of murder.

AP/Wide World Photos

Supreme Court has ruled that unanimous verdicts are not required in noncapital cases.[141] Even so, some juries are unable to agree upon any verdict. When a jury is deadlocked, it is said to be a *hung jury*. When a unanimous decision is required, juries may be deadlocked by the strong opposition of only one member to a verdict agreed upon by all the others.

In some states, judges are allowed to add a boost to nearly hung juries by recharging them under a set of instructions agreed upon by the Supreme Court in the 1896 case of *Allen* v. *U.S.*[142] The Allen Charge, as it is known in those jurisdictions, urges the jury to vigorous deliberations and suggests to obstinate jurors that their objections may be ill founded if they make no impression upon the other jurors.

PROBLEMS WITH THE JURY SYSTEM

Judge Harold J. Rothwax, a well-known critic of today's jury system, tells the tale of a rather startling 1991 case over which he presided. The case involved a murder defendant, a handsome young man who had been fired by a New York company that serviced automated teller machines (ATMs). After being fired, the defendant intentionally caused a machine in a remote area to malfunction. When two former colleagues arrived to fix it, he robbed them, stole the money inside the ATM, and shot both men repeatedly. One of the men survived long enough to identify his former coworker as the shooter. The man was arrested, and a trial ensued; but after three weeks of hearing the case the jury deadlocked. Judge Rothwax later learned that the jury had voted 11 to one to convict the defendant, but the one holdout just couldn't believe that "someone so good-looking could . . . commit such a crime."[143]

Many everyday cases, like those seen routinely by Judge Rothwax, and some highly publicized cases, like the murder trial of O. J. Simpson, which the whole world watched, have called into question the ability of the American jury system to do its job—that is, to sort through the evidence and to accurately determine the defendant's guilt or innocence. Because jurors are drawn from all walks of life, many cannot be expected to understand modern legal complexities and to appreciate all the nuances of trial court practice. Some instructions to the jury are probably poorly understood and rarely observed by even the best-intentioned jurors.[144] In highly charged cases, emotions are often difficult to separate from fact, and during deliberations, some juries are dominated by one or two members with forceful personalities. Jurors may also suffer from inattention or be unable to understand fully the testimony of expert witnesses or the significance of technical evidence.

Many such problems became evident in the trial of Raymond Buckey and his mother, Peggy McMartin Buckey, who were tried in Los Angeles in the late 1980s for allegedly molesting dozens of children at their family-run preschool.[145] The trial, which involved 65 counts of child sexual molestation and conspiracy and 61 witnesses, ran for more than three years. Many jurors were stressed to the breaking point by the length of time involved. Family relationships suffered as the trial droned on, and jurors were unable to accompany their spouses and children on vacation. Small-business owners, who were expected to continue paying salaries to employees serving as jurors, faced financial ruin and threatened their absent employees with termination. Careers were put on hold, and at least one juror had to be dismissed for becoming inattentive to testimony. The trial cost taxpayers more than $12 million but was nearly negated as jury membership and the number of alternate jurors declined due to sickness and personal problems. Ultimately, the defendants were acquitted.

Another trial in which the defendants were acquitted of the majority of the charges against them involved the state-level prosecution of the officers accused in the now-infamous Rodney King beating. Following the riots in Los Angeles and elsewhere which came on the heels of their verdict, jurors in the Rodney King trial reported being afraid for their lives. Some slept with weapons by their side, and others sent their children away to safe locations.[146] Because of the potential for harm that jurors faced in the 1993 federal trial of the same officers, U.S. District Judge John G. Davies ruled that the names of the jurors be forever kept secret. Members of the press called the secrecy order "an unprecedented infringement of the public's right of access to the justice system."[147] Similarly, in the 1993 trial of three black men charged with the beating of white truck driver Reginald Denny during the Los Angeles riots, Los Angeles Superior Court Judge John Ouderkirk ordered that the identities of the jurors not be released.

Opponents of the jury system have argued that it should be replaced by a panel of judges who would both render a verdict and impose sentence. Regardless of how well considered such a suggestion may be, such a change could not occur without modification to the Constitution's Sixth Amendment right to trial by jury.

An alternative suggestion for improving the process of trial by jury has been the call for professional jurors. Professional jurors would be paid by the government, as are judges, prosecutors, and public defenders. They would be expected to have the expertise to sit on any jury. Professional jurors would be trained to listen objectively and would be taught the kinds of decision-making skills necessary to function effectively within an adversarial context. They would hear one case after another, perhaps moving between jurisdictions in cases of highly publicized crimes.

A professional jury system offers these advantages:

1. *Dependability.* Professional jurors could be expected to report to the courtroom in a timely fashion and to be good listeners, since both would be required by the nature of the job.
2. *Knowledge.* Professional jurors would be trained in the law, would understand what a finding of guilt requires, and would know what to expect from other actors in the courtroom.
3. *Equity.* Professional jurors would understand the requirements of due process and would be less likely to be swayed by the emotional content of a case, having been schooled in the need to separate matters of fact from personal feelings.

A professional jury system would not be without difficulties. Jurors under such a system might become jaded, deciding cases out of hand as routines lead to boredom. They might categorize defendants according to whether they "fit the type" for guilt or innocence based on the jurors' previous experiences. Job requirements for professional jurors would be difficult to establish without infringing on the jurors' freedom to decide cases as they understand them. For the same reason, any evaluation of the job performance of professional jurors would be a difficult call. Finally, professional jurors might not truly be peer jurors, since their social characteristics might be skewed by education, residence, and politics.

Improving the Adjudication Process

Courts today are coming under increasing scrutiny, and well-publicized trials, such as those of Andrea Yates, O. J. Simpson, Susan Smith, and the Menendez brothers, have heightened awareness of problems with the American court system. One of today's most important issues involves reducing the number of jurisdictions by unifying courts. The current multiplicity of jurisdictions frequently leads to what many believe are avoidable

CJ Futures

[Courtrooms of the Future]

In the mid-1990s, the College of William and Mary, in conjunction with the National Center for State Courts (NCSC), unveiled Courtroom 21. At the time, it was the most technologically advanced courtroom in the United States. Courtroom 21, located in the McGlothlin Courtroom of the College of William and Mary, offers a glimpse at what American courtrooms might be like in the mid-twenty-first century. Courtroom 21 includes the following integrated capabilities:

1. *Automatic video recording of the proceedings, using ceiling-mounted cameras with voice-initiated switching.* A sophisticated voice-activation system directs cameras to tape the person speaking, to record what is said, and to tape evidence as it is being presented.

2. *Recorded and televised evidence display with optical disk storage.* Documentary or real evidence can be presented to the judge and the jury through the use of a video "presenter," which also makes a video record of the evidence as it is being presented for later use.

3. *Remote, two-way television.* The two-way television arrangement allows video and audio signals to be sent from the judge's bench to areas throughout the courtroom, including the jury box.

4. *Text-, graphics-, and video-capable jury computers.* Courtroom 21's jury box contains computers for information display and animation so that jury members can easily view documents, live or prerecorded video, and graphics, such as charts, diagrams, and pictures. Video-capable jury computers also allow for the remote appearance of witnesses—that is, for questioning witnesses who are unable or unwilling to appear in the courtroom—and for the display of crime scene reenactments via computer animation.

5. *Access to online legal research databases for the judge and for counsel on both sides.* Available databases contain an extensive selection of state and federal statutes, case law, and other precedent, allowing the judge and the attorneys to find answers to unanticipated legal questions which arise during trial.

6. *Built-in video playback facilities for out-of-court testimony.* Because an increasing number of depositions are being videotaped by attorneys in preparation for trial, Courtroom 21 has capabilities for video playback. Video depositions can be played on courtroom monitors to present expert witness testimony or to impeach a witness.

7. *Information storage with software search capabilities.* Integrated software programs provide text-searching capabilities for courtroom participants. Previously transcribed testimony and precedent-setting cases from other courts can be searched and reviewed.

8. *Concurrent (real-time) court reporter transcription.* A court reporter uses a self-contained computerized writing machine for the real-time capture of testimony in the courtroom. While the reporter writes, the computer translates strokes into English transcripts, which are immediately distributed to the judge and counsel via their personal computers. Using this technology, the judge and attorneys can mark an individual copy of the day's testimony and take it with them on their laptop computer or on a floppy disk for later review and trial preparation.

The technology demonstrated by Courtroom 21 suggests many possibilities. For one thing, attorneys could use court video equipment for filing remote motions and for other types of hearings. As one of Courtroom 21's designers puts it, "Imagine the productivity gains if lawyers no longer need to travel across a city or county for a ten-minute appearance."

Courtroom 21 designers also suggest that the innovative use of audio and video technology can preserve far more evidence and trial detail than written records, making a comprehensive review of cases easier for appellate judges. One study that has already been conducted by the NCSC showed that when a video record is available, an appellate court is less likely to reverse the original determination of the trial court. Video court records, analysts say, "might also improve the performance of attorneys and judges. By preserving matters not now apparent on a written record, such as facial expressions, voice inflections, body gestures, and the like, video records may cause trial participants to be more circumspect in their behavior than at present."

Advanced technology can also be expected to have considerable impact on the trial itself. The technology built into Courtroom 21 facilitates computer animations and crime-scene reenactments. As one of the designers of Courtroom 21 says, "*Jurassic Park* quality computer reenactment may have enormous psychological impact" on jurors.

While Courtroom 21 shows what a typical courtroom of the near future may be like, it also raises questions about the appropriate use of innovative courtroom technologies. As Fred Lederer, one of Courtroom 21's designers, points out, "Modern technology holds enormous promise for our courts. We must recognize, however, that technology's utility often depends upon how people will use it. Although we must continue to improve our courts via technology, we must be sensitive to technology's impact and work to recognize and minimize any negative consequences it might have on our system of justice."

An even more intriguing vision of courtrooms of the future is offered by the Technology of Justice Task Force in its draft report to the Pennsylvania Futures Commission. The task force predicted that by the year 2020, "there will be 'virtual courtrooms,' where appropriate, to provide hearings without the need for people to come to a physical courthouse." The task force envisions trials via teleconferencing, public Internet access to many court documents, and payments of fines by credit card.

Visit Courtroom 21 on the Web at http://www.courtroom21.net, and take a virtual tour of its facilities.

❓ DISCUSSION QUESTIONS

1. How might technologies like those discussed in this box affect the outcome of criminal trials, if at all?

2. Can you imagine types of criminal trials in which the use of high-technology courtrooms might not be appropriate? If so, what might they be?

Sources: Court Technology Bulletin, Vol. 6, No. 1 (January–February 1994); *Court Technology Bulletin,* Vol. 6, No. 2 (March–April 1994); National Center for State Courts website at http://www.ncsc.us (from which some of the material in this box is taken); Technology of Justice Task Force, "Draft Report to the Pennsylvania Futures Commission," February 21, 1997; and Courtroom 21 website at http://www.courtroom21.net, accessed October 21, 2001.

Multiculturalism and Diversity in America

[The Bilingual Courtroom]

One of the central multicultural issues facing the criminal justice system today is the need for clear communication with recent immigrants and subcultural groups that have not been fully acculturated. Many such groups hold to traditions and values that differ from those held by the majority of Americans. Such differences influence the interpretation of things seen and heard. Even more basic, however, are language differences that might prevent effective communication with criminal justice system personnel.

Techniques that law enforcement officers can use in overcoming language differences were discussed in Chapter 2. This box focuses on language differences in the courtroom and on the use of courtroom translators to facilitate effective and accurate communication. The role of the courtroom interpreter is to present neutral verbatim, or word-for-word, translations. Interpreters must provide true, accurate, and complete interpretation of the exact statements made by non-English-speaking defendants, victims, and witnesses—whether on the stand, in writing, or in court-related conferences. The Court Interpreters and Translators Association also requires, through its code of professional ethics, that translators remember their "absolute responsibility to keep all oral and written information gained completely confidential."

Although most court interpreters are actually present in the courtroom at the time of trial, telephone interpreting provides an alternative way for courts to reduce problems associated with the lack of access to qualified interpreters. Today, state court administrative offices in Florida, Idaho, New Jersey, and Washington sponsor programs through which qualified interpreters in metropolitan counties are made available to courts in rural counties by telephone.

The federal Court Interpreters Act of 1978[1] specifically provides for the use of interpreters in federal courts. It applies to both criminal and civil trials and hearings. The act reads, in part, as follows:[2]

The presiding judicial officers . . . shall utilize [an interpreter] . . . in judicial proceedings instituted by the United States, if the presiding judicial officer determines on such officer's own motion or on the motion of a party that such party (including the defendant in a criminal case), or a witness who may present testimony in such judicial proceedings—

(A) speaks only or primarily a language other than English; or

(B) suffers from a hearing impairment . . . so as to inhibit such party's comprehension of the proceedings or communication

with counsel or the presiding officer, or so as to inhibit such witness's comprehension of questions and the presentation of such testimony.

As this extract from the statute shows, translators are also required for hearing-impaired individuals who communicate primarily through American Sign Language. The act does not require that an interpreter be appointed when a party or witness suffers from a speech impairment that is not accompanied by a hearing impairment. A court is not prohibited, however, from providing assistance to such an individual if it will aid in the efficient administration of justice.

The Court Interpreters Act, because it is a federal law, does not apply to state courts. Nonetheless, most states have enacted similar legislation. A few states are starting to introduce high-standard testing for court interpreters, although most states currently conduct little or no interpreter screening. The federal government, and those states with high standards for court interpreters generally require interpreter certification. To become certified, an interpreter must pass an oral examination, such as the federal court interpreter's examination or an examination administered by a state court or by a recognized international agency, such as the United Nations.

There is growing recognition among professional court interpreters of the need for standardized interstate testing and certification programs. To meet that need, the National Center for State Courts created the Consortium for State Court Interpreter Certification. The consortium works to pool state resources for developing and administering court interpreter testing and training programs. The consortium's founding states were Minnesota, New Jersey, Oregon, and Washington, although many other states have since joined.

Because certified interpreters are not always available, even by telephone, most states have created a special category of "language-skilled interpreters." To qualify as a language-skilled interpreter, a person must demonstrate to the court's satisfaction his or her ability to interpret court proceedings from English to a designated language and from that language to English. Many states require sign language interpreters to hold a Legal Specialist Certificate, or its equivalent, from the Registry of Interpreters for the Deaf, showing that they are certified in American Sign Language. Learn more about language interpreting in the courts from the National Association of Judiciary Interpreters and Translators via **Web Extra! 9–9** at cjtoday.com.

Web EXTRA!

Sources: The National Association of Judiciary Interpreters and Translators website at http://www.najit.org, accessed October 30, 2001; Madelynn Herman and Anne Endress Skove, "State Court Rules for Language Interpreters," memorandum number IS 99.1242, National Center for State Courts, Knowledge Management Office, September 8, 1999; Madelynn Herman and Dot Bryant, "Language Interpreting in the Courts," National Center for State Courts, Web posted at http://www.ncsc.dni.us/KMO/Projects/Trends/99-00/articles/CtInterpreters.htm, accessed October 30, 2001; National Crime Prevention Council, *Building and Crossing Bridges: Refugees and Law Enforcement Working Together* (NCPC: Washington, D.C., 1994).

[1] 28 U.S.C. section 1827.

[2] Ibid., at section 1827(d)(1).

conflicts and overlaps in the handling of criminal defendants. Problems are exacerbated by the lack of any centralized judicial authority in some states which might resolve jurisdictional and procedural disputes.[148] Proponents of unification suggest the elimination of overlapping jurisdictions, the creation of special-purpose courts, and the formulation of administrative offices in order to achieve economies of scale.[149]

Court-watch citizen's groups are also rapidly growing in number. Such organizations focus on the trial court level, but they are part of a general trend toward seeking greater openness in government decision making at all levels. Court-watch groups regularly monitor court proceedings and attempt to document and often publicize inadequacies. They frequently focus on the handling of indigents, fairness in the scheduling of cases for trial, unnecessary court delays, the reduction of waiting time, the treatment of witnesses and jurors, and the adequacy of rights advisements for defendants throughout judicial proceedings.

The statistical measurement of court performance is another area which is receiving increased attention. Research has looked at the efficiency with which prosecutors schedule cases for trial, the speed with which judges resolve issues, the amount of time judges spend on the bench, and the economic and other costs to defendants, witnesses, and communities involved in the judicial process.[150] Statistical studies of this type often attempt to measure elements of court performance as diverse as sentence variation, charging accuracy, fairness in plea bargaining, evenhandedness, delays, and attitudes toward the court by lay participants.[151] Visit **Library Extra! 9–5** for more information on standards and measures in court performance.

Summary

This chapter discussed the activities and the personnel characteristic of today's criminal courts and identified the criminal trial as the hallmark of American criminal justice. The criminal trial, which owes its legacy to the development of democratic principles in Western society, builds upon an adversarial process which pits prosecution against defense. Trials have historically been viewed as peer-based fact-finding processes intended to protect the rights of the accused while disputed issues of guilt or innocence are resolved. The adversarial environment, which has served American courts for over 200 years, is now being questioned. Well-publicized trials of the last decade or two have demonstrated apparent weaknesses in the trial process. Moreover, the plethora of recent social and technological changes might at least partially supplant the role of advocacy in the fact-finding process. In many cases, new technologies which were unanticipated by the framers of our present system (such as DNA fingerprinting, which is discussed in detail in Chapter 17) hold the promise of closely linking suspects to criminal activity. Today's electronic media can rapidly and widely disseminate investigative findings. This combination of investigative technologies and readily available public information may eventually make courtroom debates about guilt or innocence obsolete. Whether the current adversarial system can continue to serve the interests of justice in an information-rich and technologically advanced society will be a central question for the twenty-first century.

Discussion Questions

1. We described participants in a criminal trial as working together to bring about a successful close to courtroom proceedings. What do you think a "successful close" might mean to the judge? To the defense attorney? To the prosecutor? To the jury? To the defendant? To the victim?
2. What are the three forms of indigent defense used throughout various regions of the United States? Why might defendants prefer private attorneys over public counsel?
3. What is an expert witness? A lay witness? What different kinds of testimony might they provide? What are some of the challenges of expert testimony?
4. What is a dying declaration? Under what circumstances might it be a valid exception to the hearsay rule? Why do most courts seem to believe that a person who is about to die is likely to tell the truth?

5. Do you think the present jury system is outmoded? Might professional jurors be more effective than the present system of peer jurors? On what do you base your opinion?

To participate in an online discussion on these topics and others, go to the Global Town Meeting electronic message board for Chapter 9 on the *Criminal Justice Today* Companion Website at cjtoday.com.

Web Quest!

Take a virtual tour of the U.S. Supreme Court building via Northwestern University's multimedia Oyez Project, available on the Web at http://oyez.nwu.edu. Once there, use the clickable "hot spots" on the QuickTime images to help you navigate the site. Take a closer look at almost any area of the building, and get a 360-degree view of almost every room by clicking on the picture (hold the mouse button down and drag it). For this assignment, make use of all of the navigational features available at the Oyez Project site to move through the Supreme Court building. As you tour the building, write down what you see, and print out the images of each room you visit. Submit these descriptions and images to your instructor if asked to do so.

To complete this Web Quest! online, go to the Web Quest! module in Chapter 9 of the *Criminal Justice Today* Companion Website at cjtoday.com.

Library Extras!

Library Extra! **9–1**   *Improving Criminal Justice Systems through Expanded Strategies and Innovative Collaborations: Report of the National Symposium on Indigent Defense* (OJP, 1999).
Library Extra! **9–2**   *National Survey of Indigent Defense Systems* (BJS, 2001).
Library Extra! **9–3**   *State-Funded Indigent Defense Services, 1999* (NIJ, 2001).
Library Extra! **9–4**   *The Convergence of Race, Ethnicity, Gender, and Class on Court Decisionmaking* (NIJ, 2000).
Library Extra! **9–5**   *Standards and Measures in Court Performance* (NIJ, 2000).

To explore these resources online, go to the Library Extras! area of the *Criminal Justice Today* Companion Website at cjtoday.com. You should also check the author's "Late Picks" online for newly released documents and updated Library Extras! You can find Late Picks at http://cjtoday.com/latepicks.htm.

Notes

1. D. Graham Burnett, "Anatomy of a Verdict: The View from a Juror's Chair," *New York Times* magazine, August 26, 2001.
2. Jill Smolowe, "The Trials of the Public Defender," *Time,* February 8, 1993, p. 46.
3. "Louisiana's Public Defender System Found Unconstitutional," *Criminal Justice Newsletter,* March 3, 1992, p. 1.
4. See, for example, Jeffrey T. Ulmer, *Social Worlds of Sentencing: Court Communities under Sentencing Guidelines* (Ithaca: State University of New York Press, 1997); and Roy B. Flemming, Peter F. Nardulli, and James Eisenstein, *The Craft of Justice: Politics and Work in Criminal Court Communities* (Philadelphia: University of Pennsylvania Press, 1993).
5. See, for example, Edward J. Clynch and David W. Neubauer, "Trial Courts as Organizations," *Law and Policy Quarterly,* Vol. 3 (1981), pp. 69–94.
6. American Bar Association, *ABA Standards for Criminal Justice,* 2d ed. (Chicago: ABA, 1980).
7. In 1940, Missouri became the first state to adopt a plan for the "merit selection" of judges based upon periodic public review.
8. National Judicial College, "About the NJC." Web posted at http://www.judges.org/about. Accessed February 2, 2000.
9. National Judicial College, "Judicial Education." Web posted at http://www.judges.org/educate. Accessed January 30, 2000.

10. Doris Marie Provine, *Judging Credentials: Nonlawyer Judges and the Politics of Professionalism* (Chicago: University of Chicago Press, 1986).

11. Town and village justices in New York State serve part-time and may or may not be lawyers; judges of all other courts must be lawyers, whether or not they serve full-time. From New York State Commission on Judicial Conduct, *2001 Annual Report*. Web posted at http://www.scjc.state.ny.us/annual.html. Accessed March 10, 2002.

12. Ibid.

13. "Defendant Claims Judge Bit Him," Associated Press wire service, June 27, 1997.

14. "Nationline: Judge—Show Legs, Pick Up Men," *USA Today*, August 16, 1996, p. 3A.

15. Aminah Franklin, "District Justice Charged with Misconduct," *Morning Call*, July 6, 1995, p. 1A.

16. Allen Baker, "Alaska Justice Steps Down," Associated Press wire service, July 3, 1997.

17. Debbie Howlett, "Impeachment Sought for 'Arrogant' Judge," *USA Today*, May 6, 1997, p. 3A.

18. Bureau of Justice Statistics, *Report to the Nation on Crime and Justice: The Data* (Washington, D.C.: U.S. Department of Justice, 1983).

19. For a discussion of the resource limitations that district attorneys face in combating corporate crime, see Michael L. Benson et al., "District Attorneys and Corporate Crime: Surveying the Prosecutorial Gatekeepers," *Criminology*, Vol. 26, No. 3 (August 1988), pp. 505–517.

20. Carol J. DeFrances and Greg W. Steadman, *Prosecutors in State Courts, 1996* (Washington, D.C.: Bureau of Justice Statistics, 1998).

21. Also known as the McDade-Murtha Law, codified at 28 U.S.C. 530A.

22. Some of the wording in this paragraph is adapted from Kim Murphy, "Prosecutors in Oregon Find 'Truth' Ruling a Real Hindrance," *Los Angeles Times*, August 5, 2001.

23. S45801, Oregon Supreme Court, August 17, 2000.

24. The ruling was based upon Disciplinary Rule 1-102 of the Oregon State Bar, which says, in part, that it is professional misconduct for a lawyer to "engage in conduct involving dishonesty, fraud, deceit or misrepresentation." The rule also prohibits a lawyer from violating this dishonesty provision through the acts of another. Also at issue was Disciplinary Rule 7-102, which prohibits a lawyer from "knowingly making a false statement of law or fact."

25. See Jeff Adler, "Ruling in Oregon Halts Federal Undercover Probes," *Washington Post*, August 9, 2001, p. A3.

26. "Nationline: Prosecutors Drop Charges against Mayor of Miami," *USA Today*, August 7, 2001, p. 3A.

27. Kenneth Culp Davis, *Discretionary Justice* (Baton Rouge: Louisiana State University Press, 1969), p. 190.

28. Barbara Borland, *The Prosecution of Felony Arrests* (Washington, D.C.: Bureau of Justice Statistics, 1983).

29. *Brady* v. *Maryland*, 373 U.S. 83 (1963).

30. *U.S.* v. *Bagley*, 473 U.S. 667 (1985).

31. *Imbler* v. *Pachtman*, 424 U.S. 409 (1976).

32. *Burns* v. *Reed*, 500 U.S. 478 (1991).

33. Ibid., complaint, p. 29.

34. Cassia Spohn, John Gruhl, and Susan Welch, "The Impact of the Ethnicity and Gender of Defendants on the Decision to Reject or Dismiss Felony Charges," *Criminology*, Vol. 25, No. 1 (1987), pp. 175–191.

35. The same is true under federal law, and in almost all of the states, of communications between defendants and members of the clergy, psychiatrists and psychologists, medical doctors, and licensed social workers in the course of psychotherapy. See, for example, *Jaffee* v. *Redmond*, 116 S.Ct. 1923 (1996).

36. Richard Carelli, "Rehnquist," Associated Press wire service, May 25, 1996.

37. *Powell* v. *Alabama*, 287 U.S. 45 (1932).

38. *Johnson* v. *Zerbst*, 304 U.S. 458 (1938).

39. *Gideon* v. *Wainwright*, 372 U.S. 335 (1963).

40. *Argersinger* v. *Hamlin*, 407 U.S. 25 (1972).

41. *In re Gault*, 387 U.S. 1 (1967).

42. Jane Fritsch, "Pataki Rethinks Promise of a Pay Raise for Lawyers to the Indigent," *New York Times*, December 24, 2001.

43. Steven K. Smith and Carol J. DeFrances, *Indigent Defense* (Washington, D.C.: Bureau of Justice Statistics, 1996).

44. Ibid.

45. Carol J. DeFrances, *State-Funded Indigent Defense Services, 1999* (Washington, D.C.: National Institute of Justice, 2001), from which the information in this paragraph is derived.

46. National Symposium on Indigent Defense, *Improving Criminal Justice Systems through Expanded Strategies and Innovative Collaborations* (Washington, D.C.: Office of Justice Programs, 2000).

47. DeFrances, *State-Funded Indigent Defense Services, 1999*.

48. Ibid.

49. Nationline: "McVeigh's Defense Cost Taxpayers $13.8 Million," *USA Today*, July 3, 2001, p. 3A.

50. Caroline Wolf Harlow, *Defense Counsel in Criminal Cases* (Washington, D.C.: Bureau of Justice Statistics, 2000); and Carol J. DeFrances and Marika F. X. Litras, *Indigent Defense Service in Large Counties, 1999* (Washington, D.C.: Bureau of Justice Statistics, 2000).

51. *Faretta* v. *California*, 422 U.S. 806 (1975).

52. Smith and DeFrances, *Indigent Defense*, pp. 2–3.

53. *Anders* v. *California*, 386 U.S. 738 (1967).

54. *People* v. *Wende*, 25 Cal. 3d 436, 600 P.2d 1071 (1979).

55. *Smith* v. *Robbins*, 528 U.S. 259 (2000).

56. *Texas* v. *Cobb*, 532 U.S. 162 (2001).

57. Details for this story come from Knight-Ridder News Service, "Lawyer's Confession Puts a Life and a Career on the Line," November 10, 2000.

58. "Killings Spotlight Lawyers' Ethics," *Fayetteville* (N.C.) *Observer-Times*, September 13, 1992, p. 11A.

59. *Nix* v. *Whiteside*, 475 U.S. 157 (1986).

60. Ibid.

61. "ABA Eases Secrecy Rules in Lawyer-Client Relationship," *USA Today*, August 7, 2001.

62. "Courtroom Killings Verdict," *USA Today*, February 15, 1993, p. 3A.

63. "How Crucial Is Courtroom Security?" *Security Management*, August 1992, p. 78.

64. "Courtroom Firebomb," *USA Today*, April 9, 1997, p. 3A.

65. President's Commission on Law Enforcement and Administration of Justice, *The Challenge of Crime in a Free Society* (Washington, D.C.: U.S. Government Printing Office, 1967), p. 129.

66. National Advisory Commission on Criminal Justice Standards and Goals, *Courts* (Washington, D.C.: U.S. Government Printing Office, 1973), Standard 9.3.

67. See, for example, Joan G. Brannon, *The Judicial System in North Carolina* (Raleigh, NC: Administrative Office of the United States Courts, 1984), p. 14.

68. *Daubert* v. *Merrell Dow Pharmaceuticals, Inc.*, 113 S.Ct. 2786 (1993).

69. Joseph L. Peterson, "Use of Forensic Evidence by the Police and Courts," *Research in Brief* (Washington, D.C.: National Institute of Justice, 1987), p. 3.
70. Ibid., p. 6.
71. Jennifer Bowles, "Simpson-Paid Experts," Associated Press wire service, August 12, 1995.
72. *California* v. *Green,* 399 U.S. 149 (1970).
73. Patrick L. McCloskey and Ronald L. Schoenberg, *Criminal Law Deskbook* (New York: Matthew Bender, 1988), Section 17, p. 123.
74. Bureau of Justice Statistics, *Report to the Nation on Crime and Justice,* 2d ed., (Washington, D.C.: BTE, 1088 p. 82. Florida Statutes (Supplement 1996), Chapter 92: "Witnesses, Records, and Documents," for example, reads, "Witnesses in all cases, civil and criminal, in all courts, now or hereafter created, and witnesses summoned before any arbitrator or master in chancery shall receive for each day's actual attendance $5 and also 6 cents per mile for actual distance traveled to and from the courts. A witness in a criminal case required to appear in a county other than the county of his or her residence and residing more than 50 miles from the location of the trial shall be entitled to per diem and travel expenses at the same rate provided for state employees."
75. *Demarest* v. *Manspeaker et al.,* 498 U.S. 184, 111 S.Ct. 599, 112 L.Ed. 2d 608 (1991).
76. BJS, *Report to the Nation on Crime and Justice,* p. 82.
77. *Williams* v. *Florida,* 399 U.S. 78, 90 S.Ct. 1893, 26 L.Ed. 2d 446 (1970).
78. *Smith* v. *Texas,* 311 U.S. 128 (1940). That right does not apply when the defendants are facing the possibility of a prison sentence less than six months in length or even when the potential aggregate sentence for multiple petty offenses exceeds six months (see *Lewis* v. *U.S.* 518 U.S. 322 [1996]).
79. *Thiel* v. *Southern Pacific Co.,* 328 U.S. 217 (1945).
80. The author was himself the victim of a felony some years ago. His car was stolen in Columbus, Ohio, and recovered a year later in Cleveland. He was informed that the person who had taken it was in custody, but he never heard what happened to him, nor could he learn where or whether a trial was to be held.
81. *Crosby* v. *U.S.,* 113 S.Ct. 748, 122 L.Ed. 2d 25 (1993).
82. *Zafiro* v. *U.S.,* 113 S.Ct. 933, 122 L.Ed. 2d 317 (1993).
83. Dale Russakoff, "N.Y. Defendant Keeps His Own Counsel; Alleged Killer of Six Commuter Train Passengers Shuns His Lawyers' Advice," *Washington Post* wire service, January 27, 1995.
84. Larry McShane, "Ferguson—Why?" Associated Press wire service, February 18, 1995.
85. *Nebraska Press Association* v. *Stuart,* 427 U.S. 539 (1976).
86. However, it is generally accepted that trial judges may issue limited gag orders aimed at trial participants.
87. *Press Enterprise Company* v. *Superior Court of California, Riverside County,* 478 U.S. 1 (1986).
88. *Caribbean International News Corporation* v. *Puerto Rico,* 508 U.S. 147 (1993).
89. Charles L. Babcock et al., "Fifty-State Survey of the Law Governing Audio-Visual Coverage of Court Proceedings." Web posted at http://www.jw.com/articles/details.cfm?articlenum=120. Accessed October 10, 2001.
90. See Radio-Television News Directors Association, "Summary of State Camera Coverage Rules." Web posted at http://www.rtnda.org/issues/cameras—summary.htm. Accessed February 9, 2000.

91. *Chandler* v. *Florida,* 499 U.S. 560 (1981).
92. Harry F. Rosenthal, "Courts-TV," Associated Press wire service, September 21, 1994. See also "Judicial Conference Rejects Cameras in Federal Courts," *Criminal Justice Newsletter,* September 15, 1994, p. 6.
93. H.R. 1281.
94. Marc G. Gertz and Edmond J. True, "Social Scientists in the Courtroom: The Frustrations of Two Expert Witnesses," in Susette M. Talarico, ed., *Courts and Criminal Justice: Emerging Issues* (Beverly Hills, CA: Sage, 1985), pp. 81–91.
95. *Klopfer* v. *North Carolina,* 386 U.S. 213 (1967).
96. *Barker* v. *Wingo,* 407 U.S. 514 (1972).
97. *Strunk* v. *U.S.,* 412 U.S. 434 (1973).
98. Speedy Trial Act, 18 U.S.C. 3161 (1974).
99. *U.S.* v. *Brainer,* 515 F. Supp. 627, 630 (D. Md. 1981).
100. *U.S.* v. *Taylor,* 487 U.S. 326, 108 S.Ct. 2413, 101 L.Ed. 2d 297 (1988).
101. *Fex* v. *Michigan,* 113 S.Ct. 1085, 122 L.Ed. 2d 406 (1993).
102. *Doggett* v. *U.S.,* 112 S.Ct. 2686 (1992).
103. William U. McCormack, "Supreme Court Cases: 1991–1992 Term," *FBI Law Enforcement Bulletin,* November 1992, pp. 28–29.
104. See, for example, the U.S. Supreme Court's decision in the case of *Murphy* v. *Florida,* 410 U.S. 525 (1973).
105. *Witherspoon* v. *Illinois,* 391 U.S. 510 (1968).
106. *Mu'Min* v. *Virginia,* 500 U.S. 415 (1991).
107. Federal Rules of Criminal Procedure, Rule 24(6).
108. "Are Juries Colorblind?" *Newsweek,* December 5, 1988, p. 94.
109. Ibid.
110. Ibid.
111. Ibid.
112. Joseph P. Fried, "Following Up: For Convicted Killer, the Battle Goes On," *New York Times* (New York Region), July 8, 2001.
113. Supreme Court majority opinion in *Powers* v. *Ohio,* 499 U.S. 400 (1991), citing *Strauder* v. *West Virginia,* 100 U.S. 303 (1880).
114. *Swain* v. *Alabama,* 380 U.S. 202 (1965).
115. *Batson* v. *Kentucky,* 476 U.S. 79, 106 S.Ct. 1712 (1986).
116. *Ford* v. *Georgia,* 498 U.S. 411 (1991), footnote 2.
117. Ibid.
118. *Powers* v. *Ohio,* 499 U.S. 400 (1991).
119. *Edmonson* v. *Leesville Concrete Co., Inc.,* 500 U.S. 614, 111 S.Ct. 2077, 114 L.Ed. 2d 660 (1991).
120. *Georgia* v. *McCollum,* 505 U.S. 42 (1992).
121. *J.E.B.* v. *Alabama,* 114 S.Ct. 1419 (1994).
122. See, for example, *Davis* v. *Minnesota,* 511 U.S. 1115 (1994).
123. Michael Kirkland, "Court Rejects Fat Jurors Case," United Press International wire service, January 8, 1996. The case was *Santiago-Martinez* v. *U.S.,* No. 95-567 (1996).
124. *Campbell* v. *Louisiana,* 523 U.S. 392 (1998).
125. Although the words *argument* and *statement* are sometimes used interchangeably in alluding to opening remarks, defense attorneys are enjoined from drawing conclusions or "arguing" to the jury at this stage in the trial. Their task, as described in the section which follows, is simply to explain to the jury how the defense will be conducted.
126. *U.S.* v. *Dinitz,* 424 U.S. 600, 612 (1976).
127. *Michigan* v. *Lucas,* 500 U.S. 145 (1991).
128. *Kotteakos* v. *U.S.,* 328 U.S. 750 (1946); *Brecht* v. *Abrahamson,* 113 S.Ct. 1710, 123 L.Ed. 2d 353 (1993); and *Arizona* v. *Fulminante,* 111 S.Ct. 1246 (1991).

129. The Court, citing *Kotteakos* v. *U.S.,* 328 U.S. 750 (1946) in *Brecht* v. *Abrahamson,* 113 S.Ct. 1710, 123 L.Ed. 2d 353 (1993).

130. *Sullivan* v. *Louisiana,* 113 S.Ct. 2078, 124 L.Ed. 2d 182 (1993).

131. *Griffin* v. *California,* 380 U.S. 609 (1965).

132. Leading questions may, in fact, be permitted for certain purposes, including refreshing a witness's memory, impeaching a hostile witness, introducing nondisputed material, and helping a witness with impaired faculties.

133. *In re Oliver,* 333 U.S. 257 (1948).

134. *Coy* v. *Iowa,* 487 U.S. 1012, 108 S.Ct. 2798 (1988).

135. *Maryland* v. *Craig,* 497 U.S. 836, 845–847 (1990).

136. "The Right to Confront Your Accuser," *Boston Globe* magazine, April 7, 1991, pp. 19, 51.

137. *Maryland* v. *Craig* (1990).

138. *Idaho* v. *Wright,* 497 U.S. 805 (1990).

139. *White* v. *Illinois,* 112 S.Ct. 736 (1992).

140. Federal Rules of Criminal Procedure, Rule 29.1.

141. See *Johnson* v. *Louisiana,* 406 U.S. 356 (1972); and *Apodaca* v. *Oregon,* 406 U.S. 404 (1972).

142. *Allen* v. *U.S.,* 164 U.S. 492 (1896).

143. Judge Harold J. Rothwax, *Guilty: The Collapse of Criminal Justice* (New York: Random House, 1996).

144. Amiram Elwork, Bruce D. Sales, and James Alfini, *Making Jury Instructions Understandable* (Charlottesville, VA: Michie, 1982).

145. "Juror Hardship Becomes Critical as McMartin Trial Enters Year Three," *Criminal Justice Newsletter,* May 15, 1989, pp. 6–7.

146. "King Jury Lives in Fear from Unpopular Verdict," *Fayetteville* (N.C.) *Observer-Times,* May 10, 1992, p. 7A.

147. "Los Angeles Trials Spark Debate over Anonymous Juries," *Criminal Justice Newsletter,* February 16, 1993, pp. 3–4.

148. Some states have centralized offices called Administrative Offices of the Courts or something similar. Such offices, however, are often primarily data-gathering agencies which have little or no authority over the day-to-day functioning of state or local courts.

149. See, for example, Larry Berkson and Susan Carbon, *Court Unification: Its History, Politics, and Implementation* (Washington, D.C.: U.S. Government Printing Office, 1978); and Thomas Henderson et al., *The Significance of Judicial Structure: The Effect of Unification on Trial Court Operators* (Alexandria, VA: Institute for Economic and Policy Studies, 1984).

150. See, for example, Thomas J. Cook et al., *Basic Issues in Court Performance* (Washington, D.C.: National Institute of Justice, 1982).

151. See, for example, Sorrel Wildhorn et al., *Indicators of Justice: Measuring the Performance of Prosecutors, Defense, and Court Agencies Involved in Felony Proceedings* (Lexington, MA: Lexington Books, 1977).

Sentencing

LEARNING OBJECTIVES

After reading this chapter, you should be able to

■ Explain the philosophy of criminal sentencing

■ Describe the five goals of contemporary criminal sentencing

■ Illustrate the difference between indeterminate and structured sentencing, and describe the different types of structured sentencing models in use today

■ Define mandatory sentencing, and explain how it came about

■ Describe truth in sentencing

■ Explain the importance of federal sentencing guidelines

■ Describe the nature and importance of the presentence investigation report

■ Describe the history of victims' rights and services, and discuss the growing role of the victim in criminal justice proceedings

■ List the four traditional sentencing options

■ Outline the arguments for and against the death penalty

POLICE LINE: DO NOT CROSS

chapter 10

[*We go between periods of romanticism and periods of idealism or realism. In sentencing, we have gone through determinate, indeterminate and back and forth in the last century. But in our time, life moves much faster. It took a hundred years from the peak of indeterminate sentencing, or the full realization of indeterminate sentencing values in the late 1870s to 1900 to wash away by the mid-1970s. . . . Is it possible that, with things happening so much faster, in just twenty or twenty-five years the cycle might once again be changing back in a different direction?*]

—Michael Tonry, Director, Institute of Criminology, Cambridge University[1]

Key Concepts

[Terms]

aggravating circumstances
capital offense
capital punishment
determinate sentencing
deterrence
equity
gain time
general deterrence
good time
incapacitation

indeterminate sentencing
just deserts
mandatory sentencing
mitigating circumstances
presentence investigation
presumptive sentencing
proportionality
rehabilitation
restoration
restorative justice

retribution
sentencing
social debt
specific deterrence
structured sentencing
truth in sentencing
victim-impact statement
voluntary/advisory sentencing guidelines
writ of *habeas corpus*

[Cases]

Booth v. *Maryland*
Coker v. *Georgia*
Coleman v. *Thompson*
Deal v. *U.S.*
Furman v. *Georgia*

Gregg v. *Georgia*
In re Kemmler
McCleskey v. *Zandt*
Mistretta v. *U.S.*
Payne v. *Tennessee*

Schlup v. *Delo*
Smith v. *U.S.*
Wilkerson v. *Utah*
Woodson v. *North Carolina*

Introduction

Hear the author discuss this chapter at **cjtoday.com**

> Putting people in prison is the single most important thing we've done [to decrease crime].
>
> —James Q. Wilson,
> Professor Emeritus,
> University of California
> at Los Angeles[i]

Some years ago, John Angus Smith traveled from Tennessee to Florida to buy cocaine. He hoped to resell it at a profit. While in Florida, he met an acquaintance, Deborah Hoag. Hoag purchased cocaine for Smith and then brought him to her motel room, where they were joined by a drug dealer. While Hoag listened, Smith and the dealer discussed Smith's MAC-10 firearm, which had been modified to operate as an automatic weapon. The MAC-10 is small, compact, and lightweight, can be equipped with a silencer, and is a favorite among criminals. A fully automatic MAC-10 can be devastating. It can fire more than 1,000 rounds per minute.[2] The dealer expressed his interest in owning a MAC-10, and Smith promised that he would discuss selling the gun if his arrangement with another potential buyer fell through.

Unfortunately for Smith, Hoag had contacts not only with narcotics traffickers but also with law enforcement officials. She was a confidential informant, and she informed the Broward County Sheriff's Office of Smith's activities. The sheriff's office responded quickly, sending an undercover officer to Hoag's motel room to pose as a pawnbroker. Several other officers were assigned to keep the motel under surveillance. Smith presented the undercover officer with a proposition: He had an automatic MAC-10 and silencer with which he might be willing to part if a good price could be arranged. The officer examined the gun and asked Smith what he wanted for it. Rather than asking for money, however, Smith asked for drugs. He was willing to trade his MAC-10, he said, for two ounces of cocaine. The officer told Smith that he was just a pawnbroker and did not distribute narcotics. Nonetheless, he indicated that he wanted the MAC-10 and would try to get the cocaine.

> Punishment, that is justice for the unjust.
>
> —Saint Augustine
> (A.D. 354–430)

The undercover officer then left, promising to return within an hour, and went to the sheriff's office to arrange for Smith's arrest. But Smith did not wait. The officers who were conducting surveillance saw him leave the motel room carrying a gun bag; he climbed into his van and drove away. When law enforcement authorities tried to stop Smith, he led them on a high-speed chase, which ended in his apprehension. Smith, it turned out, was well armed. A search of his van revealed the MAC-10, a silencer, ammunition, and a "fast-feed" mechanism. In addition, police found a MAC-11 machine gun, a loaded .45-caliber pistol, and a .22-caliber pistol with a scope and a homemade silencer. Smith also had a loaded 9-millimeter handgun in his waistband.

A grand jury for the Southern District of Florida returned an indictment charging Smith with, among other offenses, two drug-trafficking crimes: conspiracy to possess cocaine with intent to distribute and attempt to possess cocaine with intent to distribute. More importantly, the indictment alleged that Smith knowingly used the MAC-10 and its silencer during and in relation to a drug-trafficking crime. Under federal law, a defendant who so uses a firearm must be sentenced to five years' incarceration. And where, as here, the firearm is a machine gun or is fitted with a silencer, the sentence is 30 years. The jury convicted Smith on all counts.

This story is taken from the majority opinion in the 1993 U.S. Supreme Court case of *Smith* v. *U.S.*,[3] which held that "[a] criminal who trades his firearm for drugs 'uses' it within the meaning" of federal sentencing guidelines. The plain language of the statute, the high court explained, imposes no requirement that the firearm be used as a weapon. Smith's appeal of his 30-year sentence was denied.[4]

Sentencing is the imposition of a penalty upon a person convicted of a crime. Most sentencing decisions are made by judges, although in some cases, especially where a death sentence is possible, juries may be involved in a special sentencing phase of courtroom proceedings. The sentencing decision is one of the most difficult made by any judge or jury. Not only does it involve the future, and perhaps the very life, of the defendant, but society looks to sentencing to achieve a diversity of goals, some of which may not be fully compatible with one another.

This chapter examines sentencing in terms of both philosophy and practice. We will describe the goals of sentencing as well as the historical development of various sentencing models in the United States. The role of victims in contemporary sentencing practices will also be discussed. This chapter contains a detailed overview of victimization and victims' rights in general, especially as they relate to courtroom procedure and to sentencing practice. Federal sentencing guidelines and the significance of presentence investigations are also described. For a good overview of sentencing issues, visit the Sentencing Project via **Web Extra! 10–1** at cjtoday.com.

sentencing

The imposition of a criminal sanction by a judicial authority.

The Philosophy and Goals of Criminal Sentencing

Traditional sentencing options have included imprisonment, fines, probation, and—for very serious offenses—death. Limits on the range of options available to sentencing authorities are generally specified by law. Historically, those limits have shifted as understanding of crime and the goals of sentencing have changed. Sentencing philosophies, or the justifications upon which various sentencing strategies are based, are manifestly intertwined with issues of religion, morals, values, and emotions.[5] Philosophies which gained ascendancy at a particular point in history usually reflected more deeply held social values. Centuries ago, for example, it was thought that crime was due to sin and that suffering was the culprit's due. Judges were expected to be harsh. Capital punishment, torture, and painful physical penalties served this view of criminal behavior.

An emphasis on equitable punishments became prevalent around the time of the American and French Revolutions, brought about, in part, by Enlightenment philosophies. Offenders came to be seen as highly rational beings who intentionally and somewhat carefully chose their course of action. Sentencing philosophies of the period stressed the need for sanctions which outweighed the benefits to be derived from criminal activity. Severity of punishment became less important than quick and certain penalties.

Recent thinking has emphasized the need to limit offenders' potential for future harm by separating them from society. We still also believe that offenders deserve to be punished, and we have not entirely abandoned hope for their rehabilitation. Modern sentencing practices are influenced by five goals, which weave their way through widely disseminated professional and legal models, continuing public calls for sentencing reform, and everyday sentencing practice. Each goal represents a quasi-independent sentencing philosophy, since each makes distinctive assumptions about human nature and holds implications for sentencing practice. These are the five goals of contemporary sentencing:

■ Retribution
■ Incapacitation

- ■ Deterrence
- ■ Rehabilitation
- ■ Restoration

Retribution

retribution

The act of taking revenge upon a criminal perpetrator.

Retribution is a call for punishment based upon a perceived need for vengeance. Retribution is the earliest known rationale for punishment. Most early societies punished offenders whenever they could catch them. Early punishments were immediate—often without the benefit of a hearing—and they were often extreme, with little thought given to whether the punishment "fit" the crime. Death and exile, for example, were commonly imposed, even for relatively minor offenses. The Old Testament dictum of "an eye for an eye, a tooth for a tooth"—often cited as an ancient justification for retribution—was actually intended to reduce the severity of punishment for relatively minor crimes.

just deserts

A model of criminal sentencing that holds that criminal offenders deserve the punishment they receive at the hands of the law and that punishments should be appropriate to the type and severity of the crime committed.

In its modern guise, retribution corresponds to the **just deserts** model of sentencing. The just deserts model holds that offenders are responsible for their crimes. When they are convicted and punished, they are said to have gotten their "just deserts." Retribution sees punishment as deserved, justified, and even required[6] by the offender's behavior. The primary sentencing tool of the just deserts model is imprisonment, but in extreme cases capital punishment (that is, death) becomes the ultimate retribution.

Although it may be an age-old goal of criminal sentencing, retribution is still in the forefront of public thinking and political policy making today. During the 1990s, as the public-order perspective, with its emphasis on individual responsibility, gained ascendancy, public demands for retribution-based criminal punishments became loud and clear. In 1994, for example, the Mississippi legislature, encouraged by then-Governor Kirk Fordice, voted to ban prison air conditioning, remove privately owned television sets from prison cells and dormitories, and prohibit weight lifting by inmates. Governor Fordice sent a "get tough" proposal to the legislature, which was quickly dubbed the "Clint Eastwood Hang 'em High Bill"[7] and required inmates to wear striped uniforms with the word *CONVICT* stamped on the back. State Representative Mac McInnis explained the state's retribution-inspired fervor this way: "We want a prisoner to look like a prisoner, to smell like a prisoner."[8] As critics note, however, none of these measures are likely to deter crime, but that is beside the point. The goal of retribution, after all, is not deterrence, but satisfaction.[9]

Incapacitation

incapacitation

The use of imprisonment or other means to reduce the likelihood that an offender will be capable of committing future offenses.

Incapacitation, the second goal of criminal sentencing, seeks to protect innocent members of society from offenders who might do them harm if not prevented in some way. In ancient times, mutilation and amputation of the extremities were sometimes used to prevent offenders from repeating their crimes. Modern incapacitation strategies separate offenders from the community to reduce opportunities for further criminality. Incapacitation, sometimes called the "lock 'em up approach," forms the basis for the movement toward prison "warehousing" discussed in Chapter 12.

Unlike retribution, incapacitation requires only restraint—and not punishment. Hence, advocates of the incapacitation philosophy of sentencing are sometimes also active prison reformers, seeking to humanize correctional institutions. Innovations in confinement are now offering ways to achieve the goal of incapacitation without imprisonment. Electronic confinement (discussed in Chapter 11) and biomedical intervention (such as "chemical castration") may offer alternatives to imprisonment.

Deterrence

deterrence

A goal of criminal sentencing that seeks to inhibit criminal behavior through the fear of punishment.

Deterrence uses the example or threat of punishment to convince people that criminal activity is not worthwhile. Its overall goal is crime prevention. **Specific deterrence** seeks to reduce the likelihood of recidivism (repeat offenses) by convicted offenders, while **general deterrence** strives to influence the future behavior of people who have not yet been arrested and who may be tempted to turn to crime.

specific deterrence

A goal of criminal sentencing that seeks to prevent a particular offender from engaging in repeat criminality.

general deterrence

A goal of criminal sentencing that seeks to prevent others from committing crimes similar to the one for which a particular offender is being sentenced by making an example of the person sentenced.

Deterrence is one of the more "rational" goals of sentencing. It is rational because it is an easily articulated goal and because it is possible to investigate objectively the amount of punishment required to deter. Jeremy Bentham's hedonistic calculus, discussed in Chapter 3, laid the groundwork for many later calculations of just how harsh punishments need to be to deter effectively. It is generally agreed today that harsh punishments can virtually eliminate many minor forms of criminality.[10] Few traffic tickets would have to be written,

Inmates in a California prison learning how to repair computer equipment. Skills acquired through such prison programs might translate into productive, noncriminal careers. Rehabilitation is an important, but infrequently voiced, goal of modern sentencing practices.
Courtesy of Robert W. Winslow

for example, if minor driving offenses were punishable by death. A free society like our own, of course, is not willing to impose extreme punishments on petty offenders, and even harsh punishments are not demonstrably effective in reducing the incidence of serious crimes, such as murder and drug running.

Deterrence is compatible with the goal of incapacitation, since at least specific deterrence can be achieved through incapacitating offenders. Hugo Adam Bedau, however, points to significant differences between retribution and deterrence.[11] Retribution is oriented toward the past, says Bedau. It seeks to redress wrongs already committed. Deterrence, in contrast, is a strategy for the future. It aims to prevent new crimes. But as H. L. A. Hart has observed, retribution can be the means through which deterrence is achieved.[12] By serving as an example of what might happen to others, punishment may have an inhibiting effect.

Rehabilitation

Rehabilitation seeks to bring about fundamental changes in offenders and their behavior. As in the case of deterrence, the ultimate goal of rehabilitation is a reduction in the number of criminal offenses. Whereas deterrence depends upon a fear of the consequences of violating the law, rehabilitation generally works through education and psychological treatment to reduce the likelihood of future criminality.

The term *rehabilitation*, however, may actually be a misnomer for the kinds of changes that its supporters seek. Rehabilitation literally means to return a person to his or her previous condition. Hence, medical rehabilitation programs seek to restore functioning to atrophied limbs, to rejuvenate injured organs, and to mend shattered minds. In the case of criminal offenders, however, it is unlikely that restoring many to their previous state will result in anything other than a more youthful type of criminality.

In the past, rehabilitation as a sentencing strategy was applied primarily to youths. One of the first serious efforts to reform adult offenders was begun by the Pennsylvania Quakers, who developed the late-eighteenth-century penitentiary. The penitentiary, which attempted to combine enforced penance with religious instruction, proved to be something of an aberration. Within a few decades, it was firmly supplanted by a retributive approach to corrections.

It was not until the 1930s that rehabilitation achieved a primary role in the sentencing of adult offenders in the United States. At the time, the psychological theories of therapists

rehabilitation

The attempt to reform a criminal offender. Also, the state in which a reformed offender is said to be.

such as Sigmund Freud were entering popular culture. Psychology held out, as never before, the possibility of a structured approach to rehabilitation through therapeutic intervention. The rehabilitative approach of the mid-1900s became known as the *medical model of corrections* since it was built around a prescriptive approach to the treatment of offenders which provided at least the appearance of clinical predictability.

The primacy of the rehabilitative goal in sentencing fell victim to the "nothing-works" doctrine in the late 1970s. The nothing-works doctrine was based upon studies of recidivism rates which consistently showed that rehabilitation was more an ideal than a reality.[13] With as many as 90% of former convicted offenders returning to lives of crime following release from prison-based treatment programs, public sentiments in favor of incapacitation grew. Although the rehabilitation ideal has clearly suffered in the public arena, emerging evidence has begun to suggest that effective treatment programs do exist and may be growing in number.[14] See **Library Extra! 10–1** at cjtoday.com to read more about treatment programs that work.

Restoration

Victims of crime or their survivors are frequently traumatized by their experiences. Some victims are killed, and others receive lasting physical injuries. For many, the world is never the same. The victimized may live in constant fear—reduced in personal vigor and unable to form trusting relationships. **Restoration** is a sentencing goal that seeks to address this damage by making the victim and the community "whole again."

A U.S. Department of Justice report explains restoration this way: "Crime was once defined as a 'violation of the State.' This remains the case today, but we now recognize that crime is far more. It is—among other things—a violation of one person by another. While retributive justice may address the first type of violation adequately, **restorative justice** is required to effectively address the latter. . . . Thus [through restorative justice] we seek to attain a balance between the legitimate needs of the community, the . . . offender, and the victim."[15] The "healing" of all parties involves many aspects, ranging from victim-assistance initiatives to legislation supporting victims' compensation.

The Bureau of Justice Assistance has identified four guidelines for people working in restorative justice:[16]

1. *Recognize that communities are victims.* Quality-of-life crimes damage communities. If unaddressed, low-level offenses erode communal order, leading to disinvestment and neighborhood decay and creating an atmosphere in which more serious crime can flourish.

2. *Use punishment to pay back the community.* Standard sentences that involve jail, fines, and probation may punish offenders, but they do little to make restitution for the damage caused by crime. Restorative justice requires offenders to compensate neighborhoods through community service.

3. *Combine punishment with help.* By permanently altering the behavior of chronic offenders, social service programs can play an important role in crime control. Encouraging offenders to deal with their problems honors a community's ethical obligation to people who break its laws because they have lost control of their lives.

4. *Give the community a voice in shaping restorative sanctions.* The most effective restorative justice projects develop a dialogue with neighbors, seeking their input in developing appropriate community service projects. A community advisory board can offer residents an institutionalized mechanism for interacting with anyone who is planning a restorative justice–oriented project.

Sentencing options that seek to restore the victim have focused primarily on restitution payments which offenders are ordered to make, either to their victims or to a general fund, which may then go to reimburse victims for suffering, lost wages, and medical expenses. In support of these goals, the 1984 Federal Comprehensive Crime Control Act specifically requires, "If sentenced to probation, the defendant must also be ordered to pay a fine, make restitution, and/or work in community service."[17]

Texas provides one example of a statewide strategy to utilize restitution as an alternative to prison.[18] The Texas Residential Restitution Program operates community-based centers that house selected nonviolent felony offenders. Residents work at regular jobs in the community, pay for the support of their families, make restitution to their victims,

---

restoration

A goal of criminal sentencing that attempts to make the victim "whole again."

restorative justice

A sentencing model that builds upon restitution and community participation in an attempt to make the victim "whole again."

To make punishments efficacious, two things are necessary. They must never be disproportioned to the offense, and they must be certain.

—William Sims (1806–1870)

and pay for room and board. During nonworking hours, they are required to perform community service.

Vermont, which in 1995 began a new Sentencing Options Program built around the concept of reparative probation, provides a second example. According to state officials, the Vermont reparative options program, which "requires the offender to make reparations to the victim and to the community, marks the first time in the United States that the Restorative Justice model has been embraced by a state department of corrections and implemented on a statewide scale."[19] Vermont's reparative program builds upon "community reparative boards" consisting of five or six citizens from the community where the crime was committed and requires face-to-face public meetings between the offender and board representatives. Keeping in mind the program's avowed goals of "making the victim(s) whole again" and having the offender "make amends to the community," board members determine the specifics of the offender's sentence. Options include restitution, community service work, victim-offender mediation, victim-empathy programs, driver improvement courses, and the like.

Some advocates of the restoration philosophy of sentencing point out that restitution payments and work programs which benefit the victim can also have the added benefit of rehabilitating the offender. The hope is that such sentences may teach offenders personal responsibility through structured financial obligations, job requirements, and regularly scheduled payments. Learn more about restorative justice by visiting **Library Extra! 10–2** and **Web Extra! 10–2** at cjtoday.com.

> We will not punish a man because he hath offended, but that he may offend no more; nor does punishment ever look to the past, but to the future; for it is not the result of passion, but that the same thing be guarded against in time to come.
>
> —Seneca (4 B.C.–A.D. 65)

Indeterminate Sentencing

While the *philosophy* of criminal sentencing is reflected in the goals of sentencing we have just discussed, different sentencing *practices* have been linked to each goal. During most of the twentieth century, for example, the rehabilitation goal was influential. Since rehabilitation required that individual offenders' personal characteristics be closely considered in defining effective treatment strategies, judges were generally permitted wide discretion in choosing from among sentencing options. Although incapacitation is increasingly becoming the sentencing strategy of choice today, many state criminal codes still allow judges to impose fines, probation, or widely varying prison terms, all for the same offense. These sentencing practices, characterized primarily by vast judicial choice, constitute an **indeterminate sentencing** model.

Indeterminate sentencing has both a historical and a philosophical basis in the belief that convicted offenders are more likely to participate in their own rehabilitation if participation will reduce the amount of time they have to spend in prison. Inmates on good behavior will be released early, while recalcitrant inmates will remain in prison until the end of their terms. For that reason, parole generally plays a significant role in states which employ the indeterminate sentencing model.

Indeterminate sentencing relies heavily upon judges' discretion to choose among types of sanctions and to set upper and lower limits on the length of prison stays. Indeterminate sentences are typically imposed with wording such as this: "The defendant shall serve not less than five and not more than twenty-five years in the state's prison, under the supervision of the state department of correction." Judicial discretion under the indeterminate model also extends to the imposition of concurrent or consecutive sentences when the offender is convicted on more than one charge. Consecutive sentences are served one after the other, while concurrent sentences expire simultaneously.

The indeterminate model was also created to take into consideration detailed differences in degrees of guilt. Under this model, judges can weigh minute differences among cases, situations, and offenders. All of the following can be considered before sentence is passed: (1) whether the offender committed the crime out of a need for money, for the thrill it afforded, out of a desire for revenge, or for the "hell of it"; (2) how much harm the offender intended; (3) how much the victim contributed to his or her own victimization; (4) the extent of the damages inflicted; (5) the mental state of the offender; (6) the likelihood of successful rehabilitation; and (7) the degree of the offender's cooperation with authorities.

Under the indeterminate sentencing model, the inmate's behavior (while incarcerated) is the primary determinant of the amount of time served. State parole boards wield great discretion under the model, acting as the final arbiters of the actual sentence served.

indeterminate sentencing

A model of criminal punishment that encourages rehabilitation via the use of general and relatively unspecific sentences (such as a term of imprisonment of from one to ten years).

A few states employ a partially indeterminate sentencing model. They allow judges to specify only the maximum amount of time to be served. Some minimum is generally implied by law but is not under the control of the sentencing authority. General practice is to set one year as a minimum for all felonies, although a few jurisdictions assume no minimum time at all, making offenders eligible for immediate parole.

Critiques of Indeterminate Sentencing

Indeterminate sentencing is still the rule in many jurisdictions, including Georgia, Hawaii, Iowa, Kentucky, Massachusetts, Michigan, Nevada, New York, North Dakota, Oklahoma, Rhode Island, South Carolina, South Dakota, Texas, Utah, Vermont, West Virginia, and Wyoming.[20] By the 1970s, however, the model had come under fire for contributing to inequality in sentencing. Critics claimed that the indeterminate model allowed judges' personalities and personal philosophies to produce a wide range of sentencing practices from very lenient to very strict. The indeterminate model was also criticized for perpetuating a system under which offenders might be sentenced, at least by some judges, more on the basis of social characteristics, such as race, gender, and social class, rather than culpability.

Because of the personal nature of judicial decisions under the indeterminate model, offenders often depend upon the advice and ploys of their attorneys to appear before a judge who is thought to be a good sentencing risk. Requests for delays are a commonly used defense strategy in indeterminate sentencing states, where they are used in attempts to manipulate the selection of the judge involved in the sentencing decision.

Another charge leveled against indeterminate sentencing is that it tends to produce "dishonesty" in sentencing. Because of sentence cutbacks for good behavior and other reductions available to inmates through involvement in work and study programs, time served in prison is generally far less than sentences would seem to indicate. An inmate sentenced to five to ten years, for example, might actually be released in a couple of years after all **gain time**, **good time**, and other special allowances have been calculated. (Some of the same charges can be leveled against determinate sentencing schemes under which correctional officials can administratively reduce the time served by an inmate.) A recent survey by the Bureau of Justice Statistics found that even violent offenders released from state prisons during the study period served, on average, only 51% of the sentences they originally received.[21] Nonviolent offenders served even smaller portions of their sentences. Table 10–1 shows the percentage of an imposed sentence that an offender sentenced to state prison in 1996 could expect to serve.

To ensure long prison terms in indeterminate jurisdictions, some court officials have gone to extremes. In 1994, for example, a judge in Oklahoma sentenced convicted child molester Charles Scott Robinson, 30, to 30,000 years in prison.[22] Judge Dan Owens, complying with the jury's efforts to ensure that Robinson would spend the rest of his life behind bars, sentenced him to serve six consecutive 5,000-year sentences. Robinson had 14 previous felony convictions.

gain time

The amount of time deducted from time to be served in prison on a given sentence for participation in special projects or programs.

good time

The amount of time deducted from time to be served in prison on a given sentence for good behavior.

TABLE 10–1	PERCENTAGE OF SENTENCE TO BE SERVED—BY NEW COURT COMMITMENTS TO STATE PRISON	
Offense Type		**Percentage**
Violent		51
Property		46
Drug		46
Public-order		49
Average for all felonies		49

Source: Paula M. Ditton and Doris James Wilson, *Truth in Sentencing in State Prisons* (Washington, D.C.: Bureau of Justice Statistics, 1999).

Structured Sentencing

Until the 1970s, all 50 states used some form of indeterminate (or partially indeterminate) sentencing. Eventually, however, calls for equity and proportionality in sentencing, heightened by claims of racial disparity in the sentencing practices of some judges,[23] led many states to move toward closer control over their sentencing systems.

Critics of the indeterminate model called for the recognition of three fundamental sentencing principles: **proportionality**, **equity**, and **social debt**. Proportionality refers to the belief that the severity of sanctions should bear a direct relationship to the seriousness of the crime committed. Equity is based upon a concern with social equality and means that similar crimes should be punished with the same degree of severity, regardless of the general social or personal characteristics of offenders. According to the principle of equity, for example, two bank robbers in different parts of the country, who use the same techniques and weapons, with the same degree of implied threat, should receive roughly the same kind of sentence even though they are tried under separate circumstances. The equity principle needs to be balanced, however, against the notion of social debt. In the case of the bank robbers, the offender who has a prior criminal record can be said to have a higher level of social debt than the one-time robber, where all else is equal. Greater social debt, of course, would suggest a heightened severity of punishment or a greater need for treatment.

Beginning in the 1970s, a number of states moved to address these concerns by developing a different model of sentencing, known as **structured sentencing**. One form of structured sentencing, called **determinate sentencing**, requires that a convicted offender be sentenced to a fixed term that may be reduced by good time or earned time. Determinate sentencing states eliminated the use of parole and created explicit standards to specify the amount of punishment appropriate for a given offense. Determinate sentencing practices also specify an anticipated release date for each sentenced offender.

In a 1996 report that traced the historical development of determinate sentencing, the National Council on Crime and Delinquency (NCCD) observed that "the term 'determinate sentencing' is generally used to refer to the sentencing reforms of the late 1970s. In those reforms, the legislatures of California, Illinois, Indiana, and Maine abolished the parole release decision and replaced the indeterminate penalty structure with a fixed (flat) sentence that could be reduced by a significant good-time provision. The only state that has adopted a true determinate sentencing system since 1980 is Arizona, which enacted a 'truth in sentencing law' on January 1, 1994. These five states have retained their determinate sentencing models, although no other states have adopted such a structured sentencing scheme."[24] The NCCD report continues, "In three of the states (California, Illinois, and Indiana), the legislators provided presumptive ranges of confinement. But those in Illinois and Indiana were so wide that they provided the court with extensive discretion on sentence length. For many offenses, there was no presumptive lead as to whether the sentence should be for, or against, incarceration. Thus, courts were left with extensive discretion in deciding both whether to incarcerate and the length of incarceration. It is arguable that the discretion attacked in these reforms was mainly that of parole boards and that the discretion lost by parole boards was largely shifted to the courts or to the prosecutors who control the charging function."[25]

In response to the then-growing determinate sentencing movement, a few states developed **voluntary/advisory sentencing guidelines**. Such guidelines consist of recommended sentencing policies that are not required by law. They are usually based upon past sentencing practices and serve as guides to judges. Voluntary/advisory sentencing guidelines may build upon either determinate or indeterminate sentencing structures. Florida, Maryland, Massachusetts, Michigan, Rhode Island, Utah, and Wisconsin all experimented with voluntary/advisory guidelines during the 1980s. Voluntary/advisory guidelines constitute a second form of structured sentencing.

A third model of structured sentencing employs what NCCD calls "commission-based **presumptive sentencing** guidelines." Presumptive sentencing schemes became common in the 1980s as states began to experiment with sentencing guidelines developed by sentencing commissions. These models differed from both determinate and voluntary/advisory guidelines in three respects. First, presumptive sentencing guidelines were not developed by the legislature but by a sentencing commission that often represented a diverse array of criminal justice and sometimes private interests. Second, presumptive sentencing guidelines were explicit and highly structured, typically relying on a quantitative scoring instrument to classify the offense for which a person was to be

Margin glossary

proportionality

A sentencing principle that holds that the severity of sanctions should bear a direct relationship to the seriousness of the crime committed.

equity

A sentencing principle, based upon concerns with social equality, that holds that similar crimes should be punished with the same degree of severity, regardless of the social or personal characteristics of the offenders.

social debt

A sentencing principle that holds that an offender's criminal history should objectively be taken into account in sentencing decisions.

structured sentencing

A model of criminal punishment that includes determinate and commission-created presumptive sentencing schemes, as well as voluntary/advisory sentencing guidelines.

determinate sentencing

A model of criminal punishment in which an offender is given a fixed term that may be reduced by good time or gain time. Under the model, for example, all offenders convicted of the same degree of burglary would be sentenced to the same length of time behind bars.

voluntary/advisory sentencing guidelines

Recommended sentencing policies that are not required by law.

presumptive sentencing

A model of criminal punishment that meets the following conditions: (1) The appropriate sentence for an offender convicted of a specific charge is presumed to fall within a range of sentences authorized by sentencing guidelines that are adopted by a legislatively created sentencing body, usually a sentencing commission. (2) Sentencing judges are expected to sentence within the range or to provide written justification for departure. (3) The guidelines provide for some review, usually appellate, of the departure.

sentenced. Third, the guidelines were not voluntary/advisory in that judges had to adhere to the sentencing system or provide a written rationale for departures. NCCD observes, "As in the move to determinate sentencing and voluntary/advisory guidelines, the driving forces stimulating presumptive sentencing guidelines were issues of fairness (including disparity, certainty, and proportionality) and prison crowding. These concerns provided the impetus for states to adopt guidelines, replace indeterminate sentencing with determinate sentencing, and abolish or curtail discretionary parole release."[26]

The first four states to adopt presumptive sentencing guideline systems were Minnesota (1980), Pennsylvania (1982), Washington (1983), and Florida (1983). The Minnesota model in particular, with its focus on controlling prison population growth, has often been cited as a successful example of controlling disparity and rising corrections costs through sentencing guidelines. The American Bar Association (ABA) has endorsed commission-based sentencing guidelines through its Criminal Justice Standards Committee's Sentencing Alternatives and Procedures (adopted by the ABA House of Delegates). In making such an endorsement, the Standards Committee relied heavily upon the system of presumptive sentencing pioneered in Minnesota.

The federal government and 16 states have now established commission-based sentencing guidelines. Ten of the 16 states use presumptive sentencing guidelines. The remaining six have voluntary/advisory guidelines. As a consequence, sentencing guidelines authored by legislatively created sentencing commissions are now the most popular form of structured sentencing. Learn more about sentencing reform via **Library Extra! 10–3** at cjtoday.com.

Guideline jurisdictions, which specify a presumptive sentence for a given offense, generally allow for "aggravating" or "mitigating" circumstances—indicating greater or lesser degrees of culpability—which judges can take into consideration in imposing a sentence somewhat at variance from the presumptive term. **Aggravating circumstances** are those which appear to call for a tougher sentence and may include especially heinous behavior, cruelty, injury to more than one person, and so on. In death penalty cases, however, the U.S. Supreme Court has held that aggravating factors must "provide specific and detailed guidance and make rationally reviewable the death sentencing process. . . . In order to decide whether a particular aggravating circumstance meets these requirements, a federal court must determine whether the statutory language defining the circumstance is itself too vague to guide the sentencer."[27]

Mitigating circumstances, or those which indicate that a lesser sentence is called for, are generally similar to legal defenses, although in this case they only reduce criminal responsibility, not eliminate it. Mitigating circumstances include such things as cooperation with the investigating authority, surrender, good character, and so on. Common aggravating and mitigating circumstances are listed in CJ Today Exhibit 10–1.

---

aggravating circumstances

Circumstances relating to the commission of a crime which cause its gravity to be greater than that of the average instance of the given type of offense.

mitigating circumstances

Circumstances relating to the commission of a crime which may be considered to reduce the blameworthiness of the defendant.

Rapper Eminem (left), whose real name is Marshall Mathers, standing before Judge Denise Langford Morris in Oakland County Circuit Court in Pontiac, Michigan. Mathers was arrested in 2000 and charged with carrying a concealed weapon. He was found guilty, sentenced to two years' probation, fined $2,500, and ordered to pay court costs of $5,000. Under the terms of his probation, Mathers is banned from possessing a firearm, cannot use drugs or become inebriated, and cannot travel abroad without the court's permission. If he violates those terms, Mathers could be sent to prison for as long as five years.

Newsmakers, Getty Images, Inc.

Critiques of Structured Sentencing

Structured sentencing models, which have generally sought to address the shortcomings of indeterminate sentencing by curtailing judicial discretion in sentencing, are not without their critics. Detractors charge that structured sentencing is overly simplistic, based upon a primitive concept of culpability, and incapable of offering hope for rehabilitation and change. For one thing, they say, structured sentencing has built-in limitations which render it far less able to judge the blameworthiness of individual offenders. Legislatures and sentencing commissions, say critics, simply cannot anticipate all the differences that individual cases can present. Aggravating and mitigating factors, while intended to cover most circumstances, will inevitably shortchange some defendants who don't fall neatly into the categories they provide.

A second critique of structured sentencing is that while it reduces judicial discretion substantially, it does nothing to hamper the huge discretionary decision-making power of prosecutors.[28] In fact, federal sentencing reformers, who have adopted a structured sentencing model, have specifically decided not to modify the discretionary power of prosecutors, citing the large number of cases which are resolved through plea bargaining. Such a shift in discretionary authority, away from judges and into the hands of prosecutors, say critics, is misplaced.

Another criticism of structured sentencing questions its fundamental purpose. Advocates of structured sentencing inevitably cite greater equity in sentencing as the primary benefits of the model. Reduced to its essence, this means that "those who commit the same crime get the same time." Sentencing reformers have thus couched the drive toward structured sentencing in progressive terms. Others, however, have pointed out that the philosophical underpinnings of the movement may be quite different. Albert W. Alschuler, for example, suggests that structured sentencing is a regressive social policy which derives from American weariness with considering offenders as individuals.[29] Describing

> The root of revenge is in the weakness of the Soul; the most abject and timorous are the most addicted to it.
>
> —Akhenaton (circa 1375 B.C.)

CJ Today Exhibit 10–1

[Aggravating and Mitigating Circumstances]

Listed here are typical aggravating and mitigating circumstances which judges may consider in arriving at sentencing decisions in presumptive-sentencing jurisdictions.

Aggravating Circumstances

- The defendant induced others to participate in the commission of the offense.
- The offense was especially heinous, atrocious, or cruel.
- The defendant was armed with or used a deadly weapon during the crime.
- The defendant committed the offense to avoid or prevent a lawful arrest or to escape from custody.
- The offense was committed for hire.
- The offense was committed against a current or former law enforcement or correctional officer while engaged in the performance of official duties or because of the past exercise of official duties.
- The defendant took advantage of a position of trust or confidence to commit the offense.

Mitigating Circumstances

- The defendant has no record of criminal convictions punishable by more than 60 days of imprisonment.
- The defendant has made substantial or full restitution.
- The defendant has been a person of good character or has had a good reputation in the community.
- The defendant aided in the apprehension of another felon or testified truthfully on behalf of the prosecution.
- The defendant acted under strong provocation, or the victim was a voluntary participant in the criminal activity or otherwise consented to it.
- The offense was committed under duress, coercion, threat, or compulsion that was insufficient to constitute a defense but that significantly reduced the defendant's culpability.
- The defendant was suffering from a mental or physical condition that was insufficient to constitute a defense but that significantly reduced the defendant's culpability for the offense.

❓ DISCUSSION QUESTIONS

1. What aggravating circumstances, if any, might you add to the list in this box? Why?
2. What mitigating circumstances, if any, might you add to the list in this box? Why?

this kind of thinking, Alschuler writes, "Don't tell us that a robber was retarded. We don't care about his problems. We don't know what to *do* about his problems, and we are no longer interested in listening to a criminal's sob stories. The most important thing about this robber is simply that he *is* a robber."[30] A different line of thought is proposed by Christopher T. Link and Neal Shover, who found in a study of state-level economic, political, and demographic data that structured sentencing may ultimately be the result of declining economic conditions and increasing fiscal strain on state governments rather than any particular set of ideals.[31]

A final critique of structured sentencing centers on its alleged inability to promote effective rehabilitation. Under indeterminate sentencing schemes, offenders have the opportunity to act responsibly and thus to participate in their own rehabilitation.[32] Lack of responsible behavior results in denial of parole and extension of the sentence. Structured sentencing schemes, by virtue of dramatic reductions in good-time allowances and parole opportunities, leave little incentive for offenders to participate in educational programs, to take advantage of opportunities for work inside of correctional institutions, to seek treatment, or to contribute in any positive way to their own change.

While these critiques may be valid, they will probably do little to stem the rising tide of structured sentencing. The growth of structured sentencing over the past few decades represents the ascendancy of the "just deserts" perspective over other sentencing goals. In a growing number of jurisdictions, punishment, deterrence, and incapacitation have replaced rehabilitation and restitution as the goals which society seeks to achieve through sentencing practices.

Mandatory Sentencing

mandatory sentencing

A structured sentencing scheme that allows no leeway in the nature of the sentence required and under which clearly enumerated punishments are mandated for specific offenses or for habitual offenders convicted of a series of crimes.

Mandatory sentencing, another form of structured sentencing, deserves special mention.[33] **Mandatory sentencing** is just what its name implies: a structured sentencing scheme which mandates clearly enumerated punishments for specific offenses or for habitual offenders convicted of a series of crimes. Mandatory sentencing, because it is truly *mandatory*, differs from presumptive sentencing, which allows at least a limited amount of judicial discretion within ranges established by published guidelines. Some mandatory sentencing laws require only modest mandatory prison terms (for example, three years for armed robbery), while others are much more far-reaching.

Typical of far-reaching mandatory sentencing schemes are "three-strikes" laws, discussed in CJ Today Exhibit 10–2. Three-strikes laws (and, in some jurisdictions, two-strikes laws) require mandatory sentences (sometimes life in prison without the possibility of parole) for offenders convicted of a third serious felony. Such mandatory sentencing enhancements are aimed at deterring known and potentially violent offenders and are intended to incapacitate convicted criminals through long-term incarceration.

Three-strikes laws impose longer prison terms than most earlier mandatory minimum sentencing laws. California's three-strikes law, for example, requires that offenders who are convicted of a violent crime and who have had two prior convictions serve a minimum of 25 years in prison. The law doubled prison terms for offenders convicted of a second violent felony.[34] Three-strikes laws also vary in breadth. The laws of some jurisdictions stipulate that both of the prior convictions and the current one be for violent felonies; others require only that the prior convictions be for violent felonies. Some three-strikes laws count only prior adult convictions, while others permit consideration of juvenile crimes.

By passing mandatory sentencing laws, legislators convey the message that certain crimes are deemed especially grave and that people who commit them deserve, and should expect, harsh sanctions. These laws are sometimes passed in response to public outcries following heinous or well-publicized crimes.

Mandatory sentencing has had significant consequences that deserve close attention. Among them are its impact on crime and on the operation of the criminal justice system. The possible consequences for certain groups of people also bears examination. Evaluations of mandatory sentencing have focused on two types of crimes: those committed with handguns and those related to drugs (the offenses most commonly subjected to mandatory minimum penalties in state and federal courts). An evaluation of a Massachusetts law that imposed mandatory jail terms for possession of an unlicensed handgun, for example, concluded that the law was an effective deterrent of gun crime—at least in the short term.[35] Studies of similar laws in Michigan[36] and Florida,[37] however, found no evidence that crimes committed with firearms had been prevented by similar laws. An evaluation of mandatory gun-use sentencing enhancements in six large cities (Detroit,

Jacksonville, Tampa, Miami, Philadelphia, and Pittsburgh) indicated that such laws deterred homicide but not other violent crimes.[38] A similar assessment of New York's Rockefeller drug laws was unable to support claims for their efficacy as a deterrent to drug crime.[39] None of the studies, however, examined the incapacitation effects of these laws on individual offenders.

Mandatory sentencing has also been evaluated in terms of its impact on the criminal justice system. Traditionally, criminal courts have relied on a high rate of guilty pleas to speed case processing and to avoid logjams. Officials have been able to offer inducements (by way of lowered sentences) to defendants to obtain bargained pleas. Mandatory sentencing laws, it has been found, can disrupt established plea-bargaining patterns by preventing a prosecutor from offering a short prison term in exchange for a guilty plea. However, unless policymakers enact long-term mandatory sentences that apply to many related categories of crimes, prosecutors can usually shift strategies and bargain on charges rather than on sentences, thus retaining plea bargaining as a valid option in most courtrooms.

Research findings on the impact of mandatory sentencing laws on the criminal justice system have been summarized by Michael Tonry.[40] Tonry found that under mandatory sentencing, officials tend to make earlier and more selective arrest, charging, and diversion decisions. They also tend to bargain less and to bring more cases to trial. Specifically, Tonry found the following: (1) Criminal justice officials and practitioners (police, lawyers, and judges) exercise discretion to avoid the application of laws they consider unduly harsh. (2) Arrest rates for target crimes tend to decline soon after mandatory sentencing laws take effect. (3) Dismissal and diversion rates increase during the early stages of case processing after mandatory sentencing laws become effective. (4) For defendants whose cases are not dismissed, plea-bargain rates decline and trial rates increase. (5) For convicted defendants, sentencing delays increase. (6) When the effects of declining arrests, indictments, and convictions are taken into account, the enactment of mandatory sentencing laws has little impact on the probability that offenders will be imprisoned. (7) Sentences become longer and more severe. Mandatory sentencing laws may also occasionally result in unduly harsh punishments for marginal offenders who nonetheless meet the minimum requirements for sentencing under such laws.

In an analysis of federal sentencing guidelines, other researchers found that blacks receive longer sentences than whites, not because of differential treatment by judges, but because they constitute the large majority of those convicted of trafficking in crack cocaine[41]—a crime Congress has singled out for especially harsh mandatory penalties. This pattern can be seen as constituting a "disparity in results," and partly for this reason, in 1999 the U.S. Sentencing Commission recommended to Congress that it eliminate the legal distinction between crack and regular cocaine for purposes of sentencing (a recommendation that Congress rejected).

An alternative to mandatory minimum sentencing provisions which would protect sentencing policy, preserve legislative control, and still toughen sentences for repeat violent offenders is the use of presumptive sentences. Other possibilities include (1) directing mandatory sentencing laws at only a few especially serious crimes and requiring "sunset" provisions (for example, requiring that geriatric inmates who have reached a specified age be released after serving a certain minimum); (2) subjecting long mandatory sentences to periodic administrative review to determine the advisability of continued confinement in individual cases; (3) building a funding plan into sentencing legislation to ensure awareness of and responsibility for the costs of long-term imprisonment; and (4) developing policies that make more effective and systematic use of intermediate sanctions.

Truth in Sentencing

In 1984, with passage of the Comprehensive Crime Control Act, the federal government adopted presumptive sentencing for nearly all federal offenders.[42] The act also addressed the issue of truth in sentencing. Under the old federal system, a sentence of ten years in prison might actually have meant only a few years behind bars before the offender was released. On average, good-time credits and parole reduced time served to about one-third of the actual sentence.[43] At the time, the sentencing practices of most states reflected the federal model. While sentence reductions may have benefited offenders, they often outraged victims, who felt betrayed by the sentencing process. The 1984 act nearly eliminated good-time credits[44] and began the process of phasing out federal parole and eliminating

> When I walked out of that execution chamber that night, I felt like I had been given my life back. It could not bring Cary back, but it gave us our life back.
>
> —Charlotte Stout, the mother of eight-year-old Cary Medlin, who was kidnapped, raped, and killed by Robert Glen Coe in 1979, after witnessing Coe's execution in 2000[ii]

[Three Strikes and You're Out: A Brief History of the "Get Tough on Crime" Movement]

In the spring of 1994, California legislators passed the state's now-famous "three strikes and you're out" bill. Amid much fanfare, Governor Pete Wilson signed the "three-strikes" measure into law, calling it "the toughest and most sweeping crime bill in California history."[1]

California's law, which is retroactive in that it counts offenses committed before the date the legislation was signed, requires a 25-year-to-life sentence for three-time felons with convictions for two or more serious or violent prior offenses. Criminal offenders facing a "second strike" can receive up to double the normal sentence for their most recent offense. Parole consideration is not available until at least 80% of the sentence has been served.

Today, about half the states have passed three-strikes legislation, and other states may still be considering it. At the federal level, the Violent Crime Control and Law Enforcement Act of 1994 contains a three-strikes provision, which mandates life imprisonment for federal criminals convicted of three violent felonies or drug offenses.

Questions remain, however, about the effectiveness of three-strikes legislation, and many are concerned about its impact on the justice system. One year after it was signed into law, the California three-strikes initiative was evaluated by the RAND Corporation.[2] RAND researchers found that, in the first year, more than 5,000 defendants were convicted and sentenced under the law's provisions. The large majority of those sentenced, however, had committed nonviolent crimes, causing critics of the law to argue that it is too broad. Eighty-four percent of two-strikes convictions and nearly 77% of three-strikes convictions resulted from nonviolent, drug, or property crimes. A similar 1997 study of three-strikes laws in 22 states, conducted by the Campaign for an Effective Crime Policy (CECP), concluded that such legislation results in clogged court systems and crowded correctional facilities while encouraging three-time felons to take dramatic risks to avoid capture.[3] A 1998 study found that only California and Georgia were making widespread use of three-strikes laws.[4] Other states, the study found, have narrowly written laws that are applicable to repeat offenders only in rare circumstances. A 2001 study of the original California legislation and its consequences concluded that three-strikes laws are overrated.[5] According to the study, "California's three-strikes law has increased the number and severity of sentences for nonviolent offenders—and contributed to the aging of the prison population—but has had no significant effect on the state's decline in crime." The study found that declines in California crime rates that are often attributed to the legislation are consistent with nationwide declines in the rate of crime and would mostly have occurred without the law. "Crime had been declining for several years prior to the enactment of the three-strikes law, and what's happening in California is very consistent with what's been happening nationally, including in states with no three-strikes law," said Marc Mauer, an author of the study.

Supporters of three-strikes laws argue that those convicted under them are career criminals who will be denied the opportunity to commit more violent crimes. "The real story here is the girl somewhere that did not get raped," said Mike Reynolds, a Fresno, California, photographer whose 18-year-old daughter was killed by a paroled felon. "The real story is the robbery that did not happen," he added.[6]

Practically speaking, California's three-strikes law has had a dramatic impact on the state's criminal justice system. By 1999, more than 40,000 people had been sentenced under the law. But the law has its critics. "'Three strikes and you're out' sounds great to a lot of people," says Alan Schuman, President of the American Probation and Parole Association. "But no one will cop a plea when it gets to the third time around. We will have more trials, and this whole country works on plea bargaining and pleading guilty, not jury trials," Schuman said at a meeting of the association.[7] Some California district attorneys have responded by choosing to prosecute fewer misdemeanants and to concentrate on the more serious three-strikes defendants. According to RAND, full enforcement of the law could cost as much as $5.5 billion annually—or $300 per California taxpayer.

Researchers at RAND conclude that while California's sweeping three-strikes legislation could cut serious adult crime by as much as one-third throughout the state, the high cost of enforcing the law may keep it from ever being fully implemented. In 1996, the California three-strikes controversy became even more complicated following a decision by the state supreme court (in *People* v. *Superior Court of San Diego—Romero*[8]) that California judges retain the discretion to reduce three-strikes sentences and to refuse to count previous convictions at sentencing "in furtherance of justice." As this book goes to press, the law remains firmly in place, although proposals to amend it are being made. Some want stricter language written into the law which would require judges to follow it, while others suggest that three-strikes sentences should only be imposed on offenders who commit violent crimes, such as murder, rape, armed robbery, and certain types of arson.

❓ DISCUSSION QUESTIONS

1. Do you think three-strikes laws serve a useful purpose? If so, what is that purpose? What other sentencing arrangements, if any, might meet that purpose?
2. How will three-strikes laws affect state and federal spending on the criminal justice system? Do you think that such shifts in spending can be justified? If so, how?

[1]Michael Miller, "California Gets 'Three Strikes' Anti-Crime Bill," Reuters wire services, March 7, 1994.

[2]Dion Nissenbaum, "Three-Strikes First Year Debated," United Press International wire services, northern edition, March 6, 1995.

[3]Campaign for an Effective Crime Policy, *The Impact of Three Strikes and You're Out Laws: What Have We Learned?* (Washington, D.C.: CECP, 1997).

[4]Walter Dickey and Pam Stiebs Hollenhorst, "Three-Strikes Laws: Massive Impact in California and Georgia, Little Elsewhere," *Overcrowded Times,* Vol. 9, No. 6 (December 1998), pp. 2–8.

[5]Tamar Lewin, "3-Strikes Law is Overrated in California, Study Finds," *The New York Times,* August 23, 2001.

[6]Bruce Smith, "Crime Solutions," Associated Press wire services, January 11, 1995.

[7]Ryan S. King and Marc Mauer, *Aging Behind Bars: "Three Strikes" Seven Years Later* (Washington, D.C.: The Sentencing Project, August 2001).

[8]*People* v. *Superior Court of San Diego—Romero,* 13 Cal. 4th 497, 917 P.2d 628.

the U.S. Parole Commission.[45] The emphasis on **truth in sentencing** created, in effect, a sentencing environment of "what you get is what you serve."

More recently, the movement toward truth in sentencing has accelerated. Truth in sentencing, described as "a close correspondence between the sentence imposed upon those sent to prison and the time actually served prior to prison release,"[46] has become an important policy focus of many state legislatures and the U.S. Congress. The Violent Crime Control and Law Enforcement Act of 1994 set aside $4 billion in federal prison construction funds (called Truth in Sentencing Incentive Funds) for states which adopt truth-in-sentencing laws and are able to guarantee that certain violent offenders will serve 85% of their sentences. By 1999, 27 states and the District of Columbia had met the 85% requirement.[47] Although most other states are moving toward practices which support truth in sentencing, there are some notable exceptions. Texas and Maryland, for example, retain 50% requirements for violent offenders, and Nebraska and Indiana require all offenders to serve only 50% of their sentences.

truth in sentencing

A close correspondence between the sentence imposed upon an offender and the time actually served prior to release from prison.[iii]

Federal Sentencing Guidelines

Title II of the Comprehensive Crime Control Act, called the Sentencing Reform Act of 1984,[48] established the nine-member U.S. Sentencing Commission. The commission comprises presidential appointees, including three federal judges. The Sentencing Reform Act limited the discretion of federal judges by mandating the creation of federal sentencing guidelines, which federal judges are required to follow. The sentencing commission was given the task of developing structured sentencing guidelines to reduce disparity, promote consistency and uniformity, and increase fairness and equity in sentencing. To guide the commission, Congress specified the purposes of sentencing to include (1) deterring criminals, (2) incapacitating and/or rehabilitating offenders, and (3) providing "just deserts" in punishing criminals. Congress established mandatory minimum sentences for certain federal crimes, including drug offenses, and asked the commission for a system which would permit flexibility in the face of mitigating or aggravating circumstances.

While developing federal sentencing guidelines, the commission analyzed thousands of past cases and enacted a scale of punishments considered typical for given types of offenses.[49] It came up with a series of federal guidelines intended to provide predictability in sentencing, but individual judges are allowed to deviate from the guidelines when specific aggravating or mitigating circumstances are present. The commission also considered relevant federal law, parole guidelines, and the anticipated impact of changes upon federal prison populations. One boundary was set by statute: In creating the Sentencing Commission, Congress had specified that the degree of discretion available in any one sentencing category could not exceed 25% of the basic penalty for that category, or six months, whichever might be greater.

The guidelines established by the Commission took effect in November 1987 but quickly became embroiled in a series of legal disputes, some of which challenged Congress's authority to form the Sentencing Commission. In January 1989, in the case of *Mistretta* v. *U.S.*,[50] the U.S. Supreme Court held that Congress had acted appropriately in establishing the Sentencing Commission and that the guidelines developed by the commission could be applied in federal cases nationwide. The federal Sentencing Commission continues to meet at least once a year to review the effectiveness of the guidelines it created. Visit the U.S. Sentencing Commission via **Web Extra! 10–3** at cjtoday.com.

Federal Guideline Provisions

For each criminal offense, federal sentencing guidelines specify a sentencing range from which judges must choose. If a particular case has "atypical features," judges are allowed to depart from the guidelines. Departures are generally expected to be made only in the presence of mitigating or aggravating circumstances—a number of which are specified in the guidelines.[51] Aggravating circumstances may include the possession of a weapon during the commission of a crime, the degree of criminal involvement (whether the defendant was a leader or a follower in the criminal activity), and extreme psychological injury to the victim. Punishments also increase when a defendant violates a position of public or private trust, uses special skills to commit or conceal offenses, or has a criminal history. Defendants who express remorse, cooperate with authorities, or willingly make restitution may have their sentences reduced under the guidelines. Any departure from the guidelines may, however, become the basis for appellate review concerning the reasonableness of the sentence imposed, and judges who deviate from the guidelines must provide written reasons for doing so.

Federal sentencing guidelines are built around a table containing 43 rows, each corresponding to one offense level. The penalties associated with each level overlap those of the levels above and below to discourage unnecessary litigation. A person convicted of a crime involving $11,000, for example, is unlikely to receive a penalty substantially greater than if the amount involved had been somewhat less than $10,000—a sharp contrast to the old system. A change of six levels roughly doubles the sentence imposed under the guidelines, regardless of the level at which one starts. Because of their matrixlike quality, federal sentencing provisions have been referred to as *structured*. The federal sentencing table is available at **Web Extra! 10–4** at cjtoday.com.

The sentencing table also contains six rows corresponding to the criminal history category into which an offender falls. Criminal history categories are determined on a point basis. Offenders earn points for previous convictions. Each prior sentence of imprisonment for more than one year and one month counts as three points. Two points are assigned for each prior prison sentence over six months, or if the defendant committed the offense while on probation, parole, or work release. The system also assigns points for other types of previous convictions and for offenses committed less than two years after release from imprisonment. Points are added together to determine the criminal history category into which an offender falls. Thirteen points or more are required for the highest category. At each offense level, sentences in the highest criminal history category are generally two to three times as severe as for the lowest category.

Defendants may also move into the highest criminal history category (VI) by virtue of being designated a career offender. Under the sentencing guidelines, a defendant is a career offender if "(1) the defendant was at least 18 years old at the time of the . . . offense, (2) the . . . offense is a crime of violence or trafficking in a controlled substance, and (3) the defendant has at least two prior felony convictions of either a crime of violence or a controlled substance offense."[52]

According to the U.S. Supreme Court, an offender may be adjudged a career offender in a single hearing, even when previous convictions are lacking. In *Deal* v. *U.S.* (1993),[53] the defendant, Thomas Lee Deal, was convicted in a single proceeding of six counts of carrying and using a firearm during a series of bank robberies which occurred in the Houston, Texas, area. A federal district court sentenced him to 105 years in prison as a career offender—five years for the first count and 20 years for each of the five other counts, with sentences to run consecutively. In the words of the Supreme Court, "We see no reason why [the defendant should not receive such a sentence], simply because he managed to evade detection, prosecution, and conviction for the first five offenses and was ultimately tried on all six in a single proceeding."

Plea Bargaining under the Guidelines

Plea bargaining plays a major role in the federal judicial system. Approximately 90% of all federal sentences are the result of guilty pleas,[54] and the large majority of those stem from plea negotiations. In the words of former Sentencing Commission Chairman William W. Wilkins, Jr., "With respect to plea bargaining, the Commission has proceeded cautiously. . . . The Commission did not believe it wise to stand the federal criminal justice system on its head by making too drastic and too sudden a change in these practices."[55]

Although the commission allowed plea bargaining to continue, it does require that the agreement (1) be fully disclosed in the record of the court (unless there is an overriding and demonstrable reason why it should not) and (2) detail the actual conduct of the offense. Under these requirements, defendants are no longer able to hide the actual nature of their offense behind a substitute plea. The thrust of the federal rules concerning plea bargaining is to reduce the veil of secrecy that had previously surrounded the process. Information on the decision-making process itself is available to victims, the media, and the public.

In 1996, in the case of *Melendez* v. *U.S.*,[56] the U.S. Supreme Court held that a government motion requesting that a trial judge deviate from the federal sentencing guidelines as part of a cooperative plea agreement does not permit imposition of a sentence below a statutory minimum specified by law. In other words, while federal judges may depart from the guidelines, they cannot accept plea bargains which would result in sentences lower than the minimum required by law for a particular type of offense. Read about what the future may hold for federal sentencing guidelines at **Library Extra! 10–4** at cjtoday.com.

CJ Today News

[Does "Scarlet Letter" Judge Cross the Line?]

CORPUS CHRISTI, Tex.—First, state District Judge J. Manuel Banales imposed a unique probation condition on Robert Torres, a 19-year-old sex offender: no sex until he is married.

Then, Banales ordered other sex offenders in this city of 381,000 to post signs in their yards and on their automobiles that warn of their offenses.

Now, the State Commission on Judicial Conduct, which considers complaints against judges, is scrutinizing Banales' actions, according to Gerald Rogen, Torres' attorney.

Rogen, president of the Coastal Bend Criminal Defense Lawyers Association, says he will ask the 13th Court of Appeals this week to overturn Banales' ruling on the signs. He's also asking the court to recuse Banales from Torres' case and to modify the conditions of his probation—life in prison if he violates the no-sex order.

Banales, 50, touched off a wave of controversy—and earned the sobriquet "the Scarlet Letter judge"—on May 18 [2001]. After reviewing probationers' statuses, he ordered 14 of about 45 registered sex offenders to place 18- by 24-inch warning signs in their yards: "DANGER: Registered Sex Offender Lives Here." Banales ordered them to put similar signs in automobiles they ride in and bumper stickers on cars they own.

"I think a lot of people here think, hey, that's really kind of going out of line," says Douglas Tinker, a lawyer who has known Banales for 15 years.

Banales, a 14-year veteran of the bench in Nueces County, says he's simply following the law. He says it authorizes a judge to require a sex offender on probation to notify the public of the crime he or she committed.

Judge Mike Westergren has known Banales for more than 20 years. He says the sign order came shortly after a man with a prior sexual-offense conviction was found guilty in Westergren's courtroom of attempted sexual assault. The man lured a 12-year-old girl into his house, which was along her route to school, and attempted to sexually assault her.

Banales "said she wouldn't have gone in the house if there had been signs," Westergren says.

Banales' critics say he has overstepped the law and is creating a setting ripe for public harassment and vigilantism against sex offenders on probation. They also say the signs will result in declining property values.

"Judge Banales went outside the scope of the state Legislature in defining what sex offender notification should entail and created his own method of notification that violates these individuals' First Amendment rights," says Diana Philip, a board member of the American Civil Liberties Union of Texas. The ACLU is providing legal assistance to Rogen.

Banales, one of eight judges in Nueces County, is the only one to implement such orders. He says he doesn't know whether he's being inves-

Courting controversy. Critics say that Judge J. Manuel Banales has overstepped the law by making sex offenders place signs outside their homes announcing their presence in the community.

AP/Wide World Photos

A sign warning of the presence of a registered sex offender in front of a residence in Corpus Christi, Texas.

AP/Wide World Photos

(continued)

tigated, and he declines to comment on whether his rulings will withstand appeals. "It would be inappropriate for me to comment," he says.

The State Commission on Judicial Conduct does not confirm or deny investigations of judges, says Seana Willing, the commission's general counsel. The commission is made up of 11 members and one investigator. It investigated 1,200 complaints against Texas' 3,550 judges in fiscal year 2000. On average, she says, inquiries take four to six months.

The commission may dismiss a case, reprimand a judge privately, censure him or her publicly or recommend that a judge be suspended or removed, Willing says.

Robert Dawson, law professor at the University of Texas—Austin and an expert on state legal matters, says Banales was well within his legal rights to order the signs. "It's not illegal, it's just dumb," he says. "I believe doing it was more for the publicity than in an honest belief that it deters future crime."

Exactly one month before he issued the sign order, Banales ordered Torres not to have sex until he gets married. Torres had been sentenced in 1999 to five years' probation after pleading guilty to having sex with a 13-year-old. The girl told authorities that Torres was her boyfriend.

During a probation revocation hearing on April 18, Banales learned that Torres had fathered a daughter with a 16-year-old girl and had impregnated a 17-year-old while on probation. Torres violated probation by drinking beer, smoking marijuana and visiting his 1-year-old daughter. Banales sentenced him to five more years' probation, 30 days in jail and no sex.

Banales says he was concerned that Torres was involved "with so many women, two of them were girls, and getting them pregnant without supporting them. I felt he needed some stability, and a marriage contract is one way of showing that he is truly committed."

Banales' supporters applaud him for tackling the problem of teen pregnancy in a creative manner.

"Our county has one of the highest rates of teen pregnancy in Texas and probably the U.S., and he's trying to address that in a creative way," says retired district judge Robert Pate of Corpus Christi. "People here . . . congratulate him out of the blue for his character, courage and conviction."

Others have a different opinion.

"Judges have done some weird things," Dawson says. "Sometimes I think the dye in those black robes is toxic, and it seeps into their skin and causes judicial dementia."

For the latest in crime and justice news, visit the Talk Justice news feed at http://www.crimenews.info.

Source: Larry Copeland, "Does 'Scarlet Letter' Judge Cross the Line? Some Applaud Texas Jurist for Taking Creative Approach to Sentencing Sex Offenders," *USA Today,* July 10, 2001. Copyright 2001, *USA Today.* Reprinted with permission.

Innovations in Sentencing

> If you want a small prison population, make punishment certain. If you want a large prison population, make punishment uncertain.
>
> —Former House Speaker Newt Gingrich

In 2001, two Coshocton, Ohio, men were forced to parade down the main street of their hometown dressed as women. The men, Jason Householder, 23, and John Stockum, 21, had been convicted of criminal damage for throwing beer bottles at a woman. Coshocton County Municipal Judge David Hostetler ordered the men to march through the center of Coshocton (population 12,000) for an hour wearing women's dresses, wigs, and makeup.[57] The judge told the men that they could either comply with his order or go to jail for 60 days. He also fined them $250 each. Hostetler, who is known for his habit of imposing unusual sentences, says he does so because of overcrowding in the Coshocton County Jail.

In an ever-growing number of cases, innovative judges have begun to use the wide discretion in sentencing available to them under the law of certain jurisdictions to impose truly unique punishments. In Memphis, Tennessee, for example, Judge Joe Brown escorted burglary victims to thieves' homes, inviting them to take whatever they wanted.[58] An Arkansas judge made shoplifters walk in front of the stores they stole from, carrying signs describing their crimes. At least one Florida court began ordering those convicted of drunk driving to put a "Convicted DUI" sticker on their license plates. Similarly, two years ago, Thomas Jache, a Manchester, New Hampshire, child molester who admitted his guilt, got two years of a minimum five-year sentence suspended but was ordered to place an advertisement in two local newspapers that included his picture, an apology, and a plea for other potential molesters to get help. In 1997, Boston courts began ordering men convicted of the crime of "sexual solicitation" to spend four hours sweeping the streets of Chinatown, an area known for prostitution. The public was invited to watch men sentenced to the city's "John Sweep" program clean up streets and alleyways littered with used condoms and sexual paraphernalia.

A common theme of individualized sentencing innovations such as these is that of public shaming. The rise in shame-as-punishment harks back to "scarlet letter" days, when sentences were meant not only to punish, but also to deter wrongdoers through public humiliation. Some of today's innovative judges, faced with prison overcrowding, high incarceration costs, and public calls for retribution, have begun to employ the kinds of shaming strategies described here.

Shaming as a crime reduction strategy finds considerable support in criminal justice literature. Australian criminologist John Braithwaite, for example, found shaming to be a particularly effective strategy because, he said, it holds the potential to enhance moral awareness among offenders, thereby building conscience and increasing inner control.[59] Braithwaite distinguishes, however, between "disintegrative (or stigmatic) shaming" and "reintegrative" shaming. Disintegrative shaming, says Braithwaite, treats offenders like outcasts, while reintegrative shaming includes communal forgiveness and attempts to reintegrate the offender back into the community. Reintegrative shaming, which Braithwaite says is inherent in Japanese culture but not in American society, is said to be more effective at reducing recidivism. The results of a 1997 Australian study by Braithwaite and others, called the Reintegrative Shaming Experiments (RISE), appear to show that reintegrative shaming can be far more effective at producing feelings of guilt and shame in offenders than traditional criminal court processing. The experiments induced feelings of shame in offenders through the use of diversionary conferencing, a technique that builds upon an intensive form of moderated interaction between victim and offender.[60]

Braithwaite is quick to point out that judges in American society are far more likely to employ disintegrative shaming techniques than reintegrative ones. Perhaps for that reason, critics argue that contemporary efforts at shaming in the United States don't work. "It's an embarrassment to the criminal justice system and all done in the guise of law and order to appease the victims," says Knoxville lawyer Jim A. H. Bell.[61] Bell, who serves on the board of the National Association of Criminal Defense Lawyers, says, "It's all done for shock value."

> Developing a sentencing system that provides appropriate types and lengths of sentences for all offenders is a challenging task.
>
> —National Conference of State Legislatures

CJ Futures

[Is Chemical Castration a Valid Sentencing Option?]

In September 1996, then-Governor Pete Wilson signed legislation making California the first state in the nation to require regular hormone injections for convicted child molesters upon their release from prison. "Chemical castration," which went into effect in the state on January 1, 1997, requires twice-convicted child molesters to receive weekly injections of a synthetic female hormone known as Depo-Provera. The laboratory-manufactured chemical is said to lower the sex drive in males. Under the law, judges can also mandate injections for first offenders. Treatment is to continue until state authorities determine that it is no longer necessary.

Georgia, Texas, Montana, and Florida have similar legislation in place, and some other states are considering enacting chemical castration laws. California Assemblyman Bill Hoge, author of the California legislation, has encouraged other states to pass castration legislation. "We have now set the stage for America—and we hope you are listening, America," Hoge said. "We can do this all over the country. This is going to have the biggest impact on this horrible, horrible crime of any legislation ever seen."

If chemical castration survives continuing court challenges, it may establish itself in the mid-twenty-first century as a widely used form of alternative sentencing. Opposition to the new law, however, is plentiful. After the California law was enacted, a spokeswoman for the American Civil Liberties Union (ACLU) said that the group was considering a legal challenge because the legislation supposedly mandates an unproven remedy for child molestation and is a violation of civil rights. "There is no evidence, absolutely no evidence, that chemical castration will alleviate the problem," said Ann Bradley, a Los Angeles ACLU spokeswoman. "We see this as a violation of prisoners' civil liberties," she said.

Proponents of the legislation, on the other hand, cite studies in Canada and Europe where repeat offender rates of more than 80% were reduced to less than 4% among criminals treated with Depo-Provera. "I would have to say to the ACLU that there is no right to molest a child," Governor Wilson replied.

Sources: "Castration 1998–2001." Web posted at http://members.aol.com/USCCCN/FAQ-Castration.index.html. Accessed February 20, 2001; and Dave Lesher, "Molester Castration Measure Signed: California Becomes the First State to Require That Offenders Get Periodic Injections to Suppress Sex Drive," *Los Angeles Times,* September 18, 1996.

On the other hand, Dan Kahan, a professor at the University of Chicago Law School, points out that "shame supplies the main motive why people obey the law, not so much because they're afraid of formal sanctions, but because they care what people think about them."[62]

Whether public shaming will continue to grow in popularity as an alternative sentencing strategy is unclear. What is clear, however, is that the American public and an ever-growing number of judicial officials are now looking for workable alternatives to traditional sentencing options.

Questions about Alternative Sanctions

As prison populations continue to rise, alternative sentencing strategies are likely to become increasingly attractive. Many questions must be answered, however, before most alternative sanctions can be employed with confidence. These questions were succinctly stated in a RAND Corporation study authored by Joan Petersilia.[63] Unfortunately, while the questions can be listed, few definitive answers are yet available. Here are some of the questions Petersilia poses:

■ Do alternative sentencing programs threaten public safety?

■ How should program participants be selected?

■ What are the long-term effects of community sanctions on people assigned to these programs?

■ Are alternative sanctions cost-effective?

■ Who should pay the bill for alternative sanctions?

■ Who should manage stringent community-based sanctions?

■ How should program outcomes be judged?

■ What kinds of offenders benefit most from alternative sanctions?

The Sentencing Environment

A number of studies have attempted to investigate the decision-making process that leads to the imposition of a particular sentence. Early studies found a strong relationship between the informal influence of members of the courtroom work group and the severity, or lack thereof, of sentences imposed.[64] A number suggested that minorities ran a much greater risk of imprisonment.[65] Other studies found that sentencing variations are influenced by extralegal conditions[66] and that public opinion can play a role in the type of sentence handed down.[67] If these findings about public opinion are true, they might explain some of the increase in prison populations. A public opinion study conducted by Bowling Green State University, for example, found that 71% of respondents identified incarceration as the preferred punishment for serious offenses.[68]

More recent analyses, especially in structured sentencing jurisdictions, however, have begun to show that sentences in a number of jurisdictions are becoming more objective and, hence, more predictable. A California study of racial equity in sentencing, for example, found that the likelihood of going to prison was increased by[69]

■ Having multiple current conviction counts, prior prison terms, and juvenile incarcerations

■ Being on adult or juvenile probation or parole at the time of the offense

■ Having been released from prison within 12 months of the current offense

■ Having a history of drug or alcohol abuse

■ Being over 21 years of age

■ Going to trial

■ Not being released prior to trial

■ Not being represented by a private attorney

The study concluded that, perhaps partly because of the 1977 California Determinate Sentencing Act, "California courts are making racially equitable sentencing decisions."[70] The findings applied only to the crimes of assault, robbery, burglary, theft, forgery, and drug abuse but held for sentences involving both prison and probation. Similarly, no disparities were noted in the lengths of sentences imposed.[71] Other studies have found that female felons are not treated much differently by sentencing authorities than their male counterparts.[72]

The Presentence Investigation Report

Before imposing sentence, a judge may request information on the background of a convicted defendant. This is especially true in indeterminate sentencing jurisdictions, where judges retain considerable discretion in selecting sanctions. Traditional wisdom has held that certain factors increase the likelihood of rehabilitation and reduce the need for lengthy prison terms. These factors include a good job record, satisfactory educational attainment, strong family ties, church attendance, no prior arrests for violent offenses, and psychological stability.

Information about a defendant's background often comes to the judge in the form of a **presentence investigation** report. The task of preparing presentence reports usually falls to the probation or parole office. Presentence reports take one of three forms: (1) a detailed written report on the defendant's personal and criminal history, including an assessment of present conditions in the defendant's life (often called the *long form*); (2) an abbreviated written report summarizing the information most likely to be useful in a sentencing decision (the *short form*); and (3) a verbal report to the court made by the investigating officer based on field notes but structured according to established categories. A presentence report is much like a résumé, except that it focuses on what might be regarded as negative as well as positive life experiences.

A typical long form is divided into ten major sections: (1) personal information and identifying data describing the defendant; (2) a chronology of the current offense and the circumstances surrounding it; (3) a record of the defendant's previous convictions, if any; (4) home life and family data; (5) educational background; (6) health history and current state of health; (7) military service; (8) religious preference; (9) financial condition; and (10) sentencing recommendations made by the probation or parole officer completing the report.

The data on which a presentence report is based come from a variety of sources. Since the 1960s, modern computer-based criminal information clearinghouses, such as the Federal Bureau of Investigation's National Crime Information Center (NCIC), have simplified at least a part of the data-gathering process. The NCIC, begun in 1967, contains information on people wanted for criminal offenses throughout the United States. Individual jurisdictions also maintain criminal records repositories which can provide comprehensive files on the criminal history of persons processed by the justice system.

Sometimes the defendant is a significant source of much of the information which appears in the presentence report. When such is the case, efforts must be made to corroborate the defendant's information. Unconfirmed data are generally marked on the report as "defendant-supplied data" or simply "unconfirmed."

In a presentence report, almost all third-party data are subject to ethical and legal considerations. The official records of almost all agencies and organizations, though often an ideal source of information, are protected by state and federal privacy requirements. In particular, the federal Privacy Act of 1974[73] may limit records access. Investigators must first check on the legal availability of all records before requesting them and must receive in writing the defendant's permission to access the records. Other public laws, among them the federal Freedom of Information Act,[74] may make the presentence report itself available to the defendant, although courts and court officers have generally been held to be exempt from the provision of such statutes.

The final section of a presentence report is usually devoted to the investigating officer's recommendations. A recommendation may be made in favor of probation, split sentencing, a term of imprisonment, or any other sentencing option available in the jurisdiction. Participation in community service programs may be recommended for probationers, and drug- or substance-abuse programs may be suggested as well. Most judges are willing to accept the report writer's recommendation because they recognize the professionalism of presentence investigators and because they know that the investigator may well be the supervising officer assigned to the defendant should a community alternative be the sentencing decision.

Jurisdictions vary in their use of presentence reports. Federal law mandates presentence reports in federal criminal courts and specifies 15 topical areas which each report must contain. The 1984 federal Determinate Sentencing Act directs report writers to include information on the classification of the offense and of the defendant under the offense-level and criminal history categories established by the statute. Some states require presentence reports only in felony cases, and others require them in cases where the defendant faces the possibility of incarceration for six months or more. Other states have no requirement for presentence reports beyond those ordered by a judge.

presentence investigation

The examination of a convicted offender's background prior to sentencing. Presentence examinations are generally conducted by probation or parole officers and are submitted to sentencing authorities.

Report writing, rarely anyone's favorite task, may seriously tax the limited resources of probation agencies. In 1998, New York City Department of Probation officers wrote more than 52,000 presentence investigation reports for adult offenders and 7,000 reports for juvenile offenders—averaging over 40 reports per probation officer per month.

The Victim—Forgotten No Longer

Thanks to a grassroots resurgence of concern for the plight of victims which began in this country in the early 1970s, the sentencing process now frequently includes consideration of the needs of victims and their survivors.[75] In times past, the concerns of victims were often forgotten. Although victims might testify at trial, the criminal justice system frequently downplayed other aspects of the victimization experience, including the psychological trauma engendered by the victimization process itself. That changed in 1982, when the President's Task Force on Victims of Crime gave focus to a burgeoning victims' rights movement and urged the widespread expansion of victim-assistance programs during what was then their formative period.[76] Victim-assistance programs today offer services in the areas of crisis intervention and follow-up counseling and help victims secure their rights under the law.[77] Following successful prosecution, some victim-assistance programs also advise victims in the filing of civil suits to recoup financial losses directly from the offender. In the mid-1990s, the National Institute of Justice conducted a survey of 319 full-service victim-assistance programs based in law enforcement agencies and prosecutors' offices.[78] The survey found that "the majority of individuals seeking assistance were victims of domestic assault and the most common assistance they received was information about legal rights." Other common forms of assistance included help in applying for state victim-compensation aid and referrals to social service agencies.

About the same time, voters in California approved Proposition 8, a resolution which called for changes in the state's constitution to reflect concern for victims. A continuing goal of victim-advocacy groups is an amendment to the U.S. Constitution, which such groups say is needed to provide the same kind of fairness to victims that is routinely accorded to defendants. The National Victims' Constitutional Amendment Network (NVCAN), for example, has sought to add a phrase—"likewise, the victim, in every criminal prosecution, shall have the right to be present and to be heard at all critical stages of judicial proceedings"—to the Sixth Amendment. NVCAN now advocates the addition of a new amendment to the U.S. Constitution. Visit NVCAN via **Web Extra! 10–5** at cjtoday.com.

In September 1996, a victims' rights constitutional amendment—Senate Joint Resolution 65—was proposed by a bipartisan committee in the U.S. Congress.[79] Although the plan had the support of President Bill Clinton, problems of wording and terminology prevented its passage. A revised amendment was proposed in 1998,[80] but its wording was too restrictive for it to gain endorsement from victims' organizations.[81] In 1999, a new amendment was proposed by the Senate Judiciary Committee's Subcommittee on the Constitution, Federalism, and Property, but it did not make it to the Senate floor. The U.S. Department of Justice, which had previously supported the measure, reversed its position due to a provision in the proposed amendment that gives crime victims the right to be notified of any state or federal grant of clemency. The U.S. attorney general apparently believed that the provision would impede the power of the president. The legislation also lacked the support of President Clinton and was officially withdrawn by its sponsors in 2000. The amendment may still have a future, however, as President George W. Bush expressed support for the measure when he was governor of Texas,[82] and 39 state attorneys general have publicly endorsed its adoption.[83] The text of the proposed amendment, known as Senate Joint Resolution 3, is reproduced in CJ Today Exhibit 10–3.

Although a victims' rights amendment to the federal Constitution may not yet be a reality, more than 30 states have passed their own victims' rights amendments,[84] and significant federal legislation has already been adopted. The 1982 Victim and Witness Protection Act (VWPA),[85] for example, requires judges to consider victim-impact statements at federal sentencing hearings and places responsibility for their creation on federal probation officers. In 1984, the federal Victims of Crime Act (VOCA) was enacted with substantial bipartisan support. VOCA authorized federal funding to help states establish victim-assistance and victim-compensation programs. Under VOCA, the U.S. Department of Justice's Office for Victims of Crime provides a significant source of both funding and information for victim-assistance programs. The rights of victims were further strengthened under the Violent Crime Control and Law Enforcement Act of 1994, which created a federal right of allocution for victims of violent and sex crimes, permitting victims to speak at the sentencing of their assailants. The 1994 law also requires sex offenders and child molesters convicted under federal law to pay restitution to their victims and prohibits the diversion of federal victims' funds to other programs. Other provisions of the 1994 law provide civil rights remedies for victims of felonies motivated by gender bias and extend "rape shield law" protections to civil cases and to all criminal cases as a bar to irrelevant inquiries into a victim's sexual history. A significant feature of the 1994 law can be found in a subsection titled the Violence Against Women Act (VAWA). VAWA provides financial support for police, prosecutors, and victims' services in cases involving sexual violence or domestic abuse.

Much of the philosophical basis of today's victims' movement can be found in the restorative justice model, which was discussed briefly earlier in this chapter. Restorative justice emphasizes offender accountability and victim reparation. Restorative justice also provides the basis for victim-compensation programs, which are another means of recognizing the needs of crime victims. (See Table 10–2 for a comparison of retributive justice and restorative justice.) Today, all 50 states have passed legislation providing for monetary payments to victims of crime. Such payments are primarily designed to compensate victims for medical expenses and lost wages. All existing programs require that applicants meet certain eligibility criteria, and most set limits on the maximum amount of compensation that can be received. Generally disallowed are claims from victims who are significantly responsible for their own victimization.

In 2001, the USA PATRIOT Act amended the Victims of Crime Act of 1984 to make victims of terrorism and their families eligible for victim-compensation payments.[86] It also created an antiterrorism emergency reserve fund to help provide compensation to victims of terrorism.

> Nobody gets rehabilitated. Well, I shouldn't say no one; some of them die.
>
> —Former Los Angeles Police Chief Daryl Gates

DIFFERENCES BETWEEN RETRIBUTIVE AND RESTORATIVE JUSTICE	**TABLE 10–2**

Retributive Justice	Restorative Justice
Crime is an act against the state, a violation of a law, an abstract idea.	Crime is an act against another person or the community.
The criminal justice system controls crime.	Crime control lies primarily with the community.
Offender accountability is defined as taking punishment.	Offender accountability is defined as assuming responsibility and taking action to repair harm.
Crime is an individual act with individual responsibility.	Crime has both individual and social dimensions of responsibility.
Victims are peripheral to the process of resolving a crime.	Victims are central to the process of resolving a crime.
The offender is defined by deficits.	The offender is defined by the capacity to make reparation.
The emphasis is on adversarial relationships.	The emphasis is on dialogue and negotiation.
Pain is imposed to punish, deter, and prevent.	Restitution is a means of restoring both parties; the goal is reconciliation.
The community is on the sidelines, represented abstractly by the state.	The community is the facilitator in the restorative process.
The response is focused on the offender's past behavior.	The response is focused on harmful consequences of the offender's behavior; the emphasis is on the future and on reparation.
There is dependence upon proxy professionals.	There is direct involvement by both the offender and the victim.

Source: Adapted from Gordon Bazemore and Mark S. Umbreit, *Balanced and Restorative Justice: Program Summary* (Washington, D.C.: Office of Juvenile Justice and Delinquency Prevention, 1994), p. 7.

CJ Today Exhibit 10-3

[Is the Victims' Rights Amendment Dead?]

In 1999, Senators Dianne Feinstein of California and Jon Kyl of Arizona proposed a victims' rights amendment to the U.S. Constitution in the form of Senate Joint Resolution (SJR) 3. SJR 3 was the third attempt to pass such an amendment in recent times. The bill, which lacked support from the president, had to be withdrawn the next year. The text of the Kyl-Feinstein resolution follows.

Joint Resolution 3

Proposing an amendment to the Constitution of the United States to protect the rights of crime victims

Resolved by the Senate and the House of Representatives of the United States of America in Congress assembled (two-thirds of each House concurring therein), That the following article is proposed as an amendment to the Constitution of the United States, which shall be valid for all intents and purposes as part of the Constitution when ratified by the legislatures of three-fourths of the several States within seven years from the date of its submission by the Congress:

Article—

Section 1. A victim of a crime of violence, as these terms may be defined by law, shall have the rights:

■ to reasonable notice of, and not to be excluded from, any public proceedings relating to the crime;

■ to be heard, if present, and to submit a statement at all such proceedings to determine a conditional release from custody, an acceptance of a negotiated plea, or a sentence;

■ to the foregoing rights at a parole proceeding that is not public, to the extent those rights are afforded to the convicted offender;

■ to reasonable notice of a release or escape from custody relating to the crime;

■ to consideration of the interest of the victim that any trial be free from unreasonable delay;

■ to an order of restitution from the convicted offender;

■ to consideration for the safety of the victim in determining any conditional release from custody relating to the crime; and

■ to reasonable notice of the rights established by this article.

Section 2. Only the victim or the victim's lawful representative shall have standing to assert the rights established by this article. Nothing in this article shall provide grounds to stay or continue any trial, reopen any proceeding or invalidate any ruling, except with respect to conditional release or restitution or to provide rights guaranteed by this article in future proceedings, without staying or continuing a trial. Nothing in this article shall give rise to or authorize the creation of a claim for damages against the United States, a State, a political subdivision, or a public officer or employee.

Section 3. The Congress shall have the power to enforce this article by appropriate legislation. Exceptions to the rights established by this article may be created only when necessary to achieve a compelling interest.

Section 4. This article shall take effect on the 180th day after the ratification of this article. The right to an order of restitution established by this article shall not apply to crimes committed before the effective date of this article.

Section 5. The rights and immunities established by this article shall apply in Federal and State proceedings, including military proceedings to the extent that the Congress may provide by law, juvenile justice proceedings, and proceedings in the District of Columbia and any commonwealth, territory, or possession of the United States.

Source: Senate Joint Resolution 3, 106th Congress.

Victim-Impact Statements

victim-impact statement

The in-court use of victim- or survivor-supplied information by sentencing authorities wishing to make an informed sentencing decision.

Another consequence of the national victims' rights movement has been a call for the use of **victim-impact statements** prior to sentencing. A victim-impact statement generally takes the form of a written document describing the losses, suffering, and trauma experienced by the crime victim or the victim's survivors. Judges are expected to consider such statements in arriving at an appropriate sanction for the offender.

The drive to mandate inclusion of victim-impact statements in sentencing decisions, already required in federal courts by the 1982 Victim and Witness Protection Act, was substantially enhanced by the "right of allocution" provision of the Violent Crime Control and Law Enforcement Act of 1994. Victim-impact statements played a prominent role in the sentencing of Timothy McVeigh, who was convicted of the 1995 bombing of the Murrah Federal Building in Oklahoma City and was executed in 2001. Some states, however, have gone the federal government one better. In 1984, the state of California, for example, passed legislation giving victims a right to attend and participate in sentencing and parole hearings.[87] Approximately 20 states now have laws mandating citizen involvement in sentencing, and all 50 states and the District of Columbia "allow for some form of submission of a victim impact statement either at the time of sentencing or to be contained in the presentence investigation reports" made by court officers.[88] Where written victim-impact statements are not available, courts may invite the victim to testify directly at sentencing. An alternative to written impact statements and to the appearance of victims at sentencing hearings is the victim-impact video.

Hearing from victims, however, does not guarantee that a sentencing court will be sympathetic. On April 3, 1995, for example, a court in Berlin, Germany, refused to imprison Guenter Parche, the unemployed German machinist who stabbed 19-year-old tennis superstar Monica Seles in the back with a kitchen knife at the 1993 Hamburg Open. Even though Seles told the court that Parche "ruined" her life and ended her career "as the world's best tennis player,"[89] the judge ruled that a suspended sentence was appropriate because the man apparently had not intended to kill Seles; he just wanted to disable her so that German star Steffi Graf could regain the number one world ranking in women's tennis. At the hearing, Seles's American psychologist had testified that Seles "felt like a bird trapped in a cage and was terrified that Parche would strike again."[90] Seles was not able to play professional tennis for more than two years following the attack and has never regained full championship standing.

One study of the efficacy of victim-impact statements found that sentencing decisions are rarely affected by them. In the words of the study, "These statements did not produce sentencing decisions that reflected more clearly the effects of crime on victims. Nor did we find much evidence that—with or without impact statements—sentencing decisions were influenced by our measures of the effects of crime on victims, once the charge and the defendant's prior record were taken into account."[91] The authors concluded that victim-impact statements have little effect upon courts because judges and other officials "have established ways of making decisions which do not call for explicit information about the impact of crime on victims."

THE CONSTITUTIONALITY OF VICTIM-IMPACT STATEMENTS

In 1987, the constitutionality of victim-impact statements was called into question by the U.S. Supreme Court in the case of *Booth* v. *Maryland*.[92] The case involved Irvin Bronstein, 78, and his wife, Rose, 75, who were robbed and brutally murdered in their home in Baltimore, Maryland, in 1983. The killers were John Booth and Willie Reid, acquaintances of the Bronsteins who were caught stealing to support their heroin habits. After being convicted of murder, Booth decided to allow the jury (rather than the judge) to set his sentence. As required by state law, the jury considered a victim-impact statement which was part of a presentence report prepared by probation officers. The victim-impact statement used in the case was a powerful one, describing the wholesome personal qualities of the Bronsteins and the emotional suffering their children had experienced as a result of the murders.

After receiving a death sentence, Booth appealed to the U.S. Supreme Court. The Court overturned his sentence, reasoning that victim-impact statements, at least in capital cases, violate the Eighth Amendment ban on cruel and unusual punishments. In a close (5-to-4) decision, the majority held that information in victim-impact statements leads to the risk that the death penalty might be imposed in an arbitrary and capricious manner.

In a complete about-face, affected in no small part by the gathering conservative majority among its justices, the Supreme Court held in the 1991 case of *Payne* v. *Tennessee*[93] that the *Booth* ruling had been based upon "a misreading of precedent."[94] The *Payne* case began with a 1987 double murder, in which a 28-year-old mother and her two-year-old daughter were stabbed to death in Millington, Tennessee.[95] A second child, three-year-old Nicholas Christopher, himself severely wounded in the attack, witnessed the deaths of his mother and young sister. In a trial following the killings, the prosecution claimed that Pervis Tyrone Payne, a 20-year-old retarded man, had killed the mother and child after the woman resisted his sexual advances. Payne was convicted of both murders. At the sentencing phase of the trial, Mary Zvolanek, Nicholas's grandmother, testified that the boy continued to cry out daily for his dead sister. Following *Booth*, Payne's conviction was upheld by the Tennessee Supreme Court in an opinion which did little to disguise the Tennessee court's contempt for the precedent set by *Booth*.

This time, however, the Supreme Court agreed with the Tennessee justices, holding that "[v]ictim impact evidence is simply another form or method of informing the sentencing authority about the specific harm caused by the crime in question, evidence of a general type long considered by sentencing authorities." As Chief Justice William H. Rehnquist wrote for the majority, "[C]ourts have always taken into consideration the harm done by the defendant in imposing sentence." In a concurring opinion, Justice Antonin Scalia held that "*Booth* significantly harms our criminal justice system" and had been decided with "plainly inadequate rational support."

Traditional Sentencing Options

Sentencing is fundamentally a risk-management strategy designed to protect the public while serving the ends of rehabilitation, deterrence, retribution, and restoration. Because the goals of sentencing are difficult to agree upon, so too are sanctions. Lengthy prison terms do little for rehabilitation, while community-release programs can hardly protect the innocent from offenders bent on continuing criminality.

Assorted sentencing philosophies continue to permeate state-level judicial systems. Each state has its own sentencing laws, and frequent revisions of those statutes are not uncommon. Because of huge variation from one state to another in the laws and procedures which control the imposition of criminal sanctions, sentencing has been called "the most diversified part of the Nation's criminal justice process."[96]

There is at least one common ground, however. It can be found in the four traditional sanctions which continue to dominate the thinking of most legislators and judges. The four traditional sanctions are fines, probation, imprisonment, and death. Fines and the death penalty are discussed in this chapter, while probation is described in Chapter 11, and prisons in Chapters 12 and 13.

In the case of indeterminate sentencing, fines, probation, and imprisonment are widely available to judges. The option selected generally depends upon the severity of the offense and the judge's best guess as to the likelihood of future criminal involvement on the part of the defendant. Sometimes two or more options are combined, as when an offender is fined and sentenced to prison or placed on probation and fined in support of restitution payments.

Jurisdictions that operate under presumptive sentencing guidelines generally limit the judge's choice to only one option and often specify the extent to which that option can be applied. Dollar amounts of fines, for example, are rigidly set, and prison terms are specified for each type of offense. The death penalty remains an option in a fair number of jurisdictions, but only for a highly select group of offenders.

A 2001 report by the Bureau of Justice Statistics on the sentencing practices of trial courts found that state courts convicted 927,717 felons in 1998.[97] Another 50,494 felony convictions occurred in federal courts. The report also found the following for offenders convicted of felonies in state courts (Figure 10–1):

■ Forty-four percent were sentenced to active prison terms.

■ The average sentence length for those sent to state prisons has decreased since 1990 (from six years to slightly less than five years).

■ Felons sentenced in 1998 were likely to serve more of their sentence before release (47%) than those sentenced in 1990 (33%).

■ Twenty-four percent received jail sentences, usually involving less than a year's confinement.

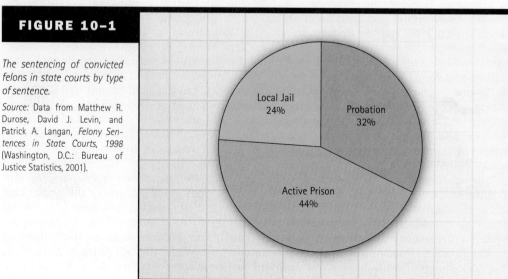

FIGURE 10–1

The sentencing of convicted felons in state courts by type of sentence.

Source: Data from Matthew R. Durose, David J. Levin, and Patrick A. Langan, *Felony Sentences in State Courts, 1998* (Washington, D.C.: Bureau of Justice Statistics, 2001).

Local Jail 24%

Probation 32%

Active Prison 44%

- Those sent to jail received an average sentence of six months.
- Thirty-two percent were sentenced to probation with no jail or prison time to serve.
- The average probation sentence was 40 months.
- Fines were imposed on 21% of convicted felons.
- One percent of those convicted of murder were sentenced to death.

Although the percentage of felons who receive active sentences may seem low to some, the number of criminal defendants receiving active prison time has increased dramatically. Figure 10–2 shows that the number of court-ordered prison commitments has increased nearly eightfold in the past 40 years.

Fines

The fine is one of the oldest forms of punishment, predating even the Code of Hammurabi.[98] Until recently, however, the use of fines as criminal sanctions suffered from built-in inequities and a widespread failure to collect them. Inequities arose when offenders with vastly different financial resources were fined similar amounts. A fine of $100, for example, can place a painful economic burden upon a poor defendant but is only laughable when imposed on a wealthy offender.

Today, fines are once again receiving attention as a serious sentencing alternative. One reason for the renewed interest is the stress placed upon state resources by burgeoning prison populations. The extensive imposition of fines not only results in less crowded prisons, but can contribute to state and local coffers and can lower the tax burden of law-abiding citizens. There are other advantages:

- Fines can deprive offenders of the proceeds of criminal activity.
- Fines can promote rehabilitation by enforcing economic responsibility.
- Fines can be collected by existing criminal justice agencies and are relatively inexpensive to administer.
- Fines can be made proportionate to both the severity of the offense and the ability of the offender to pay.

A National Institute of Justice (NIJ) survey found that an average of 86% of convicted defendants in courts of limited jurisdiction receive fines as sentences, some in combination with another penalty.[99] Fines are also widely used in courts of general jurisdiction,

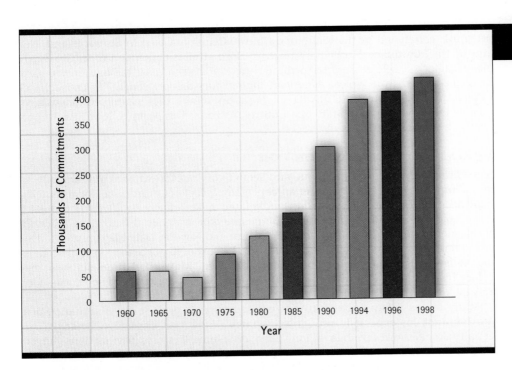

FIGURE 10-2

Court-ordered prison commitments, 1960–1998.

Source: Data from Matthew R. Durose, David J. Levin, and Patrick A. Langan, *Felony Sentences in State Courts, 1998* (Washington, D.C.: Bureau of Justice Statistics, 2001), and other years.

where the NIJ study found judges imposing fines in 42% of all cases which came before them for sentencing. Some studies estimate that over $1 billion in fines are collected nationwide each year.[100]

Fines are often imposed for relatively minor law violations, such as driving while intoxicated, reckless driving, disturbing the peace, disorderly conduct, public drunkenness, and vandalism. Judges in many courts, however, report the use of fines for relatively serious violations of the law, including assault, auto theft, embezzlement, fraud, and the sale and possession of various controlled substances. Fines are much more likely to be imposed, however, where the offender has both a clean record and the ability to pay.[101]

Opposition to the use of fines is based upon the following arguments:

- Fines allow the release of convicted offenders into the community but do not impose stringent controls on their behavior.

- Fines are a relatively mild form of punishment and are not consistent with the "just deserts" philosophy.

- Fines discriminate against the poor and favor the wealthy. Indigent offenders are especially subject to discrimination since they lack the financial resources with which to pay fines.

- Fines are difficult to collect.

A number of these objections can be answered by procedures which make available to judges complete financial information on defendants. Studies have found, however, that courts of limited jurisdiction, which are the most likely to impose fines, are also the least likely to have adequate information on offenders' economic status.[102] Perhaps as a consequence, judges are sometimes reluctant to impose fines. Two of the most widely cited objections by judges to the use of fines are (1) that fines allow more affluent offenders to "buy their way out" and (2) that poor offenders cannot pay fines.[103]

A solution to both objections can be found in the Scandinavian system of day fines. The day-fine system is based upon the idea that fines should be proportionate to the severity of the offense but also need to take into account the financial resources of the offender. Day fines are computed by first assessing the seriousness of the offense, the defendant's degree of culpability, and his or her prior record as measured in "days." The use of days as a benchmark of seriousness is related to the fact that, without fines, the offender could be sentenced to a number of days (or months or years) in jail or prison. The number of days an offender is assessed is then multiplied by the daily wages that person earns. Hence, if two people are sentenced to a five-day fine, but one earns only $20 per day and the other $200 per day, the first would pay a $100 fine and the second $1,000.

In the early 1990s, the National Institute of Justice reported on experimental day-fine programs conducted by the Richmond County Criminal Court in Staten Island, New York, and by the Milwaukee Municipal Court.[104] Both studies concluded that "the day fine can play a major . . . role as an intermediate sanction"[105] and that "the day-fine concept could be implemented in a typical American limited-jurisdiction court."[106] Those conclusions were supported by a 1996 RAND Corporation report that examined ongoing day-fine demonstration projects in Maricopa County, Arizona; Des Moines, Iowa; Bridgeport, Connecticut; and four counties in Oregon.[107]

Death: The Ultimate Sanction

Some crimes are especially heinous and seem to cry out for extreme punishment. In 1996, for example, in what some saw as an especially atrocious murder, a Norman, Oklahoma, man decapitated his neighbor and then walked naked down an alleyway to toss the victim's head into a trash Dumpster.[108] Witnesses who watched the accused killer, 33-year-old Cameron Smith, throw the head of 44-year-old Roydon Dale Major into the Dumpster called police. Responding officers discovered the rest of Major's body in a room at a boarding house where both Smith and Major had lived. Major had been stabbed repeatedly before his head was severed from his body. Smith was still naked when police found him and took him into custody.

Many states today have statutory provisions that provide for a sentence of **capital punishment** for especially repugnant crimes (known as **capital offenses**). The death penalty itself, however, has a long and gruesome history. Civilizations have almost always put criminals to death for a variety of offenses. As times changed, so did accepted methods of execution. Under the Davidic monarchy, for example, biblical Israel institu-

> Retribution is the implementation of justice.
>
> —Prosecutor Vincent Bugliosi

capital punishment

The death penalty. Capital punishment is the most extreme of all sentencing options.

capital offense

A criminal offense punishable by death.

tionalized the practice of stoning convicts to death.[109] The entire community could participate in dispatching the offender. As an apparent aid to deterrence, the convict's body might be impaled on a post at the gates of the city or otherwise exposed to public view.[110]

Athenian society, around 200 B.C., was progressive by the standards of its day. The ancient Greeks restricted the use of capital punishment and limited the suffering of the condemned through the use of poison derived from the hemlock tree. Socrates, the famous Greek orator, accused of being a political subversive, died this way.

The Romans were far less sensitive. They used beheading most often, although the law provided that arsonists should be burned alive and false witnesses thrown from a high rock.[111] Suspected witches were clubbed to death, and runaway slaves were strangled. Even more brutal sanctions included drawing and quartering; and social outcasts, Christians, and rabble-rousers were thrown to the lions or crucified. Although many people think that crucifixion was a barbarous practice that ended around the time of Christ, it survives into the present day. In 1997, for example, courts in Yemen (a country at the southern tip of the Arabian peninsula) sentenced two convicted murderers to be publicly crucified. It was the second time in three months that Yemeni courts imposed crucifixion sentences in an effort to combat a spate of violent crimes.[112]

After the fall of the Roman Empire, Europe was plunged into the Dark Ages, a period of superstition marked by widespread illiteracy and political turmoil. The Dark Ages lasted from A.D. 426 until the early thirteenth century. During the Dark Ages, executions were institutionalized through the use of ordeals designed to both judge and punish. Suspects were submerged in cold water, dumped in boiling oil, crushed under huge stones, forced to do battle with professional soldiers, or thrown into bonfires. Theological arguments prevalent at the time held that innocents, protected by God and heavenly forces, would emerge from any ordeal unscathed, while guilty parties would perish. Trial by ordeal was eliminated through a decree of the Fourth Lateran Council of 1215, under the direction of Pope Innocent III, after later evidence proved that many who died in ordeals could not have committed the crimes of which they were accused.[113]

Following the Fourth Lateran Council, trials, much as we know them today, became the basis for judging guilt or innocence. The death penalty remained in widespread use. As recently as a century and a half ago, 160 crimes were punishable in England by death.[114] The young received no special privilege. In 1801, a child of 13 was hung in Tyburn, England, for stealing a spoon.[115]

Sophisticated techniques of execution were in use by the nineteenth century. One engine of death was the guillotine, invented in France around the time of the French Revolution. The guillotine, described by its creator, Dr. Joseph-Ignace Guillotin, as "a cool breath on the back of the neck,"[116] was widely used in eliminating opponents of the revolution.

In America, hanging became the preferred mode of execution. It was especially popular on the frontier, since it required little by way of special materials and was a relatively efficient means of dispatch. By the early 1890s, electrocution had replaced hanging as the dominant form of capital punishment. The appeal of electrocution was that it stopped the heart without visible signs of gross bodily trauma.

EXECUTIONS: THE GRIM FACTS

Since 1608, when records began to be kept on capital punishment, estimates are that more than 18,800 legal executions have been carried out in the United States.[117] Although capital punishment was widely used throughout the eighteenth and nineteenth centuries, the mid-twentieth century offered a brief respite in the number of offenders legally executed in the United States. Between 1930 and 1967, when the U.S. Supreme Court ordered a nationwide stay of pending executions, nearly 3,800 people were put to death. The years 1935 and 1936 were peak years, with nearly 200 legal killings each year. Executions declined substantially every year thereafter. Between 1967 and 1977, a *de facto* moratorium existed, with no executions carried out in any U.S. jurisdiction. Following the lifting of the moratorium, executions resumed (Figure 10–3). In 1993, 38 offenders were put to death, while 56 were executed nationwide in 1995. 1999 set a modern record for executions, with 98 executions—35 in Texas alone. Substantially fewer persons (66) were executed in 2001.

Today, 38 of the 50 states and the federal government have capital punishment laws.[118] All but New York permit execution for first-degree murder, while treason, kidnapping, the murder of a police or correctional officer, and murder while under a life sentence are punishable

[Unless the Constitution is amended] we will never correct the existing imbalance in this country between [a] defendant's irreducible constitutional rights and the current haphazard patchwork of victims' rights.

—Former U.S. Attorney General
Janet Reno

Of all the initiatives that this Congress could undertake, few will touch the heart of Americans as dearly as the measure seeking to ensure that the judicial process is just and fair for the victims of crime.

—Senator Orrin Hatch

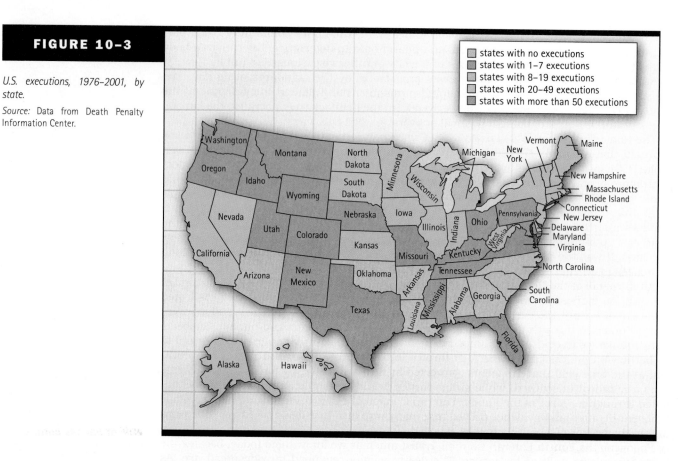

U.S. executions, 1976–2001, by state.

Source: Data from Death Penalty Information Center.

States with no executions
States with 1–7 executions
States with 8–19 executions
States with 20–49 executions
States with more than 50 executions

by death in selected jurisdictions.[119] New York allows for the imposition of a death sentence in cases involving the murder of law enforcement officers, judges, and witnesses and their families and also applies the punishment to serial killers, terrorists, murderers-for-hire, and those who kill while committing another felony such as robbery or rape.

The list of crimes punishable by death under federal jurisdiction increased dramatically with passage of the Violent Crime Control and Law Enforcement Act of 1994 and was expanded still further by the 2001 USA PATRIOT Act, a federal law that focuses on fighting terrorism. The list now includes a total of about 60 offenses. State legislators have also worked to expand the types of crime for which a sentence of death can be imposed. In 1997, for example, the Louisiana Supreme Court upheld the state's year-old child rape statute, which allows for the imposition of a capital sentence when the victim is under 12 years of age. The case involved an AIDS-infected father who raped his three daughters, ages five, eight, and nine. In upholding the father's death sentence, the Louisiana court ruled that child rape is "like no other crime."[120]

A total of 3,717 offenders were under sentence of death throughout the United States on July 1, 2001.[121] The latest statistics show that 98.5% of those on death row are male, 46% are white, 9% are Hispanic, 43% are African-American, and 2% are of other races (mostly Native American and Pacific Islander).

Methods of imposing death vary by state. The majority of death penalty states authorize execution through lethal injection. Electrocution is the second most common means of dispatch, while hanging, the gas chamber, and firing squads have survived, at least as options available to the condemned, in a few states. For the most current statistical information on capital punishment, visit the Death Penalty Information Center at **Web Extra! 10-6** at cjtoday.com.

HABEAS CORPUS REVIEW

The legal process through which a capital sentence is carried to conclusion is fraught with problems. One serious difficulty centers on the fact that automatic review of all death sentences by appellate courts and constant legal maneuvering by defense counsel often lead to a dramatic delay between the time the sentence is passed and the time it is carried out. Today, an average of ten years and ten months passes between the time a sentence of death is imposed and the time it is carried out.[122] Such lengthy delays, compounded by uncertainty over whether a sentence will ever be finally imposed, directly contravene the generally accepted notion that punishment should be swift and certain.

In a typical case, in April 1995, the Louisiana Supreme Court granted two-time killer Antonio James his fourteenth stay of execution just four hours before he was scheduled to die by lethal injection. The 39-year-old James had been sentenced to death 15 years earlier for shooting 70-year-old Henry Silver in the head during an armed robbery on New Year's Day in 1979.[123] He was later sentenced to 99 more years in prison for killing Alvin Adams, 74, during an armed robbery two weeks after the Silver killing. In granting the stay, the Louisiana Supreme Court ruled that a state district court had erred a few days earlier by not granting a hearing on new evidence James's attorneys said would prove that he was not the triggerman in either killing. Before the court's ruling, Governor Edwin Edwards had refused to block the execution. James was finally executed in 1996. He had been on Louisiana's death row since 1981.

Delays in the imposition of capital sanctions have been the source of much anguish for condemned prisoners as well as for the victims and the families of both. In a final statement just before his client was executed, for example, the attorney for 30-year-old Dorsie Johnson-Bey told witnesses, "If the jury trying this case could see what has happened to him in the 11 years he's been on death row, they would say that he certainly doesn't pose a continuing threat to society."[124] A few minutes later, Johnson-Bey was put to death by lethal injection at the Walls Unit in Huntsville, Texas. A one-time janitor in the West Texas community of Colorado City, he had been sentenced to die for the March 1986 murder of Jack Huddleston, a 53-year-old convenience store clerk who had been shot in the head with a .25-caliber pistol after being forced to lie in the store's cooler. Huddleston had been robbed of $161 and cigarettes.

In a speech before the American Bar Association in 1989, Chief Justice William Rehnquist called for reforms of the federal *habeas corpus* system, which, at the time, allowed condemned prisoners virtually limitless opportunities for appeal. **Writs of *habeas corpus*** (Latin for "you have the body"), which require that a prisoner be brought into court to determine if he or she is being legally held, form the basis for many federal appeals made by prisoners on state death rows. In 1968, Chief Justice Earl Warren called the right to file *habeas* petitions, as guaranteed under the U.S. Constitution, the "symbol and guardian of individual liberty." Twenty years later, however, Rehnquist claimed that writs of *habeas corpus* were being used indiscriminately by death-row inmates seeking to delay executions even where grounds for such delay do not exist. "The capital defendant does not need to prevail on the merits in order to accomplish his purpose," said Rehnquist. "He wins temporary victories by postponing a final adjudication."[125]

In a move to reduce delays in the conduct of executions, the U.S. Supreme Court, in the case of *McCleskey* v. *Zandt* (1991),[126] limited the number of appeals a condemned person may lodge with the courts. Saying that repeated filing for the sole purpose of delay promotes "disrespect for the finality of convictions" and "disparages the entire criminal justice system," the Court established a two-pronged criterion for future appeals. According to *McCleskey*, in any petition beyond the first filed with the federal court, a capital defendant must (1) demonstrate good cause why the claim now being made was not included in the first filing and (2) explain how the absence of that claim may have harmed the petitioner's ability to mount an effective defense. Two months later, the Court reinforced *McCleskey* when it ruled, in *Coleman* v. *Thompson* (1991),[127] that state prisoners could not cite "procedural default," such as a defense attorney's failure to meet a state's filing deadline for appeals, as the basis for an appeal to federal court.

In 1995, in the case of *Schlup* v. *Delo*,[128] the Court continued to define standards for further appeals from death-row inmates, ruling that before appeals based upon claims of new evidence could be heard, "a petitioner must show that, in light of the new evidence, it is more likely than not that no reasonable juror would have found him guilty beyond a reasonable doubt." A "reasonable juror" was defined as one who "would consider fairly all of the evidence presented and would conscientiously obey the trial court's instructions requiring proof beyond a reasonable doubt."

Opportunities for federal appeals by death-row inmates were further limited by the Antiterrorism and Effective Death Penalty Act (AEDPA) of 1996, which sets a one-year postconviction deadline for state inmates filing federal *habeas corpus* appeals. The deadline is six months for state death-row inmates who were provided a lawyer for *habeas* appeals at the state level. The act also requires federal courts to presume that the factual

writ of *habeas corpus*

A writ that directs the person detaining a prisoner to bring him or her before a judicial officer to determine the lawfulness of the imprisonment.

There is only one basic human right, the right to do as you please unless it causes others harm. With it comes the only basic human duty, the duty to take the consequences.

—P. J. O'Rourke

Anti-death penalty activist Sister Helen Prejean (left) hugging Karla Faye Tucker. The 1998 execution of Tucker by Texas authorities made her the first woman to be legally put to death in the United States in nearly 14 years. Tucker's execution led to questions about whether the death penalty makes sense when apparently nonthreatening individuals are executed years after their crimes.

Picture Quest, Vienna

> Too often, we bend over backward to protect the rights of criminals, but pay no attention to those who are hurt the most. Victims should have a voice in trial and other proceedings. Their safety should be a factor in the sentencing and release of their attackers. They should be notified when an offender is released back into their community. And they should have a right to compensation from their attacker.
>
> —Former Vice President Al Gore

findings of state courts are correct, does not permit the claim of state court misinterpretations of the U.S. Constitution as a basis for *habeas* relief unless those misinterpretations are "unreasonable," and requires that all petitioners must show, prior to obtaining a hearing, facts sufficient to establish by clear and convincing evidence that but for constitutional error, no reasonable fact finder would have found the petitioner guilty. The act also requires approval by a three-judge panel before an inmate can file a second federal appeal raising newly discovered evidence of innocence. In 1996, in the case of *Felker* v. *Turpin*,[129] the U.S. Supreme Court ruled that limitations on the authority of federal courts to consider successive *habeas corpus* petitions imposed by the Antiterrorism and Effective Death Penalty Act of 1996 are permissible since they do not deprive the U.S. Supreme Court of its original jurisdiction over such petitions.

Some recent statements by Supreme Court justices have indicated that long delays in carrying out executions that are caused by the government may render the punishment unconstitutionally cruel and unusual. One example comes from the 1998 case of *Elledge* v. *Florida*,[130] where the execution of William D. Elledge had been delayed for 23 years. Although the full Court refused to hear the case, Justice Stephen Breyer observed that "[t]wenty-three years under sentence of death is unusual—whether one takes as a measuring rod current practice or the practice in this country and in England at the time our Constitution was written." Moreover, wrote Breyer, execution after such a long delay could be considered cruel because Elledge "has experienced that delay because of the State's own faulty procedures and not because of frivolous appeals on his own part."

OPPOSITION TO CAPITAL PUNISHMENT

Thirty years ago, David Magris, who was celebrating his twenty-first birthday with a crime spree, shot Dennis Tapp in the back during a holdup, leaving Tapp a paraplegic. Tapp had been working a late-night shift, tending his father's quick-serve gas station. Magris went on to commit more robberies that night, killing 20-year-old Steven Tompkins in a similar crime. Although sentenced to death by a California court, the U.S. Supreme Court overturned the state's death penalty law in 1972, opening the door for Magris to be paroled in 1985. Long before Magris was freed from prison, however, Tapp had already forgiven him. A few minutes after the shooting happened, Tapp regained consciousness, dragged himself to a telephone, and called for help. The next thing he did was ask "God to forgive the man who did this to me."[131] Today, both men are staunch death-penalty opponents. And Tapp and Magris, who is president of the Northern California Coalition to Abolish the Death

Penalty, have become friends. They are united by a crime that happened 30 years ago and by a heartfelt need to fight against capital punishment. "Don't get me wrong," says Tapp, "David has a good personality. What he did was wrong. . . . He did something stupid and he paid for it."[132]

Because of the strong emotions that state-imposed death wrings from the hearts of varied constituencies, many attempts have been made to abolish capital punishment since the founding of the United States. The first recorded effort to abolish the death penalty occurred at the home of Benjamin Franklin in 1787.[133] At a meeting there on March 9 of that year, Dr. Benjamin Rush, a signer of the Declaration of Independence and a leading medical pioneer, read a paper against capital punishment to a small but influential audience. Although his immediate efforts came to naught, his arguments laid the groundwork for many debates which followed. Michigan, widely regarded as the first abolitionist state, joined the Union in 1837 without a death penalty. A number of other states, including Massachusetts, West Virginia, Wisconsin, Minnesota, Alaska, and Hawaii, have since spurned death as a possible sanction for criminal acts. As noted earlier, it remains a viable sentencing option in 38 of the states and in all federal jurisdictions. As a consequence, arguments continue to rage over its value.

Today, six main rationales for abolishing capital punishment are heard:

1. The death penalty can and has been inflicted on innocent people.
2. The death penalty is not an effective deterrent.
3. The imposition of the death penalty is, by the nature of our legal system, arbitrary.
4. The death penalty discriminates against certain ethnic and racial groups.
5. The death penalty is far too expensive to justify its use.
6. Human life is sacred, and killing at the hands of the state is not a righteous act, but rather one which is on the same moral level as the crimes committed by the condemned.

The first five abolitionist claims are pragmatic; that is, they can be measured and verified or disproved by looking at the facts. The last claim is primarily philosophical and therefore not amenable to scientific investigation. Hence, we shall briefly examine only the first five.

The Death Penalty Information Center claims that 98 people in 22 states have been freed from death row between 1973 and 2001 after it was determined that they were innocent of the capital crime of which they had been convicted.[134] One study of felony convictions that used analysis of DNA to provide postconviction evidence of guilt or innocence found 28 cases in which defendants had been wrongly convicted and sentenced to lengthy prison terms. The study, *Convicted by Juries, Exonerated by Science*, effectively demonstrated that the judicial process can be flawed.[135] (Read more about the study and the forensic use of DNA evidence in Chapter 17.) DNA testing can play a critical role in identifying wrongful convictions because, as Barry Scheck and Peter Neufeld point out, "Unlike witnesses who disappear or whose recollections fade over time, DNA in biological samples can be reliably extracted decades after the commission of the crime. The results of such testing have invariably been found to have a scientific certainty that easily outweighs the eyewitness identification testimony or other direct or circumstantial proof that led to the original conviction."[136] "Very simply," say Scheck and Neufeld, "DNA testing has demonstrated that far more wrongful convictions occur than even the most cynical and jaded scholars had suspected."[137]

A 2000 study by Columbia Law School professors James S. Liebman and Jeffrey Fagan examined 4,578 death penalty cases in state and federal courts from 1973 to 1995.[138] Liebman and Fagan found that appellate courts overturned the conviction or reduced the sentence in 68% of the cases examined. In 82% of the successful appeals, defendants were found to be deserving of a lesser sentence, while convictions were overturned in 7% of such appeals. According to the study's authors, "Our 23 years worth of findings reveal a capital punishment system collapsing under the weight of its own mistakes." You may read the Liebman-Fagan report in its entirety at **Library Extra! 10–5** at cjtoday.com.

Claims of innocence are being partially addressed today by recently passed state laws that mandate DNA testing of all death-row confinees in situations where DNA testing might help establish guilt or innocence (that is, in cases where blood or semen from the perpetrator is available for testing).[139] In 2000, Illinois Governor George Ryan announced that he was suspending all executions in his state indefinitely. Ryan's proclamation came after

> There can be no doubt that the taking of the life of the President creates much more societal harm than the taking of the life of a homeless person.
>
> —Tennessee Attorney General Charles Burson, arguing before the U.S. Supreme Court in *Payne* v. *Tennessee* (1991)

Northwestern University journalism students (from left) Shawn Armbrust, Cara Rubinsky, Tom McCann, and Erica LeBorgne talking with their professor, David Protess. The students investigated a controversial Illinois death-row case and found evidence that led to the release of inmate Anthony Porter.

AP/Wide World Photos

DNA testing showed that 13 Illinois death-row prisoners could not have committed the capital crimes of which they were convicted. Also in 2000, the American Bar Association issued a formal request asking states holding death-row inmates to use DNA tests to minimize the risk that innocent people would be executed.

During the 1970s and 1980s, the deterrent effect of the death penalty became a favorite subject for debate in academic circles.[140] Studies of states which had eliminated the death penalty failed to show any increase in homicide rates.[141] Similar studies of neighboring states, in which jurisdictions retaining capital punishment were compared with those which had abandoned it, also failed to demonstrate any significant differences.[142] Although death penalty advocates remain numerous, few any longer argue for the penalty based on its deterrent effects. One study that *has* found support for use of the death penalty as a deterrent was reported in 2001 by Hashem Dezhbakhsh and his colleagues at Emory University.[143] According to Dezhbakhsh, "Our results suggest that capital punishment has a strong deterrent effect. . . . In particular, each execution results, on average, in 18 fewer murders. . . .[144] According to Dezhbakhsh, most other studies in the area have not only been methodologically flawed, but have failed to consider the fact that a number of states sentence select offenders to death but do not carry out executions. Dezhbakhsh writes, "If criminals know that the justice system issues many death sentences but the executions are not carried out, then they may not be deterred by an increase in probability of a death sentence."[145]

The third abolitionist claim, that the death penalty is arbitrary, is based upon the belief that access to effective representation and to the courts themselves is differentially available to people with varying financial and other resources. The notion of arbitrariness also builds upon beliefs that differences in jury composition, judges' personal dispositions and backgrounds, varying laws and procedures, and jurisdictional social characteristics may lead to varying sentences and could mean that a person who might be sentenced to die in one place might receive a lesser sentence elsewhere.

Access to the courts, which some see as more dependent upon a changing legal environment than fair standards of due process, is another area in which arbitrariness can play a role. In recent years, access to appellate courts has been restricted by a number of new state and federal laws (discussed in greater detail in Chapter 13). Such restrictions led the American Bar Association's House of Delegates in 1997 to cite what it called "an erosion of legal rights of death row inmates" and to urge an immediate halt to executions in the United States until the judicial process could be overhauled.[146] ABA delegates were expressing concerns that over the past decade, Congress and the states have unfairly limited death-row appeals through restrictive legislation. The ABA resolution also called for a halt to executions of people under 18 years old and of those who are mentally retarded.

The claim that the death penalty is discriminatory is harder to investigate. Although past evidence suggests that blacks and other minorities in the United States have been

> Evolving standards of human decency will finally lead to the abolition of the death penalty in this country.
>
> —Former U.S. Supreme Court Justice William Brennan

disproportionately sentenced to death,[147] more recent evidence is not as clear. At first glance, disproportionality seems apparent: 45 of the 98 prisoners executed between January 1977 and May 1988 were black or Hispanic; 84 of the 98 had been convicted of killing whites.[148] A 1996 Kentucky study found that blacks accused of killing whites in that state between 1976 and 1991 had a higher-than-average probability of being charged with a capital crime and of being sentenced to die than did homicide offenders of other races.[149] For an accurate appraisal to be made, however, any claims of disproportionality must go beyond simple comparisons with racial representation in the larger population and must somehow measure both frequency and seriousness of capital crimes between and within racial groups. Following that line of reasoning, the Supreme Court, in the 1987 case of *McCleskey* v. *Kemp*,[150] held that a simple showing of racial discrepancies in the application of the death penalty does not constitute a constitutional violation. A 2001 study of racial and ethnic fairness in federal capital punishment sentences attempted to go beyond mere percentages in its analysis of the role played by race and ethnicity and in capital punishment sentencing decisions.[151] Although the study, which closely reviewed 950 capital punishment cases, found that approximately 80% of federal death-row inmates are African-American, researchers found "no intentional racial or ethnic bias in how capital punishment was administered in federal cases."[152] Underrepresented groups were more likely to be sentenced to death, "but only because they are more likely to be arrested on facts that could support a capital charge, not because the justice system acts in a discriminatory fashion," the report said.[153] The study was initiated by former Attorney General Janet Reno and was concluded during the first year of George W. Bush's administration. Read the entire report at **Library Extra! 10–6** at cjtoday.com.

Another 2001 study, this one by New Jersey Supreme Court Special Master David Baime, found no evidence of bias against black defendants in capital cases in New Jersey during the period studied (August 1982 through May 2000). The study concluded, "Simply stated, we discern no sound basis from the statistical evidence to conclude that the race or ethnicity of the defendant is a factor in determining which cases advance to a penalty trial and which defendants are ultimately sentenced to death. The statistical evidence abounds the other way—it strongly suggests that there are no racial or ethnic disparities in capital murder prosecution and death sentencing rates."[154]

The fifth claim, that the death penalty is too expensive, is difficult to explore. Although the "official" costs associated with capital punishment are high, many death penalty supporters argue that no cost is *too* high if it achieves justice. Death penalty opponents, on the other hand, point to the huge costs associated with judicial appeals and with the executions themselves. According to the Death Penalty Information Center (DPIC), which maintains a national database on such costs, "The death penalty costs North Carolina $2.16 million per execution *over* the costs of a non-death penalty murder case with a sentence of imprisonment for life."[155] The DPIC also says that an average execution in Florida costs $3.2 million to carry out, and that "in Texas, a death penalty case costs an average of $2.3 million—about three times the cost of imprisoning someone in a single cell at the highest security level for 40 years."

> There is no evidence of racial bias in the administration of the federal death penalty.
>
> —U.S. Attorney General John Ashcroft[iv]

Demonstrators protesting the execution of convicted bomber Timothy McVeigh on June 11, 2001, outside the Terre Haute, Indiana, federal correctional facility only hours before McVeigh was scheduled to die.

© Reuters, Jim Bourg, CORBIS

Capital punishment supporters gathering outside the Terre Haute, Indiana, federal correctional facility where convicted bomber Timothy McVeigh awaited execution.

AP/Wide World Photos

> Life is sacred. It's about the only sacred thing on earth—and no one has a right to do away with it.
>
> —Aldona DeVetsco, mother of a murder victim, commenting on the execution of her son's killer

JUSTIFICATIONS FOR CAPITAL PUNISHMENT

Shortly before Christmas 1996, New York State Judge Thomas Demakos sentenced 23-year-old Joshua Torres to 58 years to life in prison, saying he wished that he could impose the death penalty. Torres had been convicted of abducting and burning 20-year-old Kimberly Antonakos alive after he and his partners bungled an attempt to extort ransom from the young woman's father. The father failed to respond to the kidnappers' $75,000 ransom demand because his answering machine didn't record the call. According to witnesses, Torres tied the college student to a pole, doused her with gasoline, lit a match, and set her on fire. At sentencing, Judge Demakos told those gathered in the courtroom, "I must admit that hearing this testimony [about how Kimberly was set afire] almost brought me to tears."[156] Demakos said that although the case cried out for the death penalty, he could not impose it because it was not in effect in New York State at the time the murder took place.

Judge Demakos, like many others in today's society, feels that "cold-blooded murder" justifies a sentence of death. Justifications for the death penalty are collectively referred to as the *retentionist position.* The three retentionist arguments are (1) revenge, (2) just deserts, and (3) protection. Those who justify capital punishment as revenge attempt to appeal to the idea that survivors, victims, and the state are entitled to "closure." Only after execution of the criminal perpetrator, they say, can the psychological and social wounds engendered by the offense begin to heal.

The just deserts argument makes the simple and straightforward claim that some people deserve to die for what they have done. Death is justly deserved; anything less cannot suffice as a sanction for the most heinous crimes. As Justice Potter Stewart once wrote, "The decision that capital punishment may be the appropriate sanction in extreme cases is an expression of the community's belief that certain crimes are themselves so grievous an affront to humanity that the only adequate response may be the penalty of death."[157]

The third retentionist claim, that of protection, asserts that offenders, once executed, can commit no further crimes. Clearly the least emotional of the retentionist claims, the protectionist argument may also be the weakest, since societal interests in protection can also be met in other ways, such as incarceration. In addition, various studies have shown that there is little likelihood of repeat offenses among people convicted of murder and later released.[158] One reason for such results, however, may be that murderers generally serve lengthy prison sentences prior to release and may have lost whatever youthful propensity for criminality they previously possessed. For an intriguing dialogue between two U.S. Supreme Court justices over the constitutionality of the death penalty, see **Web Extra! 10–7** at cjtoday.com.

THE FUTURE OF THE DEATH PENALTY

Because of the nature of the positions that both sides advocate, there is little common ground even for discussion between abolitionists and retentionists. Foes of the death penalty hope that its demonstrated lack of deterrent capacity will convince others that it should be abandoned. Their approach, based as it is upon statistical evidence, appears on the surface to be quite rational. However, it is doubtful that many capital punishment opponents could be persuaded to support the death penalty even if statistics showed it to be a deterrent. Likewise, the tactics of death penalty supporters are equally instinctive.

Drug smugglers executed in China. Signs describe the offenders' crimes.

Xinhua, Getty Images, Inc.

Retentionists could probably not be swayed by statistical studies of deterrence, no matter what they show, since their support is bound up with emotional calls for retribution.

The future of the death penalty rests primarily with state legislatures. Short of renewed Supreme Court intervention, the future of capital punishment may depend more upon popular opinion than it does on arguments pro or con. Because their careers lie in the hands of their constituencies, legislators are likely to follow the public mandate. Hence, it may be that studies of public attitudes toward the death penalty may be the most useful in predicting the sanction's future. At the moment, it appears that the American public, as a whole, favors the imposition of capital punishment in the case of heinous crimes. Support for the death penalty, however, varies considerably from state to state and from one region of the country to another.[159]

THE COURTS AND THE DEATH PENALTY

The U.S. Supreme Court has for some time served as a sounding board for issues surrounding the death penalty. One of the Court's earliest cases in this area was *Wilkerson* v. *Utah* (1878),[160] which questioned shooting as a method of execution and raised Eighth Amendment claims that firing squads constituted a form of cruel and unusual punishment. The Court disagreed, however, contrasting the relatively civilized nature of firing squads with the various forms of torture often associated with capital punishment around the time the Bill of Rights was written.

In similar fashion, the Court supported electrocution as a permissible form of execution in *In re Kemmler* (1890).[161] In *Kemmler*, the Court defined cruel and unusual methods of execution as follows: "Punishments are cruel when they involve torture or a lingering death; but the punishment of death is not cruel, within the meaning of that word as used in the Constitution. It implies there is something inhuman and barbarous, something more than the mere extinguishing of life."[162] Almost 60 years later, the Court ruled that a second attempt at the electrocution of a convicted person, when the first did not work, did not violate the Eighth Amendment.[163] The Court reasoned that the initial failure was the consequence of accident or unforeseen circumstances and not the result of an effort on the part of executioners to be intentionally cruel.

It was not until 1972, however, in the landmark case of *Furman* v. *Georgia*,[164] that the Court recognized "evolving standards of decency"[165] which might necessitate a reconsideration of Eighth Amendment guarantees. In a 5-to-4 ruling, the *Furman* decision invalidated Georgia's death penalty statute on the basis that it allowed a jury unguided discretion in the imposition of a capital sentence. The majority of justices concluded that the Georgia statute, which permitted a jury to decide issues of guilt or innocence while it weighed sentencing options, allowed for an arbitrary and capricious application of the death penalty.

Many other states with statutes similar to Georgia's were affected by the *Furman* ruling but moved quickly to modify their procedures. What evolved was the two-step procedure used today in capital cases. In the first stage, guilt or innocence is decided. If the defendant is convicted of a crime for which execution is possible, a second, or penalty, phase ensues. The penalty phase generally permits the introduction of new evidence that may have been irrelevant to the question of guilt but which may be relevant to punishment, such as drug use or childhood abuse. In most death penalty jurisdictions, juries determine the punishment. However, in Arizona, Idaho, Montana, and Nebraska, the trial judge sets the sentence in the second phase of capital murder trials, and Alabama, Delaware, Florida, and Indiana allow juries only to recommend a sentence to the judge.

The two-step trial procedure was specifically approved by the Court in *Gregg* v. *Georgia* (1976).[166] In *Gregg*, the Court upheld the two-stage procedural requirements of Georgia's new capital punishment law as necessary for ensuring the separation of the highly personal information needed in a sentencing decision from the kinds of information reasonably permissible in a jury trial where issues of guilt or innocence alone are being decided. In the opinion written for the majority, the Court for the first time recognized the significance of public opinion in deciding upon the legitimacy of questionable sanctions.[167] Its opinion cited the strong showing of public support for the death penalty following *Furman* to mean that death was still a socially and culturally acceptable penalty.

Post-*Gregg* decisions set limits upon the use of death as a penalty for all but the most severe crimes. In 1977, in the case of *Coker* v. *Georgia*,[168] the Court struck down a Georgia law imposing the death penalty for the rape of an adult woman. The Court concluded that capital punishment under such circumstances would be "grossly disproportionate" to the crime. A year earlier, in the 1976 case of *Woodson* v. *North Carolina*,[169] a law requiring mandatory application of the death penalty for specific crimes was overturned.

In two 1990 rulings, *Blystone* v. *Pennsylvania*[170] and *Boyde* v. *California*,[171] the Court upheld state statutes which had been interpreted to dictate that death penalties must be imposed where juries find a lack of mitigating factors that could offset obvious aggravating circumstances. In the 1990 case of R. Gene Simmons, an Arkansas mass murderer convicted of killing 16 relatives during a 1987 shooting rampage, the Court granted inmates under sentence of death the right to waive appeals. Prior to the *Simmons* case, any interested party could file a brief on behalf of the condemned—with or without their consent.

Recently, death-row inmates, and those who file cases on their behalf to test the boundaries of statutory acceptability, have been busy bringing challenges to state capital punishment laws. Most such challenges focus upon the procedures involved in sentencing decisions. In 1995, for example, in *Harris* v. *Alabama*,[172] the U.S. Supreme Court upheld Alabama's capital sentencing system, which allows juries to recommend sentences but judges to decide them. A challenge to the constitutionality of California's capital sentencing law, which requires the jury to consider, among other things, the circumstances of the offense, prior violent crimes by the defendant, and the defendant's age, was rejected in *Tuilaepa* v. *California* (1994).[173]

The majority on today's high court seems largely convinced of the constitutionality of a sentence of death. Open to debate, however, is the constitutionality of questionable *methods* for its imposition. In a 1993 hearing, *Poyner* v. *Murray*,[174] the U.S. Supreme Court hinted at the possibility of reopening questions first raised in *Kemmler*. The case challenged Virginia's use of the electric chair as a form of cruel and unusual punishment. Syvasky Lafayette Poyner, who originally brought the case before the Court, lost his bid for a stay of execution and was electrocuted in March 1993. Nonetheless, in *Poyner*, Justices David H. Souter, Harry A. Blackmun, and John Paul Stevens wrote, "The Court has not spoken squarely on the underlying issue since *In re Kemmler* . . . and the holding of that case does not constitute a dispositive response to litigation of the issue in light of modern knowledge about the method of execution in question." In a still more recent ruling, members of the Court questioned the constitutionality of hanging, suggesting that it may be a form of cruel and unusual punishment. In that case, *Campbell* v. *Wood* (1994),[175] the defendant, Charles Campbell, raped a woman, got out of prison, then went back and murdered her. His request for a stay of execution was denied since the law of Washington State, where the murder occurred, offered Campbell a choice between various methods of execution and, therefore, an alternative to hanging. Similarly, in 1996, the Court upheld California's death penalty statute, which provides for lethal injection as the primary method of capital punishment in that state.[176] The constitutionality of the statute had been challenged by two death-row inmates who claimed that a provision in the law which permitted condemned prisoners the choice of lethal gas in lieu of injection brought the statute within the realm of allowing cruel and unusual punishments.

Questions about the constitutionality of electrocution as a means of execution again came to the fore in 1997, when flames shot from the head and the leather mask covering the face of Pedro Medina during his Florida execution. Similarly, in 1999, blood poured from behind the mask covering Allen Lee "Tiny" Davis's face as he was put to death in Florida's electric chair. State officials claimed that the 344-pound Davis suffered a nosebleed brought on by hypertension and the blood-thinning medication that he had been taking. Photographs of Davis taken during and immediately after the execution showed him grimacing while bleeding profusely onto his chest and neck. In 2001, the Georgia Supreme Court declared electrocution to be unconstitutional, ending its use in that state.[177] The Georgia court cited testimony from lower court records showing that electrocution may not result in a quick death or in an immediate cessation of consciousness. By the time of the court's decision, however, the Georgia legislature had already passed a law establishing lethal injection as the state's sole method of punishment for capital crimes. Following the decision, only two states, Alabama and Nebraska, still use electrocution as their sole method of execution.[178]

In 2001, in the case of *Penry* v. *Johnson*,[179] the U.S. Supreme Court found that a state trial court in Texas had failed to allow a jury to properly consider a murder defendant's mental retardation and childhood abuse as mitigating factors when it found that his crime warranted the death penalty rather than life in prison. This was the second time that the Court had ordered a new sentencing hearing for Johnny Paul Penry, who was first convicted of brutally raping and murdering Pamela Carpenter on October 25, 1979, and had twice been sentenced to die.[180] In both cases, the Court found fault with Texas jury instructions and the system for their implementation, which restricted jurors from effectively weighing Penry's mental retardation as a mitigating circumstance in their sentencing decision. Shortly after the Court's decision, Texas Governor Rick Perry vetoed legislation that would have banned the execution of mentally retarded death-row inmates throughout the state.[181]

Some death penalty opponents had hoped that the age of a capital defendant at the time the crime was committed might provide grounds for appeal. However, in 2001, a closely divided U.S. Supreme Court refused to stay the execution of Texan Napoleon Beazley, who was 17 years old when he shot a man to death while stealing his sedan from his driveway in 1994.[182] Twenty-three states continue to permit the execution of murderers who kill before reaching the age of 18. Among the 726 people put to death between January 1973 and August 2001, 17 had committed their crimes as juveniles.[183]

> We've never had a doubt about the guilt of Timothy McVeigh. But, we needed more than a guity defendant. We needed an innocent system.
>
> —U.S. Attorney General, John Ashcroft[v]

WHAT WOULD YOU DO?

The CD-ROM scenario for Chapter 10 discusses the constitutionality of the death penalty, especially as it relates to the issue of cruel and unusual punishment. Use the CD-ROM found in the back of your textbook to work through this scenario. Playing the role of a state legislator, you must decide what kinds of procedural requirements for capital punishment might best meet the needs of your state as well as the requirements of the U.S. Constitution.

Summary

The goals of criminal sentencing are many and varied, and they include retribution, incapacitation, deterrence, rehabilitation, and restoration. The just deserts model, with its emphasis on retribution and revenge, may be the most influential sentencing philosophy in the United States today. Many citizens, however, still expect sentencing practices to provide for the other general sentencing goals. This ambivalence toward the purpose of sentencing reflects a more basic cultural uncertainty regarding the root causes of crime, the true nature of justice, and the fundamental goals of the criminal justice system.

Structured sentencing, embodied in the Federal Sentencing Guidelines and in many state sentencing programs of today, is a child of the just deserts philosophy. The structured sentencing model, however, while apparently associated with a reduction in biased and inequitable sentencing practices which had characterized previous sentencing models, may not be the panacea it once seemed. Inequitable practices under the indeterminate model may never have been as widespread as opponents of that model claimed them to be. Worse still, the practice of structured sentencing may not reduce sentencing discretion but merely move it out of the hands of judges and into the ever-widening sphere of plea bargaining. Doubly unfortunate, structured sentencing, by deemphasizing parole, weakens incentives among the correctional population for positive change and tends to swell prison populations until they're overflowing. Even so, as society-wide sentiments and the social policies they support swing further in the direction of social responsibility, the interests of crime victims and the concerns of those who champion them will increasingly be recognized.

Discussion Questions

1. Outline the various sentencing goals discussed in this chapter. Which of these goals do you find most acceptable as the primary goal of sentencing? How might your choice of goal vary with the type of offense? Can you envision any circumstances which might make your choice less acceptable?
2. In your opinion, is the return to just deserts consistent with the structured sentencing model? Explain.
3. Trace the differences between determinate and indeterminate sentencing. Which model holds the best long-term promise for crime reduction? Why?
4. Are you a supporter of capital punishment or an opponent? Explain your position.

To participate in an online discussion on these topics and others, go to the Global Town Meeting electronic message board for Chapter 10 on the *Criminal Justice Today* Companion Website at cjtoday.com.

Web Quest!

Visit the U.S. Sentencing Commission (USSC) on the Web at http://www.ussc.gov. Review the most recent publications and reports to Congress available at that site, and identify the most current issues in federal sentencing today. List and describe these issues. Also view the USSC employment opportunities listed at the site, and read the information about the Judicial Fellows Program.

Now visit the Sentencing Project at http://www.sentencingproject.org. (You may also use the Cybrary to find sites that have moved since they were listed in this book.) What is the mission of the Sentencing Project? How does that mission coincide with the interests of the National Association of Sentencing Advocates and the Campaign for an Effective Crime Policy? (Hint: Sites for both of these organizations should be listed on the Sentencing Project home page, or you can find them through the Cybrary.) Summarize what you have learned, and submit your findings to your instructor if asked to do so.

To complete this Web Quest! online, go to the Web Quest! module in Chapter 10 of the *Criminal Justice Today* Companion Website at cjtoday.com.

Library Extras!

Library Extra! 10–1 *Preventing Crime: What Works, What Doesn't, What's Promising* (NIJ, 1997).

Library Extra! 10–2 *What Future for "Public Safety" and "Restorative Justice" in Community Corrections* (NIJ, 2001).

Library Extra! 10–3 *Thirty Years of Sentencing Reform: The Quest for a Racially Neutral Sentencing Process* (NIJ, 2000).

Library Extra! 10–4 *Sentencing Guidelines: Reflections on the Future* (NIJ, 2001).

Library Extra! 10–5 *A Broken System: Error Rates in Capital Cases* (Columbia University School of Law, 2000).

Library Extra! 10–6 *The Federal Death Penalty System: Supplementary Data, Analysis and Revised Protocols for Capital Case Review* (USDOJ, 2001).

To explore these resources online, go to the Library Extras! Area of the *Criminal Justice Today* Companion Website at cjtoday.com. You should also check the author's "Late Picks" online for newly released documents and updated Library Extras! You can find Late Picks at http://cjtoday.com/latepicks.htm.

Marginal Notes

i. "The Crime Bust." *U.S. News & World Report,* May 25, 1998.

ii. Laura Goodstein, "Death Penalty Falls from Favor as Some Lose Confidence in Its Fairness," *The New York Times,* June 17, 2001.

iii. Lawrence A. Greenfeld, "Prison Sentences and Time Served for Violence," *Bureau of Justice Statistics Selected Findings,* No. 4 (April 1995).

iv. As quoted in *Criminal Justice Newsletter,* Vol. 31, No. 13 (2000), p. 1.

v. "Judge Refuses to Delay McVeigh Execution," *The New York Times,* June 6, 2001.

Notes

1. Michael Tonry, "Implementing, Changing, and Maintaining Sentencing Guidelines in the Political Climate of the 1990's." Web posted at http://students.washington.edu/ths123/state.htm. Accessed January 3, 2002.

2. View a .9mm MAC-10 machine-pistol at http://www.securityarms.com/20010315/galleryfiles/orig/mac10.htm.

3. *Smith* v. *U.S.,* 113 S.Ct. 1178, 122 L.Ed. 2d 548 (1993).

4. This case, and others like it, turns upon the interpretation of the phrase "uses or carries a firearm" during and in relation to a "drug trafficking crime" (18 U.S.C. Section 924[c][1]). In the case of *Bailey* v. *U.S.* (516 U.S. 137 [1995]), the U.S. Supreme Court held that mere "proximity and accessibility of the firearm to drugs or drug proceeds is not alone sufficient to support a conviction for 'use.'" In *Bailey, use* was interpreted to mean "active use," connoting more than mere possession of a firearm. In the later case of *Muscarello* v. *U.S.* (524 U.S. 125 [1998]), however, the Court held that "the phrase 'carries a firearm' applies to a person who knowingly possesses and conveys firearms in a vehicle, including in the locked glove compartment or trunk of a car, which the person accompanies."

5. For a thorough discussion of the philosophy of punishment and sentencing, see David Garland, *Punishment and Modern Society: A Study in Social Theory* (Chicago: University of Chicago Press, 1990). See also Ralph D. Ellis and Carol S. Ellis, *Theories of Criminal Justice: A Critical Reappraisal* (Wolfeboro, NH: Longwood Academic, 1989); and Colin Summer, *Censure, Politics, and Criminal Justice* (Bristol, PA: Open University Press, 1990).

6. Punishment is said to be required because social order (and the laws that represent it) could not exist for long if transgressions went unsanctioned.

7. "Back to the Chain Gang," *Newsweek,* October 17, 1994, p. 87.

8. Ibid.

9. For an excellent review of the "get tough" attitudes that influenced sentencing decisions during the 1990s, see Tamasak Wicharaya, *Simple Theory, Hard Reality: The Impact of Sentencing Reforms on Courts, Prisons, and Crime* (Albany: State University of New York Press, 1995).

10. For a thorough review of the literature on deterrence, see Raymond Paternoster, "The Deterrent Effect of the Perceived Certainty and Severity of Punishment: A Review of the Evidence and Issues," *Justice Quarterly,* Vol. 4, No. 2 (June 1987), pp. 174–217.

11. Hugo Adam Bedau, "Retributivism and the Theory of Punishment," *Journal of Philosophy,* Vol. 75 (November 1978), pp. 601–620.

12. H. L. A. Hart, *Punishment and Responsibility: Essays in the Philosophy of Law* (Oxford: Clarendon Press, 1968).

13. The definitive study during this period was Douglas Lipton, Robert Martinson, and J. Woks, *The Effectiveness of Correctional Treatment: A Survey of Treatment Valuation Studies* (New York: Praeger Press, 1975).

14. See, for example, Lawrence W. Sherman et al., *Preventing Crime: What Works, What Doesn't, What's Promising* (Washington, D.C.: National Institute of Justice, 1997).

15. Gordon Bazemore and Mark S. Umbreit, foreword to *Balanced and Restorative Justice: Program Summary* (Washington, D.C.: Office of Juvenile Justice and Delinquency Prevention, 1994).

16. Adapted from John Feinblatt and Greg Berman, *Creating a Community Court,* a Bureau of Justice Assistance bulletin (Washington, D.C.: BJA, February 2001).

17. 18 U.S.C. 3563 (a) (2).

18. See Joan Petersilia, *Expanding Options for Criminal Sentencing* (Santa Monica, CA: RAND Corporation, 1987).

19. E-mail communications with the Office of Reparative Programs, Department of Corrections, State of Vermont, July 3, 1995.

20. Donna Hunzeker, "State Sentencing Systems and 'Truth in Sentencing,'" *State Legislative Report,* Vol. 20, No. 3 (Denver: National Conference of State Legislatures, 1995).

21. Paula M. Ditton and Doris James Wilson, *Truth in Sentencing in State Prisons* (Washington, D.C.: Bureau of Justice Statistics, 1999).

22. "Oklahoma Rapist Gets 30,000 Years," United Press International wire service, southwest edition, December 23, 1994.

23. For a historical consideration of alleged disparities, see G. Kleck, "Racial Discrimination in Criminal Sentencing: A Critical Evaluation of the Evidence with Additional Evidence on the Death Penalty," *American Sociological Review,* No. 46 (1981), pp. 783–805; and G. Kleck, "Life Support for Ailing Hypotheses: Modes of Summarizing the Evidence for Racial Discrimination in Sentencing," *Law and Human Behavior,* No. 9 (1985), pp. 271–285.

24. National Council on Crime and Delinquency, *National Assessment of Structured Sentencing* (Washington, D.C.: Bureau of Justice Administration, 1996).

25. Ibid.

26. Ibid.

27. *Arave* v. *Creech,* 113 S.Ct. 1534, 123 L.Ed. 2d 188 (1993). See also *Richmond* v. *Lewis,* 113 S.Ct. 538, 121 L.Ed. 2d 411 (1992).

28. For an early statement of this problem, see Franklin E. Zimring, "Making the Punishment Fit the Crime: A Consumer's Guide to Sentencing Reform," in Gordon Hawkins and F. E. Zimring, eds., *The Pursuit of Criminal Justice* (Chicago: University of Chicago Press, 1984), pp. 267–275.

29. Albert W. Alschuler, "Sentencing Reform and Prosecutorial Power: A Critique of Recent Proposals for 'Fixed' and 'Presumptive' Sentencing," in Sheldon L. Messinger and Egon Bittner, eds., *Criminology Review Yearbook,* Vol. 1 (Beverly Hills, CA: Sage, 1979), pp. 416–445.

30. Ibid., p. 422.

31. Christopher T. Link and Neal Shover, "The Origins of Criminal Sentencing Reforms," *Justice Quarterly,* Vol. 3, No. 3 (September 1986), pp. 329–342.

32. For a good discussion of such issues, see Hans Toch, "Rewarding Convicted Offenders," *Federal Probation* (June 1988), pp. 42–48.

33. Much of the material in this section is derived from Dale Parent et al., *Mandatory Sentencing,* NIJ Research in Action Series (Washington, D.C.: National Institute of Justice, 1997).

34. In mid-1996, the California Supreme Court ruled the state's three-strikes law an undue intrusion on judges' sentencing discretion, and California judges now use their own discretion in evaluating which offenses "fit" within the meaning of the law.

35. G. L. Pierce and W. J. Bowers, "The Bartley-Fox Gun Law's Short-Term Impact on Crime in Boston," *Annals of the American Academy of Political and Social Science,* Vol. 455 (1981), pp. 120–132.

36. Colin Loftin, Milton Heumann, and David McDowall, "Mandatory Sentencing and Firearms Violence: Evaluating an Alternative to Gun Control," *Law and Society Review,* Vol. 17 (1983), pp. 287–318.

37. Colin Loftin and David McDowall, "The Deterrent Effects of the Florida Felony Firearm Law," *Journal of Criminal Law and Criminology,* Vol. 75 (1984), pp. 250–259.

38. David McDowall, Colin Loftin, and Brian Wiersema, "A Comparative Study of the Preventive Effects of Mandatory Sentencing Laws for Gun Crimes," *Journal of Criminal Law and Criminology,* Vol. 83, No. 2 (summer 1992), pp. 378–394.

39. Joint Committee on New York Drug Law Evaluation, *The Nation's Toughest Drug Law: Evaluating the New York Experience—A Project of the Association of the Bar of the City of New York, the City of New York and the Drug Abuse Council, Inc.* (Washington, D.C.: U.S. Government Printing Office, 1978).

40. Michael Tonry, *Sentencing Reform Impacts* (Washington, D.C.: National Institute of Justice, 1987).

41. D. C. McDonald and K. E. Carlson, *Sentencing in the Courts: Does Race Matter? The Transition to Sentencing Guidelines, 1986–90* (Washington, D.C.: Bureau of Justice Statistics, 1993).

42. As discussed later in this chapter, federal sentencing guidelines did not become effective until 1987 and still had to meet many court challenges.

43. U.S. Sentencing Commission, *Federal Sentencing Guidelines Manual* (Washington, D.C.: U.S. Government Printing Office, 1987), p. 2.

44. A maximum of 54 days per year of good-time credit can still be earned.

45. The Parole Commission Phaseout Act of 1996 requires the attorney general to report to Congress yearly as to whether it is cost-effective for the Parole Commission to remain a separate agency or whether its functions (and personnel) should be assigned elsewhere. Under the law, if the attorney general recommends assigning the Parole Commission's functions to another component of the Department of Justice, federal parole will continue as long as necessary without respect to the November l, 2002, expiration date provided elsewhere in the legislation.

46. Lawrence A. Greenfeld, *Prison Sentences and Time Served for Violence* (Washington, D.C.: Bureau of Justice Statistics, April 1995).

47. Ditton and Wilson, *Truth in Sentencing in State Prisons.*

48. For an excellent review of the act and its implications, see Gregory D. Lee, "U.S. Sentencing Guidelines: Their Impact on Federal Drug Offenders," *FBI Law Enforcement Bulletin,* May 1995, pp. 17–21.

49. U.S. Sentencing Commission, *Federal Sentencing Guidelines Manual,* p. 10.

50. *Mistretta* v. *U.S.,* 488 U.S. 361, 371 (1989).

51. For an engaging overview of how mitigating factors might be applied under the guidelines, see *Koon* v. *U.S.,* 116 S.Ct. 2035, 135 L.Ed. 2d 392 (1996).

52. U.S. Sentencing Commission, *Federal Sentencing Guidelines Manual,* p. 207.

53. *Deal* v. *U.S.,* 113 S.Ct. 1993, 124 L.Ed. 2d 44 (1993).

54. U.S. Sentencing Commission, *Federal Sentencing Guidelines Manual,* p. 8.

55. National Institute of Justice, *Sentencing Commission Chairman Wilkins Answers Questions on the Guidelines,* NIJ Research in Action Series (Washington, D.C.: NIJ, 1987), p. 7.

56. *Melendez* v. *U.S.,* 117 S.Ct. 383, 136 L.Ed. 2d 301 (1996).

57. "Judge Sentences Two Ohio Men to Dress as Women," Reuters wire service, October 27, 2001.

58. Much of the information in this section is taken from Haya El Nasser, "Paying for Crime with Shame: Judges Say 'Scarlet Letter' Angle Works," *USA Today,* June 26, 1996, p. 1A.

59. John Braithwaite, *Crime, Shame, and Reintegration* (Cambridge, England: Cambridge University Press, 1989).

60. Four papers have been released in the RISE series to date. They are Lawrence W. Sherman and Heather Strang, *The Right Kind of Shame for Crime Prevention* (Canberra, Australia: Australian National University, 1997); Heather Strang and Lawrence W. Sherman, *The Victim's Perspective* (Canberra, Australia: Australian National University, 1997); Lawrence W. Sherman and Geoffrey C. Barnes, *Restorative Justice and Offenders' Respect for the Law* (Canberra, Australia: Australian National University, 1997); and Lawrence W. Sherman

and Heather Strang, *Restorative Justice and Deterring Crime* (Canberra, Australia: Australian National University, 1997).

61. Haya El Nasser, "Paying for Crime with Shame: Judges Say 'Scarlett Letter' Angle Works," *USA Today,* June 26, 1996, p. 1A.

62. Such evidence does, in fact, exist. See, for example, Harold G. Grasmick, Robert J. Bursik, Jr., and Bruce J. Arneklev, "Reduction in Drunk Driving as a Response to Increased Threats of Shame, Embarrassment, and Legal Sanctions," *Criminology,* Vol. 31, No. 1 (1993), pp. 41–67.

63. Joan Petersilia, *House Arrest,* A National Institute of Justice Crime File Study Guide (Washington, D.C.: NIJ, 1988).

64. James Eisentein and Herbert Jacob, *Felony Justice* (Boston: Little, Brown, 1977).

65. Joan Petersilia, *Racial Disparities in the Criminal Justice System* (Santa Monica, CA: RAND Corporation, 1983).

66. Anthony J. Ragona and John P. Ryan, *Beyond the Courtroom: A Comparative Analysis of Misdemeanor Sentencing—Executive Summary* (Chicago: American Judicature Society, 1983).

67. James H. Kuklinski and John E. Stanga, "Political Participation and Government Responsiveness: The Behavior of California Superior Courts," *American Political Science Review,* Vol. 73 (1979), pp. 1090–1099.

68. See Joseph Jacoby and Christopher Dunn, *National Survey on Punishment for Criminal Offenses—Executive Summary* (Washington, D.C.: Bureau of Justice Statistics, 1987). For a critique of this survey, see Barry Krisberg, "Public Attitudes about Criminal Sanctions," *Criminologist,* Vol. 13, No. 2 (March/April 1988), pp. 12, 16.

69. Stephen P. Klein, Susan Turner, and Joan Petersilia, *Racial Equity in Sentencing* (Santa Monica, CA: RAND Corporation, 1988). See also S. Klein, J. Petersilia, and S. Turner, "Race and Imprisonment Decisions in California," *Science,* Vol. 247 (February 1990), pp. 812–816.

70. Klein, Turner, and Petersilia, *Racial Equity in Sentencing,* p. 11. For additional information on race as it affects the justice system, see David Cole, *No Equal Justice: Race and Class in the American Criminal Justice System* (New York: New Press, 1999).

71. Ibid.

72. William Wilbanks, "Are Female Felons Treated More Leniently by the Criminal Justice System?" *Justice Quarterly,* Vol. 3, No. 4 (December 1986), pp. 517–529.

73. Privacy Act of 1974, 5 U.S.C.A. 522a, 88 Statute 1897, Public Law 93-579, December 31, 1974.

74. Freedom of Information Act, 5 U.S.C. 522, and amendments. The status of presentence investigative reports has not yet been clarified under this act to the satisfaction of all legal scholars, although state and federal courts are generally thought to be exempt from the provisions of the act.

75. For a good review of the issues involved, see Robert C. Davis, Arthur J. Lurigio, and Wesley G. Skogan, *Victims of Crime,* 2d ed. (Thousand Oaks, CA: Sage, 1997); and Leslie Sebba, *Third Parties: Victims and the Criminal Justice System* (Columbus: Ohio State University Press, 1996).

76. President's Task Force on Victims of Crime, *Final Report* (Washington, D.C.: U.S. Government Printing Office, 1982).

77. Peter Finn and Beverly N. W. Lee, *Establishing and Expanding Victim-Witness Assistance Programs* (Washington, D.C.: National Institute of Justice, 1988).

78. National Institute of Justice, *Victim Assistance Programs: Whom They Service, What They Offer* (Washington, D.C.: NIJ, 1995).

79. Senate Joint Resolution (SJR) 65 is a major revision of an initial proposal, SJR 52, which Senators Kyl and Feinstein introduced on April 22, 1996. Representative Henry Hyde introduced House Joint Resolution 174, a companion to SJR 52, and a similar proposal, House Joint Resolution 173, on April 22, 1996.

80. Senate Joint Resolution 44, 105th Congress.

81. See the National Center for Victims of Crime's critique of the 1998 amendment at http://www.ncvc.org/law/Ncvca.htm. Accessed January 10, 2000.

82. "Gov. Bush Supports VRA," National Victims' Constitutional Amendment Network, April 7, 2000. Web posted at http://www.nvcan.org/news.htm. Accessed January 22, 2002.

83. "Attorneys General Strongly Support S.J. Res. 3," National Victims' Constitutional Amendment Network, April 21, 2000. Web posted at http://www.nvcan.org/news.htm. Accessed January 22, 2002.

84. See the National Victims' Constitutional Amendment Network news page at http://www.nvcan.org/news.htm. Accessed January 10, 2002.

85. Public Law 97-291.

86. USA PATRIOT Act of 2001, Section 624.

87. Proposition 8, California's Victim's Bill of Rights.

88. National Victim Center, Mothers Against Drunk Driving, and American Prosecutors Research Institute, *Impact Statements: A Victim's Right to Speak; A Nation's Responsibility to Listen* (Washington, D. C.: OVC, July 1994).

89. Rick Atkinson, "Seles Says Attacker Has 'Ruined My Life': Retrial of Parche Aims at Tougher Sentence," *Washington Post,* March 22, 1995.

90. Rick Atkinson, "Suspended Sentence Upheld for Seles' Attacker," *Washington Post,* April 4, 1995.

91. Robert C. Davis and Barbara E. Smith, "The Effects of Victim Impact Statements on Sentencing Decisions: A Test in an Urban Setting," *Justice Quarterly,* Vol. 11, No. 3 (September 1994), pp. 453–469.

92. *Booth* v. *Maryland,* 107 S.Ct. 2529 (1987).

93. *Payne* v. *Tennessee,* 501 U.S. 808 (1991).

94. "Supreme Court Closes Term with Major Criminal Justice Rulings," *Criminal Justice Newsletter,* Vol. 22, No. 13 (July 1, 1991), p. 2.

95. See "What Say Should Victims Have?" *Time,* May 27, 1991, p. 61.

96. Bureau of Justice Statistics, *Report to the Nation on Crime and Justice,* 2d ed. (Washington, D.C.: U.S. Government Printing Office, 1988), p. 90.

97. Matthew R. Durose, David J. Levin, and Patrick A. Langan, *Felony Sentences in State Courts, 1998* (Washington, D.C.: Bureau of Justice Statistics, 2001).

98. Sally T. Hillsman et al., "Fines as Criminal Sanctions," National Institute of Justice, *Research in Brief* (September 1987), p. 1.

99. Ibid., p. 2.

100. Sally T. Hillsman, Joyce L. Sichel, and Barry Mahoney, *Fines in Sentencing* (New York: Vera Institute of Justice, 1983).

101. Ibid., p. 2.
102. Ibid., p. 4.
103. Ibid.
104. Douglas C. McDonald, Judith Greene, and Charles Worzella, *Day Fines in American Courts: The Staten Island and Milwaukee Experiments* (Washington, D.C.: National Institute of Justice, 1992).
105. Ibid., p. 56.
106. Laura A. Winterfield and Sally T. Hillsman, *The Staten Island Day-Fine Project* (Washington, D.C.: National Institute of Justice, 1993), p. 1.
107. S. Turner and J. Petersilia, *Day Fines in Four U.S. Jurisdictions* (Santa Monica, CA: RAND Corporation, 1996).
108. "Man Decapitates Neighbor, Tosses Head in Dumpster," Reuters wire service, May 25, 1996.
109. Herbert A. Johnson, *History of Criminal Justice* (Cincinnati: Anderson, 1988), pp. 30–31.
110. Ibid., p. 31.
111. Ibid., p. 36.
112. "Yemeni Court Upholds Crucifixions," Associated Press wire service, August 31, 1997.
113. Johnson, *History of Criminal Justice,* p. 51.
114. Arthur Koestler, *Reflections on Hanging* (New York: Macmillan, 1957), p. xi.
115. Ibid., p. 15.
116. Merle Severy, "The Great Revolution," *National Geographic,* July 1989, p. 20.
117. Capital Punishment Research Project, University of Alabama Law School.
118. Death Penalty Information Center, "State-by-State Death Penalty Information." Web posted at http://www.deathpenaltyinfo.org/firstpage.html. Accessed February 12, 2002.
119. U.S. Department of Justice, *Capital Punishment,* 1993 (Washington, D.C.: U.S. Government Printing Office, 1995).
120. Richard Willing, "Expansion of Death Penalty to Nonmurders Faces Challenges," *USA Today,* May 14, 1997, p. 6A.
121. Death Penalty Information Center, "Death Row Inmates by State," from which the statistics in this paragraph come. Web posted at http://www.deathpenaltyinfo.org/DRowInfo.html#year. Accessed November 16, 2001.
122. Tracy L. Snell, *Capital Punishment, 2000* (Washington, D.C.: Bureau of Justice Statistics, 2001), p. 1.
123. "Killer Spared 14th Date with Execution in Louisiana," Reuters wire service, April 18, 1995.
124. Allan Turner, "Texas Executes Third and Fourth Prisoners in a Week," *Houston Chronicle* via Simon & Schuster's NewsLink service, June 5, 1997.
125. "Chief Justice Calls for Limits on Death Row *Habeas* Appeals," *Criminal Justice Newsletter,* February 15, 1989, pp. 6–7.
126. *McCleskey* v. *Zandt,* 499 U.S. 467, 493–494 (1991).
127. *Coleman* v. *Thompson,* 501 U.S. 722 (1991).
128. *Schlup* v. *Delo,* 115 S.Ct. 851, 130 L.Ed. 2d 808 (1995).
129. *Felker* v. *Turpin, Warden,* 117 S.Ct. 30, 135 L.Ed. 2d 1123 (1996).
130. *Elledge* v. *Florida,* No. 98-5410 (1998).
131. Michelle Locke, "Victim Forgives," Associated Press wire services, May 19, 1996.
132. Ibid.
133. Koestler, *Reflections on Hanging,* p. xii.
134. Death Penalty Information Center, "Innocence: Freed from Death Row." Web posted at http://www.deathpenaltyinfo.org/Innocentlist.html. Accessed November 16, 2001.
135. Edward Connors et al., *Convicted by Juries, Exonerated by Science: Case Studies in the Use of DNA Evidence to Establish Innocence after Trial* (Washington, D.C.: National Institute of Justice, 1996).
136. Barry Scheck and Peter Neufeld, "DNA and Innocence Scholarship," in Saundra D. Westervelt and John A. Humphrey, *Wrongly Convicted: Perspectives on Failed Justice* (New Brunswick, NJ: Rutgers University Press, 2001), p. 248–249.
137. Ibid., p. 246.
138. James S. Liebman, Jeffrey Fagan, and Simon H. Rifkind, *A Broken System: Error Rates in Capital Cases, 1973–1995* (New York: Columbia Law School, 2000). Web posted at http://justice.policy.net/jpreport/finrep.PDF. Accessed March 3, 2002.
139. See, for example, Jim Yardley, "Texas Retooling Criminal Justice in Wake of Furor on Death Penalty," *New York Times,* June 1, 2001.
140. Studies include S. Decker and C. Kohfeld, "A Deterrence Study of the Death Penalty in Illinois: 1933–1980," *Journal of Criminal Justice,* Vol. 12, No. 4 (1984), pp. 367–379; and S. Decker and C. Kohfeld, "An Empirical Analysis of the Effect of the Death Penalty in Missouri," *Journal of Crime and Justice,* Vol. 10, No. 1 (1987), pp. 23–46.
141. See, especially, W. C. Bailey, "Deterrence and the Death Penalty for Murders in Utah: A Time Series Analysis," *Journal of Contemporary Law,* Vol. 5, No. 1 (1978), pp. 1–20; and W. C. Bailey, "An Analysis of the Deterrent Effect of the Death Penalty for Murder in California," *Southern California Law Review,* Vol. 52, No. 3 (1979), pp. 743–764.
142. B. E. Forst, "The Deterrent Effect of Capital Punishment: A Cross-State Analysis of the 1960's," *Minnesota Law Review,* Vol. 61, No. 5 (1977), pp. 743–767.
143. Hashem Dezhbakhsh, Paul Rubin, and Joanna Mehlhop Shepherd, "Does Capital Punishment Have a Deterrent Effect? New Evidence from Post-Moratorium Panel Data," Emory University Web document. Web posted January 2001. Accessed November 13, 2001.
144. Ibid., abstract.
145. Ibid., p. 19.
146. "Attorneys Call for Halt to U.S. Executions," Reuters wire service, February 4, 1997.
147. As some of the evidence presented before the Supreme Court in *Furman* v. *Georgia,* 408 U.S. 238 (1972), suggested.
148. *USA Today,* April 27, 1989, p. 12A.
149. Thomas J. Keil and Gennaro F. Vito, "Race and the Death Penalty in Kentucky Murder Trials: 1976–1991," *American Journal of Criminal Justice,* Vol. 20, No. 1 (1995), pp. 17–36 (published December 1996).
150. *McCleskey* v. *Kemp,* 481 U.S. 279, 107 S.Ct. 1756, 95 L.Ed. 2d 262 (1987).
151. *The Federal Death Penalty System: Supplementary Data, Analysis and Revised Protocols for Capital Case Review* (Washington, D.C.: Department of Justice, 2001).
152. David Stout, "Attorney General Says Report Shows No Racial and Ethnic Bias in Federal Death Sentences," *New York Times,* June 7, 2001. Web posted at http://college1.nytimes.com/guests/articles/2001/06/07/850513.xml.

153. "Expanded Study Shows No Bias in Death Penalty, Ashcroft Says," *Criminal Justice Newsletter,* Vol. 31, No. 13 (June 18, 2001), p. 4.

154. Mary P. Gallagher, "Race Found to Have No Effect on Capital Sentencing in New Jersey," *New Jersey Law Journal* (August 21, 2001), p. 1.

155. Death Penalty Information Center website, http://www. essential.org/dpic. Accessed March 20, 2000.

156. "Judge Gives Max in Burned Alive Case," United Press International wire service, northeast edition, December 10, 1996.

157. Justice Potter Stewart, as quoted in *USA Today,* April 27, 1989, p. 12A.

158. Koestler, *Reflections on Hanging,* pp. 147–148; and Gennaro F. Vito and Deborah G. Wilson, "Back from the Dead: Tracking the Progress of Kentucky's Furman-Commuted Death Row Population," *Justice Quarterly,* Vol. 5, No. 1 (1988), pp. 101–111.

159. For the latest information on public opinion polls, visit the Death Penalty Information Center online at http://www.essential.org/dpic.

160. *Wilkerson* v. *Utah,* 99 U.S. 130 (1878).

161. *In re Kemmler,* 136 U.S. 436 (1890).

162. Ibid., p. 447.

163. *Louisiana ex rel. Francis* v. *Resweber,* 329 U.S. 459 (1947).

164. *Furman* v. *Georgia,* 408 U.S. 238 (1972).

165. A position first adopted in *Trop* v. *Dulles,* 356 U.S. 86 (1958).

166. *Gregg* v. *Georgia,* 428 U.S. 153 (1976).

167. Ibid., p. 173.

168. *Coker* v. *Georgia,* 433 U.S. 584 (1977).

169. *Woodson* v. *North Carolina,* 428 U.S. 280 (1976).

170. *Blystone* v. *Pennsylvania,* 494 U.S. 310 (1990).

171. *Boyde* v. *California,* 494 U.S. 370 (1990).

172. *Harris* v. *Alabama,* 513 U.S. 504, 115 S.Ct. 1031, 130 L.Ed. 2d 1004 (1995).

173. *Tuilaepa* v. *California,* 114 S.Ct. 2630, 129 L.Ed. 2d 750 (1994).

174. *Poyner* v. *Murray,* 113 S.Ct. 1573, 123 L.Ed. 2d 142 (1993).

175. *Campbell* v. *Wood,* 114 S.Ct. 1337, 127 L.Ed. 2d 685 (1994).

176. *Director Gomez, et al* v. *Fierro and Ruiz,* U.S. Supreme Court, No. 95-1830, (1996).

177. The court issued its decision after reviewing two cases: *Dawson* v. *State* and *Moore* v. *State.*

178. "Georgia Court Finds Electrocution Unconstitutional," *Criminal Justice Newsletter,* Vol. 31, No. 18 (October 15, 2001), pp. 3–4.

179. *Penry* v. *Johnson,* U.S. Supreme Court, No. 00-6677 (decided June 4, 2001).

180. Penry's first death sentence was overturned in *Penry* v. *Lynaugh,* 492 U.S. 302 (1989).

181. Jim Yardley, "Two Groups Help Sway Texas Governor on Veto," *New York Times,* June 19, 2001. Web posted at http://college1.nytimes.com/guests/articles/2001/ 06/19/852692.xml. Accessed November 13, 2001.

182. Tony Mauro, "Following Three Recusals, Divided High Court Denies Stay in Texas Death Penalty Case," *American Lawyer Media,* August 14, 2001. The case was unusual because the victim was the father of a federal appellate court judge.

183. See Richard Willing, "Execution Case Revives Age Issue," *USA Today,* August 10, 2001, p. 3A.

part four

Individual Rights versus Public Order Concerns

■ Rights of the Convicted and Imprisoned

Common law, constitutional, statutory, and humanitarian rights of the convicted and imprisoned:

- A right against cruel or unusual punishment
- A right to protection from physical harm
- A right to sanitary and healthy conditions of confinement
- A limited right to legal assistance while imprisoned
- A limited right to religious freedom while imprisoned
- A limited right to freedom of speech while imprisoned
- A limited right to due process prior to denial of privileges

These individual rights must be effectively balanced against these public order concerns:

- Punishment of the guilty
- Safe communities
- The reduction of recidivism
- Secure prisons
- Control over convicts
- The prevention of escape
- Rehabilitation
- Affordable prisons

How does our system of justice work toward balance?

Corrections

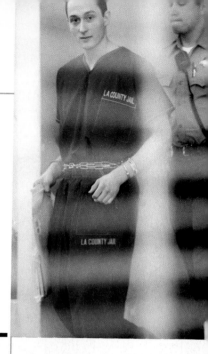

Punishment—Justice for the Unjust?

The great Christian writer C. S. Lewis (1898–1963) once remarked that if satisfying justice is to be the ultimate goal of Western criminal justice, then the fate of offenders cannot be dictated merely by practical considerations. "The concept of just desert is the only connecting link between punishment and justice," Lewis wrote. "It is only as deserved or undeserved that a sentence can be just or unjust," he concluded.

Once a person has been arrested, tried, and sentenced, the correctional process begins. Unlike Lewis's exhortation, however, the contemporary American correctional system—which includes probation, parole, jails, prisons, capital punishment, and a variety of innovative alternatives to traditional sentences—is tasked with far more than merely carrying out sentences. We also ask our correctional system to ensure the safety of law-abiding citizens, to select the best alternative from among the many available for handling each offender, to protect those under its charge, and to guarantee fairness in the handling of everyone it encounters.

This part of *Criminal Justice Today* details the development of probation, parole, community corrections, and imprisonment as correctional philosophies; describes the nuances of prison and jail life; discusses special issues in contemporary corrections (including AIDS, geriatric offenders, and female inmates); and summarizes the legal environment which both surrounds and infuses the modern-day practice of corrections. Characteristic of today's correctional emphasis is a society-wide push for harsher punishments. The culmination of that strategy, however, is dramatically overcrowded correctional institutions, the problems of which are also described. As you read through this part of the book, encountering descriptions of various kinds of criminal sanctions, you might ask yourself, "When would this punishment be deserved?" In doing so, remember to couple that thought with another question: "What are the ultimate consequences (for society and for the offender) of this kind of correctional program?" Unlike Lewis, you may also want to ask, "Can we afford it?"

Probation, Parole, and Community Corrections

OUTLINE

LEARNING OBJECTIVES

After reading this chapter, you should be able to

■ Explain the difference between probation and parole, and describe the history of each

■ Describe in detail the legal environment surrounding the use of probation and parole, including the names of significant court cases

■ Describe the federal probation system

■ Explain the nature of the job of probation and parole officers

■ List the advantages of intermediate sanctions over more traditional forms of sentencing

■ Describe the likely future of probation and parole

chapter 11

[*Accepting released offenders into the community without
a period of supervised release is morally unsatisfying; they
have not yet earned their place at our table.*]

**—Jeremy Travis, former Director of the
National Institute of Justice[1]**

[*Community corrections is an integral part of the criminal justice system
and should be fully implemented and promoted in order to save expensive
and scarce jail and prison space for violent and serious offenders.*]

**—National Association of Counties, Justice and
Public Safety Steering Committee[2]**

Key Concepts

[Terms]

caseload
community corrections
community service
conditions of parole (probation)
home confinement
intensive probation supervision (IPS)
intermediate sanctions

mixed sentence
parole
parole board
parole (probation) violation
parole revocation
probation
probation revocation

restitution
revocation hearing
shock incarceration
shock probation
split sentence

[Cases]

Bearden v. *Georgia*
Gagnon v. *Scarpelli*
Greenholtz v. *Nebraska*

Griffin v. *Wisconsin*
Mempa v. *Rhay*
Minnesota v. *Murphy*

Morrissey v. *Brewer*
U.S. v. *Knights*

Introduction

Hear the author
discuss this chapter
at **cjtoday.com**

In September 2001, Patrick Collier won $1 million in a McDonald's giveaway.[3] Collier had purchased a 99-cent breakfast sandwich and walked out of the fast-food restaurant in Ormond Beach, Florida, with the winning coupon. Months before winning the prize, Collier and his 29-year-old fiancée, Sandy Fabian, had been homeless and were sleeping on cardboard boxes. Within hours of claiming the prize, Collier was arrested and charged with aggravated battery against Fabian. Although he quickly posted bail, Orange County authorities soon took him back into custody for violating probation stemming from a forged check conviction a year earlier. A check of his records showed that Collier had been arrested 14 times in central Florida between 1994 and September 2001.

Patrick Collier, with his fiancée, Sandy Fabian. Collier was one of five winners in a McDonald's giveaway in 2001. Shortly after winning $1 million, he was arrested and charged with aggravated battery against his 29-year-old fiancée. Collier was released on bail but was soon back in jail, charged with violating probation.

AP/Wide World Photos

Donta Paige (left) being escorted to a courtroom in the Denver City and County Building on the opening day of the death-penalty stage of his murder trial. Paige was on supervised release from a prison in Maryland when he raped and viciously killed aspiring interior designer Peyton Tuthill (right) as she returned to her apartment while he was burglarizing it. The case led state officials from around the nation to work on a plan to track parolees between jurisdictions.

Glen Martin, The Denver Post (left); Karl Gehring, The Denver Post (right)

Like Collier, many probationers and parolees find themselves in continuing trouble with the law. In May 2001, for example, 25-year-old murderer Donta Paige made headlines, leading state officials from around the country to work on a plan to track parolees.[4] Paige had served two years of a ten-year sentence for a series of violent armed robberies before being released early by a Maryland judge, who also ordered him into a drug-treatment program in Denver. Within a few months, however, Paige was kicked out of the program. Planning to head back to Maryland, Paige was looking for money when he broke into an apartment near the drug-treatment center. When the resident, 24-year-old Peyton Tuthill, returned home, Paige raped and killed her. Tuthill, an aspiring interior designer, died from 18 stab wounds to her chest and a slashed throat. In 2001, Paige was convicted of Tuthill's murder and was sentenced to life in prison. What most concerned those working on the new parolee-tracking agreement was that Maryland officials had never notified authorities in Colorado that Paige was headed their way.

In a similar story, parolee Justin James Roberts, 24, of Gaylord, Michigan, was arrested in late 2001 and charged with attempted murder, kidnapping, first-degree criminal sexual conduct, and two counts of third-degree criminal sexual conduct after he allegedly forced a 14-year-old girl into the woods, then raped and strangled her, leaving her for dead.[5] The girl eventually regained consciousness, however, and was able to get to a nearby house. Roberts, who was well known to the police, was arrested an hour later. As investigators already knew, Roberts had a history of criminal activity. In 1999, he had been convicted of possession of marijuana with intent to deliver and was sentenced to 90 days in jail and given 36 months' probation. In 2000, Roberts was convicted of forgery for helping friends counterfeit $100 bills and was also convicted of burglary and being a felon in possession of a firearm—crimes for which he was given a 2- to 6-year sentence. After a brief stint in a prison "boot camp" program, however, Roberts was placed back on probation.

In August 1999, the shocking case of white supremacist Buford O. Furrow, Jr., splashed across television screens, Internet sites, and newspapers. Brandishing an assault weapon, Furrow attacked a Jewish day-care center in Los Angeles, wounding five people, including three children. He also killed a postal worker whom he encountered following the shootings. Afterward, authorities learned that Furrow had been on probation following a conviction for second-degree assault in the attack of a nurse at a psychiatric

community corrections

The use of a variety of officially ordered program-based sanctions that permit convicted offenders to remain in the community under conditional supervision as an alternative to active prison sentences.

probation

A sentence of imprisonment that is suspended. Also, the conditional freedom granted by a judicial officer to a convicted offender, as long as the person meets certain conditions of behavior.

hospital in Washington State. As a condition of probation, Furrow had been barred from owning guns. An investigation soon revealed that the probation officer had never checked to see if Furrow had complied with the judge's order and had not made recommended visits to Furrow's home.[6]

Stories like these, appearing frequently in the media, have cast a harsh light on the early release and poor supervision of criminal offenders. This chapter takes a close look at the realities behind the practice of what we call **community corrections**. Community corrections, also called *community-based corrections,* is a sentencing style that depends less on traditional confinement options and more on correctional resources available in the community. Community corrections includes a wide variety of sentencing options, such as probation, parole, home confinement, the electronic monitoring of offenders, and other new and developing programs—all of which are covered in this chapter. Learn more about community corrections by visiting the International Community Corrections Association via **Web Extra! 11–1** at cjtoday.com.

What Is Probation?

Probation, one aspect of community corrections, is "a sentence served while under supervision in the community."[7] Like other sentencing options, probation is a court-ordered sanction. Its goal is to retain some control over criminal offenders while using community programs to help rehabilitate them. Most of the alternative sanctions discussed later in this chapter are, in fact, predicated upon probationary sentences in which the offender is ordered to abide by certain conditions—such as participation in a specified program—while remaining free in the community. Although the court in many jurisdictions can impose probation directly, most probationers are sentenced first to confinement but then immediately have their sentences suspended and are remanded into the custody of an officer of the court—the probation officer.

Probation has a long history. By the fourteenth century, English courts had established the practice of "binding over for good behavior,"[8] in which offenders could be entrusted into the custody of willing citizens. John Augustus (1784–1859) is generally recognized as the world's first probation officer. Augustus, a Boston shoemaker, attended sessions of criminal court in the 1850s and offered to take carefully selected offenders into his home as an alternative to imprisonment.[9] At first, he supervised only drunkards, but by 1857 Augustus was accepting many kinds of offenders and devoting all his time to the service of the court.[10] Augustus died in 1859, having bailed out more than 2,000 convicts. In 1878, the Massachusetts legislature enacted a statute which authorized the city of Boston to hire a salaried probation officer. Missouri followed suit in 1897, along with Vermont (1898) and Rhode Island (1899).[11] Before the end of the nineteenth century, probation had become an accepted and widely used form of community-based supervision. By 1925, all 48 states had adopted probation legislation. In that same year, the federal government enacted legislation enabling federal district court judges to appoint paid probation officers and to impose probationary terms.[12]

The Extent of Probation

Today, probation is the most common form of criminal sentencing in the United States. Between 20% and 60% of those found guilty of crimes are sentenced to some form of probation. Figure 11–1 shows that 59% of all offenders under correctional supervision in the United States as of January 1, 2001, were on probation. Not shown is that the number of offenders supervised yearly on probation has increased from slightly over 1 million in 1980 to well over 3.8 million today—almost a 300% increase.[13]

Even violent offenders stand about a one in five chance of receiving a probationary term, as Figure 11–2 shows. A Bureau of Justice Statistics study of felony sentences found that 5% of people convicted of homicide were placed on probation, as were 21% of convicted sex offenders.[14] Twelve percent of convicted robbers and 30% of those committing aggravated assault were similarly sentenced to probation rather than active prison time. In one example, 47-year-old Carrie Mote of Vernon, Connecticut, was sentenced to probation for shooting her fiancé in the chest with a .38-caliber handgun after he called off their wedding.[15] Mote, who faced a maximum of 20 years in prison, claimed to be suffering from diminished psychological capacity at the time of the shooting because of the emotional stress brought on by the canceled wedding.

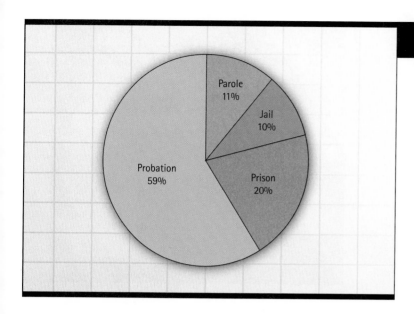

FIGURE 11-1

Offenders under correctional supervision in the United States, by type of supervision.

Source: National Correctional Population Reaches New High (Washington, D.C.: Bureau of Justice Statistics, 2001)

At the beginning of 2001, a total of 3,839,532 adults were on probation throughout the nation.[16] Individual states, however, make greater or lesser use of probation. North Dakota authorities, with the smallest probationary population, supervise only 2,521 people, while Texas reports 425,789 offenders on probation. On a per capita basis, Kentucky has the lowest rate of probation—410 for every 100,000 residents, while Delaware has the highest (3,225 for every 100,000 residents).[17] The national average is 1,649 for every 100,000 residents. Sixty-two percent of probationers successfully complete their probationary terms, while a small percentage (about 2%) abscond, and another 3% are convicted of new crimes

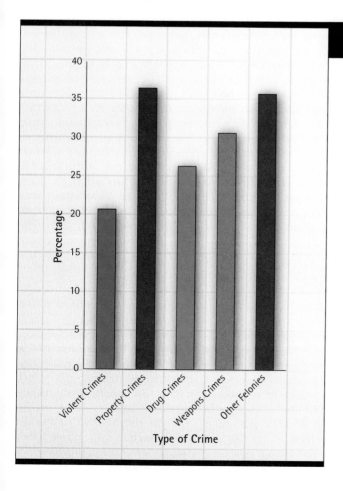

FIGURE 11-2

Percentage of convicted felony offenders receiving probation, by type of crime.

Source: Jodi M. Brown and Patrick A. Langan, Felony Sentences in the United States, 1996 (Washington, D.C.: Bureau of Justice Statistics, 1999)

A probation officer meeting with a client near a Los Angeles County school. Home, office, and school visits help officers gain substantial insights into the needs and lifestyles of the probationers and parolees they supervise.

A. Ramey, Stock Boston

while on probation.[18] See more statistics describing community corrections at **Library Extra! 11–1** at cjtoday.com.

Probation Conditions

probation revocation

A court order in response to a violation of conditions of proba-tion, taking away a person's pro-bationary status and usually withdrawing the conditional free-dom associated with that status.

Those sentenced to probation must agree to abide by court-mandated conditions of proba-tion. A violation of conditions can lead to **probation revocation**. Conditions are of two types: general and specific. General conditions apply to all probationers in a given juris-diction and usually require that the probationer obey all laws, maintain employment, remain within the jurisdiction of the court, possess no firearms, allow the probation officer to visit at home or at work, and so forth. As a general condition of probation, many proba-tioners are also required to pay a fine to the court, usually in a series of installments, that is designed to reimburse victims for damages and to pay lawyers' fees and other court costs.

Special conditions may be mandated by a judge who feels that the probationer is in need of particular guidance or control. Depending upon the nature of the offense, a judge may require that the offender surrender his or her driver's license; submit at reasonable times to warrantless and unannounced searches by a probation officer; supply breath, urine, or blood samples as needed for drug or alcohol testing; complete a specified number of hours of community service; or pass the general equivalency diploma (GED) test within a speci-fied time. The judge may also dictate special conditions tailored to the probationer's situa-tion. Such individualized conditions may prohibit the offender from associating with named others (a codefendant, for example); they may require that the probationer be at home after dark; or they may demand that the offender complete a particular treatment program within a set time.

What Is Parole?

parole

The status of an offender who has been conditionally released from prison by a paroling authority prior to the expiration of his or her sentence, is placed under the supervision of a parole agency, and is required to observe conditions of parole.

parole board

A state paroling authority. Most states have parole boards that decide when an incarcerated offender is ready for conditional release and that may also func-tion as revocation hearing panels.

Parole is the supervised early release of inmates from correctional confinement. It differs from probation in both purpose and implementation. Whereas probationers generally avoid serving time in prison, parolees have already been incarcerated. Whereas probation is a sentencing option available to a judge who determines the form probation will take, parole results from an administrative decision by a legally designated paroling authority. Whereas probation is a sentencing strategy, parole is a correctional strategy whose pri-mary purpose is to return offenders gradually to productive lives. By making early release possible, parole can also act as a stimulus for positive behavioral change.

States differ as to the type of parole decision-making mechanism they use, as well as the level at which it operates. Two major models prevail: (1) **Parole boards** grant parole based on their judgment and assessment. The parole board's decisions are termed *discretionary parole.* (2) Statutory decrees produce mandatory parole, with release dates usually set near

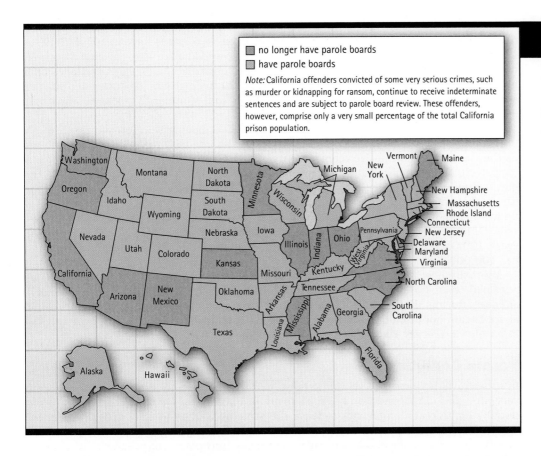

FIGURE 11–3

States that have eliminated parole boards.

Source: Timothy A. Hughes, Doris James Wilson, and Allen J. Beck, *Trends in State Parole, 1990–2000* (Washington, D.C.: Bureau of Justice Statistics, 2001)

the completion of the inmate's prison sentence, minus time off for good behavior and other special considerations. By the beginning of 2001, 15 states had entirely abolished discretionary release from prison by a parole board for all offenders (Figure 11–3). Another five states had abolished discretionary parole for certain violent offenses or other crimes against a person. As a result of the movement away from release by parole boards, statutory release (mandatory parole) became the most common method of release from prison.[19]

States that do not have parole boards can still have substantial parole populations. California, for example, one of the states that no longer uses parole boards for release decisions, has the largest population of parolees in the country.[20] (Although it does not have a parole board, California does have a Board of Prison Terms, which determines when the state's most serious offenders are ready for release from prison. These offenders, however, make up only a very small percentage of the state's prison population.)

The use of parole in this country began with New York's Elmira Reformatory in 1876. As you may recall from Chapter 10, indeterminate sentences are a key part of the rehabilitation philosophy. The indeterminate sentence was made possible by an innovative New York law advocated by leading correctional innovators. Parole was a much-heralded tool of nineteenth-century corrections. Its advocates had been looking for a behavioral incentive to motivate youthful offenders to reform. Parole, through its promise of earned early release, seemed the ideal innovation.

The Extent of Parole

Parolees make up one of the smallest of the correctional categories shown in Figure 11–1. The growing reluctance to use parole today seems to be due to the realization that correctional routines have been generally ineffective at producing any substantial reformation among many offenders prior to their release back into the community. The abandonment of the rehabilitation goal, combined with a return to determinate sentencing in many jurisdictions—including the federal judicial system—has substantially reduced the amount of time the average correctional client spends on parole.

Although discretionary parole releases are far less common than they used to be, about 25% of inmates who are freed from prison are still paroled by a paroling authority such as a parole board.[21] States operating under determinate sentencing guidelines, however, often require that inmates serve a short period of time, such as 90 days, on reentry parole—a form of mandatory release. Mandatory parole releases have increased 91% since 1990,[22] even though they typically involve either a very small amount of time on parole, or no time at all. As a result, determinate sentencing schemes have changed the face of parole in America, resulting in a dramatic reduction in the average time spent under postprison supervision, but having little impact upon the actual number of released inmates who experience some form of parole.

At the beginning of 2001, approximately 725,500 people were on parole throughout the United States.[23] States vary considerably in the use they make of parole, influenced as they are by the legislative requirements of sentencing schemes. For example, on January 1, 2001, Maine, a state that is phasing out parole, reported only 28 people under parole supervision (the lowest of all the states), North Dakota only 116, while California (the highest of all) had a parole population in excess of 117,000, and Texas officials were busy supervising more than 111,000 parolees. The rate at which parole is used varies, as well. Only 3 out of every 100,000 Maine residents are on parole, whereas 1,244 out of every 100,000 District of Columbia residents are on parole. The national average is 312 per 100,000.[24]

Approximately 42% of parolees successfully complete parole, while about 26% are returned to prison for **parole violations**, and another 12% go back to prison for new offenses during their parole period. (Others may be transferred to new jurisdictions, abscond and not be caught, or die—bringing the total to 100%.)[25] Learn more about trends in parole via **Library Extra! 11–2** at cjtoday.com.

Parole Conditions

In those jurisdictions that retain discretionary parole, the **conditions of parole** remain very similar to the conditions agreed to by probationers. General conditions of parole usually include agreement not to leave the state as well as to obey extradition requests from other jurisdictions. Parolees must also periodically report to parole officers, and parole officers may visit parolees at their homes and places of business, often arriving unannounced.

The successful and continued employment of parolees is one of the major concerns of parole boards and their officers, and studies have found that successful employment is a major factor in reducing the likelihood of repeat offenses.[26] Hence, the importance of continued employment is typically stressed on parole agreement forms, with the stricture that failure to find employment within 30 days may result in **parole revocation**. As with probationers, parolees who are working can be ordered to pay fines and penalties. A provision for making **restitution** payments is also frequently included as a condition of parole.

As with probation, special parole conditions may be added by the judge and might require the parolee to pay a "parole supervisory fee" (often around $15 to $20 per month). A relatively new innovation, the parole supervisory fee shifts some of the expense of community corrections to the offender.

Federal Parole

Federal parole decisions are made by the U.S. Parole Commission, which uses hearing examiners to visit federal prisons. Examiners typically ask inmates to describe why, in their opinion, they are ready for parole. The inmate's job readiness, home plans, past record, accomplishments while in prison, good behavior, and previous experiences on probation or parole form the basis for the examiners' report to the parole commission. The 1984 Comprehensive Crime Control Act, which mandated federal fixed sentencing and abolished parole for offenses committed after November 1, 1978, began a planned phase-out of the U.S. Parole Commission. Under the act, the commission was to be abolished by 1992. The Parole Commission Phaseout Act of 1996,[27] however, extended the life of the commission until 2002. Under the law, the U.S. attorney general must annually certify to Congress that continuation of the commission beyond 2002 is the most effective and cost-efficient method for carrying out the functions assigned to it, or the attorney general will have to propose to Congress an alternative plan for a transfer of those functions.[28] On August 5, 2000, the U.S. Parole Commission completed the assumption of authority of the District of Columbia Board of Parole, as mandated by the D.C. Revitalization Act. Visit the commission's website via **Web Extra! 11–2** at cjtoday.com.

parole (probation) violation

An act or a failure to act by a parolee (or probationer) that does not conform to the conditions of his or her parole (or probation).

conditions of parole (probation)

The general and special limits imposed upon an offender who is released on parole (or probation). General conditions tend to be fixed by state statute, while special conditions are mandated by the sentencing authority (court or board), and take into consideration the background of the offender and the circumstances surrounding the offense.

parole revocation

The administrative action of a paroling authority removing a person from parole status in response to a violation of lawfully required conditions of parole, including the prohibition against commission of a new offense, and usually resulting in a return to prison.

restitution

A court requirement that an alleged or convicted offender pay money or provide services to the victim of the crime or provide services to the community.

Probation and Parole: The Pluses and Minuses

Advantages of Probation and Parole

Probation is used to meet the needs of offenders who require some correctional supervision short of imprisonment, while providing a reasonable degree of security to the community. Parole fulfills a similar purpose for offenders released from prison. Both probation and parole provide a number of advantages over imprisonment, including these:

■ *Lower cost.* Imprisonment is expensive. Incarcerating a single offender in Georgia, for example, costs approximately $39,501 per year, while the cost of intensive probation is as little as $1,321 per probationer.[29] The expense of imprisonment in some other states may be more than three times as high as it is in Georgia. Not only do probation and parole save money, they may even help fill the public coffers. Some jurisdictions require that offenders pay a portion of the costs associated with their own supervision. Georgia, for example, charges clients $10 per month while they are being supervised, while parolees serving for violent offenses pay an additional $10 to the Georgia Crime Victims Emergency Fund.[30] Texas, in an innovative program which uses market-type incentives to encourage probation officers to collect fees, has been able to recoup more than half of what it spends on probation services annually.[31]

■ *Increased employment.* Few people in prison have the opportunity to work. Work-release programs, correctional industries, and inmate labor programs operate in most states, but they usually provide only low-paying jobs and require few skills. At best, such programs include only a small portion of the inmates in any given facility. Probation and parole, on the other hand, make it possible for offenders under correctional supervision to work full-time at jobs in the "free" economy. They can contribute to their own and their families' support, stimulate the local economy by spending their wages, and support the government through the taxes they pay.

■ *Restitution.* Offenders who are able to work are candidates for court-ordered restitution. Society's interest in restitution may be better served by a probationary sentence or parole than by imprisonment. Restitution payments to victims may help restore their standard of living and personal confidence while teaching the offender responsibility.

■ *Community support.* The decision to release a prisoner on parole or to sentence a convicted offender to probation is often partially based upon considerations of family and other social ties. Such decisions are made in the belief that offenders will be more subject to control in the community if they participate in a web of positive social relationships. An advantage of both probation and parole is that they allow the offender to continue personal and social relationships. Probation avoids splitting up families, while parole may reunite family members separated from each other by a prison sentence.

■ *Reduced risk of criminal socialization.* Prison has been called a "school in crime." Probation insulates adjudicated offenders, at least to some degree, from the kinds of criminal values that permeate prison. Parole, by virtue of the fact that it follows time served in prison, is less successful than probation in reducing the risk of criminal socialization.

■ *Increased use of community services.* Probationers and parolees can take advantage of services offered through the community, including psychological therapy, substance-abuse counseling, financial services, support groups, church outreach programs, and social services. While a few similar opportunities may be available in prison, the community environment itself can enhance the effectiveness of treatment programs by reducing the stigmatization of the offender and by allowing the offender to participate in a more "normal" environment.

■ *Increased opportunity for rehabilitation.* Probation and parole can both be useful behavioral management tools. They reward cooperative offenders with freedom and allow for the opportunity to shape the behavior of offenders who may be difficult to reach through other programs.

Disadvantages of Probation and Parole

Any honest appraisal of probation and parole must recognize that they share a number of strategic drawbacks, such as these:

■ *A relative lack of punishment.* The "just deserts" model of criminal sentencing insists that punishment should be a central theme of the justice process. While rehabilitation

> The abolition of parole has been tried and has failed on a spectacular scale. . . . The absence of parole means that offenders simply walk out the door of prison at the end of a predetermined period of time, no questions asked.
>
> —American Probation and Parole Association and the Association of Paroling Authorities International

and treatment are recognized as worthwhile goals, the model suggests that punishment serves both society's need for protection and the victim's need for revenge. Probation, however, is seen as practically no punishment at all and is coming under increasing criticism as a sentencing strategy. Parole is likewise accused of unhinging the scales of justice because (1) it releases some offenders early, even when they have been convicted of serious crimes, while some relatively minor offenders may remain in prison, and (2) it is dishonest because it does not require completion of the offender's entire sentence behind bars.

■ *Increased risk to the community.* Probation and parole are strategies designed to deal with convicted criminal offenders. The release into the community of such offenders increases the risk that they will commit additional offenses. Community supervision can never be so complete as to eliminate such a possibility, and evaluations of parole have pointed out that an accurate assessment of offender dangerousness is beyond our present capability.[32] Nonetheless, a report by the Bureau of Justice Statistics in 2001 found that only about four in every ten persons discharged from parole had successfully completed their term of supervision.[33] The rate of successful parole completion was highest among those who had been released by a parole board (54%) and lower for those whose release was required by law (33%). Parolees age 55 and older and women had higher success rates than those who were younger and male. A 1992 Bureau of Justice Statistics study—the nation's largest ever follow-up survey of felons on probation—found that 43% of probationers were rearrested for a felony within three years of receiving a probationary sentence and while still on probation.[34] Half of the arrests were for a violent crime or a drug offense. An even greater percentage of probationers, 46%, were either sent to prison or jail or had absconded.

■ *Increased social costs.* Some offenders placed on probation and parole will effectively and responsibly discharge their obligations. Others, however, will become social liabilities. In addition to the increased risk of new crimes, probation and parole increase the chance that added expenses will accrue to the community in the form of child support, welfare costs, housing expenses, legal aid, indigent health care, and the like.

The Legal Environment

Ten especially significant U.S. Supreme Court decisions provide the legal framework for probation and parole supervision. Among those cases, that of *Griffin* v. *Wisconsin* (1987)[35] may be the most significant. In *Griffin,* the U.S. Supreme Court ruled that probation officers may conduct searches of a probationer's residence without either a search warrant or probable cause. According to the Court, "A probationer's home, like anyone else's, is protected by the Fourth Amendment's requirement that searches be 'reasonable.'" However, "[a] State's operation of a probation system . . . presents 'special needs' beyond normal law enforcement that may justify departures from the usual warrant and probable cause requirements." Probation, the Court concluded, is similar to imprisonment because it is a "form of criminal sanction imposed upon an offender after a determination of guilt."

Similarly, in the 1998 case of *Pennsylvania Board of Probation and Parole* v. *Scott,*[36] the Court declined to extend the exclusionary rule to apply to searches by parole officers, even where such searches yield evidence of parole violations. In the words of the Court, "[T]he Court has repeatedly declined to extend the [exclusionary] rule to proceedings other than criminal trials. . . . The social costs of allowing convicted criminals who violate their parole to remain at large are particularly high . . . and are compounded by the fact that parolees . . . are more likely to commit future crimes than are average citizens."

In 2001, the case of *U.S.* v. *Knights*[37] expanded the search authority normally reserved for probation and parole officers to police officers under certain circumstances. Mark James Knights was a California probationer who had signed a standard state probation form agreeing to waive his constitutional protection against warrantless searches as a condition of his probation. The form did not limit such searches to probation officers but instead required that Knights submit to a search at any time, with or without a search or arrest warrant or reasonable cause, by any probation or law enforcement officer. When Knights came under suspicion of setting a fire that caused $1.5 million in damages, police officers searched his home without a warrant. The search uncovered evidence that impli-

WHAT WOULD YOU DO?

The CD-ROM scenario for Chapter 11 is built around a real-life case that involved a warrantless search of a parolee's place of residence by parole officers. Firearms were found at the parolee's home, and he was arrested based in part on that evidence. Work through the scenario using the CD-ROM found in the back of your textbook to learn more about warrantless searches by probation and parole officers.

cated Knights in the arson. A federal district court granted a motion by Knights's attorneys to suppress the evidence because the search was for police investigatory purposes, rather than for probationary purposes. The Ninth Circuit Court affirmed the lower court's decision. The U.S. Supreme Court disagreed, however, and held that the warrantless search of Knights's residence "supported by reasonable suspicion and authorized by a probation condition, satisfied the Fourth Amendment . . . as nothing in Knights' probation condition limits searches to those with a 'probationary purpose.'"

Other court cases focus on the conduct of parole or probation **revocation hearings**. Revocation is a common procedure. Annually, about 16.5% of adults on parole and 2.2% of those on probation throughout the United States have their conditional release revoked.[38] The supervising officer may request that probation or parole be revoked if a client has violated the conditions of community release or has committed a new crime. The most frequent violations for which revocation occurs are (1) failure to report as required to a probation or parole office, (2) failure to participate in a stipulated treatment program, and (3) alcohol or drug abuse while under supervision.[39] Revocation hearings may result in an order that a probationer's suspended sentence be made "active" or that a parolee return to prison to complete his or her sentence in confinement.

In a 1935 decision (*Escoe* v. *Zerbst*)[40] which has since been greatly modified, the U.S. Supreme Court held that probation "comes as an act of grace to one convicted of a crime" and that the revocation of probation without hearing or notice to the probationer is acceptable practice. In 1967, however, in the case of *Mempa* v. *Rhay*,[41] the Warren Court changed direction and declared that both notice and a hearing were required. The Court also held that the probationer should have the opportunity for representation by counsel before a deferred prison sentence could be imposed.[42]

Two of the most widely cited cases affecting parolees and probationers are *Morrissey* v. *Brewer* (1972)[43] and *Gagnon* v. *Scarpelli* (1973).[44] In *Morrissey*, the Court declared a need for procedural safeguards in revocation hearings involving parolees. After *Morrissey*, revocation proceedings would require that (1) the parolee be given written notice specifying the alleged violation; (2) evidence of the violation be disclosed; (3) a neutral and detached body constitute the hearing authority; (4) the parolee have the chance to appear and offer a defense, including testimony, documents, and witnesses; (5) the parolee have the right to cross-examine witnesses; and (6) a written statement be provided to the parolee at the conclusion of the hearing that includes the hearing body's decision, the testimony considered, and reasons for revoking parole, if such occurs.[45]

In 1973, the Court extended the procedural safeguards of *Morrissey* to probationers in *Gagnon* v. *Scarpelli*. John Gagnon had pleaded guilty to armed robbery in Wisconsin and was sentenced to 15 years in prison. His sentence was suspended, and the judge ordered him to serve a seven-year probationary term. One month later, and only a day after having been transferred to the supervision of the Cook County (Illinois) Adult Probation Department, Gagnon was arrested by police in the course of a burglary. He was advised of his rights but confessed to officers that he was in the process of stealing money and property when discovered. His probation was revoked without a hearing. Citing its own decision a year earlier in *Morrissey* v. *Brewer*, the Supreme Court ruled that probationers, because they face a substantial loss of liberty, were entitled to two hearings: (1) a preliminary hearing to determine whether there is "probable cause to believe that he has committed a violation of his parole" and (2) "a somewhat more comprehensive hearing prior to the making of the final revocation decision." The Court also ruled that probation revocation hearings were to be held "under the conditions specified in *Morrissey* v. *Brewer*."

The Court also dealt with a separate question centered on Gagnon's indigent status. While being careful to emphasize the narrowness of the particulars in this case, the Court added to the protections granted under *Morrissey* v. *Brewer*, ruling that probationers have the right to a lawyer, even if indigent, provided they claimed that either (1) they had not committed the alleged violation or (2) they had substantial mitigating evidence to explain their violation. In *Gagnon* and later cases, however, the Court reasserted that probation and parole revocation hearings were not a stage in the criminal prosecution process, but a simple adjunct to it, even though they might result in substantial loss of liberty. The difference is a crucial one, for it permits hearing boards and judicial review officers to function, at least to some degree, outside of the adversarial context of the trial court and with lessened attention to the rights of the criminally accused guaranteed by the Bill of Rights.

In 1997, the U.S. Supreme Court extended the rationale found in *Morrissey* and *Gagnon* to inmates set free from prison under early-release programs. In a unanimous decision,

revocation hearing

A hearing held before a legally constituted hearing body (such as a parole board) to determine whether a parolee or probationer has violated the conditions and requirements of his or her parole or probation.

Texas has one of the toughest parole policies in the country with the most violent offenders serving 50 percent of their sentences in actual time and capital offenders sentenced to life serving 40 years of actual time before parole consideration.

—Tony Fabelo, Executive Director of the Texas Criminal Justice Policy Council

the Court held that "an inmate who has been released under a program to relieve prison crowding cannot be reincarcerated without getting a chance to show at a hearing that he has met the conditions of the program and is entitled to remain free."[46] The case involved former Oklahoma inmate Ernest E. Harper, who had been released in 1990 after serving 15 years in Oklahoma prisons for murder. The program under which Harper had been set free was governed by a formula requiring the release of a certain number of inmates as the state's prison system approached capacity. Months after being released, Harper received a call from his parole officer at 5:30 A.M., telling him to report back to prison by ten o'clock that morning. Although Harper had been living according to the rules of the program under which he had been released, state officials argued that he was still a prisoner and said that they were only changing the conditions of his confinement by "recalling" him to an institution. The Supreme Court, however, disagreed, finding that Harper's release from prison was akin to parole—and that it "differed from parole in name alone." As in other situations, said the Court, inmates have a right to challenge, in a formal proceeding, any "grievous loss of liberty" under the Fourteenth Amendment's due process guarantee.

In 1979, the case of *Greenholtz* v. *Nebraska*[47] established that parole boards do not have to specify the evidence used in deciding to deny parole. The *Greenholtz* case focused on a Nebraska statute which required that inmates denied parole be provided with reasons for the denial. The Court held that reasons for parole denial might be provided in the interest of helping inmates prepare themselves for future review but that to require the disclosure of evidence used in the review hearing would turn the process into an adversarial proceeding.

The 1983 Supreme Court case of *Bearden* v. *Georgia*[48] established that probation could not be revoked for failure to pay a fine and make restitution if it could not be shown that the defendant was responsible for the failure. The Court also held that alternative forms of punishment must be considered by the hearing authority and be shown to be inadequate before the defendant can be incarcerated. Bearden had pleaded guilty to burglary and had been sentenced to three years' probation. One of the conditions of his probation required that he pay a fine of $250 and make restitution payments totaling $500. Bearden successfully made the first two payments but then lost his job. His probation was revoked, and he was imprisoned. The Supreme Court decision stated that "[i]f the State determines a fine or restitution to be the appropriate and adequate penalty for the crime, it may not thereafter imprison a person solely because he lacked the resources to pay it."[49] The Court held that if a defendant lacks the capacity to pay a fine or make restitution, then the hearing authority must consider any viable alternatives to incarceration prior to imposing a term of imprisonment.

A probationer's incriminating statements to a probation officer may be used as evidence if the probationer does not specifically claim a right against self-incrimination, according to *Minnesota* v. *Murphy* (1984).[50] Marshall Murphy was sentenced to three years' probation in 1980 on a charge of "false imprisonment" (kidnapping) stemming from an alleged attempted sexual attack. One condition of his probation required him to be entirely truthful with his probation officer "in all matters." Some time later, Murphy admitted to his probation officer that he had confessed to a rape and murder in conversations with a counselor. He was later convicted of first-degree murder, partially on the basis of the statements made to his probation officer. Upon appeal, Murphy's lawyers claimed that their client should have been advised of his right against self-incrimination during his conversation with the probation officer. Although the Minnesota Supreme Court agreed, the U.S. Supreme Court found for the state, saying that the burden of invoking the Fifth Amendment privilege against self-incrimination in this case lay with the probationer.

An emerging legal issue today surrounds the potential liability of probation officers and parole boards for the criminal actions of offenders they supervise or whom they have released. Some courts have held that officers are generally immune from suit because they are performing a judicial function on behalf of the state.[51] Other courts, however, have indicated that parole board members who do not carefully consider mandated criteria for judging parole eligibility could be liable for injurious actions committed by parolees.[52] In general, however, most experts agree that parole board members cannot be successfully sued unless release decisions are made in a grossly negligent or wantonly reckless manner.[53] Discretionary decisions of individual probation and parole officers that result in harm to members of the public, however, may be more actionable under civil law, especially where their decisions were not reviewed by judicial authority.[54]

CJ Today News

[Parole Denied for Radical in Fatal 1981 Robbery]

WHITE PLAINS, N.Y.—Kathy Boudin, a former member of the radical Vietnam-era group the Weather Underground, who has served nearly 20 years in prison for her role in a 1981 armed robbery that left a security guard and two policemen dead, was denied an early release today after her first hearing with members of the New York State Board of Parole.

Ms. Boudin, 58, met for 50 minutes this morning with 2 of the state's 19 Parole Board members at Bedford Hills Correctional Facility, the state prison where she is an inmate. Less than two hours afterward

Kathy Boudin has served nearly 20 years in prison for her role in an armed robbery that left three people dead. In August 2001, Boudin was denied early release.

Edward Keating, New York Times Pictures

they released a decision that she would not be released, "due to the violent nature and circumstances" of the crime. They also ruled that she would have another hearing in two years—the maximum time allowable under the law, but a fairly standard period in similar cases, said Thomas P. Grant, a spokesman for the board.

Relatives of the victims in the crime, who had spent several months campaigning against Ms. Boudin's parole, expressed their relief today, while supporters said they planned to continue their efforts to win her release.

"Justice has been served, at least for another couple of years," said Michael Paige, whose father, Peter Paige, a Brink's guard, was killed in the robbery. "Even though it's painful for the families, we'll keep going through this process so she remains in prison for the rest of her life."

Ms. Boudin's role in the crime was to serve as a decoy by sitting in the front of the getaway vehicle, a U-Haul truck, after the robbers stole $1.6 million from a Brink's truck and killed a guard, Mr. Paige.

The police stopped the U-Haul as it approached the New York State Thruway in Nyack, and after Ms. Boudin got out of the cab the robbers burst out of the back, opening fire and killing two Nyack police officers, Sgt. Edward O'Grady and Officer Waverly Brown, before they were captured.

Ms. Boudin, who was not armed, was convicted of first-degree robbery and second-degree murder, and sentenced to 20 years to life.

Several of Ms. Boudin's supporters said they were not surprised by the decision, because it is very rare for a prisoner to be released after the first parole hearing. But they said they had hoped Ms. Boudin's unusual record of achievement might win her special consideration. During her years in prison she has helped to pioneer several education and health care programs for inmates that are now national models.

For the latest in crime and justice news, visit the Talk Justice news feed at http://www.crimenews.info.

Source: Robert Worth, "Parole Denied for Radical in Fatal 1981 Robbery," *New York Times,* August 23, 2001.

The Federal Probation System

The federal probation system is nearly 80 years old.[55] In 1916, the U.S. Supreme Court, in the *Killets* case,[56] ruled that federal judges did not have the authority to suspend sentences and to order probation. After a vigorous campaign by the National Probation Association, Congress passed the National Probation Act in 1925, authorizing the use of probation in federal courts. The bill came just in time to save a burgeoning federal prison system from serious overcrowding. The prostitution-fighting Mann Act, Prohibition legislation, and the growth of organized crime all led to increased arrests and a dramatic growth in the number of federal probationers in the early years of the system.

Although the 1925 act authorized one probation officer per federal judge, it allocated only $25,000 for officers' salaries. As a consequence, only eight officers were hired to serve

> Probation and parole services are characteristically poorly staffed and often poorly administered.
>
> —President's Commission on Law Enforcement and Administration of Justice

132 judges, and the system came to rely heavily upon voluntary probation officers. Some sources indicate that as many as 40,000 probationers were under the supervision of volunteers at the peak of the system.[57] By 1930, however, Congress provided adequate funding, and a corps of salaried professionals began to provide probation services to the U.S. courts.

In the last 20 years, the work of federal probation officers has been dramatically affected by new rules of federal procedure. Presentence investigations have been especially affected. Revised Rule 32 of the *Federal Rules of Criminal Procedure,* for example, mandates that federal probation officers who prepare presentence reports must[58]

- Evaluate the evidence in support of the facts
- Resolve certain disputes between the prosecutor and the defense attorney
- Testify when needed to provide evidence in support of the administrative application of sentencing guidelines
- Utilize an addendum to the report which, among other things, demonstrates that the report has been disclosed to the defense attorney, the defendant, and government counsel

In order to conduct effective presentence investigations, probation officers must be capable of drawing objective conclusions based upon the facts they observe, and they must be able to make "independent judgments in the body of the report regarding which sets of facts by various observers the court should rely upon in imposing sentence."[59] Officers must also be effective witnesses in court during the trial phase of criminal proceedings.

The Job of Probation and Parole Officers

Correctional personnel involved in probation and parole supervision totaled 43,198 (including approximately 2,500 federal officers) throughout the United States in 1996, according to the American Correctional Association (ACA).[60] Some 15,352 of these officers supervised probationers only, while 13,833 supervised both probationers and parolees.

The tasks performed by probation and parole officers are often quite similar. Some jurisdictions combine the roles of both into one job. This section describes the duties of probation and parole officers, whether separate or performed by the same individuals. Probation/parole work consists primarily of four functions: (1) presentence investigations, (2) intake procedures, (3) needs assessment and diagnosis, and (4) client supervision.

Where probation is a possibility, intake procedures may include presentence investigations (described in Chapter 10), which examine the offender's background to provide the sentencing judge with facts needed to make an informed sentencing decision. Intake procedures may also involve a dispute-settlement process during which the probation officer works with the defendant and the victim to resolve the complaint prior to sentencing. Intake duties tend to be more common for juvenile offenders than they are for adults, but all officers may find themselves in the position of having to recommend to the judge what sentencing alternative would best answer the needs of the case.

Diagnosis, the psychological inventorying of the probation or parole client, may be done on either a formal basis involving the use of written tests administered by certified psychologists or through informal arrangements, which typically depend upon the observational skills of the officer. Needs assessment, another area of officer responsibility, extends beyond the psychological needs of the client to a cataloging of the services necessary for a successful experience on probation or parole.

Supervision of sentenced probationers or released parolees is the most active stage of the probation/parole process, involving months (and sometimes years) of periodic meetings between the officer and the client and an ongoing assessment of the success of the probation/parole endeavor in each case.

One special consideration affecting the work of all probation and parole officers is the need for confidentiality. The details of the presentence investigation, psychological tests, needs assessment, conversations between the officer and the client, and so on should not be public knowledge. On the other hand, courts have generally held that communications between the officer and the client are not privileged, as they might be between a doctor and a patient or between a social worker and his or her client.[61] Hence, incriminating evidence related by a client can be shared by officers with the appropriate authorities.

The Challenges of the Job

Perhaps the biggest challenge that probation and parole officers face is the need to walk a fine line between two conflicting sets of duties—one of which is to provide quasi–social work services and the other is to handle custodial responsibilities. In effect, two conflicting images of the officer's role coexist. The social work model stresses a service role for officers and views probationers and parolees as clients. Officers are seen as caregivers who attempt to assess accurately the needs of their clients and, through an intimate familiarity with available community services—from job placement, indigent medical care, and family therapy to psychological and substance-abuse counseling—match clients and community resources. The social work model depicts probation/parole as a "helping profession" wherein officers assist their clients in meeting the conditions imposed upon them by their sentence. The other model for officers is correctional. It sees probation and parole clients as "wards" whom officers are expected to control. This model emphasizes community protection, which officers are supposed to achieve through careful and close supervision. Custodial supervision means that officers will periodically visit their charges at work and at home, often arriving unannounced. It also means that they must be willing to report clients for new offenses and for violations of the conditions of their release.

Most officers, by virtue of their personalities and experiences, probably identify more with one of the models than with the other. They think of themselves primarily either as caregivers or as correctional officers. Regardless of the emphasis which appeals most to individual officers, however, the demands of the job are bound to generate role conflict at one time or another.

A second challenge of probation/parole work is high **caseloads**. Back in 1973, the President's Commission on Law Enforcement and Administration of Justice recommended that probation/parole caseloads average around 35 clients per officer.[62] However, caseloads of 250 clients are common in some jurisdictions today. High caseloads, combined with limited training and time constraints forced by administrative and other demands, culminate in stopgap supervisory measures. "Postcard probation," in which clients mail in a letter or card once a month to report on their whereabouts and circumstances, is an example of one stopgap measure that harried agencies with large caseloads use to keep track of their wards.

Another difficulty with probation/parole work is the lack of opportunity for career mobility. Probation and parole officers are generally assigned to small agencies serving limited geographic areas, under the leadership of one or two chief probation officers. Unless retirement or death claims a supervisor, there is little chance for other officers to advance.

Learn more about working as a probation or parole officer at the American Probation and Parole Association's website via **Web Extra! 11–3** at cjtoday.com.

> Probation and parole have essentially shifted from legitimate correctional options in their own right to temporary diversionary strategies that we are using while we are trying to figure out how to get tough on crime, [pay] no new taxes, and not pay for any prisons at all, or to pay as little as we can, or pass it off to another generation.
>
> —Dr. Charles M. Friel, Sam Houston State University

caseload

The number of probation or parole clients assigned to one probation or parole officer for supervision.

Intermediate Sanctions

In 1996, 32-year-old Sia Ye Vang, a Hmong tribesman and Vietnamese immigrant living in La Crosse, Wisconsin, was convicted of sexually molesting his young stepdaughters, aged 10 and 11. Judge Ramona Gonzalez, apparently influenced by defense arguments that sex with girls is accepted practice in Vietnam, sentenced Vang to 24 years' probation and ordered him to continue English classes and perform 1,000 hours of community service. The judge decided to allow Vang "the opportunity to continue his education, and his assimilation into our culture."[63] Vang could have received 80 years in prison.

Although Vang's case may be an extreme example, it illustrates the fact that significant new sentencing options have become available over the past few decades. Many such options are called **intermediate sanctions** because they employ sentencing alternatives which fall somewhere between outright imprisonment and simple probationary release back into the community. They are also sometimes termed *alternative sentencing strategies*. Michael J. Russell, former Director of the National Institute of Justice, says that "intermediate punishments are intended to provide prosecutors, judges, and corrections officials with sentencing options that permit them to apply appropriate punishments to convicted offenders while not being constrained by the traditional choice between prison and probation. Rather than substituting for prison or probation, however, these sanctions—which include intensive supervision, house arrest with electronic monitoring, and shock incarceration—bridge the gap between those options and provide innovative ways to ensure swift and certain punishment."[64]

intermediate sanctions

The use of split sentencing, shock probation or parole, home confinement, shock incarceration, or community service in lieu of other, more traditional, sanctions, such as imprisonment and fines.

A number of citizen groups and special-interest organizations are working to widen the use of sentencing alternatives. One organization of special note is the Washington, D.C.–based Sentencing Project. The Sentencing Project was formed in 1986[65] with support from foundation grants.[66] The project is dedicated to promoting a greater use of alternatives to incarceration and provides technical assistance to public defenders, court officials, and other community organizations.

The Sentencing Project and other groups like it have contributed to the development of over 100 locally based alternative sentencing service programs. Most alternative sentencing services work in conjunction with defense attorneys to develop written sentencing plans. Such plans are basically well-considered citizen suggestions as to appropriate sentencing in a given instance. Plans are often quite detailed and may include letters of support from employers, family members, the defendant, and even victims. Sentencing plans may be used in plea bargaining sessions or presented to judges following trial and conviction. A decade ago, for example, lawyers for country-and-western singer Willie Nelson successfully proposed an alternative option to tax court officials which allowed the singer to pay huge past tax liabilities by performing in concerts for that purpose. Lacking such an alternative, the tax court might have seized Nelson's property or even ordered the singer confined to a federal facility.

The basic philosophy behind intermediate sanctions is this: When judges are offered well-planned alternatives to imprisonment, the likelihood of a prison sentence is reduced. An analysis of alternative sentencing plans such as those sponsored by the Sentencing Project shows that they are accepted by judges in up to 80% of the cases in which they are recommended and that as many as two-thirds of offenders who receive intermediate sentences successfully complete them.[67]

Intermediate sanctions have three distinct advantages: (1) They are less expensive to operate per offender than imprisonment; (2) they are "socially cost effective" because they keep the offender in the community, thus avoiding both the breakup of the family and the stigmatization which accompanies imprisonment; and (3) they provide flexibility in terms of resources, time of involvement, and place of service.[68] Some of these new options are described in the paragraphs that follow.

Split Sentencing

split sentence

A sentence explicitly requiring the convicted offender to serve a period of confinement in a local, state, or federal facility, followed by a period of probation.

In jurisdictions where **split sentences** are an option, judges may impose a combination of a brief period of imprisonment and probation. Defendants who are given split sentences are often ordered to serve time in a local jail rather than in a long-term confinement facility. Ninety days in jail, together with two years of supervised probation, is a typical split sentence. Split sentences are frequently given to minor drug offenders and serve notice that continued law violations may result in imprisonment for much longer periods.

Shock Probation and Shock Parole

shock probation

The practice of sentencing offenders to prison, allowing them to apply for probationary release, and enacting such release in surprise fashion. Offenders who receive shock probation may not be aware that they will be released on probation and may expect to spend a much longer time behind bars.

Shock probation bears a considerable resemblance to split sentencing. The offender serves a relatively short period of time in custody (usually in a prison rather than a jail) and is released on probation by court order. The difference is that shock probation clients must *apply* for probationary release from confinement and cannot be certain of the judge's decision. In shock probation, the court in effect makes a resentencing decision. Probation is only a statutory possibility and often little more than a vague hope for the offender as imprisonment begins. If probationary release is ordered, it may well come as a "shock" to the offender who, facing a sudden reprieve, may forswear future criminal involvement. Shock probation was begun in Ohio in 1965[69] and is used today in about half the United States.[70]

New Jersey runs a model shock probation program that is administered by a specially appointed screening board composed of correctional officials and members of the public. The New Jersey program has served as an example to many other states. It has stringent selection criteria that allow only inmates serving sentences for nonviolent crimes to apply to the screening board for release.[71] Inmates must have served at least 30 days before applying, and those who have served over 60 days are ineligible. Offenders must submit a personal plan describing what they will do when released, what their problems are, what community resources they need or intend to use, and what people can be relied upon to provide assistance. Part of the plan involves a community sponsor with whom the inmate must reside for a fixed period of time (usually a few months) following release. The New Jersey program is especially strict because it does not grant outright release, but rather allows only a 90-day initial period of freedom. An inmate who successfully completes the 90-day period may request continued release.

Shock probation lowers the cost of confinement, maintains community and family ties, and may be an effective rehabilitative tool.[72] Similar to shock probation is shock parole. Whereas shock probation is ordered by judicial authority, shock parole is an administrative decision made by a paroling authority. Parole boards or their representatives may order an inmate's early release, hoping that the brief exposure to prison has reoriented the offender's life in a positive direction.

Shock Incarceration

Shock incarceration programs, which became quite popular during the 1990s, utilize military-style "boot camp" prison settings to provide highly regimented environments involving strict discipline, physical training, and hard labor.[73] Shock incarceration programs are designed primarily for young first offenders and are of short duration, generally lasting for only 90 to 180 days. Offenders who successfully complete these programs are typically returned to the community under some form of supervision. Program "failures" may be moved into the general prison population for longer terms of confinement.

Georgia established the first shock incarceration program in 1983.[74] Following Georgia's lead, more than 30 other states began their own programs.[75] The federal government and some Canadian provinces also operate shock incarceration programs. New York's program is arguably the largest, with a capacity for 1,390 participants, while programs in Rhode Island and Wyoming can handle only 30.[76] There are other differences among the states as well. About half provide for voluntary entry into their shock incarceration programs. A few allow inmates to decide when and whether they want to quit. Although most states allow judges to place offenders into these programs, some delegate that authority to corrections officials. Two states, Louisiana and Texas, give judges and corrections personnel joint authority in the decision-making process.[77] Some states, such as Massachusetts, accept female inmates into boot camp settings. The Massachusetts program, which first accepted women in 1993, requires inmates to spend nearly four months undergoing the rigors of training.

One of the most comprehensive studies to date of boot camp prison programs examined shock incarceration programs in eight states: Florida, Georgia, Illinois, Louisiana, New York, Oklahoma, South Carolina, and Texas. The report found that boot camp programs have been popular because "they are . . . perceived as being tough on crime" and "have been enthusiastically embraced as a viable correctional option."[78] The report concluded, however, that "the impact of boot camp programs on offender recidivism is at best negligible." A national study focusing on the correctional treatment of juvenile offenders compared 27 boot camps to 22 traditional institutions.[79] The study's findings were reported in 2001:

■ Despite their growth in popularity in the 1990s, correctional boot camps remain controversial. Critics question whether their military-style methods are appropriate to managing and treating juvenile delinquents and positively affecting juvenile behavior while they are confined and after their release. Boot camp advocates contend that the facilities' program structure gives staff more control over the participants and provides the juveniles with a safer environment than traditional facilities.

■ Juveniles in boot camps more frequently report positive responses to their institutional environment than do those in traditional settings. Boot camp juveniles said they were better prepared for release, were given more therapeutic programming, experienced more structure and control, and were more active than did youths in comparison facilities. The one exception was that boot camp youths were more likely to report feeling that they were in danger from the staff.

■ Staff in boot camps more frequently reported favorable perceptions of their institutional environments, such as a caring and just environment and more structure and control, than did staff in traditional facilities. Boot camp staff also more frequently reported favorable working conditions, such as less personal stress and better communication among staff.

■ Initial levels of anxiety were slightly higher for boot camp participants; initial levels of depression were higher for comparison facility juveniles. Anxiety and depression decreased over time for juveniles in both facilities. Juveniles in both types of facilities experienced decreased social bonding with family, school, and work while they were institutionalized.

shock incarceration

A sentencing option that makes use of "boot camp"–type prisons to impress upon convicted offenders the realities of prison life.

> The overarching goal of reentry, in my view, is to have returned to our midst an individual who has discharged his legal obligation to society by serving his sentence *and* has demonstrated an ability to live by society's rules.
>
> —Jeremy Travis, former Director of the National Institute of Justice

A boot camp correctional officer greeting a new arrival. Shock incarceration programs provide a sentencing alternative which gained popularity during the 1990s but whose effectiveness has recently been called into question.

R. Maiman, CORBIS, Sygma

■ In general, boot camps were more selective about the juveniles admitted to the facility than were traditional institutions. Boot camps admitted fewer juveniles who had psychological problems or were suicide risks, and they required psychological, medical, and physical evaluations before allowing juveniles to enter. In 25% of the boot camps studied, participants had to volunteer for the program.

More limited studies, such as one that focused on shock incarceration in New York State, have found that boot camp programs can be effective money savers. Such programs appear to save money in two ways: "first by reducing expenditures for care and custody" (since the intense programs reduce time spent in custody, and participation in them is the only way New York inmates can be released from prison before their minimum parole eligibility dates) and "second, by avoiding capital costs for new prison construction."[80] A 1995 study of Oregon's Summit boot camp program reached a similar conclusion. Although they did not study recidivism, the Oregon researchers found that "the Summit boot camp program is a cost-effective means of reducing prison overcrowding by treating and releasing specially selected inmates earlier than their court-determined minimum period of incarceration."[81]

Mixed Sentencing and Community Service

Some **mixed sentences** require that offenders serve weekends in jail and receive probation supervision during the week. Other types of mixed sentencing require offenders to participate in treatment or community service programs while on probation. Community service programs began in Minnesota in 1972 with the Minnesota Restitution Program, which gave property offenders the opportunity to work and turn over part of their pay as restitution to their victims.[82] Courts throughout the nation quickly adopted the idea and began to build restitution orders into suspended-sentence agreements.

Community service is more an adjunct to, rather than a type of, correctional sentence. Community service is compatible with most other forms of innovation in probation and

mixed sentence

A sentence that requires that a convicted offender serve weekends (or other specified periods of time) in a confinement facility (usually a jail) while undergoing probationary supervision in the community.

community service

A sentencing alternative that requires offenders to spend at least part of their time working for a community agency.

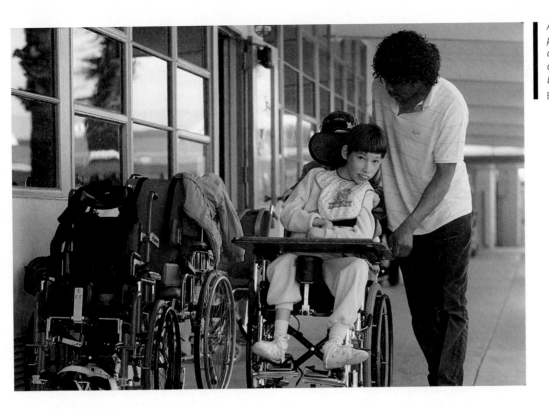

A juvenile offender works with a physically challenged child. The offender is participating in an alternative sentencing program in Bellflower, California.

Bart Bartholomew, Black Star

parole. Even with home confinement (discussed below), offenders could be sentenced to community service activities which might be performed in the home or at a job site during the hours they are permitted to be away from their homes. Washing police cars, cleaning school buses, refurbishing public facilities, and assisting in local government offices are typical forms of community service. Some authors have linked the development of community service sentences to the notion that work and service to others are good for the spirit.[83] Community service participants are usually minor criminals, drunk drivers, and youthful offenders.

One problem with community service sentences is that authorities rarely agree on what they are supposed to accomplish. Most people admit that offenders who work in the community are able to reduce the costs of their own supervision. There is little agreement, however, over whether such sentences reduce recidivism, provide a deterrent, or act to rehabilitate offenders.

> A critical assessment of probation must begin by placing its ailments within the more encompassing and deeper crisis of legitimacy affecting the entire system of justice.
>
> —Reinventing Probation Council

Intensive Supervision

Intensive probation supervision (IPS), first implemented by Georgia in 1982, has been described as the "strictest form of probation for adults in the United States."[84] IPS is designed to achieve control in a community setting over offenders who would otherwise have gone to prison. Some states have extended intensive supervision to parolees, allowing the early release of some who would otherwise serve lengthy prison terms.

The Georgia program involves a minimum of five face-to-face contacts between the probationer and the supervising officer per week, mandatory curfew, required employment, a weekly check of local arrest records, routine and unannounced alcohol and drug testing, 132 hours of community service, and automatic notification of probation officers via the State Crime Information Network when an IPS client is arrested.[85] The caseloads of probation officers involved in IPS are much lower than the national average. Georgia officers work as a team, with one probation officer and two surveillance officers supervising about 40 probationers.[86]

A study published in 2000 shows that IPS programs can be effective at reducing recidivism, especially if the programs are well planned and fully implemented.[87] The study, which compared programs in California's Contra Costa and Ventura Counties, found that the programs worked because, among other things, they used team approaches in their supervision activities and had clear missions and goals.

intensive probation supervision (IPS)

A form of probation supervision involving frequent face-to-face contact between the probationer and the probation officer.

Home Confinement and Electronic Monitoring

home confinement

House arrest. Individuals ordered confined to their homes are sometimes monitored electronically to ensure they do not leave during the hours of confinement. Absence from the home during working hours is often permitted.

Home confinement, also referred to as *house arrest,* has been defined as "a sentence imposed by the court in which offenders are legally ordered to remain confined in their own residences."[88] They may leave only to attend to medical emergencies, go to their jobs, or buy household essentials. House arrest has been cited as offering a valuable alternative to prison for offenders with special needs. Pregnant women, geriatric convicts, offenders with special handicaps, seriously or terminally ill offenders, and the mentally retarded might all be better supervised through home confinement than traditional incarceration.

Florida's Community Control Program, authorized by the state's Correctional Reform Act of 1983, is the most ambitious home confinement program in the country.[89] On any given day in Florida, as many as 5,000 offenders are restricted to their homes and are supervised by community control officers who visit unannounced. Candidates for the program are required to agree to specific conditions, including (1) restitution, (2) family support payments, and (3) supervisory fees (around $50 per month). They are also obligated to fill out daily logs about their activities. Community control officers have a minimum of 20 contacts per month with each offender. Additional discussions are held by the officer with neighbors, spouses, friends, landlords, employers, and others to allow the earliest possible detection of program violations or renewed criminality.

Florida's most serious home confinement offenders are monitored via a computerized system of electronic bracelets. Random telephone calls require the offender to insert a computer chip worn in a wristband into a specially installed modem in the home, verifying his or her presence. More modern units make it possible to record the time a supervised person enters or leaves the home, to determine whether the phone line or equipment has been tampered with, and to send or receive messages.[90] The electronic monitoring of offenders has undergone dramatic growth both in Florida and across the nation. A survey by the National Institute of Justice in 1987, as the use of electronic monitoring was just beginning, showed only 826 offenders being monitored electronically.[91] Only two years later, the number had jumped to around 6,500, and by the end of 1997 it stood at 21,375.[92] Of these, 15,373 were serving probationary sentences, and 6,002 were parolees.

In 1999, South Carolina's Probation and Parole Department began using satellites to track felons recently freed from state prisons. The satellite-tracking plan, which makes use of 21 satellites in the Global Positioning System (GPS), allows the agency's officers to keep track of every move made by convicts wearing electronic bracelets.[93] The system, which

Electronic supervision in action. Boxing's most notorious middleweight, 38-year-old Tony "El Torito" Ayala, conceals an electronic ankle bracelet under his left sock as he spars during a workout at the Zarzamore Street Gym in San Antonio prior to a scheduled fight. In 2001, the fighter pleaded guilty to burglary and was sentenced to 90 days in jail and ten years' probation. Ayala had previously served 16 years in a New Jersey prison on a 1983 rape conviction.

AP/Wide World Photos

also notifies law enforcement officers when a bracelet-wearing offender leaves his assigned area, can electronically alert anyone holding a restraint order whenever the offender goes within two miles of them.

The home confinement program in the federal court system has three components, or levels of restriction.[94] *Curfew* requires program participants to remain at home every day during certain times, usually in the evening. With *home detention*, the participant remains at home at all times except for preapproved and scheduled absences, such as for work, school, treatment, church, attorney's appointments, court appearances, and other court-ordered obligations. *Home incarceration*, the highest level of restriction, calls for 24-hour-a-day "lockdown" at home, except for medical appointments, court appearances, and other activities that the court specifically approves. Many states and the federal government view house arrest as a cost-effective response to the rising expense of imprisonment. Estimates show that traditional home confinement programs cost about $1,500 to $7,000 per offender per year, while electronic monitoring increases the costs by at least $1,000.[95] Advocates of house arrest for probationers argue that it is also socially cost-effective,[96] as it provides no opportunity for the kinds of negative socialization which occur in prison. Opponents have pointed out that house arrest may endanger the public, that it may be illegal,[97] and that it may provide little or no actual punishment.

The Future of Probation and Parole

Parole has been widely criticized in recent years. Citizen groups claim that it unfairly reduces prison sentences imposed on serious offenders. Academics allege that parole programs can provide no assurance that criminals will not commit further crimes. Media attacks upon parole have centered on recidivism and have highlighted the so-called revolving prison door as representative of the failure of parole. In 1999, for example, parole violators accounted for more than half of prison admissions in California (67%), Utah (55%), and Montana and Louisiana (both 53%). Seventy percent of parole violators in prison were arrested or were convicted of a new offense while on parole.[98]

Some years ago, the case of Larry Singleton came to represent all that is wrong with parole. Singleton was convicted of raping 15-year-old Mary Vincent, then hacking off her forearms and leaving her for dead on a California hillside.[99] When an apparently unrepentant[100] Singleton was paroled after eight years in prison, public outcry was tremendous. Communities banded together to deny him residence, and he had to be paroled to the grounds of San Quentin prison until public concern lessened. Singleton's story did not end there, however. He soon moved to Florida where, in 1997, he was charged with the murder of 31-year-old Roxanne Hayes, an alleged prostitute. Hayes's nude body was discovered in Singleton's Tampa apartment by police, who were alerted by neighbors who heard a woman screaming. She had been stabbed many times. "It's a sad commentary on the criminal justice system that a person who committed a crime this heinous was out on the street," said Tampa police spokesman Lieutenant David Gee.[101] In 1998, Singleton was found guilty of first-degree murder.[102]

Official attacks upon parole have come from some powerful corners. Senator Edward Kennedy has called for the abolition of parole, as has former Attorney General Griffin Bell and former U.S. Bureau of Prisons Director Norman Carlson.[103]

Prisoners have also challenged the fairness of parole, saying it is sometimes arbitrarily granted and creates an undue amount of uncertainty and frustration in the lives of inmates. Parolees have complained about the unpredictable nature of the parole experience, citing their powerlessness in the parole contract.

Against the pressure of official attacks and despite cases like Singleton's, parole advocates struggle to clarify and communicate the value of parole in the correctional process. As more and more states move toward the elimination of parole, advocates call for moderation. A 1995 report by the American Probation and Parole Association (APPA), for example, concludes that the states that have eliminated parole "have jeopardized public safety and wasted tax dollars." The researchers wrote, "Getting rid of parole dismantles an accountable system of releasing prisoners back into the community and replaces it with a system that bases release decisions solely on whether a prison term has been completed."[104] Some people have gone so far as to suggest a different kind of reentry system—one that would create reentry courts and use judges as reentry managers.[105] Under this model, sentencing judges might oversee an offender's sentence from the time of conviction and imprisonment through release into the community under supervision.

Probation, although it has generally fared better than parole, is not without its critics. The primary purpose of probation has always been rehabilitation. Probation is a powerful rehabilitative tool because, at least in theory, it allows the resources of a community to be focused on the offender. Unfortunately for advocates of probation, however, the rehabilitative ideal is far less popular today than it has been in the past. The contemporary demand for "just deserts" appears to have reduced the tolerance society as a whole feels for even relatively minor offenders. Also, the image of probation has not benefited from its all-too-frequent and inappropriate use with repeat or relatively serious offenders. Probation advocates themselves have been forced to admit that it is not a very powerful deterrent because it is far less punishing than a term of imprisonment.

In a series of reports issued in 1999 and 2000, the Reinventing Probation Council, a project of New York's Manhattan Institute, called for the "reinvention of probation."[106] Probation is currently in the midst of a crisis, said the council, because probationers are not being held to even simple behavioral standards and because the field of probation lacks leadership. According to the council, "Probation will be reinvented when the probation profession places public safety first, and works with and in the community." The reinvention of probation, says the council, will mean

> Probation will change when those who run probation departments are held accountable for achieving—or failing to achieve—specific outcomes.
>
> —Reinventing Probation Council

- Requiring probation officers to meet with offenders in their homes at all hours, not just in probation offices during normal business hours—a practice that the council calls "fortress probation"

- Ending the practice of allowing officers to avoid meeting at home with offenders who live in high-crime neighborhoods or dangerous locations. Avoiding dangerous neighborhoods "reduces the possibility of personal harm, but at the same time," said the council, "makes it virtually impossible to be a probation officer."

- Ending the all-too-common practice of giving probationers advance notice of when they are to take drug tests

- Reducing probation caseloads, which the council found were as high as 500 probationers per officer in some jurisdictions

- Imposing graded sanctions upon probationers who break the rules and conditions of their probation. In the words of the council, "Clearly, offenders on probation have a responsibility to comply with the conditions of supervision. When they do not, then it is up to probation to enforce compliance with such terms. It is here though that the practice of probation frequently breaks down." The council noted that "to remain out of jail, over 90% of probationers are ordered by the courts to get substance abuse counseling, remain under house arrest, perform community service, or meet other specific conditions. Unfortunately, studies have found that about half of all probationers do not comply with the terms of their sentence, and only a fifth of those who violate their sentences ever go to jail for their noncompliance." Other rule breakers include probation absconders, who don't even stay in contact with their probation officers. In many jurisdictions today, nothing is being done to apprehend these offenders, said the council. It concluded that the present system is essentially teaching probationers that there are no consequences for probation violations.

Read the council's full reports at **Library Extras! 11–3** and **11–4** at cjtoday.com.

Todd R. Clear, former President of the Academy of Criminal Justice Sciences, has taken a position similar to that of the Reinventing Probation Council.[107] Clear suggests reframing the idea of community corrections to include the notion of "a corrections of place." Clear notes that although community corrections sounds much like community policing, there are important differences. "In corrections," says Clear, "the term 'community' does not stand for the problem-solving focus but instead often merely indicates that an offender happens to be living outside a correctional facility." To develop a true corrections of place, says Clear, it is necessary to take into consideration the needs of the local community as well as the demands of the wider society for retribution, punishment, and rehabilitation. In an example from Vermont, Clear points to community boards that now assist in determining the conditions of supervision for offenders sentenced to probation or released on parole. Suggesting that correctional officials should embrace the spirit underlying the community policing movement, Clear says that "when community members feel they can shape correctional policy by direct participation, they will also feel less estranged from the decisions made by officials, and they will feel inclined to shape their participation to be meaningful rather than antagonistic."

Finally, in an intriguing American Society of Criminology task force report on community corrections, Joan Petersilia notes that the "get tough on criminals" attitude that recently swept the nation resulted in increased funding for prisons but left stagnating budgetary allotments for probation and parole services in its wake.[108] This result has been especially unfortunate, Petersilia says, because "it has been continually shown that there is a 'highly significant statistical relationship between the extent to which probationers received needed services and the success of probation.'" "As services have dwindled," she says, "recidivism rates have climbed." Some jurisdictions spend only a few hundred dollars per year on each probation or parole client, while successful treatment in therapeutic settings is generally acknowledged to cost nearly $15,000 per person per year. The investment of such sums in the treatment of correctional clients, argues Petersilia, is potentially worthwhile because diverting probationers and parolees from lives of continued crime will save society even more money in terms of the costs of crime and the expenses associated with eventual imprisonment. The solution to the crisis that now exists in community corrections, says Petersilia, is to "first regain the public's trust that probation and parole can be meaningful, credible sanctions." Petersilia concludes, "Once we have that in place, we need to create a public climate to support a reinvestment in community corrections. Good community corrections cost money, and we should be honest about that."

Learn more about recidivism and the judicious use of parole as a reentry strategy via **Library Extra! 11–5** at cjtoday.com. Learn more about the political, economic, and social consequences of community corrections via **Library Extra! 11–6** at cjtoday.com.

CJ Futures

[Probation Kiosks: High-Tech Supervision]

In 1997, probation authorities in New York City began experimenting with the use of "probation kiosks" designed to lower probation officer caseloads. Fifteen electronic kiosks, similar in design to automated teller machines, are now scattered throughout the city. They allow probationers to check in with probation officers by placing their palms on a specially designed surface and by answering questions presented on a flashing screen.

The kiosks identify probationers by the shape and size of their hands, which were previously scanned into the system. Probationers are then prompted to press "yes" or "no" in response to questions such as these: "Have you moved recently?" "Have you been arrested again?" "Do you need to see a probation officer?" Meetings with officers can be scheduled directly from the kiosk. Probation officers use a computer to monitor data sent from the kiosks and can zero in on individual probationers who are having problems, prompting more personal attention. By the time the system is fully operational, as many as 30,000 "low-risk" probationers—about one-third of New York City's total—will report through kiosks.

Kiosks have already yielded positive results, according to New York City probation officer Genée Bogans. Before the kiosks, says Bogans, she was swamped by administrative details required to track the 250 offenders in her caseload. Kiosks allow her to track nonviolent, older offenders with a minimum of time and effort, and she now focuses most of her attention on the relatively few violent youths who are also part of her caseload, meeting with them and their families twice weekly in small group sessions. Bogans even goes to family funerals and graduations, making youthful offenders feel like they are getting special attention. "But it can be done only when you have 30 cases as opposed to 200," says Bogans.

New York's use of kiosks is being watched closely by other probation and parole agencies around the country as they face swelling caseloads and shrinking budgets. Some cities have taken other steps to automate their probation systems. Denver and Seattle, for example, are using 900-numbers through which probationers can report in.

Critics charge that without personal supervision, probationers are more likely to reoffend—an assertion which is essentially untested. Others say kiosks are far removed from meaningful "punishment" and that offenders deserve stricter treatment. Supporters, on the other hand, say that kiosks and 900-numbers will soon become more commonplace. "New York City had no choice; it had to do something like that," says Todd Clear, professor of Criminal Justice at New York's John Jay College. Clear assisted the city in restructuring its probation program. "No one wants probationers reporting to kiosks, but the alternative was even more unthinkable—a system in which nobody receives quality service," said Clear.

Source: Isabelle de Pommereau, "N.Y.C. Probation Officers to Get High-Tech Helper," *Christian Science Monitor,* February 8, 1997; and Rice County, Minnesota, website.

Summary

Probation, simply put, is a sentence of imprisonment that is suspended. Parole, in contrast, is the conditional early release of a convicted offender from prison. Both probation and parole impose conditions upon offenders, requiring them to obey the law, meet with probation or parole officers, hold a job, and the like. Failure to abide by the conditions of probation or parole can result in rearrest and imprisonment.

Viewed historically, probation and parole are two of the most recent large-scale innovations in the correctional field. Both provide opportunities for the reintegration of offenders into the community through the use of resources not readily available in institutional settings. Unfortunately, however, increased freedom for criminal offenders also means some degree of increased risk for other members of society. As a consequence, contemporary "get tough" attitudes have resulted in a decreased use of probation and parole in many jurisdictions—and increased imprisonment. Until and unless probation and parole solve the problems of inaccurate risk assessment, increased recidivism, and inadequate supervision, they are likely to continue to be viewed with suspicion by a crime-weary public.

Discussion Questions

1. Do you believe that a person who commits a crime should be allowed to serve all or part of his or her sentence in the community? If so, what conditions would you impose on the offender?
2. Do you agree with those who are trying to eliminate parole? Why or why not?
3. Will ordering an offender to make restitution to the victim teach the offender to be a more responsible person? Support your opinion.
4. Do you believe that "role conflict" is a real challenge of the probation or parole officer's job? If so, do you see any way to reduce the role conflict experienced by probation and parole officers? How might you do it?
5. Is home confinement a good idea? Does it discriminate against certain kinds of offenders? What is the future of home confinement? How might it be improved?

To participate in an online discussion on these topics and others, go to the Global Town Meeting electronic message board for Chapter 11 on the *Criminal Justice Today* Companion Website at cjtoday.com.

 ## Web Quest!

Use the Cybrary to search the World Wide Web to learn as much as you can about the future of probation and parole. In particular, you might want to focus on the use of satellite technology to monitor offenders placed on probation, the use of home confinement, or public and media attitudes toward probation and parole. Also gather studies on the future of probation and parole. Group your findings under headings (for example, "Innovative Options," "Alternative Sanctions," "Probation in My Home State," and "The Future of Probation and Parole").

Also visit the American Probation and Parole Association (APPA) at www.appa-net.org. (The organization is listed in the Cybrary.) What is the mission of the APPA? What are its goals and objectives? What organizations are affiliated with it? How many of them have websites? Submit your findings to your instructor if asked to do so.

To complete this Web Quest! online, go to the Web Quest! module in Chapter 11 of the *Criminal Justice Today* Companion Website at cjtoday.com.

Library Extras!

Library Extra! **11–1** *Correctional Populations in the United States* (BJS, current volume).

Library Extra! **11–2** *Trends in State Parole, 1990–2000* (BJS, 2001).

Library Extra! **11–3** *Transforming Probation through Leadership: The "Broken Windows" Model* (Reinventing Probation Council, 2000).

Library Extra! **11–4** *"Broken Windows" Probation: The Next Step in Fighting Crime* (Reinventing Probation Council, 1999).

Library Extra! **11–5** *But They All Come Back: Rethinking Prisoner Reentry* (NIJ, 2000).

Library Extra! **11–6** *When Prisoners Return to the Community: Political, Economic, and Social Consequences* (NIJ, 2000).

To explore these resources online, go to the Library Extras! area of the *Criminal Justice Today* Companion Website at cjtoday.com. You should also check the author's "Late Picks" online for newly released documents and updated Library Extras! You can find Late Picks at http://cjtoday.com/latepicks.htm.

Notes

1. Jeremy Travis, *But They All Come Back: Rethinking Prisoner Reentry,* (Washington, D.C.: National Institute of Justice, 2000), p. 2.
2. As quoted in *Criminal Justice Newsletter,* January 19, 1993, p. 1.
3. "McDonald's $1 Million Prize Winner Arrested for Violating Probation," Associated Press wire service, September 23, 2001.
4. Toni Locy, "Murder Pushes States to Better Track Parolees," *USA Today,* May 17, 2001, p. 5A.
5. Dan Sanderson, "14-Year-Old Left for Dead after Sex Assault," *Traverse City* (Michigan) *Record-Eagle,* October 16, 2001.
6. "Report: Probation Officer Ignored Furrow's Arsenal," APB Online, August 14, 1999. Web posted at http://www.apbonline.com/911/1999/08/14/jewish0814_01.html. Accessed January 20, 2000.
7. James M. Byrne, *Probation,* National Institute of Justice Crime File Series Study Guide (Washington, D.C.: U.S. Department of Justice, 1988), p. 1.
8. Alexander B. Smith and Louis Berlin, *Introduction to Probation and Parole* (St. Paul, MN: West, 1976), p. 75.
9. John Augustus, *John Augustus, First Probation Officer: John Augustus' Original Report on His Labors—1852* (Montclair, NJ: Patterson-Smith, 1972).
10. Smith and Berlin, *Introduction to Probation and Parole,* p. 77.
11. Ibid., p. 80.
12. George C. Killinger, Hazel B. Kerper, and Paul F. Cromwell, Jr., *Probation and Parole in the Criminal Justice System* (St. Paul, MN: West, 1976), p. 25.
13. *National Correctional Population Reaches New High* (Washington, D.C.: Bureau of Justice Statistics, August 2001).
14. Jodi M. Brown and Patrick A. Langan, *Felony Sentences in the United States, 1996* (Washington, D.C.: Bureau of Justice Statistics, 1999).
15. "Woman Gets Probation for Shooting Fiancé," Associated Press wire service, April 16, 1992, p. 9A.
16. Statistics in this paragraph come from Bureau of Justice Statistics, *Probation and Parole Statistics;* and Bureau of

Justice Statistics, "National Correctional Population Reaches New High," press release, August 28, 2001.
17. Bureau of Justice Statistics, *Correctional Populations in the United States, 1997* (Washington, D.C.: BJS, 2000).
18. Ibid.
19. Adapted from Timothy A. Hughes, Doris James Wilson, and Allen J. Beck, *Trends in State Parole, 1990–2000* (Washington, D.C.: Bureau of Justice Statistics, 2001), p. 1.
20. Ibid.
21. Ibid.
22. Ibid.
23. Ibid., p. 3.
24. Ibid.
25. Bureau of Justice Statistics, "Forty-two Percent of State Parole Discharges Were Successful," press release, October 3, 2001.
26. "The Effectiveness of Felony Probation: Results from an Eastern State," *Justice Quarterly* (December 1991), pp. 525–543.
27. Public Law 104–232.
28. For additional information, see the U.S. Parole Commission website at http://www.usdoj.gov/uspc.
29. State of Georgia, Board of Pardons and Paroles, "Adult Offender Sanction Costs for Fiscal Year 2001." Web posted at http://www.pap.state.ga.us/otisweb/corrcost.html. Accessed March 1, 2002.
30. State of Georgia, Board of Pardons and Paroles, "Parolees Pay Supervision and Victim Compensation Fees." Web posted at http://www.ganet.org/pap/supv_fees.html. Accessed February 20, 2002.
31. Peter Finn and Dale Parent, *Making the Offender Foot the Bill: A Texas Program* (Washington, D.C.: National Institute of Justice, 1992); and "Benefits of Probation Fees Cited in Texas Program," *Criminal Justice Newsletter,* January 19, 1993, p. 5.
32. See Andrew von Hirsch and Kathleen J. Hanrahan, *Abolish Parole?* (Washington, D.C.: Law Enforcement Assistance Administration, 1978).
33. Bureau of Justice Statistics, "Forty-two Percent of State Parole Discharges Were Successful."

34. Patrick A. Langan and Mark A. Cunniff, *Recidivism of Felons on Probation, 1986–1989* (Washington, D.C.: Bureau of Justice Statistics, 1992).

35. *Griffin v. Wisconsin,* 483 U.S. 868, 107 S.Ct. 3164 (1987).

36. *Pennsylvania Board of Probation and Parole v. Scott,* 524 U.S. 357 (1998).

37. *U.S. v. Knights,* U.S. Supreme Court, No. 00-1260 (decided December 10, 2001).

38. Bureau of Justice Statistics, *Correctional Populations in the United States, 1997.*

39. Robyn L. Cohen, *Probation and Parole Violators in State Prison, 1991.* (Washington, D.C.: BJS, 1995).

40. *Escoe v. Zerbst,* 295 U.S. 490 (1935).

41. *Mempa v. Rhay,* 389 U.S. 128 (1967).

42. A deferred sentence involves postponement of the sentencing decision, which may be made at a later time, following an automatic review of the defendant's behavior in the interim. A suspended sentence requires no review unless the probationer violates the law or the conditions of probation. Both may result in imprisonment.

43. *Morrissey v. Brewer,* 408 U.S. 471 (1972).

44. *Gagnon v. Scarpelli,* 411 U.S. 778 (1973).

45. Smith and Berlin, *Introduction to Probation and Parole,* p. 143.

46. See Linda Greenhouse, *N.Y. Times* wire service, March 18, 1997 (no headline). The case is *Young v. Harper,* 520 U.S. 143 (1997).

47. *Greenholtz v. Inmate of Nebraska Penal and Correctional Complex,* 442 U.S. 1 (1979).

48. *Bearden v. Georgia,* 461 U.S. 660, 103 S.Ct. 2064, 76 L.Ed. 2d 221 (1983).

49. Ibid.

50. *Minnesota v. Murphy,* 465 U.S. 420 (1984).

51. *Harlow v. Clatterbuick,* 30 CLr. 2364 (VA S.Ct. 1986); *Santangelo v. State,* 426 N.Y.S. 2d 931 (1980); *Welch v. State,* 424 N.Y.S. 2d 774 (1980); and *Thompson v. County of Alameda,* 614 P. 2d. 728 (1980).

52. *Tarter v. State of New York,* 38 CLr. 2364 (NY S.Ct. 1986); *Grimm v. Arizona Board of Pardons and Paroles,* 115 Arizona 260, 564 P. 2d 1227 (1977); and *Payton v. U.S.,* 636 F. 2d 132 (5th Cir. 1981).

53. Rolando v. del Carmen; *Potential Liabilities of Probation and Parole Officers* (Cincinnati, OH: Anderson, 1986), p. 89.

54. See, for example, *Semler v. Psychiatric Institute,* 538 F. 2d 121 (4th Cir. 1976).

55. This section owes much to Sanford Bates, "The Establishment and Early Years of the Federal Probation System," *Federal Probation* (June 1987), pp. 4–9.

56. *Ex parte United States,* 242 U.S. 27 (1916).

57. Bates, "The Establishment and Early Years of the Federal Probation System," p. 6.

58. As summarized by Susan Krup Grunin and Jud Watkins, "The Investigative Role of the United States Probation Officer under Sentencing Guidelines," *Federal Probation* (December 1987), pp. 43–49.

59. Ibid., p. 46.

60. American Correctional Association, *Vital Statistics in Corrections* (Lanham, MD: ACA, 1998).

61. *Minnesota v. Murphy,* 465 U.S. 420 (1984).

62. National Advisory Commission on Criminal Justice Standards and Goals, *Task Force Report: Corrections* (Washington, D.C.: U.S. Government Printing Office, 1973).

63. "Molester Sentenced to Classes," Associated Press wire service, August 29, 1996.

64. From the introduction to James Austin, Michael Jones, and Melissa Bolyard, *The Growing Use of Jail Boot Camps: The Current State of the Art* (Washington, D.C.: National Institute of Justice, 1993), p. 1.

65. Although now an independent nonprofit corporation, the Sentencing Project has its roots in a 1981 project of the National Legal Aid and Defender Association.

66. Sentencing Project, *1989 National Directory of Felony Sentencing Services* (Washington, D.C.: Sentencing Project, 1989).

67. Sentencing Project, *Changing the Terms of Sentencing: Defense Counsel and Alternative Sentencing Services* (Washington, D.C.: Sentencing Project, no date).

68. Joan Petersilia, *Expanding Options for Criminal Sentencing* (Santa Monica, CA: RAND Corporation, 1987).

69. Ohio Revised Code, Section 2946.06.1 (July 1965).

70. Lawrence Greenfield, *Probation and Parole, 1984* (Washington, D.C.: U.S. Government Printing Office, 1986).

71. For a complete description of this program, see Petersilia, *Expanding Options for Criminal Sentencing.*

72. Harry Allen et al., *Probation and Parole in America* (New York: Free Press, 1985), p. 88.

73. For a good overview of such programs, especially as they apply to juvenile corrections, see Doris Layton MacKenzie et al., *A National Study Comparing the Environments of Boot Camps with Traditional Facilities for Juvenile Offenders* (Washington, D.C.: NIJ, 2001).

74. Doris Layton MacKenzie and Deanna Bellew Ballow, "Shock Incarceration Programs in State Correctional Jurisdictions—An Update," *NIJ Reports* (May/June 1989), pp. 9–10.

75. "Shock Incarceration Marks a Decade of Expansion," *Corrections Compendium* (September 1996), pp. 10–28.

76. Ibid.

77. MacKenzie and Ballow, "Shock Incarceration Programs in State Correctional Jurisdictions."

78. National Institute of Justice, *Multisite Evaluation of Shock Incarceration* (Washington, D.C.: NIJ, 1995).

79. MacKenzie et al., *A National Study Comparing the Environments of Boot Camps with Traditional Facilities for Juvenile Offenders.*

80. Cherie L. Clark, David W. Aziz, and Doris L. MacKenzie, *Shock Incarceration in New York: Focus on Treatment* (Washington, D.C.: National Institute of Justice, 1994), p. 8.

81. "Oregon Boot Camp Is Saving the State Money, Study Finds," *Criminal Justice Newsletter,* May 1, 1995, pp. 5–6.

82. Douglas C. McDonald, *Restitution and Community Service,* National Institute of Justice Crime File Series Study Guide (Washington, D.C.: U.S. Department of Justice, 1988).

83. Richard J. Maher and Henry E. Dufour, "Experimenting with Community Service: A Punitive Alternative to Imprisonment," *Federal Probation* (September 1987), pp. 22–27.

84. James P. Levine, Michael C. Musheno, and Dennis J. Palumbo, *Criminal Justice in America: Law in Action* (New York: John Wiley, 1986), p. 549.

85. Billie S. Erwin and Lawrence A. Bennett, "New Dimensions in Probation: Georgia's Experience with

Intensive Probation Supervision," National Institute of Justice, *Research in Brief* (1987).

86. Probation Division, State of Georgia, "Intensive and Specialized Probation Supervision." Web posted at http://www.dcor.state.ga.us/ProbationDivision/html/ProbationDivision.html. Accessed March 2, 2002.

87. Crystal A. Garcia, "Using Palmer's Global Approach to Evaluate Intensive Supervision Programs: Implications for Practice," *Corrections Management Quarterly,* Vol. 4, No. 4 (2000), pp. 60–69.

88. Joan Petersilia, *House Arrest,* National Institute of Justice Crime File Series Study Guide (Washington, D.C.: U.S. Department of Justice, 1988).

89. Ibid.

90. Ibid.

91. Marc Renzema and David T. Skelton, *The Use of Electronic Monitoring by Criminal Justice Agencies, 1989,* (Washington, D.C.: National Institute of Justice, 1990).

92. Bureau of Justice Statistics, *Correctional Populations in the United States, 1997* (Washington, D.C.: BJS, 2000).

93. "Satellites Tracking People on Parole," Associated Press wire service, April 13, 1999.

94. U.S. Probation and Pretrial Services, "Home Confinement." Web posted at http://www.uscourts.gov/misc/cchome.pdf. Accessed March 22, 2002.

95. Petersilia, *House Arrest.*

96. *BI Home Escort: Electronic Monitoring System,* advertising brochure (Boulder, CO: BI Inc., no date).

97. For additional information on the legal issues surrounding electronic home confinement, see Bonnie Berry, "Electronic Jails: A New Criminal Justice Concern," *Justice Quarterly,* Vol. 2, No. 1 (1985), pp. 1–22; and J. Robert Lilly, Richard A. Ball, and W. Robert Lotz, Jr., "Electronic Jail Revisited," *Justice Quarterly,* Vol. 3, No. 3 (September 1986), pp. 353–361.

98. Bureau of Justice Statistics, "Forty-two Percent of State Parole Discharges Were Successful."

99. "A Victim's Life Sentence," *People,* April 25, 1988.

100. Ibid., p. 40.

101. Steve Morrell, "Convicted California Rapist, Mutilator, Arrested," Reuters wire service, February 20, 1997.

102. Lisa Holewa, "Lawrence Singleton Guilty of First-Degree Murder," *Naples* (Fla.) *Daily News,* February 20, 1998. Web posted at http://www.naplesnews.com/today/florida/a38459o.htm. Accessed February 20, 2000.

103. James A. Inciardi, *Criminal Justice,* 2d ed, (New York: Harcourt Brace Javanovich, 1987) p. 664.

104. American Probation and Parole Association and the Association of Paroling Authorities International, *Abolishing Parole: Why the Emperor Has No Clothes* (Lexington, KY: APPA, 1995).

105. See, for example, Travis, *But They All Come Back.*

106. Reinventing Probation Council, *"Broken Windows" Probation: The Next Step in Fighting Crime* (New York: Manhattan Institute, 1999); and Reinventing Probation Council, *Transforming Probation through Leadership: The "Broken Windows" Model* (New York: Center for Civic Innovation at the Manhattan Institute, 2000), from which some of the quoted material in these paragraphs comes.

107. Todd R. Clear, "Toward a Corrections of Place: The Challenge of 'Community' in Corrections," *National Institute of Justice Journal* (August 1996), pp. 52–56.

108. Joan Petersilia, "A Crime Control Rationale for Reinvesting in Community Corrections," in *Critical Criminal Justice Issues: Task Force Reports from the American Society of Criminology* (Washington, D.C.: National Institute of Justice, 1997).

Prisons and Jails

LEARNING OBJECTIVES

After reading this chapter, you should be able to

■ Describe the nature and history of early punishments and their impact on modern correctional programs

■ Outline the historical development of prisons

■ Discuss the major characteristics of today's prisons

■ Explain how jails fit into the correctional framework, and discuss the issues that jail administrators currently face

■ Describe the trend toward privatization in the corrections field

chapter 12

[
To put people behind walls and bars and do little or nothing to change them is to win a battle but lose a war. It is wrong. It is expensive. It is stupid.
]

**—Former Chief Justice Warren E. Burger
(1907–1995)[1]**

[
Infinite are the nine steps of a prison cell, and endless is the march of him who walks between the yellow brick wall and the red iron gate, thinking things that cannot be chained and cannot be locked.
]

—Arturo Giovannitti (1884–1959)

Introduction

Hear the author discuss this chapter at **cjtoday.com**

prison

A state or federal confinement facility that has custodial authority over adults sentenced to confinement.

In the history of criminal justice, the 1990s may be remembered as the decade of imprisonment. As concerns with community protection reached a near crescendo and as stiff drug laws and repeat-offender statutes put more and more people behind bars, rates of imprisonment reached previously unheralded levels. Prison populations approached the breaking point, and new facilities were constructed across the nation. In the midst of this imprisonment frenzy, however, few people realized that the use of **prisons**, as places where convicted offenders serve time as punishment for breaking the law, is a relatively new development in the handling of offenders. In fact, the emphasis upon *time served* as the essence of criminal punishment is scarcely 200 years old.

Early Punishments

Prior to the development of prisons, early punishments were often cruel and torturous. An example is the graphic and unsettling description of a man broken on the rack in 1721, which is provided by Camden Pelham in his *Chronicles of Crime*.[2] The offender, Nathaniel Hawes, a domestic servant in the household of a wealthy English nobleman, had stolen a sheep in order to entertain a female friend. When the overseer of the household discovered the offense, Hawes "shot him dead." Pelham's description of what happened next follows: "For these offences, of course, he was sentenced to be broken alive upon the rack, without the benefit of the *coup de grace,* or mercy-stroke. Informed of the dreadful sentence, he composedly laid himself down upon his back on a strong cross, on which, with his arms and legs extended, he was fastened by ropes. The executioner, having by now with a hatchet chopped off his left hand, next took up a heavy iron bar, with which, by repeated blows, he broke his bones to shivers, till the marrow, blood, and splinters flew about the field; but the prisoner never uttered a groan nor a sigh! The ropes being next unlashed, I imagined him dead . . . till . . . he writhed himself from the cross. When he fell on the grass . . . he rested his head on part of the timbar, and asked the by-standers for a pipe of tobacco, which was infamously answered by kicking and spitting on him. He then begged his head might be chopped off, but to no purpose." Pelham goes on to relate how the condemned man then engaged in conversation with onlookers, recounting details of his trial. At one point he asked one of those present to repay money he had loaned him, saying, "Don't you perceive, I am to be kept alive." After six hours, Pelham says, Hawes was put out of his misery by a soldier assigned to guard the proceedings. "He was knocked on the

> Years ago I began to recognize my kinship with all living beings. . . . I said then, and I say now, that while there is a lower class I am in it; while there is a criminal element, I am of it; while there is a soul in prison, I am not free.
>
> —Eugene V. Debs, American Socialist leader (1855–1926)

head by the . . . sentinel; and having been raised upon a gallows, the vultures were busy picking out the eyes of the mangled corpse, in the skull of which was clearly discernible the mark of the soldier's musket."

This gruesome tale may seem foreign to modern readers—as though it describes an event which happened in a barbarous time long ago or in a place far away. Physical punishments, often resulting in death, however, were commonplace a mere 200 years ago in this country. Today, when we think of criminal punishment, we routinely think of prisons. Because they are so commonplace, however, we tend to forget that prisons, as correctional institutions, are relatively new. Prior to the emergence of imprisonment, convicted offenders were routinely subjected to fines, physical punishment, and often death. Corporal punishments were the most common form of criminal punishment used and generally fit the doctrine of **lex talionis** (the law of retaliation). Under *lex talionis*, the convicted offender was sentenced to suffer a punishment which closely approximated the original injury. Hence, if a person blinded another, he was blinded in return. Murderers were themselves killed, with the form of execution sometimes being tailored to approximate the method used in committing the crime.

lex talionis

The law of retaliation, often expressed as "an eye for an eye" or "like for like."

Flogging

Historically, the most widely used of physical punishments has been flogging.[3] The Bible mentions instances of whipping, and Christ himself was said to have been scourged. Whipping was widely used in England throughout the Middle Ages, and some offenders were said to have been beaten as they ran through streets and towns, hands tied behind their backs. American colonists carried the practice of flogging with them to the New World. The Western frontier provided the novel opportunity, quickly seized upon by settlers, of whipping convicted criminals as they were run out of town and into the hinterlands. Banishment, however, may have been little better than a death sentence, since it afforded little opportunity for the exiled offender to survive.

Whipping could be deadly. An infamous whip, the Russian knot, was fashioned out of leather thongs tipped with fishhook-like wires. A few stripes with the knot produced serious lacerations and often resulted in much blood loss. The cat-o'-nine-tails, another frequently used device, was made of at least nine strands of leather or rope instead of the single strip of leather which makes up most modern-day whips.

The last officially sanctioned flogging of a criminal offender in the United States happened in Delaware in 1952, when a burglar received 20 lashes.[4] The practice of whipping, however, is still with us. Amnesty International reports its use in various parts of the world for political and other prisoners; and in 1994, the flogging in Singapore of Michael Fay, an American teenager convicted of spray-painting parked cars, caused an international outcry from opponents of corporal punishment. The Fay flogging (called *caning* in Singapore because it was carried out with a bamboo rod) led to a rebirth of interest in physical sanctions in this country, especially for teenagers and vandals. In 1995, following Singapore's

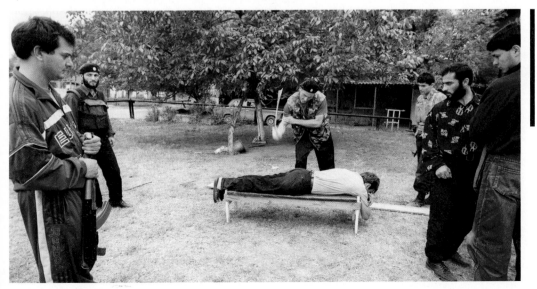

A man undergoing public punishment for an unknown transgression of the Islamic code in Grozny, Chechnya. Other than the death penalty, corporal punishment for crime has virtually disappeared in the United States, but it remains common in some Muslim nations.

AP/Wide World Photos

example, eight states entertained legislation to endorse whipping or paddling as a criminal sanction.[5] None of the proposals made it into law.

Mutilation

Flogging is a painful punishment whose memory might deter repeat offenses. Mutilation, on the other hand, was primarily a strategy of specific deterrence that made it difficult or impossible for individuals to repeat their crimes. Throughout history, various societies have amputated the hands of thieves and robbers, blinded spies, and castrated rapists. Blasphemers had their tongues ripped out, and pickpockets suffered broken fingers. Extensive mutilation, which included blinding, cutting off the ears, and ripping out the tongue, was imposed upon hunters in eleventh-century Britain who poached on royal lands.[6]

Today, some countries in the Arab world, including Iran and Saudi Arabia, still rely upon a limited use of mutilation as a penalty which incapacitates selected offenders. Mutilation also creates a general deterrent by providing potential offenders with walking examples of the consequences of crime.

Branding

In some societies, branding has been used as a lesser form of mutilation. Prior to modern technology and the advent of mechanized record keeping, branding served to readily identify convicted offenders and to warn others with whom they might come into contact of their dangerous potential.

The Romans, Greeks, French, British, and many others have all used branding at one time or another. It was not until 1829 that the British Parliament officially eliminated branding as a punishment for crime, although the practice had probably ended somewhat earlier.

Harry Elmer Barnes and Negley K. Teeters, early writers on the history of the criminal justice system, report that branding was customary in the American colonies for certain crimes, with first offenders being branded on the hand and repeat offenders receiving an identifying mark on the forehead.[7] Women were rarely marked physically, although they may have been shamed and forced to wear marked clothing. In Nathaniel Hawthorne's novel *The Scarlet Letter,* the central figure is required to wear a red letter *A* embroidered on her dress, signifying adultery.

Public Humiliation

A number of early punishments were designed to humiliate offenders in public and to allow members of the community an opportunity for vengeance. The stocks and pillory were two such punishments. The pillory closed over the head and hands and held the offender in a standing position, while the stocks kept the person sitting with the head free. A few hundred years ago, each town had its stocks or pillory, usually located in some central square or alongside a major thoroughfare. Offenders sent to the stocks or pillory found themselves captive and on public display. They could expect to be heckled and spit upon by passersby. Other citizens might gather to throw tomatoes or rotten eggs. On occasion, citizens who were particularly outraged by the magnitude or nature of the offense would substitute rocks for other less lethal missiles and would end the offender's life. Retribution remained a community prerogative, and citizens wielded the power of final sentencing. The pillory was still used in Delaware as late as 1905.[8]

The brank and ducking stool provided other forms of public humiliation. The brank was a birdcage-like device which fit over the offender's head. On it was a small door which, when closed, caused a razor-sharp blade to be inserted into the mouth. The ducking stool looked like a seesaw. The offender was tied to it and lowered into a river or lake, turning nearly upside down like a duck searching for food underwater. Both devices were used in colonial times to punish gossips and were designed to fit that crime by teaching the offender to keep a still tongue or a closed mouth.

Workhouses

The sixteenth century was a time of economic upheaval in Europe, caused partly by wars and partly by the emergence of the Industrial Revolution, which would soon sweep the continent. By mid-century, thousands of unemployed and vagrant people were scouring towns and villages seeking food and shelter. It was not long before they depleted the economic reserves of churches, which were the primary social relief agencies of the time.

In the belief that poverty was caused by laziness, governments were quick to create **workhouses** designed to instill "habits of industry" in the unemployed. The first work-house in Europe opened in 1557 in a former British palace called Saint Bridget's Well. The name was shortened to Bridewell, and *bridewell* became a synonym for *workhouse*. Bridewells taught work habits, not specific skills. Inmates were made to fashion their own furniture, build additions to the facility, and raise gardens. When the number of inmates exceeded the volume of useful work to be done, make-work projects, including treadmills and cranks, were invented to keep them busy.

Workhouses were judged successful, if only because they were constantly filled. By 1576, Parliament decreed that every county in England should build a workhouse. Although workhouses were forerunners of our modern prisons, they did not incarcerate criminal offenders—only vagrants and the economically disadvantaged. Nor were they designed to punish convicts, but served instead to reinforce the value of hard work.

workhouse

An early form of imprisonment intended to instill habits of industry in the idle.

Exile

The ancient Hebrews periodically forced a sacrificial goat symbolically carrying the tribe's sins into the wilderness, a practice which has given us the modern word *scapegoating*. Since then, many societies have banished "sinners" directly. The French sent criminal offenders to Devil's Island, and the Russians used Siberia for centuries for the same purpose.

England sent convicts to the American colonies beginning in 1618. The British pro-gram of exile, known as *transportation,* served the dual purpose of providing a captive labor force for development of the colonies while assuaging growing English sentiments opposing corporal punishments. In 1776, however, the American Revolution forced the practice to end, and British penology shifted to the use of aging ships, called *hulks,* as temporary prisons. Hulks were anchored in harbors throughout England and served as floating confinement facilities even after transportation (to other parts of the globe) resumed.

In 1787, only 17 years after Captain Cook had discovered the continent, Australia became the new port of call for English prisoners. The name of Captain William Bligh, gov-ernor of the New South Wales penal colony, survives down to the present day as a symbol of the difficult conditions and rough men and women of those times.

The Emergence of Prisons

The identity of the world's first true prison may never be known, but we do know that at some point, penalties for crime came to include incarceration. During the Middle Ages, "punitive imprisonment appears to have been introduced into Europe . . . by the Christian Church in the incarceration of certain offenders against canon law."[9] Similarly, debtors' prisons existed throughout Europe during the fifteenth and sixteenth centuries, although they housed inmates who had violated the civil law rather than criminals. John Howard, an early prison reformer, mentions prisons housing criminal offenders in Hamburg, Ger-many; Bern, Switzerland; and Florence, Italy, in his 1777 book, *State of Prisons.*[10] Early efforts to imprison offenders led to the founding of the Hospice of San Michele, a papal prison which opened in 1704, and the Maison de Force, begun at Ghent, Belgium, in 1773. The Hospice was actually a residential school for delinquent boys and housed 60 young-sters at its opening. Both facilities stressed reformation over punishment and became early alternatives to the use of physical and public punishments.

Near the end of the eighteenth century, the concept of imprisonment as punishment for crime reached its fullest expression in the United States. Soon after they opened, U.S. prisons came to serve as models for European reformers searching for ways to humanize criminal punishment. For that reason, and to better appreciate how today's prisons operate, it is important to understand the historical development of the prison movement in the United States. Figure 12–1 depicts the stages through which American prisons progressed following the introduction around 1790 of the concept of incarcera-tion as a punishment for crime. Each historical era is discussed in the pages that follow. For an online history of early prison development in England, see **Web Extra! 12–1** at cjtoday.com.

Prison Era

	The Penitentiary Era	The Mass (Congregate) Prison Era	The Reformatory Era	The Industrial Era	The Punitive Era	The Treatment Era	The Community-Based (Decarceration) Era	The Warehousing Era	The Just Deserts Era
Year	1790	1825	1876	1890	1935	1945	1967	1980	1995
Philosophy	Rehabilitation, Deterrence	Incapacitation, Deterrence	Rehabilitation	Incapacitation, Restoration	Retribution	Rehabilitation	Restoration, Rehabilitation	Incapacitation	Retribution, Incapacitation, Deterrence
Representative Institutions	Philadelphia Penitentiary, Eastern Penitentiary (Cherry Hill, PA), Western Penitentiary (Pittsburgh)	New York State Prison (Auburn, NY)	Elmira Reformatory (Elmira, NY)	Auburn (NY), Sing Sing (NY), Statesville (IL), San Quentin (CA), Attica (NY)	Alcatraz (CA)	Marion (IL)	Massachusetts Youth Services, Halfway Houses	Most Major Prisons	Characteristic of Many Prisons Today

FIGURE 12-1

Stages of prison development in the United States.

The Penitentiary Era (1790–1825)

In 1790, Philadelphia's Walnut Street Jail was converted into a penitentiary by the Pennsylvania Quakers. The Quakers, following the legacy of William Penn, intended to introduce religious and humane principles into the handling of offenders. They saw in prisons the opportunity for penance, viewing them as places wherein offenders might make amends with society and accept responsibility for their misdeeds. The philosophy of imprisonment begun by the Quakers, heavily imbued with elements of both rehabilitation and deterrence, carries over to the present day.[11]

Inmates of the Philadelphia Penitentiary were expected to wrestle alone with the evils they harbored. Penance was the primary vehicle through which rehabilitation was anticipated, and a study of the Bible was strongly encouraged. Solitary confinement was the rule, and the penitentiary was architecturally designed to minimize contact between inmates and between inmates and staff. Exercise was allowed in small high-walled yards attached to each cell. Eventually, handicrafts were introduced into the prison setting, permitting prisoners to work in their cells.

Fashioned after the Philadelphia model, the Western Penitentiary opened in Pittsburgh in 1826, and the Eastern Penitentiary opened in Cherry Hill, Pennsylvania, in 1829. Solitary confinement and individual cells, supported by a massive physical structure with impenetrable walls, became synonymous with the Pennsylvania system of imprisonment. Supporters heralded the **Pennsylvania system** as one which was both humane and provided inmates with the opportunity for rehabilitation. Many well-known figures of the day spoke out in support of the Pennsylvania system, among them Benjamin Franklin and Benjamin Rush—both of whom were influential members of the Philadelphia Society for Alleviating the Miseries of Public Prisons.[12]

The Mass Prison Era (1825–1876)

Vermont, Massachusetts, Maryland, and New York all built institutions modeled after Pennsylvania's penitentiaries. As prison populations began to grow, however, solitary confinement became prohibitively expensive. One of the first large prisons to abandon the Pennsylvania model was the New York State Prison at Auburn. Auburn introduced the congregate but silent system, under which inmates lived, ate, and worked together in enforced silence. This style of imprisonment, which came to be known as the **Auburn system**, featured group workshops rather than solitary handicrafts and reintroduced corporal punishments into the handling of offenders. Whereas isolation and enforced idleness were inherent punishments under the early Pennsylvania system, Auburn depended upon whipping and hard labor to maintain the rule of silence.[13]

Since even then, as now, there were competing ideas about which style of prison worked best and was most humane, Auburn prison was the site of an experiment in solitary confinement, which was the basis of the Pennsylvania system. Eighty-three men were placed in small solitary cells on Christmas Day of 1821 and were released in 1823 and 1824. Five

Pennsylvania system

A form of imprisonment developed by the Pennsylvania Quakers around 1790 as an alternative to corporal punishments. This style of imprisonment made use of solitary confinement and encouraged rehabilitation.

Auburn system

A form of imprisonment developed in New York State around 1820 that depended upon mass prisons, where prisoners were held in congregate fashion and were required to remain silent. This style of imprisonment was a primary alternative to the Pennsylvania system.

The Walnut Street Jail, America's first "true" prison, circa 1800.
Culver Pictures, Inc.

CJ Today Exhibit 12-1

[Chaplain James Finley's Letter
from the Ohio Penitentiary, 1850]

In 1850, James Finley, a chaplain at the Ohio Penitentiary in Columbus, Ohio, described the competing prison systems of his time, as follows:

It is true, there are yet two systems of prison discipline still in use, but both claim to have the two parties—the criminal and society—equally in view. The congregate system, going on the supposition that habits of labor and moral character are the chief desiderata among this class of men, set them to work at those trades for which their physical and mental powers, together with the consideration of their former occupations, may more especially adapt them; religious instruction is also given them by men appointed expressly for the purpose; and they are permitted to labor in large communities, where they can see but not converse with each other, as the friends of this system imagine that social intercourse, of some kind and to *some extent, is almost as necessary to man as food. The separate system, on the other hand, looking upon all intercourse between criminals as only evil in its tendency, by which one rogue becomes the instructor or accomplice of another, secludes the convicts from each other but, to atone for this defect, it encourages the visits of good men to the cells of the prisoners; and the officers of these prisons make it a particular point of duty to visit the inmates very frequently themselves. The physical habits of the imprisoned are provided for by such trades as can be carried on by individual industry; a teacher is employed to lead them on in the study of useful branches of education; while the Gospel is regularly taught them, not only by sermons on the Sabbath, but by private efforts of the chaplain in his daily rounds.*

Source: James Finley, *Memorials of Prison Life* (Cincinnati: Swormstedt and Poe, 1855).

---

of the 83 died, one went insane, another attempted suicide, and the others became "seriously demoralized."[14] Although the Auburn experiment did not accurately simulate the conditions in Pennsylvania (it allowed for no exercise, placed prisoners in tiny cells, and shunned handicrafts—which had been introduced into Pennsylvania's prisons by the time the experiment began), it provided an effective basis for condemnation of the Pennsylvania system. Partly as a result of the experiment, the Reverend Louis Dwight, an influential prison reformer of the time and the leader of the prestigious Prison Discipline Society of Boston, became an advocate of the Auburn system, citing its lower cost[15] and more humane conditions.[16] The lower cost resulted from the simpler facilities required by mass imprisonment and from group workshops which provided economies of scale unachievable under solitary confinement. Dwight also believed, in large part due to the experiment in solitary confinement, that the Pennsylvania style of imprisonment was unconscionable and inhumane. As a consequence of criticisms fielded by Dwight and others like him, most American prisons built after 1825 followed the Auburn architectural style and system of prison discipline.

About the same time, however, a number of European governments sent representatives to study the virtues of the two American systems. Interestingly, most concluded that the Pennsylvania system was more conducive to reformation than the Auburn system, and many European prisons adopted a strict separation of inmates. Two French visitors, Gustave de Beaumont and Alexis de Tocqueville, stressed the dangers of what they called "contamination," whereby prisoners housed in Auburn-like prisons could negatively influence one another.[17]

The Reformatory Era (1876–1890)

reformatory style

A late-nineteenth-century correctional model based upon the use of the indeterminate sentence and the belief in the possibility of rehabilitation, especially for youthful offenders. The reformatory concept faded with the emergence of industrial prisons around the turn of the century.

With the tension between the Auburn and Pennsylvania systems, American penology existed in an unsettled state for a half century. That tension was resolved in 1876 with the emergence of the **reformatory style**, which grew out of practices innovated by two outstanding correctional leaders of the mid-1880s: Captain Alexander Maconochie and Sir Walter Crofton.

CAPTAIN ALEXANDER MACONOCHIE AND NORFOLK ISLAND

During the early 1840s, Captain Alexander Maconochie served as the warden of Norfolk Island, a prison off the coast of Australia for "doubly condemned" inmates. English prisoners sent to Australia, who committed other crimes while there, were taken to Norfolk to be

CJ Today Exhibit 12-2

[An Early Texas Prison]

In 1860, an anonymous writer described conditions in the Texas Penitentiary at Huntsville as follows:

> By a special enactment of the Legislature, the front of the cell of any prisoner sentenced to solitary confinement for life, is painted black, and his name and sentence distinctly marked thereon. The object would seem to be to infuse a salutary dread into the minds of the other prisoners. Upon the only black-painted cell in the prison was the following inscription, in distinct white letters: William Brown, aged twenty-four years, convicted for murder in Grimes County, spring term, 1858, for which he is now suffering solitary confinement for life. Brown himself, however, was in fact at work in the factory with the other convicts! He entered the Penitentiary in May, 1859, and had been kept in close confinement in his cell, without labor, never being permitted to leave it for any purpose, until about the first of October, when his health was found to have suffered so much that, to preserve his life, he was, under a discretionary power vested in the Directors, released from the rigor of his sentence, and subjected to only the ordinary confinement of the prison. His health has since greatly improved. It is not to be wondered at that his health should decline under the strict enforcement of such a sentence. The cell in which he was confined was the same as to size, ventilation, and light as the rest; and being one of the lower tier of cells, the top of the doorway was some feet below the lower edge of the window upon the opposite side of the corridor in the outside wall. He had even less chance for fresh air than if his cell had been in almost any other location. It is the sight and knowledge of such instances of solitary unemployed confinement as this, and a willful neglect or refusal to inform themselves upon, and recognize, the very wide distinction between the terms separate and solitary, that renders many persons so violently prejudiced against, and opposed to the "Separate System."

Source: *The Journal of Prison Discipline and Philanthropy*, Vol. 15, No. 1 (January 1860), pp. 7–17.

---

segregated from less recalcitrant offenders. Prior to Maconochie's arrival, conditions at Norfolk had been atrocious. Disease was rampant on the island, fights among inmates left many dead and more injured, sanitary conditions were practically nonexistent, and the physical facilities were not conducive to good supervision. Maconochie immediately set out to reform the island prison. He is still remembered for saying, "When a man keeps the key of his own prison, he is soon persuaded to fit it to the lock."[18] In that belief, he provided incentives for prisoners to participate in their own reformation.

Maconochie developed a system of marks through which prisoners could earn enough credits to buy their freedom. Bad behavior removed marks from the inmate's ledger, while acceptable behavior added marks. The mark system made possible early release and led to a recognition of the indeterminate sentence as a useful tool in the reformation of offenders. Prior to Maconochie, inmates had been sentenced to determinate sentences specifying a fixed number of years they had to serve before release. The mark system placed responsibility for winning an early release squarely upon the inmate. Because of the system's similarity to the later practice of parole, it won for Maconochie the title "father of parole."

Opinion leaders in England, however, saw Maconochie's methods as too lenient. Many pointed out that the indeterminate sentence made possible new lives for criminals in a world of vast opportunity (the Australian continent) at the expense of the British empire, while many good citizens had to live out lives of quiet desperation and poverty back home. Amid charges that he coddled inmates, Maconochie was relieved of his duties as warden in 1844.

> Incarceration is a crash course in extortion and criminal behavior.
>
> —Vincent Schiraldi, National Center on Institutions and Alternatives

SIR WALTER CROFTON AND THE IRISH SYSTEM

Maconochie's innovations soon came to the attention of Sir Walter Crofton, head of the Irish Prison System. Crofton adapted the idea of early release to his program of progressive stages. Inmates who entered Irish prisons had to work their way through four stages. The first, or entry level, involved solitary confinement and dull work. Most prisoners in the first level were housed at Mountjoy Prison in Dublin. The second stage assigned prisoners to Spike Island, where they worked on fortifications. The third stage placed prisoners in field units, which worked directly in the community on public-service projects. Unarmed guards supervised the prisoners. The fourth stage depended upon what Crofton called the

"ticket of leave." The ticket of leave allowed prisoners to live and work in the community under the occasional supervision of a "moral instructor." It could be revoked at any time up until the expiration of the offender's original sentence.

Crofton was convinced that convicts could not be rehabilitated without successful reintegration into the community. His innovations were closely watched by reformers across Europe. But in 1862, a wave of violent robberies swept England and led to the passage of the 1863 Garotters Act, which mandated whipping for robberies involving violence and longer prison sentences for many other crimes, effectively rolling back the clock on Crofton's innovations, at least in Europe.

THE ELMIRA REFORMATORY AND THE BIRTH OF PAROLE

In 1865, Gaylord B. Hubbell, warden of Sing Sing Prison in New York, visited Great Britain and studied prisons there. He returned to the United States greatly impressed by the Irish system and recommended that indeterminate sentences be used in American prisons. The New York Prison Association, through the efforts of Theodore W. Dwight, its president, and Enoch C. Wines, its secretary, supported Hubbell and called for the creation of a "reformatory" based upon the concept of an earned early release if the inmate reformed himself.

When the new National Prison Association held its first conference in 1870 in Cincinnati, Ohio, it brought together men and women of vision. Sir Walter Crofton addressed the group, and Enoch C. Wines, the meeting's organizer, called upon "all men of good will throughout the world [to] join in a plan for an ideal prison system."[19] The association adopted a 37-paragraph Declaration of Principles that called for reformation to replace punishment as the goal of imprisonment. The most significant result of the conference, however, was the move to embody those principles in a reformatory built on American soil.

In 1876, the Elmira Reformatory opened in Elmira, New York, under the direction of Zebulon Brockway, a leading advocate of indeterminate sentencing and the former Superintendent of the Detroit House of Correction. The state of New York had passed an indeterminate sentencing bill which made possible early release for inmates who earned it. However, because reformation was thought most likely among younger people, the Elmira Reformatory accepted only first offenders between the ages of 16 and 30. A system of graded stages required inmates to meet educational, behavioral, and other goals. Schooling was mandatory, and trade training was available in telegraphy, tailoring, plumbing, carpentry, and other areas.

Unfortunately, the reformatory "proved a relative failure and disappointment."[20] Many inmates reentered lives of crime following their release, which called the success of the

reformatory ideal into question. Some authors attributed the failure of the reformatory to "the ever-present jailing psychosis"[21] of the prison staff or to an overemphasis on confinement and institutional security rather than reformation, which made it difficult to implement many of the ideals upon which the reformatory had been based.

Even though the reformatory was not a success, the principles it established remain important today. Thus, indeterminate sentencing, parole, trade training, education, and primacy of reformation over punishment all serve as a foundation for ongoing debates about the purpose of imprisonment.

The Industrial Era (1890–1935)

With the failure of the reformatory style of prison, concerns over security and discipline became dominant in American prisons. Inmate populations rose, costs soared, and states began to study practical alternatives. An especially attractive option was found in the potential profitability of inmate labor, and the era of the **industrial prison** in America was born.

Industrial prisons in the northern United States were characterized by thick, high walls, stone or brick buildings, guard towers, and smokestacks rising from within the walls. These prisons smelted steel, manufactured cabinets, molded tires, and turned out many other goods for the open market. Prisons in the South, which had been devastated by the Civil War, tended more toward farm labor and public works projects. The South, with its labor-intensive agricultural practices, used inmate labor to replace slaves who had been freed during the war.

The following six systems of inmate labor were in use by the early twentieth century:[22]

- *Contract system.* Private businesses paid to use inmate labor. They provided the raw materials and supervised the manufacturing process inside prison facilities.
- *Piece-price system.* Goods were produced for private businesses under the supervision of prison authorities. Prisons were paid according to the number and quality of the goods manufactured.
- *Lease system.* Prisoners were taken to the work site under the supervision of armed guards. Once there, they were turned over to the private contractor, who employed them and maintained discipline.
- *Public account system.* This system eliminated the use of private contractors. Industries were entirely prison owned, and prison authorities managed the manufacturing process from beginning to end. Goods were sold on the free market.
- ***State-use system.*** Prisoners manufactured only goods which could be used by other state offices, or they provided labor to assist other state agencies.
- *Public works system.* Prisoners maintained roads and highways, cleaned public parks and recreational facilities, and maintained and restored public buildings.

industrial prison

A correctional model intended to capitalize on the labor of convicts sentenced to confinement.

state-use system

A system of inmate labor in which items produced by inmates may only be sold by or to state offices. Items that only the state can sell include such things as license plates and hunting licenses, while items sold only to state offices include furniture and cleaning supplies.

Church services in Sing Sing Prison in 1906. Note the "ushers" with shotguns.

Underwood Photo Archives

Large industrial prisons that were built or converted to industrialization included San Quentin in California, Sing Sing and Auburn in New York, and the Illinois State Penitentiary at Statesville. Many prison industries were quite profitable and contributed significantly to state treasuries. Reports from 1932 show that 82,276 prisoners were involved in various forms of prison labor that year, producing products with a total value of $75,369,471—a huge amount considering the worth of the dollar 70 years ago.[23] Beginning as early as the 1830s, however, workers began to complain of being forced to compete with cheap prison labor. In 1834, mechanics in New York filed a petition with the state legislature asking that prison industries paying extremely low wages be eliminated. Labor unions became very well organized and powerful by the early part of the twentieth century, and the Great Depression of the 1930s, during which jobs were scarce, brought with it a call for an end to prison industries.

In 1929, union influence led Congress to pass the Hawes-Cooper Act, which required prison-made goods to conform to the regulations of the states through which they were shipped. Hence, states which outlawed the manufacture of free-market goods in their own prisons were effectively protected from prison-made goods which might be imported from other states. The death blow to prison industries, however, came in 1935 with the passage of the **Ashurst-Sumners Act**, which specifically prohibited the interstate transportation and sale of prison goods where state laws forbade them. In consort with the Ashurst-Sumners legislation, and because of economic pressures brought on by the Depression, most states soon passed statutes which curtailed prison manufacturing within their borders, and the industrial era in American corrections came to a close.

Ashurst-Sumners Act

Federal legislation of 1935 which effectively ended the industrial prison era by restricting interstate commerce in prison-made goods.

PRISON INDUSTRIES TODAY

Although still hampered by some federal and state laws, prison industries have begun making a comeback. Under the state-use philosophy, most states still permit the prison manufacture of goods which will be used exclusively by the prison system itself or by other state agencies or which only the state can legitimately sell on the open market. An example of the latter is license plates, whose sale is a state monopoly. North Carolina provides a good example of a modern state-use system. Its Correction Enterprises operates around 20 inmate-run businesses, each of which is self-supporting. North Carolina inmates manufacture prison clothing (at the North Carolina Correctional Center for Women in Raleigh); raise vegetables and farm animals (at the Tyrell County Work Farm) to feed inmates throughout the state; operate an oil refinery, a forestry service, and a cannery; and manufacture soap, license plates, and some office furniture. All manufactured goods other than license plates are for use within the prison system or by other state agencies. North Carolina's Corrections Enterprises pays 5% of profits to the state's crime victims' compensation fund.[24]

The federal government also operates a kind of state-use system in its institutions through a government-owned corporation called Federal Prison Industries, Incorporated (also called UNICOR).[25] The corporation was established in 1934 to retain some employment programs for federal inmates in anticipation of the elimination of free-market prison industries. Criticisms of UNICOR include charges that inmates are paid very low wages and are trained for jobs which do not exist in the free economy.[26] Even so, a long-term study by the Federal Bureau of Prisons' Office of Research and Evaluation, whose results were published in 1994, found that federal inmates participating in work experiences through UNICOR had successful postrelease employment outcomes. The study found that inmates "showed better adjustment, were less likely to be revoked at the end of their first year back in the community, and were more likely to find employment in the halfway house and community."[27] The study also found that inmates "earned slightly more money in the community than inmates who had similar background characteristics, but who did not participate in work and vocational training programs."

Free-market money-making prison industries are also staging a comeback, some funded by private-sector investment. In 1981, under the Prison Rehabilitative Industries and Diversified Enterprises, Inc., legislation, commonly called the PRIDE Act, Florida became the first state to experiment with the wholesale transfer of its correctional industry program from public to private control.[28] PRIDE industries include sugar cane processing, construction, and automotive repair. Other states have since followed suit.

Even where prison industries are not profitable, however, some states are taking steps to ensure the productive use of inmates' time and energies. In 1995, for example, prison officials in Oregon began to implement a new state constitutional amendment which requires all inmates (except those who are mentally or physically ill or who are considered too dangerous) to work full-time or to be involved in full-time education and training.[29] Since Oregon's prison regulations permit only minimum-security inmates to work outside correctional facilities, administrators have been busy creating useful job opportunities inside prison walls. The state uses inmates to answer phones for state agencies and employs a number of convicts in a prison industries program called Unigroup.

Florida and Oregon are not alone in their efforts to rebuild meaningful prison industries. In other states, a number of private firms have contracted with correctional institutions to manufacture office furniture and computer equipment and to provide telephone-answering services for motel and hotel reservations. A decade ago, the National Prison Industries Task Force, headed by former U.S. Supreme Court Chief Justice Warren E. Burger, issued a report stating five primary principles to help guide the renewal of prison industries nationwide:[30]

- The private sector should be involved in prison industries.
- Practices and regulations that impede the progress of prison industries should be rescinded, changed, or otherwise streamlined.
- Prison industries should provide meaningful and relevant work opportunities for inmates.
- Prison industries should operate in a businesslike manner.
- Prison industries should reduce inmate idleness.

The task force sought enabling legislation from the U.S. Congress and from state legislatures to permit prison industries to flourish under controlled conditions. Movement in that direction continues today.

The Punitive Era (1935–1945)

The moratorium on free-market prison industries initiated by the Ashurst-Sumners Act was to last for more than half a century. Prison administrators, left with few ready alternatives, seized upon custody and institutional security as the long-lost central purposes of the correctional enterprise, thereby ushering in an era of punitive custody. The punitive era was characterized by an emphasis on punishment and security and by the belief that prisoners owed a debt to society which only a rigorous period of confinement could repay. Writers of the period termed such beliefs the *convict bogey* and the *lock psychosis*,[31] referring to the

CJ Today Exhibit 12-3

[Alcatraz Federal Penitentiary]

Alcatraz Island in San Francisco Bay is home to one of the best-known prisons of all time. The prison, built as a fort for the U.S. Army in 1854, was used to house the Bay Area's prisoners following the great earthquake of 1906. By the 1930s, organized criminals were terrorizing the country, and Sanford Bates, the director of the federal prison system, began the call for a highly secure institution for the isolation of notorious offenders. Alcatraz Island was the obvious choice. The wide expanse of bay waters which separate the island from the coast were notorious for treacherous currents, making unaided escape a virtual impossibility.

During the early 1930s, the island prison was built on the foundation of the old fort. Some of the first prison-used metal detectors were installed, and barbed wire perimeter fences and walls were built and reinforced with armed guards in towers at strategic points.

Alcatraz Federal Penitentiary opened in 1934 with James Johnson, former warden of San Quentin and Folsom Prisons, as warden. One prisoner per cell was the rule. Cells measured 5 feet wide by 9 feet long by 7 feet high and were equipped with basic metal furniture. A rule of silence prevailed, and no newspapers or radios were permitted. Security was so strict that no original letters were delivered to inmates. Correspondence was heavily screened and retyped by the staff, who then gave only a copy to the prisoner.

Alcatraz accepted inmates only from other institutions. No direct court commitments could be made. The most difficult, dangerous, and troublesome prisoners from other facilities in the federal system were sent to Alcatraz. One of the first was Al "Scarface" Capone. George "Machine Gun" Kelly, Robert Stroud (the "Birdman of Alcatraz"), "Doc" Barker, Alvin Karpis, and many others followed.

Fourteen known escapes, involving as many as 30 men, were attempted during the time Alcatraz served as a prison. Only one attempt, involving two men—Theodore Cole and Ralph Roe—may have been successful. Cole, serving a 50-year sentence for kidnapping while on the run from McAlester Penitentiary, and Roe, a career offender sentenced to 99 years for bank robbery, cut their way through the bars on a window of the prison shop. They had picked December 16, 1937, an especially foggy and damp day. Although an extensive sea and land search was under way within a half hour following the escape, Cole and Roe were never found. Official accounts point to the strong currents of the bay (which on the day of their escape were measured as swiftly flowing toward the open sea) and wintry temperatures to conclude that the attempt must have failed.

Although not successful, the most costly escape attempt came on May 2, 1946. It resulted in a three-day hostage situation which claimed the lives of two officers and three prisoners. It ended only when U.S. Marines provided demolition grenades which were used to flush prisoners out of occupied corridors. Seventeen guards and one prisoner were wounded. Two other inmates were executed for their role in the riot.

By the 1950s, Alcatraz Penitentiary was in a state of disrepair. The salt water of the bay had contributed to an early disintegration of the concrete used in building construction, and many of the steel rods and bars had been weakened by the corrosive air. A group of local residents demanded a lessening of the environmental impact the prison was having on the bay. The final blow to Alcatraz, however, was the undermining of its purpose by a reformation-oriented society, which had moved firmly into the treatment era and away from earlier concerns with "escapeproof" institutions. As described by one now-classic textbook, "Alcatraz [was] a monument to the thesis that some criminals cannot be reformed and should be repressed and disciplined by absolute inflexibility."[1] On March 21, 1963, under the direction of Attorney General Robert Kennedy, Alcatraz Penitentiary closed its doors as a prison. Today, the island institution survives as a tourist attraction and has spawned a number of shops selling prison memorabilia.

[1]Harry Barnes and Negley Teeters, *New Horizons in Criminology,* 3d ed. (Englewood Cliffs, NJ: Prentice Hall, 1959), p. 383.
Sources: James Fuller, *Alcatraz Federal Penitentiary, 1934–1963* (San Francisco: Asteron, 1987); E. E. Kirkpatrick, *Voices from Alcatraz* (San Antonio, TX: Naylor, 1947); and James A. Johnston, *Alcatraz Island Prison* (New York: Scribners, 1949).

fact that convicts were to be both shunned and securely locked away from society. Large maximum-security institutions flourished, and the prisoner's daily routine became one of monotony and frustration. The term *stir-crazy* grew out of the experience of many prisoners with the punitive era's lack of educational, treatment, and work programs. In response, inmates created their own diversions, frequently attempting to escape or inciting riots. One especially secure and still notorious facility of the punitive era, the federal penitentiary on Alcatraz Island, is described in CJ Today Exhibit 12-3.

The punitive era was a lackluster time in American corrections. Innovations were rare, and an "out of sight, out of mind" philosophy characterized American attitudes toward inmates. Popular accounts of the time portrayed criminals as "mad dogs" and rehabilitation-oriented officials as "sob sisters" and "cream puffs."[32] Writing at the close of the punitive era, Barnes and Teeters observed, "Even earnest administrators who sincerely believe in rehabilitation are afraid to introduce a whole-hearted program that might improve treatment procedures. Such rehabilitative treatment requires flexibility and experimentation, but these increase escape risks and even the most enlightened warden realizes that his work will be

Alcatraz Federal Penitentiary. The island prison closed in 1963, a victim of changing attitudes toward corrections. It survives today as a San Francisco tourist attraction.

Paul S. Howell, Getty Images, Inc.

judged by newspapers, politicians, and the public on the basis of how successful he is in preventing escapes."[33] Correctional officers were even more single-minded in their security consciousness. Barnes and Teeters wrote, "The mental habits of the custodial staff revolve around the mania to keep prisoners either locked up or scrupulously accounted for. Considerations of reformation and humanity evaporate in the face of this inexorable and all-encompassing anxiety."[34]

The Treatment Era (1945–1967)

By the late 1940s, the mood of the nation had become euphoric. Memories of World War II were dimming, industries were productive beyond the best hopes of most economic forecasters, and America's position of world leadership was fundamentally unchallenged. Nothing seemed impossible. Amid the bounty of a postwar boom economy, politicians and the public accorded themselves the additional luxury of restructuring the nation's prisons. A new interest in "corrections" and reformation, combined with the latest in behavioral techniques, ushered in an era of treatment built around what was then a prevailing psychiatric model. Inmates came to be seen more as "clients" or "patients" than as offenders, and terms like *resident* and *group member* replaced *inmate*. The treatment era was based upon a **medical model** of corrections—one which implied that the offender was sick and that rehabilitation was only a matter of finding the right treatment.

Therapy during the period took a number of forms, many of which are still used today. Most therapeutic models assumed that the inmate had to be helped to mature psychologically and had to be taught to assume responsibility for his or her life. Prisons built their programs around both individual treatment and group therapy approaches. In individual treatment, the offender and the therapist develop a face-to-face relationship. Most individual approaches depict the offender as someone who has not developed sufficiently to manage his or her own behavior effectively. Psychological development may have been thwarted by traumatic experiences in early life, which the therapist tries to uncover to produce effective behavioral change.

Group therapy relies upon the sharing of insights, gleaned by members of the therapeutic group, to facilitate the growth process, often by first making clear to the client the emotional basis of his or her criminal behavior. What the inmate regards as personal strengths may be shown to be nothing more than excuses for the inability to "own up" to responsibility. Some group strategies are attack therapies, in which new group members are verbally and ideologically pummeled to rid them of old self-conceptions and criminal

medical model

A therapeutic perspective on correctional treatment that applies the diagnostic perspective of medical science to the handling of criminal offenders.

values so that they might accept more positive and productive images of themselves. While individual therapy may uncover past personal traumas, group therapy may itself be traumatic in its relentless destruction of all personal armor.

One of the most famous forms of group therapy was Synanon. (The name derived from a group member's attempt to say "seminar.") In the 1950s, Synanon developed into a privately owned foundation providing drug treatment for addicts in Santa Monica, California. In the 1960s, Synanon-like programs became widespread and served as models for other attack therapies.

Guided group interaction (GGI) is an example of a treatment strategy which combines elements of individual treatment with group therapy. In guided group interaction, the therapist assists the group in uncovering individual fears, hidden experiences, and anxieties which act as barriers to conventional behavior. During the 1970s, Florida and Georgia adopted GGI as their primary approach to the treatment of juvenile offenders, and many other states used it extensively.[35]

Other forms of therapy used in prisons have included behavior therapy, chemotherapy, neurosurgery, sensory deprivation, and aversion therapy. Prison programs based upon behavior therapy were structured to provide rewards for approved behavior while punishing undesirable behavior. Rewards took the form of better housing conditions, canteen allotments, or TV privileges. Chemotherapy involved the use of drugs, especially tranquilizers, to modify behavior. Neurosurgery, including the now-notorious frontal lobotomy, was used on some highly aggressive inmates to control their destructive urges. Sensory deprivation sought to calm disruptive offenders by denying them the stimulation which might set off outbursts of destructive behavior. Sensory deprivation isolated inmates in a quiet, secluded environment. Aversion therapy used drugs or electric shocks in an attempt to teach the offender to associate pain and displeasure with stimuli which had previously led to criminal behavior. Child sexual abusers, for example, were shown pictures of nude children and simultaneously given shocks, often to especially sensitive parts of their anatomy.

Inmates have not always been happy with the treatment model. In 1972, a group of prisoners at the Marion, Illinois, federal prison joined together and demanded a right to refuse treatment. The group, calling itself the Federal Prisoner's Coalition, insisted that inmates have a basic right "to resist rehabilitation techniques designed to change their attitudes, values, or personalities."[36] Supporting the inmates' refusal of treatment was the National Prison Project of the American Civil Liberties Union (ACLU). Alvin J. Bronstein, Executive Director of the National Prison Project, argued that personality-altering techniques constituted a violation of prisoners' civil rights.[37] Other suits followed. Worried about potential liability, Donald E. Santarelli, the head of the Law Enforcement Assistance Administration (LEAA), banned the expenditure of LEAA funds to support any prison programs utilizing psychosurgery, medical research, chemotherapy, and behavioral modification. Santarelli's decision was based on an LEAA report of a year earlier, which had concluded that LEAA lacked the expertise to appropriately evaluate such programs.[38]

The treatment era also suffered from attacks upon the medical model on which it was based. Academics and legal scholars pointed to a lack of evidence in support of the model[39] and began to stress individual responsibility rather than treatment in the handling of offenders. Indeterminate sentencing statutes, designed to reward inmates for improved behavior, fell before the swelling drive to replace treatment with punishment.

Any honest evaluation of the treatment era would conclude that, in practice, treatment was more an ideal than a reality. Many treatment programs existed, some of them quite intensive. Unfortunately, the correctional system in America was never capable of providing any consistent or widespread treatment because the majority of its guards and administrators were oriented primarily toward custody and were not trained to provide treatment. However, although we have identified 1967 as the end of the treatment era, many correctional rehabilitation programs survive to the present day, and new ones are constantly being developed.

The Community-Based Era (1967–1980)

Beginning in the 1960s, the realities of prison crowding combined with a renewed faith in humanity and the treatment era's belief in the possibility of behavioral change to inspire a movement away from institutionalized corrections and toward the creation of opportunities for reformation within local communities. The transition to community corrections (also called *deinstitutionalization, diversion,* and *decarceration*) was based upon the premise that rehabilitation could not occur in isolation from the free social world to which inmates must eventually return.[40] Advocates of community corrections portrayed prisons as dehumanizing, claiming that they further victimized offenders who had already been negatively labeled by society. Some states strongly embraced the movement toward decarceration. In 1972, for example, Massachusetts drew national attention when it closed all its reform schools and replaced them with group homes.[41]

Decarceration, which built upon many of the intermediate sanctions discussed in the previous chapter, used a variety of programs to keep offenders in contact with the community and out of prison. Among them were halfway houses, **work-release programs**, and open institutions. Halfway houses have sometimes been called *halfway-in* or *halfway-out houses*, depending upon whether offenders were being given a second chance prior to incarceration or were in the process of gradual release from prison. Boston had halfway houses as early as the 1920s, but they operated for only a few years.[42] It was not until 1961 that the Federal Bureau of Prisons opened a few experimental residential centers in support of its new prerelease programs focusing on juveniles and youthful offenders. Called *prerelease guidance centers*, the first of these facilities were based in Los Angeles and Chicago.[43] In 1967, the President's Commission on Law Enforcement and Administration of Justice strongly recommended the use of community-based facilities to restore ties between offenders and their families, employers, training facilities, and other social agencies.

Although the era of community corrections is now in decline, halfway houses and work-release programs still operate in many parts of the country. A typical residential treatment facility today houses 15 to 20 residents and operates under the supervision of a director, supported by a handful of counselors. The environment is nonthreatening, and residents are generally free to come and go during the workday. The building looks more like a motel or a house than it does a prison. Fences and walls are nonexistent. Transportation is provided to and from work or educational sites, and the facility retains a portion of the resident's wages to pay the costs of room and board. Residents are expected to return to the facility after work, and some group therapy may be provided.

Today's work-release programs house offenders in traditional correctional environments—usually minimum-security prisons—but permit them to work at jobs in the community during the day and to return to the prison at night. Inmates are usually required to pay a token amount for their room and board in the institution. The first work-release law was passed by Wisconsin in 1913, but it was not until 1957 that a comprehensive program created by North Carolina spurred the development of work-release programs nationwide.[44] Work release for federal prisoners was authorized by the federal Prisoner Rehabilitation Act of 1965.[45] As work-release programs grew, study release—whereby inmates attend local colleges and technical schools—was initiated in most jurisdictions as an adjunct to work release.

Work-release programs are still very much a part of modern corrections. Almost all states have them, and many inmates work in the community as they approach the end of their sentence. Unfortunately, work-release programs are not without their social costs. Some inmates commit new crimes while in the community, and others use the opportunity to escape.

The community-based format led to innovations in the use of volunteers and to the extension of inmate privileges. "Open institutions" routinely provided inmates with a number of opportunities for community involvement and encouraged the community to participate in the prison environment. Most open institutions, for example, made training available to citizens who wished to sponsor prisoners on day trips into the community for recreation, meals, and the like. Others allowed weekend passes or extended visits by family members and friends, while a few experimented with conjugal visiting and with prisons that housed both men and women ("coeducational incarceration"). Based on a merit system, conjugal visiting made possible intimate visits between male inmates and their spouses in motel-like environments constructed on the prison grounds. Some writers point to unofficial conjugal visits occurring as early as 1918 at the Mississippi State Penitentiary at Parchman.[46] It was not until 1963, however, that state funding for "red houses" authorized the practice. In 1968, the California Correctional Institute at Tehachapi initiated conjugal visits in which inmates who were about to begin parole were permitted to live with their families for three days per month in apartments on the prison grounds. The practice extended to inmates at Soledad, San Quentin, and the Rehabilitation Center at Corona. By the late 1960s, conjugal visitation was under consideration in many other states, and the National Advisory Commission on Criminal Justice Standards and Goals recommended that correctional authorities should make "provisions for family

work-release program

A prison program through which inmates are temporarily released into the community to meet job responsibilities.

It is time for the California Department of Corrections, [the governor], and others to realize that we, the families of inmates, have rights too! We work and pay taxes. And we vote. We come here today to tell you that we are fed up with being treated as second-class citizens.

—Sandra George of Pro-Family Advocates, objecting to a decision to restrict conjugal visitation in California's prisons

visits in private surroundings conducive to maintaining and strengthening family ties."[47] In 1995, however, California, which then allowed about 26,000 conjugal visits a year, moved to restrict the program, prompting an outcry from inmates' families. Nevertheless, the California Department of Corrections eliminated conjugal visits for those sentenced to death or to life without parole and for those without a parole date. Rapists, sex offenders, and recently disciplined inmates also lost conjugal privileges.

Coeducational prisons housed both men and women, allowing the sexes to join in educational programs, work tasks, and certain forms of recreation, although they slept in separate dormitories and were stringently discouraged from physical intimacy. The Federal Bureau of Prisons began experimenting with coed facilities in 1971, and the Pleasanton Youth Center in California became one of the first institutions in the nation to house both men and women. A number of coed prisons continue to exist today.

The Warehousing Era (1980–1995)

During the late 1970s and into the 1980s, public disappointment, bred of high **recidivism**[48] rates coupled with dramatic media stories of inmates who committed gruesome crimes while on release in the community, led many legislatures to curtail the most liberal aspects of educational and work-release programs. Media descriptions of institutions where inmates lounged in supposed luxury with regular visits from spouses and lovers and took frequent weekend passes infused the popular imagination with images of "prison country clubs." The failure of the rehabilitative ideal in community-based corrections, however, was due as much to changes in the individual sentencing decisions of judges as it was to citizen outrage and restrictive legislative action. Evidence points to the fact that many judges came to regard rehabilitation programs as failures and decided to implement what we earlier called the just deserts model[49] of criminal sentencing. The just deserts model, as discussed in Chapter 10, built upon a renewed belief that offenders should "get what's coming to them." It quickly led to a policy of **warehousing** serious offenders for the avowed purpose of protecting society—and led also to a rapid decline of the deinstitutionalization initiative.

Recidivism rates were widely quoted in support of the drive to warehouse offenders. One study, for example, showed that nearly 70% of young adults paroled from prison in 22 states during 1978 were rearrested for serious crimes one or more times within six years of their release.[50] The 1978 study group was estimated to have committed 36,000 new felonies within the six years following their release, including 324 murders, 231 rapes, 2,291 robberies, and 3,053 violent assaults.[51] Worse still, observed the study's authors, was the fact that 46% of recidivists would have been in prison at the time of their readmission to prison if they had served the maximum term to which they had originally been sentenced.[52] Those with long prior-arrest records (six or more previous adult arrests) were rearrested 90% of the time following release, and the younger the parolee was at first arrest, the greater the chance of a new crime violation. Equally intriguing was the finding that "the length of time that a parolee has served in prison had no consistent impact on recidivism rates."[53]

The failure of the rehabilitative model in corrections had already been proclaimed emphatically by Robert Martinson in 1974.[54] Martinson and his colleagues had surveyed 231 research studies conducted to evaluate correctional treatments between 1945 and 1967. They were unable to identify any treatment program which substantially reduced recidivism. Although Martinson argued for fixed sentences, a portion of which would be served in the community, his findings were often interpreted to mean that lengthy prison terms were necessary to incapacitate offenders who could not be reformed. About the same time, the prestigious National Academy of Sciences released a report in support of Martinson, saying, "We do not now know of any program or method of rehabilitation that could be guaranteed to reduce the criminal activity of released offenders."[55] This combined attack on the treatment model led to the **nothing-works doctrine**, which, beginning in the late 1970s, cast a pall of doubt over the previously dominant treatment philosophy.

Prison overcrowding soon resulted from a combination of the nothing-works philosophy with new sentencing schemes to whose development it contributed. Mandatory minimum sentencing provisions, truth-in-sentencing requirements, and the growing popularity of "three strikes and you're out" laws all contributed to a significant expansion in prison populations. The impact of such laws affected prison populations by substantially increasing the average time served by offenders before release. In addition to legally mandated increases in the average amount of time served, prison populations grew substantially dur-

---

recidivism

The repetition of criminal behavior. In statistical practice, a recidivism rate may be any of a number of possible counts or instances of arrest, conviction, correctional commitment, and correctional status changes related to repetitions of these events within a given period of time.

warehousing

An imprisonment strategy that is based upon the desire to prevent recurrent crime and that has abandoned all hope of rehabilitation.

nothing-works doctrine

The belief, popularized by Robert Martinson in the 1970s, that correctional treatment programs have little success in rehabilitating offenders.

ing the 1990s because of a rise in the number of parole violators returned to prison; a drop in the annual release rates of inmates; a small but growing number of inmates who will serve long terms or who will never be released; and enhanced punishments for drug offenders.[56] Average time served has continued to increase. In 1990, for example, murderers served, on average, 92 months before release. Today, a person convicted of murder can expect to serve 106 months in prison before being released—a 15% increase. During the same period, actual time served in prison for the crime of rape increased 27%, while drug offenders spent 35% more time behind bars.[57]

Much of the rise in prison populations during the warehousing era can be attributed directly to changes in sentencing laws aimed at taking drug offenders off the streets and to the resulting rapid growth in the number of incarcerated drug felons. A warehousing era report by the American Bar Association, for example, directly attributed to the huge growth in the number of inmates to what it saw as a system-wide overemphasis on drug-related offenses—an emphasis which tended to imprison mostly poor, undereducated black youths who were rarely dangerous.[58] The report pointed out that while the per capita *rate of reported crime* dropped 2.2% across the nation during the 1980s, "the *incarceration rate* increased more than 110 percent."[59]

A strong example of how drug-related incarceration led to prison overcrowding can be had in New York State's experience with enforcing its tough "Rockefeller drug laws." The laws consist of a mandatory sentencing scheme that requires judges to impose prison terms of no less than 15 years to life on anyone convicted of selling two ounces (or more) or possessing four ounces (or more) of a narcotic substance. The penalties apply without regard to the circumstances of the offense, the offender's criminal history, or the individual's character or background.[60] In 1973, the year the Rockefeller laws were passed, New York sent only 713 persons to prison for drug crimes. By 2001, as a result of the tough new laws, the state was holding more than 21,000 drug offenders in its prisons—out of a total inmate population of approximately 70,000. Moreover, the percentage of New York prisoners who are serving time for drug offenses increased from less than 9% in 1980 to well over 30% today.[61] Although minor changes were made in the Rockefeller drug laws a few years after they were passed, the statutes remained largely the same. In 2001, New York Governor George Pataki called for reform of his state's drug laws in his annual State of the State address. Referring to the Rockefeller laws, Pataki remarked, "Today, we can conclude that, however well intentioned, key aspects of those laws are out of step with both the times and the complexities of drug addiction."[62] Shortly after the governor spoke, the New York State Assembly drafted its own proposal for reform.[63] Although changes have yet to be enacted as this book goes to press, modification of the existing laws now seems all but certain.

Not only did the American prison population grow dramatically during the warehousing era (Figure 12–2), but prisons everywhere became notoriously overcrowded (Figure 12–3). A survey of 1,400 criminal justice officials conducted by the National Institute of Justice at the start of the warehousing era identified crowding in prisons and jails as the most serious problem facing the criminal justice system.[64] The problem soon got far worse. Between 1980 and 2000, state and federal prison populations more than quadrupled, from 329,000 inmates to almost 1.4 million.[65] A 1990 survey of federal prisons found them 73% overcrowded,[66] and a major program of expansion, which is only now winding down, was implemented. Although the number of people imprisoned continues to grow, new prison construction has made some inroads on the problem of overcrowding. By the beginning of 2001, overcrowding in federal prisons had dropped to approximately 31% and was running up to 15% in some state prison systems.[67]

Not only did warehousing lead to prisons that are still frighteningly overcrowded, but it also contributed to numerous administrative difficulties, many of which continue to affect prison systems throughout the nation today. By 1992, when the warehousing era was in full swing, institutions in 40 states and the District of Columbia were operating under court orders to alleviate crowded conditions.[68] Entire prison systems in nine states—Alaska, Florida, Kansas, Louisiana, Mississippi, Nevada, Rhode Island, South Carolina, and Texas—had come under court control because overcrowded conditions made it impossible for prison administrators to meet court-supported constitutional requirements related to inmate safety. Today, even more state corrections systems have become subject to federal oversight or are operating under federal consent decrees.[69] (Chapter 13 has more information.)

To meet the housing needs of burgeoning prison populations during the 1980s and 1990s, some states constructed "temporary" tent cities within prison yards. Others moved

FIGURE 12-2

U.S. prison population, 1960–2000.
Source: Bureau of Justice Statistics.

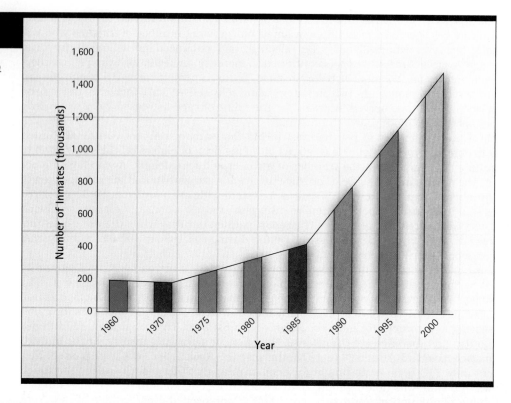

FIGURE 12-3

State and federal prison populations, inmates versus capacity, 1980–2000.

Source: Bureau of Justice Statistics, *Correctional Populations in the United States* (Washington, D.C.: Bureau of Justice Statistics, various years).

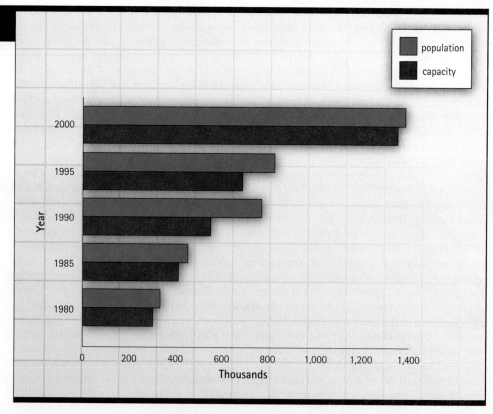

more beds into already packed dormitories, often stacking prisoners three high in triple bunk beds. A few states declared a policy of early release for less dangerous inmates and instituted mandatory diversion programs for first-time nonviolent offenders. Others used sentence rollbacks to reduce the sentences of selected inmates by a fixed amount, usually 90 days. Early parole was similarly employed by numerous states to reduce overcrowded

conditions. Most states shifted some of their correctional burden to local jails, and by 2000 34 states, the District of Columbia, and the federal government were sending prisoners to other jails because of overcrowding at their own long-term institutions.[70]

THE DIMENSIONS OF OVERCROWDING

Even though many new prisons have been built throughout the nation during the past 20 years, prison overcrowding is still very much a reality. Prison overcrowding can be measured along a number of dimensions, including these:[71]

- Space available per inmate (such as square feet of floor space)
- How long inmates are confined in cells or housing units (versus time spent on recreation and other activities)
- Living arrangements (for example, single versus double bunks)
- Type of housing (use of segregation facilities, tents, and so on in place of general housing)

Complicating the picture still further is the fact that prison officials have developed three definitions of **prison capacity**. **Rated capacity** refers to the size of the inmate population that a facility can handle according to the judgment of experts. **Operational capacity** is the number of inmates that a facility can effectively accommodate based on an appraisal of the institution's staff, programs, and services. **Design capacity** refers to the inmate population that the institution was originally built to handle. Rated capacity estimates usually yield the largest inmate capacities, while design capacity (upon which observations in this chapter are based) typically shows the highest amount of overcrowding.

Overcrowding by itself is not cruel and unusual punishment, according to the U.S. Supreme Court in *Rhodes* v. *Chapman* (1981),[72] which considered the issue of double-bunking along with other alleged forms of "deprivation" at the Southern Ohio correctional facility. The Ohio facility, built in 1971, was substantially overcrowded according to the original housing plans on which it was constructed. Designed to house one inmate per cell, the cells were small (only 63 square feet of floor space on the average). However, at the time the suit was filed, the facility held 2,300 inmates, 1,400 of whom were double-celled. Kelly Chapman, an inmate serving a sentence for armed robbery and prison escape, claimed that his portion of a cell was too small—smaller even than the space recommended by Ohio State Veterinarian Services for a five-week-old calf. Thirty-six states joined the case in support of the Ohio practice of double-celling, while the American Medical Association and the American Public Health Association took Chapman's side.[73] The Court, reasoning that overcrowding is not necessarily dangerous if other prison services are adequate, held that

prison capacity

The size of the correctional population an institution can effectively hold.[i] There are three types of prison capacity: rated, operational, and design.

rated capacity

The number of inmates a prison can handle according to the judgment of experts.

operational capacity

The number of inmates a prison can effectively accommodate based upon management considerations.

design capacity

The number of inmates a prison was intended to hold when it was built or modified.

The American public is alarmed about crime, and with good reason. For the past generation, state and federal crime control policies have been based on the belief that law enforcement can solve the problem: more police, harsher sentencing laws, greater use of the death penalty. But today, with an unprecedented number of people behind bars, we are no safer than before. We are, however, much less free.

—American Civil Liberties Union website

justice model

A contemporary model of imprisonment based upon the principle of just deserts.

prison housing conditions may be "restrictive and even harsh," for they are part of the penalty that offenders pay for their crimes.

However, overcrowding combined with other negative conditions may lead to a finding against the prison system. The American Correctional Association believes that such a totality-of-conditions approach requires the court to judge the overall quality of prison life while viewing overcrowded conditions in combination with

■ The prison's meeting of basic human needs

■ The adequacy of the facility's staff

■ The program opportunities available to inmates

■ The quality and strength of the prison management

The warehousing strategy, which is largely responsible for today's overcrowding, continues to be advocated by many who claim that while it may be financially expensive, it is less costly than turning offenders loose. Some years ago, for example, the Justice Department reported that new crimes committed by released prisoners cost society about $430,000 per year per offender for police work, court costs, and losses to victims. The report found that continued confinement, even in newly built prison cells, costs only around $25,000 per year per offender and was "not too expensive when weighed against the price of crimes that would otherwise be prevented by incapacitation."[74] A similar study by Wisconsin found that while imprisonment costs in that state were about $14,000 per inmate per year, the financial burden to the state of allowing the typical Wisconsin inmate "to freely roam the streets in search of victims" would be about $28,000 in actual losses per average offender each year.[75] Researchers who conducted the study concluded that "prison pays" and suggested that "imprisonment is a valuable corrections option from which the state cannot afford to shrink." In contrast to such findings, however, a comprehensive 1997 review of 500 crime-prevention programs across the country found that "much [existing] research on prisons was inadequate or flawed, making it impossible to measure how much crime was actually prevented or deterred by locking up more criminals."[76]

The Just Deserts Era (1995–Present)

Warehousing and prison overcrowding were primarily the result of both public and official frustration with rehabilitative efforts. In a sense, however, they were also consequences of a strategy without a clear-cut philosophy. Since rehabilitation didn't seem to work, early advocates of warehousing—not knowing what else to do—assumed a pragmatic stance and advocated separating criminals from society by keeping them locked up for as long as possible. Their avowed goal was the protection of law-abiding citizens.

Since the end of the warehousing era, however, a new philosophy based upon the second prong of the **justice model**—that is, an emphasis on individual responsibility—has become the operative principle underlying many correctional initiatives. This new philosophy is grounded squarely upon the concept of just deserts, in which imprisonment is seen as a fully deserved and proper consequence of criminal and irresponsible behavior rather than just the end result of a bankrupt system unable to reform its charges. Unlike previous correctional eras, which layered other purposes upon the correctional experience (the reformatory era, for example, was concerned with reformation, while the industrial era sought economic gain), the current era of just deserts represents a kind of return to the root purpose of incarceration: punishment.

In many ways, the current era is looking more and more like the punitive era reborn. At the start of the just deserts era, state legislatures everywhere, encouraged in large part by their constituencies, scrambled to limit inmate privileges and to increase the pains of imprisonment. In 1995, for example, Alabama became the first state in modern times to reinstitute use of the prison chain gang.[77] Under the Alabama system, shotgun-armed guards oversaw prisoners who were chained together by the ankles while they worked the state's roadsides—picking up trash, clearing brush, and filling ditches. The system, intended primarily for parole violators who must reenter prison, was tough and unforgiving. Inmates served up to 90 days on chain gangs, during which they worked 12-hour shifts and remained chained even while using portable toilet facilities.

Following Alabama's lead, in 1995 Arizona became the second state to field prison chain gangs, followed shortly by Florida.[78] Alabama chain gangs, which had expanded to include female prisoners, were discontinued in 1996 following a lawsuit against the state.

An Alabama chain gang setting out to work on the roads. In 1995, reflecting a renewed society-wide emphasis on punishment which is reminiscent of the punitive era in corrections, Alabama became the first state in modern times to revive the use of prison chain gangs.

AP/Wide World Photos

The Florida Department of Corrections continues to use restricted labor squads (its name for chain gangs) at seven correctional institutions. In 1998, a total of 179 close-custody inmates were assigned to these work squads. Florida chain gang inmates are shackled at the ankles but are not connected to each other in any way.[79]

Nationally, chain gang proponents, though dwindling in number, continue to be adamant about the purpose this punishment serves. "If a person knows they're going to be out on the highway in chains, they are going to think twice about committing a crime," says former Georgia Prison Commissioner Ron Jones.[80] Opponents of the chain gang, however, like ACLU National Prison Project spokeswoman Jenni Gainsborough, call it "a giant step backward" and "a return to the dark ages."[81]

In another example of the move toward greater punishments indicative of the just deserts era, Virginia abolished parole on January 1, 1995, increased sentences for certain violent crimes by as much as 700%, and announced that it would build a dozen new prisons by 2005.[82] Changes in state law, initiated by the administration of Governor George Allen, were intended to move the state further in the direction of truth in sentencing and to appease the state's voters, who—reflecting what appears to have been a groundswell of public opinion nationwide—demanded a "get tough" stance toward criminals. William P. Barr, a former U.S. attorney general under President George Bush and co-chairman of the Virginia commission which developed the state's plan, explained why no provisions for rehabilitation and crime prevention had been included: "The most effective method of prevention," he said, "is to take the rapist off the street for 12 years instead of four."[83]

Symptomatic of the shift in public attitudes in favor of the just deserts model of corrections was a virtual avalanche of state and federal legislation (much of it enacted in the 1990s), intended to clamp down on prison comforts, such as weight-training equipment, R-rated films, premium cable TV channels, pornographic materials by mail, miniature golf courses, individual cells with television sets and coffeepots, personally owned computers and modems, and expensive electronic musical instruments. Republican Congressman Dick Zimmer of New Jersey, a sponsor of so-called no-frills federal legislation during the mid-1990s explained that "some criminals have come to view [prison] as an almost acceptable lifestyle because amenities are better for them on the inside than on the outside. You should pay the price for your crime, not be rewarded with a vacation watching premium cable on your personal TV."[84]

As the just deserts era opened, a nationwide survey of state departments of correction conducted by *Corrections Compendium,* a publication covering all aspects of imprisonment, found that prisons "of the present and near future are being stripped of anything that can

With the huge expansion of prisons starting in the 1980s, most prison systems gave up believing they had any responsibility for changing offenders or [for] what happened after offenders were released. The objective became that prisons should be just for punishment, and politicians competed to see who could make prisons more unpleasant.

—Todd Clear, John Jay College of Criminal Justice

be considered a luxury. Prison life is becoming less and less attractive with the elimination of sacred privileges like smoking and the addition of hard labor and humiliating uniforms."[85] The survey found that 60% of the 46 states that responded reported a recent decrease in inmate privileges, including reductions in the amount or type of personal property inmates are allowed to keep, restrictions on outside purchases and food packages from home, and the elimination of cable television and rented movies. A number of prison systems reported abolishing family visits, special-occasion banquets, and the like. "The elimination of family-oriented privileges," said the publication, "reflects the extremely harsh public view towards prisoners that is currently in vogue."[86] A 2001 survey of Florida residents, however, found that sentiments supporting penal austerity do not extend to all types of amenities.[87] Survey respondents widely supported the elimination of prison pornography, including magazines (82.9%); the curtailment of cable television (78.4%); and a ban on boxing and martial arts (75.5%). But only a few respondents supported the reduced availability of books (8.5%); the elimination of job training and basic literacy programs (9%); and the cancellation of psychological counseling programs (5.5%). Only 7% of respondents wanted an end to supervised family visits.

Other "get tough" initiatives can be seen in the "three strikes and you're out" laws that swept through state legislatures everywhere in the late 1990s.[88] Three-strikes legislation, which is discussed in more detail in CJ Today Exhibit 10–2 in Chapter 10, mandates lengthy prison terms for criminal offenders convicted of a third violent crime or felony. While three-strikes laws have either been enacted or are being considered in more than 30 states and by the federal government (which requires life imprisonment for federal criminals convicted of three violent felonies or drug offenses), critics of such laws say that they will not prevent crime.[89] Jerome Skolnick, of the University of California at Berkeley, for example, criticizes three-strikes legislation because, he says, while it may satisfy society's desire for retribution to "lock 'em up and throw away the key,"[90] such a practice will almost certainly not reduce the risk of victimization—especially the risk of becoming a victim of random violence. That is so, says Skolnick, because most violent crimes are committed by young men between the ages of 13 and 23. "It follows," according to Skolnick, "that if we jail them for life after their third conviction, we will get them in the twilight of their careers, and other young offenders will take their place." Three-strikes programs, says Skolnick, will lead to the creation of "the most expensive, taxpayer-supported middle-age and old-age entitlement program in the history of the world," which will provide housing and medical care to older, burned-out law violators. Another author puts it this way: "The question . . . is whether it makes sense to continue to incarcerate aged prisoners beyond the time they would have served under ordinary sentences. This is unnecessary from the standpoint of public safety, and it is expensive."[91]

Alan Schuman, past President of the American Probation and Parole Association, feels much the same way. While building more prisons may be a popular quick fix to crime, says Schuman, such a strategy will cost millions of dollars without making streets safer. "The draconian single-level approach of merely building new institutions will cause us problems for decades," Schuman said.[92]

Criticisms like these, however, fail to appreciate the sentiments underlying the current correctional era. Proponents of "get tough" policies, while no doubt interested in personal safety, lower crime rates, and balanced state and federal budgets, are keenly focused on retribution. And where retribution fuels a correctional policy, deterrence, reformation, and economic considerations play only secondary roles. The real issue for those advocating retribution-based correctional policies is *not* whether they deter or whether they lower crime rates, but rather the overriding conviction that criminals deserve punishment. As more and more states have enacted three-strikes and other "get tough" legislation, prison populations across the nation have continued to swell, eclipsing those of the warehousing era. The just deserts era of correctional philosophy, however, now provides what has become for many an acceptable rationale for continued prison expansion. California officials, for example, estimate that by 2004, three-strikes legislation "will account for over 50% of the prison population" in that state.[93] A similar study of three-strikes laws in 22 states concluded that such legislation results in clogged court systems and crowded correctional facilities and encourages three-time felons to take dramatic risks to avoid capture.[94]

Given such studies, many now claim that the prevailing retribution-based "lock 'em up" philosophy bodes ill for the future of American corrections. "I am worried there is going to be a disaster in our prisons," says Michael Quinlan, Director of the Federal Bureau of Prisons under Presidents Ronald Reagan and George Bush.[95] The combination of burgeoning

> The first two decades of the [twenty-first] century, at least, will see a major growth in prison populations. We have an opportunity now to start doing a better job of handling the responsibilities of the criminal justice system as well as of society. I hope we take both more seriously in the future than we do currently.
>
> —Dr. Alfred Blumstein, Dean of the School of Urban and Public Affairs, Carnegie Mellon University

prison populations and restrictions on inmate privileges could have a catastrophic and disastrous effect—leading to riots, more prison violence, work stoppages, an increased number of inmate suicides, and other forms of prison disorder—says Quinlan.[96]

SELECTIVE INCAPACITATION: A STRATEGY TO REDUCE PRISON POPULATIONS

Some authors have identified the central issue of imprisonment as one of selective versus collective incapacitation.[97] Collective incapacitation, a strategy which would imprison almost all serious offenders, is still found today in states that rely upon predetermined, or fixed, sentences for given offenses or for a series of specified kinds of offenses (as in the case of three-strikes legislation). Collective incapacitation is, however, prohibitively expensive as well as unnecessary, in the opinion of many experts. Not all offenders need to be imprisoned because not all represent a continuing threat to society, but those who do are difficult to identify.[98]

In most jurisdictions where the just deserts initiative holds sway, selective incapacitation has become the rule. Selective incapacitation seeks to identify the most dangerous criminals, with the goal of selectively removing them from society. Repeat offenders with records of serious and violent crimes are the most likely candidates for incapacitation—as are those who will probably commit violent crimes in the future even though they have no records. But potentially violent offenders cannot be readily identified, and those thought likely to commit crimes cannot be sentenced to lengthy prison terms for things they have not yet done.

In support of selective incapacitation, many states have enacted career offender statutes which attempt to identify potentially dangerous offenders out of known criminal populations. Selective incapacitation efforts, however, have been criticized for yielding a rate of "false positives" of over 60%,[99] and some authors have called selective incapacitation a "strategy of failure."[100] Nevertheless, in an analysis of recidivism studies, Canadians Paul Gendreau, Tracy Little, and Claire Goggin found that criminal history, a history of preadult antisocial behavior, and "criminogenic needs"—which were defined as measurable antisocial thoughts, values, and behaviors—were all dependable predictors of recidivism.[101] The article, subtitled "What Works!" was intended as a response to Martinson's nothing-works doctrine, mentioned earlier.

Some state programs designed to reduce prison overcrowding, however, have run afoul of selective incarceration principles. In 1997, for example, the U.S. Supreme Court ordered Florida to release as many as 2,500 inmates—many of whom had been convicted of violent crimes—under a "gain time" program set up by the state in 1983.[102] Provisions of the program allowed inmates to earn as much as two months off their sentences for every month served. Although the program was originally intended to relieve overcrowding, a change in public sentiment led Florida Attorney General Bob Butterworth to revoke

Weapons confiscated from inmates being displayed at Florida State Prison during a rare media tour of the facility.

Mark Foley, AP/Wide World Photos

ex post facto

Latin for "after the fact." The Constitution prohibits the enactment of *ex post facto* laws, which make acts committed before the laws in question were passed punishable as crimes.

gain time which had already been earned. In ordering the inmates' release, however, the U.S. Supreme Court unanimously ruled that Florida had violated constitutional guarantees against **ex post facto** laws and required officials to be bound by the program's original conditions. The release of hundreds of murderers, rapists, robbers, and other felons caused a statewide uproar and media furor. Lee County Sheriff John McDougall expressed dismay at the Court's decision. "A hell of a lot of innocent people are going to be robbed, raped, and murdered," he said. "How many people are going to have to die in order to pay for this blunder?"[103]

The Florida experience, and others like it, have caused states to tighten restrictions on early-release programs. As the just deserts model continues to take center stage, it is likely that we will see the continued sentencing of violent criminals to lengthy prison stays with little possibility of release and the increased use of alternative sanctions for minor offenders.

Prisons Today

There are approximately 1,500 state prisons and 84 federal prisons in operation across the country today.[104] More are being built as both the states and the federal government continue to fund and construct new facilities. As mentioned earlier in this chapter, America's prison population has more than quadrupled since 1980, although the growth rate shows signs of slowing (Figure 12–4). On January 1, 2001, the nation's state and federal prisons held 1,381,892 inmates.[105] Slightly more than 6.6% (or 91,612) of those imprisoned were women.[106]

An examination of imprisonment statistics by race highlights the huge disparity between blacks and whites in prison. While only an estimated 1,108 white men are imprisoned in the United States for every 100,000 white men in their late 20s, the latest figures show an incarceration rate of 9,749 black men for every 100,000 black men of the same age—nine times greater than the figure for whites.[107] Worse yet, the imprisonment rate of blacks increased dramatically over the past ten years, while the rate of white imprisonment has grown far less.

The incarceration rate for state and federal prisoners sentenced to more than a year has reached a record 478 prisoners for every 100,000 U.S. residents. One out of every 109 men and one out of every 1,695 women were sentenced prisoners under the jurisdiction of state or federal authorities in 2000.[108] Many prison statistics are displayed graphically in Figures 12–5 and 12–6.

FIGURE 12–4

Change in state and federal prison populations, 1990–2000.

Source: Allen J. Beck and Paige M. Harrison, *Prisoners in 2000* (Washington, D.C.: Bureau of Justice Statistics, 2001).

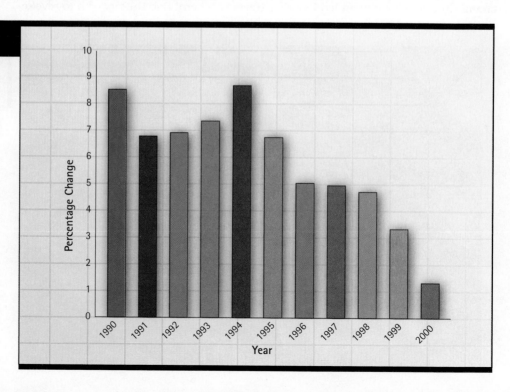

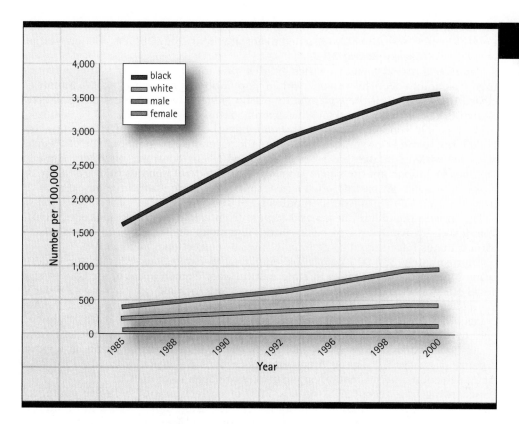

FIGURE 12–5

U.S. incarceration rates by race and sex.

Source: Bureau of Justice Statistics.

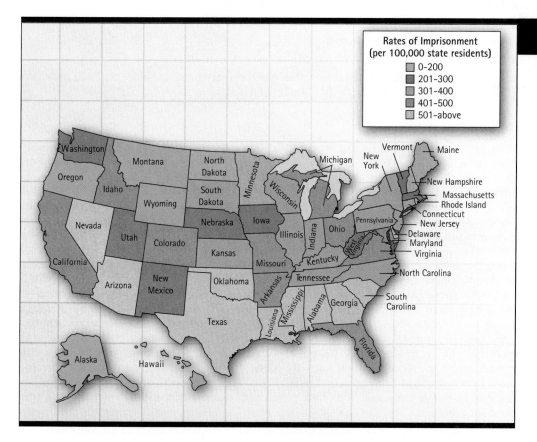

FIGURE 12–6

Rates of imprisonment in the United States.

Source: Allen J. Beck and Paige M. Harrison, *Prisoners in 2000* (Washington, D.C.: Bureau of Justice Statistics, 2001).

Federal prisons tell a similar story. On January 1, 2001, federal prisons held 145,416 inmates in facilities originally designed to accommodate only 95,374.[109] More statistics are available via **Library Extra! 12–1**.

The size of prison facilities varies greatly. One out of every four state institutions is a large, maximum-security prison, with a population approaching 1,000 inmates. A few exceed that figure, but the typical state prison is small, with an inmate population of less than 500. Community-based facilities average around 50 residents.

Most people sentenced to state prisons have been convicted of violent crimes (48%), while property and drug crimes are tied as the second most common type of offenses (21% each) for which inmates have been sentenced.[110] In contrast, prisoners sentenced for drug-law violations are the single largest group of federal inmates (61%), and the increase in the imprisonment of drug offenders accounts for more than three-quarters of the total growth in the number of federal inmates since 1980.[111]

The inmate population in general suffers from a low level of formal education, comes from a socially disadvantaged background, and lacks significant vocational skills.[112] Most adult inmates have served some time in juvenile correctional facilities.[113]

Approximately 350,000 people are employed in corrections,[114] with the majority performing direct custodial tasks in state institutions. Women account for 20% of all correctional officers, with the proportion of female officers increasing at around 19% per year.[115] In an effort to encourage the increased employment of women in corrections, the American Correctional Association (ACA) formally adopted a statement which reads, "Women have a right to equal employment. No person who is qualified for a particular position/assignment or for job-related opportunities should be denied such employment or opportunities because of gender."[116] The ACA encourages correctional agencies to "ensure that recruitment, selection, and promotion opportunities are open to women."

According to a recent ACA report, 70% of correctional officers are white, 22% are black, and slightly over 5% are Hispanic.[117] The inmate-to-staff ratio in state prisons averages around 4.1 inmates for each correctional officer. State incarceration costs an average of $57.92 per inmate per day, while the federal government spends about $59 per inmate per day.[118]

The typical prison system in relatively populous states consists of[119]

■ One high-security prison for long-term, high-risk cases

■ One or more medium-security institutions for offenders who are not high risks

■ One institution for adult women

■ One or two institutions for young adults (generally under age 25)

■ One or two specialized mental hospital–type security prisons for mentally ill prisoners

■ One or more open-type institutions for low-risk, nonviolent inmates

Security Levels

Maximum-custody prisons are the institutions most often portrayed in movies and on television. They tend to be massive old prisons with large inmate populations. Some, like Central Prison in Raleigh, North Carolina, are much newer and incorporate advances in prison architecture to provide tight security without sacrificing building aesthetics. Such institutions provide a high level of security characterized by high fences, thick walls, secure cells, gun towers, and armed prison guards. Maximum-custody prisons tend to locate cells and other inmate living facilities at the center of the institution and place a variety of barriers between the living area and the institution's outer perimeter. Technological innovations—such as electric perimeters, laser motion detectors, electronic and pneumatic locking systems, metal detectors, X-ray machines, television surveillance, radio communications, and computer information systems—are frequently used today to reinforce the more traditional maximum-security strategies. These technologies have helped to lower the cost of new prison construction. However, some people argue that prisons may rely too heavily on electronic detection devices that have not yet been adequately tested.[120] Death-row inmates are all maximum-security prisoners, although the level of security on death row exceeds even that experienced by most prisoners held in maximum custody. Prisoners on death row must spend much of the day in single cells and are often permitted a brief shower only once a week under close supervision.

Most states today have one large, centrally located maximum-security institution. Some of these prisons combine more than one custody level and may be both maximum- and medium-security facilities. Medium security is a custody level that in many ways resembles maximum security. Medium-security prisoners are generally permitted more freedom to associate with one another and can go to the prison yard, exercise room, library, and shower and bathroom facilities under less intense supervision than their maximum-security counterparts. An important security tool in medium-security prisons is the count, which is literally a head count of inmates taken at regular intervals. Counts may be taken four times a day and usually require inmates to report to designated areas to be counted. Until the count has been "cleared," all other inmate activity must cease. Medium-security prisons tend to be smaller than maximum-security institutions and often have barbed-wire-topped chain-link fences instead of the more secure stone or concrete block walls found in many of the older maximum-security facilities. Cells and living quarters tend to have more windows and are often located closer to the perimeter of the institution than is the case in maximum-security facilities. Dormitory-style housing, where prisoners live together in wardlike arrangements, may be employed in medium-security facilities. There are generally more opportunities for inmates to participate in recreational and other prison programs than in maximum-custody facilities.

Minimum-security institutions do not fit the stereotypical conception of prisons. Minimum-security inmates are generally housed in dormitory-like settings and are free to walk the yard and to visit most of the prison facilities. Some newer prisons provide minimum-security inmates with private rooms, which they can decorate (within limits) according to their tastes. Inmates usually have free access to a canteen that sells items like cigarettes, toothpaste, and candy bars. Minimum-security inmates often wear uniforms of a different color from those of inmates in higher custody levels, and in some institutions they may wear civilian clothes. They work under only general supervision and usually have access to recreational, educational, and skills-training programs on the prison grounds. Guards are unarmed, gun towers do not exist, and fences, if they are present at all, are usually low and sometimes even unlocked. Many minimum-security prisoners participate in some sort of work- or study-release program, and some have extensive visitation and furlough privileges. Counts may be taken, although most minimum-security institutions keep track of inmates through daily administrative work schedules. The primary "force" holding inmates in minimum-security institutions is their own restraint. Inmates live with the knowledge that minimum-security institutions are one step removed from close correctional supervision and that if they fail to meet the expectations of administrators they will be transferred into more secure institutions, which will probably delay their release. Inmates returning from assignments in the community may be frisked for contraband, but body-cavity searches are rare in minimum custody, being reserved primarily for inmates suspected of smuggling.

Upon entry into the prison system, most states assign prisoners to initial custody levels based upon their perceived dangerousness, escape risk, and type of offense. Some inmates may enter the system at the medium- (or even minimum-) custody level. Inmates move through custody levels according to the progress they are judged to have made in self-control and demonstrated responsibility. Serious, violent criminals who begin their prison careers with lengthy sentences in maximum custody have the opportunity in most states to work their way up to minimum security, although the process usually takes a number of years. Those who represent continual disciplinary problems are returned to closer custody levels. Minimum-security prisons, as a result, house inmates convicted of all types of criminal offenses.

The typical American prison today is medium or minimum custody. Some states have as many as 80 or 90 small institutions, which may originally have been located in every county to serve the needs of public works and highway maintenance. Medium- and minimum-security institutions house the bulk of the country's prison population and offer a number of programs and services designed to assist with the rehabilitation of offenders and to create the conditions necessary for a successful reentry of the inmate into society. Most prisons offer psychiatric services, academic education, vocational education, substance-abuse treatment, health care, counseling, recreation, library services, religious programs, and industrial and agricultural training.[121] To learn more about all aspects of contemporary prisons, visit the Corrections Connection via **Web Extra! 12–2** at cjtoday.com.

[Rural Towns Turn to Prisons to Reignite Their Economies]

SAYRE, Okla., July 27—For a town of 4,114 in western Oklahoma, Sayre has an impressive landfill. The scales to weigh the bales of crushed scrap are new. A machine for shredding trees is new. So, too, is the 60-unit apartment complex going up on the side of the road leading to the dump, the asphalt that covers that road, and the sprawling Flying J Truck Plaza nearby.

The wording on a trash-hauling bin parked near the landfill gives a hint of what is behind the revival of this withered, century-old city. It reads "North Fork Correctional Facility."

As in many other small towns around the country, a three-year-old, $37 million, 1,440-inmate, 270-employee, all-male prison is responsible for lifting Sayre's spirits and reigniting its economy.

"In my mind there's no more recession-proof form of economic development," said Jack McKennon, 52, the city manager who persuaded the Corrections Corporation of America to put its prison in Sayre. "Nothing's going to stop crime."

Sayre is not alone in its economic strategy. According to the 2000 census, prisons have been helping to revive large stretches of rural America. More than a Wal-Mart or a meat-packing plant, state, federal and private prisons, typically housing 1,000 inmates and providing 300 jobs, can put a town on solid economic footing. As communities become more and more familiar with the benefits that prisons bring, they are also becoming increasingly adept at maximizing their windfall through collecting taxes and healthy public service fees.

In the last decade, 245 prisons sprouted in 212 of the nation's 2,290 rural counties, many in Great Plains towns of Colorado, Oklahoma and Texas that had been stripped of family farms and upended by the collapse of the 1980's oil boom, said Calvin L. Beale, senior demographer at the Economic Research Service of the Agriculture Department.

Mr. Beale said an average of 25 new rural prisons opened each year in the 1990's, up from 16 in the 1980's and 4 in the 1970's. Growth followed. In the 212 prison counties, the population rose 12 percent in the 90's, far more than the rate of 1.5 percent in the preceding decade. Three small Oklahoma cities with new prisons—Hinton, Sayre and Watonga—grew more than 40 percent.

Opening a prison is a natural option for down-and-out towns, said Thomas F. Pogue, economics professor at the University of Iowa.

"It's a more stable industry for a town than a manufacturing plant," Professor Pogue said. "The wage level is a problem, but these prisons are being located where people don't have much of a choice."

The North Fork Correctional Facility, a mile and a half from downtown Sayre, is surrounded by buffalo grass and cottonwood trees. With light gray concrete walls and red metal roofs, it could pass for an immense new Comfort Inn were it not for double coils of razor wire and slotted windows. The access road for the buses that bring in new inmates is called Delivery Avenue.

The prison's economic value to Sayre is immediately apparent. The Corrections Corporation of America, a private prison management company based in Nashville, is the largest taxpayer in Beckham County, of which Sayre is the seat. The county collects $411,000 in property taxes from the prison, more than four times the amount it gets from the next largest taxpayer, the Bar-S Foods Company, a meat-processing plant. Eighty percent of the property taxes support county schools. Jody Bradley, the prison's warden, said the prison spent $2.5 million a year for goods and services in Oklahoma, largely around Sayre, and disbursed about $7 million in wages.

The prisoners are themselves cogs in Sayre's economic engine. They pay the city's 3.5 percent sales tax for the snacks and sodas they buy in the commissary. They also pay a 35 percent to 45 percent tax for the telephone calls, roughly 100 a day, all collect, all long distance. Local calls are forbidden for security reasons, not that it is much of an issue: the inmates all come from Wisconsin, which, because of a space shortage, farms out more than 4,000 prisoners to other states.

The prisoners help in other ways, too. The city has torn down the old high school and salvaged the bricks and stone work for a new City Hall. The bricks stand in stacks in the prison yard, where for no charge to the city, the inmates are cleaning them.

By any measure, Sayre, 120 miles west of Oklahoma City, was in perilous shape before the prison opened. Shattered by the oil and gas industry bust of the 1980's, it was surviving largely on federal crop support payments to its dwindling farm population, said Jack W. Ivester, the town's mayor.

At one point, officials turned off every other street light on the main commercial thoroughfare to save money. In the center of town stood a reminder of better times, a stately court house, which had been featured as a backdrop in the 1940 film "Grapes of Wrath," starring Henry Fonda.

Now Sayre can set aside 15 percent of its revenues for capital improvements. The money brought in from the telephone calls, sales taxes, water and sewer fees and landfill charges accounts for nearly all the increase in the city's budget from about $755,000 in 1996, before the prison construction began, to about $1,250,000 this year.

The money flowing into city coffers made it possible for Sayre to hire nine new employees, bringing the total to 30. Last year the city granted them $100,000 in raises. Mr. McKennon's salary has doubled to $48,000 in nine years. The police force has grown to eight officers from four, and for three years in a row, the city has been able to buy a new patrol car. Sayre has erected three new water towers, making five....

As a result, Beckham County's unemployment rate is a rock-bottom 1.7 percent, from 3.2 percent in 1998 when the prison was built, even as the nation's unemployment rate rises.

"The ones that want to work, they can go out there and get a job," said Leroy Hagerman, who operates an auto-repair shop downtown.

Mr. Hagerman's daughter got one of the best jobs, as one of six captains at the prison. "Not many places where a single woman can make $30,000 a year," he said.

While the prison's immediate economic value is clear, it remains an open question as to how deep or wide ranging its benefits will be....

For the latest in crime and justice news, visit the Talk Justice news feed at http://www.crimenews.info.

Source: Peter T. Kilborn, "Rural Towns Turn to Prisons to Reignite Their Economies," *New York Times,* August 1, 2001.

The Federal Prison System

In 1895, the federal government opened a prison at Leavenworth, Kansas, for civilians convicted of violating federal law. Leavenworth had been a military prison, and control over the facility was transferred from the Department of the Army to the Department of Justice. By 1906, the Leavenworth facility had been expanded to a capacity of 1,200 inmates, and another federal prison—in Atlanta, Georgia—was built. McNeil Island Prison in Washington State was also functioning by the early 1900s. The first federal prison for women opened in 1927 in Alderson, West Virginia. With increasing complexity in the federal criminal code, the number of federal prisoners grew.[122]

On May 14, 1930, the Federal Bureau of Prisons (BOP) was created under the direction of Sanford Bates. It was charged with providing progressive and humane care for federal inmates, professionalizing the federal prison service, and ensuring consistent and centralized administration of the 11 federal prisons in operation at the time.[123] The bureau inherited a system which was dramatically overcrowded. Many federal prisoners were among the most notorious criminals in the nation, and ideals of humane treatment and rehabilitation were all but lacking in the facilities of the 1920s. Bates began a program of improvements to relieve overcrowding and to increase the treatment capacity of the system. In 1933, the Medical Center for Federal Prisoners opened in Springfield, Missouri, with a capacity of around 1,000 inmates. Alcatraz Island began operations in 1934.

Most of the federal prison system's growth since the mid-1980s has been the result of the Sentencing Reform Act of 1984 (which established determinate sentencing, abolished parole, and reduced good time) and federal mandatory minimum sentences enacted in 1986, 1988, and 1990. From 1980 to 1989, the federal inmate population more than doubled, from just over 24,000 to almost 58,000. During the 1990s, the population more than doubled again, reaching approximately 136,000 at the start of 2000, as efforts to combat illegal drugs and illegal immigration contributed to significantly increased conviction rates. Currently, BOP is projecting dramatic population increases for the next several years as significant federal law enforcement efforts to catch and incarcerate drug offenders continue.

Today, the federal system consists of 100 institutions, six regional offices, a Central Office (headquarters), three staff-training centers, and 28 community corrections offices. The regional offices and the Central Office provide administrative oversight and support to the institutions and community corrections offices. Community corrections offices oversee community corrections centers and home-confinement programs.

The federal prison system classifies its institutions according to five security levels: (1) administrative maximum (**ADMAX**), (2) high security, (3) medium security, (4) low security, and (5) minimum security.[124] High-security facilities are called *U.S. penitentiaries* (USPs); medium- and low-security institutions are both called *federal correctional institutions* (FCIs); and minimum-security prisons are termed *federal prison camps* (FPCs).[125] Minimum-security facilities (like Eglin Air Force Base, Florida, and Maxwell Air Force Base, Alabama) are essentially honor-type camps with barracks-like housing and no fencing. Low-security facilities in the federal prison system are surrounded by double chain-link fencing and employ vehicle patrols around their perimeters to enhance security. Medium-security facilities (like those in Terminal Island, California; Lompoc, California; and Seagoville, Texas) make use of similar fencing and patrols but supplement them with electronic monitoring of the grounds and perimeter areas. High-security facilities (USPs like those in Atlanta, Georgia; Lewisburg, Pennsylvania; Terre Haute, Indiana; and Leavenworth, Kansas) are architecturally designed to prevent escapes and to contain disturbances. They also make use of armed patrols and intense electronic surveillance.

A separate federal prison category is that of administrative facilities, consisting of institutions with special missions which are designed to house all types of inmates. Most administrative facilities are metropolitan detention centers (MDCs). MDCs, which are generally located in large cities close to federal courthouses, are the jails of the federal correctional system and hold inmates awaiting trial in federal court. Another five administrative facilities, medical centers for federal prisoners (MCFPs), function as hospitals.

Federal correctional facilities exist either as single institutions or as federal correctional complexes—that is, sites consisting of more than one type of correctional institution (Figure 12–7). The federal correctional complex at Allenwood, Pennsylvania, for example, consists of a U.S. penitentiary, a federal prison camp, and two federal correctional institutions (one low and one medium security), each with its own warden. Federal institutions can be classified by type as follows: 55 are federal prison camps (holding 35% of all federal prisoners), 17

ADMAX

Administrative maximum. The term is used by the federal government to denote ultra-high-security prisons.

FIGURE 12-7

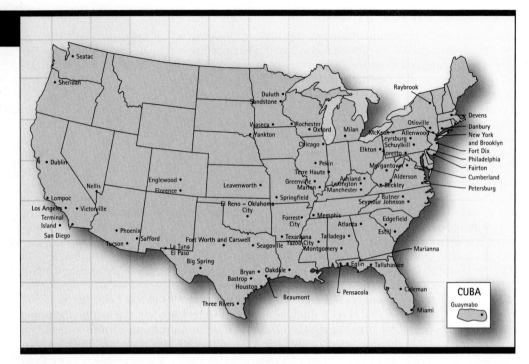

Locations of long-term confinement facilities in the federal correctional system, 2001. Note: Does not include Bureau of Prisons offices or Community Corrections Management offices.

Source: Federal Bureau of Prisons.

are low-security facilities (28%), 26 are medium-security facilities (23%), eight are high-security prisons (13%), and one is an ADMAX facility (1%).

One recent addition to the federal system is the $60 million ultra-maximum-security prison at Florence, Colorado—the federal system's only ADMAX unit. Dubbed by some "the Alcatraz of the Rockies," the new 575-bed facility was designed to be the most secure prison ever built by the government.[126] Opened in 1995, it holds mob bosses, spies, terrorists, murderers, and escape artists. Dangerous inmates are confined to their cells 23 hours per day and are not allowed to see or associate with other inmates. Electronically controlled doors throughout the institution channel inmates to individual exercise sessions, and educational courses, religious services, and administrative matters are conducted via closed-circuit television piped directly into the prisoners' cells. Remote-controlled heavy steel doors within the prison allow correctional staff to section off the institution in the event of rioting, and the system can be controlled from outside if the entire prison is compromised.

In an effort to combat rising expenses associated with a rapidly growing federal prison population, the U.S. Congress passed legislation in 1992 that imposes a "user fee" on federal inmates who are able to pay the costs associated with their incarceration.[127] Under the law, inmates may be assessed a dollar amount up to the cost of a year's incarceration—currently around $20,000. The statute, which was designed so as not to impose hardships on poor defendants or their dependents, directs that collected funds, estimated to total $48 million per year, are to be used to improve alcohol- and drug-abuse programs within federal prisons. To learn more about the Federal Bureau of Prisons, visit **Web Extra! 12-3**, or read **Library Extras! 12-2 and 12-3** at cjtoday.com.

Recent Improvements

In the midst of frequent lawsuits, court-ordered changes in prison administration, and overcrowded conditions, outstanding prison facilities are being recognized through the American Correctional Association's program of accreditation. The ACA Commission on Accreditation has developed a set of standards which correctional institutions can use in self-evaluation. Institutions that meet the standards can apply for accreditation under the program. Unfortunately, prison accreditation has few "teeth." Although unaccredited universities would not be in business long, few prisoners can choose the institution they want to be housed in.

Another avenue toward improvement of the nation's prisons can be found in the National Academy of Corrections, the training arm of the National Institute of Corrections.

The academy, located in Boulder, Colorado, offers seminars, video conferencing, and training sessions for state and local correctional managers, trainers, personnel directors, sheriffs, and state legislators.[128] Issues covered include strategies to control overcrowding, community corrections program management, prison programs, gangs and disturbances, security, and public and media relations.[129]

Jails

Jails are locally operated short-term confinement facilities originally built to hold suspects following arrest and pending trial. Today's jails also serve other purposes. Jails today[130]

- Receive individuals pending arraignment and hold them awaiting trial, conviction, or sentencing
- Readmit probation, parole, and bail-bond violators and absconders
- Temporarily detain juveniles, the mentally ill, and others pending transfer to appropriate facilities
- Hold individuals for the military, for protective custody, for contempt, and for the courts as witnesses
- Release convicted inmates to the community upon completion of their sentence
- Transfer inmates to federal, state, or other authorities
- House inmates for federal, state, or other authorities because of overcrowding in their facilities
- Operate community-based programs with day reporting, home detention, electronic monitoring, or other types of supervision
- Hold inmates sentenced to short terms (generally under one year)

A 2001 report by the Bureau of Justice Statistics found that the nation's jails held 621,149 inmates—70,414 of them women.[131] Juveniles held in local jails numbered 7,615. Fifty-six percent of jail inmates are pretrial detainees or are defendants involved in some stage of the trial process.[132] Jail authorities also supervised an additional 65,884 men and women in the community under programs that included the following: electronic monitoring (10,782), home detention without electronic monitoring (332), day reporting (3,969), community service (13,592), and weekender programs (14,523).[133]

A total of 3,365 jails operate throughout the United States today, staffed by approximately 207,600 jail employees—the equivalent of about one employee for every three jail inmates.[134] Overall, the nation's jail budget is huge, and facilities are overflowing. State

jail

A confinement facility administered by an agency of local government, typically a law enforcement agency, intended for adults but sometimes also containing juveniles, which holds persons detained pending adjudication and/or persons committed after adjudication, usually those committed on sentences of a year or less.

and local governments spend $10 billion every year to operate the nation's jails,[135] with more than $1 billion in additional monies earmarked for new jail construction and for renovation. On average, the housing of one jail inmate costs more than $14,500.[136]

Approximately 20 million people are admitted (or readmitted) to the nation's jails each year. Some jail inmates stay for as little as one day, while others serve extended periods of time. Driving under the influence is the most common charge for jailed adults 45 years of age or older (accounting for 10% of all jail inmates); while today, drug-law violations account for 22% of all those in jail.[137] Bond has been set by the court, although not yet posted, for almost nine out of ten jail inmates. Significantly, one of the fastest-growing sectors of today's jail population consists of sentenced offenders serving time in local jails because overcrowded prisons cannot accept them. Most people processed through the country's jails are members of minority groups (58%), with 41.3% of jail inmates classifying themselves as black, 15.1% as Hispanic, and 1.6% as other minorities. Nearly 42% of jail inmates classify themselves as white, and 88.6% are male.[138]

Most jails are small. Many were built to house 50 or fewer inmates. Most people who spend time in jail, however, do so in larger institutions. According to the Bureau of Justice Statistics (BJS), about 6% of jail facilities house more than half of all jail inmates in the nation.[139] Although there are many small and medium-sized jails across the country, a handful of "megajails" each house thousands of inmates. The largest such facilities can be found in Los Angeles; New York City; Cook County, Illinois; Harris County, Texas; and Maricopa County, Arizona. One such megajail is Los Angeles County's 4,000-bed Twin Towers Correctional Facility, which cost $373 million to build and opened in 1997.[140] The largest employer among these huge jails is in Cook County, Illinois, with over 1,200 personnel on its payroll.[141] On June 30, 2000, the nation's 50 largest jail jurisdictions held 33% (206,914) of all jail inmates. Twenty-one states had at least one jurisdiction which ranked in the top 50 for average daily population. States with more than one jurisdiction among the nation's 50 largest jurisdictions are California (11), Florida (8), Texas (6), Georgia (3), Ohio (3), Pennsylvania (2), Tennessee (2), and New Jersey (2). The two jurisdictions with the most inmates, Los Angeles County and New York City, together held approximately 33,300 inmates, or 5.4% of the national total.[142] More jail statistics are available via **Library Extra! 12–4** at cjtoday.com.

A correctional officer walking along a wall at Los Angeles County's $373 million Twin Towers Correctional Facility. Opened in 1997, it is one of the world's largest jails.

Damian Dovarganes, AP/Wide World Photos

CJ Today News

[Politically Correct Punishment]

The man in charge of two of San Francisco County's jails is a convicted murderer.

In 1966, when he was 18, Michael Marcum shot his abusive father to death. Nearly seven years in maximum-security prison taught him the violence and intolerance of prison culture firsthand—and after his release, he learned how terrifying freedom can be for someone set adrift, after years behind bars, with no job skills.

Deeply affected by his experience and determined to help others avoid repeating it, Marcum took a job as a counselor at the San Francisco County Jail. He made such an impression on his boss, San Francisco Sheriff Michael Hennessey, that in 1993 Hennessey over-ruled the objections of his own deputies and promoted Marcum to a top job. Now, the two men are overseeing one of the nation's most ambitious and innovative efforts at jailhouse reform.

The revolution is taking place inside Jail No. 7, an unimposing two-story building in the coastal hills south of San Francisco, and Jail No. 8, a sleek concatenation of curves and glass tucked up against Highway 101 known as the "glamor slammer." To the staff, however, they are "program facilities," and the 700-odd cons inside, who are doing time for everything from drug possession to armed robbery, are "clients." Instead of passing their time staring at their cell walls, the inmates mostly stay in open dormitories and spend up to 12 hours each day in some of over 50 separate treatment, counseling, training, and education programs.

Prisoners can join such counseling groups as Tools for Healing, Drama Therapy, and Gay Life Skills. The jail's education center offers courses in ethnic studies, women's cultural studies, and film theory, as well as basic skills. Prisoners can take a yoga and meditation class twice a week. Those in violence- or drug-treatment programs receive acupuncture to reduce their cravings for drugs or their violent impulses four days a week.

"Considering I have to be in jail, it's all right," says Bratt Woods, currently a Jail No. 7 "client" thanks to a parole violation. As a member of the Roads to Recovery drug treatment program, Woods has a busy schedule. His day starts at 8:15 A.M. with acupuncture treatment. At 9:30 A.M., it's time for literacy skills. After lunch he has computer class in the 20-terminal computer lab, followed by a meeting of his substance abuse treatment group and an "academic skills class." After dinner, it's on to a "community meeting" where inmates discuss "dorm issues." He finally gets some free time from 8 P.M. until lights-out at 10:45 P.M.

"I've been changing my life through these classes," says Woods, a father of three. He plans to participate in a post-release work program when he gets out.

The philosophy behind the program facilities is to break the cycle of violence by transforming the typical jailhouse culture of humiliation and violence into one of dignity and healing. Hennessey and Marcum say their approach is not only more humane, but also contributes more to public safety. "Tough prisons turn out tough criminals," says Hennessey. Still, even he has his limits: "I drew the line at aromatherapy," says Hennessey, with a good-natured wink.

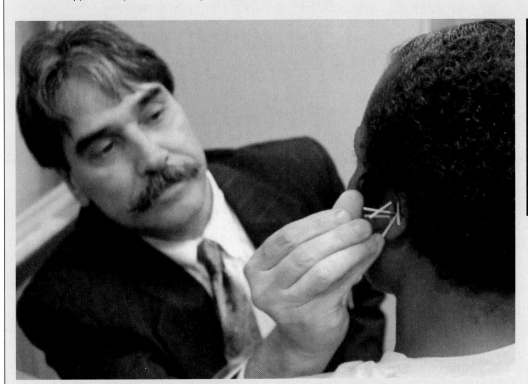

Peter Marinakis, project director of the Community Health Initiative, inserting acupuncture needles in a patient during a demonstration at the Baltimore, Maryland, City Detention Center. For seven years, female inmates at the center have been receiving acupuncture as a treatment for drug addiction. Now corrections officials have declared the program a success and are preparing a similar effort for male inmates.
AP/Wide World photos

(continued)

CJ Today News (*continued*)

"We Need to Be Able to Cry."

Their morning acupuncture finished, a group of inmates in orange sweats and plastic flip-flop sandals are seated calmly in a circle. Without prompting from the group facilitator, each in turn rattles off a list of agenda items listed on a portable bulletin board: their name, their "hit man" name (a nickname for the violent side of their personality they must learn to control), how they feel, and what they need from the group.

"My-name-is-Paul-and-I-am-a-violent-man," recites a 30ish man with a trim goatee. "My hitman is a 'premeditating-quick-reacting-bastard.'" With the formalities out of the way, Paul moves on to his feelings. "I need people to recognize what's going on inside of me. We need as men to be able to talk to one another more often. We need to be able to cry." Heads nod around the circle as a few tears slide down Paul's cheeks.

It's all part of the Resolve to Stop the Violence Program (RSVP), which aims at getting prisoners to look at themselves and what they have done, explains sheriff's program administrator Sunny Schwartz. It makes a lot more sense, she maintains, than warehousing inmates in what she calls "monster factories." On Wednesdays, RSVP participants, many of whom are charged with domestic abuse, hear female victims of violence talk about the devastation they have suffered at the hands of men like themselves. After release, the offenders are required to do something positive in the community, such as giving anti-violence talks at local schools.

The prisoners may like their yoga classes and group-therapy sessions, but the key question, of course, is this: Does it work? Do all these programs actually help reform criminals? The short answer, even according to the jail's administrators, is that the jury is still out.

A 1996 study by the University of California at San Francisco did find that the jail's flagship intensive drug-therapy program for women yielded a drop in repeat offenses from 55 to 40 percent. More encouragingly, a limited internal review of the latest version of the program, which has been running since 1997, found that recidivism among graduates had dropped to just 15 percent.

But in the seven years since Jail No. 7's programming began, a comprehensive study of the overall strategy on recidivism has yet to be conducted. The Sheriff's department recently commissioned Harvard psychiatry professor James Gilligan to conduct a thorough-

going study of the program's effectiveness at keeping violent offenders out of trouble after their release.

If nothing else, some of the programs seem to offer pragmatic advantages. Despite dire predictions of mayhem that accompanied the launch of RSVP, putting 60 violent offenders together in one dorm room with a rigorous schedule and constant supervision has been remarkably successful in reducing jailhouse violence. According to Sunny Schwartz, while the San Francisco jail system as a whole averages 6 fights a week, the RSVP dorm has had only 3 minor incidents in three years. Impressed, the notorious California state prison at Corcoran has just launched a pilot program based partly on Roads to Recovery.

In theory at least, educational and rehabilitative programs like those in Jails No. 7 and No. 8 have surprisingly wide support among corrections officials, particularly in the case of jails, where inmates are held mostly for short periods, unlike state and federal prisons. Ken Kerle, managing editor of *American Jails* magazine, has visited more than 700 jails around the country. Most jail administrators, he says, understand the value of drug and violence prevention programs like San Francisco's—but have a hard time convincing the public of their value.

Even Arizona's notorious Joe Arpaio, nicknamed "America's toughest sheriff" for such heavy-handed measures as housing prisoners in sweltering tents, putting them to work on chain gangs and forcing them to wear pink underwear, doesn't think San Francisco's approach is so off the mark. "The purpose of the jail is punishment," says Arpaio. "On the other hand, they should be given the opportunity to learn."

Ultimately, the survival of programs like San Francisco's may depend on the bottom line. The acupuncture alone costs $125,000 a year, with hundreds of thousands more going to other programs. The RSVP course is in the last year of a three-year, $600,000 grant from the Open Society Institute. If studies like Gilligan's show a dramatic drop in recidivism, the programs will pay for themselves or even save money by reducing crime, their proponents argue. But if the numbers aren't there, even in liberal San Francisco the public funds may run dry. . . .

For the latest in crime and justice news, visit the Talk Justice news feed at http://www.crimenews.info.

Source: Jeffrey Benner, "Politically Correct Punishment," Mother Jones News Service (MOJO Wire), March 16, 2000. Reprinted with permission.

Women and Jail

Although women comprise only 11.4% of the country's jail population, they are virtually the largest growth group in jails nationwide.[143] Jailed women face a number of special problems. Only 25.7% of the nation's jails report having a classification system specifically designed to evaluate female inmates,[144] and although many jurisdictions have plans "to build facilities geared to the female offender,"[145] not all jurisdictions today even provide separate housing areas for women. Educational levels are very low among jailed women, and fewer than half are high school graduates.[146] Drug abuse is another significant source of difficulty for jailed women. Over 30% of women who are admitted to jail have a substance-abuse problem at the time of admission, and in some parts of the country, that figure may be as high as 70%.[147]

Pregnancy is another problem. Nationally, 4% of female inmates are pregnant when they enter jail,[148] but in urban areas, as much as 10% of the female jail population is reported to be pregnant on any given day.[149] As a consequence, a few hundred children are born in jails each year. Not only are jailed mothers separated from their children, but they may have to pay for their support. Twelve percent of all jails in one study reported requiring employed female inmates to contribute to the support of their dependent children. Adding to the problem is the fact that substantive medical programs for female inmates, such as obstetrics and gynecological care, are often lacking. In planning future medical services for female inmates, some writers have advised jail administrators to expect to see an increasingly common kind of inmate: "an opiate-addicted female who is pregnant with no prior prenatal care having one or more sexually transmitted diseases, and fitting a high-risk category for AIDS (prostitution, IV drug use)."[150]

Female inmates are only half the story. Women working in corrections are the other. In one study, Linda Zupan, a member of the new generation of outstanding jail scholars, found that women made up 22% of the correctional officer force in jails across the nation.[151] The deployment of female personnel, however, was disproportionately skewed toward jobs in the lower ranks. Although 60% of all support staff (secretaries, cooks, and janitors) were women, only one in every ten chief administrators was female. Zupan explains this pattern by pointing to the "token-status" of female staff members in some of the nation's jails.[152] Even so, Zupan did find that female correctional employees were significantly committed to their careers and that the attitudes of male workers toward female coworkers in jails were generally positive. Zupan's study uncovered 626 jails in which over 50% of the correctional officer force consisted of women. On the opposite side of the coin, 954 of the nation's 3,316 jails operating at the time of the study had no female officers.[153] Zupan noted that "an obvious problem associated with the lack of female officers in jails housing females concerns the potential for abuse and exploitation of women inmates by male staff."[154]

Jails which do hire women generally accord them equal footing with male staffers. Although cross-gender privacy is a potential area of legal liability, few jails limit the supervisory areas which may be visited by female officers working in male facilities. In three-quarters of the jails studied by Zupan, female officers were assigned to supervise male housing areas. Only one in four jails which employed women restricted their access to unscreened shower and toilet facilities used by men or to other areas, such as sexual offender units.

The Growth of Jails

Jails have been called the "shame of the criminal justice system." Many are old, poorly funded, scantily staffed by underpaid and poorly trained employees, and given low priority in local budgets. By the end of the 1980s, many of our nation's jails had become seriously overcrowded, and court-ordered caps were sometimes placed on jail populations. One of the first such caps was imposed on the Harris County Jail in Houston, Texas, in 1990. In that year, the jail was forced to release 250 inmates after missing a deadline for reducing its resident population of 6,100 people.[155] A nationwide survey by the Bureau of Justice Statistics, undertaken around the same time, found that 46% of all jails had been built more than 25 years earlier, and of that percentage, over half were more than 50 years old.[156]

A 1983 national census revealed that jails were operating at 85% of their rated capacity (Table 12–1).[157] In 1990, however, the nation's jails were running at 104% of capacity, and new jails could be found on drawing boards and under construction across the country. By

> If you don't like the place, don't come here.
>
> —Maricopa County (Arizona) Sheriff Joe Arpaio, offering advice to inmates housed in his desert tent city

		JAIL FACTS		**TABLE 12–1**
	1983	**1988**	**1993**	**2000**
Number of jails	3,338	3,316	3,304	3,365
Number of jail inmates	223,551	343,569	459,804	621,149
Rated capacity of jails	261,556	339,949	475,224	677,787
Percentage of capacity occupied	85%	101%	97%	92%

Source: Allen J. Beck and Jennifer C. Karberg, *Prison and Jail Inmates at Midyear 2000* (Washington, D.C.: Bureau of Justice Statistics, 2001).

2000, jail capacity had increased substantially, and overall jail occupancy was reported at 92% of rated capacity. Some individual facilities, however, were still desperately overcrowded.[158] Jail jurisdictions with the largest average daily populations also reported the highest occupancy rates. At midyear 2000, occupancy was 103% of rated capacity in jail jurisdictions with an average daily population of 1,000 or more inmates, compared to 68% in those with fewer than 50 inmates.[159]

Overcrowded prisons have spilled over into jails. With the dawn of the warehousing era, some states began using jails instead of prisons for the confinement of convicted felons. In 2000, for example, approximately 63,000 inmates were being held in local jails because of overcrowding in state prisons.[160] The practice of giving jail sentences to offenders who are unable to make restitution, alimony, or child-support payments has added to jail occupancy and has made the local lockup, at least partially, a debtors' prison. Symptomatic of problems brought on by huge jail populations, the National Institute of Justice reported 328 suicides in jails across the nation during a recent year.[161] Jail deaths from all causes (which total about 930 annually) are shown in Figure 12–8.

Other factors conspire to keep jail populations high. They include the following:[162]

- The inability of jail inmates to make bond due to institutionalized bail-bond practices and lack of funding sources for indigent defendants

- Unnecessary delays between arrest and final case disposition

- Unnecessarily limited access to vital information about defendants which could be useful in facilitating court-ordered pretrial release

- The limited ability of the criminal justice system to handle cases expeditiously due to a lack of needed resources (judges, assistant prosecuting attorneys, and so on)

- Inappropriate attorney delays in moving cases through court

- Unproductive statutes requiring that specified nonviolent offenders be jailed (including mandatory pretrial jailing of those caught driving while intoxicated, minor drug offenders, second-offense shoplifters, and so on)

Some innovative jurisdictions have successfully contained the growth of jail populations by diverting arrestees to community-based programs. San Diego, California, for example, uses a privately operated detoxification reception program to divert many inebriates from the "drunk tank."[163] Officials in Galveston County, Texas, routinely divert mentally ill arrestees directly to a mental health facility.[164] Other areas use pretrial services and magistrates' offices, which are open 24 hours a day, for setting bail, making release possible. Learn more about jail overcrowding by reading **Library Extra! 12–5** at cjtoday.com.

Direct-Supervision Jails

Some authors have suggested that the problems found in many jails stem from "mismanagement, lack of fiscal support, heterogeneous inmate populations, overuse and misuse of

> We are the prisoners of the prisoners we have taken.
>
> —J. Clegg

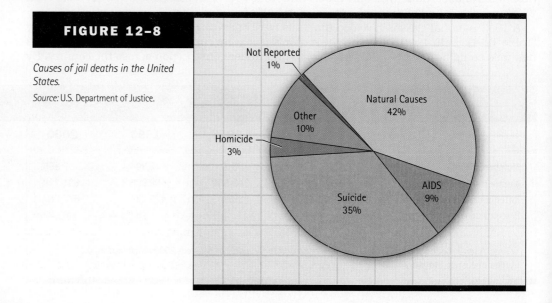

FIGURE 12–8

Causes of jail deaths in the United States.

Source: U.S. Department of Justice.

- Not Reported 1%
- Natural Causes 42%
- Other 10%
- Homicide 3%
- AIDS 9%
- Suicide 35%

detention, overemphasis on custodial goals, and political and public apathy."[165] Others propose that environmental and organizational elements inherent in traditional jail architecture and staffing have given rise to many difficulties.[166] Traditional jails, say these observers, were built upon the assumption that inmates are inherently violent and potentially destructive. They were constructed to give staff maximum control over inmates through the use of thick walls, bars, and other architectural barriers to the free movement of inmates. Such institutions, however, also limit the correctional staff's visibility and access to confinement areas. As a consequence, they tend to encourage just the kinds of inmate behavior that jails were meant to control. Today, efficient hallway patrols and expensive video technology help in overcoming the limits that old jail architecture places on supervision.

In an effort to solve many of the problems which dogged jails in the past, a new jail-management strategy emerged during the 1970s. Called **direct-supervision jail**, or podular/direct supervision (PDS) jail, this approach joined "podular/unit architecture with a participative, proactive management philosophy."[167] Often built in a system of "pods," or modular self-contained housing areas linked to one another, direct-supervision jails helped eliminate the old physical barriers that separated staff and inmates. Gone were the bars and the isolated, secure observation areas for officers. They were replaced by an open environment in which inmates and correctional personnel could mingle with relative freedom. In a number of such "new-generation" jails, large reinforced Plexiglas panels supplanted walls and served to separate activity areas, such as classrooms and dining halls, from one another. Soft furniture is the rule throughout such institutions, and individual rooms take the place of cells, allowing inmates at least a modicum of personal privacy. In today's direct-supervision jails, 16 to 46 inmates typically live in one pod, with correctional staffers present among the inmate population around the clock.

The first direct-supervision jail opened in the 1970s in Contra Costa County, California. This 386-bed facility became a model for the nation, and other new-generation jails soon opened in Las Vegas; Portland, Oregon; Reno; New York City; Bucks County, Pennsylvania; and Miami. The federal prison system opened PDS facilities in 1974 and 1975 in the metropolitan correctional centers of San Diego, New York, and Chicago.

Direct-supervision jails have been touted for their tendency to reduce inmate dissatisfaction and for their ability to deter rape and violence among the inmate population. By eliminating architectural barriers to staff-inmate interaction, direct-supervision facilities are said to place officers back in control of institutions. A number of studies have demonstrated the success of such jails at reducing the likelihood of inmate victimization. One such study, published in 1994, found that staff morale in direct-supervision jails was far higher than in traditional institutions, that inmates reported reduced stress levels, and that fewer inmate-on-inmate and inmate-on-staff assaults occurred.[168] Similarly, sexual assault, jail rape, suicide, and escape have all been found to occur far less frequently in direct-supervision facilities than in traditional institutions.[169] Significantly, new-generation jails appear to reduce substantially the number of lawsuits brought by inmates and to lower the incidence of adverse court-ordered judgments against jail administrators.

The most comprehensive study of direct-supervision jails to date, reported in 1995, found that 114 confinement facilities across the country could be classified as direct-supervision facilities.[170] The study, which attempted to survey all such jails, found that direct-supervision jails

■ Range in size from small jails with 24 inmates and 12 officers on staff to large facilities with 2,737 inmates and 600 correctional officers.

■ Average 591 inmates and 148 officers, with an inmate-to-officer ratio of 16.8 to 1 during a given shift.

■ Are podular in design, with an average of 47 inmates and one officer per pod at any given time.

■ Hold local, state, and federal prisoners. About 45% of the institutions surveyed held only local inmates, while the rest held mixed groups of inmates.

■ Varied by security level. The majority (about 59%) held mixed security levels, while 26% were maximum-security jails. About 13% described themselves as medium-security facilities, and another 2% were minimum-security.

■ Were usually unionized. About 70% of direct-supervision jails reported having unionized staffs.

direct-supervision jail

A temporary confinement facility that eliminates many of the traditional barriers between inmates and correctional staff. Physical barriers in direct-supervision jails are far less common than in traditional jails, allowing staff members the opportunity for greater interaction with, and control over, residents.

While the number of direct-supervision jails has grown rapidly, such facilities are not without their problems. In 1993, for example, the 238-bed Rensselaer County PDS jail in Troy, New York, experienced a disturbance that resulted in "a total loss of control," the removal of officers from the pods, and the escape of two inmates.[171] Somewhat later, the 700-bed San Joaquin County Jail in Stockton, California, experienced numerous problems, including the escape of seven inmates.

Some authors have recognized that new-generation jails are too frequently run by old-style managers and that correctional personnel sometimes lack the training needed to make the transition to the new style of supervision.[172] Others have suggested that managers of direct-supervision jails, especially mid-level managers, could benefit from clearer job descriptions and additional training.[173] In the words of one Canadian advocate of direct supervision, "Training becomes particularly critical in direct supervision jails where relationships are more immediate and are more complex."[174] Finally, those tasked with hiring have recommended that potential new staff members should be psychologically screened and that intensive use be made of preemployment interviews to determine the suitability of applicants for correctional officer positions in direct-supervision jails.[175]

Jails and the Future

In contrast to more visible issues confronting the justice system—such as the death penalty, gun control, the war on drugs, terrorism, and big-city gangs—jails have received relatively little attention from the media and have generally escaped close public scrutiny.[176] National efforts are under way, however, to improve the quality of jail life. Some changes involve adding crucial programs for inmates. An American Jail Association study of drug-treatment programs in jails, for example, found that "a small fraction (perhaps fewer than 10%) of inmates needing drug treatment actually receive these services."[177] Follow-up efforts were aimed at developing standards to guide jail administrators in increasing the availability of drug-treatment services to inmates.

Jail industries are another growing programmatic area. The best of them serve the community while training inmates in marketable skills.[178] In an exemplary effort to humanize its megajails, for example, the Los Angeles County Sheriff's Department opened an inmate telephone-answering service.[179] Many callers contact the sheriff's department daily, requesting information about the county's 22,000 jail inmates. These requests for information were becoming increasingly difficult to handle due to the growing fiscal constraints

Inside a direct-supervision jail. Inmates and officers can mingle in this Hillsborough County, New Hampshire, jail.

Rick Friedman, Black Star

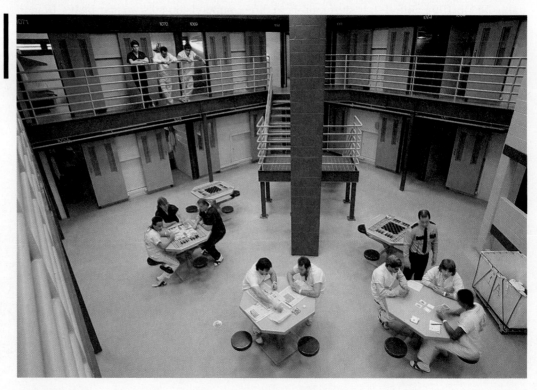

CJ Today Exhibit 12-4

[American Jail Association Code of Ethics for Jail Officers]

As an officer employed in a detention/correctional capacity, I swear (or affirm) to be a good citizen and a credit to my community, state, and nation at all times. I will abstain from all questionable behavior which might bring disrepute to the agency for which I work, my family, my community, and my associates. My lifestyle will be above and beyond reproach and I will constantly strive to set an example of a professional who performs his/her duties according to the laws of our country, state, and community and the policies, procedures, written and verbal orders, and regulations of the agency for which I work.

On the job I promise to:

Keep	The institution secure so as to safeguard my community and the lives of the staff, inmates, and visitors on the premises.
Work	With each individual firmly and fairly without regard to rank, status, or condition.
Maintain	A positive demeanor when confronted with stressful situations of scorn, ridicule, danger, and/or chaos.
Report	Either in writing or by word of mouth to the proper authorities those things which should be reported, and keep silent about matters which are to remain confidential according to the laws and rules of the agency and government.
Manage	And supervise the inmates in an evenhanded and courteous manner.

Refrain	At all times from becoming personally involved in the lives of the inmates and their families.
Treat	All visitors to the jail with politeness and respect and do my utmost to ensure that they observe the jail regulations.
Take	Advantage of all education and training opportunities designed to assist me to become a more competent officer.
Communicate	With people in or outside of the jail, whether by phone, written word, or word of mouth, in such a way so as not to reflect in a negative manner upon my agency.
Contribute	To a jail environment which will keep the inmate involved in activities designed to improve his/her attitude and character.
Support	All activities of a professional nature through membership and participation that will continue to elevate the status of those who operate our nation's jails.

Do my best through word and deed to present an image to the public at large of a jail professional, committed to progress for an improved and enlightened criminal justice system.

Source: American Jail Association, *Code of Ethics for Jail Officers,* as adopted January 10, 1991 (Hagerstown, MD: AJA, 1991). Reprinted with permission.

facing local government. To handle the huge number of calls effectively without tying up sworn law enforcement personnel, the department began using inmates specially trained to handle incoming calls. Eighty inmates were assigned to the project, with groups of different sizes covering shifts throughout the day. Each inmate staffer went through a training program to learn proper telephone procedures and how to run computer terminals containing routine data on the department's inmates. The new system now handles 4,000 telephone inquiries a day. The time needed to answer a call and provide information has dropped from 30 minutes under the old system to a remarkable 10 seconds today.

Jail boot camps, like the one run by the Harris County, Texas, probation department, are also popular. Jail boot camps give offenders who are sentenced to probationary terms a taste of confinement and the rigors of life behind bars. The Harris County Courts Regimented Intensive Probation Program (CRIPP) facility began operation in 1991 and is located in Humble, Texas. Separate CRIPP programs are run for about 400 male and 50 female probationers.[180] The most recent comprehensive study of jail boot camps found only 10 such jail-based programs in the country,[181] although current numbers are probably higher.

Capturing much recent attention are **regional jails**—that is, jails that are built and run using the combined resources of a variety of local jurisdictions and that have begun to replace smaller and often antiquated local jails in at least a few locations. One example of a regional jail is the Western Tidewater Regional Jail, serving the cities of Suffolk and Franklin and the county of Isle of Wright in Virginia.[182] Regional jails, which are just beginning to come into their own, may develop quickly in Virginia, where the state, recognizing

regional jail

A jail that is built and run using the combined resources of a variety of local jurisdictions.

the economies of consolidation, offers to reimburse localities up to 50% of the cost of building regional jails.

One final element in the unfolding saga of jail development should be mentioned: the emergence of state jail standards. Thirty-two states have set standards for municipal and county jails.[183] In 25 states, those standards are mandatory. The purpose of jail standards is to identify some basic minimum level of conditions necessary for inmate health and safety. On the national level, the Commission on Accreditation for Corrections, operated jointly by the American Correctional Association and the federal government, has developed its own set of jail standards,[184] as has the National Sheriff's Association. Both sets of standards are designed to ensure a minimal level of comfort and safety in local lockups. Increased standards, though, are costly. Local jurisdictions, already hard-pressed to meet other budgetary demands, will probably be slow to upgrade their jails to meet such external guidelines unless forced to do so. In a study of 61 jails which was designed to test compliance with National Sheriff's Association guidelines, Ken Kerle discovered that in many standards areas—especially those of tool control, armory planning, community resources, release preparation, and riot planning—the majority of jails were badly out of compliance.[185] Lack of a written plan was the most commonly cited reason for failing to meet the standards.

In what may be the best set of recommendations for the development of jails for the future, Joel A. Thompson and G. Larry Mays suggest that (1) states should provide financial aid or incentives to local governments for jail construction and renovation, (2) all states must develop mandatory jail standards, (3) mandatory jail inspections should become commonplace in the enforcement of standards, (4) citizens should be educated about the function and significance of jails to increase their willingness to fund new jail construction, (5) all jails must have written policies and procedures to be used in training and to serve as a basis for a defense against lawsuits, and (6) "communities should explore alternatives to incarceration [because] . . . many jail detainees are not threats to society and should not occupy scarce and expensive cell space."[186] Learn more about jails by visiting the American Jail Association via **Web Extra! 12–4** at cjtoday.com.

Private Prisons

Throughout our nation's history, state-run prison systems have contracted with private industries for food, psychological testing, training, and recreational and other services, and it is estimated that more than three dozen states today rely on private businesses to serve a variety of correctional needs. It was only logical, therefore, that states would at some point turn to private industry for the provision of prison space. Beginning in the early 1980s, that's exactly what they did. Although the **privatization** movement was slow to catch on, it has since grown at a rapid pace. In 1986, only 2,620 prisoners could be found in privately run confinement facilities.[187] But by 2001, privately operated correctional facilities serving as prisons and jails held over 87,000 state and federal prisoners across 31 states and the District of Columbia.[188] **Private prisons** held 5.8% of all state prisoners and 10.7% of federal prisoners at the start of 2001. One source says that the growth rate of the private prison industry has been around 35% annually[189]—comparable to the highest growth rates anywhere in the corporate sector.

According to a 2001 report by the Bureau of Justice Assistance,[190]

■ Worldwide, there are 184 privately operated correctional facilities, which hold 132,346 inmates.

■ Within the United States, a total of 158 private correctional facilities are operating in 31 states, Puerto Rico, and the District of Columbia.

■ Most private correctional facilities tend to be concentrated in the southern and western United States.

■ Texas has the most private correctional facilities (43), followed by California (24), Florida (10), and Colorado (9).

■ Another 26 private facilities operate in three other countries, with Australia (12) and the United Kingdom (10) topping the list.

■ Total revenues allocated to private prisons and jails in the United States are estimated at $1 billion.

■ Despite rapid growth in the number of private correctional facilities, they represent only a small share of the entire correctional facilities market. With jail and prison popula-

privatization

The movement toward the wider use of private prisons.

private prison

A correctional institution operated by a private firm on behalf of a local or state government.

CJ Futures

[Jails and the Future]

A number of trends are beginning to emerge as America's jails meet the needs of the twenty-first century. Among them are these:

■ A shift away from traditional, publicly run facilities to jails that are operated by private corporations under contract with local government. More information on the privatization of prisons and jails is provided in this chapter.

■ An increase in the proportion of inmates who are expected to pay for at least a portion of the expenses associated with their incarceration. In 1996, for example, pretrial inmates in the Broward County, Florida, jail system began paying a $2 per day fee for housing and meals. Charges are deducted from inmates' commissary funds, which are contributed by the inmates themselves or by family members. Inmates who feel they are unable to pay the fee are required to petition jail administrators and to demonstrate why they should not be required to pay.

■ The growing use of computer-based inmate information systems that are integrated with networks used for the administration of court schedules, for docket monitoring, and for coordination with other criminal justice agencies. One jail consultant has gone so far as to claim that, as a result of efficient and integrated information management systems, "paperwork will [soon] be a thing of the past."[1]

■ A movement toward the professionalization of jail facilities, made possible through growing opportunities for accreditation. Accreditation programs, such as those offered through the American Correctional Association, the Commission on Accreditation for Law Enforcement Agencies, and the National Commission on Correctional Health Care, are already helping shield jail administrators and local governments from the threat of lawsuits by demonstrating adherence to professional standards.

■ A movement toward the increased professionalization of jail personnel, made possible by certification programs such as the new Jail Manager Certification Program operated by the American Jail Association (AJA). Certified Jail Manager status has been available since 1997.

■ A changing public climate that may soon shift away from the "get tough" policies of the past decade toward a more pragmatic emphasis on the needs of both inmates and administrators. Inmate needs in the areas of mental health counseling, suicide prevention, and opportunities for meaningful employment will be met in an effort to facilitate institutional administration.

■ A greater use of direct-supervision jails, resulting in fewer internal problems and easier administration. The increased use of direct-supervision jails will heighten both inmate and staff morale in most locations.

■ A growing use of inmate labor, as counties, communities, the non-profit sector, and corporations begin to more fully recognize the advantages to be gained from the meaningful employment of inmates. As a consequence, more inmates will work, and those who do will be involved in an ever-widening sphere of activities. The increase in inmate labor will lead to a widening of partnerships among jails, their administrators, and other community groups. Corporate employers, for example, will begin to operate more and more training programs in jails with the goal of increasing workforce efficiency.

■ A greater use of research in the field of jail operations, which will lead to better informed and more effective programs and strategies. Research showing that a greater number of female officers means fewer assaults overall, for example, should lead to the hiring of more women in the corrections field.

Sources: Ron Carroll, "Jails and the Criminal Justice System in the Twenty-first Century," *American Jails* (March/April 1997), pp. 26–31; Susan W. McCampbell, "The Paying Prisoner," *American Jails* (March/April 1997), pp. 37–43; Cindy Malm, "AJA Jail Manager Certification Program," *American Jails* (March/April 1997), p. 99; Rod Miller, "Inmate Labor in the 21st Century," *American Jails* (March/April 1997), pp. 45–49; and Joseph R. Rowan, "Corrections in the 21st Century," *American Jails* (March/April 1997), pp. 32–36.

[1] Ron Carroll, "Jails and the Criminal Justice System in the Twenty-first Century," *American Jails* (March/April 1997), p. 31.

tions totaling approximately 1.7 million in the United States, the estimated 116,626-bed capacity of private correctional facilities makes up less than 7% of the U.S. market.

■ The number of privatized prisons is likely to increase, but not at the pace exhibited during the past decade.

■ The number of companies operating privatized prisons is likely to decrease as competition and the costs of doing business increase, forcing a consolidation of firms within the industry.

■ It is unlikely that privatized prisons will develop a strong market in the high-security market due to the recent flurry of well-publicized disturbances. However, important inroads can be expected for the private sector within low-security medical, mental health, and geriatric inmate populations.

Read the entire Bureau of Justice Assistance privatization report at **Library Extra! 12–6** on cjtoday.com.

Today's privately run prisons are operated by Cornell Corrections, Corrections Corporation of America (CCA), Correctional Services Corporation (CSC), Wackenhut Corrections Corporation, and numerous other smaller companies. Most states that use private firms to supplement their prison resources contract with such companies to provide a full range of custodial and other correctional services. State correctional administrators use private companies to reduce overcrowding, lower operating expenses, and avoid lawsuits targeted at state officials and employees.[191] But some studies have shown that private prisons may not bring the kinds of cost savings that had been anticipated.[192] A 1996 study by the U.S. General Accounting Office,[193] for example, found "neither cost savings nor substantial differences in the quality of services" between private and publicly run prisons.[194] Similar findings emerged in a 2001 report by the Bureau of Justice Assistance. That report, entitled *Emerging Issues on Privatized Prisons*, found that "private prisons offer only modest cost savings, which are basically a result of moderate reductions in staffing patterns, fringe benefits, and other labor-related costs."[195]

Many hurdles remain before the privatization movement can effectively provide large-scale custodial supervision. One of the most significant barriers to privatization lies in the fact that some states have old laws which prohibit private involvement in correctional management. Other practical hurdles exist as well. States which do contract with private firms may face the specter of strikes by guards who do not come under state laws restricting the ability of employees to strike. Moreover, since responsibility for the protection of inmate rights still lies with the state, their liability will not transfer to private corrections.[196] In today's legal climate, it is unclear whether a state can shield itself or its employees through private prison contracting, but it would appear that such shielding is unlikely to be recognized by the courts. To limit their own liability, states will probably have to oversee private operations as well as set standards for training and custody. In 1997 in the case of *Richardson* v. *McKnight*,[197] the U.S. Supreme Court made it clear that prison guards employed by a private firm are not entitled to qualified immunity from suits by prisoners charging a violation of Section 1983 of Title 42 of the U.S. Code. (See Chapter 6 for more information on 1983 lawsuits.) In the words of the Court, "While government employed prison guards may have enjoyed a kind of immunity defense arising out of their status as public employees at common law . . . [t]here is no conclusive evi-

The Corrections Corporation of America's Houston Processing Center, one of a growing number of private prison facilities across the country. Private prisons may be the way of the future.

Brett Coomer, AP/Wide World Photos

CJ Today Exhibit 12-5

[Arguments for and Against
the Privatization of Prisons]

Reasons to Privatize

1. Private operators can provide construction financing options that allow the government to pay only for capacity as needed in lieu of assuming long-term debt.
2. Private companies offer state-of-the-art correctional facility designs that are efficient to operate and that are based upon cost-benefit considerations.
3. Private operators typically design and construct a new correctional facility in half the time it takes to build a comparable government project.
4. Private companies provide government with the convenience and accountability of one entity for all compliance issues.
5. Private companies can mobilize rapidly and specialize in unique facility missions.
6. Private companies provide economic development opportunities by hiring locally and purchasing locally.
7. Government can reduce or share its liability exposure by contracting with private corrections companies.
8. Government can retain flexibility by limiting the contract's duration and by specifying the facility's mission.
9. Adding alternative service providers injects competition among both public and private organizations.

Reasons Not to Privatize

1. There are certain responsibilities that only the government should meet, such as public safety and environmental protection. The government has legal, political, and moral obligations to provide incarceration. Constitutional issues underlie both public and private corrections and involve deprivation of liberty, discipline, and preservation of the constitutional rights of inmates. Related issues include use of force, equitable hiring practices, and segregation.
2. Few private companies are available from which to choose.
3. Private operators may be inexperienced with key corrections issues.
4. A private operator may become a monopoly through political ingratiation, favoritism, and so on.
5. Government may lose the capability to perform the corrections function over time.
6. The profit motive will inhibit the proper performance of corrections duties. Private companies have financial incentives to cut corners.
7. The procurement process is slow, inefficient, and open to risks.
8. Creating a good, clear contract is a daunting task.
9. The lack of enforcement remedies in contracts leaves only termination or lawsuits as recourse.

Source: Dennis Cunningham, "Public Strategies for Private Prisons." Paper presented at the Private Prison Workshop, January 29–30, 1999, at the Institute on Criminal Justice, University of Minnesota Law School.

dence of an historical tradition of immunity for private parties carrying out these functions."[198]

Perhaps the most serious legal issues confront states that contract to hold inmates outside of their own jurisdiction. In 1996, for example, two inmates escaped from a 240-man sex-offender unit run by Corrections Corporation of America under contract with the state of Oregon. Problems immediately arose because the CCA unit was located near Houston, Texas—not in Oregon, where the men had originally been sentenced to confinement. Following the escape, Texas officials were unsure whether they even had arrest power over the former prisoners, since they had not committed any crimes in Texas. Moreover, while prison escape is a crime under Texas law, the law only applies to state-run facilities, not to private facilities where correctional personnel are not employed by the state or empowered in any official capacity by state law. Harris County (Texas) Prosecutor John Holmes explained the situation this way: "They have not committed the offense of escape under Texas law . . . and the only reason at all that they're subject to being arrested and were arrested was because during their leaving the facility, they assaulted a guard and took his motor vehicle. That we can charge them with and have."[199]

Opponents of the movement toward privatization cite these and many other issues. They claim that, aside from legal concerns, cost reductions via the use of private facilities can only be achieved by lowering standards. They fear a return to the inhumane conditions of early jails, as private firms seek to turn prisons into profit-making operations. For states which do choose to contract with private firms, the National Institute of Justice (NIJ) recommends a "regular and systematic sampling" of former inmates to appraise prison conditions, as well as annual on-site inspections of each privately run institution. State personnel serving as monitors should be stationed in large facilities, says NIJ, and a "meticulous review" of all services should be conducted prior to the contract renewal date.[200] You can learn more about prison privatization via **Web Extra! 12–5** at cjtoday.com.

Summary

Prisons are long-term secure confinement facilities in which convicted offenders serve time as punishment for breaking the law. Jails, in contrast, are short-term confinement facilities which were originally intended to hold suspects following arrest and pending trial. Differences between the two types of institutions have begun to blur, however, as large and medium-size jails across the country are increasingly being called upon to house offenders who have been convicted of relatively minor crimes and to accommodate a portion of our country's overflowing prison population.

Today's overcrowded prisons are largely the result of historical efforts to humanize the treatment of offenders. "Doing time for crime" is our modern answer to the corporal punishments of centuries past. Even so, contemporary corrections is far from a panacea, and questions remain about the conditions of imprisonment in today's correctional facilities. Many prisons are dangerously overcrowded, and new ones are expensive to build. The emphasis upon security, which is so characteristic of correctional staff members and prison administrators, leaves little room for capable treatment programs. Moreover, an end to overcrowding is nowhere in sight, and a new just deserts philosophy strongly influences today's correctional policy. The just deserts philosophy is characterized by a "get tough" attitude which continues to swell prison populations even as it reduces opportunities for change among individual inmates. It is a highly pragmatic philosophy, based as it is upon studies demonstrating the clear likelihood of recidivism among correctional clients and upon a strong belief that nothing works to rehabilitate criminal offenders.

As a result of all these considerations, today's imprisonment practices rest upon a policy of frustration. Prisons exist in a kind of limbo, continuing their role as warehouses for the untrusted and the unreformable. The return of prison industries, heightened interest in efficient technologies of secure imprisonment, and court-ordered reforms are all signs that society has given up any hope of successful large-scale reformation among inmate populations.

> We spend $60,000 building a prison cell, another $35,000 a year to keep that inmate. They have central heating and air conditioning. At the same time we spend less than $4,000 on each school student. And many of them don't have air-conditioned or centrally heated schools. Let's put the money in education. That's the only answer to crime.
>
> —Louisiana Congressman Cleo Fields

Discussion Questions

1. Trace the historical development of imprisonment, beginning with the Pennsylvania system. In what ways has correctional practice in America changed over time? What changes do you predict for the future?
2. Would a return to physical punishments and public humiliation be effective deterrents to crime in today's world? Explain.
3. Describe your vision of the future of prison industry. On what do you base your predictions?
4. What solutions, if any, do you see to the present overcrowded conditions of many prison systems? How might changes in the law help ease overcrowding? Are such changes a workable strategy? Explain.
5. Explain the pros and cons of the present just deserts model of corrections. Do you believe that new rehabilitative models will be developed which will make just deserts a thing of the past? If so, on what will they be based?
6. What is the role of private prisons today? What will be the state of private prisons two or three decades from now?

To participate in an online discussion on these topics and others, go to the Global Town Meeting electronic message board for Chapter 12 on the *Criminal Justice Today* Companion Website at cjtoday.com.

Web Quest!

Visit the Corrections Connection on the World Wide Web (http://www.corrections.com). What are some of the many features available at this site?

Explore the Legal Issues bulletin board available at the Corrections Connection to learn about the latest legal issues of concern to corrections professionals. What are some of those issues?

Participate in one of the Corrections Connections chat rooms available at the site. (The "Corrections Lobby" is often a good place to find an ongoing chat.) What topics are being discussed? If no one is in the chat room when you enter, visit the Message Boards, and list the most recent topics being discussed. Submit this information to your instructor if asked to do so.

To complete this Web Quest! online, go to the Web Quest! module in Chapter 12 of the *Criminal Justice Today* Companion Website at cjtoday.com.

Library Extras!

Library Extra! 12–1 *Prisoners in 2000* (BJS, 2001).
Library Extra! 12–2 *About the Federal Bureau of Prisons* (BOP, 2001).
Library Extra! 12–3 *The State of the Federal Bureau of Prisons* (BOP, 2001).
Library Extra! 12–4 *Census of Jails* (BJS, latest volume).
Library Extra! 12–5 *A Second Look at Alleviating Jail Crowding* (BJA, 2000).
Library Extra! 12–6 *Emerging Issues on Privatized Prisons* (BJA, 2001).

To explore these resources online, go to the Library Extras! area of the *Criminal Justice Today* Companion Website at cjtoday.com. You should also check the author's "Late Picks" online for newly released documents and updated Library Extras! You can find Late Picks at http://cjtoday.com/latepicks.htm.

Marginal Note

i. Bureau of Justice Statistics, *Prisoners in 1998* (Washington, D.C.: BJS, 1999), p. 7.

Notes

1. As cited in Gail S. Funke, *National Conference on Prison Industries: Discussions and Recommendations* (Washington, D.C.: U.S. Government Printing Office, 1986), p. 23.
2. Camden Pelham, *Chronicles of Crime: A Series of Memoirs and Anecdotes of Notorious Characters* (London: T. Miles, 1887), pp. 28–30.
3. This section owes much to Harry Elmer Barnes and Negley K. Teeters, *New Horizons in Criminology,* 3d ed. (Englewood Cliffs, NJ: Prentice Hall, 1959).
4. Ibid., p. 290.
5. See Jack Elliott, Jr., "Prison or Paddle," Associated Press wire service, February 8, 1995.
6. Barnes and Teeters, *New Horizons in Criminology,* p. 292.
7. Ibid.
8. Ibid., p. 293.
9. Arthur Evans Wood and John Barker Waite, *Crime and Its Treatment: Social and Legal Aspects of Criminology* (New York: American Book Company, 1941), p. 488.
10. John Howard, *State of Prisons* (London, 1777; reprint, New York: E. P. Dutton, 1929).
11. Although some writers hold that the Quakers originated the concept of solitary confinement for prisoners, there is evidence that the practice already existed in England prior to 1789. John Howard, for example, described solitary confinement in use at Reading Bridewell in the 1780s.
12. Vergil L. Williams, *Dictionary of American Penology: An Introduction* (Westport, CT: Greenwood, 1979), p. 200.
13. Barnes and Teeters, *New Horizons in Criminology,* p. 348.
14. Williams, *Dictionary of American Penology,* p. 29.
15. With regard to cost, supporters of the Pennsylvania system argued that it was actually less expensive than the Auburn style of imprisonment because it led more quickly to reformation.
16. Williams, *Dictionary of American Penology,* p. 30.

17. Gustave de Beaumont and Alexis de Tocqueville, *On the Penitentiary System in the United States, and Its Application in France* (Philadelphia: Carey, Lea and Blanchard, 1833).

18. As cited in Barnes and Teeters, *New Horizons in Criminology,* p. 418.

19. Frank Schmalleger, *A History of Corrections: Emerging Ideologies and Practices* (Bristol, IN: Wyndham Hall, 1986), p. 44.

20. Barnes and Teeters, *New Horizons in Criminology,* p. 428.

21. Ibid.

22. Ibid.

23. Wood and Waite, *Crime and Its Treatment,* p. 555, citing U.S. Bureau of Labor statistics.

24. See North Carolina Department of Corrections, Correction Enterprises website at http://www.doc.state.nc.us/eprise. Accessed March 2, 2002.

25. See U.S. Department of Justice, Federal Prison Industries, Inc. website at http://www.unicor.gov.

26. Robert Mintz, "Federal Prison Industry—The Green Monster, Part One: History and Background," *Crime and Social Justice,* Vol. 6 (fall/winter 1976), pp. 41–48.

27. William G. Saylor and Gerald G. Gaes, "PREP Study Links UNICOR Work Experience with Successful Post-Release Outcome," *Corrections Compendium* (October 1994), pp. 5–6, 8.

28. Criminal Justice Associates, *Private Sector Involvement in Prison-Based Businesses: A National Assessment* (Washington, D.C.: U.S. Government Printing Office, 1985). See also National Institute of Justice, *Corrections and the Private Sector* (Washington, D.C.: U.S. Government Printing Office, 1985).

29. See "Oregon Begins to Implement Full Employment for Inmates," *Criminal Justice Newsletter,* March 15, 1995, pp. 1–2.

30. Oral History Interview with Honorable Warren E. Burger, Washington, D.C., August 31, 1994 (Washington, D.C.: Bureau of Prison Archives, 1994).

31. Barnes and Teeters, *New Horizons in Criminology,* p. 355.

32. Ibid., p. 381.

33. Ibid., p. 357.

34. Ibid., p. 359.

35. Williams, *Dictionary of American Penology,* p. 90.

36. Ibid., p. 225.

37. Ibid., p. 64.

38. Ibid., p. 227.

39. Donal E. J. MacNamara, "Medical Model in Corrections: Requiescat in Pace," in Fred Montanino, ed., *Incarceration: The Sociology of Imprisonment* (Beverly Hills, CA: Sage, 1978).

40. For a description of the community-based format in its heyday, see Andrew T. Scull, *Decarceration: Community Treatment and the Deviant—A Radical View* (Englewood Cliffs, NJ: Prentice Hall, 1977).

41. Ibid., p. 51.

42. Williams, *Dictionary of American Penology,* p. 45.

43. Ibid.

44. Clemens Bartollas, *Introduction to Corrections* (New York: Harper and Row, 1981), pp. 166–167.

45. The Act also established home furloughs and community treatment centers.

46. Williams, *Dictionary of American Penology,* p. 48.

47. National Advisory Commission on Criminal Justice Standards and Goals, Standard 2.17, part 2c.

48. *Recidivism* can be defined in various ways according to the purpose the term is intended to serve in a particular study or report. *Recidivism* is usually defined as rearrest (versus reconviction) and generally includes a time span of five years, although some Bureau of Justice Statistics studies have used six years, and other studies one or two years, as definitional criteria.

49. Various advocates of the just deserts, or justice, model can be identified. For a detailed description of rehabilitation and just deserts, see Michael A. Pizzi, Jr., "The Medical Model and the 100 Years War," *Law Enforcement News,* July 7, 1986, pp. 8, 13; and MacNamara, "Medical Model in Corrections."

50. Bureau of Justice Statistics, *Annual Report, 1987* (Washington, D.C.: Bureau of Justice Statistics, 1988), p. 70.

51. Ibid.

52. Ibid.

53. Lawrence Greenfeld, *Examining Recidivism: BJS Special Report* (Washington, D.C.: U.S. Government Printing Office, 1985).

54. R. Martinson, "What Works: Questions and Answers about Prison Reform," *Public Interest,* No. 35 (1974), pp. 22–54. See also Douglas Lipton, Robert M. Martinson, and Judith Wilkes, *The Effectiveness of Correctional Treatment: A Survey of Treatment Evaluation Studies* (New York: Praeger, 1975).

55. L. Sechrest, S. White, and E. Brown, eds., *The Rehabilitation of Criminal Offenders: Problems and Prospects* (Washington, D.C.: National Academy of Sciences, 1979).

56. U.S. Department of Justice, *Office of Justice Programs Fiscal Year 2000 Program Plan: Resources for the Field* (Washington, D.C.: Office of Juvenile Justice and Delinquency Prevention, 1999).

57. Timothy A. Hughes, Doris James Wilson, and Allen J. Beck, *Trends in State Parole, 1990–2000* (Washington, D.C.: Bureau of Justice Statistics, 2001).

58. Lynn S. Branham, *The Use of Incarceration in the United States: A Look at the Present and the Future* (Washington, D.C.: American Bar Association, 1992).

59. "Reliance on Prisons Is Costly but Ineffective, ABA Panel Says," *Criminal Justice Newsletter,* April 15, 1992, p. 7.

60. See Kevin Muscoreil, "New York's Rockefeller Drug Laws," *The Razor Wire* (April/May 1998). Web posted at http://www.november.org/0704.html. Accessed January 5, 2002.

61. Aaron D. Wilson, "Rockefeller Drug Laws Information Sheet," Partnership for Responsible Drug Information website. Web posted at http://www.prdi.org/rocklawfact.html. Accessed January 30, 2002.

62. "Governor Pataki Calls for Major Reform of New York's Rockefeller Drug Laws in State of the State Address," Lindesmith Center–Drug Policy Foundation press release, January 4, 2001. Web posted at http://www.lindesmith.org/news/pr-january01-01x.html. Accessed March 2, 2002.

63. For details about the two proposals, see "The Rockefeller Drug Laws." Web posted at http://www.lindesmith.org/library/focal18.html. Accessed March 15, 2002.

64. L. A. Greenfield, *Prisoners in 1987* (Washington, D.C.: Bureau of Justice Statistics, 1988).

65. Ibid.; and Allen J. Beck and Paige M. Harrison, *Prisoners in 2000* (Washington, D.C.: Bureau of Justice Statistics, 2001). Figures as of January 1 of each year.

66. *Correctional Populations in the United States, 1990* (Washington, D.C.: Bureau of Justice Statistics, 1992).

67. Beck and Harrison, *Prisoners in 2000*.

68. *Criminal Justice Newsletter*, February 3, 1992, p. 8.

69. American Correctional Association, *Vital Statistics in Corrections* (Laurel, MD: ACA, 2000).

70. Beck and Harrison, *Prisoners in 2000*.

71. Adapted from Bureau of Justice Statistics, *Report to the Nation on Crime and Justice*, 2d ed. (Washington, D.C.: U.S. Government Printing Office, 1988), p. 108.

72. *Rhodes* v. *Chapman*, 452 U.S. 337 (1981).

73. James Lieber, "The American Prison: A Tinderbox," *New York Times Magazine*, March 8, 1981.

74. Associated Press wire service, July 4, 1988, citing James K. Stewart, Director of the National Institute of Justice.

75. Wisconsin Policy Research Institute, *Crime and Punishment in Wisconsin* (Milwaukee: Wisconsin Policy Research Institute, 1990).

76. Fox Butterfield, no headline, *New York Times* wire service, April 16, 1997, citing Office of Justice Programs, *Preventing Crime: What Works, What Doesn't, What's Promising* (Washington, D.C.: U.S. Department of Justice, 1997).

77. Although many other states require inmates to work on road maintenance, and though the inmates are typically supervised by armed guards, Alabama became the first state in modern times to shackle prisoners.

78. See "Back on the Chain Gang: Florida Becomes Third State to Resurrect Forced Labor," Associated Press wire service, November 22, 1995.

79. Florida Department of Corrections, *Corrections in Florida: 1998 Opinion Survey*. Web posted at http://www.dc.state.fl.us/pub/survey/index.html. Accessed January 24, 2001.

80. Lori Sharn and Shannon Tangonan, "Chain Gangs Back in Alabama," *USA Today*, May 4, 1995, p. 3A.

81. Ibid.

82. See Debra L. Dailey, *Summary of the 1998 Annual Conference of the National Association of Sentencing Commissions*. Web posted at http://www.ussc.gov/states/dailefsr.pdf. Accessed October 30, 2001.

83. Peter Baker, "Allen Crime Plan Ends Parole; Expensive Va. Proposal Would Strain Budget, Require More Prisons," *Washington Post* wire service, August 17, 1994.

84. "U.S. House Votes to Make Life Tougher for Prisoners," Reuters wire service, February 10, 1995.

85. "The Extinction of Inmate Privileges," *Corrections Compendium* (June 1995), p. 5.

86. Ibid.

87. Brandon K. Applegate, "Penal Austerity: Perceived Utility, Desert, and Public Attitudes toward Prison Amenities," *American Journal of Criminal Justice*, Vol. 25, No. 2 (2001), pp. 253–268.

88. The state of Washington is generally credited with having been the first state to pass a three-strikes law by voter initiative (in 1993).

89. For a good overview of the topic, see David Shichor and Dale K. Sechrest, *Three Strikes and You're Out: Vengeance as Public Policy* (Thousand Oaks, CA: Sage, 1996).

90. David S. Broder, "When Tough Isn't Smart," *Washington Post* wire service, March 24, 1994.

91. "The Klaas Case and the Crime Bill," *Washington Post* wire service, February 21, 1994.

92. Bruce Smith, "Crime Solutions," Associated Press wire service, January 11, 1995.

93. Amanda Wunder, "Corrections Systems Must Bear the Burden of New Legislation," *Corrections Compendium* (March 1995).

94. Campaign for an Effective Crime Policy, *The Impact of Three Strikes and You're Out Laws: What Have We Learned?* (Washington, D.C.: Campaign for an Effective Crime Policy, 1997).

95. Quinlan is now President of Corrections Corporation of America.

96. David Lawsky, "Prison Wardens Decry Overcrowding, Survey Says," Reuters wire service, December 21, 1994.

97. D. Greenberg, "The Incapacitative Effect of Imprisonment, Some Estimates," *Law and Society Review*, Vol. 9 (1975), pp. 541–580. See also Jacqueline Cohen, "Incapacitating Criminals: Recent Research Findings," National Institute of Justice, *Research in Brief* (December 1983).

98. For information on identifying dangerous repeat offenders, see M. Chaiken and J. Chaiken, "Selecting Career Criminals for Priority Prosecution," final report (Cambridge, MA: Abt Associates, 1987).

99. J. Monahan, *Predicting Violent Behavior: An Assessment of Clinical Techniques* (Beverly Hills, CA: Sage, 1981).

100. S. Van Dine, J. P. Conrad, and S. Dinitz, *Restraining the Wicked: The Incapacitation of the Dangerous Offender* (Lexington, MA: Lexington Books, 1979).

101. Paul Gendreau, Tracy Little, and Claire Goggin, "A Meta-Analysis of the Predictors of Adult Offender Recidivism: What Works!" *Criminology*, Vol. 34, No. 4 (November 1996), pp. 575–607.

102. *Lynce* v. *Mathis*, 519 U.S. 443 (1997).

103. "Florida Releases Prisoners, Issues Warnings to Victims," Associated Press wire service, March 12, 1997.

104. Beck and Harrison, *Prisoners in 2000*.

105. Ibid.

106. Ibid.

107. Ibid.

108. Ibid.

109. Ibid.

110. Ibid.

111. Bureau of Justice Statistics, *National Corrections Reporting Program, 1998* (Ann Arbor, MI: Interuniversity Consortium for Political and Social Research, 2001).

112. *Prisoners in 2000*.

113. Ibid.

114. American Correctional Association, "Correctional Officers in Adult Systems," in *Vital Statistics in Corrections* (Laurel, MD: ACA, 2000).

115. Ibid.

116. Ibid.

117. Ibid. "Other" minorities round out the percentages to a total of 100%.

118. Criminal Justice Institute, *The 2000 Corrections Yearbook: Adult Corrections* (Middletown, CT: Criminal Justice Institute, 2001); and e-mail correspondence with Susan Allison, Federal Bureau of Prisons, October 29, 2001.

119. Robert M. Carter, Richard A. McGee, and E. Kim Nelson, *Corrections in America* (Philadelphia: J. B. Lippincott, 1975), pp. 122–123.

120. George Camp and Camille Camp, "Stopping Escapes: Perimeter Security," *Prison Construction Bulletin* (Washington, D.C.: National Institute of Justice, 1987).

121. Adapted from G. A. Grizzle and A. D. Witte, "Efficiency in Collections Agencies," in Gordon P. Whitaker and

Charles D. Phillips, *Evaluating the Performance of Criminal Justice Agencies* (Washington, D.C.: NIJ, 1983).

122. U.S. Bureau of Prisons, *Facilities*. Web posted at http://www.bop.gov/map.html. Accessed February 2, 2002.

123. Some of the information in this section is derived from Federal Bureau of Prisons, *About the Federal Bureau of Prisons* (Washington, D.C.: BOP, 2001).

124. An older system, in which the terms *Level 1, Level 2,* and so on were used, was abandoned around 1990 and was officially replaced with the terminology used here.

125. Most of the information in this section comes from telephone conversations with and faxed information from the Federal Bureau of Prisons, August 25, 1995.

126. For additional information, see Dennis Cauchon, "The Alcatraz of the Rockies," *USA Today,* November 16, 1994, p. 6A.

127. "Congress OKs Inmate Fees to Offset Costs of Prison," *Criminal Justice Newsletter,* October 15, 1992, p. 6.

128. National Institute of Corrections website, http://www.nicic.org. Accessed March 2, 2002.

129. National Institute of Corrections website, http://www.nicic.org. Accessed March 3, 2002.

130. James J. Stephan, *Census of Jails, 1999* (Washington, D.C.: Bureau of Justice Statistics, 2001), p. 2.

131. Much of the information in this section comes from Allen J. Beck and Jennifer C. Karberg, *Prison and Jail Inmates at Midyear 2000* (Washington, D.C.: Bureau of Justice Statistics, 2001).

132. Ibid.

133. Department of Justice, "Incarceration Rate More Than Doubles in Dozen Years," press release, March 14, 1999.

134. Stephan, *Census of Jails, 1999.*

135. Ibid.

136. Ibid.

137. Caroline Wolf Harlow, *Profile of Jail Inmates, 1996* (Washington, D.C.: Bureau of Justice Statistics, 1998).

138. Beck and Karberg, *Prison and Jail Inmates at Midyear 2000.*

139. Stephan, *Census of Jails, 1999.*

140. See Gale Holland, "L.A. Jail Makes Delayed Debut," *USA Today,* January 27, 1997, p. 3A.

141. See Dale Stockton, "Cook County Illinois Sheriff's Office," *Police,* October 1996, pp. 40–43. The Cook County Department of Correction operates ten separate jails, which house approximately 9,000 inmates. The department employs more than 2,800 correctional officers.

142. Beck and Karberg, *Prison and Jail Inmates at Midyear 2000,* p. 7.

143. William Reginald Mills and Heather Barrett, "Meeting the Special Challenge of Providing Health Care to Women Inmates in the '90's," *American Jails,* Vol. 4, No. 3 (September/October 1990), p. 55.

144. Ibid.

145. Ibid., p. 21.

146. Ibid.

147. Mills and Barrett, "Meeting the Special Challenge of Providing Health Care to Women Inmates in the '90's," p. 55.

148. American Correctional Association, *Vital Statistics in Corrections.*

149. Mills and Barrett, "Meeting the Special Challenge of Providing Health Care to Women Inmates in the '90's," p. 55.

150. Ibid.

151. Linda L. Zupan, "Women Corrections Officers in the Nation's Largest Jails," *American Jails* (January/February 1991), pp. 59–62.

152. Ibid., p. 11.

153. Linda L. Zupan, "Women Corrections Officers in Local Jails," paper presented at the annual meeting of the Academy of Criminal Justice Sciences, Nashville, Tennessee, March 1991.

154. Ibid., p. 6.

155. "Jail Overcrowding in Houston Results in Release of Inmates," *Criminal Justice Newsletter,* October 15, 1990, p. 5.

156. Bureau of Justice Statistics, *Census of Local Jails, 1988* (Washington, D.C.: BJS, 1991), p. 31.

157. Kathleen Maguire and Ann L. Pastore, *Sourcebook of Criminal Justice Statistics, 1994* (Washington, D.C.: U.S. Government Printing Office, 1995).

158. Beck and Harrison, *Prisoners in 2000.*

159. Beck and Karberg, *Prison and Jail Inmates at Midyear 2000.*

160. Beck and Harrison, *Prisoners in 2000.*

161. Stephan, *Census of Jails, 1999.*

162. As identified in George P. Wilson and Harvey L. McMurray, "System Assessment of Jail Overcrowding Assumptions," paper presented at the annual meeting of the Academy of Criminal Justice Sciences, Nashville, Tennessee, March 1991.

163. Andy Hall, *Systemwide Strategies to Alleviate Jail Crowding* (Washington, D.C.: National Institute of Justice, 1987).

164. Ibid.

165. Linda L. Zupan and Ben A. Menke, "The New Generation Jail: An Overview," in Joel A. Thompson and G. Larry Mays, eds., *American Jails: Public Policy Issues* (Chicago: Nelson-Hall, 1991), p. 180.

166. Ibid.

167. Herbert R. Sigurdson, Billy Wayson, and Gail Funke, "Empowering Middle Managers of Direct Supervision Jails," *American Jails* (winter 1990), p. 52.

168. Byron Johnson, "Exploring Direct Supervision: A Research Note," *American Jails* (March/April 1994), pp. 63–64.

169. H. Sigurdson, *The Manhattan House of Detention: A Study of Podular Direct Supervision* (Washington, D.C.: National Institute of Corrections, 1985). For similar conclusions, see Robert Conroy, Wantland J. Smith, and Linda L. Zupan, "Officer Stress in the Direct Supervision Jail: A Preliminary Case Study," *American Jails* (November/December 1991), p. 36.

170. Brian Dawe and James Kirby, "Direct Supervision Jails and Minimum Staffing," *American Jails* (March/April 1995), pp. 97–100.

171. W. Raymond Nelson and Russell M. Davis, "Podular Direct Supervision: The First Twenty Years," *American Jails* (July/August 1995), p. 17.

172. Jerry W. Fuqua, "New Generation Jails: Old Generation Management," *American Jails* (March/April 1991), pp. 80–83.

173. Sigurdson, Wayson, and Funke, "Empowering Middle Managers of Direct Supervision Jails."

174. Duncan J. McCulloch and Time Stiles, "Technology and the Direct Supervision Jail," *American Jails* (winter 1990), pp. 97–102.

175. Susan W. McCampbell, "Direct Supervision: Looking for the Right People," *American Jails* (November/December 1990), pp. 68–69.

176. For a good review of the future of American jails, see Ron Carroll, "Jails and the Criminal Justice System in the Twenty-First Century," *American Jails* (March/April 1997), pp. 26–31.

177. Robert L. May II, Roger H. Peters, and William D. Kearns, "The Extent of Drug Treatment Programs in Jails: A Summary Report," *American Jails* (September/October 1990), pp. 32–34.

178. See, for example, John W. Dietler, "Jail Industries: The Best Thing That Can Happen to a Sheriff," *American Jails* (July/August 1990), pp. 80–83.

179. Robert Osborne, "Los Angeles County Sheriff Opens New Inmate Answering Service," *American Jails* (July/August 1990), pp. 61–62.

180. Robert J. Hunter, "A Locally Operated Boot Camp," *American Jails* (July/August 1994), pp. 13–15.

181. James Austin, Michael Jones, and Melissa Bolyard, *The Growing Use of Jail Boot Camps: The Current State of the Art* (Washington, D.C.: National Institute of Justice, 1993).

182. See J. R. Dewan, "Regional Jail—The New Kid on the Block," *American Jails* (May/June 1995), pp. 70–72.

183. Tom Rosazza, "Jail Standards: Focus on Change," *American Jails* (November/December 1990), pp. 84–87.

184. American Correctional Association, *Manual of Standards for Adult Local Detention Facilities*, 3d ed. (College Park, MD: ACA, 1991).

185. Ken Kerle, "National Sheriff's Association Jail Audit Review," *American Jails* (spring 1987), pp. 13–21.

186. Joel A. Thompson and G. Larry Mays, "Paying the Piper but Changing the Tune: Policy Changes and Initiatives for the American Jail," in Joel A. Thompson and G. Larry Mays, eds., *American Jails: Public Policy Issues* (Chicago: Nelson-Hall, 1991), pp. 240–246.

187. Beck and Harrison, *Prisoners in 2000*, p. 7, from which much of the information in this section is taken.

188. Ibid., p. 1.

189. Eric Bates, "Private Prisons: Over the Next Five Years Analysts Expect the Private Share of the Prison 'Market' to More than Double," *The Nation*, Vol. 266, No. 1 (1998), pp. 11–18.

190. James Austin and Garry Coventry, *Emerging Issues on Privatized Prisons* (Washington, D.C.: Bureau of Justice Statistics, 2001).

191. Gary Fields, "Privatized Prisons Pose Problems," *USA Today*, November 11, 1996, p. 3A.

192. Dale K. Sechrest and David Shichor, "Private Jails: Locking Down the Issues," *American Jails*, pp. 9–18.

193. U.S. General Accounting Office, *Private and Public Prisons: Studies Comparing Operational Costs and/or Quality of Service* (Washington, D.C.: U.S. Government Printing Office, 1996).

194. Sechrest and Shichor, "Private Jails," p. 10.

195. Austin and Coventry, *Emerging Issues on Privatized Prisons*, p. ix.

196. For a more detailed discussion of this issue, see Austin and Coventry, *Emerging Issues on Privatized Prisons*.

197. *Richardson* v. *McKnight*, 117 S.Ct. 2100, 138 L.Ed. 2d 540 (1997).

198. *Richardson* v. *McKnight*, syllabus.

199. As quoted in Thompson, "Private Prisons."

200. Judith C. Hackett et al., "Contracting for the Operation of Prisons and Jails," National Institute of Justice, *Research in Brief* (June 1987), p. 6.

Prison Life

LEARNING OBJECTIVES

After reading this chapter, you should be able to

■ Describe the realities of prison life and subculture from the inmate's point of view

■ Describe the realities of prison life from the perspective of correctional officers

■ List the stages of prison riots, and describe their causes

■ Explain the nature of the hands-off doctrine, and discuss the status of that doctrine today

■ Discuss the legal aspects of prisoners' rights, and explain the consequences of precedent-setting U.S. Supreme Court cases in the area of prisoners' rights

■ Describe the major problems and issues facing prisons today

chapter 13

Key Concepts

[Terms]

balancing test
civil death
grievance procedure

hands-off doctrine
prison argot
prisonization

prison subculture
total institutions

[Cases]

Block v. *Rutherford*
Bounds v. *Smith*
Cruz v. *Beto*
Estelle v. *Gamble*
Helling v. *McKinney*
Houchins v. *KQED, Inc.*

Hudson v. *Palmer*
Johnson v. *Avery*
Jones v. *North Carolina Prisoners' Labor Union*
Katz v. *U.S.*
Newman v. *Alabama*

Pell v. *Procunier*
Pennsylvania Department of Corrections v. *Yeskey*
Ruiz v. *Estelle*
Sandin v. *Conner*
Wolff v. *McDonnell*

Introduction

Hear the author
discuss this chapter
at **cjtoday.com**

For the first 150 years of their existence, prisons and prison life could be described by the phrase "out of sight, out of mind." Very few citizens cared about prison conditions, and those unfortunate enough to be locked away were regarded as lost to the world. By the mid-twentieth century, beginning with the treatment era, this attitude started to change. Concerned citizens began to offer their services to prison administrations, neighborhoods began accepting work-release prisoners and halfway houses, and social scientists initiated a serious study of prison life.

This chapter describes the realities of prison life today, including prisoner lifestyles, prison subcultures, sexuality in prison, prison violence, and prisoners' rights and grievance procedures. We will discuss both the inmate world and the staff world. A separate section on women in prison details the social structure of women's prisons, daily life in those facilities, and the various types of female inmates. We begin with a brief overview of early research on prison life.

Research on Prison Life—Total Institutions

In 1935, Hans Reimer, Chairman of the Department of Sociology at Indiana University, set the tone for studies of prison life when he voluntarily served three months in prison as an incognito participant-observer.[2] Reimer reported the results of his studies to the American Prison Association, stimulating many other, albeit less spectacular, efforts to examine prison life. Other early studies include Donald Clemmer's *The Prison Community* (1940),[3] Gresham M. Sykes's *The Society of Captives: A Study of a Maximum Security Prison* (1958),[4] Richard A. Cloward and Donald R. Cressey's *Theoretical Studies in Social Organization of the Prison* (1960),[5] and Cressey's edited volume, *The Prison: Studies in Institutional Organization and Change* (1961).[6]

These studies and others focused primarily on maximum-security prisons for men. They treated correctional institutions as formal or complex organizations and employed the analytic techniques of organizational sociology, industrial psychology, and administrative science.[7] As modern writers on prisons have observed, "The prison was compared to a primitive society, isolated from the outside world, functionally integrated by a delicate system of mechanisms, which kept it precariously balanced between anarchy and accommodation."[8]

Another approach to the study of prison life was developed by Erving Goffman, who coined the term **total institutions** in a 1961 study of prisons and mental hospitals.[9] Goffman described total institutions as places where the same people work, recreate, worship, eat, and sleep together daily. Such places include prisons, concentration camps, mental

total institutions

Enclosed facilities, separated from society both socially and physically, where the inhabitants share all aspects of their lives daily.

hospitals, seminaries, and other facilities in which residents are cut off from the larger society either forcibly or willingly. Total institutions are small societies. They evolve their own distinctive values and styles of life and pressure residents to fulfill rigidly prescribed behavioral roles.

Generally speaking, the work of prison researchers built upon findings of other social scientists who discovered that any group with similar characteristics, subject to confinement in the same place at the same time, develops its own subculture with specific components that govern hierarchy, behavioral patterns, values, and so on. Prison subcultures, described in the next section, also provide the medium through which prison values are communicated and expectations are made known. Learn more about prison research via **Library Extra! 13–1** at cjtoday.com.

The Male Inmate's World

Two social realities coexist in prison settings. One is the official structure of rules and procedures put in place by the wider society and enforced by prison staff. The other is the more informal but decidedly more powerful inmate world.[10] The inmate world, best described by its pervasive immediacy in the lives of inmates, is controlled by **prison subculture**. The realities of prison life—including a large and often densely packed inmate population which must look to the prison environment for all its needs—mean that prison subculture is not easily subjected to the control of prison authorities.

Prison subcultures develop independently of the plans of prison administrators, and inmates entering prison discover a social world not mentioned in the handbooks prepared by correctional staff. Inmate concerns, values, roles, and even language weave a web of social reality into which new inmates step and in which they must participate. Those who try to remain aloof soon find themselves subjected to dangerous ostracism and may even be suspected of being in league with the prison administration.

The socialization of new inmates into the prison subculture has been described as a process of "prisonization."[11] **Prisonization** refers to the learning of convict values, attitudes, roles, and even language. When the process is complete, new inmates have become "cons." The values of the inmate social system are embodied in a code whose violation can produce sanctions ranging from ostracism and avoidance to physical violence and homicide.[12] Gresham M. Sykes and Sheldon L. Messinger recognized five elements of the prison code in 1960:[13]

1. Don't interfere with the interests of other inmates. Never rat on a con.
2. Don't lose your head. Play it cool and do your own time.
3. Don't exploit inmates. Don't steal. Don't break your word. Be right.
4. Don't whine. Be a man.
5. Don't be a sucker. Don't trust the guards or staff.

Stanton Wheeler closely examined the concept of prisonization in an early study of the Washington State Reformatory.[14] Wheeler found that the degree of prisonization experienced by inmates tends to vary over time. He described changing levels of inmate commitment to prison norms and values by way of a U-shaped curve. When an inmate first enters prison, Wheeler said, the conventional values of outside society are of paramount importance. As time passes, inmates adopt the lifestyle of the prison. However, within the half year prior to release, most inmates begin to demonstrate a renewed appreciation of conventional values. Learn more about both the positive and negative impact of imprisonment at **Library Extra! 13–2** at cjtoday.com.

Different prisons share aspects of a common inmate culture;[15] prison-wise inmates who enter a new facility far from their home will already know the ropes. **Prison argot**, or language, provides one example of how widespread prison subculture can be. The terms used to describe inmate roles in one institution are generally understood in others. The word *rat*, for example, is prison slang for an informer. Popularized by crime movies of the 1950s, the term is understood today by members of the wider society. Other words common to prison argot are shown in CJ Today Exhibit 13–1.

Some criminologists have suggested that inmate codes are simply a reflection of general criminal values. If so, they are brought to the institution rather than created there. Either way, the power and pervasiveness of the inmate code require convicts to conform to the

prison subculture

The values and behavioral patterns characteristic of prison inmates. Prison subculture has been found to be surprisingly consistent across the country.

prisonization

The process whereby newly institutionalized offenders come to accept prison lifestyles and criminal values. Although many inmates begin their prison experience with only a few values supportive of criminal behavior, the socialization experience they undergo while incarcerated leads to a much wider acceptance of such values.

prison argot

The slang characteristic of prison subcultures and prison life.

Custody and security remain the primary concerns of prison staffers throughout the country—a fact seemingly belied by the apparent disregard of this posted notice.

Laima E. Druskis

worldview held by the majority of prisoners. View an online prisoner's dictionary via **Web Extra! 13–1** at cjtoday.com.

The Evolution of Prison Subcultures

Prison subcultures are constantly changing. Like any other American subculture, they evolve to reflect the concerns and experiences of the wider culture, reacting to new crime-control strategies and embracing novel opportunities for crime and its commission. The AIDS epidemic of the last two decades, for example, has brought about changes in prison sexual behavior, at least for a segment of the inmate population, while the emergence of a high-tech criminal group has further differentiated convict types. Because of such changes, John Irwin, as he was completing his classic study entitled *The Felon* (1970), expressed worry that his book was already obsolete.[16] *The Felon*, for all its insights into prison subcultures, follows in the descriptive tradition of works by Clemmer and Reimer. Irwin recognized that by 1970, prison subcultures had begun to reflect the cultural changes sweeping America. A decade later, other investigators of prison subcultures were able to write, "It was no longer meaningful to speak of a single inmate culture or even subculture. By the time we began our field research . . . it was clear that the unified, oppositional convict culture, found in the sociological literature on prisons, no longer existed."[17]

Charles Stastny and Gabrielle Tyrnauer, describing prison life at Washington State Penitentiary in 1982, discovered four clearly distinguishable subcultures: (1) official, (2) traditional, (3) reform, and (4) revolutionary.[18] Official culture was promoted by the staff and by the administrative rules of the institution. Enthusiastic participants in official culture were mostly correctional officers and other staff members, although inmates were also well aware of the normative expectations official culture imposed on them. Official culture affected the lives of inmates primarily through the creation of a prisoner hierarchy based upon sentence length, prison jobs, and the "perks" which cooperation with the dictates of official culture could produce. Traditional prison culture, described by early writers on the subject, still existed, but its participants spent much of their time lamenting the decline of the convict code among younger prisoners. Reform culture was unique at Washington State Penitentiary. It was the result of a brief experiment with inmate self-government during the early 1970s. Elements of prison life which evolved during the experimental period sometimes survived the termination of self-government and were eventually institutionalized in what Stastny and Tyrnauer called "reform culture." Such elements included inmate participation in civic-style clubs, citizen involvement in the daily activities of the prison, banquets, and inmate speaking tours. Revolutionary culture built upon the radical political rhetoric of the disenfranchised and found a ready audience among minority prisoners

CJ Today Exhibit 13-1

[Prison Argot: The Language of Confinement]

Writers who have studied prison life often comment on prisoners' use of a special language or slang termed *prison argot*. This language generally refers to the roles assigned by prison culture to types of inmates as well as to prison activities. This box lists a few of the many words and phrases identified in studies by different authors. The first group of words are characteristic of male prisons; the last few have been used in prisons for women.

Men's Prison Slang

Ace duce: Best friend
Badge (or bull, hack, the man, or screw): A correctional officer
Banger (or burner, shank, or sticker): A knife
Billy: A white man
Boneyard: The conjugal visiting area
Cat-J (or J-cat): A prisoner in need of psychological or psychiatric therapy or medication
Cellie: Cellmate
Chester: A child molester
Dog: A homeboy or friend
Fag: A male inmate who is believed to be a "natural" or "born" homosexual
Featherwood: A white prisoner's woman
Fish: A newly arrived inmate
Gorilla: An inmate who uses force to take what he wants from others
Homeboy: A prisoner from one's hometown or neighborhood

Ink: Tattoos
Lemon squeezer: An inmate who masturbates frequently
Man walking: A phrase used to signal that a guard is coming
Merchant (or peddler): One who sells when he should give
Peckerwood (or wood): A white prisoner
Punk: A male inmate who is forced into a submissive role during homosexual relations
Rat (or snitch): An inmate who squeals (provides information about other inmates to the prison administration)
Schooled: Knowledgeable in the ways of prison life
Shakedown: A search of a cell or of a work area
Tree jumper: A rapist
Turn out: To rape or make into a punk
Wolf: A male inmate who assumes the dominant role during homosexual relations

Women's Prison Slang

Cherry (or cherrie): A female inmate who has not yet been introduced to lesbian activities
Fay broad: A white female inmate
Femme (or mommy): A female inmate who plays the female role during lesbian relations
Safe: The vagina, especially when used for hiding contraband
Stud broad (or daddy): A female inmate who assumes the male role during lesbian relations

Sources: Gresham Sykes, *The Society of Captives* (Princeton, NJ: Princeton University Press, 1958); Rose Giallombardo, *Society of Women: A Study of a Woman's Prison* (New York: John Wiley, 1966); and Richard A. Cloward et al., *Theoretical Studies in Social Organization of the Prison* (New York: Social Science Research Council, 1960). For a more contemporary listing of prison slang terms, see Reinhold Aman, *Hillary Clinton's Pen Pal: A Guide to Life and Lingo in Federal Prison* (Santa Rosa, CA: Maledicta Press, 1996); Jerome Washington, *Iron House: Stories from the Yard* (Ann Arbor, MI: QED Press, 1994); Morrie Camhi, *The Prison Experience* (Boston: Charles Tuttle, 1989); and Harold Long, *Survival in Prison* (Port Townsend, WA: Loompanics, 1990).

who saw themselves as victims of society's basic unfairness. Although they did not participate in it, revolutionary inmates understood traditional prison culture and generally avoided running afoul of its rules.

The Functions of Prison Subcultures

How do social scientists and criminologists explain the existence of prison subcultures? Although people around the world live in groups and create their own cultures, in few cases does the intensity of human interaction approach the level found in prisons. As we discussed in Chapter 12, today's prisons are overcrowded places where inmates can find no retreat from the constant demands of staff and the pressures brought by fellow prisoners. Prison subcultures, according to some authors, are fundamentally an adaptation to deprivation and confinement. They are a way of addressing the psychological, social, physical, and sexual needs of prisoners living within the context of a highly controlled and regimented institutional setting.

What are some of the deprivations prisoners experience? In *The Society of Captives*, Sykes called felt deprivations the "pains of imprisonment."[19] The pains of imprisonment— the frustrations induced by the rigors of confinement—form the nexus of a deprivation model of prison subculture. Sykes said that prisoners are deprived of (1) liberty, (2) goods and services, (3) heterosexual relationships, (4) autonomy, and (5) personal security and that these deprivations lead to the development of subcultures intended to ameliorate the personal pains which accompany deprivation.

In contrast to the deprivation model, the importation model of prison subculture suggests that inmates bring with them values, roles, and behavior patterns from the outside world. Such external values, second nature as they are to career offenders, depend substantially upon the criminal worldview. When offenders are confined, these external elements shape the inmate social world.

The social structure of the prison, a concept that refers to accepted and relatively permanent social arrangements, is another element which shapes prison subculture. Clemmer's early prison study recognized nine structural dimensions of inmate society. He said that prison society could be described in terms of[20]

- Prisoner–staff dichotomy
- Three general classes of prisoners
- Work gangs and cell-house groups
- Racial groups
- Type of offense
- Power of inmate "politicians"
- Degree of sexual abnormality
- Record of repeat offenses
- Personality differences due to preprison socialization

Clemmer's nine structural dimensions are probably still descriptive of prison life today. When applied in individual situations, they designate an inmate's position in the prison "pecking order" and create expectations of the appropriate role for that person. Prison roles serve to satisfy the needs of inmates for power, sexual performance, material possessions, individuality, and personal pleasure and to define the status of one prisoner relative to another. For example, inmate leaders, sometimes referred to as "real men" or "toughs" by prisoners in early studies, offer protection to those who live by the rules. They also provide for a redistribution of wealth inside prison and see to it that the rules of the complex prison-derived economic system—based on barter, gambling, and sexual favors—are observed. To learn more about prison life, visit **Web Extra! 13–2** at cjtoday.com.

Prison Lifestyles and Inmate Types

Prison society is strict and often unforgiving. Even so, inmates are able to express some individuality through the choice of a prison lifestyle. John Irwin was the first well-known author to describe prison lifestyles, viewing them (like the subcultures of which they are a part) as adaptations to the prison environment.[21] Other writers have since elaborated on these coping mechanisms. Listed in the paragraphs that follow are some of the types of prisoners described by researchers.

- *The mean dude.* Some inmates adjust to prison by being mean. They are quick to fight, and when they fight, they fight like wild men (or women). They give no quarter and seem to expect none in return. Other inmates know that such prisoners are best left alone. The mean dude is frequently written up and spends much time in solitary confinement.

    Some prisoners occupy the mean dude role in prison as they did when they were free. Certain personality types, such as the psychopath, may feel a natural attraction to this role. On the other hand, prison culture supports the role of the mean dude in two ways: (1) by expecting inmates to be tough and (2) through the prevalence of the idea that only the strong survive inside prison.

    A psychologist might say that the mean dude is acting out against the fact of captivity, striking out at anyone he (or she) can. This role is most common in male institutions and in maximum-security prisons. It tends to become less common as inmates progress to lower security levels.

- *The hedonist.* Some inmates build their lives around the limited pleasures which can be had within the confines of prison. The smuggling of contraband, homosexuality, gambling, drug running, and other officially condemned activities provide the center of interest for prison hedonists. Hedonists generally have an abbreviated view of the future, living only for the "now." Such a temporal orientation is probably characteristic of the personality type of all hedonists, both inside the prison and out.

■ *The opportunist.* The opportunist takes advantage of the positive experiences prison has to offer. Schooling, trade training, counseling, and other self-improvement activities are the focal points of the opportunist's life in prison. Opportunists are the "do-gooders" of the prison subculture. They are generally well liked by prison staff, but other prisoners shun and mistrust them because they come closest to accepting the role which the staff defines as "model prisoner." Opportunists may also be religious, a role adaptation described below.

■ *The retreatist.* Prison life is rigorous and demanding. Badgering by the staff and actual or feared assaults by other inmates may cause some prisoners to attempt psychological retreat from the realities of imprisonment. Such inmates may experience neurotic or psychotic episodes, become heavily involved in drug and alcohol abuse, or even attempt suicide. Depression and mental illness are the hallmarks of the retreatist personality in prison. The best hope for the retreatist, short of release, is protective custody combined with therapeutic counseling.

■ *The legalist.* The legalist is the "jailhouse lawyer." Just like the mean dude, the legalist fights confinement. The weapons in this fight are not fists or clubs, however, but the legal writ. Convicts facing long sentences, with little possibility for early release through the correctional system, are most likely to turn to the courts in their battle against confinement.

■ *The radical.* Radical inmates picture themselves as political prisoners. Society and the successful conformists who populate it are seen as oppressors who have forced criminality upon many "good people" through the creation of a system which distributes wealth and power inequitably. The radical inmate speaks a language of revolution and may be versed in the writings of the "great" revolutionaries of the past.

   The inmate who takes on the radical role is unlikely to receive much sympathy from prison staff. Radical rhetoric tends to be diametrically opposed to staff insistence on accepting responsibility for problematic behavior.

■ *The colonist.* Some inmates think of prison as their home. They "know the ropes," have many "friends" inside, and may feel more comfortable institutionalized than on the streets. They typically hold either positions of power or respect (or both) among the inmate population. These are the prisoners who don't look forward to leaving prison. Most colonizers grow into the role gradually and only after having spent years behind bars. Once released, some colonizers have been known to commit new crimes to return to prison.

> Whilst we have prisons it matters little which of us occupies the cells.
>
> —George Bernard Shaw
> (1856–1950)

Convicted murderer Henry Lee Lucas. Lucas, who confessed to 600 murders, later recanted, and in 1998 his death sentence was commuted to life in prison by then-Governor George W. Bush of Texas. Prison inmates adapt diverse coping strategies, and Lucas claims to have found God.

AP/Wide World Photos

■ *The religious.* Some prisoners profess a strong religious faith. They may be "born-again" Christians, committed Muslims, or even satanists or witches (perhaps affiliated with the Church of Wicca). Religious inmates frequently attend services, may form prayer groups, and sometimes ask the prison administration to allocate meeting facilities or to create special diets to accommodate their claimed spiritual needs.

While it is certainly true that some inmates have a strong religious faith, staff members are apt to be suspicious of the overly religious prisoner. The tendency is to view such prisoners as "faking it" to demonstrate a fictitious rehabilitation and thereby gain sympathy for an early release.

■ *The realist.* The realist is a prisoner who sees confinement as a natural consequence of criminal activity. Time spent in prison is an unfortunate cost of doing business. This stoic attitude toward incarceration generally leads the realist to "pull his (or her) own time" and to make the best of it. Realists tend to know the inmate code, are able to avoid trouble, and continue in lives of crime once released.

Homosexuality in Prison

Homosexual behavior inside prisons is both constrained and encouraged by prison subculture. One Houston woman, whose son is serving time in a Texas prison, explained the path to prison homosexuality this way: "Within a matter of days, if not hours, an unofficial prison welcome wagon sorts new arrivals into those who will fight, those who will pay extortion cash of up to $60 every two weeks, and those who will be servants or slaves. 'You're jumped on by two or three prisoners to see if you'll fight,'" said the woman. "If you don't fight, you become someone's girl, until they're tired of you and they sell you to someone else."[22]

Sykes's early study of prison argot found many words describing homosexual activity. Among them were the terms *wolf, punk,* and *fag.* Wolves were aggressive men who assumed the masculine role in homosexual relations. Punks were forced into submitting to the female role, often by wolves. Fags described a special category of men who had a natural proclivity toward homosexual activity and effeminate mannerisms. While both wolves and punks were fiercely committed to their heterosexual identity and participated in homosexuality only because of prison conditions, fags generally engaged in homosexual lifestyles before their entry into prison and continued to emulate feminine mannerisms and styles of dress once incarcerated.

Prison homosexuality depends to a considerable degree upon the naïveté of young inmates experiencing prison for the first time. Even when newly arrived inmates are protected from fights, older prisoners looking for homosexual liaisons may ingratiate them-

A group of male inmates dressed as women in a California institution. Homosexuality is common in both men's and women's prisons.

Rasmussen, SIPA Press

selves by offering cigarettes, money, drugs, food, or protection. At some future time, these "loans" will be called in, with payoffs demanded in sexual favors. Because the inmate code requires the repayment of favors, the "fish" who tries to resist may quickly find himself face-to-face with the brute force of inmate society.

Prison rape represents a special category of homosexual behavior behind bars. Estimates of the incidence of prison rape are both rare and dated. Survey-based studies vary considerably in their findings. One such study found 4.7% of inmates in the Philadelphia prison system willing to report sexual assaults.[23] Another survey found that 28% of prisoners had been targets of sexual aggressors at least once during their institutional careers.[24]

While not greatly different from other prisoners, a large proportion of sexual aggressors are characterized by low education and poverty, having grown up in a broken home headed by the mother, and having a record for violent offenses. Victims of prison rape tend to be physically slight, young, white, nonviolent offenders from nonurban areas.[25] Lee H. Bowker, summarizing studies of sexual violence in prison, provides the following observations:[26]

- Most sexual aggressors do not consider themselves to be homosexuals.
- Sexual release is not the primary motivation for sexual attack.
- Many aggressors must continue to participate in gang rapes to avoid becoming victims themselves.
- The aggressors have themselves suffered much damage to their masculinity in the past.

As in cases of heterosexual rape, sexual assaults in prison are likely to leave psychological scars long after the physical event is over.[27] The victims of prison rape live in fear, may feel constantly threatened, and can turn to self-destructive activities.[28] At the very least, victims question their masculinity and undergo a personal devaluation. In some cases, victims of prison sexual attacks turn to violence. Frustrations, long bottled up through abuse and fear, may explode and turn the would-be rapist into a victim of prison homicide. Learn more about male rape in U.S. prisons at **Library Extra! 13–3** at cjtoday.com.

> We must remember always that the doors of prisons swing both ways.
>
> —Mary Belle Harris, first federal female warden

The Female Inmate's World

As Chapter 12 showed, 91,612 women are imprisoned in state and federal correctional institutions throughout the United States, accounting for 6.6% of all prison inmates.[29] Texas has the largest number of female prisoners (12,245), exceeding even the federal government.[30] Figure 13–1 provides a breakdown of the total American prison population by

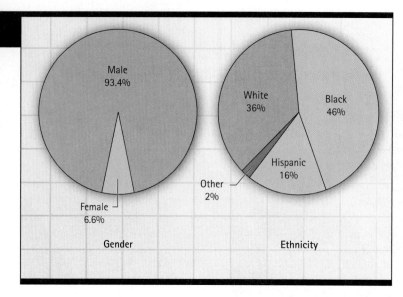

FIGURE 13-1

Prison inmates by gender and ethnicity in state and federal prisons, 2000.

Source: Allen J. Beck and Paige M. Harrison, *Prisoners in 2000* (Washington, D.C.: Bureau of Justice Statistics, 2001).

gender and ethnicity. Most female inmates are housed in centralized state facilities known as *women's prisons,* which are dedicated exclusively to incarcerating female felons. Many states, however, particularly those with small populations, continue to keep female prisoners in special wings of what are otherwise institutions for men.

While there are still far more men imprisoned across the nation than women (approximately 15 men for every woman), the number of female inmates is rising.[31] In 1981, women made up only 4% of the nation's overall prison population, but the number of female inmates nearly tripled during the 1980s and is continuing to grow at a rate greater than that of male inmates.

Some professionals working with imprisoned women attribute the rise in female prison populations largely to drugs.[32] Approximately 33% of all women in prison are there explicitly for drug offenses. Other estimates, however, say that the impact of drugs on the imprisonment of women is far greater than a simple reading of the figure indicates. Warden Robert Brennan of a New York City jail for women estimates that drugs—either directly or indirectly—account for the imprisonment of around 95% of the inmates there. Drug-related offenses committed by women include larceny, burglary, fraud, prostitution, embezzlement, and robbery, as well as other crimes stimulated by the desire for drugs. In fact, incarcerated women most frequently list (1) trying to pay for drugs, (2) attempting to relieve economic pressures, and (3) exercising poor judgment as the reasons for their arrest.[33]

Another reason for the rapid growth in the number of women behind bars may be the demise, over the last two or three decades, of the "chivalry factor." The chivalry factor, so called because it was based upon an archaic cultural stereotype that depicted women as helpless or childlike compared to men, allegedly lessened the responsibility of female offenders in the eyes of some male judges and prosecutors, resulting in fewer active prison sentences for women involved in criminal activity. Recent studies show that the chivalry factor is now primarily of historical interest. In jurisdictions examined, the gender of convicted offenders no longer affects sentencing practices except insofar as it may be tied to other social variables. In a comprehensive study of gender differences in sentencing, B. Keith Crew observes, "A woman does not automatically receive leniency because of her status of wife or mother, but she may receive leniency if those statuses become part of the official explanation of her criminal behavior (for example, she was stealing to feed her children, or an abusive husband forced her to commit a crime)."[34]

Although there may be no one typical prison for women and no perfectly average female inmate, the American Correctional Association's 1990 report by the Task Force on the Female Offender found that female inmates and the institutions which house them could be generally described as follows:[35]

■ Most prisons for women are located in towns with fewer than 25,000 inhabitants.

■ A significant number of facilities were not designed to house female inmates.

■ The number of female offenders being sent to prison is rising.

- Most facilities that house female inmates also house men.
- Few facilities for women have programs especially designed for female offenders.
- Few major disturbances or escapes are reported among female inmates.
- Substance abuse among female inmates is very high.
- Few work assignments are available to female inmates.
- The number of female inmates without a high school education is very high.

Statistics show that the average age of female inmates is 29 to 30, most are black or Hispanic (57%), most come from single-parent or broken homes, and half have other family members who are incarcerated.[36] The typical female inmate is a high school dropout (50%), who left school either because she was bored or because of pregnancy (34%). She has been arrested two to nine times (55%) and has run away from home between one and three times (65%). Thirty-nine percent report using drugs to make themselves feel better emotionally, while 28% have attempted suicide at least once. Sixty-two percent were single parents with one to three children prior to incarceration, and many have been physically or sexually abused.[37]

Eighty percent of women entering prison are mothers, and 85% of those women had custody of their children at the time of prison admission. One out of four women entering prison has either recently given birth or is pregnant. In 2000, more than 1.5 million American children had mothers who were confined in prison or jail.[38] Moreover, the number of women in prison who were parents of minor children more than doubled during the 1990s.[39]

Critics charge that female inmates face a prison system designed for male inmates and run by men. Hence, pregnant inmates, many of whom are drug users, malnourished, or sick, often receive little prenatal care—a situation that risks additional complications. Separation from their children is a significant deprivation facing incarcerated mothers.

CJ Today News

[Child Sleepovers at Prison Reviewed]

YORK, Neb. (AP)—Once a month, Jessica Davis spends five nights in a row with her 2-year-old daughter—behind prison walls.

She is just one of dozens of mother prisoners who participate in an overnight visitation program that Gov. Mike Johanns wants changed after a convicted murderer requested that her 6-year-old stay overnight with her.

Johanns said last week the policy at the Nebraska Correctional Center for Women in York will be changed to prohibit women serving life sentences from participating, and he ordered a review of the entire overnight program to begin Tuesday.

Davis, 19, serving up to two years in prison for second-degree assault, said she is bothered that some children will not be allowed to spend the night with their mothers. She and her daughter read books, watch movies, play with stuffed animals and enjoy an outdoor playground during the sleepovers.

"It's given me that chance to be able to bond with my daughter," she said. "It gives her that security knowing that I am OK."

Inmate Cherie Carter reading a book with her three-year-old daughter, Onisha, at the Nebraska Correctional Center for Women in York. Onisha was at the prison as part of an overnight visitation program that Nebraska Governor Mike Johanns wants revised. AP/Wide World Photos

But Bruce Faust doesn't want his ex-wife, Kimberly Faust, to enjoy such a luxury with their 6-year-old son. Faust was convicted in November [2000] of killing her estranged husband's girlfriend, Shannon Bluhm, and a passer-by who tried to save her.

She wants the 6-year-old to stay overnight with her at the prison, where she is serving two life sentences without the possibility of parole.

Bruce Faust has custody of the couple's two sons, ages 6 and 11. He has said he does not object to the boys visiting their mother, but does not think the 6-year-old should stay overnight.

Johanns stepped in after *Chicago Tribune* columnist Bob Greene wrote about the situation and urged people to contact the governor. Johanns received more than 1,000 e-mails, faxes and phone calls.

On Thursday, he took away Faust's right to have the son sleep over, saying the policy will no longer apply to inmates who face no possibility of parole. The move is to take effect within two weeks.

Harold Clarke, prison director, said the program was the first of its kind in the country and has a proven track record.

"Not one kid has had a bad experience in this program," Clarke said.

Of the 267 inmates at York, prison officials estimate about 40 to 50 are mothers. Clarke said more than 95 percent of the women will be leaving the prison within three years, making it important to have a program that will help them be better parents once they leave.

Johanns said the overnight program has merits for women who will be paroled.

The prison resembles a college campus. Red-brick housing units are spread out in a semicircle, inside which inmates walk freely. The entire campus is ringed by a barbed-wire fence.

Under the policy, children ages 1 to 8 are allowed to spend nights with their mothers. The rooms they share are small, with just enough space for a metal cabinet to hang clothes, a bed and cot for the child, and a night stand.

Down the hall from the rooms is a nursery equipped with all the basics—rocking chairs, playpens, swings for the children and toys.

The overnight stays are on the third floor of one of the housing units. They are isolated from inmates on the first and second floor, who are part of the general population.

In a separate building, mothers and their children can play with a variety of board games, read from a small Library of books, bake at a kitchenette, or watch videos. Outside is a playground equipped with all the basics.

"There are no bars here," said inmate Amanda Wardlow-Stubblefield, who has three children ages 2 to 13. "It seems like a small community."

For the latest in crime and justice news, visit the Talk Justice news feed at http://www.crimenews.info.

Source: Associated Press, "Child Sleepovers at Prison Reviewed," September 3, 2001. Reprinted with permission of the Associated Press.

Although husbands or boyfriends may assume responsibility for the children of imprisoned spouses or girlfriends, this outcome is the exception to the rule. Eventually, a large proportion of children are released by their imprisoned mothers into foster care or put up for adoption.

Some states do offer parenting classes for female inmates with children. In a national survey of prisons for women, 36 states responded that they provide parenting programs which deal with caretaking, reducing violence toward children, visitation problems, and related issues.[40] Some offer play areas furnished with toys, while others attempt to alleviate difficulties attending mother-child visits. The typical program studied lasts from four to nine weeks and provides for a meeting time of two hours per week.

Other meaningful prison programs for women are often lacking, perhaps because the ones which are in place were originally based upon traditional models of female roles which left little room for substantive employment opportunities. Many trade training programs still emphasize low-paying jobs, such as cook, beautician, or laundry machine operator. Classes in homemaking are not uncommon.

Social Structure in Women's Prisons

"Aside from sharing the experience of being incarcerated," says Professor Marsha Clowers of the John Jay College of Criminal Justice, "female prisoners have much in common. They are likely to be black or Hispanic, poor, uneducated, abuse survivors, single parents, and in poor health."[41] Shared social characteristics may lead to similar values and behaviors. One type of behavior identified by early prison researchers as characteristic of a fair number of incarcerated women concerns the way that female inmates construct organized pseudofamilies. Typical of such studies are D. Ward and G. Kassebaum's *Women's Prison: Sex and Social Structure* (1966),[42] Esther Heffernan's *Making It in Prison: The Square, the Cool, and the Life* (1972),[43] and Rose Giallombardo's *Society of Women: A Study of Women's Prisons* (1966).[44]

Giallombardo, for example, examined the Federal Reformatory for Women at Alderson, West Virginia, spending a year gathering data in the early 1960s. Focusing closely on the social formation of families among female inmates, she entitled one of her chapters "The Homosexual Alliance as a Marriage Unit." In it, she described in great detail the sexual identities assumed by women at Alderson and the symbols they chose to communicate those roles. Hairstyle, dress, language, and mannerisms were all used to signify "maleness" or "femaleness." Giallombardo detailed "the anatomy of the marriage relationship from courtship to 'fall out,' that is, from inception to the parting of the ways, or divorce."[45] Romantic love at Alderson was seen as being of central importance to any relationship between inmates, and all homosexual relationships were described as voluntary. Through marriage, the "stud broad" became the husband and the "femme" the wife.

Female inmates in Sheriff Joe Arpaio's "equal opportunity jail" in Maricopa County, Arizona, being inspected by a correctional officer before leaving for chain gang duty. Not all states make use of chain gangs, and only a few use female inmates on chain gangs.

Jack Kurtz, The Image Works

Studies attempting to document the extent of inmate involvement in prison "families" have produced varying results. Some have found as many as 71% of female prisoners involved in the phenomenon, while others have found none.[46] The kinship systems described by Giallombardo and others, however, extend beyond simple "family" ties to the formation of large, intricately related groups involving a large number of nonsexual relationships. In these groups, the roles of "children," "in-laws," "grandparents," and so on may be explicitly recognized. Even "birth order" within a family can become an issue for kinship groups.[47] Kinship groups sometimes occupy a common household—usually a prison cottage or dormitory area. The descriptions of women's prisons provided by authors like Giallombardo show a closed society in which social interaction—including expectations, normative forms of behavior, and emotional ties—is regulated by an inventive system of artificial relationships which mirror the outside world.

Recent studies provide additional details about the nature of homosexual behavior in women's prisons. A 1998 study of the Central California Women's Facility, for example, found that most of the staff and inmates alike claimed that "everybody was involved" in homosexual behavior. When inmates were interviewed individually, however, and asked to provide some details about the extent of their involvement in such behavior, many denied any lesbian activity.

A 2001 study of a women's correctional facility in the southeastern United States found that female inmates asked about their preincarceration sexual orientation gave answers that were quite different than when they were asked about their sexual orientation while incarcerated.[48] In general, 64% of inmates interviewed reported being exclusively heterosexual; 28% said they were bisexual; and 8% said that they were lesbians before being incarcerated. In contrast, these same women reported sexual orientations while incarcerated of 55% heterosexual; 31% bisexual; and 13% lesbian. Researchers found that same-sex sexual behavior within the institution was more likely to occur in the lives of young inmates who had had such experiences before entering prison. The study also found that female inmates tended to become more involved in lesbian behavior the longer they were incarcerated.

Types of Female Inmates

As in institutions for men, the subculture of women's prisons is multidimensional. Esther Heffernan, for example, found that three terms used by the female prisoners she studied—the *square,* the *cool,* and the *life*—were indicative of three styles of adaptation to prison life.[49] Square inmates had few early experiences with criminal lifestyles and tended to sympathize with the values and attitudes of conventional society. Cool prisoners were more likely to be career offenders. They tended to keep to themselves and generally supported inmate values. Women who participated in the life subculture were quite familiar with lives of crime. Many had been arrested repeatedly for prostitution, drug use, theft, and so on. They were full participants in the economic, social, and familial arrangements of the prison. Heffernan believed that the life offered an alternative lifestyle to women who had experienced early and constant rejection by conventional society. Within the life, women could establish relationships, achieve status, and find meaning in their lives. The square, the cool, and the life represented subcultures to Heffernan because individuals with similar adaptive choices tended to relate closely to one another and to support the lifestyle characteristic of that type.

Recently, the social structure of women's prisons has become dichotomized by the advent of "crack kids," as they are called in prison argot. Crack kids, whose existence highlights generational differences among female offenders, are streetwise young women with little respect for traditional prison values, for their elders, or even for their own children. Known for frequent fights and for their lack of even simple domestic skills, these young women quickly estrange many older inmates, some of whom call them "animalescents."

Violence in Women's Prisons

Some authors have suggested that violence in women's prisons is less frequent than it is in institutions for men. Lee Bowker observes that "except for the behavior of a few 'guerrillas,' it appears that violence is only used in women's prisons to settle questions of dominance and subordination when other manipulative strategies fail to achieve the desired effect."[50] It appears that few homosexual liaisons are forced, perhaps representing a general aversion among women to such victimization in wider society. At least one study, however, has shown the use of sexual violence in women's prisons as a form of revenge against inmates who are overly vocal in their condemnation of such practices among other prisoners.[51]

Not all abuse occurs at the hands of inmates. In 1992, 14 correctional officers, ten men and four women, were indicted for the alleged abuse of female inmates at the 900-bed Women's Correctional Institute in Hardwick, Georgia. The charges resulted from affidavits filed by 90 female inmates alleging "rape, sexual abuse, prostitution, coerced abortions, sex for favors, and retaliation for refusal to participate" in such activities.[52] One inmate who was forced to have an abortion after becoming pregnant by a male staff member said, "As an inmate, I simply felt powerless to avoid the sexual advances of staff and to refuse to have an abortion."[53]

To address the problems of imprisoned women, including violence, the Task Force on the Female Offender recommended a number of changes in the administration of prisons for women.[54] Among those recommendations were these:

- Substance-abuse programs should be available to female inmates.
- Female inmates need to acquire greater literacy skills, and literacy programs should form the basis upon which other programs are built.
- Female offenders should be housed in buildings without male inmates.
- Institutions for women should develop programs for keeping children in the facility in order to "fortify the bond between mother and child."
- To ensure equal access to assistance, institutions should be built to accommodate programs for female offenders.

Learn more about women in prison and their special needs via **Library Extras! 13–4** and **13–5** at cjtoday.com.

The Staff World

The flip side of inmate society can be found in the world of the prison staff, which includes many more people and professions than guard. Staff roles encompass those of warden, psychologist, counselor, area supervisor, program director, instructor, correctional officer, and—in some large prisons—physician and therapist. Correctional officers, generally considered to be at the bottom of the staff hierarchy, may be divided into cell-block and tower guards; others are assigned to administrative offices, where they perform clerical tasks.

Like prisoners, correctional officers undergo a socialization process that helps them function by the official and unofficial rules of staff society. In a now-classic study, Lucien X. Lombardo described the process by which officers are socialized into the prison work world.[55] Lombardo interviewed 359 correctional personnel at New York's Auburn Prison and found that rookie officers had to quickly abandon preconceptions of both inmates and other staff members. According to Lombardo, new officers learn that inmates are not the "monsters" much of the public makes them out to be. On the other hand, rookies may be seriously disappointed in their experienced colleagues when they realize that the ideals of professionalism, often emphasized during early training, rarely translate into reality. The pressures of the institutional work environment, however, soon force most correctional personnel to adopt a united front in relating to inmates.

One of the leading formative influences on staff culture is the potential threat that inmates pose. Inmates far outnumber correctional personnel in every institution, and the hostility they feel for guards is only barely hidden even at the best of times. Correctional personnel know that however friendly inmates may appear, a sudden change in institutional climate—as can happen in anything from simple disturbances on the yard to full-blown riots—can quickly and violently unmask deep-rooted feelings of mistrust and hatred.

As in years past, prison staffers are still most concerned with custody and control. Society, especially under the just deserts philosophy of criminal sentencing, expects correctional staff to keep inmates in custody; this is the basic prerequisite of successful job performance. Custody is necessary before any other correctional activities, such as instruction or counseling, can be undertaken. Control, the other major staff concern, ensures order, and an orderly prison is thought to be safe and secure. In routine daily activities, control over almost all aspects of inmate behavior becomes paramount in the minds of most correctional officers. It is the twin interests of custody and control that lead to institutionalized procedures for ensuring security in most facilities. The enforcement of strict rules; body and cell searches; counts; unannounced shakedowns; the control of dangerous items, materials, and contraband; and the extensive use of bars, locks, fencing, cameras, and alarms all support the human vigilance of the staff in maintaining security.

Types of Correctional Officers

Staff culture, in combination with naturally occurring personality types, gives rise to a diversity of correctional officer types. Like the inmate typology we've already discussed, correctional staff can be classified according to certain distinguishing characteristics. Among the most prevalent types are these:

- *The dictator.* Some officers go by the book; others go beyond it, using prison rules to enforce their own brand of discipline. The guard who demands signs of inmate subservience, from constant use of the word *sir* or *ma'am* to frequent free shoe shines, is one type of dictator. Another goes beyond legality, beating or "macing" inmates even for minor infractions or perceived insults. Dictator guards are bullies. They find their counterpart in the "mean dude" inmate described earlier.

  Dictator guards may have sadistic personalities and gain ego satisfaction through the feelings of near omnipotence which come from the total control of others. Some may be fundamentally insecure and employ a false bravado to hide their fear of inmates. Officers who fit the dictator category are the most likely to be targeted for vengeance should control of the institution temporarily fall into the hands of the inmates.

- *The friend.* Friendly officers try to fraternize with inmates. They approach the issue of control by trying to be "one of the guys." They seem to believe that they can win inmate cooperation by being nice. Unfortunately, such guards do not recognize that fraternization quickly leads to unending requests for special favors, from delivering mail to bending "minor" prison rules. Once a few rules have been "bent," the officer may find that inmates have the upper hand through the potential for blackmail.

  Many officers have amiable relationships with inmates. In most cases, however, affability is only a convenience which both sides recognize can quickly evaporate. "Friendly officers," as the term is being used here, are *overly* friendly. They may be young and inexperienced. On the other hand, they may simply be possessed of kind and idealistic personalities built on successful friendships in free society.

- *The merchant.* Contraband could not exist in any correctional facility without the merchant officer. The merchant participates in the inmate economy, supplying drugs, pornography, alcohol, and sometimes even weapons to inmates who can afford to pay for them.

  Probably only a very few officers consistently perform the role of merchant, although a far larger proportion may occasionally turn a few dollars by smuggling some item through the gate. Low salaries create the potential for mercantile corruption among many otherwise straight-arrow officers. Until salaries rise substantially, the merchant will remain an institutionalized feature of most prisons.

- *The turnkey.* The turnkey officer cares little for what goes on in the prison. Officers who fit this category may be close to retirement, or they may be alienated from their jobs for various reasons. Low pay, the view that inmates are basically worthless and incapable of changing, and the monotonous ethic of "doing time" all combine to numb the professional consciousness of even young officers.

  The term *turnkey* comes from prison argot where it means a guard who is there just to open and shut doors and who cares about nothing other than getting through his or her shift. Inmates do not see the turnkey as a threat, nor is such an officer likely to challenge the status quo in institutions where merchant guards operate.

- *The climber.* The climber is apt to be a young officer with an eye for promotion. Nothing seems impossible to the climber, who probably hopes eventually to be warden or program director or to hold some high-status position within the institutional hierarchy. Climbers are likely to be involved in schooling, correspondence courses, and professional organizations. They may lead a movement toward unionization for correctional personnel and tend to see the guard's role as a "profession" which should receive greater social recognition.

CJ Today Exhibit 13-2

[American Correctional Association Code of Ethics]

Preamble

The American Correctional Association expects of its members unfailing honesty, respect for the dignity and individuality of human beings and a commitment to professional and compassionate service. To this end, we subscribe to the following principles:

- Members shall respect and protect the civil and legal rights of all individuals.
- Members shall treat every professional situation with concern for the welfare of the individuals involved and with no intent to personal gain.
- Members shall maintain relationships with colleagues to promote mutual respect within the profession and improve the quality of service.
- Members shall make public criticisms of their colleagues or their agencies only when warranted, verifiable, and constructive.
- Members shall respect the importance of all disciplines within the criminal justice system and work to improve cooperation with each segment.
- Members shall honor the public's right to information and share information with the public to the extent permitted by law subject to individuals' right to privacy.
- Members shall respect and protect the right of the public to be safeguarded from criminal activity.
- Members shall refrain from using their positions to secure personal privileges or advantages.
- Members shall refrain from allowing personal interest to impair objectivity in the performance of duty while acting in an official capacity.

- Members shall refrain from entering into any formal or informal activity or agreement which presents a conflict of interest or is inconsistent with the conscientious performance of duties.
- Members shall refrain from accepting any gifts, service, or favor that is or appears to be improper or implies an obligation inconsistent with the free and objective exercise of professional duties.
- Members shall clearly differentiate between personal views/statements and views/statements/positions made on behalf of the agency or association.
- Members shall report to appropriate authorities any corrupt or unethical behaviors in which there is sufficient evidence to justify review.
- Members shall refrain from discriminating against any individual because of race, gender, creed, national origin, religious affiliation, age, disability, or any other type of prohibited discrimination.
- Members shall preserve the integrity of private information; they shall refrain from seeking information on individuals beyond that which is necessary to implement responsibilities and perform their duties; members shall refrain from revealing nonpublic information unless expressly authorized to do so.
- Members shall make all appointments, promotions, and dismissals in accordance with established civil service rules, applicable contract agreements, and individual merit, and not in furtherance of partisan interests.
- Members shall respect, promote, and contribute to a workplace that is safe, healthy, and free of harassment in any form.

Adopted August 1975 at the 105th Congress of Correction. Revised August 1990 at the 120th Congress of Correction. Revised August 1994 at the 124th Congress of Correction.

Source: American Correctional Association. Reprinted with permission. Visit the American Correctional Association at http://www.corrections.com/aca.

Climbers have many ideas. They may be heavily involved in reading about the latest confinement or administrative technology. If so, they will suggest many ways to improve prison routine, often to the consternation of complacent staff members.

Like the turnkey, climbers turn a blind eye toward inmates and their problems. They are more concerned with improving institutional procedures and with their own careers than they are with the treatment or day-to-day control of inmates.

- *The reformer.* The reformer is the do-gooder among officers, the person who believes that prison should offer opportunities for personal change. The reformer tends to lend a sympathetic ear to the personal needs of inmates and is apt to offer "armchair" counseling and suggestions. Many reformers are motivated by personal ideals, and some of them are highly religious. Inmates tend to see the reformer guard as naive but harmless. Because the reformer actually tries to help, even when help is unsolicited, he or she is the most likely of all the guard types to be accepted by prisoners.

The Professionalization of Correctional Officers

Correctional officers have generally been accorded low occupational status. Historically, the role of prison guard required minimal formal education and held few opportunities for professional growth and career advancement. Such jobs were typically low paying, frustrating, and often boring. Growing problems in our nation's prisons, including emerging issues of legal liability, however, increasingly require a well-trained and adequately equipped force of professionals. As correctional personnel have become better trained and more proficient, the old concept of guard has been supplanted by that of correctional officer.

Many states and a growing number of large-city correctional systems make efforts to eliminate individuals with potentially harmful personality characteristics from correctional officer applicant pools. New York, New Jersey, Ohio, Pennsylvania, and Rhode Island, for example, all use some form of psychological screening in assessing candidates for prison jobs.[56]

Although only some states utilize psychological screening, all make use of training programs intended to prepare successful applicants for prison work. New York, for example, requires trainees to complete six weeks of classroom-based instruction, as well as 40 hours of rifle range practice, followed by another six weeks of on-the-job training. Training days begin around 5 A.M. with a mile run and conclude after dark with study halls for students who need extra help. To keep pace with rising inmate populations, the state has often had to run a number of simultaneous training academies.[57]

Prison Riots

The ten years between 1970 and 1980 have been called the "explosive decade" of prison riots.[58] The decade began with a massive uprising at Attica Prison in New York State in September 1971. The Attica riot resulted in 43 deaths. More than 80 men were wounded. The "explosive decade" ended in 1980 at Santa Fe, New Mexico. There, in a riot at the New Mexico Penitentiary, 33 inmates died, the victims of vengeful prisoners out to eliminate rats and informants. Many of the deaths involved mutilation and torture. More than 200 other inmates were beaten and sexually assaulted, and the prison was virtually destroyed.

Prison riots did not stop with the end of the explosive 1970s. For 11 days in 1987, the Atlanta (Georgia) Federal Penitentiary fell into the hands of inmates. The institution was heavily damaged, and inmates had to be temporarily relocated while it was rebuilt. The Atlanta riot followed on the heels of a similar, but less intense, disturbance at the federal detention center at Oakdale, Louisiana. Both outbreaks were attributed to the dissatisfaction of Cuban inmates, most of whom had arrived in the mass exodus known as the Mariel boat lift.[59] Easter Sunday 1993 marked the beginning of an 11-day rebellion at the 1,800-inmate Southern Ohio Correctional Facility in Lucasville, Ohio—one of the country's toughest maximum-security prisons. The riot ended with nine inmates and one correctional officer dead. The officer had been hung. The close of the riot—involving a parade of 450 inmates—was televised as prisoners had demanded. Among other demands were (1) no retaliation by officials, (2) review of medical staffing and care, (3) review of mail and visitation rules, (4) review of commissary prices, and (5) better enforcement against what the inmates called "inappropriate supervision."[60]

Riots related to inmate grievances over perceived disparities in federal drug-sentencing policies and the possible loss of weight-lifting equipment occurred throughout the federal prison system in October 1995. Within a few days, the unrest led to a nationwide lockdown of 73 federal prisons. Although fires were set and a number of inmates and guards were injured, no deaths resulted. In February 2000, a riot between 200 black and Hispanic prisoners in California's infamous Pelican Bay State Prison led to the death of one inmate. Fifteen other inmates were wounded. Finally, in November 2000, 32 inmates took a dozen correctional officers hostage at the privately run Torrance County Detention Facility in Estancia, New Mexico. Two of the guards were stabbed and seriously injured, while another eight were beaten. The riot was finally quelled after an emergency response team threw tear-gas canisters into the area where the prisoners had barricaded themselves.[61]

Causes of Riots

It is difficult to explain satisfactorily why prisoners riot, despite study groups which attempt to piece together the "facts" leading up to an incident. After the riot at Attica in 1971, for example, the New York State Special Commission of Inquiry filed a report which recommended the creation of inmate advisory councils, changes in staff titles and uniforms, and other institutional improvements. The report emphasized "enhancing [the] dig-

A Broad River (South Carolina) Correctional Institution inmate being subdued following a riot in 1995. A new rule requiring collar-length hair sparked the riot, which resulted in five staff members being stabbed. Three others were taken hostage.
AP/Wide World Photos

nity, worth, and self-confidence" of inmates. In a final report on the violence at Santa Fe in 1980, the New Mexico attorney general blamed a breakdown in informal controls and the subsequent emergence of a new group of violent inmates among the general prison population.[62]

Researchers have suggested a variety of causes for prison riots.[63] Among them are these:

■ An insensitive prison administration and neglected inmates' demands. Calls for "fairness" in disciplinary hearings, better food, more recreational opportunities, and the like may lead to riots when ignored.

■ The lifestyles most inmates are familiar with on the streets. It should be no surprise that prisoners use organized violence when many of them are violent people.

■ Dehumanizing prison conditions. Overcrowded facilities, the lack of opportunity for individual expression, and other aspects of total institutions culminate in explosive situations of which riots are but one form.

■ To regulate inmate society and redistribute power balances among inmate groups. Riots provide the opportunity to "cleanse" the prison population of informers and rats and to resolve struggles among power brokers and ethnic groups within the institution.

■ "Power vacuums" created by changes in prison administration, the transfer of influential inmates, or court-ordered injunctions which significantly alter the informal social control mechanisms of the institution.

Although riots are difficult to predict in specific institutions, some state prison systems appear ripe for disorder. The Texas prison system, for example, is home to a number of gangs, among whom turf violations can easily lead to widespread disorder. Gang membership among inmates in the Texas prison system, practically nonexistent in 1983, was estimated at over 1,200 in 1992.[64] The Texas Syndicate, the Aryan Brotherhood of Texas, and the Mexican Mafia (sometimes known as La Eme, Spanish for the letter *M*) are probably the largest gangs functioning in the Texas prison system. Each has around 300 members.[65] Other gangs known to operate in some Texas prisons include Aryan Warriors, Black Gangster Disciples (mostly in midwestern Texas), the Black Guerrilla Family, the Confederate Knights of America, and Nuestra Familia, an organization of Hispanic prisoners.

Gangs in Texas grew rapidly in part because of the power vacuum created when a court ruling ended the "building tender" system.[66] Building tenders were tough inmates who were given an almost free reign by prison administrators in keeping other inmates in line, especially in many of the state's worst prisons. The end of the building tender system dramatically increased demands on the Texas Department of Criminal Justice for increased abilities and professionalism among its guards and other prison staff.

The "real" reasons for any riot are probably specific to the institution and may not allow for easy generalization. However, it is no simple coincidence that the "explosive decade" of prison riots coincided with the growth of the revolutionary prisoner subculture referred to earlier. As the old convict code began to give way to an emerging perception of social victimization among inmates, it was probably only a matter of time until those perceptions turned to militancy. Seen from this perspective, riots are more a revolutionary activity undertaken by politically motivated cliques than spontaneous and disorganized expressions stemming from the frustrations of prison life.

Stages in Riots and Riot Control

Riots are generally unplanned and tend to occur spontaneously, the result of some relatively minor precipitating event. Once the stage has been set, prison riots tend to evolve through five phases: (1) explosion, (2) organization into inmate-led groups, (3) confrontation with authority, (4) termination through negotiation or physical confrontation, and (5) reaction and explanation, usually by investigative commissions.[67] Donald Cressey points out that the early explosive stages of a riot tend to involve "binges" during which inmates exult in their newfound freedom with virtual orgies of alcohol and drug use or sexual activity.[68] Buildings are burned, facilities are wrecked, and old grudges between individual inmates and inmate groups are settled, often through violence. After this initial explosive stage, leadership changes tend to occur. New leaders emerge who, at least for a time, may effectively organize inmates into a force that can confront and resist officials' attempts to regain control of the institution. Bargaining strategies then develop and the process of negotiation begins.

In the past, many correctional facilities depended upon informal procedures to quell disturbances, often drawing upon the expertise of seasoned correctional officers who were veterans of past skirmishes and riots. Given the large size of many of today's institutions, the rapidly changing composition of inmate and staff populations, and increasing tensions caused by overcrowding and the movement toward reduced inmate privileges, the "old guard" system can no longer be depended upon to quell disturbances. Hence, most modern facilities have incident-management procedures and systems in place which are implemented in the event of a disturbance. Such systems remove the burden of riot control from the individual officer, depending instead upon a systematic and deliberate approach developed to deal with a wide variety of correctional incidents.

Prisoners' Rights

Until the 1960s, American courts took a neutral approach—commonly called the **hands-off doctrine**—toward the running of prisons. Judges assumed that prison administrators were sufficiently professional in the performance of their duties to balance institutional needs with humane considerations. The hands-off doctrine rested upon the belief that defendants lost most of their rights upon conviction, suffering a kind of **civil death**. Many states defined the concept of civil death through legislation which denied inmates the right to vote, to hold public office, and even to marry. Some states made incarceration for a felony a basis for uncontested divorce at the request of the noncriminal spouse. Aspects of the old notion of civil death are still reality in a number of jurisdictions today, and the Sentencing Project says that 3.9 million American citizens across the nation are barred from voting because of previous felony convictions.[69]

Although the concept of civil death has not entirely disappeared, the hands-off doctrine ended in 1969, when a federal court declared the entire Arkansas prison system to be

hands-off doctrine

A historical policy of nonintervention with regard to prison management that U.S. courts tended to follow until the late 1960s. For the past 30 years, the doctrine has languished as judicial intervention in prison administration has dramatically increased, although there is now some evidence of a return to a new hands-off era.

civil death

The legal status of prisoners in some jurisdictions who are denied the opportunity to vote, hold public office, marry, or enter into contracts by virtue of their status as incarcerated felons. While civil death is primarily of historical interest, some jurisdictions still limit the contractual opportunities available to inmates.

unconstitutional after hearing arguments that it constituted a form of cruel and unusual punishment.[70] The court's decision resulted from what it judged to be pervasive overcrowding and primitive living conditions. Stories about the system by longtime inmates claimed that a number of other inmates had been beaten or shot to death by guards and buried over the years in unmarked graves on prison property. An investigation did unearth some skeletons in old graves, but their origin was never resolved.

Detailed media coverage of the Arkansas prison system gave rise to suspicions about correctional institutions everywhere. Within a few years, federal courts intervened in the running of prisons in Florida, Louisiana, Mississippi, New York City, and Virginia.[71] In 1975, in a precedent-setting decision, U.S. District Court Judge Frank M. Johnson issued an order which banned the Alabama Board of Corrections from accepting any more inmates. Citing a population which was more than double the capacity of the state's system, Judge Johnson enumerated 44 standards to be met before additional inmates could be admitted to prison. Included in the requirements were specific guidelines on living space, staff-to-inmate ratios, visiting privileges, the racial makeup of staff, and food service modifications.

The Legal Basis of Prisoners' Rights

In 1974, the U.S. Supreme Court case of *Pell* v. *Procunier*[72] established a "balancing test" which, although originally addressing only First Amendment rights, eventually served as a guideline generally applicable to all prison operations. In *Pell*, the Court ruled that the "prison inmate retains those First Amendment rights that are not inconsistent with his status as a prisoner or with the legitimate penological objectives of the corrections system."[73] In other words, inmates have rights, much the same as people who are not incarcerated, provided that the legitimate needs of the prison for security, custody, and safety are not compromised. Other court decisions have declared that order maintenance, security, and rehabilitation are all legitimate concerns of prison administration but that financial exigency and convenience are not. As the **balancing test** makes clear, we see reflected in prisoners' rights a microcosm of the individual-rights-versus-public-order dilemma found in wider society.

Further enforcing the legal rights of prisoners is the Civil Rights of Institutionalized Persons Act (CRIPA) of 1980.[74] The law, which has been amended over time, applies to all adult and juvenile state or local jails, detention centers, prisons, mental hospitals, and other care facilities (such as those operated by a state, county, or city for the physically

balancing test

A principle, developed by the courts and applied to the corrections arena by *Pell* v. *Procunier* (1974), which attempts to weigh the rights of an individual, as guaranteed by the Constitution, against the authority of states to make laws or otherwise restrict a person's freedom in order to protect the state's interests and its citizens.

A jailhouse lawyer leaving his cell in Oregon State Penitentiary en route to the prison law library. Jailhouse lawyers are not formally schooled in the law but routinely assist fellow inmates in filing briefs with the court.
AP/Wide World Photos

challenged or chronically ill). Section 1997a of the act, entitled "Initiation of Civil Actions," reads as follows:

> Whenever the Attorney General has reasonable cause to believe that any State, political subdivision of a State, official, employee, or agent thereof, or other person acting on behalf of a State or political subdivision of a State is subjecting persons residing in or confined to an institution . . . to egregious or flagrant conditions which deprive such persons of any rights, privileges, or immunities secured or protected by the Constitution or laws of the United States . . . and that such deprivation is pursuant to a pattern or practice of resistance to the full enjoyment of such rights, privileges, or immunities, the Attorney General, for or in the name of the United States, may institute a civil action in any appropriate United States district court against such party for such equitable relief as may be appropriate.

Significantly, the most recent version of CRIPA also states[75]

> No action shall be brought with respect to prison conditions under section 1983 of this title, or any other Federal law, by a prisoner confined in any jail, prison, or other correctional facility until such administrative remedies as are available are exhausted.

Prisoners' rights, because they are constrained by the legitimate needs of imprisonment, can be thought of as conditional rights rather than absolute rights. The Second Amendment to the U.S. Constitution, for example, grants citizens the right to bear arms. The right to arms is, however, necessarily compromised by the need for order and security in prison, and we would not expect a court to rule that inmates have a right to weapons. Prisoner rights must be balanced against the security, order-maintenance, and treatment needs of correctional institutions.

Conditional rights, because they are subject to the exigencies of imprisonment, bear a strong resemblance to privileges, which should not be surprising since "privileges" were all that inmates officially had until the modern era. The practical difference between a privilege and a conditional right is that privileges exist only at the convenience of granting institutions and can be revoked at any time for any reason. The rights of prisoners, on the other hand, have a basis in the Constitution and in law external to the institution. Although the institution may restrict such rights for legitimate correctional reasons, those rights may not be infringed without good cause that can be demonstrated in a court of law. Mere institutional convenience does not provide a sufficient legal basis for the denial of rights.

The past two decades have seen many lawsuits brought by prisoners challenging the constitutionality of some aspect of confinement. As mentioned in Chapter 10, suits filed by prisoners with the courts are generally called writs of *habeas corpus* and formally request that the person detaining a prisoner bring him or her before a judicial officer to determine the lawfulness of the imprisonment. The American Correctional Association says that most prisoner lawsuits have been based upon "1. the Eighth Amendment prohibition against cruel and unusual punishment; 2. the Fourteenth Amendment prohibition against the taking of life, liberty, or property without due process of law; and 3. the Fourteenth Amendment provision requiring equal protection of the laws."[76] Aside from appeals by inmates which question the propriety of their convictions and sentences, such constitutional challenges represent the bulk of legal action initiated by those imprisoned. State statutes and federal legislation, however, including Section 1983 of the Civil Rights Act of 1871, provide other bases for challenges to the legality of specific prison conditions and procedures.

Precedents in Prisoners' Rights

The U.S. Supreme Court has not yet spoken with finality on a number of prisoners' rights questions. Nonetheless, high court decisions of the last few decades and a number of lower-court findings can be interpreted to identify the existing conditional rights of prisoners, as shown in Table 13–1. A number of especially significant Supreme Court decisions are discussed in the pages which follow.

COMMUNICATIONS

In the case of *Procunier* v. *Martinez* (1974),[77] the Supreme Court ruled that a prisoner's mail may be censored if it is necessary to do so for security purposes. In *McNamara* v. *Moody* (1979),[78] however, a federal court upheld the right of an inmate to write vulgar letters to his girlfriend in which he made disparaging comments about the prison staff. The court reasoned that the letters may have been embarrassing to prison officials but that

THE CONDITIONAL RIGHTS OF INMATES	TABLE 13–1

Religious Freedom

A right of assembly for religious services and groups
A right to attend services of other religious groups
A right to receive visits from ministers
A right to correspond with religious leaders
A right to observe religious dietary laws
A right to wear religious insignia

Freedom of Speech

A right to meet with members of the press[1]
A right to receive publications directly from the publisher
A right to communicate with nonprisoners

Access to Legal Assistance

A right to have access to the courts[2]
A right to visits from attorneys
A right to have mail communications with lawyers[3]
A right to communicate with legal assistance organizations
A right to consult "jailhouse lawyers"[4]
A right to assistance in filing legal papers, which should include one of the following:
- Access to an adequate law library
- Paid attorneys
- Paralegal personnel or law students

Medical Treatment

A right to sanitary and healthy conditions
A right to medical attention for serious physical problems
A right to required medications
A right to treatment in accordance with "doctor's orders"

Protection

A right to food, water, and shelter
A right to protection from foreseeable attack
A right to protection from predictable sexual abuse
A right to protection against suicide

Institutional Punishment and Discipline

An absolute right against corporal punishments (unless sentenced to such punishments)
A limited right to due process prior to punishment, including the following:
- Notice of charges
- A fair and impartial hearing
- An opportunity for defense
- A right to present witnesses
- A written decision

[1]But not beyond the opportunities afforded for inmates to meet with members of the general public.
[2]As restricted by the Prison Litigation Reform Act of 1996.
[3]Mail communications are generally designated as privileged or nonprivileged. Privileged communications include those between inmates and their lawyers or court officials and cannot legitimately be read by prison officials. Nonprivileged communications include most other written communications.
[4]Jailhouse lawyers are inmates with experience in the law, usually gained from filing legal briefs in their own behalf or in the behalf of others. Consultation with jailhouse lawyers was ruled permissible in the Supreme Court case of *Johnson v. Avery*, 393 U.S. 483 (1968), unless inmates are provided with paid legal assistance.

they did not affect the security or order of the institution. However, libelous materials have generally not been accorded First Amendment protection in or out of institutional contexts.

Concerning inmate publications, legal precedent has held that prisoners have no inherent right to publish newspapers or newsletters for use by other prisoners, although many institutions do permit and finance such periodicals.[79] Publications originating from outside of prison, such as newspapers, magazines, and special-interest tracts, have generally been protected when mailed directly from the publisher, although magazines which depict deviant sexual behavior can be banned according to *Mallery v. Lewis* (1983)[80] and other precedents. Nudity by itself is not necessarily obscene, and federal courts have held that prisons cannot ban nude pictures of inmates' wives or girlfriends.[81]

RELIGIOUS PRACTICE

The Supreme Court case of *Cruz v. Beto* (1972)[82] established that inmates must be given a "reasonable opportunity" to pursue their faith, even if it differs from traditional forms of worship. Meeting facilities must be provided for religious use when those same facilities are made available to other groups of prisoners for other purposes,[83] but no group can claim exclusive use of a prison area for religious reasons.[84] The right to assemble for religious purposes, however, can be denied to inmates who use such meetings to plan escapes or who take the opportunity to dispense contraband. Similarly, prisoners in segregation can be denied the opportunity to attend group religious services.[85]

Although prisoners cannot be made to attend religious services,[86] records of religious activity can be maintained to administratively determine dietary needs and eligibility for passes to religious services outside of the institution.[87] In *Dettmer v. Landon* (1985),[88] a federal district court held that an inmate who claimed to practice witchcraft must be provided with the artifacts necessary for his worship services. Included were items such as sea salt, sulfur, a quartz clock, incense, candles, and a white robe without a hood. The district court's opinion was later partially overturned by the U.S. Court of Appeals for the Fourth Circuit. The appellate court recognized the Church of Wicca as a valid religion but held that concerns over prison security could preclude inmates' possession of dangerous items of worship.[89]

Drugs and dangerous substances have not been considered permissible even when inmates claimed they were a necessary part of their religious services.[90] Prison regulations prohibiting the wearing of beards, even those grown for religious reasons, were held acceptable for security reasons in the 1985 federal court case of *Hill v. Blackwell*.[91]

VISITATION

Visitation and access to the news media are other areas which have come under court scrutiny. Maximum-security institutions rarely permit "contact" visits, and some have on occasion suspended all visitation privileges. In the case of *Block v. Rutherford* (1984),[92] the U.S. Supreme Court upheld the policy of the Los Angeles County Central Jail, which prohibited all visits from friends and relatives. The Court agreed that the large jail population and the conditions under which visits might take place could combine to threaten the security of the jail.

In *Pell v. Procunier* (1974),[93] discussed earlier in regard to the balancing test, the Court found in favor of a California law which denied prisoners the opportunity to hold special meetings with members of the press. The Court reasoned that media interviews could be conducted through regular visitation arrangements and that most of the information desired by the media could be conveyed through correspondence. In *Pell*, the Court also held that any reasonable policy of media access was acceptable so long as it was administered fairly and without bias.

In a later case, the Court ruled that news personnel cannot be denied correspondence with inmates but also ruled that they have no constitutional right to interview inmates or to inspect correctional facilities beyond the visitation opportunities available to others.[94] This equal-access policy was set forth in *Houchins v. KQED, Inc.* (1978) by Justice Potter Stewart, who wrote, "The Constitution does no more than assure the public and the press equal access once government has opened its doors."[95]

ACCESS TO THE COURTS AND TO LEGAL ASSISTANCE

A well-established right of prisoners is access to the courts[96] and to legal assistance. The right of prisoners to petition the court was recognized in *Bounds v. Smith* (1977),[97] which, at the time, was a far-reaching Supreme Court decision. While attempting to define "access," the Court in *Bounds* imposed upon the states the duty of assisting inmates in the preparation and filing of legal papers. Assistance could be provided through trained personnel knowledgeable in the law or via law libraries in each institution, which all states have since built. In 1996, however, in the case of *Lewis* v. *Casey*,[98] the U.S. Supreme Court repudiated part of the *Bounds* decision, saying, "[S]tatements in *Bounds* suggesting that prison authorities must also enable the prisoner to discover grievances, and to litigate effectively once in court . . . have no antecedent in this Court's pre-*Bounds* cases, and are now disclaimed." In *Lewis*, the Court overturned earlier decisions by a federal district court and by the Ninth Circuit Court of Appeals. Both lower courts had found in favor of Arizona inmates who had complained that state prison law libraries provided inadequate legal research facilities, thereby depriving them of their right of legal access to the courts, as established by *Bounds*. In turning back portions of *Bounds*, the majority in *Lewis* wrote that inmates raising such claims need to demonstrate "widespread actual injury" to their ability to access the courts, not merely "isolated instances of actual injury." "Moreover," wrote the justices, "*Bounds* does not guarantee inmates the wherewithal to file any and every type of legal claim, but requires only that they be provided with the tools to attack their sentences . . . and to challenge the conditions of their confinement."

In an earlier case, *Johnson* v. *Avery* (1968),[99] the Court had ruled that prisoners under correctional supervision have a right to consult "jailhouse lawyers" for advice when assistance from trained professionals is not available. Other court decisions have established that inmates have a right to correspond with their attorneys[100] and with legal assistance organizations. Such letters, however, can be opened and inspected for contraband[101] (but not read) by prison authorities in the presence of the inmate. The right to meet with hired counsel for reasonable lengths of time has also been upheld.[102] Indigent defendants must be provided with stamps for the purpose of legal correspondence,[103] and inmates cannot be disciplined for communicating with lawyers or requesting legal help. Conversations between inmates and their lawyers can be monitored, although any evidence obtained through such a process cannot be used in court.[104] Inmates do not, however, have the right to an appointed lawyer, even when indigent, if no judicial proceedings have been initiated against them.[105]

MEDICAL CARE

The historic Supreme Court case of *Estelle* v. *Gamble* (1976)[106] specified prison officials' duty to provide for inmates' medical care. In *Estelle*, the Court concerned itself with "deliberate indifference" on the part of the staff toward a prisoner's need for serious medical attention. "Deliberate indifference" can mean a wanton disregard for the health of inmates. Hence, while poor treatment, misdiagnosis, and the like may constitute medical malpractice, they do not necessarily constitute deliberate indifference.[107]

More recently, in *Farmer* v. *Brennan* (1994),[108] the Court clarified the concept of "deliberate indifference" by holding that it required both actual knowledge and disregard of risk of harm. The case involved Dee Farmer, a preoperative transsexual with obvious feminine characteristics who had been incarcerated with other males in the federal prison system. While mixing with other inmates, Farmer was beaten and raped by a fellow prisoner. Subsequently, he sued correctional officials, claiming that they had acted with deliberate indifference to his safety because they knew that the penitentiary had a violent environment as well as a history of inmate assaults and because they should have known that Farmer would be particularly vulnerable to sexual attack. Although both a federal district court and the U.S. Court of Appeals for the seventh circuit agreed with Farmer, the U.S. Supreme Court sent Farmer's case back to a lower court for rehearing after clarifying what it said was necessary to establish deliberate indifference. "Prison officials," wrote the justices, "have a duty under the Eighth Amendment to provide humane conditions of confinement. They must ensure that inmates receive adequate food, clothing, shelter, and medical care and must protect prisoners from violence at the hands of other prisoners. However, a constitutional violation occurs only where . . . the official has acted with 'deliberate indifference' to inmate health or safety." The Court continued, "A prison official may be held liable under the Eighth Amendment for acting with 'deliberate indifference' to inmate health or safety only if he knows that inmates face a substantial risk of serious harm and disregards that risk by failing to take reasonable measures to abate it."[109]

Two other cases, *Ruiz* v. *Estelle* (1982)[110] and *Newman* v. *Alabama* (1972)[111] have had substantial impact on the rights of prisoners to medical attention. In *Ruiz*, the Texas Department of Criminal Justice was found lacking in its correctional medical treatment programs. The court ordered an improvement in record keeping, physical facilities, and general medical care while it continued to monitor the progress of the department. In *Newman*, Alabama's prison medical services were found to be so inadequate as to be "shocking to the conscience." Problems with the Alabama program included[112]

■ Not enough medical personnel

■ Poor physical facilities for medical treatment

■ Poor administrative techniques for dispersal of medications

■ Poor medical records

■ A lack of medical supplies

■ Poorly trained or untrained inmates who provided some medical services and performed minor surgery

■ Medically untrained personnel who determined the need for treatment

Part of the issue of medical treatment is the question of whether inmates can be forced to take medication or to eat. A 1984 federal court case held that inmates could be medicated in emergency situations against their will.[113] The court did recognize that unwanted medications designed to produce only psychological effects, such as tranquilizers, might be refused more readily than life-sustaining drugs.[114] Similarly, other courts have held that inmates do not have a right to starve themselves to death.

In 1993, the U.S. Supreme Court indicated that environmental conditions of prison life which pose a threat to inmate health may have to be corrected. In *Helling* v. *McKinney*,[115] Nevada inmate William McKinney claimed that exposure to secondary cigarette smoke circulating in his cell was threatening his health, in violation of the Eighth Amendment's prohibition against cruel and unusual punishment. The Court, in ordering that a federal district court provide McKinney with the opportunity to prove his allegations, held that "an

---

CJ Today Exhibit 13-3

[Federal Oversight of the Texas Prison System: A Timeline]

1972: Inmate David Ruiz and several other prisoners file a civil rights suit against the Texas Department of Corrections (now called the Texas Department of Criminal Justice), alleging constitutional violations.

October 2, 1978–September 20, 1979: The *Ruiz* case is tried in Houston.

December 10, 1980: U.S. District Court Judge William Wayne Justice finds that confinement in the Texas prison system constitutes cruel and unusual punishment. He cites overcrowding, understaffing, brutality by guards and inmate-guards known as *building tenders*, substandard medical care, and uncontrolled physical abuse among inmates.

January 12, 1981: The judge orders improvements to be made to the system and sets deadlines.

April 19, 1981: Judge Justice appoints a special master to supervise compliance.

April 1982: The state agrees to halt the building tender system and to hire additional correctional officers.

January–June 1983: The Texas legislature passes laws intended to reduce the prison population.

November 1987: Texas voters authorize $500 million in bonds for prison construction.

March 31, 1990: The special master's office is closed.

November 1990: Texas voters approve $672 million in bonds to build 25,300 prison beds and 12,000 drug- and alcohol-treatment beds.

February 1992: Inmates' attorneys and the Texas Board of Criminal Justice reach an agreement. Texas Attorney General Dan Morales rejects it.

May 1, 1992: Morales offers a settlement proposal.

July 14, 1992: Inmates' attorneys accept the proposal.

December 11, 1992: Judge Justice signs the settlement.

January 21, 1999: Judge Justice begins a hearing to determine whether Texas prisons should be freed of federal court oversight.

March 1, 1999: Judge Justice decides to maintain oversight of the prison system.

March 20, 2001: The 5th U.S. Circuit Court of Appeals reverses Judge Justice's ruling, ending oversight but giving him 90 days to review the matter.

June 18, 2001: Judge Justice says that the Texas prison system has improved but that oversight is still needed in the areas of "conditions of confinement in administrative segregation, the failure to provide reasonable safety to inmates against assault and abuse, and the excessive use of force by correctional officers." Judge Justice discontinues federal oversight of other aspects of the prison system, including health services and staffing.

Source: Adapted from Ed Timms, "Judge to Lessen Oversight of Texas Prisons," *Dallas Morning News*, June 19, 2001. Reprinted with permission. Web posted at http://www.dallasnews.com/archive. Accessed March 12, 2002.

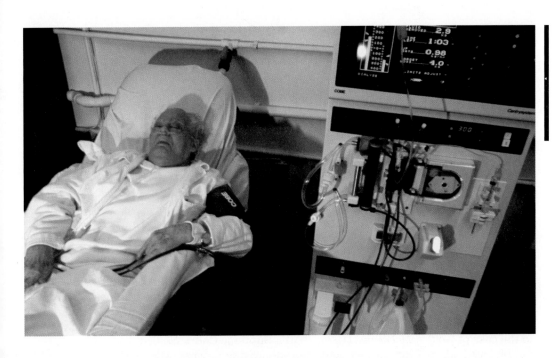

Inmate Santos Pagon undergoes kidney dialysis at Laurel Highlands Prison in Pennsylvania. Court decisions over the years have established a firm set of inmate rights. Among them is the right to necessary health care.

Mark Petersen, CORBIS/SABA Press Photos, Inc.

injunction cannot be denied to inmates who plainly prove an unsafe, life-threatening condition on the ground that nothing yet has happened to them." In effect, the *Helling* case gave notice to prison officials that they are responsible not only for "inmates' current serious health problems," but also for maintaining environmental conditions under which health problems might be prevented from developing.

In 1998, in the case of *Pennsylvania Department of Corrections* v. *Yeskey*,[116] the Supreme Court held that the Americans with Disabilities Act (ADA) of 1990[117] applies to prisons and to prison inmates. In May 1994, Ronald Yeskey was sentenced to serve 18 to 36 months in a Pennsylvania correctional facility. The sentencing court recommended that he be placed in Pennsylvania's Motivational Boot Camp for first-time offenders, the successful completion of which would have led to his release on parole in just six months. When Yeskey was refused admission because of his medical history of hypertension, he sued the Pennsylvania Department of Corrections and several state officials, alleging that his exclusion violated the ADA, Title II of which prohibits a "public entity" from discriminating against a "qualified individual with a disability" on account of that disability. Lawyers for the state of Pennsylvania argued that state prisoners are not covered by the ADA. The Supreme Court ruled, however, that "state prisons fall squarely within Title II's statutory definition of 'public entity,' which includes 'any . . . instrumentality of a State . . . or local government.'"

PRIVACY

Many court decisions, including the Tenth Circuit case of *U.S.* v. *Ready* (1978)[118] and the U.S. Supreme Court decisions of *Katz* v. *U.S.* (1967)[119] and *Hudson* v. *Palmer* (1984)[120] have held that inmates cannot have a reasonable expectation to privacy while incarcerated. Palmer, an inmate in Virginia, claimed that Hudson, a prison guard, had unreasonably destroyed some of his personal (noncontraband) property following a cell search. Palmer's complaint centered on the lack of due process which accompanied the destruction. The Court disagreed, saying that the need for prison officials to conduct thorough and unannounced searches precludes inmate privacy in personal possessions. In *Block* v. *Rutherford* (1984),[121] the Court established that prisoners do not have a right to be present during a search of their cells.

Some lower courts, however, have begun to indicate that body-cavity searches may be unreasonable unless based upon a demonstrable suspicion or conducted after prior warning has been given to the inmate.[122] They have also indicated that searches conducted simply to "harass or humiliate" inmates are illegitimate.[123] These cases may be an indication that the Supreme Court will eventually recognize a limited degree of privacy in prison cell searches, especially those which uncover legal documents and personal papers prepared by the prisoner.

GRIEVANCE AND DISCIPLINARY PROCEDURES

A major area of inmate concern is the hearing of grievances. Complaints may arise in areas as diverse as food service (quality of food or special diets for religious purposes or health regimens), interpersonal relations between inmates and staff, denial of privileges, and alleged misconduct levied against an inmate or a guard.

In 1972, the National Council on Crime and Delinquency developed a Model Act for the Protection of Rights of Prisoners, which included the opportunity for grievances to be heard. The 1973 National Advisory Commission on Criminal Justice Standards and Goals called for the establishment of responsible practices for the hearing of inmate grievances. Finally, in 1977, in the case of *Jones* v. *North Carolina Prisoners' Labor Union*,[124] the Supreme Court held that prisons must establish some formal opportunity for the airing of inmate grievances. Soon, formal grievance plans were established in prisons in an attempt to divert inmate grievances away from the courts.

grievance procedure

A formalized arrangement, usually involving a neutral hearing board, whereby institutionalized individuals have the opportunity to register complaints about the conditions of their confinement.

Today, all sizable prisons have an established **grievance procedure** whereby an inmate files a complaint with local authorities and receives a mandated response. Modern grievance procedures range from the use of a hearing board composed of staff members and inmates to a single staff appointee charged with the resolution of complaints. Inmates who are dissatisfied with the handling of their grievance can generally appeal beyond the local prison.

Disciplinary actions by prison authorities may also require a formalized hearing process, especially when staff members bring charges of rule violations against inmates which might result in some form of punishment being imposed on them. In a precedent-setting decision in the case of *Wolff* v. *McDonnell* (1974),[125] the Supreme Court decided that sanctions could not be levied against inmates without appropriate due process. The *Wolff* case involved an inmate who had been deprived of previously earned "good-time" credits because of misbehavior. The Court established that "good-time" credits were a form of "state-created right(s)," which, once created, could not be "arbitrarily abrogated."[126] *Wolff* was especially significant because it began an era of court scrutiny of what came to be called *state-created liberty interests*. State-created liberty interests were said to be based upon the language used in published prison regulations and were held, in effect, to confer due process guarantees upon prisoners. Hence, if a prison regulation said that a disciplinary hearing should be held before a prisoner could be sent to solitary confinement and that such a hearing should permit a discussion of the evidence for and against the prisoner, courts interpreted that regulation to mean that the prisoner had a state-created right to a hearing and that sending him or her to solitary confinement in violation of the regulation was a violation of a state-created liberty interest. State-created rights and privileges were also called *protected liberties* in later court decisions and were interpreted to include any significant change in a prisoner's status.

In the interest of due process, and especially where written prison regulations governing the hearing process exist, courts have generally held that inmates going before disciplinary hearing boards are entitled to (1) notice of the charges brought against them, (2) the chance to organize a defense, (3) an impartial hearing, and (4) the opportunity to present witnesses and evidence in their behalf. A written statement of the hearing board's conclusions should be provided to the inmate.[127] In the case of *Ponte* v. *Real* (1985),[128] the Supreme Court held that prison officials must provide an explanation to inmates who are denied the opportunity to have a desired witness at their hearing. The case of *Vitek* v. *Jones* (1980)[129] extended the requirement of due process to inmates about to be transferred from prisons to mental hospitals.

So that inmates can know what is expected of them as they enter prison, the American Correctional Association recommends that "a rulebook that contains all chargeable offenses, ranges of penalties and disciplinary procedures [be] posted in a conspicuous and accessible area; [and] a copy . . . given to each inmate and staff member."[130]

A Return to the Hands-Off Doctrine?

Many state-created rights and protected liberties may soon be a thing of the past. In June 1991, an increasingly conservative U.S. Supreme Court signaled the beginning of what appears to be at least a partial return to the "hands-off" doctrine of earlier times. The case, *Wilson* v. *Seiter*,[131] involved a 1983 suit brought against Richard P. Seiter, Director of the Ohio Department of Rehabilitation and Correction, and Carl Humphreys, Warden of the Hocking Correctional Facility (HCF) in Nelsonville, Ohio. In the suit, Pearly L. Wilson, a felon incarcerated at HCF, alleged that a number of the conditions of his confinement constituted cruel and unusual punishment in violation of the Eighth and Fourteenth Amendments to the U.S. Constitution. Specifically, Wilson cited overcrowding, excessive noise,

---

WHAT WOULD YOU DO?

The CD-ROM scenario for Chapter 13 is built around the issue of prisoners' rights—specifically whether inmates have a right to be informed of charges against them in a prison disciplinary hearing and whether they have a right to contribute to that procedure by presenting evidence and witnesses on their behalf. The scenario is based upon an actual U.S. Supreme Court case. Work through the scenario using the CD-ROM found in the back of your textbook to learn what the federal courts have decided in this area. Be especially attentive to the issue of state-created "liberty interests" and how they might influence the outcome of cases like this.

CJ Today News

[Male Prisoners Have Right to Procreate, Court Rules]

In the first ruling of its kind, a federal court says male prisoners have a constitutional right to procreate while they are incarcerated.

In a 2-1 decision Wednesday, a panel of the U.S. Court of Appeals for the 9th Circuit said William Gerber, 41, who's serving a 111-year sentence in California, has a "fundamental right to procreate" that is not "temporarily extinguished" while he is serving his time.

Because prisoners serving life sentences in California are barred from having conjugal visits, Gerber wants to impregnate his 46-year-old wife by artificial insemination, a procedure he and his wife say they will pay for.

Gerber filed suit 2 years ago, accusing the California Department of Corrections of violating his civil rights for refusing to allow him to send a semen sample through the mail to a Chicago medical firm, which would use the specimen to impregnate his wife.

The decision does not apply to female inmates and rejects the prison warden's concern that women prisoners would seek to be artificially inseminated if Gerber is permitted to go forward with his plans.

"Gerber does not seek to *be* artificially inseminated," Judge Myron Bright wrote. "The two sexes are not similarly situated here."

Since the 1940s, the U.S. Supreme Court has held that people have a right to procreate. The high court has ruled that prisoners have a right to marry and that they can't be sterilized because they have a right to have children once they are released from custody.

"We are heartened that the 9th Circuit has recognized that prisoners retain some semblance of rights," said Eric Balaban, staff counsel for the American Civil Liberties Union's National Prison Project.

Conservative groups criticized the ruling as another liberal decision from the 9th Circuit, a frequent target of reversals by the Supreme Court. Michael Rushford, president of the Criminal Justice Legal Foundation, said prisoners lose freedoms when they are locked up. "No babies while you're in the joint," he said. "You get those rights back when you've served your time."

The state attorney general has not decided whether to appeal.

Bright, writing for the majority, said Gerber has a right to use artificial insemination unless prison officials cite "legitimate penological interests" for rejecting the inmate's request.

In his dissent, Judge Barry Silverman said the majority opinion defied common sense. "The majority simply does not accept the fact that there are certain downsides to being confined in prison, and the interference with a normal family life is one of them," he wrote.

Silverman agreed that inmates don't lose all of their rights once they are put behind bars. "All of that," he wrote, "however, is a far cry from holding that inmates retain a constitutional right to procreate from prison via FedEx."

For the latest in crime and justice news, visit the Talk Justice news feed at http://www.crimenews.info.

Source: Toni Locy, "Male Prisoners Have Right to Procreate, Court Rules," *USA Today*, September 7, 2001, p. 2A. © 2001 *USA Today*. Reprinted with permission.

---

insufficient locker storage space, inadequate heating and cooling, improper ventilation, unclean and inadequate restrooms, unsanitary dining facilities and food preparation, and housing with mentally and physically ill inmates. Wilson asked for a change in prison conditions and sought $900,000 from prison officials in compensatory and punitive damages.

Both the federal district court in which Wilson first filed affidavits and the Sixth Circuit Court of Appeals held that no constitutional violations existed because the conditions cited by Wilson were not the result of malicious intent on the part of officials. The U.S. Supreme Court agreed, noting that the "deliberate indifference" standard applied in *Estelle* v. *Gamble* (1976)[132] to claims involving medical care is similarly applicable to other cases in which prisoners challenge the conditions of their confinement. In effect, the Court created a standard which effectively means that all future challenges to prison conditions by inmates, which are brought under the Eighth Amendment, must show "deliberate indifference" by the officials responsible for the existence of those conditions before the Court will hear the complaint.

The written opinion of the Court in *Wilson* v. *Seiter* is telling. Writing for the majority, Justice Antonin Scalia observed that "if a prison boiler malfunctions accidentally during a cold winter, an inmate would have no basis for an Eighth Amendment claim, even if he suffers objectively significant harm. If a guard accidentally stepped on a prisoner's toe and broke it, this would not be punishment in anything remotely like the accepted meaning of the word."

Although the criterion of deliberate indifference is still evolving, it is likely that such indifference could be demonstrated by petitioners able to show that prison administrators have done nothing to alleviate life-threatening prison conditions after those conditions had been called to their attention. Even so, critics of *Wilson* are concerned that the decision may excuse prison authorities from the need to improve living conditions within institutions on the basis of simple budgetary constraints. Four of the justices themselves recognized the potential held by *Wilson* for a near return to the days of the hands-off doctrine. Although concurring with the Court's majority, Justices Byron White, Thurgood Marshall, Harry Blackmun, and John Paul Stevens noted their fear that "[t]he ultimate result of today's decision [may be] that 'serious deprivations of basic human needs' . . . will go unredressed due to an unnecessary and meaningless search for 'deliberate indifference.'"

In the 1995 case of *Sandin* v. *Conner*,[133] the U.S. Supreme Court took a much more definitive stance in favor of a new type of hands-off doctrine and voted 5 to 4 to reject the argument that any state action taken for a punitive reason encroaches upon a prisoner's constitutional due process right to be free from the deprivation of liberty. The Court effectively set aside substantial portions of earlier decisions, such as *Wolff* v. *McDonnell* (1974)[134] and *Hewitt* v. *Helms* (1983),[135] which, wrote the justices, focused more on procedural issues than on those of "real substance." As a consequence, the majority opinion held, past cases such as these have "impermissibly shifted the focus" away from the nature of a due process deprivation to one based on the language of a particular state or prison regulation. "This shift in focus," the justices wrote, "has encouraged prisoners to comb regulations in search of mandatory language on which to base entitlements to various state-conferred privileges." As a result, the Court said, cases like *Wolff* and *Hewitt* "created disincentives for States to codify prison management procedures in [order to avoid lawsuits by inmates], and . . . led to the involvement of federal courts in the day-to-day management of prisons."

In *Sandin*, Demont Conner, an inmate at the Halawa Correctional Facility in Hawaii, was serving an indeterminate sentence of 30 years to life for numerous crimes, including murder, kidnapping, robbery, and burglary. Conner alleged in a lawsuit in federal court that prison officials had deprived him of procedural due process when a hearing committee refused to allow him to present witnesses during a disciplinary hearing and then sentenced him to segregation for alleged misconduct. An appellate court agreed with Conner, concluding that an existing prison regulation which instructed the hearing committee to find guilt in cases where a misconduct charge is supported by substantial evidence meant that the committee could not impose segregation if it did not look at all the evidence available to it.

The Supreme Court, however, reversed the decision of the appellate court, holding that while "such a conclusion may be entirely sensible in the ordinary task of construing a statute defining rights and remedies available to the general public, [i]t is a good deal less sensible in the case of a prison regulation primarily designed to guide correctional officials in the administration of a prison." The Court concluded that "such regulations [are] not designed to confer rights on inmates" but are meant only to provide guidelines to prison staff members. Hence, based upon *Sandin*, it appears that inmates in the future will have a much more difficult time challenging the administrative regulations and procedures imposed upon them by prison officials, even when stated procedures are not explicitly followed. "The *Hewitt* approach," wrote the majority in *Sandin*, "has run counter to the view expressed in several of our cases that federal courts ought to afford appropriate deference and flexibility to state officials trying to manage a volatile environment. . . . The time has come," said the Court, "to return to those due process principles that were correctly established and applied" in earlier times.

> The Privilege of the Writ of Habeas Corpus shall not be suspended, unless when in Cases of Rebellion or Invasion the public Safety may require it.
>
> —Article I, Section 9, Clause 2, of the U.S. Constitution

THE PRISON LITIGATION REFORM ACT OF 1996

Only about 2,000 petitions per year concerning inmate problems were filed with the courts in 1961, but by 1975 the number of filings had increased to around 17,000, and by 1996 prisoners filed 68,235 civil rights lawsuits in federal courts nationwide.[136] Some inmate-originated suits seemed patently ludicrous and became the subject of much media coverage in the mid-1990s.[137] One such suit involved Robert Procup, a Florida State Prison inmate serving time for the murder of his business partner. Procup repeatedly sued Florida prison officials—once because he got only one roll with his dinner; again because he didn't get a luncheon salad; a third time because prison-provided TV dinners didn't come with a drink; and a fourth time because his cell had no television. Two other well-publicized cases involved an inmate who went to court asking to be allowed to exercise religious freedom by attending prison chapel services in the nude and an inmate who, thinking he could become pregnant via homosexual relations, sued prison doctors who wouldn't provide him with birth-control pills. An infamous example of seemingly frivolous inmate lawsuits was one brought by inmates claiming religious freedoms and demanding that members of the Church of the New Song, or CONS, be provided steak and Harvey's Bristol Cream every

Friday in order to celebrate communion. The CONS suit stayed in various courts for ten years before finally being thrown out.[138]

The huge number of inmate-originated lawsuits in the mid-1990s created a backlog of cases in many federal courts and was targeted by the media and by some citizens' groups as an unnecessary waste of taxpayers' money. The National Association of Attorneys General, which supports efforts to restrict frivolous inmate lawsuits, estimated that lawsuits filed by prisoners cost states more than $81 million a year in legal fees alone.[139]

In 1996, the federal Prison Litigation Reform Act (PLRA) became law.[140] The PLRA is a clear legislative effort to restrict inmate filings to worthwhile cases and to reduce the number of suits brought by state prisoners in federal courts. The PLRA

- Requires inmates to exhaust their prison's grievance procedure before filing a lawsuit
- Requires judges to screen all inmate complaints against the federal government and to immediately dismiss those deemed frivolous or without merit
- Prohibits prisoners from filing a lawsuit for mental or emotional injury unless they can also show there has been physical injury
- Requires inmates to pay court filing fees. Prisoners who don't have the needed funds can pay the filing fee over a period of time through deductions to their prison commissary accounts
- Limits the award of attorneys' fees in successful lawsuits brought by inmates
- Revokes the credits earned by federal prisoners toward early release if they file a malicious lawsuit
- Mandates that court orders affecting prison administration cannot go any further than necessary to correct a violation of a particular inmate's civil rights
- Makes it possible for state officials to have court orders lifted after two years unless there is a new finding of a continuing violation of federally guaranteed civil rights
- Mandates that any court order requiring the release of prisoners due to overcrowding be approved by a three-member court before it can become effective

The PLRA has been effective in reducing the number of frivolous lawsuits filed by inmates alleging unconstitutional prison conditions. In 1997, for example, in the case of *Edwards* v. *Balisok*,[141] the Supreme Court made it harder to successfully challenge prison disciplinary convictions. The Court held that prisoners cannot sue for monetary damages under 42 U.S.C. § 1983 for loss of good-time until they sue in state court and get their disciplinary conviction set aside.[142] In *Booth* v. *Churner* (2001),[143] the U.S. Supreme Court held that, under the PLRA, "an inmate seeking only [monetary] damages must complete any prison administrative process capable of addressing the inmate's complaint and providing some form of relief [before filing his or her grievance with a federal court], even if the process does not make specific provision for monetary relief." The case involved Timothy Booth, a Pennsylvania inmate who had filed a Section 1983 action in federal district court seeking financial compensation from the state based on the claim that corrections officers had violated his Eight Amendment right to be free from cruel and unusual punishment by assaulting him, using excessive force against him, and denying him medical attention to treat his injuries.

Opponents of the PLRA fear that it might stifle the filing of meritorious suits by inmates facing real deprivations. According to the ACLU, for example, "The Prison Litigation Reform Act, passed in 1996, attempts to slam the courthouse door on society's most vulnerable members. It seeks to strip the federal courts of much of their power to correct even the most egregious prison conditions by altering the basic rules which have always governed prison reform litigation. The PLRA also makes it difficult to settle prison cases by consent decree, and limits the life span of any court judgment."[144] The ACLU is leading a nationwide effort to have many provisions of the PLRA overturned. So far, however, the effort has borne little fruit.

Issues Facing Prisons Today

Prisons are society's answer to a number of social problems. They house outcasts, misfits, and some highly dangerous people. While prisons provide a part of the answer to the question of crime control, they also face problems of their own. A few of those special problems are described here.

AIDS

Chapter 6 discussed the steps being taken by police agencies to deal with health threats represented by acquired immunodeficiency syndrome (AIDS). In 2001, the Justice Department reported finding 25,757 cases of AIDS among inmates of the nation's prisons[145]—more than a 12-fold increase over 1987, when surveys were first conducted. At the time of the most recent survey, 3.4% of all female state prison inmates tested positive for HIV infection, as did 2.1% of male prisoners. Some states have especially high rates of HIV infection among their prisoners. Almost 10% of New York prison inmates, for example, are HIV-positive. Of all HIV-positive inmates, 24% exhibit symptoms of AIDS.[146] Jail populations exhibit a similar prevalence of HIV infection. In both prisons and jails, the highest incidence of infection is found among inmates being held on drug charges (2.9%), while property offenders (2.4%) and violent criminals (1.9%) have somewhat lower rates. Those who reported having shared a needle to use drugs prior to arrest had the highest infection rate (7.7%).[147]

The incidence of HIV infection among the general population stands at 120 cases per 100,000, according to a recent report by the Centers for Disease Control. Among inmates, however, best estimates place the reported HIV-infection rate at 600 cases per 100,000[148]—five times as great. A few years ago, AIDS was the leading cause of death among prison inmates.[149] Today, however, the number of inmates who die from AIDS (or, more precisely, from AIDS-related complications like pneumonia or Kaposi's sarcoma) is much lower than it has been in the past. The introduction of drugs like protease inhibitors and useful combinations of antiretroviral therapies have reduced inmate deaths from AIDS by 75% since 1995.[150]

Some inmates are infected in prison, while others carry the HIV virus into prison with them. Authorities say the virus is spread behind bars through homosexual activity (including rape), intravenous drug use, and the sharing of tainted tattoo and hypodermic needles. The fact that inmates tend to have histories of high-risk behavior before entering prison, especially intravenous drug use, however, probably means that many are infected before coming to prison.

A report by the National Institute of Justice suggests that there are two types of strategies that correctional administrators can use to reduce the transmission of AIDS.[151] One strategy relies upon medical technology to identify seropositive inmates and to segregate them from the rest of the prison population. Mass screening and inmate segregation, however, may be prohibitively expensive. They may also be illegal. Some states specifically prohibit HIV-antibody testing without the informed consent of the person tested.[152] The related issue of confidentiality may be difficult to manage, especially when the purpose of testing is to segregate infected inmates from others. In addition, civil liability may result if inmates are falsely labeled as infected or if inmates known to be infected are not prevented from spreading the disease. Only Alabama and South Carolina still segregate all known HIV-infected inmates,[153] but more limited forms of separation are practiced elsewhere. Many state prison systems have denied HIV-positive inmates jobs, educational opportunities, visitation privileges, conjugal visits, and home furloughs, causing some researchers to conclude that "inmates with HIV and AIDS are routinely discriminated against and denied equal treatment in ways that have no accepted medical basis."[154] In 1994, for example, a federal appeals court upheld a California prison policy that bars inmates who are HIV-positive from working in food-service jobs.[155] In contrast, in 2001, the Mississippi Department of Correction ended its policy of segregating HIV-positive prisoners from other inmates in educational and vocational programs.

The second strategy is one of prevention through education. Educational programs teach both inmates and staff members about the dangers of high-risk behavior and suggest ways to avoid HIV infection. A National Institute of Justice (NIJ) model program recommends the use of simple, straightforward messages presented by knowledgeable and approachable trainers.[156] Alarmism, says NIJ, should be avoided. One survey found that 98% of state and federal prisons provide some form of AIDS/HIV education and that 90% of jails do as well—although most such training is oriented toward correctional staff rather than inmates.[157] Learn more about HIV in prisons and jails via **Library Extra! 13–6** at cjtoday.com. Inmate medical problems in general are discussed in **Library Extra! 13–7** at cjtoday.com.

Geriatric Offenders

Chapter 2 described the involvement of older people in crime. As noted in that chapter, crimes committed by the elderly, like most other crimes, have recently been on the decline. Nonetheless, the significant expansion of America's retiree population has led to an increase in the number of elderly people who are behind bars. In fact, crimes of violence are what brings most older people into the correctional system. According to one study, 52% of inmates who were over the age of 50 at the time they entered prison had committed violent crimes, compared with 41% of younger inmates.[158] On January 1, 2001, 42,300 inmates aged 55 or older were housed in state and federal prisons. The number of prisoners older than 55 increased more than 300% between 1990 and 2001.[159] Similarly, the per capita rate of incarceration for inmates aged 55 and over now stands at 164 per 100,000 residents of like age and has steadily increased for more than a decade.

Some authors have interpreted prison statistics on older inmates to presage the growth of a "geriatric delinquent" population, freed by age and retirement from jobs and responsibilities. Such people, say these authors, may turn to crime as one way of averting boredom and adding a little spice to life.[160] Prison statistics on geriatric offenders, however, probably require a more cautious interpretation. They are based upon relatively small numbers, and much of the increase in imprisonment among the elderly may be due to the rapid growth of the older population in this country; even greater increases are expected over the next three decades. Advances in health care have lengthened life expectancy and have made those added years more active than ever before. Finally, World War II baby boomers are now reaching their late middle years, which probably means that present trends in criminal involvement among the elderly can be expected to continue.

Of course, not all of today's elderly inmates were old when they entered prison. Because of harsh sentencing laws passed throughout the country in the 1990s, a small but growing number of inmates (10%) will serve 20 years or more in prison, and 5% will never be released.[161] This means that many inmates who enter prison when they are young will grow old behind bars. Hence, the "graying" of America's prison population has a number of causes: "(1) the general aging of the American population, which is reflected inside prisons; (2) new sentencing policies such as 'three strikes,' 'truth in sentencing' and 'mandatory minimum' laws that send more criminals to prison for longer stretches; (3) a massive prison building boom that took place in the 1980s and 1990s, and which has provided space for more inmates, reducing the need to release prisoners to alleviate overcrowding; and (4) significant changes in parole philosophies and practices,"[162] with state and federal authorities phasing out or canceling parole programs, thereby forcing jailers to hold inmates with life sentences until they die.

Long-termers and geriatric inmates have special needs. They tend to suffer from handicaps, physical impairments, and illnesses not generally encountered among their more youthful counterparts. Unfortunately, few prisons are equipped to deal adequately with the medical needs of aging offenders. Some large facilities have begun to set aside special sections to care for elderly inmates with "typical" disorders, such as Alzheimer's disease, cancer, or heart disease. Unfortunately, such efforts have barely kept pace with the problems that geriatric offenders present. The number of inmates requiring round-the-clock care is expected to increase dramatically over the next two decades.[163]

Even the idea of rehabilitation takes on a new meaning where geriatric offenders are concerned. What kinds of programs are most likely to be useful in providing the older inmate with the needed tools for success on the outside? Which counseling strategies hold the greatest promise for introducing socially acceptable behavior patterns into the long-established lifestyles of elderly offenders about to be released? There are few answers to these questions. Learn about some of the oldest prisoners in America via **Web Extra! 13–3** at cjtoday.com, and read a letter from William Heirens via **Web Extra! 13–4** at cjtoday.com. Heirens has been locked up for over 50 years.

Mentally Ill Inmates

The mentally ill are another inmate category with special needs. Some mentally ill inmates are neurotic or have personality problems, which increase tension in prison. Others have serious psychological disorders that may have escaped diagnosis at trial or that did not provide a legal basis for the reduction of criminal responsibility. A fair number of offenders develop psychiatric symptoms while in prison.

A 2000 Bureau of Justice Statistics (BJS) survey of public and private state-level adult correctional facilities (excluding jails) found that 51% of such institutions provide 24-hour mental health care, while 71% provide therapy and counseling by trained mental health professionals as needed.[164] A large majority of prisons distribute psychotropic medications

Elderly inmates inside the geriatric unit of Texas's Estelle Prison. Geriatric inmates are becoming an increasingly large part of the inmate population.

Andrew Lichtenstein, The Image Works

(when such medications are ordered by a physician), and 66% have programs to help released inmates obtain community mental health services. According to BJS, 13% of state prisoners were receiving some type of mental health therapy at the time of the survey, and 10% were receiving psychotropic medications (including antidepressants, stimulants, sedatives, and tranquilizers).

Unfortunately, few state-run correctional institutions have any *substantial capacity* for the in-depth psychiatric treatment of inmates who are *seriously* mentally disturbed. A number of states, however, do operate facilities that specialize in psychiatric confinement of convicted criminals. BJS reports that 12 facilities devoted exclusively to the care of mentally ill inmates are operated by state governments throughout the nation, and that another 143 prisons report psychiatric confinement as one specialty among other functions that they perform.

In the 1990 case of *Washington* v. *Harper*,[165] the U.S. Supreme Court ruled that mentally ill inmates could be required to take antipsychotic drugs, even against their wishes. The ruling stipulated that this requirement would apply when "the inmate is dangerous to himself or others, and the treatment is in the inmate's medical interest." A 1999 study by the BJS found that the nation's prisons and jails hold an estimated 283,800 mentally ill inmates (16% of those confined), and that 547,800 such offenders are on probation.[166] The government study also found that 40% of mentally ill inmates receive no treatment at all. For more details about the report, visit **Web Extra! 13–5** at cjtoday.com.

Mentally deficient inmates constitute still another group with special needs. Some studies estimate the proportion of mentally deficient inmates at about 10%.[167] Retarded inmates are less likely to complete training and rehabilitative programs successfully than are other inmates. They also evidence difficulty in adjusting to the routines of prison life. As a consequence, they are likely to exceed the averages in proportion of sentence served.[168] Only seven states report special facilities or programs for the mentally retarded inmate.[169] Other state systems "mainstream" such inmates, making them participate in regular activities with other inmates.

Texas, one state which does provide special services for retarded inmates, began the Mentally Retarded Offender Program (MROP) in 1984. Inmates in Texas are given a battery of tests that measure intellectual and social adaptability skills, and prisoners who are identified as retarded are housed in special satellite correctional units. The Texas MROP program provides individual and group counseling, along with training in adult life skills.

Learn more about prison issues in general via **Web Extra! 13–6** at cjtoday.com.

CJ Futures

[Technocorrections]

In the twenty-first century, the technological forces that have made cell phones ubiquitous will converge with the forces of law and order to create what some have called *technocorrections*. The correctional establishment—the managers of the jail, prison, probation, and parole systems and their sponsors in elected office—is seeking more cost-effective ways to increase public safety as the number of people under correctional supervision continues to grow. Technocorrections will be defined by a correctional establishment that takes advantage of all the potential offered by the new technologies to reduce the costs of supervising criminal offenders and to minimize the risk they pose to society.

Emerging technologies in three areas will soon be central elements of technocorrections: electronic tracking and location systems, pharmacological treatments, and genetic and neurobiologic risk assessments. While these technologies may significantly increase public safety, we must also be mindful of the threats they pose to democratic principles. The critical challenge will be to learn how to take advantage of new technological opportunities applicable to the corrections field while minimizing their threats.

Tracking and Location Systems

Electronic tracking and location systems are the technology perhaps most familiar to correctional practitioners today. Most states use electronic monitoring—either with the older bracelets that communicate through a device connected to telephone lines or with more modern versions based on cellular or satellite tracking. With such technology, correctional officials can continuously track offenders' locations and use that information to supervise their movements. As this technology expands, it will enable correctional officials to define geographic areas from which offenders are prohibited and to furnish tracking devices to potential victims (such as battered wives). The devices will set "safe zones" that trigger alarms or warning notices upon approach of the offender.

Tiny cameras might also be integrated into tracking devices to provide live video of offenders' locations and activities. Miniature electronic devices implanted in the body to signal the location of offenders at all times, to create unique identifiers that trigger alarms, and to monitor key bodily functions that affect unwanted behaviors are under development and are close to becoming reality.[1]

Pharmacological Treatments

Pharmacological breakthroughs—new "wonder drugs" being developed to control behavior in correctional and noncorrectional settings—will also be a part of technocorrections. Correctional officials are already familiar with some of these drugs, as many are currently used to treat mentally ill offenders. Yet these drugs could also be used to control mental conditions affecting undesirable behaviors even for offenders who are not mentally ill. Research into the relationship between levels of the neurotransmitter serotonin and violent behavior continues to be refined. Findings to date seem to indicate that people who have low levels of serotonin are more prone than others to impulsive, violent acts, especially when they abuse alcohol.[2] (See Chapter 3 for more information.) Not long ago, the National Academy of Sciences (NAS)

recommended a new emphasis in biomedical research on violence as a means to understand the biological roots of violent behavior.[3] The NAS reports that research findings from animal and human studies "point to several features of the nervous system as promising sites" for discovering reliable biological "markers" for violent behavior and designing preventive therapies.[4]

It is only a matter of time before research findings in this area lead to the development of drugs to control neurobiological processes. These drugs could become correctional tools to manage violent offenders and perhaps even to prevent violence. Such advances are related to the third area of technology that will affect corrections: genetic and neurobiological risk-assessment technologies.

Risk-Assessment Technologies

Correctional officials today are familiar with DNA profiling of offenders, particularly sex offenders. This, however, is just the beginning of the correctional application of gene-related technologies. The Human Genome Project, supported by the National Institutes of Health and the Department of Energy, is about to be completed. A map of the 3 billion chemical bases that make up human DNA will be created, and high-powered "sequencer" machines will be able to analyze the map faster than any human researcher.[5] Emerging as a powerhouse of the high-tech economy, the biotechnology industry will drive developments in this area.

Gene "management" technologies are already widely used in agriculture and are increasingly used in medicine. The progression is likely to continue, with applications in psychiatric and behavioral management. Researchers are investigating the genetic—or inherited—basis of behavior, including antisocial and criminal behavior. Studies of twins, for example, have revealed similarities in behavior attributable to a genetic effect.[6] Eventually, the genetic roots of human behavior could be profiled.

Neurobiological research is taking the same path, although thus far no neurobiological patterns specific enough to be reliable biological markers for violent behavior have been uncovered. Is it possible that breakthroughs in these areas will lead to the development of risk-assessment tools that use genetic or neurobiological profiles to identify children who have a propensity toward addiction or violence? Might they also be capable of identifying males with a propensity for sex offending? We may soon be able to link genetic and neurobiological traits with social and environmental factors to reliably predict who is at risk for addiction, sex offending, violent behavior, or crime in general.

Attempts will surely be made to develop genetic or neurobiological tests for assessing risks posed by individuals. This is already done for the risk of contracting certain diseases. Demand for risk assessments of individuals will come from correctional officials under pressure to prevent violent recidivism. Once under correctional control, specific offenders could be identified, on the basis of such testing and risk assessment, as likely violent recidivists. The group so classified could be placed under closer surveillance or declared a danger to themselves and society and be civilly committed to special facilities for indeterminate periods. In other words, incarceration could assume a more preventive role.

(continued)

CJ Futures (*continued*)

"Preventive incarceration" is already a reality for some convicted sex offenders. More than a dozen states commit certain sex offenders to special "civil commitment" facilities after they have served their prison sentences because of a behavioral or mental abnormality that makes them dangerous. This happens today with no clear understanding of the nature of the abnormality. It is not difficult to imagine what might be done to justify preventive incarceration if this "abnormal" or criminal behavior could be explained and predicted by genetic or neurobiological profiling.

Source: Adapted from Tony Fabelo, *"Technocorrections": The Promises, the Uncertain Threats* (Washington, D.C.: National Institute of Justice, 2000).

[1]"Microchip Implants Closer to Reality," *Futurist,* Vol. 33, No. 8 (October 1999), p. 9.

[2]Sheryl Stolberg, "Scientific Studies Are Generating Controversy," *Austin American-Statesman,* January 16, 1994.

[3]Albert J. Reiss, Jr., and Jeffrey A. Roth, eds., *Understanding and Preventing Violence* (Washington, D.C.: National Academy Press, 1993). Reiss and Roth call for "systematic searches for neurobiologic markers for persons with elevated potentials for violent behavior" (p. 24).

[4]Ibid., p. 12. Reiss and Roth caution, however, that "the generalizability of experimental findings from other animal species to humans is not always straightforward" (p. 116).

[5]Walter Isaacson, "The Biotech Century," *Time,* January 11, 1999, p. 42; and Michael D. Lemonick and Dick Thompson, "Racing to Map Our DNA," *Time,* January 11, 1999, p. 44.

[6]G. Carey and D. Goldman, "The Genetics of Antisocial Behavior," in D. M. Stoff et al., ed., *Handbook of Antisocial Behavior* (New York: John Wiley, 1997) pp. 243–254.

Summary

Prisons are small, self-contained societies which are sometimes described as *total institutions.* Studies of prison life have detailed the existence of prison subcultures, or inmate worlds, replete with inmate values, social roles, and lifestyles. New inmates who are socialized into prison subculture are said to undergo the process of prisonization. This involves, among other things, learning the language of prison, commonly called *prison argot.*

Prison subcultures are very influential, and both inmates and staff must reckon with them. Given the large and often densely packed inmate populations which characterize many of today's prisons, however, prison subcultures are not easily subject to the control of prison authorities. Complicating life behind bars are numerous conflicts of interest between inmates and staff. Lawsuits, riots, violence, and frequent formal grievances are symptoms of such differences.

For many years, courts throughout the nation assumed a "hands-off" approach to prisons, rarely intervening in the day-to-day administration of prison facilities. That changed in the late 1960s when the U.S. Supreme Court began to identify inmates' rights mandated by the U.S. Constitution. Rights identified by the Court include the right to physical integrity, an absolute right to be free from unwarranted corporal punishments, certain religious rights, and procedural rights, such as those involving access to attorneys and to the courts. The conditional rights of prisoners, which have repeatedly been supported by the U.S. Supreme Court, mandate professionalism among prison administrators and require vigilance in the provision of correctional services. The era of prisoners' rights was sharply curtailed in 1996, with the passage of the Prison Litigation Reform Act, spurred on by a growing recognition of the legal morass resulting from unregulated access to federal courts by inmates across the nation. The legislation, in concert with other restrictions sanctioned by the U.S. Supreme Court, has substantially limited inmate access to federal courts.

Today's prisons are miniature societies, reflecting the problems and challenges which exist in the larger society of which they are a part. HIV-infected inmates, geriatric offenders, and the mentally ill constitute special groups within the inmate population which require additional attention.

Discussion Questions

1. Explain the concept of prison subcultures. What purpose do prison subcultures serve? Why do they develop?
2. What does *prisonization* mean? Describe the U-shaped curve developed by Stanton Wheeler to illustrate the concept of prisonization. Why do you think the curve is U-shaped?
3. What are the primary concerns of prison staff? Do you agree that those concerns are important? What other goals might staff members focus on?
4. What does it mean to say that inmates have rights? Where do these rights come from? Do inmates have too many rights? Explain.
5. Explain the "balancing test" established by the Supreme Court in deciding issues of prisoners' rights. How might such a test apply to the emerging area of inmate privacy?
6. What does the term *state-created rights* mean within the context of corrections? What might be the future of state-created rights?
7. What are some of the special problems facing prisons today? What new problems might the future bring?

To participate in an online discussion on these topics and others, go to the Global Town Meeting electronic message board for Chapter 13 on the *Criminal Justice Today* Companion Website at cjtoday.com.

Web Quest!

Visit the Cybrary, and search for "jobs," "careers," and "employment." What criminal justice–related employment sites can you find? Explore some of the sites you find, and consider the possibility of a career in corrections. Document the sources you used, and list the URLs and the date you accessed each. Then answer these questions:[170]

What is the difference between a job and a career?
What career opportunities are available in corrections?
Why is career planning important? How can you develop an effective career plan?
What is the difference between education and training?
Why are education and training important to building a career in corrections?
What role might professionalism play in building your career?
What traits must you have to achieve your goals and to be successful in a career in corrections?

E-mail your answers to your instructor if asked to do so.
To complete this Web Quest! online, go to the Web Quest! module in Chapter 13 of the *Criminal Justice Today* Companion Website at cjtoday.com.

Library Extras!

Library Extra! **13–1**   *Prisons Research at the Beginning of the Twenty-first Century* (NIJ, 2001).
Library Extra! **13–2**   *Prison Use and Social Control* (NIJ, 2000).
Library Extra! **13–3**   *No Escape: Male Rape in U.S. Prisons* (Human Rights Watch, 2001).
Library Extra! **13–4**   *Women Offenders: Programming Needs and Promising Approaches* (NIJ, 1998).
Library Extra! **13–5**   *Women in Prison* (BJS, current volume).
Library Extra! **13–6**   *HIV in Prisons and Jails* (BJS, current volume).
Library Extra! **13–7**   *Medical Problems of Inmates* (NIJ, 2001).

To explore these resources online, go to the Library Extras! area of the *Criminal Justice Today* Companion Website at cjtoday.com. You should also check the author's "Late Picks" online for newly released documents and updated Library Extras! You can find Late Picks at http://cjtoday.com/latepicks.htm.

Notes

1. Web posted at http://www.whitehouse.gov/news/reports/faithbased.html. Accessed November 2, 2001.
2. Hans Reimer, "Socialization in the Prison Community," *Proceedings of the American Prison Association, 1937* (New York: American Prison Association, 1937), pp. 151–155.
3. Donald Clemmer, *The Prison Community* (Boston: Holt, Rinehart and Winston, 1940).
4. Gresham M. Sykes, *The Society of Captives: A Study of a Maximum Security Prison* (Princeton, NJ: Princeton University Press, 1958).
5. Richard A. Cloward et al., *Theoretical Studies in Social Organization of the Prison* (New York: Social Science Research Council, 1960).
6. Donald R. Cressey, ed., *The Prison: Studies in Institutional Organization and Change* (New York: Holt, Rinehart and Winston, 1961).
7. Lawrence Hazelrigg, ed., *Prison within Society: A Reader in Penology* (Garden City, NY: Anchor, 1969), preface.
8. Charles Stastny and Gabrielle Tyrnauer, *Who Rules the Joint? The Changing Political Culture of Maximum-Security Prisons in America* (Lexington, MA: Lexington Books, 1982), p. 131.
9. Erving Goffman, *Asylums: Essays on the Social Situation of Mental Patients and Other Inmates* (Garden City, NY: Anchor, 1961).
10. For a firsthand account of the prison experience, see Victor Hassine, *Life without Parole: Living in Prison Today* (Los Angeles: Roxbury, 1996); and W. Rideau and R. Wikberg, *Life Sentences: Rage and Survival behind Prison Bars* (New York: Times Books, 1992).
11. The concept of prisonization is generally attributed to Clemmer, *The Prison Community*, although Quaker penologists of the late eighteenth century were actively concerned with preventing "contamination" (the spread of criminal values) among prisoners.
12. Gresham M. Sykes and Sheldon L. Messinger, "The Inmate Social System," in Richard A. Cloward et al., *Theoretical Studies in Social Organization of the Prison* (New York: Social Science Research Council, 1960), pp. 5–19.
13. Ibid., p. 5.
14. Stanton Wheeler, "Socialization in Correctional Communities," *American Sociological Review,* Vol. 26 (October 1961), pp. 697–712.
15. Sykes, *The Society of Captives,* p. xiii.
16. Stastny and Tyrnauer, *Who Rules the Joint?* p. 135.
17. Ibid.
18. Ibid.
19. Sykes, *The Society of Captives.*
20. Clemmer, *The Prison Community,* pp. 294–296.
21. John Irwin, *The Felon* (Englewood Cliffs, NJ: Prentice Hall, 1970).
22. Joseph L. Galloway, "Into the Heart of Darkness," *U.S. News Online,* March 8, 1999. Web posted at http://www.usnews.com/usnews/issue/990308/8pris.htm. Accessed March 20, 2000.
23. Alan J. Davis, "Sexual Assaults in the Philadelphia Prison System and Sheriff's Vans," *Trans-Action,* Vol. 6 (December 1968), pp. 8–16.
24. Daniel Lockwood, "Sexual Aggression among Male Prisoners," unpublished dissertation (Ann Arbor, MI: University Microfilms International, 1978).
25. Lee H. Bowker, *Prison Victimization* (New York: Elsevier, 1980).
26. Ibid., p. 42.
27. Ibid., p. 1.
28. Hans Toch, *Living in Prison: The Ecology of Survival* (New York: Free Press, 1977), p. 151.
29. Allen J. Beck and Paige M. Harrison, *Prisoners in 2000* (Washington, D.C.: Bureau of Justice Statistics, 2001).
30. Ibid.
31. Some of the information in this section comes from the American Correctional Association, Task Force on the Female Offender, *The Female Offender: What Does the Future Hold?* (Washington, D.C.: St. Mary's Press, 1990); and "The View from behind Bars," *Time* (fall 1990, special issue), pp. 20–22.
32. Merry Morash, Timothy S. Bynum, and Barbara A. Koons, *Women Offenders: Programming Needs and Promising Approaches,* NIJ Research in Brief (Washington, D.C.: National Institute of Justice, 1998).
33. ACA, *The Female Offender.*
34. B. Keith Crew, "Sex Differences in Criminal Sentencing: Chivalry or Patriarchy?" *Justice Quarterly,* Vol. 8, No. 1 (March 1991), pp. 59–83.
35. ACA, *The Female Offender.*
36. Ibid.
37. Mary Jeanette Clement, "National Survey of Programs for Incarcerated Women," paper presented at the annual meeting of the Academy of Criminal Justice Sciences, Nashville, Tennessee, March 1991.
38. Mary K. Shilton, *Resources for Mother-Child Community Corrections* (Washington, D.C.: Bureau of Justice Assistance, 2001), p. 3.
39. Ibid.
40. Clement, "National Survey of Programs for Incarcerated Women," pp. 8–9.
41. Marsha Clowers, "Dykes, Gangs, and Danger: Debunking Popular Myths about Maximum Security Life," *Journal of Criminal Justice and Popular Culture,* Vol. 9, No. 1 (2001), pp. 22–30.
42. D. Ward and G. Kassebaum, *Women's Prison: Sex and Social Structure* (London: Weidenfeld and Nicolson, 1966).
43. Esther Heffernan, *Making It in Prison: The Square, the Cool, and the Life* (London: Wiley-Interscience, 1972).
44. Rose Giallombardo, *Society of Women: A Study of Women's Prisons* (New York: John Wiley, 1966).
45. Ibid., p. 136.
46. For a summary of such studies (including some previously unpublished), see Lee H. Bowker, *Prisoner Subcultures* (Lexington, MA: Lexington Books, 1977), p. 86.
47. Giallombardo, *Society of Women,* p. 162.
48. Mary Koscheski and Christophere Hensley, "Inmate Homosexual Behavior in a Southern Female Correctional Facility," *American Journal of Criminal Justice,* Vol. 25, No. 2 (2001), pp. 269–277.
49. Heffernan, *Making It in Prison.*
50. Bowker, *Prison Victimization,* p. 53.
51. Giallombardo, *Society of Women.*
52. "Georgia Indictments Charge Abuse of Female Inmates," *USA Today,* November 16, 1992, p. 3A.
53. Ibid.
54. ACA, *The Female Offender,* p. 39.
55. Lucien X. Lombardo, *Guards Imprisoned: Correctional Officers at Work* (New York: Elsevier, 1981), pp. 22–36.

56. Leonard Morgenbesser, "NY State Law Prescribes Psychological Screening for CO Job Applicants," *Correctional Training* (Winter 1983), p. 1.

57. "A Sophisticated Approach to Training Prison Guards," *Newsday,* August 12, 1982.

58. Stastny and Tyrnauer, *Who Rules the Joint?* p. 1.

59. See Frederick Talbott, "Reporting from behind the Walls: Do It before the Siren Wails," *The Quill* (February 1988), pp. 16–21.

60. "Ohio Prison Rebellion Is Ended," *USA Today,* April 22, 1993, p. 2A.

61. "Guards Hurt in Prison Riot," Associated Press wire service, November 11, 2000.

62. Office of the Attorney General, *Report of the Attorney General on the February 2 and 3, 1980, Riot at the Penitentiary of New Mexico* (two parts) (Santa Fe, NM: Office of the Attorney General, June and September 1980).

63. See, for example, American Correctional Association, *Riots and Disturbances in Correctional Institutions* (College Park, MD: ACA, 1981); Michael Braswell et al., *Prison Violence in America* (Cincinnati: Anderson, 1985); and R. Conant, "Rioting, Insurrectional and Civil Disorderliness," *American Scholar,* Vol. 37 (summer 1968), pp. 420–433.

64. Robert S. Fong, Ronald E. Vogel, and S. Buentello, "Prison Gang Dynamics: A Look Inside the Texas Department of Corrections," in A. V. Merlo and P. Menekos, eds., *Dilemmas and Directions in Corrections* (Cincinnati: Anderson, 1992).

65. Ibid.

66. *Ruiz* v. *Estelle,* 503 F.Supp. 1265 (S.D. Texas, 1980).

67. Vernon Fox, "Prison Riots in a Democratic Society," *Police,* Vol. 26, No. 12 (December 1982), pp. 35–41.

68. Donald R. Cressey, "Adult Felons in Prison," in Lloyd E. Ohlin, ed., *Prisoners in America* (Englewood Cliffs, NJ: Prentice Hall, 1972), pp. 117–150.

69. "Convictions Bar 3.9 Million from Voting," Associated Press wire service, September 22, 2000.

70. *Holt* v. *Sarver,* 309 F.Supp. 362 (E.D. Ark. 1970).

71. Vergil L. Williams, *Dictionary of American Penology: An Introduction* (Westport, CT: Greenwood, 1979), pp. 6–7.

72. *Pell* v. *Procunier,* 417 U.S. 817, 822 (1974).

73. Ibid.

74. Title 42 U.S.C.A 1997, Public Law 104-150.

75. Section 1997e.

76. American Correctional Association, *Legal Responsibility and Authority of Correctional Officers: A Handbook on Courts, Judicial Decisions and Constitutional Requirements* (College Park, MD: ACA, 1987), p. 8.

77. *Procunier* v. *Martinez,* 416 U.S. 396 (1974).

78. *McNamara* v. *Moody,* 606 F.2d 621 (5th Cir. 1979).

79. *Luparar* v. *Stoneman,* 382 F.Supp. 495 (D. Vt. 1974).

80. *Mallery* v. *Lewis,* 106 Idaho 227 (1983).

81. See, for example, *Pepperling* v. *Crist,* 678 F.2d 787 (9th Cir. 1981).

82. *Cruz* v. *Beto,* 405 U.S. 319 (1972).

83. *Aziz* v. *LeFevre,* 642 F.2d 1109 (2d Cir. 1981).

84. *Glasshofer* v. *Thornburg,* 514 F.Supp. 1242 (E.D. Pa. 1981).

85. See, for example, *Smith* v. *Coughlin,* 748 F.2d 783 (2d Cir. 1984).

86. *Campbell* v. *Cauthron,* 623 F.2d 503 (8th Cir. 1980).

87. *Smith* v. *Blackledge,* 451 F.2d 1201 (4th Cir. 1971).

88. *Dettmer* v. *Landon,* 617 F.Supp. 592, 594 (D.C. Va. 1985).

89. *Dettmer* v. *Landon,* 799 F.2d 929 (4th Cir. 1986).

90. *Lewellyn (L'Aquarius)* v. *State,* 592 P.2d 538 (Okla. Crim. App. 1979).

91. *Hill* v. *Blackwell,* 774 F.2d 338, 347 (8th Cir. 1985).

92. *Block* v. *Rutherford,* 486 U.S. 576 (1984).

93. *Pell* v. *Procunier,* 417 U.S. 817, 822 (1974).

94. *Houchins* v. *KQED, Inc.,* 438 U.S. 11 (1978).

95. Ibid.

96. For a Supreme Court review of the First Amendment right to petition the courts, see *McDonald* v. *Smith,* 105 S.Ct. 2787 (1985).

97. *Bounds* v. *Smith,* 430 U.S. 817, 821 (1977).

98. *Lewis* v. *Casey,* 516 U.S. 804 (1996).

99. *Johnson* v. *Avery,* 393 U.S. 483 (1968).

100. *Bounds* v. *Smith* 430 U.S. 817, 821 (1977).

101. *Taylor* v. *Sterrett,* 532 F.2d 462 (5th Cir. 1976).

102. *In re Harrell,* 87 Cal. Rptr. 504, 470 P.2d 640 (1970).

103. *Guajardo* v. *Estelle,* 432 F.Supp. 1373 (S.D. Texas, 1977).

104. *O'Brien* v. *U.S.,* 386 U.S. 345 (1967); and *Weatherford* v. *Bursey,* 429 U.S. 545 (1977).

105. *U.S.* v. *Gouveia,* 104 S.Ct. 2292, 81 L.Ed. 2d 146 (1984).

106. *Estelle* v. *Gamble,* 429 U.S. 97 (1976).

107. Ibid., pp. 105–106.

108. *Farmer* v. *Brennan,* 114 S.Ct. 1970, 128 L.Ed. 2d 811 (1994).

109. Ibid.

110. *Ruiz* v. *Estelle,* 679 F.2d 1115 (5th Cir. 1982).

111. *Newman* v. *Alabama,* 349 F.Supp. 278 (M.D. Ala. 1972).

112. Adapted from ACA, *Legal Responsibility and Authority of Correctional Officers,* pp. 25–26.

113. *In re Caulk,* 35 CrL 2532 (New Hampshire S.Ct. 1984).

114. Ibid.

115. *Helling* v. *McKinney,* 113 S.Ct. 2475, 125 L.Ed. 2d 22 (1993).

116. *Pennsylvania Department of Corrections* v. *Yeskey,* 524 U.S. 206, 209 (1998).

117. 42 U.S.C. § 12132.

118. *U.S.* v. *Ready,* 574 F.2d 1009 (10th Cir. 1978).

119. *Katz* v. *U.S.,* 389 U.S. 347, 88 S.Ct. 507, 19 L.Ed. 2ed 576 (1967).

120. *Hudson* v. *Palmer,* 468 U.S. 517 (1984).

121. *Block* v. *Rutherford,* 104 S.Ct. 3227, 3234–35 (1984).

122. *U.S.* v. *Lilly,* 576 F.2d 1240 (5th Cir. 1978).

123. *Palmer* v. *Hudson,* 697 F.2d 1220 (4th Cir. 1983).

124. *Jones* v. *North Carolina Prisoners' Labor Union,* 433 U.S. 119, 53 L.Ed. 2d 629, 641 (1977).

125. *Wolff* v. *McDonnell,* 94 S.Ct. 2963 (1974).

126. Ibid.

127. Ibid.

128. *Ponte* v. *Real,* 471 U.S. 491, 105 S.Ct. 2192, 85 L.Ed. 2d 553 (1985).

129. *Vitek* v. *Jones,* 445 U.S. 480 (1980).

130. American Correctional Association, Standard 2-4346. See ACA, *Legal Responsibility and Authority of Correctional Officers,* p. 49.

131. *Wilson* v. *Seiter et al.,* 501 U.S. 294 (1991).

132. *Estelle* v. *Gamble,* 429 U.S. 97, 106 (1976).

133. *Sandin* v. *Conner,* 63 U.S.L.W. 4601 (1995).

134. *Wolff* v. *McDonnell,* 94 S.Ct. 2963 (1974).

135. *Hewitt* v. *Helms,* 459 U.S. 460 (1983).

136. Laurie Asseo, "Inmate Lawsuits," Associated Press wire service, May 24, 1996; and Bureau of Justice Statistics, "State and Federal Prisoners Filed 68,235 Petitions in U.S. Courts in 1996," press release, October 29, 1997.

137. See, for example, "The Great Prison Pastime," *20/20,* ABC News, September 24, 1993, which is part of the video library available to instructors using this textbook.

138. Ibid.

139. Asseo, "Inmate Lawsuits."

140. Public Law 104-134. Although the PLRA was signed into law on April 26, 1996, and is frequently referred to as the Prison Litigation Reform Act of 1996, the official name of the act is the Prison Litigation Reform Act of 1995.

141. *Edwards* v. *Balisok,* 520 U.S. 641 (1997).

142. American Civil Liberties Union, *Prisoners' Rights—An ACLU Position Paper,* Fall 1999. Web posted at http://www.aclu.org/library/PrisonerRights.pdf. Accessed March 5, 2002.

143. *Booth* v. *Churner,* U.S. Supreme Court, No. 99-1964 (decided May 29, 2001).

144. American Civil Liberties Union, *Prisoners' Rights.*

145. Laura M. Maruschak, *HIV in Prisons and Jails, 1999* (Washington, D.C.: Bureau of Justice Statistics, 2001).

146. Ibid.

147. Ibid.

148. Ibid., p. 4.

149. Dennis Cauchon, "AIDS in Prison: Locked Up and Locked Out," *USA Today,* March 31, 1995, p. 6A.

150. Maruschak, *HIV in Prisons and Jails, 1999,* p. 5.

151. Theodore M. Hammett, *AIDS in Correctional Facilities: Issues and Options,* 3d ed. (Washington, D.C.: National Institute of Justice, 1988), p. 37.

152. At the time of this writing, California, Massachusetts, New York, Wisconsin, and the District of Columbia were among those jurisdictions.

153. "Mississippi Eases Policy of Separating Inmates with HIV," *Corrections Journal,* Vol. 5, No. 6 (2001), p. 5.

154. Cauchon, "AIDS in Prison."

155. See "Court Allows Restriction on HIV-Positive Inmates," in *Criminal Justice Newsletter,* Vol. 25, No. 23 (December 1, 1994), pp. 2–3.

156. Ibid.

157. Darrell Bryan, "Inmates, HIV, and the Constitutional Right to Privacy: AIDS in Prison Facilities," *Corrections Compendium,* Vol. 19, No. 9 (September 1994), pp. 1–3.

158. Lincoln J. Fry, "The Older Prison Inmate: A Profile," *Justice Professional,* Vol. 2, No. 1 (spring 1987), pp. 1–12.

159. Allen J. Beck and Paige M. Harrison, *Prisoners in 2000* (Washington, D.C.: Bureau of Justice Statistics, 2001).

160. Bennett, *Crimewarps,* p. 61.

161. Bureau of Justice Statistics, "The Nation's Prison Population Grew by 60,000 Inmates Last Year," press release, August 15, 1999.

162. Jim Krane, "Demographic Revolution Rocks U.S. Prisons," APB Online, April 12, 1999. Web posted at http://www.apbonline.com/safestreets/oldprisoners/mainpris0412.html. Accessed January 5, 2000.

163. Ronald Wikbert and Burk Foster, "The Longtermers: Louisiana's Longest Serving Inmates and Why They've Stayed So Long," paper presented at the annual meeting of the Academy of Criminal Justice Sciences, Washington, D.C., 1989, p. 51.

164. Allen J. Beck and Laura M. Maruschak, *Mental Health Treatment in State Prisons, 2000,* BJS Special Report (Washington, D.C.: Bureau of Justice Statistics, 2001), p. 1, from which most of the information in this paragraph and the next is derived.

165. *Washington* v. *Harper,* 494 U.S. 210 (1990).

166. Paula M. Ditton, *Mental Health and Treatment of Inmates and Probationers* (Washington, D.C.: Bureau of Justice Statistics, 1999).

167. Robert O. Lampert, "The Mentally Retarded Offender in Prison," *Justice Professional,* Vol. 2, No. 1 (spring 1987), p. 61.

168. Ibid., p. 64.

169. George C. Denkowski and Kathryn M. Denkowski, "The Mentally Retarded Offender in the State Prison System: Identification, Prevalence, Adjustment, and Rehabilitation, "*Criminal Justice and Behavior,* Vol. 12(1985), pp. 55–75.

170. The questions in this Web Quest! were adapted from "Building Your Career in Corrections," *Keeper's Voice,* Vol. 18, No. 1. Web posted at http://www.oict.org/public/toc.efm?series-KV. Accessed February 20, 2002.

part five

Individual Rights versus Public Order Concerns

■ Issues for the Future

Common law, constitutional, statutory, and humanitarian rights of the accused which may soon be threatened by technological advances and other developments:

- A right to privacy
- A right to be assumed innocent
- A right against self-incrimination
- A right to equal protection of the laws
- A right against cruel and unusual punishment

These individual rights must be effectively balanced against these present and emerging community concerns:

- Widespread drug abuse among youth
- The threat of juvenile crime
- Urban gang violence
- High-technology, computer, and Internet crime (cybercrime)
- Terrorism and narcoterrorism
- Occupational and white-collar crime

How does our system of justice work toward balance?

Special Issues

BETTER TO BE JUDGED BY TWELVE THAN TO BE CARRIED BY SIX

The Future Comes One Day at a Time

No one can truly say what the future holds. Will the supporters of individual rights or the advocates of public order ultimately claim the day? We cannot say for sure. This much is certain, however: Things change. The future system of American criminal justice will not be quite the same system we know today. Some of the coming changes, however, are now discernible—and hints of what is to come appear on the horizon with increasing frequency and growing clarity. A few of the more obvious changes are already upon us. They include (1) a restructuring of the juvenile justice system in the face of growing concerns about violent juvenile crime and spreading youth gang warfare; (2) the increased bankruptcy of a "war against drugs" whose promises seem increasingly hollow; (3) a growing recognition of America's international role as both victim and purveyor of worldwide criminal activity; and (4) the rapid emergence of cybercrimes, which both employ high technology in their commission and target the fruits of such technology.

This last part of *Criminal Justice Today* discusses each of these issues. It also draws your attention back to the bedrock underlying the American system of justice: the Constitution, the Bill of Rights, and the demands of due process, all of which will continue to structure the justice system well into the future.

Juvenile Justice

LEARNING OBJECTIVES

After reading this chapter, you should be able to

■ Describe the history and evolution of the juvenile justice system in the Western world

■ List and define the categories of children in today's juvenile justice system

■ Describe the nature of the problems that juveniles face in the United States today

■ Name the important U.S. Supreme Court decisions of relevance to juvenile justice, and describe their effects on the handling of juveniles by the system

■ Explain the similarities and differences between the juvenile and adult systems of justice

chapter 14

[*America's best hope for reducing crime is to reduce juvenile delinquency and youth crime.*]

—President's Commission on Law Enforcement and Administration of Justice (1967)

[*Our society's fearful of our kids. I think we don't know how to set limits on them. They begin to behave in severely outrageous ways, and nobody stops them.*]

—David York, cofounder of Toughlove International [1]

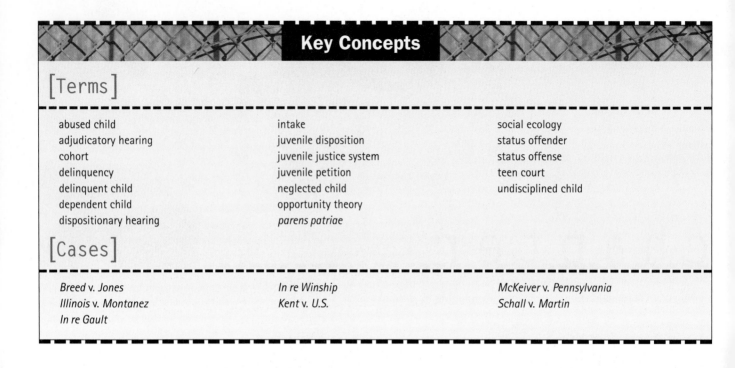

Key Concepts

[Terms]

abused child	intake	social ecology
adjudicatory hearing	juvenile disposition	status offender
cohort	juvenile justice system	status offense
delinquency	juvenile petition	teen court
delinquent child	neglected child	undisciplined child
dependent child	opportunity theory	
dispositionary hearing	*parens patriae*	

[Cases]

Breed v. *Jones*	*In re Winship*	*McKeiver* v. *Pennsylvania*
Illinois v. *Montanez*	*Kent* v. *U.S.*	*Schall* v. *Martin*
In re Gault		

Introduction

Hear the author discuss this chapter at **cjtoday.com**

> Juvenile violence is rampant, juvenile crime is exploding, juvenile killers are threatening the fabric of our society, and it's only going to get worse—much worse.
>
> —Former Senator John Ashcroft, introducing legislation to change the federal juvenile justice program

In September 2001, Tavaris Knight was convicted by a criminal court jury in Tampa, Florida, of kidnapping and raping a 43-year-old woman. Prosecutors proved that the 12-year-old Knight had used a silver toy gun to force the woman away from her four young children at a playground and into the surrounding woods. Knight raped the woman twice and beat her with the gun.[2] His fingerprints were found on the toy gun to which the victim led police. In closing arguments, prosecutor Michael Sinacore pointed to Knight, saying, "That young man is not a child. He stopped being a child when he forced [his victim] into the woods and raped her."[3] Following conviction, Knight was sentenced to 15 years in prison by Florida Circuit Judge Jack Espinosa, Jr. Knight will likely be held at a youth facility for sexual offenders until he is 21, at which time he could be transferred to another youth offender facility until the age of 25, followed by adult prison.[4]

Although the crime for which Knight was convicted may be unusual for a seventh-grader (Knight would have been in seventh grade at the time of the offense, but he had previously stopped attending school), crimes committed by preteens are not that unusual. In 2000, for example, two Kennesaw, Georgia, elementary school students, ages seven and ten, were caught by police officers ransacking a house. The pair had smashed the owner's possessions with a baseball bat and were in the process of stealing $1,000 worth of jewelry, a Samurai sword, and handgun ammunition when police arrived.[5] In another example, two 12-year-old St. Lucie County, Florida, girls were charged in 2001 with trying to drown a classmate in a lake near her home. The intended victim, 12-year-old Nicole Maines, had refused to surrender her mask and flippers—leading the other girls to jump in the water, grab her gear, and beat her.[6] When the attackers shoved Maines's head underwater, a witness, 16-year-old Hosea Rivers, jumped into the lake and pulled the girls apart. A police report showed that Maines suffered cuts and bruises all over her body.

A key finding of the Office of Juvenile Justice and Delinquency Prevention's (OJJDP) Study Group on Serious and Violent Juvenile Offenders is that most chronic juvenile offenders begin their delinquency careers before age 12, and some as early as age ten.[7] The most recent national data show that in 2000, police arrested about 140,000 children age 12 and younger.[8] These very young offenders (known as *child delinquents*) represent almost 10% of the total number of juvenile arrestees (those up to age 18).

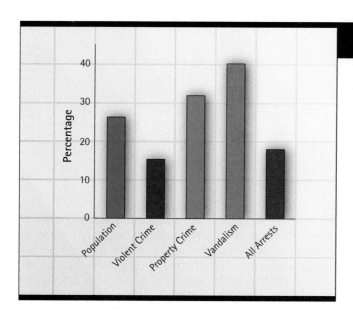

FIGURE 14–1

Juvenile involvement in crime versus system totals, 2000.

Source: Federal Bureau of Investigation, *Crime in the United States, 2000* (Washington, D.C.: U.S. Government Printing Office, 2001). *Note:* "Juvenile" refers to people younger than 18 years of age.

Although states vary as to the age at which a person legally enters adulthood, statistics on crime make it clear that young people are disproportionately involved in certain offenses. A recent report, for example, found that young people under the age of 18 account for over 15.9% of all violent crimes and 32% of all property crimes, though they make up only 26% of the population of the United States.[9] On the average, about 17% of all arrests in any year are of juveniles,[10] and people under the age of 18 have a higher likelihood of being arrested for robbery and other property crimes than do people in any other age group. Figure 14–1 shows *Uniform Crime Report* statistics on juvenile arrests for selected offense categories.

OJJDP, which was mentioned earlier, is a major source of information on juvenile justice in the United States. (Learn more about OJJDP via **Web Extra! 14–1** at

In 2002, Robert Iler, 17, who plays the role of Anthony (A. J.) Soprano (the adolescent son of mob boss Tony Soprano) on the HBO made-for-television series, The Soprano's *pled guilty to a misdemeanor charge of petty larceny in connection with a real-life New York City robbery that took place a year earlier. To some, Iler (who was arrested along with three other teenagers, and who was also charged with marijuana possession and possession of drug paraphernalia), came to symbolize the problems of youth today. Iler could have been sentenced to 15 years imprisonment on the original charges, but received three years probation as a part of the agreement.*

© Brad Rickerby, Reuters NewMedia, Inc./CORBIS

cjtoday.com.) A sweeping OJJDP report on juvenile crime and on the juvenile justice system in America found[11]

■ More than 2.8 million juveniles are arrested annually in America, an increase of 35% over the last decade.

■ Violent crime by juveniles is decreasing.

■ Younger juveniles account for a substantial proportion of juvenile arrests and the juvenile court caseload.

■ Female delinquency has grown substantially, increasing 76% in the last ten years.

■ The number of juveniles held in public facilities has increased sharply.

■ Minority juveniles are greatly overrepresented in the custody population.

■ Crowding is a serious problem in juvenile facilities.

juvenile justice system

Government agencies that function to investigate, supervise, adjudicate, care for, or confine youthful offenders and other children subject to the jurisdiction of the juvenile court.

This chapter has four purposes. First, we will describe the **juvenile justice system** from its historical beginnings to the present. The juvenile justice system has its roots in the adult system. In the juvenile system, however, we find a more uniform philosophical base and a generally clear agreement about the system's purpose. These differences may be due to the system's relative newness and to the fact that society generally agrees that young people who have gone wrong are worth salvaging. However, the philosophy which underlies the juvenile justice system in America is being increasingly called into question by "get tough" advocates of law and order, many of whom are fed up with violent juvenile crime.

Our second purpose will be to compare the juvenile and adult systems as they currently operate. The philosophy behind the juvenile justice system has led to administrative and other procedures which, in many jurisdictions, are not found in the adult system. The juvenile justice process, for example, is frequently not as open as the adult system. Hearings may be held in secret, the names of offenders are not published, and records of juvenile proceedings may be destroyed later.[12]

Our third purpose will be to describe in detail the agencies, processes, and problems of the juvenile justice system itself. Although each state may have variations, a common system structure is shared by all.

Of course, the juvenile justice system is not without its critics. As conservative attitudes began to bring changes in the adult criminal justice system over the last decade or so, the juvenile justice system remained one of the last surviving bastions of tradition. Based upon premises quite different from those of the adult system, juvenile justice has long been a separate decision-making arena, in which the best interests of the child have been accorded great importance. Near the end of this chapter, we will turn to our fourth focus and will consider some of the issues raised by critics of the current system. As we will see, substantial changes are now afoot.

*A photo of the "Trench Coat Mafia," from the Columbine High School yearbook. One of the most serious crimes committed by juveniles during the last century was the April 20, 1999, Columbine High School massacre in Littleton, Colorado. Dylan Klebold (17) and Eric Harris (18), both members of the "Mafia," perpetrated the crime. Fifteen people died and 20 were injured at the school. Learn more about the shootings via **Web Extra! 14–2** at cjtoday.com.*

Renato Rotolo, Getty Images, Inc.

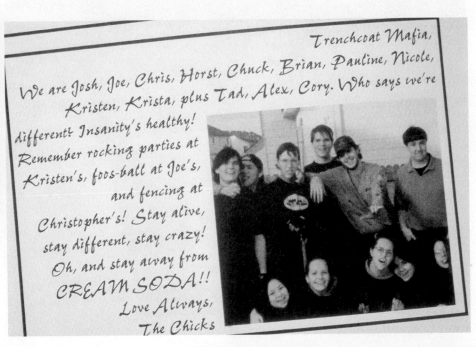

Juvenile Justice Throughout History

Earliest Times

In past centuries, children who committed crimes in the Western world could expect no preferential treatment because of their youth. They were adjudicated and punished alongside adults. The laws of King Aethelberht, the earliest legal document written in the English language (circa A.D. 600), made no special allowances for the age of the offender, and a number of recorded cases have come down through history of children as young as six or eight being hung or burned at the stake. Children were also imprisoned alongside adults. No segregated juvenile facilities existed. Neither the development of gaols (an old word for "jails") in the thirteenth century nor the early English prisons provided any leniency on the basis of age.[13] In like fashion, little distinction was made between criminality and **delinquency** or other kinds of undesirable behavior. Problems like epilepsy, insanity, retardation, and poverty were seen in the same light as crime,[14] and people suffering from these conditions were shut away in facilities shared by juveniles and adult offenders.

Court philosophy in dealing with juveniles derived from an early Roman principle called *patria postestas*. Under Roman law (circa 753 B.C.), children had membership in their family, but the father had absolute control over children, and they in turn had an absolute responsibility to obey his wishes. The power of the father extended to issues of life and death for all members of the family, including slaves, spouses, and children.[15] Roman understanding of the social role of children strongly influenced English culture and eventually led to the development of the legal principle of ***parens patriae***. *Parens patriae* allowed the king, or the English state, to take the place of parents in dealing with children who broke the law. *Parens patriae* held that the king was father of the country and thus had parental rights over all his citizens.

By the Middle Ages, social conceptions of children had become strongly influenced by Christian churches. Church doctrine held that children under the age of seven had not yet reached the age of reason and could not be held liable for spiritual transgressions. In adopting the perspective of the Church, English law of the period excepted children under the age of seven from criminal responsibility. Juveniles aged seven to 14 were accorded a special status, being tried as adults only if it could be demonstrated that they fully understood the nature of their criminal acts.[16] Adulthood was considered to begin at age 14, when marriage was also allowed.[17]

Early English institutions placed a large burden of responsibility on the family, and especially the father, who, as head of the household, was held accountable for the behavior of all family members. Children, and even wives, were almost totally dependent upon the father and had a status only slightly above that of personal property. When the father failed in his responsibility to control family members, the king, through the concept of *parens patriae*, could intervene.

The inexorable power of the king, often marked by his personal and unpredictable whims, combined with a widespread fear of the dismal conditions in English institutions to make many families hide their problem kin. The retarded, insane, and epileptic were kept in attics or basements, sometimes for their entire lives. Delinquent children were confined to the home or, if their families were wealthy enough, sent overseas to escape the conditions of asylums and gaols.

Juveniles in Early America

Early American solutions to the problems of delinquency were much like those of the English. Puritan influence in the colonies, with its heavy emphasis upon obedience and discipline, led to frequent use of jails and prisons for both juveniles and adults. Legislation reflected the biblical Ten Commandments and often provided harsh punishments for transgressors of almost any age. For example, one Massachusetts law in the seventeenth century provided, in part, that[18]

> If a man have a stubborn or rebellious son of sufficient years of understanding, viz. sixteen, which will not obey the voice of his father or the voice of his mother, and that when they have chastened him will not harken to them, then shall his father and mother, being his natural parents, lay hold on him and bring him to the magistrates assembled in Court, and testify to them by sufficient evidence that this their son is stubborn and rebellious and will not obey their voice and chastisement, but lives in sundry notorious crime. Such a son shall be put to death.

delinquency

In the broadest usage, juvenile actions or conduct in violation of criminal law, juvenile status offenses, and other juvenile misbehavior.

parens patriae

A common law principle that allows the state to assume a parental role and to take custody of a child when he or she becomes delinquent, is abandoned, or is in need of care that the natural parents are unable or unwilling to provide.

Severe punishment was consistent with Puritan beliefs that unacknowledged social evils might bring the wrath of God down upon the entire colony. In short, disobedient children had no place in a social group committed to a spiritual salvation understood as strict obedience to the wishes of the Divine.

By the end of the eighteenth century, social conditions in Europe and America began to change. The Enlightenment, a highly significant intellectual and social movement, focused on human potential and generally rejected previously held supernatural explanations in favor of scientific ones. It was accompanied by the growth of an industrialized economy, with a corresponding move away from farming. Poor laws, lower infant death rates, and social innovations born of the Enlightenment led to a reassessment of the place of children in society. In this new age, children were recognized as the only true heirs to the future, and society became increasingly concerned about their well-being.

The Institutional Era

The nineteenth century was a time of rapid social change in the United States. The population was growing dramatically, cities were burgeoning, and the industrial era was in full swing. Industrial tycoons, the new rich, and frontier-bound settlers lived elbow to elbow with immigrants eking out a living in the sweatshops of the new mercantile centers. In this environment, children took on new value as a source of cheap labor. They fueled assembly lines and proved invaluable to shop owners whose businesses needed cheap labor. Parents were gratified by the income-producing opportunities available to their offspring. On the frontier, settlers and farm families put their children to work clearing land and seeding crops.

Unfortunately, economic opportunities and the luck of the draw were not equally favorable to all. Some immigrant families became victims of the cities which drew them, settling in squalor in hastily formed ghettos. Many families, seeing only the economic opportunities represented by their children, neglected to provide them with anything but a rudimentary education. Children who did work labored for long hours and had little time for family closeness. Other children, abandoned by families unable to support them, were forced into lives on the streets, where they formed tattered gangs—surviving off the refuse of the glittering cities.

Young New York pickpockets in custody, circa 1900. Beginning in the late nineteenth century, juvenile courts had to consider what was in the child's best interests.
CORBIS

THE HOUSE OF REFUGE

An 1823 report by the Society for the Prevention of Pauperism in the City of New York called for the development of "houses of refuge" to save children from lives of crime and poverty. The society also cited the problems caused by locking up children with mature criminals. Houses of refuge were to be places of care and education, where children could learn positive attitudes about work.

In 1824, the first house of refuge opened in New York City.[19] The New York House of Refuge was intended only for those children who could still be "rescued," and it sheltered mostly young thieves, vagrants, and runaways. Other children, especially those with more severe delinquency problems, were placed in adult prisons and jails. Houses of refuge became popular in New York, and other cities quickly copied them. It was not long before overcrowding developed, and living conditions deteriorated.

The 1838 case of *Ex parte Crouse* clarified the power which states had in committing children to institutions.[20] The case involved Mary Ann Crouse, who had been committed to the Philadelphia House of Refuge by a lower court over the objections of her father. The commitment was based upon allegations made by the girl's mother that she was incorrigible—that is, beyond the control of her parents. Mary Ann's father petitioned the court to release his daughter on the grounds that she had been denied the right to trial by jury.

The decision by the appeals court upheld the legality of Mary Ann's commitment. It pointed to the state's interest in assisting children and denied that punishment or retribution played any part in her treatment. The court also focused on parental responsibilities in general and stressed the need for state intervention to provide for the moral development of children whose parents had failed them. Most important of all, the court built its decision around the doctrine of *parens patriae*, taking what had previously been an English judicial concept and applying it to the American scene. The court wrote,[21]

> The object of the charity is reformation, by training its inmates to industry; by imbuing their minds with principles of morality and religion; by furnishing them with means to earn a living; and above all, by separating them from the corrupting influence of improper associates. To this end, may not the natural parents, when unequal to the task of education, or unworthy of it, be superseded by the *parens patriae*, or common guardianship of the community?

THE CHICAGO REFORM SCHOOL

Around the middle of the nineteenth century, the child-savers movement began. Child savers espoused a philosophy of productivity and eschewed idleness and unprincipled behavior. Anthony Platt, a modern writer who recognizes the significance of the child-savers movement, suggests that the mid-nineteenth century provided an ideological framework combining Christian principles with a strong emphasis on the worth of the individual.[22] It was a social perspective which held that children were to be guided and protected.

One product of the child-savers movement was the reform school—a place for delinquent juveniles which embodied the atmosphere of a Christian home. By the middle of the nineteenth century, the reform school approach to handling juveniles was well under way. The Chicago Reform School, which opened in the 1860s, provided an early model for the reform school movement. The movement focused primarily on predelinquent youths who showed tendencies toward more serious criminal involvement. Reform schools attempted to emulate wholesome family environments to provide the security and affection thought necessary in building moral character.

The reform school movement also emphasized traditional values and the worth of hard work. The movement tended to idealize country living, apparently in the belief that the frantic pace of city life made the transition from child to adult difficult. Some early reform schools were built in rural settings, and many were farms. A few programs even tried to relocate problem children to the vast open expanses of the Western states.

The reform school movement was not without its critics. As Platt writes, "If institutions sought to replicate families, would it not have been better to place the predelinquents directly in real families?"[23] As with houses of refuge, reform schools soon became overcrowded. What began as a meaningful attempt to help children ended in routinized institutional procedures devoid of the reformer's original zeal.

In the 1870s, the Illinois Supreme Court handed down a decision that practically put the reform school movement out of business. The case of *People ex rel. O'Connell* v. *Turner*[24] centered on Daniel O'Connell, who had been committed to the Chicago Reform School under an Illinois law which permitted confinement for "misfortune." Youngsters

> The current [juvenile justice] system, a relic from a more innocent time, teaches youthful offenders that crime pays and that they are totally immune and insulated from responsibility.
>
> —National Policy Forum

classified as "misfortunate" had not necessarily committed any offense. They were, rather, ordered to reform school because their families were unable to care for them or because they were seen as social misfits. Because O'Connell had not been convicted of a crime, the Illinois Supreme Court ordered him released. The court reasoned that the power of the state under *parens patriae* could not exceed the power of the natural parents except in punishing crime. The *O'Connell* case is remembered today for the lasting distinction it made between criminal and noncriminal acts committed by juveniles.

The Juvenile Court Era

An expanding recognition of the needs of children led the state of Massachusetts to enact legislation in 1870 which required separate hearings for juveniles.[25] New York followed with a similar law in 1877.[26] The New York law also prohibited contact between juvenile and adult offenders. Rhode Island enacted juvenile court legislation in 1898, and in 1899 the Colorado School Law became the first comprehensive legislation designed to adjudicate problem children.[27] It was, however, the 1899 codification of Illinois juvenile law which became the model for juvenile court statutes throughout the nation.

The Illinois Juvenile Court Act created a juvenile court, separate in form and function from adult criminal courts. To avoid the lasting stigma of criminality, the law applied the term *delinquent* rather than *criminal* to young adjudicated offenders. The act specified that *the best interests of the child* were to guide juvenile court judges in their deliberations. In effect, the judge was to serve as an advocate for the juvenile, seeking to guide the development of the child in socially desirable directions. Concerns with guilt or innocence took second place to the betterment of the child. The law abandoned a strict adherence to the due process requirements of adult prosecutions, allowing informal procedures designed to scrutinize the child's situation. By sheltering the juvenile from the punishment philosophy of the adult system, the Illinois Juvenile Court emphasized reformation in place of retribution.[28]

> Three decades of reform have largely dissolved the traditional juvenile court, and the system that remains is rapidly losing political viability. Policy makers may soon need to devise an entirely new process for handling young offenders.
>
> —Jeffrey Butts and Adele Harrell[i]

In 1938, the federal government passed the Juvenile Court Act, which embodied many of the features of the Illinois statute. By 1945, every state had enacted special legislation focusing on the handling of juveniles, and the juvenile court movement became well established.[29]

The juvenile court movement was based upon five philosophical principles that can be summarized as follows:[30]

- The belief that the state is the "higher or ultimate parent" of all the children within its borders.

- The belief that children are worth saving and that nonpunitive procedures should be used to save the child.

- The belief that children should be nurtured. While the nurturing process is under way, they should be protected from the stigmatizing impact of formal adjudicatory procedures.

- The belief that justice, to accomplish the goal of reformation, needs to be individualized; that is, each child is different, and the needs, aspirations, living conditions, and so on, of each child must be known in their individual particulars if the court is to be helpful.

- The belief that the use of noncriminal procedures are necessary to give primary consideration to the needs of the child. The denial of due process could be justified in the face of constitutional challenges because the court acted not to punish, but to help.

Learn more about the history of juvenile justice and the juvenile court via **Library Extra! 14–1** at cjtoday.com.

CATEGORIES OF CHILDREN IN THE JUVENILE JUSTICE SYSTEM

By the time of the Great Depression, most states had expanded juvenile statutes to include the following six categories of children. These categories are still used today in most jurisdictions to describe the variety of children subject to juvenile court jurisdiction.

- **Delinquent children** are those who violate the criminal law. If they were adults, the word *criminal* would be applied to them.

- **Undisciplined children** are said to be beyond parental control, as evidenced by their refusal to obey legitimate authorities, such as school officials and teachers. They need state protection.

delinquent child

A child who has engaged in activity that would be considered a crime if the child were an adult. The term *delinquent* is applied to such a child to avoid the stigma associated with the term *criminal*.

undisciplined child

A child who is beyond parental control, as evidenced by his or her refusal to obey legitimate authorities, such as school officials and teachers.

- **Dependent children** typically have no parents or guardians to care for them or were abandoned or placed for adoption in violation of the law.
- **Neglected children** are those who do not receive proper care from their parents or guardians. They may suffer from malnutrition, may not be provided with adequate shelter, or may not be receiving a proper upbringing.
- **Abused children** include those who suffer physical abuse at the hands of their custodians. This category was later expanded to include emotional and sexual abuse.
- **Status offenders** is a special category which embraces children who violate laws written only for them.

Status offenses include behavior such as truancy, vagrancy, running away from home, and incorrigibility. The youthful "status" of juveniles is a necessary element in such offenses. Adults, for example, may decide to run away from home and not violate any law. Runaway children, however, are subject to apprehension and juvenile court processing because state laws require that they be subject to parental control.

Status offenses were a natural outgrowth of juvenile court philosophy. As a consequence, however, juveniles in need of help often faced procedural dispositions that treated them as though they were delinquent. Rather than lowering the rate of juvenile incarceration, the juvenile court movement led to its increase. Critics of the juvenile court movement quickly focused on the abandonment of due process rights, especially in the case of status offenders, as a major source of problems. Detention and incarceration, they argued, were inappropriate options where children had not committed crimes.

EXPLANATION OF DELINQUENCY

As states implemented innovative efforts to handle problem children, researchers began to investigate the causes of juvenile misbehavior. One of the first comprehensive social science explanations for delinquency, advanced by Clifford Shaw and Henry McKay in the 1920s, was known as **social ecology**.[31] The social ecology approach focused on the misbehavior of lower-class youth and saw delinquency primarily as the result of social disorganization. Whereas social order is the condition of a society characterized by social integration, consensus, smooth functioning, and lack of interpersonal and institutional conflict, social disorganization exists when a group is faced with social change, uneven development, maladaptiveness, disharmony, conflict, and lack of consensus. Geographic areas characterized by economic deprivation were said to have high rates of population turnover and cultural heterogeneity, both of which were seen as contributors to social disorganization. Social disorganization weakened otherwise traditional societal controls, such as family life, church, jobs, and schools, making delinquency more likely.

The first large-scale delinquency-prevention program grew out of the work of Shaw and McKay. Known as the Chicago Area Project, the program established self-help neighborhood centers staffed by community volunteers. Each center offered a variety of counseling services, educational programs, camps, recreational activities, and discussion groups. Programs were intended to reduce social disorganization by bringing members of the community together to work toward common goals and by providing community members with the skills needed for success.

The approach of Shaw and McKay was replaced in the 1960s by a perspective known as **opportunity theory**. Opportunity theorists saw delinquency as the result of the lack of legitimate opportunities for success available to most lower-class youth. Richard Cloward and Lloyd Ohlin described the most serious delinquents as facing limited opportunities due to their inherent alienation from middle-class institutions.[32] Others have claimed that delinquency is a natural consequence of participation in lower-class culture. Even stable lower-class communities, these authors suggest, produce delinquency as a matter of course.[33] A combination of both approaches is found in the work of Albert Cohen, who held that delinquency, especially gang-related activity, is a response to the frustration lower-class youth experience when they find they cannot share in the rewards of a middle-class lifestyle.[34] According to Cohen, vengeance and protest are major motivators among deprived youth and may account for vandalism and other seemingly senseless acts.

Opportunity theory gave rise to treatment models designed to increase chances for legitimate success among lower-class youth. Programs like New York City's Mobilization for Youth provided education, skills training, and job-placement services to young men and

dependent child

A child who has no parents or whose parents are unable to care for him or her.

neglected child

A child who is not receiving the proper level of physical or psychological care from his or her parents or guardians or who has been placed up for adoption in violation of the law.

abused child

A child who has been physically, sexually, or mentally abused. Most states also consider a child who is forced into delinquent activity by a parent or guardian to be abused.

status offender

A child who commits an act that is contrary to the law by virtue of the offender's status as a child. Purchasing cigarettes, buying alcohol, and being truant are examples of such behavior.

status offense

An act or conduct that is declared by statute to be an offense, but only when committed by or engaged in by a juvenile, and that can be adjudicated only by a juvenile court.

social ecology

A criminological approach that focuses on the misbehavior of lower-class youth and sees delinquency primarily as the result of social disorganization.

opportunity theory

A perspective that sees delinquency as the result of limited legitimate opportunities for success available to most lower-class youth.

women. Mobilization for Youth, through the federal funds it received, hired hundreds of unemployed neighborhood youths to work on community projects, such as parks conservation and building renovation.

Gresham Sykes and David Matza at least partially recognized the role of individual choice in delinquent behavior in their description of the neutralization of responsibility as a first step toward law violation.[35] The delinquent, according to Sykes and Matza, typically drifts between conformity and law violation and will choose the latter when social norms can be denied or explained away.[36]

cohort

A group of individuals sharing similarities of age, place of birth, and residence. Cohort analysis is a social science technique that tracks cohorts over time to identify the unique and observable behavioral traits that characterize them.

Cohort analysis is a useful technique for identifying the determinants of delinquency. Cohort analysis usually begins at birth and traces the development of members of a population who share common characteristics until they reach a certain age. One well-known analysis of a birth cohort, undertaken by Marvin Wolfgang during the 1960s, found that a small nucleus of chronic juvenile offenders accounted for a disproportionately large share of all juvenile arrests.[37] Wolfgang studied males born in Philadelphia in 1945 until they reached age 18. He concluded that a relatively small number of violent offenders were responsible for most of the crimes committed by the cohort. Eighteen percent of cohort members accounted for 52% of all arrests. A follow-up study found that the seriousness of offenses among the cohort increased in adulthood but that the actual number of offenses decreased as the cohort aged.[38] Wolfgang's analysis has been criticized for its lack of a second cohort, or "control group," against which the experiences of the cohort under study could be compared.[39]

Perhaps the most comprehensive study to date which has attempted to unveil the underlying causes of juvenile delinquency was begun in 1986, with results being reported on an ongoing basis. The study, named the Program of Research on the Causes and Correlates of Juvenile Delinquency, is sponsored by the U.S. Department of Justice's OJJDP.[40] The study, which is discussed in greater detail in Chapter 3, draws together data on 4,000 youths from three distinct but coordinated projects in Denver, Pittsburgh, and Rochester. The survey sampled youngsters at high risk for serious delinquency and drug use and found that (1) "the more seriously involved in drugs a youth was, the more seriously that juvenile was involved in delinquency," (2) "greater risks exist for violent offending when a child is physically abused or neglected early in life," (3) "students who were not highly committed to school had higher rates of delinquency," (4) "poor family life exacerbates delinquency and drug use," and (5) affiliation with street gangs and illegal gun ownership are both predictive of delinquency. The study also found that "peers who were delinquent or used drugs had a great impact on [other] youth."

Other studies have also indicated the importance of regular school attendance and commitment to success at school.[41] One report by OJJDP, for example, found that "chronic absenteeism is the most powerful predictor of delinquent behavior."[42] A comprehensive task force report by the American Society of Criminology similarly concluded that "strong evidence links early problem behavior to later adolescent delinquency and serious adult criminality" and suggested that early intervention is the key to preventing the development of chronic patterns of criminal behavior.[43] Authors of the task force report wrote, "There is clear indication that problem behavior often begins early in life, and there is strong evidence of substantial continuity between problem behavior in early childhood and later adolescent delinquency and serious adult criminality. 'An ounce of prevention is worth more than a pound of cure' is more than an old adage. Not only can early prevention and intervention reduce future crime and delinquency, but waiting until the mid-to-late teenage years to intervene in serious, persistent delinquency commonly results in an uphill and all too frequently fruitless battle."[44]

A more detailed explanation of the causes of crime and delinquency is available in Chapter 3. Also see **Library Extra! 14–2** at cjtoday.com, which provides an overview of OJJDP's Causes and Correlates of Delinquency Program.

The Problems of Children Today

Besides delinquency, but in some ways contributing to it, are a vast array of other problems that children face today. Many of these problems are quite different from those that existed when the juvenile court was formed.

One general problem with which many of today's children must deal is a lack of purpose. Another is frustration, especially among the urban poor. Illustrative of the latter is the "wilding" episode of a decade ago during which a young woman was raped and nearly killed by a gang of East Harlem teenagers as she jogged through New York City's Central Park.[45] The attack was just one in a series of violent crimes the gang committed. The victim, who became known as "the Central Park jogger," had been working her way through Yale Business School at the time of the attack. She suffered two skull fractures and serious brain damage. Following police questioning, the youngsters—who remained largely unrepentant—described how evenings spent "wilding" (the pack's slang term for violent mischief) had given vent to their frustrations. At the time, one psychologist noted that "feelings of frustration and alienation are widespread, particularly among lower classes."[46] "Angry adolescents" have been described as sharing these traits: (1) aggressiveness, (2) immaturity, (3) susceptibility to peer pressure, and (4) a lack of accountability.[47]

How did the angry adolescent come to be a problem in America? Over half a century ago, many of the problems encountered by juveniles grew out of their value as inexpensive laborers in the sweatshops and factories of the awakening industrial giant that was America. The economic prosperity that followed World War II, however, was based on a less labor-intensive form of production. Complicating matters still further was the need for the national economy to absorb millions of women who were entering the labor force. Juveniles, no longer needed for their labor, were thrown into a cultural limbo. Some, unable to meaningfully participate in the long educational process that was becoming necessary for future success, turned to delinquency and vandalism. For these disenfranchised youths, criminal activity became an alternative avenue to excitement and some limited sense of purpose.

By the 1960s, a self-indulgent ethic had replaced a sense of personal responsibility among many American youths. For lower-class youths, the ethic led to violence, theft, and increased participation in gangs. Middle-class youths, because they were more affluent, focused on what some authors at the time called the "automobile-alcohol-sex combination,"[48] rejecting middle-class values of social duty and personal restraint.

While much of the literature on delinquency focuses on the criminality of lower-class youths, there is evidence that middle- and upper-class youths also commit a fair number of delinquent acts. A study of the "lifetime delinquency" of Ivy League college students, for example, found "substantial levels of involvement in a variety of serious offenses."[49] According to the study, 167 students admitted to 4,100 past offenses ranging from public intoxication to forcible rape.

Regardless of class background, juveniles today face a number of common problems. They are described in the sections that follow.

Drug and Alcohol Abuse

Many of today's adolescents have experimented with illegal drugs. Statistics documenting both long-term use and experimentation are available from many sources. The Department of Health and Human Services' Monitoring the Future (MTF) survey,[50] one of the most comprehensive sources of information on juvenile drug use, annually measures drug abuse among high school and college students. The 2000 survey found that illicit drug use remains widespread among American young people. Today, over half (54%) have tried an illicit drug by the time they finish high school. If inhalant use is included in the definition of *illicit drug,* more than a third (35%) of students have done so as early as the eighth grade. Twenty-nine percent of in-school students have tried some illicit drug *other* than marijuana by the end of twelfth grade, and 20% of twelfth graders used some illicit drug other than marijuana in the past year. It is important to note that the MTF survey depends upon "self-reports of drug use among high school seniors" and "may underrepresent drug use among youth of that age because high school dropouts and truants are not included, and these groups may have more involvement with drugs than those who stay in school."[51]

The 2000 MTF survey found that marijuana continues to be the most widely used illicit drug. The annual prevalence rates (defined as having used a drug at least once during the past year) in grades 8, 10, and 12, respectively, were 16%, 32%, and 37%. There has been a steady but gradual decline in eighth-grade marijuana use since 1996, but little change in grades 10 and 12. According to 2000 MTF data, use rates for a number of other drugs were also down noticeably in all grades from their peak levels in the mid-1990s, including inhalants, LSD, crystal methamphetamine, and Rohypnol. Twelfth graders have tended to be the last to show declines in previous surveys, but they showed significant declines in their use of crack cocaine and powder cocaine during 2000. The largest increase was observed for MDMA ("ecstasy"), although steroid use among tenth graders continued to grow, and heroin use among twelfth graders increased. The 2000 MTF survey found that ecstasy use had increased at all three grade levels. While the

> There was nothing to do.
>
> —Terrance Wade, 15, on why he and his friends allegedly raped, stomped, stabbed, and ultimately murdered a Boston woman

> For the foreseeable future, American youngsters will be aware of the psychoactive potential of many drugs and, in general, will have relatively easy access to them. In the absence of reasons not to use, many are going to try them and a significant number will get into trouble with them.
>
> —Monitoring the Future survey

1999 MTF survey showed increases in ecstasy use mostly in the Northeast, increases uncovered by the 2000 MTF took place primarily in the other three regions of the country, suggesting a diffusion of the drug from the Northeast. Ecstasy is now more prevalent among American teens than cocaine.

Some young people abuse a wide variety of mind- and mood-altering substances. Surveys show that 9% of eighth graders have used inhalants at least once during the past year, while 28% of seniors, 21% of tenth graders, and 13% of eighth graders report binge drinking (defined as consuming five or more alcoholic drinks in a row).[52] According to a RAND Corporation Drug Policy Research Center study, (1) about one out of every six high school seniors averages at least one alcoholic drink every other day; (2) more than a quarter of all teenagers experience a drinking-related problem (such as missing school) on at least three occasions in any given year—or a more serious problem (such as a fight) at least once; and (3) about 25% of teenagers engage in two or more high-risk drinking activities (combining alcohol with other drugs, driving while drinking, and so on) at least once per year.[53]

As Figure 14–2 shows, drug-related arrests of juveniles have risen significantly over the past 30 years, nearly doubling between 1970 and 2000. The rise, however, has not been consistent, with peaks occurring around 1976 and 1996, with declines in between.[54] While some of the increase in the number of arrests may be due to "get tough" enforcement policies, evidence indicates that a juvenile arrested today is far more likely to be using methamphetamines ("crystal meth"), ecstasy, GHB, Rohypnol, and cocaine or crack cocaine than were juveniles in earlier periods. Likewise, heroin use has made a small but noticeable comeback. In contrast, the most commonly abused drug among young people in 1975 was marijuana.

Drug abuse can lead to other types of crime. One study, for example, found that seriously delinquent youths were regular drug users.[55] The National Institute of Justice concludes, "The involvement of adolescent users in other destructive behavior is strongly associated with the number and types of harmful substances they use; the more substances they use, the greater their chance of being involved in serious destructive or assaultive behavior."[56] Chapter 15 describes illicit drugs, drug abuse, and substance abuse laws in greater detail.

Violence

Observers of the national scene have reported a near-epidemic of violence among certain segments of the teenage population. While the numbers are small (juveniles commit approximately 800 homicides annually), violence committed both by and against children is a serious national problem. The National Center for Health Statistics lists homicide as

> Recent statistics predict a doubling in juvenile arrests for violent crime by the year 2010 if the last decade's trends continue unchecked.
>
> —Office of Juvenile Justice and Delinquency Prevention

FIGURE 14–2

Drug-related arrests of juveniles, 1960–2000.

Source: Federal Bureau of Investigation, *Crime in the United States* (Washington, D.C.: U.S. Government Printing Office, various years).

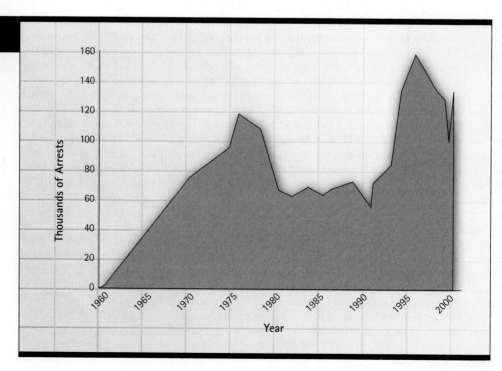

Female gang members. The values and experiences of many children today are far different from those of the past.

Robert Yager, Getty Images, Inc.

the third leading cause of death for children ages one to four and five to 14, and the second leading cause for young people 15 to 24.[57] Of the 1,300 juvenile murder victims in 2000—an average of three per day—20% were under age five.[58] Thirty-two percent were female, and 44% were African American.[59] Sixty-two percent of all juvenile murder victims and 57% of murdered youth who were 13 or older were killed with a firearm.[60] Forty percent were killed by family members, 45% by acquaintances, and only 15% by strangers.[61] The older juvenile victims, compared with those under age 13, were more likely to be male and African-American.[62] Younger victims were more likely to be killed by family members.

These statistics reflect only juvenile victimizations that were reported to the police. Only about half of the serious violent victimizations of juveniles in this country—including aggravated assault, murder, forcible rape, and robbery—are reported to police or other authorities, such as teachers and school principals.[63] Violent crimes that occur in schools, those that result in injury, and those that involve an adult rather than a juvenile perpetrator are the most likely to be reported.[64] Learn more about crimes committed against juveniles via **Library Extra! 14–3** at cjtoday.com.

Gangs

Juvenile gangs have been an inner-city phenomenon for decades. Detailed descriptions of gang activities in the United States date from the 1920s and 1930s.[65] Recent gang activities, however, differ substantially from those early reports, reflecting, perhaps, the influence of the rapid growth of cocaine markets. Whereas membership in early gangs served to provide some sense of personal identity in the immigrant's culturally diverse world, many of today's juvenile gangs have developed into financial enterprises. Their activities may center on drug running and on the acquisition and sale of stolen goods. Today's gangs rarely hesitate to use ruthless violence to protect their financial opportunities. One study of an East Coast gang of the 1930s found that the weapons of choice included milk bottles, flowerpots, and banana tree stalks.[66] In contrast, members of some large-city gangs today brandish semiautomatic weapons and Uzi submachine guns.[67]

The National Youth Gang Survey, conducted annually by OJJDP in conjunction with the National Youth Gang Center (NYGC), found 3,911 jurisdictions throughout the country with active youth gangs in 1999.[68] It was estimated that approximately 26,000 gangs and more than 840,500 gang members were active in those jurisdictions. Fifty percent of gang members in 1999 were between the ages of 18 and 24, an increase from 46% in 1998 and 37% in 1996.[69] The proportion of gang members ages 15 to 17 decreased to 26% from a high of 34% in 1996. Race-ethnicity composition, which remained similar to previous years, was as follows: Hispanic (47%), African-American (31%), White (13%), Asian (7%), and other (2%). Forty-seven percent of gangs were found to be multiethnic or multiracial.

In a question new to the 1999 survey, law enforcement agencies were asked to identify gang members by social class. Fifty percent of gang members were reported to be under-class, followed by working class (35%), middle class (12%), and upper middle class (3%). Responding jurisdictions were asked to estimate the proportion of their youth gang members who engage in specific types of serious and violent crimes. The offense types reported to be most prevalent among gang members are larceny/theft, aggravated assault, and burglary/breaking and entering. Respondents also estimated that 46% of youth gang members are involved in street drug sales to generate money for their gangs. The percentage of youth gangs that are considered drug gangs (that is, organized specifically for the purpose of trafficking in drugs) increased from 34% in 1998 to 40% in 1999.

Males were reported to be substantially more involved in gang activity than females, as females constituted only 10% of gang members throughout the country. This contrasts, however, with several recent self-report studies in which females represented approximately one-fourth to one-third of all gang members in urban adolescent samples. Read a summary of the latest National Youth Gang Survey at **Library Extra! 14–4** on cjtoday.com.

A large-scale project of the National Gang Crime Research Center (NGCRC), known as Project Gangfact, also provides a profile of gangs and gang members nationwide. The most recent Gangfact report, based on data collected by 28 researchers in 17 states, shows that (1) "gang members were significantly more likely than non-gang members to have . . . sold crack cocaine, and to be involved in organized drug dealing," (2) "gang members were less likely to come from an intact family" and more often came from a "dysfunctional family," (3) "gang members were significantly less likely than non-gang members to complete high school," and (4) gang members tended to be more predatory (that is, to be bullies in school and to be risk takers).[70] Among its dozens of intriguing findings, Gangfact also found that (1) the average age nationally for joining a gang is 12.8 years; (2) over half who joined gangs

Los Angeles gang members displaying signs of membership in front of a street mural.

A. Reininger, Woodfin Camp & Associates

CJ Today Exhibit 14–1

[What Is a Gang?]

Gangs and gang violence are of great concern today to many of our nation's citizens, law enforcement planners, and legislators. But just what is a gang? Section 186.22(f) of the California penal code provides one definition. It says a gang is:

> any ongoing organization, association, or group of three or more persons, whether formal or informal, having as one or more of its primary activities the commission of one or more

of the enumerated criminal acts [defined elsewhere as assault with a deadly weapon, robbery, homicide, drug trafficking, shooting at an occupied dwelling or occupied motor vehicle, arson, and intimidation of witnesses], which has a common name or common identifying sign or symbol, [and] whose members individually or collectively engage in or have engaged in a pattern of criminal activity.

---

have tried to quit; (3) more than two-thirds of gangs have written rules for members to follow; (4) over half of all gangs hold regular weekly meetings; (5) nearly 30% of gangs require their members to pay dues; (6) about 55% of gang members were recruited by other gang members, while the remainder sought out gang membership; (7) more than three-fourths of all gang members said they would leave the gang if given a "second chance in life"; (8) four-fifths of gang members reported that their gang sold crack cocaine; (9) 70% of gangs are not racially exclusive and consist of members of various ethnic groups; (10) one-third of gang members report that they have been able to conceal their gang membership from their parents; (11) 83% of the gangs report having female members, but few allow female members to assume leadership roles; and (12) 40% of gang members reported knowing male members of their gangs who have raped females.

Recently, the city of Chicago attempted to disrupt gang activity by passing a city ordinance prohibiting public association between criminal street gang members. The ordinance provided that people in the company of a gang member shall be ordered to disperse if their purpose is not apparent to a police officer. In 1999, however, in the case of *Chicago v. Morales*,[71] the U.S. Supreme Court invalidated Chicago's Gang Congregation Ordinance, ruling that it was impermissibly vague and failed to provide adequate standards to guide police discretion. Learn more about gangs from the National Youth Gang Center and the National Gang Crime Research Center via **Web Extras! 14–3** and **14–4** at cjtoday.com.

**Web
EXTRA!**

Runaways

The National Center for Missing and Exploited Children puts the number of children reported missing each year at more than 1.8 million.[72] An in-depth study of missing children found that the largest subgroup are runaways, while a sizable proportion are "thrownaways"—children no longer wanted by their parents.[73] Family abductions and children who are lost through accident, injury, or misadventure make up the remainder of all missing children. Although most runaway children eventually return home, there is evidence that runaway and thrownaway children are beginning to contribute to the increasing number of homeless on city streets.

Children run away for a variety of reasons. Some come from homes where there is little love and affection. Others clash with their parents over disputed activities within the home, problems in school, and difficulties with friends. Some are lured away from home by the promise of drugs or the money that drugs might bring. Official statistics show that one-third of runaways leave home because of sexual abuse,[74] while half leave because of beatings.

Whatever the reason, runaway children have become a huge problem. The Office for Juvenile Justice and Delinquency Prevention estimates that the vast majority of the children "who remain at large for a few weeks will resort to theft or prostitution as a method of self-support."[75] Of all children who do run away, only about 20% ever come into official contact with police or social service agencies.[76]

The juvenile justice system is hampered by statute in its ability to deal effectively with runaways. Running away from home is not a criminal act. Under the 1974 Juvenile Justice and Delinquency Prevention Act (as amended in 1992), runaways are designated *status offenders.* As a result, although some runaway children are placed in unguarded group homes by police officers and social service workers, neither shelter workers nor the police have any legal authority to force a child to stay in the facility.

> We know that many [youths] who are on the streets are there as a result of sound rational choices they have made for their own safety and welfare, such as avoiding physical abuse, sexual abuse, or extreme neglect at home.
>
> —National Council of Juvenile and Family Court Judges

An adolescent runaway living under a highway overpass in Hollywood, California. In recent years, the number of runaway children has become a problem of near-epidemic proportions.

Dorothy Littell, Stock Boston

Short-term solutions to the problem of runaways are being sought in clearinghouses for cataloging and disseminating information about missing and located children. The Missing Children Act of 1982 mandates that the parents, the legal guardians, or the next of kin of missing children may have information about a missing child entered into the FBI's National Crime Information Center (NCIC). The essence of these informational strategies is speed. The fast dissemination of information and the rapid reunion of family members with runaway children may provide the best hope that distraught children can be persuaded to return home.

Until the Juvenile Justice and Delinquency Prevention Act is amended to provide states and local jurisdictions with the needed authority to take runaway children into custody and safely control them, however, the problem of runaways will remain. Learn more about missing children from the National Center for Missing and Exploited Children via **Web Extra! 14–5** at cjtoday.com.

Sexual Abuse

> There are no illegitimate children—only illegitimate parents.
>
> —U.S. District Court Judge Leon R. Yankwich, in *Zipkin* v. *Mozon* (1928)

Some parents exploit their children for personal gain. In a famous case a decade ago, a mother living in Fort Lauderdale, Florida, was sentenced to a year in prison and two years of house arrest for forcing her 17-year-old daughter to work as a topless dancer.[77] The daughter committed suicide. All states have laws circumscribing the procuring of minor children for sexual performances. In recent years, the sexual exploitation of children has repeatedly made headlines.

In some parts of the country, day-care center operators have been charged with the sexual molestation of their charges, and many grade schools now routinely train young children to resist and report the inappropriate advances of adults.

The commercial sexual exploitation of children is a crime in all U.S. jurisdictions. A 2001 report by the University of Pennsylvania's Center for the Study of Youth Policy found that "child sexual abuse (CSA), child sexual assault (CSA) and child sexual exploitation (CSE) are not isolated events that are committed by a discrete group of perpetrators against a more or less clearly definable and restricted group of children. Rather, these sexual crimes against children are perpetrated by a broad segment of the American population and virtually any American child potentially can fall victim to one or another form of these abuses."[78]

The report emphasizes the existence of a *continuum of abuse* associated with child sexual abuse, child sexual assault, child sexual exploitation, and the commercial sexual exploitation of children. "While the faces of the children victimized by each form of abuse may differ," says the report, "the underlying socio-emotional-cultural dynamics responsible for all forms of child sexual abuse are the same, i.e., in every case the abuse is initiated by a more powerful offender(s), usually an adult, who exerts his or her will over [that of the] children in order to secure some sexual, economic or other benefit of value to the offender."[79] The report, which can be read at **Library Extra! 14–5** at cjtoday.com, also offers a series of recommendations for responding to the needs of sexually exploited children and youth.

Other Forms of Abuse

Most cases of child abuse are crimes that adults commit against children. For that reason, we will not discuss them in detail in this chapter. All forms of abuse, however, are damaging to children. A study conducted by the Child Welfare League of America found that "two of the surest predictors of a child likely to commit a crime [are] a child who has previously committed a crime and a child who has been victimized by child abuse and/or neglect."[80] According to the league, "9 to 12 year old youth known to the child welfare system are 67 times more likely to be arrested than 9 to 12 year old youth from the general population of children."

Some forms of abuse, such as the instance of sexual procurement mentioned earlier, may lead directly to the child's involvement in delinquency. Parental encouragement of delinquency is a problem sometimes encountered by juveniles who come from families already engaged in criminal activities. Prostitutes, for example, sometimes encourage their daughters to learn their work. In families where the theft and sale of stolen goods is a way of life, children may be recruited for shoplifting or for burglaries which require wriggling into tight spaces where an adult might not fit.

Research has shown that children who are encouraged in delinquency by adults tend to become criminals when they reach maturity. More surprising, however, is the finding that abused children have a similar tendency toward adult criminality.[81] A National Institute of Justice survey found that children "who had been abused or neglected . . . were more likely to be arrested as juveniles, as adults, and for a violent crime."[82] Although some studies have questioned the strength of the relationship, maltreatment and delinquency appear to be intertwined.[83] If so, early intervention into abusive environments may lead to an overall reduction in future criminality.

In an effort to support vigorous prosecution of child abuse cases, the National Center for the Prosecution of Child Abuse was formed in 1985.[84] The center, which serves as a national clearinghouse for legal and other information on child abuse, publishes comprehensive training manuals and materials for prosecutors and police officers to use in battling the child abuse problem. (See Figure 14–3.)

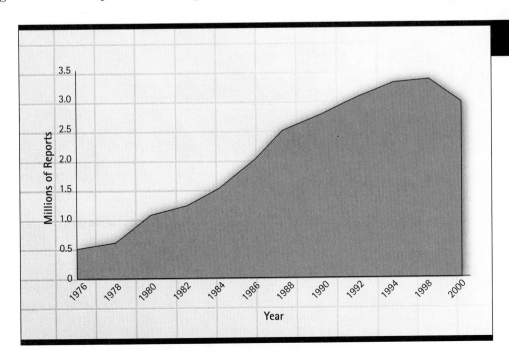

FIGURE 14-3

Reports of child abuse and neglect to child protective services agencies, 1976–2000.

Source: Based on National Clearinghouse on Child Abuse and Neglect Information.

CJ Today News

[Colorado Parents Probed in Death of Newborn]

Authorities in Colorado are investigating the death of a newborn whose parents belong to a church that relies on prayer and anointing with oil to heal its sick.

Billy Ray Reed died July 9, two days after his birth, at his home in Clifton, Colo. His parents are members of the General Assembly Church of the First Born, which does not believe in medical treatment for illness.

Six other church children have died after medical treatment was withheld. In the most recent case, church members Joshua and Mindy Glory pleaded guilty to child abuse in the death last year of their 18-day-old son. They received 16 years of probation. The child died of pneumonia as church elders prayed over him.

Most states, including Colorado, have laws that allow parents to claim religion as a defense against charges of medical neglect of their children.

In Billy's case, the boy was born at home and appeared fine until two days later, when he had trouble breathing, Mesa County Sheriff's spokeswoman Janet Prell says. Family members called 911 that night to report the child's death. Paramedics tried unsuccessfully to revive the boy.

No charges have been filed. The boy's parents, Billy Reed, 31, and Barbara Reed, 23, did not return phone messages left at their home Sunday.

In a study published in 1998 in *Pediatrics,* a medical journal, pediatrician Seth Asser examined the deaths of 172 children from 1975 through 1995 whose parents believed exclusively in faith healing. Asser found that 140 of the children died of easily treated conditions that have cure rates of greater than 90%, such as dehydration and appendicitis. Among the children was a hemophiliac infant in Philadelphia who bled to death after cutting his heel. His parents bandaged his foot with a diaper and prayed, Asser said.

"These are kids who should not have died," Asser says.

Billy died from complications of a heart defect, according to an autopsy. The county medical examiner said such a condition is not necessarily fatal. "Congenital heart disease is often recognized by professional health care providers and treated," Mesa County Coroner Rob Kurtzman said.

For the latest in crime and justice news, visit the Talk Justice news feed at http://www.crimenews.info.

Olga Worrall attempting to heal a baby at a Baltimore church. When sick children die, parents are often charged with child neglect or even more serious crimes if it can be shown that they denied their children medical help in the belief that faith healing and other alternative medical practices would cure their child.

© Roger Ressmeyer, CORBIS

Source: Donna Leinwand, "Colo. Parents Probed in Death of Newborn," *USA Today,* July 24, 2000. Copyright 2000, *USA Today.* Reprinted with permission.

Teen Suicide

In late 1998, a spate of teen suicides shocked the residents of Gallatin County, Kentucky. The first death occurred on November 5, when a 14-year-old boy shot himself in the head at his home. The boy was thought to have been depressed over his mother's death from cancer a few months earlier. Then on November 13, a 13-year-old eighth grader shot herself in the head while talking with a friend on the phone. Friends said that the girl might have been involved in an emotional relationship with the boy who had killed himself a week earlier. A third suicide took place two weeks later, when a 17-year-old Gallatin High School boy shot himself to death at his family's home.[85] The college-bound senior was a member of the school's golf team and BETA Club. He was said to have been despondent about having wrecked his Toyota Celica earlier that day.

Children today face many stressors unheard of years ago. Drugs, peer pressure, parents' insistence on success, sexual and other forms of abuse, and violent and broken homes lead some children to take their own lives. Suicide among teenagers is a quickly growing phenomenon. Only 475 teen suicides were recorded across the nation in 1960, but by 1999, up to 10,000 such deaths per year were being reported.[86] According to the American Academy of Child and Adolescent Psychiatry (AACAP), suicide has become the sixth major cause of death among five- to 14-year-old children.[87] Learn more about teen suicide from the American Foundation for Suicide Prevention at **Web Extra! 14–6** at cjtoday.com. For additional information on the problems facing children today, as well as indicators of childhood well-being, see **Library Extra! 14–6** at cjtoday.com.

What Can Be Done?

Although the problems facing children today are many and varied, there are those who believe that children in trouble share some characteristics. Broken homes, little parental supervision, poor role models, lack of educational opportunity, and poverty are seen as factors contributing to delinquency and later criminality. Recently, for example, OJJDP suggested that effective programs intended to reduce both the problems faced by children and the incidence of juvenile delinquency "must emphasize opportunities for healthy social, physical, and mental development." According to OJJDP, "Such programs must involve all components of the community, including schools, healthcare professionals, families, neighborhood groups, law enforcement, and community-based organizations."[88]

Many who have studied the problems of juveniles come back to basics, such as the quality of family life, economic conditions within neighborhoods, proper socialization, and supportive social institutions, when recommending solutions. An OJJDP "policymaker's guide," based upon the findings of a metastudy which summarized many other studies, concluded that (1) there is "a positive relationship between parental conflict and delinquency," (2) "the effect of broken homes on delinquency is real and consistent," (3) the tendency toward delinquency and other problems is enhanced for children living in low-income families, (4) "physical abuse of children leads them into violence later in life," and (5) "children who have criminal parents are at greater risk of becoming delinquent themselves."[89] The authors suggested that "a healthy home environment, one in which parents and children share affection, cohesion, and involvement, reduces the risk of delinquency" and of other childhood problems within both one- and two-parent families and that "parental rejection appears to be one of the most significant predictors of delinquency." The report concluded that "parents play a critical role in moral development" and that "the quality of [parental] supervision is consistently and strongly related to delinquency" and other childhood problems. As a consequence, said the authors, "parents must adequately monitor their children's behavior, whereabouts, and friends," and they "must reliably discipline their children for antisocial and prohibited behavior, but must do so neither rigidly nor severely."

Some also suggest that the time has come for a reevaluation of the basic philosophy underlying juvenile courts,[90] so that the decisions of such courts might be more realistic and encompass the needs of the community and of victims—as well as the needs of the children who come before them. As the National Council on Crime and Delinquency (NCCD) explains it, "We believe a more promising direction for the future of U.S. juvenile justice is the rediscovery and updating of the juvenile court's historical vision."[91] Visit NCCD via **Web Extra! 14–7** at cjtoday.com.

Some say the court must make better use of available community resources. Some years ago, for example, officials in Allegheny County, Pennsylvania, undertook a comprehensive approach to reducing juvenile crime with support from OJJDP.[92] That approach, said OJJDP Administrator Shay Bilchik, replaced "the community's fragmented response to juvenile violence with a collaborative and coordinated approach" that recognizes "that juvenile crime is a societal problem that can be solved only with the cooperation of the entire community."[93] The program, which focuses on juveniles who are at high risk of engaging in violent crimes, effectively coordinates the efforts of the law enforcement community, public and private agencies, grassroots organizations, and individual citizens. Such coordinated efforts seem to be paying off. Initial reports from the program show

> If a child cannot go to school without fear of being raped, robbed, or even murdered, then nothing else the government does really matters.
>
> —National Policy Forum

reduced rates of juvenile crime in Allegheny County, which exceed reductions in other parts of the state.

Perhaps the most comprehensive proposal yet for dealing with the problems of today's juveniles comes from the national Coordinating Council on Juvenile Justice and Delinquency Prevention (CCJJDP). The council, established by Section 206 of the Juvenile Justice and Delinquency Prevention Act, coordinates all federal programs that address juvenile delinquency, detention or care of unaccompanied juveniles, and missing and exploited children. The council's book-length report proposed an eight-point national strategy for combating juvenile delinquency, juvenile violence, and attendant problems.[94] Each point is stated in terms of an objective, as follows:

■ *Objective 1:* Provide immediate intervention and appropriate sanctions and treatment for delinquent juveniles. In support of this objective, the council recommends widespread use of preadjudicatory assessment centers which could offer a "systematic and coordinated way for youth to enter or be diverted from the system."

CJ Today Exhibit 14-2

[Parents on Trial]

Faced with a significant increase in crime among juveniles, a number of jurisdictions have responded with laws that place responsibility for children's behavior squarely on the parents. California's Street Terrorism Enforcement and Prevention Act, one of the first of its kind in the nation, subjects parents of wayward youths to arrest. Gloria Williams, the first person arrested under the law, was charged with neglecting her parental duties after her 15-year-old son was charged with rape.[1] Police said photo evidence proved that she knew her son was a gang member. Charges against her were dropped when she was able to show that she had taken a parenting course in an effort to gain better control over her son.

A number of other states have similar laws. Florida imposes a five-year prison term and a $5,000 fine on the parents of children who find and use guns left around the house, and Wisconsin makes both sets of grandparents financially liable for a child born to unmarried minor children. Wisconsin also has a law which can cause welfare parents to lose their benefits if their children are habitually truant from school.

Local jurisdictions are beginning to follow suit. In 1995, the town of Silverton, Oregon (population 6,710), began enforcing an ordinance which holds parents responsible when their children break the law. Parents of wayward children in Silverton can be fined up to $1,000. The Silverton ordinance, which is called a *parental duty law,* reads,

> A person commits the offense of failing to supervise a minor if the person is the parent, legal guardian or person with legal responsibility . . . of a child under 18 years of age and the child violates Silverton municipal code.

Soon after the Silverton law was passed, communities across the nation began asking for a copy of the ordinance.[2] Six months later, the

Oregon state legislature adopted a parental responsibility law which stipulated that, after a warning, parents of delinquent children could be fined up to $1,000 and be required to attend parenting classes.[3]

Local parental duty laws are being tailored to the specific needs of individual communities. After 25 youngsters were killed in two years of gang violence, for example, Atlanta passed an 11 P.M. curfew for anyone under 17, enforceable by a $1,000 fine with which the parents of violators can be saddled.[4] Washington, D.C., faced with a juvenile crime problem spiraling out of control, enacted a similar curfew. The law requires teenagers found in public places during curfew hours to be held at designated police-run truancy centers until a parent or guardian can claim them. Parents who are found to be permitting or aiding teens to break the curfew law are subject to fines and community service.

Supporters of these laws say they are trying to force parents to be parents. Critics claim that the statutes go "well beyond the pale of traditional law."[5] The American Civil Liberties Union (ACLU), for example, objects strenuously to the idea that people can go to prison for a crime committed by someone else. "The crime is having a kid who commits a crime," says Jay Jacobson, Director of the Arkansas section of the ACLU.

? DISCUSSION QUESTIONS

1. Do you agree with the basic philosophy of parental responsibility laws: that parents can and should be punished for the misdeeds of their minor children? Explain.
2. Do you believe that parental responsibility laws like those described in this box will be effective in reducing the incidence of juvenile delinquency in the United States? Explain.

[1]"Now, Parents on Trial," *Newsweek,* October 2, 1989, pp. 54–55.
[2]Deeann Glamser, "Communities Seek to Stem Youth Crime," *USA Today,* February 21, 1995, p. 1A.
[3]"Oregon Will Punish Delinquents' Parents," *USA Today,* July 18, 1995, p. 3A.
[4]*ABC Nightly News,* December 17, 1990.
[5]"Now, Parents on Trial," p. 55.

■ *Objective 2:* Prosecute certain serious, violent, and chronic juvenile offenders in adult criminal court. The council says that "transferring to criminal court those targeted juvenile offenders who are the most chronic and who commit the most serious and violent crimes enables the juvenile justice system to focus its efforts and resources on the much larger group of at-risk youth and less serious and violent offenders who can benefit from a wide range of effective intervention strategies."

■ *Objective 3:* Reduce youth involvement with guns, drugs, and gangs. A strong relationship exists, says the council, between delinquency and violence, gun possession, and drug use among juveniles.

■ *Objective 4:* Provide enhanced opportunities for children and youth. The council recommends the development of "comprehensive neighborhood-based programs that help children develop positive life skills and minimize risk factors."

■ *Objective 5:* Break the cycle of violence by addressing youth victimization, abuse, and neglect. "Many violent juveniles," says the council, "have themselves been victims of neglect, abuse, and violence." Hence, breaking the cycle of violence should lead to lower overall rates of offending.

■ *Objective 6:* Strengthen and mobilize communities. The council observes that "juvenile violence stems in large part from a breakdown of family and community structures." Hence, "nurturing strong families, providing social support systems, and reinforcing healthy cultural norms and values" can do much in the fight against delinquency.

■ *Objective 7:* Support the development of innovative approaches to research and evaluation. Better research should lead to more reliable and more useful information in the fight against juvenile crime, says the council.

■ *Objective 8:* Implement an aggressive public outreach campaign on effective strategies to combat juvenile violence. "A well-designed public information campaign is essential to the success of any juvenile violence reduction plan," says the council. The council recommends involving the media in creating "a public information campaign designed to persuade young people to avoid violence and dangerous lifestyles, to teach adults about proven antiviolence strategies, and to involve all segments of the community in the fight against juvenile violence."

See **Library Extra! 14–7** at cjtoday.com for an update to the CCJJDP plan.

A Concord, Massachusetts, policeman fingerprinting a young girl. Many parents, driven by a significant increase in crimes against children, make special efforts to assist in the identification of their offspring.

Bruce M. Wellman, Stock Boston

The Legal Environment

Throughout the first half of the twentieth century, the U.S. Supreme Court followed a hands-off approach to juvenile justice, much like its early approach to prisons (see Chapter 13). The adjudication and further processing of juveniles by the system was left mostly to specialized juvenile courts or to local appeals courts. Although one or two early Supreme Court decisions[95] dealt with issues of juvenile justice, it was not until the 1960s that the Court began close legal scrutiny of the principles underlying the system itself. In the pages that follow, we will discuss some of the most important U.S. Supreme Court cases relating to juvenile justice.

Kent v. *U.S.* (1966)

The U.S. Supreme Court case which ended the hands-off era in juvenile justice was *Kent* v. *U.S.*,[96] decided in 1966. The *Kent* case, which focused upon the long-accepted concept of *parens patriae,* signaled the beginning of the Court's systematic review of all lower-court practices involving delinquency hearings.

Morris Kent, Jr., age 14, was apprehended in the District of Columbia in 1959 and was charged with several house burglaries and an attempted purse snatching. Kent was placed on juvenile probation and was released into the custody of his mother. In 1961, an intruder entered a woman's apartment, took her wallet, and raped her. At the scene, police found fingerprints which matched those on file belonging to Morris Kent. At the time, Kent was 16 years old and, according to the laws of the District of Columbia, was still under the exclusive jurisdiction of the juvenile court.

Kent was taken into custody and interrogated. He volunteered information about the crime and spoke about other offenses involving burglary, robbery, and rape. Following interrogation, his mother retained counsel on his behalf. Kent was kept in custody for another week, during which time psychological and psychiatric evaluations were conducted. The professionals conducting the evaluations concluded that Kent was a "victim of severe psychopathology." Without conferring with Kent, his parents, or his lawyers, the juvenile court judge ruled that Kent should be remanded to the authority of the adult court system. He was eventually tried in U.S. District Court for the District of Columbia. The judge gave no reasons for assigning Kent to the adult court.

Kent was indicted in criminal court on eight counts of burglary, robbery, and rape. Citing the psychological evaluations performed earlier, Kent's lawyers argued that his behavior was the product of mental disease or defect. Their defense proved fruitless, and Kent was found guilty on six counts of burglary and robbery. He was sentenced to five to 15 years in prison on each count.

Kent's lawyers ultimately appealed to the U.S. Supreme Court. They argued that Kent should have been entitled to an adequate hearing at the level of the juvenile court and that, lacking such a hearing, his transfer to adult jurisdiction was unfair.

The Supreme Court, reflecting the Warren Court ideologies of the times, agreed with Kent's attorneys, reversed the decision of the district court, and ordered adequate hearings for juveniles being considered for transfer to adult court. At these hearings, the Court ruled, juveniles are entitled to representation by attorneys who must have access to their records.

Although it focused only on a narrow issue, the *Kent* decision was especially important because for the first time it recognized the need for at least minimal due process in juvenile court hearings. The *Kent* decision set the stage for what was to come, but it was the *Gault* decision, to which we now turn our attention, that turned the juvenile justice system upside down.

In re Gault (1967)

In 1964, Gerald Gault and a friend, Ronald Lewis, were taken into custody by the sheriff of Gila County, Arizona, on the basis of a neighbor's complaint that the boys had telephoned her and made lewd remarks. At the time, Gault was on probation for having been in the company of another boy who had stolen a wallet.

When Gault was apprehended, his parents were both at work. No notice was posted at their house to indicate that their son had been taken into custody, a fact which they later learned from Lewis's parents. Gault's parents could learn very little from authorities. Although they were notified when their son's initial hearing would be held, they were not told the nature of the complaint against him, nor could they learn the identity of the complainant, who was not present at the hearing.

At the hearing, the only evidence presented was statements made by young Gault and testimony given by the juvenile officer as to what the complainant had alleged. Gault was not represented by counsel. He admitted to having made the phone call but stated that after dialing the number he had turned the phone over to his friend, Lewis. After hearing the testimony, Judge McGhee ordered a second hearing, to be held a week later. At the second hearing, Mrs. Gault requested that the complainant be present so that she could identify the voice of the person making the lewd call. Judge McGhee ruled against her request. Finally, young Gault was adjudicated delinquent and remanded to the State Industrial School until his twenty-first birthday.

On appeal, eventually to the U.S. Supreme Court, Gault's attorney argued that his constitutional rights were violated because he had been denied due process. The appeal focused specifically on six areas:

- *Notice of charges.* Gault was not given enough notice to prepare a reasonable defense to the charges against him.
- *Right to counsel.* Gault was not notified of his right to an attorney or allowed to have one at his hearing.
- *Right to confront and to cross-examine witnesses.* The court did not require the complainant to appear at the hearing.
- *Protection against self-incrimination.* Gault was never advised that he had the right to remain silent, nor was he informed that his testimony could be used against him.
- *Right to a transcript.* In preparing for the appeal, Gault's attorney was not provided a transcript of the adjudicatory hearing.
- *Right to appeal.* At the time, the state of Arizona did not give juveniles the right to appeal.

The Supreme Court ruled in Gault's favor on four of the six issues raised by his attorneys. The majority opinion read, in part, as follows:[97]

> In *Kent* v. *United States*, we stated that the Juvenile Court Judge's exercise of the power of the state as *parens patriae* was not unlimited. . . . Notice, to comply with due process requirements, must be given sufficiently in advance of scheduled court proceedings so that reasonable opportunity to prepare will be afforded. . . . The probation officer cannot act as counsel for the child. His role in the adjudicatory hearing, by statute and in fact, is as arresting officer and witness against the child. There is no material difference in this respect between adult and juvenile proceedings of the sort here involved. . . . A proceeding where the issue is whether the child will be found to be "delinquent" and subjected to the loss of his liberty for years is comparable in seriousness to a felony prosecution. The juvenile needs the assistance of counsel to cope with the problems of law, to make skilled inquiry into the facts, to insist upon regularity of the proceedings, and to ascertain whether he has a defense and to prepare and submit it.

The Court did not agree with the contention of Gault's lawyers relative to appeal or with their arguments in favor of transcripts. Right to appeal, where it exists, is usually granted by statute or by state constitution—not by the Constitution of the United States. Similarly, the Court did not require a transcript because (1) there is no constitutional right to a transcript, and (2) no transcripts are produced in the trials of most adult misdemeanants.

Today, the impact of *Gault* is widely felt in the juvenile justice system. Juveniles are now guaranteed many of the same procedural rights as adults. Most precedent-setting Supreme Court decisions which followed *Gault* further clarified the rights of juveniles, focusing primarily on those few issues of due process that it had not explicitly addressed.

In re Winship (1970)

At the close of the 1960s, a New York Family Court judge found a 12-year-old boy named Samuel Winship delinquent on the basis of a petition which alleged that he had illegally entered a locker and stolen $112 from a pocketbook. The judge acknowledged to those present at the hearing that the evidence in the case might not be sufficient to establish Winship's guilt beyond a reasonable doubt. Statutory authority, however, in the form of the New York Family Court Act required a determination of facts based only on a preponderance of

> Under our Constitution, the condition of being a boy does not justify a kangaroo court.
>
> —*In Re Gault*, 387 U.S. 1 (1967)

the evidence—the same standard required in civil suits. Winship was sent to a training school for 18 months, subject to extensions until his eighteenth birthday.

Winship's appeal to the U.S. Supreme Court centered on the lower court's standard of evidence. His attorney argued that Winship's guilt should have been proved beyond a reasonable doubt—the evidentiary standard of adult criminal trials. The Court agreed, ruling that[98]

> the constitutional safeguard of proof beyond a reasonable doubt is as much required during the adjudicatory stage of a delinquency proceeding as are those constitutional guards applied in *Gault*. . . . We therefore hold . . . that where a 12 year old child is charged with an act of stealing which renders him liable to confinement for as long as six years, then, as a matter of due process . . . the case against him must be proved beyond a reasonable doubt.

As a consequence of *Winship,* allegations of delinquency today must be established beyond a reasonable doubt. The Court allowed, however, the continued use of the lower evidentiary standard in adjudicating juveniles charged with status offenses. Even though both standards continue to exist, most jurisdictions have chosen to use the stricter burden-of-proof requirement for all delinquency proceedings.

McKeiver v. *Pennsylvania* (1971)

Cases like *Winship* and *Gault* have not extended all adult procedural rights to juveniles charged with delinquency. For example, juveniles do not have the constitutional right to trial by a jury of their peers. The case of *McKeiver* v. *Pennsylvania* (1971)[99] reiterated what earlier decisions had established and legitimized some generally accepted practices of juvenile courts.

Joseph McKeiver, age 16, was charged with robbery, larceny, and receiving stolen property, all felonies in Pennsylvania. McKeiver had been involved with 20 to 30 other juveniles who chased three teenage boys and took 25 cents from them. He had no previous arrests and was able to demonstrate a record of gainful employment. McKeiver's attorney requested that his client be allowed a jury trial. The request was denied. McKeiver was adjudicated delinquent and committed to a youth development center. McKeiver's attorney pursued a series of appeals and was finally granted a hearing before the U.S. Supreme Court. There he argued that his client, even though a juvenile, should have been allowed a jury trial as guaranteed by the Sixth and Fourteenth Amendments to the Constitution.

The Court, although recognizing existent problems in the administration of juvenile justice, held to the belief that the Constitution did not mandate jury trials for juveniles. In the opinion of the Court,

> [t]he imposition of the jury trial on the juvenile court system would not strengthen greatly, if at all, the fact-finding function, and would contrarily, provide an attrition of the juvenile court's assumed ability to function in a unique manner. It would not remedy the defects of the system. . . . If the jury trial were to be injected into the juvenile court system as a matter of right, it would bring with it into that system the traditional delay, the formality, and the clamor of the adversary system and, possibly, the public trial. . . . If the formalities of the criminal adjudicative process are to be superimposed upon the juvenile court system, there is little need for its separate existence.

McKeiver v. *Pennsylvania* did not set any new standards. Rather, it reinforced the long-accepted practice of conducting juvenile adjudicatory hearings in the absence of certain due process considerations, particularly those pertaining to trial by jury. It is important to note, however, that the McKeiver decision did not specifically prohibit jury trials for juveniles. As a consequence, approximately 12 states today allow the option of jury trials for juveniles.

Breed v. *Jones* (1975)

In 1971, a delinquency complaint was filed against Jones, age 17, alleging that he committed robbery while armed with a deadly weapon. At the adjudicatory hearing, Jones was declared delinquent. A later dispositional hearing determined that Jones was "unfit for treatment as a juvenile," and he was transferred to superior court for trial as an adult. The superior court found Jones guilty of robbery in the first degree and committed him to the custody of the California Youth Authority.

In an appeal eventually heard by the Supreme Court, Jones alleged that his transfer to adult court, and the trial which ensued, placed him in double jeopardy because he had already been adjudicated in juvenile court. Double jeopardy is prohibited by the Fifth and Fourteenth Amendments to the Constitution. The state of California argued that the superior court trial was only a natural continuation of the juvenile justice process and, as a consequence, did not fall under the rubric of double jeopardy. The state further suggested that double jeopardy existed only where an individual ran the risk of being punished more than once. In the case of Jones, no punishment had been imposed by the juvenile court.

The U.S. Supreme Court did not agree that the possibility of only one punishment negated double jeopardy.[100] The Court pointed to the fact that the double jeopardy clause speaks in terms of "potential risk of trial and conviction—not punishment" and concluded that two separate adjudicatory processes were sufficient to warrant a finding of double jeopardy. Jones's conviction was vacated, clearing the way for him to be returned to juvenile court. However, by the time the litigation had been completed, Jones was beyond the age of juvenile court jurisdiction, and he was released from custody.

The *Jones* case severely restricted the conditions under which transfers from juvenile to adult courts may occur. In effect, the court mandated that such transfers as do occur must be made prior to an adjudicatory hearing in juvenile court.

Schall v. *Martin* (1984)

Gregory Martin, age 14, was arrested in New York City, charged with robbery and weapons possession, and detained in a secure detention facility for more than two weeks until his hearing. The detention order drew its authority from a New York preventive detention law which allowed for the jailing of juveniles thought to represent a high risk of continued delinquency.

Martin was adjudicated delinquent. His case eventually reached the U.S. Supreme Court, where his lawyer argued that the New York detention law had effectively denied Martin's freedom prior to conviction and that it was therefore in violation of the Fourteenth Amendment to the U.S. Constitution.

The U.S. Supreme Court, however, upheld the constitutionality of the New York statute, ruling that pretrial detention of juveniles based on "serious risk" does not violate the principle of fundamental fairness required by due process.[101] In so holding, the Court recognized that states have a legitimate interest in preventing future delinquency by juveniles thought to be dangerous. Preventive detention, the Court reasoned, is nonpunitive in its intent and is therefore not a "punishment."

While the *Schall* decision upheld the practice of preventive detention, it seized upon the opportunity provided by the case to impose procedural requirements upon the detaining authority. Consequently, preventive detention today cannot be imposed without (1) prior notice, (2) an equitable detention hearing, and (3) a statement by the judge setting forth the reason or reasons for detention.

Illinois v. *Montanez* (1996)

In 1996, in the case of *Illinois* v. *Montanez*,[102] the U.S. Supreme Court let stand a state court ruling that threw out a voluntary confession made by a juvenile suspect who had been tried as an adult. The confession was held inadmissible because it had not been made in the presence of a parent or other "concerned adult." The Chicago case involved 15-year-old Jacqueline Montanez, who admitted to participating in two execution-style slayings of rival gang members in May 1992.

According to an eyewitness, Montanez and two female companions were laughing and giggling as Montanez forced a young male member of a rival gang into a men's room at Humbolt Park. The witness described hearing a "noise like a firecracker" and seeing Montanez emerge from the men's room alone. The witness also saw the two other girls kill a second rival gang member, according to court records. Montanez was seen to then kick the body, and the three girls ran off. Both boys, members of the Latin Kings, had been shot in the back of the head at close range.

Police later arrested Montanez, who claimed to be a leader of the Maniac Latin Disciples street gang, "and two of her female gang underlings."[103] Montanez was charged as an adult and was advised of her right to remain silent and to have a lawyer present during questioning. Her mother was not allowed into the interrogation room. Montanez refused a lawyer and made three incriminating statements to police during the course of an eight-hour late-night interrogation. A videotape prepared for a local news program showed Montanez leaving the interrogation room the next morning flashing gang signs and repeating the phrase *K.K.* According to police, *K.K.* meant "King Killer," a status Montanez was said to have claimed.

Montanez was tried as an adult. Her confession was admitted at trial, and she was convicted of homicide. The Illinois Court of Appeals, however, reversed the judge's ruling, holding that since the girl's mother, a "concerned adult," was not allowed to be present at her daughter's interrogation, the confession obtained by police should have been suppressed. In refusing to hear the case, the U.S. Supreme Court indicated its agreement with the appellate court's finding.

Because the decision of the U.S. Supreme Court not to review the lower court's ruling in *Illinois* v. *Montanez* did not result in a written opinion, the case may be accorded less weight by jurists than the other cases cited here. Within the contemporary context of growing concern over violent juvenile crime, however, and given the ever-increasing number of minors throughout the nation now being charged as adults, the *Montanez* case may prove especially important in the future.

Legislation Concerning Juvenile Justice

In response to the rapidly increasing crime rates of the late 1960s, Congress passed the Omnibus Crime Control and Safe Streets Act of 1968. The act provided money and technical assistance for states and municipalities seeking to modernize their justice systems. The Safe Streets Act provided funding for youth services bureaus, which had been recommended by the 1967 presidential commission report *The Challenge of Crime in a Free Society*. These bureaus were available to police, juvenile courts, and probation departments and acted as a centralized community resource in handling delinquents and status offenders. Youth services bureaus also handled juveniles referred by schools and by young people themselves. Unfortunately, within a decade after their establishment, most youth services bureaus succumbed to a lack of continued federal funding.

In 1974, recognizing the special needs of juveniles, Congress passed the Juvenile Justice and Delinquency Prevention (JJDP) Act. Employing much the same strategy as the 1968 bill, the JJDP Act provided federal grants to states and cities seeking to improve their handling and disposition of delinquents and status offenders. Nearly all the states chose to accept federal funds through the JJDP Act. Participating states had to meet two conditions within five years:

- They had to agree to a "separation mandate," under which juveniles would not be held in institutions where they might come into regular contact with adult prisoners.

- Status offenders had to be deinstitutionalized, with most being released into the community or placed in foster homes.

Within a few years, institutional populations were cut by more than half, and community alternatives to juvenile institutionalization were rapidly being developed. Jailed juveniles were housed in separate wings of adult facilities or were removed from adult jails entirely.

When the JJDP Act was reauthorized for funding in 1980, the separation mandate was expanded to require that separate juvenile jails be constructed by the states. Studies supporting reauthorization of the JJDP Act in 1984 and 1988, however, found that nearly half the states had failed to come into "substantial compliance" with the new mandate. As a consequence, Congress modified the requirements of the act, continuing funding for states making "meaningful progress" toward removing juveniles from adult jails.[104] In 1996, however, in the face of pressures toward punishment and away from treatment for violent juvenile offenders, the Office of Juvenile Justice and Delinquency Prevention proposed new rules for jailing juveniles. The new rules allow an adjudicated delinquent to be detained for up to 12 hours in an adult jail before a court appearance and make it easier for states to house juveniles in separate wings of adult jails.[105]

The Legal Rights of Juveniles

Most jurisdictions today have statutes designed to extend the *Miranda* provisions to juveniles. Many police officers routinely offer *Miranda* warnings to juveniles in their custody prior to questioning. It is unclear, however, whether juveniles can legally waive their *Miranda* rights. A 1979 U.S. Supreme Court ruling held that juveniles should be accorded the opportunity for a knowing waiver when they are old enough and sufficiently educated to understand the consequences of a waiver.[106] A later high court ruling upheld the murder conviction of a juvenile who had been advised of his rights and waived them in the presence of his mother.[107]

An emerging area of juvenile rights centers on investigative procedures. In 1985, for example, the U.S. Supreme Court ruled in *New Jersey* v. *T.L.O.*[108] that schoolchildren have a reasonable expectation of privacy in their personal property. The case involved a 14-year-old girl who was accused of violating school rules by smoking in a high school bathroom. A vice principal searched the girl's purse and found evidence of marijuana use. Juvenile officers were called, and the girl was eventually adjudicated in juvenile court and found delinquent.

Upon appeal to the New Jersey Supreme Court, lawyers for the girl were successful in having her conviction reversed on the grounds that the search of her purse, as an item of personal property, had been unreasonable. The state's appeal to the U.S. Supreme Court resulted in a ruling which prohibited school officials from engaging in *unreasonable* searches of students or their property. A reading of the Court's decision leads to the conclusion that a search could be considered reasonable if it (1) is based upon a logical suspicion of rule-breaking actions; (2) is required to maintain order, discipline, and safety among students; and (3) does not exceed the scope of the original suspicion.

The Juvenile Justice Process Today

Juvenile court jurisdiction rests upon the offender's age and conduct. The majority of states today define a child subject to juvenile court jurisdiction as a person who has not yet turned 18. A few states set the age at 16, and several use 17. Figure 14–4 shows the upper ages of children subject to juvenile court jurisdiction in delinquency matters, by state. When they reach their eighteenth birthday, children in most states become subject to the jurisdiction of adult criminal courts.

Depending upon the laws of the state and the behavior involved, the jurisdiction of the juvenile court may be exclusive. Exclusive jurisdiction applies when the juvenile court is the only court that has statutory authority to deal with children for specified infractions. For example, status offenses like truancy normally fall within the exclusive jurisdiction of juvenile courts. Delinquency, which involves violation of the criminal law, however, is often not within the juvenile court's exclusive jurisdiction. All 50 states, the District of Columbia, and the federal government have judicial *waiver* provisions which allow juveniles who

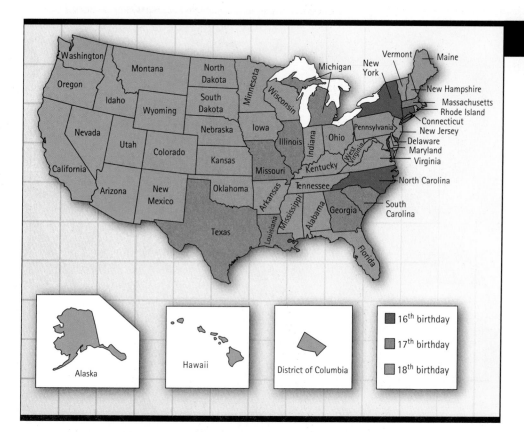

FIGURE 14–4

Limit of juvenile court jurisdiction over young offenders, by state.

> Today we are living with a juvenile justice system that was created around the time of the silent film.
>
> —John Ashcroft (1997)

commit serious crimes to be bound over to criminal court. The minimum age for transfer to criminal court in the various states is shown in Figure 14–5. In 2001, OJJDP reported that U.S. courts with juvenile jurisdiction handled nearly 1.8 million delinquency cases during 1998.[109]

Juveniles who commit violent crimes or who have prior records are among the most likely to be transferred to adult courts.[110] In a hearing which made headlines more than a decade ago, for example, Cameron Kocher, a ten-year-old Pennsylvania youngster, was arraigned as an adult for the murder of seven-year-old Jessica Carr.[111] Kocher, nine years old at the time of the crime, was alleged to have used his father's scope-sighted hunting rifle to shoot the girl from a bedroom window while she was riding on a snowmobile in a neighbor's yard. The two had argued earlier over who would get to ride on the vehicle. The case was resolved when the Pennsylvania Supreme Court overruled Kocher's arraignment as an adult, and the boy was placed on probation.

Where juvenile court authority is not exclusive, the jurisdiction of the court may be original or concurrent. Original jurisdiction means that a particular offense must originate, or begin, with juvenile court authorities. Juvenile courts have original jurisdiction over most delinquency petitions and all status offenses. Concurrent jurisdiction exists where other courts have equal statutory authority to originate proceedings. If a juvenile has committed a homicide, rape, or other serious crime, for example, an arrest warrant may be issued by the adult court.

Some states specify that juvenile courts have no jurisdiction over certain excluded offenses. Delaware, Louisiana, and Nevada, for example, allow no juvenile court jurisdiction over children charged with first-degree murder.

Adult and Juvenile Justice Compared

The court cases of relevance to the juvenile justice system that we've discussed in this chapter have two common characteristics. They all turn on due process guarantees specified by the Bill of Rights, and they all make the claim that adult due process should serve as a model for juvenile proceedings. Due process guarantees, as interpreted by the U.S. Supreme Court, are clearly designed to ensure that juvenile proceedings are fair and that the interests of juveniles are protected. However, the Court's interpretations do not offer

FIGURE 14–5

Minimum age for transfer to adult criminal court.

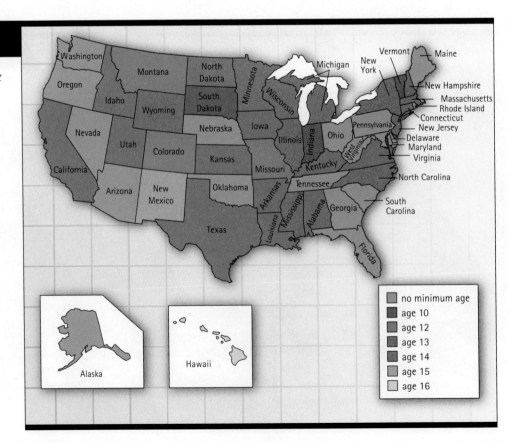

CJ Today Exhibit 14-3

[The Juvenile Justice System
Versus Criminal Case Processing]

Criminal Proceedings

Focus on criminality

Comprehensive rights against unreasonable searches of person, home, and possessions

A right against self-incrimination; a knowing waiver is possible

Assumed innocent until proven guilty

Adversarial setting

Arrest warrants form the basis for most arrests

Right to an attorney

Public trial

System goals are punishment and reformation

No right to treatment

Possibility of bail or release on recognizance

Public record of trial and judgment

Possible incarceration in adult correctional facility

Juvenile Proceedings

Focus on delinquency and a special category of "status offenses"

Limited rights against unreasonable searches

A right against self-incrimination; waivers are questionable

Guilt and innocence are not primary issues; the system focuses on the interests of the child

Helping context

Petitions or complaints legitimize apprehension

Right to an attorney

Closed hearing; no right to a jury trial

System goals are protection and treatment

Specific right to treatment

Release into parental custody

Sealed records; may (sometimes) be destroyed by specified age

Separate facilities at all levels

? DISCUSSION QUESTIONS

1. Which of the differences shown in this exhibit between the adult and juvenile justice systems do you think should be maintained or even enhanced? Why?

2. Which differences, if any, between the adult and juvenile justice systems do you think might best be eliminated or minimized? Why?

---

any pretense of providing juveniles with the same kinds of protections guaranteed to adult defendants. While the high court has tended to agree that juveniles are entitled to due process protection, it has refrained from declaring that juveniles have a right to all the aspects of due process afforded adult defendants.

Juvenile court philosophy brings with it other differences from the adult system. Among them are (1) a reduced concern with legal issues of guilt or innocence and an emphasis on the child's best interests; (2) an emphasis on treatment rather than punishment; (3) privacy and protection from public scrutiny through the use of sealed records, laws against publishing the names of juvenile offenders, and so forth; (4) the use of the techniques of social science in dispositional decision making, rather than sentences determined by a perceived need for punishment; (5) no long-term confinement, with most juveniles being released from institutions by their twenty-first birthday, regardless of offense; (6) separate facilities for juveniles; and (7) broad discretionary alternatives at all points in the process.[112] This combination of court philosophy and due process requirements has created a unique justice system for juveniles which takes into consideration the special needs of young people while attempting to offer reasonable protection to society. The juvenile justice process is diagrammed in Figure 14–6.

How the System Works

The juvenile justice system can be viewed as a process which, when carried to completion, moves through four stages: intake, adjudication, disposition, and postadjudicatory review. Though organizationally similar to the adult criminal justice process, the juvenile system is far more likely to maximize the use of discretion and to employ diversion from further formal processing at every point in the process. Each stage is discussed in the pages that follow.

INTAKE AND DETENTION HEARINGS

Delinquent juveniles may come to the attention of the police or juvenile court authorities either through arrest or through the filing of a **juvenile petition** by an aggrieved party.

juvenile petition

A document filed in juvenile court alleging that a juvenile is a delinquent, a status offender, or a dependent and asking that the court assume jurisdiction over the juvenile or that an alleged delinquent be transferred to a criminal court for prosecution as an adult.

FIGURE 14-6

The juvenile justice process.

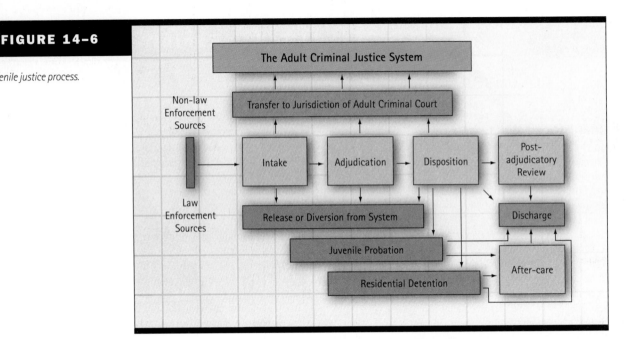

Juvenile petitions are much like criminal complaints in that they allege illegal behavior. Petitions are most often filed by teachers, school administrators, neighbors, store managers, or others who have frequent contact with juveniles. Parents who are unable to control the behavior of their teenage children are the source of many other petitions. Crimes in progress bring other juveniles to the attention of the police. Three-quarters of all referrals to juvenile court come directly from law enforcement authorities.[113]

Many police departments have juvenile officers who are specially trained in dealing with juveniles. Because of the emphasis on rehabilitation which characterizes the juvenile justice process, juvenile officers can usually choose from a number of discretionary alternatives in the form of special programs, especially in the handling of nonviolent offenders. In Delaware County, Pennsylvania, for example, police departments participate in "youth aid panels." These panels are composed of private citizens who volunteer their services to provide an alternative to the formal juvenile court process. Youngsters who are referred to a panel and agree to abide by the decision of the group are diverted from the juvenile court.

Real Justice Conferencing (RJC), another Pennsylvania program, provides another example of a diversionary program. Started in Bethlehem, Pennsylvania, in 1995, RJC has served as a model for other cities. RJC claims to be a cost-effective new approach to juvenile crime, school misconduct, and violence prevention. It makes use of family group conferences (sometimes called *community conferences*) in lieu of school disciplinary or judicial processes or as a supplement to them. The family group conference is built around a restorative justice model and allows young offenders to tell what they did, to hear from those they affected, and to participate in deciding how to repair the harm caused by their actions. Successful RJC participants avoid the more formal mechanisms of the juvenile justice process.

Even youth who are eventually diverted from the system may spend some time in custody. One juvenile case in five involves detention prior to adjudication.[114] Unlike the adult system, where jail is seen as the primary custodial alternative for people awaiting a first appearance, the use of secure detention for juveniles is acceptable only as a last resort. Detention hearings investigate whether candidates for confinement represent a "clear and immediate danger to themselves and/or to others." This judgment is normally rendered within 24 hours of apprehension. Runaways, since they are often not dangerous, are especially difficult to confine. Juveniles who are not detained are generally released into the custody of their parents or guardians or into a supervised temporary shelter, such as a group home.

Detention Hearing Detention hearings are conducted by the juvenile court judge or by an officer of the court, such as a juvenile probation officer who has been given the authority to make **intake** decisions. Intake officers, like their police counterparts, have substantial dis-

intake

- - - - - - - - - - - - - - -

The first step in decision making regarding a juvenile whose behavior or alleged behavior is in violation of the law or could otherwise cause a juvenile court to assume jurisdiction.

A teenager sitting in a cell in a juvenile detention facility in Austin, Texas. When young people are taken into custody, they are confined separately from adult offenders.

Bob Daemmrich, The Image Works

cretion. Along with detention, they can choose diversion and outright dismissal of some or all of the charges against the juvenile. Diverted juveniles may be sent to job-training programs, mental health facilities, drug-treatment programs, educational counseling, or other community service agencies. When caring parents are present who can afford private counseling or therapy, intake officers may release the juvenile into their custody with the understanding that they will provide for treatment. The National Center for Juvenile Justice estimates that more than half of all juvenile cases disposed of at intake are handled informally, without a petition, and are dismissed or diverted to a social service agency.[115]

Preliminary Hearing A preliminary hearing may be held in conjunction with the detention hearing. The purpose of the preliminary hearing is to determine if there is probable cause to believe the juvenile committed the alleged act. At the hearing, the juvenile, along with the child's parents or guardians, will be advised of his or her rights as established by state legislation and court precedent. If probable cause is established, the juvenile may still be offered diversionary options, such as an "improvement period" or "probation with adjudication." These alternatives usually provide a one-year period during which the juvenile must avoid legal difficulties, attend school, and obey his or her parents. Charges may be dropped at the end of this informal probationary period, provided the juvenile has met the conditions specified.

When a serious offense is involved, statutory provisions may allow for transfer of the case to adult court at the prosecuting attorney's request. Transfer hearings are held in juvenile court and focus on (1) the applicability of transfer statutes to the case under consideration and (2) whether the juvenile is amenable to treatment through the resources available to the juvenile justice system. Exceptions exist where statutes mandate transfer (as is sometimes the case with first-degree murder).

ADJUDICATION

Adjudicatory hearings for juveniles are similar to adult trials, with some notable exceptions. Similarities derive from the fact that the due process rights of children and adults are essentially the same. Differences include the following:

■ *No right to trial by jury.* As we discussed in our review of the U.S. Supreme Court decision in the case of *McKeiver* v. *Pennsylvania*,[116] juveniles do not have a constitutional right to trial by jury, and most states do not provide juveniles with a statutory opportunity for jury trial.[117]

Some jurisdictions, however, allow juveniles to be tried by their peers. The juvenile court in Columbus County, Georgia, for example, began experimenting with peer juries in 1980.[118] In Georgia, peer juries are composed of youths under the age of 17 who receive special training by the court. Jurors are required to be successful in school and

adjudicatory hearing

The fact-finding process wherein the juvenile court determines whether there is sufficient evidence to sustain the allegations in a petition.

may not be under the supervision of the court or have juvenile petitions pending against them. Training consists of classroomlike exposure to the philosophy of the juvenile court system, Georgia's juvenile code, and Supreme Court decisions affecting juvenile justice.[119] The county's youthful jurors are used only in the dispositional (or sentencing) stage of the court process, and then only when adjudicated youths volunteer to go before the jury.

Another early program that has served as a model for many others is the Odessa (Texas) Teen Court, started by the local Junior League in 1983. Since then, it has handled thousands of cases, with all major courtroom participants—other than the judge—coming from the ranks of local juveniles. Youngsters fill the roles of prosecutor, defense attorney, and a four-person peer jury. As in Georgia, the court does not decide guilt, but imposes sentences only. Defendants are selected by the police from among youngsters who have already pleaded guilty to relatively minor offenses. The court has been amazingly successful in reducing recidivism. Only 2% of defendants who appear before the Odessa Teen Court go on to commit another crime. As a spokesperson for the Odessa Police Department put it, "It's one peer saying to another, 'This is not acceptable behavior.' . . . The defendant cannot come back on the grown-up and say, 'You adults don't understand what I am going through.' "[120]

Today, hundreds of **teen court** programs are in operation across the country. The Office of Juvenile Justice and Delinquency Prevention notes that teen courts are "an effective intervention in many jurisdictions where enforcement of misdemeanor charges is sometimes given low priority because of heavy caseloads and the need to focus on more serious offenders."[121] Teen courts, says OJJDP, "present communities with opportunities to teach young people valuable life and coping skills and promote positive peer influence for youth who are defendants and for volunteer youth who play a variety of roles in the teen court process." Learn more about teen courts via **Web Extra! 14–8** at cjtoday.com.

teen court

An alternative approach to juvenile justice in which alleged offenders are judged and sentenced by a jury of their peers.

- ■ *Emphasis on privacy.* Another important distinctive characteristic of the juvenile system derives from its concern with privacy. Juvenile hearings are not open to the public or to the mass media. Witnesses are permitted to be present only to offer testimony and may not stay for the rest of the hearing. No transcript of the proceedings is created. One purpose of the emphasis on privacy is to prevent juveniles from being negatively labeled by the community.

- ■ *Informality.* Whereas the adult criminal trial is highly structured, the juvenile hearing borders on informality. The courtroom atmosphere may give the appearance of a friendly discussion more than an adversarial battle. The juvenile court judge takes an active role in the fact-finding process rather than serving as arbitrator between prosecution and defense.

- ■ *Speed.* Informality, the lack of a jury, and the absence of an adversarial environment promote speed. While the adult trial may run into weeks or even months, the juvenile hearing is normally completed in a matter of hours or days.

- ■ *Evidentiary standard.* Upon completion of the hearing, the juvenile court judge must weigh the evidence. If the charge involves a status offense, the judge may adjudicate the juvenile as a status offender upon finding that a preponderance of the evidence supports this finding. A preponderance of the evidence exists when evidence of an offense is more convincing than evidence offered to the contrary. If the charge involves a criminal-type offense, the evidentiary standard rises to the level of reasonable doubt.

- ■ *Philosophy of the court.* Even in the face of strong evidence pointing to the offender's guilt, the judge may decide that it is not in the child's best interests to be adjudicated delinquent. The judge also has the power, even after the evidence is presented, to divert the juvenile from the system. Juvenile court statistics indicate that only 52% of cases disposed of by juvenile courts in 1997 were processed formally. Formal processing involves the filing of a petition requesting an adjudicatory or transfer hearing. Informal cases, on the other hand, are handled without a petition. Among informally handled (nonpetitioned) delinquency cases, half were dismissed by the court. Most of the remainder resulted in voluntary probation (28%) or other dispositions (22%), but a small number (1%) involved voluntary out-of-home placements.[122]

CJ Today Exhibit 14-4

[Juvenile Courts Versus Adult Courts]

The language used in juvenile courts is less harsh than that used in adult courts. For example, juvenile courts

- Accept "petitions of delinquency" rather than criminal complaints
- Conduct "hearings," not trials

- "Adjudicate" juveniles to be "delinquent" rather than find them guilty of a crime
- Order one of a number of available "dispositions" rather than sentences.

DISPOSITION

Once a juvenile has been found delinquent, the judge will set a time for a **dispositionary hearing**, which is similar to an adult sentencing hearing. Dispositional hearings are used to decide what action the court should take relative to the child. As in adult courts, the judge may order a presentence investigation before making a dispositional decision. These investigations are conducted by special court personnel, sometimes called *juvenile court counselors*, who are, in effect, juvenile probation officers. Attorneys on both sides of the issue will also have the opportunity to make recommendations concerning dispositional alternatives.

The juvenile justice system typically gives the judge a much wider range of sentencing alternatives than does the adult system. Two major classes of **juvenile disposition** exist: to confine or not to confine. Because rehabilitation is still the primary objective of the juvenile court, the judge is likely to select the least restrictive alternative that meets the needs of the juvenile while recognizing the legitimate concerns of society for protection.

Most judges decide not to confine juveniles. Statistics indicate that in more than half (54%) of all adjudicated delinquency cases, juveniles are placed on formal probation.[123] Probationary disposition usually means that juveniles will be released into the custody of a parent or guardian and ordered to undergo some form of training, education, or counseling. As in the adult system, juveniles placed on probation may be ordered to pay fines or to make restitution. In 13% of adjudicated delinquency cases, courts order juveniles to pay restitution or a fine, to participate in some form of community service, or to enter a treatment or counseling program—dispositions that require minimal continuing supervision by probation staff. Because juveniles rarely have financial resources or jobs, most economic sanctions take the form of court-ordered work programs, as in refurbishing schools or cleaning school buses.

The Lehigh County (Pennsylvania) Juvenile Probation Office runs an innovative probation program which places juvenile probation officers in public schools. The officers function much like school counselors, paying special attention to the needs of their charges in areas like tutoring, attendance, and grades. In-school probation officers work at addressing problems as diverse as getting students to school on time (by developing personal schedules), raising grades (through improving study skills, tutoring, and sitting in on classes), and successful involvement in extracurricular activities. The program, which began a decade ago, has since been expanded through a federal grant to 29 other Pennsylvania counties.[124]

Of course, not all juveniles who are adjudicated delinquent receive probation. More than one-quarter (28%) of adjudicated cases in 1996 resulted in the youth being placed outside the home in a residential facility. In a relatively small number of cases (4%), the juvenile was adjudicated delinquent, but the case was then dismissed or the youth was otherwise released.[125]

Secure Institutions for Juveniles Juveniles who evidence the potential for serious new offenses may be ordered to participate in rehabilitative programs within a secure environment, such as a youth center or a training school. As of January 1998, approximately 125,800 young people were being held under custodial supervision in the United States.[126] Of these, 33.4% were being held for personal crimes like murder, rape, or robbery; 30.2%

dispositionary hearing

The final stage in the processing of adjudicated juveniles, in which a decision is made on the form of treatment or penalty that should be imposed upon the child.

juvenile disposition

The decision of a juvenile court, concluding a dispositionary hearing, that an adjudicated juvenile be committed to a juvenile correctional facility; be placed in a juvenile residence, shelter, or care or treatment program; be required to meet certain standards of conduct; or be released.

were being held for property crimes; 8.8% were locked up for drug offenses; 9.2% for public-order offenses (including weapons offenses); and 6.5% for status offenses. Probation and parole violations accounted for another 11.9% of those confined.[127]

Most confined juveniles are held in semisecure facilities designed to look less like prisons and more like residential high school campuses. Most states, however, operate at least one secure facility for juveniles that is intended as a home for the most recalcitrant youthful offenders. Halfway houses, boot camps,[128] ranches, forestry camps, wilderness programs, group homes, and state-hired private facilities also hold some of the juveniles reported to be under confinement. Children placed in group homes continue to attend school and live in a familylike environment in the company of other adjudicated children, shepherded by "house parents." Figure 14–7 shows juvenile custody rates by state.

The operative philosophy of custodial programs for juveniles focuses squarely on the rehabilitative ideal. Juveniles are usually committed to secure facilities for indeterminate periods of time, with the typical stay being less than one year. Release is often timed to coincide with the beginning or the end of the school year.

Most juvenile facilities are small, with 80% designed to hold 40 residents or fewer.[129] Many institutionalized juveniles are held in the approximately 1,000 homelike facilities across the nation, which are limited to ten residents or fewer.[130] At the other end of the scale are the nation's 70 large juvenile institutions, each designed to hold over 200 hard-core delinquents.[131] Residential facilities for juveniles are intensively staffed. One study found that staff members outnumber residents ten to nine on the average in state-run institutions, and by an even greater ratio in privately run facilities.[132]

Jurisdictions vary widely in their use of secure detention for juveniles. In 1995, juvenile custody populations ranged from a low of 24 in Vermont to a high of 19,567 in California.[133] This variance reflects population differences as well as economic realities and philosophical beliefs. Some jurisdictions, like California, expect rehabilitative costs to be born by the state rather than by families or local government agencies. Hence, California shows a higher rate of institutionalization than many other states. Similarly, some states have more firmly embraced the reformation ideal and are more likely to use diversionary options where juveniles are concerned.

Characteristics of Juveniles in Confinement Institutionalized juveniles are a small but special category of young people with serious problems. A recent report on insti-

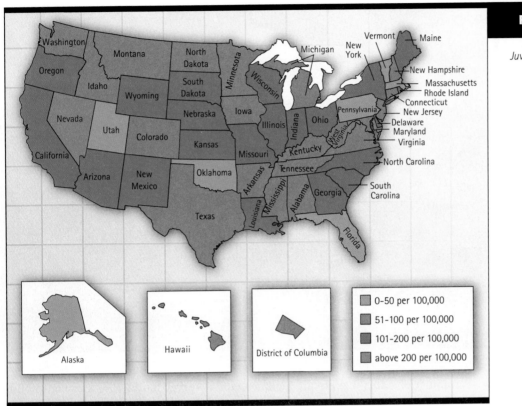

FIGURE 14-7

Juvenile custody rates, by state.

0-50 per 100,000
51-100 per 100,000
101-200 per 100,000
above 200 per 100,000

tutionalized youth by the Bureau of Justice Statistics found five striking characteristics. Of the total,[134]

- 86.5% were male
- 40% were black, 37.5% were white, and 18.5% were Hispanic
- 6.5% were institutionalized for having committed a status offense, such as truancy, running away, or violating curfew
- 42.4% were in residential facilities for a serious personal or property offense
- 2% were charged or adjudicated for homicide or murder

Overcrowding in Juvenile Facilities As in adult prisons, overcrowding exists in many juvenile institutions. In a recent survey, half of all states reported overcrowding in juvenile facilities, and 22 states were operating facilities at more than 50% over capacity.[135]

A national study of the conditions of confinement in juvenile detention facilities conducted by the Office of Juvenile Justice and Delinquency Prevention found that "there are several areas in which problems in juvenile facilities are substantial and widespread—most notably living space, health care, security, and control of suicidal behavior."[136] Using a variety of evaluative criteria, the study found that 47% of juveniles were confined in facilities whose populations exceeded their reported design capacity and that 33% of residents had to sleep "in rooms that were smaller than required by nationally recognized standards." To address the problem, the authors of the study recommended the use of alternative placement options so that only juveniles judged to be the most dangerous to their communities would be confined in secure facilities. Similarly, because injuries to residents were found to be most likely to occur within large dormitory-like settings, the OJJDP study recommended that "large dormitories be eliminated from juvenile facilities." Finally, the study recommended that "all juveniles be screened for risk of suicidal behavior immediately upon their admission to confinement" and that initial health screenings be "carried out promptly at admission." Other problems, which OJJDP found "still important enough to warrant attention," included education and treatment services. Further study of both areas is needed, OJJDP said.

A number of states use private facilities, and a survey found 13 states contracting with 328 private facilities—most of which were classified as halfway houses—for the custody of adjudicated juveniles.[137] In the past few years, admissions to private facilities (comprised primarily of halfway houses, group homes, shelters, and ranches, camps, or farms) have increased by more than 100%, compared with an increase of only about 10% for public facilities (mostly detention centers and training schools).[138] The fastest-growing category of detained juveniles comprises drug and alcohol offenders. Approximately 12% of all juvenile detainees are being held because of alcohol and drug-related offenses.[139] Reflecting widespread socioeconomic disparities, an OJJDP report found that "a juvenile held in a public facility . . . was most likely to be black, male, between 14 and 17 years of age, and held for a delinquent offense such as a property crime or a crime against a person. On the other hand, a juvenile held in custody in a private facility . . . was most likely to be white, male, 14 to 17 years of age, and held for a nondelinquent offense such as running away, truancy, or incorrigibility."[140] The report also noted that "juvenile corrections has become increasingly privatized."

POSTADJUDICATORY REVIEW

The detrimental effects of institutionalization on young offenders may make the opportunity for appellate review more critical for juveniles than it is for adults. However, federal court precedents have yet to establish a clear right to appeal from juvenile court. Even so, most states do have statutory provisions that make such appeals possible.[141]

From a practical point of view, however, juvenile appeals may not be as consequential as are appeals of adult criminal convictions. Most juvenile complaints are handled informally, while only a relatively small proportion of adjudicated delinquents are placed outside the family. Moreover, because sentence lengths are short for most confined juveniles, appellate courts hardly have time to complete the review process before the juvenile is released.

The Post–Juvenile Court Era

Extensive media coverage of violent juvenile crime in predominantly urban neighborhoods has fueled perceptions that violence committed by teenagers has reached epidemic proportions and that no community is immune to random acts of violence committed by young people—especially crimes involving a weapon. A report by the Office for Juvenile Justice and Delinquency Prevention in 1996, for example, found that the American public was vitally concerned with juvenile crime and with the seemingly increased levels of violence associated with those crimes. The OJJDP report noted that "the issue of youth violence has been at or near the top of nearly every state legislature and governor's agenda for the past several years."[142] The report's survey showed that "nearly every state has taken legislative or executive action in response to escalating juvenile arrests for violent crime and public perceptions of a violent juvenile crime epidemic. These actions have significantly altered the legal response to violent or other serious juvenile crime in this country."[143] According to OJJDP, "This level of [legislative and political] activity has occurred only three other times in our nation's history: at the outset of the juvenile court movement at the turn of the [twentieth] century; following the U.S. Supreme Court's *Gault* decision in 1967; and with the enactment of the Juvenile Justice and Delinquency Prevention Act in 1974."[144]

Jeffrey A. Butts and Ojmarrh Mitchell, members of the Program on Law and Behavior at the Urban Institute in Washington, D.C., and experts on juvenile justice, say that today, "policymakers throughout the United States have greatly dissolved the border between juvenile and criminal justice. Young people who violate the law are no longer guaranteed special consideration from the legal system. Some form of juvenile court still exists in every state, but the purposes and procedures of juvenile courts are becoming indistinguishable from those of criminal courts."[145] Butts and Mitchell also claim, "Changes in juvenile law and juvenile court procedure are slowly dismantling the jurisdictional border between juvenile and criminal justice."[146] As evidence, Butts and Mitchell note that juvenile courts across the United States are becoming increasingly similar to criminal courts in the method they use to reach conclusions and to process cases, as well as in the general atmosphere that characterizes them.

As a result of ongoing changes, some say that many states have substantially "criminalized" juvenile courts by effectively mandating the transfer of serious juvenile offenders to adult criminal courts and by reducing the confidentiality of juvenile court proceedings. In March 2000, for example, California voters endorsed sweeping changes in the state's juvenile justice system by passing Proposition 21, the Gang Violence and Juvenile Crime Prevention Act. The law reduces confidentiality in the juvenile court, limits the use of probation for young offenders, and increases the power of prosecutors to send juveniles to adult court and to put them in adult prisons. Public support for the measure was undiminished by projections that it would increase operational costs in the California juvenile justice system by $500 million annually.[147] Because laws like California's Proposition 21 are being passed at a growing rate throughout the country, a leading expert on juvenile justice notes that "the similarities of juvenile and adult courts are becoming greater than the differences between them."[148]

An OJJDP analysis of the sea change sweeping the country in the handling of serious and violent juvenile offenders found five common themes in new state laws intended to target such offenders: (1) changes in jurisdictional authority, such as legislation that removes violent juvenile offenders from the juvenile justice system so that they can be prosecuted as adults in criminal court; (2) changes in sentencing authority which mandate the imposition of specified minimum sentences, extend juvenile court jurisdiction beyond the age of majority, and allow for the imposition of "blended sentences" that mix both juvenile and adult sanctions; (3) increased pressure on correctional administrators to develop programs to serve violent juveniles; (4) a revision of traditional confidentiality provisions in favor of more open juvenile proceedings and court records; and (5) inclusion of victims of juvenile crime as "active participants" in the juvenile justice process.[149]

Proposals for further change abound. In 2001, the Task Force on Juvenile Justice Reform (TFJJR) of the American Academy of Child and Adolescent Psychiatry issued a report on juvenile justice reform. The report covered many areas, including competence to stand trial, forensic evaluations of children and adolescents, recommended standards for juvenile detention and confinement facilities, health care in the juvenile justice system, females in the juvenile justice system, disproportionate minority confinement, the educational needs of youth in juvenile justice facilities, and the transfer of juvenile cases to criminal court. Read the entire report at **Library Extra! 14–8** at cjtoday.com.

The flood of new federal and state legislation, mandated by surging public demand for personal responsibility among adolescents, is leading to significant changes in the American system of juvenile justice. Hence, the juvenile justice system of the future century may in many respects be quite different from the one we know today. Learn more about likely changes to the juvenile justice system via **Library Extra! 14–9** at cjtoday.com. For a thorough overview of the issues being debated, see **Web Extra! 14–9** at cjtoday.com.

> Eventually, the justice system may need to adapt to a new environment in which all criminal matters are referred to a single system, regardless of the offender's age.
>
> —*Jeffrey Butts and Ojmarrh Mitchell*[ii]

Summary

Children are the future hope of each mature generation, and under today's laws they occupy a special status. That status is tied closely to cultural advances that occurred in the Western world during the past 200 years, resulting in a reevaluation of the child's role.

Many children today lead privileged lives which would have been unimaginable several decades ago. Others are not as lucky, and the problems they face are as diverse as they are staggering. Some problems are a direct consequence of increased national wealth and the subsequent removal of children from the economic sphere, which has lessened expectations for responsible behavior during the childhood years. Other problems grow from the easy availability of illicit drugs—a condition which has dramatically altered the early life experiences of many children, especially in the nation's large cities. Finally, the decline of traditional institutions, the seeming plethora of broken homes throughout our country, and the immoral excesses of adult sexual predators have led to a quick abandonment of innocence by many young people today. Gang involvement, child abuse and neglect, juvenile runaways and suicides, and serious incidents of delinquency have been the result.

In the face of these massive challenges, the juvenile justice system's commitment to a philosophy of protection and restoration has begun to crumble. The present juvenile system, for the most part, still differs substantially from the adult system in the multitude of opportunities it provides for diversion and in the emphasis it places on rehabilitation rather than punishment. The "professionalization" of delinquency, however, the hallmark of which is the repeated and often violent criminal involvement of juveniles in drug-related gang activity, represents a major challenge to the idealism of the juvenile justice system. Addressing that challenge may well prove to be the most significant determinant of system change as we move through the early years of the twenty-first century.

Discussion Questions

1. Describe the six categories of children recognized by the laws of most states. Do some of the problems faced by children today necessitate the development of new categories? If so, what new categories? If not, how can existing categories handle illicit drug use by juveniles or the repeated and vicious delinquency of some inner-city gang members?

2. Is the concept of status offense still useful in our system of juvenile justice? Should laws which circumscribe status offenses be retained or abandoned? Why?

3. One explanation given in this chapter for the rise in delinquency rates is the lack of meaningful roles for juveniles in modern society. Do you agree with this explanation? Why or why not?

4. What do you think of the parental responsibility laws described in CJ Today Exhibit 14–2? Do you think these laws are useful? Are they fair? Can they achieve their desired result? Would you change them in any way? If so, how?

5. What was the impact of the *Gault* decision on juvenile justice in America? What adult rights were not accorded to juveniles by *Gault*?

6. How does the philosophy and purpose of the juvenile justice system differ from that of the adult criminal justice system? In your opinion, should children continue to receive what many regard as preferential treatment from the courts? Explain.

7. One problem with secrecy in juvenile hearings and records is that the innocent are not protected from continued delinquency. Do you think that secrecy in the juvenile justice system is justified? Or do you think that those who stand to be injured by the future delinquency of adjudicated offenders should be forewarned? Explain.

To participate in an online discussion on these topics and others, go to the Global Town Meeting electronic message board for Chapter 14 on the *Criminal Justice Today* Companion Website at cjtoday.com.

Web Quest!

Visit the National Council on Crime and Delinquency at http://www.nccd-crc.org. What are some of the areas in which NCCD is working to prevent and understand delinquency? What other areas do you think it should be exploring?

Use the Cybrary to identify other juvenile justice research and delinquency-prevention sites on the Web. Which sites contain information about school shootings? What, if anything, do they suggest can be done to reduce the incidence of these crimes? Submit your findings to your instructor if asked to do so.

To complete this Web Quest! online, go to the Web Quest! module in Chapter 14 of the *Criminal Justice Today* Companion Website at cjtoday.com.

Library Extras!

Library Extra! **14–1** *A Century of Juvenile Justice* (NIJ, 2000).
Library Extra! **14–2** *Causes and Correlates of Delinquency Programs* (OJJDP, 1999).
Library Extra! **14–3** *Characteristics of Crimes against Juveniles* (OJJDP, 2000).
Library Extra! **14–4** *1999 National Youth Gang Survey* (OJJDP, 2001).
Library Extra! **14–5** *The Commercial Sexual Exploitation of Children in the U.S., Canada and Mexico* (University of Pennsylvania, 2001).
Library Extra! **14–6** *America's Children: Key National Indicators of Well-Being, 2000* (Federal Interagency Forum on Child and Family Statistics, 2000).
Library Extra! **14–7** *Action Plan Update* (OJJDP, 2001).
Library Extra! **14–8** *Recommendations for Juvenile Justice Reform* (AACAP, 2001).
Library Extra! **14–9** *Brick by Brick: Dismantling the Border between Juvenile and Adult Justice* (NIJ, 2000).

To explore these resources online, go to the Library Extras! area of the *Criminal Justice Today* Companion Website at cjtoday.com. You should also check the author's "Late Picks" online for newly released documents and updated Library Extras! You can find Late Picks at http://cjtoday.com/latepicks.htm.

Marginal Notes

i. Jeffrey A. Butts and Adele V. Harrell, *Delinquents or Criminals: Policy Options for Young Criminals* (Washington, D.C.: Urban Institute, 1998).

ii. Jeffrey A. Butts and Ojmarrh Mitchell, "Brick by Brick: Dismantling the Border between Juvenile and Adult Justice," in Phyllis McDonald and Janice Munsterman, eds., *Criminal Justice 2000*, Vol. 2: *Boundary Changes in Criminal Justice Organizations* (Washington, D.C.: National Institute of Justice, 2000), pp. 167–213.

Notes

1. Elliot Grossman, "Toughlove Parents Scared," *Allentown* (Pa.) *Morning Call*, March 7, 1995, p. B1.
2. Many of the details for this story come from David Karp, "Boy, 13, Found Guilty of Rape," *St. Petersburg* (Fla.) *Times*, September 8, 2001.
3. Ibid.
4. "Judge Sentences 13-Year-Old to 15 Years for Daytime Park Rape," Associated Press wire service, November 9, 2001.
5. Randy Wyles, "Boys, 7 and 10, Busted for Burglary," APB News, November 1, 2000.
6. "Florida Girls Charged with Attempting to Drown Classmate," Associated Press wire service, March 14, 2001.
7. Office of Juvenile Justice and Delinquency Prevention, *OJJDP Research, 2000* (Washington, D.C.: OJJDP, 2001).
8. Federal Bureau of Investigation, *Crime in the United States, 2000* (Washington, D.C.: U.S. Government Printing Office, 2001).
9. Ibid.; and U.S. Census Bureau, *Age, 2000: A Census 2000 Brief* (Washington, D.C.: U.S. Census Bureau, 2001).

Web posted at http://www.census.gov/prod/2001pubs/c2kbr01-12.pdf. Accessed January 12, 2002.

10. Where "juvenile" refers to people under 18 years of age.

11. Office of Juvenile Justice and Delinquency Prevention, *OJJDP Research: Making a Difference for Juveniles* (Washington, D.C.: OJJDP, 1999).

12. A reform movement, now under way, may soon lead to changes in the way juvenile records are handled.

13. For an excellent review of the handling of juveniles through history, see Wiley B. Sanders, ed., *Juvenile Offenders for a Thousand Years* (Chapel Hill: University of North Carolina Press, 1970).

14. Robert M. Mennel, *Thorns and Thistles: Juvenile Delinquents in the United States, 1925–1940* (Hanover, NH: University Press of New England, 1973).

15. Arnold Binder et al., *Juvenile Delinquency: Historical, Cultural, Legal Perspectives* (New York: Macmillan, 1988), p. 45.

16. Thomas A. Johnson, *Introduction to the Juvenile Justice System* (St. Paul, MN: West, 1975), p. 1.

17. Charles E. Springer, *Justice for Juveniles*, 2d ed. (Washington, D.C.: Office of Juvenile Justice and Delinquency Prevention, 1987), p. 18.

18. Ibid., p. 50.

19. See Sanford Fox, "Juvenile Justice Reform: An Historical Perspective," in Sanford Fox, ed., *Modern Juvenile Justice: Cases and Materials* (St. Paul, MN: West, 1972), pp. 15–48.

20. *Ex parte Crouse,* 4 Whart. 9 (Pa., 1838).

21. Fox, "Juvenile Justice Reform," p. 27.

22. Anthony Platt, *The Child Savers: The Invention of Delinquency,* 2d ed. (Chicago: University of Chicago Press, 1977).

23. Ibid., p. 29.

24. *People ex rel. O'Connell* v. *Turner,* 55 Ill. 280, 8 Am. Rep. 645.

25. Johnson, *Introduction to the Juvenile Justice System,* p. 3.

26. Ibid., p. 3.

27. Ibid.

28. Fox, "Juvenile Justice Reform," p. 47.

29. Ibid., p. 5.

30. Principles adapted from Robert G. Caldwell, "The Juvenile Court: Its Development and Some Major Problems," in Rose Giallombardo, ed., *Juvenile Delinquency: A Book of Readings* (New York: John Wiley, 1966), p. 358.

31. Clifford Shaw et al., *Delinquency Areas* (Chicago: University of Chicago Press, 1929).

32. Richard A. Cloward and Lloyd E. Ohlin, *Delinquency and Opportunity: A Theory of Delinquent Gangs* (New York: Free Press, 1960).

33. Walter B. Miller, "Lower Class Culture as a Generating Milieu of Gang Delinquency," *Journal of Social Issues,* Vol. 14, No. 3 (1958), pp. 5–19.

34. Albert K. Cohen, *Delinquent Boys: The Culture of the Gang* (New York: Free Press of Glencoe, 1955).

35. David Matza, *Delinquency and Drift* (New York: John Wiley, 1964).

36. Gresham M. Sykes and David Matza, "Techniques of Neutralization: A Theory of Delinquency," *American Sociological Review,* Vol. 22 (December 1957), pp. 664–666.

37. Marvin Wolfgang, Robert Figlio, and Thorsten Sellin, *Delinquency in a Birth Cohort* (Chicago: University of Chicago Press, 1972).

38. Marvin Wolfgang, Terence Thornberry, and Robert Figlio, *From Boy to Man, From Delinquency to Crime* (Chicago: University of Chicago Press, 1987).

39. Steven P. Lab, "Analyzing Change in Crime and Delinquency Rates: The Case for Cohort Analysis," *Criminal Justice Research Bulletin,* Vol. 3, No. 10 (Huntsville, TX: Sam Houston State University, 1988), p. 2.

40. Katharine Browning et al., "Causes and Correlates of Delinquency Program," Office of Juvenile Justice and Delinquency Prevention Fact Sheet, April 1999.

41. For further information on the causes of juvenile delinquency, along with suggestions for the control of delinquency, see *Critical Criminal Justice Issues: Task Force Reports from the American Society of Criminology* (Washington, D.C.: National Institute of Justice, 1997).

42. Eileen M. Garry, "Truancy: First Step to a Lifetime of Problems," *Juvenile Justice Bulletin* (Washington, D.C.: Office of Juvenile Justice and Delinquency Prevention, 1996).

43. Marcia Chaiken and David Huizinga, "Early Prevention of and Intervention for Delinquency and Related Problem Behavior," in *Critical Criminal Justice Issues: Task Force Reports from the American Society of Criminology* (Washington, D.C.: National Institute of Justice, 1997).

44. Ibid.

45. "Going 'Wilding': Terror in Central Park," *Newsweek,* May 1, 1989, p. 27.

46. "Angry Teens Explode in Violent Wilding Sprees," *USA Today,* April 27, 1989, p. 1D.

47. Marco R. della Cava, "The Societal Forces That Push Kids Out of Control," *USA Today,* April 27, 1989, p. 6D.

48. Ruth Shonle Cavan, *Juvenile Delinquency: Development, Treatment, Control,* 2d ed. (Philadelphia: J. B. Lippincott, 1969), p. 152.

49. Alexis M. Durham III, "Ivy League Delinquency: A Self-Report Analysis," *American Journal of Criminal Justice,* Vol. 12, No. 2 (spring 1988), p. 188.

50. U.S. Department of Health and Human Services, *Monitoring the Future Survey, 2000* (Washington, D.C.: HHS, 2001).

51. Ibid.

52. Ibid.

53. Phyllis L. Ellickson et al., "Teenagers and Alcohol Misuse in the United States," *Addiction,* Vol. 91, No. 10 (1996), pp. 1489–1503.

54. Federal Bureau of Investigation, *Crime in the United States, 1996* (Washington, D.C.: U.S. Government Printing Office, 1997).

55. Cheryl Carpenter et al., *Kids, Drugs, and Crime* (Lexington, MA: Lexington Books, 1988).

56. M. R. Chaiken and B. D. Johnson, *Characteristics of Different Types of Drug-Involved Offenders* (Washington, D.C.: National Institute of Justice, 1988), p. 9, citing Delbert S. Elliott, David Huizinga, and Barbara Morse, "Self-Reported Violent Offending: A Descriptive Analysis of Juvenile Violent Offenders and Their Offending Careers," *Journal of Interpersonal Violence,* Vol. 1, No. 4 (1986), pp. 472–514.

57. S. L. Murphy, *Deaths: Final Data for 1998,* National Vital Statistics Reports, Vol. 48, No. 11 (Washington, D.C.: U.S. Department of Health and Human Services, Centers for Disease Control and Prevention, National Center for Health Statistics, 2000), p. 8.

58. FBI, *Crime in the United States, 2000,* p. 17.

59. Ibid.

60. Bureau of Justice Statistics, *Sourcebook of Criminal Justice Statistics, 1999* (Washington, D.C.: BJS, 2000), p. 297.

61. Office of Juvenile Justice and Delinquency Prevention, *Children as Victims* (Washington, D.C.: OJJDP, 2000).

62. BJS, *Sourcebook of Criminal Justice Statistics, 1999*, p. 302.

63. OJJDP, *Children as Victims*, p. 7.

64. Ibid., p. 11.

65. See, for example, Frederick M. Thrasher, *The Gang* (Chicago: University of Chicago Press, 1927); and William Foote Whyte, *Street Corner Society, the Social Structure of an Italian Slum* (Chicago: University of Chicago Press, 1943).

66. "Young Urban Terrorists," *Ohio State University Quest* (fall 1988), p. 11.

67. For a good overview of the topic, see C. Ronald Huff, *Gangs in America*, 2d ed. (Thousand Oaks, CA: Sage, 1996).

68. Office of Juvenile Justice and Delinquency Prevention, *1999 National Youth Gang Survey* (Washington, D.C.: OJJDP, 2001).

69. Ibid.

70. National Gang Crime Research Center, *Achieving Justice and Reversing the Problem of Gang Crime and Gang Violence in America Today: Preliminary Results of the Project Gangfact Study* (Chicago: NGCRC, 1996).

71. *Chicago* v. *Morales*, No. 97-1121 (1999).

72. The National Center for Missing and Exploited Children website, http://www.missingkids.com. Accessed January 12, 2000.

73. David Finkelhor, Gerald Hotaling, and Andrea Sedlak, *Missing, Abducted, Runaway, and Thrownaway Children in America* (Washington, D.C.: Office of Juvenile Justice and Delinquency Prevention, 1990).

74. "Runaway Children and the Juvenile Justice and Delinquency Prevention Act: What Is Its Impact?" *Juvenile Justice Bulletin* (Washington, D.C.: Office of Juvenile Justice and Delinquency Prevention, no date).

75. Ibid., p. 1.

76. Ibid., p. 2.

77. "Teen Stripper's Mom Gets Year in Jail," United Press International wire service, January 22, 1988.

78. Richard J. Estes and Neil Alan Weiner, *The Commercial Sexual Exploitation of Children in the U.S., Canada and Mexico* (Philadelphia: University of Pennsylvania Press, 2001), p. 67.

79. Ibid., p. 68.

80. Child Welfare League of America, *Sacramento County Community Intervention Program: Findings from a Comprehensive Study by Community Partners in Child Welfare, Law Enforcement, Juvenile Justice, and the Child Welfare League of America* (Washington, D.C.: CWLA, 1997).

81. National Committee for Prevention of Child Abuse, *Child Abuse: Prelude to Delinquency?* (Washington, D.C.: Office of Juvenile Justice and Delinquency Prevention, 1986).

82. Charles B. DeWitt, *The Cycle of Violence* (Washington, D.C.: National Institute of Justice, 1992), p. 2.

83. Matthew T. Zingraff et al., "Child Maltreatment and Youthful Problem Behavior," *Criminology*, Vol. 31, No. 2 (May 1993), pp. 173–202.

84. See "The Role of the National Center for the Prosecution of Child Abuse," *Prosecutors Perspective*, Vol. 2, No. 1 (January 1988), p. 19.

85. Gregory A. Hall, "Another Teen Suicide in Gallatin County," *Cincinnati Enquirer*, November 30, 1998.

86. "Teen Suicide Rates—Alarming News," PENpages (Pennsylvania State University). Web posted at http://www.penpages.psu.edu/reference/28507/28507493.HTML. Accessed January 10, 2000.

87. "Teen Suicide," American Academy of Child and Adolescent Psychiatry, November 1998. Web posted at http://www.aacap.org/factsfam/suicide.htm. Accessed January 15, 2000.

88. Kevin N. Wright and Karen E. Wright, *Family Life, Delinquency, and Crime: A Policymaker's Guide: Research Summary* (Washington, D.C.: Office of Juvenile Justice and Delinquency Prevention, 1994).

89. Ibid.

90. For an excellent true-to-life account of the functionings of the Los Angeles Juvenile Court, see Edward Humes, *No Matter How Loud I Shout: A Year in the Life of Juvenile Court* (New York: Simon & Schuster, 1996).

91. Barry Krisberg and James F. Austin, *Reinventing Juvenile Justice* (Newbury Park, CA: Sage, 1993).

92. Heidi M. Hsia, "Allegheny County, PA: Mobilizing to Reduce Juvenile Crime," *Juvenile Justice Bulletin* (Washington, D.C.: Office of Juvenile Justice and Delinquency Prevention, 1997).

93. Ibid.

94. Coordinating Council on Juvenile Justice and Delinquency Prevention, *Combating Violence and Delinquency: The National Juvenile Justice Action Plan* (Washington, D.C.: U.S. Government Printing Office, 1996); and CCJJDP, *Action Plan Update: Addressing Youth Victimization* (Washington, D.C.: U.S. Government Printing Office, 2001).

95. See, for example, *Haley* v. *Ohio*, 332 U.S. 596 (1948).

96. *Kent* v. *U.S.*, 383 U.S. 541 (1966).

97. *In re Gault*, 387 U.S. 1 (1967).

98. *In re Winship*, 397 U.S. 358 (1970).

99. *McKeiver* v. *Pennsylvania*, 403 U.S. 528 (1971).

100. *Breed* v. *Jones*, 421 U.S. 519 (1975).

101. *Schall* v. *Martin*, 467 U.S. 253 (1984).

102. *Illinois* v. *Montanez*, No. 95-1429 (1996), certiorari denied.

103. Michael Kirkland, "Court Rejects Juvenile Confession Case," United Press International wire service, June 10, 1996.

104. "Drug Bill Includes Extension of OJJDP, with Many Changes," *Criminal Justice Newsletter*, Vol. 19, No. 22 (November 15, 1988), p. 4.

105. See "OJJDP Eases Rules on Juvenile Confinement," *Corrections Compendium* (November 1996), p. 25.

106. *Fare* v. *Michael C.*, 442 U.S. 707 (1979).

107. *California* v. *Prysock*, 453 U.S. 355 (1981).

108. *New Jersey* v. *T.L.O.*, 105 S.Ct. 733 (1985).

109. Charles M. Puzzanchera, *Delinquency Cases Waived to Criminal Court, 1989–1998* (Washington, D.C.: Office of Juvenile Justice and Delinquency Prevention, 2001).

110. Ibid.

111. "Ten-Year-Old Faces Murder Trial as Adult," *Fayetteville* (N.C.) *Observer-Times*, August 27, 1989, p. 5A.

112. Adapted from Peter Greenwood, *Juvenile Offenders*, a Crime File Study Guide (Washington, D.C.: National Institute of Justice, no date).

113. Bureau of Justice Statistics, *Report to the Nation on Crime and Justice*, 2d ed. (Washington, D.C.: U.S. Government Printing Office, 1988), p. 78.

114. Ibid.

115. Ibid.

116. *McKeiver* v. *Pennsylvania* 403 U.S. 528 (1971).

117. Some states, such as West Virginia, do provide juveniles with a statutory right to trial.

118. Other early peer juries in juvenile court began operating in Denver, Colorado; Duluth, Minnesota; Deerfield,

Illinois; Thompkins County, New York; and Spanish Fork City, Utah, at about the same time. See Philip Reichel and Carole Seyfrit, "A Peer Jury in the Juvenile Court," *Crime and Delinquency,* Vol. 30, No. 3 (July 1984), pp. 423–438.

119. Ibid.

120. "In This Court, Teens Sit in Stern Judgment on Violators," Associated Press wire service, May 3, 1992.

121. Tracy M. Godwin, *A Guide for Implementing Teen Court Programs* (Washington, D.C.: Office of Juvenile Justice and Delinquency Prevention, 1996).

122. Office of Juvenile Justice and Delinquency Prevention, "Offenders in Juvenile Court 1997," *Juvenile Justice Bulletin* (October 2000).

123. Anne L. Stahl et al., *Juvenile Court Statistics, 1996* (Washington, D.C.: Office of Juvenile Justice and Delinquency Prevention, 1999).

124. Bethany Gardner, "Successful Pennsylvania School-Based Probation Expands," *Corrections Compendium,* Vol. 19, No. 8 (August 1994), pp. 1–3.

125. Stahl et al., *Juvenile Court Statistics, 1996.*

126. "Juvenile Offenders in Residential Placement, 1997," Office of Juvenile Justice and Delinquency Prevention Fact Sheet, March 1999. See also *OJJDP Statistical Briefing Book* online. Web posted at http://www.ojjdp.ncjrs.org/ojstatbb/html/CORRECTIONS.html.

127. Ibid.

128. See, for example, Blair B. Bourque et al., "Boot Camps for Juvenile Offenders: An Implementation Evaluation of Three Demonstration Programs," *NIJ Research in Brief* (Washington, D.C.: National Institute of Justice, 1996).

129. *Juvenile Offenders in Residential Placement, 1997,* p. 110.

130. Ibid.

131. Ibid.

132. Ibid.

133. Joseph Moone, "Juveniles in Public Facilities, 1995," Office of Juvenile Justice and Delinquency Prevention Fact Sheet, November 1997.

134. "Juvenile Offenders in Residential Placement, 1997," Office of Juvenile Justice and Delinquency Prevention Fact Sheet, March 1999.

135. Ibid.

136. Dale G. Parent et al., *Conditions of Confinement: Juvenile Detention and Corrections Facilities* (Washington, D.C.: Office of Juvenile Justice and Delinquency Prevention, 1994).

137. *Corrections Compendium* (December 1993), p. 14.

138. Ibid.

139. Ibid., p. 22.

140. Office of Juvenile Justice and Delinquency Prevention, *National Juvenile Custody Trends, 1978–1989* (Washington, D.C.: U.S. Department of Justice, 1992), p. 2.

141. Section 59 of the Uniform Juvenile Court Act recommends the granting of a right to appeal for juveniles (National Conference of Commissioners on Uniform State Laws, Uniform Juvenile Court Act, 1968).

142. Patricia Torbet et al., *State Responses to Serious and Violent Juvenile Crime* (Washington, D.C.: Office of Juvenile Justice and Delinquency Prevention, 1996).

143. Ibid., p. xi.

144. Ibid.

145. Jeffrey A. Butts and Ojmarrh Mitchell, "Brick by Brick: Dismantling the Border between Juvenile and Adult Justice," in Phyllis McDonald and Janice Munsterman, eds., *Criminal Justice 2000,* Vol. 2: *Boundary Changes in Criminal Justice Organizations* (Washington, D.C.: National Institute of Justice, 2000), p. 207.

146. Ibid., p. 167.

147. Ibid., pp. 167–213.

148. Barry C. Feld, "Abolish the Juvenile Court: Youthfulness, Criminal Responsibility, and Sentencing Policy," *Journal of Criminal Law and Criminology* (winter 1998).

149. Ibid.

Drugs and Crime

LEARNING OBJECTIVES

After reading this chapter, you should be able to

- Describe the criminal justice system's response to the drug problem in America

- Discuss the history of drug abuse and the history of antidrug legislation in America

- Identify the different types of drugs that are illegally used in this country, as well as the effects and legal classifications of each

- Explain the nature of the link between drugs and other social problems, including different forms of criminal activity

- Describe the nature of various efforts to respond to the drug problem, and assess the effectiveness of each

[*As the Republican governor of New Mexico, I'm neither soft on crime nor pro-drugs in any sense. I believe a person who harms another person should be punished. But as a successful businessman, I also believe that locking up more and more people who are nonviolent drug offenders, people whose real problem is that they are addicted to drugs, is simply a waste of money and human resources.*]

—Governor Gary E. Johnson[1]

[*The myth that anti-drug efforts do not work is refuted by the tireless, everyday efforts of our partners in this struggle: parents, teachers, coaches, and community leaders throughout the nation. They are a tribute to what works and what has kept these levels from skyrocketing.*]

—"Drug Czar" John P. Walters[2]

Key Concepts

[Terms]

club drug	drug court	narcoterrorism
controlled substance	drug czar	physical dependence
Controlled Substances Act (CSA)	forfeiture	psychoactive substance
curtilage	Harrison Act	psychological dependence
decriminalization	interdiction	Racketeer Influenced and Corrupt
drug	legalization	Organizations (RICO)
drug abuse	money laundering	recreational drug user

[Cases]

Alexander v. *U.S.*	*Oliver* v. *U.S.*	*U.S.* v. *92 Buena Vista Ave.*
Austin v. *U.S.*	*Ratzlaf* v. *U.S.*	*U.S.* v. *Oakland Cannabis Buyer's Cooperative*
California v. *Greenwood*	*U.S.* v. *Dunn*	*U.S.* v. *Ursery*

Hear the author
discuss this chapter
at **cjtoday.com**

drug abuse

Illicit drug use that results in
social, economic, psychological,
or legal problems for the user.[i]

Introduction

Some years ago, Ross Deck, Senior Policy Analyst at the Office of National Drug Control Policy (ONDCP), opened his remarks to a yearly conference on controversies in criminal justice with these words: "First of all, we are not fighting a drug war anymore. To have a war you must have enemies. In this situation, we are our own enemy. And, we cannot declare victory simply because we killed ourselves."[3] In other words, seen from the federal level, **drug abuse** is so pervasive in American society, and the values that support it have become so entrenched among large segments of the American population, that the fight against drug abuse through the application of strict criminal justice sanctions seems bound to fail. Arrest, incarceration, and a national prison system filled with drug-law violators no longer seem to hold the answer to winning the drug-control battle.

A dramatic increase in drug-related crime and the corresponding expansion of both drug laws and efforts at enforcement occurred during the last few decades, and have had a significant impact on all aspects of our justice system. In some parts of the country, court dockets have become so clogged with drug cases that criminal case processing has ground almost to a halt. Prison populations also reflect the huge increase in drug crimes. As Bill Clinton noted during his presidency, "Three quarters of the growth in the number of federal prison inmates is due to drug crimes."[4] Today, about 70% of all first offenders in the federal prisons are serving drug sentences. This is also true of 85% of the noncitizens and 66% of the women."[5] (See Figure 15–1.) Although drug crimes account for only about 20% of state prison populations, the number of men held in state prisons as a result of drug crimes has increased by almost 50% since 1990, while the number of women incarcerated for drug crimes has risen by 108%.[6]

Drug Abuse: More Than an Individual Choice

Few criminal justice textbooks devote an entire chapter to drug-related crime. Most prefer, instead, to describe a general category of social-order, or victimless, crimes. This book, however, directly addresses drug crime because it has such a pervasive and far-reaching impact, not only on the criminal justice system, but also on all of society. This is so for several reasons. Drug abuse accounts for a large proportion of present-day law violations. It contributes to many other types of criminal activity, including smuggling, theft, robbery, and murder, and it has led to a huge number of arrests, clogged courtrooms, and overcrowded prisons. As a consequence, drug abuse has placed tremendous strain on the criminal justice system, and the fight against it has become one of the most expensive activities ever undertaken by federal, state, and local governments.

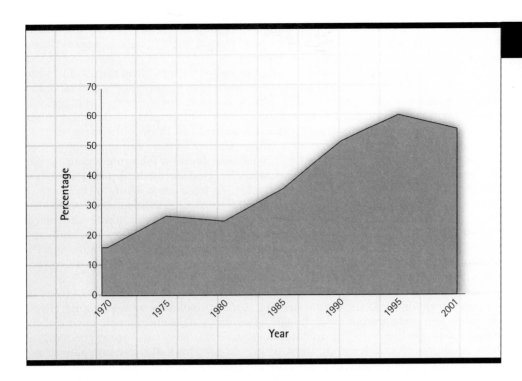

FIGURE 15-1

Percentage of federal prisoners sentenced for drug offenses, 1970–2001.

Source: Sourcebook of Criminal Justice Statistics Online, Table 6.51.

Drug crime is one of the major challenges facing the nation's criminal justice system and state and federal criminal justice policymakers today.[7] Even though drug abuse is widespread, it is only one of a great number of social-order crimes. As such, it shares a number of characteristics with other victimless crimes, like prostitution, gambling, and the diverse forms of sexual deviance which occur among consenting partners. A hallmark of such crimes is that they involve willing participants. In the case of drug-law violations, buyers, sellers, and users willingly purchase, sell, and consume illegal drugs. They do not complain to the authorities of criminal injuries to themselves or to others resulting from the illegal use of drugs. Few victimless crimes, however, are truly without an injured party. Even where the criminal participant does not perceive an immediate or personal injury, the behavior frequently affects the legitimate interests of nonparticipants. In many victimless crimes, it is society which is the ultimate victim. Prostitution, for example, may victimize the customer or his family through the spread of AIDS and other venereal diseases and through the economic cost of illicit sexual services. Prostitution has many other negative consequences, including lowered property values in areas where it regularly occurs, degradation of the status of women, victimization of the prostitute, and the seeming legitimacy it lends to interpersonal immorality of all kinds.

Drug abuse has many equally or even greater destructive consequences, including lost productivity, an inequitable distribution of economic resources among the poorest members of society, disease, wasted human potential, fragmented families, violence, and other crimes. Some evidence has even linked drug trafficking to international terrorism and to efforts to overthrow the democratic governments of the Western Hemisphere. Each of these consequences will be discussed in some detail in this chapter. We begin now with an analysis of what constitutes a drug, explore the history of drug abuse in America, and then describe the various categories of major **controlled substances**. Finally, the link between drugs and other forms of crime will be explained, and possible solutions to the problem of drug abuse will be described. See **Web Extra! 15–1** at cjtoday.com to learn more about drugs and crime.

What Is a Drug?

Before we begin any comprehensive discussion of drugs, we must first grapple with the concept of what a drug is. In common usage, a **drug** may be any ingestible substance which has a noticeable effect upon the mind or body. Drugs may enter the body via injection, inhalation, swallowing, or even direct absorption through the skin or mucous

controlled substance

A specifically defined bioactive or psychoactive chemical substance proscribed by law.

drug

Any chemical substance defined by social convention as bioactive or psychoactive.

recreational drug user
━━━━━━━━━━━━━━━━━━━━

A person who uses drugs relatively infrequently and primarily with friends and in social contexts that define drug use as pleasurable. Most addicts begin as recreational users.

membranes. Some drugs, like penicillin and tranquilizers, are useful in medical treatment, while others, like heroin and cocaine, are attractive only to **recreational drug users**[8] or to those who are addicted to them.

In determining what substances should be called "drugs," it is important to recognize the role that social definitions of any phenomenon play in our understanding of it. Hence, what Americans today consider to be drugs depends more upon social convention or agreed-upon definitions than it does upon any inherent property of the substances themselves. The history of marijuana provides a case in point. Prior to the early twentieth century, marijuana was freely available in the United States. Although alcohol was the recreational drug of choice at the time, marijuana found a following among some artists and musicians. Marijuana was also occasionally used for medical purposes to "calm the nerves" and to treat hysteria. Howard Becker, in his classic study of the early Federal Bureau of Narcotics (forerunner of the Drug Enforcement Administration, or DEA), demonstrates how federal agencies worked to outlaw marijuana in order to increase their power.[9] Federally funded publications voiced calls for laws against the substance, and movies like *Reefer Madness* led the drive toward classifying marijuana as a dangerous drug. The 1939 Marijuana Tax Act was the result, and marijuana has been thought of as a drug worthy of federal and local enforcement efforts ever since.

Both the law and social convention make strong distinctions between drugs that are socially acceptable and those that are not. Some substances with profound effects upon the mind and body are not even thought of as drugs. Gasoline fumes, chemical vapors of many kinds, perfumes, certain vitamins, sugar-rich foods, and toxic chemicals may all have profound effects. Even so, most people do not think of these substances as drugs, and they are rarely regulated by the criminal law.

Recent social awareness has reclassified substances like alcohol, caffeine, and nicotine as "drugs," although before the 1960s it is doubtful that most Americans would have applied that word to this threesome. Even today, alcohol, caffeine, and nicotine are readily available throughout the country, with only minimal controls on their manufacture and distribution. As such, they are three drugs which continue to enjoy favored status in both our law and culture. Nonetheless, alcohol abuse and addiction are commonplace in American society, and anyone who has tried to quit smoking knows the power that nicotine can wield.

Occupying a middle ground on the continuum between acceptability and illegality are substances which have a legitimate medical use and are usually available only with a prescription. Antibiotics, diet pills, and, in particular, tranquilizers, stimulants, and mood-altering chemicals (such as the popular drug Prozac®) are culturally acceptable but sometimes can only be attained legally with a physician's prescription. These substances are clearly recognized as drugs, albeit useful ones, by the majority of Americans.

Powerful drugs, those with the ability to produce substantially altered states of consciousness and with a high potential for addiction, occupy the "high ground" in social and legal condemnation. Among them are **psychoactive substances** like heroin, peyote, mescaline, LSD, and cocaine. Even here, however, legitimate uses for such drugs may exist. Cocaine is used in the treatment of certain medical conditions and can be applied as a topical anesthetic during medical interventions. LSD has been employed experimentally to investigate the nature of human consciousness, and peyote and mescaline may be used legally by members of the Native American Church in religious services. Even heroin has been advocated by some as beneficial in relieving the suffering associated with some forms of terminal illness. Hence, answers to the question of "What is a drug?" depend to a large extent on the social definitions and conventions operating at a given time and in a given place. Some of the clearest definitional statements relating to controlled substances can be found in the law, although informal strictures and definitions guide much of everyday drug use.

psychoactive substance
━━━━━━━━━━━━━━━━━━━━

A chemical substance that affects cognition, feeling, or awareness.

Alcohol Abuse

In May 2001, President Bush's 19-year-old twin daughters, Barbara and Jenna, were charged in Austin, Texas, with underage alcohol offenses, including attempting to buy alcohol with false identification and being a minor in possession of alcohol. (The minimum drinking age in Texas is 21.) They pleaded "no contest." Jenna, who had previously been arrested for another alcohol-related offense, was placed on probation. She was also fined $500, assessed $100 in court costs, required to perform 36 hours of community service, and ordered to attend a victim-impact panel to learn about alcohol's potential dangers. The judge then ordered her to surrender her driver's license for 30 days. Barbara, who was in

President George W. Bush's twin daughters, Barbara and Jenna. Both pleaded guilty to alcohol-related offenses in Texas in 2001.

George E. Mathieson, MAI, TimePix

court for her first alcohol-related offense, was ordered to serve eight hours of community service and to attend an alcohol-awareness class.[10]

Although the abuse of alcohol is rarely described in the same terms as the illegal use of controlled substances, alcohol misuse can lead to serious problems with grim consequences. In 1995, for example, a pickup truck driven by Gallardo Bermudes, 35, of Cathedral City, California, rear-ended a car carrying 11 people near Beaumont, California.[11] Most of the occupants of the car were children of Jose Luis Rodriquez and Mercedes Diaz—the only adults in the car. Eight of the children burned to death when the car flipped and caught fire after being hit. Bermudes, who fled from the scene, had been convicted of drunk driving on three previous occasions. He later told police investigators that he had had ten to 15 beers before the crash.

Recognizing the many problems attributable to the misuse of alcohol, alcohol abuse has been called "one of the nation's gravest health and social problems."[12] Indications are that it is a serious problem which shows few signs of abating. Although 30% of Americans are abstainers, surveys show that more Americans drink today than at any time since World War II, and those who drink, drink more excessively.[13] As many as 40 million Americans may be problem drinkers. According to recent polls, 93% of high school seniors have tried alcoholic beverages, and up to one-half of teenagers in the United States become intoxicated an average of once every two weeks.[14] The alcohol business in the United States is huge, with $63 billion of beer, $29.5 billion of liquor, and $11.8 billion of wine sold annually.[15]

Alcohol, sometimes in combination with other drugs, is often a factor in the commission of crimes, such as drunk driving. Most states define a blood alcohol level of 0.08% to 0.10% or more as intoxication and hold that anyone who drives with that amount of alcohol in his or her blood is driving under the influence (DUI) of alcohol.[16] In October 2000, however, an amendment to a federal highway construction bill[17] required that states lower their blood-alcohol limits for drunk driving to 0.08% by the year 2004 or lose a substantial percentage of the federal highway construction funds allocated to them.[18] Any state that adopts the new standard by 2007 will be permitted to recover any previously forfeited highway funds.

Drunk driving has been a major social concern for some time. Groups like Mothers Against Drunk Driving (MADD) and Remove Intoxicated Drivers (RID) have given impetus to enforcement efforts to curb drunk drivers. Today, approximately 1.5 million drunk driving arrests are made annually—more than for any offense other than drug abuse.[19] The average driver arrested for DUI is substantially impaired. Studies show that he or she has consumed an average of six ounces of pure alcohol (the equivalent of a dozen bottles of beer) in the four hours preceding arrest.[20] Twenty-six percent of arrestees have consumed nearly twice that amount. (Visit MADD via **Web Extra! 15-2** at cjtoday.com.)

> I keep in my house a letter from Bill O'Dwyer, who once was the mayor of New York, and who wrote to me, "There is no power on earth to match the power of the poor, who, just by sitting in their hopelessness, can bring the rest of us down." It always sounded right, but I never saw it happen until crack came along. And with it, there are no more rules in American crime. The implied agreements on which we were raised are gone. You now shoot women and children. A news reporter is safe as long as he is not there. A cop in his uniform means nothing.
>
> —Jimmy Breslin, *Crack*

Driving under the influence is costly for both offenders and society. Approximately 40% of all vehicle crashes resulting in death are alcohol-related.[21] The National Highway Traffic Safety Administration estimates that alcohol caused 16,653 traffic fatalities in 2000—the year of the largest percentage increase in alcohol-related traffic deaths.[22]

Another offense directly related to alcohol consumption is public drunkenness. During the late 1960s and early 1970s, some groups fought to decriminalize drunkenness and to treat it as a health problem. Although the number of arrests for public drunkenness reached 637,554 in 2000,[23] law enforcement officers retain a great deal of discretion in handling these offenders. Many people who are drunk in public, unless they are assaultive or involved in other crimes, are likely to receive an "official escort" home rather than face arrest.

The use of alcohol may also lead to the commission of other, very serious, crimes. Some experts have found that use of alcohol lowers inhibitions and increases the likelihood of aggression.[24] A report by the National Institute of Justice concluded that "of all psychoactive substances, alcohol is the only one whose consumption has been shown to commonly increase aggression."[25] As Figure 15–2 shows, approximately 37% of offenders consume alcohol immediately before committing a crime.[26] In cases of violent crime, the percentage of offenders under the influence of alcohol at the time of the crime jumps to 42%—and is highest for murder (44.6%).[27]

Lawmakers appear willing to deal with the problems caused by alcohol only indirectly. The American experience with Prohibition is not one that legislators are anxious to repeat. In all likelihood, future efforts to reduce the damaging effects of alcohol will continue to take the form of educational programs, legislation to raise the drinking age, and enforcement efforts designed to deter the most visible forms of abuse. Struggles in other areas may also have some impact. For example, lawsuits claiming civil damages are now being brought against some liquor companies and taverns in behalf of accident victims, cirrhosis patients, and others. We can anticipate, however, that while concern over alcohol abuse will continue, few sweeping changes in either law or social custom will occur anytime soon.

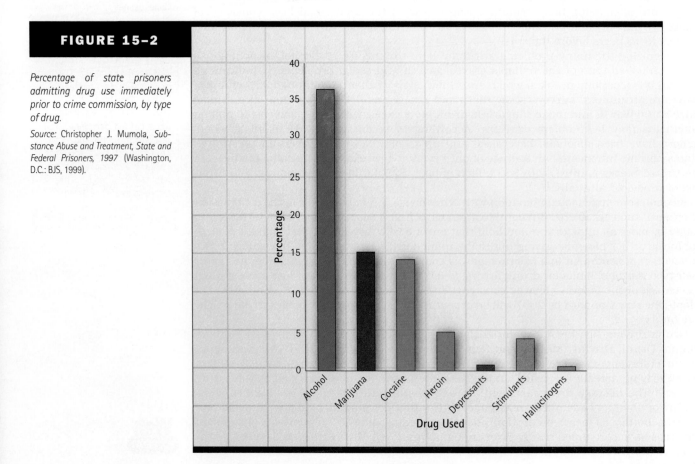

FIGURE 15–2

Percentage of state prisoners admitting drug use immediately prior to crime commission, by type of drug.

Source: Christopher J. Mumola, *Substance Abuse and Treatment, State and Federal Prisoners, 1997* (Washington, D.C.: BJS, 1999).

A Mexican federal policeman guarding a shipment of high-grade cocaine seized near Mexico City. Drug abuse is one of the most significant problems facing the criminal justice system and society today.

Miguel Castillo, MIC Photo Press, CORBIS/Sygma

A History of Drug Abuse in America

Alcohol is but one example of the many conflicting images of drug use prevalent in contemporary American society. The "war on drugs," initiated during the latter part of the twentieth century portrayed an America fighting for its very existence against the scourge of drug abuse. While many of the negative images of drugs which emanated from the "war period" may be correct, they have not always been a part of the American worldview.

Opium and its derivatives, for example, were widely available in patent medicines of the nineteenth and early twentieth centuries. Corner drugstores stocked mixtures of opium and alcohol, and traveling road shows extolled the virtues of these magical curatives. These elixirs, purported to offer relief from almost every malady, did indeed bring about feelings of well-being in most users. Although no one is certain just how widespread opium use was in the United States a hundred years ago, some authors have observed that baby formulas containing opium were fed to infants born to addicted mothers.[28]

Opium was also widely used by Chinese immigrants who came to the West Coast in the nineteenth century, often to work on the railroads. Opium dens—in which the drug was smoked—flourished, and the use of opium quickly spread to other ethnic groups throughout the West. Some of the more affluent denizens of West Coast cities ate the substance, and avant-garde poetry was written extolling the virtues of the drug.

Morphine, an opium derivative, has a similar history. Although it was legally available in this country almost since its invention, its use as a painkiller on the battlefields of the Civil War dramatically heightened public awareness of the drug.[29] In the late nineteenth century, morphine was widely prescribed by physicians and dentists, many of whom abused the substance themselves. By 1896, per capita morphine consumption peaked, and addiction to the substance throughout the United States was apparently widespread.[30]

Heroin, the most potent derivative of opium ever created, was invented as a substitute for morphine by German chemists in 1898. When first introduced, its addictive properties were unknown, and it was marketed as a nonaddictive cough suppressant. It was also said to be useful in treating morphine addiction.[31]

> The drug problem did not develop overnight; it took years and years to get to this point as a result of misguided attitudes and a mindset that drug usage, at least using cocaine and marijuana, was all right. Dealing with the drug problem involves changing attitudes, and that takes time.
>
> —Judge Reggie B. Walton

Marijuana, a considerably less potent drug than heroin, has a relatively short history in this country. Imported by Mexican immigrants around the turn of the twentieth century, marijuana use quickly became associated with nonmainstream groups. By 1930, most of the states in the Southwest had passed legislation outlawing marijuana, and some authors have suggested that antimarijuana laws were primarily targeted at Spanish-speaking immigrants who were beginning to challenge whites in the economic sector.[32] As mentioned earlier, other writers have suggested that the rapidly growing use of marijuana throughout the 1920s and 1930s provided a rationale for the development of drug legislation and the concomitant expansion of drug-enforcement agencies.[33] By the 1960s, public attitudes regarding marijuana had begun to change. The hippie generation popularized the drug, touting its "mellowing" effects upon users. In a short time, marijuana use became epidemic across the country, and books on marijuana cultivation and preparation flourished.

Another drug which found adherents among some youthful idealists of the 1960s and 1970s was LSD. LSD, whose chemical name is lysergic acid diethylamide, was first synthesized in Switzerland in 1938 and was used occasionally in this country in the 1950s for the treatment of psychiatric disorders.

Many drugs, when first "discovered," were touted for their powerful analgesic or therapeutic effects. Cocaine was one of them. An early leading proponent of cocaine use, for example, was Sigmund Freud, who prescribed it for a variety of psychological disorders. Freud was himself a user and wrote a book, *The Cocaine Papers*, describing the many ben-

An early advertisement for cocaine-laced wine. Cocaine, a controlled substance today, was commonly found in late-nineteenth-century medicines and consumer products.
CORBIS

efits of the drug. The cocaine bandwagon reached the United States in the late nineteenth century, and various medicines and beverages containing cocaine were offered to the American public. Prominent among them was Coca-Cola, which combined seltzer water, sugar, and cocaine in a new soft drink advertised as providing a real "pick-me-up." Cocaine was removed from Coca-Cola in 1910 but continued to be used by jazz musicians and artists. Beginning in the 1970s, cocaine became associated with exclusive parties, the well-to-do, and the jet set. Television shows and movies often portrayed the drug as glamorous, and cocaine soon became the drug of choice among the young and upwardly mobile. In testimony to both the cost of the drug and the economic success of some of its users, sterling silver "coke spoons" and rolled $100 bills became the preferred paraphernalia. Words like *snorting* and *freebasing* entered common usage, and it was not long before an extensive drug underworld developed, catering to the demands of affluent users. Crack cocaine, a derivative of powdered cocaine that is smoked, became popular in the 1980s and is sold today in the form of "rocks," "cookies," or "biscuits" (large pieces of crack).

Today, drugs have become a pervasive part of American culture, as evidenced by their portrayal in the contemporary media. An ONDCP study of the depiction of drugs in popular movies and music was released in 1999. The study examined the 200 most popular movie rentals and the 1,000 most popular songs from 1996 and 1997. Findings revealed that 98% of the movies studied depicted substance use (that is, drugs or alcohol), and 22% showed illicit drugs. Twenty-seven percent of the 1,000 songs contained a clear reference to either alcohol or illicit drugs.[34]

Drug Use and Social Awareness

As we have seen, drugs have long been a part of American society. There have been dramatic changes over the last century, however, in the form drug use takes and in the social consequences associated with drug involvement. Specifically, six elements have emerged which today cast drug use in a far different light than that of the past:

- The conceptualization of addiction as a physical or medical condition
- The understanding that drug use is associated with other kinds of criminal activity
- Generally widespread social condemnation of drug use as a waste of economic resources and human lives
- Comprehensive and detailed federal and state laws regulating the use or availability of drugs
- A large and perhaps still growing involvement with illicit drugs among the urban poor and the socially disenfranchised, both as an escape from the conditions of life and as a path to monetary gain
- The view that drug abuse is a law enforcement issue rather than primarily a medical problem

The last element is especially significant for what it means to the criminal justice system. In his classic study of the evolution of marijuana laws,[35] Howard Becker identified three American values which led to increased regulation of all drugs: (1) the belief "that the individual should exercise complete responsibility for what he does and what happens to him; he should never do anything that might cause loss of self-control"; (2) "disapproval of action taken solely to achieve states of ecstasy"; and (3) "humanitarianism."[36] Regarding humanitarianism, Becker said, "Reformers believed that people enslaved by the use of alcohol and opium would benefit from laws making it impossible for them to give in to their weaknesses."[37] Becker believed that these values rest upon the Protestant Ethic and strong "cultural emphases on pragmatism and utilitarianism."[38]

The contemporary situation is largely based upon the values identified by Becker. In an insightful work which clarifies the ideational basis of modern antidrug sentiments, Franklin Zimring and Gordon Hawkins examine three schools of thought which, they say, form the basis for current drug policy in the United States.[39] The first is "public health generalism," a perspective which holds that all controlled substances are potentially harmful and that drug abusers are victimized by the disease of addiction. This approach views drugs as medically harmful and argues that effective drug control is necessary as a matter of public health. The second approach, "cost-benefit specifism," proposes that drug policy be built around a balancing of the social costs of drug abuse (crime, broken families, drug-related killings, and so on) with the costs of enforcement. The third approach, the "legalist," suggests that drug-control policies are necessary to prevent the collapse of public order and of society itself. Advocates of the legalist perspective say that drug use is "defiance of lawful authority that threatens the social fabric."[40] According to Zimring and Hawkins, all recent and contemporary antidrug policies have been based upon one or the other of these three schools of thought. Unfortunately, say these authors, it may not be possible to base successful antidrug policy on such beliefs, since they do not necessarily recognize the everyday realities of drug use. Nonetheless, antidrug legislation and activities undertaken in the United States today are accorded political and ideational legitimacy via all three perspectives.

Antidrug Legislation

Antidrug legislation in the United States dates back to around 1875, when the city of San Francisco enacted a statute prohibiting the smoking of opium.[41] A number of Western states were quick to follow the city's lead. The San Francisco law and many which followed it, however, clearly targeted Chinese immigrants and were rarely applied to other ethnic groups involved in the practice.

The first major piece of federal antidrug legislation came in 1914, with the enactment of the Harrison Narcotics Act. The **Harrison Act** required anyone dealing in opium, morphine, heroin, cocaine, and specified derivatives of these drugs to register with the federal government and to pay a tax of $1.00 per year. The only people permitted to register were physicians, pharmacists, and members of the medical profession. Nonregistered drug traffickers faced a maximum fine of $2,000 and up to five years in prison.

Because the Harrison Act allowed physicians to prescribe controlled drugs for the purpose of medical treatment, heroin addicts and other drug users could still legally purchase the drugs they needed. All the law required was a physician's prescription. By 1920, however, court rulings had established that drug "maintenance" only prolonged addiction and did not qualify as "treatment."[42] The era of legally available heroin had ended.

Marijuana was not included in the Harrison Act because it was not considered a dangerous drug.[43] By the 1930s, however, government attention had become riveted on marijuana. At the urging of the Federal Bureau of Narcotics, Congress passed the Marijuana Tax Act in 1937. As the title of the law indicates, the act simply placed a tax of $100 per ounce on cannabis. Those who did not pay the tax were subject to prosecution. With the passage of the Boggs Act in 1951, however, marijuana, along with a number of other drugs, entered the class of federally prohibited controlled substances. The Boggs Act also removed heroin from the list of medically useful substances and required the removal, within 120 days, of any medicines containing heroin from pharmacies across the country.[44]

The Narcotic Control Act of 1956 increased penalties for drug trafficking and possession and made the sale of heroin to anyone under age 18 a capital offense. However, on the eve of the massive explosion in drug use which was to begin in the mid-1960s, the Kennedy administration began a shift in emphasis from the strict punishment of drug traffickers and users to rehabilitation. A 1963 presidential commission recommended the elimination of the Federal Bureau of Narcotics, recommended shorter prison terms for drug offenders, and stressed the need for research and social programs in dealing with the drug problem.[45]

THE COMPREHENSIVE DRUG ABUSE PREVENTION AND CONTROL ACT OF 1970

By 1970, America's drug problem was clear to almost everyone, and legislators were anxious to return to a more punitive approach to controlling drug abuse. Under President Richard Nixon, legislation designed to encompass all aspects of drug abuse and to permit federal intervention at all levels of use was enacted. Termed the Comprehensive Drug Abuse Prevention and Control Act of 1970, the legislation still forms the basis of federal enforcement efforts today. Title II of the Comprehensive Drug Abuse Prevention and Control Act is the **Controlled Substances Act (CSA)**. The CSA sets up five schedules which classify psychoactive drugs according to their degree of psychoactivity and abuse potential:[46]

■ Schedule I controlled substances have no established medical usage, cannot be used safely, and have great potential for abuse.[47] Federal law requires that any research employing Schedule I substances be fully documented and that the substances themselves be stored in secure vaults. Included under this category are heroin, LSD, mescaline, peyote, methaqualone (Quaaludes), psilocybin, marijuana,[48] and hashish, as well as other specified hallucinogens. Penalties for first-offense possession and sale of Schedule I controlled substances under the federal Narcotic Penalties and Enforcement

---

Harrison Act

The first major piece of federal antidrug legislation, passed in 1914.

> Wake up, America. The drug war is over. We lost.
>
> —David Nyhan,
> *Boston Globe* columnist

Controlled Substances Act (CSA)

Title II of the Comprehensive Drug Abuse Prevention and Control Act of 1970, which established schedules classifying psychoactive drugs according to their degree of psychoactivity.

Act of 1986 include up to life imprisonment and a $10 million fine. Penalties increase for subsequent offenses.

- Schedule II controlled substances are drugs with high abuse potential for which there is a currently accepted pharmacological or medical use. Most Schedule II substances are also considered to be addictive.[49] Drugs which fall into this category include opium, morphine, codeine, cocaine, phencyclidine (PCP), and their derivatives. Certain other stimulants, such as methylphenidate (Ritalin®) and phenmetrazine (Preludin®), and a few barbiturates with high abuse potential also come under Schedule II. Legal access to Schedule II substances requires written nonrefillable prescriptions, vault storage, and thorough record keeping by vendors. Penalties for first-offense possession and sale of Schedule II controlled substances include up to 20 years' imprisonment and a $5 million fine under the federal Narcotic Penalties and Enforcement Act. Penalties increase for subsequent offenses.

- Schedule III controlled substances have lower abuse potential than do those in Schedules I and II. They are drugs with an accepted medical use but which may lead to a high level of **psychological dependence** or to moderate or low **physical dependence**.[50] Schedule III substances include many of the drugs found in Schedule II but in derivative or diluted form. Common low-dosage antidiarrheals, such as opium-containing paregoric, and cold medicines and pain relievers with low concentrations of codeine fall into this category. Anabolic steroids, whose abuse by professional athletes has been subject to scrutiny, were added to the list of Schedule III controlled substances in 1991. Legitimate access to Schedule III drugs is through a doctor's prescription (written or oral), with refills authorized in the same manner. Maximum penalties associated with first-offense possession and sale of Schedule III controlled substances under federal law include five years' imprisonment and fines of up to $1 million.

- Schedule IV controlled substances have a relatively low potential for abuse (when compared to higher schedules), are useful in established medical treatments, and involve only a limited risk of psychological or physical dependence.[51] Depressants and minor tranquilizers such as Valium, Librium, and Equanil fall into this category, as do some stimulants. Schedule IV substances are medically available in the same fashion as Schedule III drugs. Maximum penalties associated with first-offense possession and sale of Schedule IV substances under federal law include three years in prison and fines of up to $1 million.

- Schedule V controlled substances are prescription drugs with a low potential for abuse and with only a very limited possibility of psychological or physical dependence.[52] Cough medicines (antitussives) and antidiarrheals containing small amounts of opium, morphine, or codeine are found in Schedule V. A number of Schedule V medicines may be purchased through retail vendors with only minimal controls or upon the signature of the buyer (with some form of identification required). Maximum federal penalties for first-offense possession and sale of Schedule V substances include one year in prison and a $250,000 fine.

Pharmacologists, chemists, and botanists are constantly discovering and creating new drugs. Likewise, street-corner "chemists" in clandestine laboratories churn out inexpensive *designer drugs*—laboratory-created psychoactive substances with widely varying effects and abuse potential. Designer drugs include substances with names like ecstasy (MDMA), GHB, ketamine, and methamphetamine (meth), which will be discussed in greater detail later in this chapter. The Controlled Substances Act includes provisions for determining which new drugs should be controlled and into which schedule they should be placed. Under the CSA, criteria for assigning a new drug to one of the existing schedules include (1) the drug's actual or relative potential for abuse; (2) scientific evidence of the drug's pharmacological effects; (3) the state of current scientific knowledge regarding the substance; (4) its history and current pattern of abuse; (5) the scope, duration, and significance of abuse; (6) risk, if any, to the public health; (7) the drug's psychic or physiological dependence liability; and (8) whether the substance is an immediate precursor of a substance already controlled.[53] Proceedings to add a new chemical substance to the list of those controlled by law or to delete or change the schedule of an existing drug may be initiated by the chief administrator of the Drug Enforcement Administration, the Department of Health and Human Services, or a petition from any interested party, including manufacturers, medical societies, or public-interest groups.[54] Access the CSA via **Library Extra! 15–1** at cjtoday.com.

psychological dependence

A craving for a specific drug that results from long-term substance abuse. Psychological dependence upon drugs is marked by the belief that drugs are needed to achieve a feeling of well-being.[ii]

physical dependence

A biologically based craving for a specific drug that results from frequent use of the substance. Dependence upon drugs is marked by a growing tolerance of a drug's effects, so that increased amounts of the drug are needed to obtain the desired effect, and by the onset of withdrawal symptoms over periods of prolonged abstinence.[iii]

> If I were king, I would find a civil way to allow citizens to sue the drug dealer for selling drugs to their children.
>
> —Samuel F. Saxton, Director, Prince George's County (Maryland) Department of Corrections

THE ANTI-DRUG ABUSE ACT OF 1988

In 1988, the country's Republican leadership, under President Ronald Reagan, capitalized upon the public's frustration with rampant drug abuse and stepped up the "war on drugs." The president created a new Cabinet-level post, naming a "drug czar" who would be in charge of federal drug-fighting initiatives through the Office of National Drug Control Policy. William Bennett, a former secretary of education, was appointed to fill the post. At the same time, Congress passed the Anti-Drug Abuse Act. The overly optimistic tenor of the act is clear from its preamble, which reads, "It is the declared policy of the United States Government to create a Drug-Free America by 1995."[55] That goal, which reflected far more political rhetoric than realistic planning, was incredibly naive.

Even so, the Anti-Drug Abuse Act of 1988 had plenty of teeth. Under the law, penalties for "recreational" drug users increased substantially,[56] and weapons purchases by suspected drug dealers became more difficult. The law also denied federal benefits, ranging from loans (including student loans) to contracts and licenses, to convicted drug offenders.[57] Earned benefits, such as Social Security, retirement, and health and disability benefits, are not affected by the legislation, nor are welfare payments or existing public housing arrangements (although separate legislation does provide for termination of public housing tenancy for drug offenses[58]). Under the law, civil penalties of up to $10,000 may be assessed against convicted "recreational" users for possession of even small amounts of drugs.

The legislation also included the possibility of capital punishment for drug-related murders. The killing of a police officer by offenders seeking to avoid apprehension or prosecution was specifically cited as carrying a possible sentence of death, although other murders by major drug dealers also fall under the capital punishment provision.[59] In May 1991, 37-year-old David Chandler, an Alabama marijuana kingpin, became the first person sentenced to die under the law.[60] Chandler had been convicted of ordering the murder of a police informant in 1990.

One especially interesting aspect of the Anti-Drug Abuse Act is its provision for designating selected areas as high-intensity drug-trafficking areas (HIDTAs), making them eligible for federal drug-fighting assistance so that joint interagency operations can be implemented to reduce drug problems. Using the law, former **drug czar** William Bennett declared Washington, D.C., a "drug zone" in 1989. His designation was based in part upon what was then the city's reputation as the murder capital of the country. At the time of the declaration, over 60% of Washington's murders were said to be drug related,[61] and legislators and tourists were clamoring for action. Bennett's plan called for more federal investigators and prosecutors and for specially built prisons to handle convicted drug dealers. The immediate results of the secretary's action, however, were squabbles between federal and city officials over who should be responsible for drug-enforcement efforts within the city. Visit ONDCP via **Web Extra! 15–3** and learn more about HIDTAs via **Web Extra! 15–4** at cjtoday.com.

drug czar

The popular name for the head of the Office of National Drug Control Policy (ONDCP), a federal Cabinet-level position that was created during the Reagan presidency to organize federal drug-fighting efforts.

OTHER FEDERAL ANTIDRUG LEGISLATION

Other significant federal antidrug legislation exists in the form of the Crime Control Act of 1990, the Violent Crime Control and Law Enforcement Act of 1994, and the Drug-Free Communities Act of 1997.[62] The Crime Control Act of 1990 (1) doubled the appropriations authorized for drug-law enforcement grants to states and local communities; (2) enhanced drug-control and education programs aimed at the nation's schools; (3) expanded specific drug-enforcement assistance to rural states; (4) expanded regulation of precursor chemicals used in the manufacture of illegal drugs; (5) sanctioned anabolic steroids under the Controlled Substances Act; (6) included provisions to enhance control over international money laundering; (7) created "drug-free school zones" by enhancing penalties for drug offenses occurring in close proximity to schools; and (8) enhanced the ability of federal agents to seize property used in drug transactions or purchased with drug proceeds.

The Violent Crime Control and Law Enforcement Act of 1994 provided $245 million for rural anticrime and drug efforts; set aside $1.6 billion for direct funding to localities around the country for anticrime efforts, including drug-treatment programs; budgeted $383 million for drug-treatment programs for state and federal prisoners; created a treatment schedule for all drug-addicted federal prisoners; required postconviction drug testing of all federal prisoners upon release; allocated $1 billion for drug court programs for nonviolent offenders with substance-abuse problems; and mandated new, stiff penalties for drug crimes committed by gangs. The act also tripled penalties for using children to deal drugs near schools and playgrounds and enhanced penalties for drug dealing in drug-free zones near playgrounds, school yards, video arcades, and youth centers. Finally, the law also expanded the federal death penalty to cover offenders involved in large-scale drug trafficking and mandated life imprisonment for criminals convicted of three violent felonies or drug offenses.

The Drug-Free Communities Act of 1997 provided support to local communities to reduce substance abuse among youth. It helped enhance broad-based community antidrug coalitions, which were previously shown to be successful at driving down casual drug use. Under the law, neighborhoods with successful antidrug programs became eligible to apply for federal grants to assist in their continued development.

The Investigation of Drug Abuse and Manufacturing

Investigation of the illegal production, transportation, sale, and use of controlled substances is a major police activity. Investigation of drug-manufacturing activities has given rise to an area of case law which supplements the plain view doctrine discussed in Chapter 7. Two legal concepts, abandonment and curtilage, have taken on special significance in drug investigations.

Abandonment refers to the fact that property, once it has been clearly thrown away or discarded, ceases to fall under Fourth Amendment protections against unreasonable search and seizure. The U.S. Supreme Court case of *California* v. *Greenwood*, (1988)[63] began when Officer Jenny Stracner of the Laguna Beach (California) Police Department arranged with a neighborhood trash collector to receive garbage collected at a suspect's residence. The refuse was later found to include items "indicative of narcotics use."[64] Based upon this evidence, Stracner applied for a search warrant, which was used in a search of the defendant's home. The search uncovered controlled substances, including cocaine and hashish. The defendant, Billy Greenwood, was arrested. Upon conviction, Greenwood appealed, arguing that the trash had been placed in opaque bags and could reasonably be expected to remain unopened until it was collected and disposed of. His appeal emphasized his right to privacy with respect to his trash.

The Supreme Court disagreed, saying that "[a]n expectation of privacy does not give rise to Fourth Amendment protection unless society is prepared to accept that expectation as objectively reasonable. . . . [I]t is common knowledge that plastic garbage bags left on or at the side of a public street are readily accessible to animals, children, scavengers, snoops, and other members of the public." Hence, the Court concluded, the property in question had been abandoned, and no reasonable expectation of privacy can attach to trash left for collection "in an area accessible to the public." The concept of abandonment extends beyond trash which is actively discarded. In *Abel* v. *U.S.* (1960),[65] for example, the Court found that the warrantless search of a motel room by an FBI agent immediately after it had been vacated was acceptable.

Curtilage, a concept which the Supreme Court clearly recognized in the case of *Oliver* v. *U.S.* (1984),[66] refers to the fact that household activity generally extends beyond the walls of a residence. People living in a house, for example, spend some of their time in their yard—an area which they probably think of as private and under the control of their household. Property within the curtilage of a residence has generally been accorded the same Fourth Amendment guarantees against search and seizure as areas within the walls of a house or an apartment. But just how far does the curtilage of a residence extend? Does it vary according to the type or location of the residence? Is it necessary for an area to be fenced for it to fall within residential curtilage?

A collateral area of concern is that of activity conducted in fields. The open fields doctrine began with the case of *Hester* v. *U.S.* (1924),[67] in which the Supreme Court held that law enforcement officers could search an open field without a warrant. The *Oliver* case extended that authority to include secluded and fenced fields posted with No Trespassing signs.

In *U.S.* v. *Dunn* (1987),[68] the U.S. Supreme Court considered a Houston-area defendant's claim that the space surrounding a barn, which was located approximately 50 yards from the edge of a fence surrounding a farmhouse, was protected against intrusion by the Fourth Amendment. The Court rejected the defendant's arguments and concluded that, even though an area may be fenced, it is not within the curtilage of a residence if it is sufficiently distant from the area of household activity which attends the residence.

Other, related decisions, have supported seizures based upon warrantless aerial observation of marijuana plants growing in the backyard of a defendant's home[69] and those

curtilage
- - - - - - - - - - - - - - -
In legal usage, the area surrounding a residence that can reasonably be said to be a part of the residence for Fourth Amendment purposes.

CJ Today Exhibit 15-1

[Drugs: What's in a Name?]

Drug names have been a source of confusion to many people attempting to grapple with the drug problem. A single drug may have a dozen or more names. Drugs may be identified according to brand name, generic name, street name, or psychoactive category.

Brand Name

The name given to a chemical substance by its manufacturer is the brand name. Brand names are registered and are often associated with trademarks. They identify a drug in the pharmaceutical marketplace and may not be used by other manufacturers. Psychoactive substances with no known medical application or experimental use are not produced by legitimate companies and have no brand name.

Generic Name

The chemical or other identifying name of a drug is the generic name. Generic names are often used by physicians in writing prescriptions because generic drugs are often less costly than brand-name drugs. Generic names are also used in most drug-abuse legislation at the federal and state levels to specify controlled substances. Generic names are sometimes applicable only to the psychoactive chemical substances in drugs and not to the "drugs" themselves. With marijuana,

for example, the chemical tetrahydrocannabinol, or THC, is the active substance.

Street Names

Street names are slang terms. Many of them originated with the pop culture of the 1960s, and others continue to be produced by modern-day drug subculture. Street names for cocaine, for example, include coke, flake, and snow; heroin is known as horse, smack, or H. Learn more about street names currently in use via **Web Extra! 15–5** at cjtoday.com.

Web EXTRA!

Psychoactive Category

Psychoactive drugs are categorized according to the effects they produce on the human mind. Narcotics, stimulants, depressants, and hallucinogens are typical psychoactive categories.

An Example

PCP and angel dust are the street names for a veterinary anesthetic marketed under the brand name Sernylan. Sernylan contains the psychoactive chemical phencyclidine, which is classified as a depressant under the Controlled Substances Act.

---

based upon naked-eye sightings from helicopters of the contents of a greenhouse.[70] The Court's reasoning in such cases is that flights within navigable airspace are common. Where no comprehensive efforts to secure privacy have been made, there can be no reasonable expectation of privacy—even within areas that might normally be considered curtilage. Were sophisticated surveillance techniques to be employed by law enforcement authorities, however—such as the use of drone aircraft, satellite, or infrared photography—the Court's decision would be in doubt because such devices extend beyond the realm of "normal flight."

The Most Common Drugs—and Who Is Using Them

The sale of illegal drugs is a $57 billion industry in the United States.[71] Some perspective can be gained on this figure by recognizing that Americans spend approximately $44 billion on alcohol products and another $37 billion on tobacco products annually.[72]

The National Household Survey on Drug Abuse (NHSDA), an annual publication of the federal Substance Abuse and Mental Health Services Administration (SAMHSA), estimates that 14 million Americans are "current" users of illegal drugs—defined as those who have used an illicit drug in the month preceding the survey.[73] Ten million people are estimated to be using marijuana, and 6 million of those are thought to be "frequent" marijuana users (defined as those who used the drug on at least 51 days during the preceding year). Around 1.75 million people are believed to use cocaine in various forms, and 608,000 are classified as "hard-core" cocaine addicts. Many users report using more than one drug, either singly or in combination, while the illegal use of inhalants, hallucinogens, and heroin and the nonmedical use of psychotherapeutics account for the remainder of the total number of reported users.

Of the 4 million estimated illicit drug users, 2.2% are 12 or 13 years old; 15.6% are 16 or 17 (which is the age range associated with the highest rate of illicit use); and 20% are 18 to 20. Rates of use decline with age, and only about 1% of those over age 50 who were surveyed reported current illicit drug use. The study also found that a total of 77 million Americans (37% of people aged 12 and older) had used an illegal drug at least once; 70 million were thought to be using marijuana, 23.5 million cocaine, 4 million crack cocaine, 2 million heroin, and 18 million hallucinogens. All these figures represent a considerable decline from 1979, the year in which the highest levels of drug abuse in the United States were reported (the number of adults estimated to be abusing drugs in 1979 was 24.3 million), although figures for recent years have shown a gradual increase in drug use (especially "occasional use"). As the Office of National Drug Control Policy points out, however, federal studies typically underestimate the number of hard-core drug abusers in the country because they fail to survey the homeless, prisoners, people living at colleges, active-duty military personnel, and those in mental and other institutions. ONDCP estimates that there are 2.1 million hard-core cocaine addicts and 600,000 heroin addicts in the country[74]—figures well above those provided by the survey. Read a summary of the latest findings from the National Household Survey on Drug Abuse via **Library Extra! 15–2** at cjtoday.com.

Another way to measure the size of the drug problem in America is to look at the dollars spent to combat it. In 1981, for example, total federal spending for all drug-control efforts, including enforcement activities, educational programs, and treatment, totaled $1.5 billion. Federal expenditures on drug-control activities stood at $16.7 billion in fiscal year 2000 and were expected to increase to $17.3 billion by 2003.[75] State budgetary allowances for drug-control activities, which are considerable, are not included in these figures.

A number of agencies report on the amount of various types of drugs which enter the country or are produced here. One such group, the National Narcotics Intelligence Consumers Committee (NNICC), was established in 1978 to coordinate the collection and analysis of foreign and domestic strategic drug-related intelligence.[76] Members of the NNICC include the DEA, the Federal Bureau of Investigation, the Central Intelligence Agency, the Internal Revenue Service, the Immigration and Naturalization Service, the Coast Guard, and other federal agencies charged with drug-law enforcement. NNICC and DEA data for each of the major drug categories are described in the paragraphs that follow. Learn more about the DEA via **Web Extra! 15–6** at cjtoday.com.

Michael Sullivan, left, and David Shull of San Francisco sharing a pipe of marijuana in a smoking lounge. Both men have AIDS, and smoking pot makes them feel better. In 1996, voters in California and Arizona passed ballot initiatives legalizing the use of marijuana for medical purposes when approved or prescribed by a doctor. In 2001, however, the U.S. Supreme Court invalidated all state medical-marijuana laws.

Fred Mertz

Marijuana

Marijuana, whose botanical name is *Cannabis sativa L.*, grows wild throughout most of the tropic and temperate regions of the world.[77] Marijuana commonly comes in loose form, as the ground leaves and seeds of the hemp plant. Also available to street-level users are stronger forms of the drug, such as sinsemilla (the flowers and the leaves of the female cannabis plant), hashish (the resinous secretions of the hemp plant), and hash oil (a chemically concentrated form of delta-9-tetrahydrocannabinol, or THC, the psychotropic agent in marijuana).

Marijuana is usually smoked, although it may be eaten or made into a "tea." A report by ONDCP found that the use of inhalants, such as spray paint and solvents, in combination with marijuana is growing in popularity.[78] Low doses of marijuana create restlessness and an increasing sense of well-being, followed by dreamy relaxation and a frequent craving for sweets.[79] Sensory perceptions may be heightened by the drug, while memory and rational thought are impaired (see Table 15–1). Marijuana's effects begin within a few minutes following use and may last for two to three hours.

Although marijuana has no officially sanctioned medical use, it may sometimes serve as a supplemental medication in cases of ongoing chemotherapy (where it seems to reduce nausea), glaucoma (where it may reduce pressure within the eye), anorexia and "AIDS wasting" (where it may increase appetite and lead to weight gain), and sleep disorders.[80] To support such use, voters in California and Arizona passed ballot initiatives in 1996 legalizing the use of marijuana for medical purposes when approved or prescribed by a doctor.

TABLE 15–1	**MAJOR CONTROLLED SUBSTANCES: THEIR USES AND EFFECTS**	
Substance	**Legitimate Use**	**Street Use**
Narcotics, including opium, morphine, heroin, codeine, Dilaudid	Pain relief, antidiarrheal, cough suppressant	Pleasure, euphoria, lack of concern, general feeling of well-being
Stimulants, including amphetamines, such as Dexedrine and Benzedrine, and other drugs like cocaine, crack, crank, methamphetamine, ice	Increased alertness, reduced fatigue, weight control	Produce excitability, feeling of competence and power
General depressants, including sedatives and tranquilizers, such as Nembutal, Seconal, Phenobarbital, Quaalude, Sopor, Valium, Librium, Thorazine, Equanil	Release from anxiety, mood elevation, treatment of psychological problems	In high doses to produce intoxication; also used to counter the effects of other drugs or in the self-treatment of withdrawal
Marijuana, including hashish, cannabis, sinsemilla, hashish oil	None fully recognized; possible use in treating nausea chemotherapy	Euphoria, relaxation, intoxication, time distortion, memory alteration, focused awareness
Hallucinogens, including LSD, mescaline, psilocybin, peyote, MDA	None	To produce hallucinations and distortions of reality
Inhalants, including nitrous oxide, gasoline, toluene, amyl nitrite, butyl nitrite	Some are used as medical sedatives	To produce a "rush" or sense of light-headedness
Anabolic steroids, including nandrolene, oxandrolene, oxymetholone, stanozolol	Weight gain; treatment of anemia, breast cancer, angioedema	To build muscle mass and increase strength (in weight lifters, professional athletes, others)

Note: Each drug may have a variety of effects or may produce different effects on individual users. Drugs used in combination may have unpredictable effects.

Source: Adapted from Drug Enforcement Administration, *Drugs of Abuse* (Washington, D.C.: U.S. Department of Justice, 1999); and U.S. Pharmacopeial Convention, *Drug Information*, 15th ed. (Rockville, MD: USP, 1995).

California's medical marijuana law was overturned, however, by a unanimous U.S. Supreme Court in the 2001 case of *U.S.* v. *Oakland Cannabis Buyer's Cooperative*.[81] In that case, the Court found that the activities of the Oakland (California) Cannabis Buyers' Cooperative, which distributed marijuana to qualified patients for medical purposes, were in violation of the U.S. Controlled Substances Act—regardless of what state law said. The Court also held that there is no medical necessity exception to the federal act's prohibitions on manufacturing and distributing marijuana. "Under any conception of legal necessity," said the justices, "the defense [of medical necessity] cannot succeed when the legislature itself has made a determination of values."[82]

Most illicit marijuana users, however, do not use cannabis for medical purposes. The majority of users are young people, many younger than 20 years old. In 2000, for example, the U.S. Department of Health and Human Services reported that past year use of marijuana was 15.6% for eighth graders, 32.2% for tenth graders, and 36.5% for twelfth graders.[83]

Intelligence shows that domestic production accounts for about 19% of all marijuana in the United States. Most marijuana brought into the United States comes from Mexico, Jamaica, and Colombia.[84] Of all the marijuana entering the country or produced domestically, approximately one-quarter, or 4,000 metric tons, is seized or lost in transit.[85]

Cocaine

Cocaine (cocaine hydrochloride [HCL]) is the most potent central nervous system stimulant of natural origin.[86] Cocaine is extracted from the leaves of the coca plant (whose botanical name is *Erythroxylon coca*). Since ancient times, the drug has been used by native Indians throughout the highlands of Central and South America, who chew the leaves of the coca plant to overcome altitude sickness and to sustain the high levels of physical energy needed for strenuous mountain farming.

Cocaine has some medical value as a topical anesthetic for use on sensitive tissues, such as the eyes and mucous membranes. Throughout the early twentieth century, physicians valued cocaine for its ability to anesthetize tissue while simultaneously constricting blood vessels and reducing bleeding. Recently, more effective products have replaced cocaine in many medical applications.

A recent report by ONDCP classifies cocaine users into three groups: "(1) the younger, often minority crack user; (2) the older injector who is combining cocaine HCL with heroin in a speedball; and (3) the older, more affluent user who is snorting cocaine HCL."[87] Cocaine generally reaches the United States in the form of a much-processed white crystalline powder. It is often diluted with a variety of other ingredients, including sugar and anesthetics such as lidocaine. Dilution allows sellers to reap high profits from small amounts of the drug.

Cocaine produces intense psychological effects, including a sense of exhilaration, superabundant energy, hyperactivity, and extended wakefulness.[88] Irritability and apprehension may be unwanted side effects. Excessive doses may cause seizures and death from heart failure, cerebral hemorrhage, and respiratory collapse. Some studies show that repeated use of cocaine may heighten sensitivity to these toxic side effects of the drug.[89]

NNICC data indicate that cocaine has become the country's most dangerous commonly used drug. During a recent year, nearly 100,000 hospital emergencies involving cocaine abuse were reported across the country.[90] In 1998, at the time of the NNICC report, cocaine was available in all major American metropolitan areas and in most small communities. The cocaine derivative crack, manufactured by numerous street-level laboratories, was available primarily in large urban areas. A DEA survey in the mid-1990s, however, found that "crack dealers are expanding their markets to target potential users in small towns and rural areas across the United States" because "crack distribution and use appears to have reached the saturation point in large urban areas."[91] The Federal Drug Seizure System reports the seizure of around 300,000 pounds of cocaine throughout the United States annually.[92]

Most cocaine enters the United States from Peru, Bolivia, or Colombia. Together, these three countries have an estimated annual production capability of around 555 tons of pure cocaine.[93] During the 1980s, most cocaine coming into the United States was controlled by the Medellín Cartel, based in Medellín, Colombia. Multinational counterdrug efforts had crippled the cartel by the start of the 1990s, however, and the Cali Cartel (based in Cali, Colombia), a loose organization of five semi-independent trafficking organizations, took over as the major illegal supplier of cocaine to this country. Arrests of the Cali Cartel's top

We cannot define what victory is. We cannot tell you which objectives to look at. We can only try to have policymakers at all levels of government working together to do what is right for this nation: reduce the impact of drug abuse and increase the strength of our families and communities. If we do that, we may still have a drug use issue, but we will have a healthier nation that can absorb that issue, that will reduce the harm of drug abuse.

—Ross Deck

leaders, Gilberto Rodriguez and his brother, Miguel, however, are said to have sounded the death knell for what may have been the world's most successful drug-trafficking organization ever.[94]

Heroin

Classified as a narcotic, heroin is a derivative of opium—itself the product of the milky fluid found in the flowering poppy plant *(Papaver somniferum)*. Opium poppies have been grown in the Mediterranean region since 300 B.C.[95] and are now produced in many other parts of the world as well. Although heroin is not used medicinally in this country, many of the substances to which it is chemically related—such as morphine, codeine, hydrocodone, naloxone, and oxymorphone—do have important medical uses as pain relievers.

Heroin is a highly seductive and addictive drug which, when smoked, injected underneath the skin ("skin popping"), or shot directly into the bloodstream ("mainlining"), produces euphoria. Because tolerance for the drug increases with use, larger and larger doses of heroin must be injected to achieve the pleasurable effects desired by addicts. Heroin deprivation causes withdrawal symptoms which initially include watery eyes, runny nose, yawning, and perspiration. Further deprivation results in restlessness, irritability, insomnia, tremors, nausea, and vomiting. Stomach cramps, diarrhea, chills, and other flulike symptoms are also common. Most withdrawal symptoms disappear within seven to ten days[96] or when the drug is readministered.

Street-level heroin varies widely in purity. It is often cut with powdered milk, food coloring, cocoa, or brown sugar. Most heroin sold in the United States is only 5% pure.[97] Because of dosage uncertainties, overdosing is a common problem for addicts. Mild overdoses produce lethargy and stupor. Larger doses may cause convulsions, coma, and death. Other risks, including infectious hepatitis and AIDS, are associated with using contaminated needles from other users. The National Institute on Drug Abuse (NIDA) notes that the number of intravenous drug users with AIDS is doubling every 14 to 16 months.[98] The Centers for Disease Control and Prevention (CDC) estimates that almost one-third of AIDS cases are associated with intravenous (IV) drug use.[99]

Heroin abuse has remained fairly constant over the past few decades. Some indicators point to an increased availability of heroin in the last few years.[100] Street-level heroin prices have declined in recent years, while nationwide heroin-related emergency room admissions have reached almost 40,000 per year.

A heroin addict shooting up. The sale and consumption of illicit drugs constitute a multibillion-dollar industry in the United States.

Alan Mercer, Stock Boston

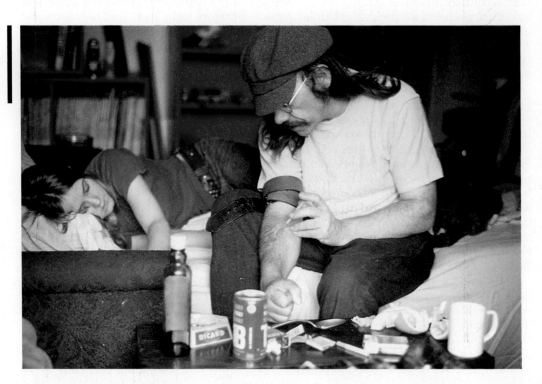

Most heroin in the United States comes from South America, Southwest Asia (Afghanistan, Pakistan, and Iran), Southeast Asia (Burma, Laos, and Thailand), and Mexico. According to data from the Heroin Signature Program (HSP), which uses chemical analysis of the trace elements in heroin supplies to identify source countries, 65% of all heroin entering the United States comes from South America.[101] The Federal Drug Seizure System reports the seizure of approximately 2,500 pounds of heroin throughout the United States annually.[102]

Evidence indicates that the heroin abuse picture is changing. Although older users still dominate heroin markets in all parts of the country,[103] increasing numbers of non-inner-city young users (under 30 years of age) are turning to the drug. Additionally, because high-purity powdered heroin is widely available in most parts of the country, new users seem to be experimenting with heroin inhalation, which often appears to lead to injection as addiction progresses. Treatment programs report that the typical heroin user is male, is over 30 years old, and has been in treatment previously.[104] Alcohol, cocaine, and marijuana remain concurrent problems for heroin users in treatment.

> We cannot go into tomorrow with the same formulas that are failing today. We must not blindly add to the body count and the terrible cost of the War on Drugs, only to learn . . . 30 years from now, that what we've been doing is wrong, terribly wrong.
>
> —Walter Cronkite

Club Drugs

In 1997, DEA officials recommended that the "date rape drug" Rohypnol (also discussed in Chapters 2 and 4) be added to the list of Schedule I controlled substances. Rohypnol is a powerful sedative manufactured by Hoffmann-LaRoche Pharmaceuticals.[105] Rohypnol is among the new "club drugs" that became popular in the mid- to late-1990s. **Club drug** is a general term used to refer primarily to synthetic psychoactive substances often found at nightclubs, bars, and "raves" (all-night dance parties). In addition to Rohypnol, club drugs include GHB, GBL, MDMA (ecstasy), methamphetamine (meth), Ketamine, and PCP. According to the Drug Enforcement Administration, the use of club drugs is increasing rapidly (see Figure 15–3).

A few years ago, the growing use of Rohypnol at fraternity parties, raves, bars, and dance clubs gave rise to the phrase *chemically-assisted date rape*, a term now generically applied to rapes in which sexual predators use drugs to incapacitate unsuspecting victims. Rohypnol (a brand name for Flunitrazepam) is a member of the benzodiazepine family of depressants and is legally prescribed in 64 countries for insomnia and as a preoperative anesthetic. Seven to 10 times more powerful than Valium, Rohypnol has become popular with some college students and with "young men [who] put doses of Rohypnol in women's drinks without their consent in order to lower their inhibitions."[106] Available on the black market, it dissolves easily in drinks and can leave anyone who unknowingly consumes it unconscious for hours, making them vulnerable to sexual assault. The drug is variously known as *ropies, roche, ruffles, roofies,* and *rophies* on the street.

club drug

A synthetic psychoactive substance often found at nightclubs, bars, "raves," and dance parties. Club drugs include MDMA (ecstasy), ketamine, methamphetamine (meth), GBL, PCP, GHB, and Rohypnol.

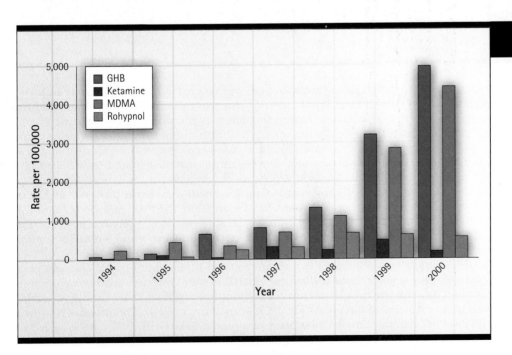

FIGURE 15–3

Estimated emergency room mentions for selected club drugs, 1994–2000.

Source: Drug Abuse Warning Network (DAWN).

CJ Today News

[Club Drugs Sending More Young People to Hospitals]

Club drugs, including Ecstasy and GHB, are sending increasing numbers of young people to the hospital with toxic reactions and overdoses, emergency-room data released Tuesday shows.

Emergency rooms in 21 metropolitan areas tracked by the Drug Abuse Warning Network reported 4,511 emergency visits involving Ecstasy in 2000. That's a 58% increase over 1999.

The network, part of a federal agency that tracks hospital admissions, also reported 4,969 visits involving the "date-rape drug" GHB, which is a 56% increase over the previous year's 3,178 cases.

Club drugs still account for only a fraction of emergency-room visits. However, the numbers indicate the drugs are becoming more widespread.

Club-drug users began arriving at emergency rooms in 1994. The drugs, including Ecstasy, GHB, an anesthetic called Ketamine and the so-called date-rape drug, Rohypnol, had grown popular at all-night rave parties and in dance clubs. That year, emergency rooms reported 56 visits for GHB and 253 visits for Ecstasy.

People ages 25 and younger account for almost a third of drug emergencies, the data show. Their share is much higher for club-drug emergencies: People 25 and younger make up 80% of Ecstasy emergencies and 60% of those involving GHB.

"We are concerned about the continued increase of club drugs among young people, which seems to be contributing to the overall increase of young people ending up in emergency rooms," says Mark Weber, spokesman for the Substance Abuse and Mental Health Services Administration in Rockville, Md., which collects the data from 466 hospitals.

For the latest in crime and justice news, visit the Talk Justice news feed at http://www.crimenews.info.

A fire juggler lighting up the night at a rave party attended by thousands in the French village of Paule, Brittany. Rave parties typically involve abundant drugs, particularly the designer drug ecstasy.

AP/Wide World Photos

Source: Donna Leinwand, "Club Drugs Sending More Young People to Hospitals," *USA Today,* July 25, 2001, p. 3A.
© 2001, *USA Today.* Reprinted with permission.

Penalties for trafficking in flunitrazepam were increased under the Drug-Induced Rape Prevention and Punishment Act of 1996,[107] effectively placing it into a Schedule I-type category for sentencing purposes. Under the act, it is a crime to give someone a controlled substance without the person's knowledge and with intent to commit a violent crime.

GHB (gamma-hydroxybutyrate), another date rape drug, has effects similar to Rohypnol. GHB, a central nervous system depressant, is now designated as a Schedule I drug but was once sold in health food stores as a performance enhancer for use by bodybuilders. Rumors that GHB stimulates muscle growth were never proven. The intoxicating effects of GHB, however, soon became obvious. In 1990, the Food and Drug Administration (FDA) banned the use of GHB except under the supervision of a physician. In 2001, federal sentencing guideline changes removed the upper limit, or "cap," on GHB sentences in cases where large amounts of the drug were sold or distributed.[108]

GBL (gamma-butyrolactone) is a chemical used in many industrial cleaners and is the precursor chemical for the manufacture of GHB. Several Internet businesses offer kits that contain GBL and the proper amount of sodium hydroxide or potassium hydroxide, along with litmus paper and directions for the manufacture of GHB. The process is quite simple and does not require complex laboratory equipment. Like GHB, GBL can be added to water and is nearly undetectable. GBL is synthesized by the body to produce GHB. As a consequence, some users drink small quantities of unmodified GBL. This often causes a severe physical reaction, usually vomiting. GBL increases the effects of alcohol and can cause respiratory distress, seizure, coma, and death.

MDMA (ecstasy), the most popular of the club drugs, is primarily manufactured in and trafficked from Europe. DEA reports indicate widespread abuse of this drug within virtually every city in the United States. Estimates from the Drug Abuse Warning Network (DAWN) show that hospital emergency department mentions for MDMA quadrupled over three years, from 1,143 in 1998 to 4,511 in 2000.[109] Although it is primarily found in urban settings, abuse of this substance also has been noted in rural communities. Prices in the United States generally range from $20 to $30 per dosage unit; however, prices as high as $50 per dosage unit have been reported in Miami. MDMA (3, 4-methylenedioxymethamphetamine) is a synthetic, psychoactive substance possessing stimulant and mild hallucinogenic properties. Known as the "hug drug" or the "feel good drug," it reduces inhibitions, produces feelings of empathy for others, eliminates anxiety, and produces extreme relaxation. In addition to chemical stimulation, the drug reportedly suppresses the need to eat, drink, or sleep. This enables club goers to endure all-night and sometimes two- to three-day parties. MDMA is taken orally, usually in tablet form, and its effects last approximately four to six hours. Often taken in conjunction with alcohol, the drug destroys both dopamine and serotonin cells in the brain. When taken at raves, the drug often leads to severe dehydration and heatstroke, since it has the effect of "short-circuiting" the body's temperature signals to the brain. An MDMA overdose is characterized by a rapid heartbeat, high blood pressure, faintness, muscle cramping, panic attacks, and, in more severe cases, seizures or loss of consciousness. One of the side effects of the drug is jaw muscle tension and teeth grinding. As a consequence, MDMA users will often use pacifiers to help relieve the tension. The most critical, life-threatening response to MDMA is hyperthermia or excessive body heat. Many rave clubs now have cooling centers or cold showers designed to allow participants to lower their body temperatures. MDMA is a Schedule I drug under the Controlled Substances Act (CSA).

The Ecstasy Anti-Proliferation Act of 2000[110] directed the U.S. Sentencing Commission to increase penalties for the manufacture, importation, exportation, and trafficking of MDMA. Under resulting emergency amendments to the U.S. Sentencing Guidelines, MDMA trafficking became a crime with serious consequences. As a result of this penalty enhancement, which became permanent in 2001, a violator convicted of trafficking 200 grams of MDMA (approximately 800 tablets) can receive a five-year prison sentence.

Another designer drug that has been attracting the attention of law enforcement agencies is methamphetamine. Known on the street as *speed, chalk, meth, crank,* and *fire,* methamphetamine is a stimulant drug chemically related to other amphetamines (like MDMA) but with stronger effects on the central nervous system. Methamphetamine is taken in pill form or is used in powdered form by snorting or injecting.[111] Crystallized methamphetamine (known as *ice, crystal,* or *glass*) is a smokable and still more powerful form of the drug. Effects of methamphetamine use include increased heart rate and blood pressure, increased wakefulness, insomnia, increased physical activity, decreased appetite, and anxiety, paranoia, or violent behavior. The drug is easily made in simple home "laboratories" from readily available chemicals, and recipes describing how to produce the substance circulate on the Internet. Methamphetamine appeals to the abuser because it increases the body's metabolism, produces euphoria and alertness, and gives the user a sense of increased energy. Methamphetamine, an increasingly popular drug at raves, is not physically addictive but can be psychologically addictive. High doses or chronic use of the drug increases nervousness, irritability, and paranoia.

Ketamine (known as *K, special K,* and *cat valium*), the last of the club drugs discussed here, produces effects that include mild intoxication, hallucinations, delirium, catatonia, and amnesia. Low doses of the drug create an experience called *K-Land,* a mellow, colorful "wonder world." Higher doses produce an effect referred to as *K-Hole,* an "out-of-body," or "near-death" experience. Use of the drug can cause delirium, amnesia, depression, long-term memory and cognitive difficulties, and fatal respiratory problems.[112]

Marketed as a dissociative general anesthetic for human and veterinary use, the only known street source of ketamine is diverted pharmaceutical products. A significant number of veterinary clinics are being robbed specifically for their ketamine stock. Ketamine liquid can be injected, applied to smokable material, or consumed in drinks. The powdered form is made by allowing the solvent to evaporate, leaving a white or slightly off-white powder that, once pulverized, looks very similar to cocaine. The powder can be put into drinks, smoked, or injected. Learn more about club drugs at **Web Extra! 15-7,** and discover more about drug abuse among young people via **Library Extra! 15-3** at cjtoday.com.

> If we fail, it means that what we have been saying is true—that drugs may represent to our civilization, to many of our cities, a life-or-death situation. If we don't get control of this drug problem, we may not go into the twenty-first century intact.
>
> —William Bennett,
> the first "Drug Czar"

Drugs and Crime

The drug problem in the United States is not simply one of drug use. The manufacture, possession, sale, and use of controlled substances are related to a variety of criminal activities and produce other large-scale social problems. Some of these problems are examined on the next few pages.

The link between drugs and crime has at least three dimensions: (1) the possession, use, or sale of controlled substances, which directly violates antidrug laws; (2) crimes committed by drug users to obtain more drugs, or crimes committed by users whose judgment is altered by drugs; and (3) organized criminal activities in support of the drug trade and associated money-laundering activities.

As Figure 15–4 shows, about 900,000 adults over the age of 18 were arrested for drug-law violations (excluding alcohol) in the United States in 2000.[113] Eighty-one percent of all arrests nationally were for possession of controlled substances; the remainder were for sale, or manufacture.[114] Arrests for heroin or cocaine possession accounted for 24.2% of all possession arrests, while 40.9% of such arrests were for marijuana possession.[115] Possession of PCP, LSD, amphetamines, and tranquilizers accounted for only a relatively small number of arrests.

After a significant decline from 1989 to 1992, the number of people arrested for drug-law violations increased from 1993 to 1996 and has remained relatively stable ever since. Moreover, as the data at the start of this chapter indicate, much of the overcrowding in federal and state prisons today is due to an accompanying increase in convictions for drug-law violations.

Drugs and crime are linked in other ways, as well. A report by the Office for National Drug Control Policy, for example, claims that 5.2% of all homicides are related to narcotic drug-law violations.[116] "Reducing drug use will have a direct and positive impact on reducing criminal activity," says ONDCP. "Drug users often commit criminal offenses, such as theft and prostitution, to support an existing drug habit."

A National Institute of Justice (NIJ) study of 201 heroin users in Central and East Harlem (New York City) found that *each* daily user committed on average about 1,400 crimes per year. Of these offenses, 1,116 were directly drug related, involving primarily drug sales and use.[117] Another 75 were relatively minor crimes, such as shoplifting, but the remaining 209 offenses committed by each user involved relatively serious violations of the law, such as robbery, burglary, theft, forgery, fraud, and the fencing of stolen goods. Another study, which examined the daily activities of 354 Baltimore heroin addicts over a nine-year period, found that they had committed a total of nearly 750,000 criminal offenses.[118]

A comprehensive effort designed to gauge the degree of drug use among criminal offenders is the NIJ's Arrestee Drug Abuse Monitoring program (ADAM). ADAM utilizes anony-

FIGURE 15–4

Adult arrests for drug-law violations, 1985–2000.

Source: Federal Bureau of Investigation, *Crime in the United States* (Washington, D.C.: U.S. Government Printing Office, various years).

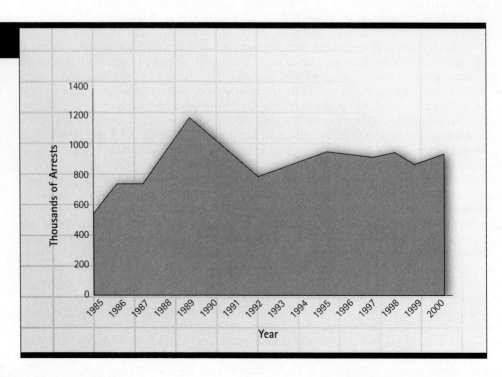

mous interviews and voluntary biological specimens from randomly selected male and female arrestees in 75 cities across the country. The median percentage of sampled arrestees testing positive for any drug, including marijuana (but not alcohol) in selected cities during 2000 was 65%.[119] Cocaine was the most widely abused drug among arrestees in most cities, with marijuana, methamphetamines, and heroin also being used frequently.

Two cautions should be held in mind when interpreting ADAM data. First, although the tendency among some who view the statistics is to conclude that drug use *causes* crime, it could be that both crime and drug use are the result of some other factor, such as poverty or socialization. Second, given the relatively high number of drug arrests, it is not entirely surprising that many arrestees have drugs in their systems, and many of those whose arrests were reported by ADAM were arrested for drug sales, possession, or use. Read the latest ADAM report at **Library Extra! 15–4,** and learn more about the dynamics of the drug-crime relationship via **Library Extra! 15–5** at cjtoday.com.

Money Laundering

Cash can flow into the hands of dealers in such huge amounts that it can be difficult for them to spend. Few people buy houses, cars, and other big-ticket items with cash, and cash transactions arouse suspicion. **Money laundering** is the name given to the process used by drug dealers to hide the source of their revenues to avoid taxes and to disguise the financial evidence of drug dealing.[120] Drug profits are laundered by converting them into other assets, such as real estate, stocks and bonds, racehorses, diamonds, gold, and other valuables. The NNICC says that millions of dollars in drug monies are laundered through commercial banks and other financial institutions each year, with major money-laundering operations flourishing in South Florida and Los Angeles.[121] Other estimates put the laundered amount as high as $300 billion.[122] The Police Executive Research Forum (PERF) estimates that profits in excess of $100 billion a year are generated in the United States through narcotics trafficking and related underworld activities.[123] PERF also points out that successful money laundering can be accomplished only with the cooperation of lawyers, accountants, stockbrokers, realtors, and other investment advisers.[124]

In the late 1980s, U.S. Customs agents in Tampa, Florida, arrested seven high-level banking executives who had been lured back into U.S. jurisdiction from other countries.[125] "The Cash Cleaners," as the men were dubbed, were arrested after allegedly laundering $14 million for narcotics agents in a "sting" operation. Estimates were that many times that amount had been laundered for real criminals.[126] Indictments named 80 individuals and the first banking company ever charged with money laundering under U.S. law. The company, Bank of Credit and Commerce International (BCCI), based in Luxembourg, was the seventh largest privately owned financial institution in the world.[127] BCCI was closed in 1991 by international banking regulators.

In an effort to catch money launderers, U.S. banking law requires financial institutions to report deposits in excess of $10,000. Traffickers attempt to avoid the law through two techniques known as *smurfing* and *structuring.*[128] Smurfers repeatedly purchase bank checks in denominations of less than $10,000, which are then sent to accomplices in other parts of the country, who deposit them in existing accounts. Once the checks have cleared, the funds are transferred to other banks or moved out of the country. Structuring is very similar and involves cash deposits to bank accounts in amounts of less than $10,000 at a time. After accounts are established, the money is withdrawn and deposited in increments elsewhere, making it difficult to trace. Countries which have secrecy laws protecting depositors are favorites for drug traffickers. Among them are Switzerland, Panama, Hong Kong, the United Arab Emirates, and the Bahamas.[129]

In 1994 in the case of *Ratzlaf* v. *U.S.,*[130] the U.S. Supreme Court made the task of catching money launderers more difficult. The Court ruled that no one can be convicted of trying to evade bank-reporting requirements unless authorities can prove that offenders knew they were violating the law.

In 2001, in an effort to enhance the amount of information received by federal regulators from banks about potential money-laundering activities, Congress passed the International Money Laundering Abatement and Anti-Terrorist Financing Act of 2001, which is Title III of the USA PATRIOT Act. The law requires banks to make considerable effort in determining the source of monies held in individual overseas accounts and provides for sanctions to be placed on nations that hinder this reporting.

Although federal law prohibits the laundering of money, relatively few states have strict laws against the practice. As a consequence, many local enforcement agencies are reluctant

money laundering

The process of converting illegally earned assets, originating as cash, to one or more alternative forms to conceal such incriminating factors as illegal origin and true ownership.[iv]

to investigate money-laundering activities in their jurisdictions. To counteract this reluctance and to facilitate interagency cooperation, the federal government created the Financial Crimes Enforcement Network (FINCEN). You can access the FINCEN home page via **Web Extra! 15–8** at cjtoday.com.

Narcoterrorism

Some authors have identified a link between major drug traffickers and terrorist groups.[131] A number of South American traffickers appear especially willing to finance the activities of terrorist groups as a way of purchasing protection for themselves and their operations. The insurgents with whom they deal have their own political agendas, including the disruption of society, the overthrow of constitutional governments, and the spread of radical political ideas. In the 1980s, for example, the Colombian government became involved in a civil war between the constitutionally elected government, on the one hand, and armed representatives of the Medellin, Cali, and Bogotá drug cartels, on the other. While the government sought to close down drug laboratories and money-laundering operations, the cartels threatened to topple the government and targeted opposing judges, newspaper editors, and government officials for assassination. By 1990, Colombian cartels had murdered 11 Colombian Supreme Court justices, over 30 other judges, two powerful newspaper editors, the country's attorney general, and hundreds of Colombian national police officers and had forced the resignation of the minister of justice.[132] In 1993, in an attempt to hide criminal activities behind a political facade, Colombian narcotics kingpin Pablo Emilio Escobar-Gaviria created an armed antigovernment revolutionary group called the Antioquian Rebellion. During the last six months of 1992, Escobar assassins killed more than 50 of the country's police officers; the drug kingpin was himself shot to death by government forces in December 1993.

narcoterrorism

━ ━ ━ ━ ━ ━ ━ ━ ━ ━ ━ ━ ━ ━

A political alliance between terrorist organizations and drug-supplying cartels. The cartels provide financing for the terrorists, who in turn provide quasi-military protection to the drug dealers.

The link between drug traffickers and insurgents has been termed **narcoterrorism**.[133] Narcoterrorism, simply defined, is the involvement of terrorist organizations and insurgent groups in the trafficking of narcotics.[134] The relationship which exists between terrorist organizations and drug traffickers is mutually beneficial. Insurgents derive financial benefits from their supporting role in drug trafficking, while the traffickers themselves receive protection and benefit from the use of terrorist tactics against foes and competitors.

The first documented instance of an insurgent force financed, at least in part, with drug money, came to light during an investigation of the virulent anti-Castro Omega 7 group in

"Drug loot" confiscated in a joint NYPD-DEA operation. The cash take from illegal drug sales must be laundered before it can enter the flow of legitimate transactions.

Nola Tully, CORBIS/Sygma

the early 1980s.[135] Clear-cut evidence of modern narcoterrorism, however, is difficult to obtain. Contemporary insurgent organizations with links to drug dealers probably include the 19th of April Movement (M-19) operating in Colombia, Sendero Luminoso (shining path) of Peru, the Revolutionary Armed Forces of Colombia, and the large Farabundo Marti National Liberation Front (FMLN), which has long sought to overthrow the elected government of El Salvador.[136]

Narcoterrorism raises a number of questions. James Inciardi summarizes them as follows:[137]

- What is the full threat posed by narcoterrorism?
- How should narcoterrorism be dealt with?
- Is narcoterrorism a law enforcement problem or a military one?
- How might narcoterrorism be affected by changes in official U.S. policy toward drugs and drug use?
- Is the international drug trade being used as a tool by anti-U.S. and other interests to undermine Western democracies in a calculated way?

Unfortunately, in the opinion of some experts, the United States is ill-prepared to combat this type of international organized crime. Testifying before the Senate's Foreign Relations Subcommittee on Terrorism, Narcotics, and International Operations, William J. Olson, a Senior Fellow at the National Strategy Information Center, told Congress that more than $1 trillion (equivalent to one-sixth of the U.S. gross national product) is generated yearly by organized criminal activities like those associated with narcoterrorism. "We must recognize that the rules of the crime game have changed," said Olson. "International criminal organizations are challenging governments, permeating societies. They're running roughshod over weak institutions and exploiting gaps in the U.S. and international response. They have the upper hand at the moment and they know it," he said.[138] Other experts testified that a comprehensive national strategy—one which goes far beyond law enforcement and criminal prosecution to include diplomacy and organized international efforts—is needed to combat international organized criminal enterprises before they can co-opt global markets and worldwide financial institutions.

Solving the Drug Problem

American drug-control strategies seem caught in a kind of limbo between conservative approaches advocating supply reduction through strict enforcement and interdiction, and innovative strategies proposing demand reduction through education, treatment, and counseling. In 2000, the White House Office of National Drug Control Policy released its new *National Drug Control Strategy*,[139] a yearly publication outlining the current drug-abuse situation in the United States and detailing a strategy intended to guide the nation's criminal justice agencies in the continuing battle against drugs. The 2000 *National Drug Control Strategy* set as its "number one goal" helping "the nation's sixty-eight million children reject drugs, alcohol and tobacco." A major portion of the strategy was built upon a $2 billion five-year federal antidrug media campaign, which is discussed in more detail later in this chapter.

Although the new federal strategy's primary focus is on education and prevention, the White House report maintains that "no single solution can suffice to deal with the multifaceted challenge that drug abuse represents." Hence, the strategy also "views law enforcement as essential to reducing drug use in the United States" and sees policing as the first line of defense against drug trafficking. The strategy "stresses the need to protect borders from drug incursion and to cut drug supply more effectively in domestic communities," seeks to curtail illegal drug trafficking via the interdiction of illicit drugs, "focuses on supply-reduction operations at the source," and "supports international efforts to curtail drug production and trafficking." Read the latest version of the *National Drug Control Strategy* in its entirety at **Library Extra! 15–6** at cjtoday.com.

Politics aside, six general types of strategies can be identified among the many methods proposed for attacking the drug problem: (1) strict enforcement, (2) asset forfeiture, (3) interdiction, (4) crop control, (5) education and treatment, and (6) legalization and decriminalization. Each of these strategies is discussed in the following pages.

The 11th Commandment: Thou shalt not end the war on drugs.

—Anonymous

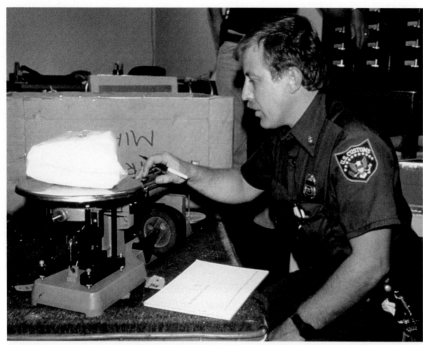

U.S. Customs officers with seized cocaine. Lower photo: Officer Rick Dallent shows how four tons of packaged cocaine were hidden in hardwood boards designed for picnic tables and shipped from Honduras to Florida.

Bob Sherman; UPI, CORBIS

Strict Enforcement

Trafficking in controlled substances is, of course, an illegal activity in the United States—and has been for a long time. Conservative politicians generally opt for a strict program of antidrug law enforcement and costly drug sentences, with the goal of removing dealers from the streets, disrupting supply lines, and eliminating sources of supply. Unfortunately, legal prohibitions appear to have done little to discourage widespread drug abuse. Those who look to strict law enforcement as a primary drug-control strategy usually stress the need for secure borders, drug testing to identify users, and stiff penalties to discourage others from drug involvement. The U.S. Coast Guard policy of "zero tolerance," for example, which was highly touted in the late 1980s, led to widely publicized seizures of multimillion-dollar vessels when even small amounts of drugs (probably carried aboard by members of the crew) were found.

But strict enforcement measures may be only a stopgap strategy and may eventually lead to greater long-term problems. As James Q. Wilson observes, "It is not clear that enforcing the laws against drug use would reduce crime. On the contrary, crime may be caused by such enforcement because it keeps drug prices higher than they would otherwise be."[140]

Some U.S. enforcement strategies attempt to enlist the help of foreign officials. Because drug exports represent extremely lucrative sources of revenue, however, and may even be thought of as valuable "foreign trade" by the governments of some of the world's major drug-producing nations, effective international antidrug cooperation is hard to come by. In 1991, for example, partly in response to pressures from cocaine-producing cartels within the country, Colombia outlawed the extradition of Colombian citizens for any purpose—making the extradition and trial of Colombian cocaine kingpins impossible. Compounding the problem, the DEA says, "the unprecedented economic, political, and social power and influence wielded by [cocaine] kingpins inside Colombia make it difficult to bring these drug lords to justice in their own country."[141]

Asset Forfeiture

Forfeiture, an enforcement strategy that federal statutes and some state laws support, bears special mention. Antidrug forfeiture statutes authorize judges to seize "all monies,

forfeiture

The authorized seizure of money, negotiable instruments, securities, or other things of value. Under federal antidrug laws, judicial representatives are authorized to seize all cash, negotiable instruments, securities, or other things of value furnished or intended to be furnished by any person in exchange for a controlled substance, as well as all proceeds traceable to such an exchange.

negotiable instruments, securities, or other things of value furnished or intended to be furnished by any person in exchange for a controlled substance . . . [and] all proceeds traceable to such an exchange."[142] Forfeiture statutes are based upon the relation-back doctrine. The relation-back doctrine assumes that because the government's right to illicit proceeds relates back to the time they are generated, anything acquired through the expenditure of those proceeds also belongs to the government.[143]

The first federal laws to authorize forfeiture as a criminal sanction were passed in 1970. They were the Continuing Criminal Enterprise (CCE) statute and the Organized Crime Control Act. A section of the Organized Crime Control Act known as the **Racketeer Influenced and Corrupt Organizations (RICO)** statute was designed to prevent criminal infiltration of legitimate businesses and has been extensively applied in federal drug-smuggling cases. In 1978, Congress authorized civil forfeiture of any assets acquired through narcotics trafficking in violation of federal law. Many states modeled their own legislation after federal law and now have similar statutes.

The newer civil statutes have the advantage of being relatively easy to enforce. Civil forfeiture requires proof only by a preponderance of the evidence, rather than proof beyond a reasonable doubt, as in criminal prosecution. In civil proceedings based upon federal statutes, there is no need to trace the proceeds in question to a particular narcotics transaction. It is enough to link them to narcotics trafficking generally.[144]

Forfeiture amounts can be huge. In one 15-month period, for example, the South Florida–Caribbean Task Force, composed of police agencies from the federal, state, and local levels, seized $47 million in airplanes, vehicles, weapons, cash, and real estate.[145] In a single investigation involving two brothers convicted of heroin smuggling, the federal government seized a shopping center, three gasoline stations, and seven homes worth over $20 million in New York City.[146]

A 1991 Virginia forfeiture case may hold special interest for college and university students. In March of that year, federal agents seized three University of Virginia fraternity houses and indicted 12 students on charges of drug distribution. The 12 were allegedly involved in a series of small sales of illegal drugs to undercover agents over the months preceding the seizure.[147] The action was part of an effort by law enforcement agencies to counter charges that enforcement activities had been focused only on inner-city areas. Following the arrests, E. Montgomery Tucker, U.S. Attorney for the Western District of Virginia, said, "[These arrests show] there are no safe havens, no safe places, to conduct illegal drug trafficking." Fraternity members were allowed to return to the houses, which are now owned by the federal government.

Although almost all states now have forfeiture statutes, prosecutions built upon them have met with less success than prosecutions based on federal law. The Police Executive Research Forum attributes the difference to three causes: (1) the fact that federal law is more favorable to prosecutors than most state laws, (2) the greater resources of the federal government, and (3) the difficulties imposed by statutory requirements that illegal proceeds be traced to narcotics trafficking.[148]

In 1993, in *U.S. v. 92 Buena Vista Ave.*,[149] the U.S. Supreme Court established an "innocent owner defense" in forfeiture cases, whereby the government was prohibited from seizing drug-transaction assets that were later acquired by a new and innocent owner. In the same year, in the case of *Austin v. U.S.*,[150] the Court placed limits on the government's authority to use forfeiture laws against drug criminals, finding that seizures of property must not be excessive when compared to the seriousness of the offense charged. Otherwise, the justices wrote, the Eighth Amendment's ban on excessive fines could be contravened. The justices, however, refused to establish a rule by which excessive fines could be judged. The *Austin* ruling was supported by two other 1993 cases, *Alexander v. U.S.* and *U.S. v. James Daniel Good Real Property*.[151] In *Alexander*, the Court found that forfeitures under the RICO statute must be limited according to the rules established in *Austin*, while in *Good*, the Court held that "absent exigent circumstances, the Due Process Clause requires the Government to afford notice and a meaningful opportunity to be heard before seizing real property subject to civil forfeiture."

Five years later, in a ruling[152] supportive of *Austin*, the Court found that $357,144 in cash confiscated by customs inspectors from an airline passenger about to leave the country had to be returned to him. The man committed no crime other than failing to report the fact that he was transporting more than $10,000 in currency out of the country, as required by law. Government prosecutors sought forfeiture of the money, but the Court

Racketeer Influenced and Corrupt Organizations (RICO)

A federal statute that allows for the federal seizure of assets derived from illegal enterprise.

> Antidrug strategies must be supported by knowledge gained from research.
>
> —The National Drug Control Strategy

Each of us has a
responsibility to work
toward reducing the
demand for drugs in this
country. We should expect
nothing less from our
government. The Congress,
the media, communities,
schools, churches,
families, and every
single citizen in this
country must make living
in a drug-free society
their top priority.

—Dr. Lee P. Brown, Former
Director, Office of National Drug
Control Policy

interdiction
- - - - - - - - - - - - - - -
The interception of drug traffic
at the nation's borders.
Interdiction is one of the many
strategies used to stem the flow
of illegal drugs into the United
States.

ruled that forfeiture of the entire $357,144 would have been "grossly disproportional to the gravity of [the] offense," since the money was lawfully owned, it was being transported to repay a lawful debt, and no other crime had been committed.

On the other hand, in 1996 the U.S. Supreme Court upheld the seizure of private property used in the commission of a crime, even though the property belonged to an innocent owner not involved in the crime. The case, *Bennis* v. *Michigan*,[153] involved the government's taking of a car that had been used by the owner's husband when procuring the services of a prostitute. In effect, the justices ruled, an innocent owner is not protected from criminal conviction–related property forfeiture.

Also in 1996, in the case of *U.S.* v. *Ursery*,[154] the U.S. Supreme Court rejected claims that civil forfeiture laws constitute a form of double jeopardy. In *Ursery*, the defendant's house had been seized by federal officials who claimed that it had been used to facilitate drug transactions. The government later seized other personal items owned by Guy Jerome Ursery, saying that they had been purchased with the proceeds of drug sales and that Ursery had engaged in money-laundering activities to hide the source of his illegal income. The Courts of Appeals, however, reversed Ursery's drug conviction and the forfeiture judgment, holding that the double jeopardy clause of the U.S. Constitution prohibits the government from both punishing a defendant for a criminal offense and forfeiting his property for that same offense in a separate civil proceeding. In reaffirming Ursery's conviction, however, the U.S. Supreme Court concluded that "civil forfeitures are neither 'punishment' nor criminal for purposes of the Double Jeopardy clause." In distinguishing civil forfeitures and criminal punishments, the majority opinion held that "Congress has long authorized the Government to bring parallel criminal actions and . . . civil forfeiture proceedings based upon the same underlying events. . . , and this Court consistently has concluded that the Double Jeopardy Clause does not apply to such forfeitures because they do not impose punishment."

Civil forfeiture laws have come under considerable fire recently as being fundamentally unfair. More than 200 forfeiture laws have been enacted across the country in recent years, many requiring only mere suspicion before items of value can be seized by government agents. Once property has been seized, getting it back can be a nightmare, even when no crime was committed. A few years ago, Illinois U.S. Representative Henry Hyde found that 80% of people whose property was seized by the federal government under drug laws were never formally charged with any crime.[155]

To address problems with federal forfeiture provisions, Congress passed the Civil Asset Forfeiture Reform Act of 2000. Under the law, federal prosecutors must meet a new burden of proof standard in forfeiture cases. They are required to establish by a *preponderance of the evidence* that the property in question was subject to forfeiture. The property owner has five years in which to make a claim on the property after the government has claimed it, but a claimant's status as a fugitive from justice is grounds for dismissal of the case contesting the forfeiture of the property. Under the new law, it is a crime to remove or destroy property to prevent seizure for forfeiture.

Interdiction

In 1989, a single Los Angeles drug bust amazed investigators with the size of their catch. In a warehouse in a quiet section of the city, police seized 20 tons of cocaine, then valued at $20 billion on the street.[156] Found along with the cocaine was $10 million in cash. Since then, other large caches have also been uncovered, including nine tons of cocaine in a house in Harlingen, Texas; six tons on a ship in the Gulf of Mexico; and more than five tons hidden in barrels of lye in New York City.[157] Annual seizures of cocaine in the United States total about 140 tons (with an estimated wholesale value of $50 billion). All such seizures reflect a failure to interdict drugs at the nation's borders.

Interdiction involves efforts aimed at stopping drugs from entering the United States. The Coast Guard, the Border Patrol, and Customs agents have played the most visible roles in interdiction efforts over the last few decades. Interdiction strategies in the fight against drugs, however, are almost doomed to failure by the sheer size of the task. Although most enforcement efforts are focused on international airports and major harbors, the international boundary of the United States extends over 12,000 miles. Rough coastline, sparsely populated desert, and dense forests provide natural barriers to easy observation and make detection of controlled substances entering the country very difficult. Add to this the fact that over 420 billion tons of goods and more than 270 million

A drug dog alerting on a bag at Moscow's international airport. Drug interdiction, which involves efforts aimed at stopping drugs from entering a country, is an international strategy.

Reuters, CORBIS

people cross over the American border annually, and the job of interdiction becomes more complicated still.[158] Because most drugs can be highly potent in even minute quantities, the interdiction strategy suffers from the proverbial "needle in the haystack" predicament.

A number of hard-line suggestions have surfaced recently on expanding interdiction efforts. Some would supplement current U.S. Border Patrol (USBP) and Coast Guard efforts with Armed Forces personnel and equipment. Advanced radar surveillance airplanes, helicopter gunships, naval vessels, and infantry soldiers could be called upon to identify, track, and search all vessels bound for the United States.

Opposition to the use of the military in the war against drugs, however, comes from many corners. One is the Posse Comitatus Act of 1878, which forbids American military forces from enforcing civilian law. The Pentagon and the Joint Chiefs of Staff are themselves opposed to military involvement in drug-interdiction activities, except for a limited role in support of law enforcement efforts. Speaking in 1995, Joint Chiefs of Staff Chairman John Shalikashvili said, "Our role is that of support to law enforcement agencies; support such as logistic support or informational support. But the issue of enforcement belongs to the properly constituted law enforcement agencies, and not the military."[159] Military estimates of costs for a full-scale interdiction operation, were it to be ordered, include $14 billion for additional surveillance aircraft and $6.2 billion yearly to physically patrol the border.[160]

Crop Control

Crop-control strategies attempt to limit the amount of drugs available for the illicit market by targeting foreign producers. Crop control in source countries generally takes one of two forms. In the first, government subsidies (often with U.S. support) are made available to farmers to induce them to grow other kinds of crops. Sometimes illegal crops are bought and destroyed. The second form of control involves aerial spraying or ground-level crop destruction.

Source country crop control suffers from two major drawbacks.[161] First, the potentially large profits which can be made from illegal acreage encourage farmers in unaffected areas to take up the production of crops which have been destroyed elsewhere. Second, it can be difficult to get foreign governments to cooperate in eradication efforts. In some parts of the world, opium and coca are major cash crops, and local governments are reluctant to undertake any action directed against them.

> A key response to drug use and drug trafficking is an aggressive and coordinated law enforcement effort. Americans have the right to feel safe in their homes and secure in their communities.
>
> —The National Drug Control Strategy

Education and Treatment

As the population of incarcerated drug offenders swelled, some state legislatures began to question the necessity of imprisoning nonviolent substance abusers who were not involved in drug sale or distribution. In 1996, as a consequence of such thinking, Arizona voters approved Proposition 200, the Drug Medicalization, Prevention and Control Act. A central purpose of the act was to expand drug treatment and education services for drug offenders and to utilize probation for nonviolent drug offenders—thereby potentially diverting many arrested drug abusers from prison. To fund the program, the Arizona law established the state's Drug Treatment and Education Fund, administered by Arizona's Office of the Courts; the fund draws revenues from the state's luxury tax on liquor.

Arizona's movement away from imprisonment and toward treatment and education for nonviolent drug offenders is based upon the Arizona Justice Model. The Arizona model can be stated as follows: "IF substance abusing offenders can be accurately and effectively assessed as to their risk/need level and degree of substance abuse problem; and if substance abusing offenders can be matched with the intervention that most effectively recognizes their special population cognitive therapeutic needs; THEN 1. substance abusing offenders' criminogenic needs and substance abusing behaviors can be reduced and/or eliminated; 2. substance abusing offenders' quality of life will improve through recovery; 3. substance abusing offenders will be less likely to commit future offenses and community safety will be increased; and 4. jails/prisons will be primarily reserved for violent and chronic offenders."[162]

A study by Arizona's Administrative Office of the Courts recently concluded that the relatively new Arizona law is "resulting in safer communities and more substance abusing probationers in recovery."[163] Moreover, said the report, the law has saved the state millions of dollars and has helped more than 75% of program participants to remain drug free.[164]

In 2000, the state of California followed Arizona's lead when voters approved Proposition 36, a sweeping initiative requiring treatment instead of imprisonment for nonviolent drug users throughout the state. The proposition, also known as the California Substance Abuse and Crime Prevention Act of 2000, contains the following passage:

SECTION 3. Purpose and Intent

The People of the State of California hereby declare their purpose and intent in enacting this Act to be as follows:

(a) To divert from incarceration into community-based substance abuse treatment programs non-violent defendants, probationers and parolees charged with simple drug possession or drug use offenses;

(b) To halt the wasteful expenditure of hundreds of millions of dollars each year on the incarceration and re-incarceration of non-violent drug users who would be better served by community-based treatment; and

(c) To enhance public safety by reducing drug-related crime and preserving jails and prison cells for serious and violent offenders, and to improve public health by reducing drug abuse and drug dependence through proven and effective drug treatment strategies.

There are many different kinds of educational and treatment programs for drug offenders. Michael Goodstadt of the Addiction Research Foundation groups drug-education and drug-treatment programs into three categories: (1) those that provide factual information about drugs; (2) those that address feelings, values, and attitudes; and (3) those that focus directly on behavior.[165] Most modern programs contain elements of all three approaches.

Drug-education programs can be found in schools, churches, and youth groups and may be provided by police departments, social service agencies, hospitals, and private citizens' groups. Project DARE (the Drug Abuse Resistance Education program), falls into Goodstadt's second category. DARE, the nation's most visible school-based antidrug education program, began as a cooperative effort between the Los Angeles Police Department and the Los Angeles Unified School District in 1983. Using uniformed law enforcement officers to conduct classes in elementary schools, the program focuses on decision-making skills, peer pressure, and alternatives to drug use.

> One of the most promising means of reducing the supply of drugs is a strong source country strategy.
>
> —The National Drug Control Strategy

A 1994 study cast the effectiveness of the DARE program into doubt, and officials in the Clinton administration were charged with refusing to recognize the study's results. The study, published in the *American Journal of Public Health,* reviewed DARE programs in six states and British Columbia and found that "the popular drug prevention program does not work well and is less effective than other drug prevention efforts targeted at students."[166] Defending the DARE program, Justice Department officials questioned the study's methodology and published their own version of the study's results, which showed that "user satisfaction" with the DARE program is high. The study, according to Justice Department interpreters, found substantial grassroots support for the DARE program and led to the conclusion that DARE "has been extremely successful at placing substance abuse education in the nation's schools."[167]

Later studies again questioned Project DARE's effectiveness. A 1997 review of numerous DARE studies concluded that the program's "effects on drug use, except for tobacco use, are nonsignificant."[168] Finally, a 1999 University of Kentucky study tracked over 1,000 Midwestern students who participated in Project DARE in the sixth grade in order to see if the level of drug abuse among them differed from those who had not been exposed to the program.[169] The study found no difference in actual drug use immediately following exposure to the program or 10 years later, when most of the former students were 20 years old.

Other studies also show that there is little evidence to support the belief that school-based anti-substance-abuse education will produce the desired effect upon problem drug users or those at risk of beginning drug use.[170] Studies analyzing state-by-state spending on school-based drug education, for example, show little relationship between the amount of money spent on drug education and the number of hard-core cocaine users.[171] To be effective, programs will probably have to acknowledge the perceived positive aspects of the drug experience, as well as cultural messages that encourage drug use.[172] Until they do, many recipients of today's messages may discount them as conflicting with personal experience. Read more about the debate over DARE at **Web Extra! 15–9** at cjtoday.com.

> The drug policy process in the United States is permeated with ideology, impervious to the lessons of history, and addicted to debating polar abstractions rather than focusing on practical alternatives to current policy.
>
> —Franklin E. Zimring and Gordon Hawkins

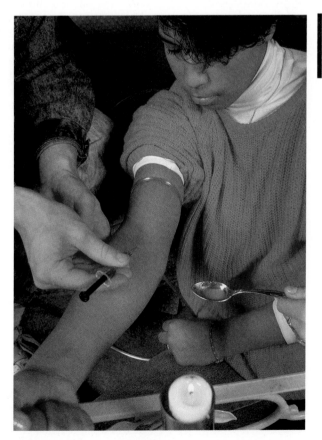

A friend helping a young woman shoot up. Drug abuse extends to all social groups and can be found among all ages.

Dennis MacDonald, PhotoEdit

Other kinds of drug-education programs may be effective, however. A recent study by the RAND Corporation's Drug Policy Research Center (DPRC), for example, found *education* to be the most efficacious alternative for dealing with drug abuse.[173] DPRC researchers focused on the use of alternative strategies for reducing cocaine abuse. Visit RAND's DPRC via **Web Extra! 15–10** at cjtoday.com.

DRUG COURTS

drug court

A special state, county, or municipal court that offers first-time substance-abuse offenders judicially mandated and court-supervised treatment alternatives to prison.

One of the most widely accepted antidrug programs operating today is the **drug court**. Drug courts focus on promoting public safety and employ a nonadversarial approach that provides defendants with easy access to a continuum of alcohol, drug, and other related treatment and rehabilitation services. Drug courts also monitor abstinence from the use of drugs on an individual basis through frequent alcohol and other drug testing. Failing to comply with court-ordered treatment, or returning to drug use, results in harsher punishments, including imprisonment.

Modern drug courts are modeled after a Dade County, Florida, innovation which became known as the *Miami Drug Court model*. An early evaluation of Miami's drug court found a high rate of success: Few clients were rearrested, incarceration rates were lowered, and the burden on the criminal justice system was lessened.[174] The success of the drug court model led to $1 billion worth of funding under the Violent Crime Control and Law Enforcement Act of 1994 for the establishment of similar courts throughout the nation. Since then, the growth in the number of drug courts serving the nation has been huge. In 2001, the National Association of Drug Court Professionals reported that nearly 1,200 drug courts were in existence or were being planned.[175]

There are special drug courts for juveniles and for drunk drivers (sometimes called *DUI courts*). The National Drug Court Institute provides training for judges and professional staff interested in today's drug court movement.[176] Learn more about drug courts via **Web Extra! 15–11** and **Library Extras! 15–7** and **15–8** at cjtoday.com.

Legalization and Decriminalization

Often regarded as the most "radical" approach to solving the drug problem, legalization and decriminalization have been proposed repeatedly, and in recent years, these ideas seem to be gaining at least a modicum of respectability. Although the words *legalization* and *decriminalization* are often used interchangeably, there is a significant difference. **Legalization** refers to the removal of all legal strictures from the use or possession of the drug in question. Manufacture and distribution might still be regulated. **Decriminalization**, on the other hand, substantially reduces penalties associated with drug use but may not eliminate them entirely. States like Oregon, which have decriminalized marijuana possession, for example, treat simple possession of small amounts of the substance as a ticketable offense similar to jaywalking or improper parking.[177] Hence, decriminalization of a controlled substance might mean that the drug "would remain illegal but the offense of possession would be treated like a traffic violation, with no loss of liberty involved for the transgressor."[178]

legalization

Elimination of the laws and associated criminal penalties that prohibit the production, sale, distribution, and possession of a controlled substance.

decriminalization

The redefinition of certain previously criminal behaviors into regulated activities that become "ticketable" rather than "arrestable."

The following arguments have been offered in support of both legalization and decriminalization:[179]

- Legal drugs would be easy to track and control. The involvement of organized criminal cartels in the drug-distribution network could be substantially curtailed.

- Legal drug sales could be taxed, generating huge revenues.

- Legal drugs would be cheap, significantly reducing the number of drug-related crimes committed to feed expensive drug habits.

- Since some people are attracted to anything taboo, legalization could, in fact, reduce the demand for drugs.

- The current war on drugs is already a failure and will be remembered as one of history's follies.[180] Prohibiting drugs is too expensive in terms of tax dollars, sacrificed civil liberties, and political turmoil.

- Drug dealers and users care little about criminal justice sanctions. They will continue their illegal activities no matter what the penalties.

- Drug use should ultimately be a matter of personal choice.

Advocates of legalization are primarily motivated by cost-benefit considerations, weighing the social costs of prohibition against its results.[181] The results, they say, have been meager at best, while the costs have been almost more than society can bear.

Opponents of legalization argue from both a moral and a practical stance. Some, like former New York City Mayor Rudolph Giuliani, believe that legalization would only condone a behavior that is fundamentally immoral.[182] Others argue that under legalization, drug use would increase, causing more widespread drug-related social problems than exist today. Robert DuPont, former head of the National Institute on Drug Abuse, for example, estimates that up to ten times the number of people who now use cocaine would turn to the substance if it were legal.[183]

A compromise approach has been suggested in what some writers call the *limitation model*. The limitation model "would make drugs legally available, but with clearly defined limits as to which institutions and professions could distribute the drugs."[184] Hence, under such a model, doctors, pharmacists, and perhaps licensed drug counselors could prescribe controlled substances under appropriate circumstances, and the drugs themselves might be taxed. Some claim that a more extreme form of the limitation model might be workable. It could be one under which drugs are sold through designated "drugstores" with distribution systems structured much like those of "liquor stores" today. Controlled substances would be sold to those of suitable age, but taxed substantially, and the use of such substances under certain circumstances (such as when operating a car) might still be illegal. The regulation and taxation of controlled substances would correspond to today's handling of alcoholic beverages.

Another example of the limitation model, already tried in some countries, is the two-market system.[185] The two-market approach would allow inexpensive and legitimate access to controlled substances for registered addicts. Only maintenance amounts (the amounts needed to forestall symptoms of drug "withdrawal") of the needed drugs, however, would be available. The two-market approach would purportedly reduce the massive profits available to criminal drug cartels while simultaneously discouraging new drug use among those who are not addicted. Great Britain provides an example of the two-market system. During the 1960s and 1970s, British heroin addicts who registered with the government received prescriptions for limited amounts of heroin, which was dispensed through medical clinics. Because of concern about system abuses, clinics in the late 1970s began to dispense reduced amounts of heroin, hoping to "wean" addicts away from the drug.[186] By 1980, heroin was replaced by methadone,[187] a synthetic drug designed to prevent the physical symptoms of heroin withdrawal. Methadone, in amounts sufficient to prevent withdrawal, does not produce a heroinlike high.

It is doubtful that the two-market system will be adopted in the United States anytime soon. American cultural condemnation of major mind-altering drugs has created a reluctance to accept the legitimacy of drug treatment using controlled substances. In addition, cocaine is much more of a problem in the United States than is heroin. The

Cher Fisher (left) of England and Henny Fou of Holland posing before the start of the sixth annual beauty pageant for inmates at the Santa Monica Women's Prison in Lima, Peru. Most women incarcerated at the Peruvian penitentiary previously worked as drug "mules" and were caught trying to smuggle cocaine out of Peru.

© AFP Photo, Jamie Razuri, CORBIS

large number of drug abusers in the country, combined with the difficulty of defining and measuring "addiction" to drugs like cocaine, would make any maintenance program impractical.

Summary

Drug crimes and drug-related crimes account for a substantial proportion of all crimes committed in this country. While the manufacture, importation, sale, and use of illegal drugs account for a substantial number of law violations, many other offenses are also linked to drug use. Among them are thefts of all kinds, burglary, assault, and murder.

Drug-related crimes derive from the fact that drugs are both expensive for users and extremely profitable for suppliers. The high cost of drugs forces many users, some of whom have little legitimate income, into the commission of property crimes to acquire the funds necessary to continue their drug habit. On the other hand, users of illicit drugs who have substantial legitimate incomes may indirectly shift the cost of drug use to society through lowered job productivity, psychological or family problems, and medical expenses.

The widespread use of illegal drugs in America today carries with it other social costs. Many criminal enterprises, for example, are supported by street-level demand for drugs. Some of these illegitimate businesses are massive international cartels which will stop at nothing to protect their financial interests. Bribery, extortion, kidnapping, torture, and murder are tools of the trade among drug kingpins in their battle to continue reaping vast profits.

Any realistic appraisal of the current situation must admit that the resources of the criminal justice system in dealing with drug crime are strained to the limit. There are simply not enough agents, airplanes, equipment, and money to entirely remove illegal drugs from American communities. The justice system faces the added problem of corruption inherent in any social-control situation where large amounts of money frequently change hands. Until attitudes that support drug use are modified or are replaced, law enforcement professionals can only hope to keep the problem of drug abuse in America from becoming worse—and to keep from losing sight of their fundamental mandates in the process.

Discussion Questions

1. Why are drugs such a big problem in the United States today? In your opinion, do particular elements of contemporary American culture support drug use? If so, what elements?
2. What commonly used legal substances might qualify as drugs, even though they are generally not recognized as such? Why do people use these substances?
3. Why does drug use tend to lead to other types of crime commission? What kinds of crimes might be involved?
4. How would you deal with the problem of illicit drug use in America today? Discuss the strategies cited in this chapter, listing the pros and cons of each.
5. What characteristics does drug use share with other social-order, or victimless, crimes? Should social-order crimes be legalized and left to individual choice? Explain.

To participate in an online discussion on these topics and others, go to the Global Town Meeting electronic message board for Chapter 15 on the *Criminal Justice Today* Companion Website at cjtoday.com.

Research drug and alcohol information on the Web using the Cybrary as a starting point. Search the Cybrary listings to find sites which contain suggestions and ideas on how to solve the drug problems facing this country.

What sources did you find? (Hint: Don't forget the *National Drug Control Strategy* available from ONDCP.) Describe the various strategies you've found. Which do you think are the most useful? Why? Submit your findings to your instructor if asked to do so.

To complete this Web Quest! online, go to the Web Quest! module in Chapter 15 of the *Criminal Justice Today* Companion Website at cjtoday.com.

Library Extra! **15–1** *The U.S. Controlled Substances Act.*
Library Extra! **15–2** *National Household Survey on Drug Abuse* (SAMHSA, current volume).
Library Extra! **15–3** *Monitoring the Future Survey* (NIDA, current volume).
Library Extra! **15–4** *ADAM Annual Report on Drug Use among Adult and Juvenile Arrestees* (ADAM, current volume).
Library Extra! **15–5** *Dynamics of the Drug-Crime Relationship* (NIJ, 2000).
Library Extra! **15–6** *The National Drug Control Strategy* (ONDCP, current volume).
Library Extra! **15–7** *Looking at a Decade of Drug Courts* (DCCTAP, 1999).
Library Extra! **15–8** *The Rebirth of Rehabilitation: Promise and Perils of Drug Courts* (NIJ, 2000).

To explore these resources online, go to the Library Extras! area of the *Criminal Justice Today* Companion Website at cjtoday.com. You should also check the author's "Late Picks" online for newly released documents and updated Library Extras! You can find Late Picks at http://cjtoday.com/latepicks.htm.

i. Bureau of Justice Statistics, *Drugs, Crime, and the Justice System* (Washington, D.C.: BJS, 1992), p. 20.
ii. Ibid., p. 21.
iii. Ibid.

iv. Clifford Karchmer and Douglas Ruch, "State and Local Money Laundering Control Strategies," *NIJ Research in Brief* (Washington, D.C.: National Institute of Justice, 1992), p. 1.

1. Gary E. Johnson, "Bad Investment," a Mother Jones.com Special Report, July 10, 2001. Web posted at http://www.motherjones.com/prisons/investment.html. Accessed January 30, 2002.
2. "New Drug Czar Targets 'Unacceptably High' Rates of Drug Use among Students," ONDCP press release, December 19, 2001. Web posted at http://www.whitehousedrugpolicy.gov/news/press01/121901.html. Accessed February 3, 2002.
3. Ross Deck, "A New Way of Looking at the Drug War," in *Enhancing Capacities and Confronting Controversies in Criminal Justice—Proceedings of the 1993 National Conference of the Bureau of Justice Statistics and the Justice Research and Statistics Association* (Washington, D.C.: Bureau of Justice Statistics, 1994), p. 12.
4. National Association of Drug Court Professionals, *The Facts: Facts on Drug Courts* (Alexandria, VA: NADCP, 2001).

5. "Who Is in Federal Prison?" *Washington Post* wire service, October 3, 1994.
6. Allen J. Beck and Paige M. Harrison, *Prisoners in 2000* (Washington, D.C.: Bureau of Justice Statistics, 2001).
7. For an excellent overview of the issues involved, see Doris Layton MacKenzie and Craig D. Uchida, *Drugs and Crime: Evaluating Public Policy Initiatives* (Thousand Oaks, CA: Sage, 1994).
8. The term *recreational user* is well established in the literature of drug abuse. Unfortunately, it tends to minimize the seriousness of drug abuse by according the abuse of even hard drugs the status of a hobby.
9. Howard Becker, *Outsiders: Studies in the Sociology of Deviance* (New York: Free Press, 1963).
10. Sentencing information is taken from Hilary Hylton, "Jenna Bush Sentenced in Alcohol Cases," Reuters wire service, July 6, 2001.

11. Jay Tokasz, "Eight of 11 People in Car Die in Crash," *USA Today,* June 20, 1995, p. 2A.

12. James B. Jacobs, *Drinking and Crime,* NIJ Crime File Study Guide (Washington, D.C.: National Institute of Justice, no date), p. 1.

13. Ibid.

14. Ibid.

15. "Shaken and Stirred: The State of the Liquor Industry," *Washington Post,* November 12, 1996.

16. In most states, individuals may also be arrested for driving under the influence of other drugs and controlled substances, including prescription medicines.

17. Fiscal year 2001 Transportation Appropriations Bill (H.R. 4475), signed by the president on October 23, 2000.

18. "Drunk Driving Limit Lowered," *Lawyers Weekly USA,* LWUSA 907 (October 16, 2000).

19. Federal Bureau of Investigation, *Crime in the United States, 2000* (Washington, D.C.: U.S. Government Printing Office, 2001).

20. Jacobs, *Drinking and Crime.*

21. *State Alcohol Estimates: Traffic Safety Facts, 2000* (Washington, D.C.: National Highway Traffic Safety Administration, 2001).

22. Ibid.

23. FBI, *Crime in the United States, 2000.*

24. Bureau of Justice Statistics, *Report to the Nation on Crime and Justice,* 2d ed. (Washington, D.C.: Department of Justice, 1988), p. 50.

25. Jeffrey A. Roth, "Psychoactive Substances and Violence," *NIJ Research in Brief* (February 1994), p. 1.

26. Christopher J. Mumola, *Substance Abuse and Treatment, State and Federal Prisoners, 1997* (Washington, D.C.: Bureau of Justice Statistics, 1999).

27. Ibid.

28. Howard Abadinsky, *Drug Abuse: An Introduction* (Chicago: Nelson-Hall, 1989), p. 32.

29. Charles E. Terry and Mildred Pellens, *The Opium Problem* (New York: Committee on Drug Addiction, 1928).

30. Ibid.

31. Ibid., p. 76.

32. David Musto, *The American Disease: Origins of Narcotic Control* (New Haven, CT: Yale University Press, 1973).

33. Becker, *Outsiders.*

34. Office of National Drug Control Policy, "New Study First to Quantify Illicit Drug and Substance Use in Movies and Music Popular among Youth." Web posted at http://www.mediacampaign.org/inthenews/mediascope.html. Accessed January 30, 2000.

35. Becker, *Outsiders.*

36. Ibid., p. 136.

37. Ibid.

38. Ibid.

39. Franklin E. Zimring and Gordon Hawkins, *The Search for Rational Drug Control* (New York: Cambridge University Press, 1992).

40. Ibid., p. 9.

41. President's Commission on Organized Crime, *Organized Crime Today* (Washington, D.C.: U.S. Government Printing Office, 1986).

42. *Webb* v. *U.S.,* 249 U.S. 96 (1919).

43. Michael D. Lyman and Gary W. Potter, *Drugs in Society: Causes, Concepts, and Control* (Cincinnati: Anderson, 1991), p. 359.

44. Drug Enforcement Administration, *Drug Enforcement: The Early Years* (Washington, D.C.: DEA, 1980), p. 41.

45. White House Conference on Drug Abuse, *Commission Report* (Washington, D.C.: U.S. Government Printing Office, 1963).

46. For a good summary of the law, see Drug Enforcement Administration, *Drugs of Abuse* (Washington, D.C.: U.S. Government Printing Office, 1997).

47. Drug Enforcement Administration, *Drug Enforcement Briefing Book* (Washington, D.C.: DEA, no date), p. 3.

48. A number of states now recognize that marijuana may be useful in the treatment of nausea associated with cancer chemotherapy, glaucoma, and other medical conditions.

49. DEA, *Drug Enforcement Briefing Book,* p. 3.

50. Ibid.

51. Ibid., p. 4.

52. Ibid.

53. DEA, *Drugs of Abuse.*

54. Ibid.

55. Anti-Drug Abuse Act of 1988, P.L. 100-690, Sec. 5251.

56. This provision became effective on September 1, 1989.

57. "Congress Gives Final OK to Major Antidrug Bill," *Criminal Justice Newsletter,* Vol. 19, No. 21 (November 1, 1988), pp. 1–4.

58. The U.S. Supreme Court upheld that legislation in the 2002 case of *Department of Housing and Urban Development* v. *Rucker* (No. 00-1770).

59. "Congress Gives Final OK to Major Antidrug Bill," p. 2.

60. "Drug Lord Sentenced to Death," *USA Today,* May 15, 1991, p. 3A.

61. Ibid.

62. Public Laws 101-647, 103-322, and 105-20.

63. *California* v. *Greenwood,* 486 U.S. 35, 108 S.Ct. 1625 (1988).

64. Ibid.

65. *Abel* v. *U.S.,* 363 U.S. 217 (1960).

66. *Oliver* v. *U.S.,* 466 U.S. 170 (1984).

67. *Hester* v. *U.S.,* 265 U.S. 57, 44 S.Ct. 445 (1924).

68. *U.S.* v. *Dunn,* 480 U.S. 294, 107 S.Ct. 1134 (1987).

69. *California* v. *Ciraolo,* 476 U.S. 207, 106 S.Ct. 1809 (1986).

70. *Florida* v. *Riley,* 488 U.S. 445, 109 S.Ct. 693, 102 L.Ed. 2d 835 (1989).

71. Office of National Drug Control Policy, "ONDCP Finds Americans Spent $57 Billion in One Year on Illegal Drugs," press release, 1997.

72. Office of National Drug Control Policy, *What America's Users Spend on Illegal Drugs* (Washington, D.C.: ONDCP, 1991), p. 4.

73. U.S. Department of Health and Human Services, *National Household Survey on Drug Abuse, 2000,* Table 1.1A: "Estimated Numbers (in Thousands) of Lifetime, Past Year, and Past Month Users of Illicit Drugs among Persons Aged 12 or Older: 1999 and 2000." Web posted at http://www.samhsa.gov/oas/nhsda/2kdetailedtabs/Vol_1_Part_1/sect1v1.htm#1.1a. Accessed February 21, 2002.

74. Carolyn Skorneck, "Drug Use," Associated Press wire service, July 20, 1994.

75. Office of National Drug Control Policy, *The National Drug Control Strategy, 1999* (Washington, D.C.: U.S. Superintendent of Documents, 1999).

76. National Narcotics Intelligence Consumers Committee, *The NNICC Report, 1998* (Washington, D.C.: Drug Enforcement Administration, 2000), preface.

77. DEA, *Drugs of Abuse,* p. 45.

78. Office of National Drug Control Policy, *Pulse Check: National Trends in Drug Abuse* (Washington, D.C.: ONDCP, 1995), p. 11.

79. Ibid.

80. See Anita Manning and Andrea Stone, "How States Will Face Regulating Marijuana as Medicine," *USA Today,* November 7, 1996, p. 3D.

81. *U.S. v. Oakland Cannabis Buyer's Cooperative,* No. 00-151. Decided May 14, 2001.

82. Ibid., syllabus.

83. Department of Health and Human Services, "2000 Monitoring the Future Survey Released: Moderating Trend among Teen Drug Use Continues," *HHS News,* December 14, 2000. Web posted at http://www. drugabuse.gov/MedAdv/00/HHS12-14.html. Accessed March 30, 2001.

84. NNICC, *The NNICC Report, 1998.*

85. Ibid.

86. Ibid.

87. ONDCP, *Pulse Check,* p. 9.

88. NNICC, *The NNICC Report, 1998.*

89. Ibid.

90. Ibid.

91. Drug Enforcement Administration, *Crack Cocaine Drug Intelligence Report, 1994* (Washington, D.C.: DEA, 1995).

92. National Institute of Justice, JUSTINFO Online, July 5, 1995.

93. NNICC, *The NNICC Report, 1998.*

94. Sam Vincent Meddis, "Arrests 'Last Rites' for Cali Cartel," *USA Today,* August 7, 1995, p. 1A.

95. DEA, *Drugs of Abuse,* p. 14.

96. Ibid., p. 12.

97. Ibid., p. 15.

98. Ibid., p. 54.

99. Office of National Drug Control Policy, *The National Drug Control Strategy: Executive Summary,* (Washington, D.C.: ONDCP, 1995), p. 13.

100. DEA, *Drugs of Abuse.*

101. NNICC, *The NNICC Report, 1998.*

102. National Institute of Justice, JUSTINFO Online, July 5, 1995.

103. Office of National Drug Control Policy, *Pulse Check: National Trends in Drug Abuse* (Washington, D.C.: ONDCP, 1997), p. 3.

104. Ibid.

105. Much of the information on club drugs in this section comes from Drug Enforcement Administration, "An Overview of Club Drugs," a Drug Intelligence Brief, February 2000. Web posted at http://www.usdoj. gov/dea/pubs/intel/20005intellbrief.pdf. Accessed March 2, 2002.

106. "'Rophies' Reported Spreading Quickly throughout the South," *Drug Enforcement Report,* June 23, 1995, pp. 1–5.

107. Public Law 104-305.

108. Sentencing enhancement information in this section comes from the Congressional Testimony of Asa Hutchinson, Administrator of the Drug Enforcement Administration, before the Senate Caucus on International Narcotics Control, December 4, 2001. Web posted at http://www.usdoj.gov/dea/pubs/cngrtest/ ct120401.html. Accessed February 3, 2002.

109. Drug Abuse Warning Network, *The DAWN Report.* Web posted at http://www.samhsa.gov/oas/dawn.htm. Accessed March 10, 2002.

110. Public Law 106-310.

111. Much of the information in this section comes from the National Institute on Drug Abuse's website at http://www.nida.nih.gov.

112. DEA, "An Overview of Club Drugs," from which some of the wording in this section is taken.

113. FBI, *Crime in the United States, 2000.*

114. Ibid.

115. Ibid. Unfortunately, UCR data combine arrests for heroin and cocaine possession into one category. They do the same for sale and manufacture arrests.

116. ONDCP, *The National Drug Control Strategy: Executive Summary,* p. 12.

117. Bernard A. Gropper, "Probing the Links between Drugs and Crime," *NIJ Research in Brief* (February 1985), p. 4.

118. J. C. Ball, J. W. Shaffer, and D. N. Nurco, *Day to Day Criminality of Heroin Addicts in Baltimore: A Study in the Continuity of Offense Rates* (Washington, D.C.: National Institute of Justice, 1983).

119. National Institute of Justice, *ADAM Preliminary 2000 Findings on Drug Use and Drug Markets* (Washington, D.C.: NIJ, 2001).

120. For a true-life account of money-laundering activities, see Nick Tosches, *Power on Earth: Michele Sindona's Explosive Story* (New York: Arbor House, 1986).

121. NNICC, *The NNICC Report, 1998.*

122. Clifford L. Karchmer and Douglas Ruch, "State and Local Money Laundering Control Strategies," *NIJ Research in Brief* (1992), p. 1.

123. Clifford L. Karchmer, *Illegal Money Laundering: A Strategy and Resource Guide for Law Enforcement Agencies* (Washington, D.C.: Police Executive Research Forum, 1988), p. iv.

124. Ibid.

125. "The Cash Cleaners," *Time,* October 24, 1988, p. 65.

126. Ibid.

127. Ibid.

128. NNICC, *The NNICC Report, 1998.*

129. Ibid.

130. *Ratzlaf* v. *U.S.,* 114 S.Ct. 655, 126 L.Ed. 2d 615 (1994).

131. Daniel Boyce, "Narco-terrorism," *FBI Law Enforcement Bulletin* (October 1987), p. 24; and James A. Inciardi, "Narcoterrorism: A Perspective and Commentary," in Robert O. Slater and Grant Wardlaw, eds., *International Narcotics* (London: Macmillan/ St. Martins, 1989).

132. The Attorney General of the United States, *Drug Trafficking: A Report to the President of the United States* (Washington, D.C.: U.S. Department of Justice, August 3, 1989), p. 19.

133. A term reportedly invented by former Peruvian President Fernando Belaunde Terry; see James A. Inciardi, "Narcoterrorism," paper presented at the 1988 annual meeting of the Academy of Criminal Justice Sciences, San Francisco, p. 8.

134. Boyce, "Narco-terrorism," p. 24.

135. Ibid., p. 25.

136. U.S. Department of State, *Terrorist Group Profiles* (Washington, D.C.: U.S. Government Printing Office, 1989).

137. Inciardi, "Narcoterrorism: A Perspective and Commentary."

138. "U.S. Government Lacks Strategy to Neutralize International Crime," *Criminal Justice International,* Vol. 10, No. 5 (September/October 1994), p. 5.

139. Office of National Drug Control Policy, *The National Drug Control Strategy, 2000* (Washington, D.C.: U.S. Government Printing Office, 2000).

140. James Q. Wilson, "Drugs and Crime," in Michael Tonry and James Q. Wilson, eds., *Drugs and Crime* (Chicago: University of Chicago Press, 1990), p. 522.

141. DEA, *The Cali Cartel,* p. 10.

142. 21 U.S.C. §881 (a) (6).

143. Michael Goldsmith, *Civil Forfeiture: Tracing the Proceeds of Narcotics Trafficking* (Washington, D.C.: Police Executive Research Forum, 1988), p. 3.

144. *U.S. v. $4,255,625.39 in Currency,* 762 F.2d 895, 904 (1982).

145. Bureau of Justice Assistance, *Asset Forfeiture Bulletin* (October 1988), p. 2.

146. Ibid.

147. Kappa Sigma Fraternity, *Drugs.* Web posted at http://www.kappasigma.org/riskmgt/drugs.html. Accessed March 8, 2002.

148. Goldsmith, *Civil Forfeiture.*

149. *U.S.* v. *92 Buena Vista Ave.,* 113 S.Ct. 1126, 122 L.Ed. 2d 469 (1993).

150. *Austin* v. *U.S.,* 113 S.Ct. 2801, 15 L.Ed. 2d 448 (1993).

151. *Alexander* v. *U.S.,* 113 S.Ct. 2766, 125 L.Ed. 2d 441 (1993); and *U.S.* v. *James Daniel Good Real Property,* 114 S.Ct. 492, 126 L.Ed. 2d 490 (1993).

152. *U.S.* v. *Bajakajian,* 524 U.S. 321 (1998).

153. *Bennis* v. *Michigan,* 116 S.Ct. 1560, 134 L.Ed. 2d 661 (1996).

154. *U.S.* v. *Ursery,* 116 S.Ct. 2135, 135 L.Ed. 2d 549 (1996).

155. Statement by the Honorable Henry J. Hyde, "Civil Asset Forfeiture Reform Act." Web posted at http://www.house.gov/judiciary/161.htm. Accessed March 10, 2002.

156. "Drug Raid Called Biggest Ever," Associated Press wire service, September 30, 1989, p. 1A.

157. "Cocaine Found Packed in Toxic Chemical Drums," *Fayetteville (N.C.) Observer-Times,* November 5, 1989.

158. Mark Moore, *Drug Trafficking,* NIJ Crime File Study Guide (Washington, D.C.: U.S. Government Printing Office, 1988), p. 3.

159. "Briefly," *Drug Enforcement Report,* March 23, 1995, p. 7.

160. "Is the War on Drugs Another Vietnam?" *Newsweek,* May 30, 1988, p. 38.

161. Moore, *Drug Trafficking.*

162. Arizona Supreme Court, *Drug Treatment and Education Fund Legislative Report for Fiscal Year 1997–1998* (Phoenix: Administrative Office of the Courts, 1999), p. 4.

163. Ibid.

164. Ibid.

165. Michael S. Goodstadt, *Drug Education,* NIJ Crime File Study Guide (Washington, D.C.: U.S. Government Printing Office, no date), p. 1.

166. "DARE Not Effective in Reducing Drug Abuse, Study Finds," *Criminal Justice Newsletter,* October 3, 1994, pp. 6–7.

167. The government version of the study was first reported as "The DARE Program: A Review of Prevalence, User Satisfaction, and Effectiveness," *National Institute of Justice Update* (October 1994). The full study, as published by NIJ, is Christopher L. Ringwalt et al., *Past and Future Directions of the DARE Program: An Evaluation Review* (Washington, D.C.: National Institute of Justice, 1995).

168. Fox Butterfield, no headline, *New York Times* wire service, April 16, 1997, citing Office of Justice Programs, *Preventing Crime: What Works, What Doesn't, What's Promising* (Washington, D.C.: U.S. Department of Justice, 1997).

169. Donald R. Lynam et al., "Project DARE: No Effects at 10-Year Follow-up," *Journal of Consulting and Clinical Psychology,* Vol. 67, No. 4 (1999).

170. Goodstadt, *Drug Education,* p. 3.

171. *USA Today,* September 6, 1990, p. 8A, citing a report by the U.S. Senate Judiciary Committee.

172. Ibid.

173. RAND Corporation's Drug Policy Research Center, *Are Mandatory Minimum Drug Sentences Cost-Effective?* (Santa Monica, CA: RAND, 1997).

174. John S. Goldkamp and Doris Weiland, "Assessing the Impact of Dade County's Felony Drug Court," *NIJ Research in Brief,* December 1993.

175. NADCP, *The Facts: Facts on Drug Courts.*

176. ONDCP, *The National Drug Control Strategy, 1999.*

177. Paul H. Blachy, "Effects of Decriminalization of Marijuana in Oregon," *Annals of the New York Academy of Sciences,* Vol. 282 (1976), pp. 405–415. For more information on the decriminalization of marijuana, see James A. Inciardi, "Marijuana Decriminalization Research: A Perspective and Commentary," *Criminology,* Vol. 19, No. 1 (May 1981), pp. 145–159.

178. Arnold S. Trebach, "Thinking through Models of Drug Legalization," *Drug Policy Letter* (July/August 1994), p. 10.

179. For a more thorough discussion of some of these arguments, see Ronald Hamowy, ed., *Dealing with Drugs: Consequences of Government Control* (Lexington, MA: Lexington Books, 1987).

180. See Kurt Schmoke (*Washington Post* editorial author), "Considering Decriminalization: War on Drugs, Policy of Folly?" reprinted in *Fayetteville (N.C.) Observer-Times,* May 16, 1988, p. 4A.

181. "Should Drugs Be Legal?" *Newsweek,* May 30, 1988, p. 36.

182. Ibid., p. 37.

183. Ibid., pp. 37–38.

184. Trebach, "Thinking through Models of Drug Legalization," p. 10.

185. For a more detailed discussion of the two-market system, see John Kaplan, *Heroin,* NIJ Crime File Study Guide (Washington, D.C.: National Institute of Justice, no date).

186. Ibid., p. 3.

187. Ibid., p. 4.

Multinational Criminal Justice

LEARNING OBJECTIVES

After reading this chapter, you should be able to

- Describe the nature of comparative criminal justice, and identify the problems inherent in cross-cultural comparisons of crime

- Describe the main characteristics of the Chinese justice system

- Describe the central features of Islamic criminal justice

- Identify the most significant characteristics of the criminal justice system in England and Wales

- Identify important international criminal justice organizations, and explain their role in international crime fighting

chapter 16

[*America's response to globalization in the criminal justice arena will necessitate major changes in both law and policy, placing greater emphasis on the education and training of practitioners at all levels of government. In addition to culture and language, tomorrow's criminal justice practitioner must have a broader understanding of the legal systems of other countries and respect for the customs and practices of immigrants, as well as an increasing number of international visitors.*]

—Richard H. Ward, Dean and Director, Criminal Justice Center,
Sam Houston State University[1]

Key Concepts

[Terms]

comparative criminologist	International Criminal Police Organization (INTERPOL)	Parliament
ethnocentric		procuratorate
European Police Office (Europol)	Islamic law	*Tazir* crime
Hudud crime	mediation committee	transnational crime

Introduction

Hear the author discuss this chapter at **cjtoday.com**

Japan greeted the year 2000 by enacting three crime bills that gave law enforcement officials limited power to wiretap phones, stiffened penalties for organized criminal activity, and increased protections for witnesses.[2] For the most part, the new laws were directed against the *yakuza*, Japan's organized crime syndicates. The laws, however, were also a sign that Japan is facing more crime than ever before and that its citizens are becoming increasingly concerned about violent crime.

Until recently, Japan had been regarded as an optimistic and relatively crime-free country. Less than a decade ago, Japan seemed safe from violent crime, and fear of crime was at the bottom of citizens' concerns. Japanese crime rates had been the lowest among developed countries since the end of World War II.

The Japanese sense of security largely disappeared in 1995, when Shoko Asahara, leader of the 10,000-member Aum Shinri Kyo (Supreme Truth) sect, was arrested and charged with masterminding a nerve gas attack on a Tokyo subway station. The attack left 12 dead and more than 5,500 injured. Intense Japanese media coverage of Asahara's arrest and pending trial made the event in some ways the Far Eastern equivalent of the 1995 O. J. Simpson trial, which received extensive coverage in American media.

Two years after the gas attacks, Japan was forced to come to terms with another shocking crime when police arrested a 14-year-old boy who confessed to beheading a fellow student and drinking the victim's blood.[3] The head of 11-year-old victim Jun Hase was discovered by a custodian at the gate of a junior high school in the city of Kobe. Hase's eyes had been gouged out, and his mouth had been slashed from ear to ear. In place of his tongue, police found a taunting note, which called investigators "fools" and boasted that the killer enjoyed seeing people die.[4] The suspect in the case, whose name was not released, told police he killed Hase, brought the severed head home, washed it in a bathroom, and hid it overnight in the attic above his room. The next morning, he carved the head on his desk, then placed it near the school. Police who later searched the boy's room found horror videos, knives, and a book about the Zodiac serial killings which took place in San Francisco in the 1960s. Investigators also reportedly found notebooks recording details of other attacks, and the boy then confessed to two assaults on young girls and to two other attacks in which one girl was beaten to death and another was stabbed.

The gruesome murder of young Hase had an especially demoralizing effect on many Japanese. Motoo Sakai, 34, a Kobe hotel doorman, was one of many upset by the beheading. "I'm worried that more and more crimes are being committed by youngsters. I just wonder where Japanese society is headed," he said.[5] Two years later, Sakai's words were supported by the annual crime statistics released by the Japanese government. The official 2002 report showed that—in contrast to reported crime in America—the number of crimes in Japan had reached new heights. Most of the increase came in areas such as muggings (up 15% in one year), nighttime store robberies (up 24%), and various property crimes (with increases ranging from 10% to 25%).[6] To most Japanese, violent crimes seemed to be everywhere. Newsworthy crimes that occurred in Japan include the gang rape and brutal beating of a 20-year-old university student by five students from the medical school at Tokyo's prestigious Keio University; the arrest of a 16-year-old boy from the town of Takane for beating his father to death; the robbery of a Tokyo jewelry store by a 14-year-old boy; the tossing of a 6-year-old boy from a condominium window by a 20-year-old man running a test in preparation for his own suicide; the arrest of a 19-year-old man for stabbing his mother to death following a discussion about his fiancée; and the arrest of a 23-year-old female teacher in Nagoya for having had sex with a 14-year-old student—all of which sound very much as if they could be crimes lifted from the pages of American tabloids.[7]

As Japanese citizens began adjusting to a lessened sense of personal security, some suggested that officials there could learn something from the experience of the United States and other industrialized countries in which criminality is rampant. A few even suggested that comparing Japanese troubles with understandings of what had historically contributed to high crime rates in America might produce effective strategies to head off further crime and social disorder in Japan.

Criminologists who study crime and criminal justice on a cross-national level are referred to as **comparative criminologists**, and their field is called *comparative criminology* or *comparative criminal justice*. Comparative criminal justice is becoming increasingly valued for the insights it provides. By contrasting native institutions of justice with similar institutions in other countries, procedures and problems which have been taken for granted under one system can be reevaluated in the light of world experience. As communications, rapid travel, and other technological advances effectively "shrink" the world, we find ourselves in the nearly ideal situation of being able to learn firsthand about the criminal justice systems of other countries and to use that information to improve our own. This chapter explains the value of comparative criminology for students of criminal justice, points to the problems which arise in comparing data from different nations, and explores three criminal justice systems in other parts of the world: Chinese, English, and Islamic criminal justice. International police agencies are also described, and the role of the United Nations in the worldwide fight against crime is discussed. Additional information on the justice systems of many countries can be found in the *World Factbook of Criminal Justice Systems*, available via **Library Extra! 16–1** at cjtoday.com. Another place to visit for international criminal justice information is the National Institute of Justice's International Center, which is accessible via **Web Extra! 16–1** at cjtoday.com.

comparative criminologist

One who studies crime and criminal justice on a cross-national level.

Ethnocentrism and the Study of Criminal Justice

Like most other human beings, we Americans often assume that the way we do things is the best way to do them. Such belief is probably part of human nature. As a consequence of this attitude, however, the study of criminal justice in the United States has been largely **ethnocentric**. Because people are socialized from birth into a particular culture, they tend to prefer their own culture's way of doing things over that of any other. Native patterns of

ethnocentric

Holding a belief in the superiority of one's own social or ethnic group and culture.

School students offering prayers and bouquets at the main gate of the Ikeda Elementary School in Japan, where eight children were stabbed to death in 2001 by a knife-wielding attacker. Once regarded as a country with a very low incidence of serious crime, Japan has recently weathered a series of traumatizing criminal episodes.

AP/Wide World Photos

behavior are seen as somehow "natural" and therefore better than foreign ones. The same is true for values, beliefs, and customs. People tend to think that the religion they were born into holds a spiritual edge over other religions, that their values and ethical sense are superior to those of others, and that the fashions they wear, the language they speak, and the rituals of daily life in which they participate are somehow better than comparable practices elsewhere. Ethnocentric individuals rarely stop to think that people elsewhere in the world cling to their own values, beliefs, and standards of behavior with just as much fervor as they do. Hence, ethnocentrism is not a uniquely American phenomenon.

Only in recent years have American students of criminal justice begun to examine the justice systems of other cultures. Unfortunately, not all cultures are equally open, and it is not always easy to explore them. In some societies, even the *study* of criminal justice is taboo. As a result, data-gathering strategies taken for granted in Western culture may not be well received elsewhere. One author, for example, has observed about China, "The seeking of criminal justice information through face-to-face questioning takes on a different meaning in Chinese officialdom than it does generally in the Western world. While we accept this method of inquiry because we prize thinking on our feet and quick answers, it is rather offensive in China because it shows lack of respect and appreciation for the information given through the preferred means of prepared questions and formal briefings."[8] Hence, most of the information available about Chinese criminal justice comes by way of officialdom, and routine Western social science practices like door-to-door interviews, participant observation, and random surveys might produce substantial problems for researchers who attempt to use these techniques in China.

Problems with Data

Similar difficulties arise in the comparison of crime rates from one country to another. The crime rates of different nations are difficult to compare because of (1) differences in the way a specific crime is defined, (2) diverse crime-reporting practices, and (3) political and other influences on the reporting of statistics to international agencies.[9]

Definitional differences create what may be the biggest problem. For cross-national comparisons of crime data to be meaningful, it is essential that the reported data share conceptual similarities. Unfortunately, that is rarely the case. Nations report offenses according to the legal criteria by which arrests are made and under which prosecution can occur. Switzerland, for example, includes bicycle thefts in its reported data on what we call "auto theft" because Swiss data gathering focuses more on the concept of personal transportation than it does upon the type of vehicle stolen. The Netherlands has no crime category for robberies, counting them as thefts. Japan classifies an assault that results in death as an assault or an aggravated assault, not as a homicide. Greek rape statistics include crimes of sodomy, "lewdness," seduction of a child, incest, and prostitution. Communist China reports only robberies and thefts which involve the property of citizens; crimes against state-owned property fall into a separate category.

Social, cultural, and economic differences among countries compound these difficulties. Auto theft statistics, for example, when compared between countries like the United States and China, need to be placed in an economic as well as demographic context. While the United States has two automobiles for every three people, China has only one car per 100 citizens. For the Chinese auto theft rate to equal that of the United States, every automobile in the country would have to be stolen nearly twice each year!

Reporting practices vary substantially between nations. The International Criminal Police Organization (INTERPOL) and the United Nations are the only international organizations which regularly collect crime statistics from a large number of countries.[10] Both agencies can only request data and have no way of checking on the accuracy of the data reported to them. Many countries do not disclose the requested information, and those that do often make only partial reports. In general, small countries are more likely to report than are large ones, and nonsocialist countries are more likely to report than are socialist nations.[11]

International reports of crime are often delayed. Complete, up-to-date data are rare since the information made available to agencies like the United Nations and INTERPOL is reported at different times and according to schedules which vary from nation to nation. In addition, official United Nations world crime surveys are conducted only infrequently. To date, five such surveys have been undertaken.

Crime statistics also reflect political biases and national values. Some nations do not accurately admit to the frequency of certain kinds of culturally reprehensible crimes.

Communist countries, for example, appear loathe to report crimes like theft, burglary, and robbery because the very existence of such offenses demonstrates felt inequities within the Communist system. After the breakup of the Soviet Union, Alexander Larin, a criminal justice scholar who worked as a Russian investigator during the 1950s and 1960s, revealed that "inside the state security bureaucracy, where statistics were collected and circulated, falsification of crime figures was the rule, not the exception. The practice was self-perpetuating," said Larin. "Supervisors in the provinces were under pressure to provide Moscow with declining crime rates. And no self-respecting investigator wanted to look worse than his neighbor. . . . From the top to the bottom, the bosses depended on their employees not to make them look bad with high crime statistics."[12]

On the other hand, observers in democratic societies showed similar biases in their interpretation of statistics following the end of the cold war. Some Western analysts, for example, reporting on declines in the prison populations of Eastern and Central Europe during that period, attributed the decline to lessened frustration and lowered crime rates brought about by democratization. In one country, Hungary, prison populations declined from 240 inmates per 100,000 residents in 1986 to 130 per 100,000 in 1993, with similar decreases in other nations.[13] The more likely explanation, however, appears to have been the wholesale post-Soviet release of political dissidents from prisons formerly run by Communist regimes. Learn more about world crime via the United Nations' *Global Report on Crime and Justice*, which is available via **Library Extra! 16–2** at cjtoday.com.

The Chinese Justice System

The People's Republic of China (PRC), with a land area of 3,691,502 square miles and a population of more than 1.2 billion people, is the largest nation on earth. Some people predict that in the twenty-first century, as the Chinese economy awakens and its massive military might makes itself felt, it will become the world's most important nation. For that reason, students of criminal justice should have some understanding of the Chinese justice system and of the cultural assumptions which underlie it.

In the spring of 1989, the world focused its attention on China, where students and workers were holding mass demonstrations calling for freedom and democracy. Tiananmen Square, in the center of Beijing, became the rallying point for protesters. The huge and famous portrait of Communist leader Mao Ze-dong, which overlooks the square, was defaced with paint. Students even constructed a small replica of the Statue of Liberty on the bricks of the square. As the world looked on, the Chinese Red Army, acting on orders of party leader Deng Xiaoping and members of the Chinese Communist Party Central Committee, moved decisively to end the demonstrations. On June 4, 1989, at least 800 people died in a hail of rifle fire directed at the protesters. It is estimated that thousands more perished in the weeks that followed.[14] Some were victims of government action to suppress continuing demonstrations, while others were summarily tried and executed for inciting riots and for plotting against the government. While the Chinese democratic revolution of 1989 did not succeed, it gives evidence of the sense of single-minded purpose so characteristic of Chinese society. It is that shared sense of purpose which underlies the Chinese legal system today.

Maoist Justice

Under Communist Party Chairman Mao Ze-dong, criminal justice in the People's Republic of China was based upon informal societal control. Mao abhorred bureaucratic agencies and procedures, and during his reign, accused offenders found themselves turned over to the populace for a hearing and punishment.[15] The infamous Chinese Cultural Revolution, from 1966 to 1973,[16] was intended to integrate Maoist teaching and principles into Chinese society. During the revolutionary period, Mao called upon his fanatical followers, known as Red Guards, to "smash the police and the courts." One of Mao's most popular sayings was, "Depend on the rule of man, not the rule of law."[17] Because of Maoist thinking, the People's Republic of China had no criminal or procedural legal codes, no lawyers, and no officially designated prosecutors until after 1978. Under Mao, the police were replaced by military control, with arrest powers residing in the People's Liberation Army.

According to the concept of class justice taught by the Cultural Revolution, the severity of punishment an offender received depended upon his or her social and political identity. Consistent with the tenor of the times, a Chinese textbook of the late 1960s proclaimed,

"The point of our criminal law is chiefly directed toward the enemies of socialism."[18] Wealthy, successful, and educated people, because of their high status under previous regimes, were automatically suspected of crimes and were often summarily tried and severely punished for the vaguest of allegations. Following Mao's death, the Cultural Revolution was denounced by the Central Committee of the Chinese Communist Party as "responsible for the most severe setback and the heaviest losses suffered by the party, the state, and the people since the founding of the People's Republic."[19]

In 1978, two years after the death of Chairman Mao, another wave of reform swept China. This time a formalized legal system, based upon codified laws, was created, and a radically revised Constitution was given life in 1982. Predictability and security, especially for the potentially most productive members of society, became the goal of the new National People's Congress. The congress sought to ensure internal stability, international commerce, and modernization through legislation. The Chinese Constitution now contains 24 articles on the fundamental rights and duties of citizens[20] and guarantees equality before the law for everyone.

The Chinese Justice System Today

The modern Chinese justice system is structured along jurisdictional lines similar to those in the United States. At the highest level, the Chinese justice system is built around four national offices: the Ministry of Public Security, the Supreme People's Court, the People's **Procuratorate**, and the Ministry of Justice. Article 5 of the Chinese Constitution specifies that the procuratorate is directly responsible for supervising the administration of criminal justice throughout the country—including the investigation of crimes and the activities of the courts, the police, and correctional institutions—and for initiating prosecution.[21]

Chinese police agencies, which fall under the authority of the Ministry of Public Security, are often regarded as technologically backward. Some, however, are beginning to apply twenty-first-century technology in the fight against crime. In 1994, for example, Chinese officials announced that police forces in more than 20 provinces had begun to use DNA fingerprinting as a method of criminal identification.[22] Also in 1994, the China Criminal Information Center, a computerized national network designed to provide police forces throughout China with rapid interprovincial information on criminal offenders, began operating in 11 provinces along China's east coast. Officials said they hoped that the new computer system will allow for improved control over China's huge migrant population,[23] estimated at between 60 and 80 million people—especially members of that group who are involved in criminal activity.

Courts in China are hierarchically organized. The Supreme People's Court is the highest court in China. It deals with cases which may have an impact on the entire country.[24] Most cases come before the court on appeal. The court is divided into three sections: criminal

procuratorate

A term used in many countries to refer to an agency with powers and responsibilities similar to those of a prosecutor's office in the United States.

CJ Today Exhibit 16-1

[Individual Rights Guaranteed Under the
Constitution of the People's Republic of China]

Right	Guaranteed by
Equality before the law	Article 33
Freedom from unlawful detention	Article 37
Right against unlawful personal searches	Article 37
Protection from unlawful arrest	Article 37
Right against unlawful searches of a residence	Article 39
Right to a public trial	Article 126
Right to defense in a criminal trial	Article 126
Right to use one's native spoken and written language in court	Article 134

Adapted December 4, 1982, by the Fifth National People's Congress, Beijing.

court, which deals with felony violations of the law, mostly on appeal, and death penalty reviews; civil affairs court; and economic court.

At the opposite judicial extreme, the Basic People's Court operates at the county level as the court with original jurisdiction over most criminal cases. Two judicial levels—the Intermediate People's Court and the Higher People's Court—stand between the Basic Court and the Supreme Court. Both function as courts of appeal, although Intermediate Courts have original jurisdiction in criminal cases with the potential for sentences involving death or life imprisonment. They also hear criminal charges brought against foreigners.

Defendants may choose to be represented in Chinese courts by an attorney, a relative, or a friend, or they may choose to represent themselves. If they desire, a lawyer will be appointed for them. Attorneys in China, however, have a far different role from that of their American counterparts. While they work to protect the rights of the defendant, attorneys have a responsibility to the court which transcends their duties to the accused. Defense lawyers are charged with helping the court render a just verdict.[25] The Chinese believe that vigorous defense strategies such as those used in the adversarial system of Western justice can lead to criminals escaping responsibility.[26]

A visit to Shanghai by a delegation of the American Bar Association determined that 78% of the workload of Chinese attorneys consisted of defending accused criminals. The remaining 22% was divided about equally between family practice (wills, divorces, adoptions, inheritance, and so on) and civil suits.[27] The legal profession in China is not, on the whole, well trained. While most lawyers probably have some formal legal education, many simply meet the conditions of Article 8 of the Chinese Constitution, which requires persons who wish to engage in the practice of law to "have the cultural level of graduates of institutions of higher learning, and be suitable to be lawyers."

The Chinese justice system has a built-in system of checks and balances which, in theory, operates to prevent abuses of power. Arrests made by the police, for example, must be approved by the local procurator's office. If a decision is made to prosecute, the court may conduct its own investigation before the trial to determine whether prosecution is warranted.

The official Chinese crime rate is astonishingly low—only 56 crimes per every 100,000 citizens (versus 5,600 per 100,000 people in the United States).[28] But official crime rates may be little more than fabrications designed for the foreign media. Asian experts say that China is now experiencing a crime wave unprecedented since the Communist revolution in 1949.[29] Drug crimes are especially problematic, with narcotics seizures in 1998 reported to be the highest in the history of Communist China. Much crime may be due to high unemployment rates. Eleven percent of the Chinese urban workforce was unemployed in 1999.[30]

One special area of concern to outsiders has been China's wholesale violation of intellectual property rights by bootleggers who reproduce foreign movies, compact discs, tapes, DVD's, and software and resell them in China and throughout Asia without paying permission fees or royalties. In 1995, U.S. industry representatives estimated that Chinese copyright, trademark, and patent violations cost American companies alone billions of dollars a year in lost sales.[31] In response to stiff international pressure, China has recently taken steps to criminalize bootlegging activities, including the establishment of special courts to prosecute those who violate laws governing intellectual property,[32] and the enforcement of new antipiracy laws seems to be increasing.

Organized crime is another problem in China. Chinese gang roots can be traced to secret societies, called *triads,* that fought to restore the Ming Dynasty, which was overthrown in 1644. Beginning in the early 1900s, the triads which survived became increasingly involved in criminal activities. In 1949, after the Communist takeover, China's gangs and underworld secret societies were either eradicated or forced into hibernation. In recent years, these "black societies" have made a strong comeback, manufacturing and selling guns, running illegal gambling operations, smuggling, forcing women into prostitution, and fighting gun battles with local police. In 1995, Chinese officials announced a major crackdown on organized crime throughout the country, vowing to execute any gang bosses who could be identified.[33]

Once arrested, suspects face a high likelihood of conviction. Records show only a 1% acquittal rate in Chinese criminal courts (versus 31% in the United States).[34] A crime problem of growing concern to the Chinese is juvenile delinquency. Juvenile gang activity is on the increase, with gang members often coming from the families of high Communist Party functionaries.[35] Some officials have also suggested that international gang-related drug trafficking is on the rise in the PRC. However, although China has had a history of problems with opium abuse, actual consumption of illicit drugs by Chinese citizens probably occurs at a rate much lower than that of the Western world.[36]

> With criminals' ability to cross international borders in a few hours, and the advances of our modern age, such as the Internet and tele-communications, crime can no longer be viewed as just a national issue.
>
> —Assistant U.S. Attorney General Laurie Robinson

A Chinese police officer questioning an elderly couple in front of the Tiananmen Gate in Beijing.

Chung Chien-min, AP/Wide World Photos

mediation committee

One of the civilian dispute-resolution groups found throughout China. Mediation committees successfully divert many minor offenders from the more formal mechanisms of justice.

MEDIATION COMMITTEES

One reason for China's low official crime rate is the Chinese system of people's **mediation committees**. By virtue of the large number of cases they resolve, mediation committees may be the most important component of justice in modern China. Mediation committees generally consist of from five to seven people, with judicial assistants assigned to them by the Bureau of Justice, the courts, and the procuratorates.[37] They are officially guided by law and by government policy. Their power, however, comes from the force of public opinion.[38] Education and persuasion are their primary tools.[39]

The committees function informally based upon the belief that minor disputes and misdemeanor offenses such as minor assaults, thefts, and vandalism can best be handled locally without unnecessary protocol. Mediation committees are also believed to play a significant role in crime prevention by resolving disputes before they evolve into serious altercations. That is why housing disputes, divorce cases, and land-sharing problems also commonly come before them.

People's mediation committees are everywhere in China—in factories, on farms, in schools, and in businesses. According to some authorities, over 800,000 Chinese mediation committees functioning on a regular basis handle over 8 million cases per year.[40] In contrast, there are only 3,000 regular courts at all levels throughout the entire country.[41] Mediation committees serve to divert a large number of people from processing by county and provincial courts. They also serve to dramatically lower the number of officially reported offenses throughout China.

CHINESE CRIMINAL PUNISHMENTS

The punishment of offenders in China can be severe in cases which go beyond mediation and enter the court system. Thirty-eight percent of convicted offenders in China are sentenced to more than five years in prison,[42] and repeat offenders are subject to harsh punishments. Widespread use of the death penalty, usually carried out with a single bullet to the back of the head soon after conviction, is characteristic of contemporary China. Executions are often preceded by a public rally during which the prisoner's name, crime, and punishment are announced to the crowd, while the prisoner is forced to stand with head bowed and hands tied. Following execution, the offender's family is routinely ordered to pay for the cost of the bullet. The number of people executed each year is a state secret. Amnesty International, however, says that more people are executed in China each year than in all of the rest of the world. The organization estimates that China's Strike Hard (Against Crime) campaigns, which began in 1983 and are revived periodically, have led to at least 19,446 executions between 1990 and 2000—an execution rate around 35 times

Female prisoners sewing in a Chinese prison.

Thomas McAninch, Ph.D.

that of the United States.[43] (See the CJ Today News box in this chapter for a description of China's 2001 Strike Hard campaign.) Amnesty International also says that a recent *Yanda*, or anticrime campaign aimed at combating major crimes, such as murder and robbery, led to 1,014 death sentences between April and June of 1996—resulting in over 800 immediate executions.[44]

In China, capital punishment can be imposed for a wide variety of crimes. One man was executed, for example, for publishing pornographic books, and four others were put to death for faking tax receipts. "The death penalty is apparently used to deter people from actions that interfere with economic development," said one Western observer.[45] Widespread use of the death penalty, while expected to deter others, is not based upon studies of the punishment's effectiveness as a deterrent. As one Chinese diplomat said, "We don't feel the death penalty is based on research but on common sense arguments and primal response."[46] Although death sentences must be reviewed by the Supreme People's Court, the court may rule on the legality of a case before a defendant is sentenced, which clears the way for speedy executions.

According to authorities there, Chinese prisons hold 1.28 million inmates in 685 prison units. Western authorities, however, doubt that official Chinese statistics are correct. Independent research into Chinese arrest and sentencing patterns, and accounts by former prisoners, lead some to conclude that as many as 16 to 20 million people are confined in 990 labor reform prisons—that is, prisons set aside for inmates whose only crime may be speaking out against the dictatorial aspects of the Chinese government.

Many Chinese prisons are notoriously primitive. Typical cells, which range in size from 36 to 60 square yards, hold 30 to 50 inmates, who sleep on hard woven mats covering the floor. Unheated in the winter, the cells are fitted with only one latrine and are lit with a single lightbulb.

For all its seeming harshness, the Chinese justice system is based upon a strong cultural belief in personal reformation. As one author has observed, "Repentance, which means reclaiming individuals for society, is at the heart of Chinese justice."[47] Confucius taught that "man is at birth by nature good,"[48] and Chinese authorities seek to build opportunities into their criminal justice system which allow offenders to change for the better.

Violation of prison rules may result in extended incarceration, solitary confinement, or "group criticism." The study of Communist policy, according to official Chinese interpretation, is required of all inmates. Such study is the focal point of prison treatment programs.[49] Political prisoners are subjected to *laogai*,[50] or "thought reform through labor," and are required to work at prison farms, factories, and the like.

Official parole eligibility comes only after the offender has shown repentance and has performed "meritoriously" while in prison. In practice, however, parole may be granted routinely

CJ Today News

[China Strikes Hard,
Hopes Crime Takes a Hit]

HONG KONG—China, caught up in one of its periodic anti-crime frenzies, has executed more than 500 people since early April [2001].

On April 11, the day the "Strike Hard" campaign officially began, 89 people were put to death.

The latest nationwide Strike Hard campaign—the first was in 1983, the most recent in 1996—is in part a reaction to rising crime. Police say the number of reported crimes shot up 50% last year. Gang-related crime increased 700%, the government says. The rise follows two decades of economic reforms that have enriched many Chinese but left millions of others unemployed and unprotected by the social benefits offered under the old communist economy. According to U.S. estimates, China's urban jobless rate hovers around 10%. Unemployment is believed to be much higher in rural areas.

"The dramatic social change taking place in China is producing a growing disadvantaged population," the government newspaper *People's Daily* noted at the beginning of the Strike Hard campaign. "This is likely to give rise to underground violent gangs."

Many see the government's efforts as a pointless ritual that does little to cut crime and much to undermine China's attempts to reform its criminal justice system. And now there is some concern that the new campaign has incited criminals to retaliate. "The evidence indicates that (executions) do not really work," says Harold Tanner, a historian and author of a book about the crackdowns, *Strike Hard!* "Campaign-style justice and enthusiastic use of the death penalty have not brought about lower crime rates. These severe tactics simply do not scare potential criminals." . . .

. . . Even before the latest Strike Hard campaign, China was the world's most enthusiastic user of the death penalty, according

to Amnesty International. From 1990 to 2000, China executed at least 19,446 people and probably many more, Amnesty says. China's population of 1.26 billion is 4 1/2 times as large as that of the USA, but China executed at least 34 1/2 times as many people in the 1990s. In the USA, 563 people were put to death over the same period.

Amnesty counted 4,367 executions during the Strike Hard year 1996, 72% more than the year before and 133% more than the year after. The number of executions is expected to be inflated again this year by the latest campaign.

Under Strike Hard, the government exhorts local prosecutors and police to crack down on specific crimes. Violent crime, gang-related crime and theft have been targeted this time, along with corruption. Criminals can be executed for organizing a prostitution ring, taking bribes or trafficking in drugs. Officials hold rallies in sports stadiums at which convicted criminals are paraded before massive crowds. Later the same day, many of the convicts get a bullet to the back of the head—the most common method of execution, though China sometimes uses lethal injection. . . .

. . . Courts and prosecutors are under enormous pressure to send criminals to jail or to the executioner, and they often ignore legal niceties in the process. Indeed, officials in Sichuan Province recently advised investigators, "Don't get entangled in details" as long as the weight of the evidence points to a suspect's guilt.

Chen Feirong, 32, a student working on a master's degree in business at Beijing's Tsinghua University, says that during Strike Hard years, criminal suspects "will be treated unfairly. The government should enforce the law, not rely on this kind of campaign."

Officers taking a female convict to the executioner immediately after a sentencing rally in Beijing.

AFP Photo

This year's effort has netted a wide variety of criminals:

- Four tax cheats in southern Guangdong Province were executed May 11 for bilking the government out of nearly $10 million in inflated tax rebates.
- A bank robber who disguised himself as a woman, wearing a wig, a dress and high-heeled shoes, was sentenced to death last month in southwestern Yunnan Province.
- An official from central Hubei Province was executed May 28 after embezzling nearly $2.4 million from two state-owned companies and blowing the money on gambling excursions to Macao.

Strike Hard might be taking the lives of more than convicts. In the city of Nanchong in Sichuan Province, four college students have been murdered. It is widely believed that they were victims of a campaign of terror by gangsters trying to intimidate the local government into refraining from executing their arrested leaders.

The gang members reportedly threatened to kill 100 students if the executions were carried out, the Information Center for Human Rights and Democracy has reported. Local officials deny any connection between the killings and Strike Hard. They say they have already arrested the murderers.

For the latest in crime and justice news, visit the Talk Justice news feed at http://www.crimenews.info.

Source: Paul Wiseman, "China Strikes Hard, Hopes Crime Takes a Hit: Many Doubt Crackdowns Are Effective," *USA Today*, June 20, 2001, p. 8A. © 2001, *USA Today*. Reprinted with permission.

after half the sentence has been served (ten years for life sentences).[51] Chinese parole follows the institutional model, in which individual confinement facilities recommend parole to the court, which then makes the final decision. Parole officers are unknown in China, but parolees are supervised by local police agencies and by citizens' groups.

The philosophy which underlies Chinese corrections is well summed up in the words of a Western observer who recently visited prisons there: "Inmates are expected to conform not to benefit themselves, but to benefit their families, villages, and even their country. Crime is not a reflection of individual failure, but instead is considered a reflection of the family, the community, and even the larger society. It is for the good of society, it is for the good of the communist structure that one must reform one's self. The individual is punished, but he is punished as a member of the group."[52] Faith in repentance, a fundamental doctrine in Chinese corrections, is apparently well placed. The official rate of recidivism in China is only 4.7% for serious offenders.[53]

In 1994, China's legislature, the National People's Congress, passed the National Prison Reform Law. The law guarantees prisoners dignity, safety, the right to a legal defense, a right of appeal, and freedom from physical abuse. The law also prohibits forced confessions and the illegal confiscation of property and holds prison officials responsible for ensuring that inmates serve their full sentences. The 1994 law officially codified a decade-old set of Chinese

A female prisoner gardening at a Chinese "reeducation center."
Xinhua, Getty Images, Inc.

administrative guidelines for prisons. The guidelines, originally approved in 1982, had been largely ignored by prison administrators and had remained unenforced—causing Chinese prisons to become the target of strong criticism from international human rights groups.

Islamic Criminal Justice

Islamic law has been the subject of much discussion in the United States since the September 11, 2001, terrorist attacks on the World Trade Center and the Pentagon and the resulting destruction of the Taliban regime in Afghanistan by American military forces. It is important for American students of criminal justice to recognize, however, that Islamic law refers to legal ideas (and sometimes entire legal systems) based on the teachings of Islam—and that it bears no intrinsic relationship to acts of terrorism committed by misguided zealots with Islamic backgrounds. Similarly, Islamic law is by no means the same thing as *jihad* (Muslim holy war) or Islamic fundamentalism. Although Americans are now much better informed about the concept of Islamic law than they were in the past, some may not be aware that various interpretations of Islam still form the basis of laws in many countries and that the entire legal systems of some nations are based on Islamic principles. Islamic law holds considerable sway in a large number of countries, including Syria, Iran, Iraq, Pakistan, Afghanistan, Yemen, Saudi Arabia, Kuwait, the United Arab Emirates, Bahrain, Algeria, Jordan, Lebanon, Libya, Ethiopia, Gambia, Nigeria, Oman, Qatar, Senegal, Tunisia, Tajikistan, Uzbekistan, and Turkey (which practices official separation of church and state).

Criminal justice professor Sam Souryal and his coauthors describe four aspects of justice in Arab philosophy and religion. Islamic justice, they say, means[54]

- A sacred trust, a duty imposed on humans to be discharged sincerely and honestly. As such, these authors say, "justice is the quality of being morally responsible and merciful in giving everyone his or her due."

- Mutual respect of one human being by another. From this perspective, a just society is one which offers equal respect for individuals through social arrangements made in the common interest of all members.

- An aspect of the social bond which holds society together and transforms it into a brotherhood in which everyone becomes a keeper of everyone else and each is held accountable for the welfare of all.

- A command from God. Whosoever violates God's commands should be subject to strict punishments according to Islamic tradition and belief.

As Souryal and his coauthors observe, "the third and fourth meanings of justice are probably the ones most commonly invoked in Islamic jurisprudence" and form the basis of criminal justice practice in many Middle Eastern countries.

The *Hudud* Crimes

Islamic law

A system of laws, operative in some Arab countries, based upon the Muslim religion and especially the holy book of Islam, the Koran.

Islamic law (or *Shari'ah* in Arabic, which means "path of God") forms the basis of theocratic judicial systems in Kuwait, Saudi Arabia, the Sudan, Iran, and Algeria. Other Arabic nations, such as Egypt, Jordan, and Iraq, recognize substantial elements of Islamic law in their criminal justice systems but also make wide use of Western and nontheocratic legal principles. Islamic law is based upon four sources. In order of importance, these sources are (1) the Koran (also spelled *Quran* and *Qur'an*), or Holy Book of Islam, which Muslims believe is the word of God, or Allah; (2) the teachings of the Prophet Mohammed; (3) a consensus of the clergy in cases where neither the Koran nor the prophet directly address an issue; and (4) reason or logic, which should be used when no solution can be found in the other three sources.[55]

Hudud crime

A serious violation of Islamic law regarded as an offense against God. *Hudud* crimes include such behavior as theft, adultery, sodomy, alcohol consumption, and robbery.

Islamic law recognizes seven **Hudud crimes**—or crimes based on religious strictures. *Hudud* (sometimes called *Hodood* or *Huddud*) crimes are essentially violations of "natural law" as interpreted by Arab culture. Divine displeasure is thought to be the basis of crimes defined as *Hudud*, and *Hudud* crimes are often said to be crimes against God (or, more specifically, God's rights). Four *Hudud* crimes for which punishments are specified in the Koran are (1) making war upon Allah and His messengers, (2) theft, (3) adultery or fornication, and (4) false accusation of fornication or adultery. Three other *Hudud* offenses are mentioned by the Koran, for which no punishment is specified: (1) "corruption on earth," (2) drinking alcohol, and (3) highway robbery—and the punishments for these crimes are determined by tradition.[56] The *Hudud* offenses and associated typical punishments are

CRIME AND PUNISHMENT IN ISLAMIC LAW: THE IRANIAN EXAMPLE	**TABLE 16-1**

Islamic law looks to the Koran and to the teachings of the Prophet Mohammed to determine which acts should be classified as crimes. The Koran and tradition specify punishments to be applied to designated offenses, as the following verse from the Koran demonstrates: "The only reward of those who make war upon Allah and His messenger and strive after corruption in the land will be that they will be killed or crucified, or have their hands and feet on alternate sides cut off, or will be expelled out of the land" (Surah V, Verse 33). Other crimes and punishments include the following.

Offense	Punishment
Theft	Amputation of the hand
Adultery	Stoning to death
Fornication	One hundred lashes
False accusation (of fornication or adultery)	Eighty lashes
Corruption on earth	Death by the sword or by burning
Drinking alcohol	Eighty lashes; death if repeated three times
Robbery	Cutting off of hands and feet on alternate sides, exile, or execution

For more information, see Sam S. Souryal, Dennis W. Potts, and Abdullah I. Alobied, "The Penalty of Hand Amputation for Theft in Islamic Justice," *Journal of Criminal Justice*, Vol. 22, No. 3 (1994), pp. 249–265; and Parviz Saney, "Iran," in Elmer H. Johnson, ed., *International Handbook of Contemporary Developments in Criminology* (Westport, CT: Greenwood, 1983), pp. 356–369.

shown in Table 16–1. "Corruption on earth" is a general category of religious offense, not well understood in the West, which includes activities like embezzlement, revolution against lawful authority, fraud, and "weakening the society of God."

The religious aspect of Islamic law makes for strict punishment of moral failure. Sexual offenders, even those who engage in what would be considered to be essentially victimless crimes in Western societies, are subject to especially harsh treatment. The Islamic penalty for fornication, for example, is 100 lashes. Men are stripped to the waist, women have their clothes bound tightly, and flogging is carried out with a leather whip. Adultery carries a much more severe penalty: flogging and stoning to death.

Under Islamic law, even property crimes are firmly punished. Thieves who are undeterred by less serious punishments may eventually suffer amputation of the right hand. In a reputedly humane move, Iranian officials recently began the use of an electric guillotine, specially made for the purpose, which can sever a hand at the wrist in one-tenth of a second. For amputation to be imposed, the item stolen must have value in Islam. Pork and alcohol, for example, are regarded as being without value, and their theft is not subject to punishment. Islamic legal codes also establish a minimum value for stolen items which could result in a sentence of amputation. Likewise, offenders who have stolen because they are hungry or are in need are exempt from the punishment of amputation and receive fines or prison terms.

Slander and the consumption of alcohol are both punished by 80 lashes. Legal codes in strict Islamic nations also specify whipping for the crimes of pimping, lesbianism, kissing by an unmarried couple, cursing, and failure of a woman to wear a veil. Islamic law provides for the execution, sometimes through crucifixion, of robbers. Laws stipulate that anyone who survives three days on the cross may be spared. Depending upon the circumstances of the robbery, however, the offender may suffer the amputation of opposite hands and feet, or simply exile.

Rebellion, or revolt against a legitimate political leader or established economic order, which is considered an aspect of "corruption on earth," is punishable by death. The offender may be killed outright in a military or police action or, later, by sentence of the court. The last of the *Hudud* crimes is rejection of Islam. The penalty, once again, is death, and can be imposed for denying the existence of God or angels, denying any of the prophets of Islam, or rejecting any part of the Koran.

In 1995, a court in Tehran, Iran, sentenced a man to death for what is believed to be the biggest bank fraud case in Iranian history.[57] The defendant, Fazel Khodadad, was convicted of embezzling $21.7 million from state-run Bank Saderat. Khodadad was sentenced under Islamic laws, which allow capital punishment for "sabotaging the country's economic system." He was also sentenced to 50 lashes for other illegal activities, including drug abuse, and 99 lashes for an illegal sexual relationship with a woman that involved "touching, kissing, and lying next to each other." The woman, identified only as M.H., received a sentence of 99 lashes, which was suspended for two years.

Souryal and coauthors observe that *Hudud* crimes can be severely punished because "punishment serves a three-tiered obligation: (1) the fulfillment of worship, (2) the purification of society, and (3) the redemption of the individual." However, they add, the interests of the individual are the least valuable component of this triad and may have to be sacrificed "for the wholesomeness and integrity of the encompassing justice system."[58]

The *Tazir* Crimes

Tazir crime

A minor violation of Islamic law that is regarded as an offense against society, not God.

All crimes other than *Hudud* crimes fall into an offense category called *tazirat*. **Tazir crimes** are regarded as any actions not considered acceptable in a spiritual society. They include crimes against society and against individuals, but not against God. *Tazir* crimes may call for *quesas* (retribution) or *diya* (compensation or fines). Crimes requiring *quesas* are based on the Arabic principle of "an eye for an eye, a nose for a nose, a tooth for a tooth" and generally require physical punishments up to and including death. *Quesas* offenses may include murder, manslaughter, assault, and maiming. Under Islamic law, such crimes may require the victim or his representative to serve as prosecutor. The state plays a role only in providing the forum for the trial and in imposing punishment. Sometimes victims' representatives dole out punishment. In 1997, for example, 28-year-old taxi driver Ali Reza Khoshruy, nicknamed "The Vampire" because he stalked, raped, and killed women at night after picking them up in his cab, was hung from a yellow crane in the middle of Tehran, the Iranian capital.[59] Before the hanging, prison officials and male relatives of the victims cursed Khoshruy and whipped him with thick leather belts as he lay tied to a metal bed. The whipping was part of a 214-lash sentence.

Islamic Courts

Islamic courts typically exist on three levels.[60] The first level hears cases involving the potential for serious punishments, including death, amputation, and exile. The second level deals with relatively minor matters, such as traffic offenses and violations of city ordinances. Special courts, especially in Iran, may hear cases involving crimes against the government, narcotics offenses, state security, and corruption. Appeals within the Islamic court system are only possible under rare circumstances and are by no means routine. A decision rendered by second-level courts will generally stand without intervention by higher judicial authorities.

Under Islamic law, men and women are treated very differently. Testimony provided by a man, for example, can be heard in court. The same evidence, however, can only be provided by two virtuous women; one female witness is not sufficient.

While Islamic law may seem barbaric to many Westerners, Islamic officials defend their system by pointing to low crime rates at home and by alleging near anarchy in Western nations. An early criticism of Islamic law was offered by Max Weber at the start of the twentieth century.[61] Weber said that Islamic justice is based more upon the moral conceptions of individual judges than upon any rational and predictable code of laws. He found that the personality of each judge, what he called "charisma," was more important in reaching a final legal result than was the written law. Weber's conclusion was that a modern society could not develop under Islamic law because enforcement of the law was too unpredictable. Complex social organizations, he argued, could only be based upon a rational law which is relatively unchanging from place to place and over time.[62]

More recent observers have agreed that "Islamic justice is based on philosophical principles which are considered alien, if not unconscionable, to the Western observer." However, these same writers note, strict punishments such as hand amputation "may not be inconsistent with the fundamentals of natural law or Judeo-Christian doctrine. The imposition of the penalty in specific cases and under rigorous rules of evidence—as the principle requires—may be indeed justifiable, and even necessary, in the Islamic context of sustaining a spiritual and peaceful society."[63]

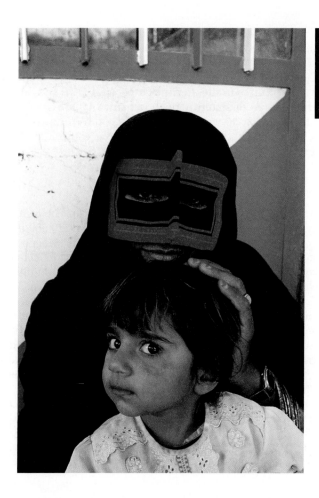

A woman in Oman wearing a style of dress strongly influenced by Islamic tradition and law. Islamic law is based upon the teachings of the Koran and the sayings of the Prophet Mohammed.

A. Johannes, CORBIS/Sygma

Criminal Justice in England and Wales

The country of England is quite small—only a little larger than the state of New Jersey—but it has a population of around 40 million people. One of the original participants in the Industrial Revolution, it remains a highly industrialized nation. England is linked closely to its neighbors—Wales, Scotland, and Northern Ireland—an alliance which created the political entity of Great Britain and which today is known as the United Kingdom.

Our American heritage, both legal and cultural, has been strongly influenced by Great Britain. Chapter 4 describes the way in which British common law formed the basis of our own legal traditions, and Chapter 5 shows how American police forces and other criminal justice agencies in their formative periods drew upon earlier English experience. Because England is a much more open society than either China or Iran, a far greater amount of descriptive detail is available about the criminal justice system there.

Crime Rates

British crime surveys mirror their American counterparts, and the Research and Statistics Department of the Home Office makes reports of crime freely available to researchers. Major crimes in England and Wales are termed "notifiable offenses," the counterpart of Part I or index offenses in the United States. Such crimes, when recorded by the police, appear in the annual Home Office publication *Criminal Statistics for England and Wales.*

Another measure of British crime is the annual British Crime Survey (BCS), which is similar to the National Crime Victimization Survey in the United States in that it depends upon household surveys rather than reports to the police. According to the BCS, 12,899,000 crimes were committed against adults living in households in England and Wales in 2000.[64] Of these, 2,618,000 were violent crimes, and 7,672,000 were thefts of various kinds. Given the size of the British population, which stood at nearly 60 million in 2000, these statistics mean that fully 4,470 of every 100,000 people in England and

Wales were violently victimized in 2000 (as opposed to 506 per 100,000 in the United States). As in the United States, victimization in Britain varies by age. Young men aged 16 to 24 were most at risk, and 18.8% of men in that age range were victims of violent crime in 1999 and 2000. While per capita crime rates in England and Wales are considerably higher than those of the United States in most crime categories, BCS-recorded levels of household and personal crime have consistently declined since 1995. The decrease in crime that occurred between 1999 and 2000 was 12%—the largest ever annual decline measured by the BCS. Table 16–2 shows the number of crimes estimated to have occurred in England and Wales in 2000. View the British Crime Survey via **Library Extra! 16–3** at cjtoday.com.

The British Political System

England is a country without a constitution in the strict sense of the word. The legal basis of English government, however, can be found in at least three significant documents: (1) the Magna Carta, (2) the Bill of Rights, and (3) the Act of Settlement. The Magna Carta, written in 1215, was forced upon the king by English nobility and the upper classes. It guarantees a number of legal rights to British citizens accused of crimes, including the right to due process of law and a hearing before one's peers. The English Bill of Rights, passed by **Parliament** in 1688, established the two houses of Parliament (the House of Lords and the House of Commons), guaranteed free elections, and placed Parliamentary authority in statutory matters over that of the sovereign. As a consequence, although modern England still has a royal family whose members perform ceremonial functions, the real power to make laws and to run the nation lies in the hands of the two houses of Parliament and the prime minister. In 1700, the Act of Settlement reinforced the powers of Parliament and made clear the authority of judges and other officials.

As Richard Terrill points out, at least three major differences can be found between the British and American systems of government, all of which bear significance for the administration of criminal justice:[65]

- The British system, unlike the American, makes no provision for judicial review of Parliamentary action. Acts of Parliament are the law of the land and cannot be overruled by any court.

- In Britain, a unity of powers, rather than a separation of branches, characterizes the government. Executive, legislative, and judicial authority all ultimately rest in Parliament.

- England is a unified nation. No separate state legislatures or state governmental offices exist. Parliamentary law applies at both the national and local levels.

Parliament

The British legislature, the highest lawmaking body of the United Kingdom.

TABLE 16–2	**ESTIMATED NUMBER OF CRIMES IN ENGLAND AND WALES, 2000**
Vandalism (against vehicles and other private property)	2,608,000
All property thefts	7,672,000
All burglaries	1,063,000
All vehicle-related thefts	2,619,000
Bicycle thefts	377,000
Other household thefts	1,616,000
Other personal property thefts and stealth thefts	1,997,000
All violence	2,618,000
Mugging (robbery and snatch thefts)	312,000
Wounding	417,000
Common assault	1,890,000
All BCS crime	12,899,000

Note: Subtotals do not add up to total due to rounding.
Source: Home Office, *The 2001 British Crime Survey* (London: Home Office, 2001). Web posted at http://www.homeoffice.gov.uk/rds/bcs1.html.

Modern Criminal Law in Britain

In 1967, Parliament passed the Criminal Law Act, a sweeping piece of legislation which substantially altered English criminal procedure. The old distinction between "felonies" and "misdemeanors" was eliminated in favor of two new offense categories: "arrestable" (or indictable) and "nonarrestable" (or summary) offenses. Under English common law, the arrest powers of the police without a warrant were limited to treason, felonies, and breaches of the peace. The Criminal Law Act broadened arrest powers in the absence of a warrant to all offenses "for which [a] sentence is fixed by law" and to attempts to commit such offenses. The 1967 act also gave private citizens the power to arrest offenders they caught engaging in criminal activity or whom they had reasonable suspicion to believe had committed an arrestable offense.

In November 1994, a powerful nationwide conservative emphasis led to passage of the Criminal Justice and Public Order Act. The 1994 Criminal Justice Act (CJA) marked a return to a "get tough" English anticrime policy. British Home Secretary Michael Howard explained why the bill was passed in these words: "In the last 30 years the balance in the criminal justice system has been tilted too far in favor of the criminal and against the protection of the public. The time has come to put that right."[66]

The CJA selectively criminalized what had previously been especially serious violations of the civil law, made it easier to catch and convict criminals, made it harder for repeat offenders to get bail, and restricted, at least to some degree, the rights of criminal defendants. Prior to the new legislation, for example, police officers in England were required to caution detained suspects with the admonishment: "You do not have to say anything unless you wish to do so, but anything you say may be given as evidence." Criticisms of the British right to silence were effectively promoted in the national media by law enforcement agencies, which cited difficulties in obtaining convictions when a suspect's silence went unquestioned. Such criticisms influenced the 1994 legislation, and English courts are now permitted to draw "such inferences as are appropriate" from a suspect's silence. Today, an English police officer arresting someone is required to say, "You do not have to say anything, but it may harm your defense if you do not mention, when questioned, something which you later rely on in court. Anything you say may be used as evidence." When preparing to question a suspect, officers are enjoined to admonish, "I must warn you that if from now on you refuse to account for a fact, a court may draw their own conclusions why you have not done so." Hence, under modern British law, a suspect's refusal to answer questions (specifically to account for his or her presence at a given location or to account for the possession of objects, substances, and bodily injuries) can be used later by a court to infer the suspect's guilt. The CJA also gave British courts wider powers to sentence persistent offenders between the ages of 12 and 14 and effectively doubled the maximum possible sentence youthful offenders could receive.

The Sex Offenders Act of 1997 imposed a registration requirement on newly convicted offenders, including those supervised in the community or released from prison. The duration of the registration requirement depends on sentence length, type of offense, age of the offender, and age and gender of the victim. Under the act, convicted sex offenders are required to keep the police informed of their current address.

In 1998, the Crime and Disorder Act, passed by the British Parliament, received royal assent. The purpose of the act, in the words of the British Home Office, "is to tackle crime and disorder and help create safer communities."[67] It builds upon the theme of establishing local partnerships between the police and the local community to cut crime. The act places a statutory obligation on local authorities and the police to conduct a "crime audit" of levels and patterns of crime in their area; to analyze the results of the audit; to hold consultations on the results; to prepare a strategy to reduce levels of crime and disorder; to implement and monitor the effectiveness of that strategy; and to repeat the process every three years.

Finally, in 2001, Parliament passed the Anti-terrorism, Crime and Security Act, which became law after receiving royal assent shortly afterward. The wide-ranging legislation, modeled after the 2001 USA PATRIOT Act, includes (1) new police powers for the purpose of monitoring terrorist groups, (2) a provision for detention without trial for suspected international terrorists even when they cannot be deported (British law does not allow deportation of criminal suspects to countries with the death penalty), and (3) a new offense of knowingly causing a nuclear explosion.[68] Like its American cousin, the Anti-terrorism, Crime and Security Act contains a sunset provision, meaning that some significant provisions of the law will have to be periodically renewed by Parliament.

Powerful international criminal groups now work outside national or international law. They include traffickers in drugs, money laundering, the illegal trade in arms—including trade in nuclear materials—and the smuggling of precious metals and other commodities. These criminal elements exploit both the new liberal international economic order and the different approaches and practices of States. They command vast sums of money, which they use to suborn State officials. Some criminal "empires" are richer than many poorer States. These problems demand a concerted, global response.

—*Former UN Secretary-General Boutros Boutros-Ghali*[i]

The British Police

The historical development of police forces in nineteenth-century Britain is described in Chapter 5. By World War II, 183 police departments—some large, some very small—existed throughout England and Wales.[69] Each was headed by a chief constable, and jurisdictional disputes between departments were common. Major efforts to consolidate police departments culminated in the Police Acts of 1946 and 1964, to which contemporary British policing owes its structure. The Local Government Act of 1972 further reduced the number of police forces throughout England and Wales until the combined forces numbered just 43. The smallest police agency in Britain today has over 600 officers—a good-sized department by American standards. Approximately 128,000 sworn police officers are employed throughout Britain, and 55,000 civilians serve police forces there.[70]

The police of Britain are subject to civilian control through local commissions called *police authorities*. Two-thirds of the members of each police authority are elected civilians; the others are judicial officers elected by fellow magistrates. Each police authority appoints a local chief constable—with overall authority for the daily operations of the police—and an assistant chief constable. In 1994, Parliament passed the Police and Magistrates Courts Act, legislation which emphasizes the important role local communities play in setting the goals of police service. In tones reminiscent of the American emphasis on community policing, British Home Secretary Michael Howard described the new law this way: "I believe that an active partnership between government, the public, and the police is the way forward. The Police and Magistrates Courts Act gives us the framework for the future."[71]

Beyond the local level, the British home secretary has statutory authority to intervene in police administration, police discipline, and suspected cases of corruption and mismanagement. The home secretary also coordinates police services throughout Britain, runs the Police College and local police training centers, maintains forensic laboratories, and is ultimately responsible for information management, including national databases and telecommunications.

Britain does not have a national police force.[72] The Metropolitan Police District, with 26,000 members,[73] however, serves many centralized functions. The Metropolitan Police District encompasses 32 boroughs and portions of four counties surrounding London. Headquartered at New Scotland Yard, perhaps the most famous address of any police force in the world, the Metropolitan Police serve as a national repository for information on crime statistics, criminal activity, fingerprints, missing persons, and wayward and delinquent juveniles. The agency also maintains links with INTERPOL and handles requests for information from police agencies in other countries.

In 1992, the National Criminal Intelligence Service (NCIS), charged with intelligence gathering and record keeping, began operation in England.[74] Likened by some to the Federal Bureau of Investigation, few real similarities exist, primarily because NCIS agents do not have an operational role but function only as staff officers to exchange information on criminal activity with other police agencies throughout England.

In 1948, the Police College opened at Ryton-upon-Dunsmore. The Police College was designed to enhance professionalism among the nation's constables. The training it provided made possible professional advancement within police ranks. In 1960, the college relocated to Bramshill. Known today by its new name, the Police Staff College at Bramshill serves as an international model for police management training.[75]

Traditionally, British police officers have gone on patrol unarmed, except for a nightstick. Events in the 1980s, especially terrorist attacks on civilian targets including London's Heathrow Airport, led to a reassessment of traditional policy. That reassessment continues today, although most beat constables remain unarmed. Weapons are kept on hand in local police stations and can be issued upon the order of senior police personnel. Officers who routinely patrol highly congested areas, including those with considerable international traffic, such as major airports, are now armed with handguns and automatic weapons as a precaution against terrorist attack. In emergencies, local chief constables are authorized to call upon the military for armed assistance. Even so, support continues to grow for British police to routinely carry sidearms as part of their everyday equipment. However, former Scotland Yard chief Ken Hyder warns that "carrying guns as a normal part of equipment will lead to accidental shootings of bystanders as well as suspects. Arming the police in a routine way," he says, "would have two other effects—it would distance them from the public, whom they need to provide them with information and support, and it would encourage more villains to arm themselves."[76]

Evidentiary standards, such as the American exclusionary rule, do not apply to the British police. Unlike their American counterparts, British courts have not utilized precedent-setting decisions to carve out individual rights for citizens who face apprehension and criminal prosecution. What they have done, through judicial conferences, is draw up "directions" for acceptable police procedure. A key document to emerge from judicial conferences was the *Judges' Rules and Administrative Directions*, drawn up in 1964. Rules like these have the weight of law even though they are technically only administrative regulations. Although offenders may not be released when incriminating evidence is gathered inappropriately, as happens in the United States, improper actions by police officers can be grounds for reprimand or dismissal.

In 1995, British police began using the world's first national DNA database, which was hailed as the biggest advance in the fight against crime since the use of fingerprints. Although the database, which may have uses other than in the field of criminal investigation, currently holds only around 135,000 records, plans are to expand it to more than 5 million records within a decade. Records in the database will come from convicted criminals and from unsolved crimes. The 1994 CJA gives police officers the authority to collect and retain "nonintimate" biological specimens, without consent, from anyone charged with a crime.

The British Courts

Nonarrestable (summary) offenses are minor matters which are tried in magistrates' courts. Magistrates are members of the local community; they are unpaid and are not required to have formal training in the law. Magistrates sit as a body, usually in groups of three or more, and hear cases without a jury. While they generally try less serious cases in summary fashion, criminal defendants charged with certain major crimes may waive the right to trial by jury and be tried in a magistrates' court. It has been estimated that the approximately 900 magistrates' courts throughout Great Britain handle 98% of all criminal cases in the kingdom.[77] Within the magistrates' courts, certain courts are designated "youth courts" and process the majority of youthful offenders who are apprehended for criminal law violations. Although English common law originally provided for hearings before a grand jury, Parliament abolished the grand jury system in 1933. Magistrates' courts have taken over some of the functions of the grand jury, including binding over serious offenders for trial by higher courts. Magistrates are limited in their sentencing

A British judge looking over the heads of his colleagues, all of whom are wearing the traditional wig and robe during a formal procession from Westminster Abbey to the Houses of Parliament. True to tradition, English judges still wear the formal garb of centuries past.

Jacqueline Arzt, AP/Wide World Photos

authority to a maximum of six months' imprisonment. In serious cases, however, they can refer convicted defendants to higher courts for sentencing.

Arrestable (indictable) offenses involve more serious crimes. They require a preliminary hearing in front of magistrates who decide whether there is substance to the charges against the defendant. If the magistrates issue an indictment, then the defendant appears before a Crown court and may be tried before a jury. Created in 1971, Crown courts are headed by justices appointed by the monarch on the recommendation of the lord chancellor. Twelve-member juries hear Crown court cases. Conviction requires only a majority consensus, not unanimous agreement among jurors.

A third offense category is that of "mixed offenses." Mixed offenses involve certain cases of theft, burglary, and other crimes which are less serious than indictable offenses. Depending upon the circumstances, mixed offenses may be tried by a jury in a Crown court or before magistrates.

Tradition dictates considerable formality at all court levels. Crown court judges and counsel both wear white powdered wigs and black flowing robes. Verbal give-and-take is highly structured and polite. Sharp exchanges between the bench and counsel almost never occur, and lawyers are expected to treat one another with respect.

Crown courts also hear appeals from magistrates' courts. Appeals are heard without a jury. Petitions from magistrates' courts which concern questions of law sometimes go directly to an appellate court called the *high court*. The high court is divided into three divisions: (1) the Queen's Branch, (2) Family Court, and (3) the Chancery. The Chancery Division deals with matters of inheritance, trusts, property, and so on, while the Family Court concerns itself with marriages, divorces, adoption, and the like. The section of the high court which focuses on criminal matters is the Queen's Branch. Like other divisions of the high court, the Queen's Branch sits without a jury when hearing criminal appeals.

Another intermediate appellate court occupies a level above the high court. Called the *court of appeals*, it has two branches: one civil and one criminal. The court of appeals consists of 16 lord justices of appeal and is headed by a judge called the *master of the rolls*. Criminal appeals not resolved by the high court may go to the court of appeals. Appeals involving sentencing decisions made by magistrates' or Crown courts can go directly to the criminal division of the court of appeals.

At the apex of the appellate process stands the House of Lords, one of the houses of Parliament. The House of Lords may hear appeals from both the Queen's Branch and the criminal division of the court of appeals. An appeal to the House will be heard only by those

CJ Today Exhibit 16-2

[Judicial Officers in Britain]

The court system in the United Kingdom is highly dependent upon tradition. Three principal judicial officers ensure the effective functioning of the courts:

■ *The lord chancellor.* The lord chancellor is appointed by the monarch upon the recommendation of the prime minister. Tradition calls for an appointee who is well versed in the law. The lord chancellor presides over the House of Lords, one of the two houses of the British Parliament. Because the House of Lords is the highest English court, the lord chancellor is also the highest judicial officer in the kingdom. The lord chancellor recommends for appointment all members of the judiciary.

■ *The attorney general.* Appointed by the prime minister, the attorney general is legal adviser to the monarch and to Parliament. The attorney general officially serves as "guardian of the public interest" and handles most controversial legal issues affecting the government—both criminal and civil.

■ *The director of public prosecutions.* The director of public prosecutions is charged with advising police agencies involved in criminal investigations and with coordinating the activities of prosecutors throughout the kingdom. Appointed by the home secretary and supervised by the attorney general, the director is a lawyer in charge of a staff of professional "solicitors" who specialize in criminal law and procedure.

Source: Julia Fionda, *Public Prosecutors and Discretion: A Comparative Study* (Oxford: Clarendon Press, 1995); and Richard J. Terrill, *World Criminal Justice Systems: A Survey* (Cincinnati: Anderson, 1984).

members who specialize in the appeals process. Although the House of Lords is the highest appellate court in Britain, it has nothing like the power of the U.S. Supreme Court. Acts of Parliament are inviolate and cannot be "struck down" or significantly modified by judicial interpretation.

British Corrections

The British correctional system operates under the Prison Act of 1964 and the Young Offenders Institution Statutory Instrument, passed in 1988. The correctional system is under the administrative control of the home secretary, who makes appointments to the national Prison Board, which in turn sets policy for the Prison Department. The Prison Department oversees the activities of the nation's prisons, the parole board, and probation and after-care services. A separate agency, the Board of Visitors, permits lay volunteers to serve on hearing boards attached to individual prisons. Each Board of Visitors is empowered to hear alleged violations of prison regulations and is expected to prepare a yearly report on prison conditions.

Three kinds of prisons exist in England: short term, medium term, and long term. Short-term institutions house offenders serving less than 18 months, while medium-term institutions hold those sentenced to between 18 months and four years. Long-term prisons hold offenders sentenced to more than four years. Inmates in all British prisons are expected to work, although meaningful work programs are not available for everyone.[78]

In the face of growing crime fears, members of Parliament have come under increasing pressure to require longer and more frequent prison sentences for many offenders. Growing crime rates, high levels of unemployment, increased drug use, and the development of poverty-ridden ghettolike areas in many of the nation's large cities have all contributed to a public perception of unnecessary leniency in the criminal justice system. The 1994 CJA, passed in response to growing public concerns about crime, mandated increased sentences for a variety of crimes and the building of six new privately run prisons.

As in the United States, which sports the highest incarceration rate among democratic nations (see Figure 16–1), the call for longer sentences has come up against the reality of prison crowding. The British prison population on September 30, 2001 was 67,470 inmates, the highest level ever recorded and an increase of 4% over the previous year.[79] Of the total, 3,960 were women. The Home Office estimates that prisons throughout England and Wales will hold somewhere between 76,700 and 83,500 inmates by 2008.[80] Learn more about crime and justice in the United Kingdom by visiting the Home Office Internet Service via **Web Extra! 16–2** at cjtoday.com.

FIGURE 16-1

Incarceration rates for selected countries.

Source: Sentencing Project, "U.S. Continues to Be World Leader in Rate of Incarceration," news release, no date; and Roy Walmsley, *World Prison Population List,* 2d ed. (London: Home Office, 2000).

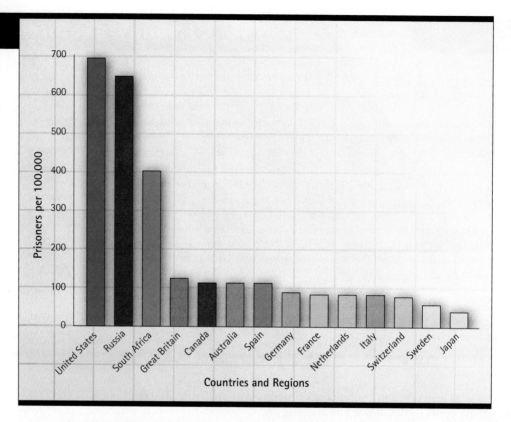

International Criminal Justice Organizations

The first international conference on criminology and criminal justice met in London in 1872.[81] It evolved out of emerging humanitarian concerns about the treatment of prisoners. Human rights, the elimination of corporal punishment, and debates over capital punishment occupied the conference participants. Although other meetings were held from time to time, little agreement could be reached among the international community on criminal etiology, justice paradigms, or the philosophical and practical bases for criminal punishment and rehabilitation. Finally, in 1938, the International Society for Criminology (ISC) was formed to bring together people from diverse cultural backgrounds who shared an interest in social policies relating to crime and justice. In its early years, membership in the ISC consisted mostly of national officials and academics with close government ties.[82] As a consequence, many of the first conferences (called *international congresses*) sponsored by the ISC strongly supported the status quo and were devoid of any significant recommendations for change or growth.

Throughout the 1960s and 1970s, the ISC was strongly influenced by a growing worldwide awareness of human rights. About the same time, a number of international organizations began to press for an understanding of the political and legal processes through which deviance and crime come to be defined. Among them were the Scandinavian Research Council for Criminology (formed in 1962), the Criminological Research Council (created in 1962 by the Council of Europe), and other regional associations concerned with justice issues.

A number of contemporary organizations and publications continue to focus world attention on criminal justice issues. Perhaps the best-known modern center for the academic study of cross-national criminal justice is the International Center of Comparative Criminology at the University of Montreal. Established in 1969, the center serves as a locus of study for criminal justice professionals from around the world and maintains an excellent library of international criminal justice information. The Office of International Criminal Justice (OICJ), based in Chicago at the University of Illinois, has also become a well-known contributor to the study of comparative criminal justice. In conjunction with the university's Center for Research in Law and Justice, the OICJ publishes the newsletter

Criminal Justice International and sponsors study tours of various nations. Visit OICJ via **Web Extra! 16–3** at cjtoday.com.

In 1995, Mitre Corporation in McLean, Virginia, began an Internet service that provides information about the United Nations Crime Prevention Branch. The United Nations Online Justice Information System (UNOJUST) holds much promise as an online provider of international criminal justice information. Visit UNOJUST via **Web Extra! 16–4** at cjtoday.com. Similarly, the World Justice Information Network (WJIN), sponsored by the National Institute of Justice and the U.S. Department of State, provides a members-only forum for the discussion of justice issues around the globe. Apply for membership in WJIN via **Web Extra! 16–5** at cjtoday.com. Finally, the United Nations Centre for International Crime Prevention, in conjunction with the World Society of Victimology, sponsors the International Victimology Website, available via **Web Extra! 16–6** at cjtoday.com.

The Role of the United Nations in Criminal Justice

The United Nations (UN), composed of 185 member states and based in New York City, is the largest and most inclusive international body in the world. From its inception in 1945, the United Nations has been very interested in international crime prevention and world criminal justice systems. A UN resolution entitled the International Bill of Human Rights supports the rights and dignity of everyone who comes into contact with the criminal justice system.

One of the best-known specific UN recommendations on criminal justice is its Standard Minimum Rules for the Treatment of Prisoners, adopted in 1955 at the first UN Congress on the Prevention of Crime and the Treatment of Offenders. The rules call for the fair treatment of prisoners, including recognition of the basic humanity of all inmates, and set specific standards for housing, nutrition, exercise, and medical care. Follow-up surveys conducted by the United Nations have shown that the rules have had a considerable influence upon national legislation and prison regulations throughout the world.[83] Although the rules do not have the weight of law unless adopted and enacted into local legislation, they carry the strong weight of tradition, and at least one expert claims that "there are indeed those who argue that the rules have entered the *corpus* of generally customary human rights law, or that they are binding . . . as an authoritative interpretation of the human rights provisions of the UN charter."[84]

A more recent, but potentially significant, set of recommendations can be found in the UN Code of Conduct for Law Enforcement Officials. The code calls upon law enforcement officers throughout the world to be cognizant of human rights in the performance of their duties. It specifically proscribes the use of torture and other abuses.

The UN World Crime Surveys, which report official crime statistics from nearly 100 countries, provide a global portrait of criminal activity. Seen historically, the surveys have shown that crimes against property are most characteristic of nations with developed economies (where they constitute approximately 82% of all reported crime), while crimes against the person occur much more frequently in developing countries (where they account for 43% of all crime).[85] Complementing the official statistics of the World Crime Surveys are data from the International Victim Survey (IVS), which is conducted in approximately 50 countries. To date, three IVS surveys have been conducted—in 1989, 1992, and 1996–1997. The International Victimization Survey can be viewed as **Library Extra! 16–4** at cjtoday.com.

Through its Crime Prevention and Criminal Justice Program, the United Nations continues to advance the cause of crime prevention and to disseminate useful criminal justice information. The program provides forums for ongoing discussions of justice practices around the world. It has regional links throughout the world, sponsored by supportive national governments which have agreed to fund the program's work. The European Institute for Crime Prevention and Control (HEUNI), for example, provides the program's regional European link in a network of institutes operating throughout the world. Other network components include the UN Interregional Crime and Justice Research Institute (UNICRI) in Rome; an Asian regional institute (UNAFEI) in Tokyo; ILANUE, based in San Jose, Costa Rica, which focuses on crime problems in Latin America and the Caribbean; an African institute (UNAFRI) in Kampala, Uganda; Australia's AIC in Canberra; an Arabic institute (ASSTC) in Riyadh, Saudi Arabia; and other centers in Siracusa, Italy, and in Vancouver and Montreal, Canada.[86]

At its formation, the Crime Prevention and Criminal Justice Program announced these goals: "1) the prevention of crime within and among states; 2) the control of crime both

CJ Today Exhibit 16-3

[Vienna Declaration on Crime and Justice]

We the Member States of the United Nations,

Concerned about the impact on our societies of the commission of serious crimes of a global nature and convinced of the need for bilateral, regional and international cooperation in crime prevention and criminal justice,

Concerned in particular about transnational organized crime and the relationships between its various forms,

Convinced that adequate prevention and rehabilitation programmes are fundamental to an effective crime control strategy, and that such programmes should take into account social and economic factors which may make people more vulnerable to, and likely to engage in criminal behaviour,

Stressing that a fair, responsible, ethical and efficient criminal justice system is an important factor in the promotion of economic and social development and of security,

Aware of the promise of restorative approaches to justice that aim to reduce and promote the healing of victims, offenders and communities,

Having assembled at the Tenth United Nations Congress on the Prevention of Crime and the Treatment of Offenders in Vienna from 10 to 17 April 2000 to decide to take effective concerted action, in a spirit of cooperation, to combat the world crime problem,

Declare as follows:

■ We emphasize the responsibility of each State to establish and maintain a fair, responsible, ethical and efficient criminal justice system.

■ We recognize the necessity of closer coordination and cooperation among States in combating the world crime problem, bearing in mind that action against it is a common and shared responsibility. . . .

■ We undertake to strengthen international cooperation in order to create a conducive environment for the fight against organized crime, promoting growth and sustainable development and eradicating poverty and unemployment.

■ We also commit ourselves to the development of action-oriented policy recommendations based on the special needs of women as criminal justice practitioners, victims, prisoners and offenders.

■ We commit ourselves to the development of more effective ways of collaborating with one another with a view to eradicating the scourge of trafficking in persons, especially women and children, and the smuggling of migrants. . . .

■ We also commit ourselves to the enhancement of international cooperation and mutual legal assistance to curb illicit manufacturing of and trafficking in firearms, their parts and components and ammunition, and we establish 2005 as the target year for achieving a significant decrease in their incidence worldwide.

■ We reaffirm that combating money-laundering and the criminal economy constitutes a major element of the strategies against organized crime. . . .

■ We decide to develop action-oriented policy recommendations on the prevention and control of computer-related crime. . . . We also commit ourselves to working towards enhancing our ability to prevent, investigate and prosecute high-technology and computer-related crime.

■ We note that acts of violence and terrorism continue to be of grave concern. In conformity with the Charter of the United Nations and taking into account all the relevant General Assembly resolutions, we will together, in conjunction with our other efforts to prevent and to combat terrorism, take effective, resolute and speedy measures with respect to preventing and combating criminal activities carried out for the purpose of furthering terrorism in all its forms and manifestations. . . .

■ We also note that racial discrimination, xenophobia and related forms of intolerance continue and we recognize the importance of taking steps to incorporate into international crime prevention strategies and norms measures to prevent and combat crime associated with racism, racial discrimination, xenophobia and related forms of intolerance.

■ We affirm our determination to combat violence stemming from intolerance on the basis of ethnicity and resolve to make a strong contribution, in the area of crime prevention and criminal justice. . . .

■ We also recognize the importance of prison reform, the independence of the judiciary and the prosecution authorities, and the International Code of Conduct for Public Officials. . . .

■ We shall endeavour, as appropriate, to use and apply the United Nations standards and norms in crime prevention and criminal justice in national law and practice. . . .

■ We further recognize with great concern that juveniles in difficult circumstances are often at risk of becoming delinquent or easy candidates for recruitment by criminal groups, including groups involved in transnational organized crime, and we commit ourselves to undertaking countermeasures to prevent this growing phenomenon. . . .

■ We recognize that comprehensive crime prevention strategies at the international, national, regional and local levels must address the root causes and risk factors related to crime and victimization through social, economic, health, educational and justice policies. . . .

■ We commit ourselves to according priority to containing the growth and overcrowding of pre-trial and detention prison populations, as appropriate, by promoting safe and effective alternatives to incarceration.

■ We decide to introduce, where appropriate, national, regional and international action plans in support of victims of crime, such as mechanisms for mediation and restorative justice. . . .

■ We encourage the development of restorative justice policies, procedures and programmes that are respectful of the rights, needs and interests of victims, offenders, communities and all other parties. . . .

Source: Excerpted from the Tenth United Nations Congress on the Prevention of Crime and the Treatment of Offenders, *Vienna Declaration on Crime and Justice: Meeting the Challenges of the Twenty-first Century,* Vienna, Austria, April 10–17, 2000.

nationally and internationally; 3) the strengthening of regional and international cooperation in crime prevention, criminal justice, and the combating of transnational crime; 4) the integration and consolidation of the efforts of member states in preventing and combating transnational crime; 5) more efficient and effective administration of justice, with due respect for the human rights of all those affected by crime and all those involved in the criminal justice system; and 6) the promotion of the highest standards of fairness, humanity, justice and professional conduct."[87]

In 1995, the United States signed an agreement with the United Nations Crime Prevention and Criminal Justice Branch, intended to facilitate the international sharing of information and research findings.[88] Under the agreement, the National Institute of Justice joined 11 other criminal justice research organizations throughout the world as an associate UN institute.

Continuing a tradition begun in 1885 by the former International Penal and Penitentiary Commission, the United Nations holds an international congress on crime every five years. The first UN crime congress met in Geneva, Switzerland, in 1955. Crime congresses provide a forum via which member states can exchange information and experiences, compare criminal justice practices between countries, find solutions to crime, and take action at an international level. The Tenth United Nations Congress on the Prevention of Crime and the Treatment of Offenders was held in Vienna, Austria, in 2000. Topics discussed at the meeting included (1) promoting the rule of law and strengthening the criminal justice systems of various nations, (2) the need for international cooperation in combating transnational crime, and (3) the need for a fair, ethical, and effective system of criminal justice in the promotion of economic and social development. See CJ Today Exhibit 16–3 in this chapter for additional details.

Transnational Crime

Transnational crime, or transnational organized crime, and the internationally organized criminal groups that support it promise to be one of the most pressing challenges of the early twenty-first century. In a recent conference in Seoul, Korea, Assistant Attorney General Laurie Robinson addressed the issue of transnational crime, saying, "The United States recognizes that we cannot confront crime in isolation. . . . It is clear crime does not respect international boundaries. It is clear crime is global. As recent economic trends demonstrate, what happens in one part of the world impacts all the rest. And crime problems and trends are no different."[89]

The post–cold war world is more dangerous and less stable than when power was balanced among superpowers. The power vacuum created in many parts of the world by the fall of the Soviet Union has led to a number of new threats. According to Robert Gelbard, U.S. Assistant Secretary for International Narcotics and Law Enforcement Affairs, "The main threat now is transnational organized crime. It comes in many forms: drug trafficking, money laundering, terrorism, alien smuggling, trafficking in weapons of mass destruction, fraud and other forms of corruption. These problems all have one critical element in common," says Gelbard. "They threaten the national security of all states and governments—from our closest allies to those that we find most repugnant. No country is safe. International criminal organizations all seek to establish pliant governments that can be manipulated through bribery and intimidation. They respect no national boundaries and already act with virtual impunity in many parts of the world."[90]

Worse still, entire nations may become rogue countries, or quasi-criminal regimes where criminal activity runs rampant and wields considerable influence over the national government. As this book goes to press, Russia, for example, appears to be quickly approaching this status through an intertwining of the goals of organized criminal groups and official interests that run to the top levels of government. The number of organized criminal groups operating in Russia is estimated to be over 12,000.[91] Emilio Viano, professor of criminology at American University and an expert on Russian organized crime, notes that "what we have is an immense country practically controlled by organized crime. These groups are getting stronger and stronger and using Russia as a base for their global ventures—taking over everything from drugs and prostitution to currency exchange and stealing World Bank and IMF [International Monetary Fund] loans."[92] In 1999, federal authorities discovered that more than $10 billion had passed through the Bank of New York in a major money-laundering scheme run by Russian organized crime.[93] Much of the money may have come from loans made to Russia by the IMF almost a year earlier.

transnational crime

Unlawful activity undertaken and supported by organized criminal groups operating across national boundaries.

WHAT WOULD YOU DO?

The CD-ROM scenario for Chapter 16 asks whether the constitutional protections offered by the Bill of Rights apply to searches conducted by American law enforcement officers of property owned by non-citizens and located outside of the United States. This scenario is derived from an actual incident involving international drug trafficking. The real-life case eventually found its way to the U.S. Supreme Court. Use the CD-ROM found in the back of your textbook to work through this scenario.

Palestinian boys holding toy rifles as a girl holds a poster of Osama bin Laden in Gaza City during a demonstration at Al Azhar University to honor suicide bombers. The school was organized by members of the Islamic Jihad. The children are being socialized into the culture of international terrorism. Terrorist activities, in which these children may later participate, fall under the heading of "transnational crime."

AP/Wide World Photos

The globalization of crime has necessitated the enhanced coordination of law enforcement efforts in different parts of the world and the expansion of American law enforcement activities beyond national borders. U.S. police agencies routinely send agents to assist law enforcement officers in other countries who are involved in transnational investigations. Another tool in the fight against transnational crime is extradition. Not all countries, however, are willing to extradite suspects wanted in the United States. As Kevin Ryan observes, "The globalization of United States law enforcement policy has also entailed the abduction of fugitives from abroad to stand trial when an asylum nation refuses an extradition request."[94] For additional information on transnational organized crime, see **Web Extra! 16–7** at cjtoday.com.

INTERPOL and Europol

International Criminal Police Organization (INTERPOL)

An international law enforcement support organization that began operations in 1946 and today has 137 members.

The **International Criminal Police Organization (INTERPOL)**, headquartered in Lyons, France, traces its origins back to the first International Criminal Police Congress of 1914, which met in Monaco.[95] The theme of that meeting was international cooperation in the investigation of crimes and the apprehension of fugitives. INTERPOL, however, did not officially begin operations until 1946, when the end of World War II brought about a new spirit of international harmony.

Today, 176 nations belong to INTERPOL.[96] The U.S. INTERPOL unit is called the U.S. National Central Bureau (USNCB) and is a separate agency within the U.S. Department of Justice. USNCB is staffed with personnel from 12 federal agencies, including the Drug Enforcement Administration, the Secret Service, and the Federal Bureau of Investigation (FBI). Through USNCB, INTERPOL is linked to all major U.S. computerized criminal records repositories, including the FBI's National Crime Information Index, the State Department's Advanced Visa Lookout System, and the Immigration and Naturalization Service's Master Index.

INTERPOL's primary purpose is to act as a clearinghouse for information on offenses and suspects who are believed to operate across national boundaries. The organization is committed to promoting "the widest possible mutual assistance between all criminal police authorities within the limits of laws existing in . . . different countries and in the spirit of the Universal Declaration of Human Rights."[97] INTERPOL does not intervene in religious, political, military, or racial disagreements in participant nations. As a consequence, a number of bombings and hostage situations were not officially investigated until 1984, when INTERPOL pledged itself to the fight against international terrorism.

In late 2001, INTERPOL's Seventieth General Assembly unanimously adopted the Budapest Anti-terrorism Resolution. The resolution calls for greater police cooperation in fighting international terrorism. As a follow-up to the resolution, INTERPOL'S Sixteenth Annual Symposium on International Terrorism, took place at the organization's headquarters.

INTERPOL does not have its own field investigators. The agency has no powers of arrest or of search and seizure in member countries. Instead, INTERPOL's purpose is to facilitate, coordinate, and encourage police cooperation as a means of combating international crime. It draws upon the willingness of local and national police forces to lend support to its activities. The headquarters staff of INTERPOL consists of around 250 individuals, many with prior police experience, who direct data-gathering efforts around the world and who serve to alert law enforcement organizations to the movement of suspected offenders within their jurisdiction. Learn more about INTERPOL via **Web Extra! 16–8** at cjtoday.com.

The members of the European Union agreed to the establishment of the **European Police Office (Europol)** in the Maastricht Treaty of February 7, 1992. Based in The Hague, The Netherlands, Europol started limited operations in 1994 in the form of the Europol Drugs Unit. Over time, other important law enforcement activities were added to the Europol agenda. The Europol Convention was ratified by all member states in 1998, and Europol commenced full operations the next year. Europol's mission is to improve the effectiveness and cooperation of law enforcement agencies within the member states of the European Union with the ultimate goal of preventing and combating terrorism, illegal drug trafficking, illicit trafficking in radioactive and nuclear substances, illegal money laundering, trafficking in human beings (including child pornography), and other serious forms of international organized crime. Europol and INTERPOL are committed to interagency cooperation, and they work with one another in developing information on international terrorism, drug trafficking, and trafficking in human beings.[98] Learn more about Europol via **Web Extra! 16–9** at cjtoday.com.

The International Criminal Court

On April 12, 2000, the International Criminal Court (ICC) was created under the auspicies of the United Nations. The ICC was intended to be a permanent criminal court

European Police Office (Europol)

The integrated police-intelligence gathering and dissemination arm of the member nations of the European Union.

The Palace of Justice in Brussels, Belgium. The Belgian court system has become a kind of international criminal court, prosecuting cases of genocide or crimes against humanity, no matter where in the world the incidents occur. The court may soon be replaced by a proposed International Criminal Court sponsored by the United Nations.

Topham, The Image Works

for trying individuals (not countries) who commit the most serious crimes of concern to the international community, such as genocide, war crimes, and crimes against humanity—including the wholesale murder of civilians, torture, and mass rape. The ICC will be a global judicial institution with international jurisdiction complementing national legal systems around the world. Needed support for the ICC was developed through the United Nations, where more than 70 countries approved the court's creation by ratifying what is known as the Rome Statute of the International Criminal Court.

The ICC initiative began after World War II, with unsuccessful efforts to establish an international tribunal to try individuals accused of war crimes.[99] In lieu of such a court, military tribunals were held in Nuremberg, Germany, and Tokyo to try those accused of war crimes. Although the 1948 Genocide Convention called for an international criminal court, efforts to establish a permanent court were delayed for decades by the cold war and by the refusal of some national governments to accept the court's proposed international legal jurisdiction.

In December 1948, the UN General Assembly (GA) adopted the Universal Declaration of Human Rights and the Convention on the Prevention and Punishment of the Crime of Genocide. It also called for criminals to be tried "by such international penal tribunals as may have jurisdiction." A number of member states soon asked the United Nation's International Law Commission (ILC) to study the possibility of establishing an ICC.

Development of an ICC was delayed by the cold war that took place between the world's superpowers—none of which were willing to subject their military personnel or commanders to international criminal jurisdiction in the event of a "hot" war. In 1981, however, the United Nation's General Assembly asked the International Law Commission to consider creation of an international Code of Crimes.

The 1992 War in Bosnia-Herzegovina, which involved clear violations of the Genocide and Geneva Conventions, heightened world interest in the establishment of a permanent ICC. A few years later, 160 countries participated in the UN Diplomatic Conference of Plenipotentiaries on the Establishment of an International Criminal Court,[100] which was held in Rome. At the end of that conference, member states voted overwhelmingly in favor of the Rome Statute, calling for establishment of an ICC.

The United States, however, has expressed concern about the ICC, saying that members of the American military could become subject to ICC jurisdiction. That concern led to U.S. efforts to delay the court's creation. On December 7, 2001, for example, the U.S. Senate approved the American Servicemembers' Protection Act (ASPA) proposed by North Carolina Senator Jesse Helms. The act was proposed as an amendment to the Defense Appropriations Act.[101] If approved by the full Congress and signed by the president, it will prohibit U.S. cooperation with the ICC and will authorize the president to use "all means necessary and appropriate" to release U.S. or Allied personnel from detention by the Court. As this book goes to press, European leaders are expressing strong disapproval of the pending American legislation. Visit the Coalition for an International Criminal Court via **Web Extra! 16–10** at cjtoday.com.

Prior to the existence of a true international criminal court, Belgium made its courts available to the rest of the world.[102] The country's legal system, in essence, took on the role of global prosecutor. Under a 1993 Belgian law, which is regarded by many as the world's most expansive statute against genocide and crimes against humanity, Belgian justices were called upon to enforce the country's criminal laws on a global scale. Other investigations focused on enforcing the 1949 Geneva Convention governing the conduct of war and the treatment of refugees. Belgian law specifically provides for the criminal prosecution of individuals who are not Belgian citizens, and it provides no immunity to prosecution for foreign leaders. In 2001, a Brussels jury convicted four people, including two Catholic nuns, of contributing to ethnic violence in the central African nation of Rwanda in 1994.

Currently, Belgian authorities are investigating more than a dozen complaints involving current and former state officials, including Ariel Sharon (prime minister of Israel), Saddam Hussein (president of Iraq), Hissene Habre (former dictator of Chad), Hashemi Rafsanjani (former president of Iran), Driss Basri (former interior minister of Morocco), Denis Sassou Nguesso (president of Congo-Brazzaville), and Fidel Castro (leader of Cuba). Cuban exiles charged Castro in Brussels's criminal court in October 2001 with false imprisonment, murder, torture, and other crimes against humanity. As a result of its ongoing investigations, Belgium has experienced strained relationships with a number of countries, and the nation's officials have begun to question the wisdom of charging sitting heads of state with violations of the criminal law.

Summary

The international perspective has much to contribute to the study of American criminal justice. Law enforcement agencies, court personnel, and correctional officials in the United States can benefit from exposure to innovative crime-prevention and investigative and treatment techniques found in other parts of the world. Through a study of foreign legal codes and the routine practice of criminal justice in other countries, policymakers can acquire a fresh perspective on upcoming decisions in the area of law and justice.

A number of barriers, however, continue to limit the applicability of cross-national studies. One is the continuing unavailability of sufficiently detailed, up-to-date, and reliable international information on crime rates, victimization, and adjudication. Another, more difficult limit is imposed by ethnocentrism. Ethnocentrism, a culturally determined hesitancy on the part of some people to consider any personal or professional viewpoints other than their own, reduces the likelihood for serious analysis of even the limited international information which is available in the area of criminal justice.

Given enough time, most barriers are overcome. Although political, economic, and ideological differences will remain dominant throughout the world for many years, the globe is shrinking. Advances in communications, travel, and the exchange of all types of information are combining with an exponential growth in technology to produce a worldwide interdependence among nations. As new international partnerships are sought and formed, barriers to understanding will continue to fall.

Discussion Questions

1. What are the benefits of studying criminal justice systems in other countries? Are there any potentially negative consequences of such study?
2. If you were to study the criminal justice systems of other countries, which nations would you select for analysis? Why?
3. What is ethnocentrism? How does it develop, and what purpose does it serve? How can it be overcome? Should it be?
4. What are some of the limitations imposed on the international study of criminal justice today? Do you see any way to overcome those limitations?
5. Should police in England carry guns, like their American counterparts? Explain.

To participate in an online discussion on these topics and others, go to the Global Town Meeting electronic message board for Chapter 16 on the *Criminal Justice Today* Companion Website at cjtoday.com.

Web Quest!

Use the Cybrary to identify countries other than the United States that make information on their criminal justice system available on the Web. What countries do so? List the sites that you find, and describe the justice system of each nation.

Then use the Cybrary to identify countries other than the United States that make crime statistics available on the Web. What countries are those? List the statistics sites that you find for each country, and include a summary of the statistics available for each. Submit your findings to your instructor if asked to do so.

To complete this Web Quest! online, go to the Web Quest! module in Chapter 16 of the *Criminal Justice Today* Companion Website at cjtoday.com.

Library Extras!

Library Extra! 16–1 *World Factbook of Criminal Justice Systems* (BJS, various years).
Library Extra! 16–2 *Global Report on Crime and Justice* (UN, current volume).
Library Extra! 16–3 *The British Crime Survey* (Home Office, current volume).
Library Extra! 16–4 *The International Crime Victimization Survey* (Home Office, current volume).

To explore these resources online, go to the Library Extras! area of the *Criminal Justice Today* Companion Website at cjtoday.com. You should also check the author's "Late Picks" online for newly released documents and updated Library Extras! You can find Late Picks at http://cjtoday.com/latepicks.htm.

Marginal Notes

i. UN Department of Public Information, "The United Nations versus Transnational Crime," April 1995. Web posted at http://www.un.org/ecosocdev/geninfo/crime/dpi1644e.htm. Accessed January 15, 2000.

Notes

1. Richard H. Ward, "The Internationalization of Criminal Justice," in Phyllis McDonald and Janice Munsterman, eds., *Criminal Justice 2000:* Vol. 2 *Boundary Changes in Criminal Justice Organizations* (Washington, D.C.: National Institute of Justice, 2000), p. 267.

2. "Japanese Parliament Approves Wiretap Law," Associated Press wire service, August 13, 1999. The legislation became effective in 2000.

3. Martin Fackler, "Coverage of Brutal Murder Ignites Media Debate in Japan," Associated Press wire service, February 27, 1998.

4. Joji Sakurai, "Arrest Made in Japan Beheading," Associated Press wire service, June 28, 1997.

5. Shizuo Kambayashi, "Beheading Arrest Shocks Japan," Associated Press wire service, June 29, 1997.

6. Japanese Ministry of Public Management, Home Affairs, Posts and Telecommunications, *Japan Statistical Yearbook 2002* (Tokyo: Japan Statistics Bureau, 2002).

7. "Juvenile Crime," *Mainichi Daily News.* Web posted at http://www3.justnet.ne.jp/matudasy/ikai/eng-news3.html. Accessed February 2, 2000.

8. Robert Lilly, "Forks and Chopsticks: Understanding Criminal Justice in the PRC," *Criminal Justice International* (March/April 1986), p. 15.

9. Adapted from Carol B. Kalish, "International Crime Rates," *BJS Special Report* (Washington, D.C.: Bureau of Justice Statistics, 1988).

10. Ibid.

11. Ibid.

12. Lee Hockstader, "Russia's War on Crime: A Lopsided, Losing Battle," *Washington Post* wire service, February 27, 1995.

13. Roy Walmsley, *Developments in the Prison Systems of Central and Eastern Europe,* HEUNI papers no. 4 (Helsinki, 1995).

14. "China: The Hope and the Horror," *Reader's Digest,* September 1989, p. 75.

15. This section draws heavily upon Shao-Chuan Leng and Hungdah Chiu, *Criminal Justice in Post-Mao China: Analysis and Documents* (Albany: State University of New York at Albany Press, 1985).

16. Various authorities give different dates for the ending of the Cultural Revolution. We have chosen 1973 because it represents the date when military control over law enforcement finally ended.

17. *China Mainland Magazine,* No. 625, September 3, 1968, p. 23.

18. Central Political-Judicial Cadre's School, *Lectures on the General Principles of Criminal Law in the People's Republic of China* (Peking, 1957), as cited by Leng and Chiu, *Criminal Justice in Post-Mao China,* p. 21.

19. "On Questions of Party History," *Beijing Review,* Vol. 24, No. 27 (July 6, 1981), p. 20, as quoted in Leng and Chiu, *Criminal Justice in Post-Mao China.*

20. Leng and Chiu, *Criminal Justice in Post-Mao China,* p. 42.

21. For an excellent review of the role of the prosecutor in China, see He Jiahong and Jon R. Waltz, *Criminal Prosecution in the PRC and the USA: A Comparative Study,* English edition (Beijing: China Procuratorial Press, 1995).

22. "China Uses Technology to Tackle Soaring Crime," Reuters wire service, December 18, 1994.

23. Ibid.

24. Zhenxiong (Joseph) Zhou, "An Introduction to the Present Legal System of the People's Republic of China," *North Carolina Criminal Justice Today,* Vol. 4, No. 6 (Salemburg, NC: N.C. Justice Academy, 1987), pp. 8–15.

25. Lilly, "Forks and Chopsticks," pp. 14–15.

26. Ibid., p. 14.

27. Leng and Chiu, *Criminal Justice in Post-Mao China,* p. 75.

28. Benjamin Kang Lim, "China Declares War on Organized Crime," Reuters wire service, February 23, 1995.

29. John Pomfret, "Chinese Crime Rate Soars as Economic Problems Grow," *Washington Post*, January 21, 1999, p. A19.

30. Ibid.

31. "Shenzhen Cracks Down Hard on Piracy," *People's Daily* (China), January 24, 2002.

32. "China Cracking Down on Piracy of DVDs," *People's Daily* (China), November 26, 2001.

33. Lim, "China Declares War on Organized Crime."

34. Statistics on arrest, conviction, and imprisonment in China are taken from Robert Elegant, "Everyone Can Be Reformed," *Parade*, October 30, 1988, pp. 4–7.

35. Leng and Chiu, *Criminal Justice in Post-Mao China*, pp. 141–142.

36. Zhu Entao, "A Perspective on Drug Abuse," *Criminal Justice International* (January/ February 1987), pp. 5–6.

37. Zhou, "An Introduction to the Present Legal System of the People's Republic of China," p. 13.

38. Ibid.

39. For more information, see Lening Zhang et al., "Crime Prevention in a Communitarian Society: *Bang-Jiao* and *Tiao-Jie* in the People's Republic of China," *Justice Quarterly*, Vol. 13, No. 2 (June 1996), pp. 199–222.

40. Ibid.

41. Leng and Chiu, *Criminal Justice in Post-Mao China*, p. 64.

42. Elegant, "Everyone Can Be Reformed," p. 5.

43. Amnesty International, death penalty information page. Web posted at http://www.web.amnesty.org/ rmp/dplibrary.nsf/other?openview. Accessed January 8, 2002.

44. Amnesty International, "At Least 1000 People Executed in 'Strike Hard' Campaign against Crime," October 2, 1997. Web posted at http://www.amnesty.org. Accessed January 10, 1998.

45. "Executions an Every Day Event in China," Reuters wire service, March 17, 1995.

46. Ibid.

47. Elegant, "Everyone Can Be Reformed," p. 6.

48. Ibid.

49. E. Eugene Miller, "Corrections in the People's Republic of China," in American Correctional Association, *International Corrections: An Overview* (College Park, MD: American Correctional Association, 1987), p. 69.

50. Harry Wu, "A Prisoner's Journey," *Newsweek*, September 23, 1991, p. 30.

51. Miller, "Corrections in the People's Republic of China," pp. 65–71.

52. Jeff Sanders and Thomas McAninch, "A Communist Prison Experience," *American Jails* (November/December 1994), p. 87.

53. Elegant, "Everyone Can Be Reformed," p. 5.

54. Sam S. Souryal, Dennis W. Potts, and Abdullah I. Alobied, "The Penalty of Hand Amputation for Theft in Islamic Justice," *Journal of Criminal Justice*, Vol. 22, No. 3 (1994), pp. 249–265.

55. Parviz Saney, "Iran," in Elmer H. Johnson, ed., *International Handbook of Contemporary Developments in Criminology* (Westport, CT: Greenwood, 1983), p. 359.

56. This section owes much to Matthew Lippman, "Iran: A Question of Justice?" *Criminal Justice International* (1987), pp. 6–7.

57. Sharif Imam-Jomeh, "Iran Court Sentences Man to Death for Bank Fraud," Reuters wire service, August 22, 1995.

58. Souryal, Potts, and Alobied, "The Penalty of Hand Amputation for Theft in Islamic Justice."

59. Afshin Valinejad, "Iran Flogs, Hangs Serial Killer Known as 'The Vampire,'" *USA Today*, August 14, 1997, p. 11A.

60. For additional information on Islamic law, see Adel Mohammed el Fikey, "Crimes and Penalties in Islamic Criminal Legislation," *Criminal Justice International* (1986), pp. 13–14; and Sam S. Souryal, "Shariah Law in Saudi Arabia," *Journal for the Scientific Study of Religion*, Vol. 26, No. 4 (1987), pp. 429–449.

61. Max Weber, in Max Rheinstein, ed., *On Law in Economy and Society* (New York: Simon & Schuster, 1967), translated from the 1925 German edition.

62. Ibid.

63. Souryal, Potts, and Alobied, "The Penalty of Hand Amputation for Theft in Islamic Justice."

64. Home Office, *The 2001 British Crime Survey* (London: Home Office, 2001). Web posted at http://www. homeoffice.gov.uk/rds/pdfs/bcs1.html. Accessed January 25, 2002.

65. Richard Terrill, *World Criminal Justice Systems* (Cincinnati: Anderson, 1984), p. 3.

66. Alan Wheatley, "Howard Promises Crackdown on Crime," Reuters wire service, October 6, 1994.

67. Home Office, *The Crime and Disorder Act: Introductory Guide*. Web posted at http://www.homeoffice.gov.uk/ cdact/cdaint2.htm. Accessed March 23, 2000.

68. Information in this section is derived from "Q&A: Anti-terror Bill," BBC News online. Web posted at http://newsvote.bbc.co.uk/hi/english/uk_politics/ newsid_1708000/1708097.stm. Accessed December 15, 2001.

69. Philip John Stead, *The Police of Britain* (New York: Macmillan, 1985), p. 94.

70. Home Office, Research and Statistics Department.

71. "Police and Magistrates Court Act Aids British Service," *Criminal Justice International* (May/June 1995), p. 7.

72. Exceptions might include the Transport Police, who supervise the operation of the nation's ports, and secretive intelligence gathering agencies like M.I.5.

73. "An Interview with Sir Kenneth Newman, Commissioner of the Metropolitan Police," *Criminal Justice International* (November/ December 1986), p. 17.

74. "New Intelligence Service Begins Operation," *Criminal Justice International* (July/August 1992), p. 3.

75. For a good discussion of the curriculum at Bramshill, see Dennis Rowe, "On Her Majesty's Service: Policing England and Wales," *Criminal Justice International* (November/December 1986), pp. 9–16.

76. Ken Hyder, "Beware LA Law," *Criminal Justice International* (May/June 1995), pp. 10–11.

77. Stead, *The Police of Britain*, p. 147.

78. Terrill, *World Criminal Justice Systems*, p. 71.

79. Mike Elkins, Carly Gray, and Keith Rogers, *Prison Population Brief—England and Wales: September 2001* (London: Home Office, 2001), p. 1. Web posted at http://www.homeoffice.gov.uk/rds/pdfs/prissep01. pdf. Accessed March 5, 2002.

80. Ibid., p. 20.

81. Paul Friday, "International Organization: An Introduction," in Elmer H. Johnson, ed., *International Handbook of Contemporary Developments in Criminology* (Westport, CT: Greenwood, 1983), p. 31.

82. Ibid., p. 32.

83. Gerhard O. W. Mueller, "The United Nations and Criminology," in Elmer H. Johnson, ed., *International Handbook of Contemporary Developments in Criminology* (Westport, CT: Greenwood, 1983), pp. 74–75.

84. Roger S. Clark, *The United Nations Crime Prevention and Criminal Justice Program: Formulation of Standards and Efforts at Their Implementation* (Philadelphia: University of Pennsylvania Press, 1994).

85. Ibid., pp. 71–72.

86. "International News," *Corrections Compendium* (June 1995), p. 25.

87. Resolutions adopted on the reports of the Third Committee at the Forty-sixth Session of the United Nations General Assembly.

88. Khaled Dawoud, "U.N. Crime Meeting Wants Independent Jail Checks," Reuters wire service, May 6, 1995.

89. Laurie Robinson, address given at the Twelfth International Congress on Criminology, Seoul, Korea, August 28, 1998.

90. Robert S. Gelbard, "Foreign Policy after the Cold War: The New Threat—Transnational Crime," address at St. Mary's University, San Antonio, Texas, April 2, 1996.

91. Barbara Starr, "A Gangster's Paradise," ABC News Online, September 14, 1998. Web posted at http://more.abcnews.go.com/sections/world/dailynews/russiacrime980914.html. Accessed January 22, 2000.

92. Ibid.

93. Raymond Bonner and Timothy L. O'Brien, "Activity at Bank Raises Suspicions of Russia Mob Tie," *New York Times*, August 19, 1999, p. 1A.

94. Kevin F. Ryan, "Globalizing the Problem: The United States and International Drug Control," in Eric L. Jensen and Jurg Gerber, eds., *The New War on Drugs: Symbolic Politics and Criminal Justice Policy* (Cincinnati: Anderson, 1997).

95. See "INTERPOL: Extending Law Enforcement's Reach around the World," *FBI Law Enforcement Bulletin,* December 1998, pp. 10–16.

96. U.S. Department of Justice, "INTERPOL Member Countries." Web posted at http://www.usdoj.gov/usncb/countrytext.htm. Accessed January 19, 2000.

97. "INTERPOL at Forty," *Criminal Justice International* (November/December 1986), pp. 1, 22.

98. ICPO-Interpol General Assembly Resolution No. AG-2001-RES-07.

99. Much of the information and some of the wording in this section is adapted from "The ICC International Criminal Court Home Page," Web posted at http://www.iccnow.org/index.html; and the ICC "Timeline," Web posted at http://www.iccnow.org/html/timeline.htm. Accessed April 12, 2002.

100. The conference was officially known as the Conference of Plenipotentiaries on the Establishment of an International Criminal Court. *Plenipotentiaries* is another word for "diplomats."

101. Coalition for the International Criminal Court, "American Servicemember's Protection Act Receives Senate Approval," press release, December 11, 2001.

102. Much of the information in this paragraph and the next comes from David J. Lynch, "Belgium Plays Global Prosecutor," *USA Today,* July 16, 2001, p. 7A; and Katie Nguyen, "Cubans Use Belgian Law to File Case Against Castro," Reuters wire service, October 4, 2001.

The Future
of Criminal Justice

LEARNING OBJECTIVES

After reading this chapter, you should be able to

■ Explain the important role that technology has played, and will continue to play, in the fight against crime and the quest for justice

■ Explain the nature of high-technology crime, and list some forms that such crime might take

■ Discuss the historical roots of terrorism, what motivates terrorists, and the government's attempts to prevent and control the spread of terrorism

■ Identify the threats to individual rights inherent in the increased use of advanced technology

chapter **17**

[*At some point, we can do away with cybercrime laws because most crimes will involve computers in some way, and all crime will be cybercrime.*]

—Computer crime expert Donn Parker[1]

[*The rise of a new kind of America requires a new kind of law enforcement system.*]

—Alvin Toffler

[*Terrorism is going to join the omnipresence of crime as one of the things we have to worry about in American cities.*]

—Bruce Hoffman, RAND

Key Concepts

[Terms]

ballistics	DNA profiling	international terrorism
computer crime	domestic terrorism	occupational crime
computer virus	expert system	protected computer
corporate crime	foreign terrorist organization (FTO)	smart card
criminalist	forensic anthropology	software piracy
criminalistics	forensic entomology	terrorism
cyberterrorism	hacker	white-collar crime
Daubert standard	identity theft	

[Names]

Alphonse Bertillon	Henry Faulds	William Herschel
James Coleman	Sir Francis Galton	William Tafoya

[Cases]

Daubert v. *Merrell Dow Pharmaceuticals, Inc.*	*Holt* v. *Sarver*	*Reno* v. *ACLU*

Introduction

Hear the author discuss this chapter at **cjtoday.com**

In August 2001, police investigators in Farmingdale, New York, announced that they had made three arrests in the case of a 15-year-old girl who had allegedly been kidnapped by a man she met through the Internet.[2] Officers said that the girl had been exchanging e-mail messages with James Warren, 41, of Hampton Bays, New York, for months and that she decided to run away from home with him. The teenager rendezvoused with Warren at a mall in Wrentham, Massachusetts, and then drove off in a car with him, police said. Warren allegedly took her to a home on Long Island where she was beaten, handcuffed, tied up in a closet, and sexually assaulted by Warren and two other people for a week. Finally, after her abductors left the house, the teenager managed to free herself and called police. Arrested along with Warren were Beth Loschin, 46, of Farmingdale, and Michael Montez, 35, of New York City. All face multiple charges, including kidnapping, sodomy, sexual abuse, sexual assault, and rape. Officials also suspect the three of running a child pornography ring, which may have been Internet-based.

One week before the Warren conspirators were taken into custody, U.S. Attorney General John Ashcroft announced the arrests of more than 100 people resulting from an undercover investigation into the largest commercial child pornography business ever uncovered.[3] The investigation, known by the code name Operation Avalanche, involved a two-year probe by the U.S. Postal Inspection Service, the Federal Bureau of Investigation (FBI), the U.S. Customs Service, and the Dallas Police Department of an online child pornography business. Run by Thomas Reedy, 37, and his wife, Janice, 32, of Fort Worth, the website served 250,000 to 300,000 subscribers around the world who each paid $29.95 a month for access to online photos and videos. In late 2001, a federal judge sentenced Thomas Reedy to 1,335 years in prison—15 years for each of the 89 counts of trafficking in child pornography of which he had been convicted. Janice Reedy was sentenced to serve 14 years in prison. As this book goes to press, the second phase of Operation Avalanche is getting under way. It involves rounding up the site's suppliers and customers, many of whom were identified after law enforcement agents took over the Reedys' business following their arrest. Agents continued to run the site for almost a year in an effort to snare regular users. As a result of the online sting, federal authorities have already conducted 144 searches in 37 different states.

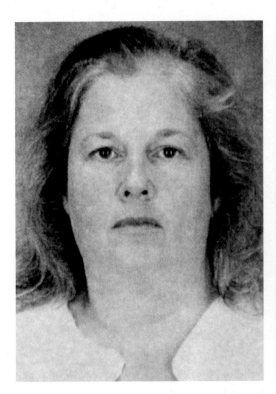 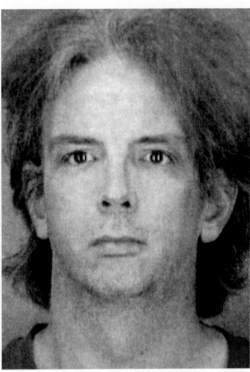

Beth Loschin, 46, and James Warren, 41, two of the three suspects arrested in connection with the alleged abduction and sexual abuse of a 15-year-old girl by a man she met over the Internet. The two face charges of kidnapping, sodomy, rape, first-degree sexual abuse, and child abuse.

AP/Wide World Photos

Technology and Criminal Justice

Rapidly expanding technologies, including computer networking, the Internet, wireless services of all kinds, and simple access to relatively anonymous forms of electronic communication, signal a new era for the American justice system. A generation ago, many crimes committed through the use of, or facilitated by, today's high-technology were impossible—if not unthinkable. Already, legislative activity at both the state and federal levels, designed to control socially undesirable and harmful activity made possible by new technologies, has resulted in the definition of new crimes like software piracy, illegal access to computers, electronic security violations (that is, computer viruses and worms), e-fraud, and the electronic theft of digital information.

On the other hand, law enforcement access to high-technology investigative tools has produced enormous amounts of information on crimes and suspects, and the use of innovative investigative tools like DNA fingerprinting, keystroke captures, laser vision technologies, and thermography are beginning to shape many of the practical aspects of the twenty-first-century criminal justice system. There are even laptop computers, vehicles, and other devices that call police to report themselves stolen and that provide satellite-based tracking information so authorities can determine their whereabouts. A number of rental car companies, for example, now have cars equipped with systems that can be instructed from a central location to prevent the car from starting and that can also track the car as it moves. No doubt the future will see a race between technologically sophisticated offenders and law enforcement authorities to determine who can wield the most advanced technical skills in the age-old battle between crime and justice.[4]

Nonetheless, the criminal justice system of the near future will look much like the system we know today. It will rest upon constitutional mandates and will be responsive to court precedent. The system itself will remain recognizable through its backbone of subsystems: the police, the courts, and corrections. Deterrence, apprehension, and reformation will continue to serve as the philosophical triad guiding the day-to-day operations of criminal justice agencies. New issues will arise, but most of them will be resolved within the context of the question which has guided American criminal justice since its inception: how to ensure public order and safety while guaranteeing individual rights and social justice in a free society.

Attorney General John Ashcroft, at a Washington, D.C., news conference in 2001, standing before a display of Web-based banner advertisments used to lure customers looking for child pronography on the Internet. Ashcroft was announcing the arrests of 100 people as part of an undercover sting into the largest commercial child pornography operation ever found.

AP/Wide World Photos

> Technology throughout history has been a double-edged sword, equally capable of enhancing or endangering democratic values.
>
> —John H. Gibbons, Director of the Office of Technology Assessment, U.S. Congress

Many demographic, ideological, and behavioral transformations, such as widespread illegal drug use and a greater social acceptance of certain victimless crimes, have already occurred and are now firmly rooted in substantial segments of American society. Less clear, however, are changes yet to come—changes we can only now begin to discern. This chapter attempts to identify some of these coming changes and to predict what practical impact they will have on American criminal justice. Perhaps the two most significant sources of change will be technology and the continuing evolution of society. Throughout history, the interplay between technology and culture has been weighted in favor of cultural norms and ideals. Scientific advances often came before society was ready for them. When they did, they were denied or suppressed. Today, however, the situation is reversed. Technology is now often the prime mover, unable to be easily denied, forcing social change when it occurs. Because technology may be the most important harbinger of change in the modern world, this chapter focuses on the opportunities and threats that technology represents to the justice system.

A Brief History of Criminal Justice Technologies

We live in a world governed by rapid change. Technology and science are the modern-day engines of change, and they continue to run relentlessly forward. The impact of change on all areas of human life has been dramatic. The automobile and the airplane have made the world a smaller place, and journeys that would have required months a century ago can now be made in a day or less. Radio, television, and the Internet have transformed the planet into a "global village" in which every human being can be in touch with events of importance as they happen anywhere around the globe. Computers have dramatically altered the rate at which information is being produced, so much so that precedence is given today to storing and securing information rather than using it. Coming software, it is hoped, will do a better job of sorting through terabytes of accumulated information, distinguishing the significant from the mundane and permitting us to make use of that which is of interest.

Technological advances throughout history have signaled both threats and opportunities for the justice field. By the turn of the twentieth century, for example, police call boxes were standard features in many cities, utilizing the new technology of telephonic communications to pass along information on crimes in progress or to describe suspects and their activities. A few years later, police departments across the nation adapted to the rapid growth in the number of private automobiles and the laws governing their use. Over the years, motorized patrol, VASCAR devices, radar, laser speed detectors, and police helicopters and aircraft were all called into service to meet the need for a rapid response to criminal activity. Today's citizens band radios, often monitored by local police and highway patrol agencies, and cell phones with direct numbers to police dispatchers are continuing the trend of adapting advances in communications technology to police purposes.

Technology affects criminal justice in many areas. The National Law Enforcement Technology Center (NLETC) performs yearly assessments of key technological needs and opportunities facing the justice system. The center is responsible for helping to identify, develop, manufacture, and adopt new products and technologies designed for law enforcement, corrections, and other criminal justice applications.[5] NLETC concentrates on four areas of advancing technology: (1) communications and electronics, (2) forensic science, (3) transportation and weapons, and (4) protective equipment.[6] Once opportunities for improvement are identified in any area, referrals are made to the Law Enforcement Standards Laboratory—a part of the National Bureau of Standards—for the testing of available hardware. The Justice Technology Information Network (JUSTNET), a service of NLETC, acts as an information gateway for law enforcement, corrections, and criminal justice technology and notifies the justice community of the latest technological advances. JUSTNET, accessible via the World Wide Web, lists the websites of technology providers.

While federal justice technology assessment programs concentrate primarily on facilitating suspect apprehension and the protection of enforcement personnel, some authors have pointed to the potential held by emerging technologies in the area of offender treatment. Some have suggested, for example, that novel forms of biomedical intervention, building upon the earlier practices of castration, psychosurgery, and drug treatment, will continue to be adapted from advances in the biological sciences and will serve as innovative treatment modalities.[7] The possibilities are limited only by the imagination.[8] Chemical substances to reform the offender, drugs to enhance the memories of witnesses and victims, recombinant DNA behavioral therapy, and microchip extensions of the personality all appear to be on the horizon.

Criminalistics: Past, Present, and Future

The use of technology in the service of criminal investigation is a subfield of criminal justice referred to as **criminalistics**. Criminalistics applies scientific techniques to the detection and evaluation of criminal evidence. Police crime-scene analysts and laboratory personnel who use these techniques are referred to as **criminalists**. Modern criminalistics began with the need for the certain identification of individuals. Early methods of personal identification were notoriously inaccurate. In the nineteenth century, for instance, one day of the week was generally dedicated to a "parade" of newly arrested offenders; experienced investigators from distant jurisdictions would scrutinize the convicts, looking for recognizable faces.[9] By the 1840s, the Quetelet system of anthropometry was making itself known.[10] The Quetelet system depended upon precise measurements of various parts of the body to give an overall "picture" of a person for use in later identification.

The first "modern" system of personal identification was created by Alphonse Bertillon.[11] Bertillon was the director of the Bureau of Criminal Identification of the Paris Police Department during the late nineteenth century. The Bertillon system of identification was based upon the idea that certain bodily aspects, such as eye color, skeletal size and shape, and ear form, did not change substantially after physical maturity. The system combined physical measurements with the emerging technology of photography. Although photography had been used previously in criminal identification, Bertillon standardized the technique by positioning measuring guides beside suspects so that their physical dimensions could be calculated from their photographs and by taking both front views and profiles.

Fingerprints, produced by contact with the ridge patterns in the skin on the fingertips, became the subject of intense scientific study in the mid-1840s. While their importance in criminal investigation today seems obvious, it was not until the 1880s that scientists began to realize that each person's fingerprints were unique and unchangeable over a lifetime. Both discoveries appear to have come from the Englishmen William Herschel and Henry Faulds, who were working in Asia.[12] Some writers, observing that Asiatic lore about finger ridges and their significance extends back to antiquity, suggest that Herschel and Faulds must have been privy to such information.[13] As early as the Tang Dynasty (A.D. 618–906), inked fingerprints were being used in China as personal seals on important documents, and there is some evidence that the Chinese had classified patterns of the loops and whorls found in fingerprints and were using them for the identification of criminals as far back as 1,000 years ago.[14]

The use of fingerprints in identifying offenders was popularized by Sir Francis Galton[15] and was officially adopted by Scotland Yard in 1901. By the 1920s, fingerprint identification was in use in police departments everywhere, having quickly replaced Bertillon's anthropometric system. Suspects were fingerprinted, and their prints were compared with those lifted from a crime scene. Those comparisons typically required a great deal of time and a

criminalistics

The use of technology in the service of criminal investigation; the application of scientific techniques to the detection and evaluation of criminal evidence.

criminalist

A police crime-scene analyst or laboratory worker versed in criminalistics.

bit of luck to produce a match. Over time, as fingerprint inventories in the United States grew huge, including those of everyone in the armed services and in certain branches of federal employment, researchers looked for a rapid and efficient way to compare large numbers of prints. Until the 1980s, most effective comparison schemes depended upon manual classification methods which automatically eliminated large numbers of prints from consideration. As late as 1974, one author lamented, "Considering present levels of technology in other sciences . . . [the] classification of fingerprints has profited little by technological advancements, particularly in the computer sciences. [Fingerprint comparisons are] limited by the laborious inspection by skilled technicians required to accurately classify and interpret prints. Automation of the classification process and potentially comparison as well, would open up fingerprinting to its fullest potential."[16]

Within a decade, advances in computer hardware and software made possible CAL-ID, the automated fingerprint identification system (AFIS) of the California State Department of Justice. The system used optical scanning and software pattern matching to compare suspects' fingerprints. Such computerized systems have grown rapidly in capability, and links between systems operated by different agencies are now routine. Modern technology employs proprietary electro-optical scanning systems which digitize live fingerprints, eliminating the need for traditional inking and rolling techniques.[17] Other advances in fingerprint identification and matching are also being made. The use of lasers in fingerprint lifting, for example, allowed the FBI to detect a 50-year-old fingerprint of a Nazi war criminal on a postcard.[18] Other advances now make it possible to lift latent fingerprints from the skin of crime victims and even from bodies that have been submerged underwater for considerable periods of time.[19]

Computerization and digitization have improved accuracy and reduced the incidence of "false positives" in fingerprint comparisons.[20] The Los Angeles Police Department, which uses an automated fingerprint identification system, estimates that fingerprint comparisons which in the past would have taken as long as 60 years can now be performed in a single day.[21] Computerized fingerprint identification systems took a giant step forward in 1986 with the introduction of a new electronic standard for fingerprint data exchange.[22] This standard makes it possible to exchange data between different automated fingerprint identification systems. Prior to its invention, the comparison of fingerprint data between AFISs was often difficult or impossible. Using the standard, cities across the nation can share and compare fingerprint information over telephone lines linking their AFISs.[23] Recently, the FBI announced plans to develop an integrated automated fingerprint identification system (IAFIS) as part of NCIC—2000 (see Chapter 5). IAFIS will integrate state fingerprint databases and automate search requests from police agencies throughout the country.

ballistics

The analysis of firearms, ammunition, projectiles, bombs, and explosives.

forensic anthropology

The use of anthropological principles and techniques in criminal investigation.

forensic entomology

The study of insects to determine issues such as a person's time of death.

Modern criminalistics also depends heavily upon **ballistics**, to analyze weapons, ammunition, and projectiles; medical pathology, to determine the cause of injury or death; **forensic anthropology**, to reconstruct the likeness of a decomposed or dismembered body; **forensic entomology**, to determine issues such as the time of death; forensic dentistry, to help identify deceased victims and offenders; the photography of crime scenes (now often done with video or digital cameras); plaster and polymer castings of tire tracks, boot prints, and marks made by implements; polygraph (the "lie detector") and voiceprint identification; as well as a plethora of other techniques. Many criminal investigative practices have been thoroughly tested and are now accepted by most courts for the evidence they offer. Polygraph[24] and voiceprint identification techniques are still being refined, however, and have not won the wide acceptance of the other techniques mentioned.

Emerging Technologies in Criminalistics

Law enforcement practitioners of the future will be aided in their work by a number of technologies, some of which are still in their infancy. They include

- DNA profiling and new serological/tissue identification techniques
- Online databases and clearinghouses for the sharing of criminal justice information
- Computer-generated psychological profiles and computer-aided crime-scene analysis
- Computer enhancements of photographs, images, and other types of evidence
- Forensic animation (computer simulations of criminal activity)
- Chemical and microscopic examination of fibers and other materials using advanced techniques

Forensic anthropologist Frank Bender explaining how he makes forensic models at his studio in Philadelphia. Bender, who describes himself as "the recomposer of the decomposed," has helped police identify dozens of murder victims and, in some cases, find their killers.

AP/Wide World Photos

Brief descriptions of these technologies, including their current state of development and the implications they hold for the future, is provided in the paragraphs that follow.

DNA PROFILING

In March 2000, a man known only by his genetic makeup was indicted and charged with a series of sexual assaults in Manhattan.[25] Authorities said that it was the first indictment based on a DNA profile. No arrest has yet been made. The man, dubbed the "East Side Rapist" and named in the indictment as "John Doe, an unidentified male," followed by his DNA profile, was charged with two sexual assaults in 1995 and one in 1997. He is alleged to have sexually attacked 16 women since 1994.

DNA evidence (also discussed in Chapter 10), which is increasingly preferred as a method of positive identification, sometimes works in favor of defendants. In December 2001, for example, Marvin Lamond Anderson, a Virginia parolee, was cleared of rape charges stemming from a 1982 crime for which he had served 15 years in prison.[26] Anderson received assistance from the Innocence Project, a volunteer organization specializing in the use of DNA technology to investigate and challenge what it regards as dubious convictions. A Virginia law passed in 2000, which allows felons to seek exoneration and expungement of their convictions on the basis of modern DNA testing, helped Anderson prove that he could not have committed the crime of which he had been convicted. DNA taken from a 19-year-old cotton swab was compared to the state's DNA database of more than 100,000 convicted felons and conclusively demonstrated that Anderson had not committed the crime. Learn more about the Innocence Project via **Web Extra! 17–1.**

The U.S. Department of Justice notes that "DNA evidence is playing a larger role than ever before in criminal cases throughout the country, both to convict the guilty and to exonerate those wrongly accused or convicted."[27] **DNA profiling**, also termed *DNA fingerprinting*, makes use of human DNA for purposes of identification. DNA (deoxyribonucleic acid) is a nucleic acid found in the center of cells. It is the principal component of chromosomes, the structures that transmit hereditary characteristics between generations. Each DNA molecule is a long, two-stranded chain made up of subunits called *nucleotides*, coiled in the form of a double helix. Because genetic material is unique to each individual (except in the case of identical twins or clones), it can provide a highly reliable source of suspect identification. DNA profiling was originally used as a test for determining paternity.

DNA profiling

The use of biological residue, found at the scene of a crime, for genetic comparisons in aiding the identification of criminal suspects.

DNA profiling requires only a few human cells for comparison. One drop of blood, a few hairs, a small amount of skin, or a trace of semen usually provide sufficient genetic material. Because the DNA molecule is very stable, genetic tests can be conducted on evidence taken from crime scenes long after fingerprints have disappeared. The process, diagrammed in Figure 17–1, involves the use of a highly technical procedure called *electrophoresis*, which has not yet been universally accepted in American courts, although courts in 49 states have admitted DNA evidence in hundreds of trials and hearings.[28] Many of those trials, however, have involved civil suits. Maine, Rhode Island, North Dakota, and Utah have yet to fully accept DNA evidence in criminal trials.[29]

Forensic use of DNA technology in criminal cases began in 1986 when British police asked Dr. Alec J. Jeffreys (who coined the term *DNA fingerprints*[30]) of Leicester University to verify a suspect's confession that he was responsible for two rape-murders in the English Midlands. DNA tests proved that the suspect could not have committed the crimes. Police then began obtaining blood samples from several thousand male inhabitants in the area in an attempt to identify a new suspect.[31]

In a 1987 British case, 32-year-old Robert Melias became the first person ever convicted of a crime on the basis of DNA evidence.[32] Melias was convicted of raping a 43-year-old disabled woman, and the conviction came after genetic tests of semen left on the woman's clothes positively identified him as the perpetrator.[33]

In the civil case of *Daubert* v. *Merrell Dow Pharmaceuticals, Inc.* (1993),[34] the Supreme Court revised the criteria for the admissibility of scientific evidence by rejecting a previous admissibility standard established in the 1923 case of *Frye* v. *U.S.*[35] The *Daubert* Court ruled that the older *Frye* standard requiring "general acceptance" of a test or procedure by the relevant scientific community "is not a necessary precondition to the admissibility of scientific evidence." The baseline rule for the admissibility of scientific evidence, said the Court, is established by Rule 402 of the *Federal Rules of Evidence,* which was published after *Frye* and supersedes it. Rule 402 says that, in a trial, "all relevant evidence is admissible, except as otherwise provided by the Constitution of the United States, by Act of Congress, by these Rules, or by other rules prescribed by the Supreme Court pursuant to statutory authority." The Court went on to say that although "the Frye test was displaced by the Rules of Evidence, [that] does not mean . . . that the Rules themselves place no limits on the admissibility of purportedly scientific evidence. Nor is the trial judge disabled from screening such evidence. To the contrary, under the Rules the trial judge must ensure that any and all scientific testimony or evidence admitted is not only relevant, but reliable." The real test for the admissibility of scientific expert testimony, said the Court, is for the trial judge to decide "at the outset . . . whether the expert is proposing to testify to (1) scientific knowledge that (2) will assist the trier of fact to understand or determine a fact in issue." The Court concluded that the task of the trial judge is one of "ensuring that an expert's testimony both rests on a reliable foundation and is relevant to the task at hand. Pertinent evidence based on scientifically valid principles," said the Court, "will satisfy those demands."

Daubert standard

A test of scientific acceptability applicable to the gathering of evidence in criminal cases.

The plaintiffs in *Daubert* did not argue the merits of DNA testing, but claimed, instead, that the drug Bendectin caused birth defects. Nonetheless, the **Daubert standard** eased the criteria for the introduction of scientific evidence at both civil and criminal trials, effectively clearing the way for the use of DNA evidence in the courtroom.[36] Specifically, the *Daubert* Court found that the following factors may be used to determine whether any form of scientific evidence is reliable:[37]

- Whether it has been subject to testing
- Whether it has been subject to peer review
- Known or potential rates of error
- The existence of standards controlling application of the techniques involved

In 1994, the DNA Identification Act[38] provided substantial funding to improve the quality and availability of DNA analyses for law enforcement identification. The act also provided for the establishment of a "DNA index" for law enforcement purposes which has now been developed (see Chapter 5 for more information). The index allows investigators to produce quick matches with DNA samples already on file. The law limits accessibility of DNA samples to investigators, court officials, and personnel authorized to evaluate such samples for the purposes of criminal prosecution and defense.

In 1996, the most comprehensive report to date on the applicability of DNA testing to criminal case processing was released by the National Institute of Justice (NIJ). The report,

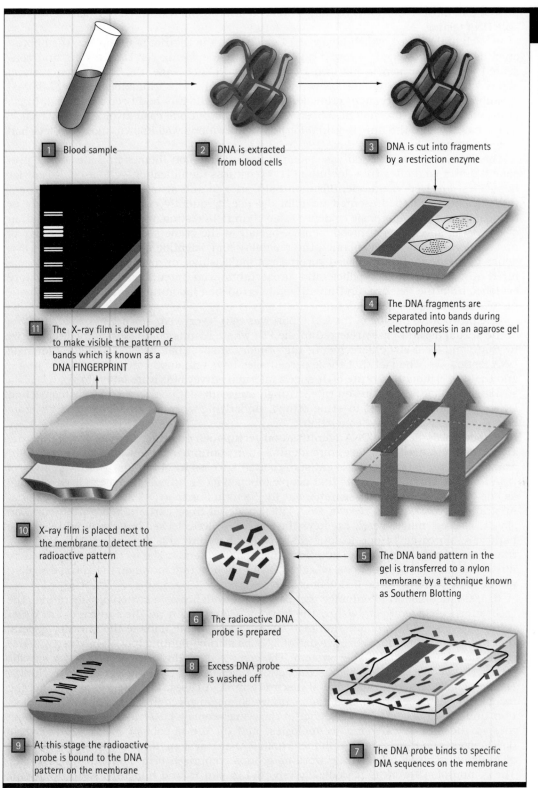

FIGURE 17–1

The DNA fingerprinting process.
Source: Cellmark Diagnostics. Reprinted with permission.

1 Blood sample

2 DNA is extracted from blood cells

3 DNA is cut into fragments by a restriction enzyme

11 The X-ray film is developed to make visible the pattern of bands which is known as a DNA FINGERPRINT

4 The DNA fragments are separated into bands during electrophoresis in an agarose gel

10 X-ray film is placed next to the membrane to detect the radioactive pattern

5 The DNA band pattern in the gel is transferred to a nylon membrane by a technique known as Southern Blotting

6 The radioactive DNA probe is prepared

8 Excess DNA probe is washed off

9 At this stage the radioactive probe is bound to the DNA pattern on the membrane

7 The DNA probe binds to specific DNA sequences on the membrane

entitled *Convicted by Juries, Exonerated by Science,*[39] called DNA testing "the most important technological breakthrough of twentieth-century forensic science" and provided a detailed review of 28 cases in which postconviction DNA evidence exonerated defendants who had been sentenced to lengthy prison terms. The cases were selected on the basis of a detailed examination of records which indicated that the convicted defendants might have actually been innocent. The men in the study had served, on average, seven years in prison, and most had been tried and sentenced prior to the widespread availability of reliable DNA testing.

In each of the cases, which involved 14 states and the District of Columbia, the imprisoned defendant obtained, through an attorney, case evidence for DNA testing and consented to a comparison to his own DNA sample. In each case, the results conclusively showed the lack of matching DNA, and the defendant was ultimately set free. Sexual assault was the most frequent crime for which the defendants had been sentenced. In six of the cases, the victims had also been murdered. All but one case involved a jury trial.[40] Of the cases where the time required for jury deliberations was known, most verdicts had been returned in less than a day.

The 28 wrongful conviction cases shared several common themes in the evidence presented during and after trial, including (1) eyewitness identification—all cases, except for homicides, involved victim identification both prior to and at trial; (2) an alibi defense—most defendants had presented an alibi defense, frequently corroborated by family or friends; (3) the use of forensic evidence other than DNA testing, including the examination of nonvictim specimens of blood, semen, or hair at the crime scene; (4) the testimony of prosecution experts who explained the reliability and scientific strength of non-DNA evidence to the jury; and (5) alleged government malfeasance or misconduct, including perjured testimony at trial, police and prosecutors who intentionally kept exculpatory evidence from the defense, and intentionally erroneous laboratory tests and expert testimony admitted at trial as evidence.

One provocative finding of the NIJ report was that "every year since 1989, in about 25% of the sexual assault cases referred to the FBI where results could be obtained (primarily by State and local law enforcement), the primary suspect has been excluded by forensic DNA testing. . . . The fact that these percentages have remained constant for seven years, and that the National Institute of Justice's informal survey of private laboratories reveals a strikingly similar 26% exclusion rate, strongly suggests that postarrest and postconviction DNA exonerations are tied to some strong, underlying systemic problems that generate erroneous accusations and convictions."

As standards develop, DNA identification techniques continue to evolve. Notably, the amount of DNA needed for accurate identification continues to grow smaller. In 1997, for example, Australian forensic scientists reported success in obtaining useful amounts of DNA from the surface of objects that people touched for as little as five seconds as long ago as one year. In their tests, researchers at the Victoria Forensic Science Center in Victoria, Australia, used swabs to recover DNA-laden material from partial fingerprints found on gloves, glasses, mugs, pens, car keys, briefcases, knives, locker handles, and telephone handsets. Moreover, in one in four cases, they also were able to recover DNA that was transferred from one person to another while shaking hands. The technique developed by Australian forensic scientists uses "naked DNA," such as that found on the surface of skin, rather than the DNA found inside of cells.[41]

In 1998, in an effort to enhance the use of DNA evidence as a law enforcement tool, the U.S. Attorney General established the National Commission on the Future of DNA Evidence. The task of the commission is to submit recommendations to the attorney general that will help ensure more effective use of DNA as a crime-fighting tool and to foster its use throughout the criminal justice system. The commission addresses issues in five specific areas: (1) the use of DNA in postconviction relief cases, (2) legal concerns, including *Daubert* challenges and the scope of discovery in DNA cases, (3) criteria for training and technical assistance for criminal justice professionals involved in the identification, collection, and preservation of DNA evidence at the crime scene, (4) essential laboratory capabilities in the face of emerging technologies, and (5) the impact of future technological developments on the use of DNA in the criminal justice system. Each topic will be the focus of in-depth analysis by separate working groups comprised of prominent professionals. The commission's work is periodically reported in papers and bulletins. Keep up-to-date with the work of the commission via **Web Extra! 17–2** at cjtoday.com.

In 2000, San Diego officials decided to offer postconviction DNA testing to people convicted prior to 1992 of serious crimes in which DNA evidence was available but was not used at trial (generally because DNA testing had not yet reached a credible level of scientific acceptability within the legal community).[42] Members of the San Diego County Bar Association and district attorneys for San Diego County reviewed 561 such cases, but found only three instances in which DNA testing might have exonerated convicts. In two of those cases, however, one involving a murder and the other a sexualt assault, the convicts refused the free tests without explanation. As this book goes to press, prosecutors are waiting for an answer from the third inmate. Finally, in what may have been a decision based in part on the results of the San Diego experiment, the U.S. Department of Justice announced at the end of 2001 that it was scrapping plans to offer $500,000 in federal grants to states and local agencies to pay for the postconviction DNA testing of certain serious offenders so that prosecutors "could verify their convictions."[43] Learn more about the forensic uses of DNA testing via **Library Extra! 17–1** at cjtoday.com.

ONLINE DATABASES AND CLEARINGHOUSES

Computerized information systems and the personnel who operate them are an integral part of most police departments today. Police department computers assist with such routine tasks as word processing, filing, record keeping, printing reports, and scheduling personnel, equipment, and facilities. Computers that serve as investigative tools, however, have the greatest potential to affect criminal justice in the near future. The automated fingerprint technology discussed earlier is but one example of information-based systems designed to help in identifying offenders and solving crimes. Others include the nationwide National Crime Information Center (NCIC and NCIC—2000) and the Violent Criminal Apprehension Program (VICAP) databases; state-operated police identification networks; specialized services like METAPOL, an information-sharing network run by the Police Executive Research Forum; and the FBI's Combined DNA Index System (CODIS), which allows law enforcement agencies to compare DNA profiles in their possession with other DNA profiles that have been entered into local, state, and national databases in order to identify a suspect or to link serial crimes. NCIC and police information networks furnish a 24-hour channel to information on suspects, stolen vehicles, and other data and can be accessed through computers installed in patrol cars.

In 1993, William Sessions, then Director of the FBI, announced the creation of the Criminal Justice Information Services (CJIS) Division within the FBI.[44] The CJIS mission today is to "reduce criminal activity by maximizing the ability to provide timely and relevant criminal justice information to the FBI and to qualified law enforcement, criminal justice, civilian, academic, employment, and licensing agencies concerning individuals, stolen property, criminal organizations and activities, and other law enforcement related data."[45] View the CJIS website at **Web Extra! 17–3** at cjtoday.com.

Increasingly, law enforcement agencies are making criminal database information available to the public via the Internet. Among the most common forms of information available are sex-offender registries, although the FBI's "Most Wanted" list and the "Most Wanted" lists of various states can be viewed online. In 1998, Texas became the first state to make its entire criminal convictions database available on the Internet.[46] View the sex offender registries for a number of states via **Web Extra! 17–4** at cjtoday.com, and see the FBI's "Most Wanted" list at **Web Extra! 17–5.**

COMPUTER-AIDED INVESTIGATIONS

Some police agencies use large computer databases that can cross-reference specific information about crimes to determine patterns and to identify suspects. One of the earliest of these programs was HITMAN, developed by the Hollywood (California) Police Department in 1985. HITMAN has since evolved into a department-wide database that helps detectives in the entire Los Angeles Police Department (LAPD) solve violent crimes. The LAPD uses a similar computer program to track a target population of approximately 60,000 gang members.[47]

The developing field of artificial intelligence uses computers to make inferences based upon available information and to draw conclusions or to make recommendations to the system's operators. **Expert systems**, as these computer models are often called, depend upon three components: (1) a user interface or terminal, (2) a knowledge base containing information on what is already known in the area of investigation, and (3) a computer program known as an *inference engine* which compares user input and stored information according to established decision-making rules.

A number of expert systems already exist. One is being used by the FBI's National Center for the Analysis of Violent Crime (NCAVC) in a project designed to profile violent serial criminals. The NCAVC system depends upon computer models of criminal profiling to provide a theoretical basis for the development of investigative strategies. A number of other systems have been developed, including some which focus on serology analysis, narcotics interdiction, serial murder and rape, and counterterrorism.[48]

expert system

Computer hardware and software which attempts to duplicate the decision-making processes used by skilled investigators in the analysis of evidence and in the recognition of patterns which such evidence might represent.

Similar to expert systems are relational databases, which permit fast and easy sorting of large records. Perhaps the best known early criminal justice database of this sort was called Big Floyd. It was developed in the 1980s by the FBI in conjunction with the Institute for Defense Analyses. Big Floyd was designed to access the more than 3 million records in the FBI's Organized Crime Information System and to allow investigators to decide which federal statutes apply in a given situation and whether investigators have enough evidence for a successful prosecution.[49] In the years since Big Floyd, other "bad-guy" relational databases targeting malfeasants of various types have been created, including computer systems to track deadbeat parents and quack physicians. In 1996, President Bill Clinton ordered the Department of Justice to create a computerized national registry of sex offenders.[50] The national sex-offender registry, developed as part of an overhaul of the FBI's computer systems, went online in 1999.

Some systems are even more problem-specific. For example, ImAger, a product of Face Software, Inc., uses computer technology to artificially age photographs of missing children. The program has been used successfully to identify and recover a number of children. One of them was only six months old when he disappeared and was found after ImAger created a photo of what the child would look like at age five. The child was recognized by viewers who called police after the photo was broadcast on television.[51] Another composite imaging program, Compusketch by Visatex Corporation, is used by police artists to create simulated photographs of criminal suspects.[52]

COMPUTER–BASED TRAINING

Computers provide an ideal training medium for criminal justice agencies. They allow users to work at their own pace, and they can be made available around the clock to provide on-site instruction to personnel whose job requirements make other kinds of training difficult to implement. Computer-based training (CBT) is already well established as a management-training tool, and has begun to be used in the field of law enforcement. CBT has the added advantage of familiarizing personnel with computers so that they will be better able to use them in other tasks.

Some of the more widely used computer-training programs include shoot/no-shoot decision-based software and police-pursuit driving simulators. The Atari Mobile Operations Simulator (AMOS), firearms training simulation (FATS), and ROBBEC'S JUST (Judgment Under Stress Training) are just a few of the products available to police-training divisions. Recent innovations in the field of virtual reality (a kind of high-tech-based illusion) have led to the creation of realistic computer-based virtual environments in which law enforcement agents can test their skills.[53] Other high-technology-based training is available via the Law Enforcement Satellite Training Network (LESTN), a privately owned company operating out of Carrollton, Texas.

Some of the most prominent uses of technology in criminal justice have been mentioned, but they are by no means all of them. Laser fingerprint-lifting devices, space age photography, video camera–equipped patrol cars, satellite and computerized mapping,[54] advanced chemical analysis techniques, chemical sniffers, and hair and fiber identification are all contemporary crime-fighting techniques. Field test kits for drug analysis, chemical sobriety checkers, and handheld ticket-issuing computers have also made the transition from costly high technology to widespread and relatively inexpensive use. As one expert has observed, "Police agencies throughout the world are entering an era in which high technology is not only desirable but necessary in order to combat crime effectively."[55] Learn more about information technology innovations in criminal justice via **Library Extras! 17–2** and **17–3** at cjtoday.com.

> More money has been stolen at the point of a fountain pen than at the point of a gun.
>
> —Woody Guthrie (1912–1967)

Library EXTRA!

Problems in Implementing New Technologies

Technological innovations do not represent all smooth sailing for several reasons. First, the speed with which justice agencies successfully adapt to the opportunities offered by technology may be limited. Some writers have observed that "law enforcement has been slow to utilize new technology,"[56] and a study by the International Association of Chiefs of Police found that only 10% of police departments are innovative in their use of computers.[57] As anyone knows who has bought a computer recently, technology changes rapidly, quickly making equipment obsolete. Just the sheer amount of choice involved may also be daunting, as can the dependability of some high-technology vendors' claims about their products. And line staff and decision makers within police departments may lack the personal experience and knowledge to use technology effectively. Equally sig-

nificant, the future legal acceptability and social applicability of specific technologies is uncertain.[58]

A second area of concern arises from the "supersleuth" capabilities of some high-technology items. As high-tech gadgetry becomes more commonplace in criminal justice agencies, we can be sure that the courts will watch for potential violations of individual rights. The use of photographic techniques developed for the space program, for example, which permit enlargement of details never before thought possible, or the use of superlistening devices, such as those now used to isolate and amplify the voices of referees and quarterbacks on weekend television, may extend investigative capabilities beyond previous understandings of limited search and seizure.

Finally, it must be recognized that the investigative and other opportunities created by technology for the agents of criminal justice have their flip side in the threats represented by the products of modern science in the hands of criminals.

Cybercrime: The New White-Collar Crime

The flip side of high technology, as far as the justice system is concerned, is the potential it creates for committing old crimes in new ways or for committing new crimes never before imagined. Sometimes in today's high-tech world, it's even difficult to tell when a crime has occurred. In 1995, for example, University of Michigan student Jacob Alkhabaz (aka Jake A. Baker), 20, became the first person ever indicted for writing something on the Internet. He was arrested by the FBI and charged with five counts of interstate transmission of threats.[59] Alkhabaz had posted a series of stories on the Internet about his fantasy of torturing, raping, and murdering a female classmate. One of his messages contained these words: "Just thinking about it anymore doesn't do the trick. I need to do it." Another story read, "Torture is foreplay, rape is romance, snuff (killing) is climax."[60]

Although he might have been punished by a sentence of up to five years in prison, Detroit U.S. District Judge Avern Cohn threw out the charges after Alkhabaz had spent 29 days in jail.[61] Cohn ruled that Alkhabaz's violent-sounding Internet writings were protected under the free speech clause of the U.S. Constitution. In contrast, the government had argued that true threats are not so protected, and it had maintained that Alkhabaz's naming of a specific woman had raised the threats to the level required for violation of federal criminal law. Under the law, however, federal prosecutors had to prove that Alkhabaz intended to carry out his threats, something the judge did not believe they could do.

WHITE-COLLAR CRIME

Because of the skill and knowledge required by their crimes, most, but not all, of today's high-tech offenders can aptly be labeled white-collar criminals. The term **white-collar crime** was

white-collar crime

- - - - - - - - - - - - -

Nonviolent crime for financial gain committed by means of deception by offenders with professional status or specialized technical skills during the everyday pursuit of their business endeavors.

coined by Edwin Sutherland in his 1939 presidential address to the American Sociological Society.[62] Sutherland later defined the term to include crimes committed by those in authority during the normal course of their business transactions. White-collar crimes include embezzlement, bribery, political corruption, price fixing, misuse and theft of company property, corporate tax evasion, fraud, and money laundering. White-collar crimes tend to be committed by financially secure, well-educated, middle- or upper-class people. Sutherland claimed that the prevalence of white-collar crimes shows that "the theories of criminologists that crime is due to poverty or to psychopathic and sociopathic conditions statistically associated with poverty are invalid."[63] Anyone is capable of committing a crime, said Sutherland, but many crimes are overlooked when committed by powerful people.

We will use a broader and somewhat more modern definition of white-collar crime: non-violent crime for financial gain committed by means of deception by people with professional status or specialized technical skills, during the everyday pursuit of their business endeavors.[64] The insider trading *scam* of stock market tycoon Ivan Boesky, which was estimated to have netted $250 million for Boesky and his friends in the late 1980s,[65] and the $600 million *fine* levied against junk bond king Michael Milken in 1990 for securities fraud provide two examples of white-collar crime. Another can be found in the savings and loan (S&L) fiasco of the late 1980s and early 1990s, which has been called "the biggest white-collar crime in history."[66]

A more recent white-collar crime appears to have been involved in the bankruptcy of Canadian gold prospector Bre-X Minerals Ltd. In the mid-1990s, Bre-X officials claimed that assayed ore from the company's Busang Mine in Indonesia proved that it owned what was likely to be the world's largest gold reserve. In what some have called "the greatest stock fraud of the [twentieth] century," shares of the company's stock soared from pennies to a value of $206 each. After a number of debacles, including the suspicious death of the company's chief geologist, who fell from a helicopter over the Indonesian jungle, Bre-X admitted in 1997 the truth of an independent report which showed that the company's claims were based on falsified data.[67] Bre-X shareholders were left with worthless stock certificates, while the company's vice president of exploration filed for residency status in the Cayman Islands, where he owned about $6 million worth of beachfront homes.

No industry is immune to white-collar crime. In 1999, for example, two executives with Nashville-based Columbia/HCA Healthcare Corporation were convicted of defrauding Medicare and other government health insurance programs of nearly $3 million. Jay Jarrell and Robert Whiteside, both executives at the nation's largest hospital chain, were found guilty of conspiring to defraud and defrauding tax-supported health insurance programs.[68] The case was the largest health care criminal investigation ever conducted in terms of its scope and the amount of money taken.

A few months later, money manager Martin Frankel was arrested at his posh hotel in Hamburg, Germany, where he had been staying with a young American woman. Frankel had fled his Connecticut mansion carrying diamonds in a private jet and leaving behind burning documents including a "to-do" list that said "launder money."[69] He stands accused of money laundering and wire fraud charges involving activities that may have netted him as much as $915 million. Most of that money disappeared from insurance companies which invested money through Frankel. Another $1.98 billion was also reported missing from the St. Francis of Assisi Foundation, a fund established by Frankel in the British Virgin Islands in August 1998.[70] Frankel was sentenced to three years in prison in Germany on unrelated charges. Halfway through that sentence, he was extradited to the United States to face fraud charges and, as this book goes to press, is awaiting trial in Mississippi.

White-collar criminals tend to be punished less severely than other offenders. In the 1930s and 1940s, Edwin Sutherland studied the 70 largest corporations of his time and found that 547 adverse court and regulatory agency decisions had been made against them—an average of 7.8 decisions per corporation.[71] Although this should have been evidence of routine corporate involvement in white-collar criminality, almost no corporate executives were sentenced to prison. More recent studies have shown that about 40% of convicted federal white-collar offenders are sentenced to prison versus 54% of non-white-collar criminals.[72] When prison sentences are imposed, white-collar offenders are sentenced to only 29 months on average, versus 50 months for other inmates.[73] As other authors have noted, "For some reason our system has seen nothing unjust in slapping an 18-year-old inner-city kid with a 20-year prison sentence for robbing a bank of a couple of thousand dollars while putting a white-collar criminal away for just two years in a 'prison camp' for stealing $200 million through fraud."[74]

OCCUPATIONAL AND CORPORATE CRIME

Criminologists were quick to realize that if people of high socioeconomic status could commit crimes during the course of their business, then so could people of lower social standing.[75] The term **occupational crime** was coined to describe the on-the-job illegal activities of employees. Thefts of company property, vandalism, the misuse of information, software piracy that occurs in the workplace, and many other activities come under the rubric of occupational crime. The employee who uses a company phone for personal calls, the maintenance worker who steals cleaning supplies for home use, and the store clerk who lifts items of clothing or jewelry provide other examples of occupational criminality. The Council of Better Business Bureaus estimates that one-third of all plant and office workers steal from their employers.[76] Total losses are said to be in the range of $10 to $20 billion per year.[77] The council believes that one-third of all business failures are directly attributable to employee crime.[78]

In his book on occupational crime, Gary Green defines *occupational crime* as "any act punishable by law which is committed through opportunity created in the course of an occupation that is legal."[79] Green has developed the following typology, which considerably broadens the classification of occupational criminality: "(a) crimes for the benefit of an employing organization (organizational occupational crime); (b) crimes by officials through the exercise of their state-based authority (state authority occupational crime); (c) crimes by professionals in their capacity as professionals (professional occupational crime); and (d) crimes by individuals as individuals (individual occupational crime)."[80]

James Coleman provides a further distinction between types of white-collar crime.[81] Coleman points out that some white-collar crimes affect only property, while others endanger the safety and health of people. The knowing sale of tainted food products or medicine is an example of the latter type of crime. Coleman has also suggested that the term *organizational crime* is useful to distinguish those offenses which are designed to further the goals of corporate entities from business-related crimes committed by individuals to further their own interests.[82] Organizational crimes are the "crimes of big business." Sometimes, however, it pays to remember that all crimes are committed by people and not by institutions.

Some authors maintain that occupational and **corporate crime** are a way of life in American businesses.[83] Examples abound.[84] Government investigations in the late 1950s revealed that the General Electric Company was heavily involved in price fixing.[85] In 1975, Allied Chemical Corporation was fined $5 million and agreed to donate another $8 million to a cleanup fund after it was revealed that former Allied employees had arranged to establish a small, seemingly independent business to supply Allied with the highly toxic chemical Kepone.[86] Workers in the Kepone manufacturing facility became seriously ill, and the Saint James River near the plant was badly contaminated. Most readers of this volume will recognize the acronym *PCBs* and the role of such chemicals in cases of criminal contamination of the environment. A few may have heard of the infamous "Love Canal incident" or the exploding gas tanks on Ford Pintos which were manufactured between 1971 and 1976. There is evidence that Ford executives may have known of the defects before the Pinto was even put into production.[87] The Ford Motor Company ultimately paid more than $100 million in recall fees and civil settlements directly related to the gas tank coverup.[88]

Other examples of corporate crime are the $10 billion 1985 mail and wire fraud scheme of E. F. Hutton[89] and the 1988 stock fraud case of Wall Street giant Drexel Burnham Lambert, Incorporated. In 1988, Drexel agreed to pay $650 million in fines and restitution and pleaded guilty to six felony counts involving securities law violations.[90] Government prosecutors used the case to prove other wrongdoings on the part of some of the nation's best-known corporate traders.[91] On May 20, 1999, two companies, Hoffman-LaRoche, Ltd., and BASF AG, agreed to plead guilty to charges of fixing the prices of vitamins A, B_2, B_5, C, and E and beta-carotene. The companies agreed to pay a $500 million fine—the largest antitrust criminal fine ever imposed. They paid another $225 million as part of a plea bargain agreement.[92]

White-collar, occupational, and corporate crime are the subject of the National White Collar Crime Center (NWCCC). Formed in 1992, the NWCCC provides a national support system for the prevention, investigation, and prosecution of multijurisdictional economic crimes, including investment fraud, telemarketing fraud, securities fraud, commodities fraud, and advanced-fee loan schemes. Today, the center provides training, research, and information sharing (computer database) services to local and state law enforcement, prosecution, and regulatory agencies throughout the United States. The center also provides

occupational crime

Any act punishable by law that is committed through opportunity created in the course of a legitimate occupation.

corporate crime

A violation of a criminal statute by a corporate entity or by its executives, employees, or agents acting on behalf of and for the benefit of the corporation, partnership, or other form of business entity.[i]

specialized training at locations across the country on a variety of white-collar crime topics. The National White Collar Crime Center, which is located in Morgantown, West Virginia, is funded by the federal Bureau of Justice Assistance. Visit the NWCCC via **Web Extra! 17–6** at cjtoday.com.

COMPUTER AND HIGH-TECHNOLOGY CRIME

During Sutherland's time, political corruption and corporate bribery were serious concerns. Although both offenses exist today, computer crimes are rapidly becoming the white-collar crime par excellence in the modern world. **Computer crimes**, sometimes called *cybercrimes*, use computers and computer technology as tools in crime commission. Thefts of computer equipment, although sometimes spectacular, are not computer crimes but are instead classified as larcenies. In 1995, for example, armed robbers clad in sports coats and ties tied up employees at Centon Electronics, a computer chip distributor based in California's Silicon Valley, and stole more than $12 million in computer chips.[93] At the time of the heist, the stolen chips, consisting primarily of 32-megabyte memory modules, were worth more per pound than gold.

"True" computer criminals, however, go beyond the theft of hardware, focusing instead on the information stored in computer systems and manipulating it in a way which violates the law. In 1995, for example, the arrest of computer expert Kevin Mitnick, then known as the "FBI's most wanted **hacker**,"[94] alarmed security experts because of the potential for harm that Mitnick's electronic intrusions represented. The 31-year-old Mitnick broke into an Internet service provider's computer system and stole more than 20,000 credit card numbers. Although Mitnick was apparently arrested before the numbers were sold or clandestinely distributed, experts feared that others with similar high-tech skills might be tempted to enact copycat schemes, costing credit card–issuing companies millions of dollars. Mitnick was caught with the help of Tsutoma Shimomura, whose home computer Mitnick had also attacked and who assisted FBI experts in tracking him through telephone lines and computer networks to the computer in his Raleigh, North Carolina, apartment. In March 1999, Mitnick pleaded guilty to seven federal counts of computer and wire fraud. He was sentenced to 46 months in prison but was released on parole in January 2000. Under the terms of his release, Mitnick was barred from access to computer hardware and software and from any form of wireless communication for a period of three years.[95] In an interview after his release, Mitnick pointed out that "malicious hackers don't need to use stealth computer techniques to break into a network. . . . Often they just trick someone into giving them passwords and other information."[96] According to Mitnick, "People are the weakest link. . . . You can have the best technology, firewalls, intrusion-detection systems, biometric devices . . . and somebody can call an unsuspecting employee. That's all she wrote, baby. They got everything."

Many of today's cybercrimes involve prostitution, child pornography, and copyright infringement, as well as fraud. Some computer criminals offer to sell illegal goods and services through the Web. In 1999, for example, Diana Deveaux, 41, of Fort Smith, Arkansas, was arrested by an undercover police vice officer she had met on the Internet and was charged with soliciting sex—a misdemeanor under state law. Deveaux, who advertised herself on her website as a "private escort," told police she had been meeting men through the Internet since the beginning of the year. Deveaux explained that she needed the money and had gotten the idea from other women on the Internet.[97]

U.S. Customs Service Senior Special Agent Donald Daufenbach, an international expert in child pornography and the Internet, points out that "the Internet is like anything else: It can be bent or perverted for nefarious purposes. . . . The Internet has absolutely changed the way people communicate with each other, changed the way people conduct commerce, changed the way people do research, changed the way people entertain themselves and changed the way people break the law."[98] Daufenbach added, "It's just a new version of what the mails or what the telephones used to be. . . . People are catching on pretty quick, but law enforcement is lagging behind miserably in this whole endeavor."

Another form of cybercrime, the unauthorized copying of software programs, also called **software piracy**, appears rampant. According to the Software Industry Information Association (SIIA), global losses from software piracy totaled nearly $12.2 billion in 1999.[99] According to the SIIA, 38% of all software in use in the world has been copied illegally.

---

computer crime

Any crime perpetrated through the use of computer technology. Also, any violation of a federal or state computer crime statute. The first portion of this definition highlights the manner in which a crime is committed rather than the target of the offense. Hence, using that portion of the definition, the physical theft of a computer or of a floppy disk would not be a computer crime, but the use of computer software to analyze a company's security operations prior to committing a robbery might be.

hacker

A computer hobbyist or professional, generally with advanced programming skills. Today, the term *hacker* has taken on a sinister connotation, referring to hobbyists who are bent on illegally accessing the computers of others or who attempt to demonstrate their technological prowess through computerized acts of vandalism.

software piracy

The unauthorized duplication of software or the illegal transfer of data from one storage medium to another. Software piracy is one of the most prevalent computer crimes in the world.

Some countries have especially high rates of illegal use. Of all the computer software in use in Vietnam, for example, SIIA estimates that 97% has been illegally copied, while 95% of the software used in China and 92% of the software used in Russia is thought to be pirated—resulting in a substantial loss in manufacturers' revenue.

An especially important characteristic of cybercrime is that it can easily be cross-jurisdictional or international. That is, a cyberoffender sitting at a keyboard in Australia, for example, can steal money from a bank in Russia and then transfer the digital cash to a bank in Chile. For investigators, the question may be, "What laws were broken?" Complicating matters is the fact that each country mentioned here has a set of fragmented computer crime laws—or (as with Russia[100]) laws that are particularly ineffective.

According to researchers at McConnell International, a Washington, D.C.–based consulting firm, only one of 52 countries surveyed in 2000—the Philippines—has effective computer crime legislation in effect.[101] The Philippines had enacted new cybercrime laws that year after the creator of the highly damaging "Love Bug" computer virus, a 23-year-old Philippine student named Onel de Guzman, could not be prosecuted under the country's existing laws.[102] De Guzman was finally charged with theft and violation of a law that was created to deter credit card fraud, the new cybercrime law could not be applied to him retroactively.

In an effort to enhance similarities in the computer crime laws of different countries, and to provide a model for national law-making bodies concerned with controlling cybercrimes, the 43-nation Council of Europe approved a cybercrime treaty in November 2001.[103] The treaty outlaws specific online activities, including fraud and child pornography, and outlines what law enforcement officials in member nations may and may not do in enforcing computer crime laws. The goal of the treaty is to standardize both legal understandings of cybercrime and cybercrime laws in member nations. It also allows police officers to detain suspects wanted in other countries for cybercrimes and facilitates the gathering of information on such crimes across national borders. In addition to the council's member states, the treaty was also signed by the United States, Canada, Japan, and South Africa.[104] Visit the Council of Europe's Treaty Office via **Web Extra! 17–7** at cjtoday.com, and click on "New Treaties" to find the full text of the council's cybercrime treaty. Learn more about cybercrime from the President's Working Group on Unlawful Conduct on the Internet via **Library Extra! 17–4** at cjtoday.com.

Criminal defense lawyer Jennifer Granick in her San Francisco office. Granick specializes in defending computer hackers and crackers. Tougher cybercrime laws are keeping her busy, and her desk is cluttered with software-piracy and unauthorized-access cases. Douglas Adesko, Koko Represents.

Photo originally published in *WIRED*.

COMPUTER VIRUSES AND OTHER TYPES OF COMPUTER CRIME

While a comprehensive typology of computer-based crime has yet to be developed,[105] Peter Grabosky of the Australian Institute of Criminology suggests that most such crimes fall into one of the following broad categories:[106] (1) theft of services, such as telephone or long-distance access; (2) communications in furtherance of criminal conspiracies—for example, the e-mail communications said to have taken place between members of Osama bin Laden's Al Qaeda terrorist network;[107] (3) information piracy and forgery—that is, the stealing of trade secrets or copyrighted information; (4) the dissemination of offensive materials, such as child pornography, including extortion threats, such as those made against financial institutions by hackers claiming the ability to destroy their electronic records; (5) electronic money laundering and tax evasion (through electronic funds transfers that conceal the origin of financial proceeds); (6) electronic vandalism and terrorism, including computer viruses, worms, Trojan horses, and cyberterrorism, which is discussed later in this chapter; (7) telemarketing fraud (including investment frauds and illegitimate electronic auctions); (8) illegal interception of telecommunications—that is, illegal eavesdropping; and (9) electronic funds-transfer fraud (specifically, the illegal interception and diversion of legitimate transactions).

Computer viruses have become a special concern of the general computer user over the past several years, especially as more people have connected to the Internet. Computer viruses were brought to public attention in 1988, when the Pakistani virus (or Pakistani brain virus) became widespread in personal and office computers across the United States.[108] The Pakistani virus was created by Amjad Farooq Alvi and his brother Basit Farooq Alvi, two cut-rate computer software dealers in Lahore, Pakistan. The Alvi brothers made copies of costly software products and sold them at low prices to mostly Western shoppers looking for a bargain. Motivated by convoluted logic, the brothers hid a virus on each disk they sold to punish buyers for seeking to evade copyright laws.

A more serious virus incident affected sensitive machines in the National Aeronautics and Space Administration (NASA), nuclear weapons labs, federal research centers, and universities across the United States in late 1988.[109] The virus did not destroy data. Instead, it made copies of itself and multiplied so rapidly that it clogged and effectively shut down computers within hours after invading them. Robert Morris, creator of the virus, was sentenced in 1990 to 400 hours of community service, three years' probation, and a fine of $10,000.[110] Since then, many other virus attacks have made headlines, including the infamous Michelangelo virus in 1992; the intentional distribution of infected software on an AIDS-related research CD-ROM distributed about the same time; the Kournikova virus in 2000, and the Sircam, Nimda, and Code Red worms—all of which made their appearance or were substantially modified by their creators in 2001.

computer virus

A computer program designed to secretly invade systems and either modify the way in which they operate or alter the information they store. Viruses are destructive software programs that may effectively vandalize computers of all types and sizes.

Tennis superstar Anna Kournikova. Kournikova served as inspiration for Jan de Wit, 20, of Sneek, Netherlands, creator of the "Kournikova computer virus." In 2001, Wit was convicted of violating Holland's law against spreading data into a computer network with the intention of causing damage and was sentenced to 150 hours of community service.

AP/Wide World Photos

Computer viruses have become increasingly sophisticated. Although early viruses were relatively easy to detect with hardware or software scanning devices which looked for virus "signatures," new viruses called *stealth viruses* and *polymorphic viruses* change form with each new "infection" and are much more difficult to locate and remove. Moreover, while older viruses infected only executable programs, or those that could be run, newer viruses (such as the Word for Windows Macro virus, also called the Concept virus) attach themselves to word-processing documents and to computer codes that are routinely distributed via the World Wide Web (including Java and Active-X components used by Web browsers). In 1998, the world's first HTML virus was discovered. The virus, named HTML.Internal, infects computers whose users are merely viewing Web pages.[111] Later that year, the first JAVA-based virus, named Strange Brew, made its appearance.[112] Learn more about cyber-crime and efforts to combat it at **Web Extra! 17–8** at cjtoday.com.

PROSECUTION OF COMPUTER AND HIGH-TECHNOLOGY CRIME

A generation ago, computer crimes were virtually unheard of, and as recently as a decade ago, few states had computer crime laws. Crimes using computer technology had to be prosecuted, if at all, under laws intended for other purposes. Burglary laws sometimes served to prosecute illegal entry into computer systems, laws against theft were applied to the stealing of digitized information, and embezzlement statutes were applied to illegal electronic fund transfers. Thirty years ago, for example, an employee of Texas Instruments Corporation who stole more than 50 typewritten copies of software programs was convicted of theft under Texas law.[113] Had the software been stolen in electronic form or through the use of a modem, prosecution under the state larceny statute would have been much more difficult. In another early case, Wisconsin authorities found themselves at a loss as to how to prosecute the "414 gang"—a teenage group of computer hackers based in Milwaukee who had infiltrated the computers of 60 businesses, including government computer systems, the Los Alamos National Laboratory, the Sloan-Kettering Cancer Center, and the Security Pacific National Bank in Los Angeles.[114] At the time of the offense (1983), neither Wisconsin nor the federal government had specific legislation applicable to the hackers' activity, and they had to be arraigned under a law pertaining to telephone mischief.

Because existing laws were often not adequate in the prosecution of computer crimes, most states and the federal government moved rapidly to create computer and high-technology criminal statutes. In 1984, the first federal computer crime law was enacted.[115] The Computer Fraud and Abuse Act (CFAA), made unauthorized access to government computers or to computers containing information protected under the Federal Privacy Act a crime.[116] It also made unauthorized interstate entry into any computer illegal. In 1986, Congress modified the Computer Fraud and Abuse Act,[117] expanding the penalty for illegal access to federal-interest computers—or those which represent a "unique federal interest." (The term *federal-interest computer* has since been replaced by **protected computer**.) Under the CFAA, which has been revised a number of times since it was first passed, convicted offenders face penalties of up to ten years' imprisonment and fines which can extend to twice the amount of the "unlawful gain."

Today, high-tech criminals may be prosecuted under a variety of other federal statutes. In addition to the Computer Fraud and Abuse Act, applicable Federal statutes include the Computer Abuse Amendments Act of 1994 (a part of the Violent Crime Control and Law Enforcement Act); aspects of the Electronic Communications Privacy Act of 1986; the National Stolen Property Act;[118] the Federally Protected Property Act;[119] the Federal Trade Secrets Act;[120] the amended Copyright Act of 1980;[121] the No Electronic Theft Act of 1997 (NETA);[122] the Digital Millennium Copyright Act of 1998;[123] the Digital Theft Deterrence and Copyright Damages Improvement Act of 1999;[124] and various federal wire, mail, and bank fraud statutes.[125] All can support prosecutions of high-tech offenders.

In December 2000, the Computer Crime Enforcement Act was signed into law. The act established a grant program within the U.S. Department of Justice to help state and local law enforcement officers and prosecutors improve education, training, enforcement, and prosecution of computer crimes. The funds could be used to assist state and local law enforcement agencies enforce laws relating to computer crime; educate and train law enforcement officers and prosecutors to conduct investigations, forensic analyses of evidence, and prosecutions of computer crime; acquire computers and other equipment to conduct investigations and forensic analysis of evidence of computer crimes; and facilitate and promote the sharing of federal law enforcement expertise and

protected computer

Under federal law, a computer exclusively for the use of a financial institution or the U.S. government, or, in the case of a computer not exclusively for such use, used by or for a financial institution or the U.S. government; or which is used in interstate or foreign commerce or communication.

information about the investigation, analysis, and prosecution of computer crimes with state and local law enforcement officers and prosecutors, including the use of multi-jurisdictional task forces.

Following the lead of the federal government, most states have developed their own computer crime laws. New York's Computer Crime Act is an example of such legislation.[126] Enacted in 1986, it created six crime categories involving software and computer misuse. The law specifically prohibits the duplication of copyrighted software and makes the possession of illegally duplicated software a felony. Other activities defined as illegal under the law include the unauthorized use of a computer, computer trespass, and theft of computer services. The New York bill also created sweeping amendments to existing laws. Theft laws were modified to specifically include "computer program" and "computer data" under the definition of "property," and computer terminology was incorporated into forgery laws. Most state computer crime laws impose punishments proportional to the damage done, although California bases penalties on the number of violations.

Identity Theft

In March 2000, a 28-year-old data-entry clerk was arrested in Tampa, Florida, and accused of stealing the identities of more than 350 people. Elnetta Denise Brown apparently lived lavishly using other people's credit. She was arrested after allegedly trying to use a fraudulently obtained credit card at a Sears store.[127] Following the arrest, police discovered 350 "complete identities" in the new car Brown was driving—including the names, Social Security numbers, dates of birth, and addresses of victims. After an investigation, Brown was charged with 35 counts of fraudulently using an identity to get credit cards. Her story didn't end there, however. While out on bail and awaiting trial, Brown was hired at an American Automobile Association (AAA) office in Tampa, and she used her position to gain access to AAA's national database of members. "She was working in the insurance division (of AAA), checking people's backgrounds," Detective Skip Pask said, "and writing down names, addresses, dates of birth and Social Security numbers on scrap pieces of paper and taking them home."[128] Brown allegedly used the information to open lines of credit at stores like JC Penney and Target, then purchased store gift certificates, which she sold at half price in area malls. Police say Brown told purchasers that she was doing a promotion for the stores. As this book goes to press, she stands accused of stealing the identities of an unknown number of AAA members.

identity theft

A crime in which an imposter obtains key pieces of information, such as Social Security and driver's license numbers, to obtain credit, merchandise, and services in the name of the victim. The victim is often left with a ruined credit history and the time-consuming and complicated task of repairing the financial damages.[ii]

Identity theft became a federal crime in 1998, with the passage of the Identity Theft and Assumption Deterrence Act.[129] The law makes it a crime whenever anyone "knowingly transfers or uses, without lawful authority, a means of identification of another person with the intent to commit, or to aid or abet, any unlawful activity that constitutes a violation of federal law, or that constitutes a felony under any applicable state or local law."

Anyone can fall prey to identity theft, even celebrities. In 2000, for example, golfer Tiger Woods learned that his identity had been stolen and that credit cards taken out in his name had been used to steal $17,000 worth of merchandise, including a 70-inch TV, stereos, and a used luxury car. In 2001, the thief, 30-year-old Anthony Lemar Taylor, who looks nothing like Woods, was convicted of falsely obtaining a driver's license using the name of Eldrick T. Woods (Tiger's given name), Wood's Social Security number, and his birth date. Because Taylor already had 20 previous convictions of all kinds on his record, he was sentenced to 200 years in prison under California's three-strikes law.[130]

Like Woods, most victims of identity theft do not even know that their identities have been stolen until they receive bills for merchandise they haven't purchased. According to the National White Collar Crime Center, identity thieves use several common techniques. Some engage in "Dumpster diving," going through trash bags, cans, or Dumpsters to get copies of checks, credit card and bank statements, credit card applications, or other records that typically bear identifying information. Others use a technique called "shoulder surfing." It involves simply looking over the victim's shoulder as he or she enters personal information into a computer or on a written form. Eavesdropping is another simple, yet effective, technique that identity thieves often use. Eavesdropping can occur when the victim is using an ATM machine, giving credit card or other personal information over the phone, or dialing the number for their telephone calling card. The Internet is also a place where criminals obtain personal identifying information from potential victims. Some Internet users, for example, reply to "spam" (unsolicited e-mail) that promises them all sorts of attractive benefits but which also requests identifying data, such as checking account or credit card numbers and expiration dates, along with the victim's name and

World-renowned professional golfer Tiger Woods. In 2000, Woods became the victim of identity theft when 29-year-old Anthony Lemar Taylor of Sacramento, California, allegedly used Woods's identity to charge $17,000 on the golfer's charge cards.

AP/Wide World Photo

address.[131] Learn more about identity thieves and how they operate via **Web Extra! 17–9** and **Library Extra! 17–5** at cjtoday.com.

One technology that seems to hold promise in the fight against identity theft, and which may also be a useful tool in the battle against terrorism and other crimes, is the smart card. **Smart cards** are technologically advanced credit card–like devices that can store a considerable amount of unalterable information about the cardholder.

Smart cards can be used for a variety of purposes. They can store detailed records of a person's medical history or banking transactions. They can enable the holder to purchase goods and services, to enter restricted areas (both real and virtual), or to perform other operations. Smart cards can even be designed so that they can be tracked from orbiting satellites, which can report a card's location to within ten feet anywhere on the earth's surface. Most of today's smart cards are tailored for a variety of limited uses, however. A number of universities, for example, have adopted modified versions of smart cards for use as student identification cards. Credit card companies have also begun to make use of at least certain aspects of smart card technology. One of the most widely carried smart cards today is Blue, an "intelligent" credit card available through American Express.

Smart cards were developed independently in Germany in 1967, in Japan in 1970, in the United States in 1972, and in France in 1974.[132] The term, *smart card* was not coined, however, until 1980, when France initiated a major campaign to export smart card technology.

Today's smart cards may feature a tamper-resistant hologram of the intended bearer, along with a miniature nonalterable computer memory chip containing unalterable digitized information such as name, home address, social security number, birth date, gender, ethnicity, telephone number, e-mail address, office address, frequent flyer numbers, or bank account and credit card numbers. Some cards also include a plastic strip encoded with read-only laser-imprinted information that may contain something as complex as the intended bearer's DNA code. None of today's smart cards hold all of the information described here, although cards capable of doing so can readily be made. Currently being tested by the U.S. military and by governments in Italy and Singapore, smart cards are already used in some industries to enhance access security in the workplace. It is estimated that over 3 billion smart cards had been issued by 2000.[133] Learn more about smart cards and smart card technology via **Web Extra! 17–10** at cjtoday.com.

smart card

A plastic card or similar device containing a computer chip and other sources of nonalterable information (such as a hologram or a laser-encoded memory strip) used to provide highly secure personal identification.

Smart cards and smart card readers. These bank cards contain microchips allowing for enhanced security and ease of use. The chips in these cards keep track of how much money is available in the holder's account, and permit a wide variety of secure transactions tied to that account. Smart cards are being developed for a variety of purposes. They can store details of a person's medical history, allow the holder access to restricted areas (both real and virtual), authenticate the holder's identify (through embedded DNA code, stored and unalterable retinal images, and so on), or be tracked from orbiting satellites—which can report a card's location to within a few feet anywhere on the earth's surface. Most of today's smart cards, however, are tailored for more limited uses.

AP/Wide World Photos

Terrorism

As midnight struck and the ball fell in New York City's Time Square, ushering in 2002, many among the half million warmly dressed revelers felt thankful for the enhanced police presence keeping a watchful eye over them. Few knew, however, that a handful of the 7,000 police officers spread out among the celebrating crowd were carrying radiation-monitoring devices on loan from the federal government. The devices were capable of detecting the presence of even small amounts of radioactive materials, such as might be used to make "dirty bombs." These devices use a conventional explosive to disperse fine nuclear materials into the air, poisoning people and rendering miles of real estate uninhabitable for decades.[134]

Terrorism, as a criminal activity, and the prevention of further acts of terrorism became primary concerns of American justice system officials following the September 11, 2001, attacks on the World Trade Center and the Pentagon. There is, however, no single uniformly agreed-upon definition of terrorism that is applicable to all places and all circumstances. Some definitions are statutory in nature, while others were created for such practical purposes as gauging success in the fight against terrorism. Still others relate to specific forms of terrorism, such as cyberterrorism (discussed later in this section), and many legislative sources speak only of "acts of terrorism" or "terrorist activity" rather than terrorism itself because it is easier to legislate against acts than against concepts.

The federal Foreign Relations Authorization Act[135] defines *terrorism* in terms of four primary characteristics. The act says that terrorism is (1) premeditated, (2) politically motivated (3) violence (4) committed against noncombatant targets.[136] The FBI, on the other hand, defines terrorism as "a violent act or an act dangerous to human life in violation of the criminal laws of the United States or of any state to intimidate or coerce a government, the civilian population, or any segment thereof, in furtherance of political or social objectives."[137] Among the laws that define certain forms of human activity as terrorism, the Immigration and Nationality Act provides one of the most comprehensive and widely used definitions. That definition is shown in CJ Today Exhibit 17–1.

According to criminologist Gwynn Nettler, all forms of terrorism share six characteristics:[138]

■ *No rules.* There are no moral limitations upon the type or degree of violence which terrorists can use.

■ *No innocents.* No distinctions are made between soldiers and civilians. Children can be killed as easily as adults.

- *Economy.* Kill one, frighten 10,000.
- *Publicity.* Terrorists seek publicity, and publicity encourages terrorism.
- *Meaning.* Terrorist acts give meaning and significance to the lives of terrorists.
- *No clarity.* Beyond the immediate aim of destructive acts, the long-term goals of terrorists are likely to be poorly conceived or impossible to implement.

Moreover, notes Nettler, "Terrorism that succeeds escalates."[139]

Types of Terrorism

It is important to distinguish between two major forms of **terrorism**: domestic and international. Such distinctions are generally made in terms of the origin, base of operations, and objectives of a terrorist organization. **Domestic terrorism** refers to the unlawful use of force or violence by a group or an individual who is based and operates entirely within the United States and its territories without foreign direction and whose acts are directed at elements of the U.S. government or population.[140] **International terrorism**, in contrast, is the unlawful use of force or violence by a group or an individual who has some connection to a foreign power or whose activities transcend national boundaries, against people or property to intimidate or coerce a government, the civilian population, or any segment thereof, in furtherance of political or social objectives.[141] International terrorism is sometimes mistakenly called *foreign terrorism*, a term that, strictly speaking, refers only to acts of terrorism that occur outside of the United States.

DOMESTIC TERRORISM

Throughout the 1960s and 1970s, domestic terrorism in the United States required the expenditure of considerable criminal justice resources. The Weathermen, Students for a Democratic Society, the Symbionese Liberation Army, the Black Panthers, and other radical groups routinely challenged the authority of federal and local governments. Bombings, kidnappings, and shoot-outs peppered the national scene. As overt acts of domestic terrorism declined in frequency in the 1980s, international terrorism took their place. The war in Lebanon; terrorism in Israel; bombings in France, Italy, and Germany; and the many violent offshoots of the Iran-Iraq and Gulf wars occupied the attention of the media and of much of the rest of the world. Vigilance by the FBI, the Central Intelligence Agency (CIA), and other agencies largely prevented the spread of terrorism to the United States.

terrorism

A violent act or an act dangerous to human life in violation of the criminal laws of the United States or of any state to intimidate or coerce a government, the civilian population, or any segment thereof, in furtherance of political or social objectives.[iii]

domestic terrorism

The unlawful use of force or violence by a group or an individual who is based and operates entirely within the United States and its territories without foreign direction and whose acts are directed at elements of the U.S. government or population.[iv]

international terrorism

The unlawful use of force or violence by a group or an individual who has some connection to a foreign power or whose activities transcend national boundaries, against people or property to intimidate or coerce a government, the civilian population, or any segment thereof, in furtherance of political or social objectives.[v]

CJ Today Exhibit 17-1

[What Is Terrorist Activity?]

Federal law enforcement efforts directed against agents of foreign terrorist organizations derive their primary authority from the Immigration and Nationality Act, found in Chapter 12 of the U.S. Code. The act defines *terrorist activity* as follows:

(ii) "Terrorist activity" defined

As used in this chapter, the term "terrorist activity" means any activity which is unlawful under the laws of the place where it is committed (or which, if committed in the United States, would be unlawful under the laws of the United States or any State) and which involves any of the following:

(I) The highjacking or sabotage of any conveyance (including an aircraft, vessel, or vehicle).

(II) The seizing or detaining, and threatening to kill, injure, or continue to detain, another individual in order to compel a third person (including a governmental organization) to do or abstain from doing any act as an explicit or implicit condition for the release of the individual seized or detained.

(III) A violent attack upon an internationally protected person (as defined in section 1116(b)(4) of title 18) or upon the liberty of such a person.

(IV) An assassination.

(V) The use of any—

(a) biological agent, chemical agent, or nuclear weapon or device, or

(b) explosive or firearm (other than for mere personal monetary gain), with intent to endanger, directly or indirectly, the safety of one or more individuals or to cause substantial damage to property.

(VI) A threat, attempt, or conspiracy to do any of the foregoing.

(iii) "Engage in terrorist activity" defined

As used in this chapter, the term "engage in terrorist activity" means to commit, in an individual capacity or as a member of an organization, an act of terrorist activity or an act which the actor knows, or reasonably should know, affords material support to any individual, organization, or government in conducting a terrorist activity at any time, including any of the following acts:

(I) The preparation or planning of a terrorist activity.

(II) The gathering of information on potential targets for terrorist activity.

(III) The providing of any type of material support, including a safe house, transportation, communications, funds, false documentation or identification, weapons, explosives, or training, to any individual the actor knows or has reason to believe has committed or plans to commit a terrorist activity.

(IV) The soliciting of funds or other things of value for terrorist activity or for any terrorist organization.

(V) The solicitation of any individual for membership in a terrorist organization, terrorist government, or to engage in a terrorist activity.

Worrisome today are domestic underground survivalist and separatist groups and potentially violent special-interest groups, each with its own vision of a future America. In 1993, for example, a confrontation between David Koresh's Branch Davidian followers and federal agents left 72 Davidians (including Koresh) and four federal agents dead in Waco, Texas.

Exactly two years to the day after the Davidian standoff ended in a horrific fire that destroyed the compound, a powerful terrorist truck bomb devastated the Alfred P. Murrah Federal Building in downtown Oklahoma City. One hundred sixty-eight people died, and hundreds more were wounded. The targeted nine-story building had housed offices of the Social Security Administration, the Drug Enforcement Administration, the Secret Service, the Bureau of Alcohol, Tobacco, and Firearms, and a day-care center called America's Kids. The fertilizer-and-diesel-fuel device used in the attack was estimated to have weighed about 1,200 pounds and had been left in a rental truck on the Fifth Street side of the building. The blast, which left a crater 30 feet wide and 8 feet deep and spread debris over a ten-block area, demonstrated just how vulnerable the United States is to terrorist attack.

In 1997, a federal jury found 29-year-old Timothy McVeigh guilty of 11 counts, ranging from conspiracy to first-degree murder, in the Oklahoma City bombing. Jurors concluded that McVeigh had conspired with Terry Nichols, a friend he had met while both were in the Army, and with unknown others to destroy the Murrah Building. Prosecutors made clear their belief that the attack was intended to revenge the 1993 assault on the Branch Davidian compound. McVeigh was sentenced to death, and was executed by lethal injection at the U.S. penitentiary in Terre Haute, Indiana, in 2001.[142] McVeigh was the first person under federal jurisdiction to be put to death since 1963. Terry Nichols was later convicted of conspiracy in the bombing and of eight counts of involuntary manslaughter. In 2001, Oklahoma County District Attorney C. Wesley Lane II announced that he planned to charge Nichols with an additional 160 counts of first-degree murder and that he would seek the death penalty.[143]

Some experts believe that the Oklahoma City attack was modeled after a similar bombing described in the *Turner Diaries*, a novel used by extremist groups to map their rise to power.[144] Just as Hitler's biography *Mein Kampf* served as a call to arms for Nazis in Europe during the 1930s, the *Turner Diaries* describes an Aryan revolution which occurs in the United States during the 1990s in which Jews, blacks, and other minorities are removed from positions of influence in government and society. Unsolved as of this writing is the 1996 Olympic Centennial Park bombing in which one person died and 111 were injured—an attack which many antiterrorism experts believe was the work of a separatist organization.

Active fringe groups include those espousing a nationwide "common law movement," under which the legitimacy of elected government officials is not recognized. An example is the Republic of Texas separatists who took neighbors hostage near Fort Davis, Texas, in 1997 to draw attention to their claims that Texas was illegally annexed by the United States in 1845. While not necessarily bent on terrorism, such special-interest groups may turn to violence if thwarted in attempts to reach their goals.

Sometimes individuals can be as dangerous as organized groups. In 1996, for example, 52-year-old Theodore Kaczynski, a Lincoln, Montana, recluse, was arrested and charged in the Unabomber case. The Unabomber (so called because the bomber's original targets were universities and airlines) had led police and FBI agents on a 17-year-long manhunt through a series of incidents which involved as many as 16 bombings, resulting in three deaths and 23 injuries. Kaczynski pleaded guilty to federal charges in 1998 and was sentenced to life in prison without possibility of parole.

INTERNATIONAL TERRORISM

After incidents like the terrorist attacks on Rome's Leonardo da Vinci Airport in 1987 and the bombing of Pan American's London–New York flight in 1988, Americans began to realize that international terrorism was knocking on their door. Pan American flight 103 was destroyed over Scotland by a powerful two-stage bomb as it reached its cruising altitude of 30,000 feet, killing all of the 259 passengers and crew members aboard. Another 11 people on the ground were killed, and many others injured as flaming debris from the airplane crashed down on the Scottish town of Lockerbie. Any doubts that Americans are being targeted by terrorists were dispelled by the 1996 truck bomb attack on U.S. military barracks in Dhahran, Saudi Arabia. Nineteen U.S. Air Force personnel were killed and more than 250 others injured in the blast that destroyed the Khobar Towers housing complex. A 40-person Pentagon task force headed by retired U.S. Army General Wayne Downing later concluded that the Pentagon had failed to take terrorist threats seriously.

The 1993 bombing of the World Trade Center in New York City and the 1995 conviction of Sheik Oma Abdel-Rahman and eight other Muslim fundamentalists on charges of plotting to start a holy war and of conspiring to commit assassinations and bomb the United Nations[145] indicated to many that the threat of international terrorism was becoming a part of daily life in America. According to some terrorism experts, the 1993 bombing of the World Trade Center, which killed four people and created a 100-foot hole through four subfloors of concrete, ushered in an era of serious terrorist threats at home. In late 1999, the Second U.S. Circuit Court of Appeals upheld the convictions of the sheik and his co-conspirators.

Terrorist groups are active throughout the world, and the United States is not their only target. Terrorist groups operate in South America, Africa, the Middle East, Latin America, the Philippines, Japan, India, Ireland, England, Nepal, and some of the now independent states of the former Soviet Union.

In 2001, Muslim terrorist Osama bin Laden showed the world how easy it can be to strike at American interests on U.S. soil when members of his organization allegedly attacked the World Trade Center and the Pentagon using commandeered airliners, killing approximately 3,000 people. In previous attacks in 1998, bin Laden's agents struck American embassies in Nairobi, Kenya, and Dar es Salaam, Tanzania, killing 257 people, including 12 Americans.

The current situation leads many observers to conclude that the American justice system is not fully prepared to deal with the threat represented by domestic and international terrorism. Prior intelligence-gathering efforts focused on such groups have largely failed, leading to military intervention in places like Afghanistan. Such failures are at least partially understandable, given that many terrorist organizations are tight-knit and very difficult for intelligence operatives to penetrate.

Terrorism and Technology

The technological sophistication of *state-sponsored* terrorist organizations is rapidly increasing. Handguns and even larger weapons are now being manufactured out of plastic polymers and ceramics. Capable of firing Teflon-coated armor-piercing bullets, such weapons are extremely powerful and impossible to uncover with metal detectors. Evidence points to the black market availability of other sinister items, including liquid metal embrittlement (LME). LME is a chemical which slowly weakens any metal it contacts. It could easily be applied with a felt-tipped pen to fuselage components in domestic aircraft, causing delayed structural failure.[146] Backpack-type electromagnetic pulse generators may soon be available to terrorists. Such devices could be carried into major cities, set up next to important computer installations, and activated to wipe out billions of items of financial, military, or other information now stored on magnetic media. International terrorists, along with the general public, have easy access to maps and other information which could be used to cripple the nation. The approximately 500 extremely high-voltage (EHV) transformers on which the nation's electric grid depends, for example, are entirely undefended but specified with extreme accuracy on easily available power network maps.

It is now clear that at least some terrorist organizations have at their disposal weapons of mass destruction, which the firepower and tactical mobility of law enforcement agencies cannot hope to match. Even more frightening is the prospect of nuclear terrorism. The collapse of the Soviet Union at the close of the 1980s led to very loose internal control over nuclear weapons and weapons-grade fissionable materials held in the former Soviet republics. Evidence of this continues to surface. In 1997, for example, German police were surprised to find that a gritty substance confiscated from the garage of an accused counterfeiter in the small town of Tengen-Weichs in southwestern Germany was superpure plutonium 239, a key ingredient in the manufacture of atomic bombs. Officials were able to determine through the identification of "chemical footprints" unique to the material that it had come from one of three top-secret Russian nuclear weapons laboratories that had been among the most strictly guarded sites in the former Soviet Union.[147] Experts say that oil-rich Middle Eastern countries controlled by fanatical and dictatorial regimes are willing to pay as much as $100 million for the plutonium needed to make one bomb—and this amount of plutonium can be smuggled out of a supposedly secure area in a briefcase or even in the pocket of an overcoat.

Another new kind of terrorism, called **cyberterrorism**, is lurking on the horizon. Cyberterrorism makes use of high technology, especially computers and the Internet, in the planning and carrying out of terrorist attacks. The term was coined in the 1980s by Barry Collin, a senior research fellow at the Institute for Security and Intelligence in California, who used it to refer to the convergence of cyberspace and terrorism.[148] It was later popularized by a 1996 RAND report that warned of an emerging "new terrorism" being implemented by the way in which terrorist groups organize, and by the way in which they use technology. The report warned of a coming "netwar," or "infowar," consisting of coordinated cyberattacks on our nation's economic, business, and military infrastructure.[149] A year later, FBI Agent Mark Pollitt offered a working definition of *cyberterrorism*, saying that it is "the premeditated, politically motivated attack against information, computer systems, computer programs, and data which results in violence against noncombatant targets by subnational groups or clandestine agents."[150]

Following the report by RAND, President Bill Clinton announced the formation of the President's Commission on Critical Infrastructure Protection (PCCIP) to study the critical infrastructures that constitute the life-support systems of the nation, to determine their vulnerabilities to a wide range of threats, and to propose a strategy for protecting them in the future. Eight infrastructures were identified: telecommunications, banking and finance, electrical power, oil and gas distribution and storage, water supply, transportation, emergency services, and government services.[151] Concerned over the threat of cyberterrorism to the nation's critical infrastructure, the president said,[152]

> In less than one generation, the information revolution and the introduction of the computer into virtually every dimension of our society has changed how our economy works, how we provide for our national security, and how we structure our everyday lives. . . .
>
> Yet this new age of promise carries within it peril. All computer-driven systems are vulnerable to intrusion and destruction. A concerted attack on the computers of any one of our key economic sectors or governmental agencies could have catastrophic effects.
>
> We know that the threat is real. Where once our opponents relied exclusively on bombs and bullets, hostile powers and terrorists can now turn a laptop computer into a potent weapon capable of doing enormous damage. If we are to continue to enjoy the benefits of the Information Age, preserve our security, and safeguard our economic well-being, we must protect our critical computer-controlled systems from attack.

Scenarios describing cyberterrorism possibilities are imaginative and diverse. Some have suggested that a successful cyberterrorist attack on the nation's air traffic control system might cause airplanes to collide in midair or that an attack upon food and cereal processing plants that drastically altered the levels of certain nutritional supplements might sicken or kill a large number of our nation's young children. Other such attacks might cause the country's power grid to collapse or might muddle the records and transactions of banks and stock exchanges. Possible targets in such attacks are almost endless. Although no large-scale and disruptive acts of cyberterrorism have yet been reported, the fact that critical systems are potentially vulnerable to such attack was demonstrated by a recent exercise conducted by the National Security Agency (NSA).[153] Code named Eligible Receiver, the simulated exercise targeted the U.S. Pacific Command in Hawaii, which oversees 100,000 U.S. troops. Attackers were able to penetrate military computers and divert supplies, disrupt troop movements, and control critical Department of Defense computer systems.

To assist in developing protection for the nation's critical infrastructure, President George W. Bush created the Office of Homeland Security in 2001, making its director a Cabinet member. Similarly, in an effort to protect vital interests from future acts of terrorism, the U.S. government is said to be considering the idea of building a whole new Internet of its own. Dubbed GOVNET, the service would provide secure voice and data communication by remaining physically and electronically separate from existing Internet routers and gateways. The idea for GOVNET was first offered by Richard Clarke, President Bush's cybersecurity adviser in 2001. "We'll be working . . . to secure our cyberspace from a range of possible threats, from hackers to criminals to terrorist groups, to foreign nations, which might use cyber war against us," Clarke said.[154] Visit the Office of Homeland Security via **Web Extra! 17–11**, and view **Library Extra! 17–6** at cjtoday.com to learn more about ways of protecting the nation's critical information infrastructure from attacks by cyberterrorists, criminals, and vandals.

cyberterrorism

A form of terrorism that makes use of high technology, especially computers and the Internet, in the planning and carrying out of terrorist attacks.

And say, finally, whether peace is best preserved by giving energy to the government, or information to the people—this last is the most certain, and the most legitimate engine of government. Educate and inform the whole mass of the people.

—Inscription, FBI National Academy

CJ Today News

[Student Cyber Corps Tackles Terrorism]

When [the September 11, 2001] terrorist attack struck, computer science professor Sujeet Shenoi was at a Department of Defense meeting not far from the Pentagon to talk about a program aimed at countering cyberterrorism.

"We wondered if they were going to take down the telephone systems in New York and Washington," says Shenoi, of the University of Tulsa. "My fear is for the next time this happens."

Computer security experts have long warned that systems controlling everything from the phones and air traffic to the Internet are vulnerable—and that there are too few experts to deal with problems should they occur.

But Shenoi is part of a pilot program to train more computer experts. Known as Cyber Corps, it's officially the Federal Cyber Service: Scholarship for Service program.

As in the Reserve Officer Training Corps (ROTC), the government pays for students to study computer security for up to two years. In return, they work for the government—in computer security, of course, for the same amount of time they were subsidized. They also do a summer internship.

The National Science Foundation (NSF) is funding the fall program with a grant of $11.2 million. So far, 32 students from six participating universities have received approval for the first year; 60 are anticipated next year. . . .

"Our computer communications infrastructures are riddled with security and reliability vulnerabilities," says Peter Neumann, a security expert who is frequently called to testify before Congress. "We clearly need more people who understand the risks and threats and security problems."

But the pay disparity between government and private firms makes it hard both to recruit and to get students to work for the government. "It's a desperate problem," says the NSF's Andrew Bernat. "There's no easy solution."

Still, even before the Sept. 11 attack, students were signing up.

Don McGillen, who runs the NSF program at Carnegie Mellon University in Pittsburgh, expected little interest in the program. Last year, when the high-tech economy was booming, "there was a question whether people would want to get a degree like that and go into government service." They initially planned for only two scholarships, increased it to three, and then ended up giving out nine the first year. "I've been impressed that they all do have a strong sense of patriotism," he says. . . .

Other participating schools are the Naval Postgraduate School in Monterey, Calif.; Iowa State University in Ames; Purdue University in West Lafayette, Ind.; and the University of Idaho in Moscow. The government pays tuition, room, board and a stipend. Students can get a bachelor's or master's degree.

Although students do not have to go through government security checks, they must be U.S. citizens, Bernat says.

Shenoi looks for more than just intellectual ability. "They have to be clever, articulate and natural leaders," he says. He also looks for diversity—in age, gender, and ethnicity. Shenoi's students this year include Howard Barnes, a 62-year-old former aerospace engineer from Wichita, Kan., and Julie Evans, a 42-year-old mother of three. . . .

For the latest in crime and justice news, visit the Talk Justice news feed at http://www.crimenews.info.

Source: Janet Kornblum, "Cyber Corps Tackles Terrorism: Students Learning to Take Down Hackers," *USA Today,* September 18, 2001, p. 12C.

Combating Terrorism

Terrorism represents a difficult challenge to all societies. The open societies of the Western world, however, are potentially more vulnerable than are totalitarian regimes like dictatorships. Democratic ideals of the West restrict police surveillance of likely terrorist groups and curtail luggage, vehicle, and airport searches. Press coverage of acts of terrorism encourage copycat activities by other fringe groups and communicate information on workable techniques. Laws designed to limit terrorist access to technology, information, and physical locations are stopgap measures at best. The federal Terrorist Firearms Detection Act of 1988 is an example. Designed to prevent the development of plastic firearms by requiring handguns to contain at least 3.7 ounces of detectable metal,[155] it applies only to weapons manufactured within U.S. borders.

In 1996, the Antiterrorism and Effective Death Penalty Act (AEDPA) became law. The act

■ Bans fund-raising and financial support within the United States for international terrorist organizations

■ Provides $1 billion for enhanced terrorism-fighting measures by federal and state authorities

■ Allows foreign terrorism suspects to be deported or to be kept out of the United States without the disclosure of classified evidence against them

- Permits a death sentence to be imposed upon anyone committing an international terrorist attack in the United States in which a death occurs

- Makes it a federal crime to use the United States as a base for planning terrorist attacks overseas

- Orders identifying chemical markers known as *taggants* to be added to plastic explosives during manufacture

- Orders a feasibility study on marking other explosives (except gunpowder)

More than a year before the events of September 11, 2001, the National Commission on Terrorism released its report, *Countering the Changing Threat of International Terrorism.*[156] The commission, created by House and Senate leaders in 1998 in response to the bombings of U.S. embassies in Kenya and Tanzania, was led by former U.S. Ambassador-at-Large for Counter-Terrorism L. Paul Bremer. The commission's report, which now seems to have presaged the attacks on the World Trade Center and the Pentagon, began with these words: "International terrorism poses an increasingly dangerous and difficult threat to America." The report identified Afghanistan, Iran, Iraq, Sudan, and Syria as among state sponsors of terrorism and concluded that "the government must immediately take steps to reinvigorate the collection of intelligence about terrorists' plans, use all available legal avenues to disrupt and prosecute terrorist activities and private sources of support, convince other nations to cease all support for terrorists, and ensure that federal, state, and local officials are prepared for attacks that may result in mass casualties." Some of the report's recommendations are shown in CJ Today Exhibit 17–2. A number of those recommendations were implemented only *after* the terrorist attacks of 2001.

Following the 2001 attacks, Congress enacted, and the president signed, the USA PATRIOT Act. The act, which is discussed in some detail in Chapter 1, created a number of new crimes, such as terrorist attacks against mass transportation and harboring or concealing terrorists. Those crimes were set forth in Title VIII of the Act, titled "Strengthening the Criminal Laws Against Terrorism." Title VIII can be found in CJ Today Exhibit 17–3. Learn more about countering terrorist threats at **Library Extra! 17–7** at cjtoday.com.

Foreign Terrorist Organizations

The U.S. Department of State has the authority to designate any group outside the United States as a **foreign terrorist organization (FTO)**. The process involves an exhaustive interagency review process in which all evidence of a group's activity, from both classified and open sources, is scrutinized. The State Department, working closely with the Justice and Treasury Departments and the intelligence community, prepares a detailed "administrative record" which documents the organization's terrorist activity.

Federal law requires that any organization considered for FTO designation must meet three criteria: (1) It must be foreign; (2) it must engage in terrorist activity as defined in Section 212 (a)(3)(B) of the Immigration and Nationality Act;[157] and (3) the organization's activities must threaten the security of U.S. nationals or the national security (national defense, foreign relations, or economic interests) of the United States. Table 17–1 lists 28 FTOs, as designated by the U.S. Department of State. For more detailed descriptions of these organizations, see the State Department publication *Patterns of Global Terrorism,* which can be accessed via **Library Extra! 17–8** at cjtoday.com.

Under federal law, FTO designations are subject to judicial review. In the event of a challenge to a group's FTO designation in federal court, the U.S. government relies upon the administrative record to defend the designation decision. These administrative records contain intelligence information and are therefore classified. FTO designations expire in two years unless renewed.

Once an organization has been designated as an FTO, a number of legal consequences follow. First, it becomes unlawful for a person in the United States or subject to the jurisdiction of the United States to provide funds or other material support to a designated FTO. Second, representatives and certain members of a designated FTO, if they are aliens, can be denied visas or kept from entering the United States. Finally, U.S. financial institutions must block funds of designated FTOs and their agents and must report the blockage to the Office of Foreign Assets Control within the U.S. Department of the Treasury.

Foreign Terrorist Organization (FTO)

A foreign organization that engages in terrorist activity which threatens the security of U.S. nationals or the national security of the United States and which is so designated by the U.S. secretary of state.

CJ Today Exhibit 17-2

[Recommendations of the National Commission on Terrorism]

■ CIA (Central Intelligence Agency) guidelines adopted in 1995 restricting recruitment of unsavory sources should not apply when recruiting counterterrorism sources.

■ The Attorney General should ensure that the FBI (Federal Bureau of Investigation) is exercising fully its authority for investigating suspected terrorist groups or individuals, including authority for electronic surveillance.

 —Funding for counterterrorism efforts by the CIA, NSA (National Security Agency), and FBI must be given higher priority to ensure continuation of important operational activity and to close the technology gap that threatens their ability to collect and exploit terrorist communications.

 —The FBI should establish a cadre of reports officers to distill and disseminate terrorism-related information once it is collected.

■ U.S. policies must firmly target all states that support terrorists.
 —Iran and Syria should be kept on the list of state sponsors until they stop supporting terrorists.

 —Afghanistan should be designated a sponsor of terrorism and subjected to all the sanctions applicable to state sponsors.

 —The President should impose sanctions on countries that, while not direct sponsors of terrorism, are nevertheless not cooperating fully on counterterrorism. Candidates for consideration include Pakistan and Greece.

■ Private sources of financial and logistical support for terrorists must be subjected to the full force and sweep of the U.S. and international laws.
 —All relevant agencies should use every available means, including the full array of criminal, civil, and administrative sanctions to block or disrupt nongovernmental sources of support for international terrorism.

 —Congress should promptly ratify and implement the International Convention for the Suppression of the Financing of Terrorism to enhance international cooperative efforts.

 —Where criminal prosecution is not possible, the Attorney General should vigorously pursue the expulsion of terrorists from the United States through proceedings which protect both the national security interest in safeguarding classified evidence and the right of the accused to challenge that evidence.

■ A terrorist attack involving a biological agent, deadly chemicals, or nuclear or radiological material, even if it succeeds only partially, could profoundly affect the entire nation. The government must do more to prepare for such an event.

 —The President should direct the preparation of a manual to guide the implementation of existing legal authority in the event of a catastrophic terrorist threat or attack. The President and Congress should determine whether additional legal authority is needed to deal with catastrophic terrorism.

 —The Department of Defense (DOD) must have detailed plans for its role in the event of a catastrophic terrorist attack, including criteria for decisions on transfer of command authority to DOD in extraordinary circumstances.

 —Senior officials of all government agencies involved in responding to a catastrophic terrorism threat or crisis should be required to participate in national exercises every year to test capabilities and coordination.

 —Congress should make it illegal for anyone not properly certified to possess certain critical pathogens and should enact laws to control the transfer of equipment critical to the development or use of biological agents.

 —The President should establish a comprehensive and coordinated long-term research and development program for catastrophic terrorism.

 —The Secretary of State should press for an international convention to improve multilateral cooperation on preventing or responding to cyber attacks by terrorists.

■ The President and Congress should reform the system for reviewing and funding departmental counterterrorism programs to ensure that the activities and programs of various agencies are part of a comprehensive plan.

 —The executive branch official responsible for coordinating counterterrorism efforts across the government should be given a stronger hand in the budget process.

 —Congress should develop a mechanism for a comprehensive review of the President's counterterrorism policy and budget.

Source: National Commission on Terrorism, *Countering the Changing Threat of International Terrorism* (Washington, D.C.: U.S. Department of State, 2000). Distributed by the Office of International Information Programs, U.S. Department of State. Website: http://usinfo.state.gov.

The State Department also has the authority to designate selected foreign governments as state sponsors of international terrorism. As of early 2002, Iran, Iraq, Syria, Libya, Cuba, North Korea, and Sudan continued to be the seven governments that the State Department has designated as state sponsors of international terrorism. According to the State Department, Iran "remained the most active state sponsor of terrorism in 2000."[158] According to the State Department, the Iranian government provided increasing support to numerous terrorist groups during 2000, including the Lebanese Hizballah, HAMAS, and the Palestine Islamic Jihad (PIJ), all of which seek to undermine Middle East peace negotiations through the use of terrorism. Iraq provided safe haven and support to a variety of

CJ Today Exhibit 17-3

[The USA PATRIOT Act of 2001]

Title VIII of the USA PATRIOT Act of 2001 created two new federal crimes of terrorist activity: (1) terrorist attacks against mass transportation systems and (2) harboring or concealing terrorists. The following excerpt from the act describes these offenses.

Title VIII—Strengthening the Criminal Laws Against Terrorism

Sec. 801. Terrorist Attacks and Other Acts of Violence Against Mass Transportation Systems.

Chapter 97 of title 18, United States Code, is amended by adding at the end the following:

§ 1993. Terrorist attacks and other acts of violence against mass transportation systems

(a) GENERAL PROHIBITIONS.—Whoever willfully—

(1) wrecks, derails, sets fire to, or disables a mass transportation vehicle or ferry;

(2) places or causes to be placed any biological agent or toxin for use as a weapon, destructive substance, or destructive device in, upon, or near a mass transportation vehicle or ferry, without previously obtaining the permission of the mass transportation provider, and with intent to endanger the safety of any passenger or employee of the mass transportation provider, or with a reckless disregard for the safety of human life;

(3) sets fire to, or places any biological agent or toxin for use as a weapon, destructive substance, or destructive device in, upon, or near any garage, terminal, structure, supply, or facility used in the operation of, or in support of the operation of, a mass transportation vehicle or ferry, without previously obtaining the permission of the mass transportation provider, and knowing or having reason to know such activity would likely derail, disable, or wreck a mass transportation vehicle or ferry used, operated, or employed by the mass transportation provider;

(4) removes appurtenances from, damages, or otherwise impairs the operation of a mass transportation signal system, including a train control system, centralized dispatching system, or rail grade crossing warning signal without authorization from the mass transportation provider;

(5) interferes with, disables, or incapacitates any dispatcher, driver, captain, or person while they are employed in dispatching, operating, or maintaining a mass transportation vehicle or ferry, with intent to endanger the safety of any passenger or employee of the mass transportation provider, or with a reckless disregard for the safety of human life;

(6) commits an act, including the use of a dangerous weapon, with the intent to cause death or serious bodily injury to an employee or passenger of a mass transportation provider or any

other person while any of the foregoing are on the property of a mass transportation provider;

(7) conveys or causes to be conveyed false information, knowing the information to be false, concerning an attempt or alleged attempt being made or to be made, to do any act which would be a crime prohibited by this subsection; or

(8) attempts, threatens, or conspires to do any of the aforesaid acts, shall be fined under this title or imprisoned not more than twenty years, or both, if such act is committed, or in the case of a threat or conspiracy such act would be committed, on, against, or affecting a mass transportation provider engaged in or affecting interstate or foreign commerce, or if in the course of committing such act, that person travels or communicates across a State line in order to commit such act, or transports materials across a State line in aid of the commission of such act.

(b) AGGRAVATED OFFENSE.—Whoever commits an offense under subsection (a) in a circumstance in which—

(1) the mass transportation vehicle or ferry was carrying a passenger at the time of the offense; or

(2) the offense has resulted in the death of any person, shall be guilty of an aggravated form of the offense and shall be fined under this title or imprisoned for a term of years or for life, or both.

Sec. 803. Prohibition Against Harboring Terrorists.

(a) IN GENERAL.—Chapter 113B of title 18, United States Code, is amended by adding after section 2338 the following new section:

§ 2339. Harboring or concealing terrorists

(a) Whoever harbors or conceals any person who he knows, or has reasonable grounds to believe, has committed, or is about to commit, an offense under section 32 (relating to destruction of aircraft or aircraft facilities), section 175 (relating to biological weapons), section 229 (relating to chemical weapons), section 831 (relating to nuclear materials), paragraph (2) or (3) of section 844(f) (relating to arson and bombing of government property risking or causing injury or death), section 1366(a) (relating to the destruction of an energy facility), section 2280 (relating to violence against maritime navigation), section 2332a (relating to weapons of mass destruction), or section 2332b (relating to acts of terrorism transcending national boundaries) of this title, section 236(a) (relating to sabotage of nuclear facilities or fuel) of the Atomic Energy Act of 1954 (42 U.S.C. 2284(a)), or section 46502 (relating to aircraft piracy) of title 49, shall be fined under this title or imprisoned not more than ten years, or both.

(b) A violation of this section may be prosecuted in any Federal judicial district in which the underlying offense was committed, or in any other Federal judicial district as provided by law.

(b) TECHNICAL AMENDMENT.—The chapter analysis for chapter 113B of title 18, United States Code, is amended by inserting after the item for section 2338 the following: "2339. Harboring or concealing terrorists.".

TABLE 17-1	**DESIGNATED FOREIGN TERRORIST ORGANIZATIONS**
Abu Nidal Organization (ANO)	Palestine Liberation Front (PLF)
Abu Sayyaf Group	Palestine Islamic Jihad (PIJ)
Armed Islamic Group (GIA)	Popular Front for the Liberation of Palestine (PFLP)
Aum Shinri Kyo	
Basque Fatherland and Liberty (ETA)	PFLP-General Command (PFLP-GC)
Gama'a al-Islamiyya (Islamic Group)	Al Qaeda (also al-Qaeda, al-Qa'ida)
HAMAS (Islamic Resistance Movement)	Real IRA
Harakat ul-Mujahidin (HUM)	Revolutionary Armed Forces of Colombia (FARC)
Hizballah (Party of God)	
Islamic Movement of Uzbekistan (IMU)	Revolutionary Nuclei (formerly ELA)
al-Jihad (Egyptian Islamic Jihad)	Revolutionary Organization 17 November
Kahane Chai (Kach)	Revolutionary People's Liberation Army/Front (DHKP/C)
Kurdistan Workers' Party (PKK)	
Liberation Tigers of Tamil Eelam (LTTE)	Shining Path (Sendero Luminoso, SL)
Mujahedin-e Khalq Organization (MEK)	United Self-Defense Forces of Colombia (AUC)
National Liberation Army (ELN)	

For more detailed descriptions of these organizations, see the State Department publication *Patterns of Global Terrorism*, which can be accessed via Library Extra! 17–8 at cjtoday.com.

Palestinian terrorist groups, as well as bases, weapons, and protection to the Mujahedin-e Khalq (MEK), an Iranian terrorist group that opposes the current Iranian regime. Syria provided safe haven and support to several terrorist groups, some of which oppose the Middle East peace negotiations. At the time of the State Department report, Libya was attempting to mend its international image following its surrender in 1999 of two Libyan suspects for trial in the Pan Am 103 bombing. In early 2001, one of those suspects was convicted of murder, and judges in the case found that he had acted "in furtherance of the purposes of . . . Libyan Intelligence Services." In 2000, Cuba provided safe haven to several terrorists and U.S. fugitives and maintained ties to state sponsors of terrorism and Latin American insurgents. North Korea harbored several hijackers of a Japanese Airlines flight to North Korea in the 1970s and maintained links to other terrorist groups. Finally, at the start of 2002, Sudan continued to provide a safe haven for members of Al Qaeda, the Lebanese Hizballah, Gama'a al-Islamiyya, Egyptian Islamic Jihad, the PIJ, and HAMAS, although it has been engaged in a counterterrorism dialogue with the United States since mid-2000. Learn more about terrorism from the Terrorism Research Center via **Web Extra! 17–12** at cjtoday.com. Visit the State Department's Counterterrorism Office via **Web Extra! 17–13** at cjtoday.com.

Technology and Individual Rights

The Office of Technology Assessment of the U.S. Congress noted that "what is judicially permissible and socially acceptable at one time has often been challenged when technology changes."[159] When agencies of the justice system use cutting-edge technology, it inevitably provokes fears of a future in which citizens' rights are abrogated in favor of advancing technology. Individual rights, equal treatment under the law, and due process issues all require constant reinterpretation as technology improves. However, because some of the technology available today is so new, few court cases have yet to directly address the issues involved. Even so, it is possible to identify areas which hold potential for future dispute.

Technology and the First Amendment

One of the most revered covenants in the U.S. Constitution protects free speech. Found in the First Amendment, the relevant phrase reads, "Congress shall make no law . . .

abridging the freedom of speech, or of the press." In 1996, amidst fierce debate, the U.S. Congress passed and President Clinton signed a law intended to control the availability of obscene materials on the Internet. Entitled the Communications Decency Act (CDA),[160] the new law was part of the Telecommunications Act of 1996. The CDA made it a federal offense for anyone to distribute "indecent" or "patently offensive" material to minors (anyone under 18 years of age) over computer networks like the Internet or commercial online services. The law provided for prison terms of up to two years and a $250,000 fine for breaking the law.

Opponents of the law claimed that it unconstitutionally restricted free speech because it is not technologically possible for providers of access or content on the Internet to prevent minors from obtaining indecent materials intended for adults. "The senders . . . have no ability to ensure that their messages are only available to adults," said Harvard University computer consultant Scott Bradner.[161] "It is also not possible for an Internet service provider . . . to screen out all or even most content that could be deemed 'indecent' or 'patently offensive,'" he added.

That year, a three-judge federal panel agreed with opponents of the CDA and issued a preliminary injunction barring enforcement of portions of the act. The unanimous decision held that speech over the Internet should be given the broadest possible constitutional protections—much like that now accorded to newspapers and magazines—as opposed to the tighter restrictions on broadcast media, such as television. "As the most participatory form of mass speech yet developed, the Internet deserves the highest protection from governmental intrusion," said U.S. District Judge Stewart Dalzell, a member of the judicial panel.[162] "Just as the strength of [the] Internet is chaos, so the strength of our liberty depends upon the chaos and cacophony of the unfettered speech the First Amendment protects," Dalzell wrote.

In 1997, in the landmark case of *Reno* v. *ACLU*,[163] the U.S. Supreme Court upheld the lower court's ruling, effectively invalidating enforcement provisions of the CDA. Writing for the majority, Justice John Paul Stevens said, "It is true that we have repeatedly recognized the governmental interest in protecting children from harmful materials. But that interest does not justify an unnecessarily broad suppression of speech addressed to adults." The ruling effectively accorded Internet content the same level of constitutional protection previously afforded print media, such as newspapers and magazines.

Technology and the Second Amendment

The Second Amendment to the U.S. Constitution reads, "A well regulated Militia, being necessary to the security of a free State, the right of the people to keep and bear Arms, shall not be infringed." Many interpret the words of this amendment as a complete and total ban on gun control by the federal government. The National Rifle Association (NRA), a long-time proponent of gun ownership, is the strongest, most vocal, and best organized group in the nation opposing gun control. The NRA claims that efforts to legislate controls over gun ownership, and specifically the Brady Handgun Violence Prevention Act of 1993, are unconstitutional. The Brady law, named after former President Ronald Reagan's White House press secretary Jim Brady, who was shot in the head during John Hinckley's 1981 attempted assassination of Reagan, created a national criminal background checking system which gun dealers must contact before selling any firearm. Under the law, firearms dealers must register with the federal government and must refuse to sell handguns to felons, to those awaiting trial on felony charges, and to fugitives. The Brady Handgun Violence Prevention Act is discussed in greater detail in Chapter 2.

Opponents of gun control, many of whom continue to be quite vocal today, are not convinced it will reduce crime. They believe, instead, that a waiting period and other controls impose burdens only on those who obey the law and that even an assault weapons ban contravenes liberties guaranteed under the Second Amendment.

In the area of gun control, as in many others, technology and individual rights have the potential for conflict. While government agents fear the manufacture of nondetectable handguns and other weapons, makers of such guns have been quick to fight government restrictions on the manufacturing process. As mentioned in this chapter's terrorism section, handguns and even larger weapons which are capable of firing nonmetallic projectiles are now being manufactured out of plastic polymers and ceramics, especially overseas, where legislative controls are lax. Such weapons can be extremely powerful and impossible to find with metal detectors. Agencies of control, which would ban the manufacture, importation, and possession of such easy-to-hide weapons, have suggested the

> The Internet threatens to give every child a free pass into the equivalent of every adult bookstore and every adult video store in the country.
>
> —U.S. Justice Department attorney Seth P. Waxman, arguing before the U.S. Supreme Court in *Reno* v. *ACLU* (1997)

A National Rifle Association member demonstrating in support of the Second Amendment's guarantee that "the right of the people to keep and bear Arms, shall not be infringed." Many people worry that government intrusion may reduce rights otherwise supported by the Constitution.

Donna Binder

adoption of international treaties requiring gun manufacturers to embed special transponder chips in each weapon made for civilian use so that it could be tracked anywhere in the world. Such miniaturized computer chips would be detectable by a variety of high-tech means, as well as through a network of geosyncronous satellites circling the earth, which could pinpoint the location of a specific weapon to within ten feet.

Advocates of gun ownership are bothered by such suggestions since they see efforts at further control as an infringement upon Second Amendment rights. As both technology and efforts at control advance, advocates of both gun ownership and gun control will find themselves in the midst of an ideational and political fray which will probably last for years.

Technology and the Fourth Amendment

The Fourth Amendment to the U.S. Constitution guarantees "[t]he right of the people to be secure in their persons, houses, papers, and effects, against unreasonable searches and seizures." Given the electronic network which permeates contemporary society, today's "houses" are far less secure from prying eyes than were those of the eighteenth century. Modern dwellings are linked to the outside world through phone lines, modems, fax machines, electronic mail, and even direct radio and television communications. One highly significant question centers on where the "security" of the home ends and the public realm begins.

Complicating matters still further are today's "supersnoop" technologies, which provide investigators with the ability to literally hear through walls (using vibration detectors), listen to conversations over tremendous distances (with parabolic audio receivers), record voices in distant rooms (via laser readings of windowpane vibrations), and even look through walls (using forward-looking infrared [FLIR] devices, which can detect temperature differences of as little as two-tenths of one degree). As discussed in Chapter 7, law enforcement use of FLIR for certain kinds of investigative activity was effectively banned by the U.S. Supreme Court in 2001 in the Case of *Kyllo* v. *U.S.*[164] Although not every one of the supersnoop technologies mentioned here has undergone Supreme Court scrutiny, *Kyllo* provides a clear indication of the direction the Court is likely to take with regard to most such technologies. In *Kyllo*, the Court held that "Where, as here, the government uses a device that is not in general public use, to explore details of a private home that would previously have been unavailable without physical intrusion, the surveillance is a Fourth Amendment 'search,' and is presumptively unreasonable without a warrant."[165]

Another question concerns the Fourth Amendment's guarantee of secure "papers and effects." The phrase "papers and effects" takes on a much wider meaning when we enter the world of modern technology. Although the framers of the Constitution could not envision electronic databases, their admonition would seem to apply to such records. Databases may already be the repositories of more information than is routinely stored on paper. Tax listings, records of draft registrants, Social Security rolls, health reports, criminal histories, credit bureau ratings, and government and bank logs all contain billions of items of information on almost every man, woman, and child in the country. Most agree that official access to such information should be limited.

A third question centers on the privacy of various kinds of information, the proper legal steps to be used in acquiring information for investigative purposes, and the types of information that can appropriately be stored in criminal justice data repositories. The kinds of information which can be appropriately stored, along with considerations of who should have access to the data, are both legal and ethical questions. In 1974, the Justice Department established the "one-year rule," prohibiting the FBI from disseminating criminal records that are more than a year old. The department was concerned about the potential for inaccuracy in older files.

Even "official" records may be misleading or incomplete. A study of FBI criminal record databases, for example, concluded that about 50% of arrest entries do not show the disposition of cases.[166] Inquiring agencies using such records could be falsely misled into prejudging the guilt of an offender against whom earlier charges had been dropped. The same study also found that as many as 20% of the arrest-dispositional data contained in FBI records may be erroneous. Evidence seized as the result of an arrest based upon inaccurate NCIC information can be suppressed.[167] Half of all requests for criminal records made to the FBI, however, are from employers and licensing agencies. If an applicant is refused employment or is rejected for licensing (or bonding) on the basis of criminal record inaccuracies, he or she may needlessly suffer.

The U.S. Supreme Court has not yet directly addressed database management in criminal justice agencies (see, however, the case of *Arizona* v. *Evans* in Chapter 7). A number of lower courts have held that criminal justice agencies have a duty to maintain accurate and reliable records.[168] In one important decision, *Menard* v. *Saxbe* (1974), the Federal Court of Appeals for the District of Columbia found that the FBI has a duty to be more than a "mere passive recipient" of records. The court held that the FBI should avoid unnecessary harm to people listed in its files.[169]

Technology and the Fifth Amendment

As we have discussed throughout this book, the Fifth and Fourteenth Amendments to the Constitution require that an accused receive "due process of law" prior to the imposition of any criminal sanction. Due process necessitates a presumption of innocence, and lawful prosecutions must proceed according to the standards of the Sixth Amendment.

What may be the greatest potential threat to the due process guarantee comes not from the physical sciences but from psychology, sociology, and other social scientific approaches to the study and prediction of human behavior. Social science research generally involves the observation of large numbers of individuals, often in quasi-experimental settings. Many studies produce results of questionable validity when applied in other settings. Even so, the tendency has been for social scientists to create predictive models of behavior with widely claimed applicability. Worse still, legislatures and criminal justice decision makers have often been quick to adopt them for their own purposes. Behavioral models, for example, are now used to tailor sophisticated law enforcement investigations, such as those based on the FBI's criminal profiling program. Statutory guidelines,[170] including the Federal Sentencing Guidelines,[171] are written with an eye to predictive frameworks which allegedly measure the danger potential of certain types of offenders. The justice system's growing use of behavioral models demonstrates a growing faith in the reliability of the social sciences, but it also holds the danger of punishment in anticipation of a crime.

The major threat from the social sciences to individual rights comes from the tendency they create to prejudge individuals based upon personal characteristics rather than facts—a process akin to racial profiling (discussed in Chapter 6). Persons designated as dangerous as the result of a scientifically based conceptual profile may be subject to investigation, arrest, conviction, and harsh sentences solely on the basis of identified characteristics thought to be associated with certain kinds of misbehavior. In effect, some social scientific models could produce a veiled form of discrimination. This is especially

> The principle all . . . moralists out there should remember is that when you erode one individual's rights, it can come back to attack you and your family at a later time.
>
> —Sandra Craig, following her conviction on 53 counts of assault, child abuse, and perverted sexual practices

true when the predictive factors around which they are built are mere substitutions for race, ethnicity, or gender.

As an example, some early predictive models from studies of domestic violence tended to show that, among other things, the typical offender was male, was unemployed or had a record of spotty employment, was poorly educated, and was abused as a child or came from a broken home. Because many of these characteristics also describe a larger proportion of the nation's black population than they do whites, they created a hidden tendency to strongly accuse black males suspected of such offenses—and sometimes to suspect them even when they were not accused.

With these considerations in mind, social scientific models may nonetheless prove to be useful tools. The most acceptable solution would treat individuals on a case-by-case basis, looking to the general predictive models of social science only for guidance once all the facts became known.

The Fifth Amendment raises a second issue—this one outside the purview of social science. The amendment reads, "No person shall be held to answer for a capital, or otherwise infamous crime, unless on a presentment or indictment of a Grand Jury, . . . nor shall be compelled in any criminal case to be a witness against himself."

Statements made under hypnosis or during psychiatric examination are generally protected by court decision and are not available as evidence at trial.[172] However, modern technological procedures appear to make self-incrimination a possibility even in the absence of any verbal statements. The Supreme Court, for example, has held that suspects must submit to blood-alcohol tests under certain circumstances[173] and that samples of breath, semen, hair, and tissue may also be taken without consent when the procedures used do not "shock the conscience."[174] Technological advances over the next few decades are anticipated to increase the potential for incriminating forms of nontestimonial evidence.

Technology and the Sixth Amendment

> Computers can be broken into. If they're on the Internet, [they] might as well have a welcome mat.
>
> —Kevin Mitnick[vi]

In late 2001, the White House announced that it would try some captured Al Qaeda leaders in military tribunals created especially for that purpose. The Sixth Amendment, however, guarantees the right to a public trial by an impartial jury. The amendment is generally held to apply only to U.S. citizens facing criminal charges under federal or state law, and not to prisoners of war or foreign combatants captured by U.S. military forces. The trial of the "American Taliban" John Walker Lindh, which is about to begin as this book goes to press, appears to meet Sixth Amendment guarantees. Of greater significance for this discussion, however, is the fact that the meaning of the words *public* and *impartial* has been rendered ambiguous by advancing technology. A famous author once coined the term *global village* to describe how advances in communications technology have increased the ready availability of information for us all. Are public trials ones in which TV cameras should be allowed? Would broadcasts of trials be permissible? Although (as discussed in Chapter 9) courts in some jurisdictions now allow video recordings of trials with great public interest, courts at higher levels have yet to address the question.

Also at issue is the expanding use of scientific jury-selection techniques, which are discussed briefly in Chapter 9. This new "technology" attempts to predict the outcome of jury deliberations based upon an assessment of the economic, social, cultural, and demographic characteristics of individual jurors.[175] Using jury-selection techniques, some lawyers attempt to choose jurors likely to be predisposed to a finding in favor of their client.[176] The high court has yet to decide the constitutional merits of scientific jury-selection techniques.

The Sixth Amendment allows an accused person to "be confronted with the witnesses against him." Some courts now permit only an indirect confrontation, through the use of television, videotapes, and the like. Abused juveniles, for example, appear to jurors in some jurisdictions only on television screens to spare them the trauma and embarrassment of the courtroom. Although such strategies may appear to be an end run around the Sixth Amendment, they are complicated by claims that justice is better served by an articulate witness rather than a frightened one and by the fact that most such testimonial strategies involve juveniles as witnesses.

Technology and the Eighth Amendment

The Eighth Amendment is the most concise statement in the Bill of Rights. It reads, "Excessive bail shall not be required, nor excessive fines imposed, nor cruel and unusual punishments inflicted."

Modern technology brings with it the possibility of a host of new treatments for the criminal offender. Most of these treatments can also be considered punishments because the courts impose them upon unwilling subjects. Examples of unusual "punishments" today might include drug and hormone therapy or the use of electronic bracelets to monitor the public movements of convicted offenders. In 1992, authorities in Arapahoe County, Colorado, decided to experiment with an electronic system that alerts the potential victim via an alarm when a convicted stalker approaches.[177] Although similar bracelets have been used to monitor compliance with probationary sentences of home confinement, some claim that the public use of such devices lends credence to the "brave new world" form of authoritarianism feared by many as undue governmental intrusion on privacy.

Drug therapy is another area under scrutiny. Two drugs already in use are Antabuse® and Depo-Provera.® Antabuse is utilized in the treatment of alcoholics. It produces nausea and vomiting when alcohol is ingested. Depo-Provera is the trade name given by the Upjohn Company to its brand of medroxyprogesterone acetate, a synthetic form of the female hormone progesterone. Depo-Provera has been shown to reduce the male sex drive and is sometimes administered to sex offenders by court order. In 1997, California became the first state to require twice-convicted child molesters to get weekly injections of Depo-Provera upon release from prison. (See the box in Chapter 11 on chemical castration.)

Drugs like Antabuse and Depo-Provera and surgical procedures like castration and lobotomy may soon run afoul of the Eighth Amendment's ban on cruel and unusual punishment. In most cases where these innovative treatments are contemplated by the court, criminal offenders are offered a choice between prison or a chemical or surgical remedy. The American Civil Liberties Union, however, has argued that the use of Depo-Provera and other drugs in the treatment of criminal offenders is a form of coercion. The ACLU claimed that the offered alternative, prison, is so dangerous as to force acceptance of any other choice.[178]

As with many emerging issues, drugs like Antabuse and Depo-Provera have not yet been subject to Supreme Court scrutiny. However, a few lower-court cases have begun to provide some general guidance in judging what treatments are permissible. For example, in the 1970 case of *Holt* v. *Sarver*,[179] the federal court for the Eastern District of Arkansas defined cruel and unusual punishment to be that which is "shocking to the conscience of reasonably civilized people." Whether "chemical castration" falls into such a category and whether the U.S. Supreme Court will apply the *Holt* standard to such cases are questions that remain unanswered.

Technology and the Fourteenth Amendment

Section One of the Fourteenth Amendment to the U.S. Constitution concludes with the phrase, "No State shall . . . deny to any person within its jurisdiction the equal protection of the laws." Modern technology, because it is expensive and often experimental, is not always equally available. Criminal justice programs which depend upon technology that is limited in its availability may contravene this Fourteenth Amendment provision. Court-ordered confinement, for example, which utilizes electronic monitoring and house arrest is an alternative much preferred by offenders. The technology supporting this confinement is expensive, however, which dramatically limits its availability. Although the Supreme Court has yet to address this particular topic, it has ruled that programs that require the offender to bear a portion of the cost of confinement are unconstitutional when their availability is restricted to only those offenders who can afford them.[180]

Learn more about what the American criminal justice system of the future may be like via **Library Extra! 17–9** at cjtoday.com.

Summary

Old concepts of criminality, and of white-collar crime in particular, have undergone significant revision as a result of emerging technologies. Science-fiction-like commercial products that are now widely available have brought with them a plethora of possibilities for new high-stakes crimes, including computer crimes. The well-equipped technologically advanced offender in tomorrow's world will be capable of property crimes involving dollar amounts undreamed of only a few decades ago. At the same time, the ability of law enforcement agencies to respond to everyday crimes will be enhanced by the use of cutting-edge technology.

Terrorism, a significant criminal justice issue in its own right, brings with it the threat of cyberterrorism and the potential for attacks upon information-management segments of our nation's critical infrastructure. Attacks by cyberterrorists could theoretically shut down or disable important services like electricity, food processing, military activity, and even state and federal governments.

Barring global nuclear war or world catastrophe, advances in technology will continue to occur. Citizens of the future will regard as commonplace much of what is only fantasy today. Gradual lifestyle modifications will accompany changes in technology and will result in taken-for-granted expectations foreign to today's world. Within that changed social context, the "reasonableness" of technological intrusions into personal lives will be judged according to standards tempered by the new possibilities technology has to offer.

Coming social changes, combined with powerful technologies, threaten to produce a new world of challenges for criminal justice agencies. Domestic and international terrorism, widespread drug running, and changing social values will evolve into a complex tangle of legal and technological issues which will confront the best law enforcement minds of the future. It appears safe to predict that the American criminal justice system of the twenty-first century will continue to be buffeted by the expanding power of politically oriented domestic and international groups with radical and unlawful agendas. Only through a massive infusion of funds to support the purchase of new equipment and the hiring and training of technologically sophisticated personnel can tomorrow's enforcement agencies hope to compete with technologically adept criminals.

Discussion Questions

1. How has technology affected the practice of criminal justice in America over the past 100 years?
2. What future benefits and threats to the practice of criminal justice can you imagine emanating from the technological advances which are bound to occur over the next few decades? What new forms of cybercrime do you envision?
3. What are the major differences between white-collar crime and occupational crime? How have advances in technology created new opportunities for white-collar and occupational criminals? What is the criminal justice system's best hope for coping with these criminal threats?
4. Has criminal law kept pace with the opportunities for dishonest behavior created by advancing technology? What modifications in current laws defining criminal activity might be necessary to meet the criminal possibilities inherent in technological advances?
5. Why is terrorism a law enforcement concern? How is terrorism a crime? What can the American criminal justice system do to better prepare itself for future terrorist crimes?
6. What is cyberterrorism? How do advances in technology increase the likelihood of cyberterrorism?
7. What threats to civil liberties do you imagine advances in technology might create? Will our standards as to what constitutes admissible evidence, what is reasonable privacy, and so on, undergo a reevaluation as a result of burgeoning technology?

To participate in an online discussion on these topics and others, go to the Global Town Meeting electronic message board for Chapter 17 on the *Criminal Justice Today* Companion Website at cjtoday.com.

Web Quest!

Use the Cybrary to learn about computer and high-technology crime and its link to international terrorism. Specifically, answer the following questions:

■ How can terrorists use computer technology to attack the United States?

■ How likely is such an attack?

■ What might be the potential consequences of a cyberterrorism attack?

■ How well prepared is the United States to defend itself against cyberterrorism?

■ What other forms of computer crime might international organized criminal groups engage in?

Summarize the information you've found, and submit it to your instructor if asked to do so.

To complete this Web Quest! online, go to the Web Quest! module in Chapter 17 of the *Criminal Justice Today* Companion Website at cjtoday.com.

Library Extras!

Library Extra! 17–1 *Understanding DNA Evidence* (OVC, 2001).

Library Extra! 17–2 *Criminal Justice Discovers Information Technology* (NIJ, 2000).

Library Extra! 17–3 *Criminal Justice and the Information Technology Revolution* (NIJ, 2000).

Library Extra! 17–4 *The Electronic Frontier: The Challenge of Unlawful Conduct Involving the Use of the Internet* (USGPO, 2000).

Library Extra! 17–5 *Identity Theft: When Bad Things Happen to Good People* (FTC, 2000).

Library Extra! 17–6 *Defending America's Cyberspace: National Plan for Information Systems Protection* (Critical Infrastructure Assurance Office, 2000).

Library Extra! 17–7 *Countering the Changing Threat of International Terrorism* (National Commission on Terrorism, 2000).

Library Extra! 17–8 *Patterns of Global Terrorism* (U.S. Department of State, latest release).

Library Extra! 17–9 *Creating a New Criminal Justice System for the Twenty-first Century* (BJS, 1999).

To explore these resources online, go to the Library Extras! area of the *Criminal Justice Today* Companion Website at cjtoday.com. You should also check the author's "Late Picks" online for newly released documents and updated Library Extras! You can find Late Picks at http://cjtoday.com/latepicks.htm.

Marginal Notes

i. Michael L. Benson, Francis T. Cullen, and William J. Maakestad, *Local Prosecutors and Corporate Crime* (Washington, D.C.: National Institute of Justice, 1992), p. 1.

ii. Identity Theft Resource Center. Web posted at http://www.idtheftcenter.org. Accessed April 4, 2002.

iii. FBI Counterterrorism Section, *Terrorism in the United States 1987* (Washington, D.C.: FBI, 1987).

iv. Adapted from *FBI Policy and Guidelines: Counterterrorism*. Web posted at http://www.fbi.gov/contact/fo/jackson/cntrterr.htm. Accessed March 4, 2002.

v. Ibid.

vi. Jonathan Littmann, "In the Mind of Most Wanted Hacker, Kevin Mitnick," *Computer World*, January 15, 1996, p. 87.

Notes

1. Quoted in Susan W. Brenner, "Is There Such a Thing as 'Virtual Crime'?" *California Criminal Law Review,* Vol. 4 (June 2001).

2. Details of this story come from "Three Arrested in Internet Kidnapping, Assault Case," *USA Today,* August 14, 2001.

3. Much of the material in this paragraph is adapted from "100 Arrested in Child Porn Bust," MSNBC News, August 8, 2001. Web posted at http://www.msnbc.com/news/610808.asp. Accessed October 10, 2001.

4. For an excellent overview of technology in criminal justice, see Laura J. Moriarty and David L. Carter, eds.,

Criminal Justice Technology in the Twenty-first Century (Springfield, IL: Charles C. Thomas, 1998).

5. National Law Enforcement Technology Center, electronic press release, April 7, 1995.

6. Lester D. Shubin, *Research, Testing, Upgrading Criminal Justice Technology,* National Institute of Justice Reports (Washington, D.C.: U.S. Government Printing Office, 1984), pp. 2–5.

7. Simon Dinitz, "Coping with Deviant Behavior through Technology," *Criminal Justice Research Bulletin,* Vol. 3, No. 2 (1987).

8. See, for example, Laurence P. Karper et al., "Antipsychotics, Lithium, Benzodiazepines, Beta-Blockers," in

Marc Hillbrand and Nathaniel J. Pallone, eds., *The Psychobiology of Aggression: Engines, Measurement, Control* (New York: Haworth Press, 1994), pp. 203–222.

9. Harry Soderman and John J. O'Connell, *Modern Criminal Investigation* (New York: Funk and Wagnalls, 1945), p. 41.

10. The system was invented by Lambert Adolphe Jacques Quetelet (1796–1874), a Belgian astronomer and statistician.

11. For more on Bertillon's system, see Alphonse Bertillon, *Signaletic Instructions* (New York: Werner, 1896).

12. Robert D. Foote, "Fingerprint Identification: A Survey of Present Technology, Automated Applications, and Potential for Future Development," *Criminal Justice Monograph Series,* Vol. 5, No. 2 (Huntsville, TX: Sam Houston State University Press, 1974), pp. 3–4.

13. Soderman and O'Connell, *Modern Criminal Investigation,* p. 57.

14. Ibid.

15. Francis Galton, *Finger Prints* (London: Macmillan, 1892).

16. Foote, "Fingerprint Identification," p. 1.

17. Office of Technology Assessment, *Criminal Justice: New Technologies and the Constitution: A Special Report* (Washington, D.C.: U.S. Government Printing Office, 1988), p. 18. Electro-optical systems for live fingerprint scanning were developed by Fingermatric, Inc., of White Plains, New York.

18. T. F. Wilson and P. L. Woodard, *Automated Fingerprint Identification Systems—Technology and Policy Issues* (Washington, D.C.: U.S. Department of Justice, 1987), p. 5.

19. Kristi Gulick, "Latent Prints from Human Skin," *Law and Order Magazine* Online. Web posted at http://www.lawandordermag.com/magazine/current/latentprints.html.htm. Accessed September 26, 1998.

20. Los Angeles Police Department, *Annual Report, 1985–1986,* p. 26.

21. Ibid., p. 27.

22. American National Standards Institute, *American National Standard for Information Systems—Fingerprint Identification—Data Format for Information Interchange* (New York: ANSI, 1986). Originally developed as the Proposed American National Standard Data Format for the Interchange of Fingerprint Information by the National Bureau of Standards (Washington, D.C.: NBS, 1986).

23. Dennis G. Kurre, "On-line Exchange of Fingerprint Identification Data," *FBI Law Enforcement Bulletin,* December 1987, pp. 14–16.

24. In 1998, ruling for the first time on polygraph examinations, the U.S. Supreme Court upheld the military's ban on the use of polygraph tests in criminal trials. In refusing to hear a case, Justice Clarence Thomas wrote: "[T]he aura of infallibility attending polygraph evidence can lead jurors to abandon their duty to assess credibility and guilt."

25. Details for this story come from *USA Today,* Nationline, March 16, 2000, p. 3A.

26. Francis X. Clines, "DNA Clears Virginia Man of 1982 Assault," *New York Times,* December 10, 2001.

27. U.S. Department of Justice, *Understanding DNA Evidence: A Guide for Victim Service Providers* (Washington, D.C.: DOJ, 2001).

28. John T. Sylvester and John H. Stafford, "Judicial Acceptance of DNA Profiling," *FBI Law Enforcement Bulletin,* July 1991, p. 29.

29. Edward Connors et al., *Convicted by Juries, Exonerated by Science: Case Studies in the Use of DNA Evidence to Establish Innocence after Trial* (Washington, D.C.: National Institute of Justice, 1996).

30. See Alec J. Jeffreys, Victoria Wilson, and Swee Lay Thein, "Hypervariable 'Minisatellite' Regions in Human Nature," *Nature,* No. 314 (1985), p. 67; and "Individual-Specific 'Fingerprints' of Human DNA," *Nature,* No. 316 (1985), p. 76.

31. Peter Gill, Alec J. Jeffreys, and David J. Werrett, "Forensic Application of DNA Fingerprints," *Nature,* No. 318 (1985), p. 577. See also Craig Seton, "Life for Sex Killer Who Sent Decoy to Take Genetic Test," *London Times,* January 23, 1988, p. 3. A popular account of this case, *The Blooding,* was written by crime novelist Joseph Wambaugh (New York: William Morrow, 1989).

32. Bureau of Justice Statistics, *Forensic DNA Analysis: Issues* (Washington, D.C.: BJS, 1991).

33. "Genetic Fingerprinting Convicts Rapist in U.K.," *Globe and Mail,* November 14, 1987, p. A3.

34. *Daubert* v. *Merrell Dow Pharmaceuticals, Inc.*, 509 U.S. 579, 113 S.Ct. 2786 (1993).

35. *Frye* v. *U.S.*, 54 App. D.C. 46, 47, 293 F. 1013, 1014 (1923).

36. For the application of *Daubert* to DNA technology, see Barry Sheck, "DNA and *Daubert,*" *Cardozo Law Review,* Vol. 15 (1994), p. 1959.

37. In 1999, in the case of *Kumho Tire Co.* v. *Carmichael,* 526 U.S. 137 (1999) the Court held that *Daubert* factors may also apply to the testimony of engineers and other experts who are not, strictly speaking, "scientists" and that a trial judge determining the admissibility of an engineering expert's testimony may consider one or more of the specific *Daubert* factors.

38. Violent Crime Control and Law Enforcement Act of 1994, Section 210301.

39. Connors et al., *Convicted by Juries, Exonerated by Science.*

40. The nonjury case involved a guilty plea from a defendant who had mental disabilities.

41. Stephen Strauss, "Fingerprints Leaving Fingerprints of Their Own," Simon & Schuster NewsLink, June 20, 1997.

42. National Law Enforcement Summit on DNA Technology, *Proceedings,* July 27, 2000. Web posted at http://www.ojp.usdoj.gov/nij/dnasummit/trans-5.html. Accessed March 12, 2002.

43. Richard Willing, "Inmate Genetic Testing Scrapped," *USA Today,* December 26, 2001, p. 1A.

44. William S. Sessions, "Criminal Justice Information Services: Gearing Up for the Future," *FBI Law Enforcement Bulletin,* February 1993, p. 2.

45. "The CJIS Mission." Web posted at http://www.fbi.gov/hq/cjisd/about.htm. Accessed March 15, 2002.

46. "Time Line '98," *Yahoo! Internet Life,* January 1999, p. 90. To access the database, visit http://www.publicdata.com.

47. Sessions, "Criminal Justice Information Services," pp. 181–188.

48. Office of Technology Assessment, *Criminal Justice: New Technologies and the Constitution,* p. 29.

49. Ibid., p. 29.

50. For more on the system, see Craig Stedman, "Feds to Track Sex Offenders with Database," *Computerworld,* September 2, 1996, p. 24.

51. "Saving Face," *PC Computing,* December 1988, p. 60.

52. See Dawn E. McQuiston and Roy S. Malpass, "Use of Facial Composite Systems in U.S. Law Enforcement

Agencies." Web posted at http://eyewitness.utep.edu/ Documents/McQuiston%20APLS%202000.pdf. Accessed March 5, 2002.

53. See, for example, Jeffrey S. Hormann, "Virtual Reality: The Future of Law Enforcement Training," *FBI Law Enforcement Bulletin*, July 1995, pp. 7–12.

54. See, for example, Thomas F. Rich, *The Use of Computerized Mapping Crime Control and Prevention Programs* (Washington, D.C.: National Institute of Justice, 1995).

55. Matt L. Rodriguez, "The Acquisition of High Technology Systems by Law Enforcement," *FBI Law Enforcement Bulletin*, December 1988, p. 10.

56. William L. Tafoya, "Law Enforcement beyond the Year 2000," *Futurist* (September/October 1986), pp. 33–36.

57. Ibid.

58. See Rodriguez, "The Acquisition of High Technology Systems by Law Enforcement," pp. 11–12.

59. Brian S. Akre, "Internet-Torture," Associated Press wire service, February 10, 1995.

60. Ibid.

61. Jim Schaefer and Maryanne George, "Internet User's Charges Dismissed—U.S. Criticized for Pursuing U-M Case," *Detroit Free Press* wire service, June 22, 1995.

62. James William Coleman, *The Criminal Elite: The Sociology of White Collar Crime*, 2d ed. (New York: St. Martin's Press, 1989), p. 2.

63. Edwin H. Sutherland, "White-Collar Criminality," *American Sociological Review* (February 1940), p. 12.

64. This definition combines elements of Sutherland's original terminology with the definition of *white-collar crime* found in the *Dictionary of Criminal Justice Data Terminology*, 2d ed. (Washington, D.C.: Bureau of Justice Statistics, 1981). It recognizes the fact that the socioeconomic status of today's "white-collar criminals" is not nearly as high as Sutherland imagined when he coined the term.

65. "Tennis, Anyone? Ivan Boesky Does Time," *Business Week*, April 25, 1988, p. 70.

66. Frank E. Hagan and Peter J. Benekos, "The Biggest White Collar Crime in History: The Great Savings and Loan Scandal," paper presented at the annual meeting of the American Society of Criminology, Baltimore, Maryland, 1990.

67. James Cox, "Gold Dust or Bust," *USA Today*, April 17, 1997, p. 1B.

68. "Health Executives Found Guilty of Insurance Fraud," APB Online, July 2, 1999. Web posted at http://www.apbonline.com/911/1999/07/02/hca0702_01.html. Accessed January 4, 2000.

69. *True Crimes: White Collar Crime*. Web posted at http://www.karisable.com/crwc.htm. Accessed February 12, 2002.

70. "Money Manager Frankel Is Arrested in Germany," Associated Press wire service, September 4, 1999.

71. Edwin H. Sutherland, "Is White Collar Crime Crime?" *American Sociological Review* (April 1945), pp. 132–139.

72. *White Collar Crime*, BJS Special Report (Washington, D.C.: Bureau of Justice Statistics, 1987).

73. Ibid., p. 1.

74. Stephen Pizzo, Mary Fricker, and Paul Muolo, *Inside Job: The Looting of America's Savings and Loans* (New York: McGraw-Hill, 1989), p. 284.

75. See Gilbert Geis and Robert F. Meier, eds., *White Collar Crime*, 2d ed. (New York: Free Press, 1977).

76. "The *Venture* Survey: Crime and Your Business," *Venture* (February 1986), p. 26.

77. Ibid.

78. Ibid.

79. Gary S. Green, *Occupational Crime* (Chicago: Nelson-Hall, 1990), p. 16.

80. Ibid.

81. James William Coleman, *The Criminal Elite: The Sociology of White Collar Crime* (New York: St. Martin's Press, 1989), p. 9.

82. Ibid.

83. William J. Chambliss, *Exploring Criminology* (New York: Macmillan, 1988), p. 64.

84. See, for example, M. David Ermann and Richard J. Lundman, eds., *Corporate and Government Deviance: Problems of Organizational Behavior in Contemporary Society*, 3d ed. (New York: Oxford University Press, 1987); and Stuart L. Hills, ed., *Corporate Violence: Injury and Death for Profit* (Totowa, NJ: Roman and Littlefield, 1987).

85. Gilbert Geis, "The Heavy Electrical Equipment Antitrust Cases of 1961," in Gilbert Geis and Robert F. Meier, eds., *White Collar Crime*, 2d ed. (New York: Free Press, 1977), p. 123.

86. Coleman, *The Criminal Elite*, p. 34.

87. "Ford Pinto Scored in *Coast* Magazine on Peril from Fires," *New York Times*, August 11, 1977.

88. Coleman, *The Criminal Elite*, p. 41.

89. As cited in Gwynn Nettler, *Criminology Lessons* (Cincinnati: Anderson, 1989), p. 116.

90. "After Drexel: Are Raiders Next Target?" *USA Today*, December 23, 1988, p. B1.

91. Ibid.

92. "Vitamins Price-Fixing Antitrust Litigation." Web posted at http://www.lchb.com/vitamins.htm. Accessed January 5, 2000.

93. Tom Bradford, "$12 Million High-Tech Heist One of Largest Ever," *USA Today*, May 19, 1995, p. 3A.

94. "Are You Vulnerable to Cybercrime?" *USA Today*, February 20, 1995, p. 3B.

95. "Most Wanted Hacker Released from Prison," *USA Today* online, January 21, 2000. Web posted at http://www.usatoday.com/news/ndsfri02.htm. Accessed January 21, 2000.

96. Elinor Abreu, "Kevin Mitnick Bares All," *Industry Standard*, September 28, 2000. Web posted at http://www.nwfusion.com/news/2000/0928mitnick.html. Accessed January 26, 2002.

97. Richard Zitrin, "Woman Charged with Online Prostitution," APB Online, June 10, 1999. Web posted at http://www.apbonline.com/911/1999/06/10/hooker0610_01.html. Accessed June 19, 1999.

98. Ibid.

99. Software Information Industry Association, *Report on Global Software Piracy 2000*. Web posted at http://www.siia.net/piracy/pubs/piracy2000.pdf. Accessed April 1, 2002.

100. Nikola Krastev, "East: Many Nations Lack Effective Computer Crime Laws," Radio Free Europe, December 19, 2000. Web posted at http://www.rferl.org/nca/features/2000/12/15122000153858.asp. Accessed April 8, 2002.

101. Ibid.

102. "'Love Bug' Prompts New Philippine Law," *USA Today*, June 14, 2000.

103. "Cybercrime Treaty Gets Green Light," BBC News online, November 12, 2001.

104. Details for this section come from the Council of Europe, Convention on Cybercrime signatories Web page, http://conventions.coe.int. Accessed April 8, 2002.

105. For suggested computer crime categories, see Peter Grabosky, "Computer Crime: A Criminological Overview," paper presented at the Workshop on Crimes Related to the Computer Network, Tenth United Nations Congress on the Prevention of Crime and the Treatment of Offenders, Vienna, Austria, April 15, 2000. Web posted at http://www.aic.gov.au/conferences/other/compcrime/computercrime.pdf. Accessed January 12, 2002. Also see David L. Carter, "Computer Crime Categories: How Techno-Criminals Operate," *FBI Law Enforcement Journal,* July 1995, pp. 21–26.

106. Grabosky, "Computer Crime."

107. Kevin Johnson, "Hijackers' E-mails Sifted for Clues," *USA Today,* October 11, 2001.

108. "Invasion of the Data Snatchers!" *Time,* September 26, 1988, pp. 62–67.

109. "Virus Infects NASA, Defense, University Computer Systems," *Fayetteville (N.C.) Observer-Times,* November 4, 1988, p. 19A.

110. *Raleigh News and Observer,* April 27, 1990.

111. "First HTML Virus Detected," Andover News Network. Web posted at http://www.andovernews.com/cgi-bin/news_story.pl?95529/topstories. Accessed January 6, 2000.

112. Sophos Antivirus, "The First JAVA Virus." Web posted at http://www.sophos.com/virusinfo/articles/java.html. Accessed January 5, 2002.

113. *Hancock v. State,* 402 S.W.2d 906 (Tex. Crim. Appl. 1966).

114. Stanley S. Arkin et al., *Prevention and Prosecution of Computer and High Technology Crime* (New York: Matthew Bender, 1988), §3.05.

115. The Computer Fraud and Abuse Act (Public Law no. 98-473, Title II, Section 2102 (a), October 12, 1984). The act was substantially revised in 1986 and again in 1988.

116. William J. Hughes, "Congress versus Computer Crime," *Information Executive,* Vol. 1, No. 1 (fall 1988), pp. 30–32.

117. Because of significant modifications introduced into the legislation in 1986, the law is often referred to as the Computer Fraud and Abuse Act of 1986.

118. 18 U.S.C. 2311.

119. 18 U.S.C. 641.

120. 18 U.S.C. 1905.

121. 17 U.S.C. 101, 117.

122. Public Law 106-160.

123. Public Law 105-304.

124. Public Law 105-147.

125. 18 U.S.C. 1341, 1343, and 1344.

126. N.Y. Penal Law, sections 156.30 and 156.35.

127. Some of the information in this paragraph comes from Amy Herdy, "One Woman, 375 names, 31 Charges," *St. Petersburg Times,* March 23, 2000. Web posted at http://www.sptimes.com/News/032300/TampaBay/One_woman__375_names_.shtml. Accessed March 1, 2002.

128. "The Week in Review," *St. Petersburg Times,* November 19, 2000. Web posted at http://www.sptimes.com/News/111900/Northoftampa/The_week_in_review_.shtml. Accessed March 1, 2002.

129. 18 U.S.C. Section 1028.

130. "Three Strikes, He's Out: Woods' Identity Thief Gets 200 Years-to-Life," Associated Press wire service, April 28, 2001.

131. Much of the information in this paragraph is adapted from National White Collar Crime Center, *WCC Issue: Identity Theft.* Web posted at http://www.nw3c.org/papers/Identity_Theft.pdf. Accessed April 24, 2002.

132. eEurope, *One World: Smart Cards,* p. 2. Web posted at http://eeurope-smartcards.org/Smart20Cards.pdf.

133. Thomas E. Kroll, "Year in Review, 1998: Business and Industrial Review—Microelectronics," *Encyclopedia Britannica 2000,* Deluxe Edition on CD-ROM.

134. As reported on CNN-TV, December 27, 2001.

135. Foreign Relations Authorization Act, 22 U.S.C. 2656 f (d)(2).

136. In the words of the act: "The term 'terrorism' means premeditated, politically motivated violence perpetrated against noncombatant targets by subnational groups or clandestine agents." 22 U.S.C. 2656 f (d)(2).

137. Federal Bureau of Investigation, Counterterrorism Section, *Terrorism in the United States, 1987* (Washington, D.C.: FBI, 1987), in which the full definition offered here can be found. See also *FBI Policy and Guidelines: Counterterrorism.* Web posted at http://www.fbi.gov/contact/fo/jackson/cntrterr.htm (accessed January 15, 2002), which offers a somewhat less formal definition of the term.

138. Gwynn Nettler, *Killing One Another* (Cincinnati: Anderson, 1982).

139. Ibid., p. 253.

140. Adapted from *FBI Policy and Guidelines: Counterterrorism.*

141. Ibid.

142. The death penalty was imposed for the first-degree murders of eight federal law enforcement agents who were at work in the Murrah Building at the time of the bombing. While the killings violated Oklahoma law, only the killings of the federal agents fell under federal law, which makes such murders capital offenses.

143. Jo Thomas, "Oklahoma Prosecutor to Seek Death Penalty for Bombing," *New York Times,* September 6, 2001.

144. Michael E. Wiggins, "Rationale and Justification for Right-Wing Terrorism: A Politico-Social Analysis of the *Turner Diaries,*" paper presented at the annual meeting of the American Society of Criminology, Atlanta, Georgia, October 1986.

145. Bruce Frankel, "Sheik Guilty in Terror Plot," *USA Today,* October 2, 1995, p. 1A. Sheik Abdel-Rahman and codefendant El Sayyid Nosair were both sentenced to life in prison. Other defendants received sentences of between 25 and 57 years in prison. See Sascha Brodsky, "Terror Verdicts Denounced," United Press International wire service, January 17, 1996.

146. See Steven Emerson, *American Jihad: The Terrorists Living Among Us* (NY: The Free Press, 2002).

147. Catherine Wilson, "Two Accused in Nuke Sale Sting," Associated Press wire service, June 30, 1997.

148. See Barry Collin, "The Future of Cyberterrorism," *Crime and Justice International,* March 1997, pp. 15–18.

149. John Arquilla and David Ronfeldt, *The Advent of Netwar* (Santa Monica, CA: RAND, 1996).

150. Mark M. Pollitt, "Cyberterrorism: Fact or Fancy?" *Proceedings of the 20th National Information Systems Security Conference,* October 1997, pp. 285–289.

151. As described in Dorothy E. Denning, "Activism, Hactivism, and Cyberterrorism: The Internet as a Tool for Influencing Foreign Policy," paper presented at the Internet and International Systems: Information Technology and American Foreign Policy Decisionmaking Workshop, San Francisco, December 10, 1999.

152. Critical Infrastructure Assurance Office, *Defending America's Cyberspace: National Plan for Information Systems Protection,* Version 1.0 (Washington, D.C.: U.S. Government Printing Office, 2000), from which this sentence is adapted.

153. Denning, "Activism, Hactivism, and Cyberterrorism."

154. "U.S. Plans New Secure Government Internet," Associated Press wire service, October 11, 2001.

155. The actual language of the act sets a standard for metal detectors through the use of a "security exemplar" made of 3.7 ounces of stainless steel in the shape of a handgun. Weapons made of other substances might still pass the test provided that they could be detected by metal detectors adjusted to that level of sensitivity. See "Bill Is Signed Barring Sale or Manufacture of Plastic Guns," *Criminal Justice Newsletter,* Vol. 19, No. 23 (December 1, 1988), pp. 4–5.

156. National Commission on Terrorism, *Countering the Changing Threat of International Terrorism* (Washington, D.C.: U.S. Department of State, 2000).

157. 8 U.S.C. 1-1599.

158. Information in this paragraph comes from U.S. Department of State, *Patterns of Global Terrorism 2000.* Web posted at http://www.state.gov/s/ct/rls/pgtrpt/2000/. Accessed January 2, 2002.

159. Office of Technology Assessment, *Criminal Justice: New Technologies and the Constitution,* p. 51.

160. 47 U.S.C. 151 et seq.

161. Randall Mikkelsen, "U.S. 'Cybersmut' Suit Gives Glimpse of Internet Future," Reuters wire service, March 21, 1996.

162. Randall Mikkelsen, "U.S. Court Blocks New Internet-Indecency Law," Reuters wire service, June 12, 1996.

163. *Reno* v. *ACLU* (1997), 117 S.Ct. 2329.

164. *Kyllo* v. *U.S.,* 533 U.S. 27 (2001).

165. Ibid., para. 39.

166. Office of Technology Assessment, *Criminal Justice: New Technologies and the Constitution,* p. 20.

167. *U.S.* v. *Mackey,* 387 F.Sup 1121, 1125 (D. Nev. 1975).

168. See Louis F. Solimine, "Safeguarding the Accuracy of FBI Records: A Review of *Menard* v. *Saxbe* and *Tarlton* v. *Saxbe,*" *University of Cincinnati Law Review,* Vol. 44 (1975), pp. 325, 327.

169. Office of Technology Assessment, *Criminal Justice: New Technologies and the Constitution,* p. 47.

170. The Bail Reform Act of 1996 allowed magistrates to consider elements of the offender's background, such as family ties and prior offenses, in setting bail. Factors cited by the act were based in part on social scientific findings at the time.

171. See U.S. Sentencing Commission, *Sentencing Guidelines and Policy Statements,* submitted to Congress April 13, 1987, with amendments submitted April 13, 1987.

172. *Estelle* v. *Smith,* 451 U.S. 454 (1981).

173. *Schmerber* v. *California,* 384 U.S. 757, 86 S.Ct. 1826 (1966).

174. *Rochin* v. *California,* 342 U.S. 165 (1952).

175. For a discussion of such techniques, see Patrick Moynihan, "Social Science and the Courts," *Public Interest,* No. 54 (winter 1979), pp. 12–31.

176. Arnold Urken and Stephen Traflet, "Optimal Jury Design," *Jurimetrics,* Vol. 24 (spring 1984), p. 218.

177. "Stalkers Get Electronic Guard," Associated Press wire service, September 20, 1992.

178. Office of Technology Assessment, *Criminal Justice: New Technologies and the Constitution,* p. 43.

179. *Holt* v. *Sarver,* 309 F.Sup 362 (E.D. Ark. 1970).

180. *Bearden* v. *Georgia,* 461 U.S. 660 (1983).

The first ten amendments to the U.S. Constitution are known as the Bill of Rights. These amendments, ratified in 1791, have special relevance to criminal justice and are reproduced here. The entire U.S. Constitution can be found online at http://www.prenhall.com/ schmalleger/constitution/constit.html. You can save it to your desktop or easily print the file.

Amendment I

Congress shall make no law respecting an establishment of religion, or prohibiting the free exercise thereof; or abridging the freedom of speech, or of the press; or the right of the people peaceably to assemble, and to petition the Government for a redress of grievances.

Amendment II

A well regulated Militia, being necessary to the security of a free State, the right of the people to keep and bear Arms, shall not be infringed.

Amendment III

No Soldier shall, in time of peace be quartered in any house, without the consent of the Owner, nor in time of war, but in a manner to be prescribed by law.

Amendment IV

The right of the people to be secure in their persons, houses, papers, and effects, against unreasonable searches and seizures, shall not be violated, and no Warrants shall issue, but upon probable cause, supported by Oath or affirmation, and particularly describing the place to be searched, and the persons or things to be seized.

Amendment V

No person shall be held to answer for a capital, or otherwise infamous crime, unless on a presentment or indictment of a Grand Jury, except in cases arising in the land or naval forces, or in the Militia, when in actual service in time of War or public danger; nor shall any person be subject for the same offence to be twice put in jeopardy of life or limb; nor shall be compelled in any criminal case to be a witness against himself, nor be deprived of life, liberty, or property, without due process of law; nor shall private property be taken for public use, without just compensation.

Amendment VI

In all criminal prosecutions, the accused shall enjoy the right to a speedy and public trial, by an impartial jury of the State and district wherein the crime shall have been committed, which district shall have been previously ascertained by law, and to be informed of the nature and cause of the accusation; to be confronted with the witnesses against him; to have compulsory process for obtaining witnesses in his favor, and to have the Assistance of Counsel for his defence.

Amendment VII

In suits at common law, where the value in controversy shall exceed twenty dollars, the right of trial by jury shall be preserved, and no fact tried by a jury, shall be otherwise reexamined in any Court of the United States, than according to the rules of the common law.

Amendment VIII

Excessive bail shall not be required, nor excessive fines imposed, nor cruel and unusual punishments inflicted.

Amendment IX

The enumeration in the Constitution, of certain rights, shall not be construed to deny or disparage others retained by the people.

Amendment X

The powers not delegated to the United States by the Constitution, nor prohibited by it to the States, are reserved to the States respectively, or to the people.

AACAP	American Academy of Child and Adolescent Psychiatry	DAWN	Drug Abuse Warning Network
ABA	American Bar Association	DCCTAP	Drug Court Clearinghouse and Technical Assistance Project (American University)
ACA	American Correctional Association	DEA	Drug Enforcement Administration
ACJS	Academy of Criminal Justice Sciences	DES	data encryption standard
ACLU	American Civil Liberties Union	DIRPPA	Drug-Induced Rape Prevention and Punishment Act (1996)
ADAM	Arrestee Drug Abuse Monitoring		
ADD	attention deficit disorder	DNA	deoxyribonucleic acid
ADMAX	administrative maximum	DPIC	Death Penalty Information Center
AEDPA	Antiterrorism and Effective Death Penalty Act (1996)	DPRC	Drug Policy Research Center (RAND Corporation)
AFDA	Association of Federal Defense Attorneys	DUF	Drug Use Forecasting
AFIS	automated fingerprint identification system	DUI	driving under the influence (of alcohol or drugs)
AIDS	acquired immunodeficiency syndrome		
AJA	American Jail Association	DWI	driving while intoxicated
ALI	American Law Institute	ECPA	Electronic Communications Privacy Act (1986)
AO	Administrative Office (of the United States Courts)	Europol	European Police Office
APPA	American Probation and Parole Association	FATS	firearms training simulation
ASC	American Society of Criminology	FBI	Federal Bureau of Investigation
ASIS	American Society for Industrial Security	FCC	federal correctional complex
AWDWWITK	assault with a deadly weapon with intent to kill	FCI	federal correctional institution
		FDA	Food and Drug Administration
BCS	British Crime Survey	FDSS	Federal-wide Drug Seizure System
BJA	Bureau of Justice Assistance	FGC	family group conference
BJS	Bureau of Justice Statistics	FINCEN	Financial Crimes Enforcement Network
BOP	Bureau of Prisons	FLETC	Federal Law Enforcement Training Center
BWS	battered women's syndrome	FLIR	forward-looking infrared
CAPS	Chicago's Alternative Policing Strategy	FOP	Fraternal Order of Police
CAT	computer-aided transcription	FPC	federal prison camp
CBT	computer-based training	FTCA	Federal Tort Claims Act
CCA	Corrections Corporation of America	GBMI	guilty but mentally ill
CCE	Continuing Criminal Enterprise (statute)	GGI	guided group interaction
CCJJDP	Coordinating Council on Juvenile Justice and Delinquency Prevention	HEUNI	European Institute for Crime Prevention and Control
CDA	Communications Decency Act (1996)	HIDTA	high-intensity drug-trafficking area
CDC	Centers for Disease Control and Prevention	HIV	human immunodeficiency virus
CFAA	Computer Fraud and Abuse Act (1984)	IACP	International Association of Chiefs of Police
CIA	Central Intelligence Agency	IAD	internal affairs division
CIC	children in custody	IAFIS	integrated automated fingerprint identification system (FBI)
CJA	Criminal Justice Act (England)		
CJDLC	Criminal Justice Distance Learning Consortium	IDRA	Insanity Defense Reform Act (1984)
		ILEA	International Law Enforcement Academy
CJIS	Criminal Justice Information Services (FBI)	INTERPOL	International Criminal Police Organization
CLEA	Commission on Accreditation for Law Enforcement Agencies	IPS	intensive probation supervision
		ISC	International Society for Criminology
CODIS	Combined DNA Index System (FBI)	IVS	International Victim Survey (U.N.)
COPS	Community Oriented Policing Services	JIC	Justice Information Center
CPO	Certified Protection Officer	JJDP	Juvenile Justice and Delinquency Prevention Act (1974)
CPOP	Community Police Officer Program (New York City)		
		JUSTNET	Justice Technology Information Network
CPP	Certified Protection Professional	LAPD	Los Angeles Police Department
CPTED	crime prevention through environmental design	LEAA	Law Enforcement Assistance Administration
CSA	Controlled Substances Act (1970)	LEAP	law enforcement availability pay
DARE	Drug Abuse Resistance Education	LEEP	Law Enforcement Education Program
DART	Directed Area Responsibility Teams (Houston)	LESL	Law Enforcement Standards Laboratory
		LESTN	Law Enforcement Satellite Training Network

MADD	Mothers Against Drunk Driving
MCFP	medical center for federal prisoners
MDC	metropolitan detention center
MSBP	Munchausen syndrome by proxy
MTF	Monitoring the Future (survey)
NAACP	National Association for the Advancement of Colored People
NACDL	National Association of Criminal Defense Lawyers
NADCP	National Association of Drug Court Professionals
NAP	National Assessment Program
NCAVC	National Center for the Analysis of Violent Crime
NCCD	National Council on Crime and Delinquency
NCCS	National Computer Crime Squad (FBI)
NCIC	National Crime Information Center (FBI)
NCIC 2000	National Crime Information Center 2000 (FBI)
NCIS	National Criminal Intelligence Service (England)
NCJC	National Criminal Justice Commission
NCJRS	National Criminal Justice Reference Service
NCSC	National Center for State Courts
NCTP	National Cybercrime Training Partnership
NCVS	National Crime Victimization Survey
NDAA	National District Attorneys Association
NDIS	National DNA Index System (FBI)
NETA	No Electronic Theft Act (1997)
NGCRC	National Gang Crime Research Center
NHSDA	National Household Survey on Drug Abuse
NIBRS	National Incident-Based Reporting System (FBI)
NIDA	National Institute on Drug Abuse
NIJ	National Institute of Justice
NIPC	National Infrastructure Protection Center
NLADA	National Legal Aid and Defender Association
NLECTC	National Law Enforcement and Corrections Technology Center
NLETC	National Law Enforcement Technology Center
NNICC	National Narcotics Intelligence Consumers Committee
NOBLE	National Organization of Black Law Enforcement Executives
NRA	National Rifle Association
NSA	National Sheriffs Association
NVAWS	National Violence Against Women Survey
NVC	National Victims Center
NVCAN	National Victims' Constitutional Amendment Network
NWCCC	National White Collar Crime Center
NYGC	National Youth Gang Center
NYPD	New York Police Department
OBTS	offender-based transaction statistics

OICJ	Office of International Criminal Justice (University of Illinois at Chicago)
OJARS	Office of Justice Assistance, Research, and Statistics
OJJDP	Office of Juvenile Justice and Delinquency Prevention
OLES	Office of Law Enforcement Standards
OLETC	Office of Law Enforcement Technology Commercialization
ONDCP	Office of National Drug Control Policy
PCC	Police Cadet Corps (New York City)
PCCIP	President's Commission on Critical Infrastructure Protection
PCR	police-community relations
PERF	Police Executive Research Forum
PLRA	Prison Litigation Reform Act (1996)
POST	police officer standards and training
RESTTA	Restitution Education, Specialized Training, and Technical Assistance (program)
RICO	Racketeer Influenced and Corrupt Organizations (statute)
RISE	Reintegrative Shaming Experiments (Australian Institute of Criminology)
RJC	Real Justice Conferencing (Pennsylvania)
SAMHSA	Substance Abuse and Mental Health Services Administration
SBI	State Bureau of Investigation
SEARCH	National Consortium for Justice Information and Statistics
SCU	Street Crimes Unit (New York City)
SIIA	Software Industry Information Association
SPECDA	School Program to Educate and Control Drug Abuse
SWAT	special weapons and tactics
TWGECSI	Technical Working Group for Electronic Crime Scene Investigation
UCR	Uniform Crime Reports
UNICRI	United Nations Interregional Crime and Justice Research Institute
UNOJUST	United Nations Online Justice Information System
USBP	United States Border Patrol
U.S.C.	United States Code
USNCB	United States National Central Bureau (INTERPOL)
USP	United States penitentiary
USSC	United States Sentencing Commission
VAWA	Violence Against Women Act (1994)
VCAN	Victims' Constitutional Amendment Network
VICAP	Violent Criminal Apprehension Program (FBI)
VOCA	Victims of Crime Act (1984)
VWPA	Victim and Witness Protection Act (1982)
WJIN	World Justice Information Network
WWW	World Wide Web

The 17 chapters of *Criminal Justice Today* contain hundreds of terms commonly used in the field of criminal justice. This glossary contains many more. All concepts, wherever they appear in the book, are explained whenever possible according to definitions provided by the Bureau of Justice Statistics under a mandate of the Justice System Improvement Act. That mandate was to create a consistent terminology set for use by criminal justice students, practitioners, and planners. It found its most complete expression in the *Dictionary of Criminal Justice Data Terminology*,[1] the second edition of which provides many of our definitions. Others (especially those in Chapter 2) are derived from the FBI's Uniform Crime Reporting Program and are taken from the *Uniform Crime Reporting Handbook*.[2]

Standardization is becoming increasingly important because American criminal justice agencies, justice practitioners, and involved citizens now routinely communicate over vast distances about the criminal justice system itself. For communications to be meaningful, a shared terminology is necessary. Standardization, however desirable, is not easy to achieve. In the words of the Bureau of Justice Statistics, "It is not possible to construct a single national standard criminal justice data terminology where every term always means the same thing in all of its appearances. However, it is possible and necessary to standardize the language that represents basic categorical distinctions."[3] Although this glossary should be especially valuable to the student who will one day work in the criminal justice system, it should also prove beneficial to anyone seeking a greater insight into that system.

1983 lawsuit   A civil suit brought under Title 42, Section 1983, of the U.S. Code against anyone who denies others their constitutional right to life, liberty, or property without due process of law.

abused child   A child who has been physically, sexually, or mentally abused. Most states also consider a child who is forced into delinquent activity by a parent or guardian to be abused.

acquittal   The judgment of a court, based on a verdict of a jury or a judicial officer, that the defendant is not guilty of the offense or offenses for which he or she was tried.

actus reus   An act in violation of the law. Also, a guilty act.

adjudication   The process by which a court arrives at a decision regarding a case. Also, the resultant decision.

adjudicatory hearing   In juvenile justice usage, the fact-finding process wherein the juvenile court determines whether there is sufficient evidence to sustain the allegations in a petition.

ADMAX   Administrative maximum. The term is used by the federal government to denote ultra-high-security prisons.

admission   In corrections, the entry of an offender into the legal jurisdiction of a correctional agency or into the physical custody of a correctional facility.

adult   A person who is within the original jurisdiction of a criminal court, rather than a juvenile court, because his or her age at the time of an alleged criminal act was above a statutorily specified limit.

adversarial system   The two-sided structure under which American criminal trial courts operate that pits the prosecution against the defense. In theory, justice is done when the most effective adversary is able to convince the judge or jury that his or her perspective on the case is the correct one.

aftercare   In juvenile justice usage, the status or program membership of a juvenile who has been committed to a treatment or confinement facility, conditionally released from the facility, and placed in a supervisory or treatment program.

aggravated assault (UCR)   The unlawful, intentional inflicting, or attempted or threatened inflicting, of serious injury upon the person of another. Also, the unlawful intentional causing of serious bodily injury with or without a deadly weapon.

aggravating circumstances   Circumstances relating to the commission of a crime which cause its gravity to be greater than that of the average instance of the given type of offense. See also **mitigating circumstances.**

alias   Any name used for an official purpose that is different from a person's legal name.

alibi   A statement or contention by an individual charged with a crime that he or she was so distant when the crime was committed, or so engaged in other provable activities, that his or her participation in the commission of that crime was impossible.

alter ego rule   In some jurisdictions, a rule of law that holds that a person can only defend a third party under circumstances and only to the degree that the third party could act on his or her own behalf.

alternative sanctions   See **intermediate sanctions.**

anomie A socially pervasive condition of normlessness. Also, a disjunction between approved goals and means.

Antiterrorism Act See **USA PATRIOT Act of 2001.**

appeal Generally, the request that a court with appellate jurisdiction review the judgment, decision, or order of a lower court and set it aside (reverse it) or modify it. Also, the judicial proceedings or steps in judicial proceedings resulting from such a request.

appearance (court) The act of coming into a court and submitting to its authority.

appellant The person who contests the correctness of a court order, judgment, or other decision and who seeks review and relief in a court having appellate jurisdiction. Also, the person in whose behalf this is done.

appellate court A court whose primary function is to review the judgments of other courts and of administrative agencies.

appellate jurisdiction The lawful authority of a court to review a decision made by a lower court.

arraignment Strictly, the hearing before a court having jurisdiction in a criminal case, in which the identity of the defendant is established, the defendant is informed of the charge and of his or her rights, and the defendant is required to enter a plea. Also, in some usages, any appearance in court prior to trial in criminal proceedings.

arrest The act of taking an adult or juvenile into physical custody by authority of law for the purpose of charging the person with a criminal offense, a delinquent act, or a status offense, terminating with the recording of a specific offense.

arrest (UCR) In Uniform Crime Reports terminology, each separate instance in which a person is taken into physical custody or is notified or cited by a law enforcement officer or agency, except those relating to minor traffic violations.

arrest rate The number of arrests reported for each unit of population.

arrest warrant A document issued by a judicial officer which directs a law enforcement officer to arrest an identified person who has been accused of a specific offense.

arson The intentional damaging or destruction or attempted damaging or destruction, by means of fire or explosion, of the property of another without the consent of the owner, or of one's own property or that of another with intent to defraud.

arson (UCR) The burning or attempted burning of property, with or without the intent to defraud.

Ashurst-Sumners Act Federal legislation of 1935 which effectively ended the industrial prison era by restricting interstate commerce in prison-made goods.

assault (UCR) An unlawful attack by one person upon another. Also, the unlawful, intentional inflicting, or attempted or threatened inflicting, of injury upon the person of another.

assault on a law enforcement officer A simple or aggravated assault, in which the victim is a law enforcement officer engaged in the performance of his or her duties.

atavism A condition characterized by the existence of features thought to be common in earlier stages of human evolution.

attendant circumstances The facts surrounding an event.

attorney A person trained in the law, admitted to practice before the bar of a given jurisdiction, and authorized to advise, represent, and act for others in legal proceedings. Also called *lawyer; legal counsel.*

Auburn system A form of imprisonment developed in New York State around 1820 that depended upon mass prisons, where prisoners were held in congregate fashion and were required to remain silent. This style of imprisonment was a primary alternative to the Pennsylvania system.

backlog (court) The number of cases awaiting disposition in a court which exceeds the court's capacity for disposing of them

within the period of time considered appropriate.

bail To effect the release of an accused person from custody in return for a promise that he or she will appear at a place and time specified and will submit to the jurisdiction and judgment of the court, guaranteed by a pledge to pay to the court a specified sum of money or property if the person does not appear. Also, the money or property pledged to the court or actually deposited with the court to effect the release of a person from legal custody.

bail bond A document guaranteeing the appearance of a defendant in court as required and recording the pledge of money or property to be paid to the court if he or she does not appear, which is signed by the person to be released and anyone else acting in his or her behalf.

bail bondsman A person, usually licensed, whose business it is to effect release on bail for people charged with offenses and held in custody, by pledging to pay a sum of money if the defendant fails to appear in court as required.

bailiff The court officer whose duties are to keep order in the courtroom and to maintain physical custody of the jury.

bail revocation The court decision withdrawing the status of release on bail which was previously conferred upon a defendant.

balancing test A principle, developed by the courts and applied to the corrections arena by *Pell* v. *Procunier* (1974), which attempts to weigh the rights of an individual, as guaranteed by the Constitution, against the authority of states to make laws or otherwise restrict a person's freedom in order to protect the state's interests and its citizens.

ballistics The analysis of firearms, ammunition, projectiles, bombs, and explosives.

battered women's syndrome (BWS) I. A series of common characteristics that appear in women who are abused physically and psychologically over an extended period of time by the dominant male figure in their lives. II. A pattern of psychological symptoms that develops after somebody has lived in a battering relationship. III. A pattern of responses and perceptions presumed to be characteristic of women who have been subjected to continuous physical abuse by their mates.[4]

behavioral conditioning A psychological principle that holds that the frequency of any behavior can be increased or decreased through reward, punishment, and association with other stimuli.

bench warrant A document issued by a court directing that a law enforcement officer bring a specified person before the court. A bench warrant is usually issued for a person who has failed to obey a court order or a notice to appear.

bias crime See **hate crime.**

Bill of Rights The popular name given to the first ten amendments to the U.S. Constitution, which are considered especially important in the processing of criminal defendants.

bind over To require by judicial authority that a person promise to appear for trial, appear in court as a witness, or keep the peace. Also, the decision by a court of limited jurisdiction requiring that a person charged with a felony appear for trial on that charge in a court of general jurisdiction, as the result of a finding of probable cause at a preliminary hearing held in the court of limited jurisdiction.

Biological School A perspective on criminological thought that holds that criminal behavior has a physiological basis.

***Bivens* action** A civil suit, based upon the case of *Bivens* v. *Six Unknown Federal Agents,* brought against federal government officials for denying the constitutional rights of others.

bobbies The popular British name given to members of Sir Robert (Bob) Peel's Metropolitan Police Force.

booking A law enforcement or correctional administrative process officially recording an entry into detention after arrest and identifying the person, the place, the time, the reason for the arrest, and the arresting authority.

Bow Street Runners An early English police unit formed under the leadership of Henry Fielding, magistrate of the Bow Street region of London.

broken windows thesis A perspective on crime causation which holds that physical deterioration in an area leads to increased concerns for personal safety among residents and to higher crime rates.

Bureau of Justice Statistics (BJS) A U.S. Department of Justice agency responsible for the collection of criminal justice data, including the annual National Crime Victimization Survey.

burglary By the narrowest and oldest definition, trespassory breaking and entering of the dwelling house of another in the nighttime with the intent to commit a felony.

burglary (UCR) The unlawful entry of a structure to commit a felony or a theft. Also, the unlawful entry of any fixed structure, vehicle, or vessel used for regular residence, industry, or business, with or without force, with intent to commit a felony or larceny.

capacity (legal) The legal ability of a person to commit a criminal act. Also, the mental and physical ability to act with purpose and to be aware of the certain, probable, or possible results of one's conduct.

capacity (prison) See **prison capacity.**

capital offense A criminal offense punishable by death.

capital punishment The death penalty. Capital punishment is the most extreme of all sentencing options.

career criminal In prosecutorial and law enforcement usage, a person who has a past record of multiple arrests or convictions for serious crimes or who has an unusually large number of arrests or convictions for crimes of varying degrees of seriousness. Also called *professional criminal.*

carnal knowledge Sexual intercourse, coitus, sexual copulation. Carnal knowledge is accomplished "if there is the slightest penetration of the sexual organ of the female by the sexual organ of the male."[5]

case law The body of judicial precedent, historically built upon legal reasoning and past interpretations of statutory laws, that serves as a guide to decision making, especially in the courts.

caseload (corrections) The total number of clients registered with a correctional agency or agent on a given date or during a specified time period, often divided into active supervisory cases and inactive cases, thus distinguishing between clients with whom contact is regular and those with whom it is not. Also, the number of probation or parole clients assigned to one probation or parole officer for supervision.

caseload (court) The number of cases requiring judicial action at a certain time. Also, the number of cases acted upon in a given court during a given period.

certiorari See **writ of *certiorari.***

change of venue The movement of a case from the jurisdiction of one court to another or from one location to another within the same jurisdiction.

charge An allegation that a specified person has committed a specific offense, recorded in a functional document such as a record of an arrest, a complaint, an information or indictment, or a judgment of conviction. Also called *count.*

Chicago School A sociological approach which emphasizes demographics (the characteristics of population groups) and geographics (the mapped location of such groups relative to one another) and which sees the social disorganization that characterizes delinquency areas as a major cause of criminality and victimization.

child abuse The illegal physical, emotional, or sexual mistreatment of a child by his or her parent or guardian.

child neglect   The illegal failure by a parent or guardian to provide proper nourishment or care to a child.

circumstantial evidence   Evidence that requires interpretation or that requires a judge or jury to reach a conclusion based upon what the evidence indicates. From the close proximity of a smoking gun to the defendant, for example, the jury might conclude that she pulled the trigger.

citation (to appear)   A written order issued by a law enforcement officer directing an alleged offender to appear in a specific court at a specified time to answer a criminal charge, and not permitting forfeit of bail as an alternative to court appearance.

citizen's arrest   The taking of a person into physical custody by a witness to a crime other than a law enforcement officer for the purpose of delivering him or her to the physical custody of a law enforcement officer or agency.

civil death   The legal status of prisoners in some jurisdictions who are denied the opportunity to vote, hold public office, marry, or enter into contracts by virtue of their status as incarcerated felons. While civil death is primarily of historical interest, some jurisdictions still limit the contractual opportunities available to inmates.

civil justice   The civil law, the law of civil procedure, and the array of procedures and activities having to do with private rights and remedies sought by civil action.

civil law   The branch of modern law that governs relationships between parties.

class-action lawsuit   A lawsuit filed by one or more people on behalf of themselves and a larger group of people "who are similarly situated."[6]

Classical School   An eighteenth-century approach to crime causation and criminal responsibility that grew out of the Enlightenment and that emphasized the role of free will and reasonable punishments.

clearance (UCR)   The event in which a known occurrence of a Part I offense is followed by an arrest or another decision which indicates that the crime has been solved.

clearance rate   A traditional measure of investigative effectiveness that compares the number of crimes reported or discovered to the number of crimes solved through arrest or other means (such as the death of the suspect).

clemency   An executive or legislative action in which the severity of punishment of a single person or a group of people is reduced, the punishment is stopped, or the person or group is exempted from prosecution for certain actions.

closing argument   An oral summation of a case presented to a judge, or to a judge and jury, by the prosecution or by the defense in a criminal trial.

club drug   A synthetic psychoactive substance often found at nightclubs, bars, "raves," and dance parties. Club drugs include MDMA (ecstasy), ketamine, methamphetamine (meth), GBL, PCP, GHB, and Rohypnol.

codification   The act or process of rendering laws in written form.

cohort   A group of individuals sharing similarities of age, place of birth, and residence.

comes stabuli   A nonuniformed mounted law enforcement officer of medieval England. Early police forces were small and relatively unorganized but made effective use of local resources in the formation of posses, the pursuit of offenders, and the like.

commitment   The action of a judicial officer in ordering that a person subject to judicial proceedings be placed in a particular kind of confinement or residential facility for a specific reason authorized by law. Also, the result of the action—that is, the admission to the facility.

common law   Law originating from usage and custom rather than from written statutes. The term refers to an unwritten body of judicial opinion, originally developed by English courts, that is based upon nonstatutory customs, traditions, and precedents that help guide judicial decision making.

community-based corrections   See **community corrections**.

community corrections   The use of a variety of officially ordered program-based sanctions that permit convicted offenders to remain in the community under conditional supervision as an alternative to active prison sentences. Also called *community-based corrections.*

community court   A low-level court that focuses on quality-of-life crimes that erode a neighborhood's morale, that emphasizes problem-solving rather than punishment, and that builds upon restorative principles like community service and restitution.

community policing   "A collaborative effort between the police and the community that identifies problems of crime and disorder and involves all elements of the community in the search for solutions to these problems."[7]

community service   A sentencing alternative that requires offenders to spend at least part of their time working for a community agency.

comparative criminologist   One who studies crime and criminal justice on a cross-national level.

compelling interest   A legal concept that provides a basis for suspicionless searches when public safety is at issue. (Urinalysis tests of train engineers are an example.) It is the concept upon which the Supreme Court cases of *Skinner* v. *Railway Labor Executives' Association* (1989) and *National Treasury Employees Union* v. *Von Raab* (1989) turned. In those cases, the Court held that public safety may sometimes provide a sufficiently compelling interest to justify limiting an individual's right to privacy.

compensatory damages   Damages recovered in payment for an actual injury or economic loss.

competent to stand trial   A finding by a court, when the defendant's sanity at the time of trial is at issue, that the defendant has sufficient present ability to consult with his or her attorney with a reasonable degree of rational understanding and that the defendant has a rational as well as factual understanding of the proceedings against him or her.

complaint Generally, any accusation that a person has committed an offense, received by or originating from a law enforcement or prosecutorial agency or received by a court. Also, in judicial process usage, a formal document submitted to the court by a prosecutor, law enforcement officer, or other person, alleging that a specified person has committed a specific offense and requesting prosecution.

computer crime Any crime perpetrated through the use of computer technology. Also, any violation of a federal or state computer crime statute. Also called *cybercrime*.

computer virus A computer program designed to secretly invade systems and either modify the way in which they operate or alter the information they store. Viruses are destructive software programs that may effectively vandalize computers of all types and sizes.

concurrence The coexistence of (1) an act in violation of the law and (2) a culpable mental state.

concurrent sentence One of two or more sentences imposed at the same time, after conviction for more than one offense, and served at the same time. Also, a new sentence for a new conviction, imposed upon a person already under sentence for a previous offense, served at the same time as the previous sentence.

concurring opinion An opinion written by a judge who agrees with the conclusion reached by the majority of judges hearing a case but whose reasons for reaching that conclusion differ. Concurring opinions, which typically stem from an appellate review, are written to identify issues of precedent, logic, or emphasis that are important to the concurring judge but that were not identified by the court's majority opinion.

conditional release The release by executive decision of a prisoner from a federal or state correctional facility who has not served his or her full sentence and whose freedom is contingent upon obeying specified rules of behavior.

conditions of parole (probation) The general and special limits imposed upon an offender who is released on parole (or probation). General conditions tend to be fixed by state statute, while special conditions are mandated by the sentencing authority (court or board) and take into consideration the background of the offender and the circumstances surrounding the offense.

confinement In corrections terminology, the physical restriction of a person to a clearly defined area from which he or she is lawfully forbidden to depart and from which departure is usually constrained by architectural barriers, guards or other custodians, or both.

conflict model A criminal justice perspective that assumes that the system's components function primarily to serve their own interests. According to this theoretical framework, justice is more a product of conflicts among agencies within the system than it is the result of cooperation among component agencies.

conflict perspective A theoretical approach that holds that crime is the natural consequence of economic and other social inequities. Conflict theorists highlight the stresses which arise among and within social groups as they compete with one another for resources and for survival. The social forces which result are viewed as major determinants of group and individual behavior, including crime.

consecutive sentence One of two or more sentences imposed at the same time, after conviction for more than one offense, and served in sequence with the other sentence. Also, a new sentence for a new conviction, imposed upon a person already under sentence for a previous offense, which is added to the previous sentence, thus increasing the maximum time the offender may be confined or under supervision.

consensus model A criminal justice perspective that assumes that the system's components work together harmoniously to achieve the social product we call *justice*.

constitutive criminology The study of the process by which human beings create an ideology of crime that sustains the notion of crime as a concrete reality.

containment The aspects of the social bond and of the personality which act to prevent individuals from committing crimes and which keep them from engaging in deviance.

contempt of court Intentionally obstructing a court in the administration of justice, acting in a way calculated to lessen the court's authority or dignity, or failing to obey the court's lawful orders.

controlled substance A specifically defined bioactive or psychoactive chemical substance proscribed by law.

Controlled Substances Act (CSA) Title II of the Comprehensive Drug Abuse Prevention and Control Act of 1970, which established schedules classifying psychoactive drugs according to their degree of psychoactivity.

conviction The judgment of a court, based on the verdict of a jury or judicial officer or on the guilty plea or *nolo contendere* plea of the defendant, that the defendant is guilty of the offense with which he or she has been charged.

corporate crime A violation of a criminal statute by a corporate entity or by its executives, employees, or agents acting on behalf of and for the benefit of the corporation, partnership, or other form of business entity.[8]

corpus delicti The facts that show that a crime has occurred. The term literally means "the body of the crime."

correctional agency A federal, state, or local criminal or juvenile justice agency, under a single administrative authority, whose principal functions are the intake screening, supervision, custody, confinement, treatment, or presentencing or predisposition investigation of alleged or adjudicated adult offenders, youthful offenders, delinquents, or status offenders.

corrections A generic term that includes all government agencies, facilities, programs, procedures, personnel, and techniques concerned with the intake, custody, confinement, supervision, treatment, and presentencing and predisposition investigation of alleged or adjudicated adult offenders, youthful offenders, delinquents, and status offenders.

corruption   See **police corruption**.

Cosa Nostra   A secret criminal organization of Sicilian origin. Also called *Mafia*.

counsel (legal)   See **attorney**.

count (offense)   See **charge**.

court   An agency or unit of the judicial branch of government, authorized or established by statute or constitution and consisting of one or more judicial officers, which has the authority to decide upon cases, controversies in law, and disputed matters of fact brought before it.

court calendar   The court schedule; the list of events comprising the daily or weekly work of a court, including the assignment of the time and place for each hearing or other item of business or the list of matters which will be taken up in a given court term. Also called *docket*.

court clerk   An elected or appointed court officer responsible for maintaining the written records of the court and for supervising or performing the clerical tasks necessary for conducting judicial business. Also, any employee of a court whose principal duties are to assist the court clerk in performing the clerical tasks necessary for conducting judicial business.

court disposition   I. For statistical reporting purposes, generally, the judicial decision terminating proceedings in a case before judgment is reached. II. The judgment. III. The outcome of judicial proceedings and the manner in which the outcome was arrived at.

court-martial   A military court convened by senior commanders under the authority of the Uniform Code of Military Justice for the purpose of trying a member of the armed forces accused of a violation of the code.

court of last resort   The court authorized by law to hear the final appeal on a matter.

court of record   A court in which a complete and permanent record of all proceedings or specified types of proceedings is kept.

court order   A mandate, command, or direction issued by a judicial officer in the exercise of his or her judicial authority.

court probation   A criminal court requirement that an offender fulfill specified conditions of behavior in lieu of a sentence to confinement, but without assignment to a probation agency's supervisory caseload.

court reporter   A person present during judicial proceedings who records all testimony and other oral statements made during the proceedings.

courtroom work group   The professional courtroom actors, including judges, prosecuting attorneys, defense attorneys, public defenders, and others who earn a living serving the court.

credit card fraud   The use or attempted use of a credit card to obtain goods or services with the intent to avoid payment.

crime   Conduct in violation of the criminal laws of a state, the federal government, or a local jurisdiction, for which there is no legally acceptable justification or excuse. Also, an act committed or omitted in violation of a law forbidding or commanding it, for which the possible penalties for an adult upon conviction include incarceration, for which a corporation can be penalized by fine or forfeit, or for which a juvenile can be adjudged delinquent or transferred to criminal court for prosecution.

crime-control model   A criminal justice perspective that emphasizes the efficient arrest and conviction of criminal offenders.

Crime Index (UCR)   An inclusive measure of the violent and property crime categories, or Part I offenses, of the *Uniform Crime Reports*. In UCR terminology, a set of numbers indicating the volume, fluctuation, and distribution of crimes reported to local law enforcement agencies, for the United States as a whole and for its geographic subdivisions, based on counts of reported occurrences of UCR index crimes.

crime rate   The number of Crime Index offenses reported for each unit of population.

criminal homicide (UCR)   The act of causing the death of another person without legal justification or excuse.

criminal incident   In National Crime Victimization Survey terminology, a criminal event involving one or more victims and one or more offenders.

criminalist   A police crime-scene analyst or laboratory worker versed in criminalistics.

criminalistics   The use of technology in the service of criminal investigation; the application of scientific techniques to the detection and evaluation of criminal evidence. Also, "the professional and scientific discipline dedicated to the recognition, collection, identification, and individualization of physical evidence and the application of the natural sciences to the matters of the law."[9]

criminal justice   In the strictest sense, the criminal (penal) law, the law of criminal procedure, and the array of procedures and activities having to do with the enforcement of this body of law. In its broadest sense, the aspects of social justice that concern violations of the criminal law.

criminal justice system   The aggregate of all operating and administrative or technical support agencies that perform criminal justice functions. The basic divisions of the operational aspects of criminal justice are law enforcement, courts, and corrections.

criminal law   The branch of modern law that concerns itself with offenses committed against society, its members, their property, and the social order. Also called *penal law*.

criminal negligence   Behavior in which a person fails to reasonably perceive substantial and unjustifiable risks of dangerous consequences.

criminal proceedings The regular and orderly steps, as directed or authorized by statute or a court of law, taken to determine whether an adult accused of a crime is guilty or not guilty.

criminology The scientific study of the causes and prevention of crime and the rehabilitation and punishment of offenders.

cruel and unusual punishment Punishment involving torture or a lingering death or the infliction of unnecessary and wanton pain.

culpability Blameworthiness; responsibility in some sense for an event or situation deserving of moral blame. Also, in Model Penal Code usage, a state of mind on the part of one who is committing an act which makes him or her potentially subject to prosecution for that act.

cultural defense A defense to a criminal charge in which the defendant's culture is taken into account in judging his or her culpability.

cultural pluralism See **multiculturalism.**

curtilage In legal usage, the area surrounding a residence that can reasonably be said to be a part of the residence for Fourth Amendment purposes.

custody The legal or physical control of a person or a thing. Also, the legal, supervisory, or physical responsibility for a person or a thing.

cybercrime See **computer crime.**

cyberterrorism A form of terrorism that makes use of high technology, especially computers and the Internet, in the planning and carrying out of terrorist attacks.

danger law A law intended to prevent the pretrial release of criminal defendants judged to represent a danger to others in the community.

dangerousness The likelihood that a given individual will later harm society or others. Dangerousness is often measured in terms of recidivism, or as the likelihood of additional crime commission within five years following arrest or release from confinement.

dark figure of crime Crime that is not reported to the police and that remains unknown to officials.

data encryption The encoding of computerized information.

date rape Unlawful forced sexual intercourse with a female against her will that occurs within the context of a dating relationship.

***Daubert* standard** A test of scientific acceptability applicable to the gathering of evidence in criminal cases.

deadly force Force likely to cause death or great bodily harm. Also, "the intentional use of a firearm or other instrument resulting in a high probability of death."[10]

deadly weapon An instrument designed to inflict serious bodily injury or death or capable of being used for such a purpose.

deconstructionist theory One of the emerging approaches which challenge existing criminological perspectives to debunk them and which work toward replacing them with concepts more applicable to the postmodern era.

decriminalization The redefinition of certain previously criminal behaviors into regulated activities that become "ticketable" rather than "arrestable."

defendant A person formally accused of an offense by the filing in court of a charging document.

defense (to a criminal charge) Evidence and arguments offered by a defendant and his or her attorney to show why that person should not be held liable for a criminal charge.

defense attorney See **defense counsel.**

defense counsel A licensed trial lawyer, hired or appointed to conduct the legal defense of a person accused of a crime and to represent him or her before a court of law. Also called *defense attorney.*

defensible space theory The belief that an area's physical features may be modified and structured so as to reduce crime rates in that area and to lower the fear of victimization which residents experience.

delinquency In the broadest usage, juvenile actions or conduct in violation of criminal law, juvenile status offenses, and other juvenile misbehavior.

delinquent A juvenile who has been adjudged by a judicial officer of a juvenile court to have committed a delinquent act.

delinquent act An act committed by a juvenile for which an adult could be prosecuted in a criminal court, but for which a juvenile can be adjudicated in a juvenile court or prosecuted in a court having criminal jurisdiction if the juvenile court transfers jurisdiction. Generally, a felony- or misdemeanor-level offense in states employing those terms.

delinquent child A child who has engaged in activity that would be considered a crime if the child were an adult. The term *delinquent* is applied to such a child to avoid the stigma associated with the term *criminal.*

dependent child A juvenile over whom a juvenile court has assumed jurisdiction and legal control because his or her care by a parent, guardian, or custodian has not met a legal standard of proper care. Also, a child who has no parents or whose parents are unable to care for him or her.

design capacity The number of inmates a prison was intended to hold when it was built or modified. Also called *bed capacity.*

detainee Usually, a person held in local, very short-term confinement while awaiting consideration for pretrial release or a first appearance for arraignment.

detention The legally authorized confinement of a person subject to criminal or juvenile court proceedings, until the point of commitment to a correctional facility or until release.

detention hearing In juvenile justice usage, a hearing by a judicial officer of a juvenile court to determine whether a juvenile is to be detained, is to continue to be detained, or is to be released while juvenile proceedings are pending.

determinate sentencing A model of criminal punishment in which an offender is given a fixed term that may be reduced by good time or earned time. Under the model, for example, all offenders convicted of the same degree of burglary would be sentenced to the same length of time behind bars. Also called *fixed sentencing.*

deterrence A goal of criminal sentencing that seeks to inhibit criminal behavior through the fear of punishment.

deviance A violation of social norms defining appropriate or proper behavior under a particular set of circumstances. Deviance often includes criminal acts. Also called *deviant behavior.*

diminished capacity A defense based upon claims of a mental condition that may be insufficient to exonerate the defendant of guilt but that may be relevant to specific mental elements of certain crimes or degrees of crime. Also called *diminished responsibility.*

directed patrol A police management strategy designed to increase the productivity of patrol officers through the scientific analysis and evaluation of patrol techniques.

direct evidence Evidence that, if believed, directly proves a fact. Eyewitness testimony and videotaped documentation account for the majority of all direct evidence heard in the criminal courtroom.

direct-supervision jail A temporary confinement facility that eliminates many of the traditional barriers between inmates and correctional staff. Physical barriers in direct-supervision jails are far less common than in traditional jails, allowing staff members the opportunity for greater interaction with, and control over, residents. Also called *new-generation jail; podular-direct jail.*

discharge To release from confinement or supervision or to release from a legal status imposing an obligation upon the subject person.

discretion See **police discretion.**

disposition The action by a criminal or juvenile justice agency which signifies that a portion of the justice process is complete and that jurisdiction is terminated or transferred to another agency or which signifies that a decision has been reached on one aspect of a case and a different aspect comes under consideration, requiring a different kind of decision.

dispositionary hearing The final stage in the processing of adjudicated juveniles, in which a decision is made on the form of treatment or penalty that should be imposed upon the child.

dispute-resolution center An informal hearing place designed to mediate interpersonal disputes without resorting to the more formal arrangements of criminal trial courts.

district attorney (DA) See **prosecutor.**

diversion The official suspension of criminal or juvenile proceedings against an alleged offender at any point after a recorded justice system intake, but before the entering of a judgment, and referral of that person to a treatment or care program administered by a nonjustice or private agency. Also, release without referral.

DNA profiling The use of biological residue, found at the scene of a crime, for genetic comparisons in aiding the identification of criminal suspects.

docket See **court calendar.**

domestic terrorism The unlawful use of force or violence by a group or an individual who is based and operates entirely within the United States and its territories without foreign direction and whose acts are directed at elements of the U.S. government or population.[11]

double jeopardy A common law and constitutional prohibition against a second trial for the same offense.

drug Any chemical substance defined by social convention as bioactive or psychoactive.

drug abuse Illicit drug use that results in social, economic, psychological, or legal problems for the user.[12]

drug court A special state, county, or municipal court that offers first-time substance-abuse offenders judicially mandated and court-supervised treatment alternatives to prison.

drug czar The popular name for the head of the Office of National Drug Control Policy (ONDCP), a federal Cabinet-level position that was created during the Reagan presidency to organize federal drug-fighting efforts.

drug-law violation The unlawful sale, purchase, distribution, manufacture, cultivation, transport, possession, or use of a controlled or prohibited drug. Also, the attempt to commit one of these acts.

due process A right guaranteed by the Fifth, Sixth, and Fourteenth Amendments of the U.S. Constitution and generally understood, in legal contexts, to mean the due course of legal proceedings according to the rules and forms established for the protection of individual rights.

due process model A criminal justice perspective that emphasizes individual rights at all stages of justice system processing.

electronic evidence Information and data of investigative value that are stored in or transmitted by an electronic device.[13]

element (of a crime) I. Any conduct, circumstance, condition, or state of mind which, in combination with other conduct, circumstances, conditions, or states of mind, constitutes an unlawful act. II. One of the basic components of a crime. III. In a specific crime, one of the essential features of that crime as specified by law or statute.

embezzlement The misappropriation, or illegal disposal, of legally entrusted property by the person to whom it was entrusted, with the intent to defraud the legal owner or the intended beneficiary.

emergency search A search conducted by the police without a warrant, which is justified on the basis of some immediate and overriding need, such as public safety, the likely escape of a dangerous suspect, or the removal or destruction of evidence.

entrapment An improper or illegal inducement to crime by agents of enforcement. Also, a defense that may be raised when such inducements occur.

equity A sentencing principle, based upon concerns with social equality, that holds that similar crimes should be punished with the same degree of severity, regardless of the social or personal characteristics of the offenders.

espionage The "gathering, transmitting, or losing"[14] of information related to the national defense in such a manner that the information becomes available to enemies of the United States and may be used to their advantage.

ethnocentric Holding a belief in the superiority of one's own social or ethnic group and culture.

ethnocentrism The phenomenon of "culture-centeredness," by which one uses one's own culture as a benchmark against which to judge all other patterns of behavior.

European Police Office (Europol) The integrated police-intelligence gathering and dissemination arm of the member nations of the European Union.

evidence Anything useful to a judge or jury in deciding the facts of a case. Evidence may take the form of witness testimony, written documents, videotapes, magnetic media, photographs, physical objects, and so on.

exclusionary rule The understanding, based on Supreme Court precedent, that incriminating information must be seized according to constitutional specifications of due process, or it will not be allowed as evidence in a criminal trial.

excuse A legal defense in which the defendant claims that some personal condition or circumstance at the time of the act was such that he or she should not be held accountable under the criminal law.

exemplary damages. See **punitive damages.**

Exemplary Projects Program An initiative, sponsored by the Law Enforcement Assistance Administration, designed to recognize outstanding innovative efforts to combat crime and to provide assistance to crime victims.

expert system Computer hardware and software which attempts to duplicate the decision-making processes used by skilled investigators in the analysis of evidence and

in the recognition of patterns which such evidence might represent.

expert witness A person who has special knowledge and skills recognized by the court as relevant to the determination of guilt or innocence. Unlike lay witnesses, expert witnesses may express opinions or draw conclusions in their testimony.

ex post facto Latin for "after the fact." The Constitution prohibits the enactment of *ex post facto* laws, which make acts committed before the laws in question were passed punishable as crimes.

extradition The surrender by one state to another of an individual accused or convicted of an offense in the second state.

federal court system The three-tiered structure of federal courts, comprising U.S. district courts, U.S. courts of appeals, and the U.S. Supreme Court.

felony A criminal offense punishable by death or by incarceration in a prison facility for at least one year.

feminist criminology A developing intellectual approach that emphasizes gender issues in criminology.

filing The initiation of a criminal case by formal submission to the court of a charging document, alleging that a named person has committed a specified criminal offense.

fine The penalty imposed upon a convicted person by a court, requiring that he or she pay a specified sum of money to the court.

first appearance An appearance before a magistrate during which the legality of the defendant's arrest is initially assessed and the defendant is informed of the charges on which he or she is being held. At this stage in the criminal justice process, bail may be set or pretrial release arranged. Also called *initial appearance.*

first plea See **initial plea.**

fixed sentencing See **determinate sentencing.**

fleeting targets exception An exception to the exclusionary rule that permits law enforcement offi-

cers to search a motor vehicle based upon probable cause but without a warrant. The fleeting targets exception is predicated upon the fact that vehicles can quickly leave the jurisdiction of a law enforcement agency.

force See **police use of force.**

forcible rape (UCR) The carnal knowledge of a female forcibly and against her will. See also **carnal knowledge.**

foreign terrorist organization (FTO) A foreign organization that engages in terrorist activity which threatens the security of U.S. nationals or the national security of the United States and which is so designated by the U.S. secretary of state.

forensic anthropology The use of anthropological principles and techniques in criminal investigation.

forensic entomology The study of insects to determine issues such as a person's time of death.

forfeiture The authorized seizure of money, negotiable instruments, securities, or other things of value. Under federal antidrug laws, judicial representatives are authorized to seize all cash, negotiable instruments, securities, or other things of value furnished or intended to be furnished by any person in exchange for a controlled substance, as well as all proceeds traceable to such an exchange. Also called *asset forfeiture.*

forgery The creation or alteration of a written or printed document, which if validly executed would constitute a record of a legally binding transaction, with the intent to defraud by affirming it to be the act of an unknowing second person. Also, the creation of an art object with intent to misrepresent the identity of the creator.

fraud An offense involving deceit or intentional misrepresentation of fact, with the intent of unlawfully depriving a person of his or her property or legal rights.

frivolous suit A lawsuit with no foundation in fact. Frivolous suits are generally brought by lawyers and plaintiffs for reasons of publicity, politics, or other non-law-related issues and may result in fines against plaintiffs and their counsel.

fruit of the poisoned tree doctrine A legal principle that excludes from introduction at trial any evidence later developed as a result of an illegal search or seizure.

gain time The amount of time deducted from time to be served in prison on a given sentence for participation in special projects or programs.

general deterrence A goal of criminal sentencing that seeks to prevent others from committing crimes similar to the one for which a particular offender is being sentenced by making an example of the person sentenced.

good-faith exception An exception to the exclusionary rule. Law enforcement officers who conduct a search, or who seize evidence, on the basis of good faith (that is, when they believe they are operating according to the dictates of the law) and who later discover that a mistake was made (perhaps in the format of the application for a search warrant) may still use the seized evidence in court.

good time The amount of time deducted from the time to be served in prison on a given sentence for good behavior.

grand jury A group of jurors who have been selected according to law and have been sworn to hear the evidence and to determine whether there is sufficient evidence to bring the accused person to trial, to investigate criminal activity generally, or to investigate the conduct of a public agency or official.

grievance procedure A formalized arrangement, usually involving a neutral hearing board, whereby institutionalized individuals have the opportunity to register complaints about the conditions of their confinement.

gross negligence The "intentional failure to perform a manifest duty in reckless disregard of the consequences as affecting the life or property of another."[15]

guilty but mentally ill (GBMI) A verdict, equivalent to a finding of "guilty," that establishes that the defendant, although mentally ill, was in sufficient possession of his or her faculties to be morally blameworthy for his or her acts.

guilty plea A defendant's formal answer in court to the charge or charges contained in a complaint, information, or indictment, claiming that he or she did commit the offense or offenses listed.

guilty verdict See **verdict.**

habeas corpus See **writ of** *habeas corpus.*

habitual offender A person sentenced under the provisions of a statute declaring that people convicted of a given offense, and shown to have previously been convicted of another specified offense, shall receive a more severe penalty than that for the current offense alone.

hacker A computer hobbyist or professional, generally with advanced programming skills. Today, the term *hacker* has taken on a sinister connotation, referring to hobbyists who are bent on illegally accessing the computers of others or who attempt to demonstrate their technological prowess through computerized acts of vandalism.

hands-off doctrine A historical policy of nonintervention with regard to prison management that U.S. courts tended to follow until the late 1960s. For the past 30 years, the doctrine has languished as judicial intervention in prison administration has dramatically increased, although there is now some evidence of a return to a new hands-off era.

Harrison Act The first major piece of federal antidrug legislation, passed in 1914.

hate crime A criminal offense in which the motive is hatred, bias, or prejudice based on the actual or perceived race, color, religion, national origin, ethnicity, gender, or sexual orientation of another individual or group of individuals. Also called *bias crime.*

hearing A proceeding in which arguments, witnesses, or evidence is heard by a judicial officer or an administrative body.

hearsay Something that is not based upon the personal knowledge of a witness. Witnesses who testify about something they have heard, for example, are offering hearsay by repeating information about a matter of which they have no direct knowledge.

hearsay rule The long-standing precedent that hearsay cannot be used in American courtrooms. Rather than accepting testimony based upon hearsay, the court will ask that the person who was the original source of the hearsay information be brought in to be questioned and cross-examined. Exceptions to the hearsay rule may occur when the person with direct knowledge is dead or is otherwise unable to testify.

hierarchy rule A standard *Uniform Crime Reports* scoring practice in which only the most serious offense is counted in a multiple-offense incident.

high-technology crime Violations of the criminal law whose commission depends upon, makes use of, and often targets sophisticated and advanced technology. See also **computer crime.**

home confinement House arrest. Individuals ordered confined to their homes are sometimes monitored electronically to ensure they do not leave during the hours of confinement. Absence from the home during working hours is often permitted.

homicide See **criminal homicide.**

Hudud **crime** A serious violation of Islamic law regarded as an offense against God. *Hudud* crimes include such behavior as theft, adultery, sodomy, alcohol consumption, and robbery.

hung jury A jury that, after long deliberation, is so irreconcilably divided in opinion that it is unable to reach any verdict.

hypothesis An explanation that accounts for a set of facts and that can be tested by further investigation. Also, something that is taken to be true for the purpose of argument or investigation.[16]

identity theft A crime in which an imposter obtains key pieces of information, such as Social Security and driver's license numbers, to obtain credit, merchandise, and services in the name of the victim. The victim is often left with a ruined credit history and the time-consuming and complicated task of repairing the financial damage.[17]

illegally seized evidence   Evidence seized without regard to the principles of due process as described by the Bill of Rights. Most illegally seized evidence is the result of police searches conducted without a proper warrant or of improperly conducted interrogations.

illegal search and seizure   An act in violation of the Fourth Amendment of the U.S. Constitution, which reads, "The right of the people to be secure in their persons, houses, papers, and effects, against unreasonable searches and seizures, shall not be violated, and no Warrants shall issue, but upon probable cause, supported by Oath or affirmation, and particularly describing the place to be searched, and the persons or things to be seized."

incapacitation   The use of imprisonment or other means to reduce the likelihood that an offender will be capable of committing future offenses.

inchoate offense   An offense not yet completed. Also, an offense that consists of an action or conduct that is a step toward the intended commission of another offense.

incident-based reporting   Compared with summary reporting, a less restrictive and more expansive method of collecting crime data in which all the analytical elements associated with an offense or arrest are compiled by a central collection agency on an incident-by-incident basis.

included offense   An offense that is made up of elements that are a subset of the elements of another offense having a greater statutory penalty, and the occurrence of which is established by the same evidence or by some portion of the evidence that has been offered to establish the occurrence of the greater offense.

incompetent to stand trial   In criminal proceedings, a finding by a court that, as a result of mental ill-ness, defect, or disability, a defendant is incapable of understanding the nature of the charges and proceedings against him or her, of consulting with an attorney, or of aiding in his or her own defense.

indeterminate sentence   A type of sentence to imprisonment in which the commitment, instead of being for a precise length of time, is for a range of time, such as two to five years or five years maximum and zero minimum.

indeterminate sentencing   A model of criminal punishment that encourages rehabilitation via the use of general and relatively unspecific sentences (such as a term of imprisonment of from one to ten years).

index crime   See **Crime Index.**

indictment   A formal, written accusation submitted to the court by a grand jury, alleging that a specified person has committed a specified offense, usually a felony.

individual rights   The rights guaranteed to all members of American society by the U.S. Constitution (especially those found in the first ten amendments to the Constitution, known as the *Bill of Rights*). These rights are especially important to criminal defendants facing formal processing by the criminal justice system.

individual-rights advocate   One who seeks to protect personal freedoms within the process of criminal justice.

industrial prison   A correctional model intended to capitalize on the labor of convicts sentenced to confinement.

information   A formal written accusation submitted to the court by a prosecutor, alleging that a specified person has committed a specific offense.

infraction   A minor violation of state statute or local ordinance punishable by a fine or other penalty or by a specified, usually limited, term of incarceration.

inherent coercion   The tactics used by police interviewers that fall short of physical abuse but that nonetheless pressure suspects to divulge information.

initial appearance   See **first appearance.**

initial plea   The first plea to a given charge entered in the court record by or for the defendant. The acceptance of an initial plea by the court unambiguously indicates that the arraignment process has been completed. Also called *first plea.*

insanity defense   A legal defense based on claims of mental illness or mental incapacity.

institutional capacity   The official number of inmates that a confinement or residential facility is or was intended to house.

intake   The first step in decision making regarding a juvenile whose behavior or alleged behavior is in violation of the law or could otherwise cause a juvenile court to assume jurisdiction.

intensive probation supervision (IPS)   A form of probation supervision involving frequent face-to-face contact between the probationer and the probation officer.

intent   The state of mind or attitude with which an act is carried out. Also, the design, resolve, or determination with which a person acts to achieve a certain result.

interdiction   The interception of drug traffic at the nation's borders. Interdiction is one of the many strategies used to stem the flow of illegal drugs into the United States.

interdisciplinary theory   An approach that integrates a variety of theoretical viewpoints in an attempt to explain crime and violence.

intermediate appellate court   An appellate court whose primary function is to review the judgments of trial courts and the decisions of administrative agencies and whose decisions are, in turn, usually reviewable by a higher appellate court in the same state.

intermediate sanctions   The use of split sentencing, shock probation or parole, home confinement, shock incarceration, or community service in lieu of other, more traditional, sanctions, such as imprisonment and fines. Also called *alternative sanctions.*

internal affairs The branch of a police organization tasked with investigating charges of wrongdoing involving members of the department.

International Criminal Police Organization (INTERPOL) An international law enforcement support organization that began operations in 1946 and today has 137 members.

international terrorism The unlawful use of force or violence by a group or an individual who has some connection to a foreign power or whose activities transcend national boundaries, against people or property to intimidate or coerce a government, the civilian population, or any segment thereof, in furtherance of political or social objectives.[18]

interrogation The information-gathering activities of police officers that involve the direct questioning of suspects.

Islamic law A system of laws, operative in some Arab countries, based upon the Muslim religion and especially the holy book of Islam, the Koran.

jail A confinement facility administered by an agency of local government, typically a law enforcement agency, intended for adults but sometimes also containing juveniles, which holds persons detained pending adjudication and/or persons committed after adjudication, usually those committed on sentences of a year or less.

jail commitment A sentence of commitment to the jurisdiction of a confinement facility system for adults which is administered by an agency of local government and whose custodial authority is usually limited to people sentenced to a year or less of confinement.

judge An elected or appointed public official who presides over a court of law and who is authorized to hear and sometimes to decide cases and to conduct trials.

judgment The statement of the decision of a court that the defendant is acquitted or convicted of the offense or offenses charged.

judgment suspending sentence A court-ordered sentencing alternative that results in the convicted offender being placed on probation.

judicial officer Any person authorized by statute, constitutional provision, or court rule to exercise the powers reserved to the judicial branch of government.

judicial review The power of a court to review actions and decisions made by other agencies of government.

jural postulates Propositions developed by the famous jurist Roscoe Pound that hold that the law reflects shared needs without which members of society could not coexist. Pound's jural postulates are often linked to the idea that the law can be used to engineer the social structure to ensure certain kinds of outcomes. In capitalist societies, for example, the law of theft protects property rights.)

jurisdiction The territory, subject matter, or people over which a court or other justice agency may exercise lawful authority, as determined by statute or constitution. See also **venue.**

jurisprudence The philosophy of law. Also, the science and study of the law.

juror A member of a trial or grand jury, selected for jury duty and required to serve as an arbiter of the facts in a court of law.

jury panel The group of people summoned to appear in court as potential jurors for a particular trial. Also, the people selected from the group of potential jurors to sit in the jury box, from which those acceptable to the prosecution and the defense are finally chosen as the jury.

jury selection The process whereby, according to law and precedent, members of a particular trial jury are chosen.

just deserts A model of criminal sentencing that holds that criminal offenders deserve the punishment they receive at the hands of the law and that punishments should be appropriate to the type and severity of the crime committed.

justice The principle of fairness; the ideal of moral equity.

justice model A contemporary model of imprisonment based upon the principle of just deserts.

justification A legal defense in which the defendant admits to committing the act in question but claims it was necessary in order to avoid some greater evil.

juvenile A person subject to juvenile court proceedings because a statutorily defined event or condition caused by or affecting that person was alleged to have occurred while his or her age was below the statutorily specified age limit of original jurisdiction of a juvenile court.

juvenile court A court that has, as all or part of its authority, original jurisdiction over matters concerning people statutorily defined as juveniles.

juvenile court judgment The juvenile court decision, terminating an adjudicatory hearing, that the juvenile is a delinquent, a status offender, or a dependent or that the allegations in the petition are not sustained.

juvenile disposition The decision of a juvenile court, concluding a disposition hearing, that an adjudicated juvenile be committed to a juvenile correctional facility; be placed in a juvenile residence, shelter, or care or treatment program; be required to meet certain standards of conduct; or be released.

juvenile justice The policies and activities of law enforcement and the courts in handling law violations by youths under the age of criminal jurisdiction.[19]

juvenile justice agency A government agency, or subunit thereof, whose functions are the investigation, supervision, adjudication, care, or confinement of juvenile offenders and nonoffenders subject to the jurisdiction of a juvenile court. Also, in some usages, a private agency providing care and treatment.

juvenile justice system Government agencies that function to investigate, supervise, adjudicate, care for, or confine youthful offenders and other children subject to the jurisdiction of the juvenile court.

juvenile petition A document filed in juvenile court alleging that a juvenile is a delinquent, a status offender, or a dependent and asking that the court assume jurisdiction over the juvenile or that an alleged delinquent be transferred to a criminal court for prosecution as an adult.

Kansas City experiment The first large-scale scientific study of law enforcement practices. Sponsored by the Police Foundation, it focused on the practice of preventive patrol.

kidnapping The transportation or confinement of a person without authority of law and without his or her consent, or without the consent of his or her guardian, if a minor.

Knapp Commission A committee that investigated police corruption in New York City in the early 1970s.

labeling theory An interactionist perspective that sees continued crime as a consequence of the limited opportunities for acceptable behavior which follow from the negative responses of society to those defined as offenders.

landmark case A precedent-setting court decision that produces substantial changes in both the understanding of the requirements of due process and in the practical day-to-day operations of the justice system.

larceny-theft (UCR) The unlawful taking or attempted taking, carrying, leading, or riding away of property from the possession or constructive possession of another. Motor vehicles are excluded.

latent evidence Evidence of relevance to a criminal investigation that is not readily seen by the unaided eye.

law A rule of conduct, generally found enacted in the form of a statute, that proscribes or mandates certain forms of behavior. Statutory law is often the result of moral enterprise by interest groups that, through the exercise of political power, are successful in seeing their valued perspectives enacted into law.

law enforcement The generic name for the activities of the agencies responsible for maintaining public order and enforcing the law, particularly the activities of preventing, detecting, and investigating crime and apprehending criminals.

law enforcement agency A federal, state, or local criminal justice agency or identifiable subunit whose principal functions are the prevention, detection, and investigation of crime and the apprehension of alleged offenders.

Law Enforcement Assistance Administration (LEAA) A now-defunct federal agency established under Title I of the Omnibus Crime Control and Safe Streets Act of 1967 to funnel federal funding to state and local law enforcement agencies.

law enforcement officer An officer employed by a law enforcement agency who is sworn to carry out law enforcement duties.

lawyer See **attorney.**

lay witness An eyewitness, character witness, or other person called upon to testify who is not considered an expert. Lay witnesses must testify to facts alone and may not draw conclusions or express opinions.

learning organization "An organization skilled at creating, acquiring, and transferring knowledge and at modifying its behavior to reflect new knowledge and insights."[20]

legal cause A legally recognizable cause. A legal cause must be demonstrated in court in order to hold an individual criminally liable for causing harm.

legal counsel See **attorney.**

legalistic style A style of policing marked by a strict concern with enforcing the precise letter of the law. Legalistic departments may take a hands-off approach to disruptive or problematic behavior that does not violate the criminal law.

legalization Elimination of the laws and associated criminal penalties that prohibit the production, sale, distribution, and possession of a controlled substance.

less-than-lethal weapon A weapon that is designed to disable, capture, or immobilize—but not kill—a suspect.

lex talionis The law of retaliation, often expressed as "an eye for an eye" or "like for like."

life course perspective An approach to explaining crime and deviance that investigates developments and turning points in the course of a person's life over time.

Mafia See **Cosa Nostra.**

major crimes See **Part I offenses.**

mala in se Acts that are regarded, by tradition and convention, as wrong in themselves.

mala prohibita Acts that are considered wrong only because there is a law against them.

mandatory sentence A statutorily required penalty that must be set and carried out in all cases upon conviction for a specified offense or series of offenses.

mandatory sentencing A structured sentencing scheme that allows no leeway in the nature of the sentence required and under which clearly enumerated punishments are mandated for specific offenses or for habitual offenders convicted of a series of crimes.

maximum sentence In legal usage, the maximum penalty provided by law for a given criminal offense, usually stated as a maximum term of imprisonment or a maximum fine. Also, in corrections usage in relation to a given offender, any of several quantities (expressed in days, months, or years) which vary according to whether calculated at the point of sentencing or at a later point in the correctional process and according to whether the time period referred to is the term of confinement or the total period under correctional jurisdiction.

mediation committee One of the civilian dispute-resolution groups found throughout China. Mediation committees successfully divert many minor offenders from the more formal mechanisms of justice.

medical model A therapeutic perspective on correctional treatment that applies the diagnostic perspective of medical science to the handling of criminal offenders. Rehabilitation is seen as a cure, and offenders are treated through a variety of programs to reduce their antisocial tendencies.

mens rea The state of mind that accompanies a criminal act. Also, a guilty mind.

Miranda **rights** The set of rights that a person accused or suspected of having committed a specific offense has during interrogation and of which he or she must be informed prior to questioning, as stated by the U.S. Supreme Court in deciding *Miranda* v. *Arizona* (1966) and related cases.

Miranda **triggers** The dual principles of custody and interrogation, both of which are necessary before an advisement of rights is required.

Miranda **warnings** The advisement of rights due criminal suspects by the police prior to the beginning of questioning. *Miranda* warnings were first set forth by the Supreme Court in the 1966 case of *Miranda* v. *Arizona.*

misdemeanor An offense punishable by incarceration, usually in a local confinement facility, for a period whose upper limit is prescribed by statute in a given jurisdiction, typically one year or less.

mistrial A trial that has been terminated and declared invalid by the court because of some circumstance which created a substantial and uncorrectable prejudice to the conduct of a fair trial or which made it impossible to continue the trial in accordance with prescribed procedures.

mitigating circumstances Circumstances relating to the commission of a crime which may be considered to reduce the blameworthiness of the defendant. See also **aggravating circumstances.**

mixed sentence A sentence that requires that a convicted offender serve weekends (or other specified periods of time) in a confinement facility (usually a jail) while under-

going probationary supervision in the community.

M'Naghten rule A rule for determining insanity, which asks whether the defendant knew what he or she was doing or whether the defendant knew that what he or she was doing was wrong.

Model Penal Code (MPC) A generalized modern codification considered basic to criminal law, published by the American Law Institute in 1962.

money laundering The process of converting illegally earned assets, originating as cash, to one or more alternative forms to conceal such incriminating factors as illegal origin and true ownership.[21]

moral enterprise The process undertaken by an advocacy group to have its values legitimated and embodied in law.

motion An oral or written request made to a court at any time before, during, or after court proceedings, asking the court to make a specified finding, decision, or order.

motive A person's reason for committing a crime.

motor vehicle theft (UCR) The theft or attempted theft of a motor vehicle. *Motor vehicle* is defined as a self-propelled road vehicle that runs on land surface and not on rails.

multiculturalism The existence within one society of diverse groups that maintain unique cultural identities while frequently accepting and participating in the larger society's legal and political system.[22] *Multiculturalism* is usually used in conjunction with the term *diversity* to identify many distinctions of social significance.

murder The unlawful killing of a human being. *Murder* is a generic term which in common usage may include first- and second-degree murder, manslaughter, involuntary manslaughter, and other similar offenses.

murder and nonnegligent manslaughter (UCR) Intentionally causing the death of another without legal justification or excuse. Also, causing the death of another

while committing or attempting to commit another crime.

narcoterrorism A political alliance between terrorist organizations and drug-supplying cartels. The cartels provide financing for the terrorists, who in turn provide quasi-military protection to the drug dealers.

National Crime Victimization Survey (NCVS) An annual survey of selected American households conducted by the Bureau of Justice Statistics to determine the extent of criminal victimization—especially unreported victimization—in the United States.

National Incident-Based Reporting System (NIBRS) An incident-based reporting system that collects data on every single crime occurrence. NIBRS data will soon supersede the kinds of traditional data provided by the FBI's *Uniform Crime Reports.*

natural law Rules of conduct inherent in human nature and in the natural order that are thought to be knowable through intuition, inspiration, and the exercise of reason, without the need for reference to created laws.

NCVS See **National Crime Victimization Survey.**

neglected child A child who is not receiving the proper level of physical or psychological care from his or her parents or guardians or who has been placed up for adoption in violation of the law.

negligence In legal usage, generally, a state of mind accompanying a person's conduct such that he or she is not aware, though a reasonable person should be aware, that there is a risk that the conduct might cause a particular harmful result.

negligent manslaughter (UCR) Causing the death of another by recklessness or gross negligence.

neoclassical criminology A contemporary version of classical criminology which emphasizes deterrence and retribution and which holds that human beings are essentially free to make choices in favor of crime and deviance or conformity.

new police A police force formed in 1829 under the command of Sir Robert Peel, which became the model for modern-day police forces throughout the Western world. Also called *Metropolitan Police Force.*

night watch An early form of police patrol in English cities and towns.

nolle prosequi A formal entry upon the record of the court indicating that the prosecutor declares that he or she will proceed no further in the action. The terminating of adjudication of a criminal charge by the prosecutor's decision not to pursue the case requires the approval of the court in some jurisdictions.

nolo contendere A plea of "no contest." A no-contest plea is used when the defendant does not wish to contest conviction. Because the plea does not admit guilt, however, it cannot provide the basis for later civil suits that might follow upon the heels of a criminal conviction.

not guilty by reason of insanity The plea of a defendant or the verdict of a jury or judge in a criminal proceeding that the defendant is not guilty of the offense charged because at the time the crime was committed, the defendant did not have the mental capacity to be held criminally responsible for his or her actions.

nothing-works doctrine The belief, popularized by Robert Martinson in the 1970s, that correctional treatment programs have little success in rehabilitating offenders.

no true bill The decision by a grand jury that it will not return an indictment against the person accused of a crime on the basis of the allegations and evidence presented by the prosecutor.

occupational crime Any act punishable by law that is committed through opportunity created in the course of a legitimate occupation.

offender An adult who has been convicted of a criminal offense.

offense A violation of the criminal law. Also, in some jurisdictions, a minor crime, such as jaywalking, that is sometimes described as *tick-etable.*

offenses known to police (UCR) Reported occurrences of offenses which have been verified at the police level.

opening statement The initial statement of an attorney (or of a defendant representing himself or herself) made in a court of law to a judge, or to a judge and jury, describing the facts that he or she intends to present during trial to prove the case.

operational capacity The number of inmates a prison can effectively accommodate based upon management considerations.

opinion The official announcement of a decision of a court, together with the reasons for that decision.

opportunity theory A perspective that sees delinquency as the result of limited legitimate opportunities for success available to most lower-class youth.

organized crime The unlawful activities of the members of a highly organized, disciplined association engaged in supplying illegal goods and services, including gambling, prostitution, loan-sharking, narcotics, and labor racketeering.[23]

original jurisdiction The lawful authority of a court to hear or act upon a case from its beginning and to pass judgment on the law and the facts.

parens patriae A common law principle that allows the state to assume a parental role and to take custody of a child when he or she becomes delinquent, is abandoned, or is in need of care that the natural parents are unable or unwilling to provide. It means, in effect, that the state assumes responsibility for the welfare of problem children.

Parliament The British legislature, the highest lawmaking body of the United Kingdom.

parole The status of an offender who has been conditionally released from prison by a paroling authority prior to the expiration of his or her sentence, is placed under the supervision of a parole agency, and is required to observe conditions of parole.

parole board A state paroling authority. Most states have parole boards that decide when an incarcerated offender is ready for conditional release and that may also function as revocation hearing panels. Also called *parole commission.*

parolee A person who has been conditionally released by a paroling authority from a prison prior to the expiration of his or her sentence, is placed under the supervision of a parole agency, and is required to observe conditions of parole.

parole revocation The administrative action of a paroling authority removing a person from parole status in response to a violation of lawfully required conditions of parole, including the prohibition against commission of a new offense, and usually resulting in a return to prison.

parole supervision Guidance, treatment, or regulation of the behavior of a convicted adult who is obligated to fulfill conditions of parole or conditional release. Parole supervision is authorized and required by statute, is performed by a parole agency, and occurs after a period of prison confinement.

parole supervisory caseload The total number of clients registered with a parole agency or officer on a given date or during a specified time period.

parole violation An act or a failure to act by a parolee that does not conform to the conditions of his or her parole.

paroling authority A board or commission which has the authority to release on parole adults committed to prison, to revoke parole or other conditional release, and to discharge from parole or other conditional release status.

Part I offenses A set of UCR categories used to report murder, rape, robbery, aggravated assault, burglary, larceny-theft, motor vehicle theft, and arson, as defined under the FBI's Uniform Crime Reporting Program. Also called *major crimes.*

Part II offenses A set of UCR categories used to report arrests for less serious offenses.

PATRIOT Act See **USA PATRIOT Act of 2001.**

peacemaking criminology A perspective which holds that crime-control agencies and the citizens they serve should work together to alleviate social problems and human suffering and thus reduce crime.

Peace Officer Standards and Training (POST) program The official program of a state or legislative jurisdiction through which standards for the training of law enforcement officers are set. All states set such standards, although not all use the term *POST*.

penal code The written, organized, and compiled form of the criminal laws of a jurisdiction.

penal law See **criminal law.**

penitentiary A prison. See also **Pennsylvania system.**

Pennsylvania system A form of imprisonment developed by the Pennsylvania Quakers around 1790 as an alternative to corporal punishments. This style of imprisonment made use of solitary confinement and encouraged rehabilitation.

peremptory challenge The right to challenge a juror without assigning a reason for the challenge. In most jurisdictions, each party to an action, both civil and criminal, has a specified number of such challenges and after using all peremptory challenges is required to furnish a reason for subsequent challenges.[24]

perjury The intentional making of a false statement as part of the testimony by a sworn witness in a judicial proceeding on a matter relevant to the case at hand.

perpetrator The chief actor in the commission of a crime—that is, the person who directly commits the criminal act.

petition A written request made to a court asking for the exercise of its judicial powers or asking for permission to perform some act that requires the authorization of a court.

petit jury See **trial jury.**

phenomenological criminology A perspective on crime causation that holds that the significance of criminal behavior is ultimately knowable only to those who participate in it. Central to this school of thought is the belief that social actors endow their behavior with meaning and purpose. Hence, a crime might mean one thing to the person who commits it, quite another to the victim, and something far different still to professional participants in the justice system.

phrenology The study of the shape of the head to determine anatomical correlates of human behavior.

physical dependence Dependence upon drugs marked by a growing tolerance of a drug's effects, so that increased amounts of the drug are needed to obtain the desired effect, and by the onset of withdrawal symptoms over periods of prolonged abstinence.[25] Also, a biologically based craving for a specific drug which results from long-term substance abuse. Also called *physical addiction.*

piracy See **software piracy.**

plaintiff A person who initiates a court action.

plain view A legal term describing the ready visibility of objects that might be seized as evidence during a search by police in the absence of a search warrant specifying the seizure of those objects. To lawfully seize evidence in plain view, officers must have a legal right to be in the viewing area and must have cause to believe that the evidence is somehow associated with criminal activity.

plea In criminal proceedings, the defendant's formal answer in court to the charge contained in a complaint, information, or indictment that he or she is guilty of the offense charged, is not guilty of the offense charged, or does not contest the charge.

plea bargaining The process of negotiating an agreement among the defendant, the prosecutor, and the court as to an appropriate plea and associated sentence in a given case. Plea bargaining circumvents the trial process and dramatically reduces the time required for the resolution of a criminal case.

police-community relations (PCR) An area of emerging police activity that stresses the need for the community and the police to work together effectively and that emphasizes the notion that the police derive their legitimacy from the community they serve. PCR began to be of concern to many police agencies in the 1960s and 1970s.

police corruption The abuse of police authority for personal or organizational gain.[26]

police discretion The opportunity of law enforcement officers to exercise choice in their daily activities. The decision whether to make an arrest or to release a suspect is an example of discretion in law enforcement activity.

police ethics The special responsibility to adhere to moral duty and obligation that is inherent in police work.

police management The administrative activities of controlling, directing, and coordinating police personnel, resources, and activities in the service of crime prevention, the apprehension of criminals, the recovery of stolen property, and the performance of a variety of regulatory and helping services.

police professionalism The increasing formalization of police work and the accompanying rise in public acceptance of the police.

police subculture A particular set of values, beliefs, and acceptable forms of behavior characteristic of American police with which the police profession strives to imbue new recruits. Socialization into the police subculture commences with recruit training and continues thereafter. Also called *police culture.*

police use of force The use of physical restraint by a police officer when dealing with a member of the public.[27]

police working personality All aspects of the traditional values and patterns of behavior evidenced by police officers who have been effectively socialized into the police subculture. Characteristics of the police personality often extend to the personal lives of law enforcement personnel.

Positivist School An approach to criminal justice theory that stresses the application of scientific techniques to the study of crime and criminals.

POST See **Peace Officer Standards and Training.**

postconviction remedy The procedure or set of procedures by which a person who has been convicted of a crime can challenge in court the lawfulness of a judgment of conviction, a penalty, or a correctional agency action and thus obtain relief in situations where this cannot be done by a direct appeal.

postmodern criminology A brand of criminology that developed after World War II and which builds upon the tenets inherent in postmodern social thought.

precedent A legal principle that ensures that previous judicial decisions are authoritatively considered and incorporated into future cases.

preliminary hearing A proceeding before a judicial officer in which three matters must be decided: (1) whether a crime was committed, (2) whether the crime occurred within the territorial jurisdiction of the court, and (3) whether there are reasonable grounds to believe that the defendant committed the crime.

presentence investigation The examination of a convicted offender's background prior to sentencing. Presentence examinations are generally conducted by probation or parole officers and are submitted to sentencing authorities.

presentment Historically, unsolicited written notice of an offense provided to a court by a grand jury from their own knowledge or observation. In current usage, any of several presentations of alleged facts and charges to a court or a grand jury by a prosecutor.

presumptive sentencing A model of criminal punishment that meets the following conditions: (1) The appropriate sentence for an offender convicted of a specific charge is presumed to fall within a range of sentences authorized by sentencing guidelines that are adopted by a legislatively created sentencing body, usually a sentencing commission. (2) Sentencing judges are expected to sentence within the range or to provide written justification for departure. (3) The guidelines provide for some review, usually appellate, of the departure.

pretrial detention Confinement occurring between the time of arrest or of being held to answer a charge and the conclusion of prosecution.[28]

pretrial discovery In criminal proceedings, disclosure by the prosecution or the defense prior to trial of evidence or other information which is intended to be used in the trial.

pretrial release The release of an accused person from custody, for all or part of the time before or during prosecution, upon his or her promise to appear in court when required.

prison A state or federal confinement facility that has custodial authority over adults sentenced to confinement.

prison argot The slang characteristic of prison subcultures and prison life.

prison capacity The size of the correctional population an institution can effectively hold.[29]

prison commitment A sentence of commitment to the jurisdiction of a state or federal confinement facility system for adults whose custodial authority extends to offenders sentenced to more than a year of confinement, to a term expressed in years or for life, or to await execution of a death sentence.

prisoner A person in physical custody in a state or federal confinement facility or in the personal physical custody of a criminal justice official while being transported to or between confinement facilities.

prisonization The process whereby newly institutionalized offenders come to accept prison lifestyles and criminal values. Although many inmates begin their prison experience with only a few values supportive of criminal behavior, the socialization experience they undergo while incarcerated leads to a much wider acceptance of such values.

prison subculture The values and behavioral patterns characteristic of prison inmates. Prison subculture has been found to be surprisingly consistent across the country.

private prison A correctional institution operated by a private firm on behalf of a local or state government.

private protective services Independent or proprietary commercial organizations that provide protective services to employers on a contractual basis.

private security Self-employed individuals and privately funded business entities and organizations providing security-related services to specific clientele for a fee, for the individual or entity that retains or employs them, or for themselves, in order to protect people, private property, or interests from various hazards.[30]

private security agency See **private protective services.**

privatization The movement toward the wider use of private prisons.

probable cause A set of facts and circumstances that would induce a reasonably intelligent and prudent person to believe that a particular other person has committed a specific crime. Also, reasonable grounds to make or believe an accusation.

probation A sentence of imprisonment that is suspended. Also, the conditional freedom granted by a judicial officer to an adjudicated adult or juvenile offender, as long as the person meets certain conditions of behavior.

probationer A person who is placed on probation status, is required by a court or a probation agency to meet certain conditions of behavior, and may or may not be placed under the supervision of a probation agency.

probation revocation A court order in response to a violation of conditions of probation, taking away a person's probationary status and usually withdrawing the conditional freedom associated with that status.

probation termination The ending of the probation status of a given person by routine expiration of the probationary period, by special early termination by the court, or by revocation of probation.

probation violation An act or a failure to act by a probationer that does not conform to the conditions of his or her probation.

probation workload The total set of activities required to carry out the probation agency functions of intake screening of juvenile cases, referral of cases to other service agencies, investigation of juveniles and adults for the purpose of preparing predisposition or presentence reports, supervision or treatment of juveniles and adults granted probation, assistance in the enforcement of court orders concerning family problems, such as abandonment and nonsupport cases, and other such functions assigned by statute or court order.

problem police officer A law enforcement officer who exhibits problem behavior, as indicated by high rates of citizen complaints and use-of-force incidents and by other evidence.[31]

problem-solving policing A type of policing that assumes that many crimes are caused by existing social conditions within the community and that crimes can be controlled by uncovering and effectively addressing underlying social problems. Problem-solving policing makes use of community resources, such as counseling centers, welfare programs, and job-training facilities. It also attempts to involve citizens in crime prevention through education, negotiation, and conflict management. Also called *problem-oriented policing.*

procedural defense A defense that claims that the defendant was in some significant way discriminated against in the justice process or

that some important aspect of official procedure was not properly followed in the investigation or prosecution of the crime charged.

procedural law The part of the law that specifies the methods to be used in enforcing substantive law.

procuratorate A term used in many countries to refer to an agency with powers and responsibilities similar to those of a prosecutor's office in the United States. Also called *procuracy.*

profession An organized undertaking characterized by a body of specialized knowledge acquired through extensive education and by a well-considered set of internal standards and ethical guidelines which hold members of the profession accountable to one another and to society.

professional criminal See **career criminal.**

property bond The setting of bail in the form of land, houses, stocks, or other tangible property. In the event that the defendant absconds prior to trial, the bond becomes the property of the court.

property crime A UCR offense category that includes burglary, larceny-theft, motor vehicle theft, and arson.

proportionality A sentencing principle that holds that the severity of sanctions should bear a direct relationship to the seriousness of the crime committed.

prosecution agency A federal, state, or local criminal justice agency or subunit whose principal function is the prosecution of alleged offenders.

prosecutor An attorney who is the elected or appointed chief of a prosecution agency and whose official duty is to conduct criminal proceedings on behalf of the state or the people against those accused of having committed criminal offenses. Also, any attorney deputized to assist the chief prosecutor. Also called *county attorney; district attorney (DA); state's attorney; U.S. attorney.*

prosecutorial discretion The decision-making power of prosecu-

tors, based upon the wide range of choices available to them, in the handling of criminal defendants, the scheduling of cases for trial, the acceptance of bargained pleas, and so on. The most important form of prosecutorial discretion lies in the power to charge, or not to charge, a person with an offense.

prostitution The act of offering or agreeing to engage in, or engaging in, a sex act with another in return for a fee.

protected computer Under federal law, a computer exclusively for the use of a financial institution or the U.S. government, or, in the case of a computer not exclusively for such use, used by or for a financial institution or the U.S. government; or which is used in interstate or foreign commerce or communication.

psychoactive substance A chemical substance that affects cognition, feeling, or awareness.

psychoanalysis A theory of human behavior, based upon the writings of Sigmund Freud, that sees personality as a complex composite of interacting mental entities.

psychological dependence A craving for a specific drug that results from long-term substance abuse. Psychological dependence upon drugs is marked by the belief that drugs are needed to achieve a feeling of well-being.[32] Also called *psychological addiction.*

psychological manipulation Manipulative actions by police interviewers, designed to pressure suspects to divulge information, that are based upon subtle forms of intimidation and control.

psychological profiling The attempt to categorize, understand, and predict the behavior of certain types of offenders based upon behavioral clues they provide.

Psychological School A perspective on criminological thought that views offensive and deviant behavior as the product of dysfunctional personalities. Psychological thinkers identify the conscious, and especially the subconscious, contents of the human psyche as major determinants of behavior.

psychopath A person with a personality disorder, especially one manifested in aggressively antisocial behavior, which is often said to be the result of a poorly developed superego. Also called *sociopath.*

psychopathology The study of pathological mental conditions—that is, mental illness.

psychosis A form of mental illness in which sufferers are said to be out of touch with reality.

public defender An attorney employed by a government agency or subagency, or by a private organization under contract to a government body, for the purpose of providing defense services to indigents, or an attorney who has volunteered such service. Also, the head of a government agency or subagency whose function is the representation in court of people accused or convicted of a crime who are unable to hire private counsel.

public defender agency A federal, state, or local criminal justice agency or subunit whose principal function is to represent in court people accused or convicted of a crime who are unable to hire private counsel.

public-order advocate One who suggests that under certain circumstances involving a criminal threat to public safety, the interests of society should take precedence over individual rights.

public safety department A state or local agency that incorporates various law enforcement and emergency service functions.

punitive damages Damages requested and/or awarded in a civil lawsuit when the defendant's willful acts were malicious, violent, oppressive, fraudulent, wanton, or grossly reckless.[33] Also called *exemplary damages.*

racial profiling "Any police-initiated action that relies on the race, ethnicity, or national origin rather than [1] the behavior of an individual, or [2] on information that leads the police to a particular individual who has been identified as being, or having been, engaged in criminal activity."[34]

Racketeer Influenced and Corrupt Organizations (RICO) A federal statute that allows for the federal seizure of assets derived from illegal enterprise.

radical criminology A conflict perspective that sees crime as engendered by the unequal distribution of wealth, power, and other resources, which adherents believe is especially characteristic of capitalist societies. Also called *critical criminology; Marxist criminology.*

rape Unlawful sexual intercourse, achieved through force and without consent. Broadly speaking, the term *rape* has been applied to a wide variety of sexual attacks and may include same-sex rape and the rape of a male by a female. The term *forcible rape* has a more concise meaning. See also **forcible rape; sexual battery.**

rated capacity The number of inmates a prison can handle according to the judgment of experts.

rational choice theory A perspective on crime causation which holds that criminality is the result of conscious choice and which predicts that individuals choose to commit crime when the benefits of doing so outweigh the costs of disobeying the law.

reaction formation The process whereby a person openly rejects that which he or she wants or aspires to but cannot obtain or achieve.

real evidence Evidence consisting of physical material or traces of physical activity.

reasonable doubt In legal proceedings, an actual and substantial doubt arising from the evidence, from the facts or circumstances shown by the evidence, or from the lack of evidence.[35] Also, the state of a case such that, after the comparison and consideration of all the evidence, jurors cannot say they feel an abiding conviction of the truth of the charge.[36]

reasonable doubt standard The standard of proof necessary for conviction in criminal trials.

reasonable force A degree of force that is appropriate in a given situation and is not excessive. Also, the minimum degree of force necessary to protect oneself, one's property, a third party, or the property of another in the face of a substantial threat.

reasonable suspicion The level of suspicion that would justify an officer in making further inquiry or in conducting further investigation. Reasonable suspicion may permit stopping a person for questioning or for a simple pat-down search. Also, a belief, based upon a consideration of the facts at hand and upon reasonable inferences drawn from those facts, that would induce an ordinarily prudent and cautious person under the same circumstances to conclude that criminal activity is taking place or that criminal activity has recently occurred. See also **probable cause.**

recidivism The repetition of criminal behavior.

recidivist A person who has been convicted of one or more crimes and who is alleged or found to have subsequently committed another crime or series of crimes.

reckless behavior Activity that increases the risk of harm.

recreational drug user A person who uses drugs relatively infrequently and primarily with friends and in social contexts that define drug use as pleasurable. Most addicts begin as recreational users.

reformatory style A late-nineteenth-century correctional model based upon the use of the indeterminate sentence and the belief in the possibility of rehabilitation, especially for youthful offenders. The reformatory concept faded with the emergence of industrial prisons around the turn of the century.

regional jail A jail that is built and run using the combined resources of a variety of local jurisdictions.

rehabilitation The attempt to reform a criminal offender. Also, the state in which a reformed offender is said to be.

release on recognizance (ROR) The pretrial release of a criminal defendant on his or her written promise to appear in court as required. No cash or property bond is required.

reprieve An executive act temporarily suspending the execution of a sentence, usually a death sentence. A reprieve differs from other suspensions of sentence not only in that it almost always applies to the temporary withdrawing of a death sentence, but also in that it is usually an act of clemency intended to provide the prisoner with time to secure amelioration of the sentence.

research The use of standardized, systematic procedures in the search for knowledge.

resident A person required, by official action or by his or her acceptance of placement, to reside in a public or private facility established for purposes of confinement, supervision, or care.

residential commitment A sentence of commitment to a correctional facility for adults, in which the offender is required to reside at night, but from which he or she is regularly permitted to depart during the day, unaccompanied by any official.

restitution A court requirement that an alleged or convicted offender pay money or provide services to the victim of the crime or provide services to the community.

restoration A goal of criminal sentencing that attempts to make the victim "whole again."

restorative justice A sentencing model that builds upon restitution and community participation in an attempt to make the victim "whole again."

retribution The act of taking revenge upon a criminal perpetrator.

revocation hearing A hearing held before a legally constituted hearing body (such as a parole or probation board) to determine whether a parolee or probationer has violated the conditions and requirements of his or her parole or probation.

rights of defendant The powers and privileges that are constitutionally guaranteed to every defendant.

robbery (UCR) The unlawful taking or attempted taking of property that is in the immediate possession of another by force or violence and/or by putting the victim in fear.

routine activities theory A neoclassical perspective that suggests that lifestyles contribute significantly to both the volume and the type of crime found in any society.

rule of law The maxim that an orderly society must be governed by established principles and known codes that are applied uniformly and fairly to all of its members.

rules of evidence Rules of court that govern the admissibility of evidence at a criminal hearing and trial.

runaway A juvenile who has been adjudicated by a judicial officer of juvenile court as having committed the status offense of leaving the custody and home of his or her parents, guardians, or custodians without permission and of failing to return within a reasonable length of time.

schizophrenic A mentally ill individual who suffers from disjointed thinking and possibly from delusions and hallucinations.

scientific jury selection The use of correlational techniques from the social sciences to gauge the likelihood that potential jurors will vote for conviction or acquittal.

scientific police management The application of social science techniques to the study of police administration for the purpose of increasing effectiveness, reducing the frequency of citizen complaints, and enhancing the efficient use of available resources.

search incident to an arrest A warrantless search of an arrested individual conducted to ensure the safety of the arresting officer. Because individuals placed under arrest may be in possession of weapons, courts have recognized the need for arresting officers to protect themselves by conducting an immediate search of arrestees without obtaining a warrant.

search warrant A document issued by a judicial officer which directs a law enforcement officer to conduct a search at a specific location, for specified property or person relating to a crime, to seize the property or person if found, and to account for the results of the search to the issuing judicial officer.

security The restriction of inmate movement within a correctional facility, usually divided into maximum, medium, and minimum levels.

self-defense The protection of oneself or of one's property from unlawful injury or from the immediate risk of unlawful injury. Also, the justification that the person who committed an act that would otherwise constitute an offense reasonably believed that the act was necessary to protect self or property from immediate danger.

sentence I. The penalty imposed by a court upon a person convicted of a crime. II. The court judgment specifying the penalty imposed upon a person convicted of a crime. III. Any disposition of a defendant resulting from a conviction, including the court decision to suspend execution of a sentence.

sentencing The imposition of a criminal sanction by a judicial authority.

sentencing disposition I. A court disposition of a defendant after a judgment of conviction, expressed as a penalty, such as imprisonment or payment of a fine. II. Any of a number of alternatives to actually executed penalties, such as a suspended sentence, a grant of probation, or an order to perform restitution. III. Various combinations of the foregoing.

sentencing hearing In criminal proceedings, a hearing during which the court or jury considers relevant information, such as evidence concerning aggravating or mitigating circumstances, for the purpose of determining a sentencing disposition for a person convicted of an offense.

sequestered jury A jury that is isolated from the public during the course of a trial and throughout the deliberation process.

service style A style of policing marked by a concern with helping rather than strict enforcement. Service-oriented police agencies are more likely to take advantage of community resources, such as drug-treatment programs, than are other types of agencies.

sex offense In current statistical usage, any of a broad category of varying offenses, usually consisting of all offenses having a sexual element, except forcible rape and commercial sex offenses. The category includes all unlawful sexual intercourse, unlawful sexual contact, and other unlawful behavior intended to result in sexual gratification or profit from sexual activity.

sex offense (UCR) Any of various "offenses against chastity, common decency, morals, and the like," except forcible rape, prostitution, and commercialized vice.

sexual battery Intentional and wrongful physical contact with a person, without his or her consent, that entails a sexual component or purpose.

sheriff The elected chief officer of a county law enforcement agency. The sheriff is usually responsible for law enforcement in unincorporated areas and for the operation of the county jail.

sheriff's department A local law enforcement agency, directed by a sheriff, which exercises its law enforcement functions at the county level, usually within unincorporated areas, and which operates the county jail in most jurisdictions.

shock incarceration A sentencing option that makes use of "boot camp"–type prisons to impress upon convicted offenders the realities of prison life.

shock probation The practice of sentencing offenders to prison, allowing them to apply for probationary release, and enacting such release in surprise fashion. Offenders who receive shock probation may not be aware that they will be released on probation and may expect to spend a much longer time behind bars.

simple assault (UCR) The unlawful threatening, attempted inflicting, or inflicting of less-than-serious bodily injury, without a deadly weapon.

smart card A plastic card or similar device containing a computer chip and other sources of nonalterable information (such as a hologram or a laser-encoded memory strip) used to provide highly secure personal identification.

smuggling The unlawful movement of goods across a national frontier or state boundary or into or out of a correctional facility.

"sneak and peak" search A search that occurs in the suspect's absence and without his or her prior knowledge.

social control The use of sanctions and rewards within a group to influence and shape the behavior of individual members of that group. Social control is a primary concern of social groups and communities, and it is their interest in the exercise of social control that leads to the creation of both criminal and civil statutes.

social debt A sentencing principle that holds that an offender's criminal history should objectively be taken into account in sentencing decisions.

social development theory An integrated view of human development that points to the process of interaction among and between individuals and society as the root cause of criminal behavior.

social disorganization A condition said to exist when a group is faced with social change, uneven development of culture, maladaptiveness, disharmony, conflict, and lack of consensus.

social ecology An approach that focuses on the misbehavior of lower-class youth and sees delinquency primarily as the result of social disorganization.

social justice An ideal that embraces all aspects of civilized life and that is linked to fundamental notions of fairness and to cultural beliefs about right and wrong.

social learning theory A psychological perspective that says that people learn how to behave by modeling themselves after others whom they have the opportunity to observe.

social order The condition of a society characterized by social inte-

gration, consensus, smooth functioning, and lack of interpersonal and institutional conflict. Also, a lack of social disorganization.

social-psychological theory A perspective on criminological thought that highlights the role played in crime causation by weakened self-esteem and meaningless social roles. Social-psychological thinkers stress the relationship of the individual to the social group as the underlying cause of behavior.

sociopath See **psychopath**.

software piracy The unauthorized duplication of software or the illegal transfer of data from one storage medium to another. Software piracy is one of the most prevalent computer crimes in the world.

somatotyping The classification of human beings into types according to body build and other physical characteristics.

specific deterrence A goal of criminal sentencing that seeks to prevent a particular offender from engaging in repeat criminality.

speedy trial A trial which is held in a timely manner. The right of a defendant to have a prompt trial is guaranteed by the Sixth Amendment of the U.S. Constitution, which begins, "In all criminal prosecutions, the accused shall enjoy the right to a speedy and public trial."

Speedy Trial Act A 1974 federal law requiring that proceedings against a defendant in a criminal case begin within a specified period of time, such as 70 working days after indictment. Some states also have speedy trial requirements.

split sentence A sentence explicitly requiring the convicted offender to serve a period of confinement in a local, state, or federal facility, followed by a period of probation.

stare decisis The legal principle that requires that in subsequent cases on similar issues of law and fact, courts be bound by their own earlier decisions and by those of higher courts having jurisdiction over them. The term literally means "standing by decided matters."

state-action doctrine The traditional legal principle that only government officials or their representatives in the criminal justice process can be held accountable for the violation of an individual's constitutional civil rights.

state court administrator A coordinator who assists with case-flow management, operating funds budgeting, and court docket administration.

state court system A state judicial structure. Most states have at least three court levels: generally, trial courts, appellate courts, and a state supreme court.

state highway patrol A state law enforcement agency whose principal functions are preventing, detecting, and investigating motor vehicle offenses and apprehending traffic offenders.

state police A state law enforcement agency whose principal functions usually include maintaining statewide police communications, aiding local police in criminal investigations, training police, and guarding state property. The state police may include the highway patrol.

state-use system A system of inmate labor in which items produced by inmates may only be sold by or to state offices. Items that only the state can sell include such things as license plates and hunting licenses, while items sold only to state offices include furniture and cleaning supplies.

status offender A child who commits an act that is contrary to the law by virtue of the offender's status as a child. Purchasing cigarettes, buying alcohol, and being truant are examples of such behavior.

status offense An act or conduct that is declared by statute to be an offense, but only when committed by or engaged in by a juvenile, and that can be adjudicated only by a juvenile court.

Statute of Winchester A law, written in 1285, that created a watch and ward system in English cities and towns and that codified early police practices.

statutory law Written or codified law; the "law on the books," as enacted by a government body or

agency having the power to make laws.

statutory rape Sexual intercourse with a person who is under the legal age of consent.

stay of execution The stopping by a court of the implementation of a judgment—that is, of a court order previously issued.

stolen property offense The unlawful receiving, buying, distributing, selling, transporting, concealing, or possessing of the property of another by a person who knows that the property has been unlawfully obtained from the owner or other lawful possessor.

stop and frisk The detaining of a person by a law enforcement officer for the purpose of investigation, accompanied by a superficial examination by the officer of the person's body surface or clothing to discover weapons, contraband, or other objects relating to criminal activity.

stranger violence Seemingly random violence perpetrated by assailants who were previously unknown to their victims. Stranger violence often results from rage, opportunity, or insanity.

strategic policing A type of policing that retains the traditional police goal of professional crime fighting but enlarges the enforcement target to include nontraditional kinds of criminals, such as serial offenders, gangs and criminal associations, drug-distribution networks, and sophisticated white-collar and computer criminals. Strategic policing generally makes use of innovative enforcement techniques, including intelligence operations, undercover stings, electronic surveillance, and sophisticated forensic methods.

street crime A class of offenses, sometimes defined with some degree of formality as those which occur in public locations and are visible and assaultive, that are a special risk to the public and a special target of law enforcement preventive efforts and prosecutorial attention.

strict liability Liability without fault or intention. Strict liability offenses do not require *mens rea*.

structured sentencing A model of criminal punishment that includes determinate and commission-created presumptive sentencing schemes, as well as voluntary/advisory sentencing guidelines.

subculture of violence A cultural setting in which violence is a traditional and often accepted method of dispute resolution.

subpoena A written order issued by a judicial officer or grand jury requiring an individual to appear in court and to give testimony or to bring material to be used as evidence. Some subpoenas mandate that books, papers, and other items be surrendered to the court.

substantive criminal law The part of the law that defines crimes and specifies punishments.

supermale A human male displaying the XYY chromosome structure.

superpredator A juvenile who is coming of age in actual and "moral poverty" without the benefits of parents, teachers, coaches, and clergy to teach right from wrong[37] and who turns to criminal activity. The term is often applied to inner-city youths, socialized in violent settings without the benefit of wholesome life experiences, who hold considerable potential for violence.

supervised probation Guidance, treatment, or regulation by a probation agency of the behavior of a person who is subject to adjudication or who has been convicted of an offense, resulting from a formal court order or a probation agency decision.

suspect An adult or a juvenile who has not been arrested or charged but whom a criminal justice agency believes may be the person responsible for a specific criminal offense.

suspended sentence The court decision to delay imposing or executing a penalty for a specified or unspecified period. Also called *sentence withheld*. Also, a court disposition of a convicted person pronouncing a penalty of a fine or a commitment to confinement but unconditionally discharging the defendant or holding execution of the penalty in abeyance upon good behavior.

suspicionless search A search conducted by law enforcement personnel without a warrant and without suspicion. Suspicionless searches are permissible only if based upon an overriding concern for public safety.

Tazir **crime** A minor violation of Islamic law that is regarded as an offense against society, not God.

team policing The reorganization of conventional patrol strategies into "an integrated and versatile police team assigned to a fixed district."[38]

teen court An alternative approach to juvenile justice in which alleged offenders are judged and sentenced by a jury of their peers.

TEMPEST A standard developed by the U.S. government that requires that electromagnetic emanations from computers designated as "secure" be below levels that would allow radio receiving equipment to "read" the data being computed.

terrorism A violent act or an act dangerous to human life in violation of the criminal laws of the United States or of any state to intimidate or coerce a government, the civilian population, or any segment thereof, in furtherance of political or social objectives.[39]

testimony Oral evidence offered by a sworn witness on the witness stand during a criminal trial.

theft Generally, any taking of the property of another with intent to deprive the rightful owner of possession permanently.

theory A set of interrelated propositions that attempt to describe, explain, predict, and ultimately control some class of events. A theory gains explanatory power from inherent logical consistency and is "tested" by how well it describes and predicts reality.

tort A wrongful act, damage, or injury not involving a breach of contract. Also, a private or civil wrong or injury.

total institutions Enclosed facilities, separated from society both socially and physically, where the inhabitants share all aspects of their lives daily.

transfer to adult court The decision by a juvenile court, resulting from a transfer hearing, that jurisdiction over an alleged delinquent will be waived and that he or she should be prosecuted as an adult in a criminal court.

transnational crime Unlawful activity undertaken and supported by organized criminal groups operating across national boundaries.

treason A U.S. citizen's actions to help a foreign government overthrow, make war against, or seriously injure the United States.[40] Also, the attempt to overthrow the government of the society of which one is a member.

trial In criminal proceedings, the examination in a court of the issues of fact and law in a case for the purpose of reaching a judgment of conviction or acquittal of the defendant.

trial *de novo* Literally, "new trial." The term is applied to cases that are retried on appeal, as opposed to those that are simply reviewed on the record.

trial judge A judicial officer who is authorized to conduct jury and nonjury trials but who may not be authorized to hear appellate cases. Also, the judicial officer who conducts a particular trial.

trial jury A statutorily defined number of people selected according to law and sworn to determine, in accordance with the law as instructed by the court, certain matters of fact based on evidence presented in a trial and to render a verdict. Also called *petit jury*.

truth in sentencing A close correspondence between the sentence imposed upon an offender and the time actually served prior to release from prison.[41]

UCR See **Uniform Crime Reports (UCR).**

unconditional release The final release of an offender from the jurisdiction of a correctional agency. Also, a final release from the jurisdiction of a court.

undisciplined child A child who is beyond parental control, as evidenced by his or her refusal to obey legitimate authorities, such as school officials and teachers.

Uniform Crime Reports (UCR) An annual FBI publication that summarizes the incidence and rate of reported crimes throughout the United States.

USA PATRIOT Act of 2001 A federal law (Public Law 107-56), enacted in response to terrorist attacks on the World Trade Center and the Pentagon occuring on September 11, 2001. The law, officially titled the Uniting and Strengthening America by Providing Appropriate Tools Required to Intercept and Obstruct Terrorism Act, substantially broadens the investigative authority of law enforcement agencies throughout America and is applicable to many crimes other than terrorism.

use of force See **police use of force.**

vagrancy (UCR) An offense related to being a suspicious person, including vagrancy, begging, loitering, and vagabondage.

vandalism (UCR) The destroying or damaging, or attempting to destroy or damage, public property or the property of another without the owner's consent. This definition of vandalism does not include burning.

venue The particular geographic area in which a court may hear or try a case. Also, the locality within which a particular crime was committed. See also **jurisdiction.**

verdict The decision of the jury in a jury trial or of a judicial officer in a nonjury trial.

victim A person who has suffered death, physical or mental anguish, or loss of property as the result of an actual or attempted criminal offense committed by another person.

victim-assistance program An organized program that offers services to victims of crime in the areas of crisis intervention and follow-up counseling and that helps victims secure their rights under the law.

victim-impact statement The in-court use of victim- or survivor-supplied information by sentencing authorities wishing to make an informed sentencing decision.

victimization In National Crime Victimization Survey terminology, the harming of any single victim in a criminal incident.

vigilantism The act of taking the law into one's own hands.

violation I. The performance of an act forbidden by a statute, or the failure to perform an act commanded by a statute. II. An act contrary to a local government ordinance. III. An offense punishable by a fine or other penalty but not by incarceration. IV. An act prohibited by the terms and conditions of probation or parole.

violent crime A UCR offense category that includes murder, rape, robbery, and aggravated assault.

voluntary/advisory sentencing guidelines Recommended sentencing policies that are not required by law.

warden The official in charge of the operation of a prison, the chief administrator of a prison, or the prison superintendent.

warehousing An imprisonment strategy that is based upon the desire to prevent recurrent crime and that has abandoned all hope of rehabilitation.

warrant In criminal proceedings, a writ issued by a judicial officer directing a law enforcement officer to perform a specified act and affording the officer protection from damages if he or she performs it.

watchman style A style of policing that is marked by a concern for order maintenance. Watchman policing is characteristic of lower-class communities where informal police intervention into the lives of residents is employed in the service of keeping the peace.

weapons offense The unlawful sale, distribution, manufacture, alteration, transportation, possession, or use, or the attempted unlawful sale, distribution, manufacture, alteration, transportation, possession, or use, of a deadly or dangerous weapon or accessory.

white-collar crime Nonviolent crime for financial gain committed by means of deception by offenders whose occupational status is entrepreneurial, professional, or semiprofessional and which utilizes their special occupational skills and opportunities. Also, nonviolent crime for financial gain utilizing deception and committed by anyone having special technical and professional knowledge of business and government, irrespective of the person's occupation.

Wickersham Commission Officially called the National Commission on Law Observance and Enforcement, this body issued a report in 1931 stating that Prohibition was unenforceable and carried a great potential for police corruption.

witness Generally, a person who has knowledge of the circumstances of a case. Also, in court usage, one who testifies as to what he or she has seen, heard, or otherwise observed or who has expert knowledge.

workhouse An early form of imprisonment intended to instill habits of industry in the idle. Also called *bridewell.*

work-release program A prison program through which inmates are temporarily released into the community to meet job responsibilities.

writ A document issued by a judicial officer ordering or forbidding the performance of a specified act.

writ of *certiorari* A writ issued from an appellate court for the purpose of obtaining from a lower court the record of its proceedings in a particular case.

writ of *habeas corpus* A writ that directs the person detaining a prisoner to bring him or her before a judicial officer to determine the lawfulness of the imprisonment.

youthful offender A person, adjudicated in criminal court, who may be above the statutory age limit for juveniles but is below a specified upper age limit, for whom special correctional commitments and special record-sealing procedures are made available by statute.

1. Bureau of Justice Statistics, *Dictionary of Criminal Justice Data Terminology*, 2d ed. (Washington, D.C.: U.S. Government Printing Office, 1982).

2. Federal Bureau of Investigation, *Uniform Crime Reporting Handbook* (Washington, D.C.: U.S. Department of Justice, 1984).

3. BJS, *Dictionary of Criminal Justice Data Terminology*, p. 5.

4. *People* v. *Romero*, 8 Cal. 4th 728, 735 (1994); and *People* v. *Dillard*, 96 C.D.O.S. 3869 (1996).

5. *State* v. *Cross*, 200 S.E. 2d 27, 29 (1973).

6. Gerald Hill and Kathleen Hill, *The Real Life Dictionary of the Law* (Santa Monica, CA: General Publishing Group, 2000). Online Web version posted at http://dictionary.law. com/lookup2.asp. Accessed February 21, 2002.

7. Community Policing Consortium, *What Is Community Policing?* (Washington, D.C.: Community Policing Consortium, 1995).

8. Michael L. Benson, Francis T. Cullen, and William J. Maakestad, *Local Prosecutors and Corporate Crime* (Washington, D.C.: National Institute of Justice, 1992), p. 1.

9. American Board of Criminalistics. Web posted at http://www. criminalistics.com/ABC/.

10. Sam W. Lathrop, "Reviewing Use of Force: A Systematic Approach," *FBI Law Enforcement Bulletin*, October 2000, p. 18.

11. Adapted from Federal Bureau of Investigation, *FBI Policy and Guidelines: Counterterrorism*. Web posted at http://www.fbi. gov/contact/fo/jackson/cntrterr. htm (accessed January 15, 2002).

12. Bureau of Justice Statistics, *Drugs, Crime, and the Justice System* (Washington, D.C.: BJS, 1992), p. 20.

13. Adapted from Technical Working Group for Electronic Crime Scene Investigation, *Electronic Crime Scene Investigation: A Guide for First Responders* (Washington, D.C.: National Institute of Justice, 2001), p. 2.

14. Henry Campbell Black, Joseph R. Nolan, and Jacqueline M. Nolan-Haley, *Black's Law Dictionary*, 6th ed. (St. Paul, MN: West, 1990), p. 24.

15. Black, Nolan, and Nolan-Haley, *Black's Law Dictionary*, p. 1003.

16. *The American Heritage Dictionary and Electronic Thesaurus on CD-ROM* (Boston: Houghton Mifflin, 1987).

17. Identity Theft Resource Center. Web posted at http://www.idtheftcenter. org. Accessed April 4, 2002.

18. Adapted from *FBI Policy and Guidelines: Counterterrorism*.

19. Jeffrey A. Butts and Ojmarrh Mitchell, "Brick by Brick: Dismantling the Border between Juvenile and Adult Justice," in Phyllis McDonald and Janice Munsterman, eds., *Criminal Justice 2000*, Vol. 2: *Boundary Changes in Criminal Justice Organizations* (Washington, D.C.: NIJ, 2000), p. 207.

20. David A. Garvin, "Building a Learning Organization," *Harvard Business Review* (1993), pp. 78–91.

21. Clifford Karchmer and Douglas Ruch, "State and Local Money Laundering Control Strategies," *NIJ Research in Brief* (Washington, D.C.: National Institute of Justice, 1992), p. 1.

22. Adapted from Robert M. Shusta et al., *Multicultural Law Enforcement*, 2d ed. (Upper Saddle River, NJ: Prentice Hall, 2002), p. 443.

23. The Organized Crime Control Act of 1970.

24. *Federal Rules of Criminal Procedure.*

25. BJS, *Drugs, Crime, and the Justice System*, p. 21.

26. Carl B. Klockars et al., "The Measurement of Police Integrity," *National Institute of Justice Research in Brief* (Washington, D.C.: NIJ, 2000), p. 1.

27. National Institute of Justice, *Use of Force by Police: Overview of National and Local Data* (Washington, D.C.: NIJ, 1999).

28. National Council on Crime and Delinquency, *National Assessment of Structured Sentencing* (Washington, D.C.: Bureau of Justice Statistics, 1996), p. xii.

29. Bureau of Justice Statistics, *Prisoners in 1998* (Washington, D.C.: BJS, 1999), p. 7.

30. *Private Security: Report of the Task Force on Private Security* (Washington, D.C.: U.S. Government Printing Office, 1976), p. 4.

31. Samuel Walker, Geoffrey P. Alpert, and Dennis J. Kenney, *Responding to the Problem Police Officer: A National Study of Early Warning Systems* (Washington, D.C.: National Institute of Justice, 2000).

32. BJS, *Drugs, Crime, and the Justice System*, p. 21.

33. Hill and Hill, *The Real Life Dictionary of the Law*. Accessed February 21, 2002.

34. Deborah Ramirez, Jack McDevitt, and Amy Farrell, *A Resource Guide on Racial Profiling Data Collection Systems: Promising Practices and Lessons Learned* (Washington, D.C.: Department of Justice, 2000), p. 3.

35. *Victor* v. *Nebraska*, 114 S.Ct. 1239, 127 L.Ed. 2d 583 (1994).

36. As found in the California jury instructions.

37. The term *superpredator* is generally attributed to John J. DiIulio, Jr. See John J. DiIulio, Jr., "The Question of Black Crime," *Public Interest* (fall 1994), pp. 3–12.

38. Sam S. Souryal, *Police Administration and Management* (St. Paul, MN: West, 1977), p. 261.

39. Federal Bureau of Investigation Counterterrorism Section, *Terrorism in the United States, 1987* (Washington, D.C.: FBI, 1987).

40. Daniel Oran, *Oran's Dictionary of the Law* (St. Paul, MN: West, 1983), p. 306.

41. Lawrence A. Greenfeld, "Prison Sentences and Time Served for Violence," *Bureau of Justice Statistics Selected Findings*, No. 4 (April 1995).

Help Wanted — The Administrative Office of the U.S. Courts

Typical Positions:
U.S. probation officer, pretrial services officer, statistician, defender services officer, and defense investigator.

Employment Requirements:
To qualify for the position of probation officer at the GS-5 level, an applicant must possess a bachelor's degree from an accredited college or university and must have a minimum of two years of general work experience. General experience must have been acquired after obtaining the bachelor's degree and cannot include experience as a police, custodial, or security officer unless the work involved criminal investigative experience. In lieu of general experience, a bachelor's degree from an accredited college or university in an accepted field of study (including criminology, criminal justice, penology, correctional administration, social work, sociology, public administration, or psychology) will qualify an applicant for immediate employment at the GS-5 level, provided that at least 32 semester hours or 48 quarter hours were taken in one or more of the accepted fields of study. One year of graduate study qualifies applicants for appointment at the GS-7 level, while a master's degree in an appropriate field or a law degree may qualify the applicant for advanced placement.

Other Requirements:
Applicants must be younger than 37 years of age at the time of hiring and must be in excellent physical health.

Salary:
Appointees are typically hired at GS-5 or GS-7, depending on education and work experience.

Benefits:
U.S. probation and pretrial services officers are included in the federal hazardous-duty law enforcement classification and are covered by liberal federal health and life insurance programs. A comprehensive retirement program is available to all federal employees.

Direct Inquiries To:
Administrative Office of the U.S. Courts
Personnel Office
Washington, DC 20544
Phone: (202) 273-1297
Website: http://www.uscourts.gov

Source:
Administrative Office of the U.S. Courts

Support Positions — U.S. Customs Service

Typical Positions:
Criminal investigator, special agent, customs inspector, canine enforcement officer, and import specialist. Support positions include intelligence research specialist, computer operator, auditor, customs aide, investigative assistant, and clerk.

Employment Requirements:
Applicants must (1) be a U.S. citizen, (2) pass an appropriate physical examination, (3) pass a personal background investigation, (4) submit to urinalysis testing for the presence of controlled substances, (5) have at least three years of work experience, and (6) be under 35 years of age. Appointment at the GS-7 level also requires (1) one year of specialized experience (for example, "responsible criminal investigative or comparable experience"), (2) a bachelor's degree with demonstration of superior academic achievement (a 3.0 grade point average in all courses completed at the time of application, a 3.5 grade point average for all courses in the applicant's major field of study, rank in the upper third of the applicant's undergraduate class, or membership in a national honorary scholastic society), or (3) one year of successful graduate study in a related field.

Other Requirements:
Applicants must (1) be willing to travel frequently, (2) be able to work overtime, (3) be able to work under stressful conditions, and (4) be willing to carry weapons and be able to qualify regularly with firearms.

Salary:
Successful candidates are typically hired at GS-5 or GS-7, depending on education and work experience.

Benefits:
Benefits include (1) 13 days of sick leave annually, (2) two and a half to five weeks of paid vacation and ten paid federal holidays each year, (3) federal health and life insurance, and (4) a comprehensive retirement program.

Direct Inquiries To:
U.S. Customs Service
Office of Human Resources
1301 Constitution Ave., N.W.
Washington, DC 20229
Phone: (800) 944-7725

Website: http://www.customs.treas.gov

Source:
U.S. Customs Service